New Zealand

THE ROUGH GUIDE

D0249373

There are more than one hundred Rough Guide titles
covering destinations from Amsterdam to Zimbabwe

Forthcoming titles include
Bangkok • Barbados
Japan • Jordan • Syria

Rough Guide Reference Series
Classical Music • European Football • The Internet • Jazz
Opera • Reggae • Rock Music • World Music

Rough Guide Phrasebooks
Czech • French • German • Greek • Hindi & Urdu • Hungarian • Indonesian
Italian • Japanese • Mandarin Chinese • Mexican Spanish • Polish
Portuguese • Russian • Spanish • Thai • Turkish • Vietnamese

Rough Guides on the Internet
http://www.roughguides.com

ROUGH GUIDE CREDITS

Text editor: Alison Cowan
Series editor: Mark Ellingham
Editorial: Martin Dunford, Jonathan Buckley, Samantha Cook, Jo Mead, Kate Berens, Amanda Tomlin, Ann-Marie Shaw, Paul Gray, Sarah Dallas, Chris Schüler, Helena Smith, Caroline Osborne, Kieran Falconer, Judith Bamber, Olivia Eccleshall, Orla Duane (UK); Andrew Rosenberg (US)
Production: Susanne Hillen, Andy Hilliard, Judy Pang, Link Hall, Nicola Williamson, Helen Ostick, James Morris

Cartography: Melissa Flack, Maxine Burke, Nichola Goodliffe
Picture research: Eleanor Hill
Online editors: Alan Spicer (UK); Geronimo Madrid (US)
Finance: John Fisher, Celia Crowley, Catherine Gillespie, Neeta Mistry
Marketing & Publicity: Richard Trillo, Simon Carloss, Niki Smith (UK); Jean-Marie Kelly, SoRelle Braun (US)
Administration: Tania Hummel, Alexander Mark Rogers

ACKNOWLEDGEMENTS

This book is dedicated to Guy Harper

The authors would like to thank Alison Cowan, whose deft use of the green pen and unending patience never wavered, even after relocation to sunnier climes; Jo Mead for stepping into the breach until the arrival of baby Ruby; and Kate Berens for orchestrating everything, right to the end. Special thanks also go to Carole Norris and Liza Clapp at the New Zealand Tourism Board in London and their cohorts back home. Thanks, too, to Sophie Griffiths at the New Zealand High Commission in London; Sally Durham of the Saltmarsh Partnership; Len West and Gordon Burrow at YHA New Zealand and the staff at Wellington, Christchurch and Dunedin YHAs; and to Geoff Walker, Heather Gamble and Karen Ferns at Penguin New Zealand. An amazed thank you, too, to readers who wrote to us even before there was something to read, including Al Inglis, Keith Duffy and Pauline Baxter. Finally, thanks go to Jonathan Bousfield for helping out with the editing, MicroMap (Romsey, Hants) and Maxine Burke for producing fine maps, Helen Ostick for more than keeping up with the typesetting, Rosemary Morlin for proofreading, and Eleanor Hill for picture research.

Laura and Tony: A big thank you to Dr Hank Driessen at the National Archives, Marek Bielski at Capital Television and Graham Hemming at Riccarton Bush Trust. We're also indebted to Welco, Scotties, Ace and U-Save for their help with transport, as well as TranzRail, the Interislander, InterCity and Southern Air; and, for their generosity, to Mary and Ted Creed

in Levin, Beryl and Colin Jobson at Ohiwa Harbour, Christine and Robert Koller at Stronechrubie (Mount Somers), and Sue and David Sweet at Mangaweka. Thanks also to our Kiwi friends – Robin and Jo Burleigh, Brian and Denny, and Peter Hawes and Elizabeth Barker – who nourished and entertained us. At home, we couldn't have done it without the support of our friends and families, especially Guy, Ann, Violet and Don.

Paul: Thanks to Beth Harman at the Auckland Art Gallery; Vanessa Byrnes from the Waitangi Tribunal; Jenny Ball at the Auckland Museum; Raewyn Davies at Hodder Moa Becket; Mark Profitt and Chris McKeller for advice on the Kiwi gay scene; and Amelia Fairney at The Women's Press. Special thanks too to Richard Turton; Jude Anaru for giving us a good plug; Irene Gardiner for last-minute checking and encouragement; Kate McLaren; Richard and Raewyn; Garry and Hillary Sye; Cal, a gorgeous dining companion; Mel and Ru; Darryl and Jamie; Andrew, Kerry and Anna in Hastings; John and Lyn Hawksworth in Gisborne; Stuart Devenie, Gillian and Laurel in Whangarei; and Kevin Bracey in Blackball for computer advice in an hour of desperate need. Cheers, too, to all those who shared experiences and huts on numerous tramps throughout the country, in particular Nance and Dee on the Routeburn. As ever, thanks to folk back home: James and Sarah, and Lorna and Joe in London, and Andy and Jelly for holding the fort in Manchester. Last but not least, extra special thanks go to James Griffin and Tania Stiles for letting me invade their lives and whose home became my home.

PUBLISHING INFORMATION

This first edition published April 1998 by Rough Guides Ltd, 1 Mercer St, London WC2H 9QJ. Distributed by the Penguin Group:
Penguin Books Ltd, 27 Wrights Lane, London W8 5TZ
Penguin Books USA Inc., 375 Hudson Street, New York 10014, USA
Penguin Books Australia Ltd, 487 Maroondah Highway, PO Box 257, Ringwood, Victoria 3134, Australia
Penguin Books Canada Ltd, 10 Alcorn Avenue, Toronto, Ontario, Canada M4V 1E4
Penguin Books (NZ) Ltd, 182–190 Wairau Road, Auckland 10, New Zealand
Typeset in Linotron Univers and Century Old Style to an original design by Andrew Oliver.
Printed in England by Clays Ltd, St Ives PLC
Illustrations in Part One and Part Three by Edward Briant.

Illustrations on p.1 & p.759 by Henry Iles
© Laura Harper, Tony Mudd & Paul Whitfield 1998.
No part of this book may be reproduced in any form without permission from the publisher except for the quotation of brief passages in reviews.
832pp – Includes index
A catalogue record for this book is available from the British Library
ISBN 1-85828-233-0

New Zealand

THE ROUGH GUIDE

written and researched by

Laura Harper, Tony Mudd & Paul Whitfield

THE ROUGH GUIDES

THE ROUGH GUIDES

TRAVEL GUIDES • PHRASEBOOKS • MUSIC AND REFERENCE GUIDES

 We set out to do something different when the first Rough Guide was published in 1982. Mark Ellingham, just out of university, was travelling in Greece. He brought along the popular guides of the day, but found they were all lacking in some way. They were either strong on ruins and museums but went on for pages without mentioning a beach or taverna. Or they were so conscious of the need to save money that they lost sight of Greece's cultural and historical significance. Also, none of the books told him anything about Greece's contemporary life – its politics, its culture, its people, and how they lived.

So with no job in prospect, Mark decided to write his own guidebook, one which aimed to provide practical information that was second to none, detailing the best beaches and the hottest clubs and restaurants, while also giving hard-hitting accounts of every sight, both famous and obscure, and providing up-to-the-minute information on contemporary culture. It was a guide that encouraged independent travellers to find the best of Greece, and was a great success, getting shortlisted for the Thomas Cook travel guide award,

and encouraging Mark, along with three friends, to expand the series.

The Rough Guide list grew rapidly and the letters flooded in, indicating a much broader readership than had been anticipated, but one which uniformly appreciated the Rough Guide mix of practical detail and humour, irreverence and enthusiasm. Things haven't changed. The same four friends who began the series are still the caretakers of the Rough Guide mission today: to provide the most reliable, up-to-date and entertaining information to independent-minded travellers of all ages, on all budgets.

We now publish 100 titles and have offices in London and New York. The travel guides are written and researched by a dedicated team of more than 100 authors, based in Britain, Europe, the USA and Australia. We have also created a unique series of phrasebooks to accompany the travel series, along with an acclaimed series of music guides, and a best-selling pocket guide to the Internet and World Wide Web. We also publish comprehensive travel information on our web site:

http://www.roughguides.com

HELP US UPDATE

We've gone to a lot of effort to ensure that this new edition of The Rough Guide to New Zealand is accurate and up-to-date. However, things change – places get "discovered", opening hours are notoriously fickle, restaurants and rooms raise prices or lower standards, extra buses are laid on or off. If you feel we've got it wrong or left something out, we'd like to know, and if you can remember the address, the price, the time, the phone number, so much the better.

We'll credit all contributions, and send a copy of the next edition (or any other Rough Guide if you prefer) for the best letters. Please mark letters: "Rough Guide New Zealand Update" and send to:
Rough Guides, 1 Mercer St, London WC2H 9QJ, or
Rough Guides, 375 Hudson St, 9th floor, New York NY 10014.
Or send email to: mail@roughguides.co.uk
Online updates about this book can be found on Rough Guides' Web site at http://www.roughguides.com

THE AUTHORS

Laura Harper first visited New Zealand in 1994 during a year out from book editing. She quickly fell in love with the place and its people and stayed for four months. Back in the UK, she updated the *Rough Guide to Florida* with Tony Mudd before co-writing this book. She also keeps her hand in as a freelance editor for publishers such as BBC Books, covering a wide range of topics including, of course, travel.

After a series of freelance jobs editing, writing and researching, **Tony Mudd** travelled around the world with Laura Harper in 1994, later returning to the land of the long white cloud to research the *Rough Guide to New Zealand*. His work for *Rough Guides* has been punctuated with occasional diversions into fiction and newspaper articles, inspired, at least in part, by the north Suffolk coast where he lives.

Paul Whitfield emigrated to New Zealand aged thirteen and spent ten formative years there, little suspecting that a decade or so on he would be writing this *Rough Guide* to his adopted land. Now based in England, he regularly escapes the worst of the northern winters, either in New Zealand or working on *Rough Guides* to Mexico and California. Large chunks of the summers are spent in Snowdonia, rock climbing and keeping his *Rough Guide to Wales* up to scratch.

CONTENTS

Introduction xi

PART THREE CONTEXTS 759

LIST OF MAPS

MAP SYMBOLS

——	Railway		▣	Parking
⊂◇⊃	State Highway		◉	Swimming pool
═══	Road		◔	Cave
-----	Path		▲	Peak
– – –	Ferry route		☆	Viewpoint
——	Waterway		✕	Airport
———	Chapter division boundary		☗	Lighthouse
■—■—■	International borders		✦	Ski area
■—■ ■	County boundary		⫫	Waterfall
⚲	Church (regional maps)		⨊	Marshland
⊞	Hospital		ϒ	Spring
♦	Places of Interest		⼞	Cliff
♜	Castle		ⓘ	Tourist office
∴	Ruins		⊠	Post office
♟	Museum		ⓒ	Telephone
⚘	Public Gardens		▰	Building
⚭	Winery		⊟	Church
⚠	Campsite		⁺⁺⁺	Cemetery
⌂	Lodge		▨	Park
◉	Hotel		▨	National Park
▣	Restaurant		⋯	Beach
⊡	Toilet		⊿	Glacier
★	Bus stop			

INTRODUCTION

New Zealand comes burdened with a reputation as a unique land packed with magnificent, raw **scenery**: craggy coastlines, sweeping beaches, primeval forests, snow-capped alpine mountains, bubbling volcanic pools, fast-flowing rivers and glacier-fed lakes, all beneath a brilliant blue sky. Even **Kiwis** themselves – named after the endearing, if decidedly odd, flightless bird that has become the national emblem – seem to be filled with astonishment at the stupendous vistas of what they like to think of as "Godzone" (God's own country). All of this provides a canvas for boundless **diversions**, from moody strolls along windswept beaches and multi-day tramps over alpine passes to the adrenalin-charged adventure activities of bungy jumping and whitewater rafting; in fact, some visitors take on New Zealand as a kind of large-scale assault course, aiming to tackle as many adventures as possible in the time available. The one-time albatross of isolation – even Australia is over a thousand kilometres away – has become a boon, bolstering New Zealand's clean, **green** image, which is, in truth, more an accident of geography than the result of government policy.

To a large extent New Zealand lives up to these expectations, and unfettered by the crowds you'd find elsewhere. What's more, everything is easily accessible, packed into a land area little larger than Britain and with a population of just 3.6 million, over half of it tucked away in the three largest **cities**: Auckland, the capital Wellington, and the South Island's Christchurch. Elsewhere, you can travel miles through bleak farmland and rarely see a soul, and there are even remote spots which, it's reliably contended, no human has ever visited.

Geologically, New Zealand split off from the super-continent of Gondwanaland early, developing a unique **ecosystem** in which birds adapted to fill the role normally held by mammals, many becoming flightless through lack of predators. That all changed around 1200 years ago when the arrival of Polynesian navigators made this the last major land mass to be settled by humans. On sighting the new land from their canoes, Maori named it **Aotearoa** – "the land of the long white cloud" – and proceeded to radically alter the fragile ecosystem, dispatching forever the giant ostrich-sized moa, which formed a major part of their diet. A delicate ecological balance was achieved before the arrival of *pakeha* – white Europeans, predominantly of British origin – who swarmed off their square-rigged ships full of colonial zeal.

The subsequent uneasy coexistence between **Maori** and **European** societies informs both recorded history and the current wrangles over cultural identity, land and resource rights. The British didn't invade as such, and were to some degree reluctant to enter into the 1840 **Treaty of Waitangi**, which effectively ceded New Zealand to the British Crown while guaranteeing Maori hegemony over their land and traditional gathering and fishing rights. As time wore on and increasing numbers of settlers demanded to buy ever larger parcels of land from Maori, antipathy soon surfaced, eventually escalating to hostility. Once Maori were subdued, a policy of partial integration ensured the rapid dilution of their cultural heritage and all but destroyed **Maoritanga** – the Maori way of doing things. Maori, however, were left well outside the new European order, where difference was perceived as tantamount to a betrayal of the emergent sense of nationhood. Although elements of this still exist and Presbyterian and Anglican values have proved hard to shake off, the Kiwi psyche has become infused

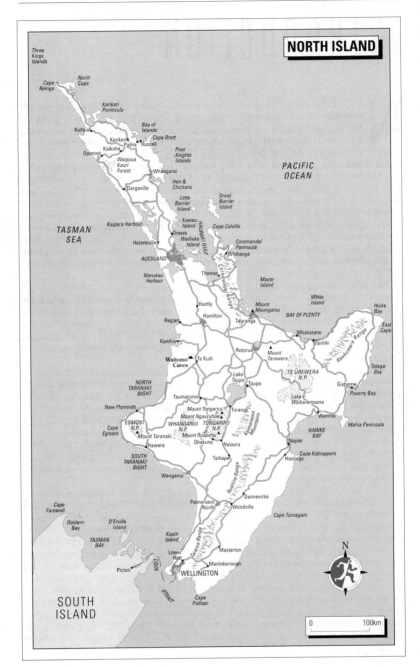

NORTH ISLAND

Three Kings Islands

North Cape

Cape Reinga

Karikari Peninsula

Kaitaia

Kerikeri
Kaikohe
Paihia
Russell

Bay of Islands
Cape Brett

Opononi

Waipoua Kauri Forest

Whangarei

Poor Knights Islands

Dargaville

Hen & Chickens

Little Barrier Island

Great Barrier Island

PACIFIC OCEAN

Kaipara Harbour

Kawau Island

HAURAKI GULF

Cape Colville

Helensville

Orewa
Waiheke Island

AUCKLAND

Coromandel Peninsula

Whitianga

TASMAN SEA

Manukau Harbour

Thames

Coromandel Range

Mayor Island

White Island

Hicks Bay

Huntly

Hamilton

Mount Maunganui

BAY OF PLENTY

East Cape

Raglan

Tauranga

Whakatane

Opotiki

Raukumara Range

Kawhia

Rotorua

Mount Tarawera

Tolaga Bay

Waitomo Caves

Te Kuiti

Lake Taupo

Taupo

TE UREWERA N.P.

Gisborne

Poverty Bay

NORTH TARANAKI BIGHT

Taumarunui

Lake Waikaremoana

New Plymouth

Mount Tongariro
Mount Ngauruhoe
Turangi

EGMONT N.P.

WHANGANUI N.P.

TONGARIRO N.P.

Kaimanawa Mountains

Wairoa

Mahia Peninsula

Cape Egmont

Mount Taranaki

Mount Ruapehu

Ohakune

Waiouru

HAWKE BAY

Hawera

Napier

Cape Kidnappers

SOUTH TARANAKI BIGHT

Taihape

Hastings

Ruahine Range

Wanganui

Dannevirke

Cape Farewell

Goldern Bay

D'Erville Island

Palmerston North

Woodville

Cape Turnagain

TASMAN BAY

Kapiti Island

Tararua Range

Masterton

Picton

COOK STRAIT

Lower Hutt

Martinborough

WELLINGTON

N

Cape Palliser

SOUTH ISLAND

0   100km

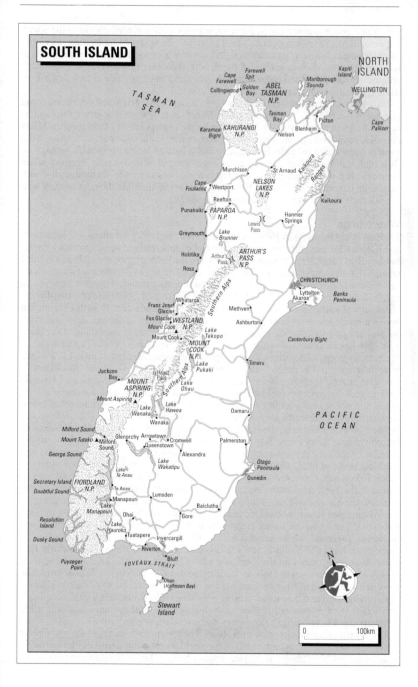

with Maori generosity and hospitality, coupled with a colonial mateyness and the unerring belief that whatever happens, "she'll be right". However, an underlying inferiority complex seems to linger: you may well find yourself interrogated as to your opinions of the country almost before you've left the airport. Balancing this out is an extraordinary enthusiasm for **sports** and **culture**, which generate a swelling pride in New Zealanders when they witness plucky Kiwis taking on the world.

Only in the last couple of decades has New Zealand come of age and developed a true national self-confidence, something partly forced on it by Britain severing the colonial apron strings in the early 1970s, and partly by the resurgence of Maori identity. Maori demands have been nurtured by a willingness on the part of most *pakeha* to redress the wrongs perpetrated over the last century and a half, as long as it doesn't impinge on their high standard of living or overall feeling of control. More recently, integration has been replaced with a policy of promoting two cultures alongside each other, but with maximum interaction. In this way New Zealand is set to head into the next century with considerable dignity and a good deal of uncertainty.

Where to go

Tourism is big business in New Zealand but even the key destinations – Queenstown and Rotorua, for example – only seem busy and commercialized in comparison with the low-key Kiwi norm. New Zealand packs a lot into the limited space available and is small enough that you can visit the main sights in a couple of weeks, but for a reasonable look around at a less than frenetic pace, reckon on at least a month. However long you've got, look at spreading your time between the North and South islands: the diverse attractions of each region are discussed fully in the introduction to each chapter, but here's a quick top-to-toe summary. Obviously, the scenery is the big draw and most people only pop into the big cities on arrival and departure – something easily done with open-jaw air tickets allowing you to fly into Auckland and out of Christchurch.

Certainly none of the cities ranks on an international scale, but in recent years they have taken on more distinct and sophisticated identities. Go-ahead **Auckland** is sprawled around sparkling Waitemata Harbour, an arm of the island-studded Hauraki Gulf. From here, most people head south, missing out on **Northland**, the cradle of both Maori and *pakeha* colonization, which comes cloaked in wonderful sub-tropical forest harbouring New Zealand's largest kauri trees. East of Auckland the coast follows the isolated greenery and long, deserted, golden beaches of the **Coromandel Peninsula**, before running down to the **Bay of Plenty** resorts. The lands immediately south are assailed by the ever-present sulphur stench of **Rotorua**, with its spurting geysers and bubbling pools of mud, and the volcanic plateau centred on the trout-filled waters of **Lake Taupo** and three snow-capped volcanoes. Cave fans will want to head west of Taupo to the eerie limestone caverns of **Waitomo**, where you can abseil into, or raft through, the blackness. From Taupo it's just a short hop to the delights of canoeing on the **Whanganui River**, a broad, emerald green waterway banked by virtually impenetrable bush, or if you don't want to get your feet wet, head for the almost perfect cone of **Mount Taranaki**, whose summit is accessible in just one day. East of Taupo lie the ranges that form the North Island's backbone, and beyond them the **Hawke's Bay wine country**, centred on the Art Deco city of Napier, and the up-and-coming wine region of Martinborough. Only an hour or so away is the capital, **Wellington**, the most self-contained of New Zealand's cities, with its centre squeezed onto reclaimed harbourside land and the suburbs slung over steep hills overlooking glistening bays. Politicians and bureaucrats give it well-scrubbed and urbane sophistication, enlivened by a burgeoning café society and after-dark scene.

The **South Island** kicks off with **Nelson**, a pretty and compact spot surrounded by lovely beaches and within easy reach of the world-renowned wineries of Marlborough. From there you've a choice of nipping around behind the 3000-metre summits of the

Southern Alps and following the West Coast to the fabulous **glaciers** at Fox and Franz Josef, or sticking to the east, passing the whale-watching territory of **Kaikoura** en route to the South Island's largest centre, straight-laced **Christchurch**, a city with its roots firmly in the traditions of England. From Christchurch it's possible to head across country to the West Coast via the famous **Arthur's Pass** scenic railway, shooting southwest from the patchwork Canterbury Plains to the foothills of the **Southern Alps** and **Mount Cook** with its distinctive drooping-tent summit.

The flatlands of Canterbury run down, via the grand architecture of **Oamaru**, to the unmistakably Scottish-influenced city of **Dunedin**, birthplace of some of the country's best rock bands and base for exploring the teeming wildlife of the **Otago Peninsula**. In the middle of the nineteenth century prospectors arrived here and rushed inland to gold strikes throughout central Otago and around stunningly set **Queenstown**, now a highly commercialized activity centre where bungy jumping, rafting, jetboating and ski-ing hold sway. This is also the tramping heartland, with the **Routeburn Track** linking Queenstown to the rain-sodden fiords, lakes and mountains of **Fiordland**, and the

CLIMATE CHART

	Jan	Feb	March	April	May	June	July	Aug	Sept	Oct	Nov	Dec
Auckland												
av. max. temp. (°C)	23	23	22	19	17	14	13	14	16	17	19	21
av. min. temp. (°C)	16	16	15	13	11	9	8	8	9	11	12	14
av. rainfall (mm)	79	94	81	97	17	137	145	117	102	102	89	79
Napier												
av. max. temp. (°C)	24	23	22	19	17	14	13	14	17	19	21	23
av. min. temp. (°C)	14	14	13	10	8	5	5	6	7	9	11	13
av. rainfall (mm)	74	76	74	76	89	86	102	84	56	56	61	58
Wellington												
av. max. temp. (°C)	21	21	19	17	14	13	12	12	14	16	17	19
av. min. temp. (°C)	13	13	12	11	8	7	6	6	8	9	10	12
av. rainfall (mm)	81	81	81	97	117	117	137	117	97	102	89	89
Christchurch												
av. max. temp. (°C)	21	21	19	17	13	11	10	11	14	17	19	21
av. min. temp. (°C)	12	12	10	7	4	2	2	2	4	7	8	11
av. rainfall (mm)	56	43	48	48	66	66	69	48	46	43	48	56
Hokitika												
av. max. temp. (°C)	19	19	18	16	14	12	12	12	13	15	16	18
av. min. temp. (°C)	12	12	11	8	6	3	3	3	6	8	9	11
av. rainfall (mm)	262	191	239	236	244	231	218	239	226	292	267	262
Queenstown												
av. max. temp. (°C)	21	21	20	7	11	9	9	11	14	18	19	20
av. min. temp. (°C)	10	10	9	7	3	1	0	1	3	5	7	10
av. rainfall (mm)	79	72	74	72	64	58	59	63	66	77	64	62
Dunedin												
av. max. temp. (°C)	19	19	17	15	12	9	9	11	13	15	17	18
av. min. temp. (°C)	10	10	9	7	5	4	3	3	5	6	7	9
av. rainfall (mm)	86	71	76	71	81	81	79	76	69	76	81	89

world-renowned **Milford Track**. The further south you travel, the more you'll feel the bite of the Antarctic winds, which reach their peak on New Zealand's third land mass, the tiny and isolated **Stewart Island**, covered mostly by dense coastal rainforest and famous for testing the patience of even the most avid trampers with its almost permanently muddy tracks.

When to go

With over a thousand kilometres of ocean in every direction, it comes as no surprise that New Zealand has a maritime climate: warm through the southern summer months of December to March and never truly cold, even in winter.

Weather patterns are strongly affected by the prevailing westerlies, which suck up moisture from the Tasman Sea and dump it on the western side of both islands. The South Island gets the lion's share, with the West Coast and Fiordland ranking among the world's wettest places. The mountain ranges running the length of both islands cast long rain shadows over the eastern lands, making them considerably drier, though the south is a few degrees cooler than elsewhere, and sub-tropical Auckland and Northland are appreciably more humid. In the North Island, warm, damp summers fade almost imperceptibly into cool, wet winters, but the further south you go the more the year divides into four distinct seasons.

Such regional variation makes it viable to visit at any time of year, provided you pick your destinations. The **summer** months are the most popular and you'll find everything open, though often packed with holidaying Kiwis from Christmas to the end of January. Accommodation at this time is at a premium. In general, you're better off joining the bulk of foreign visitors during the **shoulder seasons** – October to Christmas and February to April or May – when sights and attractions can be a shade quieter, and rooms easier to come by. **Winter** (June–Sept) is the wettest, coldest and consequently least popular time, though Northland can still be relatively balmy. The switch to prevailing southerly winds tends to bring periods of crisp, dry and cloudless weather to the West Coast and heavy snowfalls to the fine and plentiful skiing pistes of the Southern Alps and Central North Island.

PART ONE

GETTING THERE FROM BRITAIN AND IRELAND

Over a dozen airlines compete to fly you from Britain to New Zealand from as little as £600–800, remarkably cheap considering the distances involved. Going for the cheapest flight typically means sacrificing some comfort, which you may regret, given that your journey will last at least 24 hours, longer if your flight makes more than the obligatory refuelling stop. There are no direct flights to New Zealand from Ireland, and prices are proportionately higher, since the short hop to London (IR£82 return) has to be added on to the fare.

No matter how keen you are to arrive in New Zealand, it makes sense to break the journey, and most **scheduled flights** allow multiple **stopovers** either in North America and the Pacific, or Asia and Australia. The vast majority of direct scheduled flights to New Zealand depart from London's Heathrow, though Garuda Indonesia fly from London Gatwick (2 weekly), and Singapore Airlines use Manchester (4 weekly) as well as Heathrow. There are few overseas flights into Wellington, so the only real choice is between the main international airport at **Auckland**, in the north of the North Island, and the second airport at **Christchurch**, midway down the South Island. Christchurch receives far fewer direct flights, but most scheduled airlines have a code-share shuttle from Auckland at no extra cost The most desirable option, an **open-jaw ticket** (flying into one and out of the other), usually costs no more than an ordinary return.

Seasonal (Nov–March only) **charter flights** to New Zealand have been trailblazed by Britannia who fly to both Auckland and Christchurch from London Gatwick; fares are low, but flights are bound with restrictions (you must stay for a minimum of 2 weeks but no longer than 8 weeks, and stopovers are strictly limited), which can make them a less attractive option.

If you are planning on doing a lot of **travelling within New Zealand**, especially between the North and South islands, it may be worth looking into **air passes** offered by both Air New Zealand and Ansett New Zealand (see "Getting Around", p.24). In addition, if you are **combining Australia and New Zealand**, there are handy airpasses covering internal travel in each country and the joining flight. Qantas's **Boomerang Pass** is available to all international travellers (not just Qantas ticket holders), and comprises between two and ten coupons, each valid for a flight within Australasia: a one-zone coupon to fly within New Zealand or short hops in Oz costs £100, a two-zone trans-Tasman coupon costs £125. Ansett's **G'day Pass** is fundamentally the same, but has a larger number of travel zones and a wider range of prices.

FARES

The surest way to land a flight at a reasonable price is to book as far ahead as possible through a **travel agent**. These are almost invariably cheaper than buying direct from the airline, though we've given a rundown of all the carriers to show the variety of routes (see box on p.51). In the end you'll find the available flights at much the same price everywhere, the main differential being between the plusher airlines like Air New Zealand, British Airways (BA), Singapore and Thai – which offer more legroom, movies and comforting accessories – and Garuda Indonesia and United, which are generally the least expensive.

Tourists and those on short-term working visas (see p.121) are generally required by New Zealand immigration to arrive with a ticket out of the country, so **one-way tickets** are really only viable for Australian and New Zealand residents. If you've purchased a return ticket and find you

AIRLINES FLYING FROM THE UK TO NEW ZEALAND

Aerolineas Argentinas (☎0171/494 1001). Twice-weekly flights from London Heathrow via Buenos Aires to Auckland.

Air New Zealand (☎0181/741 2299). Five flights weekly to Auckland, via Los Angeles and the popular South Pacific route with a choice of stopovers in Honolulu, Fiji, Western Samoa, the Cook Islands, Tahiti and Tonga. Easy connections to Christchurch.

Britannia, book through *Austravel* (see box on p.5). Charter flights to Auckland and Christchurch (both Nov–March only), weekly from Gatwick and monthly from Manchester.

British Airways (UK reservations ☎0345/222 111, in the Republic of Ireland ☎0600/626 747). Daily flights from London Heathrow to Auckland and Christchurch, with stopovers in Asia, Australia, LA or Fiji.

Canadian Airlines International (UK reservations ☎0345/616 767, in the Republic of Ireland ☎1800/709 900). Daily flights from London Heathrow to Auckland via Toronto, Vancouver, Honolulu and Fiji.

Cathay Pacific (☎0345/581 581). Five weekly flights from Heathrow and Manchester to Auckland via Hong Kong, with connections to Christchurch.

Garuda Indonesia (☎0171/486 3011). London Gatwick and Manchester to Auckland via Abu Dhabi, Bangkok, Singapore, Jakarta and Bali.

Japanese Airlines (☎0171/408 1000). Three flights weekly from Heathrow to Auckland.

Korean Air (☎0800/413 000; in the Republic of Ireland ☎01/799 7990). Several flights a week from Heathrow to Auckland and Christchurch via Seoul, and sometimes Fiji.

Malaysian Airlines (MAS) (UK reservations ☎0171/341 2020, in the Republic of Ireland ☎01/676 1561). Three flights weekly from Heathrow to Auckland and Christchurch via Kuala Lumpur and Dubai.

Qantas (☎0345/747 767). Daily scheduled flights from Heathrow to Auckland and Christchurch, via LA, Bangkok and Singapore.

Singapore Airlines (UK reservations ☎0181/747 0007, in the Republic of Ireland ☎01/671 0722). Flights from Heathrow (daily) and Manchester (4 weekly) to Auckland and Christchurch via Singapore.

Thai International (☎0171/491 9113). Three flights weekly from Heathrow to Auckland, via Bangkok and Sydney.

United Airlines (☎0181/990 9900). Daily flights from Heathrow to Auckland, with various US stopovers.

Virgin Atlantic Airways (UK reservations ☎01293/747 747, in the Republic of Ireland ☎01/873 3388). Daily flights from Heathrow to Auckland, via LA and Fiji, plus code-share services with MAS (see above).

---

want to stay longer or head off on a totally different route, it's sometimes possible to cash in the return half of your ticket (though you'll make a loss on the deal) at the same travel agent where you bought it.

The cheapest **scheduled fare** you're likely to find is around £600 return, available during the low-season months of April, May and June; if you insist on flying with Air New Zealand, Qantas, BA or Singapore, expect to pay upwards of £650 for a flight in this off-peak period. The most expensive time to fly is in the two weeks before **Christmas**, when you'll be lucky to find anything for less than £1000 return: to stand a chance of getting one of the cheaper tickets, aim to book at least six months in advance. In between times (the **shoulder seasons** of July–Nov and Jan–March), you should expect to pay £750–850 (nearer £1000 with the prestige airlines).

The lowest **charter fares** are for stays of two weeks and start at £600 return. Standard fares for four- to eight-week stays hover around £700–800 in November, early December and most of January, rising through £900–950 over Christmas.

STOPOVERS AND RTW TICKETS

An excellent alternative to a direct flight is a **multi-stopover ticket**, often for little more than an ordinary return. Unusual routes combining the resources of two or more airlines in a **round-the-world (RTW) ticket** (usually valid for 12 months) are more expensive, but are almost infinitely variable. The best deals are along fixed routes such as the Aerolineas Argentinas/Thai combo that routes you from London through Buenos Aires, Auckland, Sydney, Perth and

FLIGHT AND TRAVEL AGENTS

Austravel, 50 Conduit St, London W1R 9FB (☎0171/734 7755), plus branches in Bournemouth, Bristol, Leeds and Manchester. Specialists in Britannia charter flights (Nov–March only), offering stopovers in Tokyo, Seoul, Singapore, LA or Fiji and costing as little as £499 return, rising to £969 at Christmas. Austravel also lays on "Focus Downunder" audio-visual presentations all over the UK to help you plan your trip.

Bridge the World, 47 Chalk Farm Rd, London NW1 8AN (☎0171/911 0900). Round-the-world ticket specialist, with good deals aimed at the backpacker market. A second office, at 4 Regents Place, Regent St, London W1R 6BH (☎0171/734 7447), deals in swankier arrangements and tours specifically to New Zealand and Australia. Agents for Kiwi Experience.

Campus Travel, 52 Grosvenor Gardens, London SW1W 0AG (☎0171/730 8111), plus branches in Birmingham, Brighton, Bristol, Cambridge, Edinburgh, Manchester and Oxford; Web site *www.campustravel.co.uk*. Student/youth travel specialists, with branches in YHA shops and on university campuses all over Britain.

Council Travel, 28a Poland St, London W1V 3DB (☎0171/437 7767). Specialize in students' fares, with good deals to New Zealand.

Cresta World Travel, 32 Victoria St, Altrincham, WA14 1ET (☎0161/929 9727). Comprehensive range of flights and round-the-world tickets to New Zealand and Australia, with good backpacker deals.

Destination Group, 41–45 Goswell Rd, London EC1V 7EH (☎0171/253 9000). Good discount fares, especially on Garuda flights; Far East and USA inclusive packages.

Flightbookers, 177–178 Tottenham Court Rd, London W1P 0LX (☎0171/757 2468). Low fares on scheduled flights.

Joe Walsh Tours, 34 Grafton St, Dublin 2 (☎01/671 8751); 69 Upper O'Connell St , Dublin 2 (☎01/872 2555); 8–11 Baggot St, Dublin 2 (☎01/676 3053); 117 St Patrick St, Cork (☎021/277 959). General budget fares agent.

Jupiter Travel, 46 Victoria Rd, Surbiton, Surrey KT6 4JL (☎0181/296 0309). Cheap and reliable agent with multi-stopover and RTW tickets to New Zealand.

London Flight Centre, 131 Earls Court Rd, London SW5 9RH (☎0171/244 6411). Long-established agent dealing in discount flights; visas and vaccinations are also on offer.

North South Travel, Moulsham Mill Centre, Parkway, Chelmsford, Essex CM2 7PX (☎01245/492 882). Friendly, competitive travel agency, offering discounted fares worldwide. Profits go to support projects in the developing world, especially the promotion of sustainable tourism.

Quest Worldwide, 10 Richmond Rd, Kingston, Surrey KT2 5HL (☎0181 547 3322). Specialists in round-the-world and Australasian discount fares, with plenty of round-the-world ideas, plus car and motorhome rental, guided Great Walks and bus tours, including Magic Bus.

STA Travel, 86 Old Brompton Rd, London SW7 3LH (☎0171/361 6262), plus branches in Birmingham, Bristol, Cambridge, Canterbury, Cardiff, Coventry, Durham, Glasgow, Leeds, Loughborough, Manchester, Nottingham, Oxford, Warwick and Sheffield; Web site *www.sta-travel.com*. Worldwide specialists in low-cost flights and tours; also good deals for students and under-26s. Experts on New Zealand travel with branches in major Kiwi cities.

Thomas Cook, 45 Berkeley St, London W1X 5AE (☎0990/666 222, Flights Direct ☎0990/101 520); 11 Donegall Place, Belfast (☎001232/242341); 118 Grafton St, Dublin 2 (☎01/677 1721), plus branches nationwide. Long-established one-stop travel agency for package holidays and scheduled flights; other services include exchange and travellers' cheques, travel insurance and car rental.

Trailfinders, 42–50 Earls Court Rd, London W8 6FT (☎0171/938 3366); 4–5 Dawson St, Dublin 2 (☎01/677 7888), plus branches in Manchester, Glasgow, Birmingham and Bristol. One of the most efficient agents for independent travellers; their quarterly magazine is worth scrutinising for round-the-world routes (call ☎0171/938 3366 for a free copy).

Travel Bag, 52 Regent St, London W1R 6DX (☎0171/287 4522). Discount flights to New Zealand, plus tours and adventure trips; agents for Kiwi Experience.

Travel Mood, 214 Edgeware Rd, London W2 1DH (☎0171/258 1234) and a branch in Dundee. Discount fares and round-the-world tickets; also car rental and bus tours, including Kiwi Experience.

Bangkok from around £1100, or Alitalia/Air New Zealand's London-based circuit through Bangkok, Singapore, Bali, Auckland, Christchurch, Sydney/Cairns and Los Angeles for a little under £1000. It is also possible to reduce your flight costs by incorporating an **overland section** into your round-the-world ticket: common land sectors include Delhi to Kathmandu, Brisbane or Sydney to Cairns, and Buenos Aires to São Paulo.

ORGANIZED TOURS

The rapid increase in long-haul package tourism in recent years hasn't passed New Zealand by, and there are now well over a dozen companies offering everything from flexible backpacker-orientated excursions through mainstream bus **tours** to no-expense-spared extravaganzas. Of course, they're not for everyone, but if time is limited and you have a fairly clear idea of what it is you want to do, there are good deals going. Even if an all-in package doesn't appeal, there may be some mileage in **pre-booking** some accommodation, tours or a rental vehicle – all things most agents listed in the box on p.5 can arrange.

Full "see-it-all" packages can work out quite expensive – to say nothing of being rather tame and controlled – but aren't bad value, considering what you'd be spending anyway. Basic **bus tours** range from 6 days around Northland for £850 to 17–21 day nationwide tours staying in four-star hotels with all meals, and various cruises and sightseeing included, costing around £3000. A number of companies, most notably Kiwi Experience and Magic Bus (see "Getting Around", p.24, for details), operate **flexible bus tours**, which you can hop off whenever you like and rejoin a day or two later when the next bus comes through.

Pretty much all the major tour operators can also book you onto **tramping trips**, including some of the guided Great Walks (see p.24); you'll still need to book way in advance, though. Mount Cook are the people to contact for **skiing** holidays in the South Island, based either at Queenstown for Coronet Peak and The Remarkables (6 days; £367), or at Methven for Mount Hutt (6 days; £290), including accommodation, transport from there to the field, ski passes and bus travel from Christchurch.

PACKAGE TOUR AND SPECIALIST OPERATORS

Most flight and travel agents can also arrange tours and accommodation – see box on p.5.

Australian Pacific Tours (☎0181/879 7444). Massive range of fully-inclusive bus tours, a 15-day national tour costing £2200 with meals, £1700 without.

Connections (☎0181/747 0333, fax 742 3045). Minibus tours for 18–35s, including all transport and most meals, but not international flights (5–16 days; £245–775).

Contiki (☎0181/290 6777). Bus tours for 18–35s "thriving on good times and loads of fun". Itineraries range from 3 days around the Bay of Islands (£139) to a 20-day grand tour (£1090), with accommodation and most meals included.

Explore Worldwide (☎01252/319 448). Small-group tours, staying in small hotels and including treks, canoeing and rafting (18–32 days; £2400–4000, around £900 less for land-only).

Journeys of Distinction (☎01695/578 140). Sedate and exclusive, fully-escorted tours (28 days; £3500).

Kuoni Worldwide (☎01306/741 111). A 20-day bus tour inclusive of flights from Britain and all accommodation (£2435–2953), as well as more flexible holidays ranging from 3 to 10 days.

Mount Cook Line (☎0181/741 5652, fax 741 2125). Major New Zealand holiday and travel company offering tame, planned-itinerary tours as well as flight and bus passes, motorhome rental and ski holidays.

Sunbeam Tours (☎01483/454 455). Bus tours, self-drive car and motorhome holidays, guided Great Walks, semi-independent tours at mid-range prices.

GETTING THERE FROM THE USA AND CANADA

Auckland is the only city in New Zealand that has direct, non-stop flights from North America. From there you will find several connections a day to the two other major airports, Wellington and Christchurch. The flying time from Los Angeles to Auckland is approximatly 12 hours 45 minutes.

The low season for fares is April 1 to August 31; shoulder season runs from September 1 to November 30 and through March; and high season is December 1 to February 28.

SHOPPING FOR TICKETS

Barring special offers, the cheapest of the airlines' published fares is usually an **Apex** ticket, although this will carry certain restrictions: you'll most likely have to book – and pay – at least 21 days before departure, spend a minimum of seven days and a maximum of one month, and you tend to get penalized if you change your schedule.

You can normally cut costs further, and possibly avoid some of the APEX restrictions, by going through a **specialist flight agent** – either a **consolidator**, who buys up blocks of tickets from the airlines and sells them at a discount, or a **discount agent**, who in addition to dealing with discounted flights may also offer special student and youth fares and a range of other travel-related services such as travel insurance, rail passes, car rentals, tours and the like. Bear in mind, though, that penalties for changing your plans can be stiff.

DISCOUNT FLIGHT AGENTS, TRAVEL CLUBS & CONSOLIDATORS

Air Brokers International, 323 Geary St, Suite 411, San Francisco, CA 94102 (☎1-800/883-3273; *www.aimnet.com/~airbrokr*). Consolidator and specialist in RTW and Circle Pacific tickets.

Airtech, 584 Broadway, Suite 1007, New York, NY 10012 (☎1-800/575-TECH). Standby seat broker; also deals in consolidator fares and courier flights.

Council Travel, 205 E 42nd St, New York, NY 10017 (☎1-800/226-8624; *www.ciee.org*), and branches in many other US cities. Student and budget travel agency.

High Adventure Travel, 353 Sacramento St, Suite 600, San Francisco, CA 94111 (☎1-800/350-0612; *www.highadv.com*). Round-the-world and Circle Pacific tickets. The Web site features an interactive database that lets you build your own RTW itinerary.

Now Voyager, 74 Varick St, Suite 307, New York, NY 10013 (☎212/431-1616; *www.nowvoyager travel.com*). Courier flight broker and consolidator.

Skylink, 265 Madison Ave, New York, NY 10016 (☎1-800/AIR-ONLY), plus branches in Chicago, Los Angeles, Montreal, Toronto, and Washington DC. Consolidator.

STA Travel, 10 Downing St, New York, NY 10014 (☎1-800/777-0112; *www.sta-travel.com*), plus branches in the Los Angeles, San Francisco and Boston areas. Worldwide discount travel firm; also student IDs, insurance, car rental and travel passes.

Travel CUTS, 243 College St, Toronto, ON M5T 1P7 (☎1-800/667-2887), and other branches all over Canada. Agent specializing in student fares, IDs and other travel services.

Worldtek Travel, 111 Water St, New Haven, CT 06511 (☎1-800/243-1723). Discount travel agency.

Some agents specialize in **charter flights**, which may be cheaper than anything available on a scheduled flight, but again departure dates are fixed and withdrawal penalties are high. If you travel a lot, **discount travel clubs** are another option – the annual membership fee may be worth it for benefits such as cut-price air tickets and car rental.

Remember that these companies make their money by dealing in bulk – don't expect them to answer lots of questions, and don't automatically assume that tickets from a travel specialist will be cheapest – once you get a quote, check with the airlines and you may turn up an even better deal. Be advised also that the pool of travel companies is swimming with sharks – exercise caution and *never* deal with a company that demands cash up front or refuses to accept payment by credit card.

FLIGHTS FROM THE USA

Air New Zealand, Qantas, and United have daily non-stop flights **from Los Angeles** to Auckland, with connections to Christchurch and Wellington, for a midweek round-trip Apex fare of $925, rising to $1337 in peak season. Expect to pay an extra $50–65 for weekend travel. Singapore Airlines fly daily from LA to Auckland via Singapore, and 4 days a week to Christchurch, again via Singapore, but their fares are significantly higher. And don't forget the discount travel companies, which sometimes offer fares for up to $200 less than those quoted above.

Flights from all **other US cities** are routed via Los Angeles. Air New Zealand and United quote **add-on fares** of $360 (from New York) or $310 (from Chicago), but shopping around the discount agents or checking out the newspapers for special offers could save you more than a few bucks.

FLIGHTS FROM CANADA

Canadian Airlines flies direct **from Vancouver** to Auckland, touching down in Hawaii, on Wednesdays and Fridays, with return flights on Fridays and Sundays. United have daily flights from Vancouver to Auckland via LA, with Air Canada connections from other Canadian cities. Depending on the season, sample Apex mid-week fares are in the following ranges: from

---

AIRLINES IN THE USA AND CANADA

Air Canada, in US ☎1-800/776-3000; in BC ☎1-800/663-3721; in Alberta, Saskatchewan and Manitoba ☎1-800/542-8940; in eastern Canada ☎1-800/268-7240
Air New Zealand, ☎1-800/262-1234, in Canada ☎1-800/663-5494
Canadian Airlines, ☎1-800/426-7000; in Canada ☎1-800/665-1177
Qantas, ☎1-800/227-4500
Singapore Airlines, ☎1-800/742-3333
United, ☎1-800/538-2929

Vancouver CAN$1489–1934; **from Toronto** CAN$1783–2228; from Montreal CAN$1909–2354. Finally, discount travel companies have been known to track down fares from Vancouver for CAN$1199, or from Toronto for CAN$1499.

RTW AND CIRCLE-PACIFIC ROUTES

If New Zealand is only one stop on a longer journey, you might want to consider buying a **Round-the-World (RTW)** ticket. A sample itinerary of LA–Fiji–Auckland–Bangkok–London–LA should cost around $1875 (low-season departure). An equally exotic option is a **Circle Pacific** ticket. Air New Zealand offer a "Pacific Escapade" ticket for $2600, valid for six months and with no limit to stopovers as long as you follow an onward circular route (no backtracking). However, a discount agent should be able to put together cheaper itineraries by combining sectors from different airlines, such as LA–Hong Kong–Bangkok– Auckland–Fiji–LA, starting from $1590.

ORGANIZED TOURS

Tour operators offer everything from luxury all-inclusive vacations to straightforward car-rental and accommodation **packages** (around $100 a day) and simple home stays (from $50 per night). There's also a seemingly infinite range of **activities** to indulge in, from wine-tasting to hanging out with miniature penguins (see box on p.9); flights, unless otherwise stated, are from Los Angeles.

SPECIALIST AGENTS AND TOUR OPERATORS

Abercrombie and Kent (☎1-800/323-7308). Upmarket operator with customized tours and set packages. Their 9-day cultural/historical sightseeing package is priced at $3024 (land costs and internal flights only).

Australian Pacific Tours (☎1-800/290-8687). Various land-only packages, including eco-tours of the national parks from $2065 (10 days) or $4595 (21 days).

Collette Tours (☎1-800/832-4656, in Canada ☎1-800/468-5955). Specialists in Australia and New Zealand travel. Their 13-day fully escorted tour of the North and South islands, including trips to glaciers and rainforests, starts at $2900 (land and air from NY).

Contiki Holidays (☎1-800/CONTIKI). Specialists in travel for 18–35s.

Different Strokes Tours (☎1-800/668-3301). Customized tours for gay travellers.

Elderhostel (☎617/426-8056). Educational and activity programmes for senior travellers. In addition to joint Australia/New Zealand packages, specialist tours include Gardens and Vineyards, Geysers and Greenstone, and Past and Present ($3340–4970, including return flights from LA).

Global Touring Inc (☎1-800/942-9399). South Pacific travel specialists. Their 12-day New Zealand Complete tour is priced at a very reasonable $1762, including airfares.

Inta-Aussie Tours (☎1-800/531-9222). North American agents catering to the cost-conscious, free-wheeling traveller: escorted tours, customized packages, transport and accommodation passes, etc.

KiwiPac Tours (☎ 650/595-2090). Options include a 12-day hiking trip for seniors (land and air from $3500) and customized packages geared to such activities as quilting, beer tasting and swimming with dolphins.

Mount Cook Tours (☎1-800/468-2665). Official agents for Air New Zealand, offering bus tours, treks, ski holidays, etc.

Newmans South Pacific Vacations (☎1-800/421-3326). Specialists in New Zealand vacations, with around 50 different package options in addition to fully independent tours. Their 21-day Overture to the South Pacific takes in Australia, Fiji and New Zealand and starts at $4929 (air and land package), while their New Zealand tours include 14-day bus tours (from $1695, land only) and a 5-day walking tour through the Fiordland National Park (from $1088, also land only).

New Zealand Travellers (☎1-800/362-2718). Backpacking and day-hiking tours of the South Island from $2200 (12 days, airfares extra).

Qantas Vacations (☎1-800/641-8772, in Canada ☎1-800/268-7525). Highly flexible packages, including fly-drives out of LA, with accommodation and one internal flight for $1680 (10 days) or $3300 (21 days).

Skylink Women's Travel (☎1-800/225 5759). Specialists in tours for lesbian travellers.

Sunbeam Tours (☎1-800/955-1818). Customized tours, along with several set packages. Their fully escorted 15-day sightseeing tour of the North and South Islands starts at $2200 (including airfare).

United Vacations (☎1-800/328-6877). Variety of fly-drives, excursions and escorted tours. A 14-day land/air package costs around $3000 (low season) or $4000 (high season).

GETTING THERE FROM AUSTRALIA

Australia–New Zealand routes are busy and competition is fierce, resulting in an ever-changing range of deals and special offers; your best bet is to check the latest with a specialist travel agent (see box on p.11). It's a relatively short hop across the Tasman: flying time from Sydney to Auckland is around 3 hours and 30 minutes.

All the fares quoted below are for travel during low or shoulder seasons; flying at **peak times** (primarily December to mid-January) can add substantially to these prices. Ultimately, the price you pay for your flight will depend on how much flexibility you want; many of the cheapest deals are hedged with restrictions – typically a maximum stay of thirty days, and an **advance-purchase** requirement. Qantas and Air New Zealand each have daily direct flights from most Australian cities to Auckland. Flights **from the eastern states** cost A$449–599, while flights **from Perth** start at A$859; flying to Wellington or Christchurch generally adds an extra A$150–200. Outside peak season, when the airlines often have surplus capacity, they may offer **promotional fares**, which can bring down prices to as low as A$399 for a 30-day return from Sydney to Auckland.

Open-jaw tickets – which let you fly into one city and out of another, making your own way between – can save a lot of backtracking, and don't add hugely to the total fare. For example, flying from eastern Australia into Auckland and out of Christchurch, or vice versa, with Qantas or Air New Zealand costs from A$699. There are also various **air passes** for internal flights available (see "Getting Around", p.24, for details).

Cruise **ships** do pass through the Pacific between November and January, but not on a regular basis; travel agents should be able to advise on which vessels are operating each season.

AIRLINES

Air New Zealand ☎13 2476.
Ansett Australia ☎13 1767.
Ansett New Zealand ☎1800/022 146.

Qantas, ☎1800/062 123.
Singapore Airlines, ☎13 1011.
United Airlines, ☎13 1777.

TRAVEL AGENTS

Anywhere Travel, 345 Anzac Parade, Kingsford, Sydney (☎02/9663 0411).

Brisbane Discount Travel, 260 Queen St, Brisbane (☎07/3229 9211).

Flight Centres Australia: 82 Elizabeth St, Sydney, plus branches nationwide (☎13 1600).

Northern Gateway, 22 Cavenagh St, Darwin (☎08/8941 1394).

STA Travel, Australia: 702 Harris St, Ultimo, Sydney; 256 Flinders St, Melbourne; other offices in state capitals and major universities (nearest branch ☎13 1776, fastfare telesales ☎1300/360 960). Web site: *www.statravelaus.com.au;* email: *traveller@statravelaus.com.au*

Thomas Cook, Australia: 175 Pitt St, Sydney; 257 Collins St, Melbourne; plus branches in other state capitals (local branch ☎13 1771, Thomas Cook Direct telesales ☎1800/063 913).

RTW TICKETS

If you're taking in New Zealand at the beginning (or end) of your **grand tour**, you can usually add a New Zealand stop at negligible extra cost, since most routes to the USA go via New Zealand gateway airports anyway. There's a vast range of **RTW routes** and your choice will largely depend on where you plan to travel after the Antipodes: sample routes from Sydney might take in Manila, Bangkok, Frankfurt, Honolulu, Fiji, Auckland and back to Sydney (from A$1745); or, starting from Adelaide, flying to Bangkok, Munich and Mexico City, then travelling overland to San Francisco, before picking up the homeward leg via Honolulu and Auckland back to Adelaide (from A$2389).

PACKAGES AND TOURS

There's a huge variety of holidays and tours to New Zealand available in Australia; call any of the travel agents listed in the box below. The holiday subsidiaries of airlines such as Air New Zealand, Ansett and Qantas package short **city-breaks** (flight and accommodation) and **fly-drive** deals for little more than the cost of the regular airfare.

If serious exploring, kayaking and tramping are high on your list, check out some of the **adventure tours**; these can be a good way of covering a lot of ground in a short time, and getting you to remote places that would otherwise be inaccessible without your own transport. A more economical option is offered by **backpacker-orientated companies** such as Kiwi Experience and Magic Bus (see "Getting Around", p.24), whose tours can be booked through STA and several other agents if you want to plan ahead.

In winter, Australians flock to the reliable snow of New Zealand's skifields, which are near enough to the eastern cities to allow for short breaks. Basic three-day airfare and accommodation **skiing** packages from Sydney start from A$634, rising to A$1084 for a seven-day trip to Queenstown, including return airfare, accommodation, lift passes and transport to the skifields.

SPECIALIST AGENTS AND TOUR OPERATORS

Adventure World (☎02/9956 7766 and 1800/221 931). Agents for Explore Worldwide's hotel and camping tours (15–29 days, A$3185–6365; airfares extra).

Kirra Tours (☎1800/888 242). Guided Great Walks, including the Milford Track (5 days, A$1350, excluding airfares), and wilderness trips to the Hollyford Valley, Fiordland and Stewart Island; also accommodation bookings.

Mount Cook Line (☎1800/221 134). Skiing packages, flightseeing, bus tours (4–14 days, A$856–1855) and all travel arrangements.

Naturally New Zealand Holidays (☎1800/331 582). Small-group eco-tours, guided walks and cycling trips (8 days around the Coromandel Peninsula, A$1695), Fiordland cruises (3 days, A$310) and tall-ship sailing holidays around the Bay of Islands and Hauraki Gulf (3–6 days, A$410–910); all land-only.

Qantas Holidays (☎1800/808 506). Fly-drive packages (3 days from A$526) and campervan holidays (5 days from A$534), plus accommodation passes and all-inclusive tours.

Pro Dive (☎02/9264 9499). Diving trips.

Value Tours (☎1800/222 001 and 02/9262 5611). Skiing and snowboarding holidays throughout New Zealand, plus airfares, car and campervan rental and accommodation passes.

VISAS AND RED TAPE

All visitors to New Zealand must have a passport and it must be valid for at least three months beyond the time you intend to stay, although if your home country has an embassy or consulate in New Zealand that can renew your passport, you can get away with one month.

On arrival, British citizens are automatically issued with a **permit** to stay for up to six months,

and a three-month permit is granted to citizens of most other European countries, Southeast Asian nations, Japan, the USA and Canada. Australian citizens and permanent residents can stay indefinitely.

Other nationalities need to obtain a **visa** from a New Zealand Embassy (see box below); a tourist visa costs the local equivalent of NZ$61 and is normally valid for three months.

The granting of a visitor permit or tourist visa is dependent upon your having evidence of **sufficient funds** to support yourself without working (about NZ$1000 a month, or NZ$400 a month if your accommodation is prepaid), in the form of a bank draft, cash, travellers' cheques, a statement from a New Zealand bank account, one of the major credit cards, or a friend or relative who is prepared to guarantee your accommodation and maintenance (although you are rarely asked to prove these things when you get off the plane). You must also have a confirmed **onward ticket** and right of entry (including any necessary visas) to your proposed destination.

Tourist visas, visitor permits and short-term work permits and study permits can be **extended** in three-month chunks up to nine months, and

---

NEW ZEALAND EMBASSIES AND CONSULATES ABROAD

Australia
High Commission: Commonwealth Avenue, Canberra, ACT 2600 (☎02/6270 4211, fax 6273 3194).
Consulates: Level 14, 1 Alfred St, Circular Quay, Sydney (☎02/9247 8567); 60 Albert Rd, Melbourne (☎03/9696 0501); Watkins Place Building, 288 Edward St, Brisbane (☎07/3221 9933).

Canada
High Commission: Suite 727, 99 Bank St, Ottawa, Ontario K1P 6G3 (☎613/238 5991).
Consulate: Suite 1200, 888 Dunsmuir St, Vancouver, British Columbia, V6C 3K4 (☎604/684 7388).

Ireland
Embassy: 46 Upper Mount Street, Dublin 2, (☎01/676 2464).

Japan
Embassy: 20–40 Kamiyama-cho, Shibuya-ku, Tokyo 150 (☎03/3467 2271/5).

Netherlands
Embassy: Carnegielaan 10, 2517 KH The Hague (☎70/346 9324).

UK
High Commission: The Haymarket, London SW1Y 4TQ (☎0171/973 0363).
Consulate: The Ballance House, 118a Lisburn Rd, Glenavy, Co. Antrim (☎01846/648 098).

USA
Embassy: 37 Observatory Circle NW, Washington, DC 20008 (☎202/328 4848, visa enquiries ☎202/328-4835).
Consulates: Suite 1150, 12400 Wilshire Boulevard, Los Angeles (☎310/207 1605); Suite 1904, 780 Third Ave, New York (☎212/832 4038).

"genuine tourists" may be able to get extensions up to a maximum stay of twelve months. Apply for extensions (each costing NZ$61) though the **New Zealand Immigration Service**, which has offices in Auckland, Christchurch, Dunedin, Hamilton, Manukau, Palmerston North and Wellington.

WORKING AND STUDYING

If working or studying is part of your plan, you're better off obtaining the **relevant visa** before entering the country. You can apply for a **short-term** work or study permit after you have entered New Zealand, but if it is granted, it will only cover the time left on your visitor permit.

British, Canadian and Japanese citizens between the ages of 18 and 30 may be able to obtain a **Working Holiday Visa**. This entitles you to undertake short-term work as you travel around the country for up to twelve months. Only two thousand such permits are granted each year, beginning in July, and are allocated on a first-come, first-served basis, so apply early.

A **long-term work permit** must be obtained before you enter New Zealand and will be granted only if you have a confirmed job offer and no New Zealand citizen is suitable and available for the post. These permits stipulate the type of employment in which you can engage and are normally valid for up to three years.

You can **study** for up to three months on a visitor permit, but to study longer you will need to obtain a study permit before you enter the country. For **further information** on the various permits and visas available, consult the *Visiting New Zealand* leaflet, which is stocked by all New Zealand embassies and consulates (see box on p.12).

CUSTOMS

In a country all too familiar with the damage that can be caused by the import of non-native plants and animals, New Zealand customs take particular care to minimize the chance of destructive foreign bodies being introduced to the delicate environment of the country. Aircraft cabins are sprayed with **insecticide** before passengers are allowed to disembark, to kill off any stowaway insects or micro-organisms; the spray is apparently harmless to humans.

It is prohibited to import certain goods into New Zealand. The following must be **declared** at customs and will either be treated or confiscated: fresh food, plants or parts of plants (dead or alive), animals (dead or alive), equipment used with animals, camping gear, golf clubs, used bicycles, biological specimens, and footwear (specifically walking boots). If your camping stuff or boots have soil deposits from other countries, they will be cleaned before being returned to you. The **duty-free allowance** is 200 cigarettes, or 250 grams of tobacco, or 50 cigars; alcohol allowances are a generous 4.5 litres of wine or beer, plus one bottle of not more than 1125ml of spirits.

There are restrictions on the **export** of wildlife, antiquities and works of art. If you're unsure, contact the nearest customs office; there are offices in Auckland, Christchurch, Dunedin, Invercargill, Napier, Nelson, New Plymouth, Tauranga, Mount Maunganui, Timaru, Wellington and Whangarei.

INSURANCE

With New Zealand's accident compensation scheme (see p.18) you may feel that the need for comprehensive travel insurance is reduced, especially if you have paid for your trip with a credit card, which may have limited levels of coverage included. Similarly, if you have a good "all risks" home insurance policy it may well cover your possessions against loss or theft even when overseas, and many private medical schemes also cover you when abroad – make sure you know the procedure and the helpline num-

ber. However, these often leave gaps in coverage and you still need a good travel insurance policy to cover the eventual costs. Premiums vary according to the level of coverage: pricier policies tend to be more comprehensive while others may cover only certain risks (accidents, illnesses, delayed or lost luggage, cancelled flights, etc). In particular, ask whether the policy pays medical costs up front or reimburses you later, and whether it provides for **medical evacuation** to your home country. Note also that very few insurers will arrange on-the-spot payments in the event of a major expense or loss; you will usually be reimbursed only after going home. In all case of loss or theft of goods, you will have to contact the local **police** to have a **report** made out so that your insurer can process the claim.

While in New Zealand you are quite likely to be participating in what are considered to be "dangerous activities" (skiing, mountaineering – even tramping qualifies under some policies), so be sure to ask whether these activities are covered: most companies – STA, Campus and others – have supplementary policies covering you for pretty much everything except bungy jumping. In the UK, Snowcard Insurance Services specialize in mountaineering and activity-holiday travel insurance.

TRAVEL INSURANCE COMPANIES

Most travel agents will arrange travel insurance at no extra charge.
The following insurance companies can be called directly.

BRITAIN AND IRELAND
American Express ☎0800/700 737.
Columbus Travel Insurance ☎0171/375 0011.
Endsleigh Insurance ☎0171/436 4451.
Snowcard Insurance Services ☎01327/262 805.
USIT Belfast ☎01232/324 073; Dublin ☎01/602 1600.
Worldwide ☎01732/773366.
Note: Good-value policies are also available through **Campus Travel** and **STA** (see p.5 for addresses).

USA AND CANADA
Access America ☎1-800/284-8300.
Carefree Travel Insurance ☎1-800/323-3149.
Desjardins Travel Insurance – Canada only ☎1-800/463-7830.
International Student Insurance Service (**ISIS**) – sold by *STA Travel* ☎1-800/777-0112.
Travel Guard ☎1-800/826-1300.
Travel Insurance Services ☎1-800/937-1387.

AUSTRALIA
Cover More ☎02/9202 8000 & 1800/251 881.
Ready Plan ☎03/9791 5077 & 1800/337 462.

BRITISH AND IRISH COVER

Most travel agents and tour operators will offer you insurance when you book your flight or holiday, and some will insist you take it. Such schemes (standard cover from around £33 a month) are sold by almost every travel agent or bank, and by specialist insurance companies (see box on p.14). These policies are usually reasonable value, but if you feel the cover is inadequate, or you want to compare prices, any travel agent, insurance broker or bank should be able to help.

If you're visiting New Zealand as part of a round-the-world, **extended trip**, Columbus does a special "Globetrotter" policy offering basic coverage (excluding baggage, money or missed departures) for £109 for 6 months or £185 for a year; more comprehensive cover for an entire year can cost as much as £360. While rates for annual **multi-trip** policies are enticing, some limit their cover to trips that last 30 days or less. However, Columbus does an annual multi-trip policy with as many trips of up to 60 days as you like for £89.50; and American Express has an annual travel insurance policy open to non-card holders for an unlimited number of worldwide trips up to 91 days (£94.95), up to a maximum of 183 days' cover.

Some insurance companies refuse to cover travellers **over 65**, and most that do charge hefty premiums; some of the best policies for older travellers are offered by Age Concern (☎01883/346 964).

AMERICAN AND CANADIAN COVER

Before buying an insurance policy, check that you're not already covered. Canadian provincial health plans typically provide some overseas **medical coverage**, although they are unlikely to

pick up the full tab in the event of a mishap. Holders of official student/teacher/youth cards are entitled to accident coverage and hospital in-patient benefits – the annual membership is far less than the cost of comparable insurance. **Students** may also find that their health coverage extends during the vacations and for one term beyond the date of last enrolment, and **homeowners'** or **renters'** insurance often covers theft or loss of documents, money and valuables while overseas.

After exhausting the possibilities above, you might want to contact a specialist **travel insurance** company; your travel agent can usually recommend one, or see the box on p.141. Note that most North American travel policies apply only to items lost, stolen or damaged while in the custody of an identifiable, responsible third party – hotel porter, airline, luggage consignment, etc. The best **premiums** are usually to be had through travel agencies – ISIS policies, for example, cost $48–69 for fifteen days (depending on level of coverage), $80–105 for a month, $149–207 for two months, $510–700 for a year.

AUSTRALIAN COVER

Travel insurance is available from most travel agents (see p.11) or direct from insurance companies (see box opposite), for periods ranging from a few days to a year or even longer. Most policies are similar in premium and coverage – but if you plan to indulge in high-risk activities such as mountaineering, bungy jumping or scuba diving, check the policy carefully to make sure you'll be covered. A typical policy covering the Pacific region (New Zealand, Bali, Fiji and Pacific islands) will cost A$85 for 2 weeks, A$125 for 1 month, and A$180 for 2 months.

TRAVELLERS WITH DISABILITIES

New Zealand is disabled-traveller-friendly, but that does not mean everything is rosy. Many public buildings, galleries and museums are accessible to disabled travellers, but as a rule restaurants and local public transport make few concessions.

Long-distance **transport** companies will generally offer disabled travellers help with boarding, but on-board access to toilets and other amenities can be difficult for wheelchair users. All **accommodation** in New Zealand should have at least one room or unit suitable for disabled travellers but the level of facilities and access varies considerably, often depending on the age of the building in ques-

tion. On the plus side, many **tour operators** are prepared to go to that extra bit of trouble to enable travellers with disabilities to participate in activities.

PLANNING A TRIP

There are **organized tours and holidays** specifically for people with disabilities – the contacts in the box below will be able to put you touch with any specialists for trips to New Zealand. If you want to be more **independent**, it's important to become an authority on where you must be self-reliant and where you may expect help, especially regarding transport and accommodation. It is also vital to be

---

BEFORE YOU LEAVE: USEFUL ORGANIZATIONS

UK

Access Travel, 16 Haweswater Ave, Astley, Lancashire M29 7BL (☎01942/888 844). Tour operator that can arrange flights, transfers and accommodation.

Holiday Care Service, 2nd floor, Imperial Building, Victoria Rd, Horley, Surrey RH6 7PZ (☎01293/774535). Provides free list of accessible accommodation in New Zealand.

RADAR (Royal Association for Disability and Rehabilitation), 12 City Forum, 250 City Rd, London EC1V 8AF (☎0171/250 3222; Minicom ☎0171/250 4119). Produces a holiday guide to long-haul destinations (£5, including p&p) every two years, devoting five pages to New Zealand.

Tripscope, The Courtyard, Evelyn Rd, London W4 5JL (☎0181/994 9294). This registered charity provides a national telephone information service offering free advice on international transport and travel for those with a mobility problem.

IRELAND

Irish Wheelchair Association, Blackheath Drive, Clontarf, Dublin 3 (☎01/833 8241). Provides information for wheelchair travellers intending to go to New Zealand, including travel, accommodation and activities.

USA

Directions Unlimited, 720 N Bedford Rd, Bedford Hills, NY 10507 (☎914/241-1700). Travel

agency specializing in custom tours for people with disabilities.

Society for the Advancement of Travel for the Handicapped (SATH), 347 5th Ave, Suite 610, New York, NY 10016 (☎212/447-7284; *www.sittravel.com*). Non-profit travel-industry referral service that passes queries on to its members as appropriate; allow plenty of time for a response.

Travel Information Service (☎215/456-9600). Telephone information and referral service.

Twin Peaks Press, Box 129, Vancouver, WA 98666 (☎360/694-2462 or 1-800/637-2256). Publisher of the *Directory of Travel Agencies for the Disabled* ($19.95), listing more than 370 agencies worldwide; *Travel for the Disabled* ($19.95); the *Directory of Accessible Van Rentals* ($9.95); and *Wheelchair Vagabond* ($14.95), loaded with personal tips.

CANADA

Jewish Rehabilitation Hospital, 3205 Place Alton Goldbloom, Chomedy Laval, Quebec H7V 1RT (☎514/688-9550, ext. 226). Guidebooks and travel information.

AUSTRALIA

ACROD (Australian Council for Rehabilitation of the Disabled), PO Box 60, Curtin, ACT 2605 (☎02/6282 4333). Provides lists of useful organizations, plus specialist travel agencies and tour operators.

honest – with travel agencies, insurance companies and travel companions. Know your limitations and make sure others know them. If you do not use a wheelchair all the time but your walking capabilities are limited, remember that you are likely to need to cover greater distances while travelling (often over rougher terrain and in hotter temperatures) than you are used to. If you use a wheelchair, have it serviced before you go and carry a repair kit.

Read your travel **insurance** small print carefully to make sure that people with a pre-exisiting medical condition are not excluded. And use your travel agent to make your journey simpler: airline or bus companies can cope better if they are expecting you, with a wheelchair provided at airports and staff primed to travel. A **medical certificate** of your fitness to travel, provided by your doctor, is also extremely useful; some airlines or insurance companies may insist on it. Make sure that you have extra supplies of drugs – carried with you if you fly – and a prescription including the generic name in case of emergency. Carry spares of any clothing or equipment that might be hard to find; if there's an association representing people with your disability, contact them early in the planning process.

Once you're **in New Zealand**, several organizations provide information for travellers with disabilities and give practical advice on where to go and how to get there (again, see box on p.16 for contact details).

ACCOMMODATION

The New Zealand Tourism Board's *Where to Stay Guide* provides a few useful pointers on disabled-friendly accommodation, with **countrywide listings**, in which disabled facilities are indicated by a wheelchair symbol.

Current New Zealand **law** stipulates that any newly built hotel, hostel or motel must have at least one room modified for disabled access and use. Much pre-existing accommodation establishments have also **converted rooms** to meet these requirements, including most YHA hostels, some motels, campsites and larger hotels. Older buildings are least likely to lend themselves to such conversions.

TRAVELLING

Few airlines, trains, ferries and buses allow complete independence. Air New Zealand provides a special wheelchair narrow enough to move around in the plane, and the rear toilet cubicles are wider than the others to facilitate access; other **domestic**

airlines will provide help, if not always extra facilities. Cook Strait **ferries** have reasonable access for disabled travellers, including physical help while boarding, if needed, and adapted toilets. If given advance warning, **trains** will provide attendants to get passengers in wheelchairs or sight-impaired travellers on board, but moving around the train in a standard wheelchair is impossible and there are no specially adapted toilets; the problems with long-distance **buses** are much the same.

Some specifically adapted **taxis** (for wheelchairs) are available in the cities, but must be pre-booked; otherwise taxi drivers obligingly deal with wheelchairs by throwing them into the boot and their occupant onto a seat. The **New Zealand Total Mobility Scheme** also allows for anyone unable to use public transport to use taxis at a subsidized rate (50 percent); a list of participating areas and companies is available from the Disabled Persons Assembly (see box below), who will also arrange for the necessary vouchers to be issued. The staff on **public buses** will endeavour to lend a hand, but buses are difficult to board. Some small **minibus** conversions are available and **shuttle buses** will help you board and stow your chair, but it pays to let the operator know beforehand of your particular needs. The Disabilities Resource Centre (again, see box below) can provide lists of companies with **rental cars** adapted for disabled travellers.

HEALTH

New Zealand is relatively free of serious health hazards and the most common pitfalls are not taking precautions or simply under-estimating the power of nature. No vaccinations are required to enter the country, but you should make sure you have adequate health cover in your travel insurance, especially if you plan to take on the Great Outdoors (see p.49 for advice on tramping health and safety).

New Zealand has a fine health service, despite recent government cuts, and medical services are reasonably cheap by world standards. Although visitors are covered by the **accident compensation scheme**, under which you can claim some medical and hospital expenses in the event of an accident, without full accident cover in your travel insurance (see p.14), you could still face a hefty bill. For more minor ailments, you can visit a **doctor** for a consultation ($30) and, armed with a prescription, buy any required medication at a reasonable price.

AIDS is as much of an issue in New Zealand as elsewhere but official attitudes are reasonably enlightened, and there are no restrictions on people with HIV or AIDS entering the country. **Support organizations** include the New Zealand AIDS Foundation, 76 Grafton Rd, Grafton, Auckland (☎09/303 3124) and the 24-hour HIV/AIDS National Hotline (☎0800/802 437).

THE SUN

The biggest health problem for visitors to New Zealand is over-exposure to the **sun**, which shines more fiercely here than in the northern hemisphere, its damaging ultra-violet rays reaching a far greater intensity. You should take extra care, especially at first, to avoid burning. New Zealand has a high rate of **skin cancer**, so it makes sense to slap on maximum-protection **sunblock**. Remember to **re-apply** every few hours as well as after swimming, and you should avoid sunbathing altogether between 11am and 3pm, when the sun is at its strongest. Keep a check on any moles on your body and if you notice any changes, during or after your trip, see a doctor right away.

BUGS AND CRITTERS

Something worth avoiding is **giardia**, a parasite that inhabits rivers and lakes in some national parks. Infection results from drinking contaminated water, with symptoms appearing several weeks later: a bloated stomach, cramps, explosive diarrhoea and wind. The Department of Conservation advises on the likely presence of giardia in national parks around the country. To minimize the risk of infection, purify **drinking water** by using iodine-based solutions or tablets (regular chlorine-based tablets aren't effective against giardia); by fast boiling water for at least seven minutes; or by using a giardia-rated filter (obtainable from any outdoors or camping shop).

The relatively rare **amoebic meningitis** is another water-borne hazard, this time contracted from hot thermal pools. The amoeba enters the body via the nose or ears, lodges in the brain, and weeks later causes severe headaches, stiffness of the neck, hypersensitivity to light, and eventually coma. If you experience any of these symptoms, seek medical attention immediately, but to avoid contamination in the first place, simply don't put your head underwater in thermal pools.

Virtually without exception, New Zealand **wildlife** is harmless. Even **shark attacks** are rare; you are more likely to be carried away by a strong tide than a great white, though it still pays to be sensible and obey any local warnings when swimming. The country is free of snakes, scorpions and other nasties, and there's only one poisonous creature: the **little katipo spider**. Mercifully rare, this 6mm-long critter (the biting female is black with a red patch), is found in coastal areas – except in the far south – and only bites if disturbed. The bite can be fatal, but antivenin is available in most hospitals, is effective up to three days after a bite and no one has died from an encounter with the spider for many years. The West Coast of the South Island in the summer is the worst place for **mosquitoes** and **sandflies**, though they appear to a lesser degree in many other places across the country. They are more irritating than dangerous and a liberal application of repellent keeps most of them at bay.

GEOLOGICAL HAZARDS

Although common in New Zealand, **earthquakes** are usually minor. If the worst happens, the best advice is to stand in a doorway or crouch under a table. If caught in the open, try to get inside; failing that, keep your distance from trees and rocky outcrops to reduce the chances of being injured by falling branches or rocks. New Zealand's **volcanoes** also have a habit of making their presence felt: vulcanologists are often able to predict periods of eruptive activity, and if warnings are issued, get as far away as possible.

INFORMATION AND MAPS

New Zealand promotes itself heavily and enthusiastically abroad through the New Zealand Tourism Board (see box below), where enquiries will trigger a deluge of glossy brochures. Much of it comprises inspirational, if rose-tinted, images of the country but is of limited practical use; specific requests can prove far more fruitful.

Many of the information centres listed below, as well as some cafés, bars and hostels, keep a supply of **free** newspapers and **magazines** orientated towards backpackers and usually filled with promotional copy, but informative nonetheless. Two of the best are the *New Zealand Backpackers News* and *TNT*.

VISITOR CENTRES

Once you arrive you'll soon be weighed down with leaflets advertising just about everything in the country. Every town of any size will have an **official visitor centre**, signified by the green Visitor Information Network (VIN) logo. These are invariably well-stocked, staffed by helpful and knowledgeable personnel and sometimes offer

NEW ZEALAND TOURISM BOARD OFFICES

The **New Zealand Tourism Board** head office can be contacted at PO Box 95, Wellington, New Zealand (☎04/472 8860, fax 478 1736).

Australia 8/35 Pitt St, Sydney, NSW 2000 (premium-rated information line ☎1902/260 558, 50¢ per minute; fax 02/9241 1136).

Canada Suite 1200-888 Dunsmuir St, Vancouver BC, V6C 3K4 (☎604/684 2117, fax 684 1265).

Germany Friedrichstrasse 10–12, 60323 Frankfurt am Main (☎069/971 2110, fax 971 2113); handles Western European and Nordic enquiries.

Japan Shinjuku Monolith 21st Floor, 2-3-1Nishi, Shinjuku-ku, Tokyo (☎03/5381 6331, fax 5381 6327).

United Kingdom New Zealand House, Haymarket, London, SW1Y 4TQ (premium-rated information line ☎0839/300 900, fax 0171/839 8929); also handles enquiries from Ireland.

USA Suite 300, 501 Santa Monica Blvd, Santa Monica, CA 90401 (☎310/395 7480 & 1800/388 5494, fax 395 5453); 780 3rd Ave, Suite 1904, New York, NY 10017-2024 (☎212/832 8482, fax 832 7602).

MAP OUTLETS

BRITAIN

Stanfords in London is the UK's largest map sellers, and operates a **mail-order service**, as do most bookshops. By far the best outlet for **New Zealand** books, **maps** and **periodicals** in Britain is Kiwifruits: The New Zealand Shop, 7 Royal Opera Arcade, Pall Mall, London SW1Y 4UY (☎071/930 4587, fax 839 0592), who also run a mail-order service.

Aberdeen Map Shop, 74 Skene St, Aberdeen AB10 1QE (☎01224/637 999).

Daunt Books, 83 Marylebone High St, London W1M 3DE (☎0171/224 2295); 193 Haverstock Hill, London NW3 4QL (☎0171/794 4006).

Heffers Map Shop, in Heffer's Stationery Department, 19 Sidney St, Cambridge CB2 3HL (01223/568 467).

John Smith and Sons, 57–61 St Vincent St, Glasgow G2 5TB (☎0141/221 7472).

National Map Centre, 22–24 Caxton St, London SW1 0QU (☎0171/222 2466).

Newcastle Map Centre, 55 Grey St, Newcastle upon Tyne NE1 6EF (☎0191/261 5622).

Stanfords, 12–14 Long Acre, London WC2E 9LP (☎0171/836 1321); maps can be ordered by phone on this number. Other branches in London are located at 52 Grosvenor Gardens, London SW1W 0AG (☎0171/730 1314), and 156 Regent St, London W1R 5TA (☎0171/434 4744).

The Travel Bookshop, 13–15 Blenheim Crescent, London W11 2EE (☎0171/229 5260).

IRELAND

Easons Bookshop, 40 O'Connell St, Dublin 1 (☎01/873 3811).

Waterstone's, Queens Bldg, 8 Royal Ave, Belfast BT1 1DA (☎01232/247 355); 7 Dawson St, Dublin 2 (☎01/679 1260); 69 Patrick St, Cork (☎021/ 276 522).

USA

Book Passage, 51 Tamal Vista Blvd, Corte Madera, CA 94925 (☎415/927-0960).

The Complete Traveller Bookstore, 199 Madison Ave, New York, NY 10016 (☎212/685-9007).

Map Link, 30 S La Petera Lane, Unit #5, Santa Barbara, CA 93117 (☎805/692-6777).

The Map Store Inc., 1636 1st St, Washington DC 20006 (☎202/628-2608).

Phileas Fogg's Books & Maps, #87 Stanford Shopping Center, Palo Alto, CA 94304 (☎1-800/533-FOGG).

Rand McNally, 444 N Michigan Ave, Chicago, IL 60611 (☎312/321-1751); 150 E 52nd St, New York, NY 10022 (☎212/758-7488); 595 Market St, San Francisco, CA 94105 (☎415/777-3131); call ☎1-800/333-0136 (ext 2111) for other locations, or for maps by mail order.

Sierra Club Bookstore, 6014 College Ave, Oakland, CA 94618 (☎510/658-7470).

CANADA

Open Air Books and Maps, 25 Toronto St, Toronto (☎416/363-0719).

Ulysses Travel Bookshop, 4176 St Denis, Montreal (☎514/843-9447).

World Wide Books and Maps, 736 Granville St, Vancouver (☎604/687-3320).

AUSTRALIA

Bowyangs, 372 Little Bourke St, Melbourne (☎03/9670 4383).

The Map Shop, 16a Peel St, Adelaide (☎08/8231 2033).

Perth Map Centre, 891 Hay St, Perth (☎08/9322 5733).

Travel Bookshop, 20 Bridge St, Sydney (☎02/9241 3554).

some form of video or slide presentation on the area. Apart from dishing out local maps and leaflets, they'll book you into accommodation, get you on trips and activities, and book onward travel, all at no extra charge. In the more popular tourist areas, you'll also come across all manner of places presenting themselves as independent **information centres**, which always follow a hidden agenda, typically promoting a number of allied adventure companies. While these can be useful, it's worth remembering that their advice won't be impartial.

Other useful resources are the **Department of Conservation offices** and field centres, usually sited close to wilderness areas and popular tramping tracks, and often serving as the local visitor centre as well. Again these are highly informative and well geared to trampers' needs, with local weather forecasts, intentions forms and maps.

Finally, drivers who are already members of motoring associations at home can generally make use of New Zealand's **Automobile Association** (AA), which provides many useful services to drivers (see p.28) and supports a nationwide network of offices (see "Listings" throughout the Guide), stocking excellent maps and providing information on accommodation.

MAPS

Specialist booksellers (see box on p.20) should have a reasonable stock of **maps of New Zealand**. The best available is the two-sided 1:1,000,000 edition produced by *International Travel Maps*, with all the important roads, and an attractive and instructive colour scheme giving a good sense of the country's terrain. The 1:2,000,000 maps produced by *GeoCentre* and *Bartholemew* come a distant joint second. **Road atlases** are widely available in New Zealand bookshops and service stations; the best are those produced by the AA, all of which indicate the type of road surface – though some roads marked as unsealed have since been tar-sealed. The AA also provide their members with simple

---

NEW ZEALAND ONLINE

Needless to say, the following list of recommended addresses won't remain current for long, but as many of the sites are well linked, you'll discover the up-and-coming sites pretty quickly.

TRAVEL SITES

New Zealand Tourism Board *www.nztb.govt.nz*
Somewhat tame official site but a fair starting point, with useful links to other Kiwi-related Web sites.

Department of Conservation *www.doc.govt.nz*
DOC's web presence with a motherlode of stuff on the environment and the latest conservation issues.

New Zealand Bed & Breakfast Guide
www.kiwihome.co.nz/stay/B-B
Electronic listing of this handy guide to most of New Zealand's B&Bs.

Budget Backpacker Hostels
www.backpack.co.nz
Net version of the "Blue Book" backpacker hostels guide, with details of all the hostels.

VIP Hostels
www.backpackers.com.au/bpnz/htm
Straightforward list of member hostels with an online reservation facility.

YHA *www.yha.org.nz/yha*
Official YHA site with everything you need to know about membership and the hostels themselves.

GENERAL INTEREST – AND FUN

Flying Nun *www.flyingnun.co.nz*
Official site of Dunedin's seminal record label, Flying Nun, with material on local-guys-made-good bands Bailterspace, The Chills and Tall Dwarfs, as well as a Kiwi-rock discography and info on the latest releases and tours.

The Press *www.press.co.nz*
Excellent site of New Zealand's best daily paper with the latest news and reviews and a good subject search facility.

Rugby *www.rugbynet.co.nz*
Heavily New Zealand-orientated rugby news with results of past games, team line-ups and the like.

Soda *www.soda.co.nz*
Website of an organization promoting Kiwi Web sites, with hot links to recent award-winners in various categories. Something for everyone.

The Wizard *www.chch.planet.org.nz/wizard*
The official site for Christchurch's eccentric Wizard, complete with his upside-down world and all sorts of other buffoonery and homespun philosophy .

but effective strip maps of major touring routes free of charge.

With a road atlas and our city plans you can't go far wrong on the roads, but more detailed maps may be required for **tramping**. All the major walks are covered by the *Trackmap* series, complete with photos ($11 from DOC offices and bookshops in New Zealand), or go for the larger scale *Topo* maps ($12.50), which cover the whole country.

NEW ZEALAND ON THE NET

Perhaps because of its geographical isolation, New Zealand has embraced the **Internet** with a vengeance and in recent years there has been a rapid proliferation of **Web sites**. Many are primarily promotional tools but are handy nonetheless: we've included a few of the most useful and entertaining in the box on p.21.

COSTS, MONEY AND BANKS

After a few years riding the crest of an economic wave, New Zealand has recently seen a slight downturn in the economy and a consequent dip in the value of the New Zealand dollar. Nonetheless, most things remain fairly expensive, though largely on a par with prices in North America and Europe. The quality of goods and standards of service you can expect are comparably high and, on balance, the country offers good value for money.

New Zealanders are a straightforward bunch and the price quoted is what you pay. In almost all cases, the 12.5 percent Goods and Service Tax (GST) is almost always included in the listed price.

The **currency** is the Kiwi dollar, or "buck", divided into 100 cents. There are $100, $50, $20, $10 and $5 paper notes, and coins in denominations of $2 and $1, and 50¢, 20¢, 10¢ and 5¢; prices are sometimes given to the nearest cent, but the final bill is rounded up or down to the nearest five cents.

SOME BASIC COSTS

New Zealand is well set up for visitors, but **budget travellers** are especially well catered for, with an extensive network of backpackers' hostels and discounts on travel and the all-too-tempting array of adventure activities that can easily wreak havoc with your spending money.

The **minimum expenditure** if you are camping, hitching or cycling, preparing most of your own food and keeping a tight rein on tours and activities would be in the region of $30 a day, rising to $40–60 if you stay in hostels, use public transport and indulge in the odd meal out. Couples staying in hostel rooms or homestays, eating at unpretentious restaurants and not skimping on attractions and activities are looking at around $70–90 each per day; and if you rent a car for at least some of your stay, sleep in comfortable B&Bs and eat well, you should reckon on at least $100 a day. All these figures can be ramped up dramatically once you start bungy jumping and jetboat riding, though this can be offset by abstemious tramping days. With the prevalence of good hostels, **single travellers** can live almost as cheaply as couples, though you'll pay around thirty percent more if you insist on having a room to yourself.

Accommodation costs from as little as a couple of dollars for a basic campsite, but an $8 per-person pitch or a $12–17 dorm bed in a hostel is more common. Simple double rooms start from as little as $35, though you'll pay $70–90 for a motel unit, $70–120 for homestays and

B&Bs, and anything from $100–250 for flash international-standard hotels. **Food** is good quality, though not especially cheap; supermarkets are reasonably priced and you can usually find a filling plateful at a pub or café for under $10. A reasonable three-course meal will cost upwards of $30, though you can save on drinks by patronizing **BYO** (Bring Your Own) restaurants, where you can drink wine you've brought with you. **Drinking** in pubs and restaurants is substantially more expensive than buying from a bottle shop or from a supermarket, though the latter only sell wine.

Given New Zealand's compact size, **transport** costs shouldn't be prohibitive, but if you find yourself moving on every couple of days it can soon add up. Though you are unlikely to return from New Zealand laden with souvenirs, you can completely blow your budget on **adventure trips** – such as a bungy jump (around $130) or tandem parachuting ($180 and up). If you've got the money, by all means spend it; if not, think carefully about how best to get the maximum enjoyment from your visit.

Student **discounts** are few and far between, but you can make substantial savings on accommodation and travel if you buy either the YHA or VIP cards (see box p.25); kids and seniors enjoy reductions of around fifty percent on most trains, buses and entry to many sights.

TRAVELLERS CHEQUES, CREDIT AND DEBIT CARDS

There are **no exchange controls** in New Zealand, so you can bring in as much in cash and travellers' cheques as you like.

The safest way to carry your money is still as **travellers' cheques**, which can be exchanged efficiently at banks and bureaux de change all over New Zealand and will be replaced if they are lost or stolen. Recognized brands – American Express, Thomas Cook, Mastercard and Visa – are accepted in all major currencies and, though cheques in New Zealand dollars relieve the uncertainty of fluctuating exchange rates, they aren't generally accepted as cash. You usually pay one to two percent commission when you buy travellers' cheques but there is seldom an additional charge when you cash them.

As a back-up, or even a primary source of funds, **credit cards** are extremly useful: Visa, Mastercard, Bankcard and, to a lesser extent,

American Express and Diners Club cards are widely accepted. You'll find more resistance at supermarkets, and many hostels, campsites and homestays will only accept cash, though YHAs do accept cards. You'll also find credit cards useful for advance booking of accommodation and trips, and with the appropriate PIN you can obtain **cash advances** through 24-hour ATMs found almost everywhere, though you should be aware that such withdrawals may accrue interest immediately or be subject to a two percent premium – check with your bank before you go too wild. Most ATMs also have the facility for **international debit card** transactions using the Plus and Cirrus networks.

CREDIT CARD HOTLINES

To report **lost** or **stolen** cards in New Zealand, call:

American Express	☎0800/656 660
Bankcard (Access/Mastercard)	☎0800/800 468
Diners Club	☎0800/652 582
Visa	☎0508/724 200

BANKS AND EXCHANGE

The best **exchange rates** are usually from **banks** – BNZ, ANZ, Westpac, Postbank and The National Bank have branches in towns of any size and are open from Monday to Friday 9.30am to 4.30pm except for public holidays, while city branches stay open on Saturday until around noon. Outside banking hours, you'll have to rely on **bureaux de change** in the big cities and tourist centres, which are typically open from 8am to 8pm daily. If you get caught short, the larger hotels will often change travellers' cheques at any time, but rates tend to be poor.

If you are spending some time in New Zealand – say a couple of months or more – it makes life a lot easier if you open a **bank account**, a surprisingly easy process, requiring only a couple of

---

EXCHANGE RATES

Exchange rates tend to be fairly stable in relation to the Australian and US dollars, less so against European currencies. The **New Zealand dollar** currently trades at NZ$2.30 for £1, NZ$1.45 for US$1 and NZ$1.10 for A$1.

pieces of ID and an address for statements. The ANZ bank seem particularly helpful and maintain an extensive network of branches and accessible ATMs.

The big advantage of having an account is that you can get money from branches and ATMs using a **cash card**, the same piece of plastic doubling as an **EFTPOS** (Electronic Funds Transfer at Point of Sale) card. This enables you to pay for stuff at shops, service stations, restaurants, in fact just about anywhere, by swiping the card and punching in your PIN (Personal Identification Number). Almost everywhere will also give you cash, so you can go for weeks without visiting a bank, which has to be a good thing.

EMERGENCY CASH

If you run out of money, or there is some kind of emergency, the best way to get money sent out is get in touch with your bank at home and have

Western Union offices

Australia	☎1800/649 565
Canada	☎1800/361 1872
Ireland	☎1800/395 395
New Zealand	☎0800/270 000
UK	☎0800/833 833
USA	☎1800/325 6000

them **wire money** to the nearest bank. Depending how much you're prepared to pay for a fast buck, this takes anything from a few minutes (around NZ$80 for a transfer of NZ$2000) to a week (roughly $25). Thomas Cook Moneygram runs a similar service, as does American Express for its members. Perhaps the most convenient of all is Western Union (see box above), with near-instantaneous transfers for comparable fees and the facility for the sender to phone the transfer through using their credit card.

GETTING AROUND

New Zealand is a relatively small country and getting around is easy, with some form of transport going to most destinations.

Although it is possible to **fly** to most destinations in New Zealand, you need to consider whether the time you save outweighs the substantial expense involved. With time to spare you will appreciate the scenery better by travelling

more slowly and at ground level. The **rail** service is fairly limited and is also quite expensive, as are the Interislander **ferries** that connect the North and South islands. The cheapest and easiest way to get around is by **bus** or **shuttle bus** but this is also the most time-consuming mode of travel. With careful planning, you can reduce your costs by **booking in advance** and taking advantage of the many special offers and **reduced fares** (see box on p.25).

For getting off the beaten track, you'll need a car. **Rental cars** are fine for short periods, but if you are staying in the country for more than a month, it's more economical to **buy** a car, provided you're not averse to some haggling and paperwork. New Zealand is renowned for its green countryside and some travellers prefer to **cycle** their way around – a fine way of seeing the country, so long as you're fit and in no great hurry.

However, you'll still need to take to the air or the water (or your feet) to reach the **offshore islands** and the more **remote** parts of the country that remain stubbornly impenetrable by road, such as Fiordland.

Regular long-distance bus, train and plane services can be found under **Travel details** at the
end of each chapter, with local buses and
trains covered in the main text.

DOMESTIC FLIGHTS

Domestic flights are generally **expensive**, but
may well be worth it if you have limited time in
the country – especially if you can bag a **standby
bargain** or tag one on to your international flight
for a little extra. The stranglehold of the major
carriers, Air New Zealand and Ansett, results in
the absurd situation whereby it is sometimes
cheaper to fly from New Zealand to Australia than
to fly between the North and South islands. There
are, however, a number of small companies (most
wholly or partly owned by ANZ or Ansett) flying
specific routes that offer good deals from time to
time; check the latest with local visitor centres.

Both Air New Zealand and Ansett offer a broad
range **fares** for domestic flights, from the usual
business and economy classes to limited-
availability **advance-purchase tickets** that are
only bookable in New Zealand; see box on p.26
for more on these and **concessionary fares**
available to backpackers and seniors. A full-fare
economy-class flight from Auckland to
Christchurch is currently about $343. Two of the
most **useful short hops** are the very scenic
Southern Air flights from Invercargill to Stewart
Island ($34–68) and the Ansett and Air New
Zealand flights to Milford Sound from
Queenstown ($150) – both places it's difficult and
time-consuming to reach by other methods.

Flights can be **booked** through travel agents,
some visitor centres or direct with an airline; special offers are widely promoted at airports or in
visitor centres around the country.

FERRIES

The ferries you're most likely to use are those plying the **Cook Strait** between the North and South
islands, but there are also ferries to Stewart
Island from the South Island and from Auckland
across the Hauraki Gulf and over to Coromandel.
Information about these short ferry trips is includ-

FARE CONCESSIONS

Backpacker discounts of 30–50 percent are available on many forms of transport to holders of YHA
or VIP cards (see box on p.36). Fare concessions are also available to **children** on provision of proof of
age, as are **seniors**' discounts – with the exception of over-60s airfares, which are only available to
New Zealand residents.

FLIGHTS
Advance-purchase fares (7–14 days) give
30–50 percent discount on all Air New Zealand,
Ansett and Mount Cook flights.
Standby fares (50 percent off) are available on
some Air New Zealand and Ansett flights to
holders of YHA and VIP cards.

FERRIES
Advance-purchase fares (7 days) give 15–50
percent discount on selected sailings.

TRAINS
Advance-purhase fares (economy, saver and
auper saver), offering discounts of 25–50 percent, are available in limited numbers; **day-
excursion** fares are discounted by 30 percent.
No Frills tickets are available in limited numbers, offering significant reductions (around 50

percent) for travelling in older, non-air-condi-
tioned carriages; call ☎0800/802 802 for details.
A discount of 30 percent is available to **YHA** and
VIP card holders.
Over 60s are entitled to a 30 percent reduction
on all services.
Blind and other **disabled travellers** are entitled
to a 50 percent discount if they present auth-
orization (from the DPA; see p.16).

BUSES
YHA and **VIP** cardholders get 30 percent off
fares with all three of the major companies
(InterCity, Newmans and Mount Cook); and 5 percent off with Kiwi Experience.
Advance-purchase fares offer 30 percent discount for tickets bought 5 days ahead of travel,
and there are a limited number of 50 percent discounts available on a first-come, first-served basis.

ed in our accounts on Invercargill (see p.608) and Auckland (see p.65).

The Interislander fleet that shuttles between **Wellington** on the North Island and **Picton** on the South Island consists of three ferries and the quicker wave-piercing catamaran called the *Lynx* (nicknamed the Vomit Comet, for all-too-obvious reasons). The **ferries** run seven days a week year-round, take around three hours, are very reliable and surprisingly comfortable in most conditions. The standard fare is $44 one-way, though this can be reduced by as much as half if you book in advance or take a night or early morning crossing; add $12 each way for a bike, $160 for a car. The *Lynx* **wave-piercer** operates between

Wellington and Picton from December to April, but is cancelled if the swell is greater than half a metre. A standard fare is $59, less if booked well in advance, or in conjunction with special offers; bikes cost an extra $15, cars another $190.

Reservations can be made for both services at travel agents or by phone or fax (☎0800/802 802, fax 0800/101 525); you'll generally get the best deal by booking direct.

TRAINS

Tranz Rail **trains** are a fast method of travel to a limited number of destinations in New Zealand, despite the fact that they seem to have been kept

NEW ZEALAND TRAVEL PASSES

Travel passes generally offer unlimited travel within a specified period. You'll probably get your money's worth if you're determined to see a lot in a limited amount of time, but if you prefer a more leisurely pace, think carefully before you buy. Most can be bought either before you leave or after you arrive, but **air passes** are usually restricted to **non-residents** of New Zealand.

FLIGHTS

Air New Zealand and Ansett **air passes** both work out at around $150 per flight; good value if you are flying between the main islands but otherwise not a great saving; Air New Zealand's pass is also valid on Mount Cook Airline services. For both passes, the minimum purchase is **3 coupons** ($450) and the maximum is **8** ($1140), each redeemable for one flight. You can get a refund on any left over coupons, so long as you apply before you leave the country.

BUSES

Bus passes either offer unlimited stops along a **fixed route**, or a fixed number of **travel days** within a certain time frame.

InterCity offer **fixed-route passes**, including the **North Island** Coromandel Loop Pass (Thames to Coromandel, Whitianga and back; $40); **Eastland Passport** (around the east coast to Gisborne and then inland to Taupo and Rotorua; $98); **North Island Value Pass** (any route between Auckland and Wellington; $95); and the **North Island Combo Pass** (which combines any two of the above for $130–180). Prices for their **South Island** passes are seasonal: options include the **West Coast Passport** (Nelson to

Queenstown; April–Oct $99, Oct–April $114); the **East Coast Explorer** (Te Anau to Picton, via Dunedin and Christchurch; $105/$120); and the **Milford Bound** (Christchurch to Milford, via Mount Cook and Queenstown; $105/$120); any combination of two of these is available as a **South Island Combo Pass** ($199/$229).

Of the passes that allow a certain number of **travel days**, Newmans **FlexiPass** is valid on services of several operators for a certain number of travel days in a three-month period. The deal is either One Island (7 days, $295; 10 days, $375; 15 days, $495; then $30 for each additional day) or Two Islands (7 days, $395; 10 days, $495; 15 days, $595 and $40 for each additional day). The best deal among the Mount Cook Landline passes is the **Southern Discovery Coach Pass**, which allows unlimited travel around the South Island – from 7 travel days over 30 days ($335) to 33 travel days over 90 days ($699).

COMBINED TRAVEL PASSES

Tranz Rail's range of travel passes combine trains, buses and planes. The **3 in 1 pass** is valid for travel on trains and InterCity buses and for one Interislander ferry crossing (5 days' travel over 10 days, $350; 22 days in 8 weeks, $690). The **4 in 1** version offers all the above plus one domestic flight on Ansett or Air New Zealand (5 travel days $580, 22 days $920).

Tranz Rail Scenic Thoroughfares are a range of fixed-itinerary tickets that connect the North and South islands, combining trains with the Interislander ferries and selected bus services, for example Wellington–Christchurch ($85), or Christchurch–Auckland ($165).

largely as a **tourist attraction**, with the exception of the **commuter services** that run into Wellington from the Hutt Valley and Palmerston North.

Most carriages are air-conditioned, with on-board phones and huge picture windows; airline-style meals (including vegetarian options) are served at your seat, and there's also a buffet car. Passengers check in on the platform before boarding (a ticket guarantees a seat) and bags are carried in a luggage van. As a contrast to the trains, stations tend to be in a depressingly run-down state.

These days **services** are limited. On the North Island, trains run from Auckland to Wellington; from Hamilton to Tauranga and Rotorua; from Palmerston North to Gisborne; from Napier to Palmerston North and on to Wellington; and from Masterton to Wellington. On the South Island, the main service operates between Picton and Invercargill along the east coast only. From Christchurch, a branch line runs to Greymouth on the west coast, while further south at Dunedin another service cuts inland to Middlemarch. These last two services are scenic trips run almost entirely for the benefit of tourists and are priced accordingly.

Tranz Rail have a multi-tier **fare** structure, with advance-purchase and concessionary fares available only within New Zealand (see box on p.26). The minimum fare is $14, no matter how short your journey, and a standard, non-discounted ticket from Auckland to Wellington is $129; Picton to Christchurch will set you back $60.

Tranz Rail also offers a range of **passes** for unlimited travel for a certain number of days within a specified period and **fixed-itinerary tickets** (see box on p.26). For further information and advance **bookings**, call Tranz Rail on ☎0800/802 802 or fax on 0800/101 525.

BUSES

Buses and **shuttle buses** (minibuses) are the cheapest form of public transport and will get you to most places. In general, they are reliable and reasonably comfortable: the larger buses are usually air-conditioned; some have toilets and show feature films and New Zealand promotional material to while away longer journeys. The three **main bus companies** are InterCity (who operate on both islands), Newmans (with services concentrated on the North Island) and Mount Cook Landline (who run between Auckland and Wellington, via Rotorua, on the North Island and serve most destinations on the South Island).

Standard **fares** with most bus companies from Auckland to Wellington are in the region of $96; Christchurch to Queenstown, $70; Queenstown to Nelson, $152; though prices often plummet during peak periods and a range of discounted fares is available (see box on p.26). Bus **bookings** can be made by phone: InterCity (Mon–Fri 7am–8pm & Sat–Sun 7am–7pm; in Auckland ☎09/357 8400, in Wellington ☎04/472 5111, in Christchurch ☎03/379 9020); Newmans (☎0800/777 707); Mount Cook Landline (☎0800/800 287, fax 0800/699 800), or at most visitor centres and travel agents. Note that once you've bought your ticket or pass, you may incur an agent's **reservation fee** of $3 unless you book bus seats direct.

SHUTTLE BUSES

A host of **shuttle bus** companies around the country fill the gaps, linking with the services of the major operators to take you off the beaten track. Some shuttle operators also compete with the big companies on the main routes – though generally cheaper, they're not as comfortable over long distances. Most major bus companies don't operate on unsealed roads, so in areas such as the remoter parts of the Coromandel Peninsula and the Catlins you'll probably have to resort to shuttle buses.

Most visitor centres carry shuttle-bus timetables, so you can compare destinations and fares. **Fares** can be as low as half the price of standard (but not discounted) bus fares, for example Christchurch to Queenstown ($35), or Queenstown to Nelson ($99), though these vary with supply and demand.

BACKPACKER BUSES AND TOURS

One of the cheapest ways to cover a lot of ground is on a **backpacker bus**, which combines the flexibility of independent travel with the convenience of a tour. The deal is that you purchase a ticket for a fixed route (valid for up to 6 months), then either stick with the one bus, or stay in some places longer and hop on a later bus. Unlike more conventional tours, the ticket does not cover the cost of accommodation, adventure activities (although these are often discounted), side-trips or food.

Kiwi Experience (Auckland ☎09/366 1665, Wellington ☎04/385 2153, Christchurch ☎03/377

0550) has something of a reputation for rowdy group-bonding, drinking and encouraging participants to do the same things, in the same place, at the same time. They offer seventeen trips (2–20 days; $104–610). **Magic Bus** (Auckland ☎09/358 5600, Wellington ☎04/387 2018, Christchurch ☎03/377 0951) trips are generally less gung-ho and target the more independently minded, offering eleven options (3–15 days; $125–449).

More along the lines of a fully fledged tour, but specifically orientated towards backpackers, **Flying Kiwi** (☎03/573 8126) offer **budget bus tours** where participants muck in with the cooking and dishes. Vehicles are equipped with bikes, canoe, windsurfer, kitchen, awning, fridge, beds, tents and hot shower. Aiming to get off the beaten track a little, their trips operate all year, with seven options available (3–24 days; $120–1200); food costs extra, and you should allow around $7 per day. An even more complete wilderness experience for anyone who is reasonably fit is on offer from **New Zealand Nature Safaris**, 52 Holborn Drive, Wellington (☎0800/NZSAFARI, fax 04/563 7324). Good-humoured and informative guides take small groups tramping, climbing and wilderness camping in virtually untouched country (9–10 days; $650–720).

A few regionally-based companies offer variations on the same theme on specific routes, and these are detailed throughout the Guide.

> New Zealand domestic **travel arrangements** can be made in advance through most **travel agents** (see boxes on pp.6, 9 and 11); some also act as agents for Kiwi Experience and others bus and train travel.

DRIVING

If your budget will stretch to it, driving is the best way to go, enabling you to get to places beyond the reach of public transport and to set your own timetable.

In order to **drive** in New Zealand you need a valid **licence** from Australia, Britain, Canada, Fiji, Germany, Namibia, The Netherlands, Switzerland or South Africa; citizens of other countries need to obtain an International Driver's Licence before they leave (available from national motoring organizations).

Road rules are similar to those in the UK, Australia and the US, but if you plan to do much

driving, you should pick up a copy of *The Road Guide* from AA offices or selected bookshops and newsagents for $14.95. The one variation peculiar to New Zealand is that you must **give way** to all traffic crossing or coming from your right; this means that if you are turning left and another car coming from the opposite direction wants to turn right into the same side-road, you must let them go first. Most importantly, **drive on the left**, and remember that **seatbelts** are compulsory for all occupants. Always **park** in the same direction as that in which you are travelling; roadside parking facing oncoming traffic is illegal.

The **speed limit** for the open road is 100km/hr, reduced to 50km/hr in built-up areas and in limited speed zones (signposted **LSZ**) when road conditions are deemed unsafe – owing to bad weather, poor visibility, crossing pedestrians, cyclists, or excessive traffic. The fine for speeding is currently $120; some drivers warn others of lurking police patrols by flashing their headlights at oncoming cars. **Drink driving** is a major problem in New Zealand: as part of a campaign to cut the death-toll, random breath tests have been introduced, and offenders are dealt with severely.

Unleaded and super unleaded **petrol** and **diesel** are available in New Zealand. Prices hover around 91¢ a litre for unleaded, 96¢ for super unleaded, and 60¢ for diesel, with predictably higher prices in more out-of-the-way places.

The New Zealand **Automobile Association (AA)** has reciprocal rights with motoring organizations from lots of other countries, so check with your home service before you leave. If you don't qualify and you'll be driving your own vehicle, consider joining the AA as an overseas visitor ($50, plus $20 joining fee), valid for six months, or as a full member ($66, plus $20 joining fee), valid for a year. Apart from free 24-hour emergency **breakdown service** (☎0800/500 222) – excluding vehicles bogged on beaches – membership entitles you to free maps, accommodation guides and legal assistance, discounts on some rental cars and accommodation, plus access to insurance and pre-purchase vehicle inspection services.

Road conditions are generally good: most roads are sealed, although a few have a "**metalled**" surface composed of an aggregate of loose chippings. Obviously, these are slower to drive along, are prone to wash-outs and landslides after heavy rain, and demand considerably more care and attention from the driver. Metalled roads are clearly marked on most maps, so plan your route carefully beforehand. Some car-rental companies **prohibit** the use of their cars on the worst metalled roads – typically those along Ninety Mile Beach, Skippers Canyon and around the Coromandel Peninsula. Always **check conditions locally** before setting off on these routes.

Compared with most parts of the world, there are relatively few cars on New Zealand's roads, but **traffic** can still be a problem around the major cities and on public holidays. Other **hazards** include flocks of sheep and slow, wide farm equipment on country roads, as well as monstrous logging trucks in forested regions.

RENTING A CAR OR CAMPERVAN

Although you can get good **rental deals** with the major international companies (Avis, Budget and Hertz all operate in NZ – see below for reservation numbers) before you leave home, if you have a few days to spare when you arrive you'll usually get cheaper rates from **local firms**. Competition is fierce, so there are always deals to be had. Your best bet is to go for mid-range firms (we've listed the more reliable outfits throughout the Guide), rather than the sometimes-unscrupulous outfits that appear to offer rock-bottom rates.

Renting a **car** in New Zealand is fairly simple: you need a full, clean driver's licence and you must be over 21; drivers under 25 often have to pay more for insurance. For most roads you won't need **four-wheel drive** and, since 4WD rental rates are steep (usually $10–20 extra per day), you'll do best to rent for specific areas rather than long term. **Daily rates** with the major companies are in the region of $80 for a small two-door hatchback, or $90 for a medium-sized four-door saloon. With mid-range and smaller companies you can get a car on the road for about $45 a day, although many advertise deceptively cheap rates, then add on extra charges for insurance and mileage up to this level. **Weekly rates** should save you around $5 or $10 per day – keep your eyes peeled for deals.

One-way rental is handy but usually incurs a large drop-off fee, which can be as much as $100–120. However, since most one-way rentals seem to go from north to south, if you're travelling in the opposite direction, you may be able to sweet-talk your way out of drop-off charges. In particular, there is often a glut of cars in Queenstown or Christchurch which the company would be glad to get dropped off in Picton; the same applies in Wellington, if you're heading upcountry to Auckland.

Remember that car rental is a **seasonal** business: from December to February business is good and prices are at their highest, but for the rest of the year the companies will be prepared to make deals rather than leave their vehicles idle, so shop around and don't be afraid to haggle. **Before signing** on the dotted line, always **check** the following points:

● The accident cover and bond. Before giving you a car, rental companies take a credit-card slip or a cash bond from you for anything up to $1000 (usually between $500 and $750). If you have an accident, the bond is used to pay for any damage: in some cases you pay anything up to the value of the bond; in others you pay the entire bond, no matter how slight the damage.

● A Value of Collision Damage Waiver will cost extra but means that if you have an accident, you won't automatically forfeit your bond.

● Check exactly how much damage you'll be liable for in the event of an accident. Although some companies only charge a $500 bond, the contract might stipulate that you are in fact liable for the first $1000 worth of damage.

● Check the car for any visible defects, so you won't end up being charged for someone else's mistakes.

● Check whether there are any restrictions on driving along certain roads.

● If you'll be driving a fair distance, avoid limited-mileage deals whereby you pay for each kilometre in excess of a set daily allowance.

● Check that insurance cover is adequate, bearing in mind any existing travel or vehicle insurance you may have.

A rented **campervan** provides independence, accommodation and a mobile kitchen. The disadvantages are its potential for isolating your from Kiwis and fellow travellers, the risk of theft – and the expense, though this is offset by savings on accommodation, especially for families and groups. Campervan-rental **rates** average about $150 a day during the high season (Oct–April), dropping to $90 the rest of the year. The two most popular rental firms are Maui and Brits: NZ (see box on p.30), but a few smaller companies in New

Zealand offer campervans and converted delivery vans at slightly cheaper rates. Freedom Campervans (☎09/275 3034 in Auckland, ☎03/379 3822 in Christchurch), who also have an office in the UK (see box), offer vans for $74–124 a day, depending on season, and Greentours (☎0800/399 935) have converted Toyota vans for $55 a day or $330 a week, year round.

Although no special licence is required to drive a campervan, some caution is needed, especially in high winds and when climbing hills and going around tight corners. Bear in mind, too, that you are not allowed to **park** a campervan in a lay-by **overnight** – though you're unlikely to be hassled in isolated areas.

BUYING A USED CAR

Buying a used car in New Zealand can be **cost-effective** if you are staying in the country for more than eight weeks or so. Reselling can recoup enough of the price to make it a cheaper option than using public transport or renting a car long term, though reselling without a guaranteed buy-back can be a lengthy process.

A decent car bought privately will **cost** anything from $1500, whereas one bought from a garage will begin at around $4000; if you pay less than this, chances are you'll be buying a petrol- and oil-guzzling disaster. Check over vehicles carefully, taking into account their age and the number of previous owners. Since the majority of people buy cars in Auckland and then try to sell them in Christchurch, as a buyer in Christchurch you often have more choice and are in a better bargaining position. For general pointers, call the premium-rated AA Techline (Mon–Fri 8.30am–5pm; ☎0900/58324, 99¢ per minute), who can fill you in on the good and bad points about a range of vehicles and their running costs, and advise on maintenance and approximate value.

The major points of entry (Auckland, Christchurch and Wellington) have plenty of **garages** falling over themselves to sell you a used car, some also offering a **buy-back service** at the end of your trip, usually paying about fifty percent of the original purchase price. This is only useful if you are returning to the city of purchase; some garages guarantee to buy back the car but also give you the option to try to sell it privately first for a better price.

If you're mechanically minded and confident of your ability to spot a lemon, you can try to pick up a cheap car at an **auction** or **fair**; they're held weekly in Auckland and Christchurch, and are advertised in the local press. Buying a car in a **private sale** is a good compromise if you don't know your big end from your steering column. Trawl the local papers or noticeboards at supermarkets and hostels for likely candidates. If you buy from a **fellow traveller**, you might be able to negotiate a canny price if their flight is imminent or get some useful extras (camping equipment and the like) thrown in. Just make sure you arrange a **vehicle inspection**, either from the AA (contact the local technical centre; numbers listed in *AA Services Handbook*) or from Car Inspection Services of Auckland (☎09/309 8084); this will set you back around $75–80, but may save you buying a wreck and/or give you enough ammunition to negotiate a significant price reduction. Finally, before you close a private sale, call **Autocheck** (☎0800/658 934), which will warn you if there's money owing on a vehicle being sold privately, a **debt** that a buyer would inherit.

Before they're allowed on the road, all vehicles must have a **Vehicle Inspection Certificate** (VIC), which is a test of its mechanical worthiness and safety. VICs are carried out and issued for specified garages and last for a year. Always check the expiry date, as the test must have been carried out no more than 28 days before you apply to register the car.

When you buy a car you have to **transfer** the vehicle **ownership** by filing a form (filled in by buyer and seller) at the post office, but it should already be registered. If it isn't, or in any case when it runs out, you'll have to pay for **registration** (6 months, $110; 12 months, $206). Next you'll need **insurance** (approximately $150 for 6 months) – shop around or use the AA if you're a member. Although it's not compulsory to have insurance in New Zealand, you'll pay through the nose if you risk it and are involved in an accident, whether it's deemed to be your fault or not.

HITCHING AND CAR SHARES

Although many travellers enthuse about **hitching** in New Zealand – and it does enjoy a reputation of relative safety – the official advice is don't. Sadly, New Zealand has its share of unpleasant individuals and, with an extensive network of affordable transport and tours at your disposal, there's really little reason to take unnecessary **risks**. If you're determined to do it regardless, hitch in pairs (no guarantee of avoiding trouble

but safer than going solo). **Women**, especially, should trust their instincts: it's better to refuse a lift than regret it later; there will always be another car. Always ask the driver where they are going, rather than telling them where you're headed, and keep your gear with you so you can make a quick get away if it becomes necessary.

Finding the best **hitching spots** around the country is generally a matter of common sense, or common knowledge on the travellers' grapevine. Some town and city hostels drop their guests at hitching spots as a matter of course; pick a spot where you can be clearly seen and drivers can stop safely.

A good compromise is **car share**, where the cost of travel is shared. You can organize this formally through organizations such as Travelpool in Auckland (daily 9am–8pm; ☎09/307 0001) and Travelshare in Wellington (daily 8am–9pm; ☎04/473 5558), to whom you pay a commission for the introduction service, before signing a contract with the driver to split the cost of the journey; obviously the more of you there are, the cheaper it gets. Casual car shares are also advertised on hostel noticeboards, which saves on commission but demands more trust on both sides.

MOTORBIKING

Although motorbikes are generally cheaper to buy than cars and more economical from a fuel point of view, bear in mind that you'll also be more **exposed** to the elements and be able to carry considerably less stuff with you. Be prepared for riding on **unsealed roads**, which can be a far-from-pleasant experience, and be sure you know what you're doing – there's nothing worse than having to push a broken-down bike a few kilometres to the nearest town. Note also that to ride a motorbike your international licence must specify motorbikes.

A worthwhile **secondhand bike** will set you back approximately $1000, and the registration procedure is the same as for cars (see p.30). Motorbikes can be **rented** or bought (outright or on a buy-back basis) from Graham Crosby Motorcycles Ltd, 299 Great North Rd, Grey Lynn, Auckland (☎09/376 2711, fax 376 5033), or through the same channels as cars (see p.30).

CYCLING

Cycling is an excellent way of appreciating the countryside, especially if you're reasonably fit and keep your time on the main highways to a minimum. Disadvantages are dealing with **unsealed roads**, which become irksome if you're on them all day and wreak havoc with your tyres (fat tyres limit the damage).

Contrary to what you might think, cycling New Zealand's mountainous **South Island** is easier than in the North Island. The South Island's north–south alpine backbone presents virtually the only geographical barrier, while the eastern two-thirds of the island comprise a flat plain. By contrast, in the **North Island** you can barely go 10km without encountering significant hills – and you have to contend with significantly more traffic, including overbearing logging trucks.

If you do get sick of pedalling, you can always hoick your bike onto a **bus** or **train** for around $10–12 per trip. Another possibility is to combine pedal power with stints on Kiwi Experience's backpacker buses, which will also cart spare gear to your next destination. With their **Wild Cycles** operation (☎09/366 1445, fax 357 0524), you get a month's bike rental for $440 and buy bus vouchers (2 for $75, 5 for $110), each good for one day's travel.

Most people seem to prefer using mountain **bikes** but since the majority of riding is on roads, touring bikes are just as good; **helmets** are required by law. If all you want to do is explore locally, some **hostels** and guesthouses have pre-loved bikes you can use for a nominal sum, or even for **free**. **Renting** bikes for more than the odd day can be an expensive option, costing anything from $15–35 a day, depending whether you want a bike with little more than pedals and brakes, a tourer, or a state-of-the-art mountain

bike. Specialist cycle shops also do economical monthly rental for around $200 for a touring bike, $300 for a full-suspension superbike.

If you plan on any long-distance cycle-touring, it's generally cheaper to **buy**, though you have to factor in the cost of transporting the bike by bus or train (see above) if you shirk the longer hauls. Hostel noticeboards are the place to look for bargains (between $150 and $300 is a reasonable deal), often accompanied by extras like wet-weather gear, lights, helmet and a pump; some cycle shops will guarantee **buy back** at the end of your trip for about fifty percent of the purchase price.

It is possible to bring **your own bike** to New Zealand by plane and if you intend to cycle a lot this is the cheapest option. On most airlines, assuming you prepare and package them appropriately, bikes simply count as a piece of luggage and don't incur any extra cost so long as you don't exceed your baggage limit. It's easy enough to find **spares** in cities and larger country towns but in the more out-of-the-way places you may have to wait some time for spares to be delivered.

Visitors with extensive cycling in mind should get in touch with **Adventure Cycles** (☎09/309 5566) or **Cycle Xpress** (☎09/379 0779), both in Auckland. If you're bringing your own bike they'll let you store the bike box you transported your machine in, help you organize an emergency package of spare parts and extra clothing to be forwarded at your request, and give your bike a final once over before you set off, all for around $20. They also operate buy-back schemes (see above), which are good value for anything longer than a two-month tour.

ACCOMMODATION

which cover the whole spectrum from a room in someone's suburban home to pampered luxury in a country mansion.

In the last decade or so, New Zealand has, together with Australia, pioneered the **backpacker hostel**, a less-regimented alternative to traditional **YHAs**, which have transformed themselves dramatically to compete. Found all over the country, hostels offer superb value to budget travellers.

Wherever you stay, you can expect unstinting **hospitality** and a truckload of valuable advice on local activities and onward travel. As far as facilities go, there is almost always some form of laundry, and tea and coffee are often provided free.

Accommodation will make up a fair chunk of your spending while in New Zealand, and while rates can seem rather high, they are matched by excellent standards. Almost every town has a motel or hostel of some description, so finding accommodation is seldom a problem – though it's advisable to book in advance from Christmas through to the end of January when Kiwis take their summer holidays, and a couple of months either side when places fill with international visitors.

Kiwis travel widely at home, most choosing to self-cater at the country's huge number of well-equipped **motor camps** and **motels**, shunning **hotels**, which cater mainly to package holiday-makers and the business community. An appealing alternative is the range of **guesthouses**, **bed & breakfasts**, **homestays** and **farmstays**,

HOTELS AND MOTELS

In New Zealand, a "**hotel**" may not be quite what you expect. The term is frequently used to describe old-style **pubs**, which were once legally obliged to provide rooms for drinkers to recuperate from their excesses. Many no longer provide accommodation, but some have transformed themselves into backpacker hostels, while others are dedicated to preserving the tradition. At their best, hotels offer comfortable rooms in characterful, historic buildings, though just as often lodgings are rudimentary. Hotel bars are frequently at the centre of smalltown social life and, at weekends in particular, they can be pretty raucous; for the asking price of around $50 a double, you may find a budget room at a hostel a better bet.

ACCOMMODATION PRICES

Accommodation listed in this guide has been categorized into one of nine price bands, as set out below. The rates quoted represent the **cheapest available** double or twin **room** (single rooms generally cost only 10–20 percent less) in **high season** – except for category ①, which are per-person rates for a **dorm bed**; fees for **tent sites** and **DOC huts** are also per-person, unless otherwise stated. In the lower categories, most rooms will be without **private bath**, though there may well be a washbasin in the room. From the ⑤ band upwards, you'll more than likely have private facilities.

Prices normally include Goods and Services Tax (**GST**), as do our codes, though some more business-orientated places may give the GST-exclusive price.

① under $20 per person	④ $60–80	⑦ $140–180
② under $40 per room	⑤ $80–100	⑧ $180–240
③ $40–60	⑥ $100–140	⑨ over $240

In the **cities** and **major resorts**, you'll also come across hotels in the conventional sense, predominantly business- or tourbus-orientated places with all the usual trappings of international-style establishments. Priced accordingly, they're seldom good value, usually costing $150–300 a room, though at quiet times and weekends there can be substantial discounts; it's always worth asking.

Most Kiwi families on the move prefer the astonishingly well-equipped **motels**, which congregate along the roads running into town, making them more convenient for drivers than for those using trains or buses. They come provided with bed linen, towels, TV, a full kitchen and tea and coffee, but are often depressingly functional concrete-block places with little to distinguish one from another. Rooms range from all-in-one-room **studios** ($60–80 for two), with beds, kettle, toaster and microwave;' through **one-bed-room units** ($70–90 for two), usually with a full and separate kitchen; to two- and three-bedroom **suites**, sleeping six or eight. Suites generally go for the same basic price as a one-bedroom unit, with each additional adult paying $12–18, making them an economical choice for groups travelling together. Anything calling itself a **motor inn** or similar will be quite luxurious, with a bar, restaurant, swimming pool and sauna but no cooking facilities.

GUESTHOUSES AND B&BS

While families might prefer the freedom and adaptability of a motel, couples are generally better served by a guesthouse or bed and breakfast (B&B). These terms are used almost interchangeably in New Zealand, though the cheaper places are more likely to call themselves **guesthouses**, offering simple rooms, usually with a bathroom down the hall and a modest continental breakfast included in the price.

A **B&B** may be exactly the same as a guesthouse, but the term also encompasses simple homestays, and luxurious colonial homes with well-furnished en-suite rooms and sumptuous home-cooked breakfasts. Those at the top end are now fashioning themselves as "**boutique hotels**" and "exclusive retreats", where standards of service and comfort are raised to extraordinary levels, with prices to match.

Roughly speaking, **rates** for a double room are around $60–80 at guesthouses, $70–120 at B&Bs, $120–250 at boutique hotels and reach stratospheric levels when it comes to the exclusive retreats, where $800 a night is not unheard of. Rates drop in the low season, and these places can often be exceptionally good value. If you're travelling alone and don't fancy hostels, B&Bs can also be a viable alternative, usually charging **lone travellers** 60–80 percent of the double room rate.

HOMESTAYS AND FARMSTAYS

Homestays usually offer a guest room or two in an ordinary house where you muck in with the owners and join them for breakfast the following morning. Staying in such places can be an excellent way to meet ordinary New Zealanders; you'll be well looked after, sometimes to the point of being overwhelmed by your hosts' generosity. Always try to book ahead, and bear in mind you'll usually have to pay in cash. Rural versions often operate as **farmstays**, where you're encouraged to stay a couple of nights and are welcome to spend the intervening day trying your hand at farm tasks: rounding up sheep, milking cows, fencing, whatever might need doing. Both homestays and farmstays charge $55–80 for a double room, including breakfast; some cook dinner on request for $15–25 per person, and you'll pay a small fee for lunch if you spend the day at the farm.

There are also places where you can **work for your keep**, typically toiling for four hours a day in return for board and lodging. FHiNZ, PO Box 99, Woodville (☎ & fax 06/376 4582), organize stays on farms, orchards and horticultural holdings for singles, couples and families, and no experience is needed. Over 120 places are listed in their booklet ($15) and accommodation ranges from basic to quite luxurious. An organization run along the same lines is the international **WWOOF** (Willing Workers on Organic Farms, PO Box 1172, Nelson; ☎ & fax 03/544 9890), which coordinates some 180 properties (booklet $20), mostly farms but also orchards, market gardens and self-sufficiency orientated smallholdings, all using organic methods to a greater or lesser degree. They'll expect a stay of at least two nights, though much longer periods are common; armed with the booklet, you then **book direct** (preferably a week or more in advance). Most hosts will work you three to four hours a day and vary the tasks to keep you interested, but there have been occasional reports of taskmasters; make sure you discuss what will be expected of you before you commit yourself. Property managers are vetted but **lone women** may feel happier seeking placements with couples or families.

HOSTELS AND BACKPACKERS

New Zealand is awash with budget, self-catering places, pretty much interchangeably known as **hostels** or **backpackers** and offering a bed for around $15. As often as not they're in superb locations – bang in the centre of town, beside the beach, close to a ski field or amid magnificent scenery in a national or forest park – and are invariably great places to meet others, hook-up to the travellers' grapevine and pick through the mass of local information, aided by genuinely helpful managers. Wherever you stay, you'll find a fully-equipped kitchen, laundry, TV and games room, a travellers' noticeboard, and a stack of tourist information. Often there'll also be a pool, barbecue area, bike and/or canoe rental and information on local work opportunities. If you **book ahead** – essential in December and January, and preferable through February and March – hostels may even pick you up from the nearest public transport.

Many hostels allow you to pitch a tent in the grounds for around $10 a person, but generally the most basic and **cheapest accommodation** is in a 6–12 bunk dorm ($12–17), with 3–4 bed "shares" usually priced a dollar or two higher. Most hostels nowadays also have double, twin and family rooms ($18–25 per adult), the more expensive ones with en-suite bathrooms. Unless you are planning on only using YHA hostels (where all bedding is provided), you can save money by carrying your own sleeping bag or sleeping sheet.

The odd **YMCA** and **YWCA** does exist but with plenty of other choices and the tendency of Ys to cater to long-termers, they are rarely the most appealing option.

YHAS

New Zealand's **YHA hostels** are some of the best of their kind in the world. They're clean, secure, well-equipped, run by trained staff, and frequently beautifully sited, though despite their best modernizing efforts some still retain an institutional feel. They've now abandoned daily chores, arcane opening hours (but office hours are still generally limited to 8–10am & 5–10pm) and strict segregation of the sexes, though there's almost always a dorm solely for women. Newer hostels have been purpose-built to reflect the YHA's environmental concerns, promoting recycling and energy conservation; older places are likely to be converted schools or large houses.

Sixty hostels are listed in the annual *YHA Accommodation Guide* (free to members) and the condensed *Good Bed Guide* version (free to all). Over half of these are **full YHA hostels** open only to members: either obtain a Hostelling International Card in your own country (see box below) or join in New Zealand, where you can stump up the $24 annual membership fee or pay $4 on top of the normal price on each of your first six nights. The rest of the hostels are affiliated **associate hostels**, where no membership card

---

HOSTELLING INTERNATIONAL OFFICES

Australia 422 Kent St, Sydney (☎02/9261 1111); 205 King St, Melbourne (☎03/9670 9611); 38 Stuart St, Adelaide (☎08/8231 5583); 154 Roma St, Brisbane (☎07/3236 1680); 236 William St, Perth (☎08/9227 5122); 69a Mitchell St, Darwin (☎08/8981 2560); 28 Criterion St, Hobart (☎03/6234 9617).

Canada Room 400, 205 Catherine St, Ottawa, ON K2P 1C3 (☎1-800/663-5777 or 613/237-7884).

England and Wales Trevelyan House, 8 St Stephen's Hill, St Albans, Herts, Al1 2DY (☎01727/855 215); London shop and information office: 14 Southampton St, London WC2 7HY (☎0171/836 1036).

Ireland 61 Mountjoy St, Dublin 7 (☎01/830 4555).

New Zealand PO Box 436, Christchurch 1 (☎03/379 9970).

Northern Ireland 22 Donegall Rd, Belfast BT12 5JN (☎01232/324 733).

Scotland 7 Glebe Crescent, Stirling, FK8 2JA (☎01786/451 181).

USA 733 15th St NW, Suite 840, PO Box 37613, Washington, DC 20005 (☎202/783 6161; *www.hostel.com*).

is required, though there is often a discount of a dollar or so for members. At full YHAs all bedding is supplied, whereas associate hostels usually charge a small additional fee if you are not using your own sleeping bag or sheet.

At the cheapest hostel, you can pay as little as $9, and in some city places as much as $19, though the majority of beds fall into the $14–17 range. You can book ahead either from another hostel (they charge $1 for the phone call) or through the YHA National Reservations Centre, PO Box 68 149, Auckland (☎09/309 2802, fax 373 5083; email *yhaakbg@yha.org.nz* Web site *www.yha.org.nz/yha*) using a credit card or bank draft; you can also make advance bookings before you leave through Hostelling International offices in your home country (see box on p.35).

BACKPACKER HOSTELS

YHAs are outnumbered five-to-one by independent **backpacker hostels**. Quality is more variable than in YHAs: a few fall well short of expected standards, with disinterested staff and cramped rooms, but the majority have excellent facilities and a warm atmosphere; some are friendly and relaxed, others are more free-spirited and raucous. Many of the best places have been specially built or converted, though some are substantially less appealing, wedged into former hotel rooms above pubs. On average, **prices** are comparable with YHAs, with the basic rate often a dollar or two less, but offset by having to supply your own bedding or renting it for $1–2 a time.

Around seventy hostels are members of VIP Backpacker Resorts (c/- Auckland Central Backpackers, 9 Fort St, Auckland; ☎09/358 4877, fax 358 1142), an umbrella organization that offers a dollar off each night's stay to people who buy the annual **VIP backpacker discount card** ($25, valid in New Zealand and at 120 hostels in Australia).

The best **guide** to backpackers throughout the country is the free *Budget Backpacker Hostels* booklet (BBH or simply "Blue Book"), which details the majority of non-YHA hostels in New Zealand (including some VIP places), currently numbering over 200. The entries don't pretend to be impartial, but each hostel is given a rating based on an annual survey of guests, and these are fairly reliable assessments of the overall tone and general appeal of the place. Brandishing the Blue Book at the VIP hostels listed will get you

VIP's dollar discount. Obtain one at visitor centres, all participating hostels, direct from Budget Backpackers Hostels NZ Ltd (c/- Rainbow Lodge, 99 Titiraupenga, St, Taupo; ☎ & fax 07/377 1568), or through their Web site, *www.backpack.co.nz* where there are also full listings and a reservation facility for hostels in Auckland and Christchurch.

MOTOR CAMPS, CAMPSITES AND CABINS

New Zealand has some of the world's best camping facilities, so even if you've never been camping before, you may well find yourself using **motor camps**, which are geared up for Kiwi families on holiday, with space to pitch tents, hook-ups for campervans and usually a broad range of rooms and dorms. Elsewhere there is more down-to-earth camping at wonderfully located DOC sites.

Camping is largely a **summer activity** (Nov–May), especially in the South Island where winters can get very cold. At worst, New Zealand is very wet, windy and plagued by voracious winged insects, so the first priority for tent campers is good-quality gear with a fly sheet which will repel the worst that the elements can dish out, and an inner tent with enough bug-proof ventilation for those hot mornings.

Busy times at motor camps fall into line with the school holidays, making Easter and the summer period from Christmas to the end of January the most hectic. **Book** as far in advance as possible at this time and a day or two before you arrive anytime through February and March. DOC sites are not generally bookable, and while this is no problem through most of the year, Christmas can be a mad free-for-all.

MOTOR CAMPS AND CABINS

Motor camps are typically located on the outskirts of towns and are invariably well-equipped, with communal kitchen, TV lounge, games area, laundry, and sometimes a swimming pool; non-residents can often get showers for $2–3. **Campers** usually get the quietest and most sylvan corner of the site and be charged $7–9 per person; there is often no distinction between tent pitches and **powered sites** set aside for campervans, which are charged an extra dollar or so per person for the use of power hook-ups and dump station.

In addition, most sites have some form of on-site accommodation: the basic dorm-style **lodge** ($10–13 per person); 2–4 berth **standard cabins** (around $30 for two, plus $10 for each extra person), often little more than a shed with bunks; larger **tourist cabins** and **tourist flats** ($40–55 for two, plus $10–12 each extra person), all with cooking facilities and some with bathrooms; and fully self-contained **motel units** ($60–80 for two, plus $13–15 per extra person), usually with a separate bedroom and a TV. In all but the motel units, blankets, sheets and towels are not generally included, so bring a sleeping bag or be prepared to pay $2–3 a night to rent bed linen.

DOC CAMPSITES

Few motor camps can match the idyllic locations of the two hundred or so **campsites** operated by the **Department of Conservation** (DOC) in national parks, reserves, maritime and forest parks, the majority beautifully set by sweeping beaches or deep in the bush. This is back-to-nature camping, low-cost and with simple facilities, though sites almost always have running water and toilets of some sort. Listed in DOC's free *Conservation Campsites* leaflet, the sites fall into one of three categories: **informal** (free), often accessible only on foot and with nothing but a water supply; the more common **standard** ($2–6 per person), all with vehicular access and many with barbecues, fireplaces, picnic tables and refuse collection; and rare **serviced** ($6–9 per person), which are similar in scope to the regular motor camps described above. At any site children aged 5–15 are charged half price, and only the serviced sites can be booked in advance.

Other possibilities for using your tent include pitching in the grounds of many backpackers (see above) and along backcountry tramps (see p.50). **Free camping** is not generally a viable option, though with huge areas of thinly populated land you can probably get away with a dusk-to-dawn stay pretty much anywhere outside the cities, though this is not strictly legal. Parking your campervan overnight in roadside rest areas is also proscribed, though many do and suffer no adverse consequences.

For advice on **backcountry camping** and **trampers' huts**, see the "Outdoor Activities" section on p.49.

FOOD AND DRINK

Forget any preconceptions you may have about "slam in the lamb" Kiwi cuisine with a pavlova for dessert, New Zealand's food scene has forged ahead in recent years – both in terms of the quality of the food and the places where it's served.

New Zealand's **gastronomic roots** were nurtured in the British tradition of overcooked meat and two nuked vegetables, an unfortunate heritage which still informs the cooking patterns of older Kiwis and hasn't been completely displaced at some farmstays and guesthouses. Indeed, it is only in the last decade or so that New Zealand's chefs have really woken up to the possibilities presented by a fabulous larder of super-fresh, top-quality ingredients, formulating what might be termed **Modern Kiwi** cuisine. Taking its culinary cues from Californian and contemporary Australian cuisine, it combines traditional elements such as steak, salmon and crayfish with flavours drawn from the **Mediterranean**, **Asia** and the **Pacific Rim**: sun-dried tomatoes, lemongrass, basil, ginger, coconut and many more. Restaurateurs feel duty-bound to fill their menu with as broad a spectrum as possible, lining up seafood linguini, couscous, sushi, Thai venison meatballs and a chicken korma alongside the rack of lamb and gourmet pizza. Sometimes this results in gastronomic overload, but more often the results are sensational.

NEW ZEALAND INGREDIENTS

New Zealanders have a taste for meat. The quality of New Zealand lamb is matched by that of other **meats**, beef, chicken and, more recently, farmed venison, which appears on menus as cervena. Farmed ostrich is also gaining fans for its leanness and superb taste, though the greasy charms of **muttonbird** remain a mystery to most. A traditional source of sustenance for Maori, each April and May these birds of the shearwater family are still plucked from their burrows on the Titi Islands, off the southwest tip of Stewart Island, and sold through fishmongers in areas with substantial Maori populations.

With the country's long coastline, it's no surprise that **fish and seafood** loom large on the culinary horizon. The white, flaky flesh of the **snapper** is the most common saltwater fish, though you'll also come across tuna, John Dory, groper (often known by its Maori name of hapuku), flounder, blue cod (a speciality from the Chatham Islands), the firm and delicately-flavoured terakihi and the moist-textured **orange roughy**. You'll also see a lot of **salmon** – but not trout, which cannot be bought or sold, though some hotel restaurants will cook your catch for you. One much-loved delicacy is **whitebait**, a tiny silvery fish mostly caught on the West Coast and eaten whole in fritters during the August to November season. Shellfish are a real New Zealand speciality, and the king of them all is the **toheroa**, a type of clam dug from the sands of Ninety Mile Beach on the rare occasions when numbers reach harvestable levels. They are usually made into soups and are sometimes substituted by the inferior and sweeter **tuatua**, also dug from Northland beaches. On menus you're more likely to come across the fabulous **Bluff oysters**, scallops and sensational **green-lipped mussels**, which have a flavour and texture that's hard to beat and are grown in the cool clear waters of the Marlborough Sounds, especially around Havelock. Pricey **crayfish** is also delicious and if you get a chance, try **smoked eel** and **smoked marlin**.

Vegetables too are generally fresh and delicious. British favourites – potatoes, carrots, peas, cabbage – along with pumpkin and squash are

KIWI FOOD AND DRINK TERMS

butternut	type of pumpkin	*muttonbird*	gull-sized sooty shearwater that was a major component of the pre-European Maori diet and is said to taste like oily and slightly fishy mutton – hence the name
capsicum	bell peppers		
cervena	farmed venison		
crayfish	a slightly sweeter and pincer-less type of lobster		
eggplant	aubergine		
entree	appetizer	*paua*	the muscular foot of the abalone
feijoa	fleshy, palm-sized fruit with an indescribable but delicious flavour	*pavlova*	sickly meringue confection topped with cream and fruit that's claimed by Kiwis as adamantly as it is by Aussies
hogget	the meat from a year-old sheep. Older and more tasty (though less succulent) than lamb, but not as tough as mutton		
		pikelets	small, thick pancakes served cold with butter and jam or whipped cream
hot dog	a rather disgusting-looking battered sausage on a stick, dipped in tomato ketchup. What the rest of the world knows as a hot dog is known here as an American hot dog	*puha*	type of watercress traditionally gathered by Maori
		saveloy	particularly revolting kind of sausage served boiled
kiwifruit	hairy brown egg-sized fruit with a juicy green centre which swept the world in the 1980s to become the garnish of choice. The New Zealand-grown variety is now marketed as *Zespri*	*silverside*	top-grade corned beef, cured in honey and often served with tangy mustard
		swede	rutabaga
		tamarillo	slightly bitter, deep-red fruit, often known as a tree tomato
kumara	particularly delicious type of sweet potato and a long-standing Maori staple; often served as kumara chips with sour cream	*Vegemite*	a dark savoury yeast-extract spread that mystifies most people but is much loved by antipodeans, who insist it is far superior to its English equivalent, Marmite
lamington	sponge cake coated in chocolate or pink icing and rolled in desiccated coconut		

common in Kiwi homes but on restaurant menus you're far more likely to encounter aubergines (eggplant), capsicums (bell peppers) and tomatoes. Pacific staples to look out for are **kumara** (sweet potato), which crops up in hangi and deep-fried as kumara chips, and the starchy taro and sweeter yam, both much more rarely seen.

New Zealanders eat a lot of **cheese**, yoghurt and ice cream, and all are first-rate. Small producers springing up all over the country – but especially around the Kapiti Coast (north of Wellington), Blenheim and Banks Peninsula (east of Christchurch) – are turning out some gorgeous individual cheeses, from the traditional hard cheddar-style to spicy pepper brie. **Ice cream** of the firm, scooped variety is something of a New Zealand institution, and is available in a vast range of flavours, including intensely fruity ones and the indulgent hokey pokey – vanilla ice cream riddled with chunks of caramel.

Fruit too is a winner, especially at harvest time when stalls line the roadsides selling apples, pears, citrus and stonefruits for next to nothing. Top-quality fruit and dairy products are the starting point for some delicious **desserts** – mostly variations on the themes of ice cream, cheesecake and pavlova.

This abundance of fresh vegetables and superb dairy food means that self-catering **vegetarians** will eat very well, though those who eat in restaurants are less well served. Outside the major centres you'll find few dedicated vegetarian restaurants, and will have to rely on the token meat-free dishes served at most regular restaurants and cafés. Pretty much everywhere you'll be able to get a salad, sandwich, or vegetarian pizza and pasta – but it can get a bit monotonous. **Vegans** can always ask for a simple stir-fry if all else fails. In terms of snacks, you may find yourself developing an unhealthy reliance on nachos (a plateful of tortilla chips with a dollop of refried beans, grilled cheese and a hearty helping of sour cream), and the ubiquitous vegeburger.

If you are taking a rafting expedition or 4WD **tour** on which food is provided, give them plenty of notice of your dietary needs – otherwise you might be left with bread and salad.

RESTAURANTS, CAFÉS AND BARS

The quality of **restaurants** in New Zealand is typically superb. Prices are comparable with those in Western Europe, and can seem high to Australians and North Americans. However, the portions are respectable and they still represent wonderful value for money – especially at **BYO** establishments, where the cost is eased if you "bring your own" wine, sometimes for a nominal corkage fee. In most restaurants you can expect to pay upwards of $15 for a main course, perhaps $30 for three courses without wine. Service tends to be unpretentious and helpful without being forced, and there is no expectation of a tip, though a reward for exceptional service is always welcomed.

New Zealand's range of **ethnic restaurants** is meagre by international standards, with only the major influx of east Asian immigrants enervating the scene and lending a strong Chinese and Japanese flavour to the larger cities, alongside a smattering of Mexican places. **Maori food** is barely represented in restaurants at all, but you shouldn't miss the opportunity to sample the contents of a hangi (see box below), an earth oven producing delectable, fall-off-the-bone meat and delicately steamed vegetables.

Often there is little ground between restaurants and the better **café/bars** which have sprung up all over the land and offer food that's just as good and a few dollars cheaper. Here, dining is less formal and you may well find yourself elbow to elbow with folk only there for the beer or coffee, but dining is very much part of the café/bar scene. Simpler **cafés** may only stretch to breakfasts, grilled focaccias stuffed with Italian-inspired fillings, salads and cakes but always produce good coffee and keep long hours.

Though common in the more cosmopolitan cities, cafés are less prevalent in the country towns, which are still ruled by traditional **tea-**

THE HANGI

In New Zealand restaurants you'll find little or no representation of **Maori** or Polynesian cuisines, but you can sample traditional cooking methods at a **hangi** (pronounced nasally as "hungi"), where meat and vegetables are steamed for hours in an earth oven then served to the assembled masses. The ideal way to experience a hangi is as a guest at a private gathering of extended families, but most people have to settle for one of the commercial affairs in Rotorua or Christchurch. Though you'll be a paying customer rather than a guest, the hangi will be no less authentic.

First the men light a **fire** and place river stones in the embers. While these are heating, they dig a suitably large pit, place the **hot stones** in the bottom and cover them with **wet sacking**. Meanwhile the women prepare lamb, pork, chicken, fish, shellfish and vegetables (particularly kumara), wrapping the morsels in leaves then arranging them in baskets (originally of flax, but now more often of steel mesh). The baskets are lowered into the cooking pit and covered with earth so that the steam and the flavours are sealed in. A couple of hours later, the baskets are disinterred, revealing fabulously tender **steam-smoked** meat and vegetables with a faintly earth flavour. A suitably reverential silence, broken only by munching and appreciative murmurs, descends.

rooms, daytime (most close around 5pm), self-service places that are low on atmosphere but high on value. Most are now equipped with a coffee machine, though espresso incompetence may mean you're better sticking with the staple of tea, usually accompanied by a cellophane-wrapped sandwich, uninspiring savouries and either "Devonshire (cream) Teas" or home-style cakes – the carrot cake and ginger crunch are generally good bets. On main tourist routes, long-distance buses usually make their comfort stops at tearooms.

Some of the more civilized bars serve **pub meals**, often the best budget eating around with straightforward plates of steak and chips, lasagne or burritos, all served with salad for around $10. One to look out for here is the nationwide *Cobb & Co.* chain, formerly used as waystations by stagecoaches and now offering reliable, if uninspired, meals and good last-all-day breakfasts.

BREAKFAST, SNACKS AND TAKEAWAYS

New Zealanders generally take a fairly light "continental" **breakfast** of juice, cereals, toast and tea or coffee. Visitors staying at a homestay or B&B may well be offered an additional "cooked breakfast" probably along the lines of the traditional English breakfast of bacon and eggs; if you're staying in motels, hostels or campsites, you'll generally have to fend for yourself. In the bigger towns, you'll often find a **bakery** selling fresh croissants, bagels and focaccia, but increasingly New Zealanders are going out for breakfast or brunch, aided by the proliferation of cafés serving anything from a bowl of fruit and muesli ($5) to stupendous platefuls of Eggs Florentine and smoked salmon ($12).

In the cities you'll also come across **food courts**, usually in shopping malls where a central seating area is surrounded by a dozen or so stalls selling bargain plates of all manner of ethnic dishes. Some have outlets for **fast food**, a market dominated by the ubiquitous *McDonalds*, *Pizza Hut*, *KFC* and *Burger King*, with local additions like the meat pie chain of *Georgie Pie*. Meat **pies** are a stalwart of Kiwi snacking: sold in bakeries and from warming cabinets in pubs everywhere, the traditional steak and mince varieties are now supplemented by bacon and egg, venison, steak and cheese, steak and oyster and many others, though there is seldom a vegetarian version.

Undeterred by US fast-food hegemony, traditional **burger bars** continue to serve constructions far removed from the limp franchise offerings: weighty buns with juicy patties, thick ketchup, a stack of lettuce and tomato and that all-important slice of beetroot. At one stage, *McDonalds* even succumbed to consumer pressure and produced a Kiwiburger laden with beetroot and not a pickle in sight.

Fish and chips (or "greasies") are also rightly popular – the fish is usually shark (euphemistically called lemon fish) and the chips (fries) are invariably thick and crisp. Look out too for paua fritters, a battered slab of minced abalone that's something of an acquired taste.

SELF-CATERING

If you're **self-catering** your best bet for supplies is the local supermarket: the warehouse-style Pak 'n' Save is cheap and found in most large towns and usually stays open until at least 8pm every day. Failing that, you'll notice a marked drop in scope and an appreciable hike in prices at the neighbourhood superette – IGA and Four Square are the biggies. Convenient corner shops (or dairies), stock the essentials, but along with shops at campsites, also tend to have inflated prices, more so if located in isolated areas or anywhere with a captive market.

DRINKING

New Zealand boasts many fine wines and beers, which can be sampled in cafés and restaurants all over the land. But for the lowest prices and a genuine Kiwi atmosphere you can't go past the **pub**, often known as a **hotel** from the days when all drinking establishments were required to have rooms for revellers to sleep off a skinful. The pub is a place where folk stop off on their way home from work, the emphasis being on consumption and back-slapping camaraderie, with ambience and decor taking a back seat. In the cities, where competition from cafés is strong, pubs are sharpening up their act and comfortable, relaxed bars are more common, but in country areas little has changed. Rural pubs can initially be daunting for strangers, but once you get chatting, barriers soon drop. Some pubs are still divided into the **public bar**, a joyless Formica and linoleum place where overalls and work boots are the sartorial order of the day, and the **lounge bar**, where you are expected to dress up and are charged more for the privilege.

There is barely any limitation on the **hours** you can drink from Monday to Friday, most bars shutting up around midnight if it is quiet, more like 3am at weekends. **Sundays** are another matter and New Zealand's arcane **licensing laws** currently stipulate that you are only allowed to buy a drink on Sunday if you have the "intention of eating" – a loophole exploited by many cafés and pubs, which blithely assume that you intend to eat and sell you a drink anyway. Traditional pubs which don't serve meals (meat pies don't count) can't open on Sunday, however, and bottle shops are also closed. Supermarkets are only licensed to sell wine, but again not on Sunday. The **drinking age** is currently 20 and police frequently raid bars to pick-up under-age drinkers; those between 18 and 20 are allowed to drink if accompanied by a parent or a spouse who's over 20.

BEER

Beer is drunk everywhere and often in New Zealand. Nearly all beer is produced by two huge conglomerates – New Zealand Breweries and DB Breweries – who market countless variations on the lager and Pilsener theme, as well as insipid, deep-brown liquid dispensed from taps and in bottles as "draught" – a distant and altogether feebler relation of British-style bitter beer. Increasingly, Kiwi beer drinkers are turning to lager, especially their beloved Steinlager, which regularly bags international awards, as well as the new fangled cold-filtered and ice beers. There really isn't a lot to choose between them except for alcohol content, normally around four percent though five percent is common for premium beers usually described as "export".

To find something truly different, seek out **boutique beers** such as those brewed near Nelson by Mac's. Try their dark and delicious stout-like Black Mac, or wait around for the Oktober Mac, a light and fresh concoction brewed in September and only available until it runs out. Nelson's Pink Elephant brewery also produces a wonderful naturally-brewed bitter of the same name which is delicious and packs a punch. Small, regional brewers and in-house micro-breweries are still fairly rare but are establishing themselves on the scene – look out for the *Loaded Hog* and *One Red Dog* restaurant/bars. Most bottle shops stock a fair range of foreign brews and the flashier bars are always well stocked with the best of international bottled beers – at a price. On tap, you will only find New

Zealand beer, except for the odd ersatz Irish bar pouring Guinness.

Measures are standard throughout the country: traditionalists buy a one-litre **jug** which is then decanted into the required number of glasses, usually a **seven** (originally seven fluid ounces, or 200mls), a **ten**, or even an elegantly fluted **twelve**. Despite twenty years under the metric system, handled "**pints**" (roughly half a litre) have now become widespread. Prices vary enormously, but you can expect to pay around $3–4 for a pint. It is much cheaper to buy in bulk from a bottle shop where beer is either sold in six-packs or cartons of a dozen ($14–18); serious drinkers go for refillable half-gallon **flagons** (2.25 litres) or their metricated variant, the two-litre **rigger**; these can be bought for around a dollar and filled for $7–9 at taps in bottle shops.

WINES AND SPIRITS

Kiwis are justifiably loyal to New Zealand winemakers, who have made great strides in recent years and now produce wines which rank alongside some of the best in the world. New Zealand is rapidly encroaching on the Loire's standing as the world benchmark for Sauvignon Blanc, and there is an increasing band of fans for the bold fruitiness of its Chardonnay and the apricot and citrus palate of its Riesling. Certainly wine menus feature few non-Kiwi **whites**, but reds are often of the hefty Aussie variety. Nevertheless, New Zealand **reds** are rapidly improving and there are some very fine young-drinking varietals using Cabernet Sauvignon, Merlot and, the great red hope, Pinot Noir. The latest drinking trend is **dessert wines**, typically made from grapes withered on the vine by the botrytis fungus.

Most bars and licensed restaurants will have a tempting range of wines, many sold by the glass ($3–6, $8 for dessert wine), while in shops the racks are groaning with bottles starting from $8 ($12–15 for reasonable quality). Nowadays, the "chateau cardboard" wine bladders are considered passé, so do yourself (and your erstwhile hosts) a favour and buy a decent bottle if invited to a barbecue or dinner.

If you want to try before you buy, visit a few **wineries**, where you are usually free to sample half a dozen different wines. Among the established wine-growing areas, **Henderson** and the **Kumeu Valley**, 15km west of Auckland, is one of the more accessible though its urban nature makes it perhaps the least appealing to tour. On the east coast of the North Island, the area around **Gisborne** is good for a tasting afternoon, but wine connoisseurs are better off in **Hawke's Bay**, where Napier and Hastings are surrounded by almost thirty vineyards open to the public. Further south, **Martinborough** has the most accessible cluster of vineyards, many within walking distance. The colder climate of the South Island effectively limits wine production to the northern part, though there are a few vineyards in **Central Otago** near Queenstown and Alexandra. The best though are in **Marlborough**, close to Blenheim, which competes with Hawke's Bay for the title of New Zealand's top wine region.

New Zealand also produces fruit **liqueurs**; some are delicious, though few visitors develop an enduring taste for the sickly sweet kiwifruit or feijoa varieties, which are mostly sold through souvenir shops. International **spirits** are widely available and their dominance is only challenged by a couple of South Island whiskies, the blended Wilson's and the ten-year-old single malt Lammelaw.

SOFT DRINKS

New Zealand coolers are stocked with just about every international brand of carbonated soft drink, but one home-grown brand to look out for is L&P – originally **Lemon and Paeroa** after the Hauraki Plains town where it was first made – a genuinely lemon-flavoured pop. **Milkshakes**, thickshakes (usually with a dollop of ice cream) and smoothies made with blended fruit are popular thirst quenchers, and almost any café worth its salt serves glasses of **spirulina**, a thick, green goo made from powdered seaweed and often mixed with the likes of apple juice and avocado. Advocates claim restorative properties when drunk the morning after a bender.

TEA AND COFFEE

Tea is usually a down-to-earth Indian blend (sometimes jocularly known as "gumboot"), though you may also have a choice of a dozen or so flavoured, scented and herbal varieties. **Coffee** drinking has been elevated to an art form in New Zealand and, after a few trip-ups, you'll soon master the Antipodean coffee terminology: an Italian-style espresso is known as a **short black**; a weaker and larger version is a **long black**, which with the addition of milk becomes a **flat white**; **cappuccinos** come regular or chocolate-laced as a **mochaccino**; while a milky **café latte** is usually sold in a glass but sometimes in a gargantuan bowl. Better places will serve all these decaffeinated, skinny and even made with soya milk.

COMMUNICATIONS AND MEDIA

Communications services in New Zealand are generally first-rate, and excellent international networks make it pretty easy to keep in touch. The standard of media coverage sometimes leaves a little to be desired, but for the most part this is a well informed country with relatively sophisticated tastes.

MAIL

Post boxes are white, black and red and found everywhere, usually with some indication of when and how often their contents are collected. Most New Zealand towns used to boast rather grand Victorian or Edwardian **post offices** in or near their centres but these days the majority have been sold off and postal services are now operated from much less picturesque, multipurpose **post shops** (Mon–Fri 9am–5pm, plus Sat 9am–12.30pm in large towns and cities).

The extremely efficient mail service operates two forms of **domestic** delivery: **Standard** (45¢, or 80¢ for larger envelopes), delivered to any destination within 2–3 days; and **FastPost** (80¢, or $1.20 for larger envelopes), delivered in 1 day from cities and 2 from rural areas. **International air mail** takes 3–6 days to reach Australia ($1), and 6–12 days to Europe, Asia and the United States ($1.80), depending on where it's posted; prices are higher for larger envelopes. **Aerogrammes** cost $1 to anywhere in the world, as do air-mail **postcards**. Make sure you send your missives by air mail, or the recipients could be in for a long wait. **Stamps** are sold at some

newsagents, garages and general stores, as well as at post offices and post shops. Call the NZ Post **information line** (☎0800/501 501) or call into any post shop for further information.

Certain post offices operate a **Poste Restante** service, where you can receive mail; you can get hold of a list of their addresses from the New Zealand Embassy or Tourism Board in your home country or any Central Post Office in New Zealand. You need a passport or other ID to collect mail, which is returned to the sender after thirty days – though you can get it redirected if you change your plans by filling in a form at any post office. Most **hostels** and **hotels** will also keep mail for you, preferably marked with your expected date of arrival. Holders of an American Express card or travellers' cheques can have mail sent to **American Express** offices, which will hold it for thirty days; addresses are given in the "Listings" sections throughout the Guide – and you can pick up a booklet of all their locations from any American Express office.

FAX AND EMAIL

Faxes can be sent from the vast majority of hostels and hotels and most motels, but are not cheap, usually costing around $5 a page overseas and $1 a page within New Zealand. The average charge for receiving a fax is $1 a page.

An inexpensive way of keeping in touch while you're travelling is via **email**. An increasing number of cafés and libraries in the main cities and larger towns now offer Internet access; existing ones are included in "Listings" sections throughout the *Guide*, but more are springing up all the time – visitor centres should be able to point you in the right direction.

PHONES

There are two **phone companies** in New Zealand: the formerly state-run **Telecom**, which still has a monopoly on public payphones and local calls, and **Clear**, which competes for long-distance and international business. There is a huge discrepancy between the rates that apply to calls made from public and private phones in New Zealand, and if at all possible you should try to use **private phones**. On a private phone, depending on the type of line rental, local calls are either free or cost 20¢ for as long as you want. Long-distance and international calls from New Zealand are considerably cheaper on certain days (Sat and Sun) and at certain times, usually after 6pm.

Public telephones are pretty easy to find: they are either blue (coin-operated and rare), green (phone-card operated and common), or yellow (credit-card phones, fairly common). Most bars also have coin-operated phones. **Coin-operated** phones accept 10¢, 20¢, 50¢, $1 and $2 coins; **cardphones** take cards for $1, $5, $10, $20, $50, which are available at post shops, newsagents, dairies, garages, visitor centres and supermarkets; **credit-card** phones deduct the price of the call from your card and accept all major credit cards. The charge rates are the same for card and credit-card phones, though there is a 85¢ once-per-call additional fee for the use of credit cards and a minimum call charge of $2 (max $100).

COSTS AND CODES

A **local call** on a public payphone costs 50¢ flat rate. Calls outside the local area are charged according to distance, from 50¢ locally to the

---

USEFUL PHONE NUMBERS

All calls to the following numbers are free:
National operator ☎010
International operator ☎0170
National directory assistance ☎018
International directory assistance ☎0172
Emergency services (police, ambulance and fire brigade) ☎111

---

maximum **nationwide** rate of $1.40 a minute. Any ☎0800 and ☎0508 numbers are a **free call** nationwide, but if you call them on a credit-card or phonecard payphone you will still have to put a valid card into the machine, though you won't be charged; in coin-phones, your coin will be returned after you are connected. Calls to **mobile phones** (numbers prefixed ☎025 and ☎021) are charged at 99¢ per minute, as are calls to **premium-rated** information lines (prefixed ☎0900).

You can make **international calls** from any phone box, though it's a good deal easier with a card; instructions are provided in all phone boxes. From a **public phone**, calls to Australia cost $2.20 a minute, to the USA and UK $3.80 a minute (international dialling codes are listed in the box

---

INTERNATIONAL DIALLING CODES

To **call New Zealand** from overseas, dial the international access code (☎00 from the UK, ☎011 from the USA and Canada, ☎0011 from Australia), followed by ☎64, the area code minus its initial zero, and then the number.

To **dial out** of New Zealand, it's ☎00, followed by the country code (see below), then the area code (without the initial zero if there is one) and the number. Remember that there'll be a time difference between your country and New Zealand, which can be substantial (check out p.62 to avoid rude awakenings).

COUNTRY CODES

Remember to dial ☎00 first, then:

Australia: 61	**Netherlands**: 31
Canada: 1	**UK**: 44
Ireland: 353	**USA**: 1

HOME COUNTRY DIRECT

The **Home Country Direct** system enables you to talk to an operator in your own country and then to make a collect call (reverse the charges) or charge your call to a credit card.

Australia: ☎00, followed by 0996 for Optus, 0961 for Telstra	**Netherlands**: ☎0931
Canada: ☎0919	**UK**: British Telecom ☎0944, Mercury ☎094
Ireland: ☎0953	**USA**: (excluding Hawaii) AT&T ☎0911, MCI ☎0912, Sprint ☎0999; Hawaii ☎0918

on p.45). The **rate** that applies to your call is automatically shown in the display when you dial a number; public phones also accept **incoming calls**.

On a **private phone**, dial ☎013 before you make a national call and the operator will call you back when you've finished to tell you the **cost**; for the same service on international calls, dial ☎0160. This service costs $3 for all calls.

There are only five **area codes** in New Zealand. The North Island is divided into four area codes, while the South Island makes do with just one; all numbers in the Guide are given with their area code. Even within the same area, you may have to dial the code if you're calling another town some distance away.

THE MEDIA

New Zealand has no **national newspaper** but it does have three pretenders: *The New Zealand Herald* from Auckland, *The Dominion* from Wellington and *The Press* from Christchurch. Each contains local and national stories, editorial comment and limited international news – usually gleaned from news agencies, with little original journalism. Of the three, *The Press* is the most highly regarded, though the difference between them is negligible. However, the standard of **local papers** varies widely: Palmerston North's *Evening Standard* showcases reporting skills and intelligence; while the *Otago Daily Times*, sometimes known as the ODDITY for its acronym and its bizarre reporting habits, makes entertaining reading, as does the extraordinarily parochial *Southland Times*.

Some **international papers** are stocked in city newsagents and in supermarkets throughout the country. In addition, there are weekly digests of daily papers compiled in the country of origin, such as *The Guardian Weekly*, *The Weekly Telegraph* and one or two incarnations of the less esteemed UK tabloids; each costs between $3 and $4 per issue.

For more in-depth analysis of international news, pick-up a copy of *Newsweek* or *Time* **magazines**, which are widely available in New Zealand. The *Listener* is an excellent weekly **current affairs** magazine, which carries a TV and radio guide, as well as international and national news and entertainment reviews. Visiting walkers and **nature** buffs might want to take a look at the quarterly *New Zealand Geographic* or the monthly *New Zealand Wilderness*. Both focus on tracks and ecology, highlighting where to go to avoid the crowds.

TELEVISION AND RADIO

Television in New Zealand isn't very thrilling, unless you thrive on a diet of sport, cheap imported programming and commercials. There are four terrestrial channels (imaginatively called One, Two, Three and Four), though reception of the last two is patchy in more remote areas. The most conservative channel, One, concentrates on New Zealand programmes and imports from the UK; it also broadcasts BBC world news at 1am. Two has mostly imported Australian and American films, dramas, soaps and sitcoms, while Three and Four screen mostly USA-made fodder. There is also Sky TV (which is piped into many motels), featuring more sport, films, MTV and CNN news.

The most informative radio station is **National Radio** (837kHz), which gives an insight into the Kiwi mindset and concerns of the day; programmes focus on news, current affairs, talk shows, plays, book readings and short stories. Also broadcasting nationally are the **BBC World Service** on 990AM, with international news and a mix of entertainment, documentary and education; and the talkback stations **Newstalk ZB** (89.4kHz) and **Radio Pacific** (95.6FM), which are generally more vapid than rabid. Of the music stations, **Concert FM** (96FM) broadcasts classical and jazz, while hundreds of local stations cater to all musical tastes. Radio frequencies and reception may vary in isolated areas, so check for tuning details in the *Listener*.

OPENING HOURS, HOLIDAYS AND FESTIVALS

Opening hours have changed in New Zealand in the last few years, and there's now a marked trend towards Sunday opening in large towns and cities. However, the further out into the wilds you go the more conservative the opening times become, with many small towns being shut up tight from Saturday lunchtime until Monday morning. Holidays result in amiable mayhem, as Kiwis hit the roads en masse.

OPENING HOURS

Banks open Monday to Friday, 9.30am to 4.30pm, with some city branches opening on Saturday mornings (until 12.30pm). **Shops** are usually open Monday to Friday, 9am to 5pm, and until noon on Saturday. **Late-night shopping** until 8 or 9pm on Thursday and Friday nights is becoming more common, and many tourist-orientated shops are open daily until 8pm as a matter of course. In larger towns and cities, many shops stay open on Saturday afternoons and **Sundays**.

An ever-increasing number of **supermarkets** (at least one in or near each major city) now open seven days a week, 24 hours a day and small **"dairies"** (corner shops or convenience stores) also keep long hours and open on Sundays. **Museums** and **sights** usually open around 9am, although small-town museums often open only in the afternoons and/or only on specific days.

HOLIDAYS

Christmas falls in the middle of summer in the southern hemisphere, during the school **summer holidays**, which run from mid-December until the end of January. The knock-on effects of this are that there are more people out and about, prices go up, and accommodation and travel can be difficult to book. To help you chart a path through the chaos, visitor centres are open for longer hours, as are some museums and many other tourist attractions. Other **school holidays** hit for a week in the middle of April, the second week in July and the first two weeks of October, though these have a less pronounced effect than **the main bout of summer madness. Public holidays** (see box on p.48) are big news in New Zealand and it can feel like the entire country has taken to the roads, so it's worth considering staying put rather than trying to travel on these days.

There are a number of **regional festivals** which celebrate characteristics of the area and are usually treated as a showcase for local businesses and artistic talent (the box on p.48 lists some worth looking out for). Cities, towns and villages also take one day a year to celebrate the **anniversary** of the founding of their community. Although this isn't a good time to actually arrive in town, if you're there already, you can join in the shenanigans. Festivities usually consist of an agricultural show, horse jumping, sheep shearing, cake baking and best-vegetable contests, plus a novelty event like wellington boot throwing – all in the salubrious surroundings of the local A&P Showground and accompanied by the acrid smell of fried onions and the excessive consumption of alcohol.

HOLIDAYS AND FESTIVALS

All the festivals listed below are covered in more detail in the relevant section of the *Guide*; **public holidays** are in bold.

JANUARY
New Year's Day (January 1).

Whaleboat Racing Regatta, Kawhia (January 1).

Public Holiday (January 2).

Mountain Rock Festival, Manawatu Gorge, between Palmerston North and Napier (second weekend).

Wellington anniversary day (January 22).

Wellington Summer Festival (January–February).

Anniversary day for Auckland, Northland, Waikato, Coromandel, Taupo and the Bay of Plenty, celebrated with a massive regatta on Auckland's Waitemata Harbour (fifth Monday in January or first Monday in February).

FEBRUARY
Nelson anniversary day (February 1).

Taste Nelson food and wine festival (first Saturday).

Garden City Festival, Christchurch (February 3–14).

Waitangi Day (February 6).

Hawke's Bay Harvest food and wine festival (Waitangi holiday weekend).

Marlborough Food and Wine Festival, Blenheim (second weekend).

Art Deco Weekend, Napier (third weekend).

Devonport Food and Wine Festival (third weekend).

International Festival of the Arts, Wellington, in even-numbered years only; roughly coinciding with this, the month-long Wellington Fringe Festival is held every year, and draws acts from all over the world (late February to early March).

MARCH
Golden Shears sheep-shearing competition in Masterton (first week).

Wildfoods Festival, Hokitika (second Saturday).

Auckland Round-the-Bays fun run (early March).

New Plymouth Festival of the Arts (throughout March).

Ngaruawahia Maori Regatta, near Hamilton (closest Saturday to March 17).

Public holiday in Dunedin, Otago and Southland, including Fiordland (third Monday).

23rd Otago and Southland anniversary day (March 23).

Taranaki Anniversary Day (March 31).

APRIL
Arrowtown Autumn Festival (week before Easter).

Good Friday and **Easter Sunday** (late March to late April).

Waiheke Jazz Festival; Royal New Zealand Easter Show, Auckland; Highland Games, Hastings (Easter week).

Gumboot day, Taihape (Easter Tuesday).

ANZAC Day (April 25).

JUNE
Queen's Birthday (first Monday).

JULY
Auckland International Film Festival (early July).

OCTOBER
Labour Day (fourth Monday).

Public holiday in Hawke's Bay, Gisborne, Marlborough, Nelson (one week after Labour Day).

NOVEMBER
Hawke's Bay and Marlborough anniversary day (November 1).

Guy Fawkes' Night fireworks (November 5).

Canterbury Show week (second weeek).

Toast Martinborough food and wine festival (third Sunday).

DECEMBER
Westland anniversary day (December 1).

16th Canterbury anniversary day (December 16).

Christmas Day (December 25).

Boxing Day (December 26).

OUTDOOR ACTIVITIES

Life in New Zealand is very much tied to the Great Outdoors, and no visit to the country would be complete without spending a fair chunk of your time in intimate contact with nature.

The lofty peaks of the Southern Alps are perfect for challenging **mountaineering** and great **skiing**, and the lower slopes are ideal for multi-day **tramps** which cross low passes between valleys choked with sub-tropical and temperate rainforests. Along the coasts there are sheltered lagoons and calm harbours for gentle **swimming** and **boating**, but also sweeping strands battered by some top-class **surf**.

Kiwis have long taken it for granted that within a few minutes' drive of their home they can find a deserted beach or piece of "bush" and wander freely through it, an attitude enshrined in the fabulous collection of **national**, **forest** and **maritime parks**. They are all administered by the **Department of Conservation (DOC)**, PO Box 10-420, 59 Boulcott St, Wellington (☎04/471 0726, fax 471 1082) which struggles to balance the maintenance of a fragile ecology with the demands of tourism. For the most part it manages remarkably well, providing a superb network of well-signposted paths studded with trampers' huts; operating visitor centres that present highly informative material about the local history, flora and fauna; and publishing excellent leaflets for the major walking tracks.

For some years New Zealand has been addicted to outdoor thrills and spills, and now promotes itself as the **adventure tourism** capital of the world. All over the country you will find places to go **bungy jumping**, whitewater or cave **rafting**, **jet boating**, tandem **skydiving**, **mountain biking**, stunt **flying**, **scuba diving**, in fact you name it and someone somewhere organizes it. The Kiwi DIY ethic reigns supreme and it sometimes seems as though every Kiwi in possession of a minibus and a mobile phone runs an adventure-tourism business. While thousands of people participate in these activities every day without incident, standards of **instructor training** do vary. It seems to be a point of honour for all male (and they are almost all male) river guides, bungy operators and tandem parachute instructors to play the macho card and put the wind up you as much as possible. Such bravado shouldn't necessarily be interpreted as a genuine disregard for **safety**, but the fact remains that there have been quite a few well publicized injuries and deaths in recent years – a tragic situation that's finally being addressed by industry-regulated codes of practice and an independent system of **accreditation**. The first accreditations should be in place by the 1998 season, and official visitor centres plan to promote only accredited companies.

Before engaging in any adventure activities, check your **insurance cover** (see p.14).

TRAMPING

Tramping, trekking, bushwalking, hiking – call it what you will, it is one of the most compelling reasons to visit New Zealand, and for many the sole objective. Even if the concept sounds appalling, you should try it once; reluctant trampers are frequently bitten by the bug.

Tramps are multi-day walks, normally taking three to five days and following a well-worn trail through relatively untouched wilderness, more often than not in one of the country's national parks. Along the way you'll be either camping out or staying in idyllically located trampers' huts, and will consequently be lugging a pack over some pretty rugged ground, so a moderate level of **fitness** is required. If this sounds daunting, you can sign up with one of the **guided tramping** companies, which maintain more salubrious huts, provide meals and carry much of your gear, but at a price, details of these are given throughout the Guide.

The main **tramping season** is in summer, from October to May. Some of the most popular tramps – the Milford, Routeburn and Kepler – are in the cooler southern half of the South Island, where the season is shorter by a few weeks at either end.

THE TRAMPS

Rugged terrain and a history of track-bashing by explorers and deer hunters has left New Zealand with a web of tramps following river valleys and linking up over passes, high above the bushline. As far as possible, we've indicated the degree of difficulty of all tramps covered in the Guide, broadly following DOC's classification system: a **path** is level, well-graded and often wheelchair-accessible; **walking tracks** and **tramping tracks** (usually marked with red and white or orange flashes on trees) are respectively more arduous affairs requiring some fitness and proper walking equipment; and a **route** requires considerable tramping experience to cope with an ill-defined trail, frequently above the bushline. DOC's estimated **walking times** can trip you up: along paths likely to be used by families, for example, you can easily find yourself finishing in under half the time specified, but on serious routes aimed at fit trampers you might struggle to keep pace. We've given estimates for moderately fit individuals and, where possible, included the distance and amount of climbing involved to further aid route planning.

Invaluable information on walking directions, details of access, huts and an adequate map are contained in the excellent DOC **tramp leaflets** (usually $1 apiece); as long as you stick to the designated route, there's really no need to fork out for specialized **maps** (see p.20), unless you're keen to identify features along the way. In any case, most trampers' huts have a copy of the local area map pinned to the wall or laminated into the table. In describing tramps we have used "**true directions**" in relation to rivers and streams, whereby the left bank (sometimes referred to as the "true left") is the left-hand side of the river looking downstream.

Eight of New Zealand's finest and most popular tramps (and a river journey) have been classified by DOC as **Great Walks**; all are covered in detail in the text. On the North Island, the gentle **Lake Waikaremoana Circuit** (3–4 days) circumnavigates one of the country's most beautiful lakes; and the **Tongariro Northern Circuit** (3–4 days) takes in the magnificent volcanic and semi-desert scenery of the central part of the island. The popular **Abel Tasman Coastal Track** (2–3 days) skirts the pristine beaches and crystal-clear bays of the northern half of the South Island and avoids the difficult logistics of the **Heaphy Track** (4–5 days), which passes through the Kahurangi National Park, balancing sub-alpine tops and surf-pounded beaches. The tramping heartland is around Queenstown and Fiordland, where there are three magnificent, alpine Great Walks: the world-famous **Milford Track** (4 days) passing through stunning glaciated scenery; the equally superb **Routeburn Track** (3 days), which spends much longer above the bushline; and the **Kepler Track** (4 days), intended to take the pressure off the other two, but no less appealing for that. Finally, there's the **Rakiura Track** (3 days) on Stewart Island, conveniently circular and partly along the coast.

Great Walks get the lion's share of DOC track spending, resulting in relatively smooth, broad walkways, with boardwalks over muddy sections and bridges over almost every stream. In short, they represent the slightly **sanitized** side of New Zealand tramping and are sometimes disparagingly referred to as hikers' highways. This is somewhat unfair since, even on the busiest tramps, by judiciously picking your departure time each morning, you can go all day hardly seeing anyone.

Access to tracks is seldom a problem in the most popular tramping regions, though it does require some planning. Most tramps finish some distance from their start, so taking your own vehicle is not much use; besides, cars parked at trailheads are an open invitation to thieves. Great Walks always have transport from the nearest town, but there are often equally stunning and barely used tramps close by which just require a little more patience and tenacity to get to – we've included some of **the best of the rest** in the Guide, all listed under "Tramps" in the index.

BACKCOUNTRY ACCOMMODATION: HUTS AND CAMPING

Going bush needn't involve too much discomfort as New Zealand's backcountry is strung with a network of almost nine hundred **trampers' huts**, sited less than a day's walk apart, frequently in beautiful surroundings. They fall into four distinct categories as defined by DOC, which maintains the majority of them, though all are fairly simple, communal affairs.

The simplest huts are the crude **Category 4** (free), mostly used by hunters and rarely encountered on the major tramps. Next up in luxury is **Category 3** ($4 per person per night), basic, weatherproof huts usually equipped with individual bunks or sleeping platforms accommodating a dozen or so, an external long-drop toilet and a water supply. There is seldom any heating and there are **no cooking facilities**. **Category 2** huts ($8) tend to be larger, sleeping twenty or more in bunks with mattresses; water is piped indoors to a sink – and flush toilets aren't unusual. Again, you'll need to bring your own stove and cooking gear, but heating is provided; if the fire is a wood-burning one, you should replace any firewood you use. Most sophisticated are **Category 1** huts ($6–30 per night), found in the most popular walking areas and along the Great Walks. These tend to have separate bunkrooms, gas rings for cooking (but no utensils), gas stoves for heating, a drying room and occasionally solar-powered lighting. Most cost a modest $12–15 a night, though fees are substantially higher on the Milford and Routeburn tracks, reflecting the extra costs involved in maintaining these fragile areas. In winter (May–Sept), these huts are often stripped of their heating and cooking facilities and revert to Category 3 status.

Hut fees are usually paid in advance at the local DOC office, visitor centre or other outlet close to the start of the track. For most tramps you buy a quantity of $4 tickets (valid for 15 months) and give the warden the appropriate number (one for a Category 3 hut, two for a Category 2 hut and so on) or post them in the hut's honesty box. You can sometimes buy tickets direct from wardens, but there is often a 25 percent premium on the price (60 percent on the Milford and Routeburn tracks). If you are planning a lot of tramping outside the Great Walks system, it may be worth buying an **Annual Hut Pass** ($58), which allows you to stay in almost all Category 2 and 3 huts; in winter it can also be used in the downgraded Great Walks huts. With the exception of the Milford and Routeburn tracks, having a ticket or an annual hut pass doesn't guarantee you a place: bunks are allocated on a **first-come, first-served** basis, so

at busy times you may find yourself in an undignified gallop along the path to stake your claim.

All the Great Walks operate under a separate system of **accommodation passes**, and in addition, the oversubscribed Milford and Routeburn tracks require **reservations** as far in **advance** as possible. The easiest way to do this from overseas is to use a booking agent or send a letter or fax, with payment, to the relevant DOC office (see *Guide* accounts of the major tramps), stating where you intend to spend each night.

Camping is allowed on all tracks except the Milford, and costs one hut ticket ($4) per night. Rules vary, but in most cases you're required to minimize environmental impact by camping close to the huts, whose facilities you're welcome to use (toilets, water and gas rings where available, but obviously not bunks).

EQUIPMENT

Tramping in New Zealand can be a dispiriting experience unless you're equipped for both hot, sunny days and wet, cold and windy weather. The best Kiwi tramps pass through some of the world's wettest regions, with parts of the Milford Track receiving over six metres of rain a year. It is essential to carry a good **waterproof**, preferably made from breathable fabric and fitted with a good hood. Keeping your lower half dry is less crucial and most Kiwis tramp in **shorts**. Early starts often involve wading through long, sodden grass, so a pair of knee-length gaiters can come in handy. Comfortable **boots** with good ankle support are a must; take suitably broken-in leather boots or lightweight walking boots, and some comfortable footwear for day's end. You'll also need a **warm jacket** or jumper and a windproof shell, plus a good sleeping bag; even the heated huts are cold at night. All this, along with lighter clothing for sunny days, should be kept inside a robust **backpack**, preferably lined with a strong **waterproof liner** such as those sold at DOC offices ($3).

Once on the tramp, you need to be totally self-sufficient. On Great Walks, you need to carry a **pan** or two, a **bowl** or plate, a **mug** and **cutlery**; on other tramps you also need a **cooking stove** and **fuel**, both available in New Zealand. **Food** can be your heaviest burden; freeze-dried meals (available from all outdoors shops) are light and reasonably tasty, but they are expensive, and many cost-conscious trampers just carry quantities of pasta or rice, dried soups for sauces, a handful of fresh vegetables, muesli (granola), milk powder, and bread or crackers for lunch. Also consider taking biscuits, trail mix (known in New Zealand as "scroggin"), tea, coffee and powdered fruit drinks (the *Raro* brand is good), and jam, peanut butter or Vegemite. All huts have a drinkable **water** supply, but DOC advise treating water taken from lakes and rivers to protect yourself from **giardia**; see p.18 for more on this and suitable water-purification methods.

You should also carry a basic **first aid kit**, moleskin to prevent blisters, **sunscreen**, **insect repellent**, a **torch** (flashlight) with spare battery and bulb, **candles**, **matches** or a lighter, and a **compass** (though few bother on the better-marked tracks). Don't forget your **camera**, and if you've an interest in New Zealand's flora and fauna you might also want to take relevant guides (see Contexts for some recommendations).

In the most popular tramping areas you can **rent** stoves, pans, sleeping bags and waterproofs. Most important of all, remember that you'll have to carry all this stuff for hours each day. Hotels and hostels in nearby towns will generally let you leave your **surplus gear** either free or for a small fee, perhaps $1 a day.

SAFETY

Most people spend days or weeks tramping in New Zealand with nothing worst than stiff legs and a few irritating sandfly bites, but **safety** is nonetheless a serious issue and every year there are cases of individuals failing to return from tramps. The culprit is usually New Zealand's **fickle weather**. It cannot be stressed too strongly that within an hour (even in high summer) a warm, cloudless day can turn bitterly cold, with high winds driving in thick banks of track-obscuring cloud. Heeding the weather forecast (posted in DOC offices) is some help, but there is no substitute for carrying warm, windproof and waterproof clothing.

Failed **river crossings** are one of the most common causes of tramping fatalities. If you are confronted with something that *looks* too dangerous to cross, then it *is*, and you should wait until the level falls (usually as quickly as it rose) or backtrack. If the worst happens and you get swept away while attempting a crossing, don't try to stand up in fast-flowing water; you may trap your leg between rocks and drown. Instead, face downstream and float feet first until you

reach a place where swimming to the bank seems feasible.

If you do get lost or injured, your chances of being found are better if you left word of your whereabouts either with a friend or with the nearest DOC office, which stock **intention forms** for you to declare your planned route and estimated finishing time. While on the tramp, fill in the hut logs as you go, so that your movements can be traced, and when you return, *don't forget* to check in with your contact or with DOC.

Animals are not a problem in the New Zealand bush. Kiwis never tire of reminding you there are no snakes, and there is only one poisonous spider, rarely encountered. You might stumble upon the odd irate wild pig but the biggest irritants are likely to be **kea**, boisterous green parrots that delight in sliding down hut roofs, pinching anything they can get their beaks into then tearing it apart. If you want to keep your boots, don't leave them outside when kea are around.

SWIMMING, SURFING AND WIND-SURFING

Kiwi life is inextricably linked with the **beach** and from Christmas to the end of March (longer in the warmer northern climes) a weekend isn't complete without a dip or a waterside barbecue – though you should never underestimate the ferocity of the southern sun (see p.18 for precautions). Some of the best beaches are in the west, open to the pounding Tasman surf and stretching away into the salt-spray. Swimming here can be hazardous, so only venture into the water at beaches patrolled by **surf lifesaving clubs** and always swim between the flags. If you get into trouble, don't fight the current, but signal for assistance by raising one arm. Spotter planes patrol the most popular beaches and warn of any **sharks** in the area: if you notice everyone heading for the safety of the beach, get out of the water.

New Zealand's tempestuous coastline offers near-perfect conditions for **surfing** and **windsurfing**. At major beach resorts there is often a kiosk or shop renting out small dinghies, catamarans, canoes and windsurfers; in regions where there is reliably good surf you might also come across boogie boards and surfboards for rent, and seaside hostels often have a couple for guests' use.

SAILING

New Zealand's numerous harbours studded with small islands and ringed with deserted bays make **sailing** one of Kiwis' favourite pursuits. Kids are often introduced to the tiny "P Class" dinghies before they're riding bikes, and many grow up to own the yachts which choke the marinas for most of the year. Unless you manage to befriend one of these fortunate folk, you'll probably be limited to commercial yacht **charters** (expensive and usually with a skipper), more reasonably priced and often excellent **day-sailing trips**, or renting a small catamaran for some inshore antics along the bay. Most of what's available is in the northern half of the North Island with Auckland's Hauraki Gulf and the Bay of Islands being the main focal points.

SCUBA DIVING AND SNORKELLING

The waters around New Zealand's coast offer some superb opportunities for **scuba diving** and **snorkelling**. What they lack in tropical warmth and fabulously colourful fish they make up for with the range of diving environments. Pretty much anywhere along the more sheltered eastern side of both islands you'll find somewhere with rewarding snorkelling, but much the best and most accessible spot is the **Goat Island Marine Reserve**, in Northland, where there's a superb range of habitats close to the shore. Northland also has world-class scuba diving at the **Poor Knights Islands Marine Reserve**, reached by boat from Tutukaka; wreck diving on the *Rainbow Warrior*, from Matauri Bay; other good spots lie close to Auckland in the **Hauraki Gulf Maritime Park** and off Great Barrier Island. In the South Island there are the crystal-clear **Pupu Springs**, and fabulous growths of **black and red corals** relatively close to the surface of the southwestern **fiords** near Milford.

For the inexperienced, the easiest way to get as taste of what's under the surface is to take a "**resort dive**" with an instructor. If you want to dive independently, you need to be PADI qualified, which demands classroom instruction and a series of dives over a minimum period of a week. For more information, pick up the free, comprehensive *Dive New Zealand: The Best Dive Sites in New Zealand* brochure from dive shops and the bigger visitor centres.

RAFTING

Whitewater rafting is undoubtedly one of the most thrilling of New Zealand's adventure activities, negotiating challenging rapids (see box on p.54 for details of grading) amid gorgeous scenery. Visitor numbers and weather restrict the main **rafting season** to October to May, and most companies set the **lower age limit** at twelve or thirteen. In general you'll be supplied with all the gear you need except for a swimming costume and an old pair of trainers. After safety instruction, you'll be placed in eight-seater rafts and guided through narrow, rock-strewn riverbeds, spending an average of a couple of hours on the water, before being ferried back for refreshments.

Thrilling though it undoubtedly is, rafting is also one of the most **dangerous** of the adventure activities, claiming a number of lives in recent years. Operators seem to be cleaning up their act with a self-imposed code of practice and independent accreditation is imminent, but there are still cowboys out there. It might seem to be stating the obvious, but fatalities happen when people fall out of rafts: heed the guide's instructions about how best to stay on board and how to protect yourself if you do get a dunking.

Each main island has its major rafting centre – **Rotorua** on the North Island and **Queenstown** on the South Island – each with an enviable selection of river runs from mildly enervating to heart-stopping. Less frequented but equally exciting rafting areas include Turangi on the North Island, and central Canterbury and the West Coast in the South Island.

In more remote areas, **helirafting** is common, with rafts and punters airlifted to otherwise inaccessible reaches by helicopter. This can involve a lot of hanging around, so make sure what you are letting yourself in for and be wary of extravagant claims – the water may be no more exciting than more accessible (and cheaper) rivers. That said, if it's a wilderness experience you are after then consider the **Landsborough**, run from Queenstown, or visit Hokitika, Greymouth and Karamea for the best West Coast rivers.

Rafts are exchanged for inner tubes to undertake cave or **blackwater rafting**, which involves a generally placid drift through underground waterways, with the emphasis on exploration and viewing glow-worms.

GRADING OF RIVERS

Both rivers and rapids are graded according to the six-level grading system below, the river grade being dictated by the grade of the most demanding rapid. This lends itself to some creative thinking, and you need to take rafting company promotional material with a pinch of salt – a river hyped as Grade V might be almost entirely Grade III with one Grade V rapid. For maximum thrills and spills, the expression to look out for is "Continuous Grade IV".

I Very easy; a few small waves.

II A flicker of interest with choppier wave patterns. Dunking potential for inexperienced kayakers but no sweat in a raft.

III Bigger but still easily ridden waves make this bouncy and fun. Good proving ground for novice rafters.

IV Huge, less predictable waves churned up by rocks midstream make this excellent fun but dramatically increase the chance of a swim.

V Serious stuff with chaotic standing waves, churning narrow channels and huge holes ready to swallow you up. Best avoided by first-time rafters but thrilling nonetheless.

VI Dicing with death; commercially unraftable and only shot by the most experienced of paddlers.

CANOEING AND KAYAKING

New Zealand is a paddler's paradise, and pretty much anywhere with water nearby has somewhere you can **rent** either canoes or kayaks. Sometimes this is simply an opportunity to muck around in boats but often there is some kind of instruction or **guided trips** available, with the emphasis being on learning new skills and soaking up the scenery.

Grade II water is pretty much the limit for novices, making the scenic **Whanganui River** a perennial favourite. Despite its riverine nature, the **Whanganui Journey** (3–5 days) operates as a Great Walk and special arrangements apply to access and accommodation (see p.51); several companies rent out all the necessary gear, often including the DOC hut passes as part of their all-inclusive price. Far shorter trips down similar water are run on the **Matukituki River** near Wanaka and the **Dart River** from Glenorchy.

Casual paddlers are much more likely to find themselves **sea kayaking** the near-landlocked harbours in Northland or the bays along the Abel Tasman Coastal Path; a perfect way to experience New Zealand's magnificent coastline and to encounter dolphins and seals.

JETBOATING

The shallow, braided rivers of the high Canterbury sheep country posed access difficulties for run-owner Bill Hamilton, who got around the problem by inventing the **Hamilton Jetboat**. His inspired invention could plane in as little as 100mm of water, reach prodigious speeds (up to 80km per hour) and negotiate rapids while maintaining astonishing turn-on-a-sixpence manoeuvrability.

The jetboat carried its first fare-paying passengers on a deep and glassy section of the Shotover River, which is still used by the pioneering Shotover Jet. Over half a dozen companies now run similar deep-water trips around Queenstown, while at nearby Glenorchy there's a wonderful wilderness trip along the shallow and twisting Dart River. Other key sites include the Wilkin River at Makarora and the Waikato River immediately below Taupo's Huka Falls.

Thrills-and-spills rides ($50–60) tend to last for around thirty eye-streaming minutes, time enough for as many 360-degree spins as anyone really needs. **Wilderness trips** ($50–100) can last two hours or longer, pacing their antics.

BUNGY JUMPING, BRIDGE SWINGING AND RAP JUMPING

For maximum adrenalin, minimum risk and greatest expense, you can't go past **bungy jumping**.

WHEN IS A KAYAK A CANOE?

In New Zealand, **canoe** seems to be the generic term for any small craft, whether it be fitted with a closed cockpit – elsewhere known as a kayak – or of the open variety paddled with a single-bladed paddle, sometimes differentiated by the term **Canadian canoe**.

To further confuse matters, some rafting companies run small **inflatable** boats akin to **mini-rafts** and paddled with a double-bladed paddle, which tend to be called **kayaks**.

Not only is New Zealand the birthplace of commercial bungy jumping, it also has some of the world's finest jump sites – bridges over deep canyons and platforms cantilevered out over rivers. It is a complete head game; there's really nothing to fear but a massive rush of wind that lasts for ten seconds and a huge surge of adrenalin that can linger in the system for days.

The craze was kicked off by Kiwi A.J. Hackett who, after a spectacular and highly-publicized jump from the Eiffel Tower in 1986, set up the first commercial operation just outside Queenstown on the **Kawerau Suspension Bridge** (43m). Its location beside the Queenstown–Cromwell highway, and the chance to be dunked in the river make this the most popular jump site, but there are a couple of other local sites above the Shotover River in **Skippers Canyon** and a handful of other sites around the country.

Wherever you jump, there'll be a boom-box cranking out the Red Hot Chili Peppers or suchlike while they strap the bungy cord to your legs. You'll be fed the jocular spiel about the bungy breaking (it won't) or not being attached properly (it will be) then you'll be chivvied into producing a cheesy (or wan) grin for a camera or three before shuffling out onto the precipice for the countdown. A swan dive is the traditional first jump, but there is often a substantial discount for second and subsequent jumps on the same day, giving jump veterans the opportunity to try The Elevator (just hopping off the platform, either forwards or backwards) or any number of variations. The pleasure is greatly enhanced by pre-jump banter and post-jump analysis, making the longer trips involving a drive into the site – the Skippers Canyon sites in particular – all the more appealing. To show how brave you've been, this will all have been captured on video; there are also souvenir strips of used bungy cord to buy and a T-shirt, sometimes included in the jump package. **Prices** range from $90–130.

There have been a couple of injuries in the past but, on balance, bungy jumping is **one of the safest** adventure activities. The bungy cords are made from latex rubber (if it's good enough for condoms...) and only used 600 times, a quarter of their expected life. Some folk have been known to notch up over 1500 jumps without adverse effects, though bloodshot eyes aren't uncommon and there have been isolated reports of detached retinas and aggravated back injuries.

A couple of close relatives of bungy jumping have hit the scene in recent years. A couple of places are now offering **bridge swinging**, which involves a gut-wrenching fall and superfast swing along a gorge while harnessed to a cable. Then there's **rap jumping**, a variation on abseiling in which you hurtle face first down a sheer surface, controlling your descent with the rope.

CANYONING AND MOUNTAINEERING

The easiest way to get your hands on New Zealand rock is to go **canyoning**, which involves following a steep and confined river gorge or streambed down chutes and over waterfalls for a few hours, sliding, jumping and abseiling all the way. This is currently only commercially available in a handful of places, the most accessible being in **Wanaka** and **Hanmer Springs**, though there are bound to be more places in the near future.

In the main, New Zealand is better suited to **mountaineering** than rock climbing, though most of what is available is fairly serious stuff, suitable only for well-equipped parties with a good deal of experience. For most people the only way to get above the snow line is to tackle the easy summit of **Mount Ruapehu**, the North Island's highest point, or pay for a guided ascent of one of New Zealand's classic peaks. Prime candidates here are the country's highest mountain, **Mount Cook** (3754m), accessed from the climbers' heartland of Mount Cook Village, and New Zealand's single most beautiful peak, the pyramidal **Mount Aspiring** (3030m), approached from Wanaka. In both areas there is a comprehensive system of climbers' huts used as bases for what are typically twenty-hour attempts on the summit.

FLYING, SKYDIVING AND PARAGLIDING

Almost every town in New Zealand seems to harbour an airstrip or a helipad, and there is inevitably someone happy to get you airborne for half an hour's **flightseeing**. The best of these cross the truly spectacular mountain scenery of the Southern Alps or the ice-sculpted terrain of Fiordland, either from Fox Glacier, Franz Josef Glacier, Mount Cook, Wanaka or Queenstown. Half an hour in a plane will set you back around $100; helicopters cost around fifty percent more and can't cover the same distances but score on manoeuvrability and the chance to land. If money is tight, you could always take a regular flight to somewhere you want to go anyway. First choice here would have to be the journey from either Wanaka or Queenstown to Milford Sound, which overflies some of the very best of Fiordland.

In **tandem skydiving**, a kind of double harness links you to an instructor, who has control of the parachute. After suitable instruction, the plane circles up to around 2500m and you leap out together, experiencing around thirty seconds of eerie freefall before the instructor pulls the ripcord. Again the Southern Alps and Fiordland are popular jumping grounds, and Taupo seems to be establishing itself as a low-cost and reliable venue, charging as little as $165 a shot; elsewhere $180–200 is more common.

A hill, a gentle breeze and substantial tourist presence and you've all the ingredients for **tandem paragliding**, where you and an instructor jointly launch off a hilltop, slung below a manoeuvrable parachute. For perhaps ten minutes of graceful gliding and stomach-churning banked turns, you pay a little over $100; Queenstown, Wanaka and Nelson are prime spots.

SKIING

New Zealand's **ski season** (roughly June to October or November) starts as northern hemisphere slopes finally melt away. This, combined with the South Island's backbone of 3000m peaks and the North Island's equally lofty volcanoes, make New Zealand an increasingly popular international ski destination. Most fields, though, are geared to the domestic downhill market – and the eastern side of the Southern Alps is littered with **club fields** sporting a handful of rope tows, simple lifts and a motley collection of private ski lodges. They're open to all-comers, but some are only accessible by four-wheel-drive vehicles, others have a long walk in, and ski schools are almost unheard of. Conversely, lift tickets are only $20–40, queues are short and there's usually a gear-rental shop not too far away. Throughout the country, there's also a dozen exceptions to this norm: **commercial resorts**, with high-speed quad chairs (lift tickets around $55), ski schools, gear rental and groomed wide-open slopes. What you won't find are massive on-site resorts of the scale found in North America and Europe; skiers commute daily to the slopes from nearby après-ski towns. **Gear rental**, either from shops in the nearest town or on the field, ranges from around $35 a day for a full set of decent equipment to around $60 for the fancy stuff or for snowboarding tackle.

The best up-to-date source of skiing information is the free, annual **Ski & Snowboard Guide** published by Brown Bear Publications, PO Box 8609, Christchurch (☎03/377 1444, fax 377 1119). For each field it gives a detailed rundown of facilities, expected season, lift ticket prices and an indication of suitability for beginners, intermediates and advanced skiers. Heliskiing is also dealt with and there's brief coverage of the main ski towns.

The main **North Island** fields include the country's two largest and most popular destinations, **Turoa** and **Whakapapa**, both on the volcanic Mount Ruapehu, which erupted during the 1995 and 1996 seasons but remained quiet in 1997. The Southern Alps give the **South Island** a great deal more scope, with the greatest concentration of commercial fields being around Queenstown – **Coronet Peak** and **The Remarkables** – and Wanaka – **Treble Cone**, **Cardrona** and the **Waiorau Nordic Ski Area**, New Zealand's only organized cross-country site. Further north, **Porter Heights** and **Mount Hutt** are within two hours' drive of Christchurch, and the Nelson region is home to New Zealand's newest commercial field, **Mount Lyford**. All these ski areas are covered in the relevant chapters of the Guide.

At weekends and school holidays the tow queues at the major fields can become unfeasibly long, and the ideal solution is **heliskiing**. Guides conversant with the routes and skilled in reading avalanche danger take small parties onto virgin slopes high among the sparkling peaks of the Southern Alps. Provided you are an intermediate skier and are reasonably proficient at skiing powder you should be able to pass the ability questionnaire, but at around $500 a day it isn't for everyone. If you can't resist, places to consider are the usual suspects of Fox Glacier, Wanaka and Queenstown; in Canterbury, you can ski the wonderful Tasman Glacier from Mount Cook Village or get a taster from the Mount Hutt skifield car park.

FISHING

Kiwis grow up fishing: virtually everyone seems to have fond memories of long days out on a small boat trailing a line for snapper, if only to stock the beachside barbecue. All around the

New Zealand **coast**, but particularly in the north of the North Island, there are low-key canoe, yacht and launch trips on which there is always time for a little **casual fishing**, but you'll also find plenty of trips aimed at more dedicated anglers. Most sea trips aim to land something of modest size with good flavour: snapper, kahawai, moki and flounder being common catches. Bigger boats might hope for hapuku, then there's a step up to the **big-game fishing** boats. From December to May these scout the seas off the northern half of the North Island for marlin, shark and tuna. This is serious business and you're looking at around $200 per person per day to go out on a boat with three others, but on the smaller boats, a day out fishing might cost as little as $60, with all tackle supplied.

Inland, the **rivers** and **lakes** are choked with rainbow and brown trout, quinnat and Atlantic salmon, all introduced for sport at the end of the nineteenth century. Certain areas have gained enviable reputations: the waters of the Lake Taupo catchment are world-renowned for the abundance and fighting quality of the rainbow trout; South Island rivers, particularly around Gore, boast the finest brown trout in the land; and braided gravel-bed rivers draining the eastern slopes of the Southern Alps across the Canterbury Plains bear superb salmon. Archaic laws prohibit the sale of **trout**, so if you want to eat some you've got to go out and catch it.

A national **fishing licence** ($58 for the year from Oct 1 to Sept 30; $23 for 7 days; $16.50 for 2 days; and $11.50 for 24 hours) covers all New Zealand's lakes and rivers except for those in the Taupo catchment area, where a local licensing arrangement applies (see p.275).

Wherever you fish, the **rules** are taken very seriously and are rigidly enforced. If you're found with an undersize catch or an over-full bag, heavy fines may be imposed and equipment confiscated. Be sure to find out the **local regulations** before you set out.

HORSE TREKKING

New Zealand's highly urbanized population leaves a huge amount of countryside available for **horse trekking**, occasionally along beaches, often through patches of native bush and tracts of farmland; there may even be an opportunity to swim the horses. There are schools everywhere and all levels of experience are catered for, but more experienced riders might prefer the greater scope of full-day or even week-long wilderness treks. We've highlighted some of the more noteworthy places and operators throughout the Guide.

MOUNTAIN BIKING

If you prefer a smaller saddle, you'll find a stack of places renting out **mountain bikes**. For a quality machine, you might be paying over $40 a day, but for that you get a bike, a helmet and a headful of advice about local routes. The main trail-biking areas around Rotorua, Queenstown, Mount Cook and Hanmer Springs will often have a couple of companies willing to take you out on **guided rides** (the going rate is about $100 a half-day), usually dropping you at the top of hill and picking you up at the bottom.

Mountain bikes aren't allowed **off-road** in national parks and reserves, and elsewhere you must respect the enjoyment of others by letting walkers know of your presence, avoiding skid damage to tracks and keeping your speed down. For more information, consult the specific biking guides available in New Zealand.

POLICE, TROUBLE AND HARASSMENT

Violent crime is still sufficiently novel in New Zealand that it is reported with relish by the media. As long as you use your common sense and don't drop your guard just because you're on holiday, you're unlikely to run into any trouble.

There are a few areas, like K' Road in Auckland, where it is unwise for **lone women** to walk late at night, but as long as you are reasonably careful you should stay out of trouble. In fact, the main source of crime in New Zealand is vehicles. **Car break-ins** are common in cities, or in car parks at the beginning of short or long walks, or even just on the roadside while you go to take a picture of a waterfall. Campervans are particularly vulnerable, since they contain all your possessions and make easy pickings. When you leave your vehicle, take your valuables with you, and put packs and bags in the boot or out of sight. If you have a particularly vulnerable vehicle, whether because of age or make, invest in a steering lock. Before setting out on long walks use a **secure car park** if possible, where your car will be kept safe for a small sum. There is rarely any **stealing** in hostels apart from the odd case of mistaken identity when it comes to food in the fridge, although it doesn't do any harm to lock away stuff if you can.

Nude and topless **sunbathing** is not something you will see in New Zealand except at naturist camps and recognized nudist beaches. Assuming someone takes the trouble to complain, naked sun worshippers on a crowded public beach may even be arrested, and **topless** women may well find themselves being asked to cover up or made to feel uncomfortable. There are, however, hundreds of isolated beaches and beauty spots in New Zealand that are so remote you can pretty much do what you like.

> ☎111 is the free emergency telephone number to summon the police, ambulance or fire service.

POLICE AND THE LAW

The **police** are perceived as friendly, mostly incorruptible and helpful which, generally speaking, they are. If you do get arrested, you will be allowed one phone call; a solicitor will be appointed if you cannot afford one and you may be able to claim legal aid. It is unlikely that your consulate will take more than a passing interest unless there is something strange or unusual about the case against you.

The laws regarding **alcohol** consumption in New Zealand are pretty lenient, and unless you are actively causing trouble, the police will give you a wide berth. The same does not apply to **drink driving** (see p.28), which is taken very seriously. Home-grown **marijuana** or "electric *puha*" (taken from the Maori, *puha* meaning watercress) has a reputation for being very potent and is pretty easily available. It is, however, **illegal** and although a certain amount of tolerance is sometimes shown towards personal use, the police and courts take a dim view of any tangles with **hard drugs**, handing out long custodial sentences.

PREJUDICE

Most New Zealanders welcome foreign visitors with open arms and, as a traveller, you're unlikely to experience overt **discrimination** to any great degree. There are few places in New Zealand where you will be refused service because of your race, colour or gender, although on rare occasions you may feel slightly **uneasy**. This can be the case for lone women in out-of-the-way **country pubs**, or for tourists who stray into predominantly Maori pubs. More often than not, the locals will be friendly but you might end up feeling like the cowboy who stops all the music and conversation when he walks through the door.

Despite constant efforts to maintain good relations between **Maori** and *pakeha* (Europeans), tensions do exist – inflamed by disproportionately high rates of unemployment and imprisonment among the Maori population. **Asian** immigrants, meanwile, often bear the brunt of prejudice from both Maori and *pakeha*.

GAY AND LESBIAN NEW ZEALAND

New Zealand has in recent years become a broadly gay-friendly country, defying the odds in what has always been perceived as a fairly macho country. Certainly there remains an undercurrent of redneck intolerance, particularly in rural areas, but it generally stays well below the surface.

All this has partly come about in response to New Zealand's admirable recent history of resistance to anti-gay bigotry. Homosexuality was decriminalized in 1986 and the **age of consent** was set at sixteen (the same as for heterosexuals). The human rights section of the **legislation**, making it illegal to discriminate against gays and people with HIV or AIDS, was passed in 1993, with none of the usual exceptions made for the military or the police. There are officially no restrictions on people with **HIV** or AIDS entering the country; see "Health", p.18, for details of support organizations.

Such is the mainstream **acceptance** that the New Zealand Symphony Orchestra is quite upfront about one of its most prominent composers, Gareth Farr, doubling as a drag queen – though not mid-concert.

WHERE TO GO

This tolerant attitude has conspired to de-ghettoize the gay community; even in **Auckland** and **Wellington**, the only cities with genuinely vibrant gay scenes, there aren't any predominantly gay areas and most venues have a mixed clientele. The gay communities of both cities cel-

GAY AND LESBIAN CONTACTS

Media express (fortnightly, $2; ☎09/376/2018, fax 376 2019), sold in almost any decent bookstore, graces the magazine racks of gay-friendly cafés and is often distributed free at gay venues; it is the best source of on-the-ground information and a good way to make contacts. Also keep your eyes skinned for the national bi-monthly *OUT!*, and the Wellington-based *Lesbian Quarterly*. By the middle of 1998, Auckland looks set to have *Triangle TV*, a community-access TV station with a substantial proportion of gay programming.

Travel information The non-profit *New Zealand Gay and Lesbian Tourism Association*, PO Box 11-582, Wellington 6001 (☎04/384 1877, fax 384 5187, email *secretariat@nzglta.org.nz*) provides travel information aimed at gay, lesbian and bisexual visitors, and vets businesses for standards of service and hospitality, working closely with the New Zealand Tourism Board. *Gaylink Travel*, PO Box 11–584, Wellington (☎04/384 1865 & 0800/429 872, fax 882 8246, email *reznz@gaylink.co.nz*) run a nationwide gay and lesbian accommodation and travel reservation service and also have a branch in Auckland.

Web sites One of the best is *www.nz.com/glb/* which gives direct access to the *New Zealand Pink Pages*, essentially a collection of linked pages on all aspects of gay and lesbian New Zealand, including what's on in the gay community and a calendar of events all over the country. Almost all sites of interest can be reached from here, though you may want to go directly to *www.nz.com/NZ/Queer/Devotion/* for information on the Devotion Festival and *www.nz.com/NZ/Queer/Hero/* for the Hero Festival.

ebrate their existence each year with a glam, over-the-top parade and associated revelry. Wellington kicks the party season off with its **Devotion Parade** in November, followed in February by Auckland's **Hero Parade**, a two-week celebration of film, theatre, dance and sport that culminates in a street parade along Ponsonby Road and an all-night dance party.

Outside the festival season, Auckland and Wellington slip back into the groove of easy-going clubbing. Auckland's scene is generally the largest and most lively, but the intimate nature of Wellington makes it more accessible and welcoming. **Christchurch** has a small number of predominantly gay venues in the inner city and the fledgling **Freedom dance party** each February; and **Nelson** has a moderately active

gay community centred on Spectrum, 42 Franklyn St (☎03/547 2827). Elsewhere it is hard to find a gay network to plug into; even Queenstown is quiet, though this is beginning to change.

Out in the sticks you'll be relying on the gay press (see box on p.59) to make contacts – unless you can time your visit to coincide with the annual **Vinegar Hill Summer Camp**, held just outside the small town of Hunterville, in the middle of the North Island, from Boxing Day to just after New Year. It is a very laid-back affair with perhaps a couple of hundred gay men and women camping out, mixing and partying. There's no charge (except a couple of dollars for camping), no tickets and no hot water, but a large river runs through the grounds and everyone has a great time. Check the gay press for details – or just turn up.

WORK

Australians don't need to undergo any formalities to work in New Zealand, but just about everyone else needs a Work Visa: apply at New Zealand embassies or consulates before you leave home (see p.12).

But be warned: given persistent **unemployment**, these are almost impossible to obtain unless you have an offer of employment from a prospective employer who can prove there are no New Zealanders available to take the job. The

only significant exception is for British, Canadian and Japanese citizens aged 18 to 30, who are eligible to apply for a **Working Holiday Visa** (again, see "Visas and Red Tape", p.12). If your application is successful and you're prepared to try anything, there are plenty of opportunities for **casual** paid work. In addition, there are organized **work programmes** – both paid and **voluntary**.

CASUAL WORK

One of the main sources of casual work is **picking fruit** or related **orchard work** such as packing or pruning and thinning. The main areas to consider are Kerikeri in the Bay of Islands for citrus and kiwifruit, Hastings in Hawke's Bay for apples, pears and peaches, Tauranga and Te Puke for kiwifruit, and Alexandra and Cromwell in Central Otago for stonefruit. Most work is available during the autumn **picking season**, which runs roughly from January to May, but this is also when there are most people looking for work so you can often find something just as easily in the off-season. In popular working areas, some hostels cater to short-term workers and these are usually the best places to find out what's going.

Picking can be hard and heavy work and is usually **paid** by the quantity gathered, rather than by the hour. When you're starting off, the poor returns can be frustrating but with persistence and application you can soon find yourself pulling in a decent wage. Don't expect to earn a fortune, but in an eight-hour day you should gross $60–90.

Finding other types of casual work is more ad hoc, with no recognized channels other than newspapers, and hostel noticeboards; just keep your ear to the ground, particularly in popular tourist areas – Rotorua, Nelson, Queenstown – where people running **cafés**, **bars** and **hostels** often need extra staff during peak periods. If you have no luck, try your chances in more out of the way locales, where there'll be fewer travellers clamouring for work.

Your earnings will be **taxed** and your employer will require you to obtain a tax number: pop along to the nearest tax office with your passport and they should issue one on the same day. The tax department rakes in twenty-four percent of your earnings and you won't be able to reclaim any of this.

WORKING HOLIDAYS

One way to reduce your travelling costs without transgressing the terms of your visitor permit is to **work for your board**, most easily achieved doing farm work through Willing Workers On Organic Farms (WWOOF; see p.34). No money changes hands, but in exchange for four hours work a day, you get free board and lodging.

The Department of Conservation's **Conservation Volunteer Programme** provides an excellent way to spend time out in the New Zealand bush while putting something back into the environment. Often you will get into areas most visitors never see and learn some skills while you're at it. Projects include bat surveys, kiwi monitoring and nest protection, as well as more rugged tasks like track maintenance, tree planting and hut repair – all detailed in a booklet available from DOC offices nationwide or direct from head office at PO Box 10-420, 59 Boulcott St, Wellington (☎04/471 0726, fax 471 1082). You can muck in for just a day or up to five days; for longer outings a small fee (around $60 for the duration) may be levied to cover food and transport.

DIRECTORY

CHILDREN New Zealand is a child-friendly place: nearly every town of any size has Plunket

Rooms, which can be used for changing nappies and sometimes host play groups; family rooms are commonly available in motels, and children are welcomed in most restaurants.

CIGARETTES AND SMOKING Smoking is outlawed on most public transport and in many public buildings, and smoking in restaurants is strongly discouraged if not banned. Cigarette advertising has long been outlawed and now sponsorship has gone the same way, with the cigarette-tax-funded Smokefree organization standing in where Rothman's and others have been ousted. Consequently cigarettes are expensive and best bought duty-free on arrival.

DATES New Zealand follows Britain's lead with dates, and 1/4/98 means April 1 not January 4.

DEPARTURE TAX A departure tax of $20 (to be paid in NZ currency) is charged to everyone over the age of 12. This is occasionally included in the air-ticket price, but more often you have to pay at the airport; keep some cash handy or pay by credit card.

ELECTRICITY New Zealand operates a 230/240volt, 50Hz AC power supply, and sockets take a three-prong, flat-pin type of plug. North American appliances require both a transformer and an adaptor, British and Irish equipment needs only an adaptor and Australian appliances need no alteration. Suitable adaptors are widely available in New Zealand and at most international airports.

EMERGENCIES Dial ☎111

FLOORS What would be called the first floor in the US is the *ground* floor in NZ, the one above is known as the first, and so on.

GST A Goods and Services Tax is charged at 12.5 percent on almost all items and services and is included in the price quoted, except for some business hotels where rates will be clearly marked GST-exclusive. GST exemption is available on more expensive items bought at shops bearing the "Duty-Free Shopping" sticker which are to be sent or taken out of the country.

MEASUREMENTS New Zealand uses the metric system of measurements. Distances are in kilometres, petrol is bought in litres, food is weighed in kilos (see conversion table below if you're struggling).

PHOTOGRAPHY Film is widely available, but at a price – and processing is expensive, too. For transparencies, Fujichrome Velvia seems to be particularly good at capturing New Zealand's intense blues and greens and costs around $27 for 36 exposures, plus $15 for processing.

SEASONS Don't forget that in the southern hemisphere the seasons are reversed. Summer lasts from November to March, and winter from June to September, with a couple of transitional months in between that pass for spring and autumn.

TIME New Zealand Standard Time (NZST) is 12 hours ahead of Greenwich Mean Time, so at noon in New Zealand, it's midnight in London, 7pm in New York, 4pm in Los Angeles, and 10am in Sydney. From the first Sunday in October to the third Sunday in March, Daylight Saving puts the clocks one hour further forward.

TIPPING There is no expectation of a tip, though reward for exceptional service is always welcomed.

METRIC CONVERSION TABLE		
	1 centimetre (cm) = 0.394in	1inch (in) = 2.54cm
		1 foot (ft) = 30.48cm
1 metre (m) = 100cm	1 metre = 39.37in	1 yard (yd) = 0.91m
1 kilometre (km) = 1000m	1 kilometre = 0.621 miles	1 mile = 1.610km
1 hectare = 10,000 square metres	1 hectare = 2.471 acres	1 acre = 0.4 hectares
	1 litre = 0.22 UK gallons	1 UK gallon (gal) = 4.55 litres
	1 litre = 0.26 US gallons	1 US gallon (gal) = 5.46 litres
1 kilogramme (kg) = 1000kg	1 gramme (g) = 0.035oz	1 ounce (oz) = 28.57g
	1 kilogramme = 2.2lb	1 pound (lb = 454g

PART TWO

THE

GUIDE

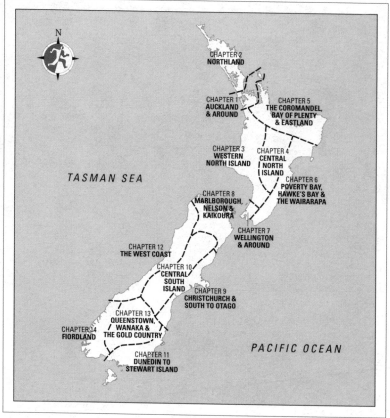

CHAPTER ONE

AUCKLAND AND AROUND

Auckland is New Zealand's largest and most cosmopolitan city and, as the site of the major international airport, is likely to be your introduction to the country. As planes bank high over the island-studded **Hauraki Gulf**, bright-spin-nakered yachts tack through the glistening waters towards this "City of Sails". Indeed, Auckland looks its best from the water, the high-rise downtown dwarfed by the brand-new Skytower and backed by the low, grassy humps of some of the fifty-odd extinct volcanoes which ring **Waitemata Harbour**. Beyond the central business district it is a low-slung city, rarely rising above two stories with prim wooden villas, each surrounded by a substantial garden, spreading off into the distance. As a consequence it is one of the least densely populated cities in the world; occupying twice the area of London and almost that of Los Angeles, it has barely more than a million inhabitants. With its attractive harbour, warm climate and the country's most exciting and vibrant cultural life, Auckland's fans rank it alongside Sydney, though it fails to live up to the claim on most counts. Look beyond the glitzy shopfronts and there's a modest small-town feel and a measured pace, though this can seem frenetic enough in comparison with the rest of the country.

Where Auckland stakes its claim to fame is as the **world's largest Polynesian city**. Almost twenty percent of the city's population claim Maori descent or are the families of migrants who arrived from Tonga, Samoa, the Cook Islands and other South Pacific islands during the 1960s and 1970s. Nevertheless, the Polynesian profile has tradi-tionally been confined to small pockets, notably the nexus of **Karangahape Road** (universally abbreviated to K' Road), and it is only fairly recently, as the second gen-eration reaches maturity, that Polynesia is making its presence felt in mainstream Auckland life, notably in the arts.

Auckland is often regarded very much as a transit place, and many visitors only stay long enough for a quick zip around the smattering of key sights before moving on to far less metropolitan locales. You could be forgiven for doing the same, but don't miss the **Auckland Museum**, with its matchless collection of Maori and Pacific Island carving and artefacts. With more time, dip into the country's strongest collection of New Zealand fine art at the **Auckland Art Gallery**, and delve into the perspex shark tunnels of **Kelly Tarlton's Underwater World**. Beyond these, the pleasure is in ambling around the fashionable inner-city suburbs of Ponsonby, Parnell and Devonport, and using the city a base for exploring what's **around Auckland** – the wild and desolate West Coast **surf beaches** an hour's drive from downtown, and the **wineries** nearby. Ferries based in the centre of the city open up the **Hauraki Gulf islands**: the botanically and geologically fascinating Rangitoto Island, the sophistic-ated city retreat of Waiheke Island and the time-warped and isolated Great Barrier Island.

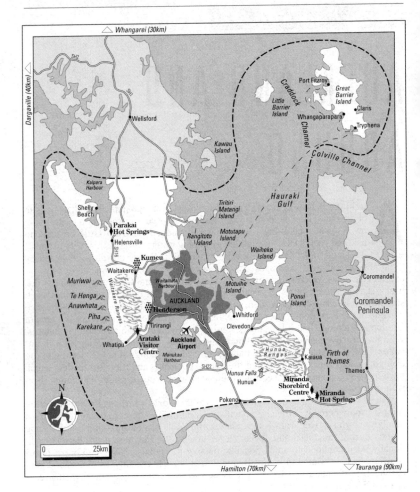

Auckland's **climate** is often described as muggy; it is never scorching hot, and the heat is always tempered by a sea breeze. Winters are generally mild but rainy.

AUCKLAND

AUCKLAND's urban sprawl completely smothers the North Island's wasp waist, a narrow isthmus where the island is all but severed by river estuaries probing inland from the city's two harbours. To the west, the shallow and silted **Manukau Harbour** opens out onto the Tasman Sea at a rare break in the long string of black-sand beaches continually pounded by heavy surf. Maori named the eastern anchorage **Waitemata Harbour** for its "sparkling waters", which constitute Auckland's deep water port and a focus for the heart of the city. Every summer weekend the harbour and adjoining Hauraki Gulf explode into a riot of brightly-coloured sails.

There could hardly be a more appropriate venue for the **Americas Cup**, which is due to be hosted in the Hauraki Gulf at the turn of the millennium (see box on p.80). As the city cranks up to the big event, it is consolidating its position as New Zealand's most **progressive city**, but its profusion of pavement cafés and trendy restaurants is somewhat at odds with dowdy streets, lack-lustre window displays and down-home trimmings. Despite Auckland's cosmopolitan bustle and harbourside setting, few fall in love with the city on short acquaintance or stick around long enough to scratch below the surface. Those who persist might just find themselves as enthusiastic about the place as Aucklanders.

Some history

The earth's crust between the Waitemata and Manukau harbours is so thin that every few thousand years, magma finds a fissure and bursts onto the surface, producing yet another volcano. The most recent eruption, some six hundred years ago, formed Rangitoto Island, to the horror of some of the region's earliest Maori inhabitants settled on adjacent Motutapu Island. Legend records their ancestors' arrival on the Tamaki Isthmus, the narrowest neck of land between Waitemata and Manukau harbours. With plentiful catches from two harbours and rich volcanic soils on a wealth of highly defensible volcano-top sites, the land, which they came to know as *Tamaki-makau-rau* ("the spouse sought by a hundred lovers"), was the prize of numerous battles over the centuries. By the middle of the eighteenth century it had fallen to **Kiwi Tamaki**, who established a three-thousand-strong pa or fortified village on *Maungakiekie* (One Tree Hill), and a satellite pa on just about every volcano in the district, but was eventually overwhelmed by rival *hapu* (sub-tribes) from Kaipara Harbour to the north.

With the arrival of musket-trading **Europeans** in the Bay of Islands around the beginning of the nineteenth century, Northland Ngapuhi were able to launch successful raids on the Tamaki Maori which, combined with the predations of smallpox epidemics, left the region almost uninhabited, a significant factor in its choice as the new capital after the signing of the Treaty of Waitangi in 1840. Scottish medic, **John Logan Campbell**, was one of few European residents when this fertile land, with easy access to major river and sea-borne trading routes, was purchased for £55 and some blankets. The capital was roughly laid out and Campbell took advantage of his early start, wheeling and dealing to achieve control of half the city, eventually becoming mayor and "the father of Auckland". After 1840, immigrants boosted the population to the extent that more land was needed, a demand which partly precipitated the **New Zealand Wars** of the 1860s (see Contexts, p.765).

During the depression that followed, many sought their fortunes in the Otago goldfields and, as the balance of European population shifted south, so did the centre of government. Auckland lost its **capital status** to Wellington in 1865 and the city slumped further, only seeing the glimpse of a recovery when prospectors flooded through on their way to the gold mines around Thames in the late 1860s. Since then Auckland has never looked back, repeatedly ranking as New Zealand's fastest growing city and absorbing waves of migrants, initially from Britain then, in the 1960s and 1970s from the Polynesian Islands of the South Pacific and, most recently, from Asian countries. Rising from the depression years of the early 1990s with its head high, Auckland is confidently leading New Zealand's renaissance as a modern nation, accepted on its own terms.

Arrival and information

As New Zealand's major gateway city, Auckland receives the bulk of **international arrivals**, a few disembarking from stately cruise ships at the dock by the Ferry Building, but the vast majority arriving by air.

Auckland International Airport is located 20km south of the city centre in the suburb of Mangere. A **taxi** into the city will set you back around $35, but there are plenty of **minibuses** vying for trade after each arrival, and most offer discounts to backpackers in possession of a YHA or student card. The Airbus (every 20mins 6.30am–8.30pm; $10 one-way, $16 return) follows a fixed route into the city, stopping in Newmarket and Parnell. Most other buses are more or less door-to-door services and charge around $15 for the first person to any one destination and $5–10 for each accompanying person (see "Listings", p.105, for operators). The well-stocked and helpful **visitor centre** (☎09/275 6467) stays open for all international arrivals and will book you into a city hotel free of charge, or you can make use of the bank of courtesy phones nearby. There's also a branch of the BNZ **bank** which changes money at reasonable rates, and some **duty-free shops**, where inbound passengers can top up their quota.

Three companies run long-distance **buses** into Auckland: InterCity and Newmans services arrive at the terminal in the Sky City casino complex on Hobson Street; Mount Cook Landlines buses pull in at the Downtown Airline Terminal on Quay Street, opposite the Ferry Building.

Trains pull in ten minutes' walk east of the centre of the city at the station on Beach Road.

Information

Auckland's main **visitor centre**, at 299 Queen St (Mon–Fri 8.30am–5.30pm, Sat & Sun 9am–5pm; ☎09/366 6888, fax 366 6893), though often crowded, is fairly efficient at booking and organizing pretty much anything you might want to do in New Zealand. At the bottom of Queen Street the **QEII Square visitor centre** (Nov–March daily 9.30am–5pm, April–Oct Mon–Fri 9.30am–5pm; ☎09/366 0691) serves much the same purpose. Both visitor centres, as well as booking agents, hotels and hostels, stock a number of advertisement-heavy **free publications**; the weekly *Auckland Tourist Times* newspaper, and two quarterlies, the *Auckland A–Z Visitors Guide* and the *Auckland What's On*. The last two both have sketch **maps** that are adequate for most purposes, or you could splash out on Wises' *Greater Auckland* fold-out sheet ($10).

The compact **Department of Conservation (DOC) office**, in the Ferry Building at 99 Quay St (Mon–Fri 8.30am–5pm, plus Nov–Feb Sat 9am–4.30pm & Dec–Jan Sun 9am–4.30pm; ☎09/366 2166), stocks DOC material for the whole country but specializes in the Auckland and Hauraki Gulf region.

City transport

Auckland's public transport is in a sorry state and periodic moves to improve it are hampered by the city's vast spread and low population density. That said, you'll find you can get to most places **on foot** (see box on p.69), by local **bus**, or with one of the city tour buses that shuttle between the major sights. Out on the harbour, **ferries** connect the city to the inner suburb of Devonport and numerous islands. **Taxis** are numerous and can be flagged down, though they seldom cruise the streets and are best contacted by phone (see "Listings", p.105, for numbers). Few visitors will find much use for the Tranz Metro suburban **train** services, which start from the station on Beach Road and call at graffiti-covered and inhospitable stations in places that are low on most visitors' must-see lists; the two lines run south through Newmarket and Ellerslie, and west through Henderson then north to Waitakere. Auckland **drivers** are reasonably courteous and **parking** isn't a major headache, but really you're better off renting a car once you're ready to leave the city. Hilly terrain and motorists' lack of

---

AUCKLAND WALKS

The most ambitious walking normally attempted in Auckland is a stroll through The Domain or a more demanding hike up to one of the volcano-top viewpoints. The best of these have been threaded together as the well-marked **Coast to Coast Walkway**, a four-hour, 13-kilometre route straddling the isthmus from the Ferry Building on Waitemata Harbour to Onehunga on Manukau Harbour. By devoting a full day to the enterprise you can take in much of the best Auckland has to offer, including excellent harbour views from The Domain and the summits of Mount Eden and One Tree Hill, the Auckland Museum, Albert Park, and numerous sites pivotal to the development of the city. All is revealed in the *Coast to Coast Walkway* leaflet, which includes information on intersecting bus routes for walkers who want to tackle shorter sections. Half a dozen **smaller-scale**, and generally less satisfying, **walks** are detailed in the *Inner City Strolling* leaflet. Both these leaflets are free and are widely available from visitor centres and some accommodation.

---

bike-awareness render **cycling** an unrealistic option through city streets, but the situation is redeemed by a few dedicated routes.

Buses

The majority of **local buses** are run by Yellow Buses, who also staff the Buz-a-Bus **timetable** helpline (☎09/366 6400 & 0800/366 640). The useful *Auckland Busabout Guide* leaflet is available free from visitor centres; other sources of bus **information** include newsagents and the Information Kiosk (Mon–Sat 7am–6.30pm, Sun 9am–5pm) at the **Downtown Bus Terminal** on Commerce Street.

The single most useful **route** is The Link (Mon–Thurs 6am–10pm, Fri 6am–11pm, Sat 7am–11pm, no Sun service; $1); these flashy white buses ply a continuous loop through the city, Parnell, Newmarket, K' Road and Ponsonby every ten minutes during the day and every half-hour in the evening. City-bound buses will be marked "Downtown" if terminating at the Downtown Bus Terminal, or "Midtown" if ending their run at the corner of Victoria Street and Queen Street.

Fares are charged according to a zonal system: the inner city, Parnell, Mount Eden and Ponsonby are covered by one zone ($1 per journey), from the city to Newmarket is two zones ($2), Henderson is five zones ($3.60), and so on. You can save ten percent by buying a **Ten-trip Ticket** (price determined by the number of zones covered), which is also valid on the trains; for short-stay visitors, a better deal is the **Busabout Day Pass** ($8 from bus drivers), which gives unlimited travel on buses and trains after 9am on weekdays and all day at weekends.

Tourist buses

The easiest way to get around the main sights is on one of the hop-on-hop-off **city tourist buses**, which run hourly between 10am and 4pm, and regale you with a commentary en route. They all follow much the same circuit from the Ferry Building on Quay Street (or opposite at the Downtown Airline Terminal), along Tamaki Drive to Kelly Tarlton's Underwater World, up to Parnell and the Auckland Museum, out to the Auckland Zoo and MOTAT, and back via Victoria Park Market and the Maritime Museum. The two main players are Bus A Bout (daily tickets $10 per person, $16 per couple; ☎09/358 1149) and the double-decker United Airlines Explorer Bus (☎0800/727 892; $15 for 1 day, $25 for a 2-day ticket); during the sumer months (Oct–April), the latter also takes in Mount Eden and the Auckland Art Gallery.

If you're really pressed for time, and don't mind the highly structured nature of a fully-fledged **bus tour**, there are plenty of companies willing to oblige (see "Listings", p.105, for details).

EXPLORING AUCKLAND'S WATERWAYS

Auckland is so water-focused that it would be a shame not to get out on the water at some point; and there is a welter of ways to do just that. The easiest and cheapest way is to hop on one of the **ferries** (see p.71), but for prolonged forays, consider one of the many **cruises** available; for a close-up perspective, a **sea-kayaking** trip offers a more intimate experience.

CRUISES

Fullers, of ferries fame, also offer a couple of **inexpensive cruises**: their Coffee Break Cruise (3–4 daily; 2hr; $22) tours the inner harbour, while the Lunch Cruise (4 daily; $38), combines a ten-minute harbour crossing with a meal at the waterside *Port o' Call* restaurant in Devonport. Comparable trips are run by Auckland Harbour Cruises (☎09/366 7000 & 0800/227 847): options include a Coffee Cruise (11am & 1pm; 1hr 30min; $25, optional seafood buffet $20 extra) and a Dinner Cruise (6pm, 1hr 30min, $65; 8pm, 2hr 30min; $75). A more **stylish** option is available on Friday and Saturday evenings courtesy of the 1904 MV *Kestrel* (hourly; $7 return), which shuttles back and forth to Devonport; on-board entertainment is provided by a jazz band, and moderately priced dinners are also served (reservations recommended, ☎09/377 1771).

Romantics might prefer a trip **under sail** on one of the Maritime Museum's fleet of yachts (☎09/373 4557); choose between the gentle half-day Morning Highlights (9.30am–2.30pm; $79) and the longer Auckland Experience (9.30am–4pm; $99), which includes a visit to Kelly Tarlton's Underwater World. On most **summer weekends**, you can help sail the *Søren Larsen* (Nov–March Sat 1–4pm, $45 & Sun 10am–4pm, $85; ☎09/411 8755), a Danish Baltic trader built of oak in 1949 and later fitted with a nineteenth-century sailing rig. This majestic vessel starred in the 1970s TV series *The Onedin Line* and led the First Fleet re-enactment that formed a part of the Australian bicentennial celebrations in 1987. Passengers are free to participate – steering, hauling sheets and climbing the rigging – though maritime instruction tends to be a larger component of the mid-week trips to Hauraki Gulf and Coromandel (2–5 nights, $450–1000).

If you want a **multi-day cruise** with a strong ornithological and botanical angle, look no further than the Adventure Cruising Co (Nov–April; ☎09/444 9342). With a **naturalist guide** aboard, the *Te Aroha*, a solid kauri trading ship dating from 1909, heads out into the gulf, visiting the Little Barrier Island wildlife sanctuary as well as Kawau Island (see p.140), Tiritiri Matangi, Rakino, Rangitoto and Motuora Island. All-inclusive itineraries range from **overnight trips** to Tiritiri Matangi ($165) to three-and four-day trips concentrating on **endangered species** and island restoration ($400 and up).

KAYAKING

Several companies around Auckland will take you **kayaking**. One of the most popular trips is with *Ferg's Kayak* (☎09/529 2230), kayaking the 7km across to Rangitoto Island (see p.117), watching sundown, then paddling back by the light of the silvery moon (Oct–March daily 5.30pm; 6hr; $45); they also do an evening trip to Devonport, stopping for a fish-and-chip supper (Oct–March daily 6pm; 4hr; $35).

The Devonport-based Little Adventure Co (☎0800/886 654) arranges less ambitious trips, guiding you along the coastline ($15 an hour), or on a sunset tours ($35), while highly-regarded paddling trips with an ecological bent are organized by Auckland Wilderness Kayaking (2 days, $315; ☎09/630 7782).

Ferries

Waitemata Harbour was once a seething mass of ferries bringing commuters in from the suburbs. Services have been rationalized over the years, but the harbour **ferries** remain a fast, pleasurable and scenic way to get around. The main destinations are the Hauraki Gulf islands (see p.116), but there are also services calling at Devonport and the Orakei Wharf, run by Fullers, the principal ferry company (☎09/367 9111, timetable information ☎09/367 9102). The **Devonport Ferry** (daily 6am–11pm; every 20min; $7 return, bikes $1) is the cheapest of the ferries and takes around fifteen minutes to cross the harbour. On Friday and Saturday evenings, the service is supplemented by the 1904 MV *Kestrel* (see box on p.70).

To explore further afield, invest in a **Harbour Explorer All Day Boat Pass** ($22), which entitles you to stop at Devonport, Orakei Wharf and Rangitoto Island. If you're here for a few days, consider a **Harbour Explorer Super Ticket** ($59), which is valid for five days, includes two All Day Boat Passes, a couple of Devonport ferry tickets, and admission to Kelly Tarlton's Underwater World (see p.88).

Driving

With many of the Auckland region's sights conveniently accessible on foot or by public transport, there isn't a huge advantage in having a car while you're in the city, though you'll need one to explore far-flung gems like the Henderson wineries and the surf beaches of the West Coast. As the main point of entry, Auckland is awash with places to **rent a car** (see 'Listings", p.105 for details of outfits in the city); and if you're planning on some serious touring, you may be interested in **buying a car** – see Basics, p.29, for some advice on the pros and cons, as well as the potential pitfalls.

Driving around Auckland isn't especially taxing, with relatively tame rush hours and few aggressive drivers. That said, on first acquaintance, Auckland's urban freeways can be unnerving, with frequent junctions and vehicles overtaking on all sides. If you are used to driving on the right, it takes that much longer to go with the flow; if you've just arrived after a long flight, consider waiting a day or so before driving. Inner-city streets are metered, which means that parking is best done in multi-storey **car parks** dotted all over the central city and reasonably well signposted (see "Listings", p.107, for locations); none are open 24 hours, so check the latest exit time – usually around midnight.

Cycling

Cycling around Auckland's hills can be a tiring and dispiriting exercise. However, a few areas lend themselves to pedal-powered exploration, most notably the harbourside Tamaki Drive east of the city centre, which forms part of a 50km **cycle route** around the city and isthmus – detailed in a free leaflet available from visitor centres. **Rental bikes** cost around $15–25 per day ($70–120 a week), depending on the sophistication of the model; see "Listings", p.105, for details of outlets. In addition, there are several companies that offer monthly rental and **buy-back schemes** for long-stayers (see Basics, p.31).

Accommodation

Auckland has a broader range of accommodation than anywhere else in the country, but that doesn't stop everywhere filling up through December, January and February, when you should definitely **book ahead**. At other times this is less critical, and through the quiet winter months from June to September you'll be spoiled for choice and will find significant discounts on room rates, particularly if you're staying for a few days; it's always worth asking.

Perhaps more than anywhere else in New Zealand, Auckland is a place where you might choose to stay outside the **city centre**. Unless you have a mind to hit the clubs or have arrangements to make in the centre, you may have little cause to spend much time there, and sightseeing can be done just as easily from the **suburbs**. Inner-city suburbs such as **Parnell**, 2km east of the centre; **Ponsonby**, a similar distance west of the centre; **Mount Eden**, 2km south of the central city; and peaceful and salubrious **Devonport**, a short ferry journey across the harbour, all make excellent alternatives. Besides, all four suburbs are well supplied with places to eat and drink, Ponsonby and Parnell's main streets ranking as the city's most vibrant.

The city centre remains the place to find international four- and five-star **hotels**, mostly geared towards business travellers and tour groups; walk-in rates are usually prohibitively high, though there are sometimes tempting weekend deals. Backpacker **hostels** also congregate in the city centre and along the narrow corridor from Parnell into Grafton and Newmarket; **B&Bs** and **guesthouses** are strongest in Devonport and the southern suburbs of Epsom and Remuera; and the widest selection of **motels** is just south of Newmarket in Epsom.

Predictably, **campsites** are much further out.

Hotels and motels

As befits New Zealand's largest city, the range of **hotels** and **motels** is second to none. Hotels pepper the city centre and inner suburbs, ranging from places little more salubrious than the hostels up to swanky five-star affairs. High city rents force motels further out and you'll see them just about everywhere, but nowhere more so than the stretch of Great South Road in Epsom, immediately south of the Newmarket shops, where there are at least a dozen places in a kilometre. We've stuck to recommending places that are relatively convenient to the centre and the main sights.

City centre

All the following hotels and motels are marked on the map on p.74.

Centra, 128 Albert St (☎09/302 1111, fax 302 3111). Serious business hotel occupying the top floors of an office block, with most rooms having great city and harbour views. Occasional weekend rates as low as ⑧, otherwise ⑨.

De Brett, cnr High St & Shortland St (☎09/303 2389, fax 303 2300). Built in the Thirties, this international-standard hotel still retains some Art-Deco features in the public areas. The spacious en-suite rooms are mostly modernized but slightly faded. ⑤.

AIRPORT ACCOMMODATION

With a choice of several efficient door-to-door shuttle services into central Auckland there is little reason to stay near the airport except, perhaps, if you have a hideously early flight to catch. There is no accommodation actually at the airport site, but a dozen places line McKenzie and Kirkbride roads in Mangere, some 5km away at the end of the approach road and close to many of the car-rental pick-up points. The pricier places have their own shuttle services, while the others rely on the airport shuttle buses which pick up and drop off for $3 per person; a taxi fare over the same distance will cost about $12.

Kiwi International Motor Inn, 150 McKenzie Rd (☎09/256 0046 & 0800/801 919, fax 256 0047). Both hotel and motel-style rooms, plus restaurant and bar facilities and free transfers. ⑤.

Oakwood Manor Motor Inn, 610 Massey Rd (☎09/275 0539 & 0800/801 555, fax 275 0534). One of the better airport places, with indoor spa, outdoor swimming pool and free transfers. ⑥.

Pacific Inn, 210 Kirkbride Road (☎09/275 1129 & 0800/504 800, fax 275 1128).

Modern and fairly spacious studio rooms with TV and tea- and coffee-making facilities, as well as a restaurant and bar downstairs. ④.

Skyway Lodge, 30 Kirkbride Rd (☎09/275 4443, fax 275 5012). Basic budget accommodation with beds in shared rooms and compact doubles. Dorms ①, doubles ③.

Traveller's International, 190 Kirkbride Rd (☎09/275 5082 & 0800/800 562, fax 256 0106). Conference-orientated motor inn with free transfers, a pool and attractive rooms. ⑤.

First Imperial, 131–139 Hobson St (☎09/357 6770, fax 357 6793). Spacious, modern and surprisingly quiet business hotel with on-site bar and restaurant and quality rooms, all with private facilities and some with good harbour views. Rooms ⑦, apartments ⑧.

Kiwi International, 411 Queen St (☎09/379 6487 & 0800/100 411, fax 379 6496). A rather characterless and ageing warren of rooms that compensates with off-street parking and low rates. The standard rooms are fairly comfortable, economy rooms come without a bathroom and there are bunks in dorms, though no self-catering facilities. Dorms ①, economy rooms ③, standard rooms ④.

Novotel, 8 Custom St (☎09/377 8920, fax 307 3739). Second-string business hotel with some nice rooms overlooking the water. Weekend specials ⑦, otherwise ⑨.

Park Towers, 3 Scotia Place (☎09/309 2800 & 0800/809 377, fax 302 1964). One of the best-value hotels in the city with excellent weekend deals. En-suite rooms are modern and airy, many have expansive views, and there's the full range of hotel facilities including bar, brasserie and off-street parking. Weekends ⑤, weekdays ⑦.

Sky City, cnr Victoria St & Federal St (☎09/912 6000 & 0800/777 711, fax 912 6032). Part of the casino complex, with all the facilities that entails: rooftop pool, gym, sauna, bars and restaurants. Rooms are standard, international-hotel style but nicely done, many with good harbour views. Rack rates start high and rise through the stratosphere, but walk-in rates (including breakfast and valet parking) are often lower, especially at weekends and in the winter. Specials ⑧, otherwise ⑨.

Stamford Plaza, Albert St (☎09/309 8888 & 0800/442 519, fax 379 6445). One of Auckland's top hotels with prices to match. A little pretentious and glitzy, but ameliorated by frequent weekend deals that include breakfast, cinema tickets, free wine and the like. Weekend specials ⑨, otherwise ⑨.

Whitaker Lodge, 21 Whitaker Place (☎09/37 3623, fax 377 3621). Very central motel tucked down in Grafton Gully and right by the motorway but surprisingly appealing. Choice of smallish rooms without cooking facilities or regular motel units. Rooms ⑤, units ⑥.

Parnell

All the following hotels and motels are marked on the map on p.99.

Parnell Inn, 320 Parnell Rd (☎ & fax 09/358 0642). Compact and simple hotel attached to *The Other Side* café right in the heart of Parnell. Rooms are fairly small, some having cooking facilities, and off-street parking is available. ⑤.

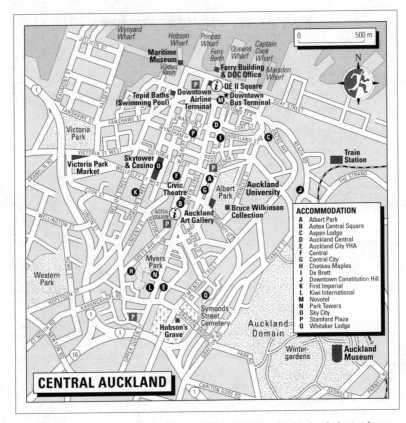

CENTRAL AUCKLAND

ACCOMMODATION

A	Albert Park
B	Aotea Central Square
C	Aspen Lodge
D	Auckland Central
E	Auckland City YHA
F	Central
G	Central City
H	Chateau Maples
I	De Brett
J	Downtown Constitution Hill
K	First Imperial
L	Kiwi International
M	Novotel
N	Park Towers
O	Sky City
P	Stamford Plaza
Q	Whitaker Lodge

Parnell Rise, 73 Parnell Rd (☎09/358 1178, fax 357 0518). Ageing but functional, clean and super-cheap motel right in Parnell and an easy walk from the city. ④.

Parnell Village, 2 St Stephen's Ave (☎09/377 1463, fax 373 4192). Slightly cramped but well-maintained motor inn opposite the cathedral with studios and self-catering units. Studios ⑤, units ⑥.

Epsom

All the following hotels and motels are marked on the map on p.86.

Green Park, 66 Great South Rd (☎09/520 3038, fax 520 4705). Renovated motel with standard and executive suites, all with separate bedrooms and full facilities. ⑤–⑥.

Hansen's, 96 Great South Rd (☎09/520 2804, fax 524 7597). One of the cheapest motels in town with small but perfectly formed self-contained studios and a nice swimming pool. ④.

Off Broadway, 11 Alpers Ave (☎09/529 3550, fax 529 3551). Brand new business-orientated hotel with air-conditioned, soundproofed en-suite rooms. Plump for the much larger studios or suites if your budget allows. Studios ⑥–⑦, suites ⑧.

Siesta, 70 Great South Rd (☎09/520 2107, fax 522 4413). Good modern motel with kitchenless studios and self-catering units. Studios ④, units ⑤.

Tudor Court, 18 Great South Rd (☎09/523 1069, fax 523 3970). Compact motel with small hotel-style rooms and slightly larger ones with kitchenettes. Spa pool on site. ④.

Ponsonby, Herne Bay and Freeman's Bay

All the following hotels and motels are marked on the map on p.100.

Abaco Spa, 59 Jervois Rd (☎09/376 0119, fax 378 7039). Mainstream motel close to Herne Bay and Ponsonby shops and restaurants, with budget kitchenless rooms, and larger motel units, some with private spas and distant harbour views. Budget rooms ④, units ⑤–⑥.

Harbour Bridge, 6 Tweed St (☎09/376 3489). Excellent-value modern motel units based around a century-old house with a peaceful garden and located in a quiet street. ④–⑤.

Unicorn, 31 Shelley Beach Rd (☎09/376 2067, fax 376 0685). Top-quality, modern, air-conditioned motel with spacious fully-equipped units, and a small pool. ⑥.

B&Bs and guesthouses

Auckland's stock of B&Bs and guesthouses is rapidly expanding. New places are continually opening, many pitching for the upper end of the market, with just a few rooms and an almost obsessive attention to the finest detail. Places are scattered widely around the **inner suburbs** on the south side of the harbour, but in recent years the choice in the North Shore suburb of **Devonport** has mushroomed. At last count there were over a dozen high-standard places, not all of them close to the ferry but all willing to pick up and drop off if you arrive that way.

City centre

All the following guesthouses are marked on the map on p.74.

Aspen Lodge, 62 Emily Place (☎09/379 6698, fax 377 7625). Compact hotel right in the heart of the city but surprisingly quiet and with a small garden and deck. Rooms aren't big and don't have private facilities but it's great value and a continental breakfast is included. ④.

Chateau Maples, 100 Grey's Ave (☎ & fax 09/358 2737). Good-value B&B on a quiet street right in the city centre with pleasant, though small, rooms with shared bathrooms, off-street parking and continental breakfast. ④.

Parnell

All the following guesthouses are marked on the map on p.99.

Chalet Chevron, 14 Brighton Rd, Parnell (☎09/309 0291, fax 373 5754). Comfortable B&B with some pokey and some spacious en-suite rooms. ⑤.

St Georges Bay Lodge, 43 St Georges Bay Rd, Parnell (☎09/303 1050, fax 303 1055). Gorgeous and welcoming B&B in one of the four original St Georges Bay villas, built in the 1890s and since tastefully and authentically renovated, fitted out in native timbers and hung with New Zealand artworks. Complimentary port and wine, and a full breakfast are all part of the package. ⑥.

Mount Eden, Epsom and Remuera

All the following guesthouses are marked on the map on p.86.

Aachen House, 39 Market Rd, Remuera (☎09/520 2329 & 0800/AACHEN, fax 524 2829). Elegant boutique B&B in an Edwardian house sumptuously decorated with antiques. Every comfort is

---

GAY-FRIENDLY ACCOMMODATION

Although Auckland doesn't have any exclusively gay or lesbian hotels, neither does it have a reputation for homophobic proprietors, so you can stay pretty much where you like. There is, however, some gay-friendly accommodation, mostly small **guesthouses**: check out *Aspen Lodge*, in the city centre; *Bavaria B&B* in Mount Eden; *Remuera House* in Remuera; *Dryden Lodge* and *The Great Ponsonby B&B* in Ponsonby; *Heathmaur Lodge* in Herne Bay – all reviewed in our main "B&Bs and guesthouses" listings, starting on p.75.

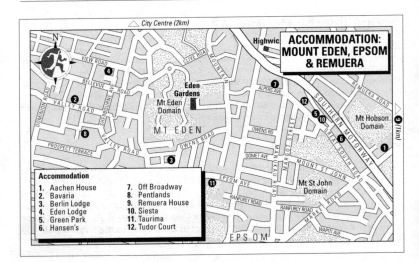

ACCOMMODATION: MOUNT EDEN, EPSOM & REMUERA

City Centre (2km)

Highwic

Eden Gardens

Mt Eden Domain

MT EDEN

Mt Hobson Domain

Mt St John Domain

EPSOM

Accommodation

1. Aachen House
2. Bavaria
3. Berlin Lodge
4. Eden Lodge
5. Green Park
6. Hansen's
7. Off Broadway
8. Pentlands
9. Remuera House
10. Siesta
11. Taurima
12. Tudor Court

catered for.: rooms are spacious, beds are huge, bathrooms are beautifully tiled and breakfasts are delicious. ⑦.

Bavaria, 83 Valley Rd, Mount Eden (☎09/638 9641, fax 638 9665). Spacious, comfortable ninety-year-old B&B villa that's popular with German speakers, and boasts a pleasant deck and garden. Buses numbered in the 250s and 260s run along Dominion Road close by. ⑤.

Pentlands, 22 Pentlands Ave, Mount Eden (☎ & fax 09/638 7031). Peaceful, low-cost B&B ten minutes' walk from Mount Eden shops with plain bathless rooms but spacious lounges and a tennis court and barbecue area out back. Continental breakfast is served. ④.

Remuera House, 500 Remuera Rd, Remuera (☎09/524 7794). Characterful, turn-of-the-century guesthouse packed with art and antiques and offering attractive double and single rooms. ④.

Taurima, 18 Epsom Ave, Epsom (☎ & fax 09/630 7710). Friendly B&B in an attractive suburban villa fifteen minutes' walk from Mount Eden and Newmarket. Only one of the rooms and the self-catering cottage in the garden are en suite, but all are nicely decorated and a formidable cooked breakfast is served. ⑤.

Devonport

All the following guesthouses are marked on the map on p.93.

Cheltenham-by-the-Sea, 2 Grove Rd (☎ & fax 09/445 9437). Devonport's cheapest B&B, right by Cheltenham Beach, twenty minutes' walk from the ferry. Rooms are spacious and simple, in a comfortable, modern home run by friendly folk. ⑤.

Devonport Villa, 46 Tainui Rd (☎09/445 8397, fax 445 9766; email *dvilla@ihug.co.nz*). Luxurious, top-class B&B near Cheltenham Beach in a lovingly restored Edwardian villa decorated with contemporary Kiwi art. There's a tastefully restrained feel to both the very comfortable en-suite rooms in the house and the colonial style cottages in the garden. Sumptuous breakfasts are served. ⑦.

The Garden Room, 23 Cheltenham Rd (☎ & fax 09/445 2472). A lovely private cottage in a leafy garden; breakfast can be served under an arbour or in your room. ⑥.

Karin's Garden Villa, 14 Sinclair St (☎09/445 8689). Very good-value B&B fifteen minutes' walk from the ferry with a self-catering kitchen and pleasant rooms, some with verandahs overlooking the large garden. Continental breakfast is served. ⑤.

Peace and Plenty Inn, 6 Flagstaff Terrace (☎09/445 2925, fax 445 2901). One of New Zealand's finest B&Bs. Elegantly restored kauri floorboards lead through to a lovely verandah, past exquisite rooms filled with fresh flowers and equipped with sherry and port. If you can bear to venture outside the bounds of the inn, you're right in the heart of Devonport. The communal breakfast is a major event, and the hosts will even take you sailing. ⑧.

Villa Cambria, 71 Vauxhall Rd (☎09/445 7899, fax 446 0508; email *villacambria@xtra.co.nz*). Beautifully decorated Victorian villa close to Cheltenham beach and fifteen minutes' walk from Devonport with friendly and attentive hosts who provide lovely breakfasts. ⑥–⑦.

Ponsonby and Herne Bay
All the following guesthouses are marked on the map on p.100.

Dryden Lodge, 27–31 Dryden St, Ponsonby (☎09/378 0892; fax 378 1282). Somewhat faded guest-house close to the Grey Lynn shops with reasonable rooms and an ardent gay and lesbian following. ④.

Freeman's B&B, 65 Wellington St, Ponsonby (☎09/376 5046, fax 376 4052). Good-value B&B well-placed midway between the city and Ponsonby with doubles, spacious self-contained apartments (without breakfast) and a secluded garden. Rooms ④, apartments ⑤.

The Great Ponsonby B&B, 30 Ponsonby Terrace, Ponsonby (☎09/376 5989, fax 376 5527). Boutique hotel in a restored 1898 villa three minutes' walk from Ponsonby Road, boldly decorated in ocean tones using native timbers and Pacific artworks and furnishings. All rooms are en-suite and come with satellite TV, there are a couple of self-catering studio units at the back. Everyone has use of the sunny lounge and shaded garden. ⑥.

Heathmaur Lodge, 75 Argyle St, Herne Bay (☎09/376 3527). Spacious B&B in a huge three-storey Edwardian house with excellent harbour views from some of the rooms, a smattering of original fittings and a spacious lounge with pool table. Basic rooms ④, en-suite rooms with views ⑤.

Hostels

Auckland has stacks of **backpacker hostels**. The scene is highly competitive, and most are very well set up for assisting new arrivals in planning their onward travel, even to the extent of having a fully staffed on-site travel service – sometimes pushing favoured trips and activities, but generally offering fair and impartial advice.

There's a definite trade off between proximity to the facilities offered by **downtown** hostels, and the relative quiet and comfort of places outside the centre. Those in the centre tend to cram in the beds and, with bars and clubs only a short stagger away, cater to party animals. The emphasis is firmly on having a wild time and the larger places have a reputation for being noisy at night; self-catering facilities seem like an afterthought and serve to encourage guests to eat out or patronize the on-site café. Hostels in the **inner suburbs** – mostly in Parnell and Mount Eden – tend to be less boisterous affairs often in old, converted houses, sometimes with gardens and always with easy parking.

As you'd expect, **prices** are a touch higher than at hostels in the rest of the country, though by squeezing ten or twelve into a dorm, hostels are still able to offer beds around the $14 mark. Small dorms and four-shares hover around $18 and most doubles and twins just edge over $40. If you are arriving during the peak summer season, try to book a couple of days in advance to be sure of getting a bed.

City centre
All the following hostels are marked on the map on p.74.

Albert Park, 27–31 Victoria St East (☎09/309 0336, fax 309 9474). Probably the best of the city centre backpackers; new, clean and fairly spacious with some large, and several smaller dorms, comfortable doubles, reasonable cooking facilities, bar and pool table. Dorms ①, rooms ②.

Aotea Central Square, 2nd Floor, 295 Queen St (☎0800/733 031). Low-key mid-town backpackers with good laundry and kitchen facilities and largish rooms. Dorms ①, rooms ③.

Auckland Central, 9 Fort St (☎09/358 4877, fax 358 4872). Auckland's biggest and rowdiest hostel, located in an eight-storey building just off Queen St. Facilities run to a cinema, a well-stocked rooftop bar and café with good-value daily specials, pool tables and video games, an outdoor-gear shop and a big travel centre. The ten-bed dorms are some of the cheapest in the centre, though the marginally more expensive four-shares are a better bet. Dorms ①, rooms ③.

Auckland City YHA, cnr City Rd & Liverpool St (☎09/309 2802, fax 373 5083). The most central of Auckland's two YHAs and, with 160 beds, the country's largest. Seven floors of mostly twin and double rooms – some with fine city views – plus well-equipped common areas and a large travel centre. Dorms ①, rooms ③.

Central City, 26 Lorne St (☎09/358 5685, fax 358 4716). Large, busy and ever-popular hostel just off Queen Street with a lively atmosphere and stacks of local information plus a travel agency and bar downstairs. Four floors of ten-bunk dorms, four-shares and doubles are well-equipped and fairly spacious. Dorms ①, rooms ③.

Downtown Constitution Hill, 6 Constitution Hill (☎09/303 4768). The smallest of Auckland's central backpackers fills a couple of houses close to the city and train station and mid-way to Parnell. It is friendly, homely, has a small garden, on-parking and fairly cramped four- and six-bunk dorms and double rooms. Dorms ①, rooms ②.

Parnell, Newmarket and Grafton
All the following hostels are marked on the map on p.86

City Garden Lodge, 25 St Georges Bay Rd, Parnell (☎09/302 0880, fax 309 8998). One of the city's smallest and finest backpackers in a spacious, well-organized villa surrounded by expansive lawns. For an extra dollar or two, the three- and five-person dorms have beds rather than bunks, and there are some lovely double and twin rooms. Dorms ①, rooms ③.

Georgia Parkside, 189 Park Rd, Grafton (☎09/309 8999). The cheapest beds in these parts, squeezed into twelve-bunk dorms and four-shares in an ageing house, but with good facilities for the price. Dorms ①, rooms ②.

International Backpackers (Alan's Place), 8 Maunsell Rd, Newmarket (☎09/358 4584). A vast, former home for the blind right by the Auckland Museum and close to Newmarket's shops and restaurants. The slightly institutional feel is easily compensated for by a well-run operation, a massive kitchen, spacious dorms and huge doubles. Dorms ①, rooms ②.

Lantana Lodge, 60 St Georges Bay Rd, Parnell (☎09/373 4546). Small, spotlessly clean and friendly hostel with good facilities. Dorms ①, rooms ②.

Parnell YHA, 2 Churton St, Parnell (☎09/379 3731, fax 358 4143). Clean, peaceful hostel on a quiet street three minutes' from Parnell with parking and a nice fenced garden. Dorms ①, rooms ②.

YWCA, 10 Carlton Gore Rd, Grafton (☎09/377 8763, fax 358 1628). Very small and secure women-only hostel with self-catering facilities and a couple of three-bed rooms let by the night or for $110 a week. ①.

Mount Eden
All the following hostels are marked on the map on p.86.

Berlin Lodge, 5a Oaklands Road, Mount Eden (☎09/638 6545). Former YHA in a big old house right by Mount Eden shops. Progressive renovation is gradually improving the standard of accommodation. Beds come in a large dorms, four-shares and doubles. Catch buses #274 or #275 from the Downtown Bus Terminal. Dorms ①, rooms ③.

Eden Lodge, 22 View Rd, Mount Eden (☎ & fax 09/630 0174). Well-run, spacious and very clean hostel with all the facilities you could ask for and lawns right around the house. The cheapest beds are in a cramped bunkhouse outside, but there are better dorms inside and well-priced doubles. Catch bus #274 or #275 from the Downtown Bus Terminal. Dorms ①, rooms ②.

Ponsonby and Grey Lynn
All the following hostels are marked on the map on p.86.

Ivanhoe Lodge, 14 Shirley Rd, Grey Lynn (☎09/846 2800, fax 846 8599). All the usual facilities, but rooms let on a weekly basis only ($160 per double, $100 per single). Take the #045 Point Chevalier bus from the Downtown Bus Terminal.

Ponsonby Backpackers, 2 Franklin Rd, Ponsonby (☎09/360 1311). Rambling hostel in a large Victorian house with off-street parking. The rooms are nothing special but the place is a good deal more peaceful than the city hostels and you're right by the Ponsonby bars and restaurants. Catch bus #15 or #16 from the train station or Queen Street. Dorms ①, rooms ②.

Campsites and motor parks
You'd have to travel a long way to find anywhere genuinely attractive to pitch a **tent**, but there are numerous well-equipped motor camps within the city limits which are

fine for **campervans** and often have bargain **cabins**. However, without your own vehicle, you'll find yourself spending a lot of time and money on buses, the costs outweighing any saving you may make over staying in town.

Avondale Motor Park, 46 Bollard Ave, Avondale (☎09/828 7228, fax 828 3344). Restful and fairly central site 6km southwest of the city and accessible by Yellow Buses #210 and #229 from Victoria St. Tent sites $9–10, on-site vans ②, cabins & flats ③.

North Shore Motels & Holiday Park, 52 Northcote Rd, Takapuna (☎09/418 2578, fax 480 0435). Well-appointed site on the North Shore, just off the northern motorway, with indoor swimming pool and extensive barbecue areas. Catch Yellow Buses #921 and #922 from the corner of Victoria and Hobson streets. Tent sites $12.50, cabins & motel units ②–⑤.

Remuera Motor Lodge and Inner City Camping Ground, 16 Minto Rd (☎09/524 5126 & freephone 0508/244244, fax 524 5639). About the most central, convenient and appealing site, 6km east of the city in a quiet, sylvan residential area. There's even a swimming pool. Buses #645 and #655 from the Downtown Bus Terminal will get you here. Sites $10, dorms ①, motel units ②–⑤.

Takapuna Beach Caravan Park, 22 The Promenade, Takapuna (☎ & fax 09/489 7909). Beachside caravan park on the North Shore overlooking Rangitoto and within five minutes' walk of the Takapuna shops and restaurants. Yellow Buses numbered in the 800s and 900s from the cnr Victoria St & Hobson St pass nearby. Tent sites $9, flats & cabins ②–③.

Tui Glen Camping Park, 56 Edmonton Rd, Henderson (☎09/838 8978). Well-equipped and pleasant site in a residential area at the foot of the Waitakere Ranges, 12km west of the city and accessible on the Henderson train line, Yellow Buses from the Downtown Bus Terminal and express Whenuapai Buses from Lower Albert St. Tent sites $8, campervan sites $20, flats & cabins ②–③.

The City

Auckland's city centre clings to the southern shores of the **Waitemata Harbour**, with **Queen Street**, the main drag, striking south through a downbeat business district largely sustained by banks and insurance companies, as the ascendant inner-city suburbs – trendy Ponsonby, affluent Parnell and go-ahead Newmarket – continually erode its mercantile dominance.

Queen Street meets the harbour at the Ferry Building, hub of ferry services to the North Shore, the maritime suburb of **Devonport** and to the islands of the Hauraki Gulf. One of the best ways to begin your exploration of the city is on foot, following the **Coast-to-Coast Walkway** which starts here and winds up through the city past many sights (see box on p.69). Skirting **Albert Park**, wedged between the **University** and the **Auckland Art Gallery**, the route then veers towards **The Domain**, an extensive blanket of parkland that represents Auckland's premiere green space, laid out around the city's most-visited attraction, the **Auckland Museum**. The Domain divides the city from the inner-eastern suburb of **Parnell**, ecclesiastical heart of the city with the **Cathedral**, one of Auckland's oldest churches and a couple of historical houses, both associated with clergymen. The walkway finishes beside Manukau Harbour, after climbing to two of Auckland's highest points, **Mount Eden** and its more diverting kin, **One Tree Hill** with its encircling **Cornwall Park**.

To the east of Parnell, the harbourside **Tamaki Drive** runs past **Kelly Tarlton's Underwater World** to the city beaches of Mission Bay and St Heliers. West of the centre, the suburbs spread out beyond the reclaimed basin of Freeman's Bay to Auckland's most concentrated cluster of superb restaurants and cafés along **Ponsonby** Road, and out to Western Springs, home to the **Auckland Zoo** and the transport museum commonly referred to by its abbreviated name, **MOTAT**.

Aucklanders with time on their hands and a penchant for thundering breakers leave the stresses of city behind and head to the surf **beaches** of the West Coast (see p.109) but there are local spots for a more impulsive dip, particularly compact and often-crowded coves along **Tamaki Drive** and the more expansive strands on the North Shore near **Takapuna**.

Downtown and The Domain

Auckland's central city street names represent a roll call of prime movers in New Zealand's early European history. The city's backbone, Queen Street, along with attendant royal acolytes, Victoria and Albert streets, forms a central grid bedded with thoroughfares commemorating the country's first Governor-General, William Hobson; Willoughby Shortland, New Zealand's first colonial secretary; and William Symonds, who chivvied along isthmus Maori chiefs reluctant to sign the Treaty of Waitangi.

The central business district butts up against **Waitemata Harbour** which, through the development of the **Maritime Museum** and the waterside rejuvenation in preparation for the defence of the **Americas Cup** at the turn of the millennium (see box below), is gradually being reconnected to the city. There's little of abiding interest right in the city centre except for the **Auckland Art Gallery**, the country's foremost showcase for fine art. The highbrow theme continues to the east at the excellent **Auckland Museum**, packed with superb Maori and Pacific Islander artefacts, which

---

THE AMERICAS CUP

For a few glorious days in May 1995 **yacht-racing** eclipsed rugby as New Zealand's premiere sport. Peter Blake, skipper of the *Black Magic* crew which wrested yachting's most valuable prize, the Americas Cup, from the Americans (for only the second time in the race's 144-year history), was feted as a national hero and the crew were welcomed down Queen Street with a ticker-tape parade.

The cup was **first contested** as the "One Hundred Guinea Cup", with fifteen British boats and one American racing to circumnavigate the Isle of Wight, off the south coast of England, as part of imperial Britain's self-congratulatory Great Exhibition in 1851. The schooner *America* romped away with the trophy and the New York Yacht Club held on to it through 23 defences, during which time the race became a battlefield for some of the world's most experienced crews and a proving ground for the latest boat designs, using space-age composite materials.

Finally, in 1983, the Perth Yacht Club's controversial winged-keel *Australia II*, showed that the Americans didn't have an inalienable right to the "Auld Mug". The Americas Cup became something of a holy grail for Kiwis, and everything eventually came together in 1995, with *Black Magic* losing only one race in the challenger series. Kiwis went nuts. When Peter Blake declared that the **red socks** he had been wearing were his lucky charm, the entire nation – Prime Minister Jim Bolger and Governor-General Catherine Tizard included – donned red socks, the proceeds of sales going to fund the *Black Magic* crew, who went on to trounce the Americans five–nil in the final series.

The victory in the seas off San Diego earned New Zealand the right to **defend the trophy** on home turf. From November 1999 the waters of the **Hauraki Gulf** will host a series of races. One between New Zealand boats will determine the defender of the trophy, and one between yachts from around the world will decide the challenger; the final race-off between the two winners will take place from February 26 to March 5, 2000. Auckland has begun to gear up for the five-month jibe-fest: **Viaduct Basin**, in downtown Auckland, will be transformed to accommodate the various crews, waterfront property-owners are turning a business eye to renting out their homes for a few months, and **Maori** groups with claims to the development sites struggle to get some remuneration from the event. For one disgruntled Maori, things came to a head in February 1997 when, driven by frustration, he smashed the cup – then on display in the Royal New Zealand Yacht Squadron's clubhouse – with a sledge hammer. The battered trophy occupied a first-class seat on the plane when it was flown to its original manufacturer, the royal jeweller Garrard's in London, for emergency repairs.

To keep abreast of the lead-up to the Americas Cup, surf *www.ac2000.co.nz* which lists race dates and links to the Web sites of challenger syndicates.

dominates **The Domain**, a vast swathe of trees and lawns sweeping down towards the harbour.

The waterfront

Auckland's waterfront is dominated by the neo-classical 1912 **Ferry Building**, which is still the hub of the Waitemata Harbour ferry services, though the chaotic bustle of the days before the construction of the harbour bridge is now a distant memory. Nonetheless, there's a constant ebb and flow of commuters and sightseers boarding speedy catamarans to Devonport, the Coromandel Peninsula and offshore to Rangitoto, Waiheke and Great Barrier islands.

The seafaring theme continues a couple of hundred metres west at the **National Maritime Museum**, Viaduct Quay, on the corner of Quay Street and Hobson Street (daily Nov–Easter 9am–6pm; Easter–Oct 9am–5pm; $9) which pays homage to the maritime history of an island nation reliant on the sea for Maori and *pakeha* colonization, trade and sport. Outrigger and double-hulled canoes from all over the South Pacific illustrate the huge variety of designs employed for fishing, lagoon sailing and ocean voyaging – the last represented by the huge 23m-long *Taratai*, which carried New Zealand photographer and writer James Siers and a crew of thirteen over 2400km from Kiribati to Fiji in 1976. Made entirely from traditional materials and propelled by an oceanic lateen sail, its intriguing method of operation is neatly demonstrated on a rig nearby. The creaking innards of a migrant ship and displays on New Zealand's coastal traders and whalers lead on to a collection of just about every class of yacht, culminating in the devotional exhibits on yacht racing – in particular, comprehensive coverage of the **Americas Cup** (see box on p.80), its history and detailed scale replicas of key entrants. Other highlights include a very early example of the Hamilton Jetboat, which was designed for shallow, braided Canterbury rivers, and a replica of a classic 1950s holiday bach and milk bar, with great archival film footage adding to the nostalgic flavour.

The Maritime Museum backs on to **Viaduct Basin**, a lively row of restaurants, bars and harbour cruise company offices, due for massive redevelopment in time for the Americas Cup defence, that makes a good spot to while away an hour in the late afternoon sun.

The city centre

The windswept **Queen Elizabeth II Square**, opposite the Ferry Building, makes an inauspicious and scruffy introduction to the city centre – not helped by the gradually decaying Neoclassical frontage of the 1910 former post office, now lying idle. South, across Customs Street lies the city's main axis, **Queen Street**, an inelegant canyon lined by shops, banks and offices threaded by arcades – notably Queen's Arcade and The Strand Arcade – running through to the parallel High, Lorne and Elliot streets. The foot of Queen Street once had a three-hundred-metre-long wharf extending out to deep water, but progressive reclamation has shifted the shoreline away from Fort Street (originally Fore Street), which, in keeping with its port-of-call past, is now downtown's red light district. Jean Batten Place runs south off Fort Street, becoming **High Street**, which is energized by bookshops and trendy clothes shops, and is the liveliest place to be on Friday and Saturday nights. Most of the action happens around the junction with the former blacksmithing street of **Vulcan Lane**, now equally well-equipped with bars and swanky stores.

One of Queen Street's few buildings of any distinction is the art nouveau **Civic Theatre**, on the corner of Wellesley Street. The talk of the town when it opened in 1929, the management went as far as to import a small Indian boy from Fiji to complement the ornate Moghul-style decor. Due to close for a major restoration, it should re-open as a theatre late in 1998; when it does, stick your head inside to see the star-strewn artificial sky and the ornate proscenium arch and flanking lions with blazing red eyes.

The next block south opens out into **Aotea Square**, overlooked by the recently refurbished Town Hall and the country's foremost concert hall, the Aotea Centre, which opened in a blaze of glory in 1990, with Kiri Te Kanawa honouring a long-standing promise to perform on the inaugural night.

The city centre is dominated by the brand new concrete **Skytower**, on the corner of Victoria Street and Federal Street (daily 8.30am–midnight; $15, plus $3 for upper viewing deck), a potent symbol for the city in the run-up to the Americas Cup. At 328m, it is New Zealand's tallest structure (just pipping the Eiffel Tower and Sydney's Centrepoint in the height stakes), and has the obligatory observation decks with stupendous views right over the city and Hauraki Gulf. It sprouts from **Harrah's Sky City Casino**, another newcomer to the city that's struggling to carve a niche for itself in a country where temperance is still revered. If you can demonstrate that you are over twenty and eschew shorts, singlets and thongs (flip-flops), you can get on to a gaming floor awash in deep blue and green decor that's supposed to represent Polynesian demi-god Maui's underwater realm. All the usual distractions intended to separate you from your money are here, along with cafés, bars, a high-roller room and Harrah's Club for those who prefer the jacket-and-tie approach. Learner classes are held most mornings.

The Art Gallery and Albert Park

From the Casino, Victoria Street runs back across Queen Street to the **Auckland Art Gallery**, which comes in two parts – one predominantly traditional, the other resolutely contemporary – which jointly make up the world's most important collection of Kiwi art.

The elaborate mock-French-styled **Heritage Gallery**, on the corner of Wellesley Street and Kitchener Street (daily 10am–5pm; free, special exhibitions $5; free guided tours daily at 2pm; infoline ☎09/309 0831), includes a small but respectable collection of quality works by internationally renowned artists – Corot, Maillol, Liechtenstein – but this is essentially a place to come to appreciate New Zealand art. Original drawings by the artists on James Cook's expeditions lead on to overwrought and often crass oils depicting Maori migrations. These romantic and idealized images of Maori life seen through European eyes frequently show composite scenes that could never have happened, contributing to a mythical view that persisted for decades. Two works show contrasting but equally misleading views: Kennett Watkins' 1912 *The Legend of the Voyage to New Zealand*, with its plump, happy natives on a still lagoon; and Charles Goldie's 1898 *The Arrival of the Maoris in New Zealand*, modelled on Géricault's *Raft of the Medusa* and showing starving, frightened voyagers battling tempestuous seas.

Much of the rest of the early collection is devoted to works by two of the country's most loved artists – both highly respected by Maori as among the few to accurately portray their ancestors. Bohemian immigrant **Gottfried Lindauer** emigrated to New Zealand in 1873 and spent his later years painting lifelike, almost documentary, portraits of *rangatira* (chiefs) and high-born Maori men and women. In the early part of the twentieth century, **Charles F. Goldie** became New Zealand's resident "old master" and earned international recognition for his painterly portraits of elderly Maori subjects regally showing off their facial tattoos, or *moko* – though they were in fact often painted from photographs (sometimes after the subject's death).

Contemporary landscape painters largely projected their European visions of beauty onto New Zealand landscapes, reducing vibrant visions of shimmering colour into subdued scenes reminiscent of English parkland, drab north European seas and Swiss Alps. It took half a century for more representative images to become the norm – an evolutionary process which continued into the 1960s and 1970s, when many works betray an almost cartoon-like quality, with heavily delineated spaces daubed in shocking colours. Look out for works by **Rita Angus**, renowned for her images of

Central Otago in the 1940s, and **Tony Fomison** (1939–1990), painter of one of the gallery's most recent and expensive works, *Study of Holbein's "Dead Christ"*. Completed in 1973, it is typical of his later, more obsessive period, combining the artist's passion for art history and his preoccupation with mortality.

Across the street, the **New Gallery**, on the corner of Wellesley Street and Lorne Street (daily 10am–5pm; $3; free guided tours daily at 1pm), has two light and spacious floors, signalling its more youthful and approachable nature. The exhibitions and site-specific installations by predominantly New Zealand, and particularly Maori artists encourage fresh ways of looking at art, with CD-ROM consoles exploring and explaining modern movements and profiling prime movers. One name to look out for is **Colin McCahon**, who died in 1987, but whose fascination with the power and beauty of New Zealand landscape informs so much recent Kiwi art. Others, such as **Gordon Walters**, draw their inspiration from Maori iconography, in Walters' case controversially employing vibrant, graphic representations of traditional Maori symbols – spirals, fern-root emblems and stylized human forms (for more on Maori design, see 'Maoritanga" in Contexts, p.773).

The gallery's works spill outside, with George Rickey's stainless-steel 1984 *Double L Gyratory* and Neil Dawson's monumental semicircular *Throwback* sculpture creeping into **Albert Park**. These formal Victorian-style gardens spread uphill to the university, and are generally thronged with sunbathing students and office workers. Originally the site of a Maori pa, the land was successively conscripted into service as Albert Barracks in the 1840s and 1850s, and then as a labyrinthine network of air-raid shelters during World War II, before relaxing into its current incarnation as peaceful parkland. The underground shelters, large enough to protect 20,000 people, still exist and there are plans to open them in the next few years. In the meantime there's just the park, filled with a century's worth of memorials, a floral clock, some beautiful trees and the 1882 former gatekeeper's cottage containing the **Bruce Wilkinson Collection** (daily 10am–5pm; free), a small display of ornate clocks and figurines amassed by an Auckland businessman and donated to the city.

Karangahape Road

At its southern end, Queen Street climbs to the ridge-top **Karangahape Road**, universally known as K' Road, formerly an uptown residential area for prosperous nineteenth-century merchants, and long associated with Auckland's Polynesian community. For twenty years now, planners have hailed a K' Road shopping renaissance but it remains determinedly downmarket. Clothes shops selling budget designer garb and clubbing gear have gradually gained a toehold, ousting some of the more dowdy shops, and Pacific culture remains strong – evidenced by a couple of agents specializing in Pacific Island travel, the Niuean consulate, a Samoan Church and the excellent *Books Pacifica*, at no. 283 (☎09/303 2349).

K' Road is much loved by those who know it and much maligned, even feared, by those who don't – chiefly on account of the notoriety associated with its western end, a hundred-metre-long corridor of massage parlours, strip clubs and gay cruising clubs. It is certainly one of the seedier parts of town, but the raunchy places are interspersed with more mainstream nightclubs and there is always a vibrant feel that is seldom intimidating, though the usual precautions should be exercised at night.

Further east, K' Road crosses Symonds Street by the little-known and overgrown **Symonds Street Cemetery**, one of Auckland's earliest burial grounds, with allocations for Jewish, Presbyterian, Wesleyan, Roman Catholic and Anglican faiths – the last two areas largely destroyed by the motorway cut through Grafton Gully in the 1960s. A patch of deciduous woodland shades the grave of New Zealand's first Governor, William Hobson (tucked away on the eastern side of Symonds Street almost under the vast concrete span of Grafton Bridge).

The Domain

Grafton Gully separates the city centre from **The Domain**, a vast swathe of semi-formal gardens draped over the low, irregular profile of an extinct volcano known to Maori as *Pukekawa* or "hill of bitter memories", a reference to the bloodshed of ancient inter-tribal fighting. In the 1840s, when Auckland was the national capital, Governor Grey set aside the core of The Domain as the city's first park, and it remains the finest, furnished with all the obligatory mid-nineteenth-century accoutrements: a band rotunda, phoenix palms, formal flower beds and spacious lawns. In summer, the scores of rugby pitches metamorphose into cricket ovals and softball diamonds, and every few weeks marquees and stages are erected in the crater's shallow amphitheatre for outdoor musical extravaganzas.

The Domain's volcanic spring was one of Auckland's original water sources and was used to farm the country's first rainbow trout in 1884, and by the Auckland Acclimatisation Society to grow European plants, thereby promoting the rapid Europeanization of the New Zealand countryside. The spirit of this enterprise lingers on in the **Winter gardens** (Nov–March Mon–Sat 9am–5.30pm, Sun 9am–7.30pm; April–Oct daily 9am–4.30pm; free), a shallow fishpond in a formal sunken courtyard flanked by two elaborate barrel-roofed glasshouses – one temperate, the other heated to mimic tropical climes – filled with neatly tended botanical specimens and some impressive two-metre-diameter lilies. Next door, a former scoria quarry has been transformed into the **Fernz Fernery** (daily 10am–4pm; open late until 7pm on Sundays Dec–March; free), a verdant dell with over a hundred types of fern in dry, intermediate and wet habitats.

Auckland Museum

The highest point on the domain is crowned by the imposing Greco-Roman-style **Auckland Museum** (*Te Papa Whakahiku*; daily 10am–5pm; donations encouraged). Built as a World War I memorial in 1929, the names of World War II battles were duly added to those of earlier bloodbaths around the outer walls. The contents of Auckland's original city museum were moved here and the holdings expanded to form one of the world's finest collections of Maori and Pacific art. For decades the museum was sadly neglected but is now in the throes of a major revamp, as the arid rows of stuffy glass cases are replaced by thoroughly modern displays; whole floors will be off limits at least until the end of 1998 and some rooms won't be finished until 2000.

When complete, the ground floor will be arranged chronologically, tracing the emergence of Oceanian cultures through the Polynesian migrations from southeast Asia to the South Pacific and on to New Zealand. The pick of the Polynesian, Melanesian and Micronesian treasures will remain on display throughout the restoration: the shell-inlaid ceremonial food bowl from the Solomon Islands; an elegant vessel for holding kava (a mildly narcotic drink brewed from roots), polished with years of use; stunning tooth and shell necklaces; ceremonial clubs; and a wonderfully resonant Fijian slit-gong. Pride of place is given to a simple yet majestic, breadfruit-wood statue from the Caroline Islands depicting **Kave**, Polynesia's malevolent and highest-ranked female deity whose menace is barely hinted at in this serene form.

The transition from purely Polynesian motifs to an identifiably Maori style is exemplified in the **Kaitaia Carving**, a piece that is Polynesian in style yet Maori in concept. Found around 1920 near Kaitaia (see p.173) and estimated to date from the twelfth or thirteenth century, this piece predates most Maori art so far discovered. The two-and-a-half-metre-wide totara carving is thought to have been designed for a ceremonial gateway – guarded by the central goblin-like figure with sweeping arms that stretch out to become lizard forms at their extremities.

The museum's prize Maori exhibits are gathered in the **Maoritanga** room, a riot of red, black and white with fern-root swirls, spirals and contorted human figures adorning almost every patch of exposed wood. As traditional Maori villages started to disappear towards the end of the nineteenth century, some of the best examples of carved panels, meeting houses and food stores were rescued. Many are currently displayed here, though some of the exhibits are claimed by Maori groups throughout the country and may ultimately be returned to their traditional owners. To gain an insight into the significance of these exemplary pieces, join one of the 45-minute **guided talks** (daily 11.15am & 12.45pm; $7), which are followed by an hour-long Maori **concert**.

The centre of the Maoritanga room is dominated by the intricately carved prow- and stern-piece of **Te Toki a Tapiri**, a 25m-long war canoe (*waka taua*), the only surviving specimen from the pre-European era. Designed to seat a hundred warriors, it was hewn from a single totara log near Wairoa in Hawke's Bay, in 1836, and donated to the museum in 1885. The canoe stands outside **Hotunui**, a large carved meeting house (*whare whakairo*), built near Thames in 1878, late enough to have a corrugated iron rather than rush roof, and re-erected here in 1929. Once again the craftsmanship is superb; the house's exterior is all grotesque faces, lolling tongues and glistening paua-shell eyes, while the interior is lined with wonderful geometric *tukutuku* panels. Elsewhere you are bombarded with magnificent work in the shape of storehouses and stand-alone statues, many of them the work of the renowned Te Arawa carvers from the Rotorua district.

The first floor is currently off-limits for a complete overhaul but by the end of 1998 it will be reborn as the **natural history galleries**, with visitors progressing from a simulated "Big Bang" through an exploration of plate tectonics and the break up of Gondwanaland, the geology and seismology of New Zealand and its flora and fauna. The idea is that at any time you will be able to divert from the main timeline to explore any topic in more detail using interactive displays.

The same multi-levelled approach is used on the top floor in the **Scars on the Heart** exhibition, an emotional exploration of how New Zealanders' involvement in war has helped shape the national identity, concentrating on personal accounts of the troops' experiences and the responses of those back home. Artefacts aren't completely abandoned, but most of the uniforms, arms and memorabilia are neatly worked into the greater fabric of the exhibition, with the exception of the boldly displayed armoury. You enter through a slightly incongruous mock-up of an 1860s Auckland street that sets the scene for the New Zealand Wars, interpreted from both Maori and *pakeha* perspectives. World War I gets extensive coverage, particularly the Gallipoli campaign in Turkey, when botched leadership led to a massacre of ANZAC –Australian and New Zealand Army Corps – troops in the trenches. Powerful visuals and rousing martial music accompany newsreel footage of the Pacific campaigns of World War II, and finally New Zealand's foray into Vietnam is documented.

If all this is a little heavy for the kids, leave them in the **Children's Discovery Centre** – and, if you're interested in buying Maori crafts while you're in New Zealand, check out the high-quality traditional and contemporary work in the museum **shop**.

Auckland Museum is on the route of the Coast-to-Coast Walkway, and both the city tour **buses** and regular buses with numbers beginning #63- and #65- from the Downtown Bus Terminal stop outside the museum.

East of the city

The Auckland Domain separates the city from the fashionable inner suburbs of **Parnell** and **Newmarket**, the former an established, moneyed district of restaurants, boutiques and galleries with a modest line in churches and historical houses, the latter a relative upstart. To the east lies Auckland's prime waterfront, traced by **Tamaki Drive**, a twisting thoroughfare that skirts eight kilometres of some of Auckland's most

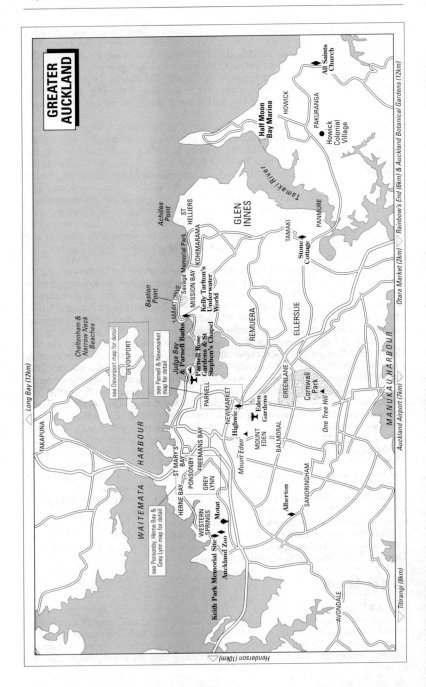

popular city beaches – **Mission Bay**, Kohimarama and **St Heliers** – and some of the city's most expensive real estate. Throughout the summer it is the favoured hangout of roller-bladers and recreational cyclists, all jockeying for position. **Kelly Tarlton's Underwater World** is the only specific sight, but the harbour views out to Rangitoto and the Hauraki Gulf are excellent both from shore level and from a couple of headland viewpoints. The gentle hills behind are peppered with the secluded mansions of leafy **Remuera**, Auckland's old-money suburb which is also home to some fine B&Bs. Further east you're well into the suburban heartland of Panmure, Pakuranga and the former "fencible" settlement of **Howick**.

Buses numbered #63- and #65- strike through the Domain to Parnell, while the 65- buses head for Newmarket.

Parnell

Thirty years ago, few would have predicted the transformation of run-down **PARNELL**, 2km east of Queen Street, into one of New Zealand's most sought-after addresses with restored kauri villas clamouring around the fashionable shops of the main thoroughfare, Parnell Road.

In fact, the district narrowly escaped the high-rise-concrete fate of many an inner-city suburb in the mid-1960s. Just as the bulldozers were closing in on the quaint but dilapidated shops and houses, eccentric dreamer **Les Harvey** managed to raise enough money to buy the properties, whisking them from under the developers' noses. In the guise of the now somewhat dated, ersatz-Victorian **Parnell Village**, the area blossomed, with rent from the shops and restaurants funding much-needed restoration. Meanwhile, Harvey successfully campaigned against New Zealand's strict trading laws, with the result that during the 1970s and much of the 1980s Parnell was the only place in Auckland where you could shop on a Saturday. Parnell Road soon established an enviable reputation for chic clothes shops and swanky restaurants and art galleries.

Even if you are not buying, Parnell makes an appealing place to spend half a day browsing, sipping cappuccinos at pavement cafés and exploring some of the marks left by Parnell's long history. At the southern end of Parnell Road stands one of the world's largest wooden churches, the **Cathedral Church of St Mary** (Mon–Fri 10am–4pm, Sat & Sun 2–5pm; free), built from native timbers in 1886. Inside, the most interesting feature is a series of photos taken on the dramatic day in 1984 when the church was rolled from its original site across Parnell Road to join its more modern (and more messy) kin, the **Auckland Cathedral of the Holy Trinity** (same hours; free). The original Gothic chancel was started in 1959 then left half-finished until the late 1980s, when an airy nave with a Swiss chalet-style roof was grafted on, supposedly in imitation of the older church alongside. The result is shambolic. Nevertheless, it is worth admiring the work in progress on the new stained-glass windows; the completed bold and bright side panels symbolize Maori and *pakeha* contributions to society. The Maori window has sea creatures frolicking in ribbed waves, while on the shore a basket of kumara is surrounded by shellfish, native birds and flowers. European influence is seen through Cook's arrival and the settlement that followed in his footsteps: the city skyline, sunbathing citizens on St Heliers Beach and cars careening along Tamaki Drive.

The Gothic flourishes of the nineteenth-century church show the influence of New Zealand's prominent missionary bishop, George Selwyn. With his favoured architect, Frederick Thatcher, Selwyn left behind a trail of trademark wooden **"Selwyn" churches**, distinguished by vertical timber battens – examples include St Stephen's Chapel, down the hill at Judges Bay (see p.88) and All Saints' at Howick (see p.90). In 1857, Selwyn commissioned Thatcher to build the nearby **Kinder House**, at 2 Ayr St (Mon–Sat 11am–3pm; $1), for the headmaster of the new grammar school – a post filled by John Kinder, an accomplished watercolourist and documentary photographer. Built of rough-hewn Rangitoto volcanic rock, the house contains some interesting photos and reproductions of Kinder's paintings of nineteenth-century New Zealand. Enthusiastic volunteers will flesh out the details both here and down the road at **Ewelme Cottage**, 14 Ayr St (Wed–Sun 10.30am–noon & 1–4.30pm; $3), a pioneer kauri house built as a family home in 1864 for Howick clergyman Vicesimus Lush, who wanted his sons to live close to the grammar school. The appeal of the place lies not so much in the house itself but in its contents: the furniture, fittings and possessions have been left just as they were when Lush's descendants finally moved out in 1968, the family heirlooms betraying a desire to replicate the home comforts of their native Oxfordshire.

Judges Bay and Newmarket

From here, you can continue south to Newmarket (see below) or north past the cathedral and down Gladstone Road to Dove-Myer Robinson Park and the **Parnell Rose Gardens** (unrestricted entry; free), where five thousand bushes are at their glorious best from October to April. The park sweeps from the rose beds down to **Judges Bay**, named for three officers of the colony's Supreme Court who lived here from 1841, commuting to the courts on Symonds Street by rowboat. Bishop Selwyn used to stay with his friend, the Chief Justice William Martin, and had **St Stephen's Chapel** (usually closed) built nearby on a prominent knoll overlooking the harbour; the waterside Judges Bay Road leads to the open-air saltwater Parnell Baths (see p.101).

The southern continuation of Parnell Road runs into Broadway, the main drag through **NEWMARKET**, a formerly run-down suburb on the eastern flanks of Mount Eden which, over the last decade, has re-invented itself with scores of fashionable shops, several excellent restaurants and numerous motels. Specific sights are few, but if you are staying over this way there are a couple of thing to do.

A short walk off Broadway up Khyber Pass Road, New Zealand's major beer manufacturer runs the **Lion Breweries Tour** (generally Tues–Thurs 10.30am & 2pm; free; information & reservations, ☎09/377 8840), with a quick buzz around the plant – and the obligatory tasting. For a more cultural experience, make for the Gothic timber mansion of **Highwic**, 40 Gillies Ave (Wed–Sun 10.30am–noon & 1–4.30pm; $5, accompanied kids free; ☎09/524 5729), which lies at the far end of Newmarket shops, almost buried under a motorway overpass. Built as a "country" property by a wealthy auctioneer and landowner in 1862, the estate, complete with its outbuildings and servants' quarters, gives a fair indication of the contrasting lives of the aristocracy and the less fortunate. From here it is a short walk to **Eden Gardens**, 24 Omana Ave (daily 9am–4.30pm; $3), a peaceful garden of mature trees, flowering shrubs and a splendid collection of camellias, azaleas and rhododendrons, all planted and lovingly tended by volunteers.

Along the Tamaki Drive waterfront

Quay Street runs east from the foot of Queen Street, soon becoming **Tamaki Drive**, which separates Waitemata Harbour from Judges Bay. Crossing the causeway to Okahu Bay brings you to one of the city's foremost attractions, **Kelly Tarlton's Underwater World and Antarctic Encounter**, 23 Tamaki Drive (daily: Oct–March 9am–9pm; April–Sept 9am–6pm; $18).

Underwater World was the brainchild of Kiwi diver, treasure hunter and salvage expert, Kelly Tarlton, who wanted to share the undersea wonders off New Zealand's shores with the non-diving public. Having failed to secure a location in his home town of Paihia in the Bay of Islands, he settled on these huge tanks which, from 1910 until 1961, flushed the city's effluent into Waitemata Harbour on the outgoing tides. Opened in 1985, the aquarium pioneered the walk-through acrylic tunnels (which have since become de rigueur for all self-respecting aquariums), a novelty which lured 100,000 visitors in the seven weeks before Tarlton's untimely death from a heart attack at the age of 47. A moving walkway glides you through two tanks, both sculpted into the gnarled rock walls: the first is dominated by flowing kelp beds, colourful reef fish and twisting eels; the second with graceful rays and smallish sharks, all appearing alarmingly close in the crystal-clear water. You can step off the walkway for closer inspection at any time.

The remaining tanks have since been converted into the **Antarctic Encounter**, a synthesis of Antarctic history and penguin-arium. An earnest video welcome from Sir Edmund Hillary introduces you to an accomplished replica of the prefabricated hut used by Robert Falcon Scott and his team on their ill-starred 1911 attempt to be the first to reach the South Pole and plant the British flag there; the original hut still stands at Scott Base, New Zealand's Antarctic foothold. Other Kiwi connections derive from the fact that Scott departed for the ice from Port Chalmers, near Dunedin, after first picking up a pianola donated by the people of Christchurch. Nor is a pianola the only unexpected thing you'll encounter in this capacious shelter. Fittings include a fully-functional laboratory and a printing press – from which the *South Polar Times* rolled every few months throughout the three long years of the expedition. Contemporary footage and tales of their exploits add to the haunting atmosphere. Seamlessly moving from the sublime to the ridiculous, the **Snow Cat** is an inept attempt at a Disney-esque ride made bearable by the close-up views of King and Gentoo penguins shooting through the water and hopping around on fake icebergs.

City tour **buses** and Yellow Buses numbered #720–759 from the Downtown Bus Terminal all stop outside and the Harbour Explorer **ferry** stops at the end of Orakei Wharf, opposite the entrance.

A little further along Tamaki Drive, Hapimana Street leads up onto the grassy range of Bastion Point and the **M.J. Savage Memorial Park**, the nation's austere Art Deco homage to its first Labour prime minister, who ushered in the welfare state in the late 1930s. More recently, **Bastion Point** was the site of a seventeen-month stand-off between police and its traditional owners, the Ngati Whatua, over the subdivision of land for housing. The occupiers were finally removed in May 1977, but the stand helped to galvanize the land-rights movement, and paved the way for a significant change in government attitude. Within a decade, the Waitangi Tribunal recommended that the land be returned, along with a compensatory cash payment.

Bastion Point looks down on **MISSION BAY**, the closest of the truly worthwhile city **beaches**, where a grassy waterside reserve is backed by an enticing row of cafés and restaurants. Swimming is best here close to high tide; at other times the water remains shallow a long way out. Similar conditions prevail at the sheltered beaches of **Kohimarama** and **St Heliers Bay**, both a short way further along Tamaki Drive, which finishes on a high note with excellent harbour views from **Achilles Point**.

Panmure and Howick

With your own transport it is easy enough to wind south from St Heliers through the low-rent suburbs of Glen Innes and Tamaki to **PANMURE**, one of four **fencible settlements** – Panmure and Howick in the east, Onehunga and Otahuhu in the south – set up around the young capital as a defence against disgruntled Maori and ambitious French. So-called "fencibles" (pensioned British soldiers) were re-enlisted to defend these sites for seven years, in return for free passage and a block of land. Skirmishes were few, and the original shipments of men and their families formed the basis of small towns, all of which were subsequently engulfed by the Auckland conurbation. Panmure has its relocated and restored **Stone Cottage**, at the corner of King's Road and Queen's

Road (Fri & Sun 1–3pm; free), but the best place to get a sense of fencible life is at the **Howick Colonial Village**, Bells Road, Lloyd Elsmore Park (daily: Jan–March 10am–5pm; April–Dec 10am–4pm; $9), ten dismal kilometres east of downtown through the numbing suburb of Pakuranga. Over thirty buildings dating from the 1850s and 1860s have been restored and re-sited from the four fencible settlements, and arranged in a believable village setting complete with a pond, a working blacksmith and market gardens. Volunteers role-play the diligently-researched lives of real 1850s characters as they amble between the tents and makeshift Maori-style *raupo* huts used on arrival, the officers' cottages, the hostelry, school hall and flower mill.

The colonial village is one kilometre off Pakuranga Road, plied by all Howick & Eastern **buses**, which take about forty minutes to get out here from the Downtown Bus Terminal.

In the last ten years, droll Kiwis have dubbed the suburb of **HOWICK**, a further 5km east, "Chowick" – on account of its Chinese inhabitants' weakness for huge, florid mansions, which have gradually marched across the former farmland to the south of town. For Aucklanders, these have become almost an attraction in their own right, mounting a challenge to Howick's more traditional sight, the distinctive, square-turreted **All Saints' Church**, the country's oldest active "Selwyn" church (see p.87), built in 1847.

West of the city

The suburbs of West Auckland developed later than their eastern counterparts, a consequence of their distance from the sea in the days when almost all travel was by ferry. The exceptions were the inner suburbs of Freeman's Bay, **Ponsonby** and Herne Bay, now enjoying renewed desirability for their proximity to the city and an unsurpassed array of the city's best restaurants, cafés and bars. Except for the flagging **Victoria Park Market**, sights are scarce until you get out to **Western Springs**, infant Auckland's major water source. The site of the springs is now part of **MOTAT**, a less than thrilling transport and technology museum, and the small but go-ahead **Auckland Zoo**. To the south stands **Alberton**, once one of the city's grandest residences, but now just a brief distraction before you hit the wineries and West Coast beaches (see "Around Auckland", p.108).

Freeman's Bay, Ponsonby and Herne Bay

Victoria Street climbs the ridge west of Queen Street and descends into **Freeman's Bay**, a flat basin long-since reclaimed from Waitemata Harbour to accommodate early saw-milling operations. The land is now given over to the popular rugby and cricket fields of Victoria Park, all overshadowed by the 38m-high chimney of Auckland's defunct incinerator, occupied since 1984 by **Victoria Park Market** (daily 9am–7pm), a knot of stalls and restaurants. Despite having lost some of its more aspirational patrons to burgeoning Ponsonby up the road, it's still an interesting enough place to mooch about for reasonably priced clothes and crafts, and a good place to break your walk out to Ponsonby. The #005 **bus** (Mon–Fri only) passes on its way to Herne Bay, and city tour buses also stop here.

Victoria Park Market is the starting point of the **Historic Ponsonby Heritage Walk** (pick up a free leaflet at the market), which winds past wisteria-draped kauri clapboard villas and grandiose civic buildings in the neighbouring suburbs of St Mary's Bay and **PONSONBY**. Early in Auckland's European history these became fashionable neighbourhoods, only moving downmarket with the arrival of trams at the turn of the century. Inner-city living conditions deteriorated dramatically in the

Depression of the 1930s, and the resulting low rents attracted large numbers of Pacific Islanders during the 1950s. Ponsonby took a bohemian turn in the Seventies and before long young professionals were moving in, restoring old houses and spending fistfuls of dollars in the cafés, restaurants and boutiques along Ponsonby Road. The street itself may not be beautiful, but the people sure are: musicians, actors and media folk congregate to lunch, schmooze and be seen in the latest fashionable haunt. There's good reason to brave the poseurs, though, for some of New Zealand's classiest shopping (particularly gorgeous ceramics) and eating.

Beyond St Mary's Bay and Ponsonby lies **HERNE BAY**, which followed its neighbours' economic ebb and flow and now ranks as Auckland's most expensive suburb, the merchants' water-view villas fetching astronomical prices. There's little to see out this way, but you may find yourself staying here or indulging at one of the restaurants and cafés along Jervois Road.

Western Springs: MOTAT and the zoo

In the late nineteenth century the burgeoning city of Auckland, with its meagre supply of unreliable streams, was heavily reliant on the waters of **Western Springs**, 4km west of the city.

The area is now devoted to attractive parkland, a major music venue and two of Auckland's more significant sights, the most prominent of which is the **Museum of Transport, Technology and Social History** (MOTAT), on Great North Road (daily 10am–5pm; $8; infoline ☎09/846 7020). This trawl through New Zealand's vehicular and industrial past in a jumble of sheds and halls feels half-baked and incomplete – and it's all too obvious that some of the displays haven't been updated in over twenty years. However it might be just the thing if you're newly arrived and have kids to entertain: hidden among the shiny cars and jet-black steam engines are a reconstruction of a Victorian Village, and the Western Springs' pumphouse whose original engine still slowly turns, albeit by electricity rather than steam. Next door, the aviation section includes a replica of the home-built plane first flown near Timaru by Richard Pearse (see p.529).

Admission includes entry to the **Sir Keith Park Memorial Site** (same hours; $4 separately), a kilometre away and linked to the main site by ancient rattling trams (every 10–20min; $1 return). This is one for aeroplane buffs, with a couple of dozen lovingly restored examples slotted into a hangar around the star attractions – one of the few surviving World War II Lancaster bombers, plus a double-decker flying boat, all decked out for dining in a more gracious age, which was used on Air New Zealand's South Pacific "Coral Route" until the mid-1960s.

The tram between the two sites also stops outside the **Auckland Zoo**, Motions Road (daily 9.30am–5.30pm; $11), which is endeavouring to overturn the ancient regime of caged bears, replacing them with naturalistic habitats and captive breeding programmes. The trailblazing Pridelands development will have lions, hippos, baboons, rhinos, giraffes, zebras and gazelles all roaming across mock savannah behind enclosing moats. Naturally, New Zealand's wildlife is well represented, with a nocturnal kiwi house, a group of tuatara which form part of conservation work on offshore islands, and a large walk-through aviary. One of the best displays features the desert-dwelling meerkats: plastic domes placed at ground level enable you to observe their super-cute behaviour at close quarters. Elsewhere, the "rainforest walk" threads its way among artificial islands inhabited by colonies of monkeys, while kids are well catered for at the Tui Farm and by keeper talks and animal-feeding sessions held throughout the day.

Western Springs is reached by Yellow Bus #045 from Custom Street East and is also on city tour **bus** routes.

Alberton

The only other diversion in the western suburbs proper is the imposing mid-Victorian mansion of **Alberton**, 100 Mount Albert Rd (daily except Thurs & Fri 10.30am–noon & 1–4.30pm; $5), 3km south of the zoo, which began life as a farmstead in 1863. Despite numerous additions, this grand old house has maintained an unusual cohesion, its framing turrets and extensive verandahs a suitable centrepiece for an estate which once stretched over much of western Auckland. Alberton was originally owned by the Kerr-Taylor family, whose furniture, possessions and nineteenth-century wallpapers still adorn many of the rooms.

The North Shore

Until the 1960s there was very little to the **North Shore**, just a handful of scattered communities linked to each other and the rest of Auckland by a web of ferries crisscrossing the harbour. The completion of the harbour bridge in 1959 provided the catalyst for development. By the early 1970s, the volume of traffic to the booming suburbs log-jammed the bridge – until a Japanese company attached a two-lane extension (affectionately dubbed "the Nippon Clip-ons") to each side. The vast urban sprawl marches inexorably towards the Hibiscus Coast (see p.108), with only the maritime village of **Devonport** to keep you from the string of excellent, calm swimming **beaches** which stretch the length of this coast. At the southern end the pick are the quiet coves of **Cheltenham** and **Narrow Neck**, both a short walk from Devonport. Further north try the more open and busier **Takapuna**, a short stroll from dozens of good cafés and reached by buses #80- and #90-, and **Long Bay** (buses #83- & 85-), with a grassy reserve and barbecue areas. All to some degree suffer from the Auckland curse of being shallow at low tide but beaches tend to be well attended throughout the summer days.

Devonport

DEVONPORT is one of Auckland's oldest suburbs, founded in 1840 and still linked to the city by a ten-minute ferry journey. The naval station was one of Devonport's earliest tenants, soon followed by wealthy merchants, who built fine kauri villas. Some of these are graced with little turrets which served as lookouts where the traders could watch for the arrival of their precious cargoes. Wandering along the peaceful streets and the tree-fringed waterfront past grand houses is the essence of Devonport's appeal, and there's no shortage of tempting cafés and restaurants along the main street to punctuate your amblings.

Devonport's former post office is now home to **Jackson's Museum**, 10 Victoria Road (Christmas–Feb daily 10am–5pm; March–Christmas Sun only 10am–5pm; $10; ☎09/445 9191), two floors overflowing with Bryan Jackson's lifetime collection of collections – a reflection of his philosophy that "more is more". This is an overwhelming hoard of just about everything imaginable: soda siphons, hot-water bottles, gramophones, aquatint postcards, kauri gum, milk bottles and much, much more, ranging from the moderately special to the unbelievably ordinary. The place is forever under threat of closure due to longstanding battles with the local council over the museum's somewhat unorthodox use of a listed building, so call before making a special journey.

Unless you have a soft spot for lifeless collections of uniforms and guns, you can blithely skip the **Navy Museum**, Spring Street (daily 10am–4.30pm; free) in favour of a stiff walk up one of the two ancient volcanoes that back Devonport. The closest, about fifteen minutes' walk, is **Mount Victoria** (*Taka-a-ranga*; unrestricted access for pedestrians; closed to vehicles from dusk on Thurs, Fri & Sat), from where you get fabulous city, harbour and gulf views. The hill was once the site of a Maori pa and fortified vil-

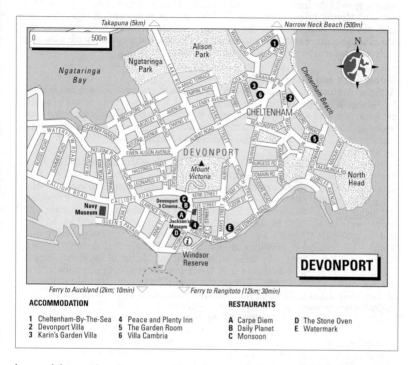

DEVONPORT

Ferry to Auckland (2km; 10min)   Ferry to Rangitoto (12km; 30min)

ACCOMMODATION

1 Cheltenham-By-The-Sea	4 Peace and Plenty Inn
2 Devonport Villa	5 The Garden Room
3 Karin's Garden Villa	6 Villa Cambria

RESTAURANTS

A Carpe Diem	D The Stone Oven
B Daily Planet	E Watermark
C Monsoon	

lage, and the remains of terraces and kumara pits can still be detected on the northern and eastern slopes. A kilometre east, the grass- and flax-covered volcanic plug of **North Head** (*Takapuna*, "rock with a spring"; daily 6am–10pm, vehicles 8am–8pm; free) guards the entrance to the inner harbour, a strategic site for Maori before it was coopted to form part of the young nation's coastal defences. In the wake of the "Russian Scares" of 1884–86, which were precipitated by the opening of the port of Vladivostok, North Head became Fort Cautley, riddled with an extensive system of concrete tunnels linking gun emplacements. Most of the tunnels remain closed to the public, but you are free to poke around some of the peripheral remains and the gulf views are unbeatable.

Devonport is best reached on the **Devonport Ferry** (daily 6am–11pm, every 20mins; $7 return, bikes $1). The ferry is met by Fullers' "Devonport Highlight Tour" (daily 10am–3pm; 1hr; $22; ☎09/357 6366), but really you're better off calling in to the **visitor centre**, Windsor Reserve, Victoria Road (daily 10am–4pm; ☎09/446 0677), picking up a free map and exploring at your own pace.

If you happen to be here over the third weekend in February, head for the **Devonport Food and Wine Festival**, when the central streets are closed to traffic and for $10 you can join winemakers, market gardeners and restaurateurs celebrating their produce.

South of the city

The southern tranche of Auckland, arcing around the eastern end of Manukau Harbour, is the most neglected by visitors, though the airport at Mangere is where most arrive. In the main there are few unmissable attractions but the city's most lofty volcano, **Mount Eden**, offers superb views, and its near-identical twin, **One Tree Hill**, has some of the best surviving examples of the terracing undertaken by early Maori inhabitants. Further south, Auckland's Polynesian community plies its wares early each Saturday morning at the **Otara Market**.

Mount Eden and One Tree Hill

At 196m, **Mount Eden** (*Maungawhau*), is Auckland's highest volcano and is named for George Eden, the first Earl of Auckland. The extensive views from the summit car park, just 2km south of the city, make it extraordinarily popular with tour buses which grind up the steep slope through the day and well into the evening, though you can walk up from Mount Eden Road or take buses #274 or #275 from Custom Street East.

More rewarding, though, is the area around **One Tree Hill** (*Maungakiekie*; 183m), 5km to the southeast. One of the city's most distinctive landmarks, One Tree Hill is indeed topped by a single ageing pine tree – and a twenty-metre-tall granite obelisk. For a century, until just before the arrival of Europeans, *Maungakiekie* ("mountain of the kiekie plant") was one of the largest pa sites in the country; an estimated 4000 people were drawn here by the proximity to abundant seafood from both harbours and the rich soils of the volcanic cone, which still bears the scars of extensive earthworks – the remains of dwellings and kumara pits. The site had already been abandoned when it was bought by the Scottish medic and "father of Auckland", Sir John Logan Campbell, who was one of only two European residents when the city was granted capital status in 1840. Through widespread land purchases and the founding of numerous shipping, banking and insurance companies, Campbell prospered, eventually becoming mayor in time for the visit of the heirs to the British throne, the Duke and Duchess of Cornwall, in 1901. To commemorate the event, he donated his One Tree Hill estate to the people of New Zealand and named it **Cornwall Park** (daily 7am–dusk; free) in honour of his distinguished guests. The park puts on its best display around Christmas time, when avenues of pohutukawa trees erupt in a riot of red blossom. Campbell is buried at the summit, next to the obelisk, which bears inscriptions in Maori and English lauding Maori–*pakeha* friendship. The summit is known in Maori as *Te Totara-i-ahua*, a reference to the single totara which originally gave One Tree Hill its name. Early settlers cut it down in 1852, and Campbell planted several pines as a windbreak; a lone pine survives, heavily stayed after a 1994 attempt by a Maori activist to avenge the loss of the totara by attacking its usurper with a chainsaw.

Free leaflets outlining a trail around the archeological and volcanic sites of the hill are available from the **visitor centre** (daily 10am–4pm), which is housed in **Huia Lodge**, originally built on the northern slopes by Campbell as a gatekeeper's house and now containing displays on the park and the man. Immediately opposite is **Acacia Cottage** (dawn–dusk; free), Campbell's original home and the city's oldest building, re-sited from central Auckland in the 1920s. Over the years, it has been heavily restored, but it's worth sticking your head in to see the simple construction and plain furnishings. Campbell devotees can round off their homage with a visit to the magisterial statue of him in mayoral garb at the northern end of the park by Manukau Road.

Fans of astronomy are better served on the southern side of One Tree Hill at the **Auckland Observatory**, on Manukau Road, where a frequently changing schedule of 45-minute multimedia programmes on the moon, and the crystalline stars and distant galaxies of the southern skies is played out on the ceiling of the **StarDome Planetarium** (Tues, Thurs, Fri, Sat & Sun 3pm, 4pm, 6.30pm, 7.30pm & 8.30pm; Wed 3pm & 4pm only; $9; infoline ☎09/625 6945). Weather permitting, the last two

Tuesday, Thursday and Saturday shows are followed by an hour of telescope viewing ($3 extra; viewing only, $4); what you see obviously varies, but the moons of Jupiter, binary stars and Saturn's rings are all possibilities.

Most of Cornwall Park is closed after dark but the observatory and the summit are accessible from the southern entrance off Manukau Road, which can be reached on **buses** numbered #300–#319 from the corner of Queen and Victoria streets.

South Auckland

Head much beyond Cornwall Park and you are venturing into **South Auckland**, the city's poorest sector and the less-then-flatteringly-depicted gangland setting for Lee Tamahori's film *Once were Warriors*. There isn't a great deal to see down here, but neither is it a no-go zone and the **Otara Market** is certainly worth a look. Each Saturday morning, stalls sprawl across the car park of the Otara Town Centre, 18km south of central Auckland. Plausibly billed as the largest Maori and Polynesian market in the world, its authenticity has been greatly diluted by an influx of market traders flogging cheap clothes and shoddy trinkets. The tat is alleviated by a displays of island-style floral print fabrics and reasonably priced Maori carvings. Your best bet for a bargain, though, is the food: the vegetable market is heavily laden with inexpensive yams and taro, and there are stalls where you can buy home-made cakes and Maori bread; there's even a van ingeniously kitted out to produce an ersatz hangi. The market gets going around 5am and runs through to noon, though by 10am things are winding down, so get there early. Take the Otara exit off the southern motorway or catch buses #487 or #497 for the fifty-minute journey from the Downtown Bus Terminal.

Parents with kids may well want to push on a few kilometres further south to **Rainbow's End**, Great South Road, Manukau City (Christmas–Jan-daily 10am–6pm, Feb–Christmas daily 10am–5pm; 24hr infoline ☎09/262 2044), New Zealand's largest theme park, with a few mega-rides – corkscrew roller coaster, log flume – supplemented by the likes of pirate ships, go-karts and flight simulators. The most taxing decision you'll be required to make is whether to go for the Minipass (any 3 rides; $15 for adults & kids) or go the whole hog with the Superpass (as many rides as you can handle; $30, kids $20). Buses numbered #3-7, #4-7 and #5-7 all come out this way.

If you have your own transport, consider a jaunt to the **Auckland Botanical Gardens**, 102 Hill Road (daily 9am–dusk; free), just by the Manurewa motorway turnoff, 27km south of the city centre. This extensive but relatively young collection of native and exotic plants opened in 1982, but came of age in 1997 when New Zealand's top horticultural show, the **Ellerslie Flower Show** (held annually in mid-Nov), was relocated here. The gardens come complete with interpretive visitor centre (daily 9am–4pm), a reference library, a café and a network of walks centred on two ornamental lakes.

Eating

Aucklanders takes their eating seriously and there is no shortage of wonderful **restaurants**, with ever more adventurous places opening all the time. They may only be following the trends of Australia or California but they're close behind and easily as good. If you're after a more casual eating experience, don't overlook the **pubs** (see "Pubs and bars" listings, starting on p.40), many offering a decent meal for under $10.

The best areas for grazing are the inner-city suburbs, chiefly along **Ponsonby Road**, Auckland's culinary crucible; **Parnell Road**, the other main eat street; and **Devonport**, with a more modest but still tempting selection. In the **city centre**, the best bets are the seafood restaurants dotted along the foreshore.

Central Auckland

The centre of Auckland is undoubtedly the best place to grab something quick during the day with dozens of places geared up to cope with the **lunchtime** press of office workers and bank staff. Among the most popular are the **food halls**, seating plazas surrounded by numerous vendors, often tucked away in the basements of the shopping arcades which spur off Queen Street. For a broad choice and a bustling atmosphere, check out the ones under the BNZ Tower at 125 Queen St; the Countrywide Bank Centre at 280 Queen St, the Atrium on Elliot Street, or the Downtown Shopping Centre at the foot of Queen Street. There's a stronger Asian influence in the spartan and spotless Food Alley, 9 Albert St, with Indonesian, Thai, Chinese and Indian offerings; and all manner of stuff at Victoria Park Market in Freeman's Bay.

Parts of the city can feel pretty dead in the evening, but if you know where to look – **High Street** and **Lorne Street** are both good hunting grounds – there are plenty of places to eat. **Karangahape Road** (usually abbreviated to K' Road) is less influenced by the daytime crowds and its small selection of quirky places can be lively at any hour.

Cafés and takeaways

Art Gallery, Kitchener St. Two excellent cafés, one in each section of the gallery, both providing sandwiches, quiches, cakes and coffee in airy and relaxing surroundings.

Brazil, 256 K' Rd. Quirky super-slim café in a mosaiced and barrel-vaulted former theatre entrance that vibrates to heavy beats and jazz grooves. Gourmet burgers and cakes are eased down by shakes or industrial-strength espressos.

Brucie's, 285 Queen St. Straightforward takeaway with a longstanding reputation for serving Auckland's best traditional burgers.

Café Verona, 169 K' Rd. Fun café that's a popular muso hangout, with pinball and occasional live music. Come to ogle the Sixties and Seventies pop decor over coffee.

DKD Café, Bledisloe Lane, behind the Civic Theatre. Longstanding and hard-to-find coffee bar, this relic from pre-café/bar days serves well-priced lunches and great cakes until late in wildly coloured surroundings.

Kettledrum Café, 41 Elliot St. Tiny, beatific vegetarian café hidden in the Elliot Mews arcade serving smoothies, pizza, quiche and baked potatoes at low, low prices.

Melba, 33 Vulcan Lane. Comfortable café in the heart of the shopping and clubbing district that's justifiably popular for breakfasts, delicious muffins and light meals all day every day.

Mezzaluna, 259 K' Rd. Low-key daytime café, breakfast and lunch bar with a selection of gourmet sandwiches, bagels and quiches, and reliably fine coffee.

Middle East Café, 23a Wellesley St. Tiny camel-themed eat-in or take-out café that's become an Auckland institution, justly celebrated for its shawarma and felafel, all ready to be cloaked in creamy garlic and spicy tomato sauce.

Simple Cottage, 50 High St. The budget vegetarian, wholesome and predominantly sugar-free food here is at its best and freshest early in the day, though the café stays open until 9pm. BYO.

White Lady Diner, cnr Queen St & Shortland St. Kerbside caravan in the club zone, open for refuelling throughout the night. Toasted sandwiches and burgers, notably the pack-in-the-works Ambassador, fit the bill – and the staff understand fluent drunk.

Restaurants

Caravanserai Tea House, 430 Queen St. Relaxed Middle Eastern place decked out in Turkish rugs and cushions around knee-high tables. The extensive range of mezze, moussaka and kebabs go for around $11, or there are lighter snacks for half that. BYO.

Cin Cin on Quay, Ferry Building, 99 Custom St (☎09/307 6966). Casual and bustling, moderately priced brasserie nicely sited next to the ferries and with particularly fine seafood lunches. Licensed.

Dynasty Chinese Restaurant, 57–59 Wakefield St. Cavernous restaurant always popular with Auckland's Chinese community especially for Sunday morning yum cha.

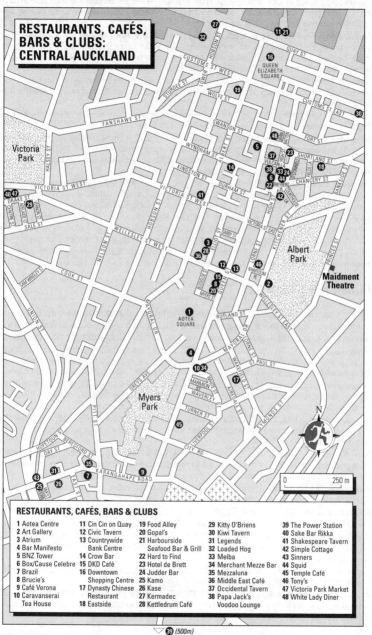

**RESTAURANTS, CAFÉS,
BARS & CLUBS:
CENTRAL AUCKLAND**

Victoria
Park

Albert
Park

Maidment
Theatre

Aotea
Square

Myers
Park

N

0   250 m

RESTAURANTS, CAFÉS, BARS & CLUBS

1 Aotea Centre	**19** Food Alley	**29** Kitty O'Briens
2 Art Gallery	**20** Gopal's	**30** Kiwi Tavern
3 Atrium	**21** Harbourside	**31** Legends
4 Bar Manifesto	Seafood Bar & Grill	**32** Loaded Hog
5 BNZ Tower	**22** Hard to Find	**33** Melba
6 Box/Cause Celebre	**23** Hotel de Brett	**34** Merchant Mezze Bar
7 Brazil	**24** Judder Bar	**35** Mezzaluna
8 Brucie's	**25** Kamo	**36** Middle East Café
9 Café Verona	**26** Kase	**37** Occidental Tavern
10 Caravanserai	**27** Kermadec	**38** Papa Jack's
Tea House	**28** Kettledrum Café	Voodoo Lounge
11 Cin Cin on Quay		**39** The Power Station
12 Civic Tavern		**40** Sake Bar Rikka
13 Countrywide		**41** Shakespeare Tavern
Bank Centre		**42** Simple Cottage
14 Crow Bar		**43** Sinners
15 DKD Café		**44** Squid
16 Downtown		**45** Temple Café
Shopping Centre		**46** Tony's
17 Dynasty Chinese		**47** Victoria Park Market
Restaurant		**48** White Lady Diner
18 Eastside		

Gopal's, 1st Floor, 145 Queen St. Serene Hare Krishna restaurant serving wholesome vegetarian lunches and early evening dinners ($5–9) Monday to Saturday – and a proselytising Sunday feast for $2 if you arrive before 6.15pm, $4 afterwards.

Harbourside Seafood Bar & Grill, 99 Quay St (☎09/307 0556). Classy but none-too-formal, award-winning Pacific Rim seafood restaurant upstairs in the Ferry Building. If it's warm, reserve a table on the harbour-view terrace, and feast on beautifully prepared and presented fish and crustaceans. Expect to part with at least $50 for a full meal. Licensed.

Hard to Find, 47 High St. Longstanding Mexican favourite tucked away in the Canterbury Arcade. Tasty and reasonably priced enchiladas, burritos, carne asada, and other favourites from south of the border. BYO.

Kamo, 382 K' Rd (☎09/377 2313). Stripped-down, rowdy restaurant serving Mediterranean and Pacific-influenced dishes at very reasonable prices. Licensed.

Kermadec, 1st Floor, Viaduct Quay, cnr Lower Hobson St & Quay St (restaurant ☎09/309 0412, brasserie and bars ☎09/309 0413). Fashionable and imaginatively decorated seafood emporium, with a large bustling brasserie for classy versions of bistro favourites and the more formal, and expensive, Pacific Room for fine dining. Licensed.

Merchant Mezze Bar, 428 Queen St, cnr Mayoral Drive (☎09/307 0349). Buzzing café with a small deck outside and Turkish rugs strewn within. Soups, salads and mezze ($6–8) served until 11pm, then drinks and coffee until midnight or later. Licensed. Closed Sun.

Sake Bar Rikka, Victoria Park Market (☎09/377 8239). Excellent Japanese restaurant: settle down to their formidable platter of tempura, miso, sushi, chicken teriyaki and more for two people (under $40) and every kind of sake known to mankind including chilled versions. Licensed.

Tony's, 32 Lorne St (☎09/373 2138). Traditional steak restaurant highly regarded for its juicy slabs of prime meat ($25–30), plus cheaper lunches and early evening specials. Licensed.

Parnell and Okahu Bay

Parnell's eating places split into two camps; established **restaurants** with the accent on fine dining, and trendier, cheaper places – including a couple of great **bakeries** and **takeaways** – catering to younger devotees, and backpackers from the nearby hostels.

Antoine's, 333 Parnell Rd, Parnell (☎09/307 9875). Fancy French dining much favoured by Parnell and Remuera blue bloods. Consistently rated among the best in Auckland, it's all very professionally, if somewhat conservatively, done. Try top-quality lamb and salmon dishes, at top-notch prices.

Hammerheads, 19 Tamaki Drive, Okahu Bay, by Kelly Tarlton's (☎09/521 4400). Popular waterfront seafood restaurant that's renowned for painfully slow service. The delectable food is worth the delay, though, and your wait is eased by dynamite cocktails. Licensed.

Iguaçu, 269 Parnell Rd, Parnell (☎09/358 4804). Flashy conservatory-style brasserie frequented by a young corporate crowd and wannabes, but worth a look in for a light meal or just a glass of wine. Licensed.

Java Room, 317 Parnell Rd, Parnell (☎09/366 1606). Intimate restaurant serving loosely Indonesian-influenced dishes but stretching to dim sum, spicy fish cakes, Szechwan prawns and whole snapper in sambal. Licensed & BYO.

Kebab Kid, 363 Parnell Rd, Parnell. Modern, Middle Eastern eat-in, takeaway and bring-to snack bar with top-of-the-league felafel and shawarma around the $7 mark.

Konditorei Boss, 305 Parnell Rd, Parnell. Bakery selling melt-in-the-mouth German pastries.

The Other Side, 320 Parnell Rd, Parnell. Bright, breezy and reasonably priced café serving good breakfasts and a typical range of Kiwi café food with German additions like bratwurst and schnitzel.

Pandoro, 427 Parnell Rd, Parnell. Bakery specializing in Italian-style loaves, stuffed pizza bread – and chocolate brownies.

Portofino, 156 Parnell Rd, Parnell (☎09/373 3740). Basic but good trattoria with pasta and pizza favourites all exceptionally well done. Licensed & BYO.

Strawberry Alarm Clock, 119 Parnell Rd, Parnell. Low-key café popular with Parnell's bright young things and perfect for breakfasts, a snack, or just hanging out over good coffee either inside or out in the rear courtyard.

La Trattoria, 259 Parnell Rd, Parnell. (☎09/379 5358). Upmarket Italian serving delicious antipasto, succulent green-lipped mussels and wonderful pasta either indoors or al fresco in an attractive courtyard. Licensed. Closed Sun.

Newmarket

Newmarket is rapidly heading the same way as Parnell, with interesting new places opening up all the time.

Appetite Café, 4 Osborne St, Newmarket (☎09/524 2371). Evening-only café that's neither strictly vegetarian nor determinedly wholesome but serves natural and organic foods such as vegetarian paella, kebabs and Scotch fillet at bargain prices. Licensed & BYO. Closed Mon.

First Floor Dining Room, 1 Teed St, Newmarket (☎09/523 3448). A meat lover's Nirvana, with the likes of roast pork belly and slow-cooked Greek-style lamb beautifully prepared and presented on beautiful old china platters. Not especially cheap ($20–25), but worth every penny. Licensed & BYO.

Kenzie, 17a Remuera Rd, Newmarket. Smart café selling pricey but delicious lunches, cakes and coffee, all beautifully presented.

Vivo, 65 Davis Crescent, Newmarket (☎09/522 0688). Gourmet pizza served in a capacious wood-floored interior or out on the pavement with the denizens of this trendy little street.

Ponsonby, Herne Bay and Grey Lynn

At the cutting edge of Auckland's foodie scene is Ponsonby Road, a street where devotion to style is as important as culinary prowess. But don't be intimidated; the food is almost invariably excellent and though prices are generally a notch above those in more downbeat parts of the city, there are several reasonably-priced places hanging in there. Again, popular daytime cafés frequently ease into more rumbustious drinking later on, often until the wee hours.

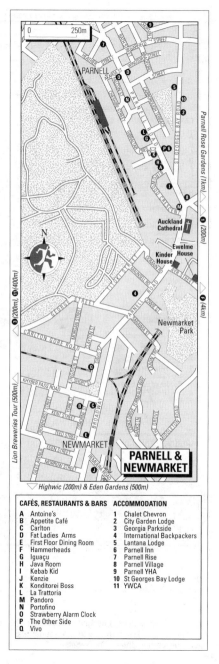

CAFÉS, RESTAURANTS & BARS	ACCOMMODATION
A Antoine's	1 Chalet Chevron
B Appetite Café	2 City Garden Lodge
C Carlton	3 Georgia Parkside
D Fat Ladies Arms	4 International Backpackers
E First Floor Dining Room	5 Lantana Lodge
F Hammerheads	6 Parnell Inn
G Iguaçu	7 Parnell Rise
H Java Room	8 Parnell Village
I Kebab Kid	9 Parnell YHA
J Kenzie	10 St Georges Bay Lodge
K Konditorei Boss	11 YWCA
L La Trattoria	
M Pandoro	
N Portofino	
O Strawberry Alarm Clock	
P The Other Side	
Q Vivo	

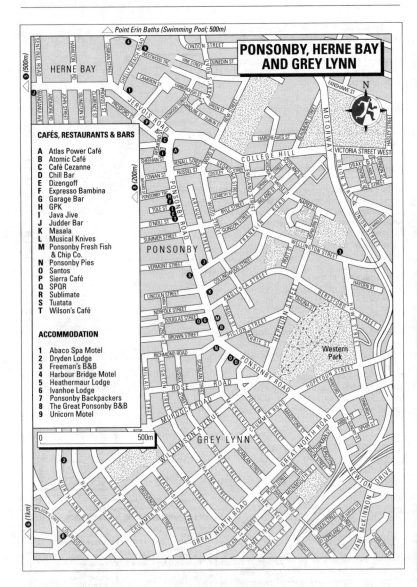

△ Point Erin Baths (Swimming Pool; 500m)

PONSONBY, HERNE BAY AND GREY LYNN

HERNE BAY

PONSONBY

GREY LYNN

Western Park

CAFÉS, RESTAURANTS & BARS

A Atlas Power Café
B Atomic Café
C Café Cezanne
D Chill Bar
E Dizengoff
F Expresso Bambina
G Garage Bar
H GPK
I Java Jive
J Judder Bar
K Masala
L Musical Knives
M Ponsonby Fresh Fish
   & Chip Co.
N Ponsonby Pies
O Santos
P Sierra Café
Q SPQR
R Sublimate
S Tuatata
T Wilson's Café

ACCOMMODATION

1 Abaco Spa Motel
2 Dryden Lodge
3 Freeman's B&B
4 Harbour Bridge Motel
5 Heathermaur Lodge
6 Ivanhoe Lodge
7 Ponsonby Backpackers
8 The Great Ponsonby B&B
9 Unicorn Motel

0 ————————— 500m

Atlas Power Café, 285 Ponsonby Rd, Ponsonby. Small modern café with a strong gay following, and pricey but delectable sandwiches and salads for around $14.

Atomic Café, 121 Ponsonby Rd, Ponsonby (☎09/376 4954). Atomic's own-roast coffee has become a byword for quality espresso all over town. Here, at their home base, the muffins reign supreme and macrobiotic and organic food dominates the blackboard. The sandpit and fluffies (cappuccino froth adorned with hundreds and thousands) make it a great place for harassed parents. Open to 5pm daily, until midnight Thurs–Sat.

Café Cézanne, 296 Ponsonby Rd, Ponsonby. This casual, ramshackle place is a welcome refuge from the glitz; great for reading the papers over hearty quiches, pizza slices and huge wedges of cake.

Dizengoff, 256 Ponsonby Rd, Ponsonby (☎09/360 0108). Unlicensed breakfast and lunch café specializing in wonderful bagels, Kosher meals and luscious char-grilled vegetables all at reasonable prices.

Expresso Bambina, 266 Ponsonby Rd, Ponsonby. Minimally decorated postage-stamp-sized sandwich bar, perfect for delicious panini, bruschetta and great coffee.

GPK, 260 Ponsonby Rd, Ponsonby (☎09/360 1113). Smart bar and restaurant wood-firing some of the tastiest pizzas in town with avant-garde toppings such as Thai green curry or octopus. They're small, considering the $16–18 price tag, but well worth it; eat in or take out. Licensed.

Masala, 169 Ponsonby Rd, Ponsonby (☎09/378 4500). Spartan Indian restaurant that's always bustling with diners eager to get their chapatis around tandoori dishes and succulent butter chicken. Licensed.

Musical Knives, 272 Ponsonby Rd, Ponsonby (☎09/376 7354). Auckland's only classy, and expensive, vegetarian restaurant serving up curry, sushi and buckwheat noodles with shiitake mushrooms. Licensed.

Ponsonby Fresh Fish and Chip Co, 127 Ponsonby Rd, Ponsonby (☎09/378 7885). One of the best basic fish, chips and burger joints around, frequently lauded in *Metro* magazine's annual readers' poll and always busy, so call ahead or trot across the road to the SPQR bar and wait.

Ponsonby Pies, 134 Ponsonby Rd, Ponsonby. Basically a takeaway with a few chairs that's great for sumptuous filled focaccia and, of course, pies: apple and pork, silverbeet and cheese, pumpkin and bacon, to name but a few.

Santos, 114 Ponsonby Rd, Ponsonby. Unbeatable cappuccinos and panini.

Sierra Café, 50 Jervois Rd, Herne Bay. Excellent café with great coffee roasted on site and a tempting range of all-day breakfasts and lunches.

Sublimate, 135 Williamson Ave, Grey Lynn. Big windowed café and bar a little off the beaten track but a personal favourite for wonderful breakfasts: avocado-mozzarella scrambled eggs and about the best salmon bagel florentine in town. Daytime snacks give way to a wine-bar atmosphere on Tues–Sat evenings. Licensed.

Tuatara, 198 Ponsonby Rd, Ponsonby (☎09/360 0098). Big, loud café and brasserie with reliable tasty food; one of the key places to see and be seen on this street full of such places. Licensed.

Devonport

Devonport's range of places to eat is more limited than elsewhere but there are several worthwhile **lunch stops** and a couple of quality restaurants for **evening dining**.

Carpe Diem, 49 Victoria Rd. Comfortable and relaxed café good at any time of the day for soups, quiches and salads or just for coffee and cake.

Monsoon, 71 Victoria Rd (☎09/445 4263). Excellent value-for-money Thai place with tasty dishes at around $12.

The Stone Oven, 3 Clarence St. Large, bustling bakery and café with a solid reputation for organic sourdough, black Russian and barley rye breads; also popular for quiches, pies, sandwiches, cakes and pastries to take away or eat in, accompanied by aromatic coffee.

Watermark, 33 King Edward Parade (☎09/446 0822). One of Devonport's finest restaurants – all bare boards and white napkins. Main evening dishes ($25) range from sashimi to tandoori chicken, and at weekends you can indulge in a decadent all-day breakfast for $12.

Drinking, nightlife and entertainment

Auckland certainly doesn't rank as a great city for nightlife but, with a million people to entertain, there is always something going on, even if it is just a night down at the local **boozer**. The best way to find out **what's on** is to pick up the *New Zealand Herald*, which has daily entertainment listings and on Thursday carries *The Voice*, a supplement with film previews and comprehensive gig and club **listings** for Auckland and much of the northern half of the North Island. The monthly *Real Groovy* magazine, available free from any record store is great for gig information, though the monthly *Rip it Up* ($2), from magazine stands and record stores, has better nationwide coverage.

New Zealand produces plenty of **bands** and at any time you should be able to find some quality local acts bashing away in a club or dedicated venue; due to New Zealand's remoteness, bands from North America or Europe are less frequent visitors. One of the best ways to see local bands is to attend one of the **free summer concerts** held in Aotea Square, Albert Park and The Domain, under the *Music in Parks* banner (mid-Dec to early Feb; infoline, ☎09/367 1077), mostly on Friday, Saturday and Sunday afternoons.

Auckland's **arts scene** is quieter, though you should be able to track down a couple of plays and perhaps some dance or opera.

Pubs and bars

In Auckland, as in much of the rest of the country, the distinction between eating and drinking places is frequently blurred, with cafés, restaurants and bars all just points along the same continuum. The factor uniting those listed below is their dedication to **drinking**: some are bars which may serve food but where drinking is the norm; others are old-time hotels in the Kiwi tradition, though even these have been dramatically smartened up and may do a sideline in inexpensive counter meals.

Apart from the curious Sunday rules (see Basics, p.41), drinking hours are almost unlimited and you will find places serving alcohol virtually round the clock. The exception is in Auckland's **"dry areas"**, where you won't find any pubs, and even licensed restaurants are scarce. **Grey Lynn**, which borders Ponsonby, has recently voted to relinquish its dry status, but **Mount Eden** remains resolutely arid.

City centre

Bar Manifesto, 315 Queen St. (☎09/303 4405). Fashionable, uptown evening-only wine and espresso bar with live Sunday-night jazz for around $5.

Civic Tavern, cnr Queen St & Wellesley St. Two-in-one pub that's good for a quick snifter before the movies across the road: choose between *Murphy's Irish Bar* downstairs and the *London Bar* upstairs with bistro meals and a hundred brands of bottled beer.

Hotel De Brett, cnr High St & Shortland St. One of the best of the downtown watering holes with several bars, including the people-watching *Corner Bar*, a wine bar popular with office workers, and the grungy *Bob's* with pool tables and DJs at weekends.

Judder Bar, cnr Vulcan Lane & High St. Compact, trendy bar, brother of the more famous establishment in Herne Bay (see below).

Kitty O'Brien's, 2 Drake St, Freeman's Bay (☎09/303 3936). Irish pub with reliable bar meals, Irish music or covers bands almost every night and an upstairs comedy venue (see p.105).

Kiwi Tavern, 3 Britomart Place (☎09/307 1717). Top-floor bar with pool tables, $5 meals and drink discounts that's predictably popular with backpackers and even has a travellers' noticeboard.

The Loaded Hog, Viaduct Basin. Vast, bustling, glass-walled bar with seating right on the quay, bar food, an impressive range of wines by the glass and four tantalizing micro-brewed beers; beware of the dress standards (no shorts, vests or thongs) enforced in the evenings.

Occidental Tavern, 8 Vulcan Lane. A slice of traditional Kiwi pub life in the middle of a trendy quarter of the city.

Shakespeare Tavern, 62 Albert St. Pub with an in-house micro-brewery producing a thirst-quenching low-alcohol ginger beer and a handful of commendable, stiffer brews – also sold in two-litre bottles to take away.

The suburbs

Carlton, cnr Broadway & Khyber Pass Rd, Newmarket. Pub and brasserie offering good-value meals but better known as a sports bar, especially for big games. Live music most weekends.

Chill Bar, 116 Ponsonby Rd, Ponsonby. Big, boozy bar with Ponsonby panache draught beer and pool tables out back. Open until around 3am at weekends.

Daily Planet, 59 Victoria Rd, Devonport. Café/bar tucked away behind the shops but worth seeking out for lively music in the bar and more relaxed tunes in the courtyard.

GAY AND LESBIAN AUCKLAND

New Zealand has a fairly small but progressive and proactive **gay culture**, and Auckland, the most vibrant of the cities, is at its centre. The two-week **Hero Festival** in late-February (booking office: PO Box 184, Auckland; ☎09/307 1057) is the community's reverential nod to Sydney's Mardi Gras. The **Lesbian and Gay Film Festival** and a number of other events lead up to the climactic **Hero Parade**, a more earnest, less frivolous and substantially smaller affair than Sydney's extravaganza, but no less committed to a good time. Ponsonby Road is closed off for the Saturday night and tens of thousands – gay, straight and voyeuristic party animals alike – line the streets to egg on the lavish floats. Once the procession is over, free buses depart Ponsonby Road and K' Road for the all-night Hero Party; tickets cost $55 and are available in person only from *Surrender Dorothy* (175 Ponsonby Rd) and *The Den* (348 K' Rd).

There's a heap of information about **what's happening** in the fortnightly *Express* magazine ($2), which can be bought from branches of *Maggazzino* and the *Out!* bookshop (see "Listings", p.106), and is available for browsing in many cafés. It's also worth tuning in to *In the Pink*, 95BFM's Sunday evening gay and lesbian interest programme (8–9pm), preceded by an hour of *The GirlsOwn Show*.

Outside of festival time, the gay **scene** is fairly low-key, gently woven into the café/bar mainstream of Ponsonby, Parnell and Newmarket, with the exception of the western end of K' Road where the strip clubs mingle freely with gay bars and cruise clubs. Among the **cafés**, *Atlas Power Café* in Ponsonby, and *Sublimate* in Grey Lynn (see p.99–101) both attract a significant gay clientele, and, in the same area, the intimate and friendly *Surrender Dorothy*, 175 Ponsonby Rd, is great for a quiet drink, though it isn't exclusively gay. Almost all the significant gay action happens along a short section of K' Road, where *The Kase*, 340 K' Rd (☎09/377 0303; closed Sun–Tues) and *Legend*, 335 K' Rd (☎09/377 6062; open nightly) are two of the hottest **clubs**, both open late and often hosting live drag acts or other entertainment. *Sinners*, 373 K' Rd (☎09/308 9985; Fri & Sat only) is another popular haunt with pool tables, a lounge area and dance floor, which on Thursdays transforms itself into *Q Bar*, Auckland's only venue catering to "women and their friends".

USEFUL CONTACTS

Gaylink Travel, 177 Parnell Rd, Auckland; postal address PO Box 37–259, Parnell, Auckland (☎09/302 0553 & 0800/429 872, fax 358 1206, email *akltravel@gaylink.co.nz*). A dedicated inbound tour operator that also deals in domestic travel, offering an information and reservation service for gay- and lesbian-friendly accommodation and rental vehicles.

Millbrook Travel, 2nd Floor, Vulcan Building, Vulcan Lane, Auckland; postal address PO Box 105–011, Auckland

(☎09/358 2220, fax 358 2221). Gay-friendly travel agency with contacts throughout the country.

Pride Centre, 33 Wyndham St, Auckland; postal address PO Box 5426, Wellesley St (☎09/302 0590, fax 303 2042). The best place to tap into the scene, with a drop-in centre (generally Mon–Fri 8am–5pm) and a good events noticeboard.

See p.75 for advice on finding **gay-friendly accommodation** in the city.

Fat Ladies Arms, 144 Parnell Rd, Parnell. Spit-and-sawdust place at odds the Parnell swank along the rest of the street. Basic bistro food and a lively atmosphere.

Garage Bar, 152 Ponsonby Rd, Ponsonby. Diminutive, smart, barstool-perching place with fine wines by the glass, plenty of top-shelf cocktails and a great window seat. Closed Sunday.

Judder Bar, 198 Jervois Rd, Herne Bay. Herne Bay's original dingy bar, equally good for a quiet drink or a session, and named after the traffic-calming bump in the road outside.

SPQR, 150 Ponsonby Rd, Ponsonby. Longstanding dimly lit bar with an excellent range of wines and beers, and fine food; a good venue for spotting off-duty rock stars and actors.

Wilson's Café, 258 Ponsonby Rd, Ponsonby (☎09/376 1279). Smart café/bar run by ex-All Black Stu Wilson and therefore the place to go to watch the match, though you'll need to book to get a table when a big game is on.

Clubs and gigs

Auckland undoubtedly has New Zealand's largest and most exciting club scene and, by sheer weight of population, gets to see more bands than anywhere else; indeed, the bigger international acts often make it no further.

Though Karangahape Road occasionally grasps the **clubbing** torch for a time, the flame usually burns brightest downtown around the junction of Vulcan Lane and High Street, where you can join the nightly flow of bright young things surging between the bars and clubs. Unless someone special is spinning the platters or a band is playing, few clubs charge admission, encouraging sporadic and unpredictable exoduses to other venues – just follow the crowds.

Many of the clubs have one area set up as a stage and on any night of the week you might find top Kiwi acts and even overseas **bands** blazing away in the corner; a few pubs may also put on a band from time to time. Bigger acts understandably opt for the larger venues; tickets can be booked through Ticketek (☎09/307 5000).

All venues listed are in the **city centre** unless otherwise specified.

Aotea Centre, Aotea Square, Queen St (☎09/307 5060). Mainstream venue hosts occasional gigs by low-key rock bands.

The Box/Cause Celebre, 35 High St (☎09/303 1336). Twin clubs, *The Box* currently noted for e-driven drum 'n' bass, while *Celebre* mixes acid jazz and smoother sounds.

Crow Bar, 26 Wyndham St. The place to go when everywhere else has shut, spinning DJ House and trance until long past sun up. Occasional cover charges around the $5 mark.

Eastside, 67 Shortland St. Womb-like late-night bar that's all maroon and dim lighting – and often quiet enough to enable conversation.

Java Jive Café, 12 Pompallier Terrace, Ponsonby (☎09/376 5870). Tiny basement bar with nightly live music. Regular acoustic, jazz and blues sessions; call or check local listings magazines for details.

Logan Campbell Centre, 217 Greenlane West, Greenlane (☎09/638 8833). Major indoor rock venue way down south and disparagingly known as the Logan Concrete Centre for its acoustically abominable interior: avoid it unless there's someone you *really* must see.

Papa Jack's Voodoo Lounge, 9 Vulcan Lane (☎09/358 4847). Big bar with a party atmosphere that's heaving at weekends when it stays open to the small hours. Mixed dance and alternative rock DJs occasionally give way to top Kiwi touring bands when there'll be a small cover charge.

The Power Station, 33 Mount Eden Rd, Mount Eden (☎09/377 3488). Sweaty venue that's usually the most happening place for alternative rock acts.

Squid, 17 O'Connell St (☎09/373 2234). Young, loud, hopelessly hip and great fun club with a strong techno/dance following, and frequent touring bands. Entry costs vary from $15 down to nothing at all. Closed Sun–Tues.

Temple Café, 486 Queen St (☎09/377 4866). Tiny café and bar with pool tables and early-evening happy hours that also sees emerging and more established Kiwi acoustic and blues acts pretty much every night. Admission ranges from free to $5.

Classical music, dance, theatre and comedy

Auckland's **theatre** scene is floundering at present; there is no professional company with a permanent venue and, with the recent closure of a couple of theatres and no immediate prospect of replacements, touring groups are having trouble finding places to play. Classical music, **opera** and **ballet** at least get a major venue in the shape of the Aotea Centre, but events are held only sporadically: the New Zealand Symphony Orchestra strikes up every month or so, the Wellington-based New Zealand Ballet calls in during its tours of the provinces from time to time, and the Auckland Opera puts on several shows a year. The **comedy** scene is livelier, with a couple of pubs hosting regular stand-up comedy, while in late April and early May theatres and pubs around town are alive with local stand-up comics and top-flight international acts for the two-week **comedy festival**.

Aotea Centre, Aotea Square, Queen St (☎09/307 5060). New Zealand's first purpose-built opera house, opened in 1990 and the home stage for New Zealand Symphony Orchestra and the New Zealand Ballet. Pick up the quarterly *Aotea Centre Events Guide*.

Kitty O'Briens, 2 Drake St, Freeman's Bay, behind Victoria Park Market (☎09/303 3936). The pick of the comedy venues – in a room above an Irish pub with an open-mike night on Wednesdays ($5), and Pro Night on Thursday ($12).

Maidment Theatre, cnr Princess St & Alfred St (☎09/308 2383). Two university theatres, with mainstream works in the larger venue and more daring stuff in the studio.

The Masonic, 28 King Edward Parade, Devonport (☎09/445 0485). The best of Kiwi stand-up every Saturday night. Cover charge around $10.

Cinema

Mainstream cinemas cluster close to the junction of Queen and Wellesley streets: try Mid-City Cinema Centre, 239 Queen St (☎09/302 0277); St James Theatre, 312 Queen St (☎09/377 4241) and Village 8 on Broadway, 77 Broadway, Newmarket (☎09/520 0806); **repertory** cinemas are more widely scattered, and are listed below. The annual **Auckland International Film Festival**, usually held in early July, presses many of these cinemas into service for arthouse and foreign screenings.

Admission is around $10, though many cinemas drop their admission to $7 before 6pm on weekdays.

Academy, 64 Lorne St (☎09/373 2761). Predominantly arthouse cinema tucked underneath the main library.

Capitol Cinema, 610 Dominion Rd, Balmoral (☎09/630 0634). Tucked away in the southern suburbs, this is the place to go for off-beat art films.

Devonport 3, 56 Victoria Rd, Devonport (☎09/445 4470). First-run Hollywood movies. Accessible from the city with Fullers' Ferry & Movie Pass for much the same price you'd pay for just the movie on Queen Street – and in a more salubrious setting.

Hollywood, 20 St Georges Rd, Avondale, 6km southwest of the city centre (☎09/828 8393). Mainstream movies through the week and classics on weekend afternoons, often with accompaniment from the Wurlitzer organ.

Listings

Abseiling Cliffhanger Adventure Tours abseil down the 110m Waitakere Falls (full-day trip; $145–165, including barbecue; ☎09/815 1851). Absolute Adrenalin Adventures offer urban rap jumping (2hr; $50; booking essential, ☎09/358 4874) down the side of the city-centre Novotel.

Airlines Air New Zealand and Air New Zealand Link, 139 Queen St (☎09/357 3000); Ansett New Zealand, 75 Queen St (☎09/302 2146); British Airways, 154 Queen St (☎09/356 8690); Canadian, 44–48 Emily Place (☎09/309 0735); Garuda, 120 Albert St (☎09/366 1855); JAL, 120 Albert St

MOVING ON FROM AUCKLAND

Moving on from Auckland is a straightforward business, with frequent **buses** following the main routes north and south to most major destinations, and **trains** leaving daily for Hamilton, Wellington and Rotorua. With your **own transport** you have a couple of alternatives if you're heading north. You can take SH1 directly over the harbour bridge Waitemata Harbour past the wineries, West Coast Beaches and Waitakere Ranges to meet up with SH1 at Wellsford. **Cyclists** must use the Devonport Ferry rather than the harbour bridge if heading directly north but will do well to take the western route, possibly riding a suburban train to Waitakere (bikes carried free outside peak hours). Southbound cyclists are better off following the Seabird Coast (see p.115) avoiding the Southern Motorway, the main route south out of the city for motorists.

The network of **ferries** and **flights** linking the islands in the Hauraki Gulf presents a few more interesting ways to get out of the city. By linking them together you can visit a few islands and continue on to the Coromandel Peninsula or Whangarei without returning to Auckland. The most useful combination is to take a ferry to Great Barrier Island (see p.125) and catch a flight from there, possibly adding Waiheke Island to your itinerary; contact Fullers (☎09/367 9111) and Great Barrier Airlines (☎09/275 9120 & 0800/275 912) for schedules and fares. If you are heading directly to the Coromandel Peninsula, consider the Coromandel Ferry Service ($26 one way; ☎09/866 7084) which runs from Hobson Wharf, near the Ferry Building, to Coromandel, though low tides often force the ferry to use a wharf 7km south of Coromandel where a bus awaits.

Finally, if you're on your way out of New Zealand, **airline** and **travel agents** are listed below –and remember to keep $20 aside for your **departure tax.**

(☎09/379 3202); Malaysian, 12th Floor, 12–26 Swanson St (☎09/373 2741); Qantas, 154 Queen St (☎09/357 8700 & 0800/808767); Singapore Airlines, cnr Albert St & Fanshaw St (☎09/379 3209); Thai, 22 Fanshawe St (☎09/377 3886); United, 7 City Rd (☎09/379 3800).

Airport There are three terminals – one international and two domestic terminals, one each for Ansett New Zealand and Air New Zealand – with a free bus shuttling between them every twenty minutes or so. For information, call ☎0800/101 048.

Airport buses Airbus (☎09/275 9396; $10) plies between the city and the airport, via Newmarket and Parnell. Door-to-door services include Johnston's Shuttle Link (☎09/275 1234 & 0800/SHUTTLE) and Super Shuttle (☎09/307 5210 & 0800/727 747).

American Express 101 Queen St (Mon–Fri 8.30am–5.30pm & Sat 9.30am–12.30pm; ☎379 8243 & 0800/262 263); 69 Symonds St (Mon–Fri 8.30am–5pm; ☎367 4384).

Automobile Association 99 Albert St (☎09/377 4660).

Ballooning *Balloon Safaris* can take you up, up and away for an hour or so ($195; ☎09/415 8289).

Banks and exchange American Express (see above); Interforex, 2 Queen St (☎09/302 3031) & 99 Quay St (☎09/302 3066); Thomas Cook (see below); Travelex, 32 Queen St (☎09/358 9173) & 75 Queen St (☎09/302 0143).

Bike rental Cycle Xpress, 11 Beach Rd (☎09/379 0779); Penny Farthing, cnr Khyber Pass Rd & Symonds St (☎09/379 2002); Pack & Pedal, 436 Broadway, Newmarket (☎09/522 2161); and Adventure Cycles, Fort Lane (☎309 5566 & 0800/335 566), who also rent tandems; daily rates range from $15–25.

Bookshops Whitcoulls, 210 Queen St (☎09/356 5400) and London Bookshops, Downtown Shopping Centre (☎09/373 5355) are the two main nationwide chains. In addition, try Books Pasifica, Samoa House, 283 K' Rd (☎09/303 2349) for the city's best selection of Maori and Pacific Island books and cassettes; Hard to Find (But Worth The Effort) Quality Secondhand Books, 171–175 The Mall, Onehunga (☎09/634 4340) for a massive selection of secondhand books; Out!, 45 Anzac Ave (☎09/377 7770) for gay-interest books and magazines; Women's Bookshop, 228 Dominion Rd (☎09/630 7162), for feminist literature and women's interest books; and Specialty Maps, 58 Albert St (☎09/307 2217) for all your cartographic needs.

Buses InterCity (☎09/357 8400) run the most comprehensive range of services to most destinations; Newmans (☎09/309 9738 & 0800/777 707) have a more skeletal but still wide coverage; and

Mount Cook Landlines (☎09/309 5395 & 0800/800 287) run to Wellington via Rotorua, Taupo and Palmerston North. Tickets for InterCity and Newmans can be bought at the office in the Sky City terminal on Hobson St, those for Mount Cook at the Downtown Airline Terminal on Quay St. See separate listings for Airport buses and Tours – and p.69 for the low-down on local bus services in Auckland.

Buying a car For general advice, consult Basics (see p.30), then peruse the noticeboards in hostels and at the main visitor centre or get along to one of the weekend car fairs, which are typically dominated by private sellers rather than dealers. The major Saturday venues are the Auckland Car Fair, Ellerslie Racecourse, Greenlane (☎09/529 2233), and the Saturday Car Fair, Beach Road, City (☎09/636 9775); on Sunday, there's the Park-n-Sell Car Fair, Manukau City Shopping Centre (☎09/358 5000). All take place in the early morning (aim to get there by 9am) and are well organized, with qualified folk on hand to check roadworthiness. Alternatively, glance through the page of cars for sale in the weekly *Auto Trader* or *Trade & Exchange* magazines, or pick up Wednesday's *New Zealand Herald* newspaper.

Camping and outdoor equipment Bivouac, 196 Queen St (☎09/366 1966) & 326 Broadway, Newmarket (☎09/529 2298) have a good selection of gear for sale or rent; Canvas City, 171 Hobson St (☎09/373 5753) stocks all the major brands; and it's also worth checking the noticeboard in Auckland's main visitor centre for offers of camping and tramping gear for sale.

Car parks Victoria Street, cnr Victoria St & Kitchener St; Downtown, cnr Customs St & Lower Hobson St; Civic Underground, Mayoral Drive; and K' Road, Mercury Lane.

Car rental The international companies all have depots close to the airport and free shuttle bus to get you to them; smaller companies, frequently offering highly competitive rates in return for older cars and a poorer back-up network, are mostly based in the city or inner suburbs. A2B Rentals, 11 Stanley St (☎09/377 0825 & 0800/222 929); Avis, 17/19 Nelson St (☎09/379 2650) & airport (☎09/275 7239); Budget, 83 Beach Rd (☎09/375 2230) & airport (☎09/256 8447); Hertz, 154 Victoria St West (☎09/309 0989) & airport (☎09/256 8690); National Car Rental, Princes Wharf (☎09/309 3336) & airport (☎09/275 0066); NZ Rent a Car, cnr Lower Hobson St & Custom St West (☎09/308 9005) & airport (☎09/275 2422); Rent-a-Dent, 105 Lower Cook St (☎09/309 0066) & airport (☎09/275 2044); Thrifty Car Rental, 79 Fanshaw St (☎09/309 0111) & airport (☎09/256 1405).

Consulates Australia, Union House, 32–38 Quay St (☎09/303 2429); Canada, 44–48 Emily Place (☎09/309 3690); Ireland, 2/87 Queen St (☎09/302 2867); Netherlands, 90 Symonds St (☎09/379 5399); UK, 17/151 Queen St (☎09/303 2973); USA, cnr Shortland St & O'Connell St (☎09/303 2724).

Cruises See p.70.

Emergencies Police, fire and ambulance, ☎111; main police station, cnr Cook St & Vincent St (☎09/379 4240).

Events Auckland Anniversary Weekend, sailing regatta on the Waitemata Harbour on the last weekend in Jan; Devonport Food and Wine Festival, third weekend in Feb; Round-the-Bays Run, a 10km fun run that attracts up to 70,000 participants, early March; Waiheke Jazz Festival, Easter week; Royal New Zealand Easter Show, Easter weekend, family entertainment Kiwi-style with equestrian events, wine tasting and arts and crafts, all held at the showgrounds along Greenlane; Auckland International Film Festival, early July.

Ferries Fullers, Ferry Building, Quay St West (☎09/367 9111, timetable information ☎09/367 9102) run most Hauraki Gulf routes, serving Devonport and the islands of Rangitoto, Waiheke, Motuihe and Great Barrier; Subritzky Shipping Line (☎09/534 5663) run to Kennedy Point on Waiheke Island from Half Moon Bay near Pakuranga in Auckland's eastern suburbs; Gulf Trans (☎09/373 4036 & 0800/GULFTRANS) run a barge from Auckland's Wynyard Wharf to Great Barrier Island; and Coromandel Ferry Service, Hobson Wharf (☎09/866 7084) run from Auckland to Coromandel.

Gay and lesbian Auckland See box on p.103.

Kayak rental Ferg's Kayaks, 12 Tamaki Drive, Okahu Bay (☎09/529 2230; $10 per hour); see also p.70 for details of organized kayaking trips.

Laundry Clean Green Laundromat, 18 Fort St (Mon–Sat 9am–8pm; ☎09/358 4370).

Left luggage Sky City Bus Terminal, Hobson St (daily 7am–8pm); Downtown Terminal, cnr Quay St & Albert St (Mon–Fri 7am–7pm, Sat & Sun 7am–6pm).

Library Auckland Public Library, 44–46 Lorne St (Mon–Thurs 9.30am–8pm, Fri 9.30am–9pm, Sat 10am–4pm, Sun 1–5pm; ☎09/377 0209); only the ground floor reading room is open on Sundays.

Medical treatment Auckland Hospital, Park Rd, Grafton (☎09/379 7440); Travelcare, 5th Floor, Dingwall Building, 87 Queen St (☎09/373 4621), offers diving medicals, physiotherapy, X-rays and dental treatment. Registered medical practitioners are listed separately at the beginning of the White Pages phone directory.

Newspapers and magazines Auckland's morning paper is the anodyne *New Zealand Herald*, the closest New Zealand gets to a national daily. International newspapers and magazines are sold at numerous outlets, including MegaMags, 58 Queen St (☎09/366 6216) and branches of Magazzino (cnr Victoria St & Kitchener St; 123 Ponsonby Rd, Ponsonby; and 3 Mortimer Passage, Newmarket). These shops also sell *Metro*, Auckland's city monthly which, if nothing else, offers an insight into the aspirations of upwardly mobile Aucklanders.

Pharmacy Seven Day Pharmacy, 202 Ponsonby Rd (daily 8am–9.30pm; ☎09/378 6075); emergency departments of hospitals (see "Medical treatment" above) have 24-hour pharmacies.

Post office Auckland's main post office and poste restante (Mon–Thurs 9am–5pm, Fri 9am–6pm, Sat 9am–noon) is just off Queen St on Wellesley St West.

Roller blading Tamaki Drive is a favourite spot, and blades can be rented for around $10 for the first hour and $5 for each subsequent hour. Cheapskates (daily summer, weekends only in winter; mobile ☎021/622 422) have a van on Tamaki Drive close to Kelly Tarlton's Underwater World; other outlets include Mission Blades, on Tamaki Drive at Mission Bay, and Ferg's Kayaks, opposite Kelly Tarlton's at Okahu Bay.

Sailing See p.80.

Swimming Central pools include the indoor Edwardian-style Tepid Baths, 102 Customs St West (☎09/379 4794), the open-air saltwater Parnell Baths, Judges Bay Rd (☎09/373 3561), and the heated outdoor Point Erin Baths, cnr Shelley Beach Rd & Sarsfield St, Herne Bay (☎09/376 6863). Otherwise, simply head for one of the beaches (see "The North Shore", p.92).

Taxis Auckland Taxi Co-op (☎09/300 3000); City Cabs (☎09/366 6666); Dial-a-Cab (☎0800/342522).

Thomas Cook Dilworth Building, cnr Customs St & Queen St (☎09/379 7799); and at 96 Queen St (☎09/377 2666).

Tours There's a wide choice of Auckland-based trips, ranging from short tours of the city (half-day and full-day, $36–99) to multi-day jaunts to the Bay of Islands, Rotorua and Waitomo (2–3 days, from $300); operators include Scenic Tours (☎09/303 3123), Grey Line (☎09/377 0904) and Great Sights (☎09/303 1170). See also "Abseiling" and "Ballooning" pp.105–6 – and the box on p.70 for details of cruises, sailing and kayaking trips.

Trains Inside the train station on Beach Road, the Tranz Rail Travel Centre (Mon–Fri 7.30am–6pm, Sat & Sun 7.30am–1pm; ☎0800/802 802) dispenses tickets for long-distance Tranz Scenic and suburban Tranz Metro train services. Long-distance services run daily to Hamilton, Wellington and Rotorua. The two suburban lines run south through Newmarket and Ellerslie, and west through Henderson then north around the end of the Waitemata Harbour to Waitakere; bikes can be taken on local trains free of charge outside peak times.

Travel agencies Auckland Central Backpackers Travel Centre, 6 Shortland St (☎09/358 4874) specializes in budget domestic travel, as does CCB Travel Shop, City Central Backpackers, 26 Lorne St (☎09/309 5724); for internal and international travel, try Budget Travel, 16 Fort St (☎09/366 0061 & 0800/808 040), STA Travel, 10 High St (☎09/309 0458), or the YHA, cnr Shortland St & Jean Batten Place (☎09/379 4224). Outside Adventure Exchange, 16 Shortland St (☎09/366 1445), is the main booking agent for Kiwi Experience's backpacker bus tours.

Women's centres Auckland Women's Centre, 63 Ponsonby Rd (Mon–Fri 9am–4pm; ☎09/376 3227) offers counselling, health advice, massage and reflexology.

AROUND AUCKLAND

For many, the best Auckland has to offer lies in the immediate vicinity, with its verdant hills, magnificent beaches and appealing seaside communities. Few would argue that the **Waitakere Ranges**, to the **west** of the city, rank among New Zealand's most spectacular landscapes, but their proximity makes them a viable break from the urban bustle. The hills also serve to deflect the prevailing westerly winds, providing shelter for the **vineyards** of the Henderson Valley and Kumeu, the base for many of the country's top winemakers, most of which offer tastings.

Although there are spectacular expanses of sand pretty much right along New Zealand's western seaboard, which can't be beaten for long moody strolls, only at the **West Coast beaches** will you find surf-lifesaving patrols in such reassuring numbers. Heading **north**, Auckland infringes on southern Northland, making the **Hibiscus Coast** a virtual suburb enormously popular with day-trippers and holiday-home owners. South of Auckland, the **Hunua Ranges** offer a few modest walks and again provide a windbreak, this time for the **Seabird Coast**, where low shingle banks and extensive mudflats provide an excellent breeding ground for dozens of migratory species.

West of Auckland

Auckland's suburban sprawl peters out some 20km west of the centre among the enveloping folds of the **Waitakere Ranges**. Despite being the most accessible expanse of greenery for almost a million people, the hills remain largely unspoiled, with plenty of trails through native bush. On a hot summer day, thousands head up and over the hills to one of half a dozen thundering **surf beaches**, all largely undeveloped but for a few holiday homes (known to most Kiwis as baches) and the odd shop. The soils around the eastern fringes of the Waitakeres nurture long established **vineyards**, mainly clustered in the Henderson Valley but also stretching north to Kumeu, just short of the Kaipara Harbour town of **Helensville** and the **hot pools** at Parakai.

You'll need your own transport to do justice to the beaches and most of the ranges, but the Tranz-Metro **trains** make it as far as Henderson and Waitakere – a boon for cyclists keen to get out of the city quickly – and city **buses** with numbers beginning #06– run through Henderson and Kumeu to Helensville.

The Henderson and Kumeu wineries

Much of New Zealand's enviable reputation as a producer of quality wine is the result of vintages emanating from West Auckland, the historical home of the country's viticulture. The bigger enterprises now grow most of their grapes in Marlborough, Gisborne and Hawke's Bay, but much of the production process is still centred around the suburban **Henderson Valley**, 20km west of the city, or 20km further north around the contiguous and equally characterless villages of **Kumeu** and **Huapai**.

As early as 1819 the Reverend Samuel Marsden planted grapes, ostensibly to produce sacramental wine, in Kerikeri in the Bay of Islands, but commercial winemaking didn't really get under way until Dalmatians turned their hand to growing grapes after the kauri gum they came to dig ceased to be profitable (see box on p.177 for the finer points of gum digging). Many of today's thriving businesses owe their existence to these immigrant families, a legacy evident in winery names such as Babich, Delegat, Nobilo and Selak. Today, the region is producing some quality wines and winning prestigious awards, usually with the key varietals of Cabernet Sauvignon, Merlot, Pinot Noir and Chardonnay.

The free *Winemakers of West Auckland* leaflet available from Auckland visitor centres details the wineries which can be visited; most offer tastings. If you are reliant on public transport, catch the Tranz Metro train out to Henderson where *Corbans*, 426–448 Great North Road (Mon–Sat 9am–6pm; ☎09/837 3390), is the most easily accessible of almost a dozen wineries and does free tours. With your own wheels, head out to the rural and broadly more appealing Kumeu where half a dozen places do tastings, notably *Coopers Creek*, SH16, Huapai (Mon–Fri 9.30am–5.30pm, Sat 10.30am–

5.30pm; ☎09/412 8560), *Kumeu River*, SH16, Kumeu (Mon–Fri 9am–5.30pm, Sat 11.30am–5.30pm; ☎09/412 8415), *Nobilo*, Station Road, Huapai (Mon–Fri 9am–5pm, Sat 10am–5pm, Sun 11am–4pm; ☎09/412 9148), and *Matua Valley*, Waimauku Valley Road, Waimauku (Mon–Fri 9am–5pm, Sat 9am–6pm, Sun 11am–4.30pm; ☎09/411 8301). At the last, reserve a table to eat at the wonderful, if pricey *Hunting Lodge* **restaurant** (lunch Fri–Sun; dinner Thurs–Sun; $25–30 for main dishes; ☎09/411 8259), which is beautifully set beside the vines.

If you plan to do some serious tasting, do yourself a favour – leave the car behind and join one of Kiwi Scene Tours' **trips** (3hr; $59; ☎09/817 2180), visiting three or four wineries.

The Waitakere Ranges and the West Coast beaches

Auckland's western limit is defined by the bush-clad **Waitakere Ranges**, which rise up to five hundred metres. At less than an hour's drive from the city, the hills are a perennially popular weekend destination for Aucklanders intent on a picnic and a bit of a stroll. The western slopes roll down to the wild, black-sand **West Coast beaches**. Pounded by heavy surf and punctuated by precipitous headlands, these tempestuous shores are a perfect counterpoint to the calm, gently shelving beaches of the Hauraki Gulf.

The Kawarau, a Maki people, knew the region as *Te Wao Nui a Tiriwa* or "the Great Forest of Tiriwa", aptly describing the kauri groves that swathed the hills before the arrival of Europeans. By the turn of the century, diggers had pretty much cleaned out the kauri gum, but logging continued until the 1940s, by which time the land was economically spent. The Auckland Regional Council bought the land, built reservoirs and designated a vast tract as the Centennial Memorial Park, with two hundred kilometres of walking tracks leading to fine vistas and some of the numerous waterfalls which cascade off the escarpment.

The easiest access to the majority of the walks and beaches is the **Waitakere Scenic Drive** (Route 24), which winds through the ranges from the dormitory suburb of **Titirangi**, in the foothills, to the informative **Arataki visitor centre** (daily 9am–5pm). From here, walkways forge into the second-growth forest, where panels identify kahikatea, rimu, rewarewa, nikau palms and a multitude of other species, all readily visible from the three nature trails (20min, 40min and 1hr) which loop around the centre, the longest visiting one of the few mature kauri stands to survive the loggers' onslaught. One recently felled kauri has been transformed by Kawerau, a Maki carver, into a striking *pou*, or guardian post, the largest of several fine carvings around the centre. Arataki is also the place to pick up **camping** permits for two vehicle-based and thirteen backpacker sites scattered through the ranges and located on the *Walking and Tramping Tracks of the Waitakere Ranges* map ($8, available from the visitor centre).

Beyond the visitor centre, the scenic drive swings north along the range, passing side roads to the **beaches**. Noted for their foot-scorching, golden-black sands and demanding swimming conditions, mountainous waves and strong tidal rips are par for the course here. Swim only in the areas between the red-and-yellow flags (patrolled Nov–Easter) and, if you get into trouble, raise one arm to attract the attention of lifeguards. A limited **bus** service (#159 from Henderson; 1 daily Mon–Fri) runs as far as Piha Beach; otherwise, you're on your own.

Whatipu and Karekare

WHATIPU is the southernmost of the West Coast surf beaches, located by the sandbar entrance to Manukau Harbour, the watery grave of many a ship. It is something of an outlier, 45km from central Auckland along the curvy Manukau Harbour shoreline. The wharf at Whatipu was briefly the terminus of the precarious coastal **Parahara Railway**, which hauled kauri from the mill at Karekare across the beach and headlands during the 1870s. The tracks were continually pounded by surf, but a second tramway from Piha covered the same treacherous expanse in the early twentieth century. Scant remains are visible, including an old tunnel which proved too tight a squeeze for a large steam engine whose boiler still litters the shore. The only sign of civilization here now is the *Whatipu Lodge* (☎09/811 8860; tent sites $8 per site, backpacker bunks ①, cabins ②). Occupying a 120-year-old former mill manager's house, the lodge is also equipped with tennis court, table tennis, snooker and a cosy library.

You can walk 5km along Whatipu Beach to **KAREKARE**, otherwise reached by a 17km road from Arataki visitor centre. Perhaps the most intimate and immediately appealing of the West Coast settlements, Karekare has regenerating manuka, pohutukawa and cabbage trees running down to a deep, smooth beach hemmed in by high promontories and only a smattering of houses more or less successfully integrated into the bush. In one hectic year, this dramatic spot was jolted out of its relative obscurity, providing the setting for beach scenes in Jane Campion's 1993 film *The Piano* and, at much the same time, the inspiration for Crowded House's *Together Alone* album. Spikes that once secured the Parahara railway tracks to the wave-cut platform around the headland to the south can still be seen from the **Gap Gallery Track** (15min each way), which winds around Korekau Point to the seemingly endless beach beyond – but beware, the track is submerged at high tide.

The Karekare Surf Club patrols a safe swimming area on summer weekends, or there is the pool below **Karekare Falls**, a five-minute walk on a track just inland from the road. Despite the presence of the fine colonial Winchelsea House, which took guests for its first fifty years, there is nowhere to stay and no facilities at Karekare.

Piha and Te Henga

For decades **PIHA**, 20km west of the visitor centre at Arataki and 40km west of Auckland, has been an icon for Aucklanders: the quintessential West Coast beach with its string of low-key weekend cottages and crashing surf that lures day-tripping families – and a youthful partying set whose New Year's Eve antics hastened in a dusk-till-dawn alcohol ban on holiday weekends. Piha feels on the brink of change; in the last couple of years, some of the quaint old-time baches have been displaced by condo-style developments, and gentrification seems inevitable.

For the time being, though, a 3km-long sweep of gold and grey sand is hemmed in by bush-clad hills and split by Piha's defining feature, the 101m **Lion Rock**. This former pa site, with some imagination, resembles a seated lion staring out to sea; the energetic climb up the steps to the summit (30–40min return) is best done as the day cools and the sun casts a gentler light. The **Tasman Lookout Track** (30–40min return) leaves the south end of the beach, climbing up to a lookout over the tiny cove of The Gap where a spectacular blowhole performs in heavy surf.

Most **swimmers** flock to South Piha, the quarter of the beach south of Lion Rock where the more prestigious of the two surf-lifesaving clubs hogs the best **surf**. North Piha Road follows the beach north of Lion Rock for 2km to the second surf club. If battling raging surf isn't your thing, head for the cool **pool** below Kitekite Falls, a three-stage plunge reached on a loop track (1hr 30min) that starts 1km up Glen Esk Road, which runs inland opposite Piha's central Domain.

Most of Piha's visitors are day-trippers so the only **place to stay** is the shadeless, year-round *Piha Domain Motor Camp* (☎09/812 8815; tent sites $9; on-site vans ②), slightly set back from the beach and best booked in advance. **Eating** possibilities are equally scanty with only a general store, a fine traditional burger bar at South Piha and the weekend-only *Lion Rock Café* inside the RSA on South Piha Road.

The smaller and much less popular **TE HENGA** (also known as Bethell's Beach) lies at the end of a long road from Waitakere 8km north along the coast. Less dramatic than Karekare, Piha or Muriwai, Te Henga is correspondingly less visited, making it good for escaping the crowds at the height of summer. There are no shops, but there is a surf club and **accommodation** – at either the elegant pohutukawa-shaded *Te Koinga Cottage*, which sleeps up to four, or *Turehu Cottage*, a smaller studio sleeping two; both have kitchen facilities (☎ & fax 09/810 9581; ④–⑥).

Muriwai

MURIWAI, the most populous of the West Coast beach settlements, lies 15km north of Piha, and 10km coastwards from the nearest bus stop (served by Helensville buses #064 and #066–069) at Waimauku. Again, there's wonderful surf and a long beach stretching 45km north to the heads of Kaipara Harbour (see p.184). The main attraction here, though, is at the southern end of the beach where a **gannet colony** occupies Motutara Island and Otakamiro Point, the headland between the main beach and the surfers' cove of Maori Bay. The gannets breed here between September and March before migrating to sunnier Australian climes, a few staying behind with the fur seals which inhabit the rocks below. Gannets normally prefer the protection of islands and this is one of the few places where they nest on the mainland, in this case right below some excellent viewing platforms from where you can observe them gracefully wheeling on the up-draughts. Short paths lead up here from near the surf club and off the road to Maori Bay. The beach, dunes and exotic planted forests to the north are best explored on **horse treks** run by the Muriwai Riding Centre, 290 Oaia Rd (☎09/411 8480; 2hr; $45).

The Waterfront **general store** serves coffee and light meals, and you can **stay** at either the *Muriwai Beach Motel*, 280 Motutara Rd (☎09/411 8780; ④), half a kilometre back from the beach, or the shaded *Muriwai Beach Motor Camp*, (☎09/411 9262; tent sites $10). For those without transport, *Bush & Beach Ltd* (☎09/478 2882) run half-day trips out here for $55.

The southern Kaipara: Helensville and Parakai

Venture beyond the vineyards of Kumeu and you'll soon find yourself in uninspiring **HELENSVILLE**, 45km from Auckland but more closely associated with Kaipara Harbour (see p.184). Like many Kaipara towns, Helensville was founded on timber which, following the completion of the rail link to Auckland in 1881, was floated here in huge rafts then loaded onto wagons. Dairying has replaced the kauri trade and Helensville potters along. Photos of busier days are displayed at the **Helensville Pioneer Museum**, on Commercial Street (daily 1–3.30pm; free) but you'll get a better idea of what the kauri logging days were like aboard the MV *Kewpie Too* (Dec to mid-March, according to demand; call☎09/420 8466 for information), which plies the waters of Kaipara Harbour, visiting kauri mills and bush camps. The four-hour Historical and Nature Cruise costs a bargain $12 and leaves from **Shelly Beach wharf**, 20km north of Helensville, while the Great West Coast Sand Safari ($35) links up with Taylor Made Tours in Dargaville (see p.186) for a half-day out on the water and a drive along Ripiro Beach.

To get to the wharf, you have to drive through **PARAKAI**, 3km north of Helensville and chiefly noted for its Aquatic Park (daily 10am–10pm; $9, private spa $5 extra per hour; ☎09/420 8980), where a series of enclosed and open pools are filled by natural hot springs; entry includes free use of several buffeting water chutes.

Practicalities

Auckland's Yellow Bus Company operate routes numbered #064 and #066–069 **buses** (no Sunday service) from the Downtown Bus Terminal to Parakai and Helensville, the latter two continuing on to Orewa (see below).

The best **place to stay** is the central *Malolo House*, 110 Commercial Rd (☎ & fax 09/420 7262; dorms ①, budget rooms ②, B&B ⑤), which operates both high-standard backpacker accommodation and a beautifully decorated B&B with lavish breakfasts; bikes are rented at $8 a day. There's a **campsite** adjacent to Parakai's Aquatic Centre (☎09/420 8980; tent sites $9, $12 including pool entry).

Helensville is basically **takeaway** land, with the notable exception of *Gallery 88*, at 88 Commercial Rd (☎09/420 7984), a superb **restaurant** open evenings and for lunch (Wed–Sun only), serving well-prepared modern dishes such as Thai chicken salad with black-bean and soy dressing for around $23.

North of Auckland

The straggling suburbs of north Auckland virtually merge into **The Hibiscus Coast**, which starts 40km north of the city and is increasingly favoured by retirees and long-distance commuters. The region centres on the suburban Whangaparaoa Peninsula, the launching point for trips to Tiritiri Matangi Island (see p.134), and the pleasant beach-side community of **Orewa**. Immediately to the north, the hot springs at **Waiwera** herald the beach-and-barbecue scene of **Wenderholm** and the wonderful **Puhoi** pub.

Orewa

The most striking of the Hibiscus Coast beaches is the three-kilometre strand backed by **OREWA**, the region's main town, which garners just about all the accommodation and restaurants. Swimming aside, there isn't a great deal to do here, though the visitor centre can point you towards pleasant bushwalks and minor diversions such as the town's stern-looking statue of Edmund Hillary.

South of Orewa, the **Whangaparaoa Peninsula** juts out 12km into the Hauraki Gulf, its central ridge traced by Whangaparaoa Road, which passes the small-time, narrow-gauge **Whangaparaoa Railway**, 400 Whangaparaoa Rd (Sat & Sun 10am–5pm, plus school holidays Mon–Fri 10am–4pm; $4) on the way to **Shakespear Regional Park** (8am–dusk; free), a pleasant enough place to swim and wander through regenerating bush spotting pukeko, red-crowned parakeets and tui. The peninsula's most enticing diversion, though, is a trip to the bird sanctuary of **Tiritiri Matangi** (see p.134), with boats leaving from the vast Gulf Harbour Marina just before Shakespear Park. Auckland's Yellow Bus Company routes #898 and #899 run along Whangaparaoa Road to Shakespear Park several times a day, passing within 2km of the Tiritiri Matangi wharf.

Practicalities

Auckland's Yellow Bus Company (☎09/366 6400) and Main Coachlines (☎09/278 8070) run a complex timetable from the Downtown Bus Terminal in Auckland to the Hibiscus Coast, often requiring a transfer at Silverdale, just south of Orewa. **Buses** stop on Puriri Street, after passing the well-stocked **visitor centre**, 214a Hibiscus Coast Hwy (Dec–March Mon–Fri 9am–5.30pm, Sat 9am–5pm & Sun 10am–4pm; April–Nov Mon–Fri 10am–5pm, Sat & Sun 10am–4pm; ☎09/426 0076, fax 426 0086).

ACCOMMODATION

Accommodation is predominantly in motels strung along Orewa's main drag, supplemented by a couple of budget places. The most convenient of the **backpackers'** places is *Pillows Travellers Lodge*, 412 Hibiscus Coast Hwy (☎ & fax 09/426 6338; dorms ①, rooms ②–③), has small modern dorms, while 2km north at Hatfields Beach, *Marco Polo Backpackers*, 2a Hammond Ave (☎09/426 8455, fax 426 6338; dorms ①, rooms ②), has rooms set around a lush garden and exudes a more relaxed atmosphere. People often stay at this peaceful retreat for a few days to learn bone carving (Mon–Fri; $30) or take a tour to the marine sanctuary of Goat Island (see p.142; 4hr; $30, including wetsuit and snorkelling gear).

Beachfront **motels** such as the *Edgewater Motel*, 387–389 Hibiscus Coast Hwy (☎09/426 5260, fax 426 3378; ⑤) and *Golden Sands*, 381 Hibiscus Coast Hwy (☎09/426 5177, fax 426 4804; ⑤) tend to be expensive, particularly during the summer months. Cheaper accommodation is available at the peaceful *Puriri Park Holiday Complex*, Puriri Avenue (☎09/426 6396; tent sites $9, cabins ②, tourist flats ③). One of the finest **homestays** in the vicinity is *The Ambers*, 149 Pine Valley Rd, Silverdale (☎09/426 5354, fax 426 3287; ⑤), 4km south of Orewa and beautifully furnished.

EATING

Inexpensive eating centres on a number of decent **café/bars** around Orewa, including *Creole Bar Brasserie*, 310 Pacific Coast Hwy, which does good nachos and the like, and stays open late at weekends, when there is usually some live entertainment. The best of the mid-range places is *Il Veneziano*, Red Beach Shopping Centre, Red Beach Road, 2km south of Orewa (☎09/426 5444; closed Mon): about the closest you can get to a genuine Venetian **restaurant** in these parts, everything is done with great verve and the menu justifiably effuses over the modern Italian dishes, priced around the $16 mark. Top-class lunches and candlelit dinners are served at the *Walnut Cottage*, 498 Hibiscus Coast Hwy (☎09/426 6523; closed Sun & Mon; BYO & licensed), a very popular restaurant in the riverside watchhouse of Orewa's oldest residence.

Waiwera and Wenderholm

The main highway north of Orewa (and bus #895) runs through the cluster of holiday and retirement homes that make up Hatfields Beach to **WAIWERA**, 6km north of Orewa, where Maori once dug holes in the sands to take advantage of the naturally hot springs. Bathing is now formalized in the **Waiwera Thermal Pools**, Waiwera Road (daily 9am–10pm; $12, kids $7), a vast complex of suicidal water slides and over twenty indoor and outdoor pools naturally heated to between 34 and 46°C.

Occupying a high headland between the estuaries of the Puhoi and Waiwera rivers, **Wenderholm Park** was the first of Auckland's regional parks and is still one of the most celebrated. Its sweeping golden beach is backed by pohutukawa-shaded swathes of grass, often packed with barbecuing families on summer weekends. Walking tracks ranging from twenty minutes to two hours wind up through nikau palm groves onto the headland and you can take a peek at **Coudrey House** (Sat & Sun 1–4pm; free), an 1860s colonial homestead. The #895 bus terminates here on summer Sundays.

Puhoi

The village of **PUHOI**, 6km north of Waiwera, is reached on a side road that passes a Calvary – evidence of the staunchly Catholic Bohemian migrants who arrived here in 1863 from Egerland, in what was then the Austro-Hungarian Empire. Their descendants still form a large proportion of Puhoi's small population. As the land was found to be poor, the settlers were forced to eke out a living by cutting the bush for timber, and the horns of some of the more famed bullock teams are still ranged around the walls of the historic **Puhoi Tavern**, a single-roomed bar festooned with all manner of pioneering paraphernalia and photos of harder times. Buy a beer, charm the bartender and you may be invited to see the side room, with its kauri table laid with numerous ancient tea services and walls hung with what is claimed to be New Zealand's largest collection of paintings of Maori chiefs and princesses. Come on the second or last Friday of each month to see ageing members of a local Bohemian band playing their accordions and supping jugs of beer.

Few visitors get much further than the pub, but there is an interesting **Puhoi Historical Society Museum** (Christmas–Easter daily 1–4pm; Easter–Christmas Sat, Sun & school holidays 1–3.30pm; donations requested) in the former Convent School. For some gentle activity, you can **kayak** along a tidal section of the river ($12 per hour) or continue downstream to Wenderholm (2hr; $25, including pick-up at the far end) with Puhoi River Canoe Hire (☎09/422 0891). Puhoi Adventure Bike Tours (☎09/422 0625) do two-hour guided **bike rides** ($24) and half-day adventures in the Puhoi valley and forest ($35).

Southeast of Auckland

Most southbound travellers hurry along Auckland's southern motorway to Hamilton or turn off to Thames at Pokeno – either way missing out on the (admittedly modest) attractions of the **Hunua Ranges** and **The Seabird Coast** on its eastern shore. For **cyclists** in particular the coast road is an excellent way into and out of Auckland, avoiding the worst of the city's traffic: follow Tamaki Drive from central Auckland then wind through Panmure, Howick and Whitford to Clevedon and the coast.

Even for Auckland day-trippers the older and more rounded Hunuas definitely play second fiddle to the more biologically rich Waitakeres, but there are a few decent walks – notably those around the **Hunua Falls**. There are greater rewards further south with excellent seabird viewing and hot pools at **Miranda**.

The Hunua Ranges

A considerable amount of rain dumps on the 700m-high **Hunua Ranges**, 50km southeast of Auckland, and flows down into a series of four dams which jointly supply sixty percent of the city's water. The bush surrounding the reservoirs was once logged for kauri but has largely regenerated, providing a habitat for birds; bellbirds, long since extinct in Auckland, can sometimes be heard here.

Access to the region is easiest through the village of **CLEVEDON**, home to Auckland's polo club (games on Sundays Dec–April; ☎09/292 8556), and with a couple of restaurants and a smattering of craft shops. Pressing on south to Hunua, you'll come across the **Hunua Ranges Park visitor centre** (daily 8am–4.30pm), which sells the *Hunua Recreation & Track Guide* ($8) – invaluable for extended walks in the ranges. The best of the walks are around the thirty-metre Hunua Falls, around 5km east, where the Wairoa River carves its way through the crater of an ancient volcano. A good day-hike, passing some lovely swimming holes, crosses the Wairoa River at the falls and follows Massey Track to Cossey's Dam and back down the Cossey Creek Track to the falls.

The Seabird Coast and Miranda

The Hunua Ranges are bounded to the east by the Firth of Thames, a sheltered arm of the Hauraki Gulf which separates South Auckland from the Coromandel Peninsula.

Its frequently windswept western littoral has become known as **the Seabird Coast**, in recognition of its international importance for migrating shorebirds; almost a quarter of all known species visit the region. During winter, the vast inter-tidal flats support huge 30,000-strong flocks of birds, with over fifty percent of the entire world population of the wrybill plover over-wintering here. During the southern summer (Sept–March), the arctic migrants are more significant – notably bar-tailed godwits and lesser knots, as well as turnstones, curlews, sandpipers and red-necked stints – who fly 15,000 kilometres from Alaska, Siberia and Mongolia.

The tidal flats butt up against the geologically significant "chenier plain" around Miranda, where the land has been built up from successive depositions of shell banks; much has been converted to farmland but newer shell banks in the making can be seen along the coast.

From Clevedon the coast road winds 35km past the small beach settlements of Kawakawa Bay and Orere Point, and the **Tapapakanga Regional Park** (primitive camping $5) to **KAIAUA**. Here you'll find the *Kaiaua Motor Camp* (☎09/232 2712; tent sites $7, cabins ②) and pub rooms at the *Bay View Hotel* (☎09/232 2717; ④), which also does a good grilled snapper. The adjacent *Kaiaua Fisheries*, has twice been voted the best **fish and chip** shop in the land.

The coast's birdlife is thoroughly interpreted at the **Miranda Shorebird Centre**, 7km south of Kaiaua (daily 9am–5pm, though the resident manager will often open later); they'll fill you in on the current hot sightings and point you in the direction of the best viewing spots. With a sunny verandah for viewing, the centre also has a good self-catering accommodation – a lodge with four-to-six-bed dorms and a flat sleeping six (☎09/232 2781; dorms ①, flat ②). A further 7km south are the slightly alkaline **Miranda Hot Springs** (daily 9am–9pm; $6, private spa $3 extra per hour), with a large warm, open pool surrounded by grassy lawns and barbecue areas with private kauri spa tubs. Entry to the pool is free if you stay at the adjacent *Miranda Holiday Park* (☎ & fax 07/867 3205 & 0800/833 144; tent sites $12, dorms ①, on-site vans ②, cabins ④).

From here it is only around twenty minutes' drive to Thames (see p.308).

ISLANDS OF THE HAURAKI GULF

One of Auckland's greatest assets is the island-studded **Hauraki Gulf**, a seventy-kilometre-square patch of ocean to the northeast of the city. In Maori, Hauraki means "wind from the north" – though the gulf is somewhat sheltered from the prevailing winds and ocean swells by the islands of Great Barrier and Little Barrier, creating benign conditions for Auckland's legions of yachties. Most are content just to sail but those who wish to strike land can choose from some of the 47 islands of the **Hauraki Gulf Maritime Park**. Administered by the Department of Conservation, the islands are designated either for recreational use, with full access, or as sanctuaries for endangered wildlife, requiring permits.

Auckland's nearest island neighbour is uninhabited **Rangitoto**, a flat cone of gnarled and twisted lava which dominates the harbourscape. The most populous of the gulf islands is **Waiheke**, increasingly a commuter suburb of Auckland – but one with sandy beaches and a delightfully slow pace, enlivened by some quality wineries and an improving range of restaurants. Such sophistication is a far cry from the largest island hereabouts, **Great Barrier**, which until recently seemed trapped in a thirty-year time warp. However, the advent of fast ferries has put its sandy surf beaches, hilly tramping tracks and exceptional fishing within easy reach of holidaying Aucklanders and international visitors, many of whom continue on to the Coromandel (see p.306). DOC's happy compromise of allowing access to wildlife sanctuaries is wonderfully demonstrated at **Tiritiri Matangi**, where a day-trip gives visitors an unsurpassed opportunity to see some of the world's rarest bird species. **Little Barrier Island** resists any such interference, and is pretty much off-limits except to researchers.

Frequent **ferries** run to the more popular islands from the wharves around Auckland's Ferry Building, at the foot of Queen Street; there's a DOC **information** centre (Mon–Fri 8.30am–5pm, plus Nov–Feb Sat 9am–4.30pm & Dec–Jan Sun 9am–4.30pm; ☎09/366 2166) conveniently located in the same complex. Around the corner is the Fullers Cruise Centre (daily 8am–5pm; bookings and enquiries ☎09/367 9111, timetable information ☎09/367 9102), which sells tickets for all island-bound boats. Several companies operate extended **cruises** around the gulf (see box on p.70).

Rangitoto and Motutapu islands

The distinctive, low, conical shape of **Rangitoto**, 10km northeast of the city centre, is a familiar sight to every Aucklander – yet few Aucklanders have actually set foot on the island. They miss out on a freakish land of fractured black lava, with the world's largest pohutukawa forest clinging precariously to the crevices. Alongside lies the much older and geologically quite distinct island of **Motutapu** or "sacred island", linked to Rangitoto by a narrow causeway.

RANGITOTO SUMMIT WALK

The best way to appreciate Rangitoto Island is on foot; but bear in mind that, though not especially steep, the terrain is rough and it can get very hot out there on the black lava. Consequently the best walks are those that follow shady paths to the summit rather than the more open roads. A favourite is the clockwise **Summit/Coastal Path loop** (12km; 5–6hr; 260m ascent) around the southeast of the island. Turn left just past the toilets at Rangitoto Wharf and follow signs for the **Kowhai Grove**, a typical Rangitoto bush area with an abundance of the yellow-flowering kowhai that blossoms in September. Turn right onto the coastal road towards Rangitoto Wharf then left into **Kidney Fern Grove**, which is packed with unusual miniature ferns that unfurl after rain. The well-worn **Summit Track** winds through patches of pohutukawa forest. Around three-quarters of the way to the summit, a side track leads to the **lava caves** (20min return), which probe deep into the side of the volcano. Further along the main track a former military observation post on the **summit** provides views down into the bush-shrouded sixty-metre-deep crater and out across Auckland city and the Hauraki Gulf.

Continue northwards to the east–west road across the island and follow it towards Islington Bay; from there, pick up the **coastal track** south, initially following the bay then cutting inland through some little-frequented forests back to Rangitoto Wharf.

A **day-trip** is enough to get a feel for Rangitoto, make the obligatory hike to the summit and tackle a few other trails, but **longer stays** are possible if you're prepared to pitch your tent at the primitive campsite at Home Bay on Motutapu.

Rangitoto is Auckland's youngest and largest **volcano**. Molten magma probably pushed its way through the bed of the Hauraki Gulf around six hundred years ago – watched by Motutapu Maori, who apparently called the island "blood red sky" after the awesome spectacle that accompanied its creation. Others attribute the name to a contraction of *Te Rangi i totongia a Tamatekapua* ("the day the blood of Tamatekapua was shed"), recalling an incident when chiefs of the Arawa and Tainui clashed at Islington Bay.

Rangitoto's youth, lack of soil and the porous nature of the rock have created unusual conditions for **plant life**, though the meagre supply of insects attracts few birds, making things eerily quiet. Pohutukawa trees seeded first, given a head start by their roots, which are able to tap underground reservoirs of fresh water up to 20 metres below the surface, then smaller and fleshier plants established themselves under the protective canopy. Harsh conditions have led to some strange botanical anomalies: both epiphytes and mud-loving mangroves are found growing directly on the lava, an alpine moss is found at sea level, and the pohutukawa has hybridized with its close relative, the northern rata, to produce a spectrum of blossoms ranging from pink to crimson. Sadly, the succulent pohutukawa leaves are a big hit with **possums**, which were introduced in the 1880s and proceeded to ravage the forests. Their eradication in 1990 has allowed the pohutukawa to rebounded with renewed vigour, and in fifty years' time Rangitoto will look completely different.

Europeans gave Rangitoto a wide berth until the Crown purchased the island for £15 in 1854, putting it to use as a military lookout point and a workcamp for prisoners. From the 1890s, areas were leased for camping and, in keeping with the defiantly anti-authoritarian streak that thrived in early New Zealand, unauthorized baches were cobbled together on the sites. By 1937, over 120 baches had sprouted, but subsequent legislation decreed that they could be neither sold nor handed down, and must be removed upon the expiry of the lease. Only thirty-three remain and, ironically, some of the finest examples are being preserved for posterity, their corrugated iron chimneys and cast-off verandah railings used as fenceposts capturing the make-do spirit of the times.

The moment you step across the **causeway** onto **Motutapu**, the landscape changes dramatically; suddenly, you are back in rural New Zealand with its characteristic grassy paddocks, ridge-top fencelines, corrugated iron barns and macrocarpa wind-breaks. DOC's plan is to gradually restore its cultural and natural landscape, replanting forests, restoring wetlands and interpreting the numerous Maori sites. Currently though Motutapu is drearier than Rangitoto: about the only thing to do is walk the Motutapu Walkway to the campsite and beach at Home Bay (6km; 1hr 30min one-way), then walk back again.

Practicalities

Fullers **ferries** (Christmas–April 3 daily; May–Christmas Mon–Fri 2 daily, Sat & Sun 3 daily; $18 return), dock at Rangitoto Wharf after a forty-minute journey from Auckland; there are also occasional departures from Devonport. At Rangitoto Wharf there is an **information kiosk**, which opens to coincide with ferry arrivals; here you'll find a few bags of potato chips, a toilet block, the island's only **drinking water**, and a sun-warmed saltwater swimming pool that's great for kids. Apart from more toilet facilities at Islington Bay there's nothing else on the island, so bring everything you need – including strong shoes to protect you from the sharp rocks, sun hat, raincoat and, if you're planning a walk, carry plenty of water. Boats are met by the only transport on the island, the **Summit Safari**, a dusty summit trip on a shaded, tractor-drawn buggy with a full and informative commentary (2hr; $17); the final 800m is on foot along a boardwalk.

DOC have intentionally done all they can to ensure that the twin islands are the preserve of day-trippers. As a concession to the hardy and determined, there is a primitive but pleasant beachside DOC **campsite** ($4), with toilets, water and a barbecue area, at Home Bay on the eastern side of Motutapu, over an hour's walk from Islington Bay and two hours' walk from Rangitoto Wharf.

Waiheke Island

Pastoral **WAIHEKE**, 20km east of Auckland, is the second-largest of the gulf islands and easily the most populous, particularly on summer weekends when Auckland day-trippers and weekenders quadruple the island's 8000 resident population. The traffic isn't all one-way, though, and a fast and frequent ferry service makes it feasible for a tenth of the islanders to leave every day for work in the city – a trend that threatens to turn Waiheke into just another suburb. For the moment Waiheke, with its chain of sandy beaches along the north coast and a climate that's slightly warmer and a lot less humid than Auckland, retains its sybaritic character – and is increasingly being discovered by international visitors in search of a peaceful spot to recover from jet lag or to idle away their last few days before flying out.

The **earliest settlers** on Waiheke trace their lineage back to the crew of the Tainui canoe who landed at Onetangi and gave the island its first name of *Te Motu-arai-Roa*, "the long sheltering island". *Waiheke*, or "cascading waters", originally referred to a particular creek but was assumed by European settlers to cover the whole island. Among the first **Europeans** to set foot on Waiheke was Samuel Marsden, who preached here in 1818 and established a mission near Matiatia. The island went through the familiar cycle of kauri logging, gum digging and clearance for farming. Gradually, the island's magnificent coastal scenery gained popularity as a setting for grand picnics, and hamper-encumbered Victorians, surreally attired in formal dress, arrived in boatloads.

Development was initially sluggish, but the availability of cheap land amid dramatic landscapes drew painters and **craftspeople** to the island's shores; others followed as access from Auckland became easier and faster. Since the mid-1980s, the city has been less than forty minutes away, and Waiheke has become increasingly **sophisticated**: dilapidated shacks have been replaced by swanky condos, cafés and restaurants are a match for many in Auckland and boutique **wineries** produce some of the finest Cabernet Sauvignon blends in the country.

Arrival, information and getting around

Fullers operate fast **ferries** (40min; $23 return, bikes $4 return) from the Ferry Building in Auckland to the Matiatia Wharf at the western end of Waiheke, 2km from the main settlement of Oneroa, every couple of hours. If you're staying for a couple of days or longer, you may find it cost-effective to bring your vehicle over using the daily **car ferry**, a flat-deck barge run by Subritzky Shipping Line (☎09/534 5663; $100 return for a car and driver, plus $20 per passenger) from Half Moon Bay near Pakuranga in Auckland's eastern suburbs to Kennedy Point. With frequent fast ferries there is little advantage in **flying** here, though if you are planning to visit Great Barrier Island and don't need to return to Auckland you can fly there twice daily with Waiheke Air Services (2 daily; $65; ☎09/372 5000). The **airport** is 3km east of Ostend and is reached by taxi (see "Listings", p.125).

Information

Waiheke's main source of information is the efficient **visitor centre**, 2 Korora Rd, Oneroa (daily: Nov–Easter 9am–5pm; Easter–Oct 9am–4pm; ☎09/372 9999, fax 372 9919), which can organize most things on the island, and stores bags for $2 apiece. **Shops**, a couple of **banks** and a post office are also clustered in Oneroa. The weekly *Gulf News* ($1) comes out on Thursday afternoons and has details of **what's on**, as well as a run-down of arts and crafts outlets. The island goes mad at Easter for the five days of the **Waiheke Island Jazz Festival**, which is held at venues and cafés all over the island.

Getting around

Ferries connect with the island's two **bus routes** – #1 to Onetangi via Oneroa, Surfdale and Ostend, and #2 to Rocky Bay via Oneroa, Little Oneroa and Palm Beach – which return in time for ferry departures. Tickets and a $7 day pass (which becomes worthwhile for return trips between Oneroa and Onetangi) are available on the bus. For more flexibility, rent a vehicle (see "Listings" on p.125 for details of outlets). A car will set you back $50 per day, a jeep $65, both plus 40¢ per kilometre; a scooter goes for $45, while bikes cost around $25 per day, though bear in mind that Waiheke is very undulating and unless you're pretty fit you'll do better on a motor-assisted mountain bike ($40 per day).

Day-trippers are well catered for by a number of **island tours**. Among those departing from Auckland, which include the return ferry trip, are Fullers Island Explorer (daily year-round; $37), which includes an hour-and-a-half island tour, plus an all-day bus pass so you can explore further on your own, and their Beyond & Back Tour (Oct–Easter daily, 10am; $47), which visits the eastern half of the island and stops for a barbecue lunch at Onetangi. If you're only here for the wine, Fullers also run a half-day Island of Wine Vineyard Explorer Tour (Wed–Sun at noon; $46) with three hours spent sightseeing and visiting the Croll and Stonyridge vineyards.

Island-based operators include WISE Shuttles (☎09/372 7756) and Wally's Waiheke Tours (☎09/372 5010), both of which run tours and **drop-offs** at accommodation

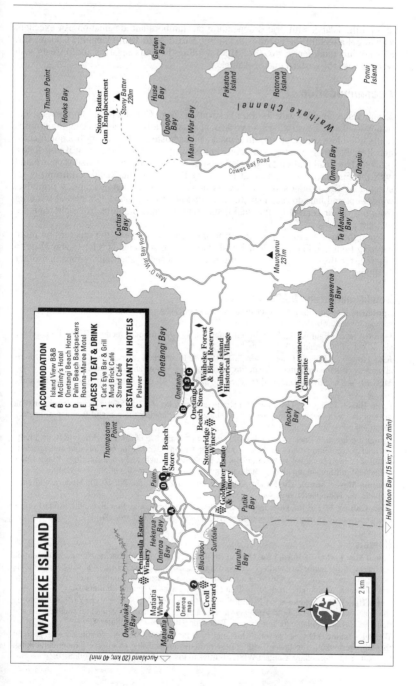

WAIHEKE ISLAND

Thumb Point

Hooks Bay

Garden Bay

Stony Batter Gun Emplacement

▲ Stony Batter 220m

Huse Bay

Oppoo Bay

Man O' War Bay

Pakatoa Island

Rotoroa Island

Ponui Island

Waiheke Channel

Cactus Bay

Cowes Bay Road

Man O' War Bay Road

▲ Maunganui 231m

Te Matuku Bay

Onaru Bay

Orapiu

Awaawaroa Bay

ACCOMMODATION
A Island View B&B
B McGinty's Hotel
C Onetangi Beach Hotel
D Palm Beach Backpackers
E Roanna-Maree Motel

PLACES TO EAT & DRINK
1 Cat's Eye Bar & Grill
2 Mud Brick Café
3 Strand Café

RESTAURANTS IN HOTELS
C Palaver

Onetangi Bay

Thompsons Point

Onetangi

E 3 C
B

Waiheke Forest & Bird Reserve

Onetangi Beach Store

Waiheke Island Historical Village

Stoneridge Winery

Whakanewanewa Campsite

Rocky Bay

D Palm Beach Store

Palm

Goldwater Estate & Winery

Putiki Bay

Peninsula Estate Winery

Owhanake Bay

Hekerua Bay

Oneroa Bay

A

Blackpool

Surfdale

Huruhi Bay

Matiatia Wharf

see Oneroa map

2

Croll Vineyard

Matiatia Bay

N

0   2 km

▷ Half Moon Bay (15 km; 1 hr 20 min)

around the island, with prices depending on numbers and destination. An excellent way to get a feel for the island is to join the **Rural Mail Run** (Mon–Fri 8.30am; 4hr; $15, not including ferry; ☎09/372 9166), visiting the houses, farms and retreats scattered across the eastern end of Waiheke.

Accommodation

If your visit coincides with the Jazz Festival, the peak Christmas and January season, or any weekend, be sure to **reserve** a room as far **in advance** as you can, though this tends to be less critical at the three backpacker hostels dotted along the north coast beaches. At other times, accommodation is fairly plentiful, especially if you follow Aucklanders' lead and go for **B&Bs**; most are registered with the visitor centre and with the Fullers Cruise Centre at the Ferry Building in Auckland. **Camping** is restricted to the grounds of the hostels at Oneroa and Onetangi and a primitive, windswept and hard-to-reach site at *Whakanewha Regional Park* ($5, permit required from the visitor centre) on the tidal Rocky Bay, a couple of kilometres walk from the nearest bus stop.

Though there's a lot to be said for basing yourself at one of the quieter and more relaxing **beaches** like Palm Beach and Onetangi, many people prefer to stay close to Oneroa, for the convenience of being near the buses, restaurants, shops and other facilities.

Hotels, motels and B&Bs

Appletree Cottage, 33 Kiwi St, Oneroa (☎09/372 6647). A simple but pleasant and inexpensive cottage for rent. ④.

Island View, 9 Hauraki Rd, Palm Beach (☎09/372 9000). A friendly, modern B&B with good sea views, but a fifteen-minute trek to the beach. ⑤.

Kiwi House, 23 Kiwi St, Oneroa (☎09/372 9123). At this sociable place, several good B&B rooms all have access to communal self-catering facilities, a TV lounge and barbecue. ⑤.

McGinty's, The Strand, Onetangi (☎ & fax 09/372 8118). Modest hotel with en-suite rooms and a bar. ⑤.

Palm Beach Lodge, 23 Tiri View Rd, Palm Beach (☎ & fax 09/372 7763). Luxurious salmon-pink guesthouse with lovely rooms, each with a balcony overlooking the sea and free use of kayaks, mountain bikes and a dinghy. ⑦.

Punga Lodge, 223 Ocean View Rd, Little Oneroa (☎ & fax 372 6675). Delightful B&B, with helpful hosts. Accommodation consists of one budget room, a range of comfortable and spacious doubles (shared facilities) with verandahs overlooking the bush, and a self-catering cottage – plus coffee and muffins on tap all day. Budget room ④, standard room ⑤, cottage ⑥.

Roanna-Maree Motel, The Strand, Onetangi (☎09/372 7051, fax 372 5056). Modern and comfortable, pool-equipped motel. ⑤.

Twin Gables, 17 Tiri Rd, Oneroa (☎09/372 9877). Another goodie, this bed and breakfast offers excellent sea views from attractive modern rooms with shared facilities. ⑤.

Hostels

Fossil Bay Lodge, 58 Korora Rd, Oneroa (☎09/372 7569). The only backpacker accommodation in Oneroa is this haphazard and very relaxed collection of huts, small dorms and self-catering units where guests can muck in with volunteers on an organic farm five minutes' walk from an all-but private beach, a kilometre from town. Tent sites $10, dorms ①, rooms ②, units ④.

Palm Beach Backpackers, 54 Palm Rd, Palm Beach (☎09/372 8662). A low-key place right by the beach with nice verandahs, grassy lawns for camping and chalets divided into small dorms and doubles. Kayaks available for guests' use. Tent sites $10, dorms ①, rooms ②.

Waiheke Island YHA, Seaview Rd, Onetangi (☎ & fax 09/372 8971). A well-run place set high on the hill overlooking the beach, with a host of activities available to guests – mountain-biking, kayaking and snorkelling. Contact WISE Shuttles to get you here. Dorms ①, rooms ②.

Around the island

The bulk of Waiheke's population inhabits the western quarter of the island, chiefly around the main town of **Oneroa**, a kilometre east of the Matiatia wharf. For many, Waiheke's finest beaches lie east of Oneroa, particularly the almost circular **Enclosure Bay** for snorkelling and **Palm Beach**, while **Onetangi** is one for the surfies.

Waiheke has no shortage of diversions once you've tired of baking on the beaches and cooling off in the surf. The lovely bays and headlands lend themselves to some short but often steep **walks** detailed in the free *Waiheke Island Walks* leaflet, available from the visitor centre in Oneroa. One of the best and most accessible coastal tracks leads from Oneroa past Little Oneroa around to Enclosure Bay, while inland there's a shady stroll through the regenerating bush of the **Waiheke Forest and Bird Reserve**, up behind Onetangi. If you're still restless, take your pick from horse riding, kayaking, sailing and so on (see "Listings" on p.125).

Oneroa and around

The settlement of **ONEROA** is draped across a narrow isthmus between the sandy sweep of Oneroa Bay – one of the best and most accessible beaches on the island – and the shallow and silty Blackpool Beach. The ridge-top main street runs up to the island's visitor centre (see above), where you can pick up a free leaflet about the *Arts & Crafts Trail* around the scattered **studios** of Waiheke's numerous artists and craftspeople; studio opening times tend to be erratic, so call ahead if you're set on visiting particular workshops (phone numbers are in the leaflet). Local artists' work is also displayed in the adjoining Artworks gallery (daily 10am–4pm; free). In the same building is the slightly eccentric **Whittaker's Musical Experience** (daily 10am–4pm; donations requested), a room full of flageolets, piano accordions, player pianos, xylophones

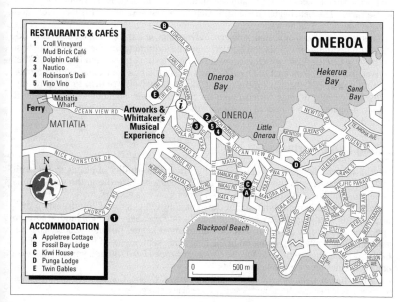

and more, some dating back two hundred years – and all ably demonstrated during the "musical experience" performance (daily except Tues 1pm; 1hr 30min; $7, $4 if you're on the Island Explorer tour). Two of Waiheke's **vineyards** are easily accessible from Oneroa: the *Peninsula Estate*, 52a Korora Rd, 1km northwest of town (free tours and tastings by appointment only; ☎09/372 7866); and the more casual *Croll Vineyard*, 2km west on Church Bay Road (daily in summer; ☎09/372 9050), where you should also investigate the attached *Mud Brick Café* (see "Eating and entertainment", p.125).

The rest of the island

What passes for a main road on Waiheke winds east from Oneroa through the contiguous settlements of Little Oneroa, Blackpool and Surfdale, and across the lagoon at Putaki Bay to **OSTEND**, the island's light-industrial heart that's far from any appealing beaches and best ignored.

A couple of Waiheke's most reputable **wineries** lie between here and Onetangi. At *Goldwater Estate*, 18 Causeway Rd (visits by appointment only; ☎09/372 7493), you can picnic in style, accompanied by one of their fine wines (price range $15–30); you'll need to bring your own provisions, but glasses are lent for free if you buy wine. The organic, hand-tended vineyards of *Stonyridge*, 80 Onetangi Rd, produce Larose, one of New Zealand's top Bordeaux-style reds. Each vintage is sold out before it is even bottled so there are often no cellar-door sales, but the **tour and tasting** ($10; by appointment, ☎09/372 8822), or coordinate your visit with the Fullers tour – generally 11.30am on summer weekends) is entertaining and you can stick around for an excellent, moderately priced al fresco meal in view of the vines, olive trees and cork oaks.

Six kilometres east of Oneroa, **PALM BEACH** takes a neat bite out of the north coast, with houses tumbling down to a small sandy beach separated by a handful of rocks from the nude bathing zone at the western end. The Palm Beach Store rents mountain bikes ($25 per day), boogie boards ($10 per day) and snorkelling gear ($10 per day). Waiheke's longest and most exposed beach is **ONETANGI**, popular in summer with surfers, board riders and swimmers, and an occasional venue for beach horse races. The beachside Onetangi Beach Store rents waveskis ($10 an hour) and boogie boards ($5 an hour).

There are no shops or restaurants east of Onetangi, just tracts of open farm land riddled with fledgling vineyards and bordered by fine swimming beaches. One of the best of these is **Cactus Bay**, which is accessible down a short track from the end of Man O' War Bay Road, 6km east of Oneroa. The two shuttle bus companies both run trips out to the road end, the start of the track (12km return; 3–4hr return) to the labyrinth of dank concrete tunnels which make up **Stony Batter**, abandoned World War II defences against the threat of Japanese attack – take a torch if you want to poke around.

Eating and entertainment

Oneroa is unchallenged on Waiheke for its **range** and **quality** of places to eat, with restaurants catering to the demands of city day-trippers. Elsewhere, the scene tends to be more ad hoc, with **beachside cafés** serving snacks and fast food.

Entertainment is more limited, but the joint jumps in Oneroa at *Nautico* when they bring bands over from the mainland (most Thurs, Fri & Sat evenings), and *Vino Vino* often has some form of **live music** on summer weekends. Beyond Oneroa, you can generally find something going on in the beachside settlements of Palm Beach (at the *Cat's Eye*) and Onetangi (head for the *Onetangi Beach Hotel*), though you may have an enforced quiet time on weekday nights.

Cat's Eye Bar & Grill, 39 Palm Rd, Palm Beach (☎09/372 7844). Good seafood meals right by the beach, plus frequent theme nights and occasional live music.

Dolphin Café, 147 Ocean View Rd, Oneroa. Fabulous gourmet hamburgers the size of dinner plates for $7. What more could you want?

Mud Brick Café, Croll Vineyard, Church Bay Road, 2km west of Oneroa (☎09/372 9050). The expensive but delicious Mediterranean-inspired meals here maintain a consistently high reputation. Lunch & dinner daily in summer; licensed.

Nautico, Pendragon Mall, Oneroa (☎09/372 8785). Opposite *Vino Vino*, and in a similar vein – but with higher prices, grander aspirations and variable results. Licensed.

Palaver, The Strand, Onetangi (☎09/372 8028). Newly refurbished place serving moderately priced pizza, pasta dishes and Mediterranean-influenced mains for around $25. Licensed.

Robinsons Deli, 153 Ocean View Rd, Oneroa. The best place in town for wholesome quiches, spicy bean pies and sumptuous cakes.

Strand Café, at the beach store, The Strand, Onetangi. Casual place, serving breakfasts, light meals and takeaways.

Vino Vino, 153 Ocean View Rd, Oneroa (☎09/372 9888). Hard to beat for light meals, extending to bruschetta, warm salads and daily blackboard specials. Eat inside, or out on the deck with fabulous views across to the Coromandel. Licensed.

Listings

Bike rental Wharf Rats Trading Co (☎09/372 7937) rent out regular bikes at the wharf, or head up to Oneroa, where Waiheke Worx (☎09/372 9914) rent motor-assisted mountain bikes.

Car and motorbike rental At Matiatia Wharf, Waiheke Rental Cars (☎09/372 8635) rents cars, motorbikes and 50cc scooters; Waiheke Worx, at Oneroa's Artworks complex (☎09/372 9914), rents out 4WD jeeps.

Ferries Fullers (☎09/367 9111); Subritzky Shipping Line (☎09/534 5663).

Horse riding Shepherd's Point Riding Centre, 91 Ostend Rd, Ostend (☎09/372 8104) will take you on a two-hour beach ride ($40), or a full day bush-and-beach session ($60, including lunch).

Kayaking Ross Adventures (☎09/372 5550) run from Matiatia and offer four-hour paddles ($45), moonlit evening trips ($50) and round-the-island camping trips (2–5 days; $110 per day). Kayak Waiheke (☎09/372 7262) take you from the wharf to wherever is most suitable for paddling that day, charging around $40 for basic instruction and use of a kayak for the rest of the day.

Sailing Gulf Island Sailing Safaris (☎0800/326 7245) and Waiheke Island Yacht Charters (☎09/372 9579) run trips to the open bird sanctuary of Tiritiri Matangi (see p.134) or over to the Coromandel Peninsula (day-trips from $85).

Taxis Dial-a-Cab (☎09/627 9666); Waiheke Taxi (☎09/372 8038).

Great Barrier Island (Aotea)

Rugged and sparsely populated **GREAT BARRIER ISLAND** (*Aotea*) lies 90km northeast of Auckland on the outer fringes of the Hauraki Gulf and, though only 30km long and 15km wide, packs in a mountainous heart which drops away to deep indented harbours in the west and eases gently to golden surf beaches in the east. It is only a two-hour ferry or half-hour plane ride from the big city but seems a world apart, almost anachronistic in its lack of mains electricity or a reticulated water supply. There are no towns to speak of, no industry and no regular public transport, lending Great Barrier that sense of peace and detachment unique to island life, enhanced by **surf beaches**, **hot springs** and **tightly packed mountains** clad in bush spared the ravages of deer and possums.

Ferries arrive in **Tryphena**, the southern harbour and major settlement, before heading up the west coast to the minuscule hamlets of **Whangaparapara** and **Port Fitzroy**, both ideal jumping-off points for tramps in the Great Barrier Forest. **Claris**, in the east, is the site of the main airport and is convenient for the best beaches at **Medlands** and **Awana Bay**.

Some history

Great Barrier is formed from the same line of extinct **volcanoes** as the Coromandel Peninsula, and shares a common geological and human past. Aotea was one of the places first populated by **Maori**, and the Ngatiwai and Ngatimaru people were occupying numerous pa sites when Cook sailed by in 1769; recognizing the calming influence of Aotea and neighbouring Hauturu on the waters of the Hauraki Gulf, Cook renamed them Great Barrier Island and Little Barrier Island. The vast stands of kauri all over the island were soon seized upon for ships' timbers, the first load being taken in 1791. Kauri **logging** didn't really get under way until the late nineteenth century but continued until 1942, outliving some early copper mining at Miners Head and sporadic attempts to extract gold and silver from a large quartz intrusion in the centre of the island. Kauri logging and gum digging were replaced by a short-lived whale-oil extraction industry at Whangaparapara in the 1950s, but the Barrier soon fell back on tilling the poor clay soils and its peak population of over 5000 dropped back to little more than 1000.

The space and tranquillity of the island appealed to budding alternative lifestylers, many of whom trickled across from the mainland in the 1960s and 1970s. Much of the Seventies idealism has been supplanted by Nineties pragmatism, but **self-sufficiency** remains. Now more of a necessity in the face of isolation than a lifestyle choice, many people grow their own vegetables; everyone has their own water supply and the load on diesel generators is eased by wind-driven turbines and solar panels. However, **agriculture** is beginning to take a back seat to **tourism** and second-home-owners – a trend resisted to some degree by islanders, who fear that the Barrier will become just another commuter suburb for Auckland. At present this seems unlikely, though the introduction of a fast ferry service in 1992 (reducing travelling time from five to two hours) and the inclusion of the Barrier within the domain of Auckland City Council in 1993 have certainly made their mark, and a new entrepreneurial spirit has resulted in dilapidated lodges being bought by ambitious owners keen to make the Barrier a real destination. An anarchic streak lingers, though: until the early 1990s, island vehicles were exempt from the usual annual mechanical checks and even today, when the Department of Transport inspectors come over, half the population stays at home and the island grinds to a halt.

Arrival, information and getting around

Points of entry are the **airport** at Claris on the east coast, the grass airstrip at Okiwi in the north, and the three main **harbours** of Port Fitzroy, Whangaparapara and Tryphena Harbour. Around the first two ports there's little more than a couple of lodges and a shop, leaving the bulk of the activity to the four main bays of Tryphena Harbour. Ferries arrive at Shoal Bay, from where shuttle buses run to Mulberry Grove, where there's a shop, a bakery and a motel, or on to Stonewall Village, where there are several places to stay and eat, and a shop. Puriri Bay is a short walk along the coast from Stonewall.

The vast majority of visitors arrive from Auckland aboard Fullers **ferries** (Nov–Easter Wed, Fri & Sun; Easter–Oct Tues, Thurs, Fri & Sun; 2hr; ☎09/367 9111), which call at each of the three main west coast harbours. A standard return **fare** costs $89–99, depending on the season, but look out for specials such as a day-return for $50, a day-return plus a two-hour minibus tour of the island for $67, and occasional backpacker discounts. Shuttle buses meet the ferry, charging around $5 to Stonewall Village, $10 to Medlands.

The surprisingly comfortable Gulf Trans **barge** ($20 each way; ☎09/373 4036 & 0800/GULFTRANS) carries passengers, cars and just about all the island's freight, leaving Wynyard Wharf in Auckland every Tuesday at 7am and takes six hours to reach Tryphena, before calling at Whangaparapara and Port Fitzroy – from where it returns to Auckland, leaving at 8am each Wednesday.

Ferries are occasionally cancelled due to bad weather, and many prefer the reliability of daily **flights**. By far the biggest operator is *Great Barrier Airlines* (☎09/275 9120 & 0800/275 912), who fly from all over the northern half of the North Island, but most frequently between Auckland and Claris ($75 each way). Shuttle buses meet *Great Barrier Airlines* flights and drop off in Medlands and Tryphena for $7 ($10 return), but there is nothing meeting the flights of airlines *Northern Air* (☎09/256 8699 in Auckland, ☎09/429 0909 on the Barrier) and *TransIsland Air* (☎09/420 7470 & ☎0800/359 7233), which are competitively priced but run less frequently and to fewer destinations.

Information

The island's main **visitor centre** (daily 8am–6pm; ☎09/429 0033, fax 429 0660) is at Claris airport, perfect for plane arrivals but little help to those disembarking at Tryphena, who are better served by the Fullers office (daily: Sept–May 8am–4pm; June–Aug 9am–3pm; ☎09/429 0004, fax 429 0469) in Stonewall Village, which has all manner of information on the island. The main **DOC office** is the well-stocked and informative Port Fitzroy Field Base (Mon–Fri 8am–4.30pm; ☎09/429 0044), ten minutes' walk west of the Port Fitzroy wharf, which is supported by a smaller and sporadically open field base at Whangaparapara. Note that there are **no banks** on the island but several places have EFTPOS facilities.

Getting around

Other than the shuttle **buses** mentioned above and a seasonal service between Tryphena and Claris (Christmas to mid-January only), there is little transport on the island. Safari Tours (☎09/429 0448) run a morning bus from Tryphena to Medlands ($10) and on to some hot springs ($15), as well as running a good all-day island **tour** ($45). Bob's Tours (☎09/420 0988; $45) do a similar trip, venturing off the beaten track a little more.

Many people **rent a car** for at least part of their stay, but rates are high, at around $90 for one day, dropping to $70 a day for longer rentals; **mountain bikes** can be rented for around $20 a day, though the hills are steep and the roads dusty and hot in summer (see "Listings", p.133, for details of car- and bike-rental outfits). A couple of tour companies also function as **taxi** services; call Barrier Travel (☎09/429 0568) or Safari Tours (☎09/429 0448).

Accommodation

Accommodation on Great Barrier is broad ranging. Walkers and campers are well catered for with some pleasant but basic campsites, a couple of trampers' **huts** and a cabin, which is well set up for groups. Most of these are towards the north of the island, close to the Great Barrier Forest: all five **DOC campsites** are marked on the map on p.129, and must be booked in advance (☎09/366 2166); note that camping is not permitted elsewhere on the island. The remainder of the accommodation is concentrated around Tryphena Harbour and ranges from a couple of backpackers' **hostels** to comfortable guesthouses and high-class **lodges**. Some of the best of the island's **self-catering cottages** are given below, but there are many more on lists held by the visitor centre and at the Fullers office; the owners often live close by and can arrange breakfast and sometimes dinner. In fact, given the dearth of places to eat, many lodges and **guesthouses** also have self-catering units.

Most places **pick up** from the harbours and airport, though those in Tryphena will expect you to catch the transport which meets each boat or plane. The island's remoteness means that accommodation is generally more **expensive** than the mainland, particularly from Labour Weekend to Easter; some places further boost their rates from Christmas to the end of January when visitor numbers are at their peak – and you'll need to **book well ahead** to stand any chance of finding a place to stay. The price codes we've given below are based on standard summer prices.

Lodges and guesthouses

Barrier Oasis Lodge, Stonewall, Tryphena (☎09/429 0021, fax 429 0034). About the best accommodation on the island, with a couple of lovely en-suite rooms with great valley views and separate self-contained unit. Rooms are normally let on a full-board basis, with delicious Asian-influenced meals included. Unit ⑤, rooms ⑦.

The Flowerhouse, Rosalie Bay (☎09/429 0464). One beautiful guest room in a retreat tucked away in a remote valley, where the emphasis is on peace and healthy living. The room is let on a full-board basis, with meals made from home-grown organic produce. ⑦.

Great Barrier Lodge, Whangaparapara Harbour (☎09/429 0488, fax 429 0197). This is pretty much all there is at Whangaparapara, and the comfortable harbourside lodge also serves as the local shop. Accommodation is in cottages in the grounds or rooms in the main building, where there is a bar and restaurant serving home-style meals. Mountain bikes are available for $15 per day, as are rental cars ($95). Rooms ⑤, cottages ⑤–⑥.

Jetty Tourist Lodge, Kairara Bay, Port Fitzroy (☎09/429 0050, fax 429 0908). Superbly sited place with bar and restaurant overlooking Kairara Bay, around 2km from Port Fitzroy Wharf. B&B accommodation is in nicely decorated, self-contained chalets. ⑥.

Medlands Lodge, Masons Rd (☎09/429 0352). Two self-contained units and a nice double room in a rural setting 2km from the beach. ⑥.

Pigeons Lodge, Shoal Bay Rd, Tryphena (☎09/429 0437, fax 429 0127). Small, comfortable and classy B&B nestled in the bush near the sea, with en-suite accommodation, a self-catering chalet and a good licensed restaurant. ⑤.

Pohutukawa Lodge, Stonewall, Tryphena (☎09/429 0211, fax 429 0117). The pick of the places around Tryphena, homely, small and welcoming, with a great bar and restaurant spilling out onto the verandah and peaceful garden. It is all conveniently close to the shop; there are international newspapers on hand, and aromatherapy massage is available. Attractive rooms are let on a B&B basis, and there are compact three-bed backpacker dorms. Dorms ①, B&B ⑤.

Tipi & Bob's Holiday Lodge, Puriri Bay, Tryphena (☎ & fax 09/429 0550). Good but pricey motel rooms, some with fine sea views, and an ageing cottage sleeping six. Cottage and units ⑤, with sea views ⑥.

Self-catering cottages

(Note: see also "Lodges and guesthouses" above)

DOC Guest Cottage, Okiwi (☎09/429 0044). Fully-equipped cottage sleeping up to ten, with gas cooking and wood supplied for barbecues. It is a little isolated but beach and forest are only thirty minutes' walk away. ③.

DOC Guest Cottage, Port Fitzroy (☎09/429 0044). Similar set-up to Okiwi above, but beautifully sited at Port Fitzroy adjacent to the DOC office and campsite and ten minutes' walk from the wharf. ③.

Fitzroy House, Glenfern Rd, Port Fitzroy (☎09/429 0091, fax 429 0492). Very comfortable self-contained cottage sleeping six on the northern shore of the inner harbour. Kayaking, guided walks and yacht charters are all available. ⑦.

Hi Look Cottage, Shoal Bay Rd, Tryphena (☎09/429 0437). Quaint, simple self-contained two-bedroom set among native bush and close to the sea. ⑤.

Kairara Bay Chalet, Kairara Bay (☎09/429 0040). Self-contained unit with fabulous views, tucked under the owners' house. ⑤.

Ollie's Cottage, Puriri Bay (☎09/429 0478). Small, old-fashioned self-catering cottage on the water's edge about twenty minutes' walk from Stonewall Village. ④.

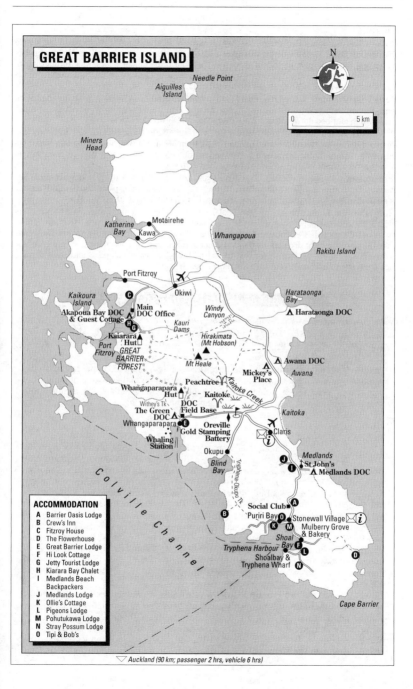

GREAT BARRIER ISLAND

Needle Point

Aiguilles Island

Miners Head

Katherine Bay
Motairehe
Kawa

Whangapoua

Rakitu Island

Port Fitzroy

Kaikoura Island
Akapoua Bay DOC & Guest Cottage
Main DOC Office
Okiwi

Harataonga Bay
Harataonga DOC

Kaiarara Hut
Port Fitzroy
GREAT BARRIER FOREST
Kauri Dams
Windy Canyon
Hirakimata (Mt Hobson)

Mt Heale
Awana DOC
Awana

Mickey's Place

Peachtree Hut
Whangaparapara Hut
Withey's Tk
The Green DOC
Kaitoke
DOC Field Base
Kanoke Creek
Kaitoka

Whangaparapara
Oreville Gold Stamping Battery

Whaling Station

Okupu
Blind Bay

Claris

Medlands
St John's
Medlands DOC

Social Club
Puriri Bay
Stonewall Village
Mulberry Grove & Bakery
Shoal Bay
Tryphena Harbour
Shoalbay & Tryphena Wharf

Cape Barrier

Colville Channel

ACCOMMODATION

A Barrier Oasis Lodge
B Crew's Inn
C Fitzroy House
D The Flowerhouse
E Great Barrier Lodge
F Hi Look Cottage
G Jetty Tourist Lodge
H Kiarara Bay Chalet
I Medlands Beach Backpackers
J Medlands Lodge
K Ollie's Cottage
L Pigeons Lodge
M Pohutukawa Lodge
N Stray Possum Lodge
O Tipi & Bob's

Auckland (90 km; passenger 2 hrs, vehicle 6 hrs)

Hostels

Crew's Inn, Schooner Bay (☎025/534134). Beautifully sited and highly characterful but simple backpacker dorm accommodation that takes a bit of effort to reach but is well worth it for the isolation and the alternative lifestyle it espouses. It's about three to four hours' walk through bushland from Stonewall or about an hour's paddle by kayak (see "Listings" on p.133). Phone for directions, and remember to bring all the food you'll need. ①.

Jetty Tourist Lodge, Kairara Bay, Port Fitzroy (☎09/429 0050, fax 429 0908). Superbly sited place with bar and restaurant overlooking the bay, around 2km from Port Fitzroy Wharf. Backpacker beds are in four-bed dorms, or there are B&B chalets. Dorms ①, chalets ⑥.

Medlands Beach Backpackers, Mason Rd (☎09/429 0320). Basic backpackers with two- and four-bed dorms on a small farm ten minutes' walk from Medlands Beach – making this place popular with surfers. There are boogie boards and snorkelling gear for guests' use, but there are no meals and no shops nearby, so bring all your food with you. ①.

Pohutukawa Lodge, Stonewall, Tryphena (☎09/429 0211, fax 429 0117). Compact three-bed backpacker dorms in a good location close to the shop. This welcoming place also has B&B rooms, a restaurant and bar, and aromatherapy massage is available. Dorms ①, rooms ⑤.

Stray Possum Lodge, Shoal Bay (☎09/429 0109, fax 429 0094). Activity-orientated backpackers with a bar and on-site evening café set in a spacious clearing in attractive bush. Beds are in four-to six-bed dorms or in well-appointed self-contained chalets ideal for groups of up to six. Daily trips visit the hot springs or drop-off for walks and horse rides, and there are mountain bikes, kayaks, snorkelling gear and surfboards for rent (see also "Tours" in Listings on p.133 for details of package deals from Auckland). Tent sites $10, dorms ①, chalets ⑤.

THE GREAT BARRIER FOREST TRAMP

The only decent walking map is the 1:50,000 Great Barrier Island Infomap ($11); the DOC also print a Track Information leaflet (50¢ from DOC offices) which will just about do, though the walk timings are a little inconsistent.

The **Great Barrier Forest**, New Zealand's largest stand of possum-free bush, offers a **unique** tramping **environment**. Because the area is so compact, in no time at all you can find yourself climbing in and out of little subtropical gullies luxuriant with nikau palms, tree ferns, regenerating rimu and kauri, up onto scrubby manuka ridges with stunning coastal and mountain views. Many of the tracks follow the routes of mining tramways past old kauri dams.

ACCESS AND HUTS

The tramp can be done equally well from Port Fitzroy or Whangaparapara, both having a reasonably well-stocked shop, a campsite and other accommodation. Both also have 24-bunk **huts** (Category 2; $8) nearby, but Port Fitzroy has the advantage of the main DOC office (Mon–Fri 8am–4.30pm; ☎09/429 0044), which sells hut **tickets** and **maps**; Whangaparapara has a sporadically open and less-well-stocked field base. In addition, Port Fitzroy's beautifully sited *Akapoua Bay* **campsite** ($6) is superior to Whangaparapara's simple site, *The Green* (donations requested).

If you have come specifically to tramp, afternoon ferry arrivals at either port dictate a short first day followed by a night spent at the nearest hut or campsite. Early afternoon departures point to a short final day from the nearest accommodation, making for a minimum **four-day trip** from Auckland.

THE TRAMP

From the wharf at **Port Fitzroy**, follow the coast road fifteen minutes south to the DOC office. From there the road climbs for half an hour over a headland with views over Kairara and Rarohara bays, to a gate. The Kairara Hut is roughly fifteen minutes on, along a 4WD track and across a couple of river fords. From **Kairara Hut to Whangaparapara Hut** (13km; 7–9hr; **800m** ascent), the track soon leaves the 4WD track and crosses the Kairara Stream several times as it climbs steeply to the first and

Campsites

Akapoua DOC Campsite, Port Fitzroy. Harbour edge site right by the DOC office and an easy walk to the harbour and shop at Port Fitzroy. It comes equipped with coin-operated barbecues, cold showers and toilets. Tent sites $6.

Awana DOC Campsite, Awana. Exposed site with separate tent and vehicle sites, all 400m from a good surf beach. Cold showers and toilets. Tent sites $6.

The Green DOC Campsite, Whangaparapara. Basic campsite with barbecues, water and toilets but without vehicular access. No showers but it's close to the sea and there's a stream to wash in. Donation requested.

Haurataonga DOC Campsite, Harataonga. Shady site 300m back from the beach, equipped with toilets and cold showers. Tent sites $6.

Medlands DOC Campsite, Medlands Beach. Attractive beach-back site that gets very crowded in the peak season. Cold showers and toilets. Tent sites $6.

Mickey's Place, Awana (☎09/429 0140). Commercial campsite 25km north of Tryphena that's less well-sited than the nearby DOC site but features hot showers, toilets and a cookhouse, all for $3.

Around the island

Places which would be regarded as sights in the usual sense are thin on the ground on Great Barrier, and most of those that do exist require some perseverance to get to.

most impressive **kauri dam** (see p.132), reached in under an hour. The well-defined path continues for another fifty minutes to one of the upper dams then begins a long and arduous series of boardwalks and wooden steps designed to keep trampers on the path and prevent the disturbance of nesting black petrels. It'll take a good thirty to forty minutes to reach the summit of the 621-metre **Hirakimata** (Mount Hobson), where you'll be amply rewarded by panoramic views.

Less extensive boardwalks extend south around the dramatic spire of Mount Heale towards the junction of **two paths**. To the right a path follows the south branch of the Kairara Stream **back to the Kairara Hut** in around an hour and a half, making a four-to-five-hour circuit from the hut. The leftmost path follows an undulating but gradually descending route into Kaitoke Creek No.1 eventually reaching the edge of Kaitoke Swamp right by the hard-to-locate **Peach Tree Hot Spring**. Originally dug by kauri loggers, the pools here are hotter than the more widely used **Kaitoke Hot Spring** – the latter reached along a ten-minute track which spurs off south twenty minutes ahead; the more attractive hollows are to be found upstream. Back on the main track, you soon reach the 4WD forest road: follow it south for a hundred metres or so, then join the signposted track to **Whangaparapara Hut**, fifteen minutes on. From here it is ten minutes' walk to the DOC field station and half an hour to the Whangaparapara Wharf.

There are two main routes from **Whangaparapara Hut to Kairara Hut**, the direct and dull route following the Pack Track due north of the hut and the 4WD forest road (11km; 5hr; 200m ascent), and the more appealing semi-coastal Kiwiriki Track (12km; 6hr; 300m ascent) which branches off the 4WD forest road just north of its junction with the Pack Track. The track cuts west from the forest road by the rocky knob of Maungapiko, leading to the picnic area at Kiwiriki Bay then climbing steeply over a ridge to Coffins Creek before a relatively gentle walk to a second picnic area at **Kairara Bay**. From here it is half an hour to Kairara Hut and another hour or so to the Port Fitzroy Wharf.

An alternative start to either route eschews the Pack Track and follows the far more interesting **Withey's Track**, which starts between the Whangaparapara DOC field base and the hut; it takes half an hour longer, but goes through some lovely bush with delightful streamside nikau groves.

Much of the pleasure here is in lazing on the beaches and striking out on foot into the **Great Barrier Forest**, a rugged chunk of regenerating bush and kauri-logging relics that takes up almost half the island between Port Fitzroy and Whangaparapara. If you're looking for more structure to your day, there are a few small-time operators keen to keep you entertained by means of various activities and tours (see "Listings", p.133, for details). Tryphena has a particular dearth of things to do, though there is the appealing **Tryphena to Okupu Walking Track** (4hr) from Puriri Bay around coastal headlands to Okupu on Blind Bay.

Most people head straight for **Medlands Beach**, a long sweep of golden sands broken by a sheltering island and often endowed with some of the Barrier's best surf – though, be warned, there is no patrolled area. The pretty blue and white **St John's Church** looks somewhat out of place – and it is, having only been moved here in 1986, making the journey from the mainland by barge before being dragged over the dunes.

North of Medlands, the road leaves the coast for the airport at **CLARIS**, where the post office runs the gimmicky **Great Barrier Pigeon-Gram Service** (summer only; $15 to send a pigeon-gram letter) in imitation of the original pigeon-mail service – said to be the world's first airmail service – set up in 1898 after it took a sobering three days to notify Auckland that the SS *Wairarapa* had been wrecked on the northwest coast. Birds took under two hours to cover the same distance, and were used until 1908 when a telephone was finally established. One or two letters are now attached to birds which fly to Auckland, where the letters are forwarded anywhere in the world.

Crossroads, 2km north of Claris, is just that – the junction of roads to Okupu, Port Fitzroy and the north of the island, and Whangaparapara. The last runs past the scant roadside remains of the **Oreville gold stamping battery** (unrestricted entry) and the start of a path to **Kaitoke Hot Springs** (4km; 1hr return; also on the Great Barrier Forest Tramp – see box on p.130), sulphurous dammed pools that aren't especially pretty but are perfect for an hour's wallowing. At Whangaparapara itself, a short stroll around the bay brings you to the foundations of a whaling station built here in the 1950s.

North from Crossroads, the Port Fitzroy road passes two excellent camping spots by the surf beach at Awana Bay, then the start of a short track to **Windy Canyon** (1km; 20–30min return), a narrow defile that gets its name from the eerie sounds produced by certain wind conditions. A narrow path winds through nikau palms and tree ferns to a viewpoint that gives a sense of the island's interior, as well as fabulous coastal views.

The island's highest point, Hirakimata, can be reached in three hours from here or a similar time from **PORT FITZROY**, whose harbour remains remarkably calm under most wind conditions, a property not lost on the dozens of yachties who flock here in summer. Apart from the shop and a few places to stay there's not a lot here, but Port Fitzroy makes the best base for **tramping** or shorter day-walks to some fine **kauri dams** (see box on p.130 for details of long and short routes). For three years from 1926, the Kauri Timber Company hacked trees out of the relatively inaccessible Kairara Valley, shunning the tramways and trestle bridges employed in more manageable terrain in favour of six kauri dams – wooden structures up to twenty metres high and spanning the valley floor. Logs were cut and rolled into the reservoirs, gradually raising the water level behind the dams. The upper dams were then tripped, followed seconds later by the lower dams; the combined releases sent a torrent of water and logs sluicing down to Kairara Bay, where they were lashed together in rafts and floated to Auckland.

Eating and drinking

The complete absence of stand-alone **restaurants** forces pretty much everywhere that provides a bed for the night to offer meals and drinks for both guests and non-residents. There's also a bakery and a couple of shops where you can get snacks and pastries when you're on the move and pick-up picnic provisions. **Drinking** tends to happen in bars attached to accommodation establishments or in the social clubs at Tryphena and Crossroads.

Barrier Oasis Lodge, Stonewall, Tryphena (☎09/429 0021). Delicious meals using local and home-grown produce, frequently with Thai, Indian or seafood themes. The luncheon platter costs $15, while evening meals are table d'hôte and will set you back around $30.

Crossroads Café & Craft, Hector Sanderson Rd, Crossroads, 2km north of Claris (☎09/429 0600). Basic shop and casual café where they cook up fine muffins, pizza bread and other baked goodies through the day.

The Flowerhouse, Rosalie Bay (☎09/429 0464). Lunches made from home-grown organic produce, including olives, their own fresh pasta and delicious cheese, for around $20. Reservations are essential and they'll pick you up from Tryphena.

Great Barrier Island Sports & Social Club, Whangaparapara Road, at the foot of the road to Medlands Beach (☎09/429 0260). Cavernous public bar with pool tables and bar meals (Wed, Fri & Sat).

Jetty Tourist Lodge, Kairara Bay, Port Fitzroy (☎09/429 0050). Spacious restaurant with a large deck and a bar overlooking the bay. Hearty Kiwi meat and seafood dishes go for around $20, and breakfasts, lunches and Devonshire teas are also served.

Great Barrier Lodge, Whangaparapara Harbour. Bar and restaurant serving home-style meals.

Mulberry Grove Bakery, Mulberry Grove. The only full-blown bakery on the island, producing excellent bread, pizzas, cakes and pies, all best early in the day. Closed Sun & Mon.

Pigeons Lodge, Shoal Bay Rd, Tryphena (☎09/429 0437). Guests and visitors alike can avail themselves of this guesthouse's charming licensed restaurant (mains around $18).

Pohutukawa Lodge, Stonewall, Tryphena (☎09/429 0211). Great bar and restaurant spilling out onto a verandah and peaceful garden. In the restaurant, mains hover around $15 though there are often lighter meals for under $10 and always a good vegetarian option.

Tipi & Bob's Holiday Lodge, Puriri Bay, Tryphena (☎09/429 0550). The rather soulless public bar and leafy garden bar are always popular spots, as is the spartan seafood restaurant serving $18–25 mains and cheaper takeaways.

Listings

Bike rental Stray Possum Lodge and Great Barrier Lodge both rent bikes to guests, and Barrier Boat Hire in Stonewall (☎09/429 0110) rent out decent bikes to all comers for around $20 a day.

Car rental On the southern half of the island, try the 4WDs of Wheels Down Under Rentals (☎09/429 0110), 4WDs and cars rented by Pegasus (based at the Stray Possum Lodge), or cars offered by Bob's Car Rental (☎09/429 0550). For car rental on the north of the island, call Aotea Tours (☎ & fax 09/429 0055).

Fishing To test Great Barrier's enviable reputation, head out for a day's fishing in the Colville Channel aboard the Tryphena-based Waiiti (daily; $60, including rod, reel and bait; ☎09/429 0468). Charter vessels cost around $400–500 a day for four people: try Stanley Marine Charters (☎09/429 0570), Hot Pursuit (☎09/429 0570) and Top Cat (☎09/429 0437).

Golf Pioneer Park, Whangaparapara Rd, Claris (☎09/429 0420; green fee $10, club rental $5), is a nine-hole par-three course surrounded by bush and with pukeko strutting across the fairways; every Thursday and Sunday the lively bar serves cheap drinks and decent meals.

Horse riding Great Barrier Island Adventure Horse Treks (☎09/429 0274) will take you out onto the beach and hinterland for $20 per hour.

Kayaking Aquaventure (☎09/429 0033) rent out basic kayaks for around $10 an hour; as do Fullers (☎09/367 9111); Aotea Sea Kayak Adventures (☎0800/767 786) run kayak trips with plenty of opportunities for snorkelling (Nov–March; half-day to 3 days; $45 a day).

Scuba diving Aquaventure (☎09/429 0033) and Barrier Boat Hire (☎09/429 0110), both in Tryphena, organize diving in some of New Zealand's best locations, with wrecks, varied undersea terrain and stacks of marine life to explore, all in conditions of good visibility (especially in autumn).

Taxis Barrier Travel (☎09/429 0568); Safari Tours (☎09/429 0448).

Tours Stray Possum (☎0800/767 786) offers the "Possum Pursuit Pass" ($45), which includes mountain biking, kayaking, trips and activities for up to a month; package deals include the pass plus ferry transport to and from Auckland ($99), or a loop from Auckland to the Barrier by ferry, a flight on to the Coromandel Peninsula then bus back to Auckland, or vice versa ($120).

Tiritiri Matangi

No one with even the vaguest interest in New Zealand's wonderful birdlife should pass up the opportunity to visit **Tiritiri Matangi**, a low scrubby island 4km off the tip of the Whangaparoa Peninsula and 30km north of Auckland. Tiritiri Matangi is run as an "open sanctuary", and visitors are free to roam through the predator-free bush where, within a couple of hours, it is quite possible to see takahe, stitchbirds, saddlebacks, whiteheads, North Island robins, parakeets and brown teals – though to stand a chance of seeing the little spotted kiwi, you'll have to be here at night.

Judging by evidence from pa sites on the island, Tiritiri Matangi was first populated by the Kawerau **Maori** and later by the Ngati Paoa, both of whom are now recognized as the land's traditional owners. They partly **cleared the island** of bush, a process continued by Europeans who arrived in the mid-nineteenth century to graze sheep and cattle. Fortunately, **predators** such as possums, stoats, weasels, deer, cats, wallabies, rats and the like failed to get a foothold on Tiritiri, so after farming became uneconomic in the early 1970s it was singled out as a prime site for helping to restore barely viable bird populations. The cacophony of birdsong in the Tiritiri bush is stark evidence of just how catastrophic the impact of these predators has been elsewhere.

When grazing stopped, a **reafforestation** programme was implemented: a quarter of a million saplings raised from seeds found on the island have been planted out to form what is currently a fairly unattractive low scrub. The **birds** seem to like it, however, and are mostly thriving – with nesting boxes standing in for decaying trees, and feeding stations equipped with video cameras and pressure-sensitive perches that weigh birds each time they alight.

Three of the species released here are among the rarest in the world, with total populations of around a couple of hundred. The most visible are the flightless **takahe**, lumbering blue-green turkey-sized birds long thought to be extinct (see Contexts p.782 for more on these ungainly critters); birds moved here from Fiordland have bred well and are easily spotted as they seem unafraid of humans and are very inquisitive. **Saddlebacks** and **stitchbirds** both stick to the bush, but often reveal themselves if you sit quietly for a few moments on some of the bush boardwalks. **Northern blue penguins** also frequent Tiritiri, and can be seen all year round – but are more in evidence in March, when they come ashore to moult, and from September to December, when they nest in specially constructed viewing boxes located along the seashore path just west of the main wharf.

Practicalities

Tiritiri Matangi is typically visited as a **day-trip**, giving over five hours on the island; you'll need to take your own lunch, as there is **no food** available. The most reliable way to get here is with Gulf Harbour Ferries (☎09/424 5561), who make the twenty-minute crossing from Gulf Harbour Marina on the Whangaparoa Peninsula, 30km north of Auckland (see p.113), every Thursday and Sunday at 9.30am ($25 return), and also run from the Auckland Ferry Building each Thursday at 8am ($30). On other weekdays, the ferry is often chartered for school trips and you are usually welcome to tag along.

An appealing alternative is to visit the island aboard the **sailboat** *Te Aroha* (see box on p.70), which gives plenty of opportunities to hear the birds at their most vocal and the possibility of seeing a kiwi in the wild. It is also worth contacting Fullers, who run Tiritiri day-trips sporadically through the summer (Jan–March, usually Wed & Sat at 10am; $30; ☎09/367 9111), linking up with a Waiheke Island Yacht Charters (☎09/372 9579) for the all-day "Twin Island Ferry and Sail" **package** ($85); Waiheke Island Yacht Charters also run trips here from Waiheke.

Visitors arriving on scheduled ferries can join extremely worthwhile **guided walks** (1hr; $5), which leave from the wharf and are led by volunteers and DOC rangers steeped in bird-lore. Otherwise, you're free to wander the island at will or indulge in a little **swimming** from Hobbs Beach, a ten-minute walk west of the wharf (turn left as you step ashore), and the only sandy strand on Tiritiri.

It's also possible to **stay overnight** in a self-contained bunkhouse near the light-house (call the rangers on ☎09/479 4490; ①), but weekends are booked months ahead and even for week nights you'll need to book at least two weeks in advance; you can also get **general information** on this phone number.

Other gulf islands

There are dozens of other islands scattered around the Hauraki Gulf, several of them privately owned but more forming part of the Hauraki Gulf Maritime Park. The most easily accessible is the DOC-managed recreation reserve of **Motuihe Island**, just 3km south of Motutapu Island, a popular day-trip destination for Aucklanders keen to laze on the sheltered sandy beaches of the northwestern peninsula and spend three or four hours exploring the easy walking trails. The majority of the island is farmland, with small patches of bush around its fringes. The northwestern end of the island, where the boats dock, has had something of a chequered history. It was used as a smallpox and influenza quarantine station from 1873 until after World War I, doubling up as prisoner-of-war camp; during World War II, the same buildings served as a naval base associated with gun emplacements built in the northern tip of the island. Motuihe can be visited on the Fullers **Mail Run** from Auckland (year-round Wed & Sun 9.30am; $18 return), which gives around six hours on the island. If you want **to stay** longer there is a well-supplied farmhouse sleeping up to twelve ($12 per person, $60 minimum nightly charge), a bunkhouse (①) and a campsite ($4). All are booked through the **kiosk** (☎09/534 8095), which is open daily for groceries and takeaways.

Very few visitors make it out to **Little Barrier Island** (*Hauturu*), 80km north of Auckland, a nature reserve barred to those without the necessary DOC permit (contact the Auckland DOC office – see p.68). Although around a third of its trees were felled for timber before the government acquired the island and set it aside as a wildlife sanctuary in 1884, mountainous Little Barrier remains largely unspoiled, its vast forests unaffected by introduced pests. Home to fascinating creatures – including giant earthworms up to a metre long, the prehistoric tuatara and a mouse-sized version of the grasshopper-like weta – once cats were eradicated in 1975, Little Barrier also became a refuge for birds under threat on the mainland, such as the kakapo, kaka, stitchbird and the kokako. The easiest way to set foot on the island is on a **nature cruise** (Nov–April; 4 days; $400; ☎ & fax 09/444 9342) aboard the Auckland-based *Te Aroha* (see box on p.70).

travel details

Trains

From Auckland to: Hamilton (4 daily; 2hr); National Park (2 daily; 5hr 30min); Ohakune (2 daily; 6hr); Palmerston North (2 daily; 8–9hr); Rotorua (1 daily; 4hr) Tauranga (1 daily; 3hr 30min); Wellington (2 daily; 11hr).

Buses

From Auckland to: Cambridge (4 daily; 3hr); Dargaville (2–3 daily; 3hr); Gisborne (1 daily; 9hr 15min); Hamilton (16–20 daily; 2hr 30min); Hastings (3 daily; 8hr); Helensville (4–6 daily; 1hr 10min); Kaitaia (2 daily; 6hr 40min); Kerikeri (4–6 daily; 5hr); Kumeu (4–6 daily; 35min); Mangonui (2 daily; 6hr); Napier (3 daily; 7hr 30min); New Plymouth (3 daily; 6–7hr); Opononi (1 daily; 7hr); Orewa (hourly; 45–60min); Paihia via Whangarei (3–7 daily; 4hr); Paihia via Opononi (1 daily; 7hr 45min); Palmerston North (2 daily; 9hr); Piha (5 weekly; 1hr 10min); Rotorua (9 daily; 4hr); Taupo (8 daily; 4–5hr); Tauranga (7–8 daily; 3hr 30min–4hr 30min); Thames (3–5 daily; 1hr 40min); Warkworth (8–10 daily; 1hr); Waipu (3–7 daily; 2hr 20min); Waitomo (3–4 daily; 3hr 30min); Whangarei (3–7 daily; 2hr 45min); Wellington (5 daily; 11–12hr).

From Helensville to: Orewa (2 Mon–Fri; 40min).

From Orewa to: Auckland (hourly; 45–60min); Helensville (2 Mon–Fri; 40min); Waiwera (hourly; 15min); Wenderholm (summer Sundays 4 daily; 15min).

Ferries

From Auckland to: Coromandel (2 daily; 2hr) Devonport (every 30min; 10min); Great Barrier (3–4 weekly; 2hr); Motuihe (2 weekly; 50min); Rakino (4 weekly; 2hr); Rangitoto (2–3 daily; 40min); Tiritiri Matangi (1 weekly; 2hr); Waiheke (7–10 daily; 40min).

From Gulf Harbour Marina to: Tiritiri Matangi Island (2 weekly; 20min).

From Half Moon Bay to: Waiheke (3–5 daily; 1hr 20min).

From Waiheke to: Auckland (7–10 daily; 40min); Coromandel (2 daily; 1hr); Rakino (3 weekly; 30min).

Flights

From Auckland to: Bay of Islands, Paihia (2–3 daily; 50min); Christchurch (25–32 daily; 1hr 20min); Dunedin (4 daily; 1hr 40min); Gisborne (5–7 daily; 1hr); Great Barrier Island (5–10 daily; 30min), Hamilton (2 daily; 35min); Kaitaia (1–2 daily; 1hr–1hr 30min), Napier (5–7 daily; 1hr); Nelson (6–7 daily; 1hr 25min); New Plymouth (5–6 daily; 50min); Palmerston North (9–12 daily; 1hr 10min); Queenstown (3 daily; 2hr 30min); Rotorua (4–6 daily; 45min); Taupo (2–4 daily; 50min); Tauranga (3–5 daily; 40min); Wanganui (2–3 daily; 1hr); Wellington (25–35 daily; 1hr); Whakatane (6–9 daily; 50min); Whangarei (5–7 daily; 40min).

Great Barrier Island: to Coromandel (1–2 daily; 20min).

From Waiheke Island to: Great Barrier Island (2 daily; 30min).

CHAPTER TWO

NORTHLAND

The narrow and staunchly Maori province of **Northland** (*Taitokerau*) thrusts 350km out from Auckland into the sub-tropical north, separating the Pacific Ocean from the Tasman Sea – two oceans which meet in the maelstrom off Cape Reinga, the North Island's most northerly accessible point. This is the "Winterless North", a name which only really holds true in the very northernmost part but rightly suggests that palms, citrus fruit and even bananas thrive here, frosts are rare, and around its shores the waters off the myriad gorgeous beaches stay warmer than elsewhere.

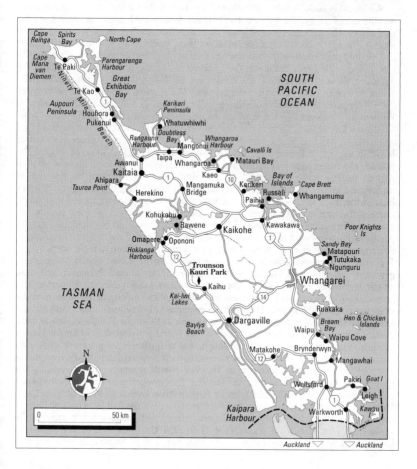

Scenically it splits down the middle. The **east coast** contorts into a labyrinth of straggling peninsulas scalloped into hidden coves between plunging headlands draped in the Christmas crimson blossom of pohutukawa trees. The beaches tend to be calm and safe, only chopping up during occasional Pacific storms, whose force is broken by clusters of protective barrier islands. The **west coast** could hardly be a greater contrast, one enormous dune-backed beach pounded by powerful Tasman breakers and occasionally broken by harbours, all with treacherous bars. Tidal rips and holes make swimming dangerous and there are no lifeguard patrols. Some beaches are even designated as roads, but are full of hazards for the unwary – and rental cars aren't insured for beach driving.

Exploration of the undulating **interior** is both hampered and enlivened by the roads: there was a time when lack of investment in infrastructure earned Northland the title of "the **roadless north**", an image it has only really shed in the last forty years or so. Furthermore, the major routes are inland and often well away from the unspoiled, deserted beaches that are the main event in these parts, leading to long forays down twisting side roads.

Northland is undoubtedly scenic, but a large part of the interest here is cultural: this was the site of most of the early contact between **Maori** and **European** settlers and the birthplace of New Zealand's most important document, the **Treaty of Waitangi**. Maori legend tells of the great Polynesian explorer Kupe discovering the Hokianga Harbour and, finding the climate and abundance of food to his liking, encouraging his people to return and settle here. But it was their ancestors in the Bay of Islands who bore the dubious honour of first contact with Europeans, as whalers plundered the seas and missionaries sought converts largely ungoverned. Maori social structure and past experience ill-prepared them for this onslaught, and their leaders petitioned Britain to step in. Without fully appreciating the implications or understanding the duplicity of the *pakeha*, the northern chiefs signed away their **sovereignty** in return for assurances on land and traditional rights, which were seldom respected. There is still a perception among Maori in the rest of the country that the five northern *iwi* gave Aotearoa away to the *pakeha*, and resentment lingers. As more fertile farmlands were found in newly settled regions further south, Northland fell into decline and the pattern became one of exploitation rather than development. Rapacious **kauri loggers** and **gum diggers** cleared the bush and, as extractive industries died away, pioneers moved in, turning much of the land to **dairy country**. Local dairy factories closed as larger semi-industrial complexes centralized processing, leaving small towns all but destitute, though planting of fast-growing exotic trees and sporadic pockets of horticulture keep places ticking over, aided by cultivation of marijuana, a major cash crop in these parts.

Finally escaping Auckland's urban sprawl, the **Kowhai Coast** begins to feel more genuinely rural and is popular with yachties sailing around Kawau Island, and snorkellers exploring the underwater world of **Goat Island Marine Reserve**. The broad sweep of **Bream Bay** runs from the Nova Scotian settlement of Waipu up to the dramatic crags of Whangarei Heads at the entrance to Northland's major port and the associated town of **Whangarei**. Off the coast here lie the **Poor Knights Islands**, New Zealand's premiere dive spot. Tourists in a hurry tend to make straight for the **Bay of Islands**, a jagged bite out of the coastline dotted with islands perfect for cruising, diving and swimming with dolphins, and steeped in early New Zealand history. Everything north of here is loosely referred to as **The Far North**, a region characterized by the quiet remoteness of the **Whangaroa Harbour**, the popular resorts of **Doubtless Bay**, and the Aupouri Peninsula, which backs **Ninety Mile Beach** all the way up to **Cape Reinga**. The west coast feels very different from the east, marked by economic neglect over the last fifty years as the kauri logging ended and dairying never successfully replaced it. First stop is the fragmented **Hokianga Harbour**, one of New Zealand's largest, with some fine sand dunes gracing **the** north head. South of here you're into

---

ACCOMMODATION PRICES

Accommodation listed in this guide has been categorized into one of nine price bands, as set out below. The rates quoted represent the **cheapest available** double or twin **room** – except for category ①, which are per-person rates for a dorm bed; fees for **tent sites** and **DOC huts** are also per-person, unless otherwise stated.

① under $20 per person	④ $60–80	⑦ $140–180
② under $40 per room	⑤ $80–100	⑧ $180–240
③ $40–60	⑥ $100–140	⑨ over $240

For more on accommodation, see p.33.

---

the **Waipoua Forest**, all that remains after the depredations of the loggers, a story best told at the excellent **Matakohe Kauri Museum** on the shores of the Kaipara Harbour.

Northland has no passenger train services so **getting around** by public transport means travelling by **bus**. Kaitaia and the Bay of Islands airports have direct **flights** to Auckland and each other, and Whangarei has flights to Auckland and Great Barrier Island, but distances are relatively short and high prices act as a deterrent. Details of frequencies and journey times are given in "Travel Details" at the end of the chapter (see p.189).

The Kowhai Coast to Bream Bay

Auckland's influence begins to wane by the time you reach the **Kowhai Coast**, a 30km stretch of shallow harbours, beach-strung peninsulas and small islands. Freed from the shackles of the city, a more individual character becomes apparent, particularly once you pass sleepy **Warkworth** and either head out to **Kawau Island**, one-time home of Governor General George Grey, or up the coast to Leigh and the snorkelling and diving nirvana of **Goat Island Marine Reserve**.

There's little to detain you on SH1 between Warkworth and Waipu as it passes through dull Wellsford and the road junction and bus interchange at **Brynderwyn**, where SH12 loops off to Dargaville, the Waipoua Kauri Forest and the Hokianga Harbour.

Northbound voyagers are better off on the coast following **Bream Bay**, named by Cook when he visited in 1770 and his crew hauled in tarakihi, which was mistaken for bream. Gently curving 20km from the modest rocky headland of Bream Tail in the south, past the entrance to Whangarei Harbour, to the dramatic and craggy Bream Head, the bay has no sizeable towns – only the small beach communities of **Mangawhai Heads** and **Waipu Cove**, looking out to the **Hen and Chicken Islands**, refuges for rare birds like the handsome wattled saddleback.

Warkworth and around

The economic focus of the **Kowhai Coast** is the easy-going small town of **WARK-WORTH**, at the head of the Mahurangi Harbour, sheltered from the sea by its eponymous peninsula. For much of the year Warkworth exudes the peace and slow pace of a pleasant Kiwi rural town, only coming to life at the peak of the summer season when thousands of yachties descend, their boats moored in the numerous estuaries and coves. From the late 1820s the languid stretch of river that flows behind the town seethed with boats shipping out kauri, initially as spars for the Royal Navy and latterly as sawn planks. A high-grade limestone deposit was discovered in 1865 and cement production became important for a while, sparking furious competition to run a ferry service to Auckland. To learn more, head 3km south to the **Warkworth and Districts Museum**, on Tudor Collins Drive (daily: Nov–Easter 9am–4pm; Easter–Oct 9am–3.30pm; $3), which explores the region's history through re-created rooms, examples of kauri gum and a 5m-long, 130-link chain carved from a single piece of kauri. The two ancient kauri outside mark the start of two well-presented twenty-minute nature trails through the **Parri Kauri Park** (9am–dusk; donations invited), a stand of bush preserved as a public amenity at the end of the nineteenth century. A couple of kilometres further south along SH1, there's the much-touted **Satellite Earth Station Visitor Centre**, Thompson Road (daily 9am–3pm; free), a blatant promotion of Telecom's satellite networks adjacent to New Zealand's first satellite dish.

Following SH1 north, it is 5km to the entertaining **Sheepworld** (daily 9am–5pm; $9), where you can observe bottle-feeding of lambs or try your hand at a little shearing. The **Dome Forest Walkway** begins 2km further north on SH1, leading up through native forest to a lookout point (40min return), continuing steeply to the summit (1hr 30min return) for superb views, and gently down to the twenty magnificent trees of the Waiwhiu Kauri Grove (3hr return).

Practicalities

Warkworth's **visitor centre**, 1 Baxter St (Christmas–Feb Mon–Fri 8.30am–5.30pm, Sat & Sun 9am–3pm; March–Christmas Mon–Fri 9am–5pm, Sat & Sun 10am–3pm; ☎09/425 9081, fax 425 7584) is right in the centre of town at the junction of Queen Street and Neville Street, where InterCity, Northliner and Gubbs buses stop.

The only budget **accommodation** is the comfortable *Boss Lodge*, 26 View Rd (☎ & fax 09/425 8185; tent sites $8, dorms ①, rooms ②), a kilometre away, initially following Queen Street; bikes ($10 a day), golf and tennis gear are available for rent. More central accommodation includes modern pub-style rooms at the *Bridge House Lodge*, Elizabeth Street (☎09/425 8351, fax 425 7410; ④) and *The Warkworth Inn*, 9 Queen St (☎09/425 8569, fax 425 9696; ③), Warkworth's original 1860 hotel, with well-priced B&B at the top end of this price category and a room-only option at the bottom end; campervans can park outside and use the facilities for $20. Among several good **B&Bs** and homestays, one stands out: *Saltings Guest House*, 1210 Sandspit Rd (☎09/425 9670, fax 425 9674; ⑤) is a standard 1970s Kiwi home exquisitely restyled along Mediterranean lines; fine breakfasts are served. *Saltings* overlooks Sandspit, 7km from Warkworth, within walking distance of the Kawau ferry wharf and the adjacent *Sandspit Motor Camp*, 1334 Sandspit Rd (☎ & fax 09/425 8610; tent sites $10, cabins ②).

Daytime **eating** is best done at *Ducks Crossing Café*, which serves good quiche, salads, cakes and coffee in the River View Plaza down by the languid river, the *Printed Word Bookshop Café*, on the corner of Queen Street and Neville Street, or the café out at the *Morris & James* pottery (see p.142). In the evening, make for the *Pizza Co*, 18 Neville St (BYO), which serves fine traditional pizza, superb vegetable soup and a spicy pepperoni Garibaldi stew.

Kawau Island

KAWAU ISLAND holds a special place in the hearts Hauraki Gulf of the yachting fraternity, as much for the safety of its rangy harbours as for the sandy coves wedged between modest cliffs. With a meagre resident population of around a hundred, the island is chiefly the preserve of **holiday homes** – some multimillion dollar affairs with helipads – which choke a shoreline bristling with jetties, virtually one for every house. And there lies the problem for the casual visitor: you can't do much without your own boat except visit the Mansion House on the unimaginatively named Mansion House Bay, and the sumptuous exotic grounds thereabouts.

Once farmed, the island is slowly reverting to kanuka scrub and is not an especially appealing place to walk. Besides, **access** is difficult to all but the DOC-managed south-western tenth of the island, where one of New Zealand's first export industries sprang up around a briefly profitable **copper trade** in the 1840s and 1850s. Mines in Dispute Cove yielded copper ore, which was processed at Smeltinghouse Bay on Bon Accord Harbour, the inlet that nearly cuts the island in two. The industry was defunct by 1862 when George Grey, then doing his second stint as New Zealand's governor, was looking for a private home and bought the mine manager's house and adjacent assay office, linking the two with his own larger-roomed extension to form the **Mansion House** (daily 10am–3.30pm; $4). Grey was an austere man and there's little flamboyance in the construction, the rooms being simply decorated using kauri and totara panels and the sole nod to his position, some kauri pillars sent to England for turning. Grey sold up in 1888, after which the house spent much of its life as a hotel, over the years sprouting ugly extensions which had to be stripped away during restoration. Apart from a collection of silverware, there is little in the house that belonged to Grey, but most of the furniture is contemporary with his tenure.

Grey's pursuit of the Victorian fashion for things exotic resulted in **grounds** stocked with flora and fauna imported from all over the world. Though much of it was ill-tended after his departure, the dell running back from the house is still a gracious place. Chilean wine palms, coral trees, Moreton Bay figs and a smattering of native species stud the formal lawns, where peacocks – one completely white – strut by, weka scurry around and rosellas screech overhead. Grey also brought in four species of **wallaby** – most easily seen in a large compound in the dell – which have overtaken the island to the extent that they are now regularly culled, and residents construct impenetrable fences to protect their gardens.

A **stroll** through the gardens runs to the tiny beach at **Lady's Bay** and on to a network of short tracks that drop down to coves on Bon Accord Harbour and to the ruins of the old copper mine (about 40min).

Practicalities

Boats to Kawau Island leave from **Sandspit** (all-day parking $5), a small road-end community on the Matakana Estuary, 8km east of Warkworth; Gubbs buses (☎09/425 8348) can generally be persuaded to run you out here. Throughout the year, Kawau Kat Cruises (☎0800/888 006) operate the **Royal Mail Run** (daily 10.30am; 4hr; $35), delivering mail (at least on Mon, Wed & Fri runs), papers and groceries to all the wharves on the island and giving you about two hours ashore at Mansion House Bay; their **direct service** (Christmas–Easter 1–3 daily; $24) gives you more time at the bay. For a cheaper and more leisurely option, try a **Coffee Cruise** on the MV *Matata* (daily: Christmas–Easter 10am; Easter–Christmas 10am & 2pm; $18; ☎ & fax 09/425 6169), which follows a similar itinerary to the Mail Run – though you'll need to go out on the early boat and come back on the later one if you want to linger on the island. Both companies run a range of other cruises in summer. Bring whatever you need to Kawau as there are only meagre supplies at the **kiosk** (Christmas–Easter daily 10am–4pm; rest of the year Sat & Sun only) in the Mansion House grounds.

There are several **places to stay** on Kawau, most, such as *St Clair Lodge*, Vivian Bay (☎09/422 8850; ⑨) and *Cottages for Couples*, Vivian Bay (☎09/422 8835; ⑧), geared to romantic weekends away with all meals included in the price. More modest accommodation includes *Pah Farm Fishing Lodge*, Moores Bay (☎09/422 8765, fax 422 8794; tent sites $10, dorms ①), and a couple of simple, self-contained **DOC houses** (☎09/422 8882; ③), *Two House Bay Cottage* and *Sunny Bay Cottage*, both within fifteen minutes' walk of the Mansion House and let for a minimum of two nights. Anyone keen to put in a week's **voluntary work** can stay free in a DOC bunkhouse at Mansion House Bay by contacting the volunteer coordinator at the Auckland Conservancy office (☎09/307 9279).

Matakana

MATAKANA, 8km northeast of Warkworth, is little more than a road junction at the heart of a fledgling grape-growing region dotted with craftspeople who have set up shop far enough from Auckland to discourage the weekend masses but close enough to lure interested buyers. The key player in the district is the **Morris & James Country Pottery**, Tongue Farm Road (daily 10am–5pm; ☎09/422 7116), which in the late 1970s exploited New Zealand's fortress economy by producing otherwise unobtainable handmade terracotta tiles and large garden pots from the local clay. Since then, its distinctive designs, executed in lustrous multi-layered salt glaze, have infiltrated ceramics shops throughout the country. In the workshop, you can watch wall tiles being hand decorated, before tucking into sumptuous Mediterranean and Pacific Rim lunches at the café/bar. The pottery is off the Leigh road just east of Matakana and almost opposite **Matakana Market Cooperative**, Matakana Valley Road (daily 10am–4pm), a quality craft, plants and produce coop in a former dairy factory that's worth a quick peek.

Half the valley seems to be **vineyards**, but there is currently only one retail outlet, *Heron's Flight*, 49 Sharp's Road (daily 10am–5pm; tastings $5; ☎09/422 7915), which produces reputable Cabernet Merlot, Chardonnay and other varietals. The attached **restaurant** does lunches daily in summer and on winter weekends.

Leigh and the Goat Island Marine Reserve

The coast-bound road runs 13km east of Matakana to **LEIGH**, a clifftop village which boasts the fine sandy bay of **Mathesons Beach**, 1km to the west, and a picturesque harbour bobbing with wooden fishing boats. The fleet's presence attests to the abundance of fish where ocean currents meet the waters of the Hauraki Gulf, though overfishing has taken its toll, something which underlines the importance of places like the **Goat Island Marine Reserve**, 4km northeast of Leigh, and so-named for its most prominent feature, a small bush-clad island 300m offshore. Established in 1975, New Zealand's first marine reserve stretches 5km along the shoreline and 800m off the coast. Two angling- and shellfishing-free decades later the undersea life is thriving, with large rock lobster and huge snapper. Feeding is discouraged but commonly practised – blue maomaos in particular seem to have developed a taste for hand-fed frozen peas and frequently mob swimmers and divers.

Easy beach access, wonderfully clear water, rock pools on wave-cut platforms, a variety of undersea terrains and relatively benign currents combine to make this an enormously popular year-round **diving** spot, as well as a summer destination for sun-seeking families. Snorkellers get a lush world of kelp forest with numerous multi-coloured fish; those who venture deeper confront more exposed seascapes with an abundance of sponges. **Gear** – mask, snorkel and fins ($11), with wetsuit and weight belt ($25) – can be rented from Seafriends (daily 9am–dusk; ☎09/422 6212), just over a kilometre up the Goat Island access road; single dives cost $60. **Non-divers** wanting a taste of what's down there can view a series of aquariums that re-create different Goat Island ecosystems, and, in fine weather, join 45-minute tours around the island with Glass Bottomed Boat Habitat Explorer (Oct–June; $18; call in advance to check times and conditions, ☎09/422 6334).

Heading north up the coast, it is possible to reach Mangawhai Heads via a string of dirt roads through steep green hills through boggy farmland and scrubby bush. It's not an especially striking journey, though, and you'll do as well to return to SH1 in Warkworth – unless you're drawn to the long, dune-backed white strand of **PAKIRI**, 10km from Leigh, where there's a couple of places to stay, and you can go **horse riding** with Pakiri Beach Horse Rides (☎ & fax 09/422 6275), a couple of kilometres further north on Rahuikiri Road. Trips head along the beach and into the forest behind ($25 an hour, $85 a day); multi-day safaris can also be arranged.

Practicalities

There's no public transport to Leigh, and the facilities are limited once you get here. Nevertheless, you can **stay** comfortably at the *Leigh Motel*, 15 Hill St (☎09/422 6179; ④), which has good two-night deals outside of January, the well-priced *Matheson Bay B&B*, 2 Grand View Rd, Matheson Bay (☎09/422 6302; ③), or pitch camp at the small and grassy *Goat Island Camping* (☎09/422 6185; tent sites $8, powered sites $10), about 1km back from the reserve. Further north **in Pakiri**, there's beachside accommodation at the *Pakiri Beach Motor Camp*, Pakiri Beach Road (☎09/422 6199; tent sites $10, cabins ②, motel units ④), or with *Pakiri Beach Horse Rides* (☎ & fax 09/422 6275; dorms ①, beach cabins ④, full-board farmstay ⑦), a couple of kilometres further north on Rahuikiri Road.

Eating is a big surprise, with the slick *Leigh Saw Mill Café*, Pakiri Road (☎09/422 6019), a vast sawmill sensitively converted into a smart café/bar serving fine gourmet pizza and a small range of well-presented dishes, often supplemented by daily specials based around an Indian, Thai or Japanese theme; weekends typically draw touring bands. Good alternatives include the café/restaurant at *Seafriends* (daily 9am–dusk; BYO & licensed), just over a kilometre up the Goat Island access road, and Leigh's takeaway, both serving excellent seafood in their own way.

Mangawhai Heads and Waipu Cove

Steering shy of the dirt roads which fan off SH1, your next chance to join the coast is at **Mangawhai Heads**, 30km north of Leigh, where the Mangawhai Harbour reaches the sea. An expanding cluster of holiday homes straggles over the hillsides behind a fine surf beach. If you want to linger and sample the surf, try the *Mangawhai Heads Hotel*, 72 Wintle St (☎09/431 4483; ④), or the *Mangawhai Heads Motor Camp*, Mangawhai Heads Road (☎09/431 4675; tent sites $10). The *Naja Garden Café*, on Molesworth Drive, serves fine salads, quiches and espresso.

You know you are getting close to the Scottish enclave of Waipu when you reach the delightful **Lang's Beach**, 12km north of Mangawhai Heads, with its tree-backed strand and the *Lochalsh* tearooms. From here it is a further 4km to the top surf beach of **Waipu Cove**, a cluster of houses by a sweeping stretch of Bream Bay, again with limited accommodation: camping at the *Waipu Cove Reserve Camp*, 897 Cove Rd (☎09/432 0410; tent sites $7, powered sites $9), and rooms at the pool-equipped *Cove Beach Motel*, 891 Cove Rd (☎09/432 0348; ④), both right by the beach.

Waipu and around

Driving through, you wouldn't pick nondescript **WAIPU** as different from any other small Kiwi town but for an Aberdeen granite monument surmounted by a Scottish lion rampant in the middle of the main street. Erected in 1914 to commemorate the sixtieth anniversary of the town's founding, the monument recalls the Scottish home of settlers who arrived here by way of Nova Scotia, following the charismatic preacher the Reverend Norman McLeod. Like numerous other crofters dispossessed by the eighteenth-century Highland clearances and enticed by stories of the New World, McLeod left Scotland in 1817 with some 400 followers and set down roots in St Ann's, Nova Scotia, where they stayed until a series of harsh winters in the late 1850s drove them out. Some went to Australia, but most decamped to Waipu, forming a self-contained and deathly strict Calvinist community that eked a living from farming and forestry. The town is proud of its heritage, and every year a child is sponsored to study pipes, drum or Scottish country dancing at The Gaelic College of Arts and Crafts in Nova Scotia, and the Nova Scotians respond by sending competitors to Waipu's annual New Year's Day **Highland Games**, in which competitors heft large stones, toss cabers and lug sheaves. The Scottish history and genealogy of the settlers is recounted in the **Waipu Museum**, on the main street (daily 9.30am–4pm; $4), which is jammed full of photos of anxious first-boat arrivees and their personal effects.

Unless you happen to coincide with the Games, there's nothing much to do in Waipu, though there's a popular excursion to the **Waipu Caves** (unrestricted entry), a 200m glow-worm-filled passage forming part of an extensive underground system in the limestone country 13km to the west. Obtain a map from the visitor centre in Waipu (see "Practicalities" below), take a couple of good torches – it's pitch-black and very disorientating inside the caves – and explore: there are no guides, so use your judgement as to how far to penetrate. The cave is signposted from Waipu Caves Road and is impenetrable when wet; you'll get muddy even in dry weather.

North from Waipu, the road runs parallel to Bream Bay, though occasional turnings give access to the long white **beach** that lies to the east. The best place to head down is at **Uretiti**, 6km north of Waipu, where there is a primitive DOC camping area ($5), with water and cold showers and an adjacent nudist beach. Four kilometres north, Ruakaka marks a turn-off for the **Marsden Point Oil Refinery** (daily 10am–5pm; free), 10km to the north, where an impressively overwrought show focuses on a vast scale model of New Zealand's only oil refinery.

Practicalities

InterCity and Northliner drop off and pick up on request and outside Bargain Buys, on the main street, which also acts as a ticket agent (☎09/432 0046). Nearby, "The House of Memories" contains the Waipu Museum (see above) and the **visitor centre** (daily 9.30am–4pm; ☎09/432 0746). The nicest budget **accommodation** is at the super-relaxed *Ebb & Flow Backpackers*, 3km south of Waipu on Johnson Point Road (☎09/432 0217; dorms ①, rooms ②); perched on the edge of the Waipu Estuary wildlife reserve, it enjoys lovely sea views out to the Hen and Chicken Islands. There are cheaper dorm beds and some more appealing units at the *Clansman Motel*, 30 Cove Rd (☎ & fax 09/432 0424; dorms ①, units ④), which also does meals – mainly grills around the $15 mark. The best **meals** for miles around are to be had at *The Last Post*, 2 Cove Rd (☎09/432 0737), a classy and fairly expensive restaurant in Waipu's former post office, with wonderfully tasty modern New Zealand cuisine served in a casual dining room or out in the garden.

Whangarei and around

On initial acquaintance, **WHANGAREI** is a bit of a disappointment. If you've come from the south, Bream Bay's sweeping coastline and the attractive Whangarei Harbour seem to promise more than Northland's provincial capital is able to deliver. Ranks of car sales yards and print shops edge into the central grid of streets, where a couple of low-rise office blocks struggle to stamp some identity onto a drab cityscape. Even the **port** that originally brought prosperity to Whangarei is several kilometres out of town and doesn't contribute any character. But Whangarei does have redeeming features, not least the new riverside **Town Basin**, where sleek yachts sit primly on their moorings outside an over-enthusiastically renovated settler-style shopping and restaurant complex. Elsewhere there's a smattering of modest museums and sights and a few pleasant walks, but Whangarei is perhaps best used as a base either for a swimming and walking day-trip out to Whangarei Heads, or for diving and snorkelling around the **Poor Knights Islands**.

Arrival, information and accommodation

Though a rail line runs from Auckland to Whangarei, no passenger trains make it this far. InterCity and Northliner **buses** pull up on Rose Street, the hub of the skeletal local service which runs on weekdays only. Daily **flights** from Auckland and Sunday flights from Great Barrier Island arrive at Onerahi Airport, 9km south and linked to town by a **shuttle bus** (☎09/437 0666; $7). The **visitor centre** lies 2km south of town on the main route from Auckland, at 92 Otaika Rd (Christmas–Jan daily 8.30am–6.30pm; Feb–Christmas Mon–Fri 8.30am–5pm, Sat & Sun 10am–3pm; ☎09/438 1079, fax 438 2943), but information on local walks is better sought at the **DOC office**, 149–151 Bank St (Mon–Fri 8am–4.30pm; ☎09/438 0299), ten minutes' walk away.

It is seldom difficult to find **accommodation** in Whangarei and, though there are few places that are really special, prices are reasonable.

Hotels, motels and B&Bs

Channel Vista Homestay, 254 Beach Rd, Onerahi, 9km south of town towards Whangarei Heads (☎ & fax 09/436 5529). Luxurious modern homestay with self-contained suites overlooking Whangarei Harbour and let on a B&B basis. ⑨.

△ **D**, Whangarei Falls (4 km) & Bay of Islands (70 km)

WHANGAREI

ACCOMMODATION
A Alpha Caravan Park
B Central Backpackers (Hatea House)
C Fountain Lodge Motel
D Hibiscus Motel
E Motel Six
F Punga Lodge
G Settlers Motor Hotel
H YHA

RESTAURANTS, CAFÉS & BARS
1 Al's Diner
2 At A Turks Café
3 Bogart's Café
4 Dickens' Inn & Oliver's Café
5 Killer Prawn
6 The Laughing Buddha
7 Red Iguana
8 Reva's on the Waterfront
9 Tastebuds Mexican Cantina

Craft Quarry

Cafler Park
Whangarei Art Museum

Margie Maddren Fernery

DOC Office

Town Basin
Clapham's Clocks

Reyburn House

Northland Breweries

Clarke Homestead & Whangarei Museum (5 km)

Whangarei Heads (25 km)

0   250 m

▽ ⓘ (2 km) & Auckland (170 km)

Fountain Lodge Motel, 17 Tarewa Rd (☎ & fax 09/438 3532, freephone 0800/999 944). Well-appointed motel close to the town centre with a couple of kitchenless studio rooms and several fully self-contained units. ④/⑤.

Hibiscus Motel, 2 Devron St (☎09/437 6312, fax 437 6229). One of Whangarei's cheapest motels yet still having comfortable rooms with TV and a swimming pool. ③.

Motel Six, 153 Bank St (☎09/438 9219, fax 438 9218). Standard, decent motel ten minutes' walk from the centre with spa pool and in-house video. ④.

Punga Lodge, 9 Punga Grove (☎09/438 3879). This is the most central homestay, but has just one double room with private bathroom and continental breakfast. ④.

Settlers Motor Hotel, 63 Hatea Drive (☎09/438 2699, fax 438 0794). Comfortable, spacious hotel style rooms in a complex with on-site bar, restaurant and swimming pool. ⑤, ④ at weekends.

Hostels and campsites

Alpha Caravan Park, 34 Tarewa Rd (☎ & fax 09/438 9867). Compact but convenient site ten minutes' walk from town. Tent sites $9, cabins ②, motel units ③.

Central Backpackers (Hatea House), 67 Hatea Drive (☎09/437 6174, fax 437 6141). This suburban house has been converted into a slightly cramped but clean hostel with dorms, doubles and a couple of compact units with fridge and stove. Guests can rent kayaks at bargain prices and all-comers can join coastal kayak trips ($35). Dorms ①, rooms & units ②.

Whangarei Falls Caravan Park, Ngunguru Rd, 6km from town near Whangarei Falls (☎09/437 0609). Although less convenient than the other campsites, the setting – on the edge of the countryside, with a pool and spa – compensates. Tent sites $9, dorms ①, cabins ②.

YHA, 52 Punga Grove Ave (☎ & fax 09/438 8954). Small and ageing hostel a fifteen-minute walk from the centre, with dorm beds, doubles and Friday night barbecues. Dorms ①, rooms ②.

The Town

Whangarei's greatest concentration of sights is around the **Town Basin**, a prettified zone of upmarket galleries, shops and restaurants based around an 1880s villa now so hidden by the lavish repainting and addition of pseudo-settler frills that it is virtually indistinguishable. Of the museums in the complex, few will be disappointed about missing **Di's Dolls Museum** (daily 10am–5pm; $2.50); likewise, only those desperate for a kitsch diversion should venture near fibreglass and stuffed specimens in the **Museum of Fishes** (daily 10am–4pm; $3.50). Make instead for **Clapham's Clocks** (daily: Dec–April 9am–8pm; May–Nov 10am–4pm; $4.50), right by New Zealand's largest sundial. Inside, one long room is packed with 1500 clocks, from mechanisms taken out of church towers to cuckoo clocks, by way of work-time recorders, domestic timepieces and all manner of ornamental clocks. Nearby, Whangarei's oldest kauri villa, **Reyburn House** (Tues–Fri 10am–4pm, Sat & Sun 1–4pm; free), hosts the Northland Society of Arts' exhibition gallery, usually containing a few quality pieces. Finally, if they have time, **Northern Breweries**, 104 Lower Dent St (☎09/438 4664) will show you around their micro-brew plant and let you sample their chemical-free brews.

On the western side of the town centre, the small but well-kept **Cafler Park** makes a pleasant place for a stroll, structured around a visit to the Rose Gardens and the adjacent **Whangarei Art Museum** (*Te Wharetaonga o Whangarei*; Tues–Fri 10am–4pm, Sat & Sun noon–4pm; donations requested), with a small permanent collection of New Zealand art and frequently changing exhibitions that showcase Kiwi artists. A footbridge crosses the stream running through Cafler Park to the restful and cool **Margie Maddren Fernery**, First Avenue (daily 10am–4pm; free), a compact collection of native ferns packed into half a dozen specially built compounds. These are flanked by two glasshouses: the **Filmy Fern House** provides a damp, draught-free environment for New Zealand's more delicate fern species, while the **Snow Conservatory** contains a steamy tropical hot-house and a desert room packed with cacti. From here, it is ten minutes' walk to the **Craft Quarry**, Selwyn Avenue (daily 8am–5pm), an artists' cooperative and something of a focus for the vibrant crafts community in this part of Northland. You are free to wander among anarchic shacks built from adobe, timber and corrugated iron, watch the artisans at work and, or course, to buy their handiwork.

Another collection of museums lies 5km southwest on SH14 in Maunu, occupying the grounds of the **Clarke Homestead** (daily 10am–4pm; $3, $7 to all three sites), a rare example of an unrestored original homestead. Built in 1886 for a Scottish doctor, Alexander Clarke, the house was at its most vibrant in the 1930s when Alexander's son, James, held high-society parties here. Much of what you see dates from that era, since James's bachelor son, Basil, took little interest in the upkeep of the place right up to his death in the 1980s. Among the accumulated possessions of the three generations, the highlight has to be Basil's unkempt, boys' own bedroom, complete with hunting gear, drum kit and an impressive shelf of medicines. In Basil's later years, he bequeathed the grounds to the **Whangarei Museum** (same hours; $3). Housed in a modern building, its collection of local history, flora and fauna is augmented by a small but strong Maori collection. Among the clubs, fishing lures and agricultural implements is a lovely feather cloak, but the prize exhibit is the *waka tupapuka*, a unique sixteenth-century wooden funerary chest decorated with bird-form carvings, as opposed to the more common human forms. The museum encourages appreciation of native fauna through the **Kiwi House** (same hours; $3), one of the best of its ilk, nicely laid out and with good visibility. On several Sundays through the summer the complex holds themed "live days", when $5 gets you the run of the place along with, say, vintage transport buffs, or log-skidding experts.

Perhaps Whangarei's greatest appeal, though, is the number of small parks and easy **walks** within a few minutes of the town, most of them outlined on the *Whangarei Walks* leaflet (available free from the visitor centre). The ugly sheet-metal war memorial atop the 240m **Mount Parahaki** can be approached by car or on foot along the steep forty-minute Ross Track from the end of Dundas Road. Understandably more popular is the twenty-minute stroll encircling the broad curtain of the **Whangarei Falls**, where the Hatea River cascades over a 26m basalt ridge into a popular swimming hole. The falls are 5km north of the town centre and Kamo-bound buses pass close by. The road out to the falls passes Whareora Road, where **A.H. Reed Park** has shady paths through native bush and, 3km further along, the fluted and weather-worn limestone formations of **Abbey Caves** (unrestricted access) invite comparison with Henry Moore sculptures. Though the caves are open to anyone, you really need some experience and confidence to enter them; the best bet is to enrol on a **guided tour** (1hr 30min–3hr; $13–35; ☎09/437 6174).

Eating and drinking

Whangarei is no great shakes for eating, but as the largest town for some distance you'll find more choice here than anywhere between Auckland and the Bay of Islands. A selection of your favourite **fast-food** franchises line Bank Street, while more imaginative **restaurants** cluster around the Town Basin and along Cameron Street. For **groceries**, *Pak 'n' Save*, on the corner of Robert Street and Curruth Street, has the best prices.

Al's Diner, cnr Walton St & Hannah St. American-style diner with reasonable burgers and the like.

At A Turks Café, 63 Bank St (☎09/438 4849). Very good Turkish restaurant where you can sit on cushions at low tables and select from a wide range of eastern Mediterranean favourites – felafel, dolmades, kebabs, spanakopitta – at around $15. BYO & licensed.

Bogart's Café, 84 Cameron St. Easy-going restaurant serving crispy gourmet pizzas and a range of appealing mains for around $17 in the evenings; also opens during the day on weekdays for coffee and snacks. BYO & licensed.

Dickens' Inn & Oliver's Café, 71 Cameron St. Spacious café/bar doing breakfast, enormous sourdough sandwiches and rich desserts at moderate prices.

Killer Prawn, 28 Bank St. Café/bar and restaurant that's the place to be seen in Whangarei, with a conservatory ambience. Prawns feature in all manner of dishes but not to the exclusion of a multitude of dishes from sashimi to steaks. Light snacks start around $5, mains $15–25.

The Laughing Buddha, 79 Walton St. Whangarei's only vegetarian café, serving wholesome well-priced dishes and great smoothies in relaxed surroundings. Open until 5pm Mon–Wed, 9pm Thurs–Sat. BYO.

Parua Bay Tavern, Parua Bay Rd (☎09/436 5856). Waterside pub 20km out of town on the road to Whangarei Heads which frequently hosts live bands; look for fly posters around town.

Reva's On The Waterfront, Town Basin (☎09/438 8969). A Whangarei institution, with breezy, quayside seating and a broad range of moderately priced daily specials from char-grilled peppers and Bream Bay seafood to gourmet pizzas.

Red Iguana, *Grand Hotel*, cnr Bank St & Rose St. Nicely modernized version of a traditional Kiwi bar mainly devoted to bar-propping, boozing and sport-watching but also serving $7 lunches and hosting live bands at weekends.

Tastebuds Mexican Cantina, 6 Vine St. Small, cheerily decorated restaurant with a basic range of filling enchiladas, burritos and nachos for around $6. Closed Sun.

Around Whangarei

The best reason to spend more than a night or two in Whangarei is to explore the surrounding area, principally those areas east and north of the town where the craggy, weathered remains of ancient volcanoes abut the sea. Half a day can be well spent around **Whangarei Heads**, the district's volcanic heartland where dramatic walks follow the coast to calm harbour beaches and windswept coastal strands. There are no roads running directly north, so you'll need to return to Whangarei to get back out to the coast at **Tutukaka** which, along with the neighbouring service village of Ngunguru, acts as the base for dive trips to the undersea wonderland around the **Poor Knights Islands**.

There is no public transport in either direction and the rugged terrain can make cycling a challenge, but dive-trip operators run vehicles out from Whangarei.

Whangarei Heads

The winding road around the northern side of Whangarei Harbour runs 35km southeast out to **Whangarei Heads**, a catch-all name for a series of small beach communities scattered around jagged volcanic mountains terminating in Bream Head, the northern limit of Bream Bay. Numerous attractive bays provide safe swimming, but there is really nothing special to see or do until the road leaves the harbour and climbs to a saddle, the start of an excellent **walk** (3km; 2hr–2hr 30min; 200m ascent) up the 430m **Mount Manaia**, the heads' most distinctive summit, crowned with five deeply eroded pinnacles shrouded in legend. One tells of a jealous dispute between two chiefs, Manaia, whose pa (fortified village) stood atop Mount Manaia, and the lesser chief, Hautatu, from across the water at Marsden Point, who was married to the beautiful Pito. Hautatu was sent away on a raid, leaving the coast clear for Manaia to steal Pito. Hautatu returned and was chasing Manaia, his two children and Pito across the hilltop when all five were struck by lightning, leaving the figures petrified on the summit. These pinnacles remain *tapu* but you can climb to their base through native bush, passing fine viewpoints.

Beyond Mount Manaia, a road forks north to **Pataua**, a family holiday village clustered around either side of a large lagoon, the two halves linked by a slender footbridge. A second road returns to the harbourside, passing the lovely McLeod's Bay on the way to **Urquarts Bay**, where a short walk (20min) leads to the white-sand **Smugglers Cove**, a longer trail (3hr return) continues to Peach Cove, and very keen walkers can press on to **Ocean Beach** (5hr one way), a wild surf beach that's also accessible by road.

Tutukaka and the Poor Knights

The Tutukaka coast means one of two things to New Zealanders, big game fishing or scuba diving – both based in **TUTUKAKA**, set on a lovely deeply incised harbour 30km northeast of Whangarei. This small coastal community is light on amenities, which are mainly provided by **NGUNGURU**, 5km back towards Whangarei. The largest settlement hereabouts, Ngunguru is strung along an attractive, sandy estuary that's fine for swimming if you dodge the jetskis.

Boats leave from Tutukaka for one of the world's premiere dive locations, the **Poor Knights Islands** marine reserve, 25km offshore, where the warm East Auckland current swirling around Cape Reinga and the lack of run-off from the land combine to create wonderfully clear water rich in New Zealand's most diverse range of sealife, including sub-tropical species found nowhere else around its shores. Two large and numerous smaller islands were cultivated by Maori but, after a nineteenth-century massacre, became *tapu* and were eventually turned into a safe haven for geckos, skinks and thousands of tuatara, the sole survivors of a branch of prehistoric lizards the rest of which became extinct 60 million years back. As land access is forbidden, interest is focused below the surface, where the volcanic forces which created the islands and subsequent changes in sea level have left a marine wonderland of near-vertical rock faces dropping down almost 100m to sand floors through a labyrinth of caves, fissures and rock arches teeming with rainbow-coloured fish, crabs, soft corals, kelp forests and shellfish. The Poor Knights even lie along the migratory routes of a number of whale species, so blue, humpback, sei and minke whales, as well as dolphins, are not uncommon.

Everything is protected within the Poor Knights reserve, but rich pickings attract free-ranging species such as marlin, shark and tuna, which stray outside the reserve and are picked off by **big game anglers** during the December to May season. Anglers wanting to rent a quarter-share of a **charter** gamefishing boat for the day will be looking at paying $200 or more: contact the Whangarei Deep Sea Anglers Club (☎09/434 3818).

PRACTICALITIES

You'll need your own wheels to get from Tutukaka to Ngunguru, where you'll find the bulk of the local **accommodation**: camping and cabins at *Ngunguru Motor Camp*, Papaka Road (☎09/434 3851; cabins ②–③), cheap but good rooms at the *Chalet Court Motel*, Main Road (☎09/434 3786; ③), and B&B at *Brimar Lodge*, 153 Ngunguru Rd (☎09/434 3951; ④). Closer to Tutukaka, try the *Sea Spray Motel*, Church Bay Road

---

DIVING AND SNORKELLING THE POOR KNIGHTS

Some prior experience opens up the best the Poor Knights have to offer, but there's plenty for novices and even snorkellers. Most of the year **visibility** is 15–20m (up to 30m Jan–Sept); in spring, the water is made murky by a profusion of plankton, but there's still lots to see.

Both Tutukaka and Whangarei, with its greater range of amenities, can be used as **diving** bases, though the **boats** all leave from Tutukaka and offer broadly the same deal – a full day out (9am–4pm) with two dives and all the equipment you need for $130–150, including **transport from Whangarei**. Divers with their own gear can expect to pay around $70 for the same two dives, and a day's **snorkelling** starts at $60. Half a dozen companies run daily trips in the main season (Nov–April), and usually at least one of them goes out most days through the rest of the year. The visitor centre in Whangarei (see p.145) has a full list of current **operators**, but the most prominent and one of the most professional in Tutukaka is Aqua Action, Marina Rd (☎09/434 3867 & 0800/689 222). In Whangarei, good deals are available at The Dive Shop, Water St (☎438 3521) and Sub Aqua Dive Centre, 41 Clyde St (☎09/438 1075).

(☎09/434 3620; ④), with plain rooms and great views over Church Bay, the next bay south from Tutukaka, or the tranquil, self-contained suites at *Pacific Rendezvous*, 73 Motel Rd (☎09/434 3847 & 0800/999 800, fax 434 3919; ⑥), which are fabulously sited on the peninsula that forms the southern arm of Tutukaka's harbour.

Eating is best done in Tutukaka at the *Schnappa Rock Café*, Marina Road (☎09/434 3774), a casual, modern place serving great burgers, gourmet sandwiches ($9), cakes and coffee plus large and tasty evening meals (around $18) in summer and on winter weekends. The *Blue Marlin Restaurant* upstairs at the Whangarei Deep Sea Anglers Club by the Tutukaka harbour unsurprisingly specializes in seafood and is generally a better bet for a meal than the nearby *Tutukaka Hotel*, which is chiefly noted as the Whangarei district's main venue for live bands.

Beaches north of Tutukaka

Settlements get smaller north of Tutukaka, most comprising a few holiday homes ranged behind the beach and little else. Day-trippers flock from Whangarei for safe swimming in gorgeous bays tucked between headlands and dotted with numerous islets. Favourites include **MATAPOURI**, 6km from Tutukaka, which backs a curving white-sand bay bounded by bushy headlands, and the pristine **Whale Bay**, 1km further north and reached by a twenty-minute bush walk off the road. The only facilities along this stretch are at Matapouri, where there's a shop and takeaway and the *Earthsea Café* (☎09/434 3662) in **Earthsea Gardens**, Clements Road (Christmas–Jan daily 10am–4pm; Feb–Christmas Sat & Sun 10am–4pm; $3 admission to gardens), an attractive subtropical dell protected from the coastal winds by stands of bamboo and harbouring a small art gallery. Heading inland from here the road is sealed most of the way to Hikurangi, where it joins SH1.

The coastal section between here and the Bay of Islands is most easily reached from Russell (see "Around Russell: Whangaruru Harbour" on p.163).

The Bay of Islands

THE BAY OF ISLANDS, 240km north of Auckland, is one of the brightest stars in New Zealand's tourism firmament, luring thousands to its beautiful coastal scenery, pattern of islands and clear blue waters. It is undoubtedly an appealing place but for scenery alone, it is really no more stunning than several other spots along the Northland coast, such as Whangaro and Hokianga harbours. What sets it apart is the ease with which you can get out among the islands, and the bay's rich history, abundantly displayed through churches, mission stations and orchards – the detritus of tentative ventures onto a new land. For this is the cradle of European settlement and a focal point for Maori, on account of the **Treaty of Waitangi** (see box on p.158) which is, despite its limitations, New Zealand's most important legal document.

It is perhaps surprising that much of your time in the Bay of Islands will in fact be spent on the mainland. There are no settlements on the islands and there is only one on which you are allowed to stay overnight. The vast majority of visitors base themselves in beachside **Paihia**, which is well geared to deal with the hordes eager to launch themselves on the various cruises, yachting trips, swimming with dolphins and the like, and is the closest town to the Treaty House at **Waitangi**. The compact town of **Russell**, a couple of kilometres across the bay by passenger ferry but distant by road, is more restrained, prettier and no less accessible to cruises. Moving away from the bay itself, **Kerikeri** is intimately entwined with early missionary history while further afield, **Waimate North** was another important mission site and still has its Mission House, though the regional focus has now moved to neighbouring **Kaikohe**.

As the main tourist centre in Northland, the Bay of Islands is forced into service as a staging post for forays further north, in particular day-long **bus tours to Cape Reinga** and Ninety Mile Beach – arduous affairs lasting eleven hours, much of it stuck inside. You're better off making your way up to Mangonui or Kaitaia and taking a trip from there, but if time is short, take your pick from the wide range of Paihia-based excursions (see box on p.154).

Some history

A warm climate, abundant seafood and deep, sheltered harbours all contributed to dense pre-European **Maori settlement** in the Bay of Islands, with every headland seeming to support a pa site. The sheltered bay was also immediately appealing to **Captain Cook**, who anchored here in 1769 and prosaically noted in his journal, "I have named it the Bay of Islands on account of the great number which line its shores, and these help to form several safe and commodious harbours". Cook landed on Motuarohia Island at what become known as Cook's Cove, where he forged generally good relations with the inhabitants. Three years later French sailor **Marion du Fresne**, en route from Mauritius to Tahiti, became the first European to have sustained contact with Maori but ultimately fared less well. He stayed three months while his crew recovered their health and the ship was refitted but a misunderstanding, probably over *tapu*, soured their initial accord and du Fresne and 26 of his crew were killed. The French retaliated, destroying a pa and killing hundreds of Maori.

Despite amicable relations between the local Ngapuhi Maori and *pakeha* whalers in the early years of the nineteenth century, the situation gradually deteriorated to the point where historian Robert Hughes described the mid-nineteenth-century Bay of Islands as "a veritable rookery of absconders ... littered with grim little communities and patriarchal clans of convicts". With increased contact, **firearms**, grog and Old World **diseases** spread and the fabric of Maori life began to break down, a process accelerated by the arrival in 1814 of Samuel Marsden, the first of many **missionaries** intent on turning Maori into God-fearing Christians. In 1833 James Busby, the British resident, was

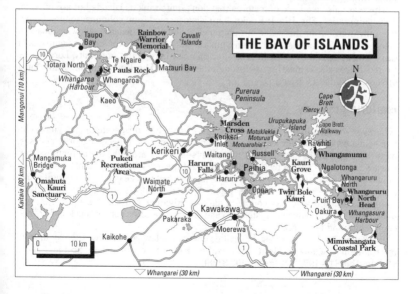

THE BAY OF ISLANDS

Taupo Bay
Rainbow Warrior Memorial
Cavalli Islands
Te Ngaire
Totara North
St Pauls Rock
Matauri Bay
Whangaroa Harbour
Whangaroa
Kaeo
Purerua Peninsula
Cape Brett
Piercy I.
Cape Brett Walkway
Marsden Cross
Motuklekle I.
Urupukapuka Island
Kerikeri Inlet
Moturua I.
Motuarohia I.
Mangonui (10 km)
Kerikeri
Waitangi
Russell
Rawhiti
Whangamumu
Mangamuka Bridge
Puketi Recreational Area
Haruru Falls
Paihia
Kauri Grove
Ngalotonga
Omahuta Kauri Sanctuary
Waimate North
Haruru
Whangaruru North
Kaitaia (80 km)
Opua
Twin Bole Kauri
Puir Bay
Whangaruru North Head
Kawakawa
Pakaraka
Oakura
Whangasura Harbour
Kaikohe
Moerewa
Mimiwhangata Coastal Park
0   10 km

▽ *Whangarei (30 km)*   ▽ *Whangarei (30 km)*

sent to secure British interests and prevent the brutal treatment meted out to the Maori by whaling captains; lacking armed back-up or judicial authority, he had little effect. The signing of the **Treaty of Waitangi** in 1840 brought effective policing, but heralded a decline in the importance of the Bay of Islands as the capital moved from its original site of Kororareka, near Russell, first to Auckland and later to Wellington.

The Bay of Islands regained some degree of world recognition in 1927 when American writer **Zane Grey** came here to fish for striped and black marlin and published photos of his exploits. Every summer since, the Bay has seen game fishing tournaments and glistening catches strung up on the jetties.

The islands

The only island to accommodate overnight guests is **Urupukapuka Island** where Zane Grey, author of best-selling westerns and avid hooker of big fish, set up his fishing resort at Otehei Bay. The resort largely burned down in 1973 but you can still stay in the accommodation units, now operating as the *Zane Grey Lodge* (☎09/403 7009; ②), with spartan rooms, full camp kitchen and optional linen rental ($5). This is behind the *Zane Grey* restaurant, a frequent stopping point for Fullers cruises, which provide regular access; lodge guests pay the concessionary $25 return fare to get out here. There are also basic DOC **campsites** in all but the western bays and there's a range of Maori pa and terrace sites, which can be explored in a few hours following signs on the island and the free *Urupukapuka Island Archeological Walk* leaflet.

Of the remaining six large islands, by far the most popular is **Motuarohia**, more commonly known as **Roberton Island** after John Roberton, who moved here in 1839. DOC manages the most dramatic central section, an isthmus almost severed by a pair of perfectly circular blue lagoons. Understandably, it is immensely popular with both private boaties and commercial cruises, and DOC have even gone to the trouble of installing an undersea nature trail for snorkellers, waymarked by inscribed stainless-steel plaques. The wildlife sanctuary of **Moturua** lies adjacent, offering a network of walks through bush alive with spotted kiwi, saddlebacks and North Island robins.

There are also a couple of features that don't quite rank as islands but are often on cruise itineraries. **The Black Rocks**, bare islets formed from columnar jointed basalt, rise only 10m out of the water but plummet a sheer 30m beneath, allowing boats to inspect at close quarters. At the outer limit of the bay there's the craggy peninsula of **Cape Brett**, named by Cook in 1769 after the then Lord of the Admiralty, Lord Piercy Brett. Cruises also regularly pass through the **Hole in The Rock**, a natural tunnel just offshore from Piercy Island.

Exploring the bay

Wherever you turn in the Bay of Islands, there are people desperate to take you yachting, scuba diving, dolphin watching, kayaking or fishing. In the vast majority of cases, trips start in **Paihia** and pick up from **Russell** wharf around fifteen minutes later. Occasionally there are no pick-ups available, but the ferry between Paihia and Russell only costs $5 return. The Bay of Islands is popular and **prices** can be quite high, especially during the summer months when demand outstrips supply and everything should be **booked** at least a couple of days **in advance**. Most hotels and motels will book these trips for you and hostels can usually arrange some sort of "backpacker" discount of around ten percent.

In addition to the water-based activities covered below you can see the bay in style on traditional seaplane **flights** offered by Paihia-based Seaplane Scenic Flights (10min–1hr; $49–195; ☎ & fax 09/402 8338).

Cruises

Without getting out onto the water you are missing the essence of the Bay of Islands. Two main companies vie for **cruise business** from the Maritime Building on Marsden Road, by the wharf in Paihia: the longstanding Fullers (daily: Oct–May 7am–9.30pm; June–Sept 7am–6.30pm; ☎09/402 7421) operates large, stable and sometimes crowded craft, while the family-run newcomers Kings (daily 7am–9.30pm; ☎09/402 8288, fax 402 7915) run faster trips in smaller boats.

For 35 years from 1919, Fullers boats collected cream from dairy farms around the perimeter of the bay, but as the infrastructure improved, the cream took to the roads and the boats began to take passengers. By the 1950s, the cream trade had died and the boat trip had been transformed into the leisurely **Cream Trip** (Oct–May daily; June–Sep Mon, Wed, Thurs & Sun; 5hr; $65), which still delivers groceries and the mail to wharves all around the bay and includes a cream tea, for old time's sake. The **Hole in the Rock Cruise** (1–2 daily; 4hr; $55) is another popular excursion, speeding out through the islands to Cape Brett and, when conditions permit, edging through the hole; by splitting your journey between the two daily summer trips, you can spend a few hours on Urupukapuka. If that's still not long enough, the **Island Experience** (Oct–May daily; $35) gives you five hours ashore. Finally, the **Supercruise** (Oct–May daily; June–Sept Mon, Wed, Thurs & Sat; 6hr; $85) visits the Hole in the Rock and spends a short time at Otehei Bay, where you get to experience **Nautilus** (included on this trip, otherwise $10), a kind of deep-hulled boat with under-sea viewing windows which putters out into the bay for twenty minutes to a spot where fish are fed.

King's, meanwhile, offers an **Express Hole in the Rock** cruise (1–2 daily; 3hr; $50), which makes no island stops, and the **See the Bay in a Day** trip (Dec–April daily; 6hr; $69), taking in the Hole in the Rock, an approximation of the Cream Trip and an island stop of the captain's choice. King's led the field with fast boats on the bay, introducing **Mack Attack** (mid-Dec to May; 5 daily; 1hr 30min; $50), an exhilarating blast out to the Hole in the Rock and back in an open catamaran. On fine days you're decked out in windproof and waterproof gear, protective glasses and life jacket; on rainy days it all gets too painful, so they don't go.

Sailing and kayaking

Fullers Northland-built **schooner** in the "tall ship" tradition, *R. Tucker Thomson*, sails out into the islands and anchors for a swim and barbecue lunch (Nov–May daily; 7hr; $75). Smaller **yachts** usually take less than a dozen passengers: competition is tight and the standards high – all have snorkelling and fishing gear on board, typically go out for six hours and include lunch.

Lack of previous experience is no impediment to going **kayaking** in either Paihia or Russell. From Paihia, Coastal Kayakers (☎09/402 8105, fax 404 0291) run half-day trips upstream to **Haruru Falls** ($40) and full-day trips ($60), which also includes paddling around **Motumaire Island**; longer excursions operate from November to June (2–5 days; $110–550). In Russell, Kaptain Kayak (☎09/403 7252) runs excellent trips around the **Russell Peninsula** (3hr; $30), open-water trips out to **Roberton Island** (5hr; $55) and full-day trips to several islands ($80). The Bay of Islands Kayak Co (☎ & fax 09/403 7672) runs similar full-day trips from Russell ($80) and tailored multi-day trips.

If you want to **go it alone**, Bay Beach Hire, at the south end of Paihia Beach (Oct–Easter; ☎09/402 7905) **rents** double and single open kayaks ($10 per hour, $35 a day), windsurfers ($25 per hour) and catamarans ($20 per hour); Coastal Kayakers (see above), based by the Waitangi Bridge in Paihia, also rent out kayaks (year-round; $15–25 per half-day, $35–40 a day) and catamarans (Dec–March; $20–30 an hour).

Dolphin watching

Relatively warm water all year round and an abundance of marine mammals makes the Bay of Islands one of the best places to go **dolphin watching**. You're likely to see bottlenose and common dolphins in pretty much any season, orca from May to August and Minke and Bryde's whales from August to January. If you don't see anything, most companies will take you out for a second chance.

Only three companies are licensed to actively search for and swim with dolphins, though that doesn't bar others from watching. Only a dozen people are allowed in the water at a time and, since most trips carry around 35 people, you can expect to be in the water about a third of the time that the dolphins are about. The pioneers, **Dolphin Discoveries**, Maritime Building ($75; ☎ & fax 09/402 8234), claim a ninety-five percent success rate, while Fullers **Dolphin Encounters** ($85) include the option of a stopover on Urupukapuka for a few hours if you take the early boat. Finally, you can swim with the dolphins off *Carino* ($60; ☎09/402 8040), a large red catamaran based in Paihia.

Diving and fishing

The main people running **scuba-diving** trips are Paihia Dive, Hire & Charter (☎09/402 7551 & 0800/107 551, fax 402 7926), who will take you **snorkelling** ($40) and diving in the Bay of Islands (from $65) or on the wreck of the *Rainbow Warrior* (see p.170; $75 and up). Russell-based Target Dive Charter (☎09/403 7971) also run competitively priced trips.

There is a wider range and greater choice of **fishing trips** than any other activity: everything from a little line fishing for snapper to big game boats in search of marlin, shark, tuna and kingfish. The best technique is to ask around and speak to the skippers to make sure you get a trip that suits; daily charter rates range from around $50 to $500 for the big game boats.

Paihia and Waitangi

PAIHIA is where it all happens. In its own way, it is just as historically important as Russell, Waitangi and Kerikeri, but this two-kilometre-long string of waterside motels, restaurants and holiday homes has been completely over-run by the demands of tourism. Its location on three flat bays looking out towards Russell and the Bay of Islands is pleasing enough and the encircling forested hills make an attractive backdrop, but the town itself could hardly be called pretty. Nevertheless, abundant well-priced accommodation, several good restaurants, a couple of boisterous bars and endless possibilities to get out on the water make this the goal of the vast majority of the Bay of Islands' visitors.

Legend has it that the town was named in 1823 by the less than accomplished Maori scholar, the Reverend Henry Williams, when he was looking for a site to establish the Church Missionary Society's third mission. He apparently exclaimed, *"pai* [good] here!"; unlikely, but it makes a nice story. At the time, Maori were overwhelmed by the influx of Europeans and looked to the missionaries to intercede on their behalf. A plaque outside the current St Paul's Anglican Church on Marsden Road marks the spot where, in 1831, the northern chiefs petitioned the British Crown for a representative to establish law and order. In 1833 King William IV belatedly addressed their concerns by sending the first British resident, James Busby. He built a house on a promontory 2km north across the Waitangi River in **WAITANGI** – the scene some seven years later of the signing of the **Treaty of Waitangi**, which ceded the nation's sovereignty to Britain in return for the protection Busby was ill-equipped to provide.

Arrival, information and transport

Northliner and InterCity **buses** arrive on the waterfront Marsden Road outside the Bay of Islands' main **visitor centre** (daily: Oct–March 7am–7pm; April–Sept 8am–5pm; ☎09/402 7345, fax 402 7301). The adjacent Maritime Building contains booking desks for all the major tour operators and stays open until around 9pm in summer, a little earlier in winter. The Bay of Islands **airport** is roughly midway between Paihia and Kerikeri, and planes are met by a shuttle bus service.

Paihia isn't big, and everywhere is within walking distance. If you've got bags to carry, engage the services of the **Paihia Tuk Tuk Shuttle Service** (☎025/866 071), who will drop up to three people pretty much anywhere in town for $5 and run up to Haruru Falls for $12. To get an overview of the district, join the **Kerikeri and Waitangi Tour** (daily; 4hr; $45), which offers lashings of historical and anecdotal information on the Treaty House, its grounds and Kerikeri.

Accommodation

Paihia abounds in good accommodation to suit all budgets. That isn't to say it is cheap, and for the couple of weeks after Christmas, motel prices can be stratospheric. B&Bs and homestays tend to vary their prices less, as do all the hostels which, though a dollar or so more expensive than other areas, maintain a very high standard. Motels and B&Bs are scattered all over, but with a central cluster in the streets opposite the wharf, and there's a kind of backpacker ghetto along Kings Road.

HOTELS, MOTELS AND B&BS

Aarangi Tui Motel, 16 Williams Rd (☎ & fax 09/402 7496, freephone 0800/453 354). One of Paihia's cheaper motels, with large, ageing fully equipped units and a barbecue area. ④.

Casa Bella, MacMurray Rd (☎09/402 7387 & 0800/800 810, fax 402 7166). Plain but decent rooms around a quiet stucco-and-Spanish-arches courtyard with a heated pool and spa. ⑤.

The Cedar Suite, 5 Sullivan's Rd (☎09/402 8516, fax 402 8555). Superb, nicely furnished and very hospitable B&B in a bush setting five minutes' walk from the beach. Rooms in the house come with cooked or continental breakfast, the apartment can be bed only or self-contained, and there's a lovely cottage with bay views sleeping up to six. ⑤–⑥.

Edgewater Motel, 10 Marsden Rd (☎09/402 7875 & 0800/833 439, fax 402 7265). Small, fully-equipped quality motel right by the beach with in-house video and a spa pool. ⑥.

Iona's Lodge, 29 Bayview Rd (☎09/402 8072). Central, self-contained B&B units with a wonderful panoramic view of the bay at very reasonable prices. ⑤.

HOSTELS

Centabay Lodge, 27 Selwyn Rd (☎09/402 7466, fax 402 8145). Central hostel situated close to beach and shops, with decent three- to five-bunk dorms, en-suite twins and doubles and motel-style self-catering studios. Guests get free use of a rowboat and kayaks, and can rent bikes for $16 a day. Dorms ①, rooms ③, studios ④.

Mayfair Lodge, 7 Puketona Rd (☎ & fax 09/402 7471). Smallish hostel at the Waitangi end of town with a friendly feel, some of the cheapest dorm beds around, a spa pool and a games room. Rooms range from spacious six-bunk dorms to twins and made-up doubles. Dorms ①, rooms ②.

The Mousetrap Backpackers, 11 Kings Rd (☎09/402 8182). Casual, friendly and idiosyncratic hostel. Every room has been individually decorated by the charismatic owners, and there are separate quiet and TV lounges. Bikes available for rent. Dorms ①, rooms ②.

Peppertree Lodge, 15 Kings Rd (☎ & fax 09/402 6122). De luxe hostel with 8-bunk dorms, 4-bunk rooms with bathroom, and en-suite doubles. The games room, TV and quiet lounges and fully-equipped kitchen are all in tip-top condition without seeming sterile. Dorms ①, rooms ③.

Tommy's, 44 Davis Crescent (☎09/402 8668). Brand new and amiably run hostel that's quieter than some of the more central places and sports super-clean facilities. Dorms ①, rooms ②.

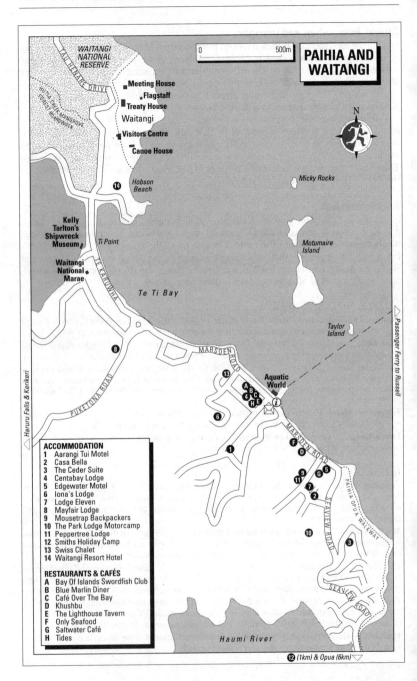

PAIHIA AND WAITANGI

0   500m

N

WAITANGI
NATIONAL
RESERVE

TAI HENUI DRIVE

HUTIA PUKA MANGROVE FOREST BOARDWALK

Meeting House
Flagstaff
Treaty House
Waitangi
Visitors Centre
Canoe House

Hobson
Beach

Micky Rocks

Kelly
Tarlton's
Shipwreck
Museum
Ti Point

Motumaire
Island

Waitangi
National
Marae

Te Ti Bay

Taylor
Island

Passenger Ferry to Russell

Haruru Falls & Kerikeri

MARSDEN ROAD

PUKETONA ROAD

Aquatic
World

MARSDEN ROAD

PAIHIA OPUA WALKWAY

SEAVIEW ROAD

SEAVIEW ROAD

Haumi River

ACCOMMODATION
1   Aarangi Tui Motel
2   Casa Bella
3   The Ceder Suite
4   Centabay Lodge
5   Edgewater Motel
6   Iona's Lodge
7   Lodge Eleven
8   Mayfair Lodge
9   Mousetrap Backpackers
10 The Park Lodge Motorcamp
11 Peppertree Lodge
12 Smiths Holiday Camp
13 Swiss Chalet
14 Waitangi Resort Hotel

RESTAURANTS & CAFÉS
A   Bay Of Islands Swordfish Club
B   Blue Marlin Diner
C   Café Over The Bay
D   Khushbu
E   The Lighthouse Tavern
F   Only Seafood
G   Saltwater Café
H   Tides

12 (1km) & Opua (6km)

CAMPSITES

Falls Motor Inn and Caravan Park, Puketona Rd (☎ & fax 09/402 7816). Tent sites down by the river opposite Haruru Falls, 4km north of Paihia, and full-blown motel units around a nice pool with commanding views. Tent sites $9, motel units ⑤.

The Park Lodge, cnr Seaview Rd & MacMurray Rd (☎09/402 7826, fax 402 8500). Average hotel backed by Paihia's most central campsite. Tent sites $10.

Smith's Holiday Camp, Opua Rd, 3km south of Paihia (☎09/402 7678). Small and peaceful waterside site with a range of cabins, and dinghies for rent. Tent sites $10, cabins ②–⑤.

Twin Pines Tourist Park, Puketone Rd (☎ & fax 09/402 7322). Attractive, well laid out and recently upgraded site by Haruru Falls, 4km north of Paihia. Tent sites $9.50, cabins & on-site vans ②–③, motel units ④.

The Town

Paihia is primarily a base for exploring the bay (see p.153), but there are a couple of diverting sights on land. The most prominent of these is **Aquatic World**, Marsden Road (daily: Dec–Feb 9am–9pm; March–Nov 9am–5pm; $6), bang next to the wharf and filled with a series of well-presented tanks full of local sea life. Visits are guided and informative, adding greatly to what could easily be just another run-of-the-mill aquarium.

Around a kilometre north, the Waitangi River separates Paihia and Waitangi and provides a mooring for the *Tui*, a three-masted barque built as a sugar lighter in 1917 and now accommodating **Kelly Tarlton's Shipwreck Museum** (daily 10am–6pm; $7). Kelly Tarlton was New Zealand's foremost wreck diver and this museum demonstrates the scale of his pioneering excavations. A salty soundtrack accompanies you through the bowels of the ship, where the expected bounty of nails, pottery and tankards is spiced up with a bottle of 1903 whisky, found by laboratory testing to be almost identical to the day it was bottled, and a collection of strangely dated-looking sunglasses and calculators from the *Mikhail Lermontov*, a Soviet cruise ship that went down in the Marlborough Sounds in 1986.

The Waitangi National Reserve

Crossing the bridge over the Waitangi River from the shipwreck museum you enter the **Waitangi National Reserve** (unrestricted access), the single most symbolic place in New Zealand for Maori and *pakeha* alike, a focal point for the modern nation's struggle for identity. For it was here in 1840 that William Hobson, Queen Victoria's representative, and approaching fifty Maori chiefs signed the Treaty of Waitangi (see box on p.158), ceding Aotearoa's sovereignty to Britain and ostensibly affording the Maori protection and guaranteeing them rights over land and resources. When the area was gifted to the people of New Zealand in 1932 by Governor-General Lord Bledisloe, the Treaty House was being used as a sheep shelter and the grounds were neglected, but a sudden desire to commemorate the 1940 centennial of the signing in fitting fashion provoked a flurry of restoration. The house is now the centrepiece of the **Waitangi Visitor Centre and Treaty House** (daily 9am–5pm; $7), where a sappy and anodyne twenty-minute video setting the historical framework is bolstered by a small exhibition of Maori artefacts, including a musket owned by Hone Heke, the first Maori chief to sign the Treaty of Waitangi, and a portrait of him blithely entitled *Johny Heke*.

The **Treaty House** itself was was built in Georgian colonial style in 1833–34; it was once described as "only a couple of rooms separated by a lobby" and is thoroughly unprepossessing, largely because Busby's superiors in Sydney failed to supply the requisite materials. The original part of the house is furnished as it would have been in Busby's time, while the wings added in the 1880s contain displays on James Busby, Waitangi life and the treaty itself. The front windows look towards Russell over sweeping lawns, where marquees were erected on three significant occasions: in 1834, when

THE TREATY OF WAITANGI

The Treaty of Waitangi is the **founding document** of modern New Zealand, a touchstone for both *pakeha* and Maori, with implications that permeate New Zealand society. Signed in 1840 between what were ostensibly two sovereign states – the United Kingdom and the United Tribes of New Zealand, plus other Maori leaders – the treaty remains central to New Zealand's **race relations**. The Maori rights guaranteed by it have seldom been upheld, and the constant struggle for recognition continues.

THE TREATY AT WAITANGI

Motivated by a desire to staunch perceived **Pacific expansionism** of the French, who were planning a settlement on the Banks Peninsula, and an obligation on the Crown to protect Maori from rapacious **land-grabbing** by settlers, the British instructed naval captain William Hobson to negotiate the **transfer of sovereignty** with "the free and intelligent consent of the natives" and to deal fairly with the Maori. Within a few days of his arrival, Hobson, with the help of Busby and others, drew up both the English Treaty and a Maori "translation". On the face of it, it is a straightforward document, but the complications of having **two versions** (see *Contexts*, p.764) and the implications of striking a deal between two peoples with widely differing views on land and resource ownership and usage have reverberated down the years. The treaty was unveiled in grand style on February 5, 1840, to a gathering of some 400 representatives of the **five northern tribes** in front of Busby's residence in Waitangi. Presented as a contract between the **chiefs** and **Queen Victoria** – someone whose role was comprehensible in chiefly terms – the benefits were amplified and the costs downplayed. As most chiefs didn't understand English, they **signed** the Maori version of the treaty, which still has *mana* ("prestige") among Maori today.

THE TREATY AFTER WAITANGI

The pattern set at Waitangi was repeated up and down the country, as seven copies of the treaty were dispatched to garner signatures and extend Crown authority over parts of the North Island that had not yet been covered, and the South Island. On May 21, before signed treaty copies had been returned, Hobson **claimed** New Zealand for Britain: the North Island on the grounds of **cession** by Maori, and the South Island by right of Cook's **"discovery"**, as it was considered to be *in terrorium nullis* (without owners), despite a significant Maori population.

Maori fears were alerted from the start, and as the settler population grew and demand for land increased, successive governments passed laws that gradually stripped Maori of control over their affairs – actions which led to the **New Zealand Wars** of the 1860s (see "History" in Contexts, p.761). Over the decades, small concessions were made, but nothing significant changed until 1973, when **Waitangi Day** (February 6) became an official national holiday. From 1971, Maori groups, supported by a small but articulate band of *pakeha*, began a campaign of **direct action**, increasingly disrupting commemorations, thereby alienating many *pakeha* and splitting Maori allegiances between angry, young, urban Maori and the *kaumatua* ("elders"), who saw the actions as disrespectful to the ancestors and an affront to tradition. Many strands of Maori society were unified by the *hikoi* ("march") to Waitangi to protest against the celebrations in 1985, a watershed year in which Paul Reeves was appointed New Zealand's first Maori Governor General and the **Waitangi Tribunal** (see Contexts, p.764) was given some teeth.

Protests have continued over the last decade – including several infamous flag-trampling, egg-pelting and spitting incidents – as successive governments have vacillated over maintaining the commemorations at Waitangi or trying to defuse the situation by promoting a parallel event at the Governor General's residence in Wellington.

Maori chiefs chose the Confederation of Tribes flag, which now flies on one yard arm of the central flagpole; the meeting a year later at which northern Maori leaders signed the Declaration of Independence of New Zealand; and, in 1840, the signing of the Treaty of Waitangi.

The northern side of the lawn is flanked by the *whare runanga* or **maori meeting house**, built between 1934 and 1940. Though proposed by Bledisloe and northern Maori chiefs, the construction of the house was a cooperative effort between all Maori and is unique in that it is pan-tribal. A short audio-visual presentation highlights and explains key elements on the richly-carved panels, introducing the major themes and legends depicted. Housed in a specially built shelter in the Treaty House grounds is another centennial project, the world's largest **war canoe** (*waka*) – the *Nga Toki Awhaorua* is named after the vessel navigated by Kupe when he discovered Aotearoa. This is undoubtedly an impressive boat, over 35m long, propelled by eighty warriors and built over two years from two huge kauri by members of the five northern tribes; it has traditionally been launched each year since 1940 on Waitangi Day, though the future of the launching, along with the Waitangi Day commemoration ceremony, remains uncertain.

The *Waitangi Resort Hotel* and the prestigious Waitangi golf course encircle the Treaty House grounds, but the Waitangi National Reserve extends beyond the fairways to the scenic viewpoint atop Mount Bledisloe, 3km away, and 2km beyond that to **Haruru Falls**, a horseshoe formed where the Waitangi River drops over a basalt lava flow. Though not that impressive by New Zealand standards, there is good swimming at the base. Haruru Falls are also accessible from outside the Treaty House grounds on the very gentle **Hutia Creek Mangrove Forest Boardwalk** (2hr).

Around Paihia

Drivers travelling between Paihia and Russell will be catching the vehicular ferry (see p.161) across the narrow Veronica Channel at **OPUA**, the Bay of Islands' major deep-water port. Fans of mangroves and estuarine scenery can tackle the gentle **Paihia–Opua Coastal Walkway** (6km; 2–3hr one-way) to get here.

The 13km stretch of railway between Opua and Kawakawa, which last carried passengers in the 1960s and saw its final freight train in 1986, is now operated as the **Bay of Islands Vintage Railway** (Christmas–Easter 3 daily; Easter–Christmas Mon, Tues, Sat & Sat 2 daily; 45min one-way; $16 return, $10 one-way; ☎09/404 0684), with steam and diesel locos hauling restored 1930s rolling stock. The highlight is the final rumble down the centre of Kawakawa's main street.

Eating and drinking

Paihia's **range** of places to eat is unmatched anywhere in the Bay of Islands and competition keeps **prices** tolerable; though none are actually on the waterfront, many have sea views and salty menus by way of compensation. The **restaurants** are also good places to stick around for post-prandial drinking, though there are a couple of more downbeat bars and an out-of-town **brewhouse** that's worth the journey.

Bay of Islands Swordfish Club, Marsden Rd. Private club which welcomes visitors outside the peak summer season for some of the cheapest drinks in town.

Blue Marlin Diner, Marsden Rd. Cheap and cheerful licensed café and takeaway, serving breakfast from $6 and, later in the day, steaks and seafood platters for $16.

Café Over the Bay, Paihia Mall, Marsden Rd. The best place for a daytime coffee on the verandah but also worth a visit for good salmon-bagel breakfasts and reasonably priced lunches and dinners with an international slant. Licensed.

Ferryman's Restaurant, Waterfront, Opua (☎09/402 7515). Well-worn, wood-panelled restaurant with an old fishing village atmosphere that's right on the ferry dock and well off the tourist trail. Fabulous, fresh seafood mains are dished up for around $18.

Khushbu, 50 Marsden Rd (☎09/402 7271). The bay's only Indian restaurant, serving a limited range of moderately priced, mainly north Indian dishes. Licensed.

The Lighthouse Tavern, upstairs in the Paihia Mall. Paihia's liveliest drinking spot, with frequent live bands in summer and drinking until late.

Saltwater Café, 14 Kings Rd (☎09/402 7783). Casual bareboards-and-steel café and restaurant serving some of the tastiest and best presented food in town, with mains of teppanyaki, Thai curry, satay and a plethora of seafood for around $15–20. BYO & licensed.

Tides, Williams Rd (☎09/402 7557). Highly regarded, innovative food with the emphasis on fresh seafood and top-quality lamb. Licensed.

Twin Pines Brew House, Puketona Rd, Haruru Falls (☎09/402 7195). Fine old villa shipped from Auckland in 1980 and refitted to micro-brew a malty ale and a clean-tasting lager, and cook a good range of bar meals. A courtesy bus runs from Paihia during the peak summer season.

The Wheelhouse, Kelly Tarlton's Shipwreck Museum, Waitangi (☎09/402 7018). Fine dining with a difference: light lunches and full-blown dinners are served either on the glassed-over exhibit tables below decks or on deck among the creaking rigging. BYO & licensed.

Russell

For much of the year the small hillside village of **RUSSELL** is a sleepy place favoured by city escapees, its isolation on a narrow peninsula with poor road but good sea access giving it an island ambience. But through the summer it is swamped with day-trippers piling off the passenger ferries from Paihia, a couple of kilometres across the water, to browse around New Zealand's most **historic** village and stroll along its appealing tree-lined waterfronts. Evenings are more peaceful – the major exception being **New Year's Eve**, when half the nation's youth seem to descend and the all-night revelry harkens back to the 1830s when **Kororareka**, as Russell was then known, was a swashbuckling town full of **whalers** and sealers with a reputation as the "Hell Hole of the Pacific".

Tales of **debauchery** may well have been exaggerated over the years, but one observer noted in 1836 that it was "notorious at present for containing, I should think, a greater number of rogues than any other spot of equal size in the universe" and a missionary found it "a dreadful place – the very seat of Satan". Savage and drunken behaviour served as an open invitation to **missionaries**, who gradually tamed a hostile congregation and left behind Russell's two oldest buildings, the church and a printing works used for producing religious tracts. By 1840, Kororareka was the largest settlement in the country, but it was deemed far too bawdy to be worthy of capital status and, after the signing of the Treaty of Waitangi, William Hobson moved his capital progressively further south.

Meanwhile, initial **Maori** enthusiasm for the Treaty of Waitangi had become tarnished: financial benefits had failed to materialize and the Confederation of Tribes flag that flew from Flagstaff Hill between 1834 and 1840 had been replaced by the Union Jack. This came to be a symbol of the **British betrayal**, and as resentment crystallized, it found a leader in Hone Heke Pokai, Ngapuhi chief and son-in-law of Kerikeri's Hongi Hika. Between July 1844 and March 1845, Hongi and his followers cut down the flagstaff four times, the last sparking the first **Maori War**, which raged for nearly a year. Kororareka was sacked and all but destroyed during the fighting, and when the rebuilding began, the authorities tried to expunge its past by **renaming** it Russell.

The new town never really flourished but grew slowly around its **beachfront** into a well laid out and peaceful place that is a delight to be in. Most Bay of Islands **cruises and trips** can be joined at Russell, but far fewer people stay here on account of the limited range of motels and budget accommodation – a consequence of ordinances designed to preserve the character of the place and to limit the strain on the town's water supply and sewage disposal, both of which struggle during the peak season. Don't let this put you off staying here, but if you are only passing through, everything can be seen comfortably in a day.

Arrival and information

Most visitors **arrive** in Russell by way of ferries. Drivers from Paihia and SH1 typically cross the narrow strait at **Opua**, 9km south of Russell, on the small **vehicle ferry** (daily 7am–9pm, Fri until 10pm; car & driver $7, passengers $1). Pedestrians and cyclists can get directly from Paihia to Russell on one of three **passenger ferries** – Fullers, the *Waimarie*, and the *Waitere* – which between them manage a boat every twenty to thirty minutes (Oct–May until 10.30pm; rest of year until 7.30pm; $3 one-way, $5–6 return); tickets are bought on the boat.

There is no fully fledged visitor centre, but information is available from **Bradley's Booking and Information**, on the end of the wharf (daily 8.30am–5pm, until 7pm Christmas–Jan; ☎09/403 7596, fax 403 7868), and, to a lesser degree, from the Fullers office, Cass Street (7.30am–5pm, until 7pm in high season; ☎ & fax 09/403 7866). For specific walking and environment information, make for DOC's **Bay of Islands Maritime & Historic Park visitor centre**, The Strand (daily: Nov–May 8.30am–5pm, June–Oct 8.30am–4pm; ☎09/403 7685, fax 403 7649), which is full of interesting displays and sells the enlightening *Russell Heritage Trails* leaflet ($1). Few places are more than half a kilometre away from the wharf, though short-stay visitors may fancy the **Russell Mini Tour** (5 daily; 1hr; $12), which leaves from outside the Fullers office and visits the major sights.

Accommodation

Accommodation in Russell is much more limited than across the water in Paihia and tends to be more upmarket, in keeping with Russell's quieter and more refined image. Beside a handful of **motels**, **hotels** and **backpacker lodges** you're in **B&B** and **homestay** territory; in addition to those listed below, Bradley's, or the visitor centre in Paihia, can help you pick one out.

Don't expect to find many vacancies in the three weeks after **Christmas**. If you will be here then, **book well ahead** and be prepared to pay a premium; **inflated rates** tend to carry on into the rest of January and February, as well.

Arcadia Lodge, Florance Ave (☎ & fax 09/403 7756). One of Russell's gems, a historic wooden house surrounded by decks overlooking luxuriant gardens, and run as both a de luxe backpackers and a B&B. Backpacker beds are in three-bed dorms, some with sea views, while B&B accommodation is in tasteful rooms, mostly with adjacent bathrooms. Everyone has access to catering facilities and there are free kayaks for guests' use. Dorms ①, rooms ⑤.

Brampton House, Wellington St (☎ & fax 09/403 7521). Two spotless, well-appointed suites in the highest house in Russell, surrounded by bush and commanding fabulous views all around. Deft touches such as complimentary wine and sumptuous breakfasts make this a treat. ⑥.

Brown Lodge, Ashby St (☎09/403 769, fax 403 7683). Richly furnished homestay in a modern all-timber house with two comfortable air-conditioned suites – one with private spa pool – and complimentary wine on arrival. ⑥.

Motel Russell, Matauwhi Bay Rd (☎09/403 7854 & 0800/240 011, fax 403 8001). Despite the lack of sea views, this is the pick of Russell's motels, with pleasant self-contained units and hotel-style rooms, an attractive pool and spa, and scooters rented at $20 a half-day. ④–⑤.

Russell Holiday Park, Longbeach Rd (☎09/403 7826, fax 403 7221). Central, well-ordered and spotless campsite with tent and powered sites, backpacker bunks and an extensive range of high-standard cabins and motel units. Tent sites $10, dorms ①, cabins & units ②–④.

Russell Lodge, cnr Chapel St & Beresford St (☎09/403 7640 & 0800/478 773, fax 403 7641). Combined backpackers and motel in a garden setting right in the heart of Russell. Backpackers get four-bunk cabins, each with a bathroom, and family units. Everyone has access to the kitchen, pool and bicycle and scooter rental. Dorms ①, studios ④, units ⑤.

Warihi, Matauwhi Rd (☎ & fax 09/403 7296). Modern, stylish and unfussy fully self-contained studio apartment below the owners' house and opening out onto a sunny deck. It sleeps up to four and is two minutes' walk from Russell wharf. Christmas–Feb ⑤, rest of year ④.

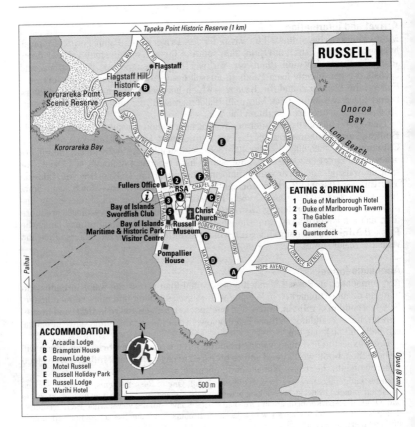

RUSSELL

Tapeka Point Historic Reserve (1 km)

Onoroa Bay

Kororareka Bay

Flagstaff Hill Historic Reserve

Kororareka Point Scenic Reserve

Long Beach

Fullers Office

Bay of Islands Swordfish Club

Bay of Islands Maritime & Historic Park Visitor Centre

Christ Church

Russell Museum

RSA

Pompallier House

EATING & DRINKING
1 Duke of Marlborough Hotel
2 Duke of Marlborough Tavern
3 The Gables
4 Gannets'
5 Quarterdeck

ACCOMMODATION
A Arcadia Lodge
B Brampton House
C Brown Lodge
D Motel Russell
E Russell Holiday Park
F Russell Lodge
G Warihi Hotel

Hope Avenue

0   500 m

Paihai

Opua (8 km)

The Town

Several historic buildings and Flagstaff Hill constitute the main sights in Russell, supplemented by a few diverting craft shops. Arriving on the passenger ferry, the single most striking building at the western end of town is **Pompallier House** (daily 10am–5pm; $5), New Zealand's oldest industrial building, dating from 1841. Built as a print shop for the French Roman Catholic bishop, Jean Baptiste François Pompallier, who had arrived three years earlier and found the Catholic word of God under siege from tracts in Maori written by Anglicans and Wesleyans. Pompallier duly imported a press and paper, installed a tannery and set about printing *Ako Marama*, a book containing a pastoral letter, prayers, hymns, psalms and a burial service in Maori. Lacking money to import all the timber needed, the missionaries built a rammed-earth structure apparently modelled on a kind of French pigeon coop, but elegant nonetheless, with its hipped roof flared to form the upper verandahs and its windows heavily shuttered to keep out prying eyes. For many years the press was kept secret, not out of religious protectionism but because of the great value of the contents; the lead type could be melted down for shot and the paper could be used for making cartridges. The printing operation only lasted until 1850 and the building changed hands several times as a domestic house, its original function being completely obliterated. Subsequent work has largely restored it to its 1841 state, an austere place of wooden boards and lime-washed walls where artisans are again producing handmade books. In the summer the processes are all amply explained in each room, while through the winter interesting fifty-minute guided tours are obligatory. Only four out of the original six thousand copies of *Ako Marama* survive, one of them in the small museum upstairs, which also charts the changes the house has undergone.

The only other building to survive Hone Heke's ransacking of Russell was the prim, white, weatherboard **Christ Church**, Robertson Road, built in 1836 and now New Zealand's oldest surviving church – earlier examples at Kerikeri and Paihia having been lost. Unlike most churches of similar vintage, it was not a mission church but was built by local settlers: an appeal for public donations loosened the purse strings of Charles Darwin, who passed through the Bay of Islands at the time, long before he fell out with the church over his theory of evolution. In the mid-nineteenth century the church was besieged during skirmishes between Hone Heke's warriors and the British, leaving several still-visible bullet holes; the neat cemetery contains some of the oldest European graves in the country and numerous headstones inscribed in Maori.

The small **Russell Museum** (*Te Whare Taonga o Kororareka*), York Street (daily: late Dec–early Feb 10am–5pm; early Feb–late Dec 10am–4pm; $2.50), contains tolerable displays on Russell's whaling days, a few Maori pieces, fishing tackle left behind by Zane Grey and an impressive one-fifth scale model of Cook's *Endeavour*, which called in here in 1769. From the museum, a stroll along The Strand passes the rooms of the prestigious Bay of Islands Game Fishing Club, which was founded in 1924, and the Duke of Marlborough hotel – the original building on this site held New Zealand's first liquor licence.

At the end of The Strand, turn left into Wellington Street for a steep climb up to **Flagstaff Hill** (*Maiki*). The current flagpole was erected in 1857, some twelve years after the destruction of the fourth by Hone Heke (see Contexts, p.765), as a conciliatory gesture by a son of one of the chiefs who had ordered the original felling. The Confederation of Tribes flag, abandoned after the signing of the Treaty of Waitangi, is now flown on twelve significant days of the year, such as the anniversary of Hone Heke's death and the final day of the first Maori War. From Flagstaff Hill it is only a further kilometre to the **Tapeka Point Historic Reserve**, a former pa site on a headland at the end of the peninsula, a wonderfully defensible position with great views and abundant evidence of terracing. Another worthwhile one-kilometre stroll from Russell is to **Oneroa Bay** (Long Beach), a gently shelving beach sheltered from the prevailing wind and safe for swimming.

Eating and drinking

The range of **restaurants** in Russell is not especially varied, and prices are relatively high. **Drinking** options are no better, though there are a number of low-cost private clubs – the *RSA* on Cass Street and the *Bay of Islands Swordfish Club* on The Strand for example – which often welcome visitors.

The Duke of Marlborough Hotel, The Strand (☎09/403 7829). Well prepared traditional food is served in New Zealand's oldest licensed establishment, now a pricey hotel. The verandahed bar is a good place to idle over a daytime coffee.

The Duke of Marlborough Tavern, York St. Unreconstructed Kiwi pub with mainstream bar meals and a lively atmosphere.

The Gables, The Strand (☎09/403 7618). Expensive waterfront restaurant serving superb French-tinged but widely varied dishes from lamb fillets to chicken quesadilla in candlelit rooms built in 1847.

Quarterdeck, The Strand (☎09/403 7761). Moderately priced, mainly seafood restaurant on the front with dining in separate booths and lively drinking at the bar. Licensed.

Around Russell: Whangaruru Harbour

To the south and east of Russell lies the mixed kauri forest of the **Ngaiotonga Scenic Reserve** and some wonderful coastline around the **Whangaruru Harbour**. The twisting and incompletely sealed Russell Road runs through the region, closely tracing the coast from Orongo Bay, just south of Russell. Just beyond the Waikare Road turn-off for Kawakawa and Paihia, a side road leads to some fine stands of kauri visited on the **Ngaiotonga Kauri Grove Walk** (1km; 20min), the **Twin Bole Kauri Walk** (5min), and the **Ngaiotonga–Russell Forest Walkway** (21km; 9hr); the last is best tackled over two days with a tent.

Continuing along Russell Road, you'll reach the junction of the road to the scattered and predominantly Maori village of **RAWHITI**, the start of the challenging but rewarding **Cape Brett Tramping Track** (20km; 8hr). This terminates at the end of the peninsula, where you turn around and come back for another eight hours. Fortunately, there's a trampers' hut at the cape (21 beds; $8; annual hut pass not valid) with gas burners but no cooking gear. The track crosses private land and a fee (currently $7) is charged: check with DOC in Russell for the latest on registration, hut bookings – and access to sections of the peninsula, where possum control is periodically undertaken. The base of the Cape Brett peninsula is crossed by the **Whangamumu Walking Track** (4km; 1hr), which starts close to the Rawhiti Road junction, and runs through forest to a beach where the remains of a 1920s whaling operation can be seen.

At **NGAIOTONGA**, 20km south of Rawhiti, a dirt road branches 8km through lumpy farmland until you round a corner revealing the broad isthmus sweep of **Bland Bay** with great beaches on both sides. You can camp at the simple *Bland Beach Motor Camp* (☎09/433 6759; tent sites $8) or press on a further 2km to **Whangaruru North Head Scenic Reserve**, with yet more lovely beaches, fine walks around the end of the peninsula and a DOC campsite ($5) with water and toilets.

The main settlement on the mainland side of the Whangaruru Harbour is **OAKURA**, 12km south of Ngaiotonga along Russell Road. Not a great deal happens here but that is exactly its appeal, with no shortage of places to swim and walk, all with lovely sea and island views. There are a few **places to stay**, including the *Whangaruru Harbour Motor Camp*, Ohawiri Road (☎09/433 6806; tent sites $8.50, cabins ②, motel units ④), and the *Oakura Bay B&B*, 24 Rapata Rd (☎ & fax 09/433 6066; dorms ①, homestay ③), which also offers evening meals for $20 and kayak rental for $15 a day.

Kerikeri

KERIKERI, 25km northwest of Paihia, is both central to the historical development and yet geographically removed from the Bay of Islands. On initial acquaintance it is a very ordinary service town, surrounded by the orchards that form Kerikeri's economic mainstay and offer abundant opportunities for casual work. Two kilometres to the east of town, the thin ribbon of the Kerikeri Inlet forces its way from the sea to its tidal limit at **Kerikeri Basin**, the site chosen by Samuel Marsden for the Church Missionary Society's second mission. John Butler, the first Anglican missionary, arrived here in 1819 but initially struggled: requiring the trust, generosity and compliance of the Ngapuhi for the mission's survival, he found himself compromised, being ethically unable to sell the Ngapuhi the muskets they so wanted. As missions opened in the new settlements that sprang up after 1840, Kerikeri's importance waned.

In the 1920s the land was planted with sub-tropical crops, which thrive here: the mainstay is citrus, supported by tamarillos, feijoas, melons, courgettes, peppers and kiwifruit. For most of the year it is possible to get **seasonal work** in the orchards, either weeding, thinning or picking the produce. Work is easiest to find during the winter (April–August), when kiwifruit and mandarins are harvested; the best contacts are the managers of the hostels (see p.165), many of which also offer good weekly rates. Kerikeri's other claim to fame is the profusion of **craft shop**s scattered among the orchards and frequently featuring on tour-bus itineraries.

Arrival, information and accommodation

Northliner and InterCity **buses** (southbound around 8am and northbound around 1.30pm) stop outside Travel Lee's (☎09/407 8013) on Cobham Road. There is no official visitor centre, but Ann's Travel, Hub Mall (usually Mon–Fri 9am–5pm, Sat 9am–noon; ☎09/407 8667) dispenses bus tickets and can provide local **information**. The **DOC office**, 34 Landing Rd (☎09/407 8474), just over the river from the Stone Store, can advise on local walks and more ambitious treks into the Puketi and Omahuta forests (see p.168). Kerikeri is fairly well endowed with **accommodation** in all categories, but is particularly strong in budget places – a consequence of the area's popularity with long-stay casual workers. Seasonal **price fluctuations** are nowhere near as marked as in Paihia, though it is still difficult to find a place in January, when places are correspondingly expensive; prices quoted here are outside this post-Christmas madness.

MOTELS AND B&BS

Abilene Motel, 136 Kerikeri Rd (☎09/407 9203, fax 407 8608). Standard, centrally located motel in a garden setting with pool and spa. ⑤.

Central Motel, 58 Kerikeri Rd (☎09/407 8921 & 0800/867 667, fax 407 8005). Aptly named motel, with some newish and some older rooms around a pleasant pool and spa. ④.

The Gables, cnr SH10 & Te Ahuahu Rd, 5km west of Kerikeri (☎09/407 7923). Comfortable rooms in a rural colonial-style house; lovely breakfasts are served. ⑤.

Kemp Lodge, 134 Kerikeri Rd (☎ & fax 09/407 8295). Three pleasant and modern self-contained cottages close to town, and complete with TV and video, solar-heated pool and spa. ④.

The Pines, 132 Kerikeri Rd (☎ & fax 09/407 6150). Appealing and stylish B&B with a bold colour scheme and a full kitchen for guests' use; rates include continental breakfast. ⑤.

The Stone Cottage, 79 Hone Heke Rd (☎09/407 6504, fax 407 6508). Attractive two-storey stone cottage equipped with pool, spa and attractively decorated rooms. Dinner available for an extra $20 per person. ⑤.

Stoneybroke, Edmonds Rd, 1km east of town beside Kerikeri Inlet (☎09/407 7371). Pleasant homestay with interesting and interested hosts. ④.

HOSTELS AND CAMPSITES

Aranga Holiday Park, Kerikeri Rd (☎09/407 9326, fax 407 9897). Large streamside site on the edge of town with a spacious area for tents, well-equipped standard cabins, self-catering tourist flats and single rooms for long-stayers at a bargain $80 a week. Friday nights feature a major barbecue, served with bread and salads. Tent sites $8, dorms ①, cabins ②, flats ③.

Hideaway Lodge, Wiroa Rd, 4km west of Kerikeri (☎ & fax 09/407 9773). Large, slightly run-down but well-appointed hostel, with bikes to get into town. Reduced weekly rates are popular with folk stopping to work around Kerikeri, who also appreciate the large pool and games room after a hard day in the orange groves. Tent sites $8, dorms ①, rooms ②–③.

Hone Heke Lodge, 65 Hone Heke Rd (☎ & fax 09/407 8170). Central hostel with six-bed dorms, each with a fridge and cooking gear, and doubles and twins, some en suite. There's also a games room and barbecue area. Tent sites $8, dorms ①, rooms ②.

Kerikeri Farm Hostel, SH10, 5km west (☎09/407 6989). Top-class hostel on an organic citrus orchard, with comfortable dorms and rooms in a lovely wooden house. Rates are high for Kerikeri but well worth it; dinner ($8–10) and breakfast also available. Dorms ①, rooms ②.

Kerikeri YHA, Main Rd (☎09/407 9391, fax 407 9328). Well-placed hostel close to the centre but showing its age. Dorms ①, rooms ②.

The Town

The only way to get a sense of Kerikeri's past importance is to make straight for **Kerikeri Basin**, nearly 2km east of the current town. It was here, in 1821, that mission carpenters started work on what is now New Zealand's oldest European-style building, **Kemp House** (daily 10am–5pm, closed Thurs & Fri May–Oct; $5), a restrained two-

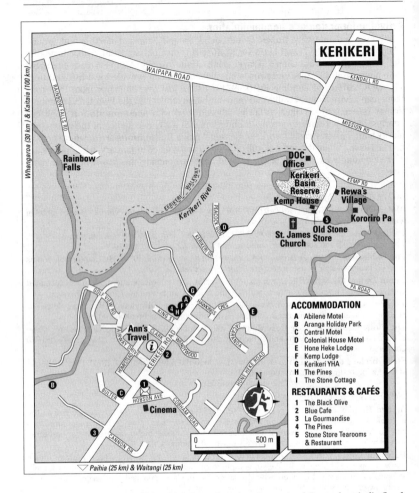

KERIKERI

WAIPAPA ROAD

KENDALL RD

MISSION RD

Whangaroa (30 km) & Kaitaia (100 km)

RAINBOW FALLS RD

Rainbow Falls

KERIKERI WALKWAY

Kerikeri River

PEACOCK GDN

KERIKERI DR

DOC Office

KEMP RD

Kerikeri Basin Reserve

Kemp House

Rewa's Village

Kororiro Pa

Old Stone Store

St. James Church

PA ROAD

GOLF VIEW RD

FAIRWAY DRIVE

HOMESTEAD RD

Ann's Travel

KING ST

CLARK

WIRINWOOD

KERIKERI ROAD

BUTLER

HAWKINS CRES

VERANDA

COBHAM ROAD

Cinema

HOBSON AVE

CANNON DR

HONE HEKE ROAD

N

ACCOMMODATION
A Abilene Motel
B Aranga Holiday Park
C Central Motel
D Colonial House Motel
E Hone Heke Lodge
F Kemp Lodge
G Kerikeri YHA
H The Pines
I The Stone Cottage

RESTAURANTS & CAFÉS
1 The Black Olive
2 Blue Cafe
3 La Gourmandise
4 The Pines
5 Stone Store Tearooms & Restaurant

0 ———— 500 m

Paihia (25 km) & Waitangi (25 km)

storey Georgian colonial affair which has miraculously survived fire and periodic flooding. The first occupants, missionary John Butler and family, soon moved on and by 1832 the house was in the hands of lay missionary and blacksmith James Kemp, who extended the three-up-three-down design.

The only other extant building from the mission station is the **Old Stone Store** (daily 10am–5pm), immediately adjacent and ranked as the country's oldest stone building, constructed mostly of local stone with keystones and quoins of Sydney sandstone. Completed in 1835 as a central provision store for the Church Missionary Society, it successively served as a munitions store for troops garrisoned here to fight Hone Heke, then a kauri trading store and a shop, before being opened to the public in 1975. Flooding and the predations of heavy passing traffic have taken their toll, forcing a major restoration project which has recently been completed.

Opposite the Old Stone Store, a five-minute path along the river leads to the well-delineated site of local chief Hongi Hika's **Kororipo Pa**, passing the site where, in the

1820s, he had a European-style house built. The pa commands a hill on a prominent bend in the river, a relatively secure base from which to launch inter-tribal attacks using their newly acquired firearms. Signs help interpret the dips and humps in the ground, but you'll get a better appreciation of pre-European Maori life from **Rewa's Village**, 1 Landing Road (daily 10am–4pm or later, honesty box entry after hours; $2), a 1969 reconstruction of a fishing village across the river from the pa site. It comes complete with marae, weapons and kumara stores, and authentic hangi site with an adjacent shell midden; the entrance kiosk screens a short video on the history of the area. Opposite is the **Kerikeri Basin Reserve** and the start of a track (1hr each way) past the swimming holes at Fairy Pools to the impressively undercut **Rainbow Falls**, which are also accessible off Waipapa Road, 3km north of the Basin.

Elsewhere Kerikeri is dominated by orchards, and the roads running between them (especially SH10 and Kerikeri Road) come studded with **craft outlets**. The free and widely available *Kerikeri Art & Craft Trail* leaflet advertises the major ones; you can easily spend a day trawling round them all. A few highly regarded establishments include The Red Barn, right in town at 127 Kerikeri Rd (☎09/407 8367), which combines local **ceramics** with predominantly Indian handicrafts; The Kauri Workshop, Kerikeri Rd, closer to SH10 (☎09/407 9196), stocks just about everything you could conceivably make out of **kauri**; Blue Gum Pottery, northwest of town on SH10, lets you watch the making of their mostly pastel-shaded **pots** at their shop a few metres from the cooperatively run Origin (☎09/407 9065). The last is probably the best of the lot, with a wide selection of **knitwear**, handmade **paper**, pottery and some fine wooden furniture.

Eating and entertainment

Kerikeri's eating options initially appear to consist of **takeaways** and unappealing **cafés**, but far better places can be found, including one of the finest **restaurants** north of Auckland. **Entertainment** is thinner on the ground but there is always the sixty-year-old and lovingly restored Cathay Cinema, on Hobson Avenue (☎09/407 9121), which shows first-run movies and has a good café attached.

The Black Olive, Kerikeri Rd. Compact eat-in and take-out pasta restaurant, which also bakes good traditional and gourmet pizza. BYO.

Blue Café, The Village Mall. Small, laid-back café tucked away in an arcade that's fine for a daytime coffee or a range of meals, including some Malaysian-inspired rice and noodle dishes.

La Gourmandise, Kerikeri Rd (☎09/407 6606). One of Northland's best restaurants, located on the outskirts of Kerikeri with an attractive verandah setting. Tuck into gorgeous European and Indonesian influenced dishes, but expect to pay $40 for three courses. Closed Tues; licensed.

The Pines Breakfast Bar & Grill, 132 Kerikeri Rd (☎ & fax 09/407 6150). Cheery, casual and well-priced restaurant serving good breakfasts and weekend brunches as well as light lunches, char-grills, and seafood and vegetarian dinners. Licensed.

Rocket Café, Kerikeri Rd, 3km west of town. Excellent modern breakfast and lunch café on the site of *Robbs Fruit Winery*, an orchard specializing in feijoa, kiwifruit and boysenberry wines and preserves. A fine range of quiches, pizzas and filo rolls stuffed with imaginative fillings, plus great coffee are served outside or in the airy interior.

Stone Store Tearooms & Restaurant, Kerikeri Basin. Good quiches, cakes and coffee in an ancient cottage or, preferably, outside on the verandah beside the Kerikeri Inlet.

Around Kerikeri

A natural progression from Kerikeri's Kemp House is **WAIMATE NORTH** and **Te Waimate Mission House** (daily except Sun 10am–12.30pm & 1.30–4.30pm; $5), New Zealand's second-oldest European building. Now pretty much in the middle of nowhere, in the 1830s this was the centre of a vigorous Anglican mission, the first to be established on an inland site chosen for its fertile soils and large Maori population. At the time, missionaries were keen to add European **agricultural techniques** to the language and religion they were teaching the Maori, and they made use of the grounds already cultivated by the missionaries' friend and Ngapuhi chief, Hongi Hika. By 1834 locally grown wheat was being milled at the river, orchards were flourishing and crops were sprouting – all duly impressing Charles Darwin, who visited the following year. Ultimately though, transport difficulties made this first European-style farm uneconomic and the mission declined. The **house** itself was built by converts in 1831–32 and almost entirely fashioned of local kauri. Though much modified over the years, it has been restored as accurately as possible to its original design and the somewhat lifeless rooms have been stocked with furniture and effects, giving some insight into the early mission lifestyle. The lush surrounding gardens are open daily during daylight hours, as is the modest mission **Church of St John the Baptist** just near by.

The nearest substantial town is **KAIKOHE**, almost equidistant from both coasts and seemingly displaced in Northland, where so much is water-focused. There's little reason to stop, but the staff at the **visitor centre**, Broadway (Dec–March daily 9am–5pm; April–Nov Mon–Fri 9am–5pm; ☎09/401 1693), will give directions to **Ngawha Springs** (daily 7am–9.45pm; $2), 7km to the east, where naturally heated waters fill Waiariki Pools, a series of eight tanks surrounded by wooden boardwalks but otherwise unfettered by tourist trappings.

The stands of the **Puketi and Omahuta native forests**, 20km north of Kaikohe, jointly comprise one of the largest continuous tracts of kauri forest in the north. The easiest and most rewarding access is to the east of the forest: head north off SH1 at Okaihau, or west off SH10 just north of Kerikeri along Pungaere Road. Both routes bring you to the **Puketi Recreation Area**, where there's a campsite and a trampers' hut at the start of the 20-kilometre **Waipapa River Track** – best done in one short (5hr) and one long (8hr) day, camping midway. This and several other worthwhile tracks are detailed in DOC's *Puketi and Omahuta Forests* leaflet (50¢) which, along with camping and hut details, can be obtained from the DOC office in Kerikeri.

North to Doubtless Bay

North of the Bay of Islands everything gets a lot quieter. There are few towns of any consequence along the coast and it is the peace and slow pace that attracts visitors to an array of glorious beaches and the lovely Whangaroa Harbour. The first stop north of Kerikeri is tiny **Matauri Bay**, where a hilltop memorial commemorates the Greenpeace flagship, *Rainbow Warrior*, which was sunk in Auckland Harbour in 1985. The wreck now lies off the coast of Motutapere Island, a site which can be dived from here. A mostly unsealed backroad continues north by way of fabulous sea views from headlands and gorgeous beaches – **Te Ngaire**, **Wainui Bay**, **Mahinepua Bay** and **Tauranga Bay** – before delivering you to the **Whangaroa Harbour**, one of the most beautiful in Northland and an excellent place to go sailing or kayaking.

Further north is the huge bite out of the coast called **Doubtless Bay**, which had two celebrated discoverers: Kupe, said to have first set foot on Aotearoa in Taipa; and Cook, who sailed past in 1769 and pronounced it "doubtless, a bay". French explorer, Jean François Marie de Surville, was also close by and, a week later, became the first European to enter the bay, though he departed in an undignified hurry after a dispute with local Maori over a missing dinghy – and it was Cook's moniker that stuck. Bounded on the west and north by the sheltering **Karikari Peninsula**, the bay offers safe boating, a boon for **Kiwi vacationers** who enjoy the abundant fish and dolphins. In January you can barely move up here and you'll struggle to find accommodation, the shoulder seasons can be surprisingly quiet and outside December, January and February the relatively high room prices drop to more affordable levels. Most of the bay's facilities cluster along the southern shore in a string of beachside settlements – **Coopers Beach**, **Cable Bay** and **Taipa Bay** – running west from picturesque Mangonui.

Matauri Bay

The high ridge behind **MATAURI BAY**, 20km north of Kerikeri and 10km off SH10, provides the dramatic first glimpse of a long curving sandy bay that stretches north to a stand of Norfolk pines and the offshore Cavalli Islands. The northern limit of the main bay is defined by Matauri Bay Hill, topped by a distinctive stone and steel memorial to the *Rainbow Warrior* (see box below), now scuttled off Motutapere Island, one of the Cavalli Islands.

Missionary Samuel Marsden first set foot in Aotearoa in 1814 at Matauri Bay, where he mediated between the Ngati Kura people – who still own the bay – and some Bay of Islands Maori, a process commemorated by the quaint wooden **Samuel Marsden Memorial Church** on the road in, and a small memorial behind the beach. The strength of Maori culture in the bay is evident from the finely carved *Mataatua II* **waka** further north along the beach: constructed in the early 1990s, its name echoes the Ngati Kura's ancestral *waka*, which lies in waters nearby. The resonance of this legendary canoe partly led the Ngati Kura to offer a final resting place to the wreck of the *Rainbow Warrior*.

FRENCH NUCLEAR TESTING IN THE PACIFIC

The French government has always claimed that nuclear testing is completely safe, but for decades has persisted in conducting its tests on the tiny Pacific atolls of **Mururoa** and Fangataufa, 15,000km from Paris and 4000km northeast of New Zealand.

In 1966 France turned its back on the 1963 **Partial Test Ban Treaty**, which outlawed **atmospheric testing**, and relocated Pacific islanders away from their ancestral villages to make way for a barrage of tests over the next eight years. The French authorities claimed that "Not a single particle of radioactive fallout will ever reach an inhabited island" – and yet radiation was routinely detected as far away as Samoa, Fiji and even New Zealand. Increasingly antagonistic public opinion forced the French to conduct their tests **underground** in deep shafts, where another 200 detonations took place, threatening the geological stability of these fragile coral atolls. Surveys with very limited access to the test sites have since revealed severe **fissuring**; there is also evidence of radioactive isotopes in the Mururoa lagoon, as well as submarine slides and subsidence.

In 1985, **Greenpeace** coordinated a New Zealand-based protest flotilla, headed by its flagship, *Rainbow Warrior*, but before the fleet could set sail from Auckland, the French secret service sabotaged the *Rainbow Warrior*, detonating two bombs below the water-line. As rescuers recovered the body of Greenpeace photographer Fernando Pereira, two **French secret service** agents posing as tourists were arrested. Flatly denying all knowledge at first, the French government was finally forced to admit to what David Lange (then Prime Minister of New Zealand) described as "a sordid act of international state-backed terrorism". The two captured agents were sentenced to ten years in jail, but France used all its international muscle to have them serve their sentences on a French Pacific island; they both served less than two years.

In 1995, to worldwide opprobrium, France announced a further series of tests. Greenpeace duly dispatched *Rainbow Warrior II*, which was impounded by the French navy on the tenth **anniversary** of the sinking of the original *Rainbow Warrior*. In early 1996 the French finally agreed to stop nuclear testing in the Pacific and it is only now that **relations** between the French and New Zealand governments are becoming more amicable. In April 1997, the two **foreign ministers** met for the first time since the bombing of the *Rainbow Warrior*.

Sculptor Chris Booth was commissioned to design the **Rainbow Warrior Memorial**, composed of a stone arch symbolizing a rainbow and the salvaged bronze propeller of the vessel, which is reached by a well-worn path from near the holiday park at the foot of the hill. Two-tank **dive trips** out to the wreck, ten minutes by boat, can be organized through Matauri Cat Charters (☎09/405 0525), also at the holiday park, who charge $135 with full gear rental. The best visibility is typically in April; from September to November plankton obscure the view.

Facilities in the bay are limited to a **shop** opposite the family-orientated *Matauri Bay Holiday Park* (☎09/405 0525; tent sites $9, on-site vans ②), and *Ocean's* (☎09/405 0417; ⑥), a self-contained **resort** with spacious units, licensed restaurant and dinghies for guests' use.

The Whangaroa Harbour

Time spent around the virtually landlocked **Whangaroa Harbour** is the perfect antidote to Bay of Islands commercialism. The scenery, albeit on a smaller scale, is easily a match for its southern cousin and, despite the limited facilities, you can still get out onto the water for a cruise or to join the big game fishers. Narrow inlets forge between cliffs and steep hills, most notably the two bald volcanic plugs, St Paul and St Peter, rising up behind the harbour's two settlements, **WHANGAROA** and **TOTARA NORTH**. The harbour wasn't always so quiet though, being among the first areas to receive the attention of pioneers, most famously those on the *Boyd*, a ship which called here in 1809 to load kauri spars for shipping to Britain. A couple of days after its arrival, all 66 crew were killed and the ship burned by local Maori in retribution for the crew's mistreatment of Tara, a high-born Maori sailor who had apparently transgressed the ship's rules. A British whaler avenged the incident by burning the entire Maori village, thereby sparking off a series of skirmishes which spread over the north for five years, substantially reducing sea captains' enthusiasm for the Whangaroa Harbour. Nonetheless, the vast stands of kauri were soon being hacked away and the harbour was said by contemporary observers to be choked with logs; some were rafted to Auckland, while others were milled at Totara North, which claims the oldest operational mill in the country.

The single best thing to do around Whangaroa is to spend a day on the *Snow Cloud* (10–11hr; $60, including meals; ☎09/405 0523), an eleven-metre **yacht** which typically sails out to the Cavalli Islands, stopping to snorkel, sunbathe and walk. Overnight **cruises** and dive trips can also be organized for small groups (4–8 people; from $500). The next best bet is to **kayak** with Northland Sea Kayaking (☎09/405 0381), on the northeastern flank of the harbour; day-trips start at $55, and include free self-catering accommodation for the number of days you spend paddling. Land-based activities primarily mean **walks**, two of the nicest being the short hike up St Paul from the top of Old Hospital Road in Whangaroa and DOC's **Lane Cove Walk** (1hr 30min–2hr each way) from Totara North past freshwater pools, mangroves and viewpoints to the Lane Cove Hut ($8) on the Pekapeka Bay. The hut has a solar-heated shower, water, toilets and plenty of sandflies, but you'll need your own cooking gear.

Practicalities

No public **transport** reaches either the small community of Whangaroa, 6km off SH10 on the southern side of the harbour, or the tiny Totara North, 4km off the highway on the northern side.

Most of the harbour's limited **accommodation** clusters along the road to Whangaroa, first up being the *Whangaroa Motor Camp* (☎09/405 0306; tent sites $8, cabins ②), 3km south of the centre. Two pricier places follow: *Truant Lodge Motel*

(☎09/405 0133; ⑤) and *Motel Whangaroa* (☎09/405 0022; ④); and there are basic rooms at Whangaroa's longstanding **pub**, the *Marlin Hotel* (☎09/405 0347; ③), right opposite the wharf. For something different, there's the luxurious *Kingfisher Lodge* (☎09/405 0164; ⑦), out towards the harbour heads and only accessible by boat. The three **hostels** close to the harbour are all excellent in their own way. In Whangaroa, the *Sunseeker Lodge*, Old Hospital Road (☎ & fax 09/405 0496; dorms ①, rooms ②), perched on the hill overlooking the harbour, benefits from a personable and helpful host and relaxed atmosphere; sea kayaks are available for guests' use. At Totara North, the bargain *Historic Gumstore Hostel* (☎09/405 1703; dorms ①, rooms ②) is a little run-down but overhangs the mangroves and is cosy enough. Just over a kilometre north of the Totara North turn-off, is the welcoming *Kahoe Farms Hostel*, on SH10 (☎09/405 1804; tent sites $10, dorms ①, rooms ②), a nicely restored homestead tucked in one corner of a working cattle farm, where people kickback for days, fuelled by Stefano's fine pizza, bread and espresso; bushwalks, kayaking through the mangroves ($30 a day), horse riding ($15 an hour) and bike riding (free) entertain guests.

Small **shops** in Whangaroa and Totara North provide for self-caterers, and the *Marlin Hotel* and the *Whangaroa Big Gamefish Club*, opposite each other in Whangaroa, serve reliable, if unexceptional, **seafood** dishes.

Mangonui and around

There's an undeniably antiquated air to **MANGONUI**, an attractive and increasingly visited village strung along a sheltered half-kilometre of harbour off Doubtless Bay. A handful of two-storey buildings with wooden, street-level verandahs have been preserved and a few trinket shops nestle between a clutch of cafés, but this is still very much a working village, with a lively fishing wharf and a traditional grocery perched on stilts over the water. It makes the most obvious stopping point on the way north, with excellent beaches nearby and a waterfront where you can successfully catch your supper over an afternoon beer and have it cooked up at one of the local restaurants.

Mangonui means "big shark", a name recalling an incident when the legendary chief Moehuri's *waka* was led into the harbour by such a fish. But it was whales and the business of revictualling **whaling** ships that made the town: one apocryphal story tells of a harbour so packed with ships that folk could cross from one side to the other by leaping between boats. As whaling diminished, the kauri trade took its place, chiefly around Mill Bay, the cove five minutes' walk to the west. While ships were being repaired and restocked at Mangonui, barrels were being fixed a couple of kilometres west beside a stream crossing the strand which became known as **COOPER'S BEACH**, a glorious and well-shaded sweep backed by a string of motels. The beach is enormously popular in January, but at other times you can pretty much have it to yourself.

Another couple of kilometres west, the smaller settlement of **CABLE BAY** owes its existence to its short-lived role as the terminus of the 1902 trans-Pacific cable; in 1912, the telegraph station was moved to Auckland. The Taipa River separates Cable Bay from the beachside village of **TAIPA**, now the haunt of sunbathers and swimmers but historically significant as the spot where Kupe, the discoverer of Aotearoa in Maori legend, first set foot on the land.

Diversions in the district are limited to visiting the **Rangikapiti Pa Historic Reserve**, off Rangikapiti Rd (unrestricted entry), chiefly noted for its fabulous bay views; **dolphin** encounters with Doubtless Bay Adventures ($75; ☎09/406 0538); and **diving** off the Karikari Peninsula and elsewhere with Crystal Coast Seabed Safaris (☎09/406 0592). Resort dives go for $75, $45 for a second on the same day; and for $135 you can dive the *Rainbow Warrior* wreck, though these trips operate only on Wednesdays and Fridays.

Practicalities

SH10 bypasses the Mangonui waterfront, which is reached on a 2km loop road plied once a day by southbound and northbound Northliner and InterCity services. **Buses** stop outside the Wilton's Garage, Beach Road (☎09/406 0024), where you can also buy tickets. The **visitor centre** (daily: Dec–May 9am–9pm; June–Nov 9am–5pm; ☎09/406 1190, fax 406 0818), a few metres along Beach Road, can point you to accommodation, both here and in Cooper's Beach.

ACCOMMODATION

Most prominent of Mangonui's places is the turn-of-the-century *Mangonui Hotel*, Beach Rd (☎09/406 0003, fax 406 0015; ④–⑤), right opposite the harbour and with an excellent upstairs verandah for whiling the day away. Rooms are fairly plain and the best ones with harbour views go quickly, so book ahead or arrive early. Further around the shore, the tastefully decorated rooms in the even more ancient *Old Oak Inn*, Waterfront Drive (☎ & fax 09/406 0665; ④), are small but characterful. Best of the **B&Bs** are the waterside *Mill House Lodge* (☎09/406 0673, fax 406 0007; ⑤), ten minutes' walk from town by the Mill Bay Cruising Club, and *Mac 'n' Mo's*, 58 Main Rd (☎ & fax 09/406 0538; ④), a little further out in Cooper's Beach.

Motels are scattered liberally among the communities. Mangonui has the *Acacia Lodge*, Mill Bay Rd (☎ & fax 09/406 0417; ④–⑥), with the more expensive rooms featuring balconies and spa baths; while Cooper's Beach has the luxurious *Beach Lodge*, 97 Main Rd (☎ & fax 09/406 0068; ⑦), right by the water and with all mod cons, and the considerably more modest *Far North Motel*, SH10 (☎09/406 0271; dorms ①, motel units ④), which also has basic backpacker dorms. The closest dedicated **hostel** is the diminutive *Coopers Beach Backpackers*, 83 SH10 (☎09/406 1024; ①), right beside Cooper's Beach.

EATING, DRINKING AND ENTERTAINMENT

Mangonui has the best range of places to eat north of Kerikeri. Besides the *Old Oak Inn*, which has a licensed and BYO **restaurant** serving tasty light lunches and evening dinners, there's good mid-priced eating at the Mangonui Hotel's *Donnybrooke Bar & Brasserie*; fine sandwiches, soups and pizzas at reasonable prices from *Café Nina* on Waterfront Drive; and the best meals for miles around at *The Slung Anchor Kitchen & Bar*, Beach Rd (☎09/406 1233), a café and restaurant which produces imaginative seafood concoctions and fine gourmet pizza to eat in or take away. Mangonui boasts the finest **fish and chips** in the north – some would say in the country – at the wharfside *Mangonui Fish Shop*, also on Beach Road. The **bar** at the Mangonui Hotel is the focus of the town's more rumbustious social life and occasionally hosts bands.

The Karikari Peninsula

Doubtless Bay to the east and Rangaunu Harbour to the west are both bounded by the crooked arm of the **Karikari Peninsula** as it strikes north, its flat forearm and lumpy fist swathed in unspoiled golden- and white-sand beaches which, at least outside the peak season, have barely a soul on them. There is no public transport, facilities are limited and, without diving or fishing gear, you'll have to resign yourself to lazing on the beaches and swimming from them – and there can be few better places to do just that.

The initial approach across a low and scrubby isthmus is less than inspiring, though it is worth stopping briefly at **Lake Ohia**, 1km off SH10, which has gradually drained to reveal the stumps of a 40,000-year-old kauri forest thought to have been destroyed by some prehistoric cataclysm. A kilometre on, the **Gum Hole Reserve** has a short trail past holes left by kauri gum diggers (see box on p.177 for more on their exploits).

Eight kilometres later, a side road leads to the peninsula's west coast and the **Puheke Scenic Reserve**, a gorgeous dune-backed beach that's desolate outside the season but popular in January. There's another fine strand nearby at the beachside hamlet of **RANGIPUTA**, with the *White Sands Motor Lodge* (☎09/408 7080; ④) and, 1km back down the road, the attractive, spa-equipped *Reef Lodge*, Rangiputa Rd (☎ & fax 09/408 7100; ⑤), set among lawns and backed by a golden beach.

The peninsula's arterial road continues past the Rangiputa junction to the community of **TOKERAU BEACH**, a cluster of houses and a couple of shops at the northern end of the grand sweep of Doubtless Bay. Here accommodation is provided by *Tokerau Beach Backpackers*, Tokerau Beach Road (☎ & fax 09/406 7943; ①), a pristine purpose-built place with free use of bikes and plenty of opportunities to go sea kayaking or fishing and diving; boat charters start at $200 a day for up to four people.

The Karikari Peninsula saves its best until last: **Maitai Bay**, 20km north off SH10, is a matchless double arc of golden sand split by a rocky knoll, all encompassed by the *Maitai Bay Campground* ($6 per adult), the largest DOC campsite in Northland. Much of the site is *tapu* to local Maori, and you are encouraged to respect the sacred areas, which is easy enough for most of the year when the site is deserted, but more problematic when the site is splitting its seams in early January.

Kaitaia and around

KAITAIA, 40km west of Mangonui, is a town of little charm and less excitement which nevertheless plays an important role as the Far North's largest commercial centre. As the starting point for some of the best bus trips to Cape Reinga and Ninety Mile Beach (see p.176), Kaitaia is on most visitors' itineraries and makes a tolerable base for ventures north, though with your own transport you might want to whizz round the sights, refuel and push on.

Kaitaia's donned its service-town mantle once the extractive industries petered out. A Maori village already flourished here when the first European missionary, Joseph Matthews, came looking for a **mission** site in 1832. The protection of the mission encouraged pastoralists who, by the 1880s, found themselves swamped by **gum diggers** keen to plunder the underground deposits around Lake Ohia (see p.172) and **Ahipara** (see p.175). Many early arrivals were young Dalmatians (mostly Croats) fleeing tough conditions in what was then part of the Austro-Hungarian Empire. The only evidence of this episode in Kaitaia's history is a telephone directory full of Croat names, a Serbo-Croat welcome at the entrance to town, and a cultural society which holds a traditional dance each year.

The Town

The best place to gain a sense of the area is the surprisingly good **Far North Regional Museum**, 6 South Rd (Christmas–Jan daily 10am–5pm; Feb–Christmas Mon–Fri 10am–5pm; $2.50), with arresting displays on pretty much every aspect of local life and history. The room of Ngati Kahu pieces is particularly strong; you enter under one of three copies of the twelfth- or thirteenth-century **Kaitaia Carving**. The carving was found around 1920 on the outskirts of Kaitaia and represents the transitional period as Polynesian art was taking on distinctly Maori elements; the original is held in the Auckland Museum (see p.84). Another rare find is a series of boards from palisades once surrounding pa sites: these were mostly burned or rotted away, but several examples survive here. Elsewhere in the room, beautifully woven and decorative flax-and-kiwi-feather cloaks contrast with utilitarian items – a carved canoe bailer, collections of clubs, spears and oratory staffs – and a complete skeleton of a juve-

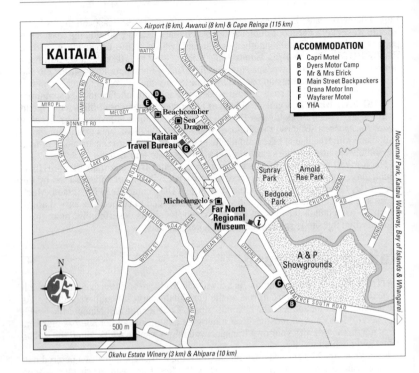

Airport (6 km), Awanui (8 km) & Cape Reinga (115 km)

KAITAIA

WATTS
GRIGG ST
JAMIESON RD
MIRO PL
MELODY
BONNETT RD
WILLIAMS ST
FOLEY
ARCHIBALD
LAKE RD
PUKEPOTO ROAD
VEGAR ST
DOMINION ROAD
RANK
WORTH ST
OKAHU RD
REDAN RD

KITCHENER ST
ALLEN
BELL DR
QUINN
MATTHEWS ST
TERENCE
PUCKEY AVE
COMMERCE SOUTH ROAD
EMPIRE
MELBA
OXFORD ST

PARKDALE

Beachcomber
Sea Dragon
Kaitaia Travel Bureau
Michelangelo's
Far North Regional Museum

Sunray Park
Arnold Rae Park
Bedgood Park
CHURCH ROAD
OKAHA ROAD
KONGAHU
TE AHU

A & P Showgrounds
COMMERCE SOUTH ROAD

N

0   500 m

ACCOMMODATION
A   Capri Motel
B   Dyers Motor Camp
C   Mr & Mrs Elrick
D   Main Street Backpackers
E   Orana Motor Inn
F   Wayfarer Motel
G   YHA

Nocturnal Park, Kaitaia Walkway, Bay of Islands & Whangarei

Okahu Estate Winery (3 km) & Ahipara (10 km)

nile kuri, the Polynesian dog brought to New Zealand by early Maori settlers, which died out around a century ago. Pride of place in the main room goes to a huge one-and-a-half-tonne anchor, the earliest European artefact to be left in New Zealand and one of three left by de Surville in 1769 when he departed in haste (see p.763). The maritime theme continues through a collection of ships in glass cases, including a fine whaler made of matchsticks, and sundry bits and pieces from the *Rainbow Warrior*. Photographs of early gum-digging operations are supported by examples of the diggers' tools and polished pieces of prize gum in shades from pale amber to deep treacle.

Dalmatians steeped in viniculture grew the first grapes in the region, though the vineyards were soon abandoned and experts have long claimed that the climate is too moist for successful wine making. Nonetheless, New Zealand's northernmost winery, **Okahu Estate**, on the corner of Okahiu Road and Pukepoto Road (Oct–May daily 10am–6pm; ☎09/408 2066), 3km out on the road to Ahipara, has managed to produce small quantities of award-winning boutique wines – and offer free tastings.

As elsewhere throughout the north, Maori people make up a large proportion of the population and influence the local culture, though on a short visit this may not be particularly evident. One way around this is to join Tall Tale Travel 'n' Tours (2hr; $20, including $5 donation to the local marae; ☎09/408 1275) on a **Maori-led visit** to the working Te Rarawa **marae**, just outside Kaitaia. Times and itineraries are flexible and the emphasis is on fostering an understanding of Maori culture, in particular marae protocol, land issues and concepts of life, death and healing.

Practicalities

Once-daily InterCity and Northliner **buses** pull up outside Kaitaia Travel Bureau, 170 Commerce St (☎09/408 0540), which handles ticket sales. Kaitaia has one of only three tarmacked runways in Northland, 6km north near Awanui, so you can arrive **by air** direct from Auckland and the Bay of Islands with Air New Zealand Link's Eagle Air arm.

Kaitaia's **visitor centre** is at Jaycee Park, South Rd (Oct–March daily 8.30am–5pm; April–Sept Mon–Fri 8.30am–5pm, Sat & Sun 8.30am–noon; ☎ & fax 09/408 0879). Car rental is available but is prohibitively expensive and, since **rental cars** can't be driven along Ninety Mile Beach, you're better off taking a **bus tour** to Cape Reinga (see p.176).

Accommodation

Even in the peak season it is seldom difficult to obtain accommodation in Kaitaia at prices considerably lower than at the coastal resorts to the east. Of the **motels**, try the basic but perfectly adequate *Capri Motel*, 5 North Rd (☎ & fax 09/408 0224; ④) and the smarter *Wayfarer Motel*, 231 Commerce St (☎09/408 2600, fax 408 2601; ④), with spa and swimming pool. The *Orana Motor Inn*, 238–242 Commerce St (☎09/408 1510, fax 408 1512; ④), is more like a hotel, with a pool but no cooking facilities, and there are a few **homestays**, such as *Mr & Mrs Elrick*, 45 South Rd (☎09/408 3053; ③).

The **budget** market is catered for by an antiquated *YHA*, 160 Commerce St (☎09/408 1840; dorms ①, rooms ②), and the *Main Street Backpackers*, 235 Commerce St (☎09/408 1275, fax 408 1100; dorms ①, rooms ②), which actively promotes itself as New Zealand's first Maori backpackers; along with a hangi three nights a week and the opportunity to hand-carve bone pendants, they rent out bikes ($10 a day), provide free sand-toboggans and rent camping gear for use at Cape Reinga; their tour arm also organizes marae visits (see p.174). **Campers** should head for *Dyer's Motor Camp*, 67 South Rd (☎09/408 0333; tent sites $9).

Eating and drinking

Kaitaia's eating options are severely limited but slowly improving. For daytime **burgers**, sandwiches, **pizza** and decent coffee, make for *Michelangelo's*, 26 Commercial St, a diner where you can eat in or take away. More substantial **meals** are better at the *Sea Dragon*, 185 Commerce St, a reasonably priced BYO Chinese restaurant and takeaway, or the pricier and marginally more formal *Beachcomber Restaurant*, 222 Commerce St (☎09/408 2010; licensed), currently Kaitaia's pinnacle of culinary achievement and predictably strong on seafood. **Drinking** happens at three pubs along the main street, all much of a muchness and all drumming up custom with local bands at weekends.

Ahipara

Bus tours along Ninety Mile Beach turn off long before its final southern curl around to **AHIPARA**, a scattered village 15km west of Kaitaia that grew up around the Ahipara gumfields. A hundred kilometres of sand recede into sea spray to the north, while to the south the high flatlands of the Ahipara Plateau tumble to the sea in a cascade of golden dunes; the southernmost bay is known as Shipwreck Bay for the paddle-shaft of the *Favourite*, wrecked in 1870, which still sticks out of the surf.

At their peak, the **gumfields**, which were worked from around 1880 until World War II, supported three hotels and two thousand people. Unlike most fields, where experimental probing and digging was the norm, here the soil was methodically excavated, washed and sieved to extract the valuable gum. None of the machinery remains on the plateau, but gum can still be found – particularly in the stream that washes down into Shipwreck Bay. An unsealed road crosses the tablelands, but to see much you really need to head **onto the dunes** with quad bikes rented from Quad Bike Hire (☎09/409 4888); on production of a current driver's licence and $70, you're set free to bounce around the dunes for a couple of hours and, if the tide is right, return around the shore. A guided version with Tua Tua Tours (☎09/409 4875) costs $105 for three hours.

Practicalities

There are a few **places to stay** at Ahipara: the lovely *Siesta Guest House*, Tasman Heights Road (☎ & fax 09/409 2011; ⑥), offers de luxe B&B in a Mediterranean-style home with courtesy transfers from Kaitaia and dinner with wine for an extra $30 per person; or there's the simple *Pine Tree Lodge Motor Camp* (☎09/409 4864; tent sites $9). *Adriaan Lodge*, Reef View Road (☎ & fax 09/409 4888; dorms ①, rooms ③–④), has attractive self-contained units, a studio and backpacker bunks, plus fine **dining** and licensed **drinking** in its *Bay View Restaurant*.

Ninety Mile Beach and Cape Reinga

Northland's final gesture is the **Aupouri Peninsula**, a narrow, 100km-long finger of consolidated and grassed-over dunes ending in a lumpy knot of 60-million-year-old marine volcanoes. To Maori, it is known as *Te Hika o te Ika* ("the tail of the fish"), recalling the legend of Maui hauling up the North Island ("the fish") from the sea while sitting in his canoe (the South Island).

The most northerly accessible point is **Cape Reinga**, a spiritually significant place for all Maori, for this is the "place of leaping", where the spirits of the dead depart. Beginning their journey by sliding down the roots of an 800-year-old pohutukawa into the ocean, they climb out again on Ohaua, the highest of the Three Kings Islands, to bid a final farewell before returning to their ancestors in Hawaiiki. The spirits reach Cape Reinga along **Ninety Mile Beach**, a wide band of sand running straight for over a hundred kilometres (actually around 64 miles) along the western side of the peninsula. Most visitors follow the spirits, but in modern buses specifically designed for belting along the hard-packed sand at the edge of the surf then negotiating the quicksands of Te Paki Stream to return to the road. The main road runs more-or-less down the centre of the peninsula, following the hilly contours and seldom glimpsing the western ocean, which is kept tantalisingly out of sight by the thin pine ribbon of the **Aupouri Forest**. The forests, and the cattle farms that cover most of the rest of the peninsula, were previously the preserve of gum diggers, who worked the area intensively early this century.

If you've made it this far north, you'll already be familiar with the paucity of facilities in rural Northland so the Aupouri Peninsula doesn't come as much of a surprise. **Accommodation** is sporadically scattered along the way and ranges from some superlative primitive camping to motels, lodges and hostels. All tend to be very reasonably priced, reflecting the tendency of most visitors to pass through without stopping; however, all are very busy immediately after Christmas. There are a few **places to eat**, though nothing stays open after around 8pm. Pukenui and Waitiki both have a shop and expensive **petrol**.

Awanui and the Kauri Kingdom

AWANUI, 8km north of Kaitaia, was formerly the site of an important radio transmitter to the outside world but has become a dilapidated rural backwater notable chiefly for the convergence of the eastern and western roads north. Almost all buses to Cape

GETTING TO THE CAPE

The best way to experience the phenomenal length and wild beauty of Ninety Mile Beach is to take one of the **bus tours** based in Kaitaia, Mangonui and Paihia in the Bay of Islands. Those from Paihia are the most numerous but are also the longest (11hr), and tours starting further north give you less time in the bus and more time to explore. Their **content** varies but in essence they do the same trip, a loop up the Aupouri Peninsula and back, travelling SH1 in one direction and Ninety Mile Beach in the other, the order being dictated by the tide. **Highlights** include leaping or tobogganing down the sand dunes that flank Te Paki Stream, and the rambling and varied collection of the Wagener Museum.

From Kaitaia, there are currently three companies running trips to the cape, all picking up from your accommodation around 9am, fitting in a bit of sand tobogganing and returning by 5pm. All three are in fierce competition and frequently undercut prices, so check the latest offers when you arrive. Harrison's Cape Runner, 123 North Rd (☎09/408 1033) have informative and entertaining small-group tours for $40, with periodic specials bringing this down to $33. Sand Safaris, 221 Commerce St (☎09/408 1778), offer well-run, slightly more formal tours and charge around $10 more, while Fun Bus 2000, 6 Taaffe St (☎09/408 2873), are the cheapest of the lot, with a "no frills" trip for $25.

From Mangonui, Nor-East Coachlines ($50; ☎09/406 0244) charge $50, including pick-up from your accommodation.

From Paihia, the two big cruise companies dominate the Cape Reinga tour market. Most trips run daily, leaving at around 7.30am and going via Kerikeri, Mangonui and Awanui in one direction and passing Kaitaia and the kauri trees of the Puketi Forest in the other. Kings (☎09/402 8288) run both the all-in Cape Reinga Scenic ($75), and the pared-down Cape Reinga Express ($60). Fullers (☎09/402 7421) operate swanky custom-designed buses on the Cape Reinga Heritage ($89), which includes a marae visit, and the more sightseeing-orientated Cape Reinga Wanderer (Oct–May only; $79), with sand tobogganning, swimming and shellfish digging. Both companies offer ten percent **discounts** if you sign up for both a cruise and a cape trip. **Smaller operators** tend to use smaller vehicles and take a less rigid approach, letting the group fine-tune the itinerary and not fussing overly if things run past the scheduled return time: Northern Exposure Tours ($60; ☎09/402 8644 & 0800/573 875) use a minibus and include a beachside picnic lunch; 4x4 Dune Rider ($75; ☎09/402 8681) make the cape trip in a four-wheel-drive so you can get right off the beaten track, will pick up in Awanui, 7km north of Kaitaia, and will also drop you off and pick you up another day at no extra cost.

If for some unfathomable reason you are intent on seeing Cape Reinga and not bothered about driving Ninety Mile Beach, you can **fly** there from Paihia with *Salt Air Paihia* ($239; ☎09/402 8338), who land at Te Paki station and cover the last section by road, or overfly the cape with Kaitaia-based Blue Sky Scenics ($250; ☎09/406 7320).

GOING IT ALONE

Rental cars are **not insured** to drive on Ninety Mile Beach – and for good reason. Vehicles frequently get **bogged** in the sand and abandoned by their occupants, who return home with salutary photos of the roof sticking out of the surf. If you are determined to take your own vehicle for a spin on the beach, **seek local advice** and prepare your long-suffering car by spraying some form of water repellent on the spark plugs – CRC is a common brand. Schedule your trip to coincide with a **receding tide**, starting two hours after high water and preferably going in the same direction as the bus traffic that day; drive close to the water's edge, avoiding any soft sand, and slow down to cross streams running over the beach – they often have deceptively steep banks. If you do get stuck in **soft sand**, lowering the tyre pressure will improve traction. There are several **access points** along the beach, but the only ones realistically available to ordinary vehicles are the ones used by the tour buses: the southern access at **Waipapakauri Ramp**, 6km north of Awanui; and the northern one along **Te Paki Stream**, which involves negotiating 3km of quicksand – start in low gear and don't stop, no matter how tempting the dunes look.

Reinga stop 1km north at the **Ancient Kauri Kingdom** (shop daily 9am–5pm, workshop Mon–Fri only; free), a defunct dairy factory now operating as a sawmill, cutting and shaping huge peat-preserved kauri logs hauled out of swamps where they have lain for between 30,000 and 50,000 years. You can wander around parts of the factory and watch slabs of wood being fashioned into hot tubs, Gothic furniture and table tops, but, predictably, the emphasis is on the shop, which peddles trinkets and some rather nasty swamp-kauri clocks.

The main southern entrance to Ninety Mile Beach, the Waipapakauri Ramp, is 5km north.

Houhora and Pukenui

The peninsula's largest concentration of facilities spreads through an area known as **HOUHORA**. Thirty kilometres north of Awanui, a 3km side road turns east to **Houhora Heads** and the **Wagener Museum Complex**, a golf course, campsite, café and twin museums that are on the itinerary of almost all the cape-bound tour buses. It was here in 1860 that Polish pioneers used locally hewn timbers and mortar made from powdered sea shells to build the **Subritzky Homestead** (Christmas–Jan 8.30am–4.30pm; rest of year opens for bus tours; $3). Although now largely restored to it original state, some rooms still reflect the style of later inhabitants, particularly the last resident, Uncle Fred, who lived here until 1960 in a simple room with a bed made of gum sacks. When descendants of the Subritzkys decided to restore the homestead in the late 1960s, they could only obtain the original furniture as part of a large purchase that included the makings of the ever-expanding **Wagener Museum** (daily: Christmas–Jan 7am–7pm; rest of year 8.30am–4.30pm; $6). This somewhat random assemblage includes one of the world's largest collection of seashells, a similarly superlative array of nearly 500 chamber pots, musical instruments, Victorian arcade games, guns, polished kauri gum, ancient washing machines and Maori artefacts.

A couple of kilometres north along SH1, the junction of Lambs Road and Wharf Road marks the centre of **PUKENUI**, a working fishing village where good catches are to be had off the wharf.

Practicalities

The area around Houhora and Pukenui has the greatest concentration of **places to stay** on the Aupouri Peninsula. The spacious A-frame chalets of the *Houhora Chalets Motor Lodge*, on the corner of SH1 and Houhora Heads Rd (☎ & fax 409 8860; ④), and the *Houhora Heads Motor Camp*, Houhora Heads Rd (☎09/409 8564; tent sites $6.50, on-site vans ②), are both close to the Wagener Museum. **In Pukenui**, the attractive *Pukenui Lodge Motel and Backpackers Hostel*, on the corner of SH1 and Wharf Road (☎09/409 8837, fax 409 8704; dorms ①, doubles ②, motel units ⑤), has a swimming pool and **bikes for rent**. Other options include the compact *Pukenui Holiday Camp*, Lambs Road (☎ & fax 09/409 8803; tent sites $9, dorms ①, on-site vans ②, flats & cabins ③), and the small, low-key *Farmstay Backpacker*, 2km west on Lambs Road (☎09/409 7863; dorms ①, room ②), which also has bikes for rent. Some 6km north, a side road winds 6km east to the excellent *North Wind Lodge Backpackers*, Otaipango Rd, **Henderson Bay** (☎ & fax 09/409 8515; dorms ①, rooms ②), a modern house not far from a fine beach with bikes for guests' use, pick-ups from Pukenui and the possibility of joining up with Cape Reinga trips.

The only places to eat are the **café** at the Wagener Museum and the *Talk of the North* **restaurant** and takeaway at Pukenui, but you can always seek refuge at New Zealand's northernmost **pub**, the waterside *Houhora Tavern*, which lies 2km north of Pukenui, just off the highway.

The Parengarenga Harbour, Te Kao and Waitiki Landing

The Houhora Harbour is the last you see of the sea before the straggling arms of the **Parengarenga Harbour**, 20km further north, a place largely forgotten by most New Zealanders until 1985, when it was identified as the drop-off point for the limpet mines (delivered by yacht from New Caledonia) that were used to sabotage the *Rainbow Warrior*. Bends in the road occasionally reveal glimpses of the silica sands of the harbour's southern headland, which are pure white except in late February and early March when hundreds of thousands of bar-tailed godwits turn the vista black as they gather for their 12,000km journey to Siberia.

This whole area is intensely Maori, with the Ngati Kuri people owning much of the land and comprising the bulk of the population, particularly in the settlement of **TE KAO**, just south of the harbour on SH1. The only reason to stop is for the twin-towered Ratana Temple, one of the few remaining houses of the Ratana religion, which combines Christian belief with elements of Maori culture and spiritual belief. There's a shady streamside DOC **campsite** nearby at *Rarawa* ($5), 4km off SH1, just back from a fine white-sand beach.

The last place of any consequence before the land sinks into the ocean is **WAITIKI LANDING**, the end of the tar seal 24km from Cape Reinga and comprising only a **café**, takeaway and **accommodation** at the *Waitiki Landing Complex*, SH1 (☎09/409 7508, fax 409 7523; tent sites $7, bunks ①, cabins ③). From here, one twisting 15km road runs to the DOC **campsite** ($4) at Kapowairua ($4) beside the gorgeous **Spirits Bay**, the other to Cape Reinga, passing the Te Paki Stream entrance to Ninety Mile Beach.

Cape Reinga

The last leg from Waitiki Landing to **Cape Reinga** runs high through the hills before revealing the Tasman Sea and the huge dunes that foreshadow it. Magnificent seascapes unfold – until you hit the Cape Reinga car park, which is surrounded by a shabby cluster of meteorological and DOC buildings that detract from the scenic grandeur and spirituality of the place without contributing much in the way of comfort. There's a souvenir shop and a post office that closes once the tour buses have gone (around 4pm in summer). Escape quickly down the well-trodden ten-minute path to the Cape Reinga **lighthouse**, dramatically perched on a headland 165m above Colombia Bank, where the waves of the Tasman Sea meet the swirling currents of the Pacific Ocean in a boiling cauldron of surf. On clear days, the view from here is stunning: east to the Surville Cliffs of North Cape, west to Cape Maria van Diemen and north to the rocky **Three Kings Islands** 57km offshore, which were named by Abel Tasman, who first came upon them on the eve of Epiphany 1643.

Several dramatic **walks** radiate from the car park. Only avid beach nuts are going to get much pleasure out of the long sandy trudge of the Cape Reinga Walkway (134km) – with limited fresh water, no facilities and a cavalcade of buses passing each day. The walkway does, however, provide the conduit for shorter strolls: west to Te Werahi Beach (30min), and steeply east to Sandy Bay (30min one-way) and **Tapotupotu Bay** (*Ngatangawhiti*; 2hr), the latter also accessible by road and a common picnic stop for tour buses.

This far north, the only place to stay is the beautifully located DOC **campsite** at *Tapotupotu Bay* ($5).

The Hokianga Harbour

The Tasman Sea burrows deep into western Northland, the narrow mangrove-flanked fissures of the **Hokianga Harbour** snaking deep inland past tiny, almost moribund, communities. For a few days' relaxation, the tranquillity and easy pace of this rural backwater are hard to beat. You are likely to spend most of your time on the southern shores, from where the striking deep blue waters beautifully set off the mountainous sand dunes of North Head. The dunes are best seen from the rocky promontory of South Head high above the treacherous Hokianga Bar, or reached by boat for a little sand tobogganing. High forest ranges immediately to the south make excellent hiking and horse-trekking territory, and the giant kauri of the Waipoua Forest are within easy striking distance, but the focus is definitely the harbour.

It was here that the great Polynesian explorer **Kupe**, guided by the stars, moon and tides, first set foot on Aotearoa, arriving from his homeland in Hawaiiki during the tenth century. Some years later, he went back to Hawaiiki and the harbour became known as *Hokianganui-a-Kupe*, "the place of Kupe's great return". His descendants returned to become the ancestors of the Ngapuhi. **Cook** saw the Hokianga Heads in 1770 but didn't realize what lay beyond, and it wasn't until a **missionary** crossed the hill from the Bay of Islands in 1819 that Europeans became aware of Hokianga Harbour. Catholics, Anglicans and Wesleyans weren't slow to convert the Ngapuhi, gaining their trust and frequently intermarrying, setting the tone for the well-integrated Maori and European communities that exist today. The Hokianga soon rivalled the pre-eminence of the Bay of Islands and notched up several **firsts**: European boat building was begun here in 1826, the first signal station opened two years later, and the first Catholic Mass was celebrated in the same year. When the Treaty of Waitangi was signed, it was considered to have little validity until the Hokianga chiefs added their marks a few days later.

With the demise of kauri felling and milling that afflicted much of Northland, Hokianga became an **economic backwater**, with little industry, high unemployment and limited facilities. Over the last couple of decades, however, city dwellers, artists and craftspeople have snapped up bargain properties and moved up here in a small and fairly inconspicuous way, settling in **Kohukohu** on the north shore, a short ferry ride away to the south, and the two larger but still small-time resorts of **Opononi** and **Omapere**, opposite the dunes near the harbour entrance.

On a practical note, you'll need to stock up with cash before exploring the Hokianga and kauri forests: there are **no banks** between Kaitaia and Dargaville, 170km away to the south, though all towns have EFTPOS facilities and the *Omapere Tourist Hotel and Motel* in the centre of Omapere will often change money, but at poor rates.

Kohukohu and the northern Hokianga

Heading south from Kaitaia, the steep and tightly twisting SH1 passes through forests draped over the Mangamuka Ranges. After forty kilometres, you'll come to **Mangamuka Bridge** (the western entrance to the Omahuta Forest; see p.168), where a narrower and equally tortuous road follows the northernmost arm of the Hokianga Harbour 25km to Narrows Landing, the northern terminus for the Rawene Vehicular Ferry (daily 8am–6pm; car and driver $8, passengers $1; ☎09/405 7829), which runs on the hour southbound and half-hour northbound.

Four kilometres before the ferry, the road passes **KOHUKOHU**, a small waterside village where even the sole pub and grocery shop barely seem to be hanging on. Once the hub of Hokianga's kauri industry, the dairying that replaced it also lapsed, consigning Kohukohu to years of decline only partly arrested by the recent influx of rat-race refugees. The upshot of all this is a low-key place with some attractive, century-old wooden houses where the delightful places to stay make a brief sojourn tempting. For some gentle exploration of the surroundings, you can go on guided **kayaking** trips through mangroves and bush with *River's Kayak Hire* (3–4hr; $40; ☎09/405 5841).

The Kohukohu area has three excellent **places to stay**, the cheapest being *The Tree*

House (☎09/405 5855; tent sites $10, dorms ①, rooms ②), at **MOTUKARAKA**, 2km west of the ferry amid organic macadamia and fruit orchards. Dorms are spacious and well designed, as are the twins and doubles scattered around the grounds; mountain bikes can be rented ($16 a day), there's bone carving and flax weaving on offer and you can even get delicious meals delivered to your abode. The tasteful and aptly-named *Harbour Views Guesthouse*, Rakautapu Rd, Kohukohu (☎09/405 5815; ④), makes a lovely spot for a peaceful night or two with shady verandahs, nicely decorated rooms and dinner for $15. Back in Motukaraka, *Catherine & John Bawden*, Hawkins Road (☎09/405 5534; ④), run a welcoming farmstay in a former schoolhouse and also serve $15 dinners.

Rawene

The vehicular ferry shuttles from near Kohukohu across to appealing **RAWENE**, a slightly livelier village occupying the tip of Herd's Point, a peninsula roughly halfway up the harbour. Though almost isolated by the mud flats at low tide, Rawene's strategic position made it an obvious choice for the location of a timber mill, which contributed material for the town's attractive wooden buildings, some perched out on stilts over the water.

On a sunny day it is a pleasant place to saunter around, the only significant distraction being **Clendon House**, Clendon Esplanade (Nov–April Sat, Sun & Mon 10am–4pm; $2), on a hillside overlooking the harbour. This was the last residence of James Clendon, a pivotal figure in the early life of the colony, serving as US honorary consul, Justice of the Peace and member of the First Legislative Council before taking up a position as resident magistrate of the Hokianga district in 1861.The house wasn't finished until 1868 and Clendon only lived there for the four years prior to his death, leaving his part-Maori second wife, Jane, and eight kids. The colonial-era contents of the two-storey house owe more to Jane than James, but nonetheless reflect the relative wealth of someone in his position with much of the stuffy furniture emanating from Britain. The upper floor has been restored as a child's playroom and schoolroom and one room beside the verandah has been retained as the post office it once was.

Practicalities

Rawene's location at the only crossing point makes it an ideal base for exploring both sides of the harbour. Parnell Street is the main thoroughfare and passes the most convenient **accommodation**, the *Masonic Hote* (☎09/405 7822, fax 401 1768; ③), with small but decent traditional hotel rooms. There are a couple of respectable homestays at *Hokingamai*, Gundry Street (☎09/405 7782; ④) and *Searell's*, Nimmo Street (☎09/405 7835; ④), off Parnell Street a kilometre from the ferry wharf and, slightly further on, the *Rawene Motor Camp*, Marmon Street (☎09/405 7720; tent sites $8, on-site vans and cabins ②), with tent sites and cabins tucked away in bush enclaves. The nearest hostel is *Rawene Backpackers*, 5km west on SH12 (☎09/405 7790; dorms ①, rooms ②), with basic beds and cooking facilities.

For such a small place you can **eat** well. First stop should be the relaxed, daytime *Boatshed Café*, on Clendon Esplanade, which is built on stilts over the water and offers a stack of magazines, light snacks and cakes and the best espresso for miles around. The *Masonic Hotel* does good bar meals and reasonably priced à la carte dinners, has a peaceful verandah to sup away the afternoon and puts on bands most summer weekends. The ritziest place is the *Harp of Erin*, on Russell Esplanade (book for dinner, ☎09/405 7713), which opens for weekend brunches and candlelit dinners on Friday, Saturday and Sunday evenings.

Opononi and Omapere

The two small-time resorts of **OPONONI** and **OMAPERE** run pretty much contiguously for 4km along the southern shore of the Hokianga Harbour, with great views across to the sand dunes on the north side. Kiwis of a certain age will be able tell you all about Opononi and the eventful summer of 1955–56 when a wild bottlenose dolphin, dubbed "Opo", took a shine to the local populace and started playing with the kids in the shallows and performing tricks with beach balls. At the time, New Zealand still had whaling factories on its shores, dolphin-watching trips were decades away and signs had to be erected discouraging people from shooting the precocious dolphin. And yet Opo's antics captivated the nation: Christmas holidaymakers jammed the narrow dirt roads; film crews were dispatched; protective laws were drafted; and bandwagon-jumping Auckland musicians Pat McMinn, Bill Langford and The Crombie Murdoch Trio cobbled together the novelty song, *Opo The Crazy Dolphin*. Written and recorded in a day, the tape arrived at the radio station for its first airing just as news of Opo's untimely death broke – the song was a hit nonetheless.

Opononi has dined out on its fifteen minutes of fame ever since, though the only concrete reminder is a statue of Opo outside the Opon.oni Resort Hotel. To get a better sense of the frenzied enthusiasm for Opo, head to Omapere – just a roadside string of clapboard houses and a few places to stay and eat – where the **local museum** inside the visitor centre (see below) shows a short videos in the classic mould of corny-yet-charming Fifties documentary footage.

Dune trips, cruises and activities

Opononi and Omapere make good bases for exploring the surrounding area. The biggest of all the kauri trees, **Tane Mahuta**, is only 15km south of Omapere and boats ply across the harbour to the **sand dunes** – though the vistas from the south side are often so striking that it is enough to visit the **viewpoints**. The most notable are the **Arai te Uru Reserve**, reached along Signal Station Road just west of Omapere, and the magical **Pakia Hill**, by SH12 further up the hill.

The **dunes** are most easily visited by boat from the Opononi wharf. Several companies, including Hokianga Express (☎09/405 8872), Harbour Explorer water taxi (☎09/405 8033) and Sierra (☎09/405 8702), will drop you off and pick you up a couple of hours later for around $12; many also supply sand toboggans. All three also run **harbour cruises** (3hr; $20) pretty much on demand. The only scheduled cruise is aboard the hundred-year-old scow *Alma* (Dec–April; ☎09/405 7704), which does the trip from Rawene at 10am on Wednesday and Opononi at 10am on Saturday. You can also take to the water on **windsurfers** (contact *Green Café Guesthouse*, ☎09/405 8193) for $18 an hour; lessons are also available. On land, Okopako Horse Trekking will take you **riding** into the bush and the hills above the treeline (2–3hr; $30–40; ☎09/405 8815).

Walks

The best and most popular of the short walks in the district is the **Waiotemarama Walk** which starts 8km southeast of Opononi along Waiotemarama Gorge Road; the starting point is conveniently marked by one of the region's better craft shops, Labyrinth Woodworks (☎09/405 4581), whose wares include carved kauri pieces and excellent woodblock prints by noted local craftsman Allan Gale. The full route through the bush to SH12 takes an entire day but most people just walk the initial short section up a lovely bush-clad valley full of ferns, nikau palms and kauri. Ten minutes' walk gets you to an attractive waterfall with a small swimming hole and in another ten minutes you reach the first kauri. Beyond there you climb higher, eventually topping out on the 680m Hauturu (5–6hr return).

Another popular outing is the **Hokianga Track** (8km; 3–4hr; 300m ascent) from Hokianga South Head along Kaikai Beach and up theWaimamaku River back to SH12. More ambitious walkers should set two or three days aside for the **Waipoua Coast Walkway**, a 50km coastal trek that continues south from the Hokianga Track to Maunganui Bluff and on to Kai Iwi Lakes (see p.186), with few facilities along the way; details are available in DOC's *Waipoua & Trounson Kauri Forests* leaflet ($1) and from visitor centres.

Practicalities

Pioneer Coachlines run daily **bus services** through the Hokianga on behalf of InterCity and Northliner, stopping by the wharf in Opononi and outside the **visitor centre** (daily 9am–5pm; ☎09/405 8869) in Omapere, where you can book and buy tickets. To explore the vicinity you can walk, or rent a scooter (available from some hostels) gutsy enough to propel you to the big trees.

ACCOMMODATION

The twin towns are well served with budget accommodation. In **Opononi** there's the small, cosy and central *House of Harmony: Te Rangimarie*, SH12 (☎09/405 8778; tent sites $8, dorms ①, rooms ②), which rents scooters at $40 per day, and a simple *YHA*, Waiotemarama Gorge Rd, Pakanae (☎09/405 8792; ①), peacefully sited 2km east of town but very likely moving to premises closer to the centre of Opononi in the near future. The beautifully sited and well-organized *Globetrekkers*, SH12 (☎ & fax 09/405 8183; tent sites $8, dorms ①, rooms ②), heads the field in **Omapere**, renting out bikes ($16 a day) and scooters ($40); but the diminutive *Green Café Guesthouse*, SH12 (☎09/405 8193; dorms ①, rooms ②), is also appealing, has a café and does good deals for windsurfers (see p.182). For something a little more upmarket, head for either the *Omapere Tourist Hotel & Motel*, SH12 (☎09/405 8738, fax 405 8801; tent and campervan sites $9, rooms ④–⑤), which is beautifully set opposite the dunes and has a heated pool, bar and restaurant; or the relaxed and friendly homestay run by *Alexa & Owen Whaley*, Signal Station Road (☎09/405 8614; ④), which is located on a smallholding with wonderful views over the harbour.

The best of the **out of town places** are *Okopako Lodge: The Wilderness Farm*, 2 Mountain Rd, 5km east of Opononi and 2km off SH12 (☎09/405 8815; tent sites $8, dorms ①, rooms ② which offers modern accommodation and horse trekking through the adjacent native bush; *Solitaire Homestay*, on SH12 in Waimamaku, 7km south of Omapere (☎ & fax 09/405 4891; ④, $20 dinners by arrangement), an attractive farmstay in a restored colonial-style house; and the nearby *Taane and Karen Thomas*, on the corner of Taita Road and SH12, Waimamaku (☎09/405 8131; ④), a Maori-run homestay that offers the chance to learn some weaving and a smattering of the language, songs and legends, as well as to partake in communal meals, all included in the price. **Campers** are best served at the hostels or the spacious, harbourside *Opononi Holiday Park*, SH12, Opononi (☎ & fax 09/405 8791; tent sites $8, powered sites $10, cabins ③).

EATING

The pick of the **places to eat** are strung along SH12 in Omapere, where you can fill up on homemade samosas, felafel and Mexican chilli beans from *Omapere Fish Supplies*; snack more healthily on organic light meals and espresso at the *Green Café Guesthouse*; sample bargain vegetable bakes, stir-fries and grills in the plastic surroundings of the *Harbourside Café*; or go for the stunning views from the *Panorama Tea Rooms*, 2km south on SH12, in Pakia Hill. The classiest dining is at the *Harbourmaster's Restaurant*, in the Omapere Tourist Hotel and Motel, where tasty bistro-style bar meals supplement more expensive à la carte dinners concentrating on local seafood.

The Kauri Forests and the northern Kaipara Harbour

Northland, Auckland and the Coromandel Peninsula were once covered in mixed forest dominated by the mighty kauri (see box on p.185), the world's second largest tree after the Californian redwoods. By the early years of the twentieth century, rapacious Europeans had nearly felled the lot, the only extensive pockets remaining in the **Waipoua and Trounson kauri forests** south of the Hokianga Harbour. Small stands of kauri occur all over Northland, but three-quarters of all the surviving mature trees grow in these two small forests, between them barely covering 100 square kilometres. **Walks** provide access to the more celebrated examples, which dwarf the surrounding tataire, kohekohe and towai, normally some of the larger forest trees.

This land is home to the Te Roroa people who, like their kin in the north, traditionally used the kauri sparingly. Simple tools made felling and working these huge trees a difficult task, and one reserved for major projects such as large war canoes. Once the Europeans arrived with metal tools, bullock trains, wheels and winches, clear felling became more manageable and most of the trees had gone by the end of the nineteenth century. The demand for ships during World War II saw renewed interest in the kauri and sparked a corresponding campaign to save something of what was left, resulting in the creation in 1952 of the Waipoua Sanctuary, which provided limited protection, since bolstered to the point where it is now illegal to fell a kauri except in specified circumstances such as culling a diseased or dying tree, or the construction of a new ceremonial canoe.

Driving through miles of farmland it is often hard to imagine the same landscape surrounded in dense forest. This is certainly true of the lands to the south around the muddy shores of the **Kaipara Harbour**, a labyrinth of mangrove-choked inlets and small beaches. This series of drowned valleys constitutes New Zealand's largest harbour, with the longest coastline and a catchment area that covers nearly half of Northland. The Kaipara once unified this quarter of Northland, the sailboats plying its waters linking the dairy farming and logging towns on its shores. Kauri was shipped out from the largest northern town, **Dargaville**, headed either for Helensville (see p.112) or out to sea, but the fragile boats all too often the foundered on the unpredictable Kaipara Bar and were eventually washed up on **Ripiro Beach**, a fabulous salty strand which just pips Ninety Mile Beach as New Zealand's longest, running for 108km. The region declined in step with the demise of harbour traffic, and modern Dargaville survives on horticulture and a constant stream of kauri-forest-bound tourists pausing to explore the beach and the windswept Kaipara Heads. If you're pushed for time, skip the town in favour of a couple of hours at the **Matakohe Kauri Museum**, 45km south, which gives the best sense of what the kauri meant to the Northland economy and their spiritual significance for Maori.

One daily **bus** in each direction runs through the kauri forests, making a brief stop to glimpse at the biggest tree; two or three buses a day run south from Dargaville, so judicious timing should enable you to see the Kauri Museum.

Waipoua and Trounson kauri forests

SH12 provides a unique opportunity to drive through nearly 20km of mature kauri forest. The road twists and turns, following the contours of the hill country and skirting around the base of the big trees so as to cause minimal damage to their fragile and shallow root system. No sooner have you entered the forest then signs indicate the three-minute path to New Zealand's mightiest tree, the 1200-year-old **Tane Mahuta**, "Lord of

KAURI LOGGERS AND GUM DIGGERS

The **kauri** (*Agathis Australis*) isn't the tallest species of tree, nor does it boast the greatest girth, but as its gargantuan trunk barely tapers from roots to crown it ranks alongside the sequoias, or redwoods, of California as one of the largest trees in existence. Unlike the redwoods, which are useless as building **timber**, kauris produce beautiful wood, thereby hastening their demise and spawning industries that dominated the economy of the young colony in the latter half of the nineteenth century.

The kauri is a type of **pine** which now grows only in New Zealand, though it once also grew in Australia and southeast Asia, where it still has close relations. Identifiable remains of kauri forests are found all over New Zealand but by the time humans arrived on the scene, its **range** had contracted to Northland, Auckland, the Coromandel Peninsula and northern Waikato. Individual trees can live up to 2000 years, reaching 50m in height and 20m in girth, finally toppling over as the rotting core become too weak to support its immense weight.

LOGGERS

Maori have long used mature kauri for dugout canoes, but it was the young "rickers" which first drew the attention of **European** kauri **loggers** since they formed perfect **spars** for sailing ships. The bigger trees didn't escape attention for long, soon earning an unmatched reputation for their durable, easy-to-work and blemish-free wood with a straight, fine grain. Loggers' ingenuity was taxed to the limit by the difficulty of getting such huge logs out of the bush. On easier terrain, **bullock wagons** with up to twelve teams were lashed together to haul the logs on primitive roads or tramways, horse-turned winches were used on steeper ground and, where water could be deployed to transport the timber, dams were constructed from hewn logs. In narrow valleys and gullies all over Northland and the Coromandel, loggers constructed **kauri dams** up to 20m high and 60m across, with trap doors at the base. Trees along the sides of the valley were felled while the dam was filling, then the dam was tripped to flush the floating trunks down the valley to inlets where the logs were rafted up and towed to the mills.

DIGGERS

Once an area had been logged, the **gum diggers** typically moved in. Like most pines, kauri exudes a thick resin to heal any wounds inflicted, and huge candle-drip accretions form on the side of trunks and in globules around the base. In pre-European times, **Maori** had chewed it as gum, made torches to attract fish at night and burned the powdered resin to form a pigment used for *moko* ("tattoos"). Once *pakeha* got in on the act, it was exported as a raw material for furniture **varnishes**, linoleum, denture moulds and the "gilt" edging on books. When it could no longer be found on the ground, diggers – Maori, Chinese and Malaysian, but mostly Dalmatian – thrust long poles into the earth and hooked out pieces with bent rods; elsewhere, the ground was turned over, loosened and sluiced to recover the gum. Almost all New Zealand gum was **exported**, but by the early twentieth century synthetic resins had captured the gum market. Kauri gum is still considered one of the finest varnishes for musical instruments, though prices don't justify collecting it; occasional accidental finds supply such specialist needs.

the Forest". A vast wall of bark rises up nearly 18m to the lowest branches, where it seems that half the forest's epiphytes have lodged in the crook. A kilometre or so further south, a car park marks the beginning of a ten-minute track to a clearing where three paths lead off to notable trees. The shortest (5min return) runs to the **Four Sisters**, relatively slender kauri all growing close together on the same mound of shed bark. A second path (30min return) twists among numerous big trees to the Big Daddy of them all, **Te Matua Ngahere**, the "Father of the Forest", ranked as the second largest tree on account of its shorter stature but, if anything, more richly festooned in epiphytes than its brothers. The third, the **Yakas Track** (6km; 3hr), leads to the Waipoua Forest visitor centre (see below); even if you don't fancy the full track, walk the first thirty minutes to Cathedral Grove, a dense conglomeration of trees, the largest being the **Yakas Kauri**, named after veteran bushman Nicholas Yakas.

In the heart of the forest, a side road leads 1km to the **Waipoua Forest visitor centre** (Mon–Fri 8am–4.30pm & Sat–Sun 10am–4pm; ☎09/439 0605), fount of all knowledge on the reserve. The grounds contain **Maxwell Cottage** (daylight hours; free), a woodcutter's cottage from 1900 built with vertical kauri paling, and a **campsite** (book through the visitor centre; tent sites $6, cabins ②). South of here the highway runs through farmland, passing the nearest formal **accommodation**, *Waipoua Lodge*, SH12 (☎ & fax 09/439 0422; ⑤), with nicely set-up self-contained doubles in a former woolshed and stables; freshly baked bread is provided each morning and there's an on-site **restaurant**, which serves moderately priced lunches and fine evening meals (main courses around $20). Nearby, the Aranga Coast Road branches west to the 460m **Maunganui Bluff**, the northern limit of Ripiro Beach (see p.187).

Another small but superb stand of kauri, the **Trounson Kauri Park**, lies 17km southeast of Waipoua and can be visited on a short track from the car park or from the simple DOC **campsite** ($6). There's more accommodation in the area, with a range of cabins and motel units nearby at *Kauri Coast Motor Camp*, Trounson Park Road (☎ & fax 09/439 0621; ②–④), and the appealing, rural *Kaihu Farm Hostel* (☎09/439 4004; dorms ①, rooms ②) on SH12 some 7km away but within easy walking distance of the forest and with good $10 meals on offer.

Kai Iwi Lakes

The **Kai Iwi Lakes**, 11km west of SH12 and 35km northwest of Dargaville, are a real change of pace, with pine woods running down to fresh, crystal-blue waters fringed by silica-white sand. All three are dune lakes – relatively common along Northland's western seaboard – fed by rainwater and with no visible outlet. Though the largest, **Taharoa**, is less than a kilometre across, and **Waikere** and **Kai Iwi** are barely a hundred metres long, they constitute the deepest and some of the largest dune lakes in the country. Families flock here in the summer to swim, fish and waterski, making use of the large and well-equipped *Pine Beach* campsite (☎09/439 8360; tent sites $6) on the gently shelving shores of Taharoa Lake; the more intimate *Promenade Point* site (☎09/439 8360; tent sites $6) has just water, toilet and cold showers. There is more substantial motel-style **accommodation** neighbouring Taharoa Lake at *Waterlea* (☎ & fax 09/439 0727; ④), which also serves meals, rents mountain bikes and canoes (around $7 an hour), takes folk water-skiing ($60 per hour) and trout-fishing ($35 an hour for 2 people).

Walkers can follow the beach north from here to Maunganui Bluff (2hr one way) and either walk back, follow Aranga Coast Road inland to pick-up a bus on SH12, or continue north along the Waipoua Coast Walkway to the Hokianga Harbour.

Dargaville and around

Sleepy **DARGAVILLE**, 30km south of Kai Iwi Lakes, is trying to shake off its cow-town image by pitching itself as the capital of the Kauri Coast, an amorphous region encompassing everywhere south from the Hokianga down and around the Kaipara. In reality, it is more a service town for the region's farming community, traditionally dairy-based but more recently burgeoning into the country's top kumara-growing district. The town was founded as a port in 1872, 64km up the strongly tidal but navigable Northern Wairoa River, by Joseph McMullen Dargaville, an Australian of Irish descent. Ships came to load kauri logs and transport gum extracted by Dalmatian settlers who, by the early part of the twentieth century, formed a sizeable portion of the community; a building on Normanby Street still proclaims itself the Yugoslav Social Hall.

The only specific sight in town is the **Dargaville Maritime Museum** (daily 9am–4pm; $3) in the hilltop Harding Park, 2km west of town and marked by two masts rescued from the *Rainbow Warrior*. Space is found for a good collection of kauri gum – including an 84kg piece reputed to be the largest found – among the extensive displays of artefacts recovered from wrecks discovered off the coast. Local experts contend that the Spaniard Juan Fernandez was the first European to visit New Zealand in 1576, a full 66 years before Abel Tasman's more widely recognized "discovery". Naturally, this is highly controversial and most of the evidence is circumstantial, but Ross Wiseman in his book "The Spanish Discovery of New Zealand in 1576" (see "Books" in Contexts) puts a strong case. Remains from later wrecks are on show along with photos of their excavation, the only pre-European artefact being the Ngati Whatua *waka* which lay buried under the sands of the North Head of the Kaipara Harbour from 1809 until 1972, and is a rare example of a canoe hewn completely using stone tools.

Ripiro Beach stretches 108km from Maunganui Bluff south to Pouto Point, the northern head of the Kaipara Harbour, and is accessible at several points, most easily at **Baylys Beach**, a conglomeration of mostly holiday homes 14km west of Dargaville. The sands of Ripiro Beach are renowned for their mobility, with several metres of beach often being shifted by a single tide, and huge areas being reclaimed over the centuries; periodically an anchor or prow of a long-lost wreck reappears through the sand. As elsewhere on the West Coast, tidal rips and holes make swimming dangerous and there are no beach patrols. Beach driving is no less fraught with danger and shouldn't be undertaken without prior local consultation; vehicles frequently get stranded. Nevertheless it's a fine place for long moody walks, digging up **tua tua**, the locally renowned shellfish, and **horse riding** with Dargaville-based Baylys Beach Horse Treks (3hhr; $25; ☎09/439 6342). Better still, sign up with Taylor Made Tours ($30; ☎09/430 1576) for a highly informative full-day trip in a specially designed 4WD truck which thunders 60km south from Dargaville along the wild, exposed beach to the disused 1884 Kaipara lighthouse. Taylor Made Tours occasionally join forces for trips with the MV *Kewpie Too* **boat** from Helensville (see p.112), combining half a day chugging around the Kaipara Harbour with a few hours of **beach-driving**.

Practicalities

Two **bus** services stop on Kapia Street in Dargaville: InterCity (operated by Pioneer) runs between Opononi and Brynderwyn, where it connects with services to Auckland; and Mainline run direct from Dargaville to Auckland. Tickets for both are available from the **visitor centre**, 65 Normanby St (Nov–March Mon–Fri 8.30am–5.30pm & Sat–Sun 9am–4pm; April–Oct Mon–Fri 8.30am–5pm & Sat 10am–3pm; ☎09/439 8360), which also has comprehensive **accommodation** listings for the region.

The best budget place to stay is *The Grenhouse Hostel*, 13 Portland St (☎09/439 6342; tent sites $8, dorms ①, rooms ②), a former schoolhouse functioning as an associate YHA **hostel**, with free use of bikes and beach equipment. Traditional **pub beds** are available at the *Northern Wairoa Hotel*, on the corner of Victoria Street and Hokianga Road (☎09/439 8923; ④), and there are reasonable **motels** such as *Dargaville Motel*, 217 Victoria St (☎09/439 7734; ④). Dargaville's grandest rooms are at the engagingly low-key *Kauri House Lodge*, Bowen Street (☎ & fax 09/439 8082; ⑥), where comfortable en-suite rooms are set in a vast kauri-built house, complete with billiard room, library and swimming pool. **Campers** can choose between *Selwyn Park Motor Camp*, Onslow Street, Dargaville (☎09/439 8296; tent sites $8, cabins ②), and the *Baylys Beach Motor Camp*, 22 Seaview Rd, Baylys Beach (☎ & fax 09/439 6349; tent sites $8, cabins ②–③).

Belushi's Café, 102 Victoria St, does cappuccino and **bagels** during the day, while the *New Asian Restaurant*, 114 Victoria St (BYO & licensed), dishes up tolerable Chinese meals. The *Northern Wairoa Hotel* is locally renowned for its bargain **pub meals** and juicy Sunday roasts, while Dargaville's fanciest restaurant, *Lorna Doone*, at the corner of Victoria Street and Gladstone Street (☎09/439 8460), turns its hand to modern Kiwi cuisine. The best value for money, though, is to be had at the *Seaview Café*, at Baylys Beach (☎09/439 4549), with shady outdoor seating for daytime coffee and tasty snacks, and an evening blackboard menu.

Matakohe and its museum

If there is one museum you must see in the north it is the **Matakohe Kauri Museum**, Church Road (Nov–Easter daily 9am–5.30pm; Easter–Oct daily 9am–5pm; $6), on the outskirts of the village of **MATAKOHE**, 45km south of Dargaville. One of the best in the country and deserving of at least a couple of hours, it focuses on the way the kauri shaped the lives of pioneers in Northland, from the makeshift settlements around logging camps and on the gumfields through to the merchants who could afford to buy the fine pieces of furniture or finely carved kauri gum. A 22m-long reconstruction of a vertical slice of a cut kauri makes an impressive start, providing a canvas for a photographic essay of its felling in 1994 after being struck by lightning. Mock-ups of the various methods of transporting the huge logs – kauri dams, wooden sleds, bullock trains and winches – lead on to a pit-saw operation and a steam-driven breaking-down mill where planks were shaped. Fine examples of cut boards surround the wall, some exhibiting the dark staining of swamp kauri where water in the peat bogs has penetrated the grain, others showing blemishes where gum climbers punctured the bark, a process which eventually killed many trees. Matakohe has the most extensive display of kauri gum anywhere, with glass cases stuffed full of everything from vast lumps of the raw material to finely worked pieces in every imaginable form down to strands braided into a plait. Rather lifeless tableaux of wealthy Victorian families at leisure in kauri-panelled rooms are perhaps the only weakness among rooms groaning with magnificently detailed furniture and fascinating photos.

Several mildly diverting wooden buildings (open during museum hours) have been moved into the museum grounds from the surrounding area: a one-room schoolhouse used for nearly a century until 1972, a 1909 post office and a diminutive pioneer church dating back to 1867. By the church is the 1950 Coates Memorial Church built in honour of locally raised Joseph Gordon Coates who, in 1925, became the country's first New Zealand-born prime minister.

It is possible to visit the museum using **public transport**, most easily done if you are heading north, when timings are more amenable. Alternatively, you can **stay** nearby in the warren of rooms at the *Old Post Office Guest House*, on SH12 in the village of Paparoa, 6km east of Matakohe (☎09/431 7453; tent sites $8; dorms ①, rooms ②); one of the double rooms is located in a renovated solid kauri nineteenth-century jail. Kayaks and bikes are free for guests' use and breakfast is available. The *Travellers Lodge*, on SH16 in Ruawai, 15km west of Matakohe (☎09/439 2283; tent sites $8, dorms ①, rooms ②), is also convenient for the museum.

travel details

Buses

Two major bus companies serve Northland. The most comprehensive operation is InterCity (☎09/357 8400), who run two routes, one up the eastern side from Auckland's Sky City Casino depot through Warkworth, Brynderwyn, Whangarei, Paihia, Kerikeri and Mangonui to Kaitaia, the other spurring off at Brynderwyn and covering Dargaville, the Waipoua Forest, Opononi and Kaikohe on the way to Paihia. Their **Northland Kauri Wanderer** pass ($80) is valid for three months and covers a loop from Auckland to Paihia and back through Opononi, the Waipoua Forest and Dargaville, or vice versa. Northliner Express (☎09/307 5873 in Auckland, ☎09/438 3206 in Whangarei), who run almost identical services with a similar frequency from Auckland's Downtown Airline Terminal. They sell three useful passes, all valid for a month and all requiring some form of backpacker or student ID: the **Bay of Islands Pass** ($49) covers Auckland to Kerikeri, the **Loop Pass** ($79) which is identical to the Northland Kauri Wanderer, and the **Northland Freedom Pass** ($109), which adds the leg up to Kaitaia. There are also two short-range operators: Gubbs (☎09/425 8348),who run from Auckland to Warkworth; and Mainline Coaches (☎09/278 8070), who also serve Warkworth and continue on to Dargaville.

From Dargaville to: Auckland (2–3 daily; 3hr); Opononi (1 daily; 2hr 40min).

From Kaitaia to: Auckland (2 daily; 6hr 40min).

From Kerikeri to: Auckland (4–6 daily; 5hr).

From Mangonui to: Auckland (2 daily; 6hr).

From Opononi/Omapere to: Auckland (1 daily; 6hr); Paihia (1 daily; 1hr 30min), Dargaville (1 daily; 2hr 40min).

From Paihia to: Auckland via Whangarei (3–7 daily; 4hr); Auckland via Opononi (1 daily; 7hr 45min); Kaitaia (2 daily; 1hr 40min); Kerikeri (4–6 daily; 20min); Mangonui (2 daily; 1hr 40min).

From Waipu to: Auckland (3–7 daily; 2hr 20min); Whangarei (3–7 daily; 40min).

From Warkworth to: Auckland (8–10 daily; 1hr);

From Whangarei to: Auckland (3–7 daily; 2hr 45min); Paihia (3–7 daily; 1hr 20min); Warkworth (3–7 daily; 1hr 45min).

Ferries

From Opua to: Okiato (every 30min; 15min).

From Paihia to: Russell (every 20–30min; 20min).

From Rawene to: Kohukohu (hourly; 20min).

Flights

From Bay of Islands (Paihia) to: Auckland (2–3 daily; 50min); Kaitaia (1 daily; 25min).

From Kaitaia to: Auckland (1–2 daily; 1hr–1hr 30min).

From Whangarei to: Auckland (5–7 daily; 40min); Great Barrier Island (1 weekly; 30min).

CHAPTER THREE

WESTERN NORTH ISLAND

Much of the **Western North Island** is ignored by visitors, who pass through the major transit centres of Hamilton and Palmerston North in a mad dash to get somewhere else. This is to do the area a disservice, however, for it contains fascinating caves; two spectacular national parks that encompass a dormant volcano and a winding river; a number of intriguing scenic reserves; a moody, isolated and rugged coast; and an extraordinary **history** of pre-European settlement and post-European conflict. This region is deeply rooted in **Maori** legend and history, for it was on the west coast at **Kawhia** that the Tainui people first landed in New Zealand. Kawhia was also the birthplace of **Te Rauparaha**, the great Maori chief who led his people from Kawhia to escape the better-armed tribes of the Waikato down the west coast to Kapiti Island and on to the South Island, pursuing his individual road to justice, fame and glory. The Waikato's **recent history** has also been a turbulent one. Containing some of the richest and most productive land in the country, it is no surprise that both Maori and *pakeha* coveted its spoils.

Spreading south from the estuary of the Waikato River is a swathe of land known as **The Waikato**, bounded to the west by the crashing waves, long beaches, bluffs and dense forests of the coast and to the east by the North Island's central plateau. Dominating the region is **Hamilton**, New Zealand's largest inland city and fourth-largest overall; poised at the intersection of two major highways (SH1 and SH3), and two rail lines, virtually everywhere on the North Island is readily accessible from this sprawling hub. The most visited seaside towns are **Raglan**, which is within easy reach of a world-class surfing beach, and **Kawhia**, the first landfall of the Tainui Maori canoe and spiritual home of its people. Both nestle in sheltered and ancient green-swathed harbours, Raglan beneath the imposing **Karioi Mountain**, just north of the dark Pirongia Forest Park, Kawhia only 4km from the black-sand of **Ocean Beach**, with its hot thermal pools. **Inland**, this rich dairying and agricultural region benefits from the fecund soil scattered by long-extinct volcanoes and the natural irrigation of plentiful streams and high rainfall, where farming settlements sit on the riverbanks, taking pride in their respective traditions. Maori cultural heritage is richest in **Ngaruawahia**, home of the Maori Queen, and **Te Awamutu**, scene of some of the bloodiest battles between Maori and *pakeha*. Nearby, tranquillity is regained at **Yarndley's Bush**, one of the few remaining stands of kahikatea trees, while **Cambridge** is redolent with the air of the English home counties.

South of the Waikato is **The King Country**, which took its name from the King Movement (see box on p.199) and was the last significant area in New Zealand to succumb to the onrush of European colonization. At one time a densely forested and inhospitable hinterland, a number of stalwart communities coexist with some extraordinary natural features – most famously the **Waitomo Caves**, which offer trav-

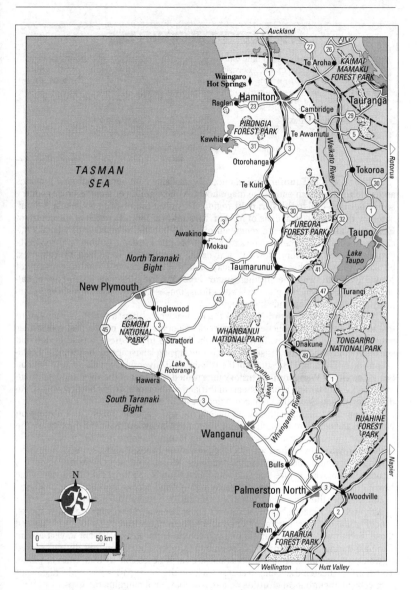

ellers the chance to explore unusual rock formations above and below ground and marvel at glow-worm-filled caverns. South of Waitomo is the small, historically significant settlement of **Te Kuiti**, where the leader of the King Movement sought refuge in the 1860s and these days, more prosaically, it relishes in the title of the sheep-shearing capital of New Zealand, but also has access to the lush, tall canopy of the **Pureora Forest Park**.

Further south is **Taumarunui**, a once-vibrant dairy community that now provides access to the northern end of the magnificent Whanganui River and the cross-country scenic heritage trail to the **Taranaki** region. This giant thumb-print peninsula is dominated by the symmetrical cone of **Mount Taranaki** (2518m). Perched at the centre of **Egmont National Park**, the mountain offers all but the terminal couch potato the chance to climb a slumbering volcano, while trout-filled streams bubble up through its granular slopes, tumbling down to a dynamic coastline characterized by estuaries, black iron-sand beaches, cliffs and rocky shores. The adjacent, coast-hugging city of **New Plymouth**, with the striking **Sugar Loaf Marine Reserve** just offshore, balanced by some stimulating cultural attractions, makes a lively base for visitors to this justly popular tramping and skiing region.

The seductive **Whanganui National Park**, meanwhile, offers a gentle river adventure that makes an ideal introduction to wilderness canoeing, as you paddle past spectacular natural features and man-made follies like the **Bridge to Nowhere**, a road bridge that speaks volumes about the resistance of this unforgiving landscape to the inroads of cultivation and civilization. The estuary of the **Whanganui River** finally spills into the Tasman Sea at the city of **Wanganui**, its history intertwined with that of the river and a talisman of the successful taming of at least part of the land, with ornate streets bordered by splendid Victorian and Edwardian edifices, a fine museum and gallery.

Another city teeming with fine architecture – and transport links – is **Palmerston North**, in the centre of the rich farming region of **Manawatu**. South of the city are the foothills of the dark, dense and moody **Tararua Range**, looming behind the coastal strip of the **Horowhenua region**, with its long windswept beaches and a string of unprepossessing retirement and commuter settlements. Museum-infested **Foxton** was once a thriving flax-weaving centre that vied with Palmerston North for regional primacy, while **Levin** is a quirky town littered with factory shops and access into the Tararua Range, which shadows the coast south towards Otaki and eventually Wellington.

Although the Western North Island does not suffer extremes of **climate**, water sports, canoeing and caving will be more enjoyable in the months leading up to Christmas and those directly after it, whereas ski and snowboard enthusiasts will want to visit Mount Taranaki during the **winter** months of June to October. The region is pretty well served by transport, and all the major destinations are easily accessible by **bus**, **train** or **plane**. To get off the beaten track and to access walks in the forest parks, you really need your own vehicle, though local **shuttles** do a reasonable job of plugging the gaps.

Hamilton

On SH1, 136km south of Auckland and 102km northwest of Rotorua, **HAMILTON** has been dubbed "The Fountain City" owing to its predilection for water-gushing ornamentation, though a more accurate moniker might be "Transit Centre". A hub of North Island air, rail and road routes, the town resembles nothing so much as a glorified interchange. A spread-out, predominantly suburban community on the banks of the languid Waikato River, with a population in excess of 110,000 and home to the University of Waikato, the city contains little of lasting interest to visitors. However, there is tranquillity to be found in **Hamilton Gardens** or on the riverbanks, perhaps an interesting half-day trawling the collections of the regional **Museum of Art and History**, and, as befits a city of Hamilton's size, a good deal of accommodation, diverse restaurants, nightlife and shopping.

Archeological evidence indicates that the **Tainui** settlement of **Kirikirioa** had existed on the current site of Hamilton for at least two hundred years before the **Europeans** muscled in on the act in the 1830s. The Europeans named their new settlement after **John Fane Charles Hamilton**, an officer of the Royal Navy who had died, either bravely or foolishly (depending whose interpretation you believe), at the battle of Gate Pa, near Tauranga, a few months earlier; a fictionalized account of the events leading up to his death appears in Maurice Shadbolt's excellent novel *The House of Strife* (see "Books" in Contexts, p.789). The **river** remained the only supply route for the city until the **railway** came in 1878, effectively opening up the country to more European immigration, farming and commercial expansion.

Arrival, information and city transport

Hamilton **airport**, 12km south, is connected to the city by the Air Shuttle, which meets all arrivals from Monday to Friday (Sat & Sun by arrangement; 20min; ☎07/847 5618; $7). The **train** station is on Fraser Street in the suburb of Frankton, a twenty-minute walk west of the city centre (bus #8). Train and bus **tickets** can be bought at the Hamilton Travel Centre, on the corner of Ward Street and Anglesea Street, where InterCity, Mount Cook Landline and Newmans **buses** drop off.

The Hamilton **visitor centre** is inside the Hamilton City Council Building, Garden Place (Mon–Fri 9am–4.30pm, Sat & Sun 10am–2pm; ☎07/839 3360 & fax 839 0794), while the **DOC office** is a few minutes' walk north at 18 London St (Mon–Fri 8.30am–4.15pm; ☎07/838 3363, fax 839 0794). Most of Hamilton's attractions are within walking distance of the centre, and other destinations can be reached by an extensive **local bus** network centred on Hamilton Travel Centre. In addition, a **free bus** trundles around the city centre loop, from Victoria Street to Knox Street, Anglesea Street and Liverpool Street, every twenty minutes (Mon–Fri 7.20am–5.20pm & Sat 9am–1.40pm).

Accommodation

There is a variety of business accommodation in Hamilton, with **motels** clustered on Ulster and Victoria streets, and in the western and eastern suburbs of the city, but few noteworthy **B&Bs** or campsites. A dearth of inexpensive centrally located accommodation means that **hostels**, which are small to start with, fill up quickly.

Hotels, motels and B&Bs

Bavaria Motel, 203–207 Ulster St (☎07/839 2520 & fax 839 2531). Large, comfortable units within eight minutes' walk of the city and conveniently close to a supermarket. ④.

Le Grand Hotel, cnr Victoria St & Collingwood St (☎07/839 1994). An elegant grand old building in the centre of town, with 38 well designed rooms, tastefully decorated and furnished. ⑤–⑦.

Home from Home B&B, 12 Galbraith Ave, Beerscourt (☎ & fax 07/849 2788). A comfortable bolt-hole in the comfortable, friendly home of a South African family, deep in suburbia, about twenty minutes' walk from Victoria Street. ④.

Manhattan Lodge Motel, 218 Grey St (☎ & fax 07/856 3785). Friendly, quiet and agreeable place set well back from the road, just a couple of minutes' walk from restaurants and shops in the suburb of Hamilton East. ④.

Mill Lodge Motor Inn, 135 Ulster St (☎07/839 3143 & fax 839 4361). Restful, self-contained studio and one- and two-bedroom units near the city centre. ⑤.

Parklands Travel Hotel/Motel, 24 Bridge St (☎07/838 2461). Simple, inexpensive and clean hotel rooms and studio-style motel units. Rooms ③, units ④.

Hostels and campsites

Flying Hedgehog Backpackers, 8 Liverpool St (☎07/839 3906). Small friendly hostel, with dorms and doubles (neither with lockable doors) but cursed with a small kitchen; free extras include an evening glass of wine or beer; videos, and lifts to hitching points. Dorms ①, rooms ②.

Hamilton East Tourist Court, 61 Cameron Rd (☎ & fax 07/856 6220). Spacious site adjacent to a food store about 3km from the city centre. Tent sites $13 for two, cabins ②, tourist flats ③.

J's Backpackers, 8 Grey St (☎07/856 8934). Amiable place with just one twin room and two dorms, run by a couple who offer highly individual tours, including kayaking on the Waikato. Dorms ①, rooms ②.

Parklands Travel Hotel/Motel, 24 Bridge St (☎07/838 2461). Basic backpacker dorms and doubles, alongside motel-style accommodation (see above). Dorms ①, backpacker doubles ②.

Silver Birches, 182 Tramway Rd (☎07/855 6260). Run by a charming German-speaking couple, who offer cosy dorms and doubles 5km from the city centre (bus #11). Dorms ①, rooms ②.

YHA Hamilton, 1190 Victoria St (☎07/838 0009, fax 838 0837). Pleasant hostel in an old, slightly run-down house with airy rooms, a large kitchen and superb grounds that lead down to the river. Dorms ①, rooms ②.

The City

The main drag is **Victoria Street**, which runs northwest to southeast along the west bank of the Waikato River, and parallel to Anglesea Street. The area immediately around Victoria Street contains almost everything of interest in Hamilton.

Much of the city is subsumed by low, suburban architecture, but a short walk along Victoria Street from its southeastern end as far as the junction with London Street reveals structures of classical splendour and endeavour. Built in 1915 of rough-cast concrete, **St Peter's Cathedral** is actually modelled on a fifteenth-century Norfolk church. As you progress north past the grand Victorian-era bank buildings (now mostly restaurants and retail outlets), the post office, some splendid old hotels and municipal buildings, you begin to discern the prosperity that farming and trade have brought to the area. The 1924 **Wesley Chambers**, on the corner of Collingwood Street, is an imposing edifice, influenced by the architecture of boomtime Chicago and embellished with wrought-iron balconies. Squeezed in between and inside these august facades are evidence of more recent economic prosperity, with run-of-the-mill plazas, malls, shopping courtyards and car parks.

Waikato Museum of Art and History

The best thing in Hamilton is the **Waikato Museum of Art and History** (daily 10am–4.30pm; $2), which occupies a challenging modern construction on Grantham Street, opposite Hood Street. The open airy spaces combine two previously separate institutions – the historic museum and the art gallery – in a functional and pleasing large-windowed building, stepping down to the river on five levels. The vast collection of Australasian paintings and photographs is augmented by objects relating to Tainui culture, including woven flax, domestic items, tools, ritual artefacts and fine examples of wood and stone carving. Among items relating to European settlement and development, one of the more interesting is the *Bullock Webster Diary*, which contains amusing cartoons of long-dead settlers and accounts of their dealings with the author/artist.

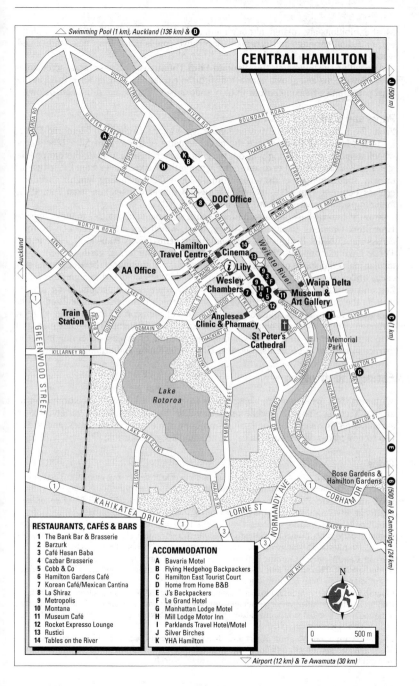

△ Swimming Pool (1 km), Auckland (136 km) & **D**

CENTRAL HAMILTON

VICTORIA STREET
RIVER ROAD
BOUNDARY ROAD
FIFTH AVE
PEACHGROVE RD

MAEROA RD

ULSTER STREET
THAMES ST
HEAPHY TERRACE
BROOKLYN RD
EAST ST

ABBOTSFORD ST
A

K
B

MILL STREET
H

ROSTREVOR ST

NORTON ROAD

KENT ST

HALLS

SEDDON ST

LONDON ST

VICTORIA STREET

ANGLESEA ST

DELTA

O'NEILL ST

LANDS RD

CLAUDE

TE AROHA ST

8 **DOC Office**

Waikato River

MEMORIAL DR

**Hamilton
Travel Centre** ◆ **Cinema**

14

13

ℹ️ **Liby**

◆ **AA Office**

WARD ST

**Wesley
Chambers**

9 ◆ **F**
10 **8**
7
6 **4** **5** **11** ◆ **Waipa Delta**

12

**Museum &
Art Gallery**

**Train
Station**

FRASERS

QUEENS AVE

LAKE RD

HILLST

COLLINGWOOD ST

WOOD

GRANTHAM ST

**Anglesea
Clinic & Pharmacy**

CLYDE ST

I

G (1 km)

DOMAIN DR

KILLARNEY RD

DOMAIN DR

THACKERAY ST

RUAKIWI RD

BRIDGE ST

**St Peter's
Cathedral**

**Memorial
Park**

HILLSBOROUGH TERR

WELLINGTON ST

G

GREY ST

G (500 m)

E

△ Auckland

GREENWOOD STREET

*Lake
Rotoroa*

PEMBROKE STREET

COBHAM DR

JELLICOE DR

MACFARLANE ST

NAYLOR ST

LAKE CRESCENT

ALISON ST

OHAUPO RD

NORMANDY AVE

**Rose Gardens &
Hamilton Gardens**

COBHAM DR

G (500 m) & Cambridge (24 km)

KAHIKATEA DRIVE

LORNE ST

BADER ST

1

3

3

FINE AVE

N

RESTAURANTS, CAFÉS & BARS

1   The Bank Bar & Brasserie
2   Barzurk
3   Café Hasan Baba
4   Cazbar Brasserie
5   Cobb & Co
6   Hamilton Gardens Café
7   Korean Café/Mexican Cantina
8   La Shiraz
9   Metropolis
10 Montana
11 Museum Café
12 Rocket Expresso Lounge
13 Rustici
14 Tables on the River

ACCOMMODATION

A   Bavaria Motel
B   Flying Hedgehog Backpackers
C   Hamilton East Tourist Court
D   Home from Home B&B
E   J's Backpackers
F   Le Grand Hotel
G   Manhattan Lodge Motel
H   Mill Lodge Motor Inn
I   Parklands Travel Hotel/Motel
J   Silver Birches
K   YHA Hamilton

▽ Airport (12 km) & Te Awamuta (30 km)

Most exhibitions are rotated, although a magnificent war canoe (*Te Winika*), contemporary Tainui carvings and *tukutuku* (decorative panels made from flax, leather and wood) are on permanent display.

Also within the building is the **Waikato Film Theatre**, which has special screenings of arthouse films and shows connected with the exhibtions, usually advertised in the local paper, and a relaxing **café** with tasty snacks (see "Eating and drinking", below).

Parks and gardens

From the museum, a pretty riverside **walk**, via Victoria Bridge and Memorial Drive, leads to **Memorial Park**, where the pitiful remains of the *Rangiriri*, an 1864 sternwheel steamer, gaze longingly at the river. In a much healthier state, the old paddle steamer *Waipa Delta* still **cruises** sedately along the Waikato River from the jetty a little way south: midday cruises run from 12.30pm ($29, including lunch); afternoon cruises begin at 3pm ($15, including tea); and dinner cruises run from 7pm ($49, including smorgasbord); call ☎07/854 9415 for details and bookings.

From Memorial Park, a footpath heads south a couple of kilometres to the extensive **Hamilton Gardens** (daily 7.30am–dusk; free), which can also be reached by road across the Cobham Bridge. The gardens' visitor centre (daily 9am–4pm), close to the Turtle Lake and opposite the café, stocks free maps. The formal gardens boast spectacular massed displays of roses, tropical plants, chrysanthemums, rhododendrons and cacti, while the authentic Japanese Garden's pavilion overlooks ordered gardens full of Zen and classic scroll features intended to encourage contemplation. Along similar lines is the intricate Chinese Scholar's Garden, which represents an idealized world characterized by walls, a courtyard, and carefully chosen combinations of plants, rock arrangements, bridges and ponds. Although equally artificial, the Turtle Lake manages to look more natural and is well worth strolling round, or at least observing from the terrace in front of the *Hamilton Gardens Café* (see "Eating and drinking", below).

Eating and drinking

With very few exceptions, the best places to eat and drink are concentrated on or around Victoria Street. In recent years Hamilton has accumulated a variety of restaurants offering quality food and value for money, some small moody cafés, and one or two trendy places where you can pay an arm and a leg for a drink.

Cafés

Café Hasan Baba, 228 Victoria St. A cheap and cheerful café serving authentic Turkish and Middle Eastern dishes. Dinner daily, plus Sun lunch; BYO.

Cobb and Co., Victoria St, near junction with Collingwood St. Predictable, reliable place for inexpensive breakfasts and simple but substantial meals. Daily 7.30am–10pm; licensed.

Hamilton Gardens Café, Cobham Drive. with. Tasty and imaginative food, such as banana yoghurt curry, lamb shanks tagine and Cajun-style fish, for under $22. Other pluses are outdoor seating, floor-to-ceiling windows and a simple modern bar. Daily 11.30am–2pm, 6pm–9.30pm.

Korean Cafe/Mexican Cantina, in the Farmers Trading Company Building, cnr Collingwood St & Alexandra St. This simple little place offers a bizarre combination of authentic Korean food for under $8 and dirt-cheap Mexican snacks. Mon–Sat 11am–7pm.

Metropolis, 211 Victoria St. A hip, black-painted all-day café that serves an eclectic range of tasty food for lunch and dinner, varying from miniature spring rolls with Thai chilli ($7), to spicy chorizo, mushroom and smoked mozzarella calzone with fresh tomato salsa ($17.50); and some good coffee and liqueurs. Licensed & BYO.

The Museum Café, Museum of Art and History, Grantham St. The food is reasonably priced Mediterranean and African influenced, the atmosphere relaxed and the setting stylish, with great views of the river. Lunch & dinner daily, plus weekend brunch.

Rocket Espresso Lounge, cnr Hood St & Victoria St. This relaxed, intimate, and truly individual coffee house has an array of ugly chairs, excellent beverages, tasty light snacks and meals from all over the globe at reasonable prices. Daily 9am–5pm.

Restaurants

The Bank Bar and Brasserie, cnr Hood St & Victoria St. An old bank has been given a new lease of life by a cleanly decorated interior with lots of wood, loud music and the feel of a big-city bistro. This is a firm favourite with local wage slaves, who relish the substantial snacks and main meals of steak, fish and grills. Sun–Thurs 11am–11pm, Fri–Sat 11am–3am.

Barzurk Gourmet Pizza Bar, 250 Victoria St. Excellent pizzas with a variety of toppings ($15–18). Lunch Wed–Sun, dinner Tues–Sun.

Cazbar Brasserie, The Marketplace, off Hood St. Stylish, dinner/night spot with more champagne chic than its neighbours. Snacks are served all day, and globally inspired dinner mains go for under $20. Live music Tues, Thurs & Sat until 3am; licensed.

Montana, 131 Victoria St. A traditional, value-for-money place popular with city-visiting farmers, sales reps and the blue-rinse brigade. What it lacks in finesse, it makes up for with excellent meat and seafood.

Rustici, Riverbank Mall, off Victoria St. One of the best places to eat lunch or dinner in Hamilton: try the rabbit pie ($21), enchilada crêpes ($15), Rigatoncini pasta ($15), fresh seafood ($18) and excellent-value specials. Licensed.

La Shiraz, 851 Victoria St (☎07/838 1960). Popular tandoori and roti restaurant (book dinner Fri & Sat), with authentic banquets for $18. Dinner daily, lunch Thurs & Fri; licensed & BYO.

Tables on the River, 12 Alam St (☎07/839 6555). Sophisticated, expensive and popular wine bar and restaurant capitalizing on the fad for "fusion" cuisine (a melting pot of Pacific-Rim, European and Asian influences).

Nightlife and entertainment

Many of the restaurants and bars double up as **drinking** venues, some branching out into live **music** and dancing on Friday and Saturday nights, while theatres often act as concert venues for bands, travelling cabaret and classical music. The Village 7 multiplex **cinema**, in the Centreplace Mall on Ward Street, shows the usual mainstream releases, while the Waikato Film Society occasionally screens arthouse and more obscure films at the Museum of Art and History, Grantham Street. Check the daily *Waikato Times* (70¢) for details of these and other happenings; comprehensive events and **entertainment listings** are in the Friday and Saturday editions.

The Bank Bar and Brasserie, cnr Hood St & Victoria St. A hugely popular nightspot on Fridays and Saturdays from around 10pm, when the DJ-instigated dancing starts.

Biddy Mulligans Irish Pub, 742 Victoria St. Live Irish-sounding bands on Fri, Sat & Sun nights, accompanied by imported and home-grown beer. Daily 11am–midnight.

Bourbon Street, 6 Bryce St. One of the most atmospheric drinking and dancing spots, this tardis-like place runs the gamut – with prolonged happy hours on Wednesdays (4pm–midnight), dancing and shows on Fridays, comedy and live music on Saturdays, and laid-back blues on Sunday.

Diggers, 17 Hood St. A real drinkers' den with a long kauri bar that's open till midnight and provides welcome respite from the trendy city bars.

Down Under, Post Office Mall, 346 Victoria St. Live rock and punk bands Thursday to Saturday and a happy hour from 5–7pm every day.

Exchange Establishment, 188 Victoria St. Live music in a cramped and bleak urban setting for connoisseurs of grunge. Daily 11am–2am; live bands Wed–Sat.

JB's, 711 Victoria St. After-business-cum-sports bar, with music from noon to midnight. Closed Sun.

Legends Nightclub, cnr Ward St & Worley St. Late-night dancing, party and booze scene.

Loaded Hog, 27 Hood St. One of the most relaxed bars in the city, this large double-gabled building is dotted with rural New Zealand memorabilia and has tables on the street out front. The usual array of excellent home-brewed ales is supplemented by a broad selection from around the country and snacky food. Dinner daily, lunch Wed–Sun; DJ-cranked dancing Fri & Sat night.

Outback Inn, The Marketplace, off Hood St. Studeny drinking hole with bare wooden floors, a good selection of beers and some alcohol-absorbing snacks. DJ at weekends.

Listings

American Express Calder and Lawson Travel Ltd, 455 Grey St (☎07/856 9009).

Automobile Association 295 Barton St (☎07/839 1397).

Banks and foreign exchange Both National and Trust Bank have branches on Victoria St, as do most of the other major national banks; all offer exchange facilities (see also listings for American Express and Thomas Cook).

Bike rental R&R Sport, 943 Victoria St (☎07/839 3755), charges $25 a day for a mountain bike.

Bookshops Dimensions Women's Bookshop, 266 Victoria St; The Government Bookshop, 33 King St; Browsers, 221 Victoria St, and Nonesuch, 192 Victoria St, both buy and sell secondhand books.

Buses Local buses run from the Hamilton Travel Centre, cnr Ward St & Anglesea St (☎07/856 4579); a full timetable (50¢) is available there or at the visitor centre. Local bus companies also run scheduled services to the neighbouring communities of Huntly, Paeroa, Raglan, Thames and Te Awamutu; Roadcat Transport (☎025 949 440) runs to and from Auckland.

Car rental Budget (☎07/838 3585); Cambridge Car Rentals (☎07/823 0990); Hertz (☎07/839 4824); Rent-a-Dent (☎07/839 1049); Waikato Car Rentals (☎07/856 9908).

Kayak rental R&R Sport, 943 Victoria St (☎07/839 3755; $25 per day).

Library The central Hamilton library is at Garden Place, Victoria St.

Medical treatment Southern Cross Hospital, cnr Von Tempsky St & Beale St; Anglesea Clinic and Pharmacy, cnr Anglesea St & Thackery St (daily 7.30am–11pm) offers consultations and fills prescriptions.

Post offices The main post office is in Post Office Mall, Victoria St; in addition, post shops are located on London St and Victoria St.

Swimming Hamilton Swimming Pool Complex, Garnett Ave (Mon–Thur, 6am–9pm, Fri–Sun, 9am–9pm; $2).

Taxis The principal taxi rank is outside the Hamilton Travel Centre, or call Dial a driver (☎07/849 0995).

Thomas Cook Garden Place (☎07/838 0149).

Trains Information and tickets are available at the train station on Fraser St, Hamilton Travel Centre (see below) and the visitor centre.

Travel agents Hamilton Travel Centre, cnr Anglesea St & Ward St (☎07/856 4579), deals with national and international travel arrangements, as does the Air New Zealand Travel Centre, 25 Ward St (☎07/839 9835).

Around Hamilton

The area north of Hamilton is largely **farmland**, with little to delay even the most inquisitive explorer, save for **Ngaruawahia**, home of the Maori monarch and scene of the signing of the Raupatu Land Settlement, whereby the New Zealand government agreed to compensate the Tainui for land confiscated in the 1860s. To the southeast of the city, the genteel English charms of **Cambridge** contrast with the turbulent history of the former garrison township of **Te Awamutu.**

The principal attraction on the sand-swathed **coast** to the west of Hamilton is **Raglan**, a surfing Mecca with a curious siren-like quality that lulls visitors into staying longer than they had intended, while further south along the robust and frowning coastline is **Kawhia**, a moribund little community on the site of the Tainui people's first landfall in Aotearoa – and still their spiritual home. The **beaches** south of Kawhia are typically black sand, steeped in isolation and lashed by wind and sea, though a little comfort can be taken in the **thermal pools** that bubble up at the shoreline close to Kawhia. Sandwiched between Raglan and Kawhia lies the **Pirongia Forest Park**, though the best access is on the landward side from the township of Te Awamutu.

South of Raglan and within the forest park, a number of **walks** lead to viewpoints atop wind-buffeted hills, from which you can truly appreciate the grisly, rough-hewn coastline to the north and south.

Ngaruawahia and around

The most interesting and culturally significant spot north of Hamilton is **NGARU-AWAHIA**, 18km away on SH1, a farming centre at the junction of the Waikato and Waipa rivers. Both rivers were important Maori canoe routes, and the area has long held great significance for Maori: it is here that the **King Movement** (see box below) has its roots, and the town is home to the current monarch, Te Arikinui Dame Te Atairangikaahu. The town's Maori character is evident in the strikingly carved and decorated **Mahinarangi House**, which houses the Maori throne; **Turongo House**, the official residence of the present queen; and the Kimi-ora Cultural Complex, with its spectacular mural and a conspicuous tetrahedral roof. The marae is open to the public only on **Regatta Day**, the closest Saturday to March 17, when a unique regatta takes place at the confluence of the two rivers, featuring traditional Maori canoe and hurdle races and a parade of great war canoes before the Maori queen. Overlooking the marae is **Turangawaewae House**, the building intended to be the Maori parliament, which was opened in 1920.

Twenty-three kilometres west of Ngaruawahia, at the junction with SH22, are the popular though slightly run-down **Waingaro Hot Springs**, Waingaro Road (daily

---

THE KING MOVEMENT

Before Europeans arrived on the scene, Maori loyalty was solely to their immediate family and tribe, but wrangles with acquisitive European settlers led many tribes to discard age-old feuds in favour of a **common crusade** against the *pakeha*. Initially a response to poor communication and administration, **Maori nationalism** hardened in the face of blatantly unjust decisions and increasing pressure to "sell" their ancestral lands.

In 1856, the influential Otaki Maori sought a chief who might **unite** the disparate tribes against the Europeans, and in 1858 the Waikato, Taupo and some other tribes (largely from the Tainui canoe) chose **Te Wherowhero** as their leader. Taking the title of Potatau I, the newly elected king established himself at **Ngarauwahia** – to this day the heartland of the **King Movement**. The principal tenet of the movement was to resist the appropriation of Maori land and to provide a basis for a degree of self-government. Whether out of a genuine misunderstanding of these aims or for reasons of pure economic expediency, the settlers interpreted the formation of the movement as an act of rebellion – despite the fact that Queen Victoria was included in its prayers – and tension heightened. The situation escalated into **armed conflict** later in 1858 when the Waitara Block near New Plymouth was confiscated from its Maori owners. The fighting spread throughout the central North Island: the King Movement won a notable victory at Gate Pa, in the Bay of Plenty, but were eventually overwhelmed at Te Ranga. Seeing the wars as an opportunity to **settle old scores**, some Maori tribes sided with the British and, in a series of battles along the Waikato, forced the kingites further and further south, until a crushing blow was struck at Orakau in 1864. The king and his followers fled south of the Puniu River into an area that, by virtue of their presence, became known as the **King Country**.

They remained there, almost devoid of all European contact, until 1881, when **King Tawhiao**, who had succeeded to the throne in 1860, made peace. Gradually the followers of the King Movement drifted back to **Ngaruawahia**. Although by no means supported by all Maori, the loose coalition of the contemporary King Movement plays an important role in the current reassessment of Maori–*pakeha* relations, and the reigning Maori queen, **Te Arikinui Dame Te Atairangikaahu**, has been the recipient of many state and royal visits.

9am–10pm; $5), a large pool complex based around a series of natural springs, which tends to get busy on summer weekends. Nearby *Worsp's Farm* (☎07/825 4515; ④), north of the springs via Matira Road, offers B&B **accommodation** and is the base for the **Hole Adventure**, an enjoyable four-hour caving and abseiling trip with a "Jurassic stroll" through prehistoric caves and ancient bushland ($95, minimum 4 people).

Continuing north, SH1 cuts an almost uninterrupted straight line to Auckland, passing through the depressing and flat town of **Huntly**, 16km further north, famous for open-cast coal mines and the largest power station in the country, whose twin 150m-high chimneys dominate the townscape.

Cambridge

About 24km east of Hamilton on SH1 is **CAMBRIDGE**, marooned in a broad agricultural belt renowned for stud farms. With a modicum of charm, Cambridge is attractive in a bucolic sort of a way, boasting a village green, tree-lined avenues and a picturesque sunken lake,**Te Koutu Lake**, five minutes' walk from the centre. Around the lakeside, reached from Albert Street, are picnic areas and tracks through stands of tall chestnut and oak trees. The most significant building in Cambridge is **St Andrew's Anglican Church**, on the corner of Victoria Street and SH1, opposite the entrance to Te Koutu Park. A Victorian construction with a tall steeple, the church hides a fine dark-wood interior and original stained-glass windows.

Another good reason to visit Cambridge is Frank Vosper's **New Zealand Horse Magic**, 6km southeast of the town on SH1, near Karapiro. Set in lush, gently rolling countryside with lots of trees and well-manicured lawns, the stud conducts interesting and educational tours (10.30am, 2.30pm & 3.30pm; 45min; $9; casual visits outside tour times, $4; ☎07/827 8118) that include a show jumping and dressage demonstration. There is also the opportunity for a short stint in the saddle.

Practicalities

Local **buses** (#20) from Hamilton stop on Duke Street in the centre of town, while both Intercity and Newmans services stop at the Cambridge Travel Centre, 74 Victoria Street. The **visitor centre** is on Queen Street, near the Victoria Street roundabout (Mon–Fri 8am–4.30pm; ☎07/827 6033, fax 827 3505).

Among the many places to eat in Cambridge, four stand out. *Alphaz*, 72 Alpha St (lunch & dinner daily), is a spacious plant-strewn **restaurant** and bar with a pleasant outdoor courtyard and excellent snacks and meals. Much more typical of Cambridge is the pleasant *Fran's Deli Café*, 62 Victoria St (Mon–Sat 11am–5pm), where you can grab simple **snacks** and light meals for under $10, while enjoying local art displayed on the walls. *Sazarac Café*, 35 Duke St (BYO), offers a selection of coffees and fresh juices, a snack menu for $10 and under, a big all-day breakfast for $8.50, and specials such as the Big-Texburger and veggie burger for around $12. The last and by far the most swanky is *Souter House*, 19 Victoria St (Nov–Feb daily lunch & dinner, March–Oct Mon–Sat dinner only; licensed; ☎07/827 3610), a sumptuous silver-service restaurant in an elegant 1878 house.

Te Awamutu and around

The small town of **TE AWAMUTU** , 30km south of Hamilton on SH3, is a placid place, surrounded by rolling hills, hedgerowed dairy pasture and peat lakes, all overlooked by mounts Pironga, Maungatautari and Kakepuku.

Local Maori trace their descent to the Tainui canoe and by the nineteenth century there was a heavy Maori presence on the land, as evidenced by the many pa sites in the loops of rivers and on steep hill tops that are still visible today. During the 1863 **New Zealand Wars**, Te Awamutu was a garrison for government forces, and one of the most famous battles of the conflict was fought at the hastily constructed Orakau pa, where 2000 soldiers were held at bay for three days by just 300 Maori, an incident touchingly remembered in the local church.

The Town

Te Awamutu is known for its extensive **rose gardens**, on the corner of Arawata Street and Gorst Avenue, which are are at their best between November and May. The town also basks in reflected glory as the birthplace of Neil and Tim Finn. Fans of Split Enz and Crowded House will be unable to resist a self-guided tour (leaflet from the visitor centre) around places of significance in the **Finn brothers**' formative years.

A poignant reminder of the New Zealand Wars can be seen in **St John's Church**, on the opposite side of Arawata Street from the rose gardens and the visitor centre (where you pick up the key; free). Built as a garrison church in 1841, St John's was spared as other European buildings burned around it, because the Maori chieftainess, Te Paea Potatau, had placed her *mana* upon it. The tribute inside the church, written in Maori and English, is from the British Regiment of Foot, the 65th, honouring their Maori enemies, many of whom crawled, under fire, onto the battlefield to give water to their wounded British foes. The church also contains one of the oldest figurative, painted stained-glass windows in New Zealand.

Te Awamutu Museum (Tues–Fri 10am–4pm, Sat & Sun 2pm–4pm; free), is on Roche Street, about ten minutes' walk west of the visitor centre. Alongside early Maori artefacts (tools, clothes, carving and household relics), there are displays the European settlers and the New Zealand Wars. The museum's pride and joy is *Uenuku*, a striking darkwood carving and sacred relic of the Tainui people, said to have been carried to New Zealand from Hawaiki in the Tainui canoe; the carving is a representation of a traditional spirit or god as a rainbow.

Around Te Awamutu

There is little to stop for along the straight highway north of town, except the atmospheric **Yarndley's Bush** (dawn–dusk; free), one of the largest remaining stands of the towering kahikatea on the North Island. To reach the bush reserve, turn off SH3 3km north of Te Awamutu, on to the Ngaroto Road and continue for 1500m to the signposted entrance. A **loop walk** (20min) winds through the reserve, past huge root buttresses, and midway along, a raised platform gives you a bird's eye view of the constantly moving canopy. The drainage of marshland for farming and the use of odourless kahikatea wood to make boxes to transport butter overseas, has hastened the demise of these magnificent native trees.

Dominating the landscape to the west of Te Awamutu is **Pirongia Mountain** (959m), scarred by redoubt trenches from the New Zealand Wars. The peak lies within the **Pirongia Forest Park**, an area traversed by a series of interesting nature **walks** described in the DOC *Pirongia Forest Park* leaflet ($1, from Te Awamutu visitor centre). Of the two best **summit tracks**, the more rewarding and easier route is the Mahaukura Track (6km; 4hr), from the education centre at the end of Grey Road, 16km west of Te Awamutu. The more direct (and steeper) Wharauroa Route (5km; 3.5hr), begins at O' Shea Road, 3km west of the township of Pirongia.

Practicalities

Trains on the main Auckland–Wellington line stop at Station Road, about 2km west of the visitor centre. All the **bus** companies drop off near the **visitor centre**, on Gorst Avenue, near the corner with Arawata Street (Mon–Fri 9am–4.30pm, Sat & Sun

10am–3pm; ☎07/871 3259), and everything in town is within ten minutes' walk of here. Te Awamutu's **accommodation** and eating options are limited, to say the least. The *Selwyn Park Motor Camp*, Gorst Ave (☎07/871 7478; tent sites $9, cabins ②–③), is a safe bet, just two minutes' walk northwest from the visitor centre, or there's clean, comfortable serviced units at the *Road Runner Motel*, 141 Bond St (☎07/871 7420; ④). Aside from the usual ranks of fast-food joints, try *Robert Harris*, Arawata Street, for a good-value **breakfast**; *Taylor's*, 414 Greenhill Drive, for a simple lunch; and either *Burns House*, upstairs at 55 Alexandra St, or the *Rose and Thorn*, 32 Arawata St, for inexpensive **dinners**.

Raglan and around

Following the gently undulating contours of the land west of Hamilton for 48km, SH23 leads to **RAGLAN**, a tiny beach town that's as far west as you can go without getting wet. The centre of the community is on Bow Street, which has a central reservation lined with palm trees and a selection of banks, shops and a garage. Raglan is famous among **surfers** for having the best left-handed break in the world, creating perfect board-riding conditions: the finest waves are generally to be found at **Manu Bay** and **Whale Bay**, 8km south of town on Whaanga Road.

Most of the settlement lies around the southern side of the large and picturesque **Raglan Harbour**, with its long sandy beaches, sparkling ocean and lush green vegetation, in the shadow of **Karioi Mountain** to the southeast. **Maori** history recounts the journey of the great migratory canoe *Tainui* south along the West Coast until Mount Karioi loomed in the far distance. They travelled towards it for a very long time, but when they reached the mouth of the harbour a bar blocked their way, so they named the harbour *Whaingaroa* ("long pursuit") and paddled on to *Aotea* (Kawhia Harbour), where they could finally land. A derivation of Whaingaroa, Whangaroa was the name used for the harbour until 1855, when it was renamed Raglan, after the officer who led the Charge of the Light Brigade.

Housed in an old police station, the **Raglan Museum**, Wainui St (Sat & Sun only 1–3.30pm; donation requested), has a modest local history collection. For a more colourful version of local lore, you'd do better to hop aboard a **Raglan Harbour Cruise** (daily 1.30pm; 90min; $15; book ahead Dec–March, ☎07/825 0300), which leaves from the jetty at the bottom of Bow Street. The skipper keeps passengers amused with a seemingly endless string of amusing facts and fictions woven around the historic sites the boat passes. The trip also takes in the so-called pancake rocks, sedimentary limestone formations which appear to be made of a pliable dough.

Walks around Raglan

In the **Karioi Range**, there are two one-day tracks to the **summit** of Mount Karioi (755m), both steep in places but well worth it for the views of the mouth of Raglan Harbour and up and down the storm-battered coast. The best place to start is at the **Te Toto Gorge** (4km; 4hr, one-way), 12km south of Raglan, off Whaanga Road. The path starts opposite an ocean-jutting point and heads up the gorge. After a strenuous and difficult climb within a cliff-lined cut to a lookout, the final walk to the summit is considerably easier. The alternative **Wairake Track** (3.5km; 3hr one-way) is shorter, steeper, and slightly less scenic, tackling the landward side of the mountain from Karioi Road.

Inland, a much easier walk leads to the **Bridal Veil Falls**, hidden in dense native bush 23km southeast of Raglan. Water plummets 55m down a sheer rock face into a green pool; some droplets evaporate before they hit the bottom, creating a shimmering veil, adorned with ethereal rainbows in sunny weather. From the Kawhia Road, a signpost indicates the track to the falls, which is about a ten-minute stroll beside a small stream.

Practicalities

Buses (#23) from Hamilton run twice daily (Mon–Sat; 1hr; $4.70; ☎07/856 7184), stopping outside the **visitor centre** at the bottom of Bow Street (Mon–Fri 10am–5pm, Sat 10am–4pm, Sun noon–3pm; ☎07/825 0556). The local **shuttle/taxi** (☎07/825 8940) will run you to the beaches or the mountain tracks, and Raglan Harbour Cruises also run a **water taxi** service (☎07/825 0300). For explorations further afield, you can **rent bikes** from Karioi Mountain Bikes, 9 Bow St (☎07/825 0003), or join one of their guided bike tours.

ACCOMMODATION

The best place to stay in town is the small and friendly *Raglan Backpackers*, 6 Nero St (☎07/825 0515; dorms ①, rooms ②), a clean and comfortable **hostel** laid out around a courtyard and backing on to a beach, a mere minute's walk from the visitor centre; they also rent kayaks for crossing the harbour ($5 for 2hr). More idiosyncratic accommodation is on offer at *Raglan Wagon Cabins*, Whaanga Rd, about 2km south of Raglan (☎07/825 8268; dorms ①, rooms ②), a collection of brightly painted, converted **train carriages** set on top of a windswept hill with panoramic views. A little off the beaten track, but with superb views, is Marcus Vernon's **farmstay** (☎07/825 6892; dorms ①, rooms ②), 334 Houchen Rd. Head 8km east of Raglan on SH23 and then about 6km up Kawhia Falls Road, turn left on to Houchen Road, and the house is about another 3km up a farm track at the end of the road; pick-ups can be arranged from the Bridal Veil Falls. Rooms are rustic but clean, and you can either go your own way or muck in with Marcus – in return for a bit of help on the farm, he will provide simple but generous dinners; horse treks are also available (2hr; $30).

EATING AND DRINKING

The steady stream of surfers and travellers have encouraged some more interesting places to eat and drink in Raglan, the best of which is the recently refurbished *Black Rock Café*, in the *Harbour View Hotel*, Bow Street (daily 11am–midnight, closed Sun May–Nov; licensed). This pleasant **café/bar** is usually lively and good bagels, **foccacia** and pasta are served, along with delicious *ikan bilis* (crisp-fried anchovies with peanuts and sweet chilli), **chilli mussels**, fresh fish, steak, Indian platters and more, with main-meal prices under $20. Alternatively, a quiet meal of good simple **country fare** can be enjoyed next door at the *Bow Street Café* (Wed–Sun dinner only; BYO). Honorary mention must also be made of *Vinnie's*, Wainui Road, near the junction with Bow Street (lunch & dinner daily; BYO), which trailblazed the café scene in Raglan. Although not what it once was, you can still enjoy good fish, **steaks** and **cakes** at agreeable prices here.

Kawhia

The sleepy, unspectacular settlement of **KAWHIA**, 55km south of Raglan, can be reached via the scenic but at times hair-raising Whaanga Road – be prepared for a 30km unsealed section – which passes the Bridal Veil Falls (see p.202), or by the more widely used inland route, which detours around the eastern edge of Pirongia Forest Park, entering town on SH31. Perched on the northern side of the large Kawhia Harbour, Kawhia's resident population of 450 swells to 4,000 in the summer, swamped by holidaying Kiwi families, who flock to the Ocean Beach and its **hot springs**.

Kawhia is the spiritual home of the **Tainui** people, whose *waka* (canoe) landed here in 1350, after the Great Migration from Hawaiki. The Tainui were members of the bird cult, *Korotangi*, represented by a carved bird on the prow of their canoe, which reputedly warned of impending disaster or misfortune. As it happened, the sea in and around Kawhia Harbour was so bountiful that the Tainui lived on its shores for some three hundred years, until tribal battles over the rich fishing grounds forced them inland. In 1821, after constant attacks by the better-armed Waikato Maori, the great Tainui chief Te Rauparaha led his people to the relative safety of Kapiti Island.

With the arrival of **European** settlers and missionaries in the 1830s, Kawhia became a highly prosperous port, providing a gateway to the fertile King Country, although its fortunes declined in the early years of the twentieth centry, owing to its unsuitability for deep-draft ships. These days the settlement is known throughout New Zealand for annual **whale-boat races** (January 1), when eleven-metre, five-crew whaling boats are rowed across the bay.

The Town & around

The town itself is little more than a couple of petrol stations, a handful of combined shops and cafés, and a quaint little museum, all strung along Jervois Street and SH31 (the only road into town). The **Kawhia Museum** (Dec–March Wed–Sun 11am–4pm; April–Nov Sat & Sun noon–4pm; free), on the waterfront beside the wharf, at the end of Jervois Street, reveals much about Maori culture and early European settlers, augmented by an extensive photographic collection. One of the highlights of the museum is an original kauri whaleboat built in the 1880s, although the whaling station it worked from was a commercial failure.

The **Tainui canoe** is buried on a grassy knoll above the beautifully carved and painted **Maketu Marae**; *Hani* and *Puna* stones mark its stern and prow. Of particular significance to the Tainui people is the pohutukawa tree, *Tangi te Korowhiti*, to which the canoe was moored when it first landed; the tree still stands at the end of the footpath where it joins Kaora Street. Maketu Marae is a short walk (about 800m) along a waterfront footpath from the museum, where you should seek permission to enter the marae.

On Ocean Beach, the **Te Puia Hot Springs** bubble up from beneath the black sand between half and low tides (check times at the museum or in any of the local stores). The protocol is to dig a hole to sit in: shovels can be borrowed from the general store for a $5 deposit, but be warned that the black sand gets very hot and can be uncomfortable on bare feet. The climb over the sand dunes on your way to the springs is rewarding in its own right, revealing views of Mount Karioi to the north and Albatross Point to the south. The car park is the end of the unsealed Taunui/Kawhia Forest Road 4km from the town.

From Kawhia it is possible to continue along the coast and then cut east through the backdoor to Waitomo (see p.206) or double back to Otorohanga and continue south on SH3 to the Waitomo turn-off.

Practicalities

The only public transport is the Kawhia Bus and Freight **bus** service from Te Awamutu (Mon–Sat). The museum (see above) acts as an unofficial **visitor centre**, dispensing free maps and details of local attractions.

The best-value **accommodation** is at the motor camps: *Beachview Motor Camp*, on the beachfront (☎07/871 0727; tent sites $7, dorms ①, cabins ②–③); or *Kopua Camping Ground*, Marine Parade (☎07/825 8283; tent sites $7, dorms ①, cabins ②, tourist flats ③, motel units ④), just a six-minute walk from the centre of town.

The best place to get a **drink** is *Lena's Bar*, Jervois Street, run by a delightfully down-to-earth woman who dishes up a variety of beers, snacks, coffee – and usually a story or some advice. Also on Jervois Street, there are two stores (opposite one another) that serve burgers, fish and chips, and a variety of other **snacks** during the day; you can also get lunches and dinners at the central *Kawhia Hotel*.

The King Country

Now characterized by a bucolic landscape given over mostly to farming, gardens and dairy cattle, the **King Country** derives its name from more uncertain times when it became the refuge of King Tawhiao and members of the **King Movement** (see box on p.199), as they were driven south in defeat during the New Zealand Wars. The area soon gained a reputation as an inhospitable **Maori stronghold**, renowned for difficult terrain and the type of welcome that meant few, if any, Europeans had the nerve to enter. However, the forest's respite was shortlived: when peace was declared in 1881, eager **loggers** descended in droves.

These days the most famous place in the King Country is **Waitomo**, a tiny village that sits at the heart of a unique and dramatic landscape, honeycombed by **limestone caves** eerily illuminated by millions of **glow-worms**, and overlaid by a geological wonderland of karst features. North of Waitomo is the small dairying town of **Otorohanga**, with the unexpected pleasure of a **kiwi house** and large aviary, while to the south is **Te Kuiti**, devoted to sheep farming – and reputedly the shearing capital of the world. In the 1860s, the town provided sanctuary for Maori rebel Te Kooti, who reciprocated with a beautifully carved **meeting house**. Further south is the **Pureora Forest Park**, an enclave of rich lowland podocarp forest that was the site of a conservation battle in the late 70s, and now provides access to some excellent **walks** and a home for the rare **kokako** bird, which seems to prefer an ungainly walk to flight. The last community in the King Country, the rather jaded town of **Taumarunui** provides access to the Whanganui River, a **historic drive** to Stratford and the spectacular **coastal road** via **Mokau**, a tiny and intriguing coastal settlement, before heading through the Taranaki coastal plains to New Plymouth.

Otorohanga

Some 30km south of Te Awamutu, **OTOROHANGA** (meaning "food for a journey") is surrounded by sheep and cattle country. Most visitors are here to see the birds at **Kiwi House Native Bird Park**, Alex Telfer Drive, off Kakamutu Road (daily: Sept–May 9.30am–5pm; June–Aug 9.30am–4pm; $7.50), five minutes' walk from the town centre. And if you do want to see kiwis, this is as good a place as any: a ten-minute film (hourly until 4pm), is followed by a guided tour through the kiwi enclosure. You're left to find your own way around the remainder of the park, which is given over to extensive walk-through aviaries and cages that house tuatara (lizard-like creatures) and geckoes.

Back on Kakamutu Road is the small **Otorohanga Museum** (Sun 2–4pm; other times by arrangement, ☎07/873 8849; donation appreciated). Prize exhibits include Maori flax weavings, dog-hair cloaks, and a splendid portrait of Wahanui Huatare, a one-time local elder, in traditional costume; a separate room houses the 110-year-old wheelbarrow used in the inaugural ceremony for the railway, which finally opened up the King Country to *pakeha* settlement.

Once you've had enough of the kiwis and local history, check out the **Karam and John Haddad Menswear Store**, 65–71 Manipoto St, the premier stockist of Swandri bushwear and Kiwi Stockman waxed coats, for men and women – vital accessories if you want to be taken seriously in rural New Zealand.

Practicalities

The **train** station, on the Auckland–Wellington line, is just behind the main street in the centre of town, while Intercity and Newmans **buses** drop off right at the **visitor centre**, 87 Maniapoto St (Mon–Fri 9am–5pm, Sat 10am–3pm, Sun 11am–2pm; ☎07/873

8951, fax 873 8398). Bill Miller, the doyen of Otorohanga Taxis (☎07/873 8214), runs **guided trips** as well as a **taxi** service; there's not much about Otorohanga that Bill doesn't know, and his enthusiasm is infectious.

Most visitors press on to Waitomo once they've crossed the kiwis off their list, but if you want to **stay**, try the *Otorohanga Backpackers*, 1 Sangro Crescent (☎07/873 6022; dorms ①, rooms ②), a small, comfortable hostel with friendly owners, or the *Otorohanga Kiwi Town Caravan Park*, Domain Road (☎07/873 8214; tent sites $6.50), a well-kept, sheltered campsite where you can hear the call of the kiwis at night. **Eating** in Otorohanga revolves around tearooms and takeaways on Maniapoto Street, a more upmarket restaurant cringeably called *La Kiwi*, also on Maniapoto Street, and the *Royal Hotel* on Te Kanawa Street. Heading south on SH3, you can't miss the **Big Apple** (daily 10am–5pm, plus evenings Fri–Sun), set in an apple and kiwi orchard just north of the Waitomo turn-off. The Big Apple viewing tower overlooks the valley and houses a four-hundred-seater restaurant, buffet, bar, and café; prices are reasonable, but it can all feel too much like a production line.

Waitomo and the caves

The tiny village of **WAITOMO**, 16km south of Otorohanga, lies 6km up the Waitomo Caves Road to the west of SH3. In addition to Waitomo's famed **caves**, the region has many other features typical of eroded limestone or **karst** areas – dry valleys, streams that disappear down funnel-shaped sinkholes, craggy limestone outcrops and fluted rocks – some of which lie just off the Te Anga Road as it heads towards the long black **beaches**, craggy bluffs and tiny wind-lashed communities of the coast.

Appropriately enough, Waitomo means "water entering shaft" and, for over a hundred years, visitors have flocked to this diminutive village to explore the surrounding caves and to marvel at a twilight world illuminated by glow-worms. The cave passages were first discovered in 1887 by Maori chief Tane Tinorau and English surveyor Fred Mace, who built a raft of flax stems and drifted along an underground stream, with candles as their only source of light. First opened to tourists in 1888, the caves were acquired by the government in 1906, but were eventually returned, in 1989, to their traditional owners, who now receive a percentage of all the revenue generated and participate in the site's management.

Arrival, information and transport

Train travellers have to get off at Otorohanga and join connecting Newmans shuttle buses to Waitomo; Newmans shuttles also meet flights at Hamilton airport. All the major **bus** companies pass through Waitomo, stopping opposite the **visitor centre** (daily 8.30am–5.30pm; ☎07/878 6219, fax 878 6184), in the Waitomo Museum of Caves in the centre of the village. As well as providing information, the centre also takes bookings for most cave trips and onward travel. The Waitomo Shuttle (☎0800/808 279) operates a **taxi** service and an air and rail pick-up service. **Regional connections** include Perry's Bus to Te Kuiti (Mon–Sat) and, between October and April, the Waitomo Wanderer to Taupo and Rotorua (3 weekly).

Accommodation

Although backpackers are well provided for in Waitomo, other options are **limited**. To make sure you get what you want, **book in advance**, particularly during December and January.

Cavelands Country Holiday Park, Waitomo Caves Rd, opposite the Museum of Caves (☎0800 400 104). Spacious campsite conveniently near the general store. Tent sites $10, dorms ①, chalets & cabins ②.

Dalziels B&B, Waitomo Caves Rd, at the eastern end of the village (☎07/878 7641). Comfortable, clean, spacious rooms and a friendly welcome. ④.

Glow-worm Motel, cnr SH3 & Waitomo Caves Rd, 8km east (☎07/873 8882). Straightforward motel with nine comfortable, fully self-contained units. ④.

Hamilton Tomo Group Lodge, 1km west (☎07/878 7442). Caving club lodge that welcomes visitors. Large and clean, if simple, dorms have access to kitchen facilities and a mine of local knowledge. ①.

Juno Hall Backpackers, Waitomo Caves Rd, 1km east (☎07/878 7649). Farmhouse-style hostel, with a courtesy bus to the village pub and THC Glow-worm Cave; the hostel is also the base for Waitomo Horse Treks (see p.209). Dorms ①, rooms ②.

THC Waitomo Caves Hotel and Hostel, up the steep hill beside the Museum of Caves (☎07/878 8227). By far the most impressive building in the area, this grand old hotel was built in 1908. Many of the rooms have recently been refurbished and are very plush, but backpackers are also catered for in an associate YHA section with simple dorms and rooms (linen $5). Dorms ③, backpacker doubles ②, hotel rooms ⑦.

The Village

Waitomo village is a small collection of buildings on either side of the Waitomo Caves Road. The dominant feature is the campsite, in a bowl opposite the general store and pub, while the THC Waitomo Caves Hotel sits atop the hill, brooding like an ancient castle over all it surveys. Passing the Glow-worm Cave, Waitomo Caves Road becomes Te Anga Road, which then forks at the Johnson Memorial Grove of trees: Te Anga Road forges west toward Te Anga and the coast; while Tumutumu Road heads southwest towards the limestone bluffs, the faultline, the Aranui Cave and the Ruakuri Natural Tunnel.

A visit to the **Museum of Caves**, on Waitomo Caves Road in the village centre (daily 8.30am–5pm; $3.50, included in Black Water Rafting & Waitomo Adventures trips), will greatly enhance your caves experience. The museum is interactive, with tight crawl holes and intelligent displays on the geology and history of the caves and their exploration, tourism and the life cycle of glow-worms and cave wetas (an insect with an other-worldly appearance, which apparently influenced the modelmakers working on the *Aliens* films). A video shown in the reception area makes a good starting point for choosing cave trips, giving you a pretty good idea of the various options.

The **Ohaki Maori Cultural Centre**, 1km east of the village on Waitomo Caves Road (daily 10am–4.30pm), contains a Maori art gallery and café. Most impressive are the demonstrations of flax weaving, which take place on selected days (check with the visitor centre). Perched on a hill above the complex is the replica Ohaki Maori Village, from where the **Opapaka Pa Bush Walk** (45min) climbs past plants and trees traditionally used in Maori medicine to the original pa site, which is thought to have been established in the 1700s.

Back towards the village, on the main road, is the **Shearing Shed** (daily 9.30am–4.30pm, shearings 1pm; free), where cute little Angora bunnies get sheared and their soft fur is made into heart-stoppingly expensive fluffy goods.

The caves

There are more than forty-five kilometres of cave passages around Waitomo, about three kilometres of which can be visited on **guided tours**; the only caves you can safely explore **independently** are the Piripiri Caves west of the village (see p.209). The caves were gouged out of Waitomo's ancient limestone when rainwater mixed with carbon dioxide in the air, forming a weak acid that flowed down cracks in the rock; as more carbon dioxide was absorbed from the soil the acid grew stronger, dissolving the limestone and enlarging the cracks and joints – eventually forming the varied caves you see today. The process continues, and each year a further seventy cubic metres of limestone (about the size of a double-decker bus) is dissolved; at the present rate, the caves will be entirely eroded in less than two million years.

The **Glow-worm Cave** has over 1300m of inter-connecting passages. Highlights include the amazing acoustics of the Cavern Cathedral and a boat ride through the cave grotto, where glow-worms shed pinpricks of ghostly pale-green light resembling constellations in the night sky of another planet. The best slot for **tours** (daily 9am–5pm; every 30min; 40min; $17.50) is the last one of the day, when most of the tourists have gone home. A **glow-worm** is the larval stage of the fungus gnat, which produces light to lure unsuspecting flying food. The **larvae** are considerably more efficient than the average light bulb – ninety percent of the power they generate is light. When the adult gnats emerge, they are mouthless and so live only a few days, during which time they frantically seek out a mate and the female lays about 120 eggs.

Aranui Cave, 3.5km east of the visitor centre, is only 250m long, but is geologically more spectacular, with high-ceilinged chambers and magnificent stalactites and stalagmites. Tickets for **tours** (daily 10am, 11am, 1pm, 2pm & 3pm; 45min; $17.50) must be bought at the visitor centre or the kiosk at the Glow-worm Cave. A two-cave combo costs $27 and a museum-and-cave special, $19.

If you want to escape the crowds, consider heading 8km south to **Mason's Limestone Caves**, Boddies Rd, Oparure (daily tours 9.30am, 3hr; $40), where a gentle trip across the farm and native bush includes a tractor drive to two very different caves, one with an impressive display of glow-worms.

Blackwater rafting, canoeing, climbing and abseiling

Most trips can be booked at the visitor centre and most operators use it as their **starting point**; the exception is Waitomo Down Under, which has an office next door where you book and join their trips. In any case, you'd do well to **book in advance**, especially around December and January. Adventure trips into the caves are well organized and you shouldn't find yourself in situations of real danger, though they're not really recommended for border-line claustrophobics. For **blackwater-rafting** trips, you'll be kitted out with a wetsuit, caver's helmet with lamp, rubber boots and – most important of all – the **inner tube** from a car tyre, which enables you to float with the current through pitch-black caverns. Heavy **rain** does sometimes lead to **cancellation**, so it pays to have a day or two to spare. The two original adventure **companies**, Black Water Rafting and Waitomo Adventures, tend to have the most experienced and well-trained staff with first aid knowledge. Waitomo Down Under is **Maorioperated** and owned, though the only tangible difference is that their tours usually begin with a visit to the local marae.

Black Water Rafting (☎07/878 6219 & 0800/247 612) run two wetsuit-clad trips. The first (3hr, 90min underground; $65) involves a bit of climbing, a jump from an underground waterfall, and an idyllic float in a glow-worm cave, while the second (5hr, 3hr underground; $125) is a little more adventurous and demanding, adding abseiling and an eerie flying fox ride into the darkness to the itinerary. Both tours end up at the *Black Water Café* for hot showers and a feed. A more off-beat proposition is **Cave Canoeing** (daily 9am & 2pm; 3–4hr; $85; ☎07/878 7640; $85): a 22-metre descent is followed by canoeing through large cave passages, with lots of glow-worms.

One of the most spectacular trips run by **Waitomo Adventures** (☎07/878 7788 & 0800/WAITOMO) is the **Lost World Adventure** (4hr; $195), involving a stomach-churning 100-metre tandem abseil into a spectacular pothole, followed by a walk through some cave formations and a climb out on a seemingly endless ladder. The best trip is the first of the morning when the light is just beginning to break into the hole – and for real cave junkies, there's also an extended version of the trip over one and a half days. Other options include Haggis Honking Holes (4hr; $125), a madcap series of abseils, climbs and crawl-throughs, and the family-orientated Pink Gum Boot ($12.50).

Waitomo Down Under (☎07/878 6577 & 0800/102 605) run four trips, ranging from glow-worm tubing to more adventurous and longer tours (3–6hr; $65–140), involving cave tubing, abseiling and rapelling. Each trip begins with a visit to the Tokikapu Marae, where visitors are given a taste of Maori protocol before preparing for the caves, and ends with a reviving hot shower and soup.

Walks and horse trekking

The **Waitomo Walkway** (10km; 3hr round-trip) starts opposite the glow-worm caves, and can be divided into three shorter walks, each with a distinct character. The last section (30min), from the car park near the Ruakuri Cave on Tumutumu Road, is the most spectacular, featuring the Raukuri Natural Tunnel and after dusk an impressive array of glow-worms. A free leaflet from the visitor outlines the various options.

Also taking advantage of the above-ground scenery, **Waitomo Horse Trekking** offers various treks (1hr, $25; half-day, $60; ☎07/878 7649).

Eating and drinking

The **range** and **quality** of food in Waitomo is surprisingly good, principally because it is such a tourist hotspot. This also means that **in winter** the options and opening times become severely restricted, though you can always adjourn to the trusty **pub**.

Black Water Café, 1km east of the village, opposite *Juno Backpackers Lodge*. Cooked breakfasts ($7), simple snacks and light meals are served from early morning to late evening. Sunday night (6.30–8.30pm) is barbecue night, with mussels, spare ribs, sausages, veggie burgers, salads and dessert for $7. Licensed.

Cavelands Café, in the general store next to the Museum of Caves. Inexpensive soups, pizza, burgers, fish and salads, plus the fearsome "Waitomo Brunch" – foccaccia, bacon, tomato, brie and avocado. Daily 8am–9pm.

Café Ohake, in the Maori Cultural Centre (☎07/878 6610). Reasonably priced burgers, toasties and the like. The café will also arrange hangis for groups (15 minimum). Daily 10am–5pm.

Roselands Farm and Garden BBQ Restaurant, Fullerton Rd, five minutes drive south of the village. Splendid buffet lunches of char-grilled meat and fish with salad and dessert ($20), served in a beautiful garden setting. Lunch only (11am–2.30pm); licensed.

THC Waitomo Caves Hotel Restaurant, up the steep hill beside the Museum of Caves. Fine European-style and Asian-influenced food for lunch and dinner in old world colonial surroundings. Prices are high here and in the attached bar.

Waitomo Caves Tavern, next to the *Museum of Caves*. This friendly pub is where everyone (locals and tourists alike) ends up. Exceptionally large evening meals include the likes of steak, egg and chips ($7) or veggie samosa and chips ($5.50), and there's occasional live music.

Around Waitomo: towards the coast

There are three particularly impressive natural sights just west of Waitomo, along Te Anga Road, though there is no public transport out this way. The **Mangapohue Natural Bridge**, 21km from the village, is signposted from a lay-by on the right-hand side of the road. An easy footpath (20min) winds through forest to an atmospheric steep-sided limestone gorge with a remarkable natural double bridge formed by the erosion of a collapsed cave. Just past the Mangapohue Bridge, the **Marakopa Tunnel Trek** (Oct–March 10.30am–4pm; 4hr; $20, including torches & picnic; ☎07/876 7865) offers a relaxed guided walk through farmland adjacent to the Marakopa River and into a grandiose tunnel that's 270m long and 50m high.

A few kilometres further on, the **Piripiri Caves** lie a short walk (30min) away, through a forested landscape full of weathered limestone outcrops. Inside the cavern (carry a torch and spare batteries), the Oyster Room contains giant fossil oysters 30 million years old. About 5km past the caves, the track to the dramatic **Marokopa Falls** (30min) leads from the roadside through a forest of tawa, pukatea and kohekohe trees. The sense of anticipation is heightened by the sound of falling water, which grows gradually louder as you approach the broad, multi-tiered cascade.

If you continue west along the road towards the coast you will come across tiny **TE ANGA**, some 30km from Waitomo. Here you'll find the characterful *Te Anga Tavern*, a relaxed place where time seems to stand still. Have an inexpensive lunch and maybe a pint or two – and if you can't tear yourself away, you can retire to the backpacker **accommodation** at nearby *Bike 'n' Hire* (☎07/876 7362; dorms ①, rooms ②), which also rents out mountain bikes for exploring the area.

Continuing southwest towards the coast, 14km further on is the hamlet of **MAROKOPA**, with its long, wild black-sand beaches – best viewed from the Marakopa Lookout, which is accessible from the Marokopa rivermouth. **Kiritehere Beach**, about 3km south of Marokopa, has a variety of unusual rock formations and a number of ancient fossils scattered among the sands.

Te Kuiti

Back on SH3, the hills narrow around the plain town of **TE KUITI**, 19km south of Waitomo. At the fulcrum of road and rail routes, from Te Kuiti you can either make for the coast along SH3 or veer inland on SH30 to Pureora Forest Park.

Te Kuiti hosts the annual **New Zealand Shearing and Wool Handling Championships**, which is held in late March or early April (depending upon Easter), and the town's primacy in the competitive world of shearing is reinforced by the seven-metre-high statue of a man shearing a sheep at the southern end of Rora Street. Te Kuiti also has a proud Maori history, for it was here that King Tawhiao and his followers fled after the battle of Rangiriri in 1864. Eight years later, Maori rebel Te Kooti (see box on p.362) also sought refuge here and lived under the Maori King's protection until he was pardoned. In return for sanctuary, Te Kooti left a magnificently carved **meeting house**, Te Tokanganui-a-noho, opposite the south end of Rora Street, on Awakino Road; ask at the visitor centre for permission to enter.

Practicalities

The **train** station lies between Rora and Carroll streets and a footbridge over the tracks takes you to the **visitor centre** on Rora Street (Mon–Fri 9am–5pm, Sat 9am–noon; ☎07/878 8077), just a few minutes' walk from *Tiffany's Restaurant*. *Tiffany's* is a focal point of life in Te Kuiti: Intercity and Newmans **buses** stop opposite, at the corner of Rora Street and Lawrence Street; the smaller operators pick up and drop off right outside; and it's here that you buy bus and train tickets. Perry's Bus run a regular **shuttle** and sightseeing **tour** to Waitomo and across to the coast, or call the local **taxi** service, King Country Cabs (☎07/878 7744).

The **DOC office**, 78 Taupiri St (Mon–Fri 8am–4.30pm), has information about the Pureora Forest Park (see p.211).

Good-value **rooms** are available at the *Panorama Motor Inn,* 59 Awakino St (☎07/878 6782; ④), and the attached restaurant serves wholesome country food, or settle for the *Domain Motor Camp*, Hinerangi Street (☎07/878 6223; tent sites $5.50, on-site vans & cabins ②), along the bank of the Mangaokewa River. Winner of the silliest name for a **bar** contest is *How Barzarre*, on the corner of King Street and Taupiri Street, where you can get snack food, great salads, booze and liqueur coffees. The most convenient places to grab a simple **snack** or meal between buses are *Tiffany's* (Mon–Thurs 8am–9.30pm, Fri–Sun 8am–10pm) and the *Te Kuiti Pie Cart* (Mon–Thurs 5pm–midnight, Fri & Sat noon–4am); both are on Rora Street.

Pureora Forest Park

The **Pureora Forest Park** straddles the Hauhungaroa Range west of Lake Taupo. Te Kuiti provides the easiest access from the west, along SH30 via the small community of Benneydale, but there is no public transport. The park narrowly escaped logging in 1978, when it became the site of a successful tree-top protest.

Along with Little Barrier Island (see p.135) and a few pockets around Rotorua, this broad-leaf forest environment is now one of the few remaining habitats of the rare North Island **kokako**. The 38cm-tall bluish-grey birds are poor fliers, preferring to walk, climb or hop; their forest habitat enables them to clamber grumpily up through the branches, but they tend to nest close to the ground, so an area free of introduced predators is vital for their survival – if you go looking for them, be careful where you tread.

The **DOC office** on Barryville Road, off SH30 46km from Te Kuiti, stocks leaflets and maps describing various short walks in the park and detailing mountain-bike access. In the vicinity of the DOC office, there are several sights worth a look: the largest recorded totara tree, the **Pouakani Tree**, is just five minutes' drive east; slightly further in, 2.5km along Pikiariki Road, the **Forest Tower**, close to the site of the landmark anti-logging protest, gives a twelve-metre-high protestor's-eye view of the surrounds. The easy **Totara Walk** (30min loop track) starts at the junction of Barryville Road and Link Road, 1km from the DOC office. This wheelchair-accessible track winds through giant podocarps, past matai, rimu, tawa, kahikatea, ferns, vines and perching plants, with a screeching accompaniment from kaka high up in the leafy canopy. A more challenging route with excellent views, the **Mount Pureora Summit Track** (2km; 3hr; 1165m ascent), starts from the Link Road car park, 10km from the DOC office.

Taumarunui

A small town in the centre of the King Country surrounded by national parks and forests, **TAUMARUNUI** sits astride SH4, 82km south of Te Kuiti, and marks the confluence of the Ongarua and Whanganui rivers. Taumarunui was one of the last places to be settled by Europeans, and didn't really take off until 1908, when the railway came to town. Upon encountering a gradient too steep for trains, the surveyor, Rochforte, curled the rail line into the **Raurimu Spiral**, thereby easing the gradient of the climb and allowing the use of the most direct route. A lookout at Raurimu, 37km south of town on SH4, and a model in the visitor centre clearly show what an amazing idea and a remarkable feat of engineering it was.

These days Taumarunui has a population of 5500 and dwindling industries have left it rather run-down. The only reason most travellers stop here is to visit the **Whanganui National Park** by canoe or jetboat (see p.231) or to follow the **Taumarunui–Stratford Heritage Trail**.

Practicalities

Both **buses** and **trains** use the train station on Hakiaha Street as their stop in town, and it also contains the **visitor centre** (Mon–Fri 9am–4.30pm, Sat & Sun 10am–4pm). The **DOC office** (Mon–Fri 8am–noon & 1–4.30pm) is in Cherry Grove, off Taumarunui Street, about fifteen minutes' walk from the visitor centre, and sells passes and hut tickets for the Whanganui National Park.

A range of **accommodation** is available at the *Alpine Inn*, an old colonial hotel on the corner of Marae Street and Miriama Street (☎07/895 7033, fax 895 7031; dorms ①, backpacker rooms ②, hotel rooms ④). On the opposite side of Marae Street, *Calverts Spa Motel*, at no. 6 (☎07/895 8500, fax 895 8400; ④), has quiet, comfortable motel rooms with free continental breakfast.

Most of the **eating** places in Tamarunui cater to the truckie trade. The 24-hour *Main Trunk Café/Café 1913*, a converted railway carriage at the east end of town on Hakiaha Street, serves filling burgers, steaks, fish, exceptional toasted sandwiches and a full cooked breakfast ($11). Sharing the same railway carriage is *Platform 2*, a daytime café where they bake their own bread, cakes and pies, and specialize in made-to-order sandwiches and rolls. The *Pinnacles Restaurant and Bar*, in the Alpine Inn, offers a broad range of straightforward dishes for under $20, including a vegetarian option, while the *Willows Restaurant*, on the first floor at 93 Hakiaha St (Tues–Fri 9am–11pm, Sat 6pm–midnight; BYO), serves a variety of steaks, seafood, pasta-dishes and liqueur coffees.

Taumarunui–Stratford Heritage Trail

This rugged 155-kilometre road (SH43), is described in the *Stratford–Taumarunui Heritage Trail* leaflet (free from visitor centres). Skirting the Whanganui National Park, the route is bordered by farmland, **scenic reserves** and some points of historic interest; you'll need to allow a minimum of three hours to travel the route, some stretches of which are unsealed – longer if you want to spend time at any of the **diversions** along the way.

The first worthwhile stop, **Maraekowhai Reserve**, is about 17km down a signposted, unsealed road. A track begins just below the car park at the road end and follows a creek to a lookout over the **Ohara Falls** (10min). Just before the falls, another track branches off to the left over a small plank bridge, climbing to a one-time stronghold of the Hau Hau (see p.345), where in 1862 they erected a war pole, **Rongo-nui**, with four arms pointing in all directions of the compass, intended to call warriors to their cause from all over the country. At the end of hostilities, a peace pole, **Rerekore**, was erected close by, and both are now preserved on this site, which is also accessible from the Whanganui River (see p.235).

Back on SH43, the road snakes through the Tangarakau Gorge, carved by the river from sedimentary limestone. Around 90km from Taumarunui is the tiny village of **WHANGAMOMONA**, a self-declared republic with a population of seventy. The centre of the community is the hotel, built in 1911, where you can get your passport stamped or buy a Whangamomonian version, while wetting your whistle. The *Whangamomona Hotel/Pub*, Ohura Road (☎06/762 5823; tent sites $8 dorms ①, cabins & rooms ②–④), also has **accommodation**, serves meals and is open daily from 11am till the barman goes to bed. This sleepy little village, which is disturbed only by one freight train a day, declared itself a republic on October 28, 1995, after the New Zealand government had altered the regional borders, taking the village out of Taranaki. The anniversary of the declaration is celebrated each year, on the closest Saturday to that date: the population swells to about 3500 (special trains run from Hamilton and Auckland), who come to witness the annual swearing in of the president, whip-cracking and gumboot-throwing competitions – and a good deal of drinking and eating.

Climbing beside steep bluffs, SH43 passes a couple of saddles with views down the valley and across the **Taranaki Plains** before descending to flat dairy pasture, eventually rolling into **Stratford** (see p.224) as the permanently snow-capped Mount Taranaki looms into view.

The coast road to Taranaki

Heading southwest from Te Kuiti, **SH3** makes a beeline for the coast, then twists its way through tiny communities, sandwiched between the spectacular **black beaches** and **cliffs** of the coast and steep inland ranges, until the scenery opens out onto **Taranaki Plains** just north of New Plymouth (see p.213).

Mokau and around

The small community of **MOKAU**, 73km from Te Kuiti, has two good surf beaches, Mokau and Rapanui (both subject to strong rips and currents), a small **museum**, the **Maniaroa Marae** and pa, and some enjoyable **river cruises**. Mokau also featured in Jane Campion's film *The Piano*, particularly in the bush scenes and the fence line, seen in silhouette, along which the daughter dances.

There is an abundance of seafood on the beaches near Mokau, including mussels, cockles, pipi and – if you know where and when (Aug 15–Nov 30) to look – whitebait. For a taste of the black-beach scenery so typical of this coastline, head for the **estuary** about ten minutes' walk from town, where a cave and waterfall are set back from the beach. From the jetty near the rivermouth, the 83-year-old historic creamboat, MV *Cygnet* (daily 11am; 3hr; $25; ☎06/752 9775), **cruises** up river via a number of points of historic interest, old coal workings and abandoned farms; weather permitting, this veteran vessel also offers an unusual candlelight bush-dining trip. Back in town, the local **museum** (daily 10am–4pm; $1), on SH3 as you enter Mokau from Awakino, charts the history of the small Maori settlements on either side of the Mokau Rivermouth and of the 1840 European settlement beside the coal-rich river. Nearby, the **Maniaroa Marae** and pa is the resting place of the Tainui canoe anchor stone from the Great Migration, a historic *waka* and some excellent wood carvings; seek permission to enter at the museum, the Te Kohatu Organic Gardens opposite the marae, or by phone (☎06/752 9792).

Continuing south down the coast, after 18km you'll come to a fascinating **sea cave** just south of the **Tongaporutu Rivermouth**. Conveniently signalled by two rock stacks on the beach opposite the entrance, the cave bears **ancient footprints** on its upper walls, about four metres up from the floor. For many years this coastal, tide-dependent route was the only access for Maori travelling between the Waikato and Taranaki districts, and this cave provided shelter. Local lore has it that the infamous chief **Te Rauparaha**, along with his most trusted female companion, rested in a sea cave to recover from a debilitating attack of boils. When the boils were lanced, the chief braced himself against the cave wall and, due to the combination of the sudden pain and his great strength, left impressions of his hands and feet in the rock. The chief was reputed to have six toes – as do eight of the foot imprints in the cave.

PRACTICALITIES

The daily C-Tours (☎06/758 1777) **bus** from Auckland to New Plymouth, via Te Kuiti, stops in Mokau at the side of the main road, opposite *KD's Café*. The museum acts as an unofficial **visitor centre**, providing maps of the local area and lists of attractions and facilities. If you're enamoured with Mokau's unassuming charms, **stay** at the *Palm House Backpackers* (☎06/752 9081; ①), a cosy, well kept hostel on SH3, right by *KD's Café*, or at the nearby, beachside *Seaview Motor Camp* (☎06/752 9708; tent sites $6, flats & cabins ②–③). **Meals** and food supplies are available at the campsite, *Mokau Roadhouse*, *KD's Café*, and the general store and post office – but be warned, almost everything in town is closed on Mondays.

New Plymouth and around

The city of **NEW PLYMOUTH** sits at the junction of SH3, linking it with Te Kuiti to the north and Wanganui to the south, and SH45, skirting the coast of the Taranaki Peninsula. Although relatively isolated, the city bustles with prosperity and bristles with a sense of its own importance: as the only deep-water international port on the west coast, **Port Taranaki**, at the edge of the city, serves as New Zealand's western gateway. Like everything else in the region, the city is dominated by **Mount Taranaki**

– though some visitors never even glimpse the summit through its cloak of low cloud, leading local wags to quip, "If you can see the mountain, it's going to rain; if you can't, it's raining already".

Captain **Cook** was the first European to sight the mountain, naming it **Egmont** after the first Lord of the Admiralty, but it was not until 1828 that a trading and **whaling station** was established by John Lowe and Richard Barrett on the Ngamotu Beach, overlooked today by the modern city. They found few **Maori** living in the area because of annual raids by the northern tribes, which forced many Te Atiawa Maori to migrate with Te Rauparaha to Kapiti Island. In 1841, the **Plymouth Company** dispatched six ships of English colonists to New Zealand; mostly from the West Country, they named their community New Plymouth. From the late 1840s many Te Atiawa people returned to their homeland and disputes arose over **land sales** to settlers, until in 1860 culminated in a ten-year armed conflict, slowing the development of the town and leaving a legacy of **Maori grievances**, some of which are still being addressed today.

Although there is no danger of the city rivalling the natural architecture of Mount Taranaki, it does boast an outstanding **gallery**, an excellent **museum** and a tranquil **public park**, as well as a lively restaurant and after-hours entertainment scene. Just offshore is the **Sugar Loaf Islands Marine Reserve**, a haven for wildlife above and beneath the sea, while 17km further south along SH45 is the surfing and windsurfing hotspot of **Oakura**. On the northeastern outskirts of the city is the **Bell Block**, home of the **Fitzroy Pole**, which commemorates one of the few instances in early New Zealand history when settlers were compelled to give back land they had taken from local Maori. Further northeast along SH3 is **Waitara**, a small settlement that effectively became the catalyst for the New Zealand Wars of the 1860s. Following SH3 as it cuts inland from the city, you'll come to the small settlement of **Inglewood**, 14km from New Plymouth and one of the main access points to the Egmont National Park.

Arrival, information and transport

The **airport** is about ten minutes' drive northeast, from where Withatruck buses shuttle into the city ($8; ☎06/751 7777). InterCity and Newmans **buses** both drop off at the Travel Centre, 32 Queen St, in the centre of the city. The **visitor centre**, on the corner of Leach Street and Liardet Street (Mon–Fri 8.30am–5pm, Sat & Sun 10am–3pm; ☎06/759 6080, fax 759 6073), stocks leaflets covering the many self-guided walks around the town, brochures and folders on the accommodation and restaurants in the area, as well as details of trips and sights. The **DOC office**, 220 Devon St West (Mon–Fri 8.30am–4.30pm), has information on Egmont National Park and sells hut tickets.

Okato Bus Lines run **local bus** services from their depot, at 32 Queen St, to all the suburbs of New Plymouth via various stops in the city; check at the visitor centre for details. There are no public buses to the mountain although some private shuttle companies do offer services (see p.222).

Accommodation

The best-value accommodation in New Plymouth is offered by the hostels and B&Bs. The majority of places are concentrated around Devon Street and in the foothills to the south.

Hotels, farmstays and B&Bs

Balconies B&B, 161 Powderham St (☎06/757 8866). A five-minute walk from the visitor centre, this large turn-of-the-century manor house offers B&B in comfortable, high-ceilinged rooms. ④.

Devon Hotel, 390 Devon St (☎06/759 9099). A smart, refurbished hotel with a range of rooms from economy to luxury, and a dining room. ④–⑤.

Henwood House B&B, 122 Henwood Rd, Bell Block, 5km east on SH3 (☎ & fax 06/755 1212). Grand 1890s wooden house nestled among trees, with spacious rooms, a lounge and sun deck; dinner by arrangement ($30). ④–⑥.

Kirkstall B&B, 8 Baring Terrace (☎06/758 3222). An intimate and friendly B&B in a 1920s house with lovely views over a garden that slopes down to the Te Henui River, about fifteen minutes' walk from the city centre, with characterful rooms; dinner by arrangement ($25). ④.

Windyglen Farmstay, Bertrand Rd, 28km northeast (☎06/752 0603). By the Waitara River, this commercial dairy farm offers comfortable rooms with shared facilities, and home-cooked meals by arrangement. ⑤.

Hostels and campsites

Belt Road Seaside Motorcamp, 2 Belt Rd (☎06/758 0228). A scenic cliff-top site, twenty minutes' walk from the city centre, with camping and cabins in a tidy sheltered area. Tent sites $8.50, cabins ②–③.

Central City Backpackers Lodge, 104 Leach St (☎06/758 0473). Has a clean dining room and kitchen, two dorms, singles and twins; linen $5, breakfast and dinner by arrangement. Dorms ①, rooms ②.

Hostel 69, 69 Mill Rd (☎06/758 7153). This small hostel is in need of attention but is cheap with cosy rooms. Located some fifteen minutes' walk uphill from the centre, close to Pukekura Park, they also offer free pick-up and drop-off. Dorms ①, rooms ②.

New Plymouth YHA, 12 Clawton St (☎06/753 5720). An ultra-friendly, comfortable hostel in a peaceful garden, reached along a gentle streamside walking track (15min) from the city centre, or by bike (rental $5 a day from the hostel). The rooms are comfortable and the facilities well kept and clean. Tent sites $8.50, dorms ①, rooms ②.

Shoestring Budget Lodge and Motel, 48 Lemon St (☎06/758 0404). Only 350m from the visitor centre, with a sauna ($4), roomy kitchen and dining room, this is one of the best places in town. Stay in the charming old house or in bargain motel units. Dorms ①, rooms ②, motel units ④.

The Whitehaven, 1518 South Rd, Oakura, 10km west on SH45 (☎ & fax 06/752 7800). Self-proclaimed home of the thrill-seeker, with clean comfortable lodging. Dorms ①, rooms ②.

The City

What New Plymouth lacks in architectural beauty it more than makes up for with energy. The centre of the city comprises a grid of broad parallel roads running north to west, complicated by a one-way system that runs the length of Leach Street (which becomes Vivian Street as it heads west) and the parallel Powderham Street (which becomes Courtney Street as it heads north). Turning its back on the coast, the city looks in on itself, the central blocks containing most of the attractions, eating and entertainment, most within ten minutes' walk of one another.

The **Govett-Brewster Art Gallery**, situated at the corner of King Street and Queen Street (daily 10.30am–5.30pm; free), benefits from a recent extension that allows the permanent display of work by the internationally renowned artist and filmmaker Len Lye. The remainder of the gallery, auditorium and concert venue are given over to travelling national and international exhibitions (check with the visitor centre). Best known for his kinetic sculptures and animated "cameraless" films, Lye developed an early fascination with movement and tribal art, which was later fuelled by his travels throughout the Pacific Islands. Applying surrealist principles to indigenous art, he experimented with sculpture, batik, painting, film and photography. Unable to secure finance for his film projects after he moved to New York in the 1950s, he returned to sculpture, finding that he could exploit the flexibility of steel rods, loops and strips to create abstract "tangible motion sculptures". These motor-driven sculptures are erratic in their movement, lending them an air of anarchy that

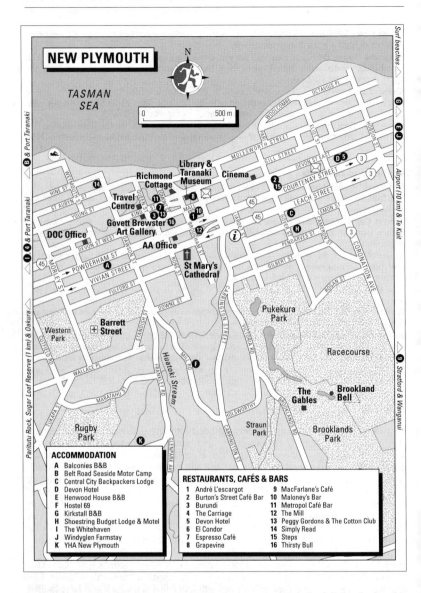

NEW PLYMOUTH

TASMAN SEA

N

0   500 m

Library & Taranaki Museum
Richmond Cottage
Cinema
Travel Centre
Govett Brewster Art Gallery
DOC Office
AA Office
St Mary's Cathedral
Barrett Street
Pukekura Park
Racecourse
The Gables
Brookland Bell
Western Park
Rugby Park
Straun Park
Brooklands Park
Huatoki Stream

Surf beaches
B & Port Taranaki
B & Port Taranaki
B & Port Taranaki
Airport (10 km) & Te Kuit
Paritutu Rock, Sugar Loaf Reserve (1 km) & Oakura
Stratford & Wanganui

ACCOMMODATION

A   Balconies B&B
B   Belt Road Seaside Motor Camp
C   Central City Backpackers Lodge
D   Devon Hotel
E   Henwood House B&B
F   Hostel 69
G   Kirkstall B&B
H   Shoestring Budget Lodge & Motel
I   The Whitehaven
J   Windyglen Farmstay
K   YHA New Plymouth

RESTAURANTS, CAFÉS & BARS

1   André L'escargot
2   Burton's Street Café Bar
3   Burundi
4   The Carriage
5   Devon Hotel
6   El Condor
7   Espresso Café
8   Grapevine
9   MacFarlane's Café
10 Maloney's Bar
11 Metropol Café Bar
12 The Mill
13 Peggy Gordons & The Cotton Club
14 Simply Read
15 Steps
16 Thirsty Bull

induces a certain primal fear – apparently, Lye was particularly delighted when his works frightened small children, considering this a litmus test of their effectiveness. Should you need some reassuring refreshment, the gallery also has a superb café.

At the bottom of King Street, in the public library building, is the **Taranaki Museum**, accessed from Ariki Street (Tues–Fri 10.30am–4.30pm, Sat & Sun 1–5pm; free). Of the permanent collection, the extensive Maori exhibition should not be missed, nor the large collection of paintings, ranging from 1834 pen-and-ink sketches through to contemporary works, including those of John Bevan Ford (see p.241). Highlights of the "Taonga Maori Treasures" include the anchor from the Tokomaru Canoe, which brought Taranaki Maori to New Zealand, and wood carvings of a style unique to Taranaki with three-dimensional figures, unlike many Maori carvings which are reliefs on a flat background.

Diagonally opposite the museum is the **Richmond Historic Cottage**, Ariki Street (Nov–May Mon, Wed & Fri 2–4pm; Sat & Sun 1–4pm; June–Oct Fri–Sun only, same hours; $1), a stone cottage built in 1854 for the Richmond family and furnished with period artefacts. Christopher William Richmond went on to become the local member of parliament.

Straight up Liardet Street, on the hill past the visitor centre, is **Pukekura Park and Brooklands** (daily dawn–dusk; free), a green, tranquil oasis in the city. The Pukekura section is dominated by water and rich plant life, with the **King Fern Gully** and fern-clad tunnels offering welcome relief from the usual rhododendron displays. Brooklands provides a glimpse of the past in **The Gables** (Jan daily 1–4pm; Feb–Dec Sat & Sun only 1–4pm; free), one of the earliest colonial hospitals (1847), now resurrected as an art gallery and medical museum. This part of the park also contains a 2000-year-old puriri tree in a stand of native bush and the **Brooklands Bowl**, an outdoor amphitheatre used for concerts and events throughout the year. Every evening from mid-December to early February, the **light festival** creates spectacular colours and magical effects in the skies above the parks after sunset.

On Vivian Street between Brougham Street and Robe Street is **St Mary's Pro Cathedral**. Designed by Frederick Thatcher and begun in 1845, this is the oldest stone church in New Zealand, a simple austere building marred by a modern annexe but worth visiting for its imposing gabled dark-wood interior and atmospheric graveyard dotted with ancient knotted trees and gravestone testaments to disease and war. Also inside the cathedral is a striking Maori memorial with carvings by John Bevan Ford and tukutuku panels by Min Crawford; unveiled in 1972, the memorial invites forgiveness for past injustices by telling the story of Raumahora and Takarangi whose love for each other united two warring *iwi*.

Another monument to the past unease between Maori and European settlers, **Fitzroy's Pole**, lies northeast of the city centre, on the corner of Devon Street East and Smart Road, on the way to Waitara. The carved pole was erected by Maori to commemorate Governor Fitzroy's 1844 decision, which forced *pakeha* settlers to give up their properties in the Bell Block area. Also at the east end of the city are several good **surfing beaches**, at the end of Octavius Place, with access by road or by following the pathway along the sea wall.

At the western end of the city and visible from the main breakwater of Port Taranaki is the massive **New Plymouth Power Station** (guided tours Sun 2pm; free), which is passed by the most scenic of many walks around the city and its outlying suburbs, the **Coastal Walkway** (7km). Running from Lake Rotomanu at the northeastern end of the city to the mouth of Herekawa Stream at the southwestern end, the walk passes the Fitzroy Seaside Park and takes in the port, power station and **Paritutu Rock**. The rock overlooks and is part of the Sugar Loaf Marine Reserve (see p.218) and is of great significance to the Maori as a border between the Taranaki and Te Atiawa territories and because it makes a near-perfect natural fortress. The twenty-minute climb up the rock, which begins beside the Survivors Outdoor Training Centre, opposite the car park on Centennial Drive, is quite arduous, with a steel rope providing guidance and support. There is another lookout point on the western side of the rock at Ngatu Road, with good views down the coast.

Around New Plymouth

The most spectacular sight around New Plymouth is the **Sugar Loaf Marine Reserve**, opposite the Paritutu Rock and reached by boat from the southern end of the city. Further south, the pretty **Carrington Road** provides a picturesque drive to some abundant and colourful formal gardens, while wilder pleasures are to be had in the surf off **Oakura**, along the coast on SH45. Heading out of the city in the opposite direction, **Waitara**, just off SH3, offers more intellectual grist, with memorials to its seminal role in the events that led to the New Zealand Wars of the 1860s (see p.765).

Sugar Loaf Marine Reserve

The **Sugar Loaf Marine Reserve** consists of a number of steep-sided rocky islands rising sharply from the sea, the Paritutu and Mataora rocks on the mainland and the Tokamapuna Reef. The reserve is DOC-administered, and a *Sugar Loaf Marine Reserve* pamphlet ($1) is available at the DOC office and the visitor centre.

The eroded remnants of an early volcanic centre, later occupied by Maori, the islands were named by Captain Cook in 1770, who was struck by Moteroa Island's similarity to sugar loaves baked in Britain at the time. These days they provide a sanctuary for rare plants, little blue penguins, petrels, sooty shearwaters and other bird species. The reserve also contains an abundance of marine life, with 67 species of fish, as well as New Zealand's most northerly breeding colony of fur seals, migrating humpback whales (Aug–Sept) and dolphins (Oct–Dec), while underwater canyons up to 30m deep are chock-full of multicoloured anemones, sponges, seaweeds and slugs.

No one is allowed to land on the islands and the best way to see the reserve is by boat. A memorable way to visit is with the eccentric but hyper-friendly **Happy Chaddy's Charters** (1hr; $20; ☎06/758 9133) in an old lifeboat launched with suitable aplomb from its shed between the Main and Lee breakwaters in the Ocean View Parade marina, off St Aubyn Street. More of a water-level view is available with **Discovery Adventure Tours** (☎06/758 0116), who offer sea kayaking (2hr; $35), snorkelling (2hr; $35) and scuba gear rental for qualified divers, as well as a straightforward boat trip out to the seal colony, picking up and emptying crab pots ($15).

Along Carrington Road

Carrington Road heads southwest out of town, skirting the mountain and passing a few attractions. At no. 548, 8km from New Plymouth, the historic **Hurworth Cottage** (daily 10am–4pm; $3.50) was originally occupied by a young lawyer, Harry Atkinson, who went on to become New Zealand's Prime Minister four times and was one of the first politicians to advocate women's suffrage and welfare benefits. Built in 1856, the cottage is the only survivor of a settlement called Hurworth, which was abandoned during the New Zealand Wars.

A few kilometres further on, the **Pouakai Zoo Park**, 590 Carrington Rd (daily 9am–5pm; $4), has an interesting walk-through bird enclosure, but the rest of the enclosures are pretty lacklustre. Around 20km from New Plymouth, **Pukeiti**, 2290 Carrington Rd (daily 9am–5pm; $6), is a rainforest garden that boasts the largest collection of rhododendrons and azaleas in New Zealand; although there are flowers in bloom all year round, the best time to visit is from November to August. There's also a restaurant in the gardens, serving light lunches, morning and afternoon teas.

Oakura

On SH45, 17km west of town, lies the surfing hotspot of **OAKURA**, with the best **windsurfing** beach in Taranaki and some good conventional boardriding. Windsurf Kiwi, 43 Pitcairn St, and Vertigo Total Surf, Main St, both **rent** learner, slalom and wave boards, and proffer information and advice on the choicest locations. While in Oakura, a visit to the **Koru pa** is well worth a brief detour: turn towards Mount Taranaki on the Wairau Road and left into Surrey Road, from which an easy walk (15min) brings you to the stronghold of the Nga Mahanga, its stone-faced ramparts now strangled by native vegetation.

Around Waitara

The small coastal settlement of **WAITARA**, 15km northeast of New Plymouth and served by local buses (Mon–Sat every 2hr), marks the beginning of the **Waitara Campaign Trail**, a 19-kilometre drive which traces the culture clash that sparked the first Taranaki Land War. The self-guided tour is described in a booklet, *The Waitara Campaign Historic Trail* (available from New Plymouth Museum; $6) and by boards and plaques along the trail.

Some 8km south of Waitara, just outside the village of **LEPPERTON**, is **Sentry Hill Winery**, Cross Road (Dec & Jan daily 9am–5pm; Feb–May & Sept–Nov Wed–Sun same hours; June–Aug Sat & Sun same hours), where you can taste the kiwi fruit and boysenberry wines, some killer golden scrumpy and hair-raising regiment gin. About 5km northeast from the winery, close to the Waitara River, is **Windyglen Horse Treks**, Bertrand Road (30min to all day, $10–85; ☎06/752 0603), offering accommodation (see p.215) and horse rides over rolling country with views of the sea and Mount Taranaki.

Eating, drinking and entertainment

The majority of the cafés, **restaurants** and clubs are on what is known as the **Devon Mile**, on Devon Street between Dawson and Eliot streets. As for **drinking**, no visit to Taranaki would be complete without a taste of the local, naturally brewed Mike's Mild Ale, an extremely tasty drop that's available in the vast majority of New Plymouth's pubs and bars.

For those of a more cultural persuasion, the **Festival of the Arts** takes over the town each March, making use of venues in Pukekura Park, the State Theatre, Govett-Brewster Art Gallery and Brooklands Bowl to showcase classical concerts, pop concerts, performance artists, comedy, parades and a searchlight tattoo. Otherwise, you can always view the natural wonders of the **night sky** on Tuesday evenings at Marshland Observatory, Marshland Hill, Robe Street (summer 8–10pm, winter 7.30–9.30pm; $2).

Cafés

El Condor, 170 Devon St East. Tiny, very simple place with value-for-money pasta and pizza.

Espresso Café, Govett-Brewster Gallery, cnr Queen St & King St. A stylish and imaginative (primarily) vegetarian café, with some meat and fish dishes (all meals under $10), a deli counter, good wine and excellent coffee. Daily 10.30am–4.30pm.

MacFarlane's Café, cnr Kelly St & Matai St, Inglewood. A popular Sunday brunch ($11.50) spot, with reasonable snacks and main meals including pasta, salads, burgers and speciality hot-chocolate drinks. Daily 9am–6pm, until 10pm Thurs–Sat; licensed.

Metropol Café Bar, cnr King St & Egmont St. A lively brasserie, with French-influenced snacks, salads and main courses, most for under $20. Daily 11am to midnight.

Simply Read, 2 Dawson St. Personable café/bookshop overlooking the beach and serving good strong coffee, a selection of teas, and wholesome sandwiches and pastries. Closed Mon & Tues.

Steps, 37 Gover St. Good-value toasted foccaccia sandwiches, veggie meals and snacks, plus Italian, Mexican, Indian and Asian main meals, followed by rich cakes and other sinful desserts. Tues–Fri 11.30am–2pm & 6–11pm; BYO.

Restaurants

André l'Escargot, 37–43 Brougham St (☎06/758 4812). Elegant institution that serves excellent French food and wine for lunch and dinner, with classics such as onion soup gratinée, half a dozen Burgundy snails, roast rabbit or côte du boeuf coming in under the $30 mark.

Burton's Street Café/Bar, *State Hotel*, cnr Gover St & Devon St. Moderately priced breakfasts, lunches, snacks and dinners, all in fearsome portions, plus drinks served in a bar bedecked with rural memorabilia.

The Carriage, Main Rd, Oakura, 17km southwest on SH45. A decorous eatery, set in an 1840 railway carriage complete with luggage racks and battered suitcases, offering reasonably priced cooked breakfasts, Greek salads, pumpkin ginger and orange soup and the like.

Devon Hotel, 390 Devon St East (☎06/759 9099). Worth a visit for its excellent evening smorgasbord ($25), with cabaret-like entertainment at the weekends, when it gets crowded.

Bars and clubs

Burundi, cnr Devon St & King St. Lively upstairs late-night bar, with dancing at weekends, serving global cuisine during the week ($10–22), all amid garish pseudo-African decor.

Grapevine Wine Bar, upstairs at 36c Currie St. Intimate relaxed bar occupied by laid-back night owls. Dinners served Mon–Sat; live music Fri.

Maloney's Bar, 1719 Devon St West. Neighbourhood Irish bar, serving quick-hit pub food, such as filled bagels with chips, for around $10; DJ Fri & Sat.

The Mill, 2 Powderham St. A massive converted flour mill with two bars for the late-night crowd, with a wide range of beers and snacks, and live bands or a DJ at weekends.

Peggy Gordon's Celtic Bar, cnr Egmont St & Devon St. With pictures of Irish and Scottish folk heroes on the walls, an extensive range of single malt whiskies, twelve beers on tap, and live Irish music on Fri & Sat, it's no surprise that this is a popular haunt of both locals and travellers. The basement Cotton Club carries on after hours (Thurs–Sat 9pm–3am), while an annual street party, held on November 16, sees thousands of revellers taking over the surrounding area.

Thirsty Bull, Devon St, opposite *Peggy Gordon's*. A large boutique brewery and bar with an open kitchen producing good continental café/bar food and snacks to accompany excellent beers naturally brewed on the premises. Daily 10am–3am; live entertainment Fri & Sat.

Listings

Automobile Association 49–55 Powderham St (☎06/757 5646).

Banks All the major banks have branches along Devon St or within one block of the city centre (see also listing for Thomas Cook).

Bike rental Coronation Cycles, 207 Coronation Ave (☎06/757 9260; $20 a day).

Camping and outdoor equipment Kiwi Outdoors, 18 Ariki St, sells work clothes, outdoor gear and camping equipment.

Car rental Avis (☎06/757 5736); Hertz (☎06/758 8189); Rent-a-dent (☎0800/736 822).

Cinema Cinema 4, 119–125 Devon St East.

Galleries Andreas Ries Art Gallery, 52 Egmont St (Tues–Fri 10am–6pm), is a small gallery showing contemporary New Zealand artists; Te Henui Vicarage, 288 Courtney St (Sat & Sun 1–4pm), displays the work of local potters.

Library There's a public library on Brougham St (Mon, Wed & Fri 9am–8.30pm, Tues & Thurs 9am–5.30pm, Sat 9am–noon).

Medical treatment Vivian Street Pharmacy, 95 Vivian St; Southern Cross Hospital, St Aubyn St (☎06/758 2338); duty doctors are listed in the *Daily News* on Fri & Sat (70¢).

Post office The main post office, with a poste restante service, is at 21 Currie St (Mon–Fri 9am–5pm).

Swimming The Aquatic Centre, Buckley Terrace, is a massive complex with indoor and outdoor pools, gym and fitness suite.

Thomas Cook 55–57 Devon St (☎06/757 5459).

Tours Cruise New Zealand (☎06/758 3222) offer a number of bus tours to points of interest around the region; Tubby's Tours (☎06/753 6306) run guided trips around the city, as well as a shuttle to Mount Taranaki (see "Trailhead transport", p.222). MacAlpine Adventure Guides, 477 St Aubyn St (☎06/751 3542), offer guided tramps, climbing and abseiling down Dawson Falls ($30); Bev Smith (☎06/758 4197) also arranges paragliding and rafting trips in the area; while Mountain Guides (☎06/758 8261) add photography, skiing and snowboarding.

Egmont National Park

In the centre of **Egmont National Park** is **Mount Taranaki**, a dormant strato-volcano that last erupted in 1755, when the layer-cake of lava flows collapsed in on itself. The crater near the summit is always filled with snow and a climb to the top of the mountain is a journey from a sub-tropical sea to an alpine summit, crossing a treeline characterized by stunted flag-form trees, lopsidedly shaped by the constant buffeting of the wind. Standing alone in relatively flat surroundings, Mount Taranaki always looks spectacular, even when partially obscured by cloud, and it's well worth making the trip to the informative visitor centres just to experience the splendid **vistas** in all directions (if the weather cooperates) – and maybe to tackle the summit track or other **walks** on its slopes.

According to **Maori**, there was a time when all the mountains on the North Island were crowded together on the central plateau. The group was dominated by chiefs Ruapehu, Tongariro, Ngaruahoe and Taranaki, while around them clustered all the smaller mountains, including the beautiful **Pihanga**, who favoured **Taranaki** among all her suitors. Challenged by the other mountains, Taranaki knocked Tongariro to his knees, striking off the top of his head to make him the shape he is today, and defeated Ngaruahoe, but when the time came to face Ruapehu, Taranaki was exhausted and badly wounded. However, Taranaki's love for Pihanga was so great that he turned his back on the other mountains and set off in the direction of the setting sun, guided by Rauhoto Tapairu, first to **Wanganui** and then west to where he stands today. The furrow Taranaki left as he made his way to Wanganui later filled with water and became the **Whanganui River**.

Park practicalities

The boundary of the national park is almost perfectly circular, enclosing a thin ribbon of **native bush** and fertile dairy farmland traversed by over 140km of **walking tracks**. Three sealed roads divide the mountain into three sections, each served by a DOC office: the **Egmont Road** and **Dawson Falls** sections of the park, which provide access to the two summit tracks and the **Pembroke Road** section, which provides access to the **Manganui Skifield** (see box on p.223).

On the north face of the mountain, the **Egmont visitor centre**, at the top of Egmont Road (Dec–March daily 8.30am–4.30pm; rest of year Wed–Sun 8.30am–4.30pm; ☎06/756 8710), is accessible from SH3 between New Plymouth and Inglewood, with various displays about the mountain, maps of all the tracks, good viewing windows and weather updates. On the south face, the smaller **Dawson Falls visitor centre**, at the top of Upper Manaia Road (Dec–March daily 8.30am–4.30pm; rest of year Wed–Sun 8.30am–4.30pm; ☎025/430 248), is accessible from the town of Manaia on SH45, or along any of the small roads that connect with the Manaia Road between Opanuake and Stratford. There is also a **DOC field centre**, Pembroke Road (☎06/765 5144), on the lower east side of the mountain, which is accessible from Stratford.

Both the DOC office and visitor centre in New Plymouth (see p.214) also have information on the park.

Accommodation and eating

The majority of visitors base themselves in New Plymouth, but there's a smattering of luxurious **accommodation** in the park itself, catering to sightseers in summer and **skiiers** in winter. The *Dawson Falls Mountain Lodge*, Upper Manaia Road (☎06/765 5457; ⑤), 45 minutes' drive from New Plymouth, is a quiet alpine-style lodge with Swiss ornamented, individually decorated rooms, stunning views, a restaurant, coffee lounge and bar. On a par is the *Mountain House Motor Lodge*, Pembroke Road (☎ & fax 06/765 6100; ⑤), a hotel/motel and restaurant at 846m above sea level, with pleasant rooms and wonderful views, all within easy reach of the skifields. A more **affordable** alternative for **trampers** wanting an early start is *The Missing Leg Backpackers*, 1082 Junction Rd (☎06/752 2570; dorms ①, rooms ②), a barn-like building next to the turning for Egmont Road, with bikes and tramping gear for rent and a shuttle service up the mountain (see below).

The licensed **restaurants** at the *Dawson Falls* and the *Mountain House* serve excellent, if expensive dinners; the Mountain House has a slight edge by virtue of having a Swiss chef who routinely prepares a daily choice of at least thirteen desserts. For lunch, the **coffee shop** in the *Dawson Falls* and the *Mountain House* **bar** both oblige with lighter, more snacky fare.

Tramping in the park

Mount Taranaki offers travellers a rare chance to climb to the **summit** of a mountain in one day with little real hardship. This is not to diminish the very real dangers posed by quick and violent weather changes: be sure to wear sturdy boots, and carry extra clothing and a plentiful supply of water and food. Always seek advice at DOC visitor centres, record your itinerary in their intentions book before setting out, and get an early start. If you want to spend longer than a day on the mountain and are happy to forgo the goal-driven dash to the summit, the spectacular and testing **Round the Mountain Circuit** might fit the bill, or try any number of **shorter walks**.

Trailhead transport – and guided walks

No public **buses** run from New Plymouth to the mountain, but several shuttle operators fill the void: Tubby's Tours (☎06/753 6306); Up The Mountain Shuttles (☎06/752 2570); and John Morton buses (☎06/758 3215). All are bookable direct or through the New Plymouth visitor centre.

If you don't want to tackle the mountain alone or aspire to go climbing or abseiling, check out the list of approved **mountain guides** at the back of the DOC leaflet, *Walks in the Egmont National Park* ($1), which is available at local visitor centres and DOC offices. Costs depend on the number of participants, but a couple of reliable outfits to try are: MacAlpine Adventure Guides, 477 St Aubyn St (☎06/751 3542), who offer summit treks, round the mountain, and abseiling down Dawson Falls; Bev Smith (☎06/758 4197); and Mountain Guides (☎06/758 8261). Finally, if you're here in February, you can join one of the local **alpine clubs**' inexpensive day climbs to the summit; book through the New Plymouth visitor centre.

Summit climbs

Of the two one-day **summit routes**, the **Northern Route** is the easier and safer of the two, though you should still allow eight hours (5hr ascent, 3hr descent). The track begins at a wooden stairway close to Tahurangi Lodge, at the top of Egmont Road, before heading over scoria slopes (rough sufaces of cooled lava) to the Lizard Ridge (2134m), which leads to the crater. After crossing the crater ice and a short scoria slope, it arrives at the summit rocks.

The ten-hour **Southern Route** (7hr ascent, 3hr descent) leaves Dawson Falls at the top of the Upper Manaia Road, climbing through bush and then making a rapid ascent up a staircase to the Lake Dive Track. From there on it is a steep series of zig-zags up scoria slopes. On a clear day, your efforts will be rewarded by panoramic **views** from the summit, taking in the central plateau, north to Hamilton and beyond, south to Kapiti Island, Wellington and the South Island, and out to sea across the Taranaki Bights and the Sugar Loaf Islands.

The Round-the-mountain circuit

The well marked **Round-the-mountain circuit**, accessible from all three sections of the mountain, is actually two tracks: the shorter, **high-level** summer **route** (Dec–Feb only; 3–4 days) and the longer, **low-level route** (year-round; 5 days). Note that although the five-day walk is easily manageable, you have be fit to do the shorter walk as the going is much more strenuous. The routes can be undertaken in either direction, but are described **clockwise** here, starting at the top of Pembroke Road. All **huts** on the circuit itself are classified as back-country (Category 2; $8), but the Camphouse at North Egmont and the Konini Lodge at Dawson Falls, both with 30-odd bunks, are relatively luxurious (Category 1; $12). Hut **tickets** must be bought in advance from local DOC offices or visitor centres.

Day one (6hr) of the **low-level route** involves a walk from the end of Pembroke Road over the Waingongoro swingbridge and joins the summit track before heading left at the Hasties Hill Walk and then onto the Lake Dive Track, crossing water courses and through forest to the **Lake Dive Hut** (18 bunks). Day two (6–7hr), the hardest, entails a traverse across difficult terrain to the **Waiaua Gorge Hut** (18 bunks), which is reached by an aluminium ladder. Day three (7–8hr), the longest, is fairly easy-going along the Oanui Track and up to Kahui Hut, before heading through scrub and tussock to the head of the Pyramid Stream Gorges and up steps to the **Holly Hut** (30 bunks). Day four (6–7hr) heads along the ridge above the Kokowai Stream and Egmont Road to the **Maketawa Hut** (18 bunks). The last day is a three-hour stroll back to the mountain house.

The shorter **high-level route** involves leaving the plateau car park at the top of Pembroke Road and heading straight to the Holly Hut; day two to the Waiaua Gorge Hut; and day three back to the plateau.

Shorter walks

On the **south side** of the mountain, at the top of Upper Manaia Road, several tracks branch off from the Dawson Falls visitor centre to places of interest. A short track to the 17m-high **Dawson Falls** (20min), which plummet over an ancient lava flow, can be extended along the **Kapuni Walk** (1hr). Another good walk leads to **Wilkies Pool** (1hr), where the waters of the Kapuni Gorge rush through a staircase of rock pools. The tougher walk to **Hasties Hill** (2hr 30min) involves crossing the flank of the mountain to a lookout and returning via the **Kaupokponui Falls.**

Short walks round the **North Egmont** section of the park, starting from the top of Egmont Road, include the unusual and atmospheric **Ngatoro Loop Track** (1hr), which winds through the hidden valley of the Goblin Forest, with its kaikawaka trees, alpine plants and gnarled trunks hung with ferns and cushiony mosses. Alternatively, the **Veronica Loop Track** (2hr) climbs up to a ridge, through mountain forest and scrub with fine views of the ancient lava flows known as Humphries Castle, New Plymouth and the coast.

MANGANUI SKIFIELD

From the top of Pembroke Road, it's just thirty minutes' walk to the **Manganui Skifield** (June–Oct daily 9am–4pm; ☎06/765 7669). A small club field with a vertical drop of 420m, the slopes are rarely crowded and the skiing and snowboarding is suitable for all levels. There are two **lifts** at the field ($30 per day), a flying fox to get skiing gear from one side of the gorge to the other, a public shelter with toilets, and a canteen. Ski and snowboard **rental** is available at the *Mountain House Motor Lodge*, Pembroke Rd (☎06/765 6100), and Up The Mountain Shuttles (☎06/752 2570) operate a **shuttle bus** ($4) to the skifields from Stratford

There are more good walking tracks around **East Egmont**, at the top of Pembroke Road, from where the **Enchanted Track** (3hr) heads for Jackson's Lookout before dropping through dense vegetation at lower altitudes, while the **Curtis Falls Track** (4hr) traces the Te Popo Stream, via steps and ladders, to the Manganui River Gorge, then follows the riverbed past two waterfalls.

New Plymouth to Wanganui

The swift, virtually uninterrupted progress of the **inland** SH3 to Hawera, 74km due south, is dull by comparison with the scenic coastal route (see below).

Just over halfway between New Plymouth and Hawera on SH3 is the small town of **STRATFORD**, which provides access to Mount Taranaki and especially the Manganui Skifield (see box on p.223). The **visitor centre** on Broadway (Mon–Fri 9am–5pm & Sat 10am–2pm; ☎06/765 6708, fax 765 7500), also acts as the Intercity and Newmans **bus** stop. There are a couple of **places to stay**, mostly patronized by the ski crowd. *Stratford Holiday Park*, 10 Page St (☎ & fax 06/765 6440; tent sites $8.50, dorms ①, cabins ②, motel units ④), has a wide range of on-site accommodation, as well as camping, in clean, well-cared-for surroundings; bike rental is also available for $20 a day. Under the same management, *Taranaki Accommodation Lodge* (☎ & fax 06/765 6440; ②) occupies a former nurses' home, with mostly twin rooms.

It takes about four hours to drive around the **coast road** (SH45) to Hawera, including stops along the way; a free map of the route is available at the New Plymouth visitor centre. At Pungarehu, Cape Road cuts west to the cast-iron tower of **Cape Egmont Lighthouse**, precariously perched on the westernmost point of the cape and overlooking Taranaki's windswept coast.

Hawera

HAWERA is situated at the confluence of SH3 and SH45 and is flat, spread out and surrounded by gently undulating farmland. With a population of 8000, Hawera is primarily a service and administration centre for the district's dairy farms, but visitors are also well provided for, with spectacular cliff-lined **surfing beaches** and one of the best museums in these parts.

The **Tawhiti Museum** (Sept–May Fri–Mon 10am–4pm, June–Aug Sun 10am–4pm; donation requested) is on Ohangi Road, near the junction with Tawhiti Road, about 4km outside Hawera. The unique exhibits really bring the past to life, recreating the social and technological heritage of both Maori and *pakeha* through the extensive use of photographs, models and dioramas. Among the most impressive are representations of pa sites, including the virtually impregnable Turuturumokai pa, and the changes to fortifications wrought by the advent of musket warfare. Other highlights include a record of the life of Chew Chong, a widely respected Chinese migrant who initiated the export of local fungi to China, a working pottery and a bush railway that trundles through displays recounting the logging history of Taranaki.

The other irresistible sight in Hawera is the **Elvis Presley Record Rooms**, 51 Argyle St (visits by appointment, ☎06/278 7624; donation requested), about ten minutes' walk from the visitor centre. K.D. Wasley's shrine to the King is his garage, which contains thousands of rare recordings, photographs and memorabilia.

Practicalities

Intercity and White Star **buses** stop at the Hawera Travel Centre on Glover Road, while Newmans drop off at the **visitor centre**, 55 High St (Mon–Fri 8.30am–5pm, Dec–Jan

Harbour Bridge, Auckland

Sheep-shearer statue, Te Kuiti,
Western North Island

Treaty House, Waitangi, Northland

Maori war canoe, Matauri Bay

Marae Hako Bay, Eastland

"Lost World" abseil, Waitomo Caves

Waiotapu Thermal Area, Rotorua

Commercial Hotel, Whakatane, Bay of Plenty

Lake Taupo

Whanarua Bay, Eastland

Tree ferns, Northland

also Sat–Sun 10am–3pm). BB Cars (☎0800 837 383) will run you out to the Tawhiti Museum and other local sights.

In town, there are comfortable units at the *Furlong Motor Inn*, 256 Waihi Rd (☎06/278 5136; ④); clean and simple rooms at the *Dominion Hotel*, Princes Street (☎06/278 7385, ④); or a range of on-site **accommodation** at the *King Edward Park Motorcamp*, Waihi Road (☎06/278 8544; tent sites $9, studios & cabins ②–④). To stay in a more scenic setting, head 4km past the Tawhiti Museum, along Ararata Road, to *Wheatley Downs* (☎06/278 6523; dorms ①, rooms ②), a friendly farmstay with views of Mount Taranaki.

When the time comes to eat, you could do worse than the licensed restaurant in the *Furlong Motor Inn*, which dishes up moderately priced **lunches** and **dinners** daily. For inexpensive snacks and meals in more stylish surroundings, try *Morrison's Café Bar*, Victoria Street (daily 11am–1am), or the BYO *East Ocean Restaurant*, 26 Union St. If you're looking for **breakfasts**, call into *Auntie's Café*, 79 High St (closed Sun), purveyor of coffee, tea, toast, bacon and eggs from early morning to late afternoon, or the value-for-money *Whistle Stop Café*, next to the Intercity bus stop.

Hawera to Wanganui

Cutting through heavily cultivated farmland, SH3 splits **PATEA**, the only major community between Hawera and Wanganui. The township has a model of the Aotea Canoe in the main street, commemorating the settlement of the area by Turi and his *hapu*, a good surfing beach at the mouth of the Patea River and a safe freshwater swimming hole, overlooked by the Manawapou Redoubt and pa site.

About 24km before Wanganui is the well-signposted turn-off for **Bushy Park Historic Homestead and Scenic Reserve**, 8km off the main road (daily 10am–5pm; $3). The park contains a large stand of native bush thick with vines, creepers and supplejack, the largest rata tree in New Zealand (3.5m in diameter and 43m tall) and a 1906 homestead. Notable features in the house include a striking stained-glass window, a carved over-mantle and fireplace and a huge five-metre chesterfield in the entrance hall; you can even **stay** and soak up the gracious surroundings (☎06/342 9879; B&B ⑥).

Wanganui and around

The city of **WANGANUI** sits by the sea on the banks of the Whanganui River, at the junction of SH3 and SH4. One of New Zealand's oldest cities and the largest community with access to the **Whanganui National Park**, Wanganui was the hub of early European commerce, by virtue of its access to the interior and coastal links with the ports of Wellington and New Plymouth. Today this clean and well-kept city has been given a facelift with an eye to the settlement's **colonial past**: the late Victorian and early Edwardian facades have been refurbished, while mock-gaslight lampposts have been installed along **cobblestone** paths. The aura of civic pride is enhanced by a profusion of **flowerbeds**, borders and hanging baskets. In addition to its pretty-as-a-post-card riverbank charm, Wanganui contains a pleasing **art gallery** and an excellent museum, both with collections of some note, along with an endearing **riverboat museum** that pays tribute to the sturdy craft that were once the city's lifeblood.

By the time **Europeans** arrived in the 1830s, the Maori population was well-established, and land rights quickly became a bone of contention. Transactions Maori perceived as a ritual exchange of gifts, the New Zealand Company took as a successful negotation for the purchase of Wanganui and a large amount of surrounding land. Settlement went ahead regardless, and it was not until the **Gilfillan Massacre** of 1847

WHANGANUI VERSUS WANGANUI

Visitors are often confused by the variant spellings of **Whanganui** (the original Maori), which is retained for the **river** and the **national park**, and **Wanganui** (the Anglicized version), which has been adopted by the **city**. Explanations of the discrepancy cite the silent "H" in spoken Maori being omitted when the name was written down, or the H being dropped over time as a result of common early English usage. A debate has been raging in the council chambers for some time about whether to restore the original Maori name to the city, but don't hold your breath.

---

that trouble erupted again. When a Maori was accidentally injured, his tribesmen took *utu* (retribution), massacring four members of the Gilfillan family. Further violent incidents culminated in a full-scale but inconclusive **battle** at St John's Hill. The next year the problems were apparently resolved by a payment of £1000 to the Maori; local tribes took no action during the wars in Taranaki, even helping European settlers by defeating Hauhau warriors at Moutoa Island in 1864 (see p.232).

In 1995 many of the old **grievances** and one or two more recent ones reached boiling point when, on Waitangi Day, Maori occupied the Moutoa Gardens, claiming it as **Maori land**. The four-month **occupation** ended peacefully in the High Court, but created much bitterness on both sides, neither of which particularly distinguished themselves during the occupation. Now, each **Waitangi Day**, the town seems to hold its breath as Maori from all over the country congregate to commemorate the incident, which is seen as a watershed in Maori–*pakeha* relations.

Arrival, information and city transport

The **airport** is ten minutes' drive southwest of the city centre and is linked by Ash Mayor Transport shuttles (☎06/343 8319; $7). **Buses** drop off at various places around town: InterCity stop at Taupo Quay, Newmans at 156 Ridgway St, and White Star at 161 Ingestre St.

The **visitor centre**, 101 Guyton St (Mon–Fri 8.30am–5pm, Sat & Sun 10am–2pm; ☎06/345 3286, fax 345 3286), provides useful leaflets and maps and acts as a booking office for trips and accommodation. The **DOC office**, 74 Ingestre St (Mon–Fri 8am–4.30pm), sells leaflets on the Whanganui National Park and the Whanganui River Road, plus hut and camping tickets. The city centre is easily manageable on foot, though Wanganui Taxi Buses (☎06/343 5555) run a limited weekday service round the city and to the beaches at the rivermouth; a timetable is available at the visitor centre.

Accommodation

Accommodation in Wanganui is plentiful but hardly varied. There are lots of motels, one central hotel/pub of note, two hostels and a couple of good motorcamps but few worthy B&Bs.

Hotels, motels and B&Bs

Acacia Park Motel, 140 Anzac Parade (☎ & fax 06/343 9093). Simple, clean rooms set in extensive grounds overlooking the river. ④.

Avenue Motor Inn, 379 Victoria Ave (☎06/345 0907). A range of rooms, from clean budget rooms to plush, spacious suites. On-site restaurant and swimming pool. ④–⑤.

Bradgate, 7 Somme Parade (☎06/345 3634). Agreeable, high-ceilinged rooms in a house overlooking the river, just eight minutes' walk from the city centre. ④.

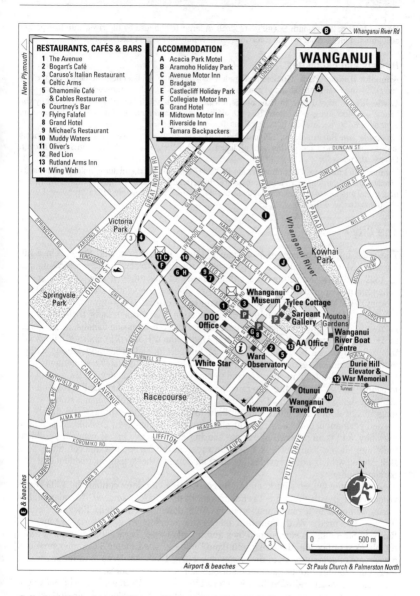

RESTAURANTS, CAFÉS & BARS
1 The Avenue
2 Bogart's Café
3 Caruso's Italian Restaurant
4 Celtic Arms
5 Chamomile Café
  & Cables Restaurant
6 Courtney's Bar
7 Flying Falafel
8 Grand Hotel
9 Michael's Restaurant
10 Muddy Waters
11 Oliver's
12 Red Lion
13 Rutland Arms Inn
14 Wing Wah

ACCOMMODATION
A Acacia Park Motel
B Aramoho Holiday Park
C Avenue Motor Inn
D Bradgate
E Castlecliff Holiday Park
F Collegiate Motor Inn
G Grand Hotel
H Midtown Motor Inn
I Riverside Inn
J Tamara Backpackers

WANGANUI

Collegiate Motor Inn, 122 Liverpool St (☎06/345 8309). Well-appointed, spacious rooms – some fully self-contained, others with only tea- and toast-making facilities. ⑤.

Grand Hotel, 99 Guyton St (☎06/345 0955). A grand old hotel indeed: built in 1927 with a number of bars, a restaurant and clean, comfortable, good-value rooms. ④.

Midtown Motor Inn, 321 Victoria Ave (☎06/345 8408, fax 345 8406). Modern, comfortable motel with a variety of budget and economy rooms, a restaurant, lounge bar and café/bar. ④–⑤.

Riverside Inn, 2 Plymouth St (☎06/347 2529). A large 1895 house by the river, with backpacker accommodation (see below) and a corridor full of comfortable, quiet B&B rooms. ④.

Hostels and campsites

Aramoho Holiday Park, 460 Somme Parade (☎06/343 8402). Well-tended site 6km from the city centre, by the river in the shade of giant trees. Tent sites $8.50, cabins & motel units ②–④.

Castlecliff Holiday Park, 1a Rangiora St, Castlecliff, 9km south (☎06/344 2227). Close by the beach, bus stop and general store, this site offers camping and a range of on-site accommodation. Tent sites $7.50, backpacker huts ①, cabins ②.

Riverside Inn Backpackers, 2 Plymouth St (☎06/347 2529). Clean, well-kept backpacker dorms and doubles at the back of this YHA-affiliated hostel, which also has B&B rooms (see above). Dorms ①, rooms ②.

Tamara Backpackers, 24 Somme Parade (☎06/347 6300), is a large historic building with plenty of space, pretty gardens, a friendly atmosphere, three minutes' walk from the city centre, offers free bike rental and lots of neat, comfortable dorms and doubles and a balcony with a river view. Dorms ①, rooms ②.

The City

The most impressive part of Wanganui is **Queens Park**, on Watt Street. On a hill known to Maori as Pukenamu, the park marks the site of the last tribal war in Wanganui in 1832 and now constitutes the cultural heart of the modern city, containing the Whanganui Regional Museum, Sarjeant Art Gallery, Alexander Library and Davis Library. The **Whanganui Regional Museum** (Mon–Sat 10am–4pm, Sun 1–4.30pm; $2), founded in 1892, has an outstanding collection of Maori artefacts, tools, weapons, garments, ornaments, musical instruments and three impressive canoes, all gathered in Te Ati Haunui-a-Paparangi, the central Maori court. Housed in another gallery off this are Lindauer's portrtaits of Maori in full ceremonial dress and tattoos. Other exhibits include a reconstruction of an early street in the *pakeha* settlement, photographs and displays on New Zealand geology and natural history. To the east of the museum, at the top of the Veteran Steps, is the **Sarjeant Art Gallery** (Mon–Fri 10.30am–4.30pm & Sat–Sun 1–4.30pm; free), a 1917 building of Oamaru stone, with a magnificent dome that filters natural light to illuminate the exhibits. The highly regarded permanent collection concentrates on contemporary New Zealand art and photography, and is augmented by various touring exhibitions. One of Wanganui's oldest buildings, dating from 1853, is **Tylee Cottage**, on the corner of Cameron Street and Bell Street, which now provides accommodation for the artists in residence at the Sarjeant Gallery.

Southwest of Queen's Park, on Hill Street, **Cook's Gardens** contain the 1903 **Ward Observatory**, with the largest refractor still in use in New Zealand (Monday nights during winter or by arrangement, ☎06/345 6113; donation requested). Back on Victoria Avenue, the pretty **Watt Fountain** marks the intersection of Victoria Avenue and Ridgway Street and is surrounded by a number of ornate classical buildings, including the old Post Office and the striking Rutland Building. The Cinema 3 Complex provides a welcome change of pace, in the shape of a stylish 1950s Art Deco exterior, foyer and mezzanine lounge, not to mention luxurious ladies' powder rooms.

At the southern end of SH3 as it enters the city is **St Paul's Memorial Church**, Anaua Street (donation requested). The church is sometimes locked, but you can get a key from the house on the corner or in a small wooden box near the church entrance. From the outside St Paul's looks like just another small whitewashed weatherboard church, but inside it is magnificently decorated with Maori *paua* carvings, a painted rib ceiling (as in Maori meeting houses), beautiful etched-glass windows and *tukutuku* panels.

Along the riverbanks

On the west bank of the river, Taupo Quay is flanked by old warehouses, stores and, at no. 1a, the **Whanganui River Boat Centre** (Mon–Fri 9am–4pm, Sat 10am–2pm, Sun 1–4pm; donation requested). Housed in an 1881 two-storey timber-framed building, the centre concentrates on the river and its history in relation to the town, with exhibits including a recently salvaged paddle steamer, the *Waimarie*, built in 1899 in London. The last working steamer to go to the upper reaches of the river, the *Waimarie* travelled the river until 1952, when it sank at its moorings.

Near the River Boat Centre, at the junction of Taupo Quay and Somme Parade, lie the historic **Moutoa Gardens**, scene of the signing of the document agreeing to the sale of Wanganui and, many years later, of a significant Maori land rights protest. Traditionally Maori had lived at Moutoa during the fishing season until it was coopted by *pakeha* settlers, who renamed the area Market Square. An ancient law prohibited the police from arresting Maori in the gardens; combined with the historical precedent, this gave the four-month occupation in 1995 great resonance.

Downstream of the City Bridge, river trips are offered by the 1907 *Otunui* **paddle wheeler** (Dec–May 10am & 2pm, rest of year 1pm; 3hr; $20; ☎06/345 3513), moored on Taupo Quay. Complimentary mulled wine is included on the trip, and you can bring your own food or use the licensed canteen on board, so kick back and listen to the amusing commentary from the skipper.

Across the City Bridge, on the east bank of the river, is the **Durie Hill Elevator and Tower** (Mon–Fri 7.30am–6pm, Sat 10am–6pm, Sun 11am–5pm; $1), where a Maori carved gateway marks the entrance to a 213-metre tunnel at the end of which a historic 1919 elevator carries passengers up through the hill to the summit, saving a 185-step climb. Once at the top of the hill there are two excellent vantage points: the lift's machinery room or atop the **Memorial Tower** (daily 8am–dusk), both granting extensive views of the city, beaches and inland.

The beaches

Adjacent to the southern jaw of the mouth of the Whanganui River is **South Beach**, a vast desolate tract of sand accessible from the old airport road, while on the northern jaw is **Castlecliff Beach**, a broad sweep of black iron-sand, with safe swimming, good surf and the usual motley collection of driftwood. South of Castlecliff Beach and accessible by walking along the beach (2hr, but check tides at the visitor centre) or by following the Rapanui Road off SH3 north for 20km, is **Mowhanu Beach**, a spectacular swimming beach surrounded by papa cliffs and renowned for good windsurfing.

Eating and drinking

Wanganui is blessed with a wide range of excellent restaurants and some rather stylish cafés. **Italian food** is a particularly good bet, owing to the presence of migrant workers who stayed on after they were brought in to work on an abortive hydroelectric scheme. The city also boasts one or two swanky **bars** and some spit-and-sawdust **pubs**, all serving tasty ale, and a couple of late-night venues that gear up at weekends.

Cafés and takeaways

The Avenue, cnr Victoria Ave & Ingestre St. Quite simply, a great fish and chip shop. Daily except Mon, 4pm till late.

Bogart's Café, in the Embassy Cinema, 34 Victoria Ave. An intimate, casual spot for snacks (under $6) and coffee. The walls are plastered with cinema posters and there's outside seating. Mon & Tues 8.30am–3pm, Wed–Fri 8.30am–10pm, Sat 11am–11pm; licensed.

Chamomile Café, 51 Victoria Ave. Renowned for excellent blackboard specials (under $20). Lunch Mon–Sat, plus Sun brunch.

The Flying Falafel, 264a Victoria Ave. Tiny café and takeaway that cooks the best and cheapest kebabs in the city. Mon–Sat 11am–10pm, Sun 3–9pm.

Muddy Waters, 9 Putiki Drive. Turn-of-the-century brick bakery overlooking the river near City Bridge, serving coffee, juices, shakes, home-made pies, sandwiches and snacks. Daily 6.30am–6.30pm.

Restaurants

Cables Restaurant, 51 Victoria Ave. The evening incarnation of the Chamomile Café, serving pasta, fresh fish, venison, osso bucco and a veggie dish ($18–24), followed by mouthwatering desserts ($8.50). Tues–Sat from 6pm; licensed & BYO.

Caruso's Italian Restaurant, 211 Wicksteed St. Stylish, modern glass-fronted café by day and restaurant by night, serving good and sensibly priced Italian food. Lunch Tues–Fri, dinner Tues–Sat; licensed.

Grand Hotel, 99 Guyton St. Cobb and Co franchise, dishing up simple food in large portions. Daily 7am–9pm.

Michael's Restaurant, 281 Wicksteed St (☎06/345 2690). Fine dining in a tastefully decorated 1911 house. Light lunches start around $8, while serious dinners (around $15–20) include the likes of lambs' brains poached in honey and stout. Closed Sun; licensed & BYO.

Olivers, Avenue Motel, 379 Victoria Ave. Gourmet pizzas and big dinners. Closed Sun; licensed.

Peppers Brasserie, Avenue Motel, 379 Victoria Ave. Snacks and meals served daily from 10am–9.30pm.

Riviera, Upokongaro, 11km north on SH4 (☎06/345 6459; book Fri & Sat dinner). The best and most authentic Italian restaurant in the area – fresh pasta, great coffee, home-made ice cream – and nothing on the menu costs more than $21. Lunch Thurs–Sun, dinner Wed–Sun; licensed.

Wing Wah, 330 Victoria St. Good-quality Chinese food at reasonable prices, with generous banquet meals for two or more, to eat in or takeaway. Daily 4.30–10pm.

Bars and clubs

Celtic Arms, 437 Victoria Ave. Bargain pub food, including fry-up breakfasts, fish'n'chips, pan-fried snapper or steak, plus live folk, jazz or rock on Fridays. Thurs–Sat noon–2am, Sun–Wed noon to midnight.

Courtneys Bar, Midtown Motor Inn, 321 Victoria Ave. Popular neon, mirror and chrome sports bar with big-screen TV, all-day bar snacks, daily happy hours (4.30–6.30pm) and an upstairs nightclub called Metro on Fri and Sat nights, with a DJ and dance music.

Red Lion, 45 Anzac Parade. An atmospheric pub with a wide selection of beers and bar meals. Daily 11am–3am.

Rutland Arms Inn, 48–52 Ridgway St. A pseudo-old-style pub, with 14 beers on tap, bar snacks, and dinners featuring olde English desserts like apple and blackberry crumble served from 5.30pm. Daily 8.30am–11pm, until 1am Thurs–Sat.

Listings

Automobile Association 78 Victoria Ave (☎06/345 4578).

Banks All the major banks are situated on Victoria Ave or within one block of it.

Buses Wanganui Taxi Buses (☎06/343 5555); Intercity (☎06/345 4433); Newmans (☎06/345 5566); White Star (☎06/347 6677); Ash's Transport (☎06/343 8319); Rivercity Tours (☎06/344 2554).

Car rental Avis (☎06/345 7612); Hertz (☎06/345 7357); Rent-a-dent (☎06/345 1505).

Cinemas Embassy 3 Cinema, 34 Victoria Ave; check local press for screenings.

Medical treatment Wanganui Hospital, cnr Heads Rd & Carlton Ave; Wanganui City Doctors Clinic, 163 Wickstead St (Mon–Fri 5–10pm & Sat–Sun 8am–10pm; ☎06/348 8333); Wicksteed After Hours Pharmacy, 214 Wicksteed St (daily 8.30am–8.30pm ☎06/345 6166).

Post office Wanganui Central Post Office, 60 Ridgway St; Mid-Avenue Post Office, Victoria Ave, between Plymouth St & Ingestre St.

Taxis Wanganui Bus Taxis (☎06/343 5555); ranks on Guyton St, Maria Place and Ridgway St.

Whanganui National Park

The emerald-green waters of the Whanganui River tumble 329km from the northern slopes of Mount Tongariro to the Tasman Sea at Whanganui, by way of 239 listed rapids. The middle reaches of the river bisect the **Whanganui National Park**, and the flow is rarely violent, making the river excellent for **canoeing**, even for people with little or no experience. The main highway from Taumaranui, SH4, mirrors the course of the river for 166km, before joining it in Wanganui.

Traditionally, **Maori** held that each bend of the river had a *kaitiaki* (guardian), who controlled the *mauri* (life force). The *mana* of each settlement depended upon the way in which the food supplies and living areas were maintained: sheltered terraces on the riverbanks were cultivated and elaborate weirs were constructed to trap eels and lamprey. The first **European** arrivals in the valley were **missionaries** who, in the 1840s, set about converting local Maori – and leaving a legacy of biblical place names along the river road. The river's isolation also attracted recluses and visionaries fleeing the excesses of the civilized world, such as poet **James K. Baxter**, who set up a commune here in the 1970s and was held in great affection by local Maori. Right up until the early 1900s, the river was the primary route to the interior of the North Island, and by 1891 a regular **boat service** carried passengers and cargo to the settlers between Pipiriki and Taumarunui, and **tourists** between Wanganui and Mount Ruapehu (see p.281). The riverboat tourist-trade ceased in the 1920s with the coming of the railway and better roads, though the boats still operated a cargo and passenger service until the 1950s.

European attempts to stamp their mark on this wild landscape has often been ill-fated. In 1917 the **Maungpurua Valley**, in the middle of the park, was opened up for settlement by servicemen returning from the first war, who little realized they were trading one battlefield for another. Plagued by **economic hardship**, remoteness and difficulty of access, many settlers had abandoned their farms by the 1920s. A bridge over the Maungpurua Valley was opened in 1936, but after a major flood in 1942, the government declined to make any further funds available for road maintenance and the bridge was cut off, the three remaining families ordered out and the valley officially closed. Today, the only signs that the valley was ever inhabited are the disappearing road, old fence lines, stands of exotic trees planted by the farmers, occasional brick chimneys and the poignant **Bridge to Nowhere**, which can be reached from the river or on the three-day Mangapurua Track.

Encompassing one of the largest remaining tracts of **lowland forest** in the North Island, Whanganui National Park sits on a bed of soft sandstone and **mudstone** (*papa*), which has been eroded to form deep gorges, sharp ridges, sheer cliffs and waterfalls. Beneath the canopy of broad-leaved podocarps and mountain beech, an understorey of tree ferns and clinging plants extends down to the riverbanks, while abundant and vociferous **birdlife** includes the kereru (native pigeon), fantail, tui, robin, grey warbler, tomtit and brown kiwi. Occupying a swathe of riverside land between Taumarunui and Wanganui, the park can be **accessed** from the west via SH43 on to the Mangaehu Road and the **Matemateaonga Track**, and from the north through Whakahoro, which is linked to SH4 by roads from Owhango and Raurimu. From **Pipiriki**, to the south, routes lead up the **Whanganui River Road** from Wanganui or down the rough 28km from Raetihi on SH4.

Whanganui River Road

The **Whanganui River Road** between **Wanganui** and **Pipiriki** is rough, partially sealed twisting, narrow and time consuming – all factors which mean you'd do well to join the **Whanganui River Mail Run**, run by Rivercity Tours ($10 one way, $25 return;

☎06/344 2554), rather than struggling along in your own vehicle. Starting in Wanganui at 7.30am, the trip takes in all the sights along the way and arrives in Pipiriki around four hours later. At Pipiriki you can join pre-arranged jetboat trips further upriver ($30–60 extra) before heading for home; tea and coffee are supplied but you need to bring your own food. If you want to go it alone, note that the route is subject to floods and landslips, and has no petrol stations.

Opened in 1934, the 78-kilometre road, bordered by river, farmland and heavily forested national park, is the supply route for the four hundred people who live along the river between Wanganui and Pipiriki. Near the start of the river road, 14km from Wanganui, is an unmanned **visitor kiosk** with a map, descriptions of sights and history relating to the route.

Aramoana to Moutoa Island

After 3km the road winds up to the summit of **Aramoana**, the starting point of the Aramoana Walkway (see p.237). Some 11km further on, you will pass **Oyster Shell Bluffs**, small roadside overhangs with oyster-shell deposits embedded in them, and **Hipango Park**, a scenic reserve on the riverbank that's only accessible from the river aboard the paddle steamer *Otunui* (see p.229) or with Rivercity jetboats (see p.235). Around 35km from Wanganui are the remains of **ATENE**, a tiny village with few occupied houses, and the start of the Atene Skyline Track (see p.237). The first real settlement of note is **KORINITI**, or Corinth, where you can see the Ngati Pamoana pa site and a 1920s meeting house. About 3km further up the river road is the well-preserved **Operiki pa site**, accessible via a stile on the left of the road and marked by a yellow sign. As you continue along the river road you will see the track to the **Kawana Flour Mill**, 56km from Wanganui. One of a number of water-powered flour mills that operated along the river road, the 1854 mill has recently been restored. A further 4km along is one of the larger settlements, **RANANA**, where there's a **campsite** (see p.234) and a Roman Catholic mission church that's still in use today. One kilometre from the church is **Moutoa Island**, scene of a famous and vicious battle in 1864 when the lower river Maori defeated the rebellious Hauhau warriors, thereby protecting the *mana* of the river and saving an untold number of settlers' lives.

Hiruharama (Jerusalem)

One of the most famous sites on the river is **HIRUHARAMA**, or Jerusalem, originally a Maori village and Catholic mission but now better known as the site of the **James K. Baxter** commune, which briefly flourished here in the early 1970s. Baxter, one of New Zealand's most (in)famous poets, attracted up to two hundred of his followers to the area. A devout Roman Catholic convert whose life followed few of the usual practices of the church, he became father to a flock of his own, the *nga moki* ("fatherless ones"), though they soon dispersed after his death in 1972. The main commune house is situated high on a hill to the right of the road, and Baxter is buried just below the house, though you'll have to fork out $5 to pay homage at his grave. Instead take ten minutes to look over the church and talk to the Sisters of Compassion, who still live in the **convent** and provide **accommodation** for visitors (see p.234). The present church was built in 1892 and features a Maori-designed and carved altar; also in the church is a photo of Mother Mary Joseph Aubert (1833–1926), who established the first community of sisters in 1829, and a portrait of Baxter, looking suitably Christ-like.

After 70km on the river road you will reach its highest point, marked by a picnic site, with excellent views of the national park and the increasingly spectacular river gorge; 2km further along is the **Omorehu Waterfall Lookout**, overlooking one of many spectacular waterfalls that cascade into the Whanganui River.

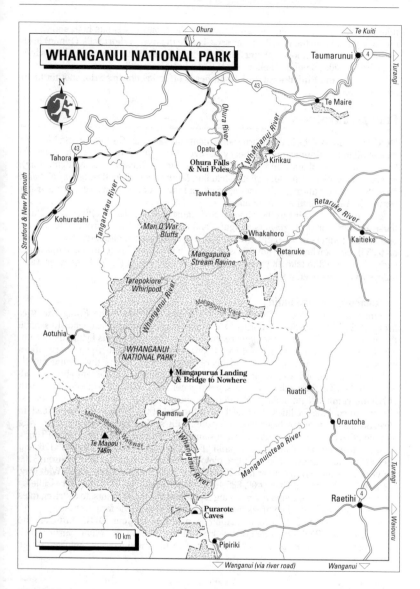

Pipiriki

The most important community on the river road is at its end: **PIPIRIKI**, some 78km from Wanganui, is the gateway to the Whanganui National Park. A **DOC office** (daily 10am–4pm) is maintained in the **Colonial House Museum** (same hours; $1), which is full of pictures, articles and information about the river. The other point of historical interest in the village is the 1904 MV *Ongarue*, the longest-serving **riverboat** on the middle reaches of the river, though these days the proud vessel sits high and dry on the riverbank. From the Pipiriki picnic area, beside the river, a short walk (15min) leads to the picturesque **Paparoa Waterfall** on the Kaitane Stream. Otherwise, there's little to Pipiriki besides a public shelter, toilets and a basic **campsite**.

From here, the **Pipiriki–Raetihi Road** heads off to Raetihi and SH4, another tortuous 28km east.

Park practicalities

DOC maintains offices in the nearby settlements of Wanganui (74 Ingestre St; Mon–Fri 8am–4.30pm), Taumarunui (Cherry Grove, off Taumarunui Street; Mon–Fri 8am–noon & 1–4.30pm), and Pipiriki (Colonial House Museum; daily 10am–4pm), where you can pick up useful leaflets, including *In and Around the Whanganui National Park* ($1). **Information** on the national park and the river is also available from visitor centres in Taumarunui and Wanganui.

All **overnight** visitors to the national park must buy a **DOC Facility User Pass**: these are valid for seven days (six nights) and cost $25 in advance from DOC offices, or $35 from rangers in the park; if you are joining an organized **canoeing trip** (see box on p.235), check whether or not this is included in the price. There are no shops in the park, so you need to take all your **supplies** with you – and don't drink the river water unless you have boiled it first.

Accommodation and eating

The most unusual place to stay in the park is in **Koriniti**, where the *Flying Fox* (☎ & fax 06/342 8160; tent sites $8, dorms ①, cabins ③), gives visitors the chance to sample the lifestyle of modern river settlers: reached across the eponymous flying fox ($2.50), which spans the river 45 minutes' drive (44km) north of Wanganui, the property offers rustic accommodation, home-brewed beers and excellent meals (by arrangement). Behind the marae at **Ranana**, the *Kauika Campsite* (☎06/342 8113; tent sites $6), adjacent to the river, has toilets, showers, fresh water and a kitchen, while further north at **Hiruharama**, accommodation is offered in the convent for $5 per person; blankets, sheets and cooking facilities are available. At the end of the Whanganui River Road, in **Pipiriki** itself, there are basic free campsites with shelter, toilets and water; during summer, there's also a hot-dog/sandwich stand clearly signposted outside Hikoi Tours.

At **Raetihi** on SH4, 28km east of Pipiriki, the *Raetihi Motor Camp* (☎06/385 4176; tent sites $10), offers camping and runs free glow-worm tours and canoeing trips (from $100 per person). About 17km upriver from Pipiriki, alongside the **Matemateaonga Walkway**, the *Ramanui Lodge and Park* (☎06/385 4995; dorms ①, rooms ④), is only accessible by tramping or by boat. Set amid regenerating native lowland forest alongside the river, rates include dinner and a cooked breakfast; wine and beer is available for purchase.

In addition, trampers' accommodation is provided by four **DOC huts** on the Matemateaonga Walkway (Category 2–3; $4–8) and one on the Mangapurua Track (Category 2; $8); all are basic back-country huts, with drinking-water supplies, stoves and toilets.

River trips

The best way to explore the Whanganui National Park is **from the river**, not least because tracks tend to get washed away or become otherwise impassable. The Whanganui, on the other hand, provides a safe and reliable route to the wilderness from November to April, and is well furnished with lodge, marae and farmstay accommodation or, better still, a number of good campsites close to the river's banks.

WHANGANUI RIVER CANOE AND JETBOAT TOUR OPERATORS

Trips **start** from various **points** along the river between Taumarunui in the north and Pipiriki in the south; few venture beyond Pipiriki, where the river broadens and becomes tidal as it flows towards its estuary at Wanganui. Although it is not a guarantee of better equipment, training or **safety-consciousness**, membership of the Whanganui River Commercial Operators Association is a good indication. Check with companies before you book – but bear in mind that many Maori operators refuse to join the *pakeha*-controlled association on principle.

TAUMARUNUI- AND WHAKAHORO-BASED TRIPS

Pioneer Jet Tours (☎07/895 8074). Jetboat trips (starting at $65), plus rental canoes for paddling from Taumarunui to Ohinepa, or right through to Wanganui.

Plateau Outdoor Adventure Guides (☎07/892 2740). Fully inclusive guided canoe, kayak and motorized raft trips (1–5 days; $95–650).

Wades Landing Outdoors (☎07/895 5995). Jetboating and canoeing trips from Whakahoro to Pipiriki (3 days; $100), plus rental canoes monitored by DOC rangers in the park.

MV Wakapai (☎06/385 4443). Gentle, comfortable trips (3 days; $550, including pick-up and drop-off) aboard a purpose-built jetboat based on the design of the old riverboats, and travelling at the same speed, which allows passengers to get up, walk about and take photographs rather than just clinging to the vessel. Trips depart at 10am on Monday, returning on Wednesday afternoon, spending one night in a remote farmstay and one aboard a purpose-built houseboat; everything except sleeping bags and pillows are provided.

Whanganui River Adventures (☎07/333 7099). Longer guided tours, again including all equipment, food, accommodation and transport (3–6 days; $395–695).

Yeti Tours (☎06/385 8197). Guided canoe/kayak trips (4–6 days; $610–715) and a canoe and jetboat combination (3 days; $625); each of the trips includes overnight accommodation in Ohakune (about 80km south of Taumarunui), where everyone must meet the night before the trip, and a farewell meal after the trip.

WANGANUI- AND PIPIRIKI-BASED TRIPS

Baldwin Adventure Tours (☎06/343 6346). Day- and overnight trips aboard a twelve-seater motorized canoe, MV *Adventurer* (1–2 days; $65–290), involving a bus ride to Koriniti for a tour of the marae, a flying fox ride, refreshments and a gentle cruise down river to Wanganui.

Bridge to Nowhere (☎06/385 4128). Popular jetboat tours (10am & 2pm; 4hr; $60) from Pipiriki to the Bridge to Nowhere, including a picnic lunch.

Hikoi Tours (☎06/345 0945). Longer trips (3 or more days; from $390), including demonstrations of traditional Maori fishing methods, an insight into the use of herbal medicines, sightseeing visits to the river and a traditional marae welcome.

Hikoi Wairua Tours (☎06/342 8140). A variety of guided canoe trips (1–2 days; $140–175), with a local Maori guide, marae visits and overnight stays.

River Spirit (☎06/342 1748). Jetboat trips to the Bridge to Nowhere, plus an overnight option, staying at the Ramanui Lodge and including dinner ($140, $250 including Wanganui pick-ups and drop-offs).

Rivercity Tours (☎06/344 2554). Ecologically friendly canoe trips (2–5 days; $250–565).

Canoeing trips (see box above for operators) range from one to five days, and most include return transport (so you only have to paddle downstream) and pretty much everything you'll need – except sleeping bags and tents for longer trips. Virtually all the companies also offer kayak and gear **rentals** for independent paddlers, with daily **rates**

averaging $30–45 for canoes. **Guided** canoe/kayak river trips can start as high up the river as Taumarunui, but the higher up you start, the longer you'll have to paddle to reach the best of the scenery, which is why many trips start in Whakahoro at the confluence with the Retaruke River. A trip starting **from Taumarunui** takes you past several spectacular water cascades and the *niu poles* of the Hauhau warriors – the latter site is also accessible from the Stratford–Taumarunui Heritage Trail (SH43; see p.212) – before you reach Whakahoro. Heading downstream **from Whakahoro** you'll see the Mangapapa Stream Ravine, the **Man-o-war Bluff** (named for its supposed resemblance to an old iron-clad battleship) and the **Tarepokiore Whirlpool**, which once completely spun a river steamer. From the **Mangapurua Landing**, you can walk to the Bridge to Nowhere (40min) before continuing past the Puraroto Caves to Pipiriki. Trips **from Wanganui** generally involve travelling by road to Pipiriki, Whakahoro or Taumarunui and paddling downstream from there.

Jetboat trips (again, see box on p.235) range from relaxed to frenetic, and tend to be more expensive; they can begin at either end of the river and take in many of same sights, depending upon time and accessibility (power boats cannot enter some of the narrow tributaries or caves).

Walks in the park

Although the national park covers a large area, there are only two walks of more than one day that are worth doing, and even they depend upon **track conditions**. The routes are predominantly through bush, leading to lookouts. The best times to go walking in the park are from **October to April** and you must buy **passes** before setting out (see "Park practicalities", p.234).

Trampers also need to arrange jetboat pick-up *before* setting out: in Wakahoro, Wades Landing Outdoors (☎07/895 5995) offer **trailhead transport** for trampers, as do Pipiriki-based Bridge to Nowhere jetboats (☎06/385 4128).

The Mangapurua Track

The **Mangapurua Track** (40km; 3 days; 663m ascent) starts from Whakahoro, heading up the Kaiwhakauka Valley before descending through the Mangapurua Valley to Mangapurua Landing, the jetboat pick-up point 30km upstream from Pipiriki. There is a **hut** near the start of the track at Whakahoro, but otherwise you stay overnight in clearly marked **camping** areas, with side streams providing water. Day one (8hr) follows old road routes and consists of easy riverside walking up the Kaiwhakauka Valley before dropping into the Mangapurua Valley, where you pitch camp. Day two (6hr) heads through bush and along sections hewn from sheer papa bluffs, but day three (6hr) is the highlight, taking in the atmospheric Bridge to Nowhere and beyond to the Mangapurua Landing, where signs mark the pick-up point and another camping spot.

Matemateaonga Walkway

The **Matemateaonga Walkway** (42km; 4 days; 732m ascent) starts just off the Upper Mangehu Road, a turning off SH43 48km from Stratford. Matemateaonga means "isolated desolation", reflecting the rugged nature and remoteness of the bush penetrated by this walk. Using old Maori trails, you are able to push deep into the dense forest before emerging at the river for a pre-arranged pick-up.

Day one (1hr 30min) heads up the Kohi Saddle overlooking the Matemeaonga Range and along to the **Omaru Hut** (Category 2; 12 bunks; $8). On day two (5hr), the track continues along the range through dense bush with occasional small clearings; after about three hours, you can take the side-track to Mount Humphries (90min return), for spectacular views across the park to mounts Taranaki and Tongariro, or continue along the main track to the **Pouri Hut** (Category 2; 12 bunks; $8). Day three (7hr) is an easy gradient along a well-defined track, mostly along a ridge crest, before ascending to a clearing where the **Otaraheke Hut** (Category 3; 2 bunks; $4) provides an ideal shelter for lunch, before the final descent to the **Puketotara Hut** (Category 2; 12 bunks; $8). The last day (1hr) comprises a steep descent from the hut to the river, where a large sign marks the pick-up point.

Short walks

The best short walks in the park are accessible from the **Whanganui River Road** (see p.231). The **Aramoana Walk** (7km; 3hr; closed Sept–Oct for lambing) is a loop, beginning and ending 17km from Wanganui at the Aramoana Summit Lookout on the river road. This easy walk heads through farmland, a plantation of pine, banks and cuttings; on a clear day, there are views of the northeast horizon dominated by Mount Ruapehu and the northwest horizon dominated by Mount Taranaki.

Further along the river road, some 35km from Wanganui, the **Atene Skyline Track** (18km; 8hr) is almost a loop, with the start and finish just 2km apart on the road. The track begins at the upriver entrance, climbing up to an old road that follows a gently ascending ridge line to a clearing, where you can get fresh water (the only point on the track). Shortly after this you reach the highest point, before skirting some impressive sandstone bluffs and descending steeply back to the river road. A shorter **nature trail** (20min) shares the same starting point, taking you past examples of the flora and fauna of the region.

Palmerston North and around

On the way to Palmerston North, you really owe it to yourself to stop at **BULLS**, 44km south of Wanganui on SH3, where the locals have let their sense of humour get the better of them. Stop off for a look at the signs outside the bank, Cash-a-Bull; the police station, Const-a-Bull; the visitor centre, Inform-a-Bull; and the fire station, Extinguish-a-Bull; then run.

Sitting on the banks of the Manawatu River, **PALMERSTON NORTH** is a thriving provincial capital, with an exuberant character and plenty to explore. Its **pivotal position** on the main north–south rail line and at the junction of road routes between Wellington and Auckland and between the west and east coasts makes it one of New Zealand's biggest interchanges. After the arrival of the rail line in the 1886, Palmerston North grew from little more than a crossroads to a city with an identity, reflected in some splendid **architecture**. An array of **cultural diversions** – an excellent museum and gallery, a visually stunning library and two theatres – in tandem with the young blood from **Massey University**, create a stimulating atmosphere – though things are noticeably duller when the students are on vacation (Dec–March). With its roots in commercial supply, the city also has an embarrassment of **shops**, malls and mega stores, along with some excellent restaurants and cafés – not to mention an inordinate number of car parks.

Arrival, information and city transport

Palmerston North **airport**, 3km northeast of the city, receives Air New Zealand and Ansett flights, and is linked to the centre by the Palmerston Shuttle (☎06/358 4499; $6). The **train station** is on Tremaine Avenue, about 1.5km northwest of the city and served by local buses #3, #5 and #7. InterCity and Newmans **buses** drop off at the Palmerston North Travel Centre, on the corner of Pitt Street and Main Street, while Mount Cook drop off in the Globe Theatre car park, opposite the travel centre.

The helpful **visitor centre**, Civic Centre Square (Mon–Fri 8.30am–5pm & Sat–Sun 9am–5pm; ☎06/358 5003), is packed to the gills with information on the area, including an excellent weekly events sheet and a range of glossy booklets detailing various aspects of the town – the *Square Walk*, *Architect's Walk* and the *Massey Historic Walk*, a guide to the university campus, are the pick of these.

The Palmerston North Travel Centre is the focal point for all **local bus** services, which run in a series of loops from the terminal to various parts of the city ($1.50); a timetable is available at the visitor centre or the travel centre. Note that services are somewhat reduced outside term time.

Accommodation

If further proof were needed that Palmerston North is a city geared to the needs of the car, then the large number of **motels**, mostly on or around Fitzherbert Avenue, and relative dearth of other good accommodation should suffice.

Hotels and motels

Acacia Court Motel, 374 Tremaine Ave (☎06/358 3471). A friendly welcome and clean, fully self-contained, ground-floor units. ④.

Albert Motor Lodge, 692–700 Main St (☎06/357 3115). Small hotel/motel with an in-house bar and restaurant, and plenty of en-suite single and double rooms with satellite TV. ④.

Birch Trees Lodge, 97 Tremaine Ave (☎06/356 1455). Six self-contained modern units and four well-kept studios, all spacious and agreeable. ④.

Empire Establishment Hotel, cnr Main St & Princess St (☎06/357 8002). Centrally located, recently refurbished hotel rooms. There's a Cobb and Co restaurant downstairs and a popular bar, which can be noisy at weekends. ④.

Illuzzions Motel, 127 Fitzherbert Ave (☎06/355 0050). Despite the awful name and its mock-Tudor appearance, this is a pretty classy establishment, with well-appointed units – and a free round of golf for each guest. ⑤.

Pioneer Motel, 632 Pioneer Hwy (☎06/357 7165). Simple and well-managed motel with twelve units, all with tea- and coffee-making facilities, bathrooms and comfortable beds. ④.

Quality Hotel, 110 Fitzherbert Ave (☎06/356 8059, fax 356 8604). A modern comfortable hotel only five minutes' walk from the square, offering a variety of accommodation largely for corporate custom. Prices drop from May–Sept and there is a lively bar often frequented by students and a reasonably priced carvery restaurant, popular with families, attached to the hotel. ⑤–⑥.

B&Bs, hostels and campsites

Emma's B&B, 250 Fitzherbert Ave (☎06/357 5143). Run by a friendly Dutch couple, who offer cosy, basic accommodation with full cooked breakfasts. Popular with students. ③.

Grey's Inn B&B, 123 Grey St (☎06/358 6928). Very comfortable rooms with their own facilities in a friendly and welcoming house. ④.

Palmerston North Holiday Park, 133 Dittmer Ave (☎06/358 0349). Campsite 2km from the central square, with a range of on-site accommodation. Tent sites $7.50, dorms ①, cabins & flats ②–③.

The Pepper Tree (YHA), 121 Grey St (☎06/355 4054). A comfortable hostel within easy walking distance of the central square. Run by a friendly and helpful folk, this is a small place, so phone ahead. Dorms ①, rooms ②.

The City

The focal point of Palmerston North is the **central square**, bordered by Broadway Avenue and Church Street. Among the mish-mash of colonial buildings that surround the square are a number of fine examples from different architectural schools: lavish classical Victorian and Edwardian edifices, the elegant lines of Art Deco-influenced

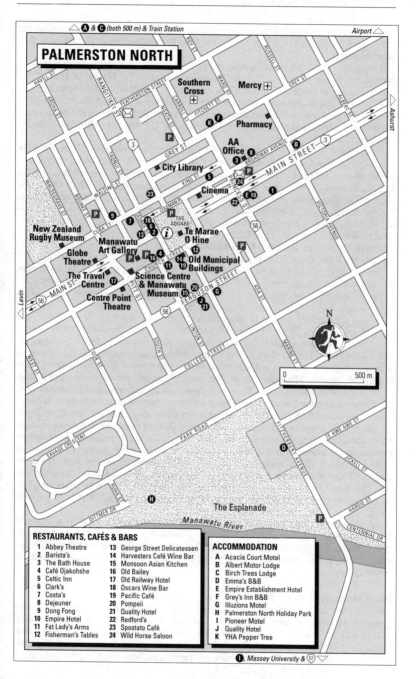

PALMERSTON NORTH

△ **A** & **C** (both 500 m) & Train Station

Airport △

△ Ashurst

HAVILL ST
ARIHA ST
RANGITIKEI STREET
FEATHERSTON STREET
NGAIA ST
CARROLL ST
FITCHETT ST
WARDS ST
BOYS ST
RUSSELL ST
GREY ST
ALBERT ST

Southern Cross ✚

Mercy ✚

K **F**

Pharmacy

3

GREY ST

AA Office

8

B

Main Street 3

BROADWAY AVENUE

City Library

3

5

KING ST

PRINCESS ST

24

Cinema

E **10**

1

22

56

23

CUBA ST

WALDING ST

BOURKE ST

WALDEGRAVE ST

9

7

18

6

13 **2**

CAMAN PL

THE SQUARE

i

Te Marae O Hine

New Zealand Rugby Museum

Manawatu Art Gallery

4

16

12

14

Old Municipal Buildings

11 **19**

Globe Theatre

GEORGE STREET

CHURCH STREET

56

P

The Travel Centre

17

Science Centre & Manawatu Museum

20

15

FERGUSON STREET

G

ADA ST

VICTORIA AVENUE

MARINE ST

Centre Point Theatre

PITT ST

56

J

21

△ Levin

56

MAIN ST

N

UNION ST

COLIX ST

SOUTH ST

WEST ST

COLLEGE STREET

0 ——— 500 m

PARK ROAD

FITZHERBERT AVENUE

TE AWE AWE ST

TICKELL ST

D

SAVAGE CRESCENT

RUHA ST

DITTMER DR

H

The Esplanade

HARDIE ST

CENTENNIAL DR

P

Manawatu River

▽ **I**, Massey University & 57 ▽

RESTAURANTS, CAFÉS & BARS

1 Abbey Theatre
2 Barista's
3 The Bath House
4 Café Ojakohshe
5 Celtic Inn
6 Clark's
7 Costa's
8 Dejeuner
9 Dong Fong
10 Empire Hotel
11 Fat Lady's Arms
12 Fisherman's Tables
13 George Street Delicatessen
14 Harvesters Café Wine Bar
15 Monsoon Asian Kitchen
16 Old Bailey
17 Old Railway Hotel
18 Oscars Wine Bar
19 Pacific Café
20 Pompeii
21 Quality Hotel
22 Redford's
23 Spostato Café
24 Wild Horse Saloon

ACCOMMODATION

A Acacia Court Motel
B Albert Motor Lodge
C Birch Trees Lodge
D Emma's B&B
E Empire Establishment Hotel
F Grey's Inn B&B
G Illuzions Motel
H Palmerston North Holiday Park
I Pioneer Motel
J Quality Hotel
K YHA Pepper Tree

structures from the late 1920s and early 1930s, and practical modern constructions like the public library, sensitively poking its nose from behind the classical facade of a much older building.

The square itself is a simple grassy expanse with trees and well-kept gardens containing the visitor centre on the southwestern side, and **Te Marae o Hine** ("The Courtyard of the Daughter of Peace") just behind it. Te Marae o Hine was the name suggested for the settlement's central square by the chief of the Ngati Raukawa in 1878, in the hope that love and peace would become enduring features in the relationship between the Manawatu Maori and incoming *pakeha*. The site is marked by the skilful carvings of John Bevan Ford.

On the southeast side of the square is the **City Library** (Mon–Thurs 10am–6pm, Sat 10am–4pm & Sun 1–4pm), an innovative building designed by Ian Athfield (see box on p.398) and opened in May 1995, which peeks out from behind the original facade of the 1927 C.M. Ross building. The interior is a challenging environment full of colour and contrast, light and texture in which all the reading materials are arranged according to "subject living rooms" furnished with armchairs and sofas. Opposite the southern corner of the square on Church Street is the old **Municipal Building**, which today houses an art centre and a couple of good cafés (see "Eating", p.241), while in the centre of the square the impressive Art Deco **Ladies Rest room** has an icing-like ornamentation and a geometric aquamarine relief surrounded by half moons above the main entrance.

You can enjoy a bird's-eye view of Palmerston North from the top of the **civic centre**, opposite the visitor centre (Mon–Fri 10am–3pm; free); from this vantage point, the city reveals itself to be sprawling and flat with a number of small green parks, like a runny omelette dotted with sprigs of parsley.

Behind the public library is **George Street**, home of Palmerston North's café society and a honey pot for the weekend-brunch bees. Around the corner from George Street is the **Science Centre**, 396 Main St (daily 10am–5pm; $6), which has imaginative displays intended to entertain and inform children, including an earthquake simulator, a section on volcanoes and exhibits covering space exploration. In the same building, the **Manawatu Museum** (daily 10am–5pm; donation requested) contains a number of highly evocative displays. One room describes the experiences of immigrants to the Manawatu region from Europe, China and India, but the most impressive area is a large Maori exhibition hall where carvings, weapons, tools, baskets and figureheads are mounted in a specially designed environment that re-creates the ambience of bush, trees, campfires and meeting houses. Local Rangitaki Maori regularly demonstrate weaving in the museum, and on the last Sunday of every month perform *The Naming of the Manawatu*; check in the foyer or at the visitor centre for details. Just across the courtyard, the **Manawatu Art Gallery**, 398 Main St (Mon–Fri 10am–5pm, Sat and Sun, 11.30am–4.30pm; free), displays *pakeha* and Maori art from its permanent collection alongside touring exhibitions; check the latest with the visitor centre or in the local press.

Northwest of the square, on the edge of the A&P Showgrounds, is the **New Zealand Rugby Museum**, 87 Cuba St (Mon–Sat 10am–noon & 1.30–4pm, Sun 1.30–4pm; $3), where die-hard rugger fans can marvel at caps, ties, blazers, jerseys, balls, cups, cartoons, photographs, a reference library of games on video and the bronzed boots of famous players.

South to the Manawatu River

Although not on most sightseeing itneraries, the leafy garden suburb of **Savage Crescent Housing Estate**, at the junction of Cook Street and College Street, is worth a quick look on your way south to The Esplanade. Faced with a severe housing shortage in the 1930s, New Zealand's first Labour government, headed by Michael Savage, funded the building of well-made houses comparable to those inhabited by more affluent Kiwis, rather than the prevalent "barracks-like workers' dwellings". Built between 1939 and 1945, Savage Crescent's modest detached houses represent the partial fulfilment of that egalitarian dream.

A couple of kilometres south of the square, the tree-filled parklands of **The Esplanade** (daily dawn to dusk; free) stretch along the north bank of the Manawutu River, with manicured lawns and flowerbeds, a miniature railway, bird aviaries, rose gardens and many excellent spots for a picnic. On the south side of the river, at the bottom of Fitzherbert Avenue, **Massey University Campus** is well worth an hour of your time. Served by local buses from the Travel Centre, the spacious leafy campus is an appealing mixture of trees and old buildings that seem to blend into a dreamy academic blur.

Around Palmerston North

Near the township of Himatangi, 38km southwest on SH56, is **Himatangi Beach**. Stretching 10km in either direction, the grey sands of this windswept beach are strewn with tangles of driftwood – and in summer with water-sports fanatics and sunbathers.

Heading northeast from the city on SH3, you'll pass the Oroua Road turning, which leads to the **Kirewood Equestrian Centre** (☎06/355 9148), 9km from Palmerston North. This is a very professional and friendly riding school, with horses to suit even the most incompetent and a range of short treks (1–2hr; $30–40), plus a moonlight ride with pick-up from Palmerston North ($50).

Back on SH3, 13km northeast of Palmerston North, is the small town of **ASHHURST**, home to the **John Bevan Ford Art Studio**, 6 Lincoln St (daily 11am–4pm), where you can where you can see work in progress. An artist of international repute, Ford produces finely wrought coloured-ink drawings on handmade watercolour paper and, more famously, sculptures and large wooden carvings using traditional Maori and more contemporary techniques. His works feature in many of New Zealand's galleries and an official archive of his work is held at the Taranaki Museum in New Plymouth; examples of his work are also held by the British Museum, Museum of Volkerkunde in Berlin, the National Art Gallery of Australia and the National Maritime Museum in Holland.

Eating and drinking

Palmerston North has some good value-for-money restaurants and bars, though the town's prosperity also means that there are a few corporate yuppie-bars which trade in expensive drinks and overpriced food. Happily, the student population moderates tendencies in this direction.

Cafés

Barista's Espresso Bar, George St. Modern minimalist café, with a corrugated-iron counter bar where they grind their own coffee and serve amazing cakes, snacky meals ($4–12), mains around the $18 mark and good bagels for breakfast. Daily 8am–11pm; licensed.

Café Ojakbashe, 41 The Square. A wonderfully eccentric café serving cheap, authentic and tasty Turkish food in a lively atmosphere. Daily 11.30am–2.30pm & 6–10pm; BYO & licensed.

Clark's, City Library, 4 The Square. Stylish café serving excellent brunches, good coffee, light snacks and more filling meals all day long.

George Street Delicatessen, cnr George St & Main St. The best espresso bar/deli in the city with sexy sandwiches, quiches, bagels, bargain breakfasts, and an excellent dinner menu that ranges through antipasto, spring salad, Greek chicken filos and Moroccan fish, all for under $16. You can also buy cheeses, other deli goods and home-made breads at the counter. Mon–Wed 7.30am–6pm, Thurs–Sat 7.30pm–midnight, Sun 8.30am–11pm.

Harvesters Café Wine Bar, in the old Municipal Building, Church St. Another stylish city venue offering café fare at reasonable prices, with a dinner menu (from 6.30pm) that includes Cajun pork and Mediterranean fish. Mon–Sat 11am–midnight; live jazz or blues every Thurs night.

Pompeii, 353 Ferguson St. The place to go for pizza, eat in or takeaway, with a broad range of toppings from the sublime to the ridiculous.

Restaurants

The Bath House, 161 Broadway Ave. A restaurant and lounge bar in a bathhouse wittily decorated in "fall of the Roman Empire" bacchanalia, plus courtyard dining. Food is suitably decadent – French- and Italian-influenced meals, finger food, and brunches.

Costa's, Cuba St, opposite the Wharehouse superstore (book Fri & Sat, ☎06/356 6383). Evening restaurant with windows looking down on the street. The food is inexpensive (mains under $20) and includes nachos, beef satay, pasta, Tex–Mex, Chinese and Thai. Licensed.

Dejeuner, 159 Broadway Ave (☎06/356 1449). Expensive French cousin of *The Bath House*, offering top-notch cuisine. Licensed & BYO.

Dong Fong, cnr Campbell St &Cuba St. Seriously good Chinese restaurant serving lunches, dinners and some inspired and extensive set menus. Licensed.

Fisherman's Table, cnr Church St & Fitzherbert Ave. No-nonsense lunches and dinners (2 courses for $12) – mostly seafood, steaks, and a salad bar.

Monsoon Asian Kitchen, 347 Ferguson St. Value-for-money Chinese, Malaysian and Singaporean cuisine. Dinner Tues–Sun; BYO.

Redford's, cnr Princess St & Main St, on the first floor. An airy, quiet restaurant serving inexpensive Kiwi dishes with a touch of Middle Eastern and European flare. Dinner daily; licensed & BYO.

Spostato Café, 213 Cuba St. Charmingly decorated, relaxed Italian restaurant, with friendly service and good authentic food at sensible prices. Dinner daily; BYO.

Drinking and entertainment

Palmerston North has more than its fair share of entertainment venues. The **Centre Point Theatre**, on the corner of Church Street and Pitt Street (☎06/359 6983), is an intimate purpose-built performance space, with a pleasant pre-show and interval bar; or take in a movie at the seven-screen **Downtown Cinema**, on Broadway Avenue between Princess Street and the square. The received wisdom regarding nightlife is that there's more fun to be had in term time – and the later you start, the better.

Bars and pubs

Celtic Inn, Regent Arcade. Primarily a late-night drinking den, with Irish food and live music Fri & Sat nights.

Empire Hotel, cnr Princess St & Main St. A recently refurbished drinking hole with a lively atmosphere and cheap food in the attached *Cobb and Co* restaurant.

Fat Lady's Arms, cnr Church St & Linton St. Part of a national chain that guarantees late nights, loud music, lots of ale, lively surroundings and affordable snacky food. Closed Mon.

Old Bailey, Grand Hotel Building, 341 Church St. A reasonable stab at an English-style pub, serving a broad range of beer and wine and generous New Zealand pub grub.

Old Railway Hotel, cnr David St & Main St. A real happening place at weekends, with three bars – the Hardrock, the Garden Bar and Legends – at least one of which has live entertainment Wed–Sat.

Oscar's Wine Bar, 1 The Square, by Coleman Mall. Unpretentious little bar, with bags of character and occasional live entertainment.

Quality Hotel, 110 Fitzherbert Ave. An excellent bar frequented by students and a reasonably priced carvery restaurant (dinner daily) that's popular with families.

Clubs and music venues

Abbey Theatre, 369 Church St. Nightclub and party venue in an old stone church, where the music ranges from heavy funk and 90s techno to 60s, 70s and 80s disco. Thurs, Fri & Sat.

Pacific Café, in the old Municipal Building, Church St. Hosts three young, local bands every Friday night (9pm–midnight; $3). Mon–Sat 8am–4pm; BYO.

Wild Horse Saloon, cnr Main St & Princess St. Pub that transmogrifies into a punk and alternative music venue on Fri and Sat nights, when things can get a little wild.

Listings

Airlines Air New Zealand, 30 Broadway Ave (☎06/351 8800); Ansett, 50 Princess St (☎06/356 5146).

Automobile Association 185 Broadway Ave (☎06/357 7039).

Banks and exchange The city has a full compliment of banks on The Square or within two blocks of it (see also listing for Thomas Cook).

Bookshops Book Mark, 292 Cuba St, has new and secondhand books; The Bookshop, 78 Broadway Ave, stocks new, rare and antiquarian books.

Car rental Avis (☎06/358 4284); Hertz (☎06/357 0921); Rent-a-dent (☎06/355 5227); Thrifty (☎06/355 4365).

Disabled travellers New Zealand Disabilities Resource Centre, 840 Tremaine Ave (☎06/356 2311, fax 355 5459), provides an information service for disabled travellers, including lists of contacts around the country.

Events The Festival of Maori Art, Craft and Culture is held annually (December 2–7), in the Pascal Street Stadium and Akers Pavilion, just off Fitzherbert Ave. Traditional and contemporary craft workshops, exhibitions, singing, dancing and storytelling keep alive what was once a purely aural culture; contact the visitor centre or Te Whare Wananga o Nga Toi Maori, 392 Ferguson St (☎06/355 3508, fax 356 5193), for details. In mid-December, the Cathedral of the Holy Spirit, 197 Broadway Ave, hosts a week-long flower and music festival, in which the aisle is carpeted with flowers and choirs give a series of recitals.

Internet/email Surfside Internet Café, 406 Main St (Mon–Fri noon–8pm, Sat 11.30am–3pm; ☎06/356 9571), offers Internet access (net surfing $5 for 15min) and email services ($5 for 30min); terminals can be booked in advance, and there's coffee, muffins and sandwiches to keep the munchies at bay.

Medical treatment City Health and Pharmacy, 22 Victoria St (daily 8am–10pm; ☎06/359 4594), has doctors available for consultation ($39) and an after-hours druggist.

Newspapers The local daily is the award-winning *Evening Standard*, (Mon–Sat, 70¢), which includes entertainment listings and has emergency information on Friday, but is worth buying just for a read; the Sunday paper is *The Tribune*.

Post offices The main post office is on Princess St, between Main St & Broadway Ave; a number of postal shops are scattered about the city.

Taxis Palmerston North Taxis (☎06/335 5333).

Thomas Cook cnr Broadway Ave & Princes St (☎06/356 4800).

Tours Adventure Aviation (☎06/351 5020), offer scenic flights in a Tiger Moth – dress warmly (15–20min; $99); a similar service in more modern and less airy planes is offered by the Manawatu Districts Aero Club (☎06/357 9244); Manawatu Wine Tours (☎06/357 1077) tour the wineries around Hawke's Bay and Martinborough; Pauline's Tours and Travel (☎06/357 0058) offer garden, mountain, wine, beach, river and volcano trips; Tui's Bus Tours (☎ & fax 06/357 4136) run half- and full-day guided tours around the area.

Travel agencies Palmerston North Travel Centre, cnr Main St & Pitt St (☎06/355 5633); Tranz Rail, Mathews Ave (☎06/351 6828).

South to Otaki

To the south of Palmerston North and the Manawatu, the peaks of the rugged and inhospitable **Tararua Mountains** corral the **Horowhenua** region into a strip along the coast. Renowned for its gentle landscape, lakes, walkways, fruit and vegetable growing, rivers and beaches, the area has a few mildly diverting settlements, but lacks any substantial attractions. Being only around ninety minutes' drive from Wellington, this is prime **commuter territory** – and also contains a high proportion of **retired** people. If you choose to stop, then the tourist-orientated **Foxton**, with a plethora of **museums** and an extraordinary long flat **beach** facing its seaside offshoot of **Foxton Beach**, and **Levin**, full of factory shops, some good eateries and with access to the mountains, are the best bets. Continuing **south to Otaki** and beyond, the natural barrier of the Tararua Mountains separates the Kapiti Coast from the Hutt Valley until you reach the outskirts of Wellington (see Chapter 7; p.389).

Archeological evidence suggests that there was a semi-nomadic **moa-hunter** culture in this area between 1400 and 1650AD, pre-dating larger tribal settlements. **Europeans** came to the area in the early 1800s and settled at the mouth of the Manawatu River, but skedaddled to Foxton owing to land-purchase problems. Foxton's early growth was based on **flax milling** and the export of flax, agricultural products and timber from its port. The opening of the Wellington–Palmerston North **rail line** in 1886 spelled the end of Foxton's commercial domination of the area; and the final ignominy was the closure of the Foxton–Palmerston North branch line in 1959.

Foxton

FOXTON is perched on the coastal plain 38km southwest of Palmerston North, reached via SH56 and SH1. The town is split in two, with the main centre beside SH1 and **Foxton Beach** 5km away on the coast, where there's a long sandy beach with good surfing, safe swimming areas and abundant birdlife around the Manawatu River estuary. The small community by the beach is full of baches for vacationing New Zealanders. Foxton is a place where you step back in time: the town has old-style shop facades, cobblestoned paving and no less than five **museums**, along with some heritage attractions and decorative murals painted on prominent buildings.

Foxton was once the flax-stripping capital of New Zealand. Maori had long relied on handmade **flax** items for their everyday needs and European immigrants followed their lead, using it for woolpacks, binder twine, fibrous plaster lashings, upholsterers' tow and carpet. In an effort to streamline the stripping and weaving processes, mills were constructed alongside swamps and on riverbanks in Manawatu and Horowhenua in the 1880s, and the history of this industry is recounted in the town's **Flax Stripper Museum**, Main Street (Tues–Sun 1–3pm; $2). Still on the flax theme, sixty-five types of green flax and their uses are marked along the riverside **flaxwalk**, which starts in Harbour Street and is described in a free leaflet available from the visitor centre or the museum.

At the north end of Main Street, in Coronation Hall, the **Museum of Audio Visual Arts and Sciences**, Avenue Road (Tues–Sun 1–3pm; $4), offers an insight into early broadcasting and home entertainment through its collection of over 14,000 records going back to the early 1890s, assorted gramophones, cameras, projectors, restored Pianola rolls, and vintage radios and televisions. Only museum addicts will want to go for a hat-trick by visiting the **Trolley Bus Museum and Gainsborough Doll Gallery**, 55 Main St (Tues–Sun 11am–4.30pm; $2), with its surreal juxtaposition of a 1953 London Bus and an assortment of ancient and modern dolls, some looking remarkably sinister.

Practicalities

The old Rail and Tram Station, 80–88 Main St, is the **bus** stop and booking office for Newmans and InterCity services. The same building houses the **visitor centre** (daily 8.30am–5pm; ☎06/363 8940), a good daytime **café** – and a horse-drawn tram that's hauled out every summer for tourist rides around town (15min; $3). When **fast-food** cravings hit, make for the *Hangi House*, Avenue Road (daily noon–9pm), offering food cooked hangi-style, fish, chips, burgers and sandwiches.

Levin and around

The small town of **LEVIN** sits at the junction of SH1 and SH57, 19km south of Foxton and 57km southwest of Palmerston North. The principal community in the Horowhenua region, Levin makes a living from horticulture and clothes-manufacturing. The town is crammed with **factory shops** flogging discount clothing and in the orchards around town, **fruit-picking** work can often be had. If neither of these grab you, you need only stay long enough to patronize the wonderful *Café Extreme* (see "Practicalities", p.244) and to take a quick spin around the nearby coast and mountains.

At the **Papaitonga Scenic Reserve**, 4km south of Levin on SH1, a gentle stroll to the Papaitonga Lookout (10min) or the Otomuiri Lookout (20min), provides great views of Lake Papaitonga and the surrounding wetlands, which provide a refuge for many rare birds, including the spotless crake, Australasian bitter, and New Zealand dabchick. Wilder scenery is the attraction at **Waitarere Beach**, 15km northwest of Levin, off SH1. This vast dune-backed, grey-sand beach boasts pounding surf and the rusted hulk of the *Hydrbad*, which was wrecked in a storm in 1878.

Tararua Forest Park

The rugged **Tararua Forest Park** is often ignored as travellers head south or north. Sandwiched between SH1 and SH2, the mountains of the Tararua Range form an almost impenetrable barrier, their exposed peaks buffeted by fog, rain, high winds and snow funnelled from the Cook Strait. The **tracks** in the area are not the broad highways of New Zealand's Great Walks, but narrow and barely distinguishable paths fraught with undulating and sometimes muddy terrain, while the **huts** on the tracks are all very basic, classified as back-country. The mountains offer a genuinely rugged and isolated experience for the keen, fit, experienced trampers, but are not for the faint-hearted – though there are some short walks accessible from Levin, Otaki (see above) and Masterton (see p.383), which give a brief taste of the range. For longer tramps, get a guide or go with someone who knows the area really well.

The Levin visitor centre (see below) can put you in touch with local tramping clubs, who will recommend a **guide** for walks in the Tararua Range. Back to Basics Guided Walks (☎06/368 6306) offer tailored trips ($50–95 a day), with an experienced guide who delights in passing on esoteric bush skills and the subtle art of navigation without benefit of a map or compass. For a taste of the park, you can reach some of the **shorter walks** in the park from Levin – such as the **Mount Thompson Track** (2–4hr), which ascends one of the smaller peaks in the range, but nonetheless offers good views of the coast and Kapiti Island. The walk begins around 100m past the Panatewaewae car park on North Manakau Road, a turning off SH1 some 10km south of Levin.

Practicalities

The **train** station backs on to Oxford Street in the centre of town, and **buses** pull into the Levin Mall car park. The **visitor centre**, in the Regent Court, Oxford Street (Mon–Fri, 8.30am–5pm, Sat, 9am–1pm), is about five minutes' walk from both the station and the bus stop.

Fantails **B&B**, 44 Queen St and 40 MacArthur St (☎ & fax 06/368 9279; ④–⑥), provide excellent, well-appointed **rooms** in two houses. A smaller operation, with just two guest rooms, is run by the ultra-friendly *Mary and Ted Creed*, 17 Stuart St (☎06/368 2706; ④), and offers dinner by arrangement ($15). **Motel** accommodation is available at the *Mountain View*, The Avenue (☎06/368 5214, fax 368 4091; ④), where most units have cooking facilities, or in the comfortable log-cabin-like units at the *Welcome Inn*, 353a Oxford St (☎ & fax 06/368 3834; ④).

The best place to **eat** in Levin is *Café Extreme*, 7 Bath St (daily 10am–11pm), with Kiwiana decor and excellent-value salads, huge steaks, deli sandwiches, gourmet burgers, veggie dishes and superb coffee. The truckers' favourite is *Raewyn's Plaze*, Oxford Street (licensed & BYO), serving good and cheap breakfasts, plus smorgasbord lunches ($12) and dinners ($22). Another safe bet is the café attached to *Fantails*, 40 MacArthur St (Wed–Sun 9am–4.30pm), which is set in pretty tree-filled gardens and has a variety of snacks, light meals and excellent ice cream.

travel details

Trains

From Hamilton to: Auckland (1 daily; 2hr 5min); Rotorua (1 daily; 2hr 6min); Tauranga (1 daily; 1hr 25min); Te Awamutu (1 daily; 19min).

From Levin to: Wellington (1 daily; 1hr 39min).

From Otorohanga to: Te Kuiti (1 daily; 16min).

From Palmerston North to: Hastings (1 daily 2hr; 46min); Levin (1 daily; 38min).

From Taumarunui to: Palmerston North (1 daily; 4hr 25min).

From Te Awamutu to: Otorohanga (1 daily; 19min).

From Te Kuiti to: Taumarunui (1 daily; 16min).

Buses

From Hamilton to: Auckland (12 daily; 2hr 15min); Cambridge (10 daily; 20min); Ngaruawahia (6 daily; 50min); New Plymouth (5 daily; 4hr 20min); Otorohanga (3 daily; 1 hr 5min); Raglan (2 daily; 45min); Te Awamutu (6 daily; 40min); Te Kuiti (4 daily; 1hr 25min); Thames (3 daily; 1hr 50min); Tauranga (3 daily; 1hr 40min); Rotorua (8 daily; 1hr 45min); Wanganui (2 daily; 6hr 15min).

From Otorohanga to: Te Kuiti (4 daily; 25min); Waitomo (6 daily; 30min).

From New Plymouth to: Wanganui (3 daily; 2hr 50min).

From Palmerston North to: Hastings (4 daily; 2hr 55min); Masterton (7 daily; 1hr 35min); Rotorua (3 daily; 5hr 30min); Wellington (8 daily; 2hr 5min).

From Taumaranui to: Wanganui (2 daily; 3hr 30min).

From Te Awamutu to: Kawhia (Mon–Sat 1; 1hr 30mins); Otorohanga (3 daily; 25mins).

From Te Kuiti to: New Plymouth (4 daily; 2hr 55min); Taumarunui (2 daily; 1hr).

From Wanganui to: Palmerston North (3 daily; 1hr 5min).

Flights

From Hamilton to: Auckland (6 daily; 30min); Christchurch (16 daily; 2hr 5min); Napier (4 daily; 2hr 55min); Nelson (17 daily; 2hr 30min); Palmerston North (6 daily; 1hr); Wellington (15 daily; 50min).

From New Plymouth to: Auckland (15 daily; 50min); Christchurch (11 daily; 2hr 5min); Tauranga (12 daily; 2hr 10min); Wellington (10 daily; 55min).

From Palmerston North to: Auckland (24 daily; 1hr 10min); Christchurch (14 daily; 1hr 25min); Nelson (12 daily; 1hr 35min); Tauranga (12 daily; 2hr 30min); Wellington (9 daily; 35min).

CHAPTER FOUR

CENTRAL NORTH ISLAND

T he landlocked **Central North Island** contains more than its fair share of New Zealand's star attractions. The area is delineated by three defining geological features: Lake Taupo, the country's largest; the Tongariro National Park, with its trio of active volcanoes; and the volcanic field that feeds colourful and fiercely active thermal areas, principally around the Arawa heartland of **Rotorua**. If you are ticking off Kiwi icons, then time is well spent around Rotorua, where **boiling mud pools** plop next to spouting **geysers** fuelled by superheated water, which is drawn off to fill the hot pools found all over town. To complete this quintessential New Zealand experience, here you'll also find the most accessible expression of Maori culture, with highly-regarded Arawa carvings and any number of groups ready to perform traditional dances and haka, and feed you with fall-off-the-bone meat cooked in a **hangi** steam oven.

The dramatic volcanic scenery is all the more striking for its contrast with the encroaching pines of the **Kaingaroa Forest**, one of the world's largest plantation forests, with serried ranks of fast-growing conifers marching to the horizon. When the country was being carved up for farming, the central North Island was all but abandoned as cattle grazed here soon contracted "bush sickness" and died. In the 1930s, scientists discovered that the disease was caused by an easily rectified deficiency of the mineral cobalt, but by this stage the free-draining pumice soils had already been planted with millions of radiata pine seedlings by gangs of convicts and Great Depression relief workers. Since then, sylviculture has continued to consolidate its position as the region's chief earner through pulp and paper mills at Kinleith, near Tokoroa, and Kawerau.

The rest of the region is loosely referred to as the **Volcanic Plateau**, a sometimes-bleak high country that is overlaid with a layer of rock and ash expelled two thousand years back when a huge volcano blew itself apart, the resultant crater being filled by **Lake Taupo**. This serene lake, and the streams and rivers feeding it, have since become a fishing mecca for anglers keen to snag brown and rainbow trout, but the area is no less appealing for the lure of its watersports and the thundering rapids of the Waikato River, which drains the lake. South of Lake Taupo rise the three majestic volcanoes of the **Tongariro National Park**, created in 1887, since when it has become a winter playground for North Island skiers and a summer destination for trampers intent on bagging a couple of magical walks.

If you're hot-footing it to this region **from Auckland**, you've got a choice of **routes**: the direct SH1 through Hamilton; or the faster, less congested and broadly more appealing journey along SH2, which branches east at Pokeno, 50km south of Auckland, then along SH27 as it cuts south across the fringes of the Hauraki Plains. The two routes converge on the small town of Tirau, where SH1 heads almost 100km

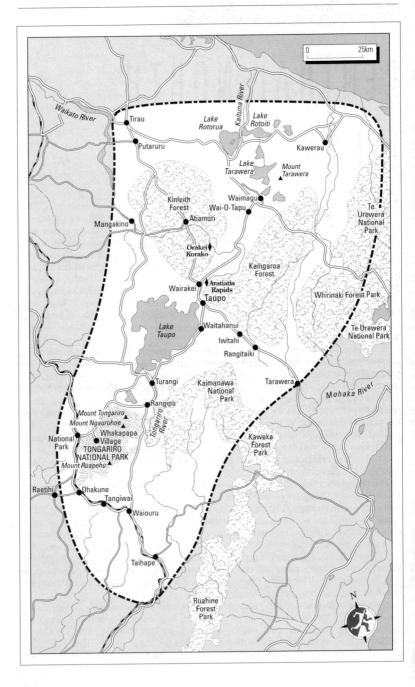

ACCOMMODATION PRICES

Accommodation listed in this guide has been categorized into one of nine price bands, as set out below. The rates quoted represent the **cheapest available** double or twin **room** – except for category ①, which are per-person rates for a dorm bed; fees for **tent sites** and **DOC huts** are also per-person, unless otherwise stated.

① under $20 per person	④ $60–80	⑦ $140–180
② under $40 per room	⑤ $80–100	⑧ $180–240
③ $40–60	⑥ $100–140	⑨ over $240

For more on accommodation, see p.33.

south to Taupo and SH5 crosses the Mamuku Plateau to Rotorua, 52km away to the east.

The **altitude** of the Volcanic Plateau lends Taupo, the Tongariro National Park and environs a refreshing crispness even in high summer, when it is a welcome retreat from the stickiness of Auckland and the north. Spring and autumn are tolerably warm and have the added advantage of freedom from the summer hordes, though the often freezing winter months from May to October are best left to winter-sports enthusiasts. The Rotorua area is more **balmy** on the whole, but can still be cool in winter, making the thermal areas steamier and the hot baths all the more appealing.

ROTORUA AND AROUND

There is little doubt that the "Sulphur City" of **Rotorua** is New Zealand's tourist destination par excellence. For this is one of the world's most concentrated and accessible geothermal areas, where twenty-metre geysers spout among kaleidoscopic mineral pools, steam wafts over cauldrons of boiling mud and terraces of encrusted silicates drip like stalactites. Everywhere you look there's evidence of **vulcanism**: birds on the lakeshore are relieved of the chore of nest-sitting by the warmth of the ground, graves in Ohinemutu and Whakarewarewa churchyards have to be built topside as digging the ground is likely to unearth a hot spring, and hotels are all equipped with geothermally-fed **hot tubs**, perfect for easing your bones after a hard day's sightseeing. Throughout the region, sulphur and heat combine to form **barren landscapes** where only the hardiest of plants brave the trickling hot streams, sputtering vents and seething fumaroles. Plant life may be absent, but there is no shortage of **colour** from iridescent mineral deposits lining the pools: bright oranges juxtaposed with emerald greens and rust reds. The underworld looms large in Rotorua's lexicon: there is no end of "The Devil's this" and "Hell's that" – a state of affairs that prompted George Bernard Shaw to ruminate on his colourful past while visiting the Hell's Gate thermal area and famously quip, "It reminds me too vividly of the fate theologians have promised me".

But hydrothermal activity is only part of Rotorua's appeal. The naturally hot water lured Maori to settle around Lake Rotorua and Lake Tarawera, using the hottest pools for cooking, bathing in cooler ones and building their *whare* (houses) on the hot ground to drive away the winter chill. Here they managed to hang on to their traditions and tribal integrity more than anywhere else in the country, forging a strong and vibrant **Maori culture** that is part of the daily life of a third of the region's people. Despite the inevitably diluting effects of tourism, there is no better place to get an introduction to Maori values and traditions, dance and song than at one of the concert and hangi evenings held all over Rotorua and on nearby marae.

Maori-owned and operated tour companies often make the most educational, not to say entertaining, ways of exploring Rotorua's surrounding area. To the south and east, the forests are punctuated by over a dozen **lakes** tucked into bush-girt hollows and overlooked by the mountainous products of ancient volcanic activity and its more recent manifestation, the shattered five-kilometre-long chasm of **Mount Tarawera**. During one cataclysmic night of eruptions in 1886 this chain of volcanoes split in two, destroying the region's first tourist attraction, the Pink and White Terraces, entombing the nearest settlement, the so-called **Buried Village**, and creating the **Waimangu Thermal Valley**. Waimangu is just one of four magnificent thermal areas open to the public; the Pohutu Geyser at **Whakarewarewa**, on the outskirts of Rotorua, and the Lady Knox Geyser at **Wai-O-Tapu**, to the south, demand particular attention.

Some history

The Rotorua region is home to the Arawa people, who trace their ancestry back to the **Arawa canoe** which struck land at Maketu, at the mouth of the Kaituna River on the Bay of Plenty, after its long journey from the Polynesian homelands of Hawaiki sometime in the fourteenth century. The leader of one of the first parties to explore the interior was the *tohunga* (priest), **Ngatoroirangi**, who made it as far as the freezing summit of Mount Tongariro, where he feared he might die from cold. His prayers to the gods of Hawaiki were answered with fire, which journeyed underground, first surfacing at the volcanic White Island in the Bay of Plenty, then at several more points in a line between there and the three central North Island volcanoes. Ngatoroirangi was saved, and he and his followers established themselves around Lake Rotorua, where they lived contentedly until another Arawa sailor, the wily **Ihenga**, duped Ngatoroirangi out of his title to the land. The victor named the lakes as he reached them along the Kaituna River: Lake Rotoiti ("small lake") and Lake Rotorua ("second lake").

In revenge for an earlier raid on an island in nearby Green Lake, the Northland Ngapuhi chief, **Hongi Hika**, led a war party here in 1823. The Arawa got wind of the attack and retreated to the sanctuary of Mokoia Island, in the middle of Lake Rotorua; undaunted, Hongi Hika and his warriors carried their canoes overland between lakes (the track between Lake Rotoiti and Lake Rotoehu still bears the name Hongi's Track). The Ngapuhi, equipped with muskets traded with Europeans in the Bay of Islands, defeated the traditionally armed Arawa then withdrew, leaving the Arawa to regroup in time for the New Zealand Wars of the 1860s, in which the Arawa supported the government. This worked in their favour when, in 1870, **Te Kooti** (see box on p.362) attacked from the east coast, and the colonial troops helped turn them back.

By this time a few **Europeans** – notably a Danish trader Philip Hans Tapsell and the missionary Thomas Chapman – had already lived for some years in the Maori villages of Ohinemutu and Whakarewarewa, but it wasn't until Te Kooti had been dispatched that Rotorua came into existence. **Tourists** began to arrive in the district to view the **Pink and White Terraces** using Ohinemutu, Whakarewarewa and Te Wairoa as staging posts. The Arawa, who up to this point had been relatively isolated from European influence, were quick to grasp the possibilities of tourism and helped turn Rotorua into what it is today.

Rotorua

You smell **ROTORUA** long before you see it. Hydrogen sulphide drifting up from natural vents in the region's thin crust means that the stench of rotten eggs lingers in the air, but after a few hours you barely notice the smell. No amount of bad odour, however, will keep visitors away from this small, ordered place clinging to the southern shores of the near-circular **Lake Rotorua**. Rotorua's northern and southern limits are defined by the two ancient villages of the Arawa sub-tribe, Ngati Whakaue. The lakeshore **Ohinemutu** and the thermal reserve of **Whakarewarewa** were the only settlements before the 1880s, when Rotorua became New Zealand's only city with its origins firmly rooted in tourism. Specifically, Rotorua was set up as a **spa town** on land leased from the Ngati Whakaue, under the auspices of the 1881 Thermal Springs Districts Act. By 1885, the fledgling Rotorua boasted the Government Sanatorium Complex, a spa designed to administer the rigorous treatments deemed beneficial to the "invalids" who came to take the waters. The original building became the Blue Baths, now closed and moribund in the oh-so-English **Government Gardens**. The gardens became the site of its successor, the **Bath House**, full of even grander baths and treatment rooms, and now a feature of the **Rotorua Museum**.

Arrival and information

InterCity and Newmans **buses** pull up outside the Tourism Rotorua complex (see below). The once-daily *Geyserland Express* **train** from Auckland and Hamilton arrives on Railway Road, 1km northwest of the centre, and is met by the Sightseeing Shuttle, which runs into town for $2. Air New Zealand, Mount Cook and Ansett **flights** from the major centres land 8km northeast of town at the lakeside airport (☎07/345 6175). The door-to-door Super Shuttle (☎07/349 3444) and the Airport Shuttle (☎07/346 2386) both charge $8 for the first passenger and $2 for each extra to the same place, and **taxis** (☎07/348 5079) run into town for around $15.

The Tourism Rotorua complex, at 67 Fenton St, contains the efficient but often busy **visitor centre** (daily 8am–5.30pm; ☎07/348 5179, fax 348 6044), and the DOC-allied Map And Track Shop (daily 8.30am–6pm; ☎ & fax 07/349 1845), which dispenses tramping information and sells hut tickets and fishing licences. If you have a specific interest in **Maori-owned and operated tours**, hangi and concerts, bustle along the street from the visitor centre to the Best of Maori Tourism, 71 Fenton St (☎07/347 4226), a souvenir and crafts shop which promotes Maori businesses and frequently offers small discounts on various activities.

For a general advert-oriented round up of what's happening around town, pick up the free weekly *Thermal Air Visitor's Guide*, and if there are two of you spending a few days sightseeing around Rotorua, you can make good savings by buying the "Things Rotorua" **discount ticket** ($25 per couple), which gives two-for-the-price-of-one deals on many of the sights and activities around town, plus discounts on movie tickets and even meals.

City transport

Reesby Coachlines (☎07/347 0098) provide the most basic level of urban **bus** transport, centred on Pukuatua Street between Tutanekai and Fenton streets. Buses leave weekdays for Ngongotaha, passing Rainbow Springs (#2 roughly hourly) and Whakarewarewa (#3 every 2hr), and costing $2 each way.

In the main, the **Sightseeing Shuttle** (☎0800/927 399) is much more convenient, completing a circuit of Whakarewarewa, the Polynesian Pools, Rainbow Springs, Skyline Skyrides, the Agrodome and the visitor centre every hour and a half or so. Half-day (8.15am–1pm or 1–5.15pm; $15) and full-day ($22) **passes** are available, as well as section fares ($3 to Whakarewarewa, $5 to the Agrodome), and there are special transport and admission deals worth considering. There are also any number of **tours**, most geared towards the more distant sights (see "Around Rotorua", p.262).

*Whakarewarewa (1km), Taupo (80km), **H** & **O** (500m)* ▽

The points visited by the Sightseeing Shuttle are mostly within 7km of central Rotorua and there are no substantial hills, so **cycling** is a viable way to go; **car-rental** rates are also fairly competitive here (see "Listings", p.262, for details of bike- and car-rental outlets).

Accommodation

Rotorua's accommodation has one big advantage: no matter how low your budget, you can stay somewhere with a **hot pool**, and for a little more you might even get a private tub in your room. In fact there is barely a place in town without a hot pool – some directly fed with mineral water, others artificially heated.

The range is wide, including a clutch of quality **hostels**, all close to the city centre, all eager to advise on local activities and many offering small discounts on trips and tours. There must be more **motels** in Rotorua than just about anywhere else in the country, most of them lining Fenton Street, which runs south towards

Whakarewarewa. It is a busy road and their visibility tends to result in higher prices, so you might be better off in motels tucked away down side roads. **B&Bs and guesthouses** come liberally scattered around Rotorua and maintain a typically high standard, while **hotels** mostly cater to bus-tour groups and charge prohibitive prices if you just walk in off the street. We've recommended some **campsites** right in town, but there are dozens of others scattered around the region; most are listed with the visitor centre, who can advise on availability.

Between Christmas and March is the busy season, when you would do well to **book** a few days **in advance**.

Hotels and motels

Amber Motel Lodge, 48 Hinemaru St (☎07/348 0595, fax 348 0795). Middle-of-the-road motel with only average rooms but well situated close to the town centre. ⑤.

Eruera Motel, 46 Hinemaru St (☎07/348 8305). Basic, central motel that's one of the cheapest in town, right at the bottom of this price code. ④.

Havana Motor Lodge, 12 Whakaue St (☎07/348 8134, fax 348 8132). Good value and very well-equipped motel close to the lakefront, with attractive units, a heated freshwater pool, private mineral pools and a play area for kids. ④.

The Princess Gate, 1 Arawa St (☎07/348 1179 & 0800/500 705, fax 348 6215). The sole survivor from the days when all of Hinemaru Street was lined with hotels catering to the ailing while they took the waters at the bathhouse across the road. This lovely old wooden hotel is now restored with en-suite rooms fronting onto lovely wide verandahs, a tennis court and in-house video. Off-peak B&B specials are sometimes available, ⑥; otherwise, ⑦.

Royal Lakeside Novotel, 9–11 Tutanekai St (☎07/346 3888, fax 347 1888). Newest and swankiest of the big hotels, with all the usual facilities, plus thermal pool and massages. ⑨.

Victoria Motel, 10 Victoria St (☎07/348 4039, fax 348 8298). Good-value motel with small studio rooms, each with private hot pool, and larger self-catering units which share a pool. ④.

B&Bs and guesthouses

Best Inn Rotorua, 8 Whakaue St (☎ & fax 07/347 9769). Pristine, modern B&B right in the centre with attractively simple, clean rooms and Japanese-style "Onsen" mineral baths. ⑤.

Devon Homestay, 54 Devon St (☎ & fax 07/346 1823). Comfortable and peaceful rimu-built homestay close to Whakarewarewa, with twins, en-suite doubles and hearty cooked breakfasts. ④.

Eaton Hall, 39 Hinemaru St (☎ & fax 07/347 0366). Dowdy but well-priced and friendly guesthouse right in the heart of town. A full cooked breakfast is served. ④.

Morihana Travellers Inn, 20 Toko St (☎ & fax 07/348 8511). Attractive B&B with nicely decorated but smallish rooms, cooked breakfast, outdoor spa and indoor mineral pool. ④.

Peacehaven, 10 Peace St (☎ & fax 07/348 3759). Suburban homestay close to Whakarewarewa with friendly hosts, comfortable rooms and a large thermally-heated pool in the back yard. ④.

Sandi's B&B, 103 Fairy Springs Rd (☎07/347 0034). Just one good-value, comfortable and nicely decorated en-suite room close to Rainbow Springs, with continental breakfast. ③.

Whanau Homestay Experience, 35 Whittaker Rd (☎ & fax 07/349 1291). Unmissable opportunity to try marae-style accommodation bundled with cultural education, an informal Maori welcome and a traditional hangi dinner. Various package deals are also available, including a two-night stay with a full-day guided tour ($138) and a three-night package with a day-trip out to the family beachhouse on the Bay of Plenty ($250). ⑥.

Hostels

Cactus Jack Downtown Backpackers, 54 Haupapa St (☎ & fax 348 3121). A snazzy paint job and enthusiastic staff add character to this ageing warren of rooms and cabins with reasonably spacious dorms, twins and doubles, and bike rental for $25 a day. Dorms ①, rooms ②.

Central Backpackers, 10 Pukuatu St (☎ & fax 07/349 3285). Small but spacious, homely and easygoing hostel in an immaculately kept, large house, with beds rather than bunks in the four- and six-bed dorms rooms. Bikes are rented at $15 a day. Dorms ①, rooms ②.

Colonial Inn YHA Hostel, cnr Eruera St & Hinemaru St (☎07/347 6810, fax 349 1426). Spacious and well-kept but somewhat characterless hostel with bunks in large dorms and four-shares, and compact doubles and twins. Dorms ①, rooms ②.

Funky Green Voyager Backpackers, 4 Union St (☎07/346 1754). Very relaxed hostel in a suburban house ten minutes' walk from town with a communal atmosphere fostered by the idiosyncratic owner. Cooking facilities in particular are excellent and there's a cosy, TV-less lounge. Dorms ①, rooms ②.

Hot Rock Backpackers, 118 Arawa St (☎07/347 9469, fax 347 8099). Large, lively and, at weekends, noisy hostel, a perennial favourite with patrons of the backpacker tour buses, kept entertained in the three mineral pools – and the Lava Bar next door. Accommodation is in four- to twelve-bunk dorms, each with private bathroom, or doubles. Dorms ①, rooms ②.

Kiwi Paka, 60 Tarewa Rd (☎07/347 0931, fax 346 3167). Huge and well-organized modern complex on the far side of Kuirau Park, with camping space and a series of accommodation blocks ranged around a pool and a low-cost café and bar. Six- and four-bunk dorms are the cheapest in town, and the doubles and chalets are a bargain too. Mountain-bike rental costs $20 a day. Tent sites $7, dorms ①, rooms ②, chalets ③.

Campsites and motor parks

Acacia Park, 137 Pukuatua St (☎07/348 1886, fax 348 1867). The closest motor camp to the city centre. A spacious camping area has tent and powered sites, basic but serviceable cabins, and more luxurious tourist flats and motel units. Tent sites $7.50, cabins ②, flats & units ③.

Cosy Cottage Holiday Park, 67 Whittaker Rd (☎07/348 3793, fax 347 9634). Excellent motor camp a couple of kilometres from town with an extensive range of comfortable cabins and motel units, powered and tent sites, some of which are on geothermally-heated ground – great in winter but less appealing in summer. Along with all the usual facilities, there's a pleasant mineral pool, naturally-fed steam boxes for hangi-style cooking, and bikes for rent ($14 a day). Tent sites $10, cabins ②, units ③.

Kiwi Paka, 60 Tarewa Rd (☎07/347 0931, fax 346 3167). Huge and well-organized modern complex with camping space and hostel-style accommodation (see above). Tent sites $7

Lakeside Thermal Holiday Park, 54 Whittaker Rd (☎ & fax 07/348 1693). Compact and slightly cramped lakefront motor camp 2km from the city, with kayaks for guests' use, a barbecue overlooking the lake and a genuine mineral-water pool. Tent sites $10, cabins ②, tourist flats ③.

The Town and Lake Rotorua

Rotorua's sights are scattered: even those around the centre of town require some form of transport, though half a day can be spent on foot visiting the fine collection of Maori artefacts in the **Rotorua Museum**, located in the former bathhouse in the formal **Government Gardens**, then strolling around the shores of **Lake Rotorua** to Ohinemutu, the city's original Maori village with its neatly carved church. For a soak in a hot pool in the slightly surreal setting of a native bird sanctuary, catch a boat out to **Mokoia Island**, the romantic setting for the tale of two lovers, Hinemoa and Tutanekai.

The majority of sights require a little more effort, though a shuttle bus (see p.251) does the rounds. Top of most sightseeing lists is **Whakarewarewa Thermal Reserve**, with its two large geysers and the fascinating carving and weaving school of the **Maori Arts and Crafts Institute**. Where Rotorua's northwestern suburbs peter out, Mount Ngongotaha rises up, providing the necessary slope for a number of gravity-driven activities at the **Skyline Skyrides**. In its shadow, **Rainbow Springs** provides a window into the life cycle of trout, with some fine specimens swimming in pools richly draped in ferns, while Rainbow Farm offers a slightly different twist on the sort of sheep-centred farmshow pioneered by the **Agrodome**, nearby.

Government Gardens and around

In the early years of the twentieth century, Rotorua was already New Zealand's premiere tourist town, a fact it celebrated in confident civic style by laying out the

Government Gardens (unrestricted entry) on a small peninsula jutting into the lake east of the town centre. A rather bizarre vision of an antipodean little England as interpreted by the colonial administrators, the gardens delight with their juxtaposition of the staid and the exotic: white-suited bowls players mill around sulphurous steaming vents; palm trees loom over rose gardens; and, commanding the centre, there's the neo-Tudor **bathhouse**, built in 1908 in a style commensurate with the expectations of patrons familiar with European spas. Heralded as the greatest spa in the South Seas, "antagonistic" waters were supplied from the nearby Rachel and Priest springs to 84 baths, all fitted with the latest balneological equipment. But this was no pleasure palace, more a state-of-the-art non-residential hospital where patients suffering from arthritis, alcoholism, nervous disorders, in fact just about anything, underwent ghoulish treatments involving electrical currents and colonic irrigation as well as the more traditional pampering. Sadly, the bathhouse opened as the era of the grand spas was coming to a close; it limped along until 1963, when a combination of low patronage and maintenance costs hiked up by corrosive hydrogen sulphide in the waters hastened its demise.

The building has gone through a number of incarnations and now houses Rotorua's **Museum of Art and History** (daily 9.30am–5pm; $4), where one of the principal attractions is the old baths themselves, complete with gloomy green and white tiling and exposed pipes. Rooms from the spa's sixty-year existence have been lovingly preserved and filled with photos of the glory days. The rest of the building is devoted to two main exhibitions, the small but exquisite and internationally significant **Te Arawa** exhibition showcasing the long-respected talents of Arawa carvers who made this area a bastion of pre-European carving traditions. The collection contains some lovely pieces, several returned from European collections, and all powerfully presented. Among the magnificent figures, dog-skin cloaks, *pounamu* (greeenstone) weapons and intricate barge-boards, prized pieces include the flute played by the legendary lover Tutanekai (see p.256), an unusually fine pumice goddess, and rare eighteenth-century carvings executed with stone tools. The photos around the walls depict faces tattooed with detailed moko, and a portrait of the Tarawera guide Sophia (see p.265) standing outside the Whakarewarewa meeting house. The remainder of the museum covers the dramatic events surrounding the **Tarawera eruption**. The somewhat dry but extensive displays include an informative relief map of the region, eye-witness accounts and reminiscences, and photos of the ash-covered Temperance Hotel at Te Wairoa and of the similarly smothered Rotomahana Hotel, both now demolished.

Immediately to the south lies the **Polynesian Spa**, Hinemoa Street (daily 6.30am–11pm; Polynesian Pools $8, Lake Spa $25) a mostly open-air complex landscaped for lake views and comprising two separate areas. The main **Polynesian Pools** section comprises thirty-odd hot mineral pools claimed to treat all manner of ailments, principally arthritis and rheumatism. The vast majority of visitors bathe in either the slightly alkaline main pool or the small and turbid Radium and Priest pools, where the acidic waters bubbling up through the bottom of the tub vary from 33°C to 43°C. Private pools (an additional $8.50 per person for 30min), where you can adjust the temperature yourself, are ranged around the Radium and Priest pools, but for real exclusivity, opt for the adjacent **Lake Spa** section, with nicely designed shallow rock pools, private relaxation lounge and bar and access to a water-jet massage (an additional $40 an hour). For that hour-long post-concert-and-hangi soak, catch the transfer bus ($5) which picks up at all the hotels.

Only if you have a passion for orchids need you go anywhere near the twin hothouses of the **Orchid Gardens**, Hinemaru Street (daily 8.30am–5.30pm; $9), which manage to lure punters with a Water Organ, seven hundred jets of water and associated coloured lights computer-choreographed to sappy tunes of the audience's choosing. A far better bet is to amble back through the Government Gardens past the lakefront to Ohinemutu (see p.256).

Lake Rotorua

From the Government Gardens it is a short walk along the waterfront to the Lakefront Jetty, the starting point for trips onto **Lake Rotorua** and out to **Mokoia Island**, 7km to the north of the jetty. New Zealand's only inland, predator-free bird sanctuary, Mokoia is the scene of a successful and longstanding breeding programme for saddlebacks and North Island robins – often spotted at the feeder stations – and a fledgling one for the little spotted kiwi. The island is better known, however, for the story of **Hinemoa and Tutanekai**, the greatest of all Maori love stories and widely considered to be more truth than legend. It tells of two lovers, the young chief Tutanekai of Mokoia Island, and his high-born paramour, Hinemoa, whose people lived along the western shores of the lake. Hinemoa's family forbade her from marrying the illegitimate Tutanekai and prevented her from meeting him by beaching their heavy *waka* (canoe), but the strains of Tutanekai's lamenting flute still wafted across the lake nightly and the smitten Hinemoa resolved to swim to him. One night, buoyed by gourds, she set off towards Mokoia, but by the time she got there Tutanekai had returned to his *whare* (house) to sleep. Hinemoa arrived at the island but, without clothes, was unable to enter the village, so she immersed herself in a hot pool. Presently Tutanekai's slave came by to collect water, and Hinemoa lured him over, smashed his gourd and sent him back to his master. An enraged Tutanekai came to investigate, only to fall into Hinemoa's embrace. The site of Tutanekai's *whare* and **Hinemoa's Pool** can still be seen, along with the grave of the first *pakeha* born in the Rotorua district, all visited on the unfortunately named Scatcat tour (4 daily; $25; ☎07/347 9852). This speedy catamaran zips across to the island in fifteen minutes for a thirty-minute guided walk and then zips back, all within an hour, though it is worth sticking around for an extended soak or to wander the trails with an eagle eye out for native birdlife, returning on a later sailing.

Several other boats ply the waters of the lake, including the leisurely *Lakeland Queen* (☎0800/862 784), a replica **paddle steamer** which runs a series of cruises: the Morning Tea Cruise (9.50am; 50min; $16), Lunch Cruise (12.30pm; 1hr; $26), Afternoon Tea Cruise (2.30pm; 1hr 30min; $18) and occasional dinner cruises. For something more exciting, check out the **thrills-and-spills rides** aboard the Aorangi Jetboat (20min; $25; ☎07/347 0100) or their five-seater Hovershuttle (15min; $25) which will take you for a scenic commentated spin around the fringes of the lake with a couple of 360-degree spins.

Ohinemutu

Before the town of Rotorua grew up around its government buildings, the principal settlement in the area was at **OHINEMUTU**, 500m northwest of the centre, on the lakeshore. Occupying a perfect site chosen for its proximity to fishing and transport on the lake, and to hot springs along its shore perfect for washing and cooking, Ohinemutu remains an overwhelmingly Maori village centred on the springs and the small wooden **St Faith's Anglican Church**. Built in 1914 to replace its 1885 predecessor, the church's simple half-timbered neo-Tudor exterior gives no hint of the gloriously rich interior where there is barely a patch of wall that hasn't been carved or covered with *tukutuku* (ornamental latticework) panels. Everything has been intricately worked, from pew ends and support beams to the entrance to the chancel, which has been made to look like the barge boards (*maihi*) of a meeting house. Even the pulpit has been inlaid with geometrically patterned cloth. Wonderful though all this is, it is treated as a sideshow to the main attraction, a window with the figure of Christ, swathed in a Maori cloak and feathers, etched into it and positioned so that he appears to be walking on the lake. Outside is a bust of Queen Victoria, which commemorates Te Arawa's loyalty to the crown during the New Zealand Wars, and the grave of Gilbert Mair, a captain in the colonial army who twice saved Ohinemutu from attacks by rival Maori and became the only *pakeha* to earn full Arawa chieftainship.

At the opposite end of the small square in front of the church stands the **Tamatekapua Meeting House**, again beautifully carved, though the best and most ancient of the work, some dating back almost two hundred years, is inside and is most easily viewed during the "Magic of the Maori" concert held nightly (see "Hangi and Maori concerts" on p.261)

Immediately south of Ohinemutu, on Ranolf Street, lies **Kuirau Park**, its northern end pockmarked by fairly modest steaming hot pools, while the southern end has some minor thrills for kids: crazy-golf, a miniature railway, play areas and the like.

Rainbow Springs, Skyline Skyrides and the Agrodome

The majority of Rotorua's attractions are heavily geared to bus tours, and none more so than the cluster of places 4km to the northwest of the city centre on SH5 to Ngongotaha. Foremost among them is **Rainbow Springs** (daily 8am–5pm; $10), an all-too-neat series of trout pools linked by nature trails which, along with the adjacent and now integrated Fairy Springs, has been admitting visitors since 1898 when a *tapu* on the springs was lifted. Fresh water flows through the crystal-clear pools, some with glass sides for superb viewing of some of the largest rainbow, brown and North American brook trout you will ever see. Adult fish all have free access to the lake, but know when they're on to a good thing and return for the near-constant supply of food tossed in by visitors. Other marginal attractions include animal pens, an aviary, a freshwater aquarium, a kiwi house and an extensive collection of ferns, but it all feels far too regimented and unless you're here early in the day it can be very crowded. You can usually escape the crush at the quieter Fairy Springs section, which has more of the same stuff. Across the road is the associated **Rainbow Farm** (shows at 10.30am, 11.45am, 1pm & 2.30pm, with extra shows at 9am & 4pm during busy times; $10, $16.50 combined with Rainbow Springs), with a huge fluffy shop and a covered area from where you can watch sheepdogs rounding up a flock, followed by a fake auction and a display of shearing prowess.

Rainbow Springs lies at the foot of Mount Ngongotaha, immediately adjacent to the **Skyline Skyrides** (daily 9am–11pm; $11), an aerial gondola that whisks you 200m up to the top station for superb views across the lake and town, scenic but uninspired dining in the restaurant and café, and a bevy of adventure activities. Among these, the most fun is the **luge**, a kind of plastic tray on wheels on which you hurtle down banked concrete tracks at speeds of up to 60km per hour. A chair lift carries you back up to the top either for another run or a ride on the **Skyline**, a five-stage flying fox (zipwire), which is exciting enough to require a body harness and fully enclosed footwear, or an easier descent on the **Sidewinder**, where you sit on a little buggy as it is guided down a gently shelving track. Tickets ($4.50 for 1 descent, $10 for 3 and $15 for 5) are interchangeable between the three rides, or you can buy a combined gondola-and-five-rides ticket for $20. Mini-golf, a flight simulator and helicopter flights complete the summit set-up.

Just about every bus touring the North Island stops 5km further north at the **Agrodome**, Western Road, Ngongotaha (shows at 9.15am, 11am & 2.30pm; show $10, farm tour $12, show & farm tour $19; ☎07/347 4350), where the star attraction, the slick 45-minute **sheep show**, is a legacy of the 1970 Osaka World's Fair. Though undoubtedly corny, the whole spectacle is oddly engaging: rams representing all nineteen of the major breeds farmed in New Zealand are enticed onto the podium and their qualities pointed out; a sheep is shorn; lambs are bottle-fed and there is an impressive display of sheep control by the two common breeds of sheepdog, the bark-as-loud-as-you-can Huntaway, and the stealthy and silent "strong-eyed" Heading Dog. Shows are followed by a sanitized 45-minute farm tour, complete with honey tasting, deer viewing and, during April, May and June, kiwifruit picking.

If you haven't yet had enough of trout, you can return to Rotorua along Paradise Valley Road past **Paradise Valley Springs**, 13km west of town (daily 9am–5pm; $10), which adds an incongruous pride of lions to the fish and native birds.

Whakarewarewa thermal reserve and forest park

To New Zealanders, mention of Rotorua immediately conjures up images of **Te Whakarewarewa Thermal Reserve**, Hemo Road, 3km south of central Rotorua (daily 8.30am–5pm; $11) – or "Whaka", as it is more commonly known – the closest thermal area to the city. Unlike the other thermal areas, Whaka is a living village founded in pre-European times and enlarged by an influx of displaced people from Te Wairoa and neighbouring villages in the aftermath of the Tarawera eruption. Running the gauntlet of souvenir shops and Maori-costumed photo opportunities, you can still see plenty of houses; many are fairly new constructions, as the hydrogen sulphide issuing from the ground tends to rot concrete. You might even see people using steam boxes for cooking, though the most common experience of geothermally cooked food is the sweetcorn stand near one entrance.

Tours have been operating here since 1875, with villagers guiding tourists past a couple of New Zealand's most spectacular geysers, the ten-metre **Prince of Wales' Feathers** and the granddaddy of them all, the thirty-metre **Pohutu** ("big splash"), which generally performs several times a day, always preceded by its neighbour. Four trails weave through the reserve, passing glooping pools of boiling mud, sulphurous springs and agglomerations of silica stalactites. A river runs through the reserve to a bridge near the exit, where kids dive for coins tossed into the sulphur-yellowed water. Ambling around is undoubtedly more appealing when the weather is good, but don't be too dismayed if the weather is poor: low barometric pressures often bring out the best in the geysers, while cool winter conditions condense the steam into thick clouds, making the place even more ethereal.

Whakarewarewa would be worth visiting if that was all there was, but it also contains a replica of a traditional Maori **village**, its entrance marked by a carving of lovers Tutanekai and Hinemoa embracing, and **The Maori Arts and Crafts Institute** (same hours; included with Whaka entry). The institute serves both to teach young Maori the traditional carving and weaving techniques and to demonstrate those same skills to visitors. Half an hour spent here can be wonderfully inspirational and informative, as skilled artisans produce flax skirts and carvings, which can be bought in the classy but expensive shop. The institute also hosts a 45-minute **lunchtime concert** (daily 12.15pm; $11, $19 including admission to the thermal reserve) and the **Maori Experience** (5.15pm; $39) of a Maori welcome, concert and barbecue.

The western fringe of the Whakarewarewa thermal area borders the **Whakarewarewa State Forest Park**, experimentally planted a century back to see which exotic species would grow well under New Zealand conditions. Redwoods were found to grow three times faster than in their native California, creating the awe-inspiring **Redwood Grove**, which is threaded by a number of short paths. Most of the rest of the forest is devoted to **mountain-biking trails** through some of the best, easily accessible off-road terrain in the country, climbing up to a fabulous viewpoint overlooking the Blue and Green lakes (see p.266). More detailed information and maps can be obtained from the **Forest Visitor Centre**, Long Mile Road (Mon–Fri 8.30am–5pm, Sat & Sun 10am–4pm; ☎07/346 2082), and bikes can be rented in town (see "Listings" p.262).

Activities

As you might expect in a place which attracts visitors in such numbers, several companies have sprung up in Rotorua to offer rafting, kayaking, flying or even fishing. The

adventure-tourism scene hasn't snowballed to the degree it has in Queenstown, but there is still plenty to keep you occupied. In addition to the activities detailed below, brochures everywhere advertise water-skiing on Blue Lake, windsurfing on Lake Rotorua, quad biking, hot-air ballooning, clay-pigeon shooting and much more.

Rafting, whitewater sledging and kayaking

Rotorua has developed a considerable reputation for its rafting trips, largely due to the Grade IV **Kaituna River**, or at least the 2km section of it after it leaves Lake Rotoiti, 20km north of Rotorua, and enters a narrow, verdant gorge. As the river twists around rocky bluffs, it periodically plummets over vertical drops, including the spectacular **Okere Falls**, where the river tumbles almost seven metres. The trip is a short one, only spending around forty minutes on the water, and everyone comes out wanting more. In the summer, the half-dozen or so companies operating out of Rotorua take several trips a day, charging around $60, and even in the depths of winter someone's bound to be running the river.

While the Kaituna is a great trip, the river to go for, if you can get the timing right, is the Grade V **Wairoa River**, 80km by road from Rotorua, on the outskirts of Tauranga, which relies on dam-releases for raftable quantities of white water (Dec–March every Sun; Sept–Nov & April–May every second Sun). This is on-the-edge rafting and one of the finest short trips in the world, negotiating a dangerous and immensely satisfying stretch of water, and shooting rapids such as Mother's Nightmare, Devil's Hole and the Toaster, which has a nasty habit of tipping rafts over immediately above the toughest rapid on the river, the Roller Coaster. This is essentially a trip for those with some rafting experience and a good appreciation of the hazards of white water; several companies do the run, charging around $70 for the six-hour trip from Rotorua (90min actually on the water), including a post-deluge barbecue. If your tastes lean more towards appreciation of the natural surroundings with a bit of a bumpy ride thrown in, opt for the Grade III **Rangitaiki River**, a full-day trip setting off from Murupara, 62km southeast, but with pick-ups in Rotorua ($75–80).

Currently over half a dozen **companies** run trips from Rotorua, all rafting the same stretches of water at pretty much the same **prices**, though it pays to ask around for special offers and backpacker discounts. For the smartest rafts and matching wetsuits, go with River Rats Rafting Adventures (☎0800/333 900), who charge a few dollars more than the likes of the Great Kiwi Whitewater Company (☎07/348 2144), Raftabout (☎07/345 4652) and Rafting Kaituna (☎07/348 0233). In addition to all the regular trips, White Water Excitement (☎07/345 7182) link up with a jetboat ride and helicopter flight for the "Kaituna Triple Tremble" ($235).

To get even more intimate with the water, go **whitewater sledging** on an exciting section of the Rangitaiki River with Whitewater Sledging New Zealand (Oct to mid-May; 1hr 30min $85, 2hr 30min $95; ☎ 07/349 6100). Still on the water, Adventure Kayaking (☎07/348 9451) run excellent **kayaking** trips: there's a relaxing day's paddle on the beautiful Lake Okataina ($75), a more ambitious overnight camping trip on Lake Tarawera (2 days; $210), a great Twilight Paddle across Lake Rotoiti to soak in the otherwise inaccessible Manupirua hot pools (2hr; $35); kayak rental ($35 a day) is also available for experienced paddlers wanting to go it alone.

Fishing

The Rotorua Lakes District has a reputation for trout fishing only matched in the North Island by the rivers and streams flowing into Lake Taupo. With eleven gorgeous lakes, the angling could hardly be more scenic and all the lakes are stocked with strong-fighting rainbow trout; a typical summer catch is around 1.5kg, though in winter this can creep up towards 3kg. The proximity of **Lake Rotorua** makes it a perennial favourite, reached by charter boats from the Lakefront Jetty (2hr minimum; $70–80 an hour, including tackle but not licences – see below).

If you are going it alone, consult the visitor centre for a set of Byzantine rules, and obtain the latest on lake and river conditions, weather reports and regulations from the free helpline (☎0800/TROUTLINE), which also gives credit-card holders the opportunity to buy the necessary **licence**. Rotorua region licences are available from the visitor centre and larger sports shops (24hr, $12; 7 days, $25); hardbitten anglers can get season licences ($62; Oct 1–Sept 30), which cover the whole country except for the Taupo fishery region. In broad terms, the fishery is open year round, though restrictions apply – particularly the streams running into Lake Rotorua (mostly closed July–Nov). For further guidance, pick up the *World Class Trout Fishing* leaflet from the visitor centre, which also lists guides who specialize in taking more experienced anglers to other lakes and into the back country to little-fished streams.

Eating, drinking and nightlife

In recent years Rotorua has made great culinary strides and there are now quite a few quality **restaurants**, most congregated along, or just off, a short strip at the lake end of Tutanekai Street. None are outrageously expensive, but the assiduously budget-conscious will fare better at less flashy places further from the main drag. Unlike the shops, which close up for much of the weekend, the restaurants and bars are generally open all week, most staying open as long as custom demands; unless you're part of a large group, there's little need to reserve a table.

Despite its exalted status as New Zealand's tourist mecca, Rotorua remains a small city and the nightlife is correspondingly limited. There are a few lively **bars** to keep you entertained, but almost everyone spends one evening of their stay attending one of the **hangi and Maori concerts** in one of the tourist hotels or, preferably, at one of the outlying marae.

Restaurants and café/bars

The Coffee Bean, 189 Tutanekai St. Better-than-average café that opens early for those pre-bus breakfasts and serves bargain snacks all day.

Copper Criollo, 61 Arawa St (☎07/348 1333). One of Rotorua's more distinctive restaurants, serving robust portions of classy Creole cooking in a cosy room arranged around a copper still. Cajun music accompanies wonderful breads, blackened chicken livers, gumbo and jambalaya. The Creole versions of traditional breakfasts are particularly good. Licensed & BYO.

Fat Dog, 69 Arawa St. Rotorua's funkiest café and bar by a long stretch, with mismatched furniture, eclectic wall hangings and great food with vegetarian leanings. Background music can be anything from jazz to drum 'n' bass. Licensed.

Freos, 117 Tutanekai St. Quality modern Kiwi café dining at reasonable prices both inside and out. Good for weekend brunch, meals all day and gourmet takeaways. Licensed & BYO.

Impromptu, 118 Tutanekai St. Minimalist café/bar and restaurant serving good coffee and cakes and a small selection of tasty meals such as prawn and coconut cream salad, and fish of the day, cooked with lemongrass, chilli and coriander. Licensed.

Kebab Café, 67 Arawa St. Plain and simple café serving lamb, beef and chicken kebabs and felafel, either in a roll for $7 or as a main meal for $15. Licensed.

Mexican Cantina, 93 Fenton St. Ever-popular Mexican eat-in and takeaway, serving hefty helpings of Tex-Mex staples at low prices.

Orchid Gardens Café, Government Gardens, Hinemaru St. Budget café serving classic Kiwi tea-room fare, nicely located at one end of a hothouse in the Orchid Gardens (see p.255).

La Pizza Forno, 31 Pukuatua St (☎07/347 9854). Eat-in and take-out pizzeria making traditionally topped pizzas on crispy bases, and serving home-style lasagne, ravioli and spag bol. Free delivery for orders over $20 (roughly two medium-sized pizzas).

Sirocco Bar and Café, 86 Eruera St (☎07/347 3388). Atmospheric café/bar and restaurant in a quiet part of town with outside seating. The Italian-inspired menu includes excellent pizzas and coffee and full meals such as *agnello in carpione*, cold lamb served with an asparagus and potato salad. Licensed.

La Vega, 38 Whakaue St. Bustling restaurant and bar concentrating on gourmet wood-fired pizzas, pasta and steaks, with $12 daytime pizza and beer deals.

Bars and clubs

Lava Bar, 118 Arawa St. A house converted into a bar that's found favour with backpackers, rafting guides and local youth. Basic meals are available and there's an early-evening happy hour, pinball machines and a pool table – if you can get to them.

La Vega, 38 Whakaue St. Popular hangout for Rotorua's cool set, with constantly changing music usually edging towards dance grooves late on. Occasional live bands.

O'Malley's, 85 Eruera St. Ersatz Irish bar with a strong line in draught Irish beers and bargain meals.

Pig & Whistle, cnr Haupapa St & Tutanekai St. Lively bar in a former police station with good locally-brewed beers on tap and excellent-value, tasty bar meals. Occasional rock and pop covers bands.

Hangi and Maori concerts

Rotorua is far and away the best place to sample food steamed to perfection in the Maori earth oven or **hangi** and watch a **Maori concert**, typically an hour-long performance of traditional dance, song and chants. Although not entirely satisfactory introductions to Maori culture, these are at least accessible and good value. Over a dozen groups vie for your custom, with offerings that fall into two distinct camps: hangi-and-concert extravaganzas laid on by Rotorua's major hotels; and packages operated and organized by Maori groups that usually involve a trip to an out-of-town marae, and exhibit a degree of authenticity with a strong sense of *Maoritanga* as a living culture. All trips run for three or four hours from 6 or 7pm, with buses picking up and dropping off at hotels and hostels around town, and cost $45–55; some of the hotels offer hangi-only or concert-only deals for about half the cost.

The three groups running **out-of-town packages** all follow largely the same format, giving instruction on marae customs and protocol (see "Maoritanga" in Contexts, p.773) as you are driven out to a Maori village, followed by a formal welcome. Rotoiti Tours ($49; ☎07/348 8969) is an engaging affair, with almost the whole *whanau* (extended family group) contributing to the proceedings, which take place in the beautifully decorated meeting house on the Rakeiao Marae at Tapuaekura Bay on the shores of Lake Rotoiti some 20km north of Rotorua. Whare Tours ($45; ☎ & fax 07/357 2023) is just as good, visiting Waiteti Marae near Ngongotaha, and Tamaki Tours ($52; ☎07/346 2823) differs slightly in that it visits a specially built Maori village rather than a genuine marae but adds a more professional flourish.

The big **hotels** take a more cabaret approach to the whole affair, usually eating first and relegating the concert to a form of after-dinner entertainment. The food is four-star-hotel standard, though in a misguided desire to present imaginative salads and precisely carved slices of meat they veer away from the more robust hangi style, sometimes resorting to steam boxes rather than traditional earth ovens. The content of the concert is almost identical to the marae-based shows but the tone is quite different, less intimate and more consciously choreographed, with sophisticated lighting and a disembodied voice commentating. There's little to choose between the hotels though the *Sheraton*, Fenton Street ($49; ☎07/349 5200) and the *THC Rotorua Hotel*, Froude Street ($47; ☎07/348 1189), both near Whakarewarewa, have good reputations.

If none of these suit, the Ohinemutu Cultural Group conduct Rotorua's original **concert-only** Magic of the Maori (8pm; $15, $13 in advance; ☎07/349 3949 & 0508/300

333) each evening inside the Tamatekapua Meeting House at Ohinemutu (see p.257), and there are daytime and evening concerts held at the Maori Arts and Crafts Institute, at Whakarewarewa (see p.258).

Listings

Airlines Air New Zealand and Mount Cook Airlines, cnr Fenton St & Hinemoa St (☎07/347 9564 & 0800/737 000); Ansett, 113 Fenton St (☎07/347 0596 & 0800/800 146).

American Express Galaxy United Travel, 411 Tutanekai St (☎07/347 9444).

Automobile Association 59 Amohau St (☎07/348 3069).

Banks and exchange ANZ, cnr Hinemoa St & Tutanekai St (☎07/348 2169); BNZ, cnr Eruera St & Tutanekai St (☎07/348 1099); National, cnr Fenton St & Hinemoa St (☎07/349 5300). See also American Express and Thomas Cook.

Bike rental Runaround bikes are available from many of the hostels, plus Lady Jane's Ice Cream Parlour, cnr Tutanekai St & Whakaue St (☎07/347 9340; $15 per day), and Rotorua Cycle Centre, 40 Hinemoa St (☎07/348 6588; $20 a day). Lady Jane's also rents mountain bikes ($28 a day), while Rotorua Cycle Centre offers full-spec machines perfect for Whakarewarewa Forest trails ($40 a day).

Bookshops London Books, 324 Tutanekai St (☎07/349 6557); Whitcoulls, Plaza Shopping Centre, Tutanekai St (☎07/348 3699).

Car rental Link, 108 Fenton St (☎07/347 8063), offers a fully-insured runabout for $59, including 100km free, per day; Budget, 116 Fenton St (☎07/348 8127), matches these rates most of the time.

Kayak rental Adventure Kayaking (☎07/348 9451) rents out kayaks for $35 per day; the same company also runs excellent kayaking trips (see p.259).

Library The public library is on Haupapa St (☎07/348 4177).

Medical treatment Rotorua Medical Centre, 9 Amohia St (☎07/347 0000), and Lakes Primecare, cnr Arawa St & Tutanekai St (☎07/348 1000), both offer accident and urgent healthcare.

Pharmacy Lakescare Pharmacy, cnr Arawa St & Tutanekai St (☎07/48 4385), is open daily 9am–9.30pm.

Police 64–98 Fenton St (☎07/348 0099).

Post office 81 Hinemoa St (☎07/349 2397).

Skydiving Should you get the urge, you can leap out of a plane with Tandem Skydiving Rotorua (☎07/345 7520) for fractionally under $200.

Thomas Cook, cnr Hinemoa St & Fenton St (☎07/347 0111).

Tours See box on p.264.

Travel agents Blackmores Galaxy United Travel, 411 Tutanekai St (☎07/347 9444); House of Travel, cnr Fenton St & Eruera St (☎07/348 4152); Rotorua Flight Centre, 304 Tutanekai St (☎07/346 3145).

Around Rotorua

Much of the best Rotorua has to offer lies outside the city among the lakes to the north and east and around the most dramatic of the volcanic zones half an hour's drive south towards Taupo. Without your own transport, you are pretty much reliant on the huge variety of **tours** run by numerous companies (see p.264), and just about any combination of sights can be packed into a full-day tour.

Travelling independently, minor sights along the eastern shore of Lake Rotorua can be quickly dispatched, leaving time for the seldom-crowded **Hell's Gate** thermal area, and the opportunity to watch terrified rafters plunging over the **Okere Falls**. Having your own boat opens up the best of lakes Rotoiti, Rotoehu and Rotama, though they're pleasing enough just to drive past on the way to Whakatane and the East Cape. Rewards are more plentiful to the east and south especially around Mount Tarawera

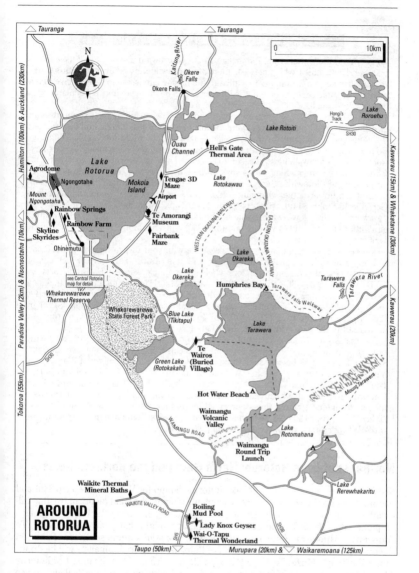

△ Tauranga △ Tauranga

0 _____ 10km

N

Hamilton (100km) & Auckland (230km)

Kaituna River

Okere Falls

Okere Falls

Lake Roroehu

Hongi's Track

Lake Rotoiti

SH30

Kawerau (15km) & Whakatane (30km)

Ouau Channel

Hell's Gate Thermal Area

Agrodome

Ngongotaha

Lake Rotorua

Mokoia Island

Tengae 3D Maze

Lake Rotokawau

Airport

Mount Ngongotaha

Rainbow Springs

Te Amorangi Museum

Paradise Valley (2km) & Nsonsotaha (10km)

Rainbow Farm

WESTERN OKATAINA WALKWAY

EASTERN OKATAINA WALKWAY

Skyline Skyrides

Fairbank Maze

Ohinemutu

Lake Okereka

Lake Okareka

see Central Rotorua map for detail

Whakarewarewa Thermal Reserve

Lake Okereka

Humphries Bay

Tarawera Falls Walkway

Tarawera Falls

Tarawera River

Kawerau (20km)

Tokoroa (55km)

SH30

Whakarewarewa State Forest Park

Blue Lake (Tikitapu)

Lake Tarawera

Green Lake (Rotokahi)

Te Wairos (Buried Village)

Hot Water Beach

Mount Tarawera

Waimangu Volcanic Valley

WAIMANGU ROAD

Lake Rotomahana

Waimangu Round Trip Launch

Lake Rerewhakaritu

Waikite Thermal Mineral Baths

WAIKITE VALLEY ROAD

Boiling Mud Pool

Lady Knox Geyser

SH5

SH38

Wai-O-Tapu Thermal Wonderland

AROUND ROTORUA

Taupo (50km) ▽ Murupara (20km) & ▽ Waikaremoana (125km)

which, in 1886, showered tonnes of ash on the **Buried Village**, where partly-interred Maori dwellings graphically illustrate the volcano's immense power. As the village and the Pink and White Terraces were being destroyed, the **Waimangu Thermal Valley** was created and now ranks as one of the finest collections of geothermal features in the region alongside kaleidoscopic **Wai-O-Tapu**, with its daily-triggered **Lady Knox Geyser** and multicoloured pools.

SIGHTSEEING TOURS FROM ROTORUA

To get out to the sights around Rotorua without your own transport, you'll have to rely on several companies, which between them offer a bewildering array of **minibus tours**, ranging from a couple of hours to a full day. All include admission to sights, have a commentary of some description and the itineraries can be quite flexible, particularly when numbers are small.

Carey's Tours (☎07/347 1197) run a vast array of trips, including the **excellent-value** Geothermal Wonderland (4hr; $55) out to Wai-O-Tapu and Waimangu. Full-day trips add the Redwood Grove and the Buried Village (8hr; $100), while the scenic Waimangu Round Trip (9hr; $140) visits the Waimangu Thermal Valley, cruising across Lake Rotomahana, bushwalking to a second cruise on Lake Tarawera, ambling around the Buried Village and finishing with a soak in the Polynesian Spa. Their **backpacker-orientated trips** – known as Carey's Capers – include lunch and a dip in natural hot pools in the bush but are otherwise almost identical. One particularly good combination is Get Volcanic (9hr; $140), which takes in Wai-O-Tapu, Waimangu and a trip up Mount Tarawera. Another low-cost favourite is The Pink Coach (☎07/345 4096), which runs a straightforward trip out to Wai-O-Tapu (3hr; $30) and a handful of other no-frills trips to Waimangu and the Buried Village.

One destination that definitely isn't accessible with your own vehicle (you need special permission) is the shattered line of craters atop **Mount Tarawera**, which can be reached on foot and on tours with four-wheel-drive companies such as Mount Tarawera 4WD Tours (half-day, $65; ☎07/348 2914) and the Maori-run Mountain Magic (half-day, also $65; ☎07/348 6399), which comes with a good helping of the history and legend of the Ngati Rangitihi and Tuhourangi people. The full-day 4WD and rafting combo run by River Deep Mountain High ($125; ☎07/357 4026), takes you up Tarawera and drops you off to raft the Rangitaiki River with River Rats (see p.259).

The majesty of Mount Tarawera is best appreciated from the air, on **fixed-wing planes** or by helicopter. Flights start from as little as $45 for a quick spin over the lake, $100 for Tarawera flights and something closer to $300 for an overflight of White Island out in the Bay of Plenty; Volcanic Wunderflights (☎07/345 6077), Volcanic Air Safaris (☎0800/800 848), and Lakeside Aviation (☎07/345 4242) all run competitive trips. **Chopper flights** will set you back a little more, and you won't get to Mount Tarawera for much under $180; try the Maori-run Kiwi Kopters (☎07/345 5459) or Tarawera Helicopters (☎07/348 1223), which also organize several combination trips, linking up with 4WD operators, rafting companies and lake cruises.

Northeast of Lake Rotorua: Hell's Gate and the northern lakes

SH30 hugs the eastern shores of Lake Rotorua, bound for Whakatane (see p.338) and passing through the region's greatest concentration of lakes and plenty of twisting hill country. Scenery aside, there isn't a great deal to stop for along the way, though fans of pioneering artefacts and relocated buildings might fancy an hour at the **Te Amorangi Museum** (Sun only 10am–4pm; donations requested), on Robinson Avenue, in Holdens Bay, 6km northeast of Rotorua. Maze traditionalists will be drawn to the **Fairbank Maze**, Te Ngae Rd, opposite the airport, 7km northeast of Rotorua (daily 10am–5pm; $4), which ranks as the largest hedge maze in New Zealand, comes arranged in concentric circles and seldom requires more than twenty minutes to negotiate. If you're after a stiffer challenge, continue 4km north to the wooden **Te Ngae 3D Maze**, Te Ngae Park (daily 9am–5pm; $4).

Immediately north of the 3D maze, SH33 cuts north to Te Puke and Tauranga, passing the Kaituna River's rafting mecca of **Okere Falls**, 8km north of the junction. From the car park, steps lead down through natural tunnels known as Tutea's Caves (formerly used as a safe haven by Maori women and children during attacks by rival groups) to a precipitous viewpoint where the tunnels penetrate the steep rock walls beside the waterfall.

Most of the traffic out this way sticks to SH30, though, the route to **Hell's Gate** (*Tikitere*; daily 9am–5pm; $10; ☎07/345 3151), 14km northeast of Rotorua. The least-visited and smallest of the major thermal areas, this is also one of the fiercest and most active, with an abundance of bubbling mud and seething gunmetal-grey waters. Its fury camouflages a lack of notable features, however, and the only real highlights are the bubbling mud of the Devil's Cauldron and the hot **Kakahi Falls**, whose soothing 38°C waters once made it a popular bathing spot (though now off-limits to bathers).

Beyond Hell's Gate lies **Lake Rotoiti**, which translates as "little lake", though it is in fact the second-largest in the region and is linked to Lake Rotorua by the narrow Ohau Channel. This passage, along with the neighbouring **Lake Rotoehu** and **Lake Rotama**, traditionally formed a part of the canoe route from the coast. A section of this route, apparently used on a raid by the Ngapuhi warrior chief Hongi Hika, is traced by **Hongi's Track** (3km; 1hr return; negligible ascent), a beautiful bushwalk which runs through to Lake Rotoehu passing the Wishing Tree, which is often surrounded by plant offerings.

Kawerau and Tarawera Falls

Around 6km beyond Lake Rotama, a good sideroad leads to the planned timber-mill town of **KAWERAU**, which sits on a flood plain of the Tarawera River at the foot of the distinctive hump of Mount Edgecombe (*Putauaki*). If the constant acrid stench from the mill isn't enough to drive you away, call in to the **visitor centre**, Plunket St (Mon–Fri 8.30am–4.30pm, Sat & Sun 11am–3pm; ☎07/323 7550), which can supply information about the local area, including the main attraction of **Tarawera Falls**, where the underground Tarawera River bursts out of a cliff face. An impressive sight in spate, when the falls appear as a solid cylinder of water, less so at other times, when they barely warrant the arduous 20km drive along a metalled forestry road, frequently being blinded by billowing clouds of dust thrown up by huge logging trucks – keep your headlights on at all times. Where the road peters out, the falls are at the end of a short bush track (15min walk).

Southeast of Rotorua

Volcanic activity again provides the main theme for attractions southeast of Rotorua, most having some association with **Lake Tarawera** and the jagged line of volcanic peaks and craters along the southeastern shore, collectively known as **Mount Tarawera**, which erupted in 1886.

Before this, Tarawera was New Zealand's premiere tourist destination, with thousands of visitors every year crossing lakes Tarawera and Rotomahana in whale boats and *waka*, frequently guided by the renowned Maori guide Sophia, to the **Pink and White Terraces**, two separate fans of silica which cascaded down the hillside to the edge of Lake Rotomahana. Boiling cauldrons bubbled away at the top of each formation, spilling mineral-rich water down the hillside where, over several centuries it formed a series of staggered cup-shaped pools, the outflow of one filling the one below. The White Terraces (*Te Tarata* or "Tattooed Rock"), were the larger, but most visitors favoured the Pink Terraces (*Otukapuarangi* or "Cloudy Atmosphere"), which were prettier and better suited to sitting and soaking. The chemical reaction which gave them the pink tint was discovered in the 1980s, since when there has been much idle talk of trying to recreate the terraces.

All this steamy bliss came to an abrupt end on the night of June 10, 1886, when the long-dormant Mount Tarawera ripped itself asunder, creating 22 craters along a 17km rift, and covering over 15,000 square kilometres in mud and scoria to a depth of 22 metres. The Pink and White Terraces were shattered by the buckling of the earth, covered by ash and lava, then submerged deep under the waters of Lake Rotomahana which, dammed by earth upheavals, grew to twenty times its previous size.

The cataclysm had been foreshadowed eleven days earlier, when two separate canoe loads of *pakeha* tourists and their Maori guides saw an ancient *waka* glide silently out of the mist, with a dozen warriors paddling furiously, then vanish just as suddenly; this was interpreted by the ancient *tohunga* (priest) Tuhoto Ariki as a sign of imminent disaster. The fallout from the eruption buried five villages, including the staging post for the Pink and White Terrace trips, **Te Wairoa**, where the *tohunga* lived. In a classic case of blaming the messenger, the inhabitants refused to rescue the *tohunga* and it wasn't until four days later that they allowed a group of *Pakeha* to dig him out. Miraculously, he was still alive, though he died a week later.

The chain of eruptions which racked the fault line during that fateful night in 1886 created an entirely new thermal valley, **Waimangu**, running southwest from the shores of the newly enlarged Lake Rotomahana. Still geothermally active, Waimangu struggles to outdo the supremely colourful thermal area of **Wai-O-Tapu**, a few kilometres further south.

Beyond the volcanic zone, the Kaingaroa Forest stretches away east to the little-visited tramping territory of the **Whirinaki Forest Park**, and the Kinleith Forest straggles west to **Tirau**, **Putaruru** and **Tokoroa**, minor way-stations on the route from Auckland to Taupo and the Tongariro National Park.

The Blue and Green lakes, the Buried Village and Lake Tarawera

To nineteenth-century tourists Rotorua was merely a staging post before they continued their journey to the shores of Lake Tarawera, 15km southeast, where canoes would take them across to view the Pink and White Terraces. Latter-day sightseers still follow the same route, passing a ridge-top viewpoint that overlooks the iridescent waters of **Blue Lake** (*Tikitapu*) and **Green Lake** (*Rotokakahi*), which get their hues from subterranean mineral activity.

The road ends close to the lake at the Te Wairoa **Buried Village** (daily: Nov–April 8.30am–5.30pm; May–Oct 9am–5pm; $9; ☎07/362 8287), the partly excavated and heavily reconstructed remains of a settlement that, at the time of the Tarawera eruption, was larger than contemporary Rotorua. Numerous houses collapsed under the weight of the two or three metres of ash that settled on Te Wairoa on June 10, 1886; others were saved by virtue of their inhabitants hefting ash off the roof to lighten the load. Much of the village was excavated in the 1930s and 1940s, though work continues slowly today. Walking around, however, there is less of a sense of an archeological dig than of a manicured orchard: half-buried *whare* and the foundations for the Rotomahana Hotel sit primly on mown lawns among European fruit trees gone to seed, marauding hawthorn and a perfect row of full-grown poplars fostered by a line of fenceposts. Many of the *whare* contain small collections of implements and ash-encrusted household goods, contrasting with the stark simplicity of other dwellings such as **Tohunga's Whare**, where the ill-fated priest lay buried alive for four days before being released from his ashen tomb. Look out too for the extremely rare, carved-stone *pataka* (storehouse), and the bow section of a *waka* once used to ferry tourists on the lake and allegedly brought to the district by Hongi Hika when he invaded in 1823.

Beyond the formal grounds, a sequence of steep steps and slippery boardwalks dives down the hill alongside **Te Wairoa Falls**, then squeezes through a small cave and climbs up through dripping, fern-draped bush on the far side. By the entrance to the Buried Village complex is a small **museum** with some fine aquatints of the Pink and White Terraces and more ash-encrusted knick-knacks.

Tarawera Landing, 2km east of the Buried Village, is the jetty for cruises across **Lake Tarawera** aboard the restored MV *Reremoana* (☎07/362 8595). Two-hour

cruises head to the southern side of the lake, giving you thirty minutes to explore the path up to Lake Rotomahana (daily 11am; $22.50), while the 45-minute option just cruises around the lake (daily 1.30pm, 2.30pm, 3.30pm & 4.30pm; $15).

Waimangu

At the southern limit of the volcanic rift blown out by Mount Tarawera lies **Waimangu Volcanic Valley** (daily 8.30am–5pm; $11, combined admission and cruise $29), 19km south of Rotorua on Waimangu Road, via SH5. Among the world's youngest thermal areas, this is also New Zealand's largest and most lushly vegetated.

A visitor centre by the entrance hints at the sights lining the streamside path, which cuts through a valley choked with scrub and native bush that has re-established itself since 1886. The regeneration process is periodically interrupted by smaller eruptions, including one in 1917 which created the 100m-diameter **Frying Pan Lake**, the world's largest hot spring. Impressive quantities of hot water welling up from the depths is the attraction of the **Inferno Crater**, an inverted cone where mesmerizing steam patterns partly obscure the powder-blue water. The water level rises and falls according to a rigid 38-day cycle – filling to the rim for 21 days, overflowing for 2 days then gradually falling to 8m below the rim over the next 15 days. More run-of-the-mill steaming pools and hissing vents line the stream, which also passes the muddy depression where, from 1900 to 1904, the **Waimangu Geyser** regularly spouted water to an astonishing height of 400m, carting rocks and black mud with it.

The path through the valley ends at the wharf on the shores of Lake Rotomahana, where the rust-red sides of Mount Tarawera dominate the far horizon. From here, frequent free shuttle buses run back up the road to the visitor centre and gentle, commentated, fifty-minute **cruises** (7 daily, included in price of admission) chug around the lake past steaming cliffs, fumaroles and over the site of the Pink and White Terraces.

Wai-O-Tapu

The tussle for Rotorua's geothermal crown is principally fought between Waimangu and the **Wai-O-Tapu Thermal Wonderland** (daily 8.30am–5pm; $9.50), 10km south of Waimangu (and 30km from Rotorua), just off SH5. This combines a vast expanse of multi-hued rocks and pools, New Zealand's largest and most impressive lake of boiling mud and the **Lady Knox Geyser**, which is ignominiously induced to perform on schedule, at 10.15am daily. Buy your entrance ticket at the main entrance then double back 1km along the road to the geyser where, as the crowds fill the serried ranks of benches, a staff member pours a packet of soap flakes into the vent. Within a few minutes, the soap reduces the water's surface tension, and superheated steam and water is released in a jet which plays initially to around 10m and continues at half that height for anything up to an hour. Everyone then bundles into their vehicles and drives back to the main site for the crawl around the hour-long walking loop track as it wends its way through a series of small lakes which have taken on the tints of the minerals dissolved in them – yellow from sulphur, purple from manganese, green from arsenic and so on. The gurgling and growling black mud of the **Devil's Ink-Pots** and a series of hissing and rumbling craters pale beside the ever-changing rainbow colours of the **Artist's Palette** pools and the gorgeous, effervescent **Champagne Pool**, a circular bottle-green cauldron wreathed in swirling steam and fringed by a burnt-orange shelf. The waters of the Champagne Pool froth over **The Terraces**, a rippled accretion of lime silicate that glistens in the sunlight.

As you drive back to the main road, follow a short detour to a huge and active **boiling mud pool** which plops away merrily, forming lovely concentric patterns. On the opposite side of SH5, Waikite Valley Road runs 6km to **Wai-Kite Thermal Mineral**

Baths (daily 10am–9.30pm; $4), a naturally-fed geothermal pool that's a good deal more low-key than the pools in Rotorua, but hardly justifies a special journey; guests at the adjacent motor camp (tent sites $8.50) get in free.

Whirinaki Forest Park and the road to Lake Waikaremoana

Midway between Waimangu and Wai-O-Tapu, some 25km south of Rotorua, SH38 spurs southeast, running arrow-straight through the regimented pines of the Kaingaroa Forest towards the jagged peaks of Te Urewera National Park, a vast tract of untouched wilderness which separates the Rotorua lakes from Poverty Bay and the East Cape. The Kaingaroa Forest finally relents 40km on, as the road crosses the Rangitikei River by the predominantly Maori timber town of **MURUPARA**. Apart from a couple of shops and takeaways, the only reason to pull over is DOC's **Te Ikawhenua Field Centre**, 1km southeast of town on SH38 (Dec–Feb daily 8am–5pm; March–Nov Mon–Fri 8am–5pm; ☎07/366 5641, fax 366 5289), with diverting displays and a stack of information on Te Urewera National Park and the Lake Waikaremoana region (see p.361).

Particular emphasis is given to the easily accessible **Whirinaki Forest Park**, a wild and wonderful slice of country which harbours some of the densest and most impressive stands of bush on the North Island: podocarps on the river flats, and native beech on the steep volcanic uplands between them, support a wonderfully rich birdlife with tui, bellbirds, parakeets and even the rare brownish-red kaka. The forest is now protected from the loggers' chainsaw, after a close shave in the late 1970s and early 1980s, when it saw one of the country's fiercest and most celebrated **environmental battles**. In early 1978, protesters had succeeded in preventing logging by occupying trees in the Pureora State Forest to the west of Lake Taupo. Anticipating similar action at Whirinaki and fearing for their livelihood, the local Ngati Whare people blockaded the road into the forest in June 1978; conflict was only avoided through intense negotiation. By 1987 logging of all native timber had ceased (except for totara cut for ceremonial-carving purposes), the mill had closed and the entire logging village of **MINGINUI**, 25km south of Murupara, was unemployed. Today, this moribund village ticks by on a trickle of tourism: even the sole community shop is only open sporadically.

River Road runs 8km south from Minginui to the Whirinaki car park, from where, in four hours or so, you can sample some of the best of the Whirinaki Forest Park – the Whirinaki Falls, where the Whirinaki River cascades over an old lava flow, and the churning Te Whaiti-nui-a-tio Canyon – on the first stretch of the **Whirinaki Track** (27km; 2 days). To penetrate deeper into the forest, you can follow the rest of this gentle track, though you'll need to carry your own cooking stove, food and sleeping bag. By linking several tracks and staying in some of the nine Category 3 **huts** ($4) that pepper the park, more robust walkers can tramp for four or five days and, if you aren't constrained by having to return to your vehicle, it is even possible to walk through to SH5, emerging close to the tiny village of Te Haroto, through which buses pass three times daily. DOC's *Whirinaki Forest Park* leaflet ($1) covers the main routes, with expanded coverage on their *Whirinaki Track* and *Te Hoe Track* leaflets (50¢ each) and on the NZMS 260 series V18 *Whirinaki* map. It is also possible to explore the area on **guided treks** with Rotorua-based Trek Whirinaki (1–2 days; $125–165; ☎07/347 6075 & 0800/801 502), which uses Maori guides and visits a local marae for a hangi feast.

PRACTICALITIES

There are buses along SH38 but no public **transport** makes it to Minginui or beyond, and it isn't advisable to leave vehicles at the Whirinaki car park, so the best bet is to enlist the assistance of *Whirinaki Forest Lodge*, on Minginui Road, 1km south of its junction with SH38 (☎ & fax 07/366 3235). As well as running a trampers' shuttle service for the Whirinaki Track (price dependent on numbers), the lodge also offers **accommodation** in comfortable dorms and motel units, or in the lodge with all meals included (dorms ①, units ②, lodge ⑥), and organizes horse treks ($13 per hour). *Jail House*, 2km south along Minginui Road (☎07/366 3234; ④), also operates track transport from their self-contained jail-turned-chalet, which sleeps up to seven. Minginui itself also has simple accommodation – in the cluster of huts which make up the *Ohu Camp* ($5) and the informal riverside *Mangamate Waterfall campsite* ($5 per tent).

West of Rotorua: Tirau, Putaruru and Tokoroa

Fifty-odd kilometres northwest of Rotorua, SH5 and SH1 meet at the small farming centre of **TIRAU**, a highwayside strip adorned with an astonishingly ugly corrugated-iron sheep housing a wool shop. There is a handful of **places to eat** along SH1, notably the *Alley Cats Espresso Café*, opposite the sheep, which serves good quiches, pizza slices and cakes. If you need to break your journey, **stay** at the well-priced *OK Tirau Motor Inn*, SH1 (☎07/883 1111, fax 883 1999; rooms ④, unit ⑤), which has modern air-conditioned rooms and large self-contained units; the budget *Backpackers Roost*, 18 Station St (☎07/883 1148; ①), with just one four-bunk room; or treat yourself to the hotel at Okoroire Hot Springs (see below).

There is little to do actually in town but Okoroire Street, beside the sheep, runs 8km to the lovely **Okoroire Hot Springs**, a series of private open-air, sandy-bottomed concrete pools located in a glade by a cascading stream, each accommodating up to twelve sybaritic souls. The pools cost $10 an hour, and can be booked at the adjacent *Okoroire Hot Springs Hotel* (☎ & fax 07/883 4876), which has regular rooms (⑤) and allows camping ($10 per tent) among the mature poplars and conifers; the hotel also has a bar, serves meals, and lets you onto their nine-hole golf course for $7.50 a day.

East of Tirau the roads split again, with SH5 forging on to Rotorua, while SH1 turns southeast towards Taupo, passing through **PUTARURU**, 8km further on, and the **Putaruru Timber Museum** (daily 9am–4pm; $5; ☎07/883 7621), a further 2km south, where the region's timber-milling heritage is pulled together in a well laid-out collection of minor historic buildings relocated from around the district. If you do nothing else, climb the totara-built 1930s fire lookout to get an inkling of just how extensive the Kaingaroa Forest really is.

SH1 continues through rolling farmland to pungent **TOKOROA**, 25km southeast, a modern place downwind of the nearby Kinleith pulp mill, the principal reason for the town's existence. There's little to stop for, but it is almost 70km to Taupo, the next place of any consequence, so **cyclists** might need to overnight at the *Glenbrook Motor Camp*, 5 Sloss Rd (☎07/886 6642; tent sites $8), at the northern entrance to town, or one of the motels dotted among the fast-food joints beside the highway. Newmans and InterCity **buses** stop outside the **visitor centre**, on SH1 (Mon–Fri 8.30am–5pm & Sat 9.30am–noon; ☎07/886 8872), and if *KFC* isn't to your taste, try *Scoffers Café* on Rosebery Street, which runs parallel to the main highway.

TAUPO AND AROUND

TAUPO, 80km south of Rotorua and slap in the centre of the North Island, is very much a Kiwi holiday resort slung around the northern shores of Lake Taupo, New Zealand's largest lake, which stretches 30km southwest towards three snow-capped volcanoes. In this magical setting, with the altitude (360m above sea level) and the reflected light from the lake's glassy surface creating an almost alpine radiance, this small town has grown up at the point where the impossibly deep-blue waters of the Waikato River ("flowing water" in Maori) start their long journey to the Tasman Sea. Both lake and river frontages are lined with parks, the pace is slow and there is an undeniably appealing tenor to the place.

For decades, Kiwi families have been descending en masse for a couple of weeks' holiday, bathing in the crisp cool waters of the lake, fishing its depths and lounging around their holiday homes that fringe the lakeshore. Although you could easily follow their lead and spend a relaxing few days here, there is no shortage of stuff to see and do, most notably around the spectacular rapids and geothermal badlands of **Wairakei Park**, immediately north of town. Thousands more come specifically for the **fishing**: the Taupo area is perhaps the most fecund trout fishery in the world, extending south to Turangi and along the Tongariro River and with an enviable reputation for the quality and fighting-spirit of its fish. Year-round, you'll see boats drifting across the lake with lines trailing and, particularly in the evenings, rivermouths choked with fly casters in chest-high waders.

Lake Taupo itself is a geological infant, born a mere two thousand years ago when a massive volcano erupted, spewing out 24 cubic kilometres of rock, debris and ash – ten times more than was produced by the eruptions of Krakatoa and Mount St Helens combined – and covering much of the North Island in a thick layer of pumice. Ash was ejected so high into the atmosphere that it was carried around the world, enabling historians to pinpoint the date of the **eruption** as 186 AD – when the Chinese noted a blackening of the sky and Romans recorded that the heavens turned blood-red. As the underground magma chamber emptied, the roof slumped, leaving a huge steep-sided **crater**, since filled by Lake Taupo. It is hard to reconcile this placid and beautiful lake with such colossal violence, though the evidence is all around: entire beaches are composed of feather-light pumice which, when caught by the wind, floats off across the lake. **Geologists** continue to study the causes and effects of the eruption and treat the lake as a kind of giant spirit-level, in which any tilting could indicate a build-up of magma below the surface that might trigger an eruption.

The local Tuwharetoa people ascribe the lake's formation to their ancestor, **Ngatoroirangi**, who cast a tree from the summit of Mount Tauhara, on the edge of Taupo, and where it struck the ground water welled up and formed the lake.

Taupo

Nowhere in Taupo's compact low-rise core is more than five minutes' walk from the waters of the Waikato River or Lake Taupo, which jointly hem in three sides. The fourth side rises up through the gentle slopes of Taupo's suburbs. Most of the commercial activity happens on, or just off, SH1, which passes through the middle of town as the main Tongariro Street and the aptly named Lake Terrace. Room for expansion is limited to the southeastern quarter, where ever more motels and timeshares are springing up along the lakeshore.

Although Taupo bears little trace of the vigorous Tuwharetoa settlement that existed into the middle of the nineteenth century, there was scant European interest in the area until the New Zealand Wars of the 1860s, when the Armed Constabulary were trying to track down **Te Kooti** (see box on p.362). They set up camp one night in June 1869 at Opepe, 17km southeast of Taupo (beside what is now SH5), and were ambushed by Te Kooti's men, who killed nine soldiers. Garrisons were subsequently established at Opepe and Taupo, but it was Taupo that flourished, enjoying a more strategic situation and being blessed with hot springs for washing and bathing. By 1877, Te Kooti had been contained, but the Armed Constabulary wasn't finally disbanded until 1886, after which several soldiers and their families stayed on, forming the nexus of European settlement.

Taupo didn't really flourish as a resort until the prosperous 1950s, when the North Island's roads had improved to the point where Kiwi families – equipped with caravans, boats and all manner of playthings – could easily drive here from Auckland,

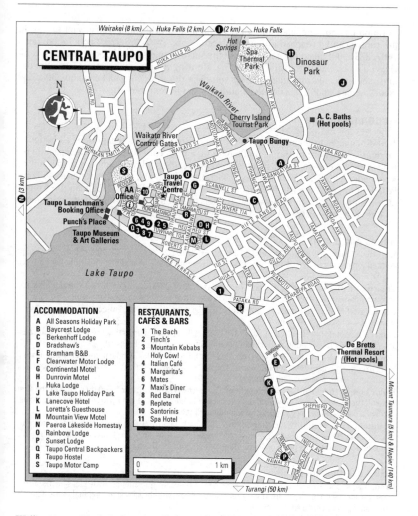

Wairakei (8 km) △ Huka Falls (2 km)△ ❶(2 km) △ Huka Falls

CENTRAL TAUPO

N

Hot Springs ● Spa Thermal Park

● ⑪ Dinosaur Park

● Ⓙ

HUKA FALLS RD

Waikato River

KAINUI RD

SPA ROAD

COUNTY AVE

NORMAN SMITH'S ST

Cherry Island Tourist Park

● A. C. Baths (Hot pools)

Waikato River Control Gates

● Taupo Bungy

LAUMARA ROAD

WAIKATO ST

SPA ROAD

MOTUTAIKO ST

RIVERSIDE

TE HEUHEU ST

TONGA ST

PIHANGA ST

TITIRAANGI ST

RUAPEHU ST

TE RANGITAIRA ST

KAIMANAWA ST

TE HEUHEU ST

PAORA HAPI ST

HOROMATANGI ST

TAMAMUTU ST

ⓈRE DOUBT

Taupo Travel Centre

●Ⓞ

⑩ AA Office ⓘ

SCANNELL ST

●Ⓖ

●Ⓐ

●Ⓒ

Taupo Launchman's Booking Office

Punch's Place

Taupo Museum & Art Galleries

Ⓡ

WHERE TIA

RUAPEHU ST

RIFLE RANGE ROAD

TAUPO VIEW RD

TAHARA-PA ROAD

MINERAL AVE

TAMATEA AVE

❻❹❾ ❷❺

Ⓓ Ⓗ

Ⓓ

HEU HEU ST

Ⓜ Ⓛ

Ⓞ❸❽❼

TUWHARE TOA

ROBERTS ST

LAKE TERRACE

TUI ST

HUIA ST

NEER RD

GILLIES AVE

RUAMOTU ST

TAHARE-PA ROAD

Lake Taupo

●Ⓘ

PATAKA RD

●Ⓑ

De Bretts Thermal Resort (Hot pools)

TAHANGA AVE

SHEPHERD RD

ARROWSMITH AVE

●Ⓔ

●Ⓚ
●Ⓕ

INGLE AVE

RICHMOND AVE

HAWAI ST

Ⓟ

HAWAI ST

ACCOMMODATION

A All Seasons Holiday Park
B Baycrest Lodge
C Berkenhoff Lodge
D Bradshaw's
E Bramham B&B
F Clearwater Motor Lodge
G Continental Motel
H Dunrovin Motel
I   Huka Lodge
J Lake Taupo Holiday Park
K Lanecove Hotel
L Loretta's Guesthouse
M Mountain View Motel
N Paeroa Lakeside Homestay
O Rainbow Lodge
P Sunset Lodge
Q Taupo Central Backpackers
R Taupo Hostel
S Taupo Motor Camp

RESTAURANTS, CAFES & BARS

1 The Bach
2 Finch's
3 Mountain Kebabs Holy Cow!
4 Italian Café
5 Margarita's
6 Mates
7 Maxi's Diner
8 Red Barrel
9 Replete
10 Santorinis
11 Spa Hotel

0   1 km

△(3 km)

Mount Taumara (5 km) & Napier (140 km)

▽ Turangi (50 km)

Wellington or Hawke's Bay. For the most part, the town just languishes by the lake, with what diversions there are limited to tacky tourist fodder, but Taupo makes a great base for exploring the natural wonders of the surrounding area.

Arrival, information and transport

Mount Cook **buses** pull up outside Taupo's **visitor centre**, Tongariro Street (daily 8.30am–5pm; ☎07/378 9000, fax 378 9003), right in the heart of town, while InterCity and Newmans buses stop at the Taupo Travel Centre **bus station**, 16 Gascoigne St. Taupo's **airport**, 10km south of the centre, is served by Air New Zealand and Mount Cook flights; shuttle buses to and from town are run by Taupo Taxis ($8; ☎07/378 5100).

Taupo has no scheduled bus service, but almost everything you'll want to visit in the centre can be reached on foot, with Stop Cabs (☎07/378 9250) and Taupo Taxis (☎07/378 5100) filling the gaps. To visit the surrounding sights without your own vehicle, you'll be reliant on **tours** (see p.277). **Renting a bike** gives greater freedom: the most sophisticated machines will set you back roughly $20 a half-day and $30 a day (see "Listings", p.277, for details of outlets – and for **car-rental**).

Accommodation

Taupo manages to maintain a very high standard of accommodation for all budgets. Finding somewhere to stay is unlikely to be a problem except when the crush is on (Christmas to end-Feb), when you should **book** several days in advance, especially at weekends. As befits a Kiwi holiday resort, there is no end of places catering to families, with much of the lakefront taken up by **motels**, and grassy spots on the fringes of town given over to **campsites**. Hostels are abundant too and uniformly good, though differing in style.

Hotels and motels

Baycrest Lodge, 79 Mere Rd (☎07/373 3838 & 0800/229 273, fax 378 4007). Luxuriously appointed top-of-the-range motel with spacious multi-room units, a heated pool, poolside bar and Sky TV. ⑥.

Clearwater Motor Lodge, 229 Lake Terrace (☎07/377 2071, fax 377 0020). Beautiful lakeside accommodation with great views, in-room spas and some rooms with small balconies. ⑥.

Continental Motel, 9 Scannell St (☎ & fax 07/378 5836). Comfortable, low-cost, central motel with small but well-maintained units. ④.

Dunrovin Motel, 140 Heu Heu St (☎07/378 7384). Older, budget units that are well-kept and characterful, being built of wood rather than the ubiquitous concrete blocks. ④.

Lanecove Hotel, 213 Lake Terrace (☎07/378 7599, fax 378 7393). Modern, top-of-the-line luxury hotel fronting the lake with elegant rooms. The more swanky rooms carry stratospheric price tags, but there are some at more reasonable rates. ⑥–⑨.

Huka Lodge, Huka Falls Rd, 4km north of Taupo (☎07/378 5791, fax 378 0427). One of the first and still the best-known of New Zealand's exclusive lodges, located just upstream from Huka Falls. It costs a cool $650 per person a night, including all meals. ⑨+.

Mountain View Motel, 12 Fletcher St (☎07/377 3076, fax 378 9366). Budget, central motel with spa pool, Sky TV, games room and kids' play area. The family units are huge, and the studios are at the bottom end of this price code. Studios ④, family units ⑤.

B&Bs and guesthouses

Bradshaw's, 130 Heu Heu St (☎07/378 8288). Good-value guesthouse with pleasant floral decorated rooms with showers, let at very reasonable rates, with breakfast an optional extra. There's also a bunkroom. Dorm ①, rooms ③.

Bramham B&B, 7 Waipahihi Ave (☎07/378 0064, fax 378 0065). Spacious homestay with expansive lake and mountain views, a couple of comfortable rooms with private facilities, and delicious breakfasts. ⑤.

Loretta's Guesthouse, 135 Heu Heu St (☎07/378 4927). Pleasant rooms in the main house and out back, all come with cooked or continental breakfast, and some come with their own bathroom. ④.

Paeroa Lakeside Homestay, 21 Te Kopua St (☎ & fax 07/378 8449). Luxurious homestay in a lush garden setting with great lake views five minutes' drive southwest of Taupo, with en-suite double and bathless twins, all with balconies. ⑥.

Hostels

Berkenhoff Lodge, 75 Scannell St (☎ & fax 07/378 4909). Bustling and slightly cramped hostel fifteen minutes' walk from the centre but with free use of bikes. The games room and on-site bar are perennially popular and they run a $5 barbecue every evening by the pool and spa. Each dorm has a bathroom, doubles and twins come with linen, and everyone gets free continental breakfast. Dorms ①, rooms ②.

Rainbow Lodge, 99 Titiraupenga St (☎07/378 5754, fax 377 1568). Spacious, relaxed and spotless purpose-built backpackers with a comfortable lounge, sauna, bikes for rent at $15 a day, a stack of local information and little touches that create a homely atmosphere. Dorms have between six and ten beds and there are spacious triples and doubles, some in self-contained cottages. Dorms ①, rooms ②.

Sunset Lodge, 5 Tremaine Ave (☎07/378 5962). Small, low-key and friendly hostel at Two Mile Bay some 3km from town but with courtesy pick-ups, free use of bikes, and daily drop-offs at the Craters of the Moon. The more capacious three-bed rooms are worth the extra dollar over the larger dorms. Dorms ①, rooms ②.

Taupo Central Backpackers, 7 Tuwharetoa St (☎07/378 3206). Taupo's principal party hostel – right in the heart of town with a rooftop bar dishing up budget-priced drinks and nightly barbecues for $7. The clean and tidy accommodation is in four- to eight-bunk dorms, each with its own bathroom, and plain doubles. Dorms ①, rooms ②.

Taupo Hostel, 56 Kaimanawa St (☎07/378 3311). Modern associate YHA hostel close to town and with good lake and mountain views from the kitchen and barbecue balcony. Dorms sleep three to five, there are doubles, and bikes can be rented for $15 a day. Dorms ①, rooms ②.

Campsites and motor parks

All Seasons Holiday Park, 16 Rangatira St (☎07/378 4272 & 0800/777 272, fax 378 1272). Compact site just over 1km from town, with tent sites scattered among nice new cabins and a range of good tourist flats. Tent sites $10, cabins ①, flats ②–③.

Lake Taupo Holiday Park, 28 Centennial Drive (☎ & fax 07/378 6860). Wonderfully spacious site 2km from town with good communal facilities and excellent range of clean and new tourist cabins, tourist flats and fully self-contained cottages, and easy access to the A.C. Baths. Tent sites $8, cabins, flats & cottages ③.

Taupo Motor Camp, 15 Redoubt Rd (☎07/377 3080). Very handy site on the banks of the Waikato River right in town. Tent sites $9, cabins & on-site vans ③.

The Town

True to its family-resort status, Taupo specializes in entertainment for the kids and adventure activities for adults. Perhaps the best all-round crowd-pleasers are the **hot pools**: marginally the pick of the two is **De Bretts Thermal Resort**, 2km southeast of the centre on SH5 (daily 7.30am–9.30pm; $6), a couple of large outdoor pools filled with natural mineral water that's oddly slippery on the skin. For an extra dollar you can also soak in one of the private mineral pools, which come in a range of temperatures, while $4 gets you as many descents as you like on the hot-water hydroslide. Without your own vehicle, you'll find it more convenient to head for the **A.C. Baths**, A.C. Baths Avenue (daily 8am–9pm; $4), where the entry fee includes use of the large freshwater hot pool and private mineral pools, but not the sauna (an extra $4 all day) or the water slides ($3). From the junction opposite the baths, Spa Road forges north to the **Spa Hotel**, site of the first hot spring used by the Armed Constabulary and now ignominiously overlooked by the thirty life-size ferro-concrete dinosaurs of the **Spa Dinosaur Valley** (daily except Tues 10am–6pm; $5). Jurassic Park it ain't, but the "realistic" dinosaur noises will probably still scare young kids witless. Just west, Spa Avenue runs down to the green swathe of **Spa Thermal Park**, where a path leads to the Waikato River past some naturally hot bathing pools (unrestricted entry) and, in an hour or so, downstream to Huka Falls (see box on p.274).

A few hundred metres upstream, the river swirls through the narrows of Hell's Gate, the 45m white cliffs providing the launch pad for **Taupo Bungy**, 202 Spa Rd (daily 9am–5pm, later in high season; $90, repeat jumps $50; ☎07/377 1135), one of

---

WALKS AROUND TAUPO

For those who just fancy a bit of a stroll, there are a few relatively easy **walks** near town. By far the most popular is the **Great Lake Walk**, which is more modest than it sounds: just follow the lakeshore east from town, covering as much of its 7km extent as you like, passing hot springs right at the water's edge.

On the northern edge of town, County Avenue leads to the **Spa Thermal Park**, where there's a pleasant thirty-minute bushwalk, which can be combined with a river-bank walk **to Huka Falls** (4km; 1hr one-way), and further extended to the Aratiatia Rapids (8km; 2hr one-way), though you've then got to get back – if you set off early, you could conceivably walk back via the Wairakei visitor centre and the Craters of the Moon (12km; 3hr).

Finally, if you have your own transport and a taste for magnificent lake and town views, try the track to the summit of **Mount Tauhara** (6km; 2–3hr return), the hill behind Taupo, which is approached on Mountain Road, which turns off SH5 to Napier after 6km.

New Zealand's finest bungy sites cantilevered 20m out from the bank. Perhaps the best spot for viewing your mates' bungy antics is the outdoor **café** adjacent to **Cherry Island Tourist Park**, Motutahae Road (daily 9am–5pm; $7.50), a feeble and over-priced display of trout, deer and exotic birds which occupies most of a tiny islet beautifully set in the clear river waters.

Few are going to want to spend long summer days indoors, but a dose of wet weather, or an abiding interest in local history, could send you scurrying back to the centre of town and the **Taupo Museum and Art Galleries**, Tongariro Park (daily 10.30am–4.30pm; free), with its varied exhibits covering pioneering days and fishing in some depth, before moving on to a curious collection of scale models of every plane which took part in World War II. On better days, there's more pleasure in lolling about outside on the pleasant grassy expanse of Tongariro Park, which sweeps down to the lakeshore and the Taupo Boat Harbour, departure-point for cruises, fishing trips and a multitude of aquatic pursuits.

Lake cruises and activities

As you would expect of Taupo, there's plenty of activities to relieve you of your holiday money. Some of the best are water-based, either cruising gently across Lake Taupo, rafting down the raging waters of the Tongariro or Rangitaiki rivers or fly-fishing the rivers and streams for trout. Taupo's magnificent scenery has also given it something of a name for tandem skydiving.

Cruises

One of the most satisfying ways to relax in Taupo is to take one of the **lake cruises**, run from the Taupo Boat Harbour and setting course for some striking modern **Maori rock carvings**, which can only be seen from the water at Mine Bay, 8km southwest of town. The carvings, dating from the late 1970s, depict a stylized image of a man's face heavy with *moko*, together with tuatara (lizard-like reptiles) and female forms draped over nearby rocks. The most characterful of the trips – as much for the sea-dog skipper as the boat – is aboard *The Barbary* (10.30am & 2pm; 2hr; $20; ☎07/378 3444), a 1926 ketch once owned by Eroll Flynn (who, it is colourfully claimed, won it in a card game) and subsequently coopted into the 1973 Greenpeace anti-nuclear-testing flotilla that sailed to Mururoa Atoll. If you're not too bothered about seeing the carvings, take the summer-time-only **sunset trip** which is a little shorter and only costs $15.

For a touch of gin-palace style, opt for the *Cruise Cat* (11.30am; 1hr 30min; $24; ☎07/378 1804 & 0800/825 825), which motors past the carvings. Different atmospherics are offered by the *Ernest Kemp* (Dec–Feb 10am, 2pm & 4.15pm; Oct–Nov & March–April 10am & 2pm; May–Sept 2pm; $20; ☎07/378 3444), a replica 1920s steamboat that chugs to the carvings and back in a couple of hours.

Trips can be **booked** either direct with operators or through the visitor centre. Bookings can be made at Punch's Place, Lakefront Terrace (daily 8am–6pm; 24hr ☎378 5596, fax 378 1747), or along the river at the Taupo Launchman's Booking Office, Redoubt Street (8am–5pm; 24hr ☎07/378 3444). Punch's Place is also the place to go for other lake-based watersports, such as **paraflying** (10min; $40), **waterskiing** ($90 per hour for up to three skiers), and **jet biking** ($45 per half hour).

Fishing

New Zealand's arcane fishing rules dictate that trout can't be sold, so if you've got a taste for their succulent flesh you'll have to catch it yourself. No one is going to guarantee you'll land a fighting rainbow or brown but the chances are better here than most places. If dinner is more of an incentive than sport, then your best approach is to **fish the lake** on a boat chartered through the visitor centre or directly from either the Taupo Launchman's Booking Office or Punch's Place (see above). Smaller **boats** go out for a minimum of two hours, but more usually three or four, and cost $65 an hour, taking up to six people with four fishing at a time. **Book in advance** from mid-December to February – and at any other time of year if you want the booking offices to help reduce your costs by matching you up with other interested parties. Boat operators have all the tackle you need and will organize a Taupo fishing licence ($9 a day, $22.50 a week, $30.50 a month and $46.50 for the full July-to-June year) for you.

The rivers flowing into Lake Taupo are the preserve of **fly-fishers**, particularly from March to September when mature rainbow trout enter the mouths of the streams and rivers and make their way upstream to shallow gravel hollows where they spawn. Brown trout are also in these waters, but they tend to be more wily. You can **rent tackle** from Sullivan's Taupo Sports Depot, Tongariro Street (☎07/378 5337) and the Fly & Gun Shop, Heu Heu Street (☎07/378 4449) and pick your own spot, but average catches are much larger if you engage the services of a **fishing guide**, which will set you back close to $200 for a full day with gear and licence.

Rafting, jumping and flying

There are no whitewater rivers right on Taupo's doorstep, but the town makes a viable base for **rafting**. The main rivers run from Taupo are the Tongariro (covered under Turangi – see p.282), the Rangitaiki and the Wairoa (both detailed on p.341), and a two-day trip on the relatively gentle upper section of the Mohaka, camping on the riverbank overnight. Rapid Sensations (☎07/378 7902 & 0800/22 RAFT) run the Tongariro for $75, Rapid Descents (☎07/377 0419 & 0800/TORAFT) shoot the Rangitaiki, also for $75, and Kiwi River Safaris (07/377 6597) organize trips to both for identical prices and also offer the Wairoa ($75) and the overnight Mohaka trip ($260, including meals). Closer to town, Bruce Webber Adventures (☎07/377 1236 & 0800/529 256) offer guided **kayaking** trips on the Waikato (2hr, $30; full day, $79), with a welcome emphasis on scenic appreciation.

Taupo has rapidly gained a reputation as one of the cheapest places to go **tandem skydiving** – and one of the best, with magnificent scenery all around, if you dare to look. Two companies, Great Lake Skydive (☎0800/373 335) and Taupo Tandem Skydive (☎07/377 0428 & 0800/2SKYDIVE), currently vie for your business, both offering jumps for $165. If you'd prefer to stay in the plane, there are fixed-wing **scenic flights** over Wairakei Thermal Area and the Huka Falls on a float plane from the Taupo Boat Harbour with ARK Aviation (10min; $30; ☎07/378 7500). An extensive range of longer flights down to the volcanoes are operated by De Bretts Aviation (☎0800/800 207; 30min–1hr 20min; $125–200). Helistar Helicopters (☎0508/554 422) offer **helicopter flights** over the Huka Falls and Craters of the Moon (10min; $75), and will combine them with a ride on the Huka Jet (see p.279) for $110.

Eating, drinking and nightlife

Taupo is a town of a hundred **tearooms** and coffee lounges, but come five o'clock eating well becomes more problematic. The better lakefront motor lodges all have pricey **restaurants**, some of them very good, and **bars** around town serve decent budget meals, leaving the middle ground somewhat rocky. However, for a small provincial town, there's a reasonable nightlife, with holidaymakers converging on several pubs and **clubs**.

Restaurants and cafés

The Bach, 2 Pataka Rd (☎07/378 7856). Modern dining in an easy-going atmosphere. Choose from wood-fired crispy pizza, a select range of $20 mains such as salmon, spinach and tomato lasagne in a champagne sauce, and an extensive selection of New Zealand wines by the bottle and glass. Dinner daily; lunch Sat & Sun, also Mon–Fri in high season. Licensed.

Finch's, 64 Tuwharetoa St (☎07/377 2425). Glass-top tables and concrete-block walls should spell disaster, but somehow it works in this least formal of Taupo's top restaurants, where you can feast on beautifully composed and presented international dishes such as grilled feta, fried artichokes and roasted garlic on naan bread with tapenade. Daily noon–midnight; licensed.

Holy Cow!, 11 Tongariro St. A bar noted for its $5 and $9 backpackers' specials – reliable favourites, including burgers, toasties, potato wedges, chicken curry and caesar salad.

Italian Café, 28 Tuwharetoa St. Reliable, if unexceptional, Italian trattoria of the gingham-table-cloth-and-Chianti-bottle ilk, with a range of traditional pizza and pasta ($12–15) and meat and fish dishes (around $20). Takeaways also available. Licensed & BYO.

Margarita's, 63 Heu Heu St. Compact bar and Mexican restaurant that's popular with backpackers (half-price discount cards are dished out at hostels around town) and locals for their burritos, enchiladas and fajitas at reasonable prices, plus steaks for a little more. Licensed.

Maxi's Diner, 38 Roberts St. Burgers, toasties and steak 'n' chips meals 24 hours a day.

Replete, 45 Heu Heu St. Taupo's finest deli and daytime café, run by a former chef from the esteemed Huka Lodge and serving excellent quiches, pizza slices, cakes and coffee until 5pm Mon–Fri, 2.30pm Sat & Sun.

Santorinis, 133 Tongariro St (☎07/377 2205). Understated white stucco and bare-boards Greek and Mediterranean café/bar serving delicious breakfasts, light lunches and dinners at very reasonable prices. Book for dinner, especially at weekends. Licensed & BYO; closed Mon.

Bars and clubs

Holy Cow!, 11 Tongariro St. The liveliest late-night bar in town, spinning an eclectic selection of rock and dance tunes and turning clubby late on.

Margarita's, 63 Heu Heu St. Convivial bar that's usually lively until late and is popular in the early evenings for drink specials.

Mates, 22 Tuwharetoa St. The place to go for the best micro-brewed beers in town, so long as you don't mind the sports-jock and cover-bands atmosphere.

Red Barrel, 4 Roberts St. Traditional beer-and-darts pub.

Spa Hotel, Spa Rd (☎07/378 4120). Cavernous beer barn with live music several nights a week, mostly at weekends.

Listings

Automobile Association 93 Tongariro St (☎07/378 6000).

Bike rental Bikes can be rented from Ski Yer Heart Out, 10 Roberts St (☎07/378 7400); R & R Sports, 17 Tamamutu St (☎07377 1585); and Rapid Sensations (☎07/378 7902). Most of the hostels have basic bikes for guests' use, and Rainbow Lodge, 99 Titiraupenga St (☎07/378 5754) also rents to non-guests. R & R Sports have motorized bikes for $40 a day.

Buses InterCity and Newmans (both booked through the Taupo Travel Centre, 16 Gascoigne St; ☎07/378 9032), have equally extensive networks, serving Rotorua, Tauranga, Hamilton, Auckland, Napier, Palmerston North and Wellington; Mount Cook (book through the visitor centre, Tongariro St; ☎07/378 9000) run north through Rotorua to Hamilton and Auckland, and south to Palmerston North and Wellington.

Car rental A1 Car Rentals, cnr Tamamutu St & Gascoigne St (☎06/378 3670), and Auto Rentals, Tuwharetoa St (☎06/378 9764), undercut the big guys.

Left-luggage Lockers are available at the Superloo, Tongariro St (daily: Dec–Jan 7.30am–9pm; Feb–Nov 7.30am–5.30pm; $1 a day).

Medical treatment Taupo Health Centre, 115 Heu Heu St (☎07/378 7060).

Pharmacy Unichem Lake Dispensary, 35–37 Heu Heu St (☎07/378 6100), is open daily until at least 6pm.

Police Story Place (☎07/378 6060).

Post office cnr Horomatangi St & Ruapehu St (☎07/378 9090).

Tours The best local sightseeing tours are Walter's Tours (☎07/378 5924), run by characterful guy with a many an anecdotal story to tell; options include the Craters of the Moon and Huka Falls (2hr; $15 for one, $10 each for two or more), while a longer trip adds Orakei Korako to the itinerary (5hr; $30/$25). Paradise Tours (☎07/378 9955) visit the same places, plus the Wairakei geothermal field and Aratiatia Rapids (2hr 30min; $25), while Rapid Sensations (☎07/378 7902) run guided bike tours around Wairakei (2–3hr; $45). Finally, Discover Taupo (☎07/377 0774) do a town tour in a 1951 London double-decker bus (Sat, Sun & school holidays; every 30min; 15min; $5), starting from the cnr Tongariro St & Lake Terrace. (See also "Lake cruises and activities", on p.274.)

Travel Agents Budget Travel, 37 Horomatangi St (☎07/378 9799); Grace United Travel, Taupo Travel Centre, 16 Gascoigne St (☎07/378 9005); James Travel Holiday Shoppe, 28 Horomatangi St (☎07/378 7065).

Around Taupo

Taupo's town attractions are limited in their appeal, but the same can't be said for region immediately to the **north**, a fabulously concentrated collection of natural wonders. Within a few minutes of each other you can find boiling mud, hissing steam harnessed by the Wairakei power station and the clear, blue Waikato River, which cuts a deep and swirling course northwards, occasionally turning wild as it squeezes through some of the country's most powerful rapids. The highlights – **Huka Falls**, **Aratiatia Rapids**, and the **Craters of the Moon** geothermal area – are all within 10km of Taupo, but you'll have to venture further to reach a second thermal park, **Orakei Korako**, 40km north. To get out this way, you'll need your own vehicle, or the services of one of Taupo's tour companies (see "Listings" above).

Moving **south** from Taupo, SH1 follows the lakeshore to Turangi (see p.282), while heading east along SH5 towards Napier (see p.366), there are a couple of things to detain you along the way.

Along Huka Falls Road

The bulk of the sights and activities around Taupo flank the Waikato River as it wends its way north, and lumped together under the collective title of **Wairakei Park**. The

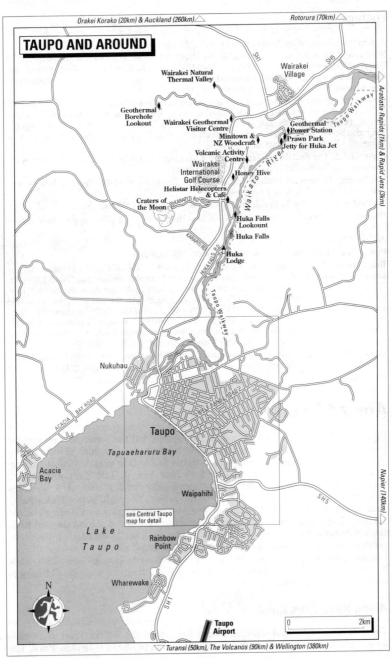

TAUPO AND AROUND

Orakei Korako (20km) & Auckland (260km) △

Rotorura (70km) △

Wairakei Village

Wairakei Natural Thermal Valley

Geothermal Borehole Lookout

Wairakei Geothermal Visitor Centre

Minitown & NZ Woodcraft

Volcanic Activity Centre

Geothermal Power Station

Prawn Park

Jetty for Huka Jet

Wairakei International Golf Course

Honey Hive

Helistar Helecopters & Café

Craters of the Moon

Huka Falls Lookount

Huka Falls

Huka Lodge

Waikato River

KARAPITI RD

HUKA FALLS RD

Taupo Walkway

Aratiatia Rapids (1km) & Rapid Jets (3km)

Napier (140km) △

Nukuhau

ACACIA BAY ROAD

GULF PANGA ROAD

Taupo

Tapuaeharuru Bay

Acacia Bay

Waipahihi

see Central Taupo map for detail

SH5

Lake Taupo

Rainbow Point

Wharewake

SH1

N

Taupo Airport

0   2km

Turansi (50km), The Volcanos (90km) & Wellington (380km) ▽

park is reached via Huka Falls Road, which loops off SH1 a couple of kilometres north of Taupo and passes the exclusive *Huka Lodge* (see p.272) en route to the first point-of-call, the impressive and justly popular **Huka Falls** (*hukanui*, or "great body of spray"). Here the full flow of the Waikato River, one of New Zealand's most voluminous rivers, funnels into a narrow chasm then plunges over an eleven-metre shelf into a seething maelstrom of eddies and whirlpools; the sheer power of some five hundred tonnes of water per second make it a far more awesome sight than its relatively short drop would suggest. A footbridge spans the channel, providing a perfect vantage point for watching the occasional mad kayaker making the descent.

The cutaway hives and educational video at the **Honey Hive** (daily 9am–5pm; free; ☎07/374 8553), 1km further north along Huka Falls, shouldn't divert you long, though they do have an excellent range of honey varieties, including the wonderful manuka. Press on to the **Volcanic Activity Centre** (Mon–Fri 9am–5pm & Sat–Sun 10am–4pm; $5), a heavyweight and highly instructional museum, which is gradually being made more interactive and fun. Currently the dense text is alleviated by striking photos, a seismograph linked to sensors on Mount Ruapehu, an earthquake simulator and a large relief map of Taupo Volcanic Zone, which extends from Mount Ruapehu to White Island.

Moving swiftly past **NZ Woodcraft** (☎ & fax 07/374 8555), essentially a shop selling turned native woods, and the adjacent and eminently missable miniature 1900s village of **Minitown** (daily 9am–5pm; $4), you'll come to the Wairakei geothermal power station. Most of the excess heat generated by the station is discharged into the river, though a portion is channelled into large open ponds, where tropical Malaysian prawns are raised in an enterprise known as the **Prawn Park** (daily 11am–4pm, tours hourly; $6). Even if the "Day in the life of a Prawn" tour of the complex doesn't stir your imagination, you can at least indulge in the scrumptious platters dished up by the *Prawn Works Bar & Grill* while seated by the deep-blue water of the Waikato.

The peace is periodically shattered by the **Huka Jet** (30min; $49; ☎07/374 8572) as it roars along the river between Huka Falls and the Aratiatia Dam. The boats leave from a **jetty** 500m upstream from the Prawn Park (courtesy bus from Taupo), and play all the usual tricks – close encounters with rock faces and 360°-spins – but if you are heading to the jetboating heartland around Queenstown, save your money until then. A more amiable way of appreciating the scenic pleasures of the river is to board the **MV Waireka** (daily 10am & 2pm; 1hr; $20; ☎07/374 8338), an ancient riverboat which leaves from the same jetty and cruises up to Huka Falls. Pleasant though these daytime cruises are, the one to go for is the Moonlight Glow Worm Cruise (daily: Nov–March 9pm; April–Oct 6pm; 1hr–1hr 30min; $20), which drifts along while spotlights pick out aquatic life and glow-worms illuminate the gorge walls.

Craters of the Moon and the Wairakei Valley

The Huka Falls loop road rejoins SH1 opposite the **Wairakei International Golf Course** (☎07/374 8152), one of the country's finest. Just south of the intersection, Karapiti Road runs west to the **Craters of the Moon** (unrestricted entry), an otherworldly geothermal area which sprang to life in the 1950s, after the construction of the Wairakei geothermal power station had drastically altered the underground hydrodynamics. What it lacks in geysers and colourful lakes, it more than makes up for in hyperactivity: the belching steam is so vigorous that the custodian on duty (8am–7pm) will insist you wear closed footwear to walk the 2km of trails that wind among roaring fumaroles and huge rumbling pits belching out pungent bad-egg smells. The culprit can only be visited vicariously through the self-promotional **Wairakei Geothermal Visitor Centre** (daily 9am–4.30pm; free), 3km north on SH1, with its relief map of the whole Tongariro and Waikato power schemes, an explanatory video shown on demand, and plenty of stuff on the intricacies of harnessing the earth's bounty. Outside, shiny high-pressure-steam pipes twist and bend the 2km to the power station from the borefield, which can be viewed from the **Geothermal Borefield Lookout** just down the road.

The same forces that created the Craters of the Moon stole the thunder of the **Wairakei Natural Thermal Valley** (daily 9am–5pm; $5), Taupo's original thermal area but now a mere shadow of its former self.

Aratiatia Rapids

Around 2km downstream from the Wairakei power station lies the first of the Waikato River's eight hydroelectric dams, the Aratiatia Dam, which holds back the Waikato immediately above the **Aratiatia Rapids**, a long series of cataracts that were one of Taupo's earliest attractions. In the 1950s, when plans to divert the waters around the rapids were revealed, public pressure succeeded in preserving the rapids. Though it's something of a hollow victory, since the rapids are left empty most of the time and only seen in their full glory during three or four thirty-minute periods each day (Oct–March 10am, noon, 2pm & 4pm; April–Sept 10am, noon & 2pm). Stand on the dam itself or at one of two viewpoints downstream and wait for the siren that heralds the bizarre spectacle of a parched watercourse being transformed into a foaming torrent of waterfalls and surging pressure waves, then easing back to a tame trickle.

Orakei Korako

There's yet more geothermal activity 40km north of Taupo at **Orakei Korako: The Hidden Valley** (daily: 8am–4.30pm in summer, 4pm in winter; $12.50), which is reached by travelling 14km east off SH1 or 23km west off SH5. The site's main distinguishing feature is its means of access, via a short shuttle-boat journey across a dammed section of the Waikato River, which drops you at the foot of a large silica terrace tinged orange, pink and green by heat-resistant algae. From here, an hour-long self-guided walking trail loops past bubbling mud pools, through an active geyser field, and down into the mouth of Ruatapu Cave, a sacred site once used by Maori women to prepare themselves for ceremonies – hence *Orakei Korako*, "a place of adorning".

You can **stay** on the opposite side of the river at *Orakei Korako Lodge* (☎07/378 3131, fax 378 0371; dorms ①) in self-catering bunk-style budget accommodation, with a big lounge, a pool table, hot tubs, and canoes for rent at $7 an hour.

The Taupo–Napier Road

Travelling beyond the immediate vicinity of Taupo, SH1 hugs the lake as it heads southwest to Turangi (see p.282), while SH5 veers southeast along the **Napier–Taupo Road**, a twisting but increasingly speedy run through some of the North Island's remotest country. Much of the early part of the journey crosses the Kaingaroa Plains, impoverished land cloaked in pumice and ash from a 186 AD volcanic eruption and of little use save for the pine plantations which stretch 100km north. The history of this route to Napier is traced by the **Napier–Taupo Heritage Trail**; pick-up a free booklet from Taupo or Napier visitor centres. Many of the 35 stops are of limited interest, but be sure to call in at **Opepe Historic Reserve**, 17km from Taupo, where a cemetery contains the graves of nine soldiers of the Bay of Plenty cavalry, killed by followers of maverick Maori leader Te Kooti in 1869. Nearby is a fine stand of totara, rimu and kahikatea and the remnants of a sawpit.

After another 11km, Clements Mill Road leads 30km south into the northern reaches of the **Kaimanawa Forest Park**, a remote rugged mountain wilderness, almost untouched, and little-visited by recreational trampers, but a perennial favourite with deer hunters and anglers. There is no public transport out this way and tracks are not well marked, but if you are experienced and determined, get hold of the detailed *Guide to Kaimanawa State Forest Park* map and set off on the remote **Te Iringa–Oamaru Circuit** (60km; 4–5 days), staying in a series of Category 3 huts ($4 per night). Some 25km southeast of the Clements Mill Road turn-off, the Waipunga River, a tributary of the Mohaka, plummets 30m over the **Waipunga Falls**, and continues beside SH5 through the lovely Waipunga Gorge, packed with tall native trees and dotted with picnic sites which double as overnight "freedom" **campsites** with no facilities but river water. Soon, the highway descends to the Mohaka River and the appealing riverside accommodation at the *Riverlands Outback Retreat*, 5km south of SH5 (☎06/834 9756; camping $8, dorms 1x, rooms 2x, self-contained units 3x), a residential multi-activity centre where the prime attractions are **horse trekking** (2hr, $30; 4hr, $40) along farm trails and down to the river; and **whitewater rafting** on Grade I–II stretches of the Mohaka (2hr, $35), or the more exciting and wonderfully scenic Grade III section (full day; $85), which runs through a narrow gorge that's just great for jumping off the cliffs either side.

Beyond the Mohaka River, the highway climbs the Titiokura Saddle before the final descent through the grape country of the **Esk Valley** into Napier (see p.366).

TONGARIRO NATIONAL PARK AND AROUND

New Zealand's highly developed network of national parks owes much to Te Heu Heu Tukino IV, the Tuwharetoa chief who, in the *pakeha* land-grabbing climate of the late nineteenth century, recognized that the only chance his people had of keeping their sacred lands intact was to donate them to the nation – on condition that they could not be settled nor spoiled. His 1887 gift formed the core of country's first major public reserve, the **Tongariro National Park**. In the north a small, outlying section of the park centres on **Mount Pihanga** and the tiny **Lake Rotopounamu**, but most visitors head straight for the main body of the park, dominated by three great volcanoes, which rise starkly from the desolate plateau to pierce the hard blue sky: the broad-shouldered ski mountain, **Ruapehu** (2290m), its squatter sibling, **Tongariro** (1968m), and, wedged between them, the conical **Ngauruhoe** (2290m).

According to the **Maori**, there used to be a lot more mountains hereabouts. All were male but for the beautiful Pihanga in the northern section of the park, whose favours were widely sought. Pihanga loved only Tongariro, the victor of numerous battles with her other suitors, and the vanquished mountains fled: Taranaki carved out the Whanganui River as he made for the west coast of the North Island; Putauaki got as far north as Kawerau; but Tauhara was reluctant to leave and continually glanced back, so that by dawn, when the mountains could no longer move, he had only reached the northern shores of Lake Taupo, where he remains to this day, "the lonely mountain".

To the local Tuwharetoa people these mountains were so **sacred** that they averted their eyes while passing and wouldn't eat or build fires in the vicinity. The *tapu* stretches back to legendary times when their ancestor **Ngatoroirangi** came to claim the centre of the island. After declaring Tongariro *tapu* he set off up the mountain, but his followers broke their vow to fast while he was away and the angry gods sent a snow storm in which Ngatoroirangi almost perished before more benevolent gods in Hawaiki saved him by sending **fire** to revive his frozen limbs.

Within the boundaries of the park is some of the North Island's most striking scenery – semi-arid plains, crystal-clear lakes and streams, steaming fumaroles, virgin rainforest, an abundance of ice and snow – and two supremely rewarding tramps, the one-day **Tongariro Crossing** and the three-to-four-day **Tongariro Northern Circuit**, one of New Zealand's Great Walks. The undulating plateau to the west of the volcanoes is vegetated by bushland and golden tussock, while on the eastern side the rain shadow of the mountains produces the **Rangipo Desert**. Although this is not a true desert, it is still an impressively bleak and barren landscape, smothered by a thick layer of volcanic ash from the 186 AD Taupo eruption. These features combine to create a unique landscape, which was designated a **World Heritage Site** in 1991.

The park captured world headlines in 1995 and again in 1996 when **Mount Ruapehu**, the highest and most massive of the three volcanoes, burst into life, blasting a plume of ash and dust 12km into the atmosphere and emptying the crater lake down the side of the mountain in great muddy deluges known as lahars. Although the eruptions drastically curtailed the ski season, they have had little lasting damage; what made them newsworthy was the dramatic contrast between the black spume of ash and the pristine snowy peak, all offset by a cloudless sky – images now endlessly recycled on the walls of local cafés and visitor centres.

The northern approach to the region is through **Turangi**, not much in itself but a reasonable base both for the Tongariro tramps and for rafting and fishing the Tongariro River. What it lacks is a sense of proximity to the mountains – something much more tangible in the service town of **National Park**, and more so again in **Whakapapa Village**, 1200m up on the flanks of Ruapehu. The southern gateway is **Ohakune**, a more appealing place than National Park but distinctly dead outside the ski season. Heading south, the Army Museum at Waiouru marks the southern limit of the Volcanic Plateau, which tails off into the pastoral southern half of the island around the agricultural town of **Taihape** and the bungy centre at **Mangaweka**.

Pretty much everyone comes to the park either to **ski** or to **tramp**, staying in one of the small towns dotted around the base of the mountains. While a **car** makes life easier, there is a reasonable network of **minibuses** plying the more useful routes and providing trailhead transport for trampers (see box on p.287). Note that this whole region is over 600m above sea level, so even in the height of summer you'll need some **warm clothing**.

Turangi

TURANGI, 50km south of Taupo, is a small, flat and characterless town planned in the mid-1960s and built almost overnight for workers toiling away at the tunnels and concrete channels of the ambitious Tongariro Power Scheme (see box on p.284). It doesn't even make the best of its location – Lake Taupo is 4km to the north and the town is separated by SH1 from its trump card, the **fishing** and **rafting** waters of the Tongariro River. Nonetheless, it works well enough as a base for a smattering of sights and activities in the immediate vicinity and for the Tongariro National Park (see p.287), just beyond the steep volcanic range to the south.

European settlement began early this century soon after trout were released into the Taupo fishery, but although the collection of fishing lodges warranted a shop and post office, no town existed until 1964 when well-paid work on the power scheme lured workers to the area, notably Italian tunnellers, many of whom subsequently settled here.

The massive popularity of trout fishing in this area makes it essential that rivers are continually restocked with fingerlings raised at fish-breeding facilities such as the **Tongariro National Trout Hatchery**, on SH1, 5km south of Turangi (daily 9am–4pm; free), set among native bush between the Tongariro River and one of its tributaries, the Waihukahuka Stream. Ever since its inception in 1927 the centre has used wild rainbow

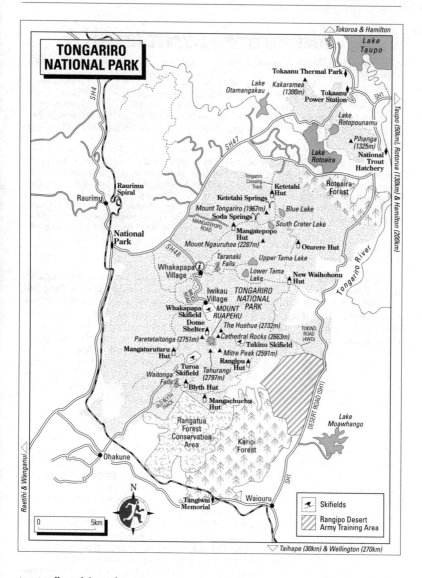

TONGARIRO NATIONAL PARK

trout collected from the stream – as opposed to the more common practice of using hatchery-raised fish – and stripped them of their eggs and milt to produce fry that are genetically more varied and disease resistant. The fish are then left to grow for around a year until they reach 150mm before being released into streams all over the country. There isn't a lot to see, but you are free to wander through buildings where tanks hold the tiniest fish, among the rearing ponds outside and into an underground viewing chamber where you can view wild trout in the Waihukahuka Stream.

THE TONGARIRO POWER SCHEME

The **Tongariro Power Scheme** provides an object lesson in harnessing the power of water with minimal impact on the environment. Its two powerhouses produce around 7 percent of the country's electricity, while the outflows that feed into Lake Taupo add flexibility to the much older chain of eight hydroelectric dams along the Waikato River (see p.575). Certainly there are those who argue it is unacceptable to tamper with such a fine piece of wilderness, and it has caused fluctuations in the levels of nutrients in the Tongariro River and erosion along some of the service tracks, but the scheme has many admirers.

In fact, if it weren't for the scale models in visitor centres and the ugly bulk of the Tokaanu power station, only astute observers would be aware of the complex system of tunnels, aqueducts, canals and weirs unobtrusively going about their business of diverting the waters of the Tongariro River and myriad streams running off the mountain slopes, back and forth around the perimeter of the national park, using modified natural lakes for storage. Mount Ruapehu poses its own unique problems: the threat of lahars is ever-present and, after the 1995 eruption, tephra (a highly abrasive volcanic ash) found its way into the turbines of the Rangipo underground powerhouse, causing an unscheduled seven-month shutdown.

Fauna in its natural state is best seen on the educational two-hour-plus **Tongariro River Delta Wetland Tour** run by Tongariro Eco Tours (around dawn & dusk; $40; ☎07/386 6409 & 0800/101 024). Aboard a specially-designed shallow-draught boat you putter around the fringes of the lake while guides well-versed in local ecosystems explain the dynamics of one of the country's largest delta wetlands, which is home to black swans, dabchicks, four species of cormorant, white-faced heron and Canada geese.

Heading away from the delta region, the **Tongariro River Walk** (10km; 3hr return) is a pleasant trail which starts from the Major Jones footbridge at the end of Koura Street on the edge of town and follows the river south to the Red Hut footbridge. Ten kilometres south of Turangi, off SH47, the **Lake Rotopounamu Circuit** (5km; 1hr 30min) encircles a pristine lake surrounded by bush alive with native birds.

Activities

Four companies offer **rafting** on the lower reaches of the Tongariro River, which runs through one of the most scenic and accessible river gorges in the country. The river's natural flow patterns have been modulated by the Tongariro Power Scheme, limiting the possibilities of a really wild time on the Grade II and Grade III rapids, but what sets the Tongariro apart is the **range of trips** you can do on one piece of water – some involving a two-hour run in traditional river rafts, some employing inflatable kayaks and some combining fishing with the rafting.

The cheapest **operators** are Rock 'n' River Adventures (☎07/386 0352), who run the Tongariro for $70, though it only costs $5 more to go with Tongariro River Rafting (☎07/386 6409 & 0800/101 024), who offer straightforward rafting, either with a guide in your craft or paddling yourselves with a guide in hailing distance, and the Tongariro Duo ($120), which spends the best part of a day careering along mountain-biking trails and rafting the river. Rapid Sensations (☎07/378 7902) also run the Tongariro ($75) and organize trips to Rotorua's Rangitaiki River ($79), while competitively priced trips on all local rivers are run by the *Club Habitat*-based River Rats (☎0800/333 900).

Big rafts make the modest scale of the lower Tongariro seem a little tame, and more fun can be had on **inflatable kayak** trips run by Eddyline Adventures (☎07/386 5081 & 0800/UKAYAK): first trips must be on the Grade II section (1hr 30min; $58), then they'll let you loose on Grade III rapids (2hr; $79).

If you're keen to try your hand at hauling a trout from Lake Taupo or one of the local rivers, the visitor centre will help pair you with a **fishing** guide to match your experience and aspirations; expect to pay around $50 an hour for gear and guiding. You can rent a boat and tackle at moderate prices from Braxmere Lodge, Little Waihi (☎07/386 7513), on the lakeshore just northwest of Turangi. The most productive months are from December to February, with the river-fishing season extending a couple of months either side of this peak and lake fishing continuing all year.

Practicalities

InterCity and Newmans **buses** pull in at the Turangi Bus & Travel Centre, Ohunga Road (Mon–Fri 8am–5pm; ☎07/386 8918, fax 386 8397), which sells tickets when open; otherwise buy them off the driver. Mount Cook buses stop just down the street outside the **visitor centre**, Ngawaka Place (daily 9am–5pm; ☎07/386 8999, fax 386 0074), which is packed with local information, including informative panels on trout fishing and a relief model of the Tongariro Power Scheme. There's also a small **DOC office**, Turanga Place (Mon–Fri 8am–5pm; ☎07/386 8607, fax 386 7086) selling walking maps, leaflets and hut tickets.

Turangi has a modest range of **accommodation**. At the cheaper end it is a toss-up between *Bellbird Lodge*, on the corner of Tautahanga Road and Rangipoia Place (☎ & fax 07/386 8281; dorms ①, rooms ②), a popular and homely backpackers with home-made cakes each evening; and *Club Habitat*, Ohuanga Road (☎07/386 7492, fax 386 0106; tent sites $7, dorms ①, rooms ③, cabins & units ④), an activity-orientated associate-YHA that comes with a spacious games, bar and dining complex, a spa and sauna, and is a favourite with the backpacker tour buses. Other options include *Creel Lodge*, 165 Taupahi Road (☎ & fax 07/386 8081; ④), a fishing-orientated cluster of self-contained units with communal games room, swimming pool and fish smoker. For more style and comfort, try *Ika Lodge*, 155 Taupahi Rd (☎07/386 5538; ⑤), a very peaceful one-time fishing lodge right by the Tongariro River, with a sauna and spa, accommodation in en-suite rooms and succulent game and fish dinners for $30.

Eating is limited to several takeaway places – the *Grand Central* on Tautahanga Street is the pick of the bunch – and a handful of licensed restaurants: the Italian *Valentino's*, Ohuanga Road (☎07/386 8812); the steak-and-pasta *Magees Restaurant & Bar*, Turangi Shopping Mall, where they'll cook your fishy catch to order; and the basic but hearty cafeteria at *Club Habitat*, which is the best place to **drink**.

Tokaanu

Turangi's smaller neighbour, **TOKAANU**, 5km west, was the main settlement in the area in pre-European times. Maori were drawn by the geothermal benefits of what is now the **Tokaanu Thermal Park** (unrestricted entry; free), a compact patch of low scrub, beautifully clear hot pools and plopping mud threaded by a fifteen-minute trail. The adjacent **Tokaanu Thermal Pools**, Mangaroa Road (daily 10am–9pm; $3), are just great for soaking your bones after a day's tramping in the national park, with an open-air public pool and hotter, partly enclosed private pools ($4 an hour).

One of Turangi's tunnellers' first jobs was getting water to the **Tokaanu Power Station**, on SH47, 2km east of Tokaanu, which can be seen on free tours conducted more-or-less on demand from the power station's visitor centre (Mon–Sat 10am–4pm; 20min; free).

To **stay** in Tokaanu, try the *Oasis Motel and Tourist Park*, SH41 (☎07/386 8569, fax 386 0694; tent sites $8, cabins ②, units ③), an extensive campsite with mineral hot pools, spa pools and simple but well priced on-site accommodation.

Whakapapa and around

Tiny **WHAKAPAPA**, the only settlement set firmly within the boundaries of the Tongariro National Park, hugs the lower slopes of Mount Ruapehu some 45km south of Turangi on SH48, which spurs off SH47. Approaching from the north, an open expanse of tussock gives distant views of the imposing form of the Grand Chateau hotel, framed by the snowy slopes of the volcano behind and overlooked by the arterial network of tows of the Whakapapa skifield.

From Whakapapa, SH48 continues as Bruce Road 6km to **IWIKAU VILLAGE** (known locally as the "Top o' the Bruce"), an ugly jumble of ski-club chalets which, from late June through to mid-November, and in exceptional circumstances as late as Christmas, becomes a seething mass of wrap-around shades and baggy snowboarders' pants. Outside the ski season, the village dies, leaving only a couple of chair lifts ($15 return) to trundle up to the *Knoll Ridge Café*, New Zealand's highest at 2020m above sea level.

Arrival and information

The only **bus services** to Whakapapa are the shuttle buses from Turangi and National Park (see box on p.287), which drop off close to DOC's helpful **visitor centre** (daily 8am–5pm; ☎07/892 3729, fax 892 3814). The centre is stocked with all the maps and leaflets you could need and is equipped with extensive displays on the park, including the tiny *Skiing on the Volcano* museum and a couple of videos that are shown on demand. *Ring of Fire* (15min; $2) is a fairly simplistic discussion of vulcanism in general and its manifestations here, while *The Sacred Gift of Tongariro* (25min; $3) deals with Maori legends surrounding Tongariro and with its bequest to the nation.

Accommodation

There's not much to Whakapapa beside a café and three **places to stay**, all within a couple of minutes' walk of each other and all often booked up in advance. You'll do well to reserve as far ahead as possible through the ski season and over the Christmas and January school holidays. The most prominent is the *Grand Chateau* (☎0800/733 944, fax 733 955; ⑥), a vast brick edifice built in 1929 and still offering by far the finest rooms and facilities in the region plus a swimming pool, tennis courts and the highest nine-hole golf course in New Zealand; the chateau also organizes the Tongariro Trek (see p.288). The only other hotel is *Skotel* (☎07/892 3719, fax 892 3777; backpacker rooms ②, standard rooms ⑤), a rambling place with a sauna and a range of rooms from self-catering hostel-style affairs (though with very limited kitchen facilities) to relatively luxurious rooms, some with views of Ngauruhoe and Tongariro. The best budget option is the *Whakapapa Holiday Park* (☎ & fax 892 3897; camping $8, dorms ①, cabins ②, flats ③), nicely set in a patch of bushland with spacious tent and powered sites, simple cabins that are let as backpacker dorms in summer, and more luxurious en-suite tourist flats. There is also the DOC's simple *Mangahuia campsite* ($4), on SH47 close to the foot of the Whakapapa access road.

Iwikau Village has no public accommodation, only ski-club lodges and a café (daytime in summer, evenings also during the ski season).

Around Whakapapa

Outside the **skiing** season (see box on p.291), Whakapapa is a lot less frenetic but is still alive with trampers, since it makes a fine base for both **short walks** and long tramps. The Tongariro Northern Circuit and the Round the Mountain Track (see "Tramping in Tongariro National Park", p.287) can both be tackled from here, but there are also easier strolls covered by DOC's *Whakapapa Walks* leaflet ($1). Three of the best of these are the **Whakapapa Nature Walk** (1km; 20–30min), highlighting the unique flora of the park; the **Taranaki Falls Walk** (6km; 2hr return), which heads through open tussock and bushland to where the Wairere Stream plunges 20m over the end of an old lava flow; and the **Silica Rapids Walk** (7km; 2hr 30min return), which follows a stream through beech forests to some creamy-coloured geothermal terraces.

Eating and drinking
When it's time to **eat**, try the lunches and snacks at *Ferguson's Café*, opposite the visitor centre, and in the evening head for *Skotel*, which has good-value bar meals and a licensed restaurant with hearty dishes. If you want to reward yourself for the successful completion of a major tramp, the *Grand Chateau* is the place to do it, with à la carte meals ($50 and up) and more manageably priced weekend buffets and brasserie meals. The Whakapapa Tavern has the cheapest **drinks** in the village.

Tramping in Tongariro National Park

The Tongariro National Park contains some of the North Island's finest walks. The **Tongariro Crossing** alone is rated as the best one-day tramp in the country, and it would be hard to dismiss the claim, but there are many longer possibilities, notably the three-to-four-day **Tongariro Northern Circuit**, which rates as one of New Zealand Great Walks; both pass through spectacular and varied volcanic terrain. Mount Ruapehu offers the arduous but rewarding **Crater Rim Walk** and a circuit, the **Round the Mountain Track**, which offers a narrower variety of terrain and sights than the Tongariro tramps, but is consequently less used.

Preliminaries
The 1:80,000 *Tongariro Park map* ($11) is ideal for these tramps, but the **DOC leaflets** ($1 each) covering the tramps separately are informative and perfectly adequate. The

---

GETTING TO – AND AROUND – TONGARIRO NATIONAL PARK

The major bus companies don't run through the Tongariro National Park, leaving several smaller companies to fill the void.

From Taupo, Kiwi Shuttles (☎025/503 654) pick up and drop off Tongariro Crossing-bound trampers ($30 return), and in winter several companies run the hour and a half down to the Whakapapa skifield in the morning and back again each evening. Contact the Taupo visitor centre or Ski Yer Heart Out, 10 Roberts St (☎07/378 7400), who also rent ski gear from $22 a day and snowboarding kit for $40 a day.

From Turangi, Alpine Scenic Tours (☎07/386 8916) do a particularly useful run three times a day, calling at Whakapapa, National Park and the start and end of the Tongariro Crossing; Bellbird Connections, based at the Bellbird Lodge (☎07/386 8281) but open to all, run a similar service but drops off at the trailhead an hour earlier than Alpine, giving you a head start on the pack; and Club Habitat (☎07/386 7492) have their own service for guests. **Fares** are very competitive – roughly $20 for the Tongariro Crossing drop-off and pick-up and around $15 one-way to either Whakapapa or National Park. All services become skifield shuttles in winter.

From Whakapapa, Tongariro Track Transport (☎07/892 3716) runs a daily shuttle from the visitor centre to the start and finish of the Tongariro Crossing ($15 return).

From National Park, shuttle buses serve the trailheads in summer and skifields in winter. Both Howard's Lodge (☎07/892 2827) and Ski Haus (☎07/892 2854) run their own all-comer buses, charging $15 for drop-off and pick-up at either end of the Tongariro Crossing or from Whakapapa, and $25 for Turoa.

main points of **access** to the walks are Mangatepopo Road and Ketetahi Road for the Tongariro Crossing and Tongariro Northern Circuit; and Whakapapa for the Tongariro Northern Circuit, the Ruapehu Crater Rim and the Round the Mountain Track. **Shuttle buses** serve the trailheads from Turangi, National Park and Whakapapa (see box on p.291); the tracks are all well maintained and comprehensively signposted, so you can judge your progress if you've a bus to catch.

Other than **accommodation** in Whakapapa Village (see p.286), the only places to stay are the **trampers huts** and adjacent **campsites**. In summer (late Oct–May), huts on the Tongariro Northern Circuit – Mangatepopo, Ketetahi, Waihohonu and Oturere – are classed as Great Walk huts ($12); in winter they lose their cooking facilities and revert to Category 2 ($8). **Hut tickets**, available from the DOC, do not guarantee a bunk, so at busy times you could still find yourself on the floor. Campers (summer $6, winter $4) stay close to the huts and use the same facilities. Huts on the Round the Mountain Track – Whakapapaiti, Mangaturuturu, Blyth, Mangaehuehu and Rangipo – are Category 2 huts all year ($8, camping $4).

There are several **organized treks**, too: the *Grand Chateau* hotel in Whakapapa Village runs the **Tongariro Trek** (mid-Dec to mid-April; $970; ☎0800/733 944), which combines the Ruapehu Crater Rim walk, the Tongariro Northern Circuit and four nights to recover from it all at the Chateau. The **Whakapapa Skifield Guided Walk** (Christmas to mid-April daily 9.30am; $40, including chair-lift ride; ☎07/892 3738) ascends to the Ruapehu Crater Rim, providing interesting commentary on the geology and flora en route.

The **weather** in the mountains is extremely changeable, and the usual provisos apply. Even on apparently scorching summer days, the increased altitude and exposed windy ridges produce a wind-chill factor to be reckoned with, and storms roll in with frightening rapidity. Any time from the end of March through to late November there can be snow on the tracks, so if you are planning a tramp during this period, enquire locally about current conditions. Always take warm **clothing** and rain gear – and if you plan to scramble up and down the volcanic cone of Mount Ngauruhoe, take gloves and long trousers for protection from the sharp scoria rock.

Tongariro Crossing

The **Tongariro Crossing** (16km; 6–8hr; 750m ascent) is by far the most popular of the major tramps in the region and for good reason. Within a few hours you climb over lava flows, cross a crater floor, skirt active geothermal areas, pass beautiful and serene emerald and blue lakes and have the opportunity to ascend the cinder cone of Mount Ngauruhoe. Even without this wealth of highlights it would still be a fine tramp, traversing a mountain massif through scrub and tussock, before descending into virgin bush for the final half-hour. It can be a long day out if you're not particularly fit, but it's not excessively arduous.

The track can be walked in either direction but most trampers are reliant on shuttle buses (see box on p.287), which are all scheduled around a west-to-east traverse, usually depositing their charges at Mangatepopo Road End, six gravel kilometres east of SH47, at around 8.30am and picking up at Ketetahi Road around 5pm. Weekdays during spring and autumn aren't especially busy, but on weekends and through the height of summer up to two hundred people complete the Crossing. To avoid the worst of the crush, steal a march on the others by choosing a shuttle operator prepared to drop-off at Mangatepopo Road a little earlier; or dawdle behind the mob and plan to stay the night at Mangatepopo Hut; or get dropped off at Ketetahi Road late in the day and sleep at Ketetahi Hut ready for a crack-of-dawn start next day.

From Mangatepopo Road End the first hour is fairly gentle, following the Mangatepopo Stream through a barren landscape and passing the Mangatepopo Hut. The track gradually steepens as you scale the fractured black lava flows towards the

Mangatepopo Saddle, passing a short side-track to the **Soda Springs**, a small wild-flower oasis in this blasted landscape. The Saddle marks the start of the high ground between the bulky and ancient Mount Tongariro and its youthful acolyte, **Mount Ngauruhoe**, which fit walkers can climb (2km return; 2hr return; 600m ascent) from here and still make the shuttle bus at the end of the day. The two-steps-forward-one-step-back ascent of this thirty-five-degree cone of red and black scoria must be one of the most exhausting and dispiriting walks in the country, but it is always popular – both for the superb views from the toothy crater rim and the thrilling headlong descent among a cascade of tumbling rocks and volcanic dust.

From the Mangatepopo Saddle, the main track crosses the flat pan of the South Crater and climbs to the rim of **Red Crater**, with fumaroles belching out steam, which obscures the banded crimson and black of the crater walls. Colours get more vibrant still as you begin the descent to the Emerald Lakes, opaque pools shading from jade to palest duck-egg, and beyond to the crystal-clear Blue Lake. Sidling around Tongariro's **North Crater**, you begin to descend steeply on golden tussock slopes to **Ketetahi Hut**, a major rest stop with views of Lake Rotoaira and Lake Taupo. Historically, one of the major attractions of this tramp was a final dip in the hot pools of Ketetahi Springs, but an ongoing dispute between the springs' *iwi* owners and the DOC has, hopefully temporarily, curtailed this activity. All that's left is the descent through cool streamside bush to the car park on Ketetahi road.

Tongariro Northern Circuit – and round the mountains

If the Tongariro Crossing appeals, but you are looking for something a little more challenging, the answer is the **Tongariro Northern Circuit** (41km; 3–4 days). From **Whakapapa to Mangatepopo Hut** (9km; 2–3hr; 50m ascent) the somewhat eroded track is relatively gentle, crossing tussock and numerous streams before meeting the Tongariro Crossing track close to Mangatepopo Hut. From **Mangatepopo Hut to Emerald Lakes** (6km; 3–4hr; 660m ascent), you follow the Tongariro Crossing (described above), then have the choice of continuing on the Crossing **to Ketetahi Hut** (4km; 2–3hr; 400m descent) and returning to this point the next day, or branching right **to Outere Hut** (5km; 1–2hr; 500m descent), descending steeply through fabulously contorted lava formations towards the Rangipo Desert. The initial section from **Outere Hut to Waihohonu Hut** (7km; 2–3hr; 250m descent) crosses open, undulating country, then descends into the beech forests before a final climb over a ridge brings you to the hut, where you can drop your pack and press on for twenty minutes to the cool and clear Ohinepango Springs. The final day's walk, from **Waihohonu Hut to Whakapapa** (14km; 5–6hr; 200m ascent), cuts between Ngauruhoe and Ruapehu, passing the Old Waihohonu Hut (no accommodation) that was built for stage coaches on the old road in 1901. The path then continues alongside Waihohonu Stream to the exposed **Tama Saddle** and, just over a kilometre beyond, a junction where side tracks lead to Lower Tama Lake (20min return) and Upper Tama Lake (1hr return), both in-filled explosion craters. It is only around two hours' walk from the saddle back to Whakapapa, so you should have time to explore the **Taranaki Falls** before ambling back through tussock to the village.

The Northern Circuit can be extended around Mount Ruapehu, a route known as the **Round the Mountain Track** (65km; 4–5 days) and most easily tackled from Whakapapa. This track can also be combined with the Northern Circuit to make a mighty five- or six-day **circumnavigation** of all three mountains.

Ruapehu Crater Rim

The ascent to the **Ruapehu Crater Rim** takes around eight hours return from the Top o' the Bruce (15km), and a much more appealing five hours from the top of the

Waterfall Express chair lift (9km), avoiding a long slog through a barren, rocky landscape. Even from the top of the chair lift, this is one of New Zealand's more gruelling walks, but the destination makes it all worthwhile. Volcanic instability makes it dangerous to go beyond the **Dome Shelter**, at 2672m the highest structure in the country and permanently surrounded in snow. It perches on the rim of the crater, with great views across the upper reaches of a small glacier to the dramatic silhouettes of Cathedral Rocks, west to Mount Taranaki and down into the crater lake, currently in the process of refilling after thousands of tonnes of water were ejected during the 1995 and 1996 eruptions. From Christmas until the first snows arrive, the ascent can usually be made in ordinary walking boots without crampons or an ice axe, but if you are in any doubt or would appreciate some commentary, join an organized trek (see "Preliminaries" p.287).

National Park

The evocative moniker attached to **NATIONAL PARK**, 15km west of Whakapapa Village, belies the overwhelming drabness of this tiny settlement – a dispiriting collection of A-frame chalets sprouting from a scrubby plain of pines, eucalypts and flax, with only the views of Ruapehu and Ngauruhoe to lend it any grace.

Arrival and information
National Park comprises a grid of half a dozen streets wedged between SH4 and the parallel rail line. **Trains** stop at the deserted platform on Station Road, while InterCity **buses** pull up outside the National Park Store, 100m north on Carroll Street, which is pretty much the hub of things in National Park, operating as the post office and selling a distinctly limited and expensive stock of food. Bus tickets can be bought across the road at *Ski Haus* or along the street from *Howard's Lodge* (see below). There are no banks or cash machines in National Park so unless you have an EFTPOS card, bring plenty of cash.

Accommodation
Accommodation is in great demand during the **ski season** – when prices will be at least one price code higher than those given here – and can fill up from Christmas to the end of January, but is otherwise plentiful. *Howard's Lodge*, on Carroll Street (☎ & fax 07/892 2827; dorms ①, rooms ②–③) is the most organized and well-equipped of the **lodges**, with a spa pool, track transport and rooms ranging from basic dorms and doubles to appreciably more modern and comfortable en-suite rooms. Kitchens are well-equipped, and mountain bikes are available to rent ($30 a day), as is tramping and climbing gear. *Ski Haus*, also on Carroll Street (☎07/892 2854; tent sites $8, dorms ①, rooms ②, B&B ④), covers similar ground, with reasonable dorms and rooms with shared bathrooms, plus gear rental and a popular bar and restaurant. Alternatives include the brand-new *Pukenui Lodge*, SH4 (☎07/892 2882, fax 892 2900; tent sites $8, dorms ①, rooms ③), with a spacious lounge, great mountain views, small dorms and plain, comfortable doubles; and the *National Park Lodge and Motel*, back on Carroll Street (☎07/892 2993 & 0800/861 861, fax 892 2846; dorms ①, units ③), offering marginally the cheapest dorms and some ageing but perfectly functional motel units.

The Town
Though initially founded as a way station on the main Auckland–Wellington train line, it owes its continued existence to skiers and trampers bound for the adjacent Tongariro National Park, and paddlers heading for the **Whanganui River Journey** (see p.231). With the limited accommodation at Whakapapa Village, visitors to

MOUNT RUAPEHU SKIFIELDS

When the snows come, two-thirds of New Zealand's skiers turn their attention to Mount Ruapehu, home to the North Island's only substantial skifields. Every weekend from around late June to early November, streams of cars pile out of Auckland and Wellington (and pretty much everywhere in between) for the four-hour drive to either **Whakapapa**, the more extensive skifield on the northwestern slopes of Mount Ruapehu, or **Turoa**, easily beaten into second place on the south side. Both fields have excellent reputations for pretty much all levels of skier and the orientation of volcanic ridges lends itself to an abundance of dreamy, natural half-pipes for snowboarding. Only club members with four-wheel-drives battle their way to the tiny **Tukino** field on the eastern flank of the mountain.

Neither of the main fields has public **accommodation** on site. Ski clubs maintain dozens of chalets at the foot of the main tows in Iwikau Village, but casual visitors (unless they can get invited to a lodge as a guest) have to stay 6km downhill at Whakapapa Village (see p.286) or 22km away at National Park (see p.290). Almost everyone skiing Turoa stays in Ohakune (see p.292).

WHAKAPAPA

With over thirty groomed runs, a dozen major chair lifts and T-bars and the dedicated learners' area of Happy Valley, **Whakapapa** is New Zealand's largest and busiest **ski area** (information ☎07/892 3738, up-to-the-minute details on the Snowphone, ☎07/892 3833). It offers the longest North Island **season** (usually late June–early Nov and sometimes through to Christmas), 675 vertical metres of snow, plus snow-making equipment, ski schools, a huge gear-rental operation, crèche ($35 a day) and a couple of cafés. **Access** is along the toll-free, sealed Bruce Road. Chains are sometimes required, in which case a fitting service miraculously appears beside the road. Car parking is free and there is a free courtesy bus from the lower car parks. Shuttle buses run from Whakapapa Village, National Park, Turangi and Taupo.

Lift passes cost $49 a day, $221 for five days, and there is a First Timer's Pack ($48) that includes gear rental, an hour-and-a-half lesson and a learners' area lift pass. On-site **ski rental** for one day costs $26–36, $47 for snowboard and boots, and there are discounts for rentals of five or more days. Several places in National Park also offer competitive rates and a wide selection of equipment.

TUROA

Turoa (information ☎06/385 8456; premium-rated Snowphone, ☎0900/99444) has developed in a much more controlled fashion than Whakapapa, and offers the country's greatest vertical drop – 720m – a skiable area almost as extensive as Whakapapa's with wide groomed trails particularly aimed at intermediate skiers and, at Ohakune, the region's best après ski. The **season** usually runs from mid- to late June through to mid-October and it is usually possible to drive straight up the sealed, toll-free, 17km **access** road from Ohakune without chains, and park for nothing. Again, the skifield operators will fit chains ($20) when needed, or you can rent from shops in Ohakune for a little less and fit them yourself. Several shuttle buses run up from Ohakune, charging $10–15 return. **Lift tickets** go for $48 a day or $208 for a five-day pass. Ski **gear** can be **rented** for $25 a day, $40 for snowboard and boots, and there is a "Learn to Ski" package ($45) that includes gear, an introductory lesson and learner tows.

Tongariro, Ngauruhoe and the northern side of Ruapehu are all but forced to stay in National Park, using shuttle buses (see box on p.287) to get to Whakapapa and the Tongariro tramps.

In National Park itself, there is precious little to do except for a few adventure activities. To go **mountain biking**, sign up with Rock Hard Mountain Bike Tours (☎07/892

2938) for their full-day Tongariro Forest Crossing ($70, with your own bike $35), designed for intermediate riders, or one of their other trips for various abilities. Go For It Tours, based in the train station (☎07/892 2705), rent out mountain bikes for $10 an hour and also operate guided trips through rivers and along muddy tracks on motor-bikes or two-rider **quad bikes** (2hr–full day; $50–246). Some 6km north of National Park, Plateau Outdoor Adventures, Uwha Road, Raurimu (☎07/892 2740) offer an astonishing range of activities, including **rafting** ($50–85), abseiling ($35–50), caving ($50) and waterfall **kayaking** ($50), to name just a few.

Eating and drinking

All lodges do **breakfast** for a small charge and *Ski Haus* also serves dinner, but for main meals you're better off at the licensed *Eivans Off Piste Café and Bar*, on the cor-ner of Carroll Street and SH4, a wayside diner that still dishes up stalwarts such as BLTs and wedges but also serves classy gourmet **sandwiches** and salmon-and-veg-etable filo, all with fab mountain views. Steaks, pub grub and dedicated drinking and pool-playing are to be had at the typically rowdy *Schnapps Bar*, on SH4, next to Pukenui Lodge, or you can get **fish 'n' chips** and a jug of beer at the *National Park Hotel* on Carroll Street.

Ohakune

OHAKUNE, 35km south of National Park, welcomes you with a huge carrot, cel-ebrating its position at the heart of one of the nation's prime market-gardening regions. This is easily forgotten once you are in town among the chalet-style lodges and ski-rental shops geared to cope with the massive influx of winter-sports enthusi-asts who descend from mid-June to early November for the **skiing** at Turoa (see box on p.291), 20km north up Ohakune Mountain Road.

Arrival and information

Ohakune is strung between two centres. There is no longer a branch line from Ohakune Junction but it retains the **train station** and a cluster of hotels and rest-aurants mostly serving the skiing fraternity. The commercial heart lies 2km to the southwest, where InterCity **buses** on the Hamilton–Taumarunui–Wanganui run (daily except Sat) stop outside the **visitor centre**, 54 Clyde Street (Nov–June Mon–Fri 9am–5pm, Sat & Sun 9am–3.30pm; July–Oct Mon–Fri 9am–5pm, Sat & Sun 10am–4pm; ☎06/385 8427, fax 385 8527), which has all the general information you'll need and sells both bus and train tickets. For more specific tramping information, the mountain weather forecast, and a detailed low-down on local flora and fauna, make for the **DOC field centre** at the foot of Ohakune Mountain Road (Mon–Fri 9am–2.30pm, until 5pm during school holidays; ☎06/385 8578, fax 385 8128).

There are no regular buses around Ohakune, so you might want to **rent a car** from Rimu Park Lodge, 27 Rimu St, for around $55 a day, or a **mountain bike** from the Powderhorn Chateau, 194 Mangawhero Terrace ($25 per half-day, $35 full-day), where you can also rent rollerblades ($5 per hour), ice axe and crampons ($20 a day), and walking boots ($15 a day).

Accommodation

Ohakune has stacks of **places to stay**, but many of them close outside the ski season and are packed once the snows arrive – when prices get hiked up by around thirty per-cent more than those quoted here. Enough places are open in summer to satisfy most budgets, starting with the *YHA*, 15 Clyde St (☎ & fax 06/385 8724; dorms ①, rooms ②), which is small, well maintained and convenient for bus travellers. Good budget beds can also be found at the *Alpine Motel Lodge*, 7 Miro St (☎ & fax 06/385 8758; lodge ②, units ④, chalets ⑤), with two-, three- and four-berth lodge rooms, studio units and fully self-contained chalets sleeping up to eight, all with access to a spa and drying room. A similar range of accommodation, but in a more appealing setting, is on offer at *Rimu Park Lodge*, 27 Rimu St (☎ & fax 06/385 9023; dorms ①, rooms ②, cabins ③, units ④, chalet ⑤), a 1914 villa containing spacious six-bunk dorms and plain but comfortable doubles; the grounds are dotted with simple cabins, en-suite units with TV and fridge but no kitchen, and a fully self-contained chalet sleeping up to four. If you are here for the skiing, some of the cheapest beds are at the excellent *Station Lodge*, 60 Thames St (ski season only; ☎06/385 8797; ①), in the former stationmaster's house right by the train station. For B&B you can't beat the very cosy and welcoming *Villa Mangawhero*, 60b Burns St (☎06/385 8076; ④), while top of the range is the *Powderhorn Chateau*, 194 Mangawhero Terrace (☎06/385 8888, fax 385 8925; ⑥), an immense log-cabin style edifice with a lovely indoor swimming pool, sun beds, and en-suite rooms, the best with balconies and mountain views.

Campers have a choice of the *Ohakune Motor Camp*, 5 Moore St (☎06/385 8561; tent sites $8, cabins ③), right on the edge of the bush but still central, and the DOC's toilets-and-water *Mangawhero Campsite* ($4), 1.5km up Ohakune Mountain Road from the field centre.

The Town and around

For four short months Ohakune comes alive, bars and restaurants swing into action, everyone makes their money for the year and then shuts up until next season. Consequently it is pretty quiet in summer, but once the snows have melted, the trails are open for tramping, mountain biking and horse trekking.

Unlike at Whakapapa, the Turoa chairlifts don't run outside the ski season, but the 17km Ohakune Mountain Road makes an impressive drive through stands of ancient rimu and provides access to a number of fine **walks**, including the Round the Mountain Track (see p.289). The pick of the shorter trails are: the **Mangawhero Forest Walk** (3km; 1hr 30min), a short and well marked loop track from opposite the DOC field centre; the **Mangawhero Falls Track** (400m; 5min) to a spectacular waterfall, starting 13km up the Mountain Road; and the **Old Blyth Track** (11km; 4–5hr), which begins 7km north of the field centre and follows a historic mountain access route through rare red beech and alpine bog to Waitonga Falls, from where you can contour around to the Ohakune Mountain Road and walk back down, or retrace your steps.

Most of the walking tracks, and any inside the bounds of the national park are off-limits for **mountain biking**, but you can coast 17km down Ohakune Mountain Road on The Ruapehu Descent (Nov–June; $25; ☎06/385 8257), or rent a bike (see "Practicalities" below) and head 12km east to the forest roads around Rangataua and the trails around Rotokura Lakes; consult the DOC or the visitor centre for more details.

A less arduous approach is to let **horses** take the strain at *Ruapehu Homestead*, 4km east on SH49 (☎06/385 8799), which runs back-country trail rides through bush and rivers (2hr; $35), as well as easier trips for the less experienced.

Eating and drinking

During the ski season, Ohakune Junction is very much the happening place to spend your evenings. In summer though, when hardly any of the half-dozen restaurants, bars and clubs bother to open, you're better off in **central Ohakune**, where you can indulge in succulent gourmet kebabs from *Mountain Kebabs*, 29 Clyde St, where chicken, lamb, seafood and vegetarian fillings are doused with a stack of tasty sauces.

Utopia, 47 Clyde St (closed Mon in summer), is the ideal spot for idling away an hour or two over great coffee and sumptuous all-day brunches, while *Sassi's*, at the *Alpine Motel Lodge*, produces standard steak, chicken and fish dishes at reasonable prices.

At the **Junction**, the *Powderhorn Chateau* harbours two restaurants: the winter-only fine-dining *Powderkeg* (☎06/385 8888; licensed), serving the likes of venison with a juniper and port glaze, and Italian-style lamb shanks; and the more modest brasserie/bar, where you can fight for a prized place on the balcony with mountain views. In winter, *Margarita's*, 5 Rimu St, do warming and tasty enchiladas, tostadas and other faux-Mexican favourites; *Bartribe*, 20 Thames St, is a justly popular hangout, and *Hot Lava*, 30 Thames St, kicks up a storm until the early hours.

South to Mangaweka

Travelling south from the Tongariro National Park along SH1, you descend from the volcanic plateau into the rich **farming country** of the Rangitikei District. Driving alongside the Rangitikei River, you seldom see the water, which has carved down through some of the youngest and softest rock in New Zealand to leave off-white cliffs as the only evidence of the river's course. This is prime farming country – a fact reflected in the character of the region's largest town, **Taihape**, an agricultural service centre of only passing interest. The only other reason to stop between Tongariro National Park and Palmerston North (see p.237) is to visit the **Army Museum** at Waiouru, 27km east of Ohakune on the fringe of the park, or to go **rafting** and **bungy jumping** at Mangaweka.

Waiouru and the Army Museum

The **Desert Road** (SH1) and the roads flanking the western side of Ruapehu, Ngauruhoe and Tongariro meet at **WAIOURU**, an uninspiring row of service stations and tearooms which has sprung up on the bleak tussock plain beside New Zealand's major army base. The serene view of the mountains from here can be fabulous but the peace is often disturbed by troop movements and even target practice.

The place to take cover is in the three concrete bunkers of the **QEII Army Memorial Museum** (daily 9am–4.30pm; $8), a showcase of national military heritage from the New Zealand Wars through the Anglo-Boer and two World Wars to New Zealand's involvement in Vietnam. Mannequins in regimental regalia set in lifeless dioramas do little to prepare you for the impact of the *Roimata Pounamu* ("Tears on Greenstone") **wall of remembrance**, where a veil of tears symbolizes mourning and cleansing as it streams down a curving bank of heavily veined greenstone tiles while the name, rank and place of death of each of the 33,000 New Zealanders who have died in the various wars is recited. A twenty-minute audio-visual presentation sets the scene for the rest of the chronologically arranged exhibits, which are brought to life by oral histories, including some heart-rending ones that recount the bungled Gallipoli campaign of World War I. The emphasis is small-scale and personal: one particularly affecting case contains artefacts made by soldiers in the trenches – cribbage boards, chess sets and a cigarette holder that completely encased the cigarette so it could be smoked without risk of the enemy seeing the telltale glow.

Taihape

For want of any more interesting features, **TAIHAPE**, 30km south of Waiouru, pronounces itself "New Zealand's one and only Gumboot City", and there is ample evidence of the said boots among the hardware stores and farm-supply shops that line the main street. Keen gardeners have been known to spend days here, visiting the four main showpiece **gardens** of Titoki, Rongoiti, Waitoka and Kiri Kiri – all within about half an hour's drive and costing around $7 entry each. Opening hours vary considerably, and your best bet is to obtain details and directions from the **visitor centre**, in the Town Hall, Hautapu Street (daily 9am–5.30pm; ☎06/388 0350, fax 388 1090).

For most it is enough to stop for a **bite to eat**, best done at the wonderful *Brown Sugar Café*, Huia Street (☎06/388 1880; closed Tues), which serves excellent light meals, cakes and coffee during the day, as well as dinner on Friday and Saturday evenings (booking advisable). If you need to **stay**, there's the *Taihape Motels*, on the corner of Kuhu Street and Robin Street (☎06/388 0456; ④), *Papa Pottery and B&B*, 24 Huia St (☎06/388 0318; ④), or the summer-only *Abba Motor Camp* (Oct–April; ☎06/388 0718; tent sites $8, cabins ②), 2km north of town on the spine-chillingly named Old Abattoir Roar Road.

Mangaweka

The weathered form of a DC3 beside SH1, 24km south of Taihape, is about the only indication that there might be a reason to stop in the dilapidated hamlet of **MANGAWEKA**, scattered across a plain high above the Rangitikei River. The *Aeroplane Café* is cheap, basic and an obvious lure, but there is more of interest at the adjacent service station, from where Rangitikei River Adventures (☎06/382 5747 & 0800/655 747) operate **bungy-jumping** and some top-quality rafting. "High Time Bungy" ($120, including T-shirt) involves a heart-stopping eighty-metre plunge from a bridge over the Rangitikei River, followed by an ascent in a water-balanced chair lift. **Rafting** ranges from family-oriented fun rafting down a gentle stretch of the river (1hr $25, half-day $40), through a full-day run down the considerably more boisterous Grade V whitewater section ($99), to an overnight camping safari that starts late in the afternoon, drifting down through the remote Utiku Gorge to a riverside campsite then paddling out next morning ($50).

Rangitikei River Adventures also run *Adventure Backpackers* (☎06/382 5747 & 0800/655 747; dorms ①), right in Mangaweka, and the riverside **accommodation** at *River Valley Lodge* (same number; dorms ①, rooms ③). To escape the rafting fraternity, make for the excellent farmstay at *Mairenui Farm Holidays*, Ruahine Road (☎ & fax 06/382 5564; old house ③, retreat ④, homestead ⑥), where you have a choice of simple rooms in the old house, self-contained accommodation among 700-year-old totara in the secluded retreat, or lovely en-suite B&B rooms in the homestead; tasty evening meals start at around $25. **Campers** should head for the *Mangaweka Motor Camp*, by the river 1.5km north of town (☎07/382 5730; $5 per tent).

travel details

Trains

From National Park to: Auckland (2 daily; 5hr 30min); Ohakune (2 daily; 30min); Palmerston North (2 daily; 3hr 30min); Waiouru (2 daily; 1hr); Wellington (2 daily; 5hr 30min).

From Ohakune to: Auckland (2 daily; 5hr 30min); Wellington (2 daily; 5hr).

From Rotorua to: Auckland (1 daily; 4hr); Hamilton (1 daily; 2hr).

Buses

From Kawerau to: Rotorua (2 daily; 45min); Whakatane (2 daily; 45 min).

From National Park to: Auckland (1 daily; 5–6hr); Ohakune (1 daily; 30min); Wellington (1 daily; 5–6hr).

From Ohakune to: Auckland (1 daily; 5–6hr); Wellington (1 daily; 5–6hr).

From Rotorua to: Auckland (9 daily; 4hr); Gisborne (2 daily; 4hr 30min); Hamilton (9 daily; 1hr 30min);

Kawerau (2 daily; 45min); Lake Waikaremoana (Mon, Wed & Fri; 3hr 15min); Murupara (Mon, Wed & Fri; 45min); Taupo (4 daily; 1hr 30min); Tauranga (4 daily; 1hr 10min); Wairoa (Mon, Wed & Fri; 4hr 15min); Whakatane (2 daily; 1hr 30min).

From Taihape to: Auckland (4 daily; 7hr); Taupo (4 daily; 2hr); Turangi (4 daily; 1hr 10min); Wellington (4 daily; 3–4hr).

From Taupo to: Auckland (8 daily; 4–5hr); Palmerston North (5 daily; 4hr); Rotorua (4 daily; 1hr 30min); Turangi (1 daily; 1hr); Wellington (5 daily; 6hr).

From Tokoroa to: Hamilton (4 daily; 1hr 40min); Taupo (4 daily; 40min).

From Turangi to: The Chateau (3 daily; 1hr).

Flights

From Rotorua to: Auckland (4–6 daily; 45min); Christchurch (3–4 daily; 2hr); Wellington (6 daily; 1hr 10min).

From Taupo to: Auckland (2–4 daily; 50min); Wellington (2 daily; 1hr 10min).

CHAPTER FIVE

THE COROMANDEL, BAY OF PLENTY AND EASTLAND

The long coastal sweep to the east of Auckland is split into three distinct areas, among them two of the most popular summer-holiday destinations on the North Island; the other is one of the least-visited parts of the country, whatever the time of year. Heading east from Auckland by road you'll first cut across at least a portion of the **Hauraki Plains**, a wedge of dairying land at the foot of the Coromondel Peninsula, its two principal towns serviced by buses. Principally a transit point to more exciting places, the area nonetheless holds a few pleasant surprises for anyone willing to dawdle for an extra day or so. In the town of **Te Aroha**, you can languish in a private **spa bath** that's fed by natural soda water in a laid-back thermal reserve at the foot of a mountain before taking in the astounding **views** from the summit; near **Paeroa** there are pleasant **walks** in the lush **Karangahake Gorge**, once the scene of intensive gold mining; and at **Waihi** you can watch a vast open-cast **gold mine** in operation or savour the golden sands on one of the country's safest oceanside **beaches**.

Directly across the Hauraki Gulf from Auckland (and accessible by road or by ferry from the city), the long and jagged **Coromandel Peninsula** is blessed with some of the country's best sandy beaches and a gorgeous climate. But if this conjures up images of overcrowding and overdevelopment, then think again. This is an outdoors kind of place, offering great coastal scenery, solitude, walks to pristine beaches, and tramps in luxuriant mountainous rainforest. The two coasts are markedly different, the

---

ACCOMMODATION PRICES

Accommodation listed in this guide has been categorized into one of nine price bands, as set out below. The rates quoted represent the **cheapest available** double or twin **room** – except for category ①, which are per-person rates for a dorm bed; fees for **tent sites** and **DOC huts** are also per-person, unless otherwise stated.

① under $20 per person	④ $60–80	⑦ $140–180
② under $40 per room	⑤ $80–100	⑧ $180–240
③ $40–60	⑥ $100–140	⑨ over $240

For more on accommodation, see p.33.

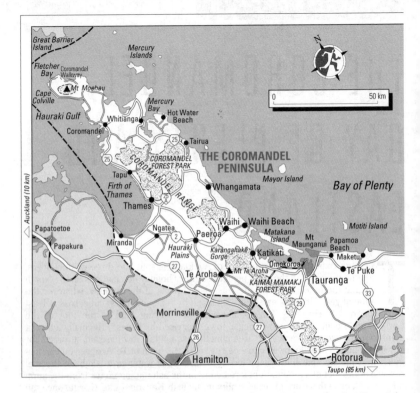

east supplying the softer, more idyllic tourist beaches and short coastal walks, while the **west** has a far more rugged and atmospheric coastline, plus easier access to the volcanic hills and ancient kauri trees of the **Coromandel Forest Park**. The scattered towns are generally less interesting than the scenery, working best as bases from which to explore the landscape. The chief access point to the peninsula from the west and south is **Thames**, a small town rich in gold mining history, while the northernmost town of any significance is the tiny **Coromandel**, set in rolling hills beside an attractive harbour. The principal towns of the east are **Whitianga**, in the north, and **Whangamata** in the south, both of which are blessed with long, luxurious, sandy beaches. Near Whitianga attractive coastal walks lead to a series of isolated beaches, among them the unusual **Hot Water Beach**, where natural thermal springs bubble up through the sand and you can create your own open-air spa pool right on the edge of the Pacific Ocean. Nearby, **Cathedral Cove Marine Reserve** acts as a playground for dolphin-spotters and snorkellers, and access point to some magnificent geological formations.

Further to the east, the broad sweep of the **Bay of Plenty** has the best climate on the North Island, making it a fertile fruit-growing region and another popular resort area. Reasonably unspoiled, it offers great surf beaches, a good variety of offshore activities and walks in the forest-clad hills of the inland **Kaimai-Mamaku Forest Park**. On top of that it's home to the country's fastest-growing city, **Tauranga** in the western Bay of Plenty, the region's most popular resort town of **Mount Maunganui**, and the historic

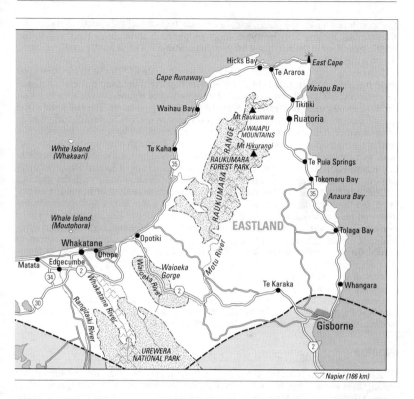

▽ Napier (166 km)

and sunny **Whakatane** to the east. Of the three, Tauranga is the most modern and vigorous, with a thriving café and bar scene, while Mount Maunganui has suffered from too much attention, becoming decidedly over-commercialized. Whakatane has the most in the way of natural features, including boat excursions to the fuming, volcanic **White Island**.

Contrasting with these two regions is the splendid, rugged and isolated **Eastland**, once a wealthy part of New Zealand but today run-down and sparsely populated. With a dramatic coastline, and a rich and varied Maori history, this region provides a taste of a secluded way of life long gone in the rest of the country. At its easternmost point – the **East Cape** – is a lighthouse that overlooks East Island, the first place in the country to see the sunrise. All of the region's small communities, each with its own distinctive personality, are dotted along the coastline, against the dramatic backdrop of the **Waiapu Mountains**.

The Hauraki Plains

From whichever direction you approach the Coromandel Peninsula by road, you'll pass through at least a part of the fertile **Hauraki Plains**, a wedge of land at the peninsula's southern end. Bordered by the Firth of Thames to the north, SH27 to the west, Waihi to the east and Te Aroha to the south, the region is a mixture of rich farmland in the west (once a swampy plain), and, in the east, transitional hill country between the Coromandel Ranges and the coast. Most people rush through on their way to the scenic splendour to the north and further east, missing out on at least a couple of sights worth a minor detour.

Journeying east from Auckland along the scenic route of "The Seabird Coast" you meet the plains at **Miranda** (see p.116), whereas approaching from the west along the more direct SH2, you'll first strike the tiny settlement of **Ngatea**, worth a fleeting visit for the curiosity value of a warehouse crammed with rock crystals. The real jewel in the crown, though, is the small and often-ignored Victorian town of **Te Aroha**, tucked away at the southern extremity of the plains. A detour here allows for a relaxing soak in natural hot springs of soda water at the foot of Mount Te Aroha after tackling a two-hour walk to the mountain's summit for breathtaking views. There's also access to tramps in the **Kaimai–Mamaku Forest Park**, which covers the rugged Kaimai Range, stretching from the Karangahake Gorge in the north almost as far as Rotorua in the south.

The hub of the plains is **Paeroa**, at the meeting-point of routes north, south, east and west, but the town has little to show for it apart from a smattering of accommodation. Between here and Waihi, though, is the scenic river valley of **Karangahake Gorge**, a leafy landscape with a few good walks along the banks of the rushing Ohinemuri River and past the skeletal remains of old gold workings, plus a short scenic train journey to **Waihi**. En route to the Bay of Plenty, Waihi is the plains' biggest town and site of a massive opencast gold mine, where huge quantities of gold-bearing quartz are still extracted. Just a few kilometres further east are the Pacific Ocean surf and golden sands of the popular **Waihi Beach**.

Getting around by public **transport** is pretty easy since the two main towns of Paeroa and Waihi are serviced daily by the major bus companies, though you might find yourself backtracking a little, depending how far south or east you go before moving on.

Ngatea

The first settlement you'll reach heading east on SH2 is tiny **NGATEA**, set amid green rolling hills some 70km from Auckland. At the junction with the southbound SH27, some 11km before the town, road signs announce the start of a scenic route to the Bay of Plenty, traversing the flat plains before tackling the hill country at the southern end of the Coromandel Range and dropping to the coast. In Ngatea itself is **Wilderness Gems**, at 13 River Rd (daily 9am–5pm; free), signposted just before the river bridge, 200m off the main road. This warehouse-type building is stuffed with rock crystals from all over the world, including those found on the nearby Coromandel Peninsula. The main room contains a wealth of polished stone and marble ornaments (candlesticks, napkin rings, ashtrays, vases, carved animals, and so on), wire baskets of rock gathered from Mexico, USA, India and Australia, plus jewellery crafted from carved jade and bone. Through a glass door and window you can catch glimpses of people at work carving and grinding in the workshop. The most interesting exhibit, though, is the dark and pokey Fluorescent Room, where you can watch a range of minerals being hit by long- and short-wave UV light, producing some curious visual effects.

From here the highway continues to Paeroa (see p.303), where you can branch off on SH26 northwards to the Coromandel Peninsula or southwards to Te Aroha.

Te Aroha

At the southern end of the plains on SH26, 45km from Ngatea and past Paeroa, is the small Victorian spa town of **TE AROHA**, with enough sights to fill a half-day or so. The town sits in the heart of dairy country at the foot of **Mount Te Aroha** (952m): sweeping views from summit, which is accessible by bus or on foot, take in the Bay of Plenty and stretch across to Mounts Ruapehu and Taranaki. To the east of town, the prominent hills of the **Kaimai-Mamaku Forest Park** are criss-crossed by gold miners' tracks.

The town itself was founded in 1880 at the furthest navigable extent of the Waihou River and the following year rich deposits of gold were found on Mount Te Aroha, sparking a full-scale **gold rush**, with the reefs of gold-bearing quartz producing handsome yields until 1921. Te Aroha's attractive hilly Domain contains a unique and low-key **thermal reserve** fed by naturally hot soda water and equipped with a series of simple modern spa baths and, within a stone's throw, an extensive museum. The only drawback is the strong and biting winds that assault the town from time to time.

The Town

Te Aroha is set amid rich farming plains beside the Waihou River, its centre and tree-filled Domain creeping up the foothills of the formidable Mount Te Aroha. The town's main street is Whitaker Street and everything of interest is close to, or on, it.

Without doubt the focal point in town is the **Hot Springs Domain**, which by the 1890s was New Zealand's most popular mineral spa, frequently compared with those of Vichy or Baden as people flocked to enjoy the therapeutic benefits of its waters, the hottest in the country at 38–41°C. Today many of the original Victorian buildings have fallen into disrepair and a restoration programme is planned for the near future, but in the meantime a modern complex of **private spa pools** and one of the original **hot pools** are open to the public (Mon–Wed 11am–9pm, Thurs–Sun 11am–10pm; 30min soak $6; booking essential, ☎07/884 8717). To find the complex, just follow your nose – a slightly smoky yet not unpleasant smell emanates from the soda baths. The **spa office** (daily noon–9pm) is next to the row of individual baths, each enclosed by a round wooden hut containing a hot shower. At one end of the line stands the rather dilapidated **No. 2 Bathhouse**, built in 1878 over a slightly cooler spring; though now rather dilapidated, you can still descend the steel-railed steps into the large communal bath. A ten-minute soak followed by a prolonged spa bath is said to extract polluting heavy metals from your system – shower first to open up your pores and be sure to drink plenty of water afterwards, to help counteract the deydrating effects of the mineral-rich water. Just above the baths is the temperamental **Mokena Geyser**, which spurts to impressive heights on good days, going off roughly every half-hour.

An old sanatorium, just below the spa baths and in front of the bowling greens, houses the town **museum** (Oct–April Sat & Sun 1–4pm; May–Sept Sat & Sun 1–3pm; other times by arrangement with visitor centre; donation requested).There are three exhibit-packed rooms and two finely decorated Royal Doulton Victorian lavatories. A large part of one room is given over to a selection of wind-up gramophones, another to a collection of black-and-white photos of the town and its people, plus a chemical analysis of the local soda water. There is also memorabilia of an old silent movie called *Tilly of Te Aroha*, made when the film industry was in its infancy, and a racy picture for its time.

Back towards the town centre from the Domain exit on Boundary Street you'll find the 1926 **St Mark's Anglican Church**, on the corner of Church Street and Kenrick Street, whose claim to fame is that it contains the oldest organ in the southern hemisphere. Built in England in 1712 by Renatus Harris, after Queen Anne petitioned Parliament to raise taxes so that the finest pipe organs of the day could be put into ten London churches, this is the sole survivor of the original ten. This particular organ has led something of a charmed life: brought to New Zealand in 1926, it was restored by an Auckland firm in 1985 to its original specification – most of the casework is English heart oak, with fine carving done at Grinling Gibbons's workshop. If you can get a group together and are prepared to make a small donation, an organ recital can be arranged through the visitor centre.

WALKS IN AND AROUND TE AROHA

Among a number of short **walks** that start in Te Aroha by far the most rewarding is the climb to the **summit** of **Mount Te Aroha**. The **Te Aroha Mountain Track** (8km return; 3hr 30min), starts from just behind the Mokena Geyser in the Domain and climbs steeply through native bush, zigzagging up a well-defined path to a viewing platform at **Whakapipi** (or Bald Spur), before dipping to a small saddle. From here, the final climb (which can be muddy and slippery after rain) becomes increasingly arduous, and you'll need to use your hands to pull yourself up in places, but the stunning views make it all worthwhile. To return, follow the **Tui Mine Track**, which drops through a stark, heavily mined landscape to link with the Tui Road back to town in one direction, and with the **Tui–Domain Track** in the other, a pleasant bushwalk past a waterfall back to the Domain. If the thought of an uphill slog right to the top is too much, the **sector** as far as the **Whakapipi Lookout** (2km; 50min) gives good views over the town and its surroundings.

Other walks of varied grades and duration lie south of Te Aroha in the **Waiorongomai Valley**, part of the **Kaimai-Mamaku Forest Park**. Formerly the scene of intense mining activity, several tracks following historic miners' trails are described in the leaflet *Guide to the Waiorongomai Valley* ($3), available from Te Aroha DOC office. Access is from a car park on the Waiorongomai Loop Road, which is signposted 4km south of town off the Shaftesbury Road – but note that this is an extremely rugged area punctuated by old mines and shafts that are dangerous to enter. **Overnight hikes** should only be attempted by experienced, fit and well equipped trampers; hut tickets can be bought from the DOC office in Te Aroha (see below).

Mount Te Aroha

Legend has it that **Mount Te Aroha** was named by a young Arawa chief, Kahumatamomoe, who climbed it after losing his way in the region's vast swamp while on his way home to Maketu in the Bay of Plenty. Delighted to see the familiar shoreline of his homeland, he called the mountain *Te Aroha*, meaning "love", in honour of his father and kinsmen. The laziest (and quickest) way to reach the **summit** is to take the **guided bus trip**, which leaves from the visitor centre on demand (Wed, Sat & Sun; 2hr; $14, minimum 10 passengers; book through visitor centre), but in fine weather only; plenty of time is allowed at the summit for a picnic and photos. The more energetic might prefer to **walk** (see box above).

Practicalities

At the Whitaker Street entrance to the Domain is the **visitor centre** (Mon–Fri 8am–5pm, Sat & Sun 10am–3pm; ☎ & fax 07/884 8052). Among the spa buildings on the Domain's top path is a well-organized **DOC office** (Mon–Fri 9am–4pm; ☎07/884 9303), which has a photographic display of Te Aroha's past and plenty of leaflets on the surrounding area.

For a small place, Te Aroha has a reasonable choice of **accommodation**. The *YHA* on Miro Street, off Burgess Street (☎07/884 8739; office open 5–8.30pm; dorms ①, room ②), about fifteen minutes' walk from the visitor centre, is in an attractive cottage on the lower slopes of Mount Te Aroha, with great views and a pretty garden. The hostel has just two bunkrooms and one twin room, and a charming kitchen stocked with plenty of basic cooking ingredients. Beside the Domain is the *Te Aroha Motel*, at 108 Whitaker St (☎07/884 9417; ④), with well-kept, comfortable units. A couple of kilometres west of town, on the way to Hamilton (SH26), is the small but modern *Four Seasons Backpackers*, 21 Waihou Rd (☎07/884 9306; dorms ①, rooms ②), while about 2km further west is the delightful *Te Aroha Holiday Park*, 217 Stanley Rd, off SH26

(☎07/884 9567; tent sites $8.50, on-site vans ②, cabins & flats ③), set among well-established oak trees with a few free-range chickens strutting around and free use of bikes.

The best **restaurant** in town is the *Domain House Restaurant*, in the Domain, where lunch and dinner is served in a lovely 1906 colonial building with broad verandahs; dishes such as chicken breast filled with camembert on fettuccine and pork fillets on wild rice with prune and red wine sauce go for $20–25. If this sounds a little rich, try the cosmopolitan *Café Banco*, 174 Whitaker St (daily 10am–5pm), which occupies a magenta-coloured former bank building. **Italian flatbreads** form the basis of most meals, dressed with a range of ingredients and rounded off with good, strong coffee. On Friday nights, things are livened up by jam sessions and there's **live jazz** on Sunday afternoons. The low-key *Mokena Restaurant*, in a rambling old wooden hotel at 6 Church St (☎07/884 8038; licensed), is a big hit with locals, offering evening **smorgasbords** (from 6pm; $25; book ahead) of fresh, home-cooked fare.

Finally, if you're cooking for yourself, take a short trip west to the **Swiss Sausage Co.**, Stanley Road, signposted from SH26 (Mon–Sat 10am–5pm). Here, in a cheery blue wooden villa with yellow trim, a Swiss family produce and cure their own meat to make a range of gourmet sausages.

Paeroa and the Karangahake Gorge

Heading north again, routes to the Coromandel Peninsula and the Bay of Plenty converge at **PAEROA**, 21km from Te Aroha and 32km south of Thames. A small, rather dreary town straddling the banks of the Ohinemuri River, Paeroa was once a significant port, marking the farthest point that ships from Auckland could travel inland along the Waihou and Ohinemuri rivers. There are few reminders of this illustrious history, and these days its claim to fame is as the place of origin of New Zealand's ubiquitous soft drink, **Lemon and Paeroa** (L & P), exploiting a source of natural mineral water discovered here in the nineteenth century. Undaunted by the harsh reality that the local bottling plant has closed and the product sold today is an artificial version made in Auckland, a giant brown L & P bottle stands at the junction of SH2 and SH26, greeting those entering town from the south.

On the main road, opposite the junction with Hall Street is the pleasant but limited **Paeroa Museum** (Mon–Fri 10.30am–3pm; $2), run by the local historical society. Avoiding the usual mind-boggling clutter, its neatly displayed exhibits cover the town's history, early shipping and gold mining in the Karangahake Gorge. Of particular interest is a huge collection of Royal Albert bone china, while among the few Maori artefacts is a stack of collection drawers containing tools and ornaments: stone adzes, cutting tools, bone fish-hooks and carved *tiki* (pendants).

Best given a wide berth, and certainly not worth the $4 admission fee, is the well-publicized **Maritime Museum**, a desultory collection near the site of the original jetty whose dubious attractions are exemplified by the rotting remains of an old paddle steamer, inexplicably marooned on a riverbank within the grounds.

Karangahake Gorge

With a car, a far better use of your time is a detour into the leafy tranquillity of the magnificent **Karangahake Gorge**, scene of the Coromandel's first gold rush in 1875. Independent miners, armed only with picks and sluice pans, were quickly superseded by large companies that could afford the powerful equipment needed to extract the metal. Today it's hard to envisage such frenetic activity in this scenic spot. The steep-sided gorge begins 8km east of Paeroa along the narrow, snaking continuation of SH2 as it traces the Ohinemuri River to Waihi. The **Karangahake Gorge Historic Walkway** covers 7km, but you can also tackle shorter sections of 2km and 5km; all these routes are described in a leaflet ($1) that's available from Paeroa visitor centre (see below). Accessed from three entry points along the gorge (each with a car park), the walkway follows parts of the old rail line, passing a waterfall and remnants of the gold fields.

At the eastern end of the gorge is the tiny village of **WAIKINO**, where an information centre (daily 10am–4.30pm), next door to the old train station, has displays on local history and walks in the area. From here you can also take a short scenic train trip to Waihi and back through the upper reaches of the Karangahake Gorge, on the Goldfields Vintage Railway (see p.305 for details).

Eight kilometres south of the Karangahake Gorge lies another entry point to the scenic **Kaimai-Mamaku Forest Park**, this time through the rugged **Waitawheta Valley**, whose own dramatic gorge was extensively logged for majestic kauri around the turn of the century. Access to the valley is along the Waitawheta Camp Road, which branches off from the Owharoa Falls midway along the Karangahake Gorge. At the end of the road turn into Franklin Road, which culminates in a car park, from where tracks follow old logging routes and rivers through a diverse mix of regenerating bush and podocarp forest, all described in DOC's *Guide to the Waitawheta Valley* leaflet. The moderately easy **Kauri Loop Track** (8km; 2hr 30min) climbs through forest to two giant kauri trees that somehow escaped the axe, before descending steeply past dramatic bluffs to the car park.

Practicalities

Paeroa's **main street** is Belmont Road (SH2) and the town centre is concentrated into a small area wedged between the Domain and the junction with SH26. InterCity **buses** between Thames and Hamilton (daily except Sat) drop-off near the **visitor centre**, at 1 Belmont Rd (Oct–April Mon–Fri 9am–5pm, Sat & Sun 10am–3pm; May–Sept Mon–Fri 9am–5pm; ☎07/862 8636). The office is well stocked with bumf on the Coromandel Peninsula, and takes bus bookings. You can also buy a can of L & P here.

There are a couple of reasonable **places to stay**. The *Paeroa Hotel*, on Belmont Road, opposite the visitor centre (☎07/862 7099; ③), is a big nineteenth-century wooden building with twenty clean and simple rooms, each with a washbasin; the hotel also has its own café and bar. There's little to choose between the motels, but try the pleasant *Casa Mexicana Motel*, two minutes' drive away on the western fringes of town, at 71 Puke Rd (☎07/862 8216; ④), which has six spacious units and a spa bath.

For a bite to eat you're limited to fairly standard, inexpensive cafés and takeaways. *Delanie's*, in the *Paeroa Hotel*, serves lunch and dinner (closed Mon), with **pasta** dishes for under $10 and other mains for under $20. The licensed *Tui Coffee Lounge*, 18 Belmont Rd, dishes up hearty **breakfasts** and lunches (Mon–Sat) and dinners (Fri only), including delicious country-fried chicken. The *Four Seasons*, 70 Belmont Road (closed Mon), is a regular Chinese and Kiwi takeaway which also has a BYO restaurant (lunch Thurs & Fri, dinner Tues–Sun). Two doors down is the small and very cheap *Rosie's Coffee Shop* (daily 6am–4.30pm), proffering standard Kiwi fare and hearty breakfasts, but for a substantial feed of **steak** and veggies (around $12.50), head for *The Steakhouse*, at 136 Normanby Rd, the eastern continuation of Belmont Road/SH2 (lunch Wed–Sat; dinner daily except Tues; BYO).

Waihi and Waihi Beach

The town of **WAIHI** lies at the intersection of SH25 and SH2, 21km east of Paeroa. Principally a mining town of 5000 inhabitants, Waihi is built around a huge opencast gold mine that began operations in 1892, ceased in 1952, but has cranked up again in recent years. The town also has a good **museum**, a scenic train ride through the nearby **Karangahake Gorge** and a couple of great places to eat.

And, if you're in need of some light relief, the popular surf beach of **WAIHI BEACH** lies 12km east of town, off SH2: its long, thin strip of golden sand stretches for 8km and is one of the safest ocean beaches in the country.

The Town

Gold was first discovered at Waihi in 1878, in a reef of gold-bearing quartz, but it was not until 1889 that a boom began, with the first successful trials in extracting gold using cyanide solution at Karangahake. By 1908 Waihi was the fastest-growing town in the Auckland Province.

At the eastern end of town, **Martha Hill Mine** still produces gold (and silver) to the value of about one million dollars a week, and is one of the few working mines in New Zealand that you can visit. **Guided tours** (Mon–Fri, according to demand; 75–90min; free; book ahead through Waihi visitor centre – see below) take visitors around the opencast gold mine and processing areas, providing background history and details of the environmental work the company is supposedly doing.

Even if you decide against the gold mine tour, it's worth taking five minutes to follow the short **Gold mine Walkway**, signposted beside the visitor centre. Passing the imposing 1901 concrete pump house – which once housed the steam engines and machinery needed to continuously pump water away from the workings as they sunk to a depth of nearly 600m – a gentle climb leads to a lookout with an eerie bird's-eye view over the vast rust-coloured pit, etched by tunnels and shafts. Laden trucks wind their way up and down, dwarfed by the sheer scale of the earthworks to the size of Dinky toys, while the noise of the mechanical diggers labouring at the bottom are strangely muffled by the distance. Meanwhile, out of sight, a two-kilometre-long conveyor belt transports about 15,000 tonnes of ore a day through a tunnel to the treatment plant just outside town.

Heading back along the main road towards Paeroa, you'll come across the **Gold-mining Museum & Art Gallery** (Mon–Fri 10am–4pm, Sat & Sun 1.30–4pm; $2), on Kenny Street, just off the roundabout. More than anything else, this is a showcase for the fine and intricately detailed models on mining themes that were made between 1976 and 1986 by Tom Morgan, a ship's engineer, in his spare time. You can't help but admire the effort that went into the working model of a miniature stamp battery, which makes almost as much racket as the original, or the delightful working model of Waihi's pump house. There are also some evocative dioramas depicting miners at work, interesting ephemera about their lives, and historical accounts of the seminal Waihi Strike of 1912. The small art gallery in the same building exhibits the work of local and invited artists.

At the western end of town, the ramshackle wooden station at the end of Wrigley Street is home to the **Goldfields Vintage Railway**, which operates scenic rail trips in summer to Waikino in the Karangahake Gorge (daily 11am & 2pm, with extra services on Sun, returning from Waikino 45min later; 20min each way; $5 one-way, $8 return; ☎07/863 8251). An old steam engine pulls 1930s carriages over a stretch of track built between 1900 and 1905 by gold-mining companies; travelling alongside SH2, you get spectacular views of the Ohinemuri River.

Practicalities

InterCity **buses** pull up at Rosemont Road Service Station, as do Whangamata Tours (☎07/865 7088) shuttle services. The **visitor centre** is at the eastern end of Seddon Street, right by the mine and beside an old creeper-covered pump house on a hill (daily: Oct–April 9am–5pm; May–Sept 9am–4.30pm; ☎07/863 6715). There are several **places to stay** in Waihi itself and a few others at the beach (see p.306). A five-minute walk from town, the *Waihi Motor Camp*, 6 Waitete Rd, off Seddon Rd (☎07/863 7654; tent sites $9, cabins & flats ②–③), enjoys a quiet creekside setting, while the *Waihi Motel*, on Tauranga Road/SH2 (☎07/863 8095; ④), two minutes' walk south of the centre, has good-sized units and a spa pool; and the central *Chez Nous B&B*, 41 Seddon Ave (☎07/863 7538; ③), offers quiet rooms in a pleasant modern house, and dinner by arrangement.

At the western end of town, on Waitete Road, the pleasant *Waitete Orchard* **winery** and **café** (daily 8.30am–5.30pm, later in summer) serves great-value, freshly cooked snacks, light meals, fresh fruit juices and naturally brewed beer; they use organic produce wherever possible and sell organic fruit and vegetables, too. A favourite is their authentic Indian samosas, served with salad ($3.50), while on summer evenings they organize **barbecues**, supplying food which you cook yourself on a terrace overlooking the orchard ($10). Just up the road is an excellent licensed and BYO **restaurant**, *Grandpa Thorn's*, 4 Waitete Rd (evenings only: Oct–April Tues–Sun; May–Sept Tues–Sat; book ahead, ☎07/863 8708); diners travel from as far afield as Tauranga and Hamilton to eat high-quality country-style Kiwi cuisine (around $20 a main course), such as rack of lamb with leek and mint compôte, in this log-cabin setting.

At **Waihi Beach** there's another **visitor centre** at 33 Wilson Rd (☎07/863 5349; Mon–Fri 9am–5pm, Sat & Sun 10am–4pm) and a few **accommodation** places strung along the waterfront Seaforth Road. Try the small *Shalmar Motel*, 40 Seaforth Rd (☎07/863 5439; ⑤), near the shops, or the secluded *Bowentown Holiday Park* (☎07/863 5381; tent sites $9, cabins & flats ②–③), which sits right at the southern end of the beach.

The Coromandel Peninsula

A long, broad thumb jutting out between Auckland and the Pacific Ocean, the **Coromandel Peninsula** is a rugged region of scenic splendour, fringed with beautiful surf and swimming beaches that bask in a balmy climate. The forested mountainous interior is sparsely populated and a haven for tramping and horse trekking, while the northern section of the peninsula is a world apart – a virtually uninhabited, craggy landscape of long-deserted dairy farms reverting to bush, traced by a three-hour **coastal track**. The two coasts are starkly different: on the **west** coast, cliffs drop sharply to the sea; while the gentler **east** coast harbours sweeping white-sand beaches and sheltered coves ripe for exploration. The wild character of the west has protected it, leaving it relatively untouched, but the east is marred by pockets of over-development. The whole region is distinguished by the **pohutakawa** trees that line the west coast, erupting in a blaze of rich red from October to December, and a **rock** of a gorgeous deep-rose colour, commonly known as **Coromandel Pink** and most noticeable on exposed bluffs.

Despite this scenic splendour, there's not a hell of a lot to do here, though it's easy to spend a few days exploring the forested **Kauaeranga Valley** behind Thames; **Mercury Bay** on the east coast, which bags some of the best coves and sandy beaches, including Hot Water Beach, along with the **Cathedral Cove Marine Reserve** and the **Mercury Islands**, where you can snorkel, dive or swim with dolphins in crystal-clear water, and the **Coromandel Walkway** at the northernmost point. For a change of pace, take a ride on the narrow-gauge **Driving Creek Railway**, near Coromandel township. Cultural pursuits are limited to an excellent **bone-carving** course in Whitianga and historical displays of the region's **gold-mining history** in museums on the west coast. The peninsula is only lightly populated, with a few small towns scattered along each coast, chiefly **Thames**, the southern gateway from Auckland and rich in gold-mining history, and the smaller **Coromandel township** on the west coast; **Whitianga**, on Mercury Bay, and the surfie hangout of **Whangamata** on the east.

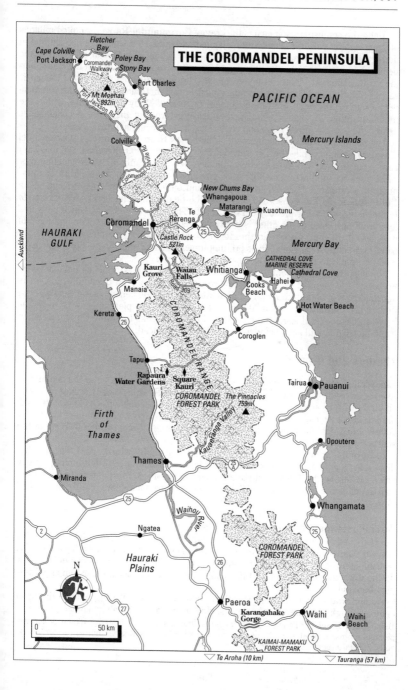

Along the peninsula's spine runs the craggy **Coromandel Range**, sculpted millions of years ago by volcanic activity into a jagged and contorted skyline, since clothed in dense rainforest. To Maori, the range represents a canoe, with **Mount Moehau**, at the peninsula's northern tip, as its prow, and Mount Te Aroha (see p.302) in the south, bordering the Hauraki Plains, as its sternpost. The **summit** area of Mount Moehau is sacred Maori-owned land, the legendary burial place of Tama Te Kapua, the commander of one of the Great Migration canoes, *Te Arawa*. Many of the **walks** within the mountain range are badly maintained and overgrown, but there are excellent ones nearer the coast, a mix of bush and coastal tracks of varying length.

The peninsula is accessible by road, air and ferry **from Auckland**. Air Coromandel flies to Whitianga, while the Coromandel Ferry Service (☎09/866 7084; $26 one-way) runs from Hobson Wharf to Coromandel town (or 7km south, with a connecting bus, when tides are too low). InterCity **buses** provides a regular loop service from Thames, north to Coromandel, across to Whitianga and back down and across to Thames: a **Peninsula Loop Pass** costs $40, including shuttle to Hahei; the fare from Auckland to Rotorua, incorporating the loop service is $79. The main road, SH25, which runs in a loop from one coast to the other is twisty but generally in good condition and most of it is sealed. Beyond Colville in the north, **roads** are poorly maintained and can be treacherous (most car-rental firms prohibit travel on these roads); you'll probably have a better time travelling by bus or on an organized tour.

Not surprisingly, the peninsula is one of the North Island's principal holiday spots, becoming the scene of frenetic activity **around Christmas**, but thankfully more manageable the rest of the summer. During **winter** much of the peninsula is deserted, even though the **climate** remains mild for most of the year. The pleasantest time to visit is between October and April, but try to avoid the two weeks following Christmas when it can be hard to find accommodation – or book well ahead.

Thames and around

Sandwiched between the Firth of Thames and the Coromandel Range is the peninsula's main service town, the small and rather dull **THAMES**, which mostly serves as a transit place, with a variety of accommodation and a few reasonable places to eat. Its gold-mining heyday having long since passed, Thames supports a population of just under 7000, a good deal of employment being supplied by the Toyota assembly plant at the southern end of town.

Most of the attractions within the town relate to its **gold-mining past**. The first big discovery of gold-bearing quartz was made in a creek bed in 1867, but mining activity tailed off during the 1880s, and none remained after 1913. More interestingly, within easy reach is the **Kauaeranga Valley**, a popular centre for visitors to the Coromandel Forest Park and often busy at weekends.

Arrival, information and accommodation

InterCity and Newmans **buses** drop off outside the **visitor centre**, which is in the Old Railway Station on Queen Street (Oct–April daily 8.30am–5pm; May–Sept Mon–Fri 8.30am–5pm, Sat & Sun 9am–4pm; ☎07/868 7251). The centre has stacks of literature on the town and the Coromandel Peninsula, and deals with accommodation and transport bookings.

Accommodation in Thames is rather scattered, most of it lying outside the town centre, though it's generally of a good standard and there's plenty of choice.

Brian Boru Hotel, cnr Pollen St & Richmond St (☎07/868 6523). Impressive 1868 building with plentiful rooms, many of them themed and most sharing facilities. Regular murder-mystery weekends. Standard rooms ③, suites ④.

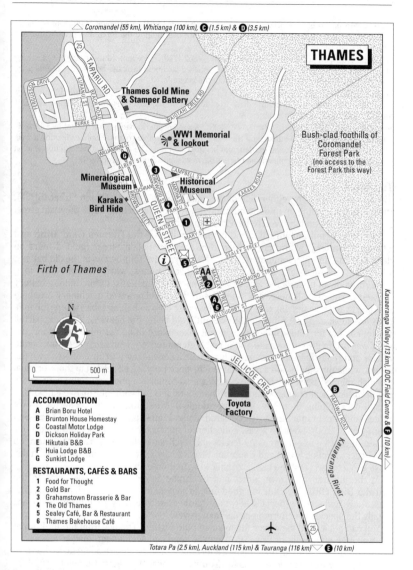

Coromandel (55 km), Whitianga (100 km), **C** (1.5 km) & **D** (3.5 km)

THAMES

Thames Gold Mine
& Stamper Battery

WW1 Memorial
& lookout

Bush-clad foothills of
Coromandel
Forest Park
(no access to the
Forest Park this way)

Mineralogical
Museum

Historical
Museum

Karaka
Bird Hide

Firth of Thames

N

*Kauaeranga Valley (13 km), DOC Field Centre & **F** (10 km)*

0   500 m

Toyota
Factory

ACCOMMODATION
A Brian Boru Hotel
B Brunton House Homestay
C Coastal Motor Lodge
D Dickson Holiday Park
E Hikutaia B&B
F Huia Lodge B&B
G Sunkist Lodge

RESTAURANTS, CAFÉS & BARS
1 Food for Thought
2 Gold Bar
3 Grahamstown Brasserie & Bar
4 The Old Thames
5 Sealey Café, Bar & Restaurant
6 Thames Bakehouse Café

Totara Pa (2.5 km), Auckland (115 km) & Tauranga (116 km)   **E** (10 km)

Brunton House Homestay, 210 Parawai Rd (☎07/868 5160). A fine, large Victorian villa within easy walking distance of the centre. Three rooms share one guest bathroom. Other facilities include swimming pool and tennis court. Dinner is also available ($20); room rates are at the lower end of this price code. ⑤.

Dickson Holiday Park, Victoria St (☎ & fax 07/868 7308). Large and well-run campsite in a pretty valley 3.5km north of the centre. Excellent facilities and bus pick-up from Thames. Tent sites $8, backpacker cabins ①, flats & units ②–④.

Coastal Motor Lodge, on SH25, 1.5km north (☎0800/843 663). A complex of pleasant "cottage" units and modern A-frame chalets (all self-contained), overlooking the Firth. Predictably, the best views are from the pricier chalets. ⑤–⑥.

Hikutaia B&B, on SH26, about 10km south (☎07/862 4710). Excellent-value, grand yet welcoming old country house with four big double rooms (shared facilities) near the bottom end of this price code. Full cooked breakfast; swimming pool in the grounds. ④.

Huia Lodge B&B, 62 Kauaeranga Valley Rd (☎07/868 6557). Peaceful setting right in the valley, amid bush and pasture, a 10-minute drive from town. Two modern en-suite units, dinner available for $15. Free transport from Thames. ④.

Sunkist Lodge, 506 Brown St (☎07/868 8808). An atmospheric backpacker hostel in a historic building; dorms hold 4–10 bunks, and there are also a few double rooms. Facilities include a well-equipped kitchen, sun deck and garden, and baggage storage. The owner is a mine of information on both the Coromandel Peninsula and Great Barrier Island. Dorms ①, rooms ②.

The Town

The town is laid out on either side of the main shopping street, Queen Street (SH25), the buildings heading up into the hills and down to the shoreline. Since the main street is only about 1.5km long, you're never far from the centre.

The most significant attraction within the town itself is the **Thames Gold Mine and Stamper Battery**, at the northern end of town on Pollen Street (guided tours on demand Oct–March; minimum of 2; $5). The informative tour begins in the old battery, where the machines are fired up for about two minutes, which is more than long enough (you can understand why deafness was an occupational hazard among battery workers). The place is noisy and smelly, with the diesel-powered machinery crushing the quartz and transferring tiny particles by water onto a shaking table, where the minerals are separated according to their weight, gold being the heaviest. The next part of the tour is not for claustrophobics, since it takes place in an old mine next door: the shaft was originally cut by hand and is just high enough to clear a miner's head. Sound effects and realistic-looking mannequins create a convincing portrayal of life down the mines, while the guides add a personal touch, since they are all related to those original Cornish miners. Back outside, the complex also contains a photo museum with over a hundred historical photographs of the Thames miners, all with informative captions.

Still on a mining theme is the **Mineralogical Museum**, on the corner of Brown Street and Cochrane Street (Oct–March daily 11am–4pm; rest of year Tues–Sun 11am–3pm; $2.50), housing a vast collection of quartz, crystals, rocks and fossils displayed in cases – one for geology freaks only. Neither is the **Historical Museum**, on the corner of Pollen Street and Cochrane Street (daily 1–4pm; $2), and stuffed with displays of Victoriana and the like, anything to write home about.

At the junction of Brown Street and Cochrane Street, a boardwalk leads to the **Karaka Bird Hide**: high tide is a good time to spot migratory birds such as knots, godwits, shags and terns, especially between October and February. An information board details the species which frequent the mangroves.

You can get a good view over the town and the Firth of Thames from the **lookout** at the war memorial; walk or drive up Waiotahi Road and Monument Road to a car park just below the monument, then follow a short flight of stone steps leading up to the viewpoint. Another excellent lookout is the **Totara pa**, near the Totara Cemetery on SH25 at the southern end of town. This was a stronghold of the Ngati Maru *iwi* (tribe) until 1821, when a party of 2000 warriors, led by the infamous Hongi Hika, outwitted them by pretending to retreat and then re-attacking, thus catching the defenders by surprise.

Kauaeranga Valley

The steep-sided **Kauaeranga Valley**, to the east of town and reached along a scenic road snaking beside the river, gives access to walks in the Coromandel Range. A shuttle **bus** leaves from the visitor centre (daily 1pm; $34 return) or you can take a taxi (see "Listings" below). To get here **by car**, head out of the southern end of Thames, along Parawai Road, which becomes Kauaeranga Road. Thirteen kilometres along you reach the **DOC office** (daily 8am–4pm; ☎07/868 6381), where you can stock up on maps, buy hut tickets and examine displays on early kauri logging in the valley. From here a loop track (4km; 1hr) leads to a working **scale model** of a kauri driving dam, the type once used extensively in this forest. A further 9km brings you to the road-end, where several walks (20min–2 days) begin, all linked to the **Kauri Trail**, which spans a spectacular landscape of pinnacles, bluffs and gorges, and leading through varied stands of forest (including some original giants such as rata, rimu and the occasional kauri) to old and rickety kauri dams. Note that some tracks are closed because of their dangerous state of repair, so check with DOC before setting off. For more information, consult the *Kauaeranga Kauri Trail* DOC leaflet ($1).

The shortest track is to **Billygoat Landing** (1.5km return; 20min), giving excellent views of the 180-metre Billygoat Falls. The best and most accessible walk is to the **Pinnacles** (6km one way; 3–4hr), involving quite a bit of steep climbing through regenerating bush to a jagged summit (759m) with great views of the bush, mountains and southern Coromandel coastline, and serviced by the enormous **Pinnacles Hut** (Category 2; 80 bunks; $12). There are also a couple of remote, basic DOC **campsites**: one near the Pinnacles Hut and another at Billygoat Clearing (both $6).

Eating and entertainment

Central Thames is packed with inexpensive but pleasant places to **eat** (most of them open daily), while a couple of friendly **bars** provide musical entertainment over the weekends, but that's as far as the nightlife goes.

Food for Thought, 574 Pollen St. A cheap café for continental cuisine and vegetarian dishes – mostly pastries, cakes and pastizzi (Lebanese pies). Mon–Fri 7.30am–5pm.

Gold Bar, 404 Pollen St. The place in town for a night out. There's a good selection of wine, plus an all-day menu of snacks, salads and pasta for under $10, and rustic dinners for about $20. Occasional live jazz, blues or rock on Fri & Sat evenings.

Grahamstown Brasserie & Bar, 719 Pollen St (☎07/868 9178). Popular, friendly and airy, with eclectic food and a garden bar. The menu ranges from light snacks to reasonably priced dinners. Lunch & dinner daily; book ahead for Sun brunch; DJ or live music Fri & Sat nights.

The Old Thames, cnr Pollen St & Pahau St. Licensed restaurant popular among families for its broad range of moderately priced seafood, steaks, pizzas and generous desserts. Daily from 5pm.

Sealey Café/Bar & Restaurant, 109 Sealey St. Laid-back place in an attractive, high-ceilinged house with a pleasant courtyard. Light lunches (under $10) and dinner mains (around $20) revolve around generous helpings of steak, meat and fish. Daily from 11am; BYO.

Thames Bakehouse Café, 326 Pollen St. Another inexpensive place for snacks, light meals – and cooked breakfasts for around $7.50. Mon–Fri 7am–4.30pm, Sat & Sun 7am–3.30pm.

Listings

Airlines Air Coromandel (☎07/866 4016) fly twice daily between Auckland and Whitianga, calling at Thames, Coromandel town, Pauanui and Matarangi, plus Great Barrier Island and Tauranga.

Banks All major banks have branches along Pollen St, with ATMs.

Bike rental and repairs Paki Paki Bike Shop, 710 Pollen St (☎07/868 8311), will supply plenty of advice about cycling on the peninsula and sometimes have bikes for rent at reasonable rates.

Buses Newmans (☎0800/777 707) links Thames with Auckland, Tauranga and Whitianga; InterCity (☎0800/686 862) serves these destinations plus Rotorua, Hamilton, Coromandel town and Whangamata.

Car rental Rent-a-Dent (☎07/868 8838) allow their budget cars onto the peninsula's roughest roads.

Medical treatment Thames Hospital, Mackay St (☎07/868 6550); Thames Medical Centre, 817 Rolleston St (☎07/868 9444).

Petrol Mobil, Queen St; Mackay St Motordome, 401 Mackay St.
Police 730 Queen St (☎07/868 6040).
Post office Pollen St, between Sealey St & Mary St.
Swimming Thames Pool is on the corner of Pollen St & Grey St ($2.50; ☎07/868 8441).
Taxis Thames Gold Cabs (☎07/868 6037).

North to Coromandel

From Thames, SH25 snakes 55km along the grey rocky shoreline of the **"Pohutukawa Coast"** past a series of tiny, sandy bays, most with little more than a few houses and maybe a campsite. Hills and, occasionally, sand-coloured cliffs rise dramatically from the roadside.

The first point of interest is reached from the small community of **TAPU**, 19km from Thames. At the far end of town is a turn-off along the narrow, unsealed but manageable **Tapu–Coroglen Road**, one of the most scenic routes in the country, traversing the Coromandel Range on its way to the east coast. A refreshing stop at any time of the year, the extensive **Rapaura Water Gardens** (daily 10am–5pm; $6) lie hidden away against a backdrop of bush, 6.5km along the road. Numerous paths meander through this lush, cleverly landscaped "wilderness" of bush and blooms, punctuated by ponds, a stream and a waterfall. Here and there, philosophical messages urge you to stop and think awhile, and it's easy enough to spend a day doing just that – though you could get around most of the gardens in about ninety minutes. One of the highlights is a three-tiered waterfall, reached by a well-kept track from the car park at the entrance (15min); picnicking is confined to the car parking area (which has plenty of trees, grass and space away from the cars), and a broad grassland area around a large pond, on the way to the waterfall. The road continues 3km on to the (easily missed) **"square kauri"** signpost near the road's summit, opposite a rough lay-by and just before a small bridge. Steep steps through bush (175m; 10min) lead to this giant of a tree (1200 years old, just over 41m high and 9m wide), whose unusual, angular shape saved it from loggers. From here it's another rough and windy 19km **across the peninsula** to Coroglen, linking with the main road between Whitianga and Whangamata, or 9.5km back to Tapu and the continuation of SH25 north.

Back on SH25 the road lurches inland soon after Kereta (about 12km from Tapu), snaking over hills to the roadside **Manaia-Kereta Lookout** (206m), which has great views of the northern peninsula: the majestic Moehau Range and Coromandel Harbour. Beyond, Great Barrier Island may be visible on a clear day – a giant block of rock with vertical cliffs rising from the sea. Ducking and diving in and out from the rocky shoreline and the blue-green vistas of the Firth of Thames, SH25 continues for 20km to the turn-off to **Road 309**, 3km south of Coromandel, which cuts **across to Whitianga** by way of a few roadside attractions, all within 8km of Coromandel (see "East to Whitianga", p.316).

Coromandel Town

The last town of any substance heading north is the small but atmospheric **CORO-MANDEL**, huddling beneath high, craggy hills at the head of Coromandel Harbour and known to most visitors simply as the jumping-off point for the **Coromandel Walkway** (see box on p.315), 57km away at the peninsula's northern tip. It's worth taking time, though, to enjoy this atmospheric old gold town with its **scenic rail trip** into the local hills. Even if you don't intend tackling the walkway, Coromandel makes a good base from which to explore the jagged landscape of the **northern peninsula**, either on your own or on a guided trip.

The town is named after a British Admiralty supply ship that called into the harbour in 1820 to obtain **kauri** spars and masts and to extend Captain Cook's brief survey of the Hauraki Gulf. A more mercenary European invasion was precipitated by the 1852 discovery of **gold**, near Driving Creek, in the northern part of town, but modern visitors will be more interested in the discovery of three **supermarkets**, a BNZ bank, a cluster of **cafés** and a broad range of **accommodation**.

The sights, though, are few, and Coromandel is really little more than a staging post en route to the more rugged country further north, or a stopover before striking **east to Whitianga**, via the continuation of SH25 (see p.316) past the deserted beaches of Whangapoua and Kuaotunu, or the more rugged Road 309 (see p.316).

Arrival, information and transport

Buses pull into the car park opposite the visitor centre on Kapanga Road. The Coromandel Ferry Service (☎09/866 7084) runs from downtown Auckland to Coromandel Harbour, or when the tides are too low, to Te Kouma, ten minutes' drive away and linked by buses. The combined **visitor centre** and **DOC office** is at the northern end of Kapanga Road, just over the bridge (Mon–Fri 9am–5pm, Sat & Sun 10am–noon; ☎07/866 8598, fax 866 7285).

Carter Tours (☎07/866 8045) run reasonably priced **guided trips** to local points of interest, or will drop you at your chosen destination; see box on p.315 for details of transport to the start of the Coromandel Walkway at Fletcher Bay. The only **car-rental** firm in town is Rent-a-Dent, 5 Kapanga Rd (around $40 a day; ☎07/866 8822), which also allows its cars onto the unsealed roads north of Colville; if the office is closed, enquire at the *Pepper Tree Restaurant* next door.

Accommodation

For a small place, Coromandel offers a good range of **places to stay**, from a campsite in the town centre through to a luxurious lodge in an idyllic setting a few kilometres north. Most are within easy walking distance of the town centre.

Buffalo Lodge, Buffalo Rd, signposted north of town past the Gold Stamper Battery (☎ & fax 07/866 8960). Luxurious, award-winning accommodation in an architect-designed house set high up in the bush, with superb views across the Hauraki Gulf. Run by two Swiss artists, the decor in the three en-suite double rooms is modern and elegant; two of them have private decks. There's also an exceptional restaurant here (see "Eating and entertainment", p.315). ⑦.

Celadon House Motel & B&B, 5 Oxford Terrace, about 1km from town (☎07/866 8058). This charming self-contained A-frame on a bush-clad hillside, with town and harbour views, operates as a motel. There are three double rooms and a 2-bed bunkroom. The separate B&B section has three en-suite rooms (two with sun decks). Motel ⑤, B&B ④.

Coromandel Colonial Cottages, 1737 Rings Rd, 1.5km north of town (☎07/866 8857). Tranquil, luxury cottages sleeping 2–6. Excellent facilities include a swimming pool and BBQ area. Good value for money. ⑤.

Jacaranda, 3km south on SH25 (☎07/866 8002). A modern house in farmland offering backpacker accommodation (in dorms and rooms), plus B&B. Rooms are extremely comfortable and spacious, breakfasts are made from organic ingredients, and dinner is available on request ($25). Backpacker dorms ①, rooms ②; B&B ④.

Rose Cottage B&B, Pagitt St (☎07/866 7047). Good value and fairly central place opposite the Historical Museum. Stay in the attractive, old kauri homestead (shared bathroom facilities) or in an en-suite double in a pleasant separate building. ③.

Tidewater Tourist Park, 270 Tiki Rd (☎07/866 8888). The best and most central campsite in town, incorporating a YHA associate hostel and set in large, leafy grounds by the harbour. Tent sites $6, backpacker dorms ①, cabins, flats & units ②–④.

Tui Lodge, 600 Whangapoua Rd, just off SH25 (☎07/866 8237). A ten-minute walk from town, this is the best-value backpackers in town. Set in a relaxed, rambling house by an orchard, perks include free linen, laundry, tea and coffee, fruit (in season), and use of bikes. Tent sites $6, dorms ①, chalet & rooms ②.

The **White House Backpackers**, cnr Rings Rd & Frederick St, 1km north of visitor centre (☎07/866 8468). Small and friendly, this hostel occupies two attractive white houses in bushland. Daily bus tours to peninsula attractions can be arranged, plus bike rental and horse treks. Dorms ①, rooms ②.

The Town and around

The town centre, such as it is, spreads along the main road, with a few old buildings left from gold-mining days. From the south, SH25 becomes Tiki Road and then splits into two: to the left is Wharf Road, which skirts the harbour; to the right you immediately enter the heart of the town, on Kapanga Road, lined with shops and cafés. A couple of blocks further on, it becomes Rings Road, before heading northwards out of town as Colville Road.

About 300m north of the visitor centre is the small **Coromandel Historical Museum**, at 841 Rings Rd (Oct–March daily 10am–4pm; rest of year Sat & Sun only 1.30–4pm, plus weekdays on request, ☎07/866 7251; $2). Based in the old School of Mines (1898), this is a mishmash of domestic items and mining memorabilia, including a number of evocative black-and-white photographs from early mining days.

The main attraction in the immediate vicinity is **Driving Creek Railway**, Driving Creek Road, 2.5km north of town (daily 10am & 2pm, extra trains during holidays; 1hr return; $9; book ahead on ☎ 07/866 8703). Built mostly by hand over twenty years, this is the country's only narrow-gauge mountain railway, the brainchild of an eccentric local potter and rail enthusiast who wanted access into the clay-bearing hills. The track is only 381mm wide and carries specially designed, articulated diesel trains, which climb 120m over a distance of about 3km. The rewards of this leisurely, commentated trip are spectacular views and extraordinary feats of engineering, including a series of viaducts, spirals and tunnels, a zigzag section, and a unique steel "double-decker" viaduct straddling a deep ravine, which you cross no fewer than four times, as well as embankments built of wine and beer bottles. At the end of the line is a lookout point with panoramic views of Coromandel town, over the Hauraki Gulf and Waiheke Island, and across the Firth of Thames to the Hunua Ranges. The journey starts and ends at the workshops, kilns and sheds, where you can see various types of pottery: stoneware and earthenware items for the home and garden, and sculptures made from terracotta that has been wood-fired to produce a variety of subtle colours.

Around 1.5km south is the turn-off to the **Gold Stamper Battery**, another 500m or so along Buffalo Road (Oct–April daily 10am–5pm; May–Sept Mon–Fri 10am–4pm; guided tour $4), where the 100-year-old machinery is operated briefly to demonstrate the processing of gold. Outside is a pleasant garden scattered with old bits of machinery and picnic tables by a stream where, for an extra $5, you can try your hand at gold panning.

Eating and entertainment

Eating out on a budget is hardly difficult in Coromandel, with several good **cafés** touting for your business. The well-heeled are also catered for by the upmarket **gourmet** dinner **restaurant** at *Buffalo Lodge*. Evening **entertainment** is restricted to live bands (summer weekends only) at the *Pepper Tree* bar.

Buffalo Lodge, Buffalo Drive (☎07/866 8960). This outstanding, prize-winning restaurant serves international and vegetarian dishes in an elegant and relaxed setting. A three-course meal will set you back around $55. Thurs–Sun evenings only, from 6pm; bookings essential; BYO.

Coromandel Café, 36 Kapanga Rd, opposite the *Pepper Tree*. Cheap snacky place, pretty standard but pleasant enough. Dec–March daily 8am–4.30pm, rest of year closed weekends.

Karmic Enchilada Café, 24 Wharf Rd, near junction with Tiki Rd. Small and laid-back, with tasty pizza, salads, Mexican and vegetarian meals. Good espresso and a small peaceful garden to sit in. Oct–April 8.30am–9pm; May–Sept 9am–5pm.

Pepper Tree, 31 Kapanga Rd. A very popular bar and restaurant, with main courses for around $20 and an all-day snack menu ($10 or less); eat indoors or on the verandah. Open daily; live bands on weekend nights in summer.

The Success Café, Kapanga Rd, next door to *Coromandel Café*. An intimate place with smart white tablecloths and covered outdoor dining at the back. Plenty of seafood and steak, mostly around the $20 mark. Open all day; licensed & BYO.

Top Pub, *Coromandel Hotel*, 611 Kapanga Rd, cnr Te Tiki St. An evening bistro, known for its seafood, but also serving steaks and other meat dishes as a set three-course meal for under $20. Closed Sun in winter (May–Sept).

North to Fletcher Bay and Port Charles

The landscape **north of Coromandel** is even more rugged than the rest of the penin-sula, its green hills dropping down to seemingly endless beaches, clean blue sea and white surf. The route is lined with ancient pohutukawa trees, creating a blaze of red blooms from the end of October until just after Christmas. **Camping** is prohibited along this stretch of coast, except in a few commercial sites between Coromandel and Colville and the odd official DOC campsite in bayside recreation reserves.

From Coromandel, the road snakes for some 20km along the coast, passing the idyl-lic *Shelly Beach Holiday Park* (☎07/866 8988; tent sites $6, dorms ①, cabins, flats & units ②–④), on a sheltered beach 5km from Coromandel and just off the main road,

---

THE COROMANDEL WALKWAY

The **Coromandel Walkway** (7km; 3hr one-way) begins at the far end of the beach in Fletcher Bay, and is pretty easy going, with posts clearly marking the route. The most scenic section of the walk is between Poley Bay and Stony Bay, and a popular option is to be dropped off at **Stony Bay** for a **return walk to Poley Bay** (10km return; 3hr).

TRAILHEAD TRANSPORT
Carter Tours (☎07/866 8045) operate daily minibus **drop-offs** from Coromandel town to Fletcher Bay or Stony Bay for around $35, as well as walkway **day-trips** ($50), dropping you at Fletcher Bay, then collecting you at the other end in Stony Bay some three hours later, or as arranged. The only regular **shuttle bus** from Coromandel to Fletcher Bay is run by *TheWhite House* (Oct–March only: Mon, Wed & Fri at noon; $14 each way; book-ings essential on ☎07/866 8468, or through the visitor centre).

ACCOMMODATION
Accommodation at **Fletcher Bay** consists of a DOC **campsite** ($4), with flush toilets, cold showers and a short sweep of sandy beach (safe for swimming); and a small, com-fortable **hostel**, *Fletcher Bay Backpackers* up on a hill overlooking the beach (bookings essential, ☎07/866 8989; ①). At the other end of the walkway, there's another DOC **campsite** in a beachside reserve at **Stony Bay** ($4), also with flush toilets and cold showers.

THE ROUTE
The track from **Fletcher Bay** heads off into a no-man's-land, first following gentle coastal hills that alternate between pasture and bush, then giving way to wilder terrain as you head further south, past a series of tiny bays. Several hilltop **vantage points** punctuate the walk, yielding spectacular vistas of the coast and Pacific Ocean beyond, before the track dips once more into pockets of dense bush. From the pretty, rocky inlet of **Poley Bay** a steep, short climb out cuts through regenerating bush to **Stony Bay**, a sweep of pebbles with a bridge across an estuary and safe swimming.

equipped with a camp store and dinghies for rent. Then it cuts inland, where the tiny settlement of **COLVILLE** is set in a quiet green valley surrounded by spectacular hills. These days it has little more than a post office and a combined general store and BYO café, which serves snacks and evening meals, and makes a good place to stock up on food for the Coromandel Walkway and to check on the state of the road north of Port Jackson.

Beyond Colville the road is unsealed, and becomes narrower, rougher and dustier the further north you go. You're also likely to encounter cattle trucks and their trailers en route, though your nail-biting moments will be compensated for by glimpses of tiny bays flanked by shelves of volcanic grey rock. The scenery becomes even more dramatic as you approach **PORT JACKSON**, with the hills rising straight from the shore. Port Jackson has only two houses and a one-kilometre sandy crescent of beach, safe for swimming and backed by a grassy DOC reserve, where you can **camp** ($4). From here the road really deteriorates and is subject to landslides, so seek local advice before heading out this way. Some 35km from Colville, the road finally rolls into **FLETCHER BAY**, the starting point of the **Coromandel Walkway** (see box on p.315).

PORT CHARLES and **Stony Bay** on the tip's eastern shore, are serviced by two perilously twisty gravel roads – one across the Coromandel Range from Coromandel, the other traversing the Moehau Range from just beyond Colville – but both are best travelled on a **guided tour** from Coromandel with Carter Tours (☎07/866 8045). At Port Charles, 6km south of Stony Bay, is a tiny hillside **hostel** overlooking the bay, *Paradise Backpackers* (☎07/866 6922; dorms ①, rooms ②), with free use of mountain bikes and a fishing boat; you can also get here by boat from *Fletcher Bay Backpackers* (see p.315).

East to Whitianga

Two highly **scenic roads** cross the mountains from Coromandel east to Whitianga: the more direct snaking, gravel **Road 309** (33km) branches off 3km south off town, while the main **SH25** climbs through forested hills before switchbacking down to the coast, 46km away.

The first stop along **Road 309** is a track to **Castle Rock**, signposted 5km from Coromandel, just around the corner from the unmissable Waiau Waterworks park. A steep climb (2km; 1hr 30min) to the 521-metre summit of this old volcanic core is rewarded by fantastic views of Whangapoua peninsula on the east coast and, just offshore, the Mercury Islands. A further 2.5km along Road 309, the **Waiau Falls** crash over a rockface into a pool below. Finally, about 500m further is a car park and easy bush track to the magnificent **Kauri Grove** (1km; 10min). If you're pressing on to Whitianga but want to break your journey, there's relaxing riverside **accommodation** at *Honey Cottage*, about 12km short of Whitianga (☎07/866 5151; tent sites $6, rooms ②).

From Coromandel town, **SH25** follows an attractive route through lush native forest, also plied by **buses** and passing a couple of isolated but pretty beachside settlements with campsites. About 14km from Coromandel is the 5-kilometre turn-off (where buses also stop) to the secluded village and beach of **WHANGAPOUA**, whose long stretch of white sand is lined by baches and a single general store/petrol station. At the end of the road is a pleasant walk to the idyllic sandy beach of **New Chums Bay** (4km return; 1hr): from the beach, cross the estuary and follow the bushline around the headland to a saddle; on the other side is New Chums Bay (accessible at low tide only). A basic but scenic **campsite**, *Whangapoua Beach Camping Ground* (tent sites $6), lies 300m along the left fork as you enter town. Continuing along SH25, about 34km from Coromandel, you drop down to the attractive seaside village of **KUAOTUNU**, with a shady and well-equipped **campsite**, on Bluff Road (☎07/866 5628; tent sites $9, on-site vans & cabins ②–③, cottage ④), and a general store/gas station that runs **guided quad-bike safaris** (daily 8am & 1pm; 4hr; $120 per single or double bike; ☎07/866 2034) through hilly, remote bush trails, explaining the local scenery and legends. About 4km past Kuaotunu, on SH25, is Twin Oaks Riding Ranch, the base for extremely **scenic horse treks** (daily 10am & 2pm, plus twilight trek at 6pm Nov–March; 2hr; $25; book ahead on ☎07/866 5388), offering breathtaking views of Mercury Bay and the northern Coromandel; transport from Whitianga can also be arranged. From here, SH25 continues through farmland to Whitianga and the stunning expanse of Mercury Bay.

Whitianga and around

The attractive **WHITIANGA** sits at the foot of hills, stretching out along the sandy western shores of the impressive **Mercury Bay**, which takes its name from the planet whose transit Captain Cook and his party of scientists observed during their stay here on board the *Endeavour* in 1769. A popular summer-holiday destination, the population of about 3000 swells dramatically during January, as vacationers flock to the town's **Buffalo Beach**, a long sweep of surf-pounded white sand.

Whitianga makes a good base from which to make a series of half-day and **day trips** to some wonderfully secluded spots, so allow a couple of days here. Just across the narrow harbour mouth and strung along Mercury Bay's eastern shore are several unusual beaches, reached by passenger ferry to **Ferry Landing**, from where you can catch a **bus** or strike out along scenic coastal tracks. The area is also served by roads branching off the southbound SH25, which loops around the deeply indented harbour. Two gems here are **Cathedral Cove**, a stunning geological formation, and **Hot Water Beach**, renowned for its natural hot-water springs bubbling beneath the sand. Bordering part of the eastern shore is **Cathedral Cove Marine Reserve**, whose protected waters are a great spot for snorkelling and scuba diving. In addition, **boat trips** to the outer reaches of Mercury Bay and the volcanically formed **Mercury Islands**, 25km offshore, explore pristine waters and shoreline – and search for bottlenose **dolphins** and **whales**. Whitianga is also the best place in New Zealand to try your hand at **bone carving**, creating your very own *tiki* (pendant) in as little as half a day, while 10km north of town you can enjoy astounding views of the whole region on a **scenic horse trek** (see above).

Arrival, information and transport

InterCity and Newmans **buses** drop off outside the visitor centre, right in the middle of town. Air Coromandel (☎07/866 4016) flies twice daily from Auckland to Whitianga (around $100 one way); the **airport** is 3km south of the town centre and is served by a free airline shuttle bus.

The **visitor centre** is at the corner of Albert Street and Blacksmith Lane (Oct–April daily 9am–5pm, May–Sept Mon–Fri 9am–5pm & Sat 9am–1pm; ☎07/866 5555).

The surrounding **beaches** are served by ferry and buses. The **passenger ferry** to Ferry Landing (daily 7.30am–noon & 1–6.30pm, until midnight in summer; $1 single, $1.75 return) takes a mere three minutes and leaves from the end of the marina, past the harbour master's office. Hot Water Beach Conxtions (book a day ahead if possible, ☎07/866 2478) run hop-on, hop-off **excursion buses** from Ferry Landing to Cooks Beach, Cathedral Cove, Hahei and Hot Water Beach (3–5 daily; $20), with some services continuing to Delmany Corner on SH25 for connection with buses to Auckland and Whitianga.

Accommodation

As one of the Coromandel's main tourist centres, Whitianga itself has plenty of **accommodation** to suit all tastes. Further out, beside the secluded **beaches** of Mercury Bay,

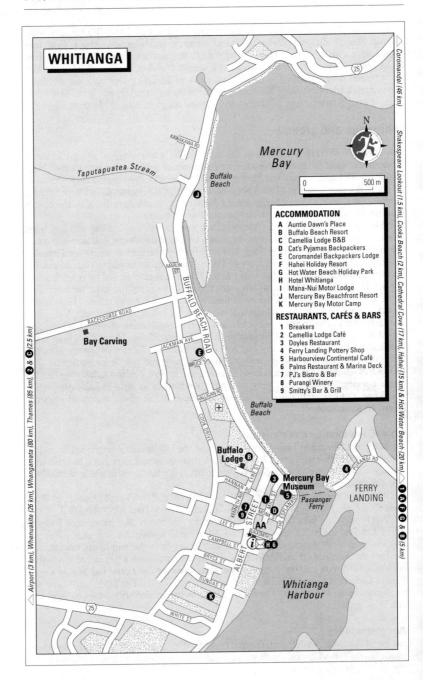

WHITIANGA

Coromandel (46 km)

Shakespeare Lookout (1.5 km), Cooks Beach (2 km), Cathedral Cove (17 km), Hahei (15 km) & Hot Water Beach (20 km)

Airport (3 km), Whenuakite (26 km), Whangamata (80 km), Thames (85 km), ② & ③ (2.5 km)

Mercury Bay

Taputapuatea Stream

KAWAKAWA RD

Buffalo Beach

N

0   500 m

ACCOMMODATION

A Auntie Dawn's Place
B Buffalo Beach Resort
C Camellia Lodge B&B
D Cat's Pyjamas Backpackers
E Coromandel Backpackers Lodge
F Hahei Holiday Resort
G Hot Water Beach Holiday Park
H Hotel Whitianga
I Mana-Nui Motor Lodge
J Mercury Bay Beachfront Resort
K Mercury Bay Motor Camp

RESTAURANTS, CAFÉS & BARS

1 Breakers
2 Camellia Lodge Café
3 Doyles Restaurant
4 Ferry Landing Pottery Shop
5 Harbourview Continental Café
6 Palms Restaurant & Marina Deck
7 PJ's Bistro & Bar
8 Purangi Winery
9 Smitty's Bar & Grill

MARLIN ST

BUFFALO BEACH ROAD

RACECOURSE ROAD

Bay Carving

JACKMAN AVE

BRUCE ST

HALLIGAN RD

COOK DRIVE

Buffalo Beach

Buffalo Lodge

HANNAN RD

KENNEDY PARK

TYR ST

MILL ST

MONK ST

THE ESPLANADE

PURANGI RD

FERRY LANDING

Mercury Bay Museum

Passenger Ferry

LEE ST

ALBERT STREET

CAMPBELL ST

BRYCE ST

DUNDAS ST

WHITE ST

AA

Whitianga Harbour

is a small selection of perfect places to unwind, mostly at Hot Water Beach and Hahei. During January, places get booked up about two months beforehand, so **book as far ahead** as possible if your visit coincides with this peak period, and be prepared for **higher prices** than on the rest of the peninsula.

HOTELS AND MOTELS

Hotel Whitianga, The Esplanade (☎ & fax 07/866 5818). Pleasant, refurbished harbourside hotel with nine well-tended rooms, most of them en-suite and all with TV and washbasin. Can get noisy on a Fri or Sat nights, with live music in bar. ④, en-suite ⑤.

Mana-Nui Motor Lodge, 20 Albert St (☎ & fax 07/866 5599). Centrally located, comfortable and well-kept motel with seven fully self-contained units. ⑥.

Mercury Bay Beachfront Resort, 111–113 Buffalo Beach Rd (☎07/866 5637). A motel with eight excellent spacious units overlooking the beach, about a ten-minute walk from the centre. ④.

Tatahi Lodge, Grange Rd, Hahei (☎07/866 3992, fax 866 3993). Several luxurious self-contained wooden units set in bush and gardens; courtesy van. ⑥.

GUESTHOUSES AND B&BS

Auntie Dawn's Place, Radar Rd, Hot Water Beach (☎07/866 3707, fax 866 3701). Tranquil modern hillside house overlooking the beach. Comfortable, fully self-contained apartments, plus backpacker beds in summer only (Oct–April). Backpacker beds ①, apartments ④.

Camellia Lodge B&B, cnr Golf Rd & SH25, near the airport (☎ & fax 07/866 2253). An attractive modern house in extensive well kept gardens, run by extremely friendly and helpful hosts, with four comfortable guest rooms; regular BBQs on summer evenings; swimming pool and spa. Dinner on request ($20). ④.

HOSTELS AND CAMPSITES

Auntie Dawn's Place, Radar Rd, Hot Water Beach (☎07/866 3707, fax 866 3701). Beachside house with backpacker beds in summer only (Oct–April). Dorms ①.

Buffalo Beach Resort, Eyre St (☎07/866 5854). Extremely well-equipped campsite adjacent to the beach, in shaded parkland a three-minute walk from the town centre. Tent sites $10, chalets & units ②–④.

Cat's Pyjamas Backpackers, 4 Monk St (☎ & fax 07/866 4663). Small, friendly and clean place with two dorms and two doubles, just a two-minute walk from the wharf. Perks include free linen, seafood, tea and coffee, fresh fruit – and sometimes home brew. Dorms ①, rooms ③.

Coromandel Backpackers Lodge, 46 Buffalo Beach Rd (☎ & fax 07/866 5380). Ten minutes' walk from town, overlooking the bay, this is an excellent, friendly and well-equipped hostel, with free use of kayaks and bikes to rent. Dorms ①, rooms ②.

Hahei Holiday Resort, Harsant Ave, Hahei Beach (☎ & fax 07/866 3889). Located on half a kilometre of beachfront and within an easy walk of Cathedral Cove, this spacious site is close to a shop and restaurant. Tent sites $9, dorms ①, flats & units ②–④.

Hot Water Beach Holiday Park, adjacent to the general store, Hot Water Beach (☎07/866 3735). Well-kept site right by the beach. Tent sites $9, plus $2 for a power hook-up.

Mercury Bay Motor Camp, 121 Albert St (☎07/866 5579). Large, sheltered and well-equipped site about 400m from the town centre with kayak and bike rental ($10 a half-day). Tent sites $9, cabins & flats ②–④.

Tatahi Lodge, Grange Rd, Hahei (☎07/866 3992, fax 866 3993). Extremely pleasant modern complex set in bush and gardens. Self-contained units, plus backpacker accommodation in dorms and doubles, with free linen; courtesy van. Backpacker dorms ①, rooms ②; units ⑥.

The Town

The town's **main street** is Buffalo Beach Road (SH25, where it hits the beach), becoming Albert Street as it forks south through the town centre and heads on out of town. The Esplanade branches off from Buffalo Beach Road and leads to the wharf.

One of the best things to do in Whitianga is the excellent and increasingly popular **bone-carving course**, where, with guidance, you can produce a *tiki* (pendant), in half a day or so. Bay Carving is at Aotearoa Lodge, Racecourse Rd, in the northern part of town (daily 8am–10pm; $25–40, dependent on size of carving; phone the day before, ☎07/866 4021); the cost is the same no matter how long you take to complete your masterpiece, and there's free tea and coffee (plus soup in winter). Choose your design from over a hundred (either traditional Maori or contemporary) and set to work on a specially prepared hunk of cow bone. Dentists' drills and plenty of sanding by hand transform the bone into a glossy, white pendant. If you lack patience, you might do better to check out the ready-carved pieces for sale at the workshop at very reasonable prices. For around $30 you can also **paint your own T-shirt** in an adjoining workshop, using batik techniques.

The big **Mercury Bay Museum**, down by the wharf in an old butter factory (Oct–April daily 10am–4pm; May–Sept Tues, Thurs & Sun 11am–2pm; $2), won't detain you for long. It focuses mainly on colonial history with the usual slight nod to Maori artefacts. Points of interest are an extensive exhibition on Captain Cook and his discovery of the peninsula; also informative displays on kauri-gum digging (including carved blackjack gum), minerals and local shipwrecks.

Ferry Landing and the beaches

The beaches across the estuary are accessible by passenger ferry to **Ferry Landing**, where buses continue to the beaches (see p.317 for details); by boat (see "Exploring Mercury Bay", p.321); or by car from Whitianga. The longer **road route** travels south along SH25, skirting the harbour and cutting inland through hill country to a signposted turn-off at Whenuakite, 26km from Whitianga, which strikes north towards Mercury Bay.

From Ferry Landing the first point of interest is **Shakespeare Lookout**, signposted 1.5km along the road, and reached after another kilometre uphill to a car park. From the lookout are panoramic views to the east of Cooks Beach, Mercury Bay and its islands; to the west of Buffalo Beach; and to the north of Mount Maungatawhiri. A memorial plaque commemorates James Cook's anchorage in Mercury Bay in 1769. From the car park, signposted tracks lead to the secluded Lonely Bay and on to **Cooks Beach** (2km one way; 20min), which is also accessible from the main road 2km further east. This popular family beach has a good one-way **walk to Cathedral Cove** (5km; 1hr), following a rock shelf only exposed at low tide (check times with Whitianga visitor centre before setting out), but once again, you can also get here via the main road (see below). About 3km east of Cooks Beach on the main road is **Purangi Winery and Wine Bar** (Oct–April lunch & dinner daily; May–Sept lunch only Mon–Fri, lunch & dinner Sat & Sun), a great place to dawdle, while soaking up the rustic atmosphere and a free tasting of their fruit wines and liqueurs made from kiwifruit and plums. They also offer a blackboard menu of reasonably priced snacks and meals, served indoors or outside under the vines; choose from steak, seafood or a simple cheeseboard with salad and French bread.

About 3km further east along the main road is the turn-off to the tiny beachside community of **HAHEI**, a further 6.5km along Hahei Beach Road, and its hilly coastal **track to Cathedral Cove** (45min), which starts from the car park at the road's end. The walk is very steep in places, with patches of pine-dominated bush, and affords great views out to sea, culminating in a sheltered long, sandy beach overshadowed by striking white cliffs and an impressive rock arch – after which the cove is named. A walk through the arch reveals another delightful beach on the other side, while offshore the remains of several arches are stranded at sea. Bring a towel and a picnic, sink into the sand and relax to the deceptively gentle sound of the waves. This is also a great place to **snorkel**, because the rich waters here are part of the protected **Cathedral Cove Marine Reserve**.

One of the most famous places on the Coromandel peninsula is **Hot Water Beach**, the last place you'll come to from Ferry Landing and the first you'll reach arriving by road from Whitianga via SH25. Either way, access is along the 5-kilometre Hot Water Beach Road, off the main road 5km south of Hahei Beach Road and 2km from the Whenuakite turn-off. The beach itself is beyond the car park at the end of the road. Be sure to visit one hour either side of **low tide**; check tide times at the visitor centre or in the local paper. The beach is renowned for a hot-water spring about 220m along the shore, past the shop and adjacent to several large rocky outcrops jutting from the sand. Dig a hole and you can sit in the hot water while being cooled by the incoming sea water, which makes for a strangely refreshing experience. In summer, the springs area will be pockmarked by other visitors' diggings, but if no one has been here before you, you'll need to **rent a spade** from the **general store** (daily 9am–5pm; $2 for 2 hours, plus $20 deposit); the store also sells burgers, toasted sandwiches, hot dogs, tea and coffee, ice cream and milk shakes.

Exploring Mercury Bay

You can combine exploring Mercury Bay and **swimming with dolphins** through Mercury Bay Seafaris (book through visitor centre; enquiries only, ☎07/866 2213), who run three highly informative boat trips **from Whitianga** wharf. You need to bring warm clothes and swimming gear; they supply wetsuits, snorkelling gear and hot drinks; you should also contact them the night before to check on sea conditions. Their Dolphin Quest (Oct–April daily 8am; 3–4hr; $75) takes you to Mercury Bay's outer reaches in a high-speed vessel, aiming to spot dolphins, orca and other whales. The Seven-Island Seafari (daily: Oct–April 3pm; May–Sept 9am; 3–4hr; $70) is a **scenic cruise** around the Mercury Islands, visiting caves, pristine beaches, island sanctuaries and bush-clad bays; there's great snorkelling among these volcanic islands, and you may also have the chance to swim with bottlenose dolphins. If you'd rather not get wet, join their glass-bottom boat trip (year-round, times according to demand; 1hr 30min; $30), which follows the coast to Cathedral Cove and the marine reserve. Good **boat trips** also run **out of Hahei**: the Hahei Explorer (book previous evening or before 9am on the day, ☎07/866 3910) is the only set-up with a DOC licence to land at Cathedral Cove; they specialize in cave trips, visiting a blowhole between Cathedral Cove and Hot Water Beach in their rigid-hull inflatable (year-round; 1hr; $32.50), and guided snorkelling trips (Nov to end-May; 3hr; $45), with gear and wetsuits provided.

The fastest way to see the bay is by **jetboat** with Mercury Bay Scenic Jet (1hr; $30; (book at visitor centre or, after hours, call ☎07/866 4125), which leaves from Whitianga wharf for an adrenalin–pumping spin to Cathedral Cove. More leisurely exploration is afforded by **guided sea kayak tours**, equally enjoyable in summer or winter. Based in Whitianga, Mercury Bay Sea Kayaks (☎07/866 2358) offer a range of trips, from half-day to multi-day adventures (day-trips start at $40), taking in Cathedral Cove, the caves of offshore islands and snorkelling. Coromandel Safaris (☎025/394 597) run kayaking trips for similar prices, but also organize dive trips and door-to-door transport from Auckland, Hamilton, Tauranga and Rotorua. **Scuba diving** in Cathedral Cove Marine Reserve can be arranged through Hahei-based Cathedral Cove Dive (☎07/866 3955): a one-dive trip costs $70, two-dives $110, less if you have your own gear. **Non-divers** can learn basic scuba skills ($90), and they also run other PADI courses, from beginners to advanced.

Eating and entertainment

As you'd expect from such a happening spot, Whitianga and its surrounds have a good choice of places to **eat**. Having said that, entertainment options are sadly limited to the *Hotel Whitianga*, with live **bands** once a week (Fri or Sat) in summer, and *PJ's Bistro & Bar*, which has in-house **karaoke** and live music at weekends after 9.30pm.

Breakers, Beach Rd, Hahei. A highly recommended, relaxing restaurant and bar in a peaceful spot, with an attractive enclosed verandah, large windows, and jasmine growing overhead. Scallops collected from a local bay are a speciality; a popular option is to go for two starters instead of a main – the latter mostly variations on a steak and seafood theme for $20 and under. Evenings only: daily Dec–Easter; closed Mon during Nov & Mon–Wed Easter–Oct.

Camellia Lodge Café, cnr Golf Road & SH25, Whitianga (near the airport). Inexpensive daytime snacks and light meals are served in this small café in beautiful tree-shaded gardens. Terrific Greek salad and ploughman's lunch (with salami and fresh fruit).

Doyles Restaurant, 21 The Esplanade. Fairly upmarket dining from a pleasant first-floor vantage point overlooking the beach. The menu consists of seafood and steak, with prices starting at $20 for a main dish. Breakfast, lunch & dinner Oct–April; dinner only May–Sept.

Ferry Landing Pottery Shop, Purangi Rd, Ferry Landing. About 100m up the hill from the wharf, this attractive garden café is perfect for light meals, coffee, and a rest among flowers and greenery. Daily from 10am until late afternoon.

Harbourview Continental Café, 10 The Esplanade (☎07/866 4263). A good lunch and dinner spot that's popular with locals – not least for its generous portions; an all-day breakfast is also on offer, with yummy pancakes. Lunches cost around $12, dinners (book ahead) $20. Licensed & BYO ($5 corkage).

Palms Restaurant & Marina Deck, in the *Hotel Whitianga*, The Esplanade. An airy, comfortable restaurant that's especially good for dinner, with main courses costing $18–25. There are also a couple of bars serving snacks all day. Daily Oct–April, closed Sun May–Sept. Licensed.

PJ's Bistro & Bar, 31 Albert St, opposite Monk St. Cheerful family bistro, specializing in stir-fries, seafood and vegetarian meals. Indoor and outdoor seating, with mains priced around $15–22, bar snacks for about $6 and bistro meals for $10 and under.

Purangi Winery, 450 Purangi Rd. Rustic, secluded restaurant in a picturesque setting proffering high-quality snacks, barbecued steak, seafood and yummy sausages, all for $20 and under. Oct–April all day; May–Sept closed Mon–Fri evenings. Licensed.

Smitty's Bar & Grill, 37 Albert St. A family-orientated hacienda-style bar, serving well-priced snacks, lunches and dinners daily from 11am. Grilled meats are the speciality here, but they make a few concessions to vegetarians. Dine in the barn-like interior, or out on the deck.

Listings

Airlines Air Coromandel (☎07/866 4016) flies twice daily to and from Auckland (around $100).

Buses Newmans (☎0800/777 707) link Whitianga with Thames, Auckland and Tauranga; InterCity (☎0800/686 862) serves Thames, Coromandel town, Opoutere, Whangamata, Tauranga, Rotorua and Auckland.

Medical treatment Mercury Bay Medical Centre, 87 Albert St (☎07/866 5911).

Pharmacy Emergency after-hours service, ☎07/866 4146 or 866 2026.

Scenic flights Air Coromandel (☎07/866 2434) offer flightseeing, with prices in the range of $30–99.

Taxis Mercury Bay Taxis (☎07/866 5643); also runs a shuttle between Whitianga and Coromandel town.

Water taxis Hahei Explorer (☎07/866 3910) operates a water-taxi service between Hahei and Cathedral Cove (on demand; 10min; $25 return).

South to Whangamata

There are a few points of interest along SH25 **south to Whangamata**, despite the sad fact that a section of this coast has been spoiled by over-development. This is especially true of **Tairua**, the midway point, and even more so of its neighbour across the harbour, the luxury retirement and holiday resort of **Pauanui**. Reminiscent of the worst excesses of Florida, this is best avoided altogether. However, hidden in an attractive valley not far from there (but not served by public transport), you'll find a great **restaurant** in an unusual resort, where you can also get stuck into some **river kayaking** or scenic **horse trekking**. Off the beaten track and mercifully unscathed is the delightful **Opoutere**, a tiny harbourside retreat at the foot of a mountain, with a wild sweep of beach and a beautifully situated hostel. From here, you're best off making a beeline for Whangamata.

Tairua

On SH25, 16km south of the turn-off to Hot Water Beach and 42km from Whitianga, **TAIRUA** is a small but overdeveloped beachside town at the mouth of the Tairua River, backed by tall, pine-forested hills. Its surf and sheltered estuary beaches draw hordes of tourists in the summer. With time on your hands, you could stop briefly for a couple of interesting activities and some good eating, or to link up with one of the several extremely informative and light-hearted **eco-tours** run by Kiwi Dundee Adventures (see p.325), who'll enlighten you on various aspects of the Coromandel Pensinsula and beyond.

The best thing to do in Tairua itself is the fifteen-minute walk up **Mount Paku**, at the town's eastern end and accessible along a track at the end of Paku Drive. From the summit you get a spectacular panoramic view of the town, its harbour and beaches, and the dreaded Pauanui.

Otherwise, your best bet is to head for *Duck Creek Farm and Holiday Resort*, about 8km along the turn-off to Pauanui. Hidden in a secluded valley on the other side of the harbour, this cooperative venture offers various activities: in the grounds is a heated indoor swimming pool and the resort runs **horse treks** (1–2hr; $25–40; bookings essential, ☎07/864 7787) and **kayaking trips** ($10 per hour). The guided horse treks cater to any level of experience and take you along beach and through forests, while kayakers paddle from the inlet into Duck Creek, through wetlands with plenty of native bush, on to Tairoa River and upstream.

PRACTICALITIES

Newmans **buses** from Whitianga drop off at Tairua post office at 2pm daily, but there's no other tranport here, or to Pauanui. If you do decide to stay (and have your own wheels), the *Duck Creek Farm and Holiday Resort* (see above; ☎07/864 7787; dorms ①, chalets & cabins ④–⑤) has an attractive range of **accommodation** – from comfortable, Spanish-style bunkrooms with terracota-tiled floors to fully equipped split-level chalets and cabins. Back in town, the small and pretty *Tairua Backpackers*, 200 Main Rd (☎ & fax 07/864 8345; dorms ①, rooms ②), is set among trees near the water's edge and across the river bridge. There's free use of windsurfers and canoes, plus sightseeing tours to local points of interest. Also on the main road, 500m north of the shops, is *The Flying Dutchman* (☎07/864 8448; tent sites $7, dorms ①, rooms ②), a clean and cosy place with a garden, barbecue and free use of boogie boards; canoes and mountain bikes are also available for rent.

The best-value **eating** option is *Accents Brasserie*, in the Tairua Shopping Centre, Main Road, a fully licensed and BYO ($3 corkage) dinner restaurant with a bar at the back; seafood is their speciality and is served in huge portions ($11–20). Meanwhile, there's no getting away from the *Duck Creek Farm and Resort*, where the rustic, licensed *Duck Creek Inn* caters to healthy outdoor appetites, with European country-style food – German pea soups, Hungarian goulash, French onion soup and the like – all at $16.80. Once a week (days vary) they cook lamb or pork on a spit, and occasionally they have theme evenings such as a country night with **line dancing** and a band, or a tea dance in gumboots.

Opoutere

Twelve kilometres south of Tairua is the turn-off to **Opoutere**, the road hugging the shoreline of Wharekawa Harbour, fringed by pohutukawa trees and overlooked by pine-covered hills towering above. This tiny settlement comprises only a handful of houses, a campsite and a hostel, all strung along the single road. People come here to enjoy the tranquillity, birdlife, plentiful shellfish – and a four-kilometre expanse of **wild** white-sand **beach** protected from development by the forest reserve that backs it. It's the sort of place you plan to visit for a day and wind up staying a week. Swimming on the beach is reasonably safe but there can be a strong undertow, and in the estuary the swirling currents make it plain dangerous. The wetlands flanking the estuary, however, yield delicious shellfish – so long as you don't mind getting your feet wet – and provide good bird-watching spots.

There are a also couple of good **walks**. Just outside the hostel gate is the start of a summit track up **Mount Maungaruawahine** (1km one way; 20min). The track goes through tall coastal bush and the climb to the summit is quite steep, passing elderly, gnarled pohutuakawa and other native trees. The **summit** gives excellent views on the seaward side across the Mayor and Aldermen islands, the estuary-harbour mouth, the length of the beach and the green flats just inland.

Further down the road are two tracks to **Ocean Beach**, starting at a small arched bridge over the Wahitapu Stream. Beyond the bridge the track forks: the **right-hand track** (1.25km one way; 15min) emerges from pine forest to follow the estuary before venturing out on to a sandspit (a bird sanctuary and breeding ground for New Zealand dotterels, oystercatchers and various species of tern; roped off during the Nov–March breeding season); crossing the spit brings you to the white sand and roaring surf of Ocean Beach, from where you can loop back through bush and back over the bridge to the car park. The **left-hand fork** is a more direct track (800m one way; 10min) that passes through pines, lupin and mingimingi, before reaching the beach.

PRACTICALITIES
Whangamata **Buses** (☎07/865 8613) from Whangamata, Waihi, Tauranga, Thames and Auckland drop-off and pick up from Opoutere *YHA* hostel (see below), and there are onward connections with InterCity services in Waihi.

By far the best place to stay is at the **YHA**, set back from the main road at the harbourmouth end and signposted at its gate (☎07/865 9072; dorms ①, rooms ②), which enjoys one of the finest sites of any hostel in New Zealand. Overlooking the river estuary, the hostel sits in a dip at the foot of the mountain, wallowing in its own mild microclimate. As if this idyllic situation wasn't enough, there's also the chance of seeing glowworms on your nocturnal wanderings, and canoes are available for guests' use (on the estuary only). The small and simple **campsite**, *Opoutere Park Beach Resort* (☎07/865 9152; tent sites $9, flats & chalet ②–④), is about 800m up the road towards the beach.

There's no general store in Opoutere, but the campsite and hostel both have basic **provisions** for sale.

Whangamata

Lying on SH25 towards the southern end of the Coromandel Peninsula is the long, straggling resort of **WHANGAMATA**, its single-storey buildings wedged between two river estuaries in one direction and hills and harbour in the other. Primarily a **surfie** Mecca, whose population of 4000 increases as much as tenfold in January, it boasts the four-kilometre **Ocean Beach**, a crescent of white sand that curves from the harbour entrance to the mouth of the **Otahu River** and has an excellent break by the bar at the harbour end.

Continuing **south of here**, SH25 peters out at the inland gold town of Waihi (see p.304), 29km away, where SH2 strikes out northwest to Auckland and southeast to the Bay of Plenty.

Arrival, information and accommodation

Buses from Whitianga and Opoutere drop off daily outside the centrally located visitor centre, with daily (except Sun) onward connections to Auckland, while Whangamata Tours (☎07/865 7088) continue south to Waihi for around $12. The **visitor centre** is on

Port Road, beside the BNZ (Oct–April Mon–Fri 9am–5pm, Sat 9am–4pm, Sun 10am–4pm; May–Sept Mon–Sat 10am–4pm, Sun 10am–1pm; ☎07/865 8340), and most places are within easy walking distance of here.

As a tourist centre, Whangamata has plenty of **accommodation**, most of it pricier than elsewhere on the peninsula, especially over the two weeks following Christmas, when rates can shoot up by as much as fifty percent. Wherever you stay, you won't be far from the town centre.

Bedshed, cnr Port Rd and Mayfair Ave (☎0800/659 580). An immaculate backpackers, motel and tourist lodge. The well equipped hostel section has small dorms and one double room; linen costs $2.50 extra, but there's free use of surfboards and transport to walks. The serviced lodge has double rooms, while the well-appointed motel units are new and spacious. Backpacker dorms ①, room ②; lodge ③; motel ⑤.

Bushland Park Lodge at Nickel Strausse, in the Wentworth Valley, 7km southwest of town (☎ & fax 07/865 7468). An exclusive but well priced hideaway in private grounds beside a high-quality German winery restaurant (see "Eating and drinking" p.326). There are three immaculate and cheerfully decorated en-suite doubles, a special Black Forest-style breakfast of bread, cheese and ham is served – and there's a sauna, spa pool and glow-worm grotto. ⑤.

Cedarwood Motor Hotel, 413–419 Port Rd (☎ & fax 07/865 9211). The biggest motel in town, offering fairly modern, spacious units sleeping up to eight. Facilities include a BBQ, several bars, a bistro and tennis courts. ⑤.

Luise's Lodge B&B, 103 Casement Rd (☎07/865 7074). Extremely friendly and centrally located only a 3min walk to the beach. Four airy doubles share facilities, and the continental breakfast includes home-made German bread. ⑤.

Pinefield Holiday Park, at the southern end of Port Rd (☎07/865 8791). An excellent, shady site that gets very busy over summer weekends. On-site accommodation comes well-equipped; there's a BBQ and a large swimming pool. Tent sites $10; cabins, flats & units ②–④.

The Town and around

Kiwis flock to this small town during their summer holidays, booking it out during the first two weeks after Christmas, but it's pretty quiet for the rest of the year. The **main street** is Port Road, which runs straight through the small town centre, linking it with the highway.

Surfies should make straight for the well-stocked Whangamata Surf Shop (daily 9am–5pm), Port Road, opposite *Ginger's Health Food Café*. Owned by surfing legend Bob Davie, this shop has heaps of designer gear to keep the coolest of customers happy, and is the only place in town where you can **rent a surfboard** ($10 per hr, $18 half-day, $25 full-day) or a **boogie board** ($5 per hr, $12 half-day, $16 full-day); they also rent out wetsuits and fins for $5 per day. The Windsurfing School, up the harbour past the boat ramp (☎07/865 8186), operates daily during summer holidays for up to three hours either side of high tide (and throughout the year on bookings); **sailboard** rental costs $20 per hour, a group lesson $25, and a private lesson $30.

Aside from enjoying the surf, there are only a couple of other diversions. One is a pleasant **walk to Wentworth Falls** (5km one way; 1hr) in the nearby Wentworth Valley. Take SH25 south for 2km to the signposted turn-off to Wentworth Valley Road; at its end (4km) is a campsite and the start of the track. The other reason to come here is to join one of the extremely popular **eco-tours** run by Kiwi Dundee Adventures (book as far ahead as possible, ☎ & fax 07/865 8809). For twenty years, the passionate conservationist Doug Johansen (popularly known as "Kiwi Dundee") has been getting his message across in his own distinctive way, generally accompanied by a good deal of showmanship. Operating year-round, the company offers a variety of tours, taking small groups off the beaten track for a day or more to explain history, geology, Maori medicines and natural history, with departures from Tairua, Pauanui and Whangamata.

Eating and drinking

Port Road is lined with several **tearooms**, takeaways and **restaurants**, but few stand out, so you might want to venture further afield for more inspiring fare.

Captain's Table, cnr Port Rd & Aicken Rd (☎07/865 8292). The most upmarket place in town, specializing in seafood for $20–30 (Oct–March, evenings only; closed Mon). The restaurant also functions as a food and hospitality training centre, serving incredibly cheap 4-course lunches on Tues and Thurs all year (apart from the Christmas period when the regular chef steps in), prepared to a high standard by trainees and served 12–2pm; book ahead for lunch. Licensed.

Cedarwood Motor Hotel, Port Rd. Popular bistro-style restaurant that serves lunches for under $15 and dinner for under $20. The *Beach Bar* also has light meals of trendy, snacky food for under $10, and there's also a sports bar and garden bar.

Ginger's Health Food Café, 601 Port Rd. Reasonably priced veggie place, open daily from morning until mid-afternoon. Great muffins. BYO.

Nickel Strausse, 7km southwest of town on the Wentworth Valley Road, off SH25 (☎07/865 7468). Excellent and good-value dining in an intimate winery restaurant set in rural surroundings. A charming German couple serve typical Bavarian lunches ($5–15) and dinners (set menu $35–45), including exquisite Black Forest gateau made fresh daily. Licensed, with an international wine list. Book ahead for Sat; closed Mon.

The Bay of Plenty

The **BAY OF PLENTY** sweeps down from the base of the Coromandel Peninsula (at Waihi Beach) in the west to Opotiki in the east, punctuated by an outstanding sequence of golden beaches and great surf, and traced along its length by the Pacific Coast Highway (SH2), which links Auckland with Gisborne. The **coast**, though popular with Kiwi holidaymakers, has remained relatively unspoiled, especially further east, while the vast bay's sheltered waters are frequented by dolphins and whales. Inland, the **western** Bay of Plenty is bordered by the craggy slopes of the Kaimai Range, clothed by the **Kaimai-Mamaku Forest Park** and giving way just north of Rotorua to the Volcanic Plateau. This rugged landscape was created about five million years ago when vast quantities of lava, scoria and ash were spewed across the region, forming a chain of large **volcanic cones**. At around the same time, thick lava was forced out of other vents, to build steep-sided **domes** like that of Mount Maunganui. The **eastern** Bay of Plenty has three major **rivers** that course down the inland forested slopes of the vast **Te Urewera National Park** towards the sea. The powerful rivers of **Motu**, **Wairoa** and **Rangitaiki** are noted for their **whitewater-rafting** opportunities, from Grade I to the near-suicidal Grade V, and trips operate from Tauranga, Whakatane and Opotiki.

The Bay of Plenty has two main centres, the lively port city of **Tauranga** in the west, which is linked by a harbour bridge to the beachside resort of **Mount Maunganui**, blessed with not only one of the North Island's two best surf beaches, but also an excellent vantage point for far-reaching views of the whole region. Both have attractions that are largely water-based, as does the smaller, more relaxed town of **Whakatane**, 83km to the east and boasting its own pretty surf beach at nearby **Ohope**. Out to sea are the seabird havens of Mayor and Whale **islands**, and the easily accessible retreat of Matakana Island, near Tauranga. Further offshore is New Zealand's only active marine volcano, **White Island**, which you can visit on memorable guided trips from Whakatane. The easternmost town of **Opotiki** is the gateway to Eastland in one direction and to Gisborne in the other, as well as providing access to some interesting walks in the hills to the south and to trips on the mighty **Motu River**.

Some of the first **Maori** to reach New Zealand arrived here in their great *waka* (war canoes) – in fact Whakatane is sometimes known as the birthplace of Aotearoa, for it was here that the Polynesian navigator **Toi te Huatahi** first landed. The Bay of Plenty earned its name from **Captain Cook**, who sailed in on the *Endeavour* in 1769 and was struck by the number of thriving Maori settlements living off the abundant resources, as well as by the generous supplies they gave him. This era of peace and plenty was shattered by the **New Zealand Wars** of the 1860s, as fierce fighting led to the establishment of **garrisons** at both Whakatane and Tauranga, and the easternmost town of Opotiki gained notoriety as the scene of the death of a European missionary – allegedly murdered by a Maori prophet. Today a more healthy **cultural exchange** is possible at two welcoming marae, one near Tauranga and the other near Opotiki, where you're encouranged not only to watch but also to participate in Maori crafts and traditions.

The region's glorious sunny **climate** makes it a rich fruit-growing area, particularly known for citrus and kiwifruit, and roadside stalls are a common sight. The Bay of Plenty is served by major **bus** companies, and the **trains** get as far southeast as Tauranga, while Air New Zealand **fly** into airports at Tauranga and Whakatane.

Although, strictly speaking, **Rotorua** lies in the Bay of Plenty, it is covered along with the rest of the volcanic plateau region in Chapter Four, starting on p.247.

Tauranga

The Bay of Plenty's heart is the prosperous, glittering port city of **TAURANGA** ("safe anchorage"), at its western end, sprawling beside an attractive sweeping harbour and backed by the stunning backdrop of the forested Kaimai Range. The long **harbour** is formed by a large and unusual estuary: protected from the open ocean by **Matakana Island**, a 24-kilometre-long barrier of dune sand, it has two narrow mouths, one at Bowentown Heads, near Katikati, and the other at **Mount Maunganui**, the distinctive cone-shaped mountain across the bridge from Tauranga.

As New Zealand's **fastest-growing city**, Tauranga is vibrant yet relaxed, a city of parks, gardens and waterfronts. Nearby is the sandy beach of Omokoroa and the popular surf **beaches** of Mount Maunganui. No surprise, then, that the area's a big draw for Kiwi **holiday-makers** throughout January and on summer weekends, when Tauranga and the increasingly commercialized resort of Mount Maunganui can be rather overwhelming and accommodation hard to come by. The benefits are a flourishing **restaurant** and **bar scene** in a compact city centre, two attractive **wineries** and a couple of excellent full-day **sailing trips**, one confined to the harbour's beaches and islands; the other a dolphin-encounter trip in the beckoning Bay of Plenty. A rewarding cultural experience can also be had at the laid-back **marae**, while at Easter the city hosts a **jazz festival**. Finally, Tauranga is in a **kiwifruit picking region**, but be warned, it's tough and prickly work and you must commit yourself to a minimum of three weeks (if this doesn't put you off, check out "Listings" on p.332).

Arrival, information and transport

InterCity and Newmans **buses** pull in at the visitor centre (see below), while the daily *Kaimai Express* from Auckland pulls into the centrally located **train station** on The Strand. The **airport** receives daily Air New Zealand flights from Auckland and Wellington, and lies 3km from the city centre, across the harbour and just outside Mount Maunganui, connected by regular shuttles ($8).

The **visitor centre** is at 80 Dive Crescent (Oct–April Mon–Fri 7.30am–5pm, Sat & Sun 9am–5pm; May–Sept Mon–Fri 7.30am–5pm, Sat & Sun 9am–3pm; ☎07/578 8103), on the harbourside, sells *Minimaps* ($3) and handles transport and accommodation bookings. The local **DOC** office is at 13 McLean St (Mon–Fri, 8am–4.40pm). For further information on the town and entertainment **listings**, as well as emergency phone numbers, buy the *Bay of Plenty Times* (every Fri; 60¢).

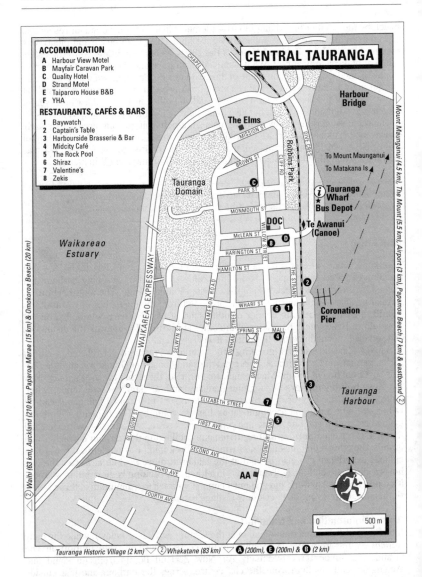

ACCOMMODATION
A Harbour View Motel
B Mayfair Caravan Park
C Quality Hotel
D Strand Motel
E Taiparoro House B&B
F YHA

RESTAURANTS, CAFÉS & BARS
1 Baywatch
2 Captain's Table
3 Harbourside Brasserie & Bar
4 Midcity Café
5 The Rock Pool
6 Shiraz
7 Valentine's
8 Zekis

CENTRAL TAURANGA

Harbour Bridge

The Elms

Tauranga Domain

Waikareao Estuary

Robbins Park

To Mount Maunganui
To Matakana Is

Tauranga Wharf Bus Depot

Te Awanui (Canoe)

DOC

Coronation Pier

Tauranga Harbour

AA

N

0   500 m

Two **local bus** services (Bayline, ☎07/578 3113, and Newloves, ☎07/578 6453) run weekday services that cover most places in the immediate vicinity; pick up timetables at the visitor centre. There's a **taxi** stand in The Strand and several local radio-cab companies (see "Listings", p.332), but for **bike rental**, you'll have to go to Mount Maunganui (see p.333). **Parking** restrictions operate in the city, with a one-hour limit within the centre (bordered north–south by Hamilton Street and First Avenue, and west–east by Cameron Road and The Strand), and two hours outside it.

Accommodation

Accommodation in Tauranga is cheap and plentiful, mostly within walking distance of the waterfront, but a bus ride from the nearest beaches. A plethora of **motels** line Fifteenth Avenue, some offering good deals at slack times of year. At Omokaroa there's a beachside **campsite** and near Papamoa Beach a delightful **B&B**. For accommodation at Mount Maunganui, see p.333.

HOTELS AND MOTELS

Ambassador Motel, 9 Fifteenth Ave (☎07/578 5665, fax 578 5226). Well-appointed motel a short drive from the city centre and near the harbour. Popular well equipped budget units and more luxurious ones, each with a spa and some with water views; swimming and spa pools. ④–⑥.

Harbour View Motel, 7 Fifth Ave East (☎07/578 8621, fax 578 7123). Small, quiet and fairly simple place a stone's throw from the bay. Rates are at the lower end of this price code ⑤.

Quality Hotel, cnr Willow St & Park St (☎07/578 9119 & 0800/808 228). The only hotel in town, this place is big and central, with Sky TV and other perks of international chain-dom. ⑥.

Strand Motel, cnr The Strand & McLean St (☎07/578 5807). Budget, central and near the waterfront, but on a noisy corner. Sea views from most of the fully equipped units. ④.

B&BS AND GUESTHOUSES

Bent Hills Farm, 1162 Welcome Bay Rd, 2.5km from Papamoa Beach (☎ & fax 07/542 0972). Attractive house and great company on a large, secluded farm, a ten-minute drive from Tauranga. The house contains two comfortable doubles (one en-suite), both with TV, fresh flowers and a sundeck. Full breakfast; dinner by arrangement ($25, including wine). Free horse ride and target shoot. ⑤.

Taiparoro House, cnr Devonport Rd & Fifth Ave (☎07/577 9607). Beautiful colonial house surrounded by gardens and trees, a five-minute walk from the centre. Five nostalgically styled rooms with private facilities, plus phone, bathrobes and CD player; sumptuous breakfasts. ⑥.

HOSTELS AND CAMPSITES

Bell Lodge, 39 Bell St, off Waihi Rd (☎07/578 6342). A clean, modern and comfortable backpacker hostel in parkland 3km from the centre. Excellent facilities; free daily pick-ups and transport to Mount Maunganui; free bikes; BBQ. Tent sites $8, dorms ①, rooms ②.

Just the Ducks Nuts, 6 Vale St (☎07/576 1366). A small backpackers just over 2km from the centre, with great views of the harbour and the Mount, and bikes for rent. Dorms ①, rooms ②.

Mayfair Caravan Park, Mayfair St, off Fifteenth Ave (☎07/578 3323, fax 5910). The closest campsite to the city centre (2.5km away, beside the harbour). Large, sheltered and tranquil, with well equipped cabins; linen $5. Tent sites $9, cabins ②.

Omokoroa Tourist Park, 165 Omokoroa Rd (☎07/548 0857). A quiet beachside setting with a camp store. Tent sites $9, cabins & chalets ②–③, motel units ④.

YHA, 171 Elizabeth St (☎07/578 5064). Modern, well equipped and extremely friendly, this hostel lies in secluded grounds a 5min walk from the centre. BBQ, volleyball, minigolf; bikes and bodyboards for rent. Tent sites $8, dorms ①, rooms ②.

The City

The flat **city centre** is concentrated between Cameron Road (SH2) and the harbourside Devonport Road (which becomes The Strand and Dive Crescent as it heads north), bordered by Elizabeth and McLean Streets. Feeding into The Strand at its southern end is a short pedestrianized street called The Mall (but known locally as "Red Square"), a focal point for cafés and evening entertainment, while the rest of the city sprawls onto the other side of the Waikareao Estuary, and back towards Waimapu Estuary.

The ornately carved traditional **war canoe**, *Te Awanui*, stands proudly in a shelter on the corner of Dive Crescent and McLean Street, and is used on ceremonial occasions on the harbour. About one block up and entered from Cliff Street, is **Robbins Park** (dawn–dusk; free), an attractive swathe of green equipped with a rose garden and

THE BATTLE OF GATE PA

In 1864 the tiny community of Tauranga became the scene of the **Battle of Gate Pa**, one of the most decisive engagements of the **New Zealand Wars**. In January the government sent troops here to build two redoubts, hoping to prevent supplies and reinforcements from reaching the followers of the Maori King (see box on p.199), who were fighting in the Waikato. Most of the local Ngaiterangi hurried back from the Waikato and challenged the soldiers from a pa they quickly built near an entrance to the mission land, which became known as Gate Pa. In April, government troops surrounded the pa and pounded it with artillery. Nonetheless, the British lost about a third of their assault force and at nightfall the Ngaiterangi slipped through the British lines to fight again in the Waikato.

begonia house, and boasting fine views across to Mount Maunganui. At the northern end of The Strand is Mission Street and "**The Elms**" (1838–47), one of the country's oldest homes, which was built by an early missionary, Archdeacon A.N. Brown, who tended the wounded of both sides during the **Battle of Gate Pa** (see box above). The house itself is closed, but for the best view of it, walk around the pretty **garden** (dawn–dusk; free), which includes an English oak planted by Brown in 1838 and a reconstruction of the original chapel. Inside is a dining table at which Brown entertained several British officers on the eve of the Battle of Gate Pa, little suspecting that over the next few days he would bury most of them.

Only worth the trek if you have children in tow, is **Tauranga Historic Village**, 155 17th Ave West (daily 9am–5pm; $6), at the southern end of town, just off Cameron Road. This collection of well restored old buildings, dating from 1844 onwards, is laid out as a fake village and is patrolled most days in the summer by volunteers in period costume. Among the curiosities are a mock cemetery with the headstones of British soldiers killed in the New Zealand Wars of 1864 and a tiny horse-drawn post office that used to be dragged from farm to farm.

The marae and the beaches

The local marae welcomes cultural exchange, is well-organized and mercifully free of rampant commercialism. **Paparoa Marae**, Paparoa Road, is on the western outskirts of Tauranga, about 15km away, near Te Puna: follow SH2 westwards to Te Puna, where you branch off on to Te Puna Road, turning onto Borell Road and finally onto Papaparoa Road. Without a car, the only way to reach it is on an organized tour run by the YHA (see "Tours" in "Listings", p.332). The marae regularly runs organized afternoon and evening events for groups (around $40). These involve a traditional *wero* (challenge) at the gate, a visit to the simple meeting-house, where the carvings are explained, and a display of Maori crafts – in return for teaching a craft of your own. On an evening visit you can partake in a hangi followed by a haka and other entertainment, involving some audience participation. As long as you phone ahead (Karen Nicholas, ☎07/552 5796), you can visit independently, or join an event or a cultural-exchange group – where you learn how to make something Maori in return for teaching a craft.

About 20km west of the city but off the public-transport route, lies the pretty **Omokoroa Beach**, a safe swimming beach accessed off SH2 near the town of Omokoroa and backed by a grassy reserve. From the point are excellent views across the water to Mount Maunganui and Matakana Island. Twenty kilometres east of Tauranga along the Pacific Highway (SH2) is **Papamoa Beach**, the continuation of Mount Maunganui's stunning Ocean Beach and backed by the dramatic Papamoa Hills; Newloves **buses** come out here (Mon–Fri only; $4).

Wineries

There are two excellent **wineries** outside the city that are worth a visit. On SH2 heading west, 6km or so from the city centre, is *Mills Reef*, Moffat Road, Bethlehem, which markets wine under three different labels, Mere Road Selection, Reserve, and Elspeth ranges; their most popular wines are the Reserve Chardonnay and Elspeth Chardonnay, though they also produce Rieslings, Sauvignons, some sparkling wines and Cabernet Sauvignons. An elegant, art deco-style building in an elevated position overlooks the vines, and contains the **tasting rooms** (daily 10am–5pm; free; phone ahead for details of tours – 45min, $5; 1hr, $10; ☎07/576 8800) and **restaurant** (see "Eating", below); you can also test your skills in a post-prandial game of pétanque in the grounds. Without your own transport, the only way to get here is with the guided YHA tour on Saturdays (see p.333).

Around 30km west of Tauranga and 5km from Katikati, also on SH2, is the charming *Morton Estate*, with its South African, **Cape Dutch-style** winery (sales and tastings daily 10.30am–5pm) and restaurant ringed by mountains and standing at the foot of a sloping vineyard with roses planted at the end of each row, in classic French tradition. The Morton Estate Chardonnay has become a New Zealand classic and they also make good sparkling wines.

Boat trips on the bay

A leisurely day out at sea, with the option of **swimming with dolphins**, is run by Gemini Galaxsea (full day; $65–75, take your own lunch; book a day ahead, ☎07/578 3197). The skipper, Butler, is a real character, a good-natured sea dog and militant greenie who has a high success rate of finding dolphins. His secret is to allow plenty of time, so don't be surprised if you're out well into the evening; if there's time you also get to snorkel around a reef. Trips run most of the year, but only in good weather conditions. Another very good **boat trip**, concentrating on beaches within the confines of the harbour, is aboard the *Slipstream* catamaran (full day; $25–30; ☎07/576 1841), a sleek and highly advanced 8.5-metre sailing craft that can drop anchor almost anywhere and is a great thrill to sail.

For details of trips to **Matakana** and **Mayor islands**, see p.336.

Eating

There's the whole gamut of eating places in Tauranga, most of them within the city centre, though there are also good restaurants nearby at two major, fairly upmarket **wineries**.

Baywatch, cnr Wharf St & The Strand. A big continental-style brasserie and bar decorated in French blue, with great first-floor views over the harbour. Food with flair, including a wide range of fresh seafood, with light meals for under $15, mains for $20 upwards. Licensed.

Bluebiyou, right on the beach at Papamoa, a 10min drive east of Tauranga. Mid-range nautically themed bar, café and restaurant, serving light meals all day, lunch, dinner and Sunday brunch. A covered deck leads right on to sand and surf. Licensed.

Captain's Table, Coronation Pier, The Strand. An inexpensive café on the water's edge by the pier, serving typical simple Kiwi fare, from 7.30am to 4pm. A good stop for breakfast ($7–9) or fish and chips ($6). Closed Mon.

Crowded Muffins, 22 Devonport Rd. Great, cheap muffins to takeaway or munch here over a coffee. Daily 7am–5pm.

Harbourside Brasserie & Bar, under the railway bridge at the southern end of The Strand. A big, airy building right on the harbour, with great views and a sizeable deck built over the water; in summer, boats moor alongside. Lively cosmopolitan ambience and food, with mains for $20–25 and cheaper light meals. Licensed.

Midcity Café, "Red Square". Run by a Dutch couple, this place has become a real hangout, offering good-quality, cheap European-style food and a wide range of coffees. Eat indoors or at tables on the street. Mon–Sat: Oct–April 8am–7pm; May–Sept 8am–5pm.

Mills Reef, Moffat Rd, Bethlehem, 6km west of Tauranga on SH2 (☎07/576 8844). Relaxing winery restaurant where you can eat indoors overlooking the vineyard, or outdoors under canvas. Lunches for $10–18, dinners for $20–25, plus Sunday brunch served all day (about $10). Daily 11am–3pm & 6pm–late.

The Rock Pool, 64 Devonport Rd. A cheerful, inexpensive BYO café and wine bar, serving great Mediterranean-style food. Breakfast and lunch daily, dinner Wed–Sat.

Shiraz, cnr Wharf St & The Strand (☎07/577 0059). Tasty Middle Eastern and Mediterranean food, excellent service and reasonable prices for lunch (under $15) and dinner (under $20) make this a popular and often packed place; reservations recommended. Leisurely eating in a small café and covered courtyard. Closed Sun.

Somerset Cottage, 30 Bethlehem Rd (☎07/576 6889). Extremely popular, reliable restaurant that oozes charm, a five-kilometre drive west of town along SH2. Excellent value at around $25 for mains. Licensed.

Valentine's, cnr Devonport Rd & Elizabeth St. A bargain for big appetites, this all-you-can-eat buffet restaurant (breakfast $13.95, lunch $15.95, dinner $24.50) is a local institution. Breakfast Fri–Sun only, lunch (noon–2.30pm) & dinner (several sittings 5.30–8.15pm) daily. Licensed.

Zekis, 15 Harington St (☎07/578 6828). Relaxed, trendy and modern brasserie-style restaurant, serving great breakfasts for under $10 (Mon–Fri from 7am), snacks and salads for under $15 and dinner mains for $16–25. Separate bar area and outdoor courtyard. Closed Sun.

Drinking, nightlife and entertainment

Most of the **bars** and **nightclubs** are within two blocks of each other near **the waterfront**. Sunday is a quiet day in Tauranga, and that generally goes for the evening too. **Films** are shown at the Cinema 5 Complex on Elizabeth Street; screening times are listed in the local press.

Abbey Road, 22 Devonport Rd. A wine bar and café (Mon & Tues from 3pm, Wed–Fri from 11.30am, Sat from 4pm), with regular live music Thurs–Sat.

Astrolabe, 82 Maunganui Rd, Mount Maunganui. A large and popular diner-cum-drinking hole and nightclub, serving lunch and dinner, salads and pasta, as well as char-grilled steak and fish; a large range of beers and some late-night boogie.

Flanagan's Irish Pub, Hamilton St, next to *Harbour View*. A big and friendly Irish pub where live bands play on Fri & Sat nights.

The Groove, 47 The Strand. A late-night, hip café, with live music some weekends. Wed & Thurs 7pm–1am, Fri & Sat 7pm–4.30am, Sun 2–11pm.

Harington's, 10 Harington St. A bar-cum-nightclub, usually packed by midnight. Mostly dance music (every night Oct–April; rest of the year Thurs–Sat 9pm–5am). During the summer holidays they often hold theme evenings and beach parties.

Midcity, "Red Square", above the *Midcity Café*. A barn-like nightclub that hots up late on Fri and Sat, with a party atmosphere, dancing and DJ.

Nowhere, 132 Devonport Rd. Bar open from 11am daily, becoming a nightclub later and open till 5am. Live bands sometimes, usually a DJ. Bistro and bar snacks. Pool bar.

The Parallel Bar, 40 Wharf St. This "alternative" bar is decorated with a curious mixture of art and masks from around the world, especially South America, and serves naturally brewed beers from the local *Pilot Bay Brewing Company*. A crowd of regulars indulge in bar snacks, dancing and general mischief. Tues–Sat 5pm–3am.

Roma, 65 The Strand. One of the more upmarket bars, open from 4pm, serving gourmet pizzas until 2am or so, and often with live jazz, plus dancing on Fri and Sat nights. Closed Mon.

Listings

Automobile Association cnr First Ave & Devonport Rd (☎07/578 2222).

Bike rental Available in Mount Maunganui (see p.333).

Buses InterCity (☎0800 686 862) run several daily services to Mount Maunganui, Auckland, Hamilton, Rotorua, Thames and Whitianga, while Newmans (☎07/578 0000) operate regular daily services to Mount Maunganui, Auckland, Hamilton, Rotorua and Thames (via Katikati, Waihi and Paeroa).

Canoeing Waimarino Canoe Centre, Taniwha Place, about 5km west on SH2 towards Katikati, runs guided overnight canoe trips on the Wairoa River ($80), plus abseiling and climbing (from $25; ☎07/576 4233).

Car rental Avis, cnr First Ave & Cameron Rd (☎07/578 4204); Hertz, 150 Elizabeth St West (☎07/578 9143); Rent-a-Dent (☎07/578 1772).

Horse riding Bent Hills Farm, 2km from Papamoa Beach, offers spectacular horse treks up to an ancient pa site, with panoramic views over the Bay of Plenty ($20 per hour; ☎ 07/542 0972).

Kiwifruit picking The *YHA* can help you to find work, or you can approach the orchards direct (see p.327). The best time for picking is late April to mid-June, but pruning is also necessary from mid-June to early Sept and again from end-Oct to Jan. For picking, you're paid by the bin, so speed is of the essence; an average rate is $70 a day, but quick workers can earn $100.

Medical treatment After-hours medical care and an emergency pharmacy is available at the Baycare Medical Service Centre (Mon–Fri 5pm–8am & Sat–Sun 24hrs, ☎07/578 8111), cnr Edgecumbe St & Tenth Ave.

Post office cnr Spring St & Grey St (Mon–Fri 9am–5pm, Sat 9am–12.30pm).

Taxis Citicabs (☎07/577 0999); Coast Line (☎07/571 8333); Tauranga Taxis (☎07/578 6086).

Thomas Cook 63 Devonport Rd (☎07/578 3119).

Tours Some of the better local bus tours are run by Danny, manager of the *YHA* (☎07/578 5064), who runs a different trip every day, from Monday's full day in Rotorua ($80) to Saturday's half-day Marae visit, including a hangi and winery stop-off ($65).

Trains The *Kaimai Express* runs once daily to Auckland; information and bookings at the visitor centre.

Whitewater rafting Woodrow Rafting tackle the rapids of the Wairoa, Motu, Rangitaiki and Mohaka rivers (90min on the water; $65; ☎07/576 2628).

Around Tauranga

Long sandy beaches lie across the harbour bridge from Tauranga, in the thriving resort of **Mount Maunganui**, which is dominated by a cone-shaped mountain that marks the eastern harbour entrance, but has been spoiled beyond redemption by the relentless march of high-rise development. Once you've sampled the delights of its popular, sixteen-kilometre **surf beach** and hot saltwater pools, and savoured the views over the bay from the eponymous mount's **summit**, you'd do best to head on.

Tauranga also serves as a base for visiting several tranquil offshore **islands**, while a guided tour of the massive **kiwifruit orchard** at Te Puke, 31km southeast of Tauranga provides a brief diversion, as does **Katikati**, 36km northwest on SH2, which is renowned for its murals. Also worth visiting from Tauranga is the **Kamai-Mamuka Forest Park**, a broad sweep of demanding mountains and tree-clad hills honeycombed with long tramps for the fit and competent, and shorter day walks for the less adventurous.

Mount Maunganui

From the end of the 3.5km-long Tauranga Harbour Bridge, you still have to travel 5km through the town's southern suburbs and a big industrial estate of cement works and a bitumen plant on your way into **MOUNT MAUNGANUI** – not an auspicious omen. Despite its natural attributes, this has evolved into a rather unpleasant beachside **resort** and party town, with most of the activity centred a few streets near the beach and mountain: the main Maunganui Road (SH29) is lined with cafés and take-aways, where everyone gravitates for sundowners.

The big draw is the mountain itself, affectionately called "The Mount", which you can **walk** around or **climb** up up to the summit (232m), with views of Matakana Island and along the coast. Starting at the hot pools on Adams Way (see p.335), the wide track **around the base** (4km; 1hr) is quite easy as it winds from the ocean to the harbour, giving broad vistas of the entire region, while the **summit track** (2km; 1hr) is tough going towards the

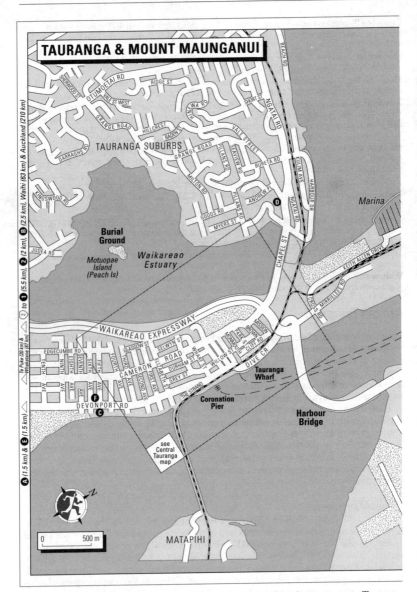

top but in good condition and well worth the effort. Guarding the entrance to Tauranga Harbour, The Mount was once an island but is now connected to the mainland by a narrow neck of dune sand (a tombolo). The shore is an unbroken sweep of sand stretching 15km from The Mount to Papamoa Beach and beyond, with long, golden **beaches**, habitually sun-kissed in the summer and consequently very popular, as is the good **surfing** (premium-rated surf hotline, ☎0900/90098). The other reason people flock to Mount Maunganui

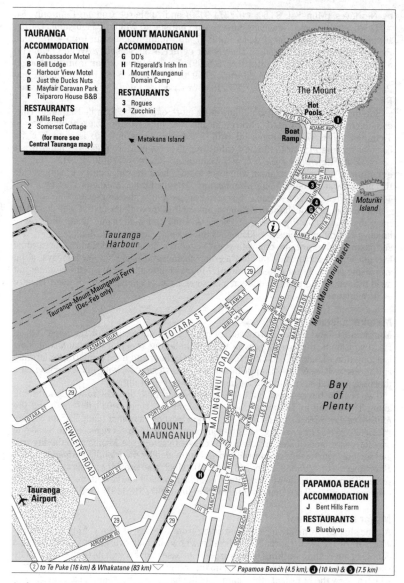

TAURANGA
ACCOMMODATION
A Ambassador Motel
B Bell Lodge
C Harbour View Motel
D Just the Ducks Nuts
E Mayfair Caravan Park
F Taiparoro House B&B

RESTAURANTS
1 Mills Reef
2 Somerset Cottage

(for more see
Central Tauranga map)

MOUNT MAUNGANUI
ACCOMMODATION
G DD's
H Fitzgerald's Irish Inn
I Mount Maunganui
   Domain Camp

RESTAURANTS
3 Rogues
4 Zucchini

Matakana Island

Tauranga
Harbour

Tauranga–Mount Maunganui Ferry
(Dec–Feb only)

The Mount

Hot
Pools

Boat
Ramp

Moturiki
Island

Bay
of
Plenty

TOTARA ST

TASMAN QUAY

HEWLETTS ROAD

MAUNGANUI ROAD

MOUNT
MAUNGANUI

Tauranga
Airport

PAPAMOA BEACH
ACCOMMODATION
J Bent Hills Farm
RESTAURANTS
5 Bluebiyou

to Te Puke (16 km) & Whakatane (83 km)   Papamoa Beach (4.5 km), J (10 km) & 5 (7.5 km)

is the **hot saltwater pools**, Adams Way (daily 8am–10pm; public pool $2.50, private $3.50; use of towel $1, togs $1), in a complex at the base of the mountain.

PRACTICALITIES

The **harbour bridge** to Mount Maunganui carries a $1 **toll** each way for cars, but is free for cyclists and pedestrians. **Shuttle buses** from Tauranga to The Mount are run by Newloves (Mon–Sat; $3.50; ☎07/574 9459) and Appletree Cottage (Sun only; $4; ☎07/576 7404); some Newmans buses also continue to Mount Maunganui. During summer, there's also a **ferry** (Oct–April; $7) to Mount Maunganui from Coronation Pier on The Strand in Tauranga. The **visitor centre** is on Salisbury Avenue (Mon–Fri 8.30am–5pm & Sat 9am–3pm; ☎07/575 5099). You can **rent a car** from the budget Johnny's Rentals, 111 Hewletts Rd (☎07/575 9204), or a **bike** ($15 a day) from Bike and Pack Warehouse, 1 Dee St (☎07/575 2189), or Gravity's Edge Cycles, 229 Maunganui Rd (☎07/575 8997).

Staying in Mount Maunganui tends to be more **expensive** than in Tauranga. This, combined with the **limited choice**, means that most visitors base themselves in Tauranga. *DD's*, 87 Maunganui Rd (☎07/575 0960; dorms only ①) is a small, clean backpacker **hostel** near to the best eating places in town. More creature comforts are on offer at *Fitzgerald's Irish Inn*, 463 Maunganui Rd (☎07/575 4013; ④), a friendly **guesthouse** run by an Irishman who loves to talk about the old country. Finally, beside the hot saltwater pools, *Mount Maunganui Domain Camp*, 1 Adams Way (☎07/575 4471; tent sites $14) is a sizeable, terraced **campsite** in a pleasant spot.

For reasonably priced **food**, ranging from curries, through pasta, to Cajun-style fish, head for *Rogues*, on the corner of Pacific Avenue and Maunganui Road: they serve lunches and dinners, plus breakfasts in high season. *Zucchini*, 79 Maunganui Rd, is a seriously good **espresso bar** with great vegetarian lunches and dinners, occasional live music and a bar, plus mouth-watering champagne brunches on Sundays, all at affordable prices. As for **entertainment**, Mount Maunganui is busy in the summer but dead the rest of the time; if you're at a loose end, catch a movie at the Regent Theatre on Maunganui Road.

Matakana Island

Matakana Island makes a great retreat from the commercialism of Tauranga. It is, in fact, two islands, the tiny **Rangiwea** and the sheltering sweep of Matakana. Matakana is a long thin island, nestled close to Tauranga Harbour and used primarily for farming and forestry. It also has 24km of **beach** on its eastern side, with great **surfing**, and there's a general store and pub for more mundane requirements.

Two regular **barges** head out to the island: *Forest Lady* departs from Sulphur Point, along The Strand in Tauranga (Mon–Fri 6.45am & 3.45pm; ☎025/937 426); and the *Matakana Ferry* leaves from Omokoroa, 20km west of Tauranga (daily 7.45am & 4pm; ☎025/927 251). The crossing takes fifteen minutes and both services charge $2.50 one way for passengers; bikes are carried free. Most visitors see Matakana on a **day-trip** and the only worthwhile **accommodation** is provided by the friendly *Matakana Island Backpackers* (☎07/577 1922, fax 548 1917; ①), which also provides meals at reasonable prices. There are expensive tours of the island but frankly you're better off finding your own way about; call the island's **information** line (☎07/548 1181) for further details.

Mayor Island (Tuhua)

A cone-shaped dormant volcano protruding from the Bay of Plenty, **Mayor Island** is 40km off the coast of Tauranga. The crater is now virtually overgrown and there are a couple of interesting **walking tracks** around its base and through its centre. The north-western edge of the island is now a **marine reserve** and provides a good spot from which to view the birds and other animals of the bay area. The island is particularly well endowed with **wasps**, so anyone allergic to stings should pack medication or just not risk it.

The island is **privately owned** by the Tuhua Trust Board, and all visitors are charged a **landing fee** ($10 for day-trips, $6 per night to stay), payable at the board's office at Opo Bay (all enquiries ☎07/577 0531). **Transport** to the island is either from Tauranga,

Mount Maunganui or Whakatane to Opo Bay, at the south end of the island and the only landing site – though sailings are often cancelled in rough weather. Regular services operate in high summer (Dec 26 to mid-Feb), but the rest of the year you may need to charter a boat; contact Tauranga visitor centre for details and the going rates. The **crossing from Tauranga** or **Mount Maunganui** usually takes two hours and a day trip costs $40; a stopover trip (including one night's accommodation) costs $60, and is offered by MV *Manutere* (☎07/544 3072) or MV *Te Kuia* (☎07/578 7119). Transport **from Whakatane** can be arranged on MV *Te RA* (☎07/865 8681) or MV *Tawa* (☎07/865 6651).

Your only option for **staying** on the island is the *Tuhua Campsite*, at Opo Bay (☎07/577 0531; tent sites $6, bunkroom ①), which sits beneath tall pohutukawa trees behind an idyllic bay, and has showers, toilets, a cooking block and a shop with a limited range of goods.

Katikati

The fairly ordinary little town of **KATIKATI**, 36km northwest of Tauranga on SH2, has sharpened up its act with colourful and well-painted murals on its buildings. Reflecting the heritage of the original settlers from Ulster and the growth of the town, the murals are celebrated with abandon during the annual **Mural Festival** (February 17–24), when local arts and crafts folk make the most of a chance to showcase their talents. More information on the town and its murals is available in the volunteer-staffed **visitor centre** (Mon–Fri 10am–4pm & Sat–Sun 10am–2pm; ☎07/549 1658) in Cherry Court on Main Road (SH2). And while you're here, drop by the *Morton Estate* **winery**, just south of Katikati on SH2 (see "Wineries", p.331, for details).

Kaimai–Mamaku Forest Park

Rising up just south of the Paeroa–Waihi Road (see p.303), the broad spine of the **Kaimai-Mamaku Forest Park** extends south for 70km past Tauranga as far as the mid-point on SH5 between Tirau and Lake Rotorua. Although not the most hospitable nor accessible of the forest parks it contains some **tracks** worthy of exploration, scenic lookouts and a network of back-country **huts**, which can be reached either from the landward side (Te Aroha; see p.300) or from Tauranga. The northern sector of the park is an extension of the Coromandel Range and has been intensively mined for gold and logged for its kauri, while the southern sector is largely plateau country, much of it dissected by deep streams.

From Tauranga **access** to the park is either north on SH2 and then west along one of the side roads that cut across to the base of the Kaimai Range, or south along SH2 and then west up SH29. Two of the easiest spots to get to are the **McLaren Falls** in the upper Wairoa Valley, 11km along SH29, and the nine cascades of the **Kaiate Falls**, signposted from the Welcome Bay Road south of Tauranga, although the walk up to the **Wairere Falls**, some 60km from Tauranga, is more spectacular. DOC produce a useful leaflet on the area ($1), as well as several booklets detailing walks in the park.

Te Puke

The "kiwifruit capital of the world", **Te Puke**, is 31km southeast of Tauranga on SH2. Not surprisingly, this is home to **Kiwifruit Country**, a further 6km past Te Puke (daily 9am–5pm; 30–40min guided tours $8). This massive orchard and processing plant also operates as a horticultural theme park, its gateway surreally decorated with a giant slice of kiwifruit. The complex is as tacky and commercialized as you would expect, but it's the only place to be if you're curious about how these little green, furry fruits grow and are harvested. The "Kiwi Kart" guided tours tell you everything you ever wanted to know about them (and much more besides). Watch out for the busloads of tourists and avoid the overpriced souvenirs and café.

Next door to Kiwifruit Country is the **Vintage Auto Barn** (daily 9am–5pm; $5), literally a big barn of old and not-so-old cars, all kept in exceptional condition. One of the more touching exhibits is The Beast, a racing car hand-built in the late 1950s by a young man dying of cancer; for his "final fling", he sped around the streets of Pirionga (near Te Awamutu) in this jalopy. Among the older models is a 1912 Model C Renault in pristine condition, complete with wooden-spoked wheels. Car fanatics might easily lose a few hours in the extensive library, which is thoughtfully equipped with seating.

From Te Puke it's 66km along SH2 to Whakatane, the road hugging the coast for much of the way, but with no sights worth breaking your journey for.

Whakatane

The main town of the Eastern Bay of Plenty is **WHAKATANE**, with a population of more than 17000. For the most part, it's a rather uninteresting single-storey urban sprawl across flat farmland, until you reach the centre, which stands confined on the flat plains between the last convulsions of the Whakatane River, before it spills into the sea, and bushy hills. Apart from an excellent **museum** and **gallery** the only other notable feature in the town is the **Pohaturoa** rock outcrop. The real attractions lie outside, in the shape of lovely beaches and bays like **Ohope Beach**, which is one of the most popular in the entire region. The main spine of the hills that overshadow the town runs out to **Kohi Point**, where there is an excellent lookout over the entire region.

The Whakatane area seems to have had more than its fair share of dramatic events. The **Maori** word Whakatane means "to act as a man" and comes from a legendary incident when the women of the *Mataatua* canoe were left aboard while the men went ashore; the canoe began to drift out to sea, but touching the paddles was *tapu* for women. Undeterred, the high-spirited Wairaka took matters into her own hands and paddled back to the safety of the shore, shouting *Ka Whakatane Au i Ah au* ("I will act as a man"), and a statue at Whakatane Heads commemorates her heroic act. The first **Europeans** to set foot in the area, apart from a brief sortie by Cook, were flax traders in the early 1800s and a trader called Philip Tapsell, who established a store in 1830. The next turning point in Whakatane's history came when, in March 1865, missionary **Carl Volkner** was killed at Opotoki, and a government agent, **James Falloon**, arrived to investigate. At this unwelcome intrusion, supporters of a fanatical Maori sect, the Hauhau, attacked Falloon's vessel, killing him and his crew. In response, the government declared **martial law**, and by the end of the year a large part of the Bay of Plenty had been confiscated and Whakatane was being peopled by military settlers. The memory of this led **Te Kooti** (see box on p.362) to choose Whakatane as his target for a full-scale attack by his Maori force in 1869, burning and looting buildings before being driven back into the hills of Urewera. In more **recent times**, the Whakatane has led a relatively quiet life as a trading area and service town for the surrounding regions, and as a tourist attraction with access to many areas of natural beauty.

Unsurprisingly, most activities in Whakatane revolve around the sea, with the most exciting trips being to **White Island**, a live volcanic outcrop billowing white plumes of smoke far from the shore, though you can opt for the more soothing charms of **Whale Island**, a DOC-controlled wildlife reserve teeming with birds, or the more intimate pleasures of **swimming with dolphins**. Inland, **jetboating** and **whitewater rafting** trips take on the Motu River or venture into Te Urewera National Park, while on the riverbanks anglers cast for the massive **trout** and salmon for which the area is renowned.

From Whakatane, you could continue with SH2 **to Opotoki**, the easternmost town in the Bay of Plenty, or take the more **scenic route** over the hills from The Strand on the old Ohope Road. Once in Ohope, you can skirt the Ohiwa Harbour by the quiet beaches and through the lovely green valleys before rejoining SH2 just outside Opotoki.

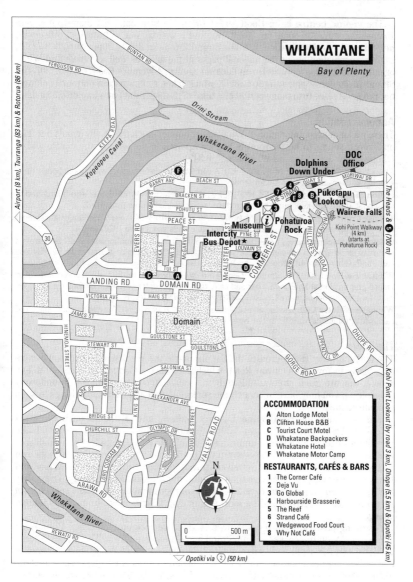

WHAKATANE
Bay of Plenty

Orini Stream

Whakatane River

Kopeopeo Canal

FERGUSON RD

BUNYAN RD

KEPA ROAD

Airport (8 km), Tauranga (83 km) & Rotorua (86 km)

BARRY AVE

BEACH ST

BRACKEN ST

POHUTU ST

PEACE ST

BRABANT ST

EVERS RD

WEKA ST

KIWI ST

TUI ST

McGARVEY ST

McALISTER ST

PYNE ST

LOUVAIN ST

COMMERCE ST

WAIEWE ST

HILLCREST ROAD

MURIWAI DR

QUAY ST

THE STRAND

OHANGA ST

Dolphins Down Under

DOC Office

Puketapu Lookout

Wairere Falls

Kohi Point Walkway (4 km) (starts at Pohaturoa Rock)

Museum

Intercity Bus Depot ★

Pohaturoa Rock

30

LANDING RD

DOMAIN RD

VICTORIA AVE

HAIG ST

JAMES ST

HINEMOA STREET

STEWART ST

GOULSTONE ST

GOULSTONE ST

SALONIKA ST

GARAWAY ST

KING STREET

KIRK ST

ALEXANDER AVE

BRIDGE ST

OLYMPIC DR

DOUGLAS STREET

CHURCHILL ST

CUTLER CR

LORD CORRAN AVE

ARAWA RD

REWATU RD

Whakatane River

Domain

GORGE ROAD

APPENBEL DR

OHOPE RD

VALLEY ROAD

The Heads & 5 (700 m)

Kohi Point Lookout (by road 3 km), Ohope (5.5 km) & Opotiki (45 km)

N

0   500 m

ACCOMMODATION
A Alton Lodge Motel
B Clifton House B&B
C Tourist Court Motel
D Whakatane Backpackers
E Whakatane Hotel
F Whakatane Motor Camp

RESTAURANTS, CAFÉS & BARS
1 The Corner Café
2 Deja Vu
3 Go Global
4 Harbourside Brasserie
5 The Reef
6 Strand Café
7 Wedgewood Food Court
8 Why Not Café

▽ Opotiki via ② (50 km)

Arrival and information

Daily Air New Zealand **flights** from Auckland and Wellington land at Whakatane **airport**, 8km north of town, and Whakatane Taxis (☎07/307 0388) runs a drop-off and pick-up service on demand ($10), as well as the usual **taxi** service (around $20). InterCity **buses** drop off in Pyne Street at the Bay Coachlines office, from where virtually everywhere in town is within walking distance.

The **visitor centre** is on Boon Street (Mon–Fri 9am–5pm, Sat 9am–1pm & Sun 10am–2pm; ☎07/308 6058, fax 307 0718), and is a small but well-stocked office with helpful staff. The **DOC office**, 236 The Strand (Mon–Fri 8am–4.30pm, ☎07/308 7213), carries information about the national parks in the area, as well as Whale and White islands. There's also a privately run booking agency, Adventure East Tourism, 207 The Strand (daily 8am–5pm; ☎07/308 8886), which takes a commission on tour bookings, but is a good place to arrange **rental** of a **bike** ($16–26 per day) or a **kayak** ($35 a day).

Accommodation

There's a lot of accommodation in Whakatane, but not much that really stands out. The preference seems to be for **motels** and **campsites** to the west of the centre and at Ohope Beach (see "Around Whakatane", p.342).

Alton Lodge, 76 Domain Rd (☎07/307 1003). A comfortable modern motel with eleven luxury units with full kitchens and good value for money. ④–⑤.

Clifton House B&B, 5 Clifton Rd (☎07/307 2145). Lovely, friendly old home with a large swimming pool, three well-kept guest rooms and two self-contained tourist flats. ④–⑤.

Tourist Court Motel, 50 Landing Rd (☎07/687 099, fax 670 821). A very friendly establishment with eight fully self-contained, clean and comfortable units and a retro 1970s feel. ④.

Whakatane Backpackers, 11 Merritt St (☎07/308 0406). A charming homestead set back from a suburban street about a ten-minute walk from the centre of town. You're guaranteed a friendly welcome and plenty of useful advice. Dorms ①, rooms ②.

Whakatane Hotel, cnr The Strand & George Rd (☎07/308 8199, fax 307 0489). A recently refurbished grand colonial hotel with a bar and café, right in the centre of town. Comfortable, serviced value-for-money rooms, as well as backpacker accommodation. Dorms ①, rooms ③.

Whakatane Motor Camp, at the end of McGarvey Rd (☎07/308 8694). A well-equipped, sheltered campsite ten minutes' walk from The Strand. Tent sites $9, cabins ②.

The Town

The main highway (SH2) crosses the flat plains and the Whakatane River to arrive triumphantly in town as Domain Road, which then meets Commerce Street and The Strand, the two main streets. Although the architecture of Whakatane is uniformly uninspiring, you only have to scratch the surface to find any number of things to keep you entertained.

You can't miss the **Whakatane District Gallery and Museum** on Boon Street (Mon–Fri 10am–4.30pm, Sat 11am–1.30pm & Sun 2pm–4pm; $2); it's the modern building with a steam engine from Tunnicliffe's Sawmill outside. The gallery is a small area that caters for travelling exhibitions, but the museum is more interesting, with its own archives, research library and well-conceived displays on geological, Maori and European history, particularly as they relate to the Eastern Bay of Plenty. The collection is rich and varied, with over 25,000 photographs and an important collection of Maori *taonga* (records) from the local *iwi*, tracing their descent from the *Mataatua* canoe.

A striking physical feature of the town is the large rock outcrop called **Pohaturoa** ("long rock"), on the corner of The Strand and Commerce Street. The place is sacred to Maori and the small park surrounding the rock contains a canoe, carved benches and a black marble monument to Te Hurinui Apanui, a great chief who propounded the virtues of peace and is mourned by *pakeha* and Maori alike. This site was once a shrine where rites were performed by Maori priests, and the seed that grew into the karaka trees at its base are said to have arrived on the *Mataatua* canoe.

Walks around Whakatane

A scenic one-kilometre **walk** from the eastern end of The Strand out to the heads is rewarded by the sight of the bronze statue of Wairaka on top of the rock, often behatted by local wags after a good night out. But one of the most interesting walks in the area is to **Kohi Point Lookout** (8km return; 3hr 30min), combining part of the Whakatane Town Centre Walk with the Nga Tapuwae o Toi ("Sacred Footsteps of Toi") Walkway, which traverses the domain of the great chieftain Toi, and ends at Kohi Point with panoramic views of Whakatane, Whale and White islands and Te Urewera National Park.

The walk starts in Commerce Street, from where you turn right between the escarpment and Pohaturoa, climb the steps to Hillcrest Road, then cross over to Seaview Road, where you will find the track leading to **Ka-pu-Terangi**, which passes the head of the **Wairere Falls**, a cool and peaceful spot. From here you walk through regenerating bush to the **Toi pa**, reputedly the oldest in New Zealand. The track continues along the cliff top past a number of other pa sites and food pits through more bushland, including honeysuckle and pohutukawa, before emerging onto flax and scrub towards the Kohi Point. If you wish, you can continue from here along the headlands to **Otarawairere Bay**, an excellent swimming and picnic spot; the steep walk down to the bay is quite beautiful, as is the bay itself. From here you can press **on to Ohope**, but the scenery doesn't get any better and the return journey makes for a long and tiring day.

There are a number of other walks in the area, all detailed in the *Walks Around Whakatane* booklet from the visitor centre or DOC office ($1).

Activities

To go **swimming with dolphins**, contact Dolphins Down Under, 19 Quay St (3–4hr; $75–85; book at least 2 days ahead in the high season of Dec–Feb; ☎07/308 4636, fax 308 0359), but you should avoid April, when dolphins make themselves scarce – and note that in winter (April–Oct), trips run according to demand. If you can face an early start, you're likely to be rewarded by calm seas and light winds. All gear is supplied and the company has a high success rate of finding dolphins; there is a resident pod of common dolphins in the area and other types occasionally visit. If you see nothing at all, you get a voucher for 25 percent of the fee to spend in their rather tacky gift shop. In the afternoons, they also run a **seal swimming** trip to Whale Island (1–2hr; $35–40), subject to weather conditions.

The best **rafting** trips in the region are on the **Motu River**, which is hidden deep in the mountain terrain of the remote Raukumara Ranges, with long stretches of white water plunging through gorges and valleys to the Bay of Plenty coast, and rafting this river is a magical and eerie experience. Whakatane Raft Tours (☎07/308 7760) run a number of day-trips on the Motu, reaching the river by helicopter ($330) or four-wheel drive ($270), including all food and equipment; they also offer cheaper trips on the Wairoa, Rangitiki, Waioeka and Waimana rivers (1hr 30min; $45–80). A swifter and cheaper, though noisier, way of enjoying the rivers is by **jetboat**. Kiwi Jet Boat Tours (1hr 15min; $55; ☎07/307 0663) is run by an ex-world champion jetboat racer, who takes you onto the Rangitaiki River, from the Matahina Dam to the beautiful Aniwhenua Falls, over a number of stomach-churning whitewater sections. If you've got your heart set on the thrills and spills of the Motu River, you can join up with a jetboat tour out of Opotiki (see p.344). There are also innumerable **fishing** guides, mostly working on a charter basis from the local marina; check at Whakatane visitor centre for the best deals.

Eating, drinking and entertainment

There are a number of good **eating** options in Whakatane, with a few reasonable **drinking** dens. There's virtually no entertainment, except for the **Cinema 3**, a multiplex on The Strand; check the local paper for screening times.

The Corner Café, 208–210 The Strand. A simple, daytime chips-with-everything cafe. Mon–Fri 7.30am–5pm, Sat 9.30am–2.30pm.

Deja Vu, 64 Commercial St. Restaurant and wine bar with authentic Italian fare. Main dishes range from $17–23, or there's pizzas for $15. Licensed & BYO.

Go Global, cnr The Strand & Commercial St. A pleasant first-floor bistro-style place with balcony views. Fully licensed and BYO ($4 corkage), open Mon–Sat for lunch and daily for dinner from 6pm. They serve bar snacks and main meals with an international bent for around $20, and a good range of fresh seafood.

Harbourside Brassiere, 62 The Strand (☎07/308 6721). A light and airy, popular family restaurant (reservations recommended), serving the biggest and meanest steaks in town at reasonable prices. Also a selection of lamb and poultry dishes of equally large proportions. Daily 11.30am–2.30pm & 5.30–10pm; licensed.

Reef, The Heads, Muriwai Drive, overlooking Whakatane Harbour entrance. A good licensed restaurant in an excellent location, about a 10min walk from the centre. Open daily for à la carte lunches and dinners, with a good-value and impressive smorgasbord on Sundays.

The Strand, 214 The Strand. The best place to eat in town at any time of the day. A relaxed licensed BYO café with simple, colourful decor and reasonable prices. A variety of excellent breakfasts, snacks and main courses such as lamb kebabs, seafood and steaks, as well as mouth-watering desserts.

Wedgewood Food Court, The Strand, opposite junction with Commercial St. Without doubt the cheapest place in town, with breakfasts, lunches and snacks for practically no money at all. Daily 8am–midnight.

Why Not Café, in the *Whakatane Hotel*, cnr The Strand & George St. A friendly and welcoming little eatery and bar, serving lunches and dinners ($15–23), including steaks and delicious seafood fettucine. Daily 11am–midnight.

Around Whakatane

One of New Zealand's premier beach resorts, **Ohope**, lies just to the east of Whakatane, while just off the coast are the twin pearls of White and Whale islands. The active volcanic **White Island**, stranded way out to sea in the Bay of Plenty, is the more spectacular, and a cruise here is one of the region's principal excursions. **Whale Island**, much nearer the shore, is the remainder of a volcanic cone which has eroded, leaving two peaks and hydrothermal activity, in the form of hot springs; it is also a wildlife sanctuary and the site of a pa.

Ohope

Nine kilometres east of Whakatane, the tiny settlement of **OHOPE** extends along the beach in a thin ribbon to the entrance of **Ohiwa Harbour**. Ohiwa ("a place of watchfulness"), is the site of a natural shellfishery for pipi and cockles, and a place of numerous pa sites, signifying the importance of a convenient and renewable food source to the Maori way of life.

When you've had enough of lazing on the unremarkable beach, reinvigorate yourself with half a day's abseiling or **rock climbing** ($40), or a full day's guided tramping, **mountain biking** or **sea kayaking** ($65), with Big Buzz Adventure (☎07/312 4308). Ohope's **accommodation** is crammed to bursting between December and February – when you'll be lucky to find anything and will probably have to retreat to Whakatane – but is quiet the rest of the year. *Ohope Beach Resort*, 5 West End (☎07/312 4692; Dec–Feb ⑤, rest of the year ④) is a complex containing spacious motel units, restaurant, bar and nightclub, all just a stone's throw from the beach and sea. The beachside housing of Ohope merges indistinguishably 4km into Port Ohope, where *Ohope Beach Holiday Park*, Harbour Road (☎ & fax 07/312 4460; tent sites $11, cabins & motel units ②–④), is a popular site overlooking the beach.

Casual resort-style bars and diners are the focus of Ohope's eating and drinking scene, and most of them are to be found at the northwestern end of the community where the road from Whakatane enters it. The *Pink Caddie Shack*, Pohutukawa Avenue, serves reasonably priced fish and chips, burgers and ice cream in a small American-style **diner**. Opposite, at no. 19, is *Café Aubergine*, a stylish **wine bar** with eclectic cuisine (mains $8–24). The liveliest place to while away an evening is at the *Ohope Beach Resort*, where the *Kauri Café* dishes up straightforward but generous food at reasonable prices, with a predominance of fresh seafood; the **pub** upstairs isn't bad either, but give the disco a miss. Finally, if you're after fresh **seafood**, stop off at the *Ohiwa Oyster Farm* (daily 10am–7pm), on the road between Ohope and Opotiki, which runs alongside Ohiwa Harbour.

Whale Island

Whale Island (*Motohora*), 10km offshore, is a DOC-controlled haven free of introduced animals and provides a safe home for grey-faced petrels, sooty shearwaters, little blue penguins, dotterels, oystercatchers, three species of lizard – geckos, and speckled and copper skinks; there are also occasional visits made by the North Island kaka and falcon, as well as fur seals. Once the site of a **pa**, the island's inhabitants sent out several canoes when Cook was tacking near its coastline and some **trading** took place. The history of the island is quiet from then until 1829, when a trading schooner, *Haweis*, was attacked by the Nga Tiwawa chief, who wanted to get hold of the muskets aboard the ship to defend himself against neighbouring *iwi*. The attack took place while some members of the crew were ashore on the island, salting pork. Noticing something was amiss, they rowed for their lives to Tauranga, where they met the schooner *New Zealander*, which duly sailed back and regained control of the *Haweis*.

Access to the island is on one of only ten **guided tours** a year (between Dec and Feb), which depart from Whakatane and can be arranged through DOC for around $35 per person; further information is available from the DOC office in Whakatane (see p.340).

White Island

Many people ignore Whale Island in favour of the more obvious and spectacular attractions of **White Island** (*Whaakari*), so named by Cook, for its permanent shroud of mist and steam. Over twice the size of Whale Island, White Island lies a sometimes-rough 50km offshore. Neither this nor its seething vulcanism deters visitors, who flock to appreciate its desolate, other worldly landscape, with its billowing towers of gas, steam and ash, spewing from a crater lake sixty metres below sea level, and to marvel at the smaller fumaroles surrounded by garish yellow and white crystal deposits that re-form in new and bizarre shapes each day.

Whaakari is the living remnant of a shift in the Pacific Plate, which was driven beneath the Indo-Australian Plate two million years ago. This resulted in the thrust upwards of super-heated rock through the ocean floor and created a massive **volcanic** structure. **Sulphur**, for use in fertilizer manufacture, was sporadically mined on the island from the 1880s and a concrete-processing works was established in 1924, but both enterprises were plagued by catastrophic eruptions, landslides and economic misfortune. The island was abandoned in 1934, and these days is home only to 60,000 sooty **shearwaters**.

An excellent **guided trip** to White Island is run from Whakatane by Pee Jays (daily 8am; 5hr; $95, including lunch; ☎07/312 9075), weather permitting; allow at least a couple of days, so as not to be disappointed. After a fairly precarious transfer to the shallow-water jetty, the two-hour tour of the island begins at the site of the 1924 factory, which is gradually being eaten away by the high sulphur content of the atmosphere, and progresses to the open-sided crater. Here, amid pools of bubbling mud and skyscraper pillars of smoke and steam, you get the chance to stand in the wind-driven clouds (with a gas mask on) and experience a spooky and disorienting white-out.

With plenty of cash and clement weather, you can also visit White Island by **helicopter** with Vulcan Helicopters (3hr; $275, including a walking tour of the island; ☎0800/804 354). Bell Air (☎07/308 6656) and East Bay Flight Centre (☎07/308 8446) operate a number of **scenic flights** over White Island (45min; $95; minimum 2 passengers).

Opotiki

The small settlement of **OPOTIKI**, 60km from Whakatane, is the easternmost town in the Bay of Plenty and the gateway to Eastland. Sitting at the junction of SH2 and SH35, the town is a useful stopping-off point from which to explore its beautiful surroundings and a good place to stock up on supplies and petrol before heading on.

From Opotiki, **SH2** strikes inland **to Gisborne**, while, **SH35** meanders along the more circumspect roads around the perimeter of **Eastland**, never straying far from its rugged and windswept coastline.

Arrival, information and accommodation

InterCity **buses** from Whakatane and Gisborne drop off at the Elliott Street bus station; Super Shuttles from Gisborne also stop off here en route to Rotorua. The combined Opotiki **visitor centre** and **DOC office**, on the corner of St Johns Street and Elliott Street (Mon–Fri 8.30am–4.30pm, plus Nov–Feb Sat & Sun 9am–5pm) is a good place to pick up information and advice.

The *Magnolia Court Motel*, on the corner of Bridge Street and Nelson Street (☎07/315 8490; ④) has thirteen clean, comfortable and modern **motel** units, but for a more intimate place to stay, head for the *Fantail Cottage* **B&B**, 318 Ohiwa Harbour Rd, 9km west of Opotiki (☎07/315 4981; ④, dinner by arrangement $20), in a quiet location with panoramic views of the harbour, an outdoor spa, and one of the friendliest welcomes in New Zealand. The *Opotiki Backpackers*, 30 King St (☎07/315 5165; dorms ①, rooms ②), is a small but friendly **hostel** in a hundred-year-old renovated kauri villa, where delicious fresh-baked German bread is often on offer. The *Opotiki Holiday Park*, corner of Potts Avenue and Grey Street (☎ & fax 07/315 6050; tent sites $8, on-site vans & cabins ②–③), close to the town centre, at the junction of the Waioweka and Otara rivers, is a sheltered and well-kept **campsite**, with excellent facilities.

The Town and around

The small settlement of Opotiki has few sights of interest to keep you before you head on around Eastland or cut across to the bright lights of Gisborne, but it does have some lush countryside and beaches around it. The main street is Church Street, which contains all the historic buildings of note and most of the eateries.

The **Opotiki Museum**, 123 Church St (Mon–Sat 10am–3.30pm & Sun 1.30pm–4pm; $2), is right in the historical centre of Opotiki, opposite St Stephen's Church. The museum stands on the site of the livery stables once used by the overland stagecoach to Whakatane, and its collection is garnered from the local area, resulting in the usual ill-assorted domestic, farming, and military bric-a-brac, here ameliorated by an extensive range of black and white photographs. Opposite, the innocent-looking **St Stephen's Church**, set among trees and chirruping birds, was once the scene of a notorious murder, for it was here, in March 1865, that local missionary **Carl Volkner** was allegedly killed by a prophet, Kereopa Te Rau, from the militant Hau Hau sect (see box on p.345). The case is far from clear-cut, however: at the time, many Maori believed that missionaries doubled as spies, duly reporting their findings to the settlers and military, and it appears that Volkner had indeed written many letters to Governor Grey espousing settlers' land-grabbing ambitions. Local Maori claim Volkner was justly executed after

THE HAU HAU

Missionaries encouraged many Maori to abandon their belief structure in favour of a zealous **Christianity**, but as land disputes with settlers escalated they increasingly perceived the missionaries as agents for land-hungry Europeans.

When **war** broke out and the recently-converted Maori suffered defeats, they felt betrayed not only by the Crown but also by their newly acquired god, and some formed the revivalist **Hau Hau** movement, based on the Old Testament. Dedicated to routing the interlopers, disciples danced around *nui* poles, chanting for the *pakeha* to leave the country. The name is derived from the **battle cry** of the warriors, who flung themselves at their enemies with their right arms raised to protect them from bullets, believing that true faith prevented them from being shot. The movement began in 1862 and by 1865, having capitalized on widespread Maori unrest at the land situation, there was a *nui* pole in most villages of any size from Wellington to the Waikato. The Hau Hau were some of the most feared **warriors** and involved in the bloodiest and bitterest battles, but the movement began to fade after their **leader** and founder, Te Ua Haumene, was captured in 1866. Some of the sect's ideas were **revitalized** when the infamous rebel **Te Kooti** (see box on p.362) based parts of his **Rangatu** movement on Hau Hau doctrine.

being confronted with the evidence and denounced as a traitor. Whatever the truth, the settlers used the story as propaganda, fuelling intermittent skirmishes over the next three years.

The small and unspoiled **Opotoki (Hukutaia) Domain** (dawn–dusk; free), is full of native palms, lianas and trees, including an ancient puriri tree once used as a burial tree by local Maori. There is also a good lookout over the Waioeka Valley and a series of short but interesting rainforest tracks. To get to the domain, head south from the centre of town on Church Street as far as the Waioweka River Bridge, cross it and then bear left along Woodlands Road for 7km.

Tours and activities

One of the most interesting attractions in the area is the **Maori Marae Cultural Experience**, at the Maromahue Marae, about 18km west of Opotiki in the Waiotahe Valley (☎07/315 4630). This offers the chance to share and participate in Maori traditions and activities, including gathering seafood, fishing, bushwalking, weaving with flax, learning Maori *Waiata* (songs), and preparing and eating a hangi. The complete experience includes an overnight stay on the marae (9am–3pm the following day; $95); the tour is only available for groups of ten or more, but there may be a possibility of tagging along with an existing party if you phone ahead.

Bay of Plenty Horse Treks (1hr–overnight; $20–80; ☎07/315 7784), 20km south of Opotiki, along the Otara Road, run **horse treks** in this excellent riding country with plenty of hills and promontories. The overnight trips include a barbecue dinner, hut accommodation and breakfast, and are good value if you can stand being in the saddle for that long.

The much-lauded **Motu River** surges through the hills to the east of Opotiki, and two **jetboat** operators rise to the challenge: Motu River Jet Boat Tours (daily 10am, 1pm & 3.30pm; 2hr; $85; booking essential, ☎07/315 8107), and East Cape River Jets (2hr; $65; ☎07/315 5557), who offer either hard-core whitewater activity or informative nature and pleasure trips.

Eating

There are a number of small, strikingly similar, daytime **cafés** in town, the best of which are the *Flying Pig* and *Aggie's*, both on Church Street. For **evening meals** try the *Elliott*

Street Bar and Brasserie, 10 Elliot St (lunch & dinner daily), about the best place to get some food and amenable company over a drink. The *Masonic Hotel*, a large colonial-style building on Church Street, is also passable, but in fine weather you could do a lot worse than a newspaper full of **fish and chips** from the *Opotiki Fish and Chip Shop* on Church Street.

The Inland Route to Gisborne

From Opotiki, **SH2** strikes out south to **Gisborne** (137km away), dotted with tiny settlements as it twists its way through the scenic and bush-clad **Waioeka Gorge**. Following the river for 30km, the route becomes increasingly narrow and steep before emerging onto rolling pastureland on the Gisborne side and dropping to plains. From there it runs straight as an arrow through orchards, vineyards and sheep farms to Gisborne (covered in Chapter Six; see p.352) . The only part of the route worth breaking your journey for, or exploring from Opotiki, is the first 72-kilometre stretch to Matawai, along which a number of interesting **walks** branch off either side of the road. Ten scenic tracks through forest, ranging from fifteen minutes to ten hours one-way, are described in the DOC leaflet *Walks in Waioeka and Urutawa* ($1), available at Opotiki visitor centre.

Eastland

The corner of land jutting out into the South Pacific, to the east of Opotiki and Gisborne, **Eastland**, is one of the most sparsely populated areas in New Zealand, rarely visited and something of a backwater lost in time. Curving around the peninsula, its scenic main road (SH35) hugs the **rugged coastline** most of the way, twisting in and out of small bays and providing spectacular views out to sea on a fine day. **Inland**, a central core of mountains runs through Eastland: the inhospitable **Waiapu Mountains**, encompassing the northeastern Raukumara Range and the typical native flora of the Raukumara Forest Park. The isolated and rugged peaks of Hikurangi, Whanokao, Aroangi, Wharekia and Tatai provide a spectacular backdrop to the coastal scenery, but are only accessible through **Maori land** and **permission** must be sought (further information is available at the DOC offices in Gisborne and Opotiki). **Raukumara Forest Park** was gazetted in 1979 and covers just over 1150 square kilometres, including the upper catchments of several rivers that drain into the Bay of Plenty. The desolate terrain and limited access discourage most visitors from exploring the park, but the tough, full-day trek up **Mount Hikurangi** (the highest peak, at 1752m) is quite popular, offering the early riser the opportunity of being among the first in New Zealand to see the sunrise.

Soon after entering the region you'll notice a **change of pace**, epitomized from time to time by the sight of a lone horseback rider clopping along the road. This is one of the most unspoiled parts of the North Island, steeped in **Maori** history (see box on p.347) and not to be rushed. Contemporary Maori, who make up a significant percentage of Eastland's population, draw on their strong culture to cope with the hardships of this untamed landscape and uncertain economic prospects.

A reminder of how New Zealand once was, the response to strangers splits into two camps: warm and friendly, or downright hostile. As for the **climate**, it tends towards extremes – hot in summer, wet in winter, and extremely changeable at any time of year. The road is sealed all the way around the coast, but the further around you go, the fewer the **services**, including food stores and petrol pumps. **Driving** can be particularly hazardous on dole days, which are associated with a good deal of drunken driving and abandoned vehicles; note, too, that **theft** from parked cars is also a big problem in Eastland, both within communities and in car parks at the start of walks. **Campervans** are particularly vulnerable because thieves know they contain everything their occupants have

---

LEGENDS OF THE EASTLAND MAORI

According to legend, a great *ariki* (leader) from Eastland was drowned by rival tribes-men and his youngest daughter swore vengeance: when she gave birth to a son called **Tuwhakairiora**, she hoped he would make good her promise. As a young man, Tuwhakairiora travelled and encountered a young woman named **Ruataupare**; she took him to her father, who happened to be the local chief. A thunderstorm broke, signalling to the people that they had an important visitor among them, and Tuwhakairiora was allowed to marry Ruataupare and live in Te Araroa. When he called upon all the *hapu* of the area to gather and avenge the death of his grandfather, many warriors travelled to Whareponga and sacked the pa there. Tuwhakairiora became renowned as a famous warrior, dominating the area from **Tolaga Bay** to Cape Runaway, and all Maori families in the region today trace their descent from him.

Ruataupare, meanwhile, grew jealous of her husband's influence. While their children were growing up, she constantly heard them referred to as the offspring of the great Tuwhakairiora, yet her name was barely mentioned. She returned to her own *iwi* in **Tokumaru Bay**, where she summoned all the warriors together and started a war against rival *iwi*; victorious, Ruataupare became chieftainess of Tokomaru Bay.

The other legend that has shaped this wild land is one of **rivalry** between two students – **Paoa**, who excelled at navigation, and **Rongokaka**, who was renowned for travelling at great speed by means of giant strides. At the time, a beautiful maiden, Muriwhenua, lived in Hauraki and many set off to claim her for their bride. Paoa set off early but his rival took only one step and was ahead of him; this continued up the coast, with Rongokaka leaving huge footprints as he went – his imprint in the rock at Matakaoa Point, at the northern end of Hicks Bay, is the most clearly distinguishable. En route, they created the **Waiapu Mountains**: Paoa, flummoxed by Rongokako's pace, set a snare for his rival at Tokomaru Bay, lashing the crown of a giant totara tree to a hill; recognizing the trap, Rongokako cut it loose. The force with which the tree sprang upright caused such vibration that Mount Hikurangi partly disintegrated, forming the other mountain peaks. Finally, Rongokaka stepped across the Bay of Plenty and up to Hauraki, where he claimed his maiden.

---

taken on holiday with them; try to lock valuables out of sight, or else take them with you.

Public transport in Eastland is limited, though a few **shuttle bus** services exist. Apanui Pony Express (Oct–April Mon–Sat; May–Sept Mon, Wed & Fri; ☎07/325 2700) departs Opotiki at 11.15am, and goes to Omaio, Te Kaha, Waihau Bay and Hicks Bay ($15–37, depending on length of journey); in the other direction, it departs Hicks Bay at 6.30am. *Hicks Bay Lodge* (☎06/864 4731) operates a shuttle service right round the cape between Opotiki and Gisborne, on demand. Linking up with the other end of the cape, Fastway Couriers (☎06/868 9421; $15, on demand) run regular services from Gisborne as far as Hicks Bay.

Waihau Bay

The road from Opotiki to **WAIHAU BAY** covers 103km, sticking close to the shore, twisting tightly from one tiny bay to another, climbing each headland in turn. The first bay of any size is **Te Kaha**, 66km away and a typically beautiful crescent shape, with spectacular headlands and a deserted beach strewn with driftwood. You can swim safely here and nearby there's the *Te Kaha Holiday Park* (☎07/325 2894; tent sites $8.50), a **campsite** with a store and petrol pump as well as access to the shoreline. Waihau Bay is another sweeping crescent of sand and grass, and on a clear day you can see White Island smoking in the distance. The bay is safe for swimming, surfing and kayaking, with an abundance of shellfish and flat fish encouraging you to forage or sling a line in to land a tasty supper. If you choose to break your journey here, the best place to **stay** is *Waihau*

Bay Homestays B&B (☎07/325 3674; ④), at the far end of the bay. They offer self-contained accommodation in a house overlooking the beach, with a very friendly and welcoming atmosphere, and a superb seafood dinner by arrangement (approximately $15).

Hicks Bay

Sheltered between headlands and rock bluffs about halfway along SH35 is the small coastal township of **HICKS BAY** (*Wharekahika*), 44km from Waihau Bay. A black volcanic beach gives way to a sandy bay, which is safe for swimming and popular in summer with campers. Named after Lieutenant Zachariah Hicks of Cook's *Endeavour* expedition, who was the first to sight it, there are numerous pa sites in the Hicks Bay region in varying states of repair, some of which were modified for musket fighting during the 1860 Hau Hau uprising.

Guided **horse treks** in and around Hicks Bay are run by Te Puna Frontier (☎06/864 4862). Options include short treks and twilight rides to Tohuroa Plateau, overlooking the bay, followed by mugs of manuka tea (2hr; $25); all-day rides along the Wharekahia River with a campfire lunch, returning happy and saddle sore to a wholesome hangi ($85); and an overnight tour ($105).

Practicalities

Accommodation in the area is provided by the sizeable *Hicks Bay Motel Lodge*, on the main road at Hicks Bay (☎06/864 4880 & fax 864 4708; ④–⑤), with scenic views over the bay. There are 27 units without cooking facilities but otherwise well-equipped, and 12 fully self-contained ones; the motel also has a licensed **restaurant** (meals around $15–20) and house **bar** (daily 4pm–1am). Behind it, overlooking Horseshoe Bay, is a glow-worm grotto, which you're welcome to visit in the evenings. About 1.5km from the township, overlooking the bay, *Hicks Bay Lodge* (☎06/864 4731; dorms ①, rooms ②) is a pleasant little **backpacker hostel** with comfortable rooms – and a variety of canoes, bikes, fishing lines and wave skis to keep you amused. They also operate shuttle buses north and south around the coast (see p.347) and special sunrise trips to the East Cape Lighthouse (departing 4 or 5am; $15).

Te Araroa and the East Cape Lighthouse

Past the turn off to Lottin Point is **TE ARAROA** (meaning "long pathway"), virtually midway between Opotiki and Gisborne, on the foreshore of Kawakawa Bay. The bay is long and magnificent, with a broad beach and good surfing at either end. In the grounds of the local school stands a giant pohutukawa tree, reputedly the largest in New Zealand. Te Araroa was once the domain of the famous Maori warrior Tuwhakairiora and of the legendary figure of Paikea, who is said to have arrived here on the back of a whale. Ironically, the first Europeans in the area occupied a **whaling station** not far from the present township. These days the settlement contains little more than a pub, garage, store and takeaway.

About 20km from Te Araroa and off the main road, following a mostly unsealed and rough road, is the East Cape proper, where the **East Cape Lighthouse** marks the most easterly point of the New Zealand mainland. From Te Araroa, turn right at the old Postbank and follow the signs to the car park, then clamber up the 500 or so steep steps. The lighthouse looks out over East Island, just offshore, and the grey-shelved promontory (140m) provides great views of the inland mountain ranges – all in all, an atmospheric spot that's well worth the bumpy trip out here. Along the road to the lighthouse is **Coastal Arts** (☎06/864 4890), run by Prue Davis, a painter and ceramic artist who produces robust, expressive works that reflect the landscape in flowing shapes and bright colours; painted plates (around $40) and tiles ($25 or so) make good buys.

Practicalities

The best place to **stay** in the bay is the excellent *Te Araraoa Holiday Park* (☎06/864 4873, fax 864 4473; tent sites $8, cabins & flats ②–③), 6km south on SH35 from Te Araraoa township. The camp has lots of facilities, including a shop (7am–7pm), and runs early-morning trips to the lighthouse (5am; minimum of 4 people; $15). Best of all, though, the site has a small indoor **cinema**; ask at the shop for programme details and tickets. It's also worth taking a sunset walk through the field behind the holiday park and out onto the beach, for an unforgettable display of colours on a clear night. For food, simply tuck into some spanking fresh **fish and chips** from the takeaway on the right-hand side of the main street as it runs towards the beach.

Tikitiki and Waiapu Bay

From Te Araroa the road cuts inland through sheep-farming country, before reaching the coastal town of **TIKITIKI** after 23km. There is little reason to stop here, except to peek inside the modest wood and pebble-dashed Anglican **church**, on a rise as you enter the town. The plain exterior hides a treasure trove of elaborate and fine Maori design, *tukutuku* and carving; unusually, the stained glass is also in Maori designs, and the rafters painted in the colours of a Maori meeting-house.

To satisfy less spiritual cravings, stop by the *Kaui Kart*, near the Barry Avenue petrol station, for a **pie** or a burger; or at the *Mountain View* café, on the left-hand side of SH35 as it heads southwest out of town. Open for lunch, afternoon teas and dinners, this licensed and BYO café serves hearty portions of simple but well prepared food at bargain prices – **steak** or fish for $10, mixed grill $16, or treat yourself to crumbed **oysters** ($21).

At Tikitiki, a well-signposted turning northeast off the main road (SH35), takes you along a rough unsealed road to **Waiapu Bay** – a busy port in its heyday, but now a beautiful and secluded inlet. Around the headland at Waiapu Bay is one of the most remote places to **stay** in Eastland: the welcoming *Waikawa Lodge Backpackers* (☎06/864 6719; dorms ①, rooms ②) asks that you phone ahead for directions or to arrange a pick-up; in return, they offer accommodation with stupendous views in a unique bush setting where you can muck in, or cater for yourself.

Te Puia and Tokomaru Bay

Back on SH35 to Tokomaru Bay you pass the small settlement of **TE PUIA**, which has **hot springs** (public pool Dec–March, $1; private pool daily, $2), behind the *Hot Springs Hotel*. The water is rich in sulphur and other minerals and first gained popularity during the early 1900s as a way of easing aching bones.

TOKOMARU BAY, 68km from Te Araroa and affectionately known as "Toko", sits at the base of steep green hills overlooking the **beach** – a broad expanse of sand, dotted with driftwood and pounded by surf. At the northern end, against the picturesque backdrop of a rocky headland, is a long wooden wharf and the shells of buildings that testify to a once-prosperous and busy port, which now gets by on the merest hint of a craft industry, with locals making possum-fur hats and slippers, painting pictures and shaping pottery.

The Maori who settled here trace their descent to Toi te Huatahi, the great navigator and the first to arrive from the ancestral home of Hawaiki. In 1865 the Mawhai Pa was the scene of several attacks by a party of Hau Hau, but they were repulsed by a small garrison of old men and women.

The turn-of-the-century Te Puka Hotel was destroyed by a cyclone in 1988, as were many of Tokomaru Bay's historic buildings. The town now has a **tavern** (built on the site of the original Te Puka Hotel), a **supermarket** (Mon–Fri 9am–5pm & Sat 10am–1pm) and, opposite the fire station on Waitangi Street, a **craft shop** (irregular hours) with some particularly fine Maori craftwork: woven flax goods such as *kete* (baskets), hats and sometimes *pupu* (skirts).

There is little to do here except take long walks on the beach or the short **waterfall walk** (3.5km; 45min) through regenerating bush – take the road along the beach towards the wharf, cross the concrete bridge and go through the gate on the other side, then follow the river round to the start of the track. If you tire of surfing and swimming, you can **explore on horseback** with Brian, the manager of the *House of the Rising Sun* (☎06/864 5858), who runs a series of treks (3hrs–2 days; $30–200) and knows the country like the back of his hand.

Practicalities

In **Te Puia**, the *Hot Springs Hotel* (☎06/864 6755; tent sites $8, backpackers ①, hotel rooms ④) serves a variety of reasonable meals and offers simple accommodation for the weary traveller.

Most things that happen in **Tokomaru Bay** happen at the *Te Puka Tavern*, on Beach Road (backpacker accommodation ①, motel units ④), which has two bars (daily 9am–3am; live bands on Saturday nights), pool tables and great views over the bay. **Accommodation** is functional but clean, and inexpensive **meals** consist largely of steak, pork or seafood, served in hefty portions. The *House of the Rising Sun*, Potae Street (☎06/864 5858; dorms ①, rooms ②), is a backpacker hostel that occupies a charming wooden house, and has cheap rental bikes. The **campsite**, on Waitangi Road (☎06/864 5843; tent sites $7.50, cabins ②), is conveniently located beside the general store (which also contains the campsite office) and petrol station, opposite the supermarket. For a complete change of pace, try David and Missy Jefferd's *Tironui* **farmstay** (☎06/864 5619; ⑥, including dinner), on the Mata Road off SH35, 6km south of Tokomaru Bay, about 3km after the tar seal, marked by a small easy-to-miss sign. Guest rooms are in an attractive house, and your hosts are a pleasant and practical couple who'll take you around the farm if you show an interest.

Anaura Bay

Continuing from Tokomaru, you'll pass the turning to rugged **Anaura Bay**, 6km off SH35 along an unsealed road. This is one for surfies, with a broad sweep of sand and jagged headlands. At the north end of the bay is the **Anaura Scenic Reserve**, a large area of bush that has mixed broadleaf trees and is famous for its large puri trees and a wealth of native birds. Starting near the end of the road, and signposted to the west by the reserve is the **Anaura Bay Walkway** (3.5km loop; 2hr), which follows the course of the Waipare Stream into thick green bush, up a gently climbing valley and then out into scrubland before turning back towards the bay and a lookout point with magnificent views.

Just beyond the start of this walk (about 100m) is a very basic DOC **campsite** (free), beside the beach. At the opposite end of the bay, the *Anaura Bay Motorcamp* (office open daily 9am–6pm; ☎06/862 6380; tent sites $8) has a store selling essentials and frozen food, heaps of local information, and can arrange a visit to the local marae.

Tolaga Bay

TOLAGA BAY (*Uawa*), 36km from Tokomaru, has street names resonant with the history of Captain Cook, who visited in 1769. Once again the beach is enclosed by rugged headlands. The town itself, with a population of six hundred, is one of the larger and better-serviced communities in Eastland.

Captain Cook, coming ashore to replenish his stocks of food and water, misnamed the bay "Tolaga", owing to a misinterpretation of the Maori name for the prevailing wind (correctly called *teraki*). One character who stayed a little longer – and may well have provided the historical basis for the character played by Harvey Keitel in the film *The Piano* – was an early flax trader called Barnet Burns. He wore full *moko* (facial tattoos), and stayed in the bay for three years, marrying a Maori woman and fathering three sons, before decamping; his wife, Amotawa, went on to marry the great Maori chief Te Kani-a-Takirau.

Heading south on the main road through town (SH35) and over the Uawa River bridge you will come to a signposted turn-off to the wharf (after about 1km). About 1km down this sealed road is the start of the **Cooks Cove Walkway** (2.6km; 45min), which involves a steep and often muddy climb through bush and birdlife, rewarding the effort with good views across the bay. About another kilometre along the sealed road is the long concrete **wharf** itself, jutting out past steep sandstone cliffs, and providing a picturesque spot for a picnic.

Practicalities

In town, the *First Light Motel*, Solander Street (☎ & fax 06/862 6425; backpacker accommodation ①, motel section ④) has four good-sized units, plus laundry and cooking facilities. Close to the beach, and sporting an incongruous mock-Tudor facade, is the *Tolaga Bay Inn*, Cook Street (☎06/862 6856; ③). **Rooms** are bright and cheerful, with access to a balcony overlooking town, while the public areas have a very relaxed and friendly atmosphere. Bar and restaurant **meals** are served (12–2pm & 6–8pm), with prices in the region of $15 for generous and filling steaks, fresh fish, roasts and stodgy puddings; there's also a bottle shop – and occasional live music (Fri & Sat nights). The beachfront *Tolaga Bay Motor Camp*, Wharf Road (☎06/862 6716; tent sites $8.50, cabins & cottages ②–③), has a store and great views.

Tolaga Bay to Gisborne

The 47-kilometre stretch from Tolaga Bay to Gisborne, via the small settlement of **Whangara**, becomes both tamer and bleaker the further south you travel, the land despoiled by clearance for farming. The road climbs in and out of more small bays, occasionally providing panoramic vistas of sea and close-ups of the slate-grey rock shelves that characterize this coast. Eventually, the comparatively enormous town of **Gisborne** (see p.354) looms into view.

travel details

Trains

From Tauranga to: Hamilton (1 daily; 1hr 25min).

Buses

From Coromandel to: Thames (1 daily; 2hr).

From Opotoki to: Gisborne, via SH2 (2 daily; 2hr), via SH35 (1 daily; 5hr).

From Tauranga to: Rotorua (2 daily; 1hr 25min); Te Kuiti (2 daily; 3hr 10min).

From Thames to: Auckland (4 daily; 2hr); Hamilton (2 daily; 1hr 45min); Tauranga (5 daily; 1 hr 45min).

From Whakatane to: Opotoki (2 daily; 55min); Rotorua (2 daily; 1hr 30min).

From Whitianga to: Thames (5 daily; 1hr 30min).

Flights

From Tauranga to: Auckland (13 daily; 30min); Blenheim (10 daily; 3hr 35min), Christchurch (18 daily; 3hr 45min); Gisborne (8 daily; 2hr); Napier (10 daily; 2hr 30min); Palmerston North (11 daily; 2hr 5min); Wellington (12 daily; 1hr 20min).

From Whakatane to: Auckland (10 daily; 40min); Blenheim (9 daily; 3hr 10min); Christchurch (11 daily; 3hr 20min); Napier (7 daily; 2hr 10min).

From Whitianga to: Auckland (2 daily; 30min).

Ferries

From Coromandel to: Auckland (Nov–May 2 daily; 1hr 30min).

CHAPTER SIX

POVERTY BAY, HAWKE'S BAY AND THE WAIRARAPA

From the tip of the East Cape, the North Island's mountainous backbone runs 650km southwest to the outskirts of Wellington, defining and isolating the **East Coast**. A region comprising the characteristically dry and sunny provinces of Poverty Bay, Hawke's Bay and the Wairarapa, this is sheep country, with large stations commanding the rich pastures of the expansive Heretaunga Plains around central Hawke's Bay and the sharp-ridged hill country to the north, frequently contoured into small terraces, hallmarks of a young land eroded by overgrazing. But the region isn't all pastoral: the contiguous Raukumara, Kaweka, Ruahine, Tararua and Rimutaka mountain ranges protect much of the coast from the prevailing westerlies and cast a long rain shadow, the bane of farmers who watched their land become parched dirt, the grass leached to a dusty brown. Increasingly, these rain-shadow pastures are being given over to viticulture, and all three provinces are now noted **wine regions**. Any tour of the wineries would have to take in **Poverty Bay**, a major grape-growing region where the main centre of **Gisborne**, is both the first city in the world

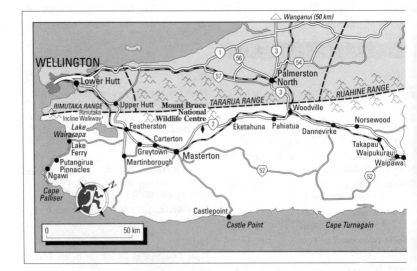

to see the light of the new day – a big millennial selling point – and was the first part of New Zealand sighted by Cook's expedition in 1769. Finding little but apparently hostile natives, he named it Poverty Bay and sailed off south across Hawke's Bay – named after Admiral Sir Edward Hawke, a boyhood hero of Cook's – to a second disastrous encounter with Maori at **Cape Kidnappers**, now the location of an impressive gannet colony.

The surrounding region of **Hawke's Bay** has long been dubbed "the fruit bowl of New Zealand", famed for orchard boughs sagging under the weight of prime apples, pears and peaches. In recent years the torch has passed to grapes, which have been producing the sort of fine vintages that enhance the Hawke's Bay wine country's reputation as one of the foremost in the country. The district is best visited from **Napier**, the single most appealing city on the East Coast, as much for its seafront location and range of minor attractions as for the wealth of Art Deco buildings constructed after the city was flattened by a massive earthquake in 1931. Nearby **Hastings** suffered much the same fate and wove Spanish Mission-style buildings into the Art Deco fabric, though this won't delay you long from pressing on south through the uninspiring "Scandinavian" towns of southern Hawke's Bay. These run almost seamlessly into the similarly lacklustre settlements in the sheep lands of the **Wairarapa**, which takes its name from Lake Wairarapa ("glistening waters"), the eye in the Maori-legend fish that is the North Island. Unless you've a taste for the competitive sheepmanship of the Golden Shears competition in **Masterton**, the main goal here is **Martinborough**, surrounded by another collection of fine vineyards, most of which can be visited on foot.

Access to the mountainous **interior** of this region is limited, with only six roads winding over or cutting through the full length of the ranges. The most tortuous and one of the most scenic of these is SH38, which forges northwest from the small town of Wairoa, midway between Gisborne and Napier, to Rotorua. En route it wends its way through the remote wooded mountains of **Te Urewera National Park**, past

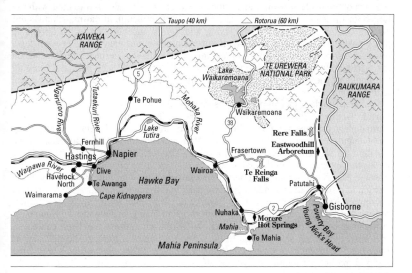

ACCOMMODATION PRICES

Accommodation listed in this guide has been categorized into one of nine price bands, as set out below. The rates quoted represent the **cheapest available** double or twin **room** – except for category ③, which are per-person rates for a dorm bed; fees for **tent sites** and **DOC huts** are also per-person, unless otherwise stated.

① under $20 per person	④ $60–80	⑦ $140–180
② under $40 per room	⑤ $80–100	⑧ $180–240
③ $40–60	⑥ $100–140	⑨ over $240

For more on accommodation, see p.33.

---

beautiful Lake Waikaremoana, which is encircled by the four-day **Lake Waikaremoana Circuit** tramping route, as well as many appealing shorter lakeside strolls.

The East Coast is privileged to have the North Island's most appealing summertime **climate**: the grape-ripening heatwaves come with just enough sea breeze to make vigorous activity tolerable. The slight chill of spring and autumn mornings has its advocates, but winter can be cold and damp. As elsewhere, the **Christmas** and January **madness** packs out the motor camps and motels, but even Napier, the most-visited destination, is manageable at this time.

Gisborne and around

The small city of **GISBORNE**, near the junction of the inland SH2, which straddles the Raukumara Range, and SH35 which skirts Eastland, is New Zealand's easternmost city – and the first in the world to see the light of the new day. As a consequence, its citizens are bracing themselves for the cacophony of popping champagne corks at the turn of the **millennium**: preparations are already well under way to cope with the hoped-for invasion. Those who leg it as soon as the millennium dawns will miss out on one of New Zealand's more relaxing and gently appealing cities, an agreeable place not overly endowed with brash entertainments, but easy-going enough for a peaceful day or so. Broad streets come lined with prim weatherboard houses, which are warmed by long hours of sunshine, and are interspersed with parkland hugging the flanks of the Pacific, the harbour and three rivers – the Taruheru, Turanganui and Waimata.

Gisborne holds a special place in the European history of New Zealand, for it was here in October 1769 that **James Cook** first set foot on the soil of Aotearoa – and immediately ran into conflict with local Maori, killing several before sailing away empty-handed. He named the landing site **Poverty Bay**, since "it did not afford a single item we wanted, except a little firewood". The fertility of the surrounding lands belies the appellation, but the name stuck and looks set to prevail, despite the wishes of some **Maori** who would rename it *Turanganui a Kiwa* – in honour of a Polynesian navigator, rather than continually harking back to that unfortunate first Maori–*pakeha* encounter. Early-nineteenth-century Poverty Bay remained staunchly Maori and few *pakeha* moved here, discouraged by both the Hau Hau rebellion and Te Kooti's uprising (see box on p.362). It wasn't until the 1870s, when these had been contained, that **Europeans** felt safe enough to flock here in numbers to farm the rich alluvial river flats. A decent port wasn't constructed until the 1920s, after which sheep farming and market gardening really took off, activities only recently challenged by the ascendant grape harvest.

Arrival, information and accommodation

A Canadian totem pole donated to the town in 1969 on the bicentennial of Cook's landing, heralds Gisborne's **visitor centre**, 209 Grey St (daily: Nov–March 7.30am–7pm; April–Oct 7.30am–5pm; ☎06/868 6139, fax 868 6138), and most **buses** drop off just outside. Flights arrive at Gisborne **airport** on the western edge of town around 2km west of the town centre, which can be reached by taxi. **Getting around** most of the city is easily done on foot, though **rental bikes** from Maintrax Cycles, on the corner of Gladstone Road and Roebuck Road ($10 a day; ☎06/867 4571) are good for a spin around the wineries.

Despite the huge number of motels, chiefly along the main Gladstone Road and the waterfront Salisbury Road, **accommodation** can sometimes be hard to come by, particularly during the month or so after Christmas when booking is advisable and prices rise a little from their normally modest levels. Campsites also tend to be full of holidaying families at this time, but you should be able to get into one of the hostels. B&Bs are relatively rare, with a few small-scale homestays scattered around the city and a real gem further afield.

Motels

Blue Pacific, 90 Salisbury Rd (☎06/868 6099, fax 867 0481). Presentable beachfront motel with fully-equipped units, a sauna and spa pool. ⑤.

Endeavour Lodge Motel, 525 Gladstone Rd (☎06/868 6075, fax 868 6074). One of Gisborne's cheapest motels, but maintained to a high standard and equipped with a nice pool. ④.

Whispering Sands, 22 Salisbury St (☎06/867 1319, fax 867 6747). Beachfront motel with large modern units, all with great sea views. ⑤.

B&Bs and homestays

Fawnridge, 29 Richardson Ave (☎06/868 8823, fax 867 6902). Very comfortable, hillside homestay with just one double room, great views over the city and a spa pool. ⑤.

Repongaere, Lavenham Rd, Patutahi (☎ & fax 06/862 7717). This peaceful, large kauri homestead 18km west of Gisborne is one of the region's most appealing B&Bs, and comes complete with tennis court, swimming pool and lovely rooms. Breakfasts are delicious and evening meals for around $30 are served. ⑥.

Thomson Homestay, 159 The Esplanade (☎ & fax 06/868 9675). Modest homestay with pleasant rooms, some with good river views and all sharing bathrooms; substantial breakfasts feature home-preserved fruit. Canoe available for guests' use. ④.

Tudor Lodge, 573 Aberdeen Rd (☎06/867 7577). Bargain B&B in an attractive house with a garden running down to the Taruheru River. The rooms aren't flash but are perfectly good, breakfast is a communal, continental affair and there are kayaks for guests' use. ③.

Hostels

Flying Nun, 147 Roebuck Rd (☎06/868 0461). Fifteen minutes' walk from town, this vast and well-kept former convent boasts a pool table in the chapel, where sofas take the place of the altar and the confessionals have become phone booths. Some of the spacious dorms front on to verandahs, and singles cost little more than dorm beds; doubles tend to be a bit cramped, but you can camp in the extensive grounds. Tent sites $7, dorms ①, rooms ②.

Gisborne Backpackers, 690 Gladstone Rd (☎06/868 1000, fax 868 4000). Somewhat sterile former orphanage with good, clean facilities fifteen minutes' walk from the centre. Doubles are especially capacious, dorms less so, and there's plenty of camping space in the grounds. Tent sites $8, dorms ①, rooms ②.

YHA, 32 Harris St (☎06/868 3269). Substantially run-down hostel in a large old house that is at least set conveniently close to town, and new management promises better things to come. Tent sites $9, dorms ①, twins and doubles ③.

Campsites

Showgrounds Park Motor Camp, Main Rd (☎06/867 5299). The more distant of the two campsites, but with perfectly reasonable facilities and rock-bottom prices. Tent sites $11 for two, cabins
②.

Waikanae Beach Holiday Park, Grey St (☎06/867 5634, fax 867 9765). Wonderfully-sited motor
park right by Gisborne's main beach and five minutes' walk from town, with tennis courts and comfortable cabins and flats. Tent sites $8, cabins ②, flats ③.

The Town

Perhaps more than any other East Coast town, Gisborne makes the best of its location,
with almost everywhere in this compact city an easy stroll from the excellent and popular swimming and sunbathing strand of **Midway Beach**. Elsewhere, pleasant parks
and green spaces run along the three rivers which converge at the largely disused harbour, below the steep hummock of Kaiti Hill.

Most of Gisborne's sights are connected in some way to the historical accident of
Cook's landing and the dynamic between Maori and *pakeha* cultures it engendered.
The first of James Cook's crew to spy the mountains of Aotearoa, a couple of days
before the first landing, was the twelve-year-old surgeon's boy, Nick Young, who thereby claimed the gallon of rum Cook had offered as a reward. Honouring a second
pledge, Cook recorded this white-cliffed promontory, 10km south of Gisborne across
Poverty Bay, on his chart as Young Nick's Head. Young's keen eyes are commemorated with a pained-looking statue on the western side of the rivermouth in
Gisborne, and on the opposite bank, an obelisk marks **Cook's landing site**, now a
couple of hundred metres inland following reclamation for the harbour facilities.
Cook's botanist also gets recognition nearby in **Banks' Garden**, full of species – especially low-growing varieties such as ngaio, tutu, karo and puriri – that he and his
accomplice Solander collected here and at Anaura Bay and Tolaga Bay as they sailed
north. Behind, Titirangi Domain climbs the side of **Titirangi** (Kaiti Hill) to the Cook

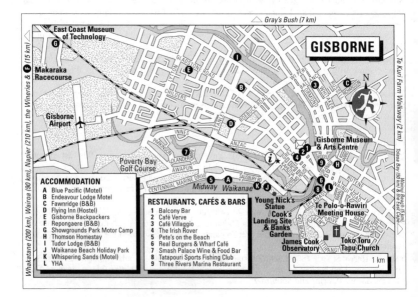

△ Gray's Bush (7 km)

GISBORNE

East Coast Museum of Technology

Makaraka Racecourse

Gisborne Airport

Poverty Bay Golf Course

Gisborne Museum & Arts Centre

Young Nick's Statue

Cook's Landing Site & Banks Garden

James Cook Observatory

Te Polo-o-Rawiri Meeting House

Toko Toru Tapu Church

Midway Waikanae

Te Kuri Farm Walkway (2 km)

Whakatane (200 km), Wairoa (90 km), Napier (210 km), the Wineries & Makaraka (15 km)

Wainui Beach (5 km) & the East Cape

Tolaga Bay (50 km) & the East Cape

ACCOMMODATION
A Blue Pacific (Motel)
B Endeavour Lodge Motel
C Fawnridge (B&B)
D Flying Inn (Hostel)
E Gisborne Backpackers
F Repongaere (B&B)
G Showgrounds Park Motor Camp
H Thomson Homestay
I Tudor Lodge (B&B)
J Waikanae Beach Holiday Park
K Whispering Sands (Motel)
L YHA

RESTAURANTS, CAFÉS & BARS
1 Balcony Bar
2 Café Verve
3 Café Villaggio
4 The Irish Rover
5 Pete's on the Beach
6 Real Burgers & Wharf Café
7 Smash Palace Wine & Food Bar
8 Tatapouri Sports Fishing Club
9 Three Rivers Marina Restaurant

0 _____ 1 km

Bicentenary Plaza, designed around a satisfied-looking Cook, with his back turned on the spot where he first set foot on New Zealand, now a log storage area. The highest point of the hill is occupied by the James Cook Observatory, which runs public stargazing nights on Tuesdays (Nov–March 8.30pm; April–Oct 7.30pm; $2).

Behind Titirangi lies the **Te Poho-o-Rawiri Meeting House**, which is among the largest in the country. The interior is superb, being almost completely covered in fine ancestor carvings, interspersed with wonderfully varied geometric *tukutuku* (woven panels). At the foot of the two support poles, ancient and intricately carved warrior statues provide a fine counterpoint to the bolder work on the walls. This is one of the most easily accessible working **marae**, but it is still necessary to arrange to be welcomed on to and guided around the site (☎06/868 5364 or 867 2835), preferably a day or two beforehand, and a *koha* (donation) is appreciated. Adjacent is the small and decorative **Toko Toru Tapu Church**, though this is seldom open.

Ten minutes' walk north of here, across the Waimata River, is the **Gisborne Museum and Arts Centre** (*Te Whare Taonga o Tairawhiti*), at 18 Stout St (Mon–Fri 10am–4pm & Sat–Sun 1.30–4pm; $3.50). Frequently changing shows augment extensive displays on East Coast Maori and a strong line in contemporary arts. Several disused buildings from around the region are clustered outside, notably the six-room, 1872 **Wyllie Cottage** (same hours; donation requested), the oldest extant house in town, and the **Sled House**, built on runners at the time of the Hau Hau uprising (see box on p.345), so that it could be hauled away by a team of bullocks at the first sign of unrest. The museum site incorporates the riverside **Star of Canada Maritime Museum** (same hours; admission included in entry fee), originally the wheelhouse and captain's quarters of the 12,000-tonne *Star of Canada*, which ran aground on the reef off Gisborne's Kaiti Beach in 1912. Most of the ship was scuttled but the bridge was turned into Gisborne's most distinctive house, a role it fulfilled for seventy years before being bequeathed to the city and moved to its present site. The photos of the shipwreck take pride of place, along with a room dedicated to Cook's voyages and the fully restored captain's cabin.

Around Gisborne

Winery visits with free tasting, easy walks and a smattering of specific attractions make a day spent around Gisborne an agreeable prospect, though with no tours specifically geared to this kind of thing and public transport of little use, you are pretty much on your own. If you don't have a car, rent a bike and head out on the flat roads to the wineries before retiring to one of the short walks just north of the city.

Before settling into some serious tippling of the local vintages, pay a visit to the **East Coast Museum of Technology**, Main Road, Makaraka, 5km northwest of the city (daily 9.30am–4.30pm; $2), where a former dairy factory has been used to hoard just about every imaginable piece of discarded household, industrial or agricultural junk. Little is labelled, let alone interpreted, but the enthusiasm of the staff is infectious and everyone should find something of interest among the ancient petrol pumps, early photocopiers and VCRs and Coke cans through the years. A couple of kilometres further northwest along SH2 lies the diminutive wooden **Matawhero Presbyterian Church**, the only building left standing by Te Kooti's raids in 1868.

Wineries

Further west along SH2 you are well into highly fertile wine country. Most of the wineries you can visit are **small concerns** that open according to demand; hours given below are a guideline only, and you'd do well to **call in advance**.

Occupying a free-draining alluvial plain, in the lee of the Raukumara Range and blessed with long hours of strong sun with warm summer nights, these wineries have made Gisborne the country's self-professed Chardonnay capital. The region has earned itself a reputation as a viticultural workhorse, churning out vast quantities of Chardonnay, Riesling, Müller-Thurgau and Gewürtztraminer grapes to be blended into cheerful wines for everyday glugging. The national giants of Corban's and Montana account for over eighty percent of the regional production, but their factory-style operations are off-limits, restricting visits to the more interesting boutique wineries. Many of these are striving to break the Hawke's Bay and Marlborough stranglehold on international sales, which has led some commentators to predict that Gisborne will be the Next Big Thing. One of the closest and longest-established wineries is **Matawhero**, Riverpoint Road, 8km west of Gisborne (Mon–Fri 9am–4pm, Sat 11am–5pm; ☎06/868 8366) and renowned for its Gewürtztraminer, but there is more interest at **Millton Winery**, Papatu Road, Manutuke, 7km further west (Oct–Easter daily 10am–5pm; rest of the year by appointment; ☎06/862 8680). This is one of New Zealand's few certified **organic** wineries, and possibly the only one to apply the **biodynamic** principles espoused by Rudolf Steiner to all aspects of wine production. The timing of planting, harvesting and bottling are dictated by the phases of the moon, which conspires to produce some delicious wines that can apparently be enjoyed even by those who experience adverse reactions to other wines. Considering the intricacy of such wine making, prices are surprisingly reasonable, so grab a bottle of Chardonnay, indulge in a picnic among the vines and a leisurely game of petanque. While most wineries concentrate on whites, reds are beginning to make inroads, notably at the youthful **Shalimar Estate Winery**, Ngatapa Road, Patutahi, 15km west of Gisborne on SH36 (daily 10am–5pm; ☎06/862 7776), which is gradually building a reputation for **quality reds**, and has already won medals for its Merlot and Pinot Gris, both of which can be sampled, along with some bargain whites.

Trees and walks

A bottle of wine tucked under your arm and a groaning picnic hamper is the most conducive way to enjoy New Zealand's largest collection of northern-hemisphere vegetation at **Eastwoodhill Arboretum**, Ngatapa–Rere Road, 35km northwest of Gisborne (daily 9am–5pm; $5). The parched hills surrounding the Poverty Bay plains stand in stark contrast to the arboretum's lush glens and formal lawns. Planting began in 1910, inspired by William Douglas Cook, who had grown to love British gardens and parks while recuperating from wounds sustained in World War I. Numerous trails thread through a unique mixture of over 3500 species – magnolias, oaks, spruce, maples, cherries – brought together in an unusual microclimate in which both hot- and cold-climate trees flourish.

Walks are not Gisborne's strong suit, but there are a couple of walks detailed in DOC leaflets available from the visitor centre. The closest is **Te Kuri Farm Walkway** (5km; 2hr), off Shelley Road, 4km north of the centre of Gisborne. Apart from a lovely panorama over the city from a ridge-top section of pastoral land, this isn't a particularly exciting route – though you do get to walk the land owned by cartoonist Murray Ball, who immortalized this terrain in his archetypal Kiwi cartoon, *Footrot Flats*, which features "the Dog", or Te Kuri. On a hot day, a better bet is the walk through the cool kahikatea, puriri and nikau woodlands of **Gray's Bush**, 9km northeast of the city, and the largest remnant of the tall forests that once covered the Poverty Bay flats.

Eating and drinking

For its size, Gisborne is surprisingly well supplied with decent **cafés** and **restaurants** to suit all budgets, many of them making good use of their locations on the city's beach, rivers or harbour by means of large glass doors thrown open at any hint of sun. Those same features make the restaurants the best bet for an evening **drink**, though there are several traditional pubs for straightforward beer consumption.

Cafés and restaurants

Pete's on the Beach, Midway Beach (☎06/867 5861). A la carte dining from a fairly traditional and expensive menu, but worth a splurge for its wonderful position overlooking the beach; also a great place for an early-evening drink. Licensed.

Real Burgers, Harbour Wharf. Upmarket takeaway with traditional and gourmet burgers, tables outside on the wharf and good coffee.

Three Rivers Marina Restaurant, Marina Park, Vogel St (☎06/868 5919). One of Gisborne's finest restaurants with a glass-sided, dining room bedecked in crisp white linen and overlooking the confluence of the Taruheru and Waimata rivers. Food is of the modern Kiwi persuasion, along the lines of hapuku (fish) mousse followed by venison with roasted pepper sauce. Expect to pay around $50 for a full meal with wine. Closed Sun; licensed.

Café Verve, 121 Gladstone St. Gisborne's grooviest all-day café and restaurant, with sofas and magazines at the back, Internet access, and gorgeous moderately priced food that extends to Moroccan vegetable tajine and a fabulous chicken curry.

Café Villaggio, 57 Balance St (☎06/868 1611). Award-winning casual restaurant set in a suburban Art Deco house and spilling over into the courtyard. A great place for weekend brunch, lunches or simple yet delicious evening meals for around $20. Licensed.

Wharf Café, Harbour Wharf. Light and airy harbourside café serving good lunches with an excellent selection of salads, and gourmet pizzas in the evening. Licensed.

Pubs and bars

Balcony Bar, 5th floor, Post Office Building, Grey St. Drab bar redeemed by a great view from its vantage point on the top floor of Gisborne's only tall building. This is the liveliest place midweek and sometimes has live bands, but is often closed for functions on Saturday nights – and, be warned, Thursday night is karaoke night.

The Irish Rover, 69 Peel St. A place of simple charms: Guinness and occasional live bands.

Smash Palace Wine & Food Bar, 24 Banks' St. Wonderfully oddball bar where overalls from the surrounding industrial area rub shoulders with suits in a corrugated-iron barn adorned with all manner of junk, from old bits of driftwood to a long-grounded DC3. The bar occasionally hosts theme evenings, and is also an outlet for some fine local plonk: *Parker MC*, an excellent fizz; and "First Light Red", a Beaujolais Nouveau-style wine. Food is basically snacks, a favourite being the nachos flame-toasted with a blow torch.

Tatapouri Sports Fishing Club, The Esplanade. Barn-like pub right on the wharf with outside seating for the consumption of ham steaks, chicken and squid, all at under $12 a plate.

Gisborne to Wairoa

All roads south of Gisborne involve lengthy travel through vast swathes of farmland, which are sparsely scattered with nowhere villages that offer little incentive to linger. There are **two routes**: the faster SH2, which sticks close to the coast before veering around Hawke's Bay; and the inland SH36, which sees very little traffic – and no public transport.

From Gisborne, SH36 winds 70km through the interior over the steep slopes of the 360m Gentle Annie hill to **Te Reinga Falls**, where the Hangaroa and Raikituri rivers join forces to plunge into a river-sculpted ravine. A loop track (4km; 1hr 30min) follows a dry riverbed past towering limestone bluffs to an excellent viewpoint, though you should ask permission at the nearby marae for access – instructions are posted in the car park. If you're short of time, a ten-minute-return path leads to a less spectacular viewpoint. Continuing 25km south, SH36 joins SH38 at **FRASERTOWN**, where you can turn coastwards for Wairoa or turn inland to Lake Waikaremoana (see p.361). Budget travellers bound for Lake Waikaramenoa could do a lot worse than Frasertown's relaxed and very well-set-up *Tipi Backpackers*, on SH38 (☎06/838 7960; tipi & dorms ①, rooms ②), with backpacker bunks either in a lovely wooden-floored house graced with sunny verandahs or outside in the garden tipi; doubles are either in the house or in a self-contained house-truck in the grounds. Trampers can rent all their gear at reasonable rates and, on days when no scheduled bus operates to the lake, a shuttle bus goes up to the trailhead ($15); trips are also run to Te Reinga Falls and other local sights.

Following the alternative **coastal route** of SH2 from Gisborne, the Poverty Bay vineyards soon give way to the hill country of the Wharerata State Forest, where the first real diversion is provided by **Morere Hot Springs** (Dec–April Mon–Fri 10am–5pm, Sat & Sun 10am–8pm; May–Nov Mon–Fri 10am–5pm, Sat & Sun 10am–7pm; $4, private pools an extra $2 for 30min), 60km south of Gisborne. Ancient sea water has been heated and concentrated along the fault line deep underground to form highly saline, iron-rich waters that well up along a small stream as it trickles down through one of the East Coast's last remaining tracts of native coastal forest. Grassy barbecue areas surround the pools and form the nucleus of numerous trails that radiate out through stands of tawa, rimu, totara and matai; a short streamside walk (10min) takes you to the Nikau Plunge Pools, where steel soaking tanks are surrounded by groves of nikau palms.

The adjacent settlement of **MORERE** has a shop and a couple of **places to stay**, both on SH2 as it passes through the village. The appealing *Peacock Lodge* (☎ & fax 06/837 8824; dorms ①, rooms ②) is a spacious and broad-verandahed house that's well set up for families and small groups alike, with beds in small dorms and nice doubles; there's also accommodation at *Morere Springs Tearooms & Camping Ground* (☎06/837 8792; tent sites $8, dorms ①, cabins ②).

Mahia Peninsula

At **NUHAKA**, 8km south of Morere, the road flirts briefly with the sea before turning sharp right for Wairoa. A side road spurs east to the pendulous **Mahia Peninsula**, a distinctive high promontory which separates Hawke's Bay from Poverty Bay. Linked to the mainland by a narrow sandy isthmus, surfers make good use of the rougher windward side, while the calmer beaches on the leeward side offer safe bathing and boating for the hundreds of families who descend each summer to swim, fish for snapper and hapuku, dive and generally chill out. Outside the mad month after Christmas it makes a relaxing place to break your journey, or to stretch your legs on the 4km loop track through the **Mahia Peninsula Scenic Reserve**.

At the northern end of the Hawke's Bay side of the isthmus is **OPUATAMA**, little more than a shop and the pine-surrounded *Blue Bay Holiday Resort* (☎06/837 5867, fax 837 5516; tent sites $8, cabins ②–③). The peninsula's main settlement of **MAHIA BEACH** lies at the southern end of the five-kilometre strand, where there is a takeaway, a café and the well-appointed *Mahia Beach Motel & Motor Camp* (☎ & fax 06/837 5830; tent sites $8, cabins ②, units ④) with spacious camping, simple tourist cabins and flashier motel units. You can also stay just over the hill, closer to the surfie beaches, at tiny **TE MAHIA**, in the log-built *Cappamore Lodge*, 435 Mahia East Coast Rd (☎ & fax 06/837 5523; dorm ①, unit ⑤), where there's just one motel unit with cooking facilities and a bunkroom in the loft. Note that though there are shops, there are no bottle shops or pubs on the peninsula, so come prepared for those all-important sundowners.

Wairoa

Sleepy **WAIROA**, some 30km west of the Nuhaka junction, hugs the banks of the broad willow-lined Wairoa River a couple of kilometres from its mouth, where ships once entered to load the produce of the dairying and sheep-farming country all around. Today the riverside wharves have all but disappeared, but the remnants make for a pleasant enough stroll if you have a few hours to wait for bus connections inland to Lake Waikaremoana and Te Urewera National Park.

The only real point of interest in town is the 1877 kauri lighthouse, which was relocated here in 1958 from Portland Island, off the southern tip of the Mahia Peninsula. If you are staying a bit longer, try to visit the highly decorative **Takitimu Marae**: trips can be organized through the **visitor centre**, centrally located on the corner of Paul Street and Queen Street (Oct–March daily 9am–5pm; April–Sept Mon–Fri 9am–5pm; ☎ & fax 06/838 7440).

Close by is the Wairoa Holiday Shop, on Marine Parade (☎06/838 7574), which sells tickets for InterCity and Newmans **bus** services to Gisborne and Napier, and also for the InterCity buses to Rotorua via Lake Waikaremoana. If an early-morning bus necessitates an **overnight stay**, head for the *Riverside Motor Camp* on Marine Parade (☎06/838 6301; tent sites $7, cabins ③), the *Riverside Homestay*, 48 Kopu Rd (☎06/838 7346; ④), or the *Three Oaks Motel*, on the corner of Campbell Street and Clyde Road (☎ & fax 06/838 8204; ④); alternatively, potential Waikaremoana Circuit trampers can use Frasertown as a staging post (see p.359).

Te Urewera National Park

Te Urewera National Park, 50km northwest of Wairoa, straddles the North Island's mountainous backbone and encompasses the largest untouched expanse of native bush outside of Fiordland. Unusually for New Zealand, it is almost completely covered in vegetation; even the highest peaks – some approaching 1500m – barely poke through this dense cloak of primeval forests whose undergrowth is trampled by deer and wild pigs, and whose cascading rivers are alive with trout. One road, SH38, penetrates the interior, but the way to get a true sense of the place is to go tramping. For hardy types, this means the **Lake Waikaremoana Circuit**, which is among the finest four-day tramps in the country, encircling a steep-sided lake at the southern end of the park. Created little more than two thousand years ago, **Lake Waikaremoana**, the "Sea of Rippling Waters", is the undoubted jewel of the park, its deep clear waters fringed by white sandy beaches and rocky bluffs, making it ideal for swimming, diving, fishing and kayaking.

Habitation is very sparse. The Tuhoe people, the "Children of the Mist", still live in the interior of the park around the tramping base of **Ruatahuna**, but most visitors make straight for **Waikaremoana**, which is barely a settlement at all, just a motor camp and a visitor centre right on the lake shore. Immediately to the south, the former hydro-electrical development town of **Tuai** provides some additional basic services, including the closest pub; but otherwise you're on your own.

Lake Waikaremoana

The magnificent, bush-girt **Lake Waikaremoana** fills a huge scalloped bowl at an altitude of over 585m, precariously held back by the Panekiri and Ngamoko ranges which, at the slightest opportunity, seem ready to part and spill the contents down the pastoral valley towards Wairoa. The lake came into being around 2200 years ago when a huge bank of sandstone boulders was dislodged from the Ngamoko range, blocking the rivers that once drained the valleys and thereby forming the lake. Maori have a less prosaic explanation of the lake's creation, pointing to the work of Hau-Mapuhia, the recalcitrant daughter of Mahu, who was drowned by her father and turned into a *taniwha*, or water spirit. In a frenzied effort to get to the sea, she charged in every direction, thereby creating the various arms of the lake. As she frantically ran south toward Onepoto, the dawn caught her, turning her to stone at a spot where the lake is said to ripple from time to time, in a watery memory of her titanic struggle.

TE KOOTI

Te Kooti Rikirangi was one of the most celebrated of Maori "rebels", a thorn in the sides of the colonial government throughout the New Zealand Wars of the late 1860s and early years of the 1870s. Depicted, at least in *pakeha*-biased school books, as a ruthless guerrilla leader and the wildest outlaw in Maori history, in truth he was a mild-mannered man with a neatly-trimmed beard and moustache rather than the more confrontational *moko* (facial tattoos). An excellent fighter and brilliant **strategist**, Te Kooti kept the mountainous spine of the North Island on edge for the best part of a decade, eluding the biggest manhunt in New Zealand's history.

Though not of chiefly rank, Te Kooti could trace his ancestry back to the captains of several canoes and was born near Gisborne into a respected family around 1830, though little else is known of his early years. By the middle of the 1860s, he was fighting for the government against the **Hau Hau** (see box on p.345), a fanatical, pseudo-Christian cult which started in Taranaki in 1862. The cult spread to the East Coast where, in 1866, Te Kooti was unjustly accused of being in league with its devotees. Denied the trial he so often demanded, he was subsequently imprisoned on the Chatham Islands, along with 300 of his supposed allies. In 1867, he was brought close to death by a fever, but rose again, claiming a divine revelation and establishing a new religion, **Ringatu** ("the uplifted hand"), which still has some 6000 believers today. Ringatu took its cues from the Hau Hau, but developed into a uniquely Maori version of Christianity, drawing heavily on the Old Testament. Some say Te Kooti saw himself as a Moses figure, called to lead his people to freedom, and he was certainly charismatic in his approach – apparently given to dousing his uplifted hand in phosphorus so that it glowed in the dim meeting houses.

After two years on the Chathams, Te Kooti and his fellow prisoners commandeered a ship and enacted a dramatic escape, returning to Poverty Bay. Te Kooti sought the rugged safety of the **Urewera Range**, with the Armed Constabulary in hot pursuit, relentlessly tailing him through snow, mud and heat on horseback and on foot. Nonetheless, Te Kooti conducted successful campaigns, exacting revenge against government troops at Whakatane on the Bay of Plenty, Mohaka in Hawke's Bay and at Rotorua. The government posted a reward of £1000 on his head, but he was always able to stay ahead of the game and it was never claimed. With the end of the New Zealand Wars in 1872, Te Kooti took refuge in the Maori safe haven of the **King Country**. He was eventually pardoned in 1883, and in 1891 was granted a plot of land near Whakatane, where he lived out the last two years of his life.

Drivers can skirt the lake's eastern shores and get to the **Papakorito Falls**, a twenty-metre-wide curtain of water just over a kilometre east of the visitor centre, but to really see and get a feel for the place you'll need to **walk**. DOC's *Waikaremoana Walks* leaflet ($1) details all the routes, including the Lake Waikaremoana Circuit (see p. 363) – and a number of more manageable excursions, such as the stroll to the double-drop **Aniwaniwa Falls** (1km; 15min return), starting from beside the visitor centre, or the **Black Beech Track** (2km; 30min one-way), which follows the old highway from the visitor centre to the motor camp. With the best part of a day to spare, take on the **Waipai–Ruapani–Waikareiti Round Trip** (15km; 6hr), which starts 200m north of the visitor centre and winds up through dense beech forest past the grassy-fringed Lake Ruapani to the beautiful and serene **Lake Waikareiti**, where you can rent rowboats ($10 per half day, $40 deposit), though you'll need to plan ahead, as the key is held at Aniwaniwa visitor centre. Return down the Waikareiti Track or head on around to the northern side of the lake (3hr one way) and stay at **Sandy Bay Hut** (Category 3; $4; 18 bunks).

Other ways to explore the lake include **kayaking** with Bay Kayaks (☎06/837 3737), based at *Waikaremoana Motor Camp*, who rent out kayaks ($35 per half-day, $45 a day, $175 for 5 days), lead guided trips on the lake (1 day $90, 2 days $250) and run tramp-

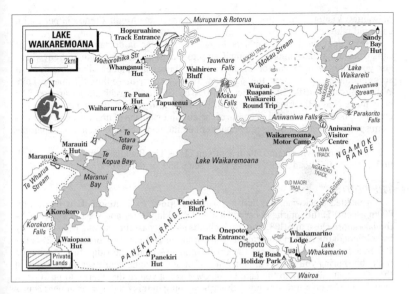

ing and paddle combos; or **horse trekking** with *Big Bush Holiday Park*, at Tuai, 3km south of Onepoto ($50 per half-day; ☎06/837 3777).

The Lake Waikaremoana Circuit

The **Lake Waikaremoana Circuit** (46km; 3-4 days; 900m ascent) undoubtedly ranks among the finest multi-day tramps in New Zealand, and is often compared with the South Island's Routeburn and Milford tracks. But with the exception of an exhausting climb on the first day, this is a much gentler affair; well-paced and mostly hugging the lakeshore, the tramp offers plenty of opportunities to fish and swim, as well as to simply admire the majestic scenery and listen to the cacophonous birdlife. This is the most popular multi-day tramp in the North Island, so you'll need to choose your time to avoid the crowds: school holidays, especially the six weeks after Christmas, are always busy and the winter months (June–Sept) can be cold and wet, making spring and autumn the best times.

DOC's *Lake Waikaremoana Track* leaflet ($1) provides all the information you need to walk the track, though **map** enthusiasts may fancy the 1:100,000 *Urewera Parkmap*. The walk is normally done in four days, spending nights in three of the five **huts** or six **campsites** scattered around the lakeshore. Huts and campsites all cost $6 per night if bought in advance from the visitor centre or motor camp, $8 if bought from a warden on the track. Each hut is supplied with drinking water, toilets and a heating stove, but a cooking stove and fuel must be carried. Most people prefer to walk clockwise around the lake, getting the challenging but panoramic ascent of Panekiri Bluff over with on the first day, though if the weather looks bad there's no reason why you shouldn't go anti-clockwise in the hope that it will improve on subsequent days.

TRAILHEAD TRANSPORT

Access to the start and finish of the Waikaremoana Circuit is either by shuttle bus or by boat: whichever way you walk, you can be on the track by 9am, and you need to finish your last day's walk by 2pm. Vehicles and clobber are best left in the car park at

Aniwaniwa Visitor Centre (free) or at the Waikaremoana Motor Camp ($3 per night, bags and bikes $4).

A **ferry service** (3 daily mid-Dec to Jan, rest of year on demand; $20 round-trip) runs from the Waikaremoana Motor Camp to Onepoto, Hopuruahine and anywhere else you might want to start or finish your walk (prices dependent on numbers). Most accommodation in or near the park can book you on to Anthony Tamati's Lake Waikaremoana **shuttle bus** service (☎06/837 3836) to the trailhead for around $25; or contact Noel Hinemoa (☎07/837 3727), who also runs a **water-taxi** service – enabling you to walk shorter sections of the circuit by means of pre-arranged pick-ups from specified beaches. Costs are dependent on numbers, but are broadly comparable with the regular ferries.

From **Frasertown**, around 50km south on SH38, Tipi Backpackers also runs a shuttle bus to the trailhead for its guests ($15; see p.359 for details).

THE ROUTE

When tackled clockwise, the first leg from **Onepoto to Panekiri Hut** (9km; 5hr; 600m ascent) is the toughest; carry plenty of drinking water and start at a shelter by the lakeshore close to SH38. The track climbs steeply past the site of a redoubt set up by soldiers of the Armed Constabulary in pursuit of Te Kooti (see box on p.362) to the Pukenui trig point, from where the track undulates along the ridge top. Steps up a rocky bluff bring you to the Panekiri Hut (36 bunks), magnificently set on the brink of the cliffs that fall away to the lake far below. Even if you've the energy to push on, it would be a shame not to stay here, though camping in this fragile environment is prohibited. Committed campers must press on to Waiopaoa, a whopping nine hours' walk from the start.

From **Panekiri Hut to Waiopaoa Hut** (7.5km; 3–4hr; 600m descent) you lose the height gained the previous day, slowly at first along the descending ridge, then very rapidly through an often-muddy area where protruding tree roots provide welcome hand-holds. Occasional lake views and the transition from beech forests to rich podocarp woodlands makes this an appealing, if tricky, section of track down to the hut (22 bunks) and campsite.

Pressing on beyond **Waiopaoa Hut to Marauiti Hut** (11km; 4–5hr; 100m ascent), you largely follow the lakeshore, initially across grassland and through kanuka scrub where a side track leads to the impressive 20m Korokoro Falls (25min return) and, just beyond the junction, the Korokoro campsite (1hr 30min from Waiopaoa Hut). Meanwhile, the main track climbs slightly above the lake past barely accessible bays, eventually reaching the Maraunui campsite and, after climbing the low Whakaneke Spur, descends to the waterside Marauiti Hut (18 bunks). From **Marauiti Hut to Te Puna Hut** (7km; 2hr 30min–3hr; 100m ascent) the track passes the lovely white-sand Te Kopua Bay and climbs an easy saddle, before dropping down to Te Totara Bay and following the lake to Waiharuru campsite and on to Te Puna Hut (18 bunks).

For most trampers, the last day covers the following two sections: **Te Puna Hut to Whanganui Hut** (5.5km; 2hr; 50m ascent), which crosses a broad neck of land to the Tapuaenui campsite then follows the shore to the nicely sited Whanganui Hut (18 bunks); and **Whanganui Hut to Hopuruahine** (5km; 2–3hr; 50m ascent), which skirts the lake and follows grassy flats beside the Hopuruahine River and across a suspension bridge to the access road.

Waikaremoana practicalities

SH38 from Wairoa runs around the eastern side of Lake Waikaremoana to the **Aniwaniwa visitor centre** (daily 8am–5pm; ☎06/837 3803), the main source of information on Lake Waikaremoana and Te Urewera National Park, with excellent and extensive displays on the social history, geology and ecology of the region and a stack of brochures detailing the numerous walks in the area. The only scheduled transport, the thrice-weekly InterCity **bus** between Wairoa and Rotorua, stops outside the visitor centre: Wairoa-bound services pass through at around 6pm, Rotorua-bound buses at 9am.

At some point you'll need **accommodation**, which for most means the well-equipped *Waikaremoana Motor Camp*, on SH38, 1.5km south of the visitor centre (☎06/837 3826; tent sites $7.50, bunkhouse ①, cabins ②, chalets & units ③), with a compact but grassy camping area, a perfectly serviceable bunkhouse, cabins and more luxurious self-contained chalets and units; showers are available for non-guests at $2 a time. Other accommodation options are **in Tuai**, 3km south of Onepoto, where there's the *Big Bush Holiday Park* (☎ & fax 06/837 3777; tent sites $8, on-site vans ①), with a daytime café selling tasty sandwiches and good coffee. Tuai also has the former construction workers' quarters of *Whakamarino Lodge*, Rotten Row (☎ & fax 06/837 3876; dorms ①, rooms & flats ③), which is rather short on character, despite being wonderfully sited right on the shores of the trout-filled Lake Whakamarino; meals are available on request and the Waikaremoana Shuttle provides lake access.

You'll largely have to fend for yourself when it comes to **eating**. Apart from the **café** at Tuai's *Big Bush Holiday Park*, the only food in the park is the limited range at the grocery shop in the *Waikaremoana Motor Camp*.

Beyond Lake Waikaremoana: the heart of the park

Beyond Lake Waikaremoana, SH38 twists and turns for two hours before regaining the tar seal at Murupara, almost 100km northwest of the lake and just an hour (62km) short of Rotorua. The road, which took 45 years to build and wasn't completed until 1930, makes a tortuous journey through the heart of Te Urewera National Park, the ancestral home of the Tuhoe people.

Historically, the Tuhoe had limited contact with Europeans; even today, they live in relative isolation in ramshackle roadside villages such as **RUATAHUNA**, 48km from Waikaremoana, which also serves as a base for a couple of little-used tracks into beautiful and remote country north of SH38. These are most often used by anglers and hunters, but are excellent for tramping, too, with Category 3 huts ($4) at regular intervals. Two DOC leaflets (50¢ each) cover these tramps, the easiest of which is the **Whakatane River Round Trip**, a three-to-five-day walk suitable for most levels of fitness through varied scenery encompassing river valleys, native forest, grassy flats and farmland. For tougher specimens, there's the **Upper Waikare River Guide**, an amalgam of several tracks, many of them following riverbeds (seek local advice on the likelihood of flooding) and enabling various route combinations (2–4 days). If you'd rather go on **horseback**, Te Urewera Adventures (1–5 days, $120–780; ☎07/366 3969) run **treks** from their Mataatua Marae in Ruatahuna, with overnight accommodation in permanently erected tents.

In the village, the *Ruatahuna Motel* (☎07/366 3393; dorms ①, units ③) offers a four-berth backpacker room with linen and towels provided, simple budget **motel** units, and breakfast and packed lunches on request; the motel also has a **takeaway** and sells the only **petrol** before Murupara. At Te Whaiti, 5km before Ruatahuna, there's a free **camping** area beside the highway.

The **northward continuation** of SH38 beyond the border of the Te Urewera National Park is covered under "Whirinaki Forest Park and the road to Lake Waikaremoana" on p.268.

Wairoa to Napier

Travelling by bus, or even by car, there is little to justify stopping in the inland farming country that lines the highway between Wairoa and Napier, though **cyclists** may want to break this 120km stretch. The most sensible place to do just that is halfway at *Bec's Backpackers and Bums*, on SH2 (☎06/839 7341; tent sites $5, dorms ①, rooms ②), a rustic, budget **farmstay** in a shed converted with a sense of fun and an eye for the offbeat, which seduces many to stay longer than their planned overnight stop. An equally appealing alternative lies 30km further on at *Glenview Farm Hostel*, Aropaoanui Road, 2km east off SH2 (☎06/836 6232; dorms ①, rooms ②, B&B ④), a small and well-organized backpackers with bargain dorm beds and self-contained rooms; a separate homestay section, 2km down the road, features an elaborate breakfast – and there's **riding** ($25 per half-day, $35 a day) that includes swimming the horses in the river.

A few kilometres further south, the highway passes the small **Lake Tutira** and its diminutive neighbour, Lake Waikopiro, neither worthy of much attention though if you want breath of air you could tackle one of three farmland loop walks (20min, 2hr and 5hr). On a hot day you might prefer the shade offered by **White Pine Bush Scenic Reserve**, 10km south, a dense clump of kahikatea, rimu and other podocarps, where loop tracks (30min and 1hr) thread through the bush alongside the Kareaara Stream. From here it is just 25km to Napier.

Napier and around

The port city of **NAPIER** is Hawke's Bay's largest, but with its beautiful seafront position, a Mediterranean climate and a population barely touching 50,000, it is an easy place to come to terms with. Factor in the world's finest collection of small-scale Art Deco buildings, heaps of amusements for kids and a burgeoning café society, and you have one of New Zealand's most likeable regional centres. There are even better reasons to stick around the Napier area, not least for the trip out to the gannet colony at Cape Kidnappers, and to tour the barrel-load of excellent **wineries** on the surrounding plains.

In 1769, James Cook sailed past **Ahuriri**, the current site of Napier, noting the seagirt Bluff Hill linked to the mainland by two slender shingle banks and backed by a superb saltwater lagoon – the only substantial sheltered mooring between Gisborne and Wellington. Nonetheless, he anchored just to the south, off what came to be known as Cape Kidnappers, on account of a less-than-cordial encounter with the native Ngati Kahungunu people. Some thirty years later, when early whalers followed in Cook's tracks, Ahuriri was all but deserted, the Ngati Kahungunu having been driven out by rivals equipped with guns – the dubious contribution of European settlers in the Bay of Islands. During the uneasy peace of the early colonial years, Maori returned to the Napier area, which weathered the **New Zealand Wars** of the 1860s relatively unscathed and profited from the peace sustained by the guiding hands of men like the missionary printer William Colenso and Land Commissioner Donald McLean, both staunch supporters of sheep farming in Hawke's Bay. The port boomed, but by the early years of the twentieth century all the available land was used up and Napier had begun to stagnate.

Everything changed in two-and-a-half minutes on the morning of February 3, 1931, when the city was rocked by the biggest **earthquake** in New Zealand's recorded history, measuring a massive 7.9 on the Richter scale. More than six hundred aftershocks followed over the next two weeks, hampering efforts to rescue the 258 people who perished throughout Hawke's Bay, 162 of them in Napier alone. The centre of the city was completely devastated: almost all the brick-built shops and offices crumbled into a heap of smouldering rubble; the more flexible wooden buildings survived the initial tremor only to be consumed by the ensuing fire, which was fanned by a stiff sea breeze. The land twisted and buckled, finding a new equilibrium more than two metres higher; the sea drained out of the Ahuriri Lagoon, leaving trawlers high and dry and fish floundering on the mud flats. Three hundred square kilometres of new land was wrested from the grip of the ocean – enough room to site the Hawke's Bay airport, establish new farms and expand the city; cast your eye inland and you can still pick out a stranded line of sea cliffs a couple of kilometres away.

All this happened in the midst of the Great Depression, but Napier grasped the opportunity to start afresh: out went the trams; telephone wires were laid underground; the streets were widened; and buildings were required to have cantilevered verandahs, obviating the need for unsightly support poles. In the spirit of the times, almost everything was designed according to the precepts of the **Art Deco** movement, the simultaneous reconstruction giving Napier a stylistic uniformity rarely seen – and ranking it alongside Miami Beach as one of the largest collections of Art Deco buildings in the world.

Arrival, information and transport

Napier is the northern terminus of the *Bay Express* **train** from Wellington, which pulls in to the Napier Travel Centre, Munroe Street (☎06/834 2720), where InterCity and Newmans long-distance **buses** also drop off. **Flights** touch down at Hawke's Bay Airport, 5km north of town on SH2, where they are met by the Super Shuttle (☎06/879 9766), which charges $7 into town.

The large and informative **visitor centre**, 100 Marine Parade (daily: Christmas–Jan 9am–8pm; Feb–Christmas 9am–5pm; ☎06/834 1911, fax 835 7219), is on the seafront, just along from Napier's former courthouse, which now houses the **DOC office**, 59 Marine Parade (Mon–Fri 9am–4.15pm; ☎06/834 3111, fax 834 4869), where you can consult tide tables for the Cape Kidnappers walk (see p.373), pick up some free and mildly diverting heritage trail leaflets, and find out about walks into the remote Kaweka and Ruahine ranges to the west.

Getting around Napier's central sights is easily done on foot. Visiting the gannets and the wineries and is a different matter: **tours** are an excellent way to go, but if you like a bit more freedom you'll need to **rent a car** (try Avis, ☎06/835 1828; Hertz, ☎06/835 6169; or Rent-a-Dent, ☎06/834 1420) or a **bike** from one of the hostels (see p.368). The Nimbus **local bus** services (Mon–Fri only) to Napier's outlying districts leave from Dalton Street, between Dickens and Thackeray streets, but aren't a great deal of use except for getting to Hastings.

Accommodation

Apart from the usual shortage of rooms during the month of so after Christmas, and to a lesser extent during February and March, you should have little trouble finding accommodation in Napier. In Kiwi-seaside fashion, there are dozens of **motels** around town, the greatest concentration being in Westshore, a beachfront suburb a few kilometres from the centre beside SH2 heading north. Right in the thick of things, Marine Parade has both low-cost backpacker **hostels** and classy **B&Bs**, but for homestays look no further than Bluff Hill. Predictably, none of the **campsites** are especially central.

Hotels and motels

Albatross Motel, 56 Meeanee Quay, Westshore (☎06/835 5991, fax 835 5949). Large and good-value motel close to Westshore Beach, with a pool, spa, studio units and self-catering rooms. Units ③, rooms ④.

The County Hotel, 12 Browning St (☎06/835 7800, fax 835 7797). Combined business and tourist hotel in the Edwardian former council offices building, one of the few to survive the earthquake. Rooms all come with en-suite facilities, Sky TV and writing desks. ⑧.

Gardner Court Motel, 16 Nelson Crescent (☎ & fax 06/835 5913). Quiet and reasonably central motel with a heated outdoor pool and standard motel rooms at bargain prices. ④.

B&Bs and homestays

Madeira B&B, 6 Madeira Rd (☎06/835 5185). Wonderfully central homestay with just one small-ish double room and breakfast on the verandah overlooking the town. ④.

Mon Logis Guesthouse, 415 Marine Parade (☎ & fax 06/835 2125). Classy and sumptuously furnished boutique hotel with a French theme. Some rooms in this lovely two-storey wooden house overlook the sea. The tariff includes a delicious breakfast, but you'll have to stump up $50 for the superb five-course table d'hôte dinner. ⑦.

Parsons Garden Loft, 29 Cameron Rd (☎06/835 1527). Attractive and excellent-value homestay with just one en-suite double room set in the leafy grounds of a fine homestead on Bluff Hill, five minutes' steep walk up steps from Dalton Street, beside the Municipal Theatre. Choice of breakfast. ④.

Sea Breeze B&B, 281 Marine Parade (☎06/835 8067, fax 835 0512). Low-cost B&B with smallish but pleasant rooms, some with sea views, and a self-service continental breakfast. ④.

Hostels

Aqua Lodge Backpackers, 53 Nelson Crescent (☎06/835 4523, fax 843 3931). Homely hostel with dorms and doubles shoehorned into a suburban house in a quiet area close to the train and bus station. There's a pool, good facilities and welcoming hosts. Dorms ①, rooms ②.

Criterion Backpackers Inn, 48 Emerson St (☎06/835 2059). A converted hotel with large communal areas, a friendly atmosphere. Accommodation is in cramped 6–8 bed dorms at rock-bottom prices, more spacious triple and quad dorms, and double rooms. Dorms ①, rooms ②.

Stables Backpackers, 321 Marine Parade (☎06/835 6242). Attractive, small modern hostel tucked behind the Earthquake 31 building with good cooking facilities, a barbecue area in the central courtyard and bike rental for $15 a day. Dorms ①, rooms ②.

YHA, 277 Marine Parade (☎ & fax 06/835 7039). Well-run and recently revamped rabbit warren of a hostel with interested and interesting staff, a view of the sea and a good standard of facilities. Bikes are rented out at $15 a day and there are small dorms, doubles, twins and a family room. Dorms ①, rooms ②.

Campsites

Kennedy Park Complex, Storkey St, off Kennedy Rd (☎06/843 9126, fax 843 6113). The most central of Napier's campsites, 3km from the city centre, and with a pool and barbecue area. Tent sites $9, cabins ②, flats ③, units ④.

Westshore Holiday Camp, 1 Main Rd, Westshore (☎06/835 9456). Located midway along Westshore Beach, 6km north of town, this site is a little less formal than the Kennedy Park Complex, but still has all the facilities you're likely to need. Tent sites $8, cabins ②, flats ③.

The Town

Napier is blessed with a fine location, neatly tucked under the skirts of **Bluff Hill** (*Mataruahou*), a 3km-long outcrop festooned with the twisting roads of the eponymous and highly desirable suburb. At its eastern summit is **Bluff Hill Domain Lookout** (daily 7am–dusk), offering views of Cape Kidnappers to the west, and right across to the distant Mahia Peninsula in the east.

On Bluff Hill's southern flank, steep roads and even steeper steps switchback down to the grid pattern of the **Art Deco commercial centre** where, at the whim of mid-

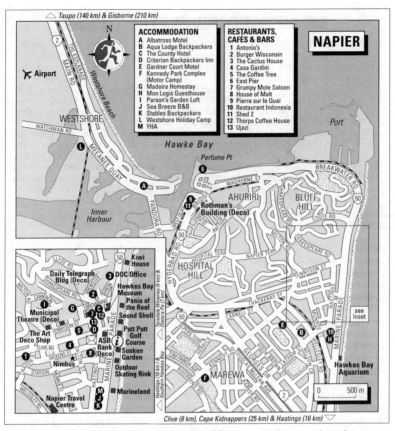

△ Taupo (140 km) & Gisborne (210 km)

NAPIER

ACCOMMODATION
A Albatross Motel
B Aqua Lodge Backpackers
C The County Hotel
D Criterion Backpackers Inn
E Gardner Court Motel
F Kennedy Park Complex
   (Motor Camp)
G Madeira Homestay
H Mon Logis Guesthouse
I Parson's Garden Loft
J Sea Breeze B&B
K Stables Backpackers
L Westshore Holiday Camp
M YHA

RESTAURANTS, CAFÉS & BARS
1 Antonio's
2 Burger Wisconsin
3 The Cactus House
4 Casa Gardini
5 The Coffee Tree
6 East Pier
7 Grumpy Mole Saloon
8 House of Malt
9 Pierre sur le Quai
10 Restaurant Indonesia
11 Shed 2
12 Thorps Coffee House
13 Ujazi

Clive (8 km), Cape Kidnappers (25 km) & Hastings (16 km) ▽

eighteenth-century Land Commissioner, Alfred Domett, streets were given the names of literary luminaries – Tennyson, Thackeray, Byron, Dickens, Shakespeare, Milton and more. Bisecting it all is the partly-pedestrianized main thoroughfare of Emerson Street, whose terracotta paving and palm trees run from Clive Square, one-time site of a makeshift "Tin Town" while the city was being rebuilt after the earthquake, to the pine-fringed **Marine Parade**. Around the northeastern side of Bluff Hill lies the original settlement site of **Ahuriri**, long since abandoned to factories and car sales yards, but recently resurgent, with some of its warehouses being tarted up and a handful of trendy café/bars taking their chances.

Art Deco Napier

If the dark cloud of the 1931 earthquake had a silver lining, it was the chance it gave Napier to rebuild from scratch, not just with more quake-resistant materials but to completely re-invent itself. Drawing on contemporary themes, Napier fell for **Art Deco** in a big way. A reaction against the organic and naturalistic themes of Art Nouveau, Deco embraced modernity, glorifying progress, the machine age and the Gatsby-style high-life, expressed by means of elaborate friezes featuring Adonis-like men, dancing women and springing gazelles. The onset of the **Great Depression** at

ART DECO NAPIER: TOURS AND TRAILS

Keen observers will find classic Art Deco everywhere, but for a systematic exploration of Napier's Art Deco revival, begin at **The Art Deco Shop**, in the Desco Centre, 163 Tennyson St (daily 9am–5pm), where you can watch a twenty-minute introductory video (shown on request, donations appreciated) and buy a leaflet for the self-guided "Art Deco Walk" ($1.50). Dedicated Deco buffs can also join the **Art Deco Walking Tour** (Dec 26–March only Wed, Sat & Sun 2pm; 2hr; $10), which sets off from the Desco Centre and whose anecdote-laden patter brings Thirties Napier to life; the tour offers access to some of the finer buildings and gives you the chance to gaze around the interiors of shops and banks without feeling quite so self-conscious. The **Self-Drive Art Deco Tour** (leaflet $2.50) presents a broader sweep of the district's distinctive architecture, reverentially trawling through Napier's far-flung Deco buildings, Hastings' Spanish Mission structures, the totally non-Deco Havelock North and the former Taradale Hotel, now a McDonald's but tastefully remodelled after the multinational was successfully petitioned by the Art Deco Trust. For real Deco fanatics, there's also the self-guided **Marewa Meander** (leaflet $1.50), covering the less-sexy domestic architecture in Napier's principal Art Deco suburb.

the end of the 1920s pared down these excesses, not least because the key American exponents of the style, Louis Sullivan and Frank Lloyd Wright, were restrained by Chicago and New York statutes which dictated that tall buildings had to be stepped back to let the sun penetrate the dark canyons below. Necessity became the mother of invention, and the recurring theme of ziggurats was introduced.

Napier's version of Art Deco was informed by the privations of this austere era. At the same time, the architects looked for inspiration to California's similarly sun-drenched and earthquake-prone **Santa Barbara** which, just six years earlier, had suffered the same fate as Napier, and had risen from the ashes. They adopted fountains (a symbol of renewal), sunbursts, chevrons, lightning flashes and stylized fluting, embedding them in highly formalized but asymmetric designs. What emerged was a palimpsest of early-twentieth-century design, combining elements of the Arts and Crafts movement, the Californian Spanish Mission style, Egyptian and Mayan motifs, the stylized floral designs of Art Nouveau, the blockish forms associated with Charles Rennie Mackintosh, and even **Maori imagery**. For the best part of half a century, Napier's residents went about their lives, unaware of the architectural harmony all around them and merrily daubing everything in grey or muted blue paint. Fortunately this meant that when a few visionaries recognized the city's potential in the mid-1980s and formed the **Art Deco Trust**, everything was still there. The trust continues to promote the preservation of buildings and provides funding for shopkeepers to pick out distinctive architectural detail in pastel colours.

Visitors with only a tangential interest in architecture can get a sense of what the fuss is about by wandering along the half-dozen streets in the city centre, notably Emerson Street, with its particularly homogeneous run of upper-floor frontages. Worth special attention here is the **ASB Bank**, on the corner of Hastings Street, its exterior adorned with fern shoots and a mask form from the head of a *taiaha* (a long fighting club), while its interior has a fine Maori rafter design. On Tennyson Street, look for the flamboyant **Daily Telegraph** building with stylized fountains capping the pilasters; and the **Municipal Theatre**, built in the late 1930s and exhibiting a strikingly geometric and streamlined form.

The only building to merit a foray outside the centre is the **Rothman's Building** (interior Mon–Fri 9am–5pm only), on the corner of Bridge Street and Osian Street, in Ahuriri, whose entrance is probably the single most frequently-used image of Deco

Napier and exhibits a decorative richness seldom seen on industrial buildings. The facade merges Deco asymmetry and the classic juxtaposition of cubic shapes and arches with the softening Art Nouveau motifs of roses and raupo (a kind of Kiwi bulrush).

Along Marine Parade

Napier's Art Deco finery may earn it a place on the world stage, but its defining feature is undoubtedly **Marine Parade**, a 2km-long boulevard lined with stately Norfolk pines and fashioned in the British seaside tradition. A restrained and faintly elegant promenade strung with attractions; entrance to three of the more major attractions – the Kiwi House, Marineland and the Aquarium – as well as Hastings' Fantasyland (see p.379), is included in the SuperPass **concession card** ($15), which is valid for a month and saves $4 if you visit all three, more if Fantasyland is on your itinerary.

Marine Parade starts by Napier's port and passes the foot of Bluff Hill, where native and exotic trees have been cultivated in **Centennial Gardens** (unrestricted entry), a former prison quarry backed by a picturesque waterfall. Pushing south, the first of the paying attractions on Marine Parade is the **Kiwi House** (daily 11am–3pm; $3), features a morepork (native owl) and a beautifully marked night heron, in addition to the usual nocturnal critters; try to time your visit for 1pm, when a kiwi is brought out for close-up inspection as part of a fifteen-minute talk.

Stroll past the outdoor swimming pool, floral clock and the ornamental Tom Parker Fountain, to the bronze cast of the curvaceous **Pania of the Reef**, a siren of Maori legend who lived on land with her lover until forcibly restrained in the briny depths by her kin when she paid them a final visit. Opposite, the **Hawke's Bay Museum**, 65 Marine Parade (daily 10am–4.30pm; $4), contains small but well chosen and competently presented exhibits, notably *taonga* (treasures) of the Ngati Kahungunu, including some exquisite clubs and fish-hooks. Downstairs there's detailed coverage of Hawke's Bay's colonial history, a photo display of the damage wrought by the 1931 earthquake, and an excellent and manageable trawl through a century of design, from Art Nouveau and Art Deco through to the Philippe Starck-influenced Nineties.

Assorted seafront constructions line the next piece of the promenade: the curving colonnade of the Veronica Sun Bay and the stage known as the Sound Shell give way to a putting course and some sunken gardens. Beyond the outdoor skating rink, you reach **Marineland** (daily 10am–4.30pm; dolphin & seal shows 10.30am & 2pm; $15), which is one for the kids really, with performing dolphins and seals put through their paces, followed by a tour of the small marine zoo, which houses a leopard seal, sea lions and penguins – many of them recovering from injuries sustained in the wild. During the summer months you should try to book a couple of days in advance (a couple of weeks immediately after Christmas) if you fancy an hour-long **Swim with the Dolphins** ($35, plus $10 for the near-essential wetsuit; ☎06/834 4027); they can usually be persuaded to play ball.

There's little need to cross the road to the **Stables Complex**, 321 Marine Parade (daily 9am–5pm; $6), a lifeless series of waxwork dioramas depicting trades from pioneering days, plus photos from the earthquake and an embarrassingly inept 'quake simulation. Instead stick with the seafront side, passing the go-karts and boating lake, to reach the **Hawke's Bay Aquarium** (Christmas–Jan daily 9am–9pm; Feb–Christmas 9am–5pm; $7.50; ☎06/834 4196), one of the finest in the country, built around a central oceanarium teeming with Hawke's Bay aquatic life: rays, sharks, eels and fish of all sizes. At 3.15pm every day a diver jumps in to hand-feed them, and for $20 (and an additional $20 if you need to rent dive gear), certified divers can join them; book as far in advance as possible. Smaller tanks and reconstructions of inter-tidal zones and rock pools contain all manner of sea creatures and amphibians, including a hawk-billed turtle, terrapins, rainbow-coloured tropical fish and the native tuatara.

Again, you can feed these critters by booking a day or so in advance for the behind the scenes tour (daily 2.30–3.15pm; $12).

Eating and drinking

As elsewhere in New Zealand, Napier's dining scene has improved markedly over recent years and, while no match for larger centres, there are enough places to keep you well fed and watered for a few days. If you've got your own transport, it is worth eating at least one lunch at one of the **wineries** around about (see p.375), but there are plenty of **cafés** and **restaurants** scattered around the centre and several more in the upper price bracket in waterside Ahuriri.

It is rare to find any really exciting entertainment, unless you hit town at **festival time** (see box on p.373), but a couple of the **bars** host live music at weekends and when touring bands pass through. Straightforward drinking happens along Hastings Street, mostly between Browning and Emerson streets, where packs of revellers surge between any of half a dozen popular bars.

Antonio's, cnr Carlyl St & Craven St. Unpretentious and good-value eat-in and takeaway pizzeria with some budget pasta dishes. Closed Mon. Licensed.

Burger Wisconsin, 10 Shakespeare Rd. One of a handful of these franchised eat-in and take-out burger joints, serving huge and well-built specimens stuffed with imaginative fillings – satay, avocado and bacon – and good coffee too.

The Cactus House, 39 Marine Parade. Pseudo-Mayan-painted house with a large restaurant and bar, cranking out reasonably priced and reliable nachos and burritos, and providing live music at weekends. Closed Mon. Licensed.

Casa Gardini, 77 Dalton St (☎06/835 3846). Classy and relaxed upstairs bar and restaurant with a deck at the back for balmy evening supping and a spartan dining room serving the likes of asparagus and salmon terrine or wild mushroom ravioli. Licensed & BYO.

The Coffee Tree, 20 Dalton St. Unassuming magazines-and-mismatched-tables café serving breakfasts at reasonable prices, light snacks and tasty cakes and coffee.

East Pier, Hardinge Rd (☎06/834 0035). Modern and breezy waterfront café/bar that's great for just relaxing by the water or dining on Thai whitebait fritters ($12) and chicken and seafood paella ($23), or cheaper bar snacks. Licensed.

Grumpy Mole Saloon, cnr Hastings St & Tennyson St. Napier's most jumping party bar, styled in Wild West mode and with nightly drinks specials.

House of Malt, Hastings St. Lively town bar with an extensive range of beers on tap and speciality bottled brews, live music at weekends and above-average pub food at prices to match.

Restaurant Indonesia, 409 Marine Parade (☎06/835 8303). Compact seafront restaurant dishing up Indonesian dishes at around $17 and a choice of rijsttafel spreads, including a vegetarian version ($24 to $32 a head). Licensed & BYO.

Pierre sur le Quai, 62 West Quay, Ahuriri (☎06/834 0189). The place for that romantic dinner for two, exuding French provincial style and serving fabulous and expensive seafood. Expect to pay around $40 a head, without wine. Closed Sun & Mon; licensed.

Shed 2, cnr West Quay & Lever St, Ahuriri (☎06/835 2202). Currently the pick of Napier's trendy restaurant/bars, spreading in the spacious stripped-boards-and-corrugated-iron interior of a former woolshed overlooking the harbour. Saunter in for an afternoon coffee, beer or something from their huge selection of wines by the glass, then stick around for wood-fired pizza in the bar, or retreat next door for beef and chicken fajitas, or fish of the day in ginger and champagne sauce for less than $20. DJs spin platters at weekends and there's occasional live jazz or stand-up comedy.

Thorps Coffee House, 40 Hastings St. Excellent eat-in and takeaway build-your-own sandwich place also serving good cakes, shakes and coffee; the interior features fine Art Deco details.

Ujazi Café, 28 Tennyson St. Lovely little daytime café with a vaguely alternative feel and largely vegetarian quiches, pies sandwiches and salads, plus scrumptious juices and good strong coffee. Closed Sun.

HAWKE'S BAY FESTIVALS

During January and February, Napier and nearby Hastings flip into festive mode, most events falling under the banner of the six-week **Hawke's Bay Summer Festival** (☎0800/737 800). Small-time events take place in January, but the first of the major events is the hyperbolically-titled **Harvest Hawke's Bay Wine and Food Extravaganza** (first weekend in Feb), when food and wine lovers from around the country flock to the Hawke's Bay Racing Centre, Prospect Rd, Hastings, for music, food and wine. Proceedings reach fever pitch for the Charity Wine auction, which is followed by a Sunday drive around the wineries and a black-tie dinner. The Summer Festival traditionally culminates with the **Mission Vineyard Concert** (second weekend in Feb), when an internationally famous vocalist – Kiri Te Kanawa, Ray Charles and Dionne Warwick in recent years – performs outdoors at the Mission Estate Winery to an audience of around 20,000.

No sooner has the Hawke's Bay Summer Festival wound up, than Napier gears up for the **Art Deco Weekend** (third weekend in Feb; ☎06/835 1191), five light-hearted days of merriment, extending to guided walks, open-house tours of domestic Art Deco, bicycle tours, Thirties-dress picnics, champagne breakfasts, dress balls, silent movies and the like.

Around Napier

Though appealing in itself, Napier's surroundings reward exploration: the **gannet colony** at Cape Kidnappers and the thirty-odd **wineries** strung out between Eskdale, 12km north of Napier, and the banks of the Tukituki River, some twenty-odd kilometres to the south.

Heading towards Cape Kidnappers, Marine Parade passes the windswept **Waitangi Mission site**, 9km south of Napier, where a plaque records the establishment of Hawke's Bay's first mission station by William Colenso in 1844. A couple of kilometres further on, is the village of **CLIVE**, where the **Juke Box Museum**, 158 Main Rd (daily 9.30am–5pm; $3), holds a lovingly assembled hoard of radios, gramophones and over twenty working jukeboxes. Some are repro-classics, but most are originals, including one with a built-in slide projector and a mock-up milk-bar booth with an operational wall-box console. Each juke box plays records carefully matched to its era, and it's easy to get carried away by the owner's tremendous enthusiasm for his collection.

Cape Kidnappers

After James Cook's ill-starred initial encounter with Maori at Gisborne, he sailed south to the southern limit of Hawke's Bay and anchored off the jagged peninsula known to the Ngati Kahungunu as *Te Matua-a-maui*, "the fishhook of Maui" – a reference to the origin of the North Island, which was dragged from the oceans by Maui. Here, Cook experienced a second unfortunate meeting. This time Maori traders noticed two young Tahitian interpreters aboard the *Endeavour*; believing them to be held against their will, the traders captured one of them and paddled away. The boy escaped back to the ship, but Cook subsequently marked the point on his chart as **Cape Kidnappers**.

Neither James Cook nor Joseph Banks, both meticulous in recording flora and fauna, mentioned any gannets on the peninsula's final shark-tooth flourish of pinnacles. However, a hundred years later, twenty-odd pairs were recorded, and now there are four thousand pairs – making this the world's largest mainland **gannet colony**. Gannets are big birds, members of the booby family distinguished by their gold-and-black head markings and their apparent lack of fear of humans. The birds start arriving at Cape Kidnappers for nesting in June, laying their eggs from early July through to October, with the chicks hatching some six weeks later. Once fledged, at around fifteen weeks, the young gannets embark on their inaugural flight, a marathon and as-yet-unexplained 3000km journey to Australia, where they spend a couple of years before flying back to spend the rest of their life in New Zealand, returning to their place of birth to breed each year.

PRACTICALITIES

During the breeding season (July–Oct), the cape is closed to the public, and the largest colony, "the saddle", is always reserved for scientific study. At other times you can get within a metre or so of the remaining two sites: "the plateau", a few hundred metres back from the saddle, where 1100 chattering pairs nest beak-by-jowl; and the beachside "black reef", a couple of kilometres back from the tip of the peninsula, where there are a further 1800 pairs.

There are six ways to **visit the gannets**: four are tide-dependent, travelling to the colony along the beach below unstable hundred-metre cliffs; the fifth gains access overland through Summerlee Station; and the last takes to the seas in kayaks. All start from well-signposted points in the adjacent settlements of **CLIFTON** and **TE AWANGA**, 20km southeast of Napier, both reached from the Napier or Hastings visitor centres with Kiwi Shuttle ($15 return; booking essential, ☎06/843 1939).

The least expensive way to get to the gannets is simply to **walk** the 8km along the beach from Clifton; no permits are needed, but you'll need to check tide tables with DOC or the Hastings or Napier visitor centres and plan to leave between three and four hours after high tide. The traditional way is aboard tractor-drawn **trailers** along the beach with Gannett Beach Adventures (Oct to late-April daily; 4hr; $18; ☎ 06/875 0898), whose pace and approach give plenty of opportunities to appreciate the geology along the way and observe the birds at close quarters. For more comfort and protection from the elements, opt for the near-identical but shorter tours in robust **all-terrain vehicles** with Unimog Adventure Tours (Oct–June daily; 3hr from Clifton, $17.50; 4–5hr from Napier or Hastings, $30; ☎06/835 4446). Also jockeying for position on the beach are **quad bikes** from Quadventures (Oct to late April daily; 3–4hr; $95 one rider, $140 for two riders on one bike; ☎06/836 6652), whose trips include complimentary wine to accompany a BYO picnic.

All these end at a DOC shelter, from where you face a twenty-minute uphill slog to "the plateau", where you'll have half an hour to admire the birds. One way to avoid this slog is to go on three-hour **overland** trips with Gannet Safaris (Oct–June daily 1.30pm; $38; ☎06/875 0511) through Summerlee Station in air-conditioned 4WD minibuses. The last option is to go with Hawke's Bay Sea Kayaking Adventures (Oct–April; ☎06/875 0341), who run customized **kayaking** trips all around Hawke's Bay and along the southern coast, including full-day trips to Cape Kidnappers ($85) and multi-day trips, camping overnight at the cape ($80 per day) and giving you some quality time with the gannets.

Hawke's Bay wine country

The twin centres of Napier and Hastings are almost entirely encircled by the Hawke's Bay's wine country, one of New Zealand's largest and most exalted grape-growing regions. The **Hawke's Bay wine trail** wends its way past some 25 wineries, most of which offer free **tastings**, and many also provide grassy picnic areas among the vines where you are encouraged to while away a blissful afternoon over a game of petanque and a bottle or two from their cellars. Some have taken the marriage of fine wine and food one step further, and lunch at one of the **vineyard restaurants** is undoubtedly a Hawke's Bay highlight.

Hawke's Bay is largely the province of boutique producers, with an unshakeable domestic reputation and an international standing challenged only by the South Island's Marlborough region. One of New Zealand's most classically well suited areas for viticulture, with a climatic pattern similar to that of the great Bordeaux vineyards, Hawke's Bay produces fine Chardonnay and Cabernet Sauvignon. As scientific studies unravel the complexity of the local soils and microclimates, growers have begun to diversify into Merlot, which has gained a foothold north of Napier along the Esk Valley, while others predict that Hawke's Bay may one day topple Marlborough's Sauvignon Blanc primacy. Hawke's Bay is New Zealand's longest-established wine-growing region: vines were first planted in 1851 by French Marist missionaries, ostensibly to produce sacramental wine. The excess was sold, and the commercial aspect of the operation continues today as the Mission Estate Winery. Some fifty-odd years later, other wineries began to spring up, initially favouring the fertile plains, but as

HAWKE'S BAY WINERIES – THE PICK OF THE BUNCH

With over 25 wineries in the region, we can't hope to give comprehensive coverage, but we've listed a few **favourites** below, concentrating on those that make good **lunch spots** or feature some sort of attraction other than the obligatory wine tasting.

Napier's closest wineries are 8km to the southwest in the suburb of **Taradale**, en route to a couple more wineries in the western foothills of the Kaweka Range along Dartmoor Road. Closer to Hastings, there are clusters 10km west near **Fernhill**, with its enviable reputation for fine wines, and outside **Havelock North**, 9km east of Hastings.

NAPIER AND AROUND

Mission Estate Winery, cnr Church Rd and Avenue Rd, Taradale (Mon–Sat 8.30am–5.30pm, Sun 1–4pm). Worth a visit for its pivotal position in the development of the Hawke's Bay's wine industry alone, but it hasn't rested on its laurels, offering well organized, free guided tours (Mon–Sat 10.30am & 2pm) and a tasting room lined with ancient wine casks brimming with fortified wines.

McDonald Winery, 150 Church Rd, next door to Mission Estate (Mon–Sat 9am–5pm, Sun 11am–4pm). A tolerably interesting wine-making museum (free), some excellent bottles to sample – notably the Church Road Chardonnay – and a restaurant (☎06/844 2053) that spills out into the gardens, serving Mediterranean-style dishes at reasonable prices.

Sacred Hill Winery, Dartmoor Rd, 20km west of Taradale. A lengthy excursion for a few sips of wine, but worthwhile for delicious and deservedly popular, moderately priced lunches (bookings recommended, ☎06/844 0138), served on rustic tables under olive trees, along with their superb wines, most notably Sauvignon Blanc.

AROUND HASTINGS

Clearview Estate Winery, Clifton Rd, Te Awanga (Nov–Easter Mon & Thurs–Sun 10am–5pm; Easter–Oct Fri–Sun 11am–4pm). Some of New Zealand's most highly rated wines are produced here, in tiny quantities and sold only from the vineyard. You do pay a premium for this sort of attention to detail, but the wines are superb, especially when enjoyed with the Clearview restaurant's equally classy southern Mediterranean lunches outside in the restaurant (☎06/875 0150). Can be combined with a visit to Cape Kidnappers (see p.373).

Ngatarawa Wines, Ngatarawa Rd, near Fernhill (daily 11am–5pm). A good first stop, with tastings of quality wines in a century-old stable complex with attractive picnic areas all about.

Te Mata Estate, Te Mata Rd, Havelock North (Mon–Fri 9am–5pm, Sat 10am–5pm, Sun 11am–4pm). Produces some reputable wines but is on most people's itinerary for the highly distinctive house adjoining the winery, designed by controversial architect Ian Athfield (see box on p.398).

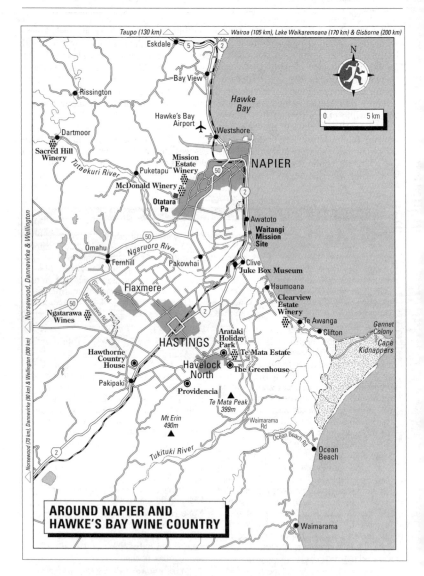

Taupo (130 km) △ △ Wairoa (105 km), Lake Waikaremoana (170 km) & Gisborne (200 km)

N

0   5 km

Eskdale

Rissington

Bay View

Hawke Bay

Hawke's Bay Airport

Dartmoor

Sacred Hill Winery

Westshore

Tutaekuri River

Mission Estate Winery

Puketapu

NAPIER

McDonald Winery

Otatara Pa

Awatoto

Waitangi Mission Site

Omahu

Ngaruroro River

Fernhill   Pakowhai

Clive

Juke Box Museum

Flaxmere

Haumoana

Clearview Estate Winery

Gimblett Rd

Ngatarawa Rd

Ngatarawa Wines

Te Awanga

Clifton

Gannet Colony

Cape Kidnappers

HASTINGS

Arataki Holiday Park

Te Mata Estate

Hawthorne Country House

Havelock North

The Greenhouse

Pakipaki

Providencia

Te Mata Peak 399m

Waimarama Rd

Mt Erin 490m

Ocean Beach Rd

Tukituki River

Ocean Beach

AROUND NAPIER AND HAWKE'S BAY WINE COUNTRY

Waimarama

◁ Norsewood, Dannevirke & Wellington

◁ Norsewood (70 km), Dannevirke (90 km) & Wellington (300 km)

tastes became more sophisticated, such sites were forsaken for the open-textured gravel terraces alongside the Tutaekuri, Ngaruroro and Tukituki rivers, which retain the day's heat and are free from moist sea breezes.

If you have your own **transport**, head for the hills with a copy of the *Hawke's Bay Wineries* leaflet (free from Napier and Hastings visitor centres), which lists wineries open to the public, along with current opening hours and facilities – and see box on p.375 for the pick of the bunch. If you can't locate an abstemious driver, take a **wine**

tour, most of which visit four or five wineries over the course of an afternoon. Jenne's Wine Tours (☎06/843 6953) are very popular, offering a basic four-stop tour (daily 1pm; $32.50) and a five-stop lunch tour (daily 11.30am; $40, food not included), and will pick up from Hastings or Havelock North for an additional $23 per booking. For a more intimate experience, opt for Vince's Wine Tour (daily at 1pm; $30; ☎06/836 6705), which benefits from chatty enthusiasm and a stack of local knowledge.

Hastings and around

As little as ten years ago, inland **HASTINGS**, 20km south of Napier, was a rival to its northern kin as Hawke's Bay's premiere city, buoyed by the wealth generated by the surrounding farmland and orchards. In recent years, shifting economic patterns, the closure of Hastings' two huge freezing works (abattoirs) and Napier's ascendancy as a tourist destination have put Hastings firmly in second place.

The city centre is all but moribund, with suburban malls usurping the functions of the inestimably more handsome central buildings that were erected after the same 1931 earthquake that rocked Napier. Hastings was saved from the worst effects of the ensuing fires, which were quenched using the artesian water beneath the city before they could take hold. Nonetheless, the centre had to be rebuilt. As in Napier, **Art Deco** predominates and, though Hastings lacks the flamboyance and overall exuberance of its neighbour, there are some unusually harmonious townscapes along Russell, Eastbourne and Heretaunga streets. Hastings also enthusiastically embraced the **Spanish Mission** style, and two exemplary buildings warrant a brief visit.

Hastings is at the heart of the wonderful Hawke's Bay **wine country** (see p.374), though the proliferation of Napier-based tours and its easy charms make that city a better base. Long before grapes were big business, Hastings relied on apples, pears and peaches, all still grown in huge quantities. The harvest, which begins in February and lasts three or four months, provides casual **orchard work** for those willing to thin, pick or pack fruit; the hostels (see p.378) are the best sources of work and up-to-the-minute information.

As Hastings steadily declines, neighbouring **HAVELOCK NORTH**, 3km east at the foot of the striking ridge-line of **Te Mata Peak**, becomes increasingly appealing. There isn't much to it and the only diversion is a drive up the peak, but the cobbled central streets give it a village atmosphere and the proliferation of tranquil **B&Bs** in the vicinity make good bases for exploring the central Hawke's Bay area.

Arrival and information

Trains startle shoppers as they rumble right through the centre of town, stopping at the Hastings Travel Centre, Caroline Street (☎06/878 0213), which is also used by both Newman's and InterCity **buses** on the Napier to Wellington run. Local bus operator Nimbus (☎06/877 8133) runs to Napier and Havelock North (Mon–Fri only) from the corner of Eastbourne Street East and Russell Street. Also on Russell Street, conveniently positioned between the Travel Centre and the Nimbus bus stop, is Hastings' **visitor centre** (Mon–Fri 8.30am–5pm, Sat & Sun 10am–3pm; ☎06/878 0510, fax 878 0512).

Accommodation

Hastings' **accommodation** situation is greatly affected by the harvest: from mid-February to May, there is precious little chance of finding a bed at any of the cheaper places, which meet the demand for self-catering and longer stays. If you're hoping to secure a bed for the **fruit-picking season**, plan to arrive early in February and

expect to pay around $80 a week for a bunk in a cramped room. Occupancy in the more expensive places is dictated by the normal summer-holiday pattern, and it's advisable to **book** a few days ahead if you'll be here between December and February. Some of the nicest places to stay are scattered through the countryside around Havelock North, where exclusive **B&Bs** and swanky self-catering houses are the mainstay.

Hastings

AJ's Backpackers Lodge, 405 Southland Rd (☎06/878 2302). The pick of the hostels, this pleasant Edwardian villa is popular with orchard workers but usually keeps a bed or two for overnighters, and has bikes for guests' use. Dorms ①, rooms ②.

Hastings Backpackers Hostel, 505 Lyndon Rd East (☎06/876 5888). Comfortable house near the centre, with good facilities, but full of pickers in the season. Dorms ①, rooms ②.

Hastings Holiday Park, Windsor Ave (☎06/878 6692, fax 878 6267). Appealing campsite on the edge of Windsor Park, with tent sites and a range of modern units, though it does get busy over the fruit-picking season. Tent sites $9, cabins ②, tourist flats ③.

Travellers Bakpak Hostel, 606 St Aubyn St West (☎06/878 7108). Suburban house, with a sauna and garden, that's reasonably spacious and comfortable, but is effectively closed to overnighters during the Feb–May season. Tent sites $9, dorms ①, rooms ②.

Woodbine Cottage, 1279 Louie St (☎06/876 9388). B&B in an attractive cottage on the outskirts of Hastings with a large garden, tennis court and pool, and pleasant sunny rooms. ④.

Havelock North and around
All the following places to stay are marked on the map on p.376.
Arataki Holiday Park, Arataki Rd (☎ & fax 06/877 7479). One of the few inexpensive places around here that doesn't take fruit pickers, so you should be able to find space even during the harvest. Tent sites $9, cabins ②, flats ③, motel units ④.
The Greenhouse, Te Mata Rd (☎06/877 4904, fax 877 4598). Superbly equipped self-catering cottage, surrounded by beautiful vineyards and sleeping up to four. ⑧.
Hawthorn Country House, 420 SH2, 7km west (☎ & fax 06/878 0035). Beautiful and very welcoming B&B in an Edwardian villa surrounded by croquet lawns and farmland. Huge en-suite rooms are decorated with understated elegance and the breakfasts are delicious. ⑦.
Providencia, Middle Rd, 3km south (☎ & fax 06/877 2300). One of the region's finest B&Bs, this beautifully preserved homestead was built in 1903 and is set among orchards and vineyards. Everything is immaculate, including wonderful cooked or continental breakfasts and optional five-course dinners at $50 a head. ⑦.

The Town

After the 1931 earthquake, Hastings looked to the Californian-inspired **Spanish Mission** style of architecture. The result lacks the homogeneity of Napier, but a couple of key buildings set the tone, with rough-cast stucco walls, arched windows, small balconies, barley-twist columns and heavily overhung roofs clad in terracotta tiles. All the finest examples can be seen in an hour or so, using the self-guided *Historic Hastings* walk leaflet ($1.50 from the visitor centre), but if time is short, limit your wanderings to Heretuenga Street East, where the **Westerman's Building**, on the corner of Russell Street, is adorned with gorgeous bronzework and sumptuous leadlighting. The **Municipal Theatre**, on the corner with Hastings Street, was actually built fifteen years before the earthquake, but was remodelled to create the region's finest Spanish Mission facade. Also worth a quick look is the **Hawke's Bay Exhibition Centre**, on the corner of Eastbourne Street and Karamu Road (Mon–Fri 10am–4.30pm, Sat & Sun noon–4.30pm; admission fees depend on exhibition), which hosts all manner of local, national and international art shows.

Desperately trying to find something to promote their city, Hastings' civic leaders have singled out its profusion of pleasant parks. None really justify the hype, though families may well find themselves in **Windsor Park**, chiefly for **Fantasyland**, Grove Road ($3, kids free; ☎06/876 9856), a theme park writ small, centred on a replica Disney-like castle and offering a welter of amusements – merry-go-round, go-karts, crazy golf, rowboats and the like. Beer fans might fancy a tour of the industrial **Hawke's Bay Brewery**, 304–308 Ellison Rd (Mon, Wed & Fri 10.30am; $2), with the obligatory tasting to finish.

Te Mata Peak

Driving from Hastings to Havelock North, the long ridge of limestone bluffs which make up the 399m **Te Mata Peak** looms into view. The ridge is held to be the supine form of a Maori chief, Rongokako, who choked on a rock as he tried to eat through the hill – just one of many Herculean feats with which he attempted to woo the beautiful daughter of a Heretaunga chief. The long and winding Te Mata Peak Road climbs the hill to a wonderful vantage point overlooking the fertile plains, north across Hawke's Bay and Cape Kidnappers, and east to the surf-pounded strands of Ocean Beach and Waimarama, the main swimming **beaches** for Hastings and Havelock North.

Overcome with grief at her father's death, Rongokako's own daughter threw herself off the peak – something you can emulate with one of the **tandem paragliding** operators. These use the thermals and winds off the Pacific to carry you along the ridge and back for at least fifteen minutes: both Tandem Paragliding (☎025/480 480) and Peak Paragliding (☎021/645 643) offer this for $90; while Peak Hang Gliding (☎06/877 7864) offer similarly hair-raising experiences slung under a rigid frame for $60–95.

Eating and drinking

As in most other things, Hastings **dining** and entertainment doesn't really rate alongside that of its northern neighbour, though keep an eye out for Hawke's Bay Summer Festival happenings (see box on p.373). Nonetheless you'll find a few reasonable places to eat both here, and in Havelock North, where they congregate conveniently near the centre.

Hastings

Cat & Fiddle Ale House, 502 Karamu Rd. A traditional English-style pub with a huge range of tap and bottled beers and bargain chips-with-everything meals; the theme is flogged to death by a London taxi used as a courtesy car.

Corn Exchange, Maraekakaho Rd. The trendiest of Hastings' restaurant/bars, converted from an ageing grain store on the northern fringes of the city and serving $20 brasserie meals, or just drinks.

Dominion Restaurant, 229 Heretaunga St East. Very basic fish-and-grills daytime restaurant with a Deco exterior, a faded Sixties interior and a good feed for under $10.

Picollo's, cnr Lyndon Rd & Nelson St (☎06/878 1188). Modern Kiwi and Pacific Rim cuisine extending to Szechuan kangaroo, lamb sweetbreads and Cajun chicken, all served indoors or outside in the garden. Closed Sat lunch and all day Sun & Mon; licensed & BYO.

Rush Munro's, 704 Heretaunga St West. A small ice-cream garden and takeaway that's been packing in the locals for some seventy years. Its sumptuous and intensely fruity natural ice cream is fashioned into distinctive, peaked cones. New fangled concoctions of coffee, chocolate and nut are now available, but it is hard to beat the traditional fruit flavours – feijoa is particularly scrumptious, though something of an acquired taste.

St Vinee's, Market St South. Well-regarded wine bar and café in the centre of Hastings, serving a fairly traditional selection of $17 meat-and-veg mains, plus potato wedges, nachos, venison sausages and light lunches.

Vidal's Winery Brasserie, 913 Aubyn St East (☎06/876 8105). Café and restaurant attached to a winery; a pleasant place to hang out and sup good wine, though the food is nothing special.

Havelock North

Café Diva, Napier Rd (☎06/877 5149). Casual daytime café and evening restaurant with a blackboard menu of tasty mains from around $18; al fresco dining out the back. Licensed.

Rose & Shamrock, Napier Rd. A fair attempt at an English/Irish pub with Guinness, draught ales and occasional Irish folk bands.

Southern Hawke's Bay

South of Hastings, the main road (SH2) give the coast a wide berth, taking you through the relentless sheep stations of **Southern Hawke's Bay**, a region uncluttered by places of genuine interest. Small farming towns stand as fitting memorials to the steadfast pioneers who tamed the region, spending the latter half of the nineteenth century clearing the huge totara trees of Seventy Mile Bush, pushing through communication links, and then establishing sheep runs on the rich plains.

None of the towns are especially interesting and if time is short you'd do as well to push straight on through, but with a little more leisure, the "Scandinavian" settlements of **Norsewood** and **Dannevirke** warrant a brief stop. The New Zealand Wars of the 1860s had discouraged British immigrants and, as new areas were opened up for colonization, the authorities took their search for settlers elsewhere, briefed to find rugged folk with string ties to the land. In 1872, Danes, Norwegians and a few Swedes answered the call, arriving in Napier ill-prepared for the hardship ahead of them. Their promised plots of land turned out to be tracts of impenetrable bush; the wages paid to construction workers who toiled to build road and rail links barely covered exorbitant food costs; and when the government demanded that the settlers repay their passage, many promptly upped sticks for North America, leaving little trace of their brief sojourn.

Almost all traffic follows SH2, but visitors in search of the esoteric might want to stray along **SH52**, which loops east towards the rugged coastline from dull **Waipukurau**, 50km south of Hastings, re-emerging at Masterton in the Wairarapa (see p.683). Fifty kilometres south of Waipukurau, a sign marks the hill known as **Taumatawhakatangihangakoauauotamateaturipukakapikimaungahoro-nukapokaiwhenuakitanatahu**, which, unsurprisingly, rates as the world's longest place name; roughly, this mouthful translates as "the hill where Tamatea, circumnavigator of the lands, played the lute for his lover".

Norsewood

Some 85km south of Hastings, SH2 enters a cutting which bisects the hilltop village of **NORSEWOOD**, invisible from the highway and easily missed. Predominantly settled by Norwegians, it manages to retain a mildly Scandinavian tenor. Like most southern Hawke's Bay towns, it was carved out of the forest, but in 1888 the bush bit back, and a raging bushfire virtually razed the place. Some regarded the devastation as an act of God precipitated by a local plebiscite that ended temperance – but, as the local paper noted, "the church was burnt down and the pub was saved".

The village is in two parts. In Upper Norsewood, the quaint and deathly quiet main street runs past a glassed-in boathouse containing the fishing boat *Bindalsfareing*, a gift from the Norwegian government on the occasion of Norsewood's centenary, and the **Pioneer Museum** (daily 8.30am–4.30pm; $1), a cottage museum full of reminders of pioneering days housed in an 1888 house. Kiwis are more familiar with Lower Norsewood, 1km to the south, which is home to Norsewear, a company famed for its hard-wearing woollen garments in rustic Scandinavian designs; the socks in particular last for years. If a chill wind is swooping down from the Ruahine Range, check for bargains in the **seconds shop** (Mon–Fri 8.30am–5pm, Sat & Sun 9am–4pm); aficionados of knitting machinery can even take a brief, ad hoc factory tour at no charge.

InterCity **buses** stop on SH2 at the turn-off for town. There are daytime **cafés** in both the upper and lower village, and you can stay at *The Beahive*, Arthur Rd, 500m east of Upper Norsewood (Nov–April only; ☎06/374 0849; ①), a self-contained bunkhouse with reasonably priced meals available on request.

Dannevirke

There's no reason for more than the briefest of stops in **DANNEVIRKE**, a small farming town 20km south of Norsewood, that struggles to play up its heritage, with little more than a rather unpleasant modern windmill along the main street to support its cause. Records and artefacts amassed in the **Gallery of History**, Gordon Street (Mon–Fri 9.30am–4pm, Sat & Sun 1.30–4pm; free), provide comprehensive coverage of the founding of the town in 1872, when the forest was hacked away to create Dannevirke

("Dane's Work") – a name recalling both the ninth-century defensive earthwork constructed across the waist of the Jutland peninsula in their homeland and the task ahead, the forging of a road from Wellington to Napier. Early photos give a sense of the hard life that drove away many of the Danes, their place taken by British migrants lured by the opening of the Napier–Wellington railway in 1884. The few Danes who remained were soon outnumbered; only a flick through the telephone directory or a glance at some of the shops and street signs betray Dannevirke's Scandinavian heritage.

Napier–Wellington **trains** and **buses** all stop in town not far from the **visitor centre**, 156 High St (Mon–Fri 8.30am–5pm; ☎06/374 8983), and there's the usual selection of tearooms, plus *State of the Art*, 21 High St, a reputable café and **espresso bar**. Should you want to **stay** the night here, check out the *Dannevirke Motor Camp*, George Street (☎06/374 7625; tent sites $7, cabins ②), which is beautifully set in a dell surrounded by a few remnants of bush; or the surreally-named *Viking Lodge Motel*, 180 High St (☎06/374 6669, fax 374 6686; ④).

South of Dannevirke, SH2 runs 25km to Woodville, the junction of SH3, which strikes west through the Manawatu Gorge to Palmerston North (see p.237), and SH2, which continues south into the Wairarapa.

The Wairarapa

The Wairarapa is self-effacing enough to promote itself as New Zealand's least-visited region, a claim that is both believable and justly earned. This is archetypal Kiwi sheep country, with white-flecked green hills etched sharply behind towns which share much in common with the workaday service centres of southern Hawke's Bay. But the Wairarapa is increasingly trying to align itself with Wellington, a source of free-spending day-trippers mostly bound for **Martinborough**, the region's wine capital and far-and-away its most appealing town.

The Wairarapa is separated from the capital by the Rimutaka Range, a persistent barrier to communication that kept the region relatively isolated for decades, until the spell was broken by the establishment of New Zealand's earliest sheep station close to present-day Martinborough. Soon the rich alluvial lands were selected for development by the **Small Farm Association** (SFA), a brainchild of Joseph Masters, a Derbyshire cooper and a long-time campaigner against the "Wakefield Scheme" of settlement, which promoted the separation of landowner and labourer. Aided and abetted by liberal governor George Grey, Masters founded the progressive association, which had the express aim of giving disenfranchised settlers the opportunity to become smallholders. At Grey's suggestion, SFA representatives sallied forth in 1853, persuading Maori to sell land for the establishment of two towns – Masterton and Greytown.

Initially **Greytown** prospered, and it retains an air of antiquity rare in New Zealand towns, but the routing of the rail line favoured **Masterton**, which soon became the main town, famed chiefly for the annual Golden Shears shearing competition. North of Masterton, the **Mount Bruce National Wildlife Centre** provides a superb opportunity to witness ongoing bird conservation work; to the south, **Featherstone** is a base for walks up the bed of the Rimutaka Incline Railway. Back on the coast, **Castlepoint** is the place for swimming, **Cape Palliser** for blustery mind-clearing walks and dramatic coastal scenery.

Mount Bruce

The northern half of the Wairarapa is very much a continuation of southern Hawke's Bay, with rolling grasslands stretching away either side of SH2, which is strung with unexceptional service towns. Leave a couple of hours in your schedule, though, for **Mount Bruce National Wildlife Centre**, 50km south of Woodville (daily 9am–4pm; $6), undoubtedly one of the best places in the country to view endangered native birds and a pioneer in the field of captive-breeding programmes. Visitors are treated to the sight of some of the world's rarest birds – kokako, saddleback, kea, kakapo, kiwi and takahe – and the lizard-like tuatara, in spacious aviaries set along a 1km trail through the last remnant of the Forty Mile Bush, lowland forest which once covered northern Wairarapa. The generous size of the cages and the thick foliage often make the birds hard to spot, so you'll need to be patient; more immediate gratification comes in the form of abundant aquatic life on the duck pond, a stand of Californian redwoods, a nocturnal kiwi house and a closed-circuit camera trained on a kokako nest.

Tranzit **buses** between Palmerston North and Masterton drop off and pick up outside the centre, and there's a small tearoom in the complex.

Masterton and around

As the Wairarapa's largest town, workaday **MASTERTON**, nestled at the foot of the Tararua Mountains some 30km south of Mount Bruce, makes a tolerable base for exploring a few minor sights. Despite boasting the only cinema in the Wairarapa, you'll find the town itself dull and lifeless – unless your visit coincides with the annual **Golden Shears** shearing competition, effectively the Olympiad of all things woolly. Contestants flock from many lands to demonstrate their prowess with the broad-blade handset; a top shearer can remove a fleece in under a minute, though for maximum points it must be done with skill as well as speed and leave a smooth and unblemished, if shivering, beast. Sideshows include wool-pressing and wool-handling competitions, and even a wool-inspired fashion parade. Held on the three days leading up to the first Saturday in March, proceedings are centred on the War Memorial Stadium, opposite the visitor centre; tickets go for $8–15 for the preliminary heats on Thursday and Friday, $20 for the Saturday finals, and $100 for the wind-up dinner and cabaret (bookings through the visitor centre).

If you front up the last Sunday in February, make for the large, formal Queen Elizabeth Park, immediately east of the centre, where local winemakers and restauranteurs ply their wares as part of the **Wairarapa Wine and Food Festival**. Across the road, the **Wairarapa Arts Centre**, Bruce Street, (Mon–Fri 10am–4.30pm, Sat & Sun 11am–4pm; free), presents temporary exhibitions that are usually worth a peek, and has a lovely café and wine bar.

Draped over the hills to the west of town, the **Tararua Forest Park**, while not among New Zealand's tramping hotspots, offers some excellent walking through beech and podocarp forests to the sub-alpine tops, where the weather is notoriously fickle. Serious trampers should consider the **Holdsworth–Jumbo Tramp**, a twelve-hour circuit that can be broken down into two or more manageable days by staying at **huts** (two Category 2, $8, & two Category 3, $4) evenly spaced along the route. The track starts at the backcountry-hut style *Holdsworth Lodge* (tent sites $4, lodge $8), 25km west of Masterton at the end of Norfolk Road (accessible only by taxi, ☎06/378 2555), where day-trippers can undertake easy riverside walks (1–2hr) and bathe in the cool waters.

For details of all these tramps, pay a visit to the Masterton DOC field centre (see p.384).

Practicalities

Masterton's commercial heart is strung along the parallel Chapel, Queen and Dixon streets. Tranzit **buses** (☎06/377 1227 in Masterton & 04/387 2018 in Wellington) pull up on Queen Street, between Russell and Smith streets, around 300m from the **visi-**

tor centre, at 5 Dixon St (Nov–March Mon–Fri 8.30am–5.30pm & Sat–Sun 9.30am–4pm; April–Oct Mon–Fri 9am–5pm & Sat–Sun 10am–4pm; ☎06/378 7373, fax 378 7042), which backs on to Queen Elizabeth Park. Tranz Metro run commuter services from Wellington to the **train station**, at the end of Perry Street, a fifteen-minute walk from the centre, or call Masterton Radio Taxis (☎06/378 2555). For trampers, DOC maintain a **field centre** (Mon–Fri 8am–5pm; ☎06/378 2061), opposite the aerodrome on South Road, the continuation of Queen Street. Without your own transport, getting around the Wairarapa's sights can be frustrating and time-consuming, but Tranzit make it easier with **tours** to Mount Bruce ($34 from Wellington, $18 from Masterton, Greytown or Carterton), Cape Palliser ($65/$50), and Martinborough ($30/$20).

Masterton is littered with motel **accommodation** and has numerous homestays around about. Budget accommodation is at the relaxed and friendly but slightly dilapidated *Masterton Backpackers*, 22 Victoria St (☎06/377 2228; tent sites $10, dorms ①, rooms ②), an associate YHA located in a suburban house. Opposite is *Victoria House*, 15 Victoria St (☎ & fax 06/377 0186; ④), a two-storey colonial house with original fittings and a couple of comfortable rooms. Central, en-suite hotel rooms can be had at the *Empire Lodge*, 94 Queen St (☎06/377 1902, fax 377 2298; ③), while campers should make for the spacious and attractive *Mawley Park Motor Camp*, 15 Oxford St (☎ & fax 06/378 6454; tent sites $9, cabins ②), ten minutes' walk north of the centre. If proximity to town is less of an issue, try the lovely *Lyndor Homestay*, Lees-Pakaraka Road (☎06/378 8105; ④), which occupies a modern house by a small vineyard ten minutes' drive from Masterton.

Budget eating is best at either the *Slug and Lettuce*, 94 Queen St, an ersatz English pub with bargain steaks and lasagne-type meals from as little as $6, or at *Fettuccini's*, 5 Church St (closed all-day Mon & Tues lunch; BYO), which serves hearty helpings of Italian favourites at modest prices. For Masterton's best food, or just a good strong coffee, head upstairs to *Bloomfields*, on the corner of Chapel Street and Lincoln Road (☎06/377 4305; closed Sun & Mon; licensed), which turns out the likes of pork medallions with figs, mango and mint coulis for around $20.

Castlepoint

The 300km of coastline from Cape Kidnappers, near Napier, south to Cape Palliser is bleak, desolate and almost entirely inaccessible – except for **CASTLEPOINT**, 65km east of Masterton, where early explorers found a welcome break in the "perpendicular line of cliff". A commanding lighthouse presides over a rocky knoll which is linked to the mainland by a thin hourglass double **beach** that encloses a sheltered pool known as The Basin. Nearby is a small settlement where Wairarapa families retreat for summer fun in the calm **lagoon**, walking to the lighthouse or the cave at its foot, riding the breakers or surfcasting from a huge rock platform. Castlepoint is at its most frenetic around the third or fourth Saturday in March, when there's an informal **horse race** along the beach – a somewhat unorthodox betting set-up requires punters to bet "blind" on numbers before they are allocated to particular horses.

You can **stay** here at the *Castlepoint Holiday Park* (☎06/372 6705, fax 372 6717; tent sites $8, cabins ②) or the *Castlepoint Motel and Cabins* (☎ & fax 06/372 6637; cabins ②, units ④).

Carterton

Once you've shaken free of the outskirts of Masterton, a string of small towns guide you towards the Rimutaka Range and over into the Hutt Valley. Staunchly conservative **CARTERTON**, 15km south of Masterton, hides a treat for lovers of kitsch souvenirs.

The **Paua Shell Factory**, at 54 Kent St (Mon–Fri 8am–5pm, Sat & Sun 9am–5pm; free), is an Aladdin's Cave of tacky objects fashioned from this beautiful rainbow-swirled seashell. Superbly polished examples of the shells themselves retail for up to $50, but other essential items, such as ashtrays inset with New Zealand coinage and kiwi birds cast in a kind of terrazzo paua-shell effect, can be yours to treasure for a much more modest sum. The factory supplies just about every tourist knick-knack shop in the country and, if you can't resist, you can even take a brief, free tour to see how the stuff is made.

Some 5km south of Carterton, a road runs 15km west into the foothills of the Tararua Range to **Waiohine Gorge**, a picturesque chasm that's ideal for picnics and safe swimming.

Greytown

There's a more traditional appeal to **GREYTOWN**, 9km south of Carterton. Laid out in 1853, the town still retains something of its Victorian feel, despite the traffic that now trundles between the rows of two-storey wooden buildings. Until the end of the nineteenth century, this was the Wairarapa's main settlement, but railway planners diverted the new line around the flood-prone environs and set the seal on a gradual decline that was only arrested by the development of profitable orchards and market gardens in the latter half of the twentieth century.

The real appeal here is the selection of **cafés** along Main Street, notably the excellent and moderately priced *Main Street Deli*, at no. 86 (☎06/304 9022; licensed & BYO), which provides reason enough to stop in Greytown for lunch, coffee and cakes, or even for dinner (Fri & Sat only). If you feel you need to earn your lunch, spend an hour among the re-sited Victorian buildings and stagecoach paraphernalia at the **Cobblestones Museums**, 169 Main St (Mon–Sat 9am–4.30pm, Sun 10am–4.30pm; $2.50), or join one of the **historical walks** (Sat & Sun at noon; 1hr; $5; booking essential, ☎06/304 9465), which leave from 123 Main St.

Featherstone and the Rimutaka Incline

The last of the Wairarapa towns before SH2 climbs west over the Rimutakas is **FEATHERSTONE**, 13km south of Greytown, where the **visitor centre**, on Fitzherbert Street (Mon–Fri 10am–3pm & Sat–Sun 9.30am–3pm; ☎06/308 8051), stands in front of the town's pride and joy. The **Fell Engine Museum**, Lyon Street (Oct–April Sat & Sun 10am–4pm; May–Sept Sat 10am–4pm, Sun 1–4pm; other times by prior arrangement, ☎06/308 9777; donations appreciated) contains what, to the casual observer, appears to be an ordinary old railway engine. Nevertheless, steam buffs cross the country to this last surviving example of the locos which, for 77 years (until the boring of a new tunnel in 1955), climbed the 265m, one-in-fifteen slope of the Rimutaka Incline over the range into the Hutt Valley, gaining purchase by gripping a central rail.

The rails have long been pulled up, but you can follow the trackbed on the **Rimutaka Incline Walkway** (17km; 6hr; 300m ascent), which starts 10km south of Featherstone at Cross Creek, passes old shunting yards and shuffles through the 576-metre summit tunnel, before descending to Kaitoke. A free leaflet from the visitor centre details the route, provides background information and pinpoints three basic, grassy campsites along the way. Many walk just an hour or two from either end and back, but if you fancy the full trek, contact South Wairarapa Tours (☎06/308 9352), who will organize **pick-ups** (cost depends on numbers). There's no public transport to Cross Creek, but Masterton–Wellington **buses** pass within 1km of the Kaitoke end of the walkway.

Buses also stop 3km north of the end of the walkway near *The Black Stump YHA Hostel*, Marchant Road, Kaitoke (☎04/526 4626; ③), a basic 10-bunk place in the tradition of youth hostels of yore; bring all the supplies you need.

Martinborough and its wineries

In the last ten years tiny **MARTINBOROUGH**, 18km southeast of Featherstone, has been transformed from a small and obscure farming town into the centre of a compact wine region synonymous with some of New Zealand's finest red wines. Being within easy striking distance of the capital, weekends see the arrival of the smart set, ready to lunch at the handful of appealing cafés and restaurants and load up their shiny land-cruisers at the dozen-or-so wineries that hem in the town. Go midweek, though, and Martinborough is a beguiling place – so small that you immediately feel at ease and with a number of excellent vineyards within easy strolling distance of the centre (see box below).

The town was initially laid out in the 1870s by patriotic landowner John Martin, who named the streets after cities he had visited on his travels and arranged the core in the form of a Union Jack centred on a leafy square. Martinborough languished as a minor agricultural centre for over a century until the first four wineries – Ata Rangi, Dry River, Chifney and Martinborough (all of which produced their first vintages in 1984) – re-invented Martinborough as the coolest, driest and most wind-prone of the North Island's grape-growing regions. With the aid of shelter belts that slice the horizon, the wineries, which now number almost twenty, produce some outstanding Pinot Noir, very good Cabernet Sauvignon (though it is losing favour as the grapes fail to fully ripen in poor years), crisp and fruity Sauvignon Blanc and wonderfully aromatic Riesling.

Martinborough is no slouch at promoting its viticultural prowess, and the best time to visit is during one of its **festivals**. The first of the summer is **Toast Martinborough** (third Sun in Nov), a specifically wine-orientated affair with all the vineyards open, free buses doing the rounds, and top Wellington and local restaurants selling their produce; it is an exclusive event and tickets ($40; contact the visitor centre) are hard to

---

MARTINBOROUGH WINERIES

For visitors, Martinborough has the edge over other wine regions in that ten of its wineries are accessible **on foot**, and half a dozen more are easily reached by **car** or a **bike** rented from Pedalpushers (☎06/306 9364; $10 a day). The best guide is the free *Winemakers of Martinborough* brochure (from the visitor centre on Kitchener St), which details the hours and facilities of the sixteen wineries that conduct **tastings**.

Here's our pick of the wineries to kick-start your explorations.

Martinborough Vineyard, Princess St (daily 11am–5pm). A Martinborough original and still one of the largest, producing top-quality Pinot Noir and Chardonnay. Picnicking is encouraged.

Muirlea Rise, Princess St, across the road from Martinborough. Top-quality Pinot Noir to go with a ploughman's lunch and lovely coffee.

Nga Waka, Kitchener St (from Nov while stocks last, Sat & Sun 1–5pm;

☎06/306 9832). One of the small, young boutique wineries known for their bone-dry whites with elegant fruit.

Te Kairanga, Martins Rd, 5km southeast (daily 10am–5pm). A consistent award-winner which produces some delicious small-volume reserve wines; tastings are held in a 130-year-old pit-sawn-plank cottage moved to the vineyard from Martinborough.

obtain. There's a considerably more egalitarian feel to the two **Martinborough Fairs** (first Sat in Feb & March), a huge country fête, during which the streets radiating from the central square are lined with stalls selling all manner of arts and crafts.

Practicalities

Tranzit **buses** (✆06/377 1227 in Masterton, ✆04/387 2018 in Wellington) meet most **trains** at Featherstone (there are no direct buses) and run to Martinborough along Kitchener Street, past the small but informative **visitor centre** (daily 10am–4pm; ✆06/306 9043), to the central Memorial Square.

The range of **accommodation** leans heavily towards mid- and upper-price B&Bs, of which *Oak House Homestay*, 45 Kitchener St (✆06/306 9198, fax 306 8198; ⑤), is one of the best, with attractive rooms in a Californian-style bungalow, substantial breakfasts and often a glass or two of wine from Te Kairanga, where Chris is the wine maker. *Olivo* (✆06/306 9074; ⑤), 3km from town on RD4 and surrounded by olive groves, is another good bet, with continental breakfast brought to your room; and for real luxury, stay at the sumptuously refurbished two-storey colonial *Martinborough Hotel*, on the corner of Kitchener Street and Memorial Square (✆06/306 9350, fax 306 9345; ⑧). At the cheaper end, try the central *Martinborough Motel*, 43 Strassburg St (✆06/306 9408; dorms ①, units ④), which has the only backpacker beds in town, or the *Martinborough Camping Ground*, Princess Street (✆06/306 9336; $10 per site).

Martinborough caters to discerning diners with half a dozen **restaurants** on, or close to, Memorial Square, all charging city prices. Accolades are heaped on the *Martinborough Bistro*, at the Martinborough Hotel, with beautifully prepared and presented dishes drawing on traditional French and modern Mediterranean cuisines at around the $20 mark, and there is simpler and cheaper fare at the daytime, wholefood *Woodlands Café*, at 48 Oxford St, five minutes' walk east of the square, which makes a great place for lunch or coffee and prepares picnic hampers (order on ✆06/306 9331) to take around the wineries.

Cape Palliser

The low-key cosmopolitanism of Martinborough stands in dramatic contrast to the bleak and windswept coast around **Cape Palliser**, 60km south. The southernmost point on the North Island, the cape was named in honour of James Cook's mentor, Rear Admiral Sir Hugh Palliser. Apart from a few gentle walks and the opportunity to observe fur seals at close quarters, there's not a lot to do out here, but it'll soon blow away the cobwebs.

From Martinborough, a sealed road leads 25km south to **LAKE FERRY**, a tiny surfcasting settlement that once had a ferry service on the coastal route to Wellington before the Rimutaka Road was completed. From a road junction just before Lake Ferry, the Cape Palliser road twists for 10km through the coastal hills until it meets the sea near the **Putangirua Pinnacles**, dozens of grey soft-rock spires and fluted cliffs up to 50m high, formed by wind and rain selectively eroding the surrounding silt and gravel. The pinnacles lie within the little-visited Aorangi (Haurangi) Forest Park, and can be reached along an easy streambed path (1hr return) from the roadside Putangirua Scenic Reserve, where there are barbecue areas and a primitive **campsite** ($5).

From here, the partly-metalled road hugs the rugged, exposed coastline for 15km to **NGAWI**, a small fishing village where all manner of bulldozers grind out their last days, hauling fishing boats up the steep gravel beach. It is five rough kilometres on to the Cape proper, where the only well-established **fur-seal colony** on the North Island lies right beside the road, overlooked by the century-old Cape Palliser **lighthouse**, standing on a knoll 60m above the sea at the top of a long flight of some 250 steps. It is easy enough to get within 20m of the seals, but you should keep your distance from any pups – and their protective parents.

travel details

Trains

The main train line runs from Wellington and Palmerston North through the Manawatu Gorge to Woodville and up through the southern Hawke's Bay towns to Hastings and Napier; a branch line, but no passenger services, continues to Gisborne.

Passenger services to the Wairarapa also originate in Wellington, and terminate in Masterton; no trains link Masterton with Woodville.

From Hastings to: Dannevirke (1 daily; 1hr 50min); Napier (1 daily; 20min); Palmerston North (1 daily; 3hr); Wellington (1 daily; 5hr).

From Masterton to: Carterton (2–5 daily; 15min); Featherston (2–5 daily; 30min); Wellington (2–5 daily; 1hr 30min).

From Napier to: Dannevirke (1 daily; 2hr 10min); Hastings (1 daily; 20min); Palmerston North (1 daily; 3hr 20min); Wellington (1 daily; 5hr 30min).

Buses

InterCity run most of the bus services through the region, with a service connecting Gisborne with all the Hawke's Bay towns, Palmerston North and Wellington; one linking Gisborne to Rotorua via Whakatane; one running from Napier and Hastings to Auckland via Taupo; and another joining Palmerston North, Masterton and Wellington. Newmans run a smaller number of comparable services, and Tranzit connect Wellington with the main Wairarapa towns.

Local Gisborne buses ply SH35 around Eastland to Opotiki; see Chapter Five for full coverage of this area.

From Gisborne to: Auckland (1 daily; 9hr 15min); Hastings (3 daily; 4hr–4hr 30min); Napier (3 daily; 3hr 30min–4hr); Hicks Bay (1–2 daily; 3–4hr); Rotorua (2 daily; 4hr 30min); Wairoa (3 daily; 1hr 40min).

From Hastings to: Auckland (3 daily; 8hr); Dannevirke (4 daily; 1hr 30min); Gisborne (3 daily; 4hr–4hr 30min); Napier (Mon–Fri 16 daily & Sat–Sun 4–5 daily; 30–45min); Norsewood (4 daily; 1hr 10min); Taupo (3 daily; 3hr); Wellington (4 daily; 4hr).

From Masterton to: Carterton (2 daily; 25min); Greytown (2 daily; 40min); Featherstone (2 daily; 45min); Palmerston North (4 daily; 2hr 30min); Wellington (2 daily; 2hr 20min).

From Napier to: Auckland (3 daily; 7hr 30min); Dannevirke (4 daily; 2hr); Gisborne (3 daily; 3hr 30min–4hr); Hastings (Mon–Fri 16 daily & Sat–Sun 4–5 daily; 30–45min); Norsewood (4 daily; 1hr 40min); Taupo (3 daily; 2hr 30min); Wellington (4 daily; 4hr 30min).

From Wairoa to: Gisborne (3 daily; 1hr 40min); Lake Waikaremoana (3 weekly; 1hr); Murupara (3 weekly; 3hr 30min); Napier (3 daily; 2hr); Rotorua (3 weekly; 4hr 15min).

Flights

From Gisborne to: Auckland (5–7 daily; 1hr); Hamilton (1–2 daily; 55min); Napier (1 daily; 40min); Palmerston North (1 daily; 1hr 10min); Wellington (3–4 daily; 50min).

From Napier to: Auckland (5–7 daily; 1hr); Wellington (5–6 daily; 55min).

CHAPTER SEVEN

WELLINGTON AND AROUND

ying at the southwestern tip of the North Island, at the junction of SH1 and SH2, **Wellington** is the capital city of New Zealand and the seat of government. With a population of 328,000, it is also the country's second-largest city and enjoys a scenic **setting**, wedged between steep hills and the broad harbour of **Port Nicholson**. An engaging and friendly place to explore, Wellington boasts plenty of outdoor activities, a decorative and bustling **waterfront**, a stimulating combination of historical and modern **architecture**, and an exuberant **café society** and nightlife, complemented by a buzzing entertainment and cultural scene. However, Wellington lives up to its nickname of **"the windy city"**, lashed most days by air funnelled through Cook Strait, an effect that's amplified by the city's high-rise buildings, which create wind tunnels. The **harbour**, on the other hand, remains relatively sheltered and is a perfect spot from which to appreciate the cityscape. With its **ferry** terminal and airport, Wellington is the principal departure point for the **South Island**, but the city warrants much more than just a fleeting glimpse. You're best off allowing three to four days to explore the sights concentrated within the central city and to make the most of the harbour, the beaches and bays, and Somes Island.

East of Wellington, where the **Rimutaka Range** separates the Hutt Valley from the Wairarapa (see p.382), a forest park offers several popular bushwalks that make for a pleasant day away from the city. The meagre attractions of the **commuter-belt communities** of the Hutt Valley and Porirua, on the other hand, don't really warrant a special trip. To the north, the **Kapiti Coast** is a pretty thirty-kilometre stretch of silvery beach scattered with tiny communities full of holiday and retirement homes, bowling greens and golf courses, with the region's most significant attraction just offshore: the long thin **Kapiti Island**, a bird sanctuary that you can visit on a day-trip from Paraparaumu Beach. Finally, Wellington is well placed for exploration of New Zealand's

---

ACCOMMODATION PRICES

Accommodation listed in this guide has been categorized into one of nine price bands, as set out below. The rates quoted represent the **cheapest available** double or twin **room** – except for category ①, which are per-person rates for a dorm bed; fees for **tent sites** and **DOC huts** are also per-person, unless otherwise stated.

① under $20 per person	④ $60–80	⑦ $140–180
② under $40 per room	⑤ $80–100	⑧ $180–240
③ $40–60	⑥ $100–140	⑨ over $240

For more on accommodation, see p.33.

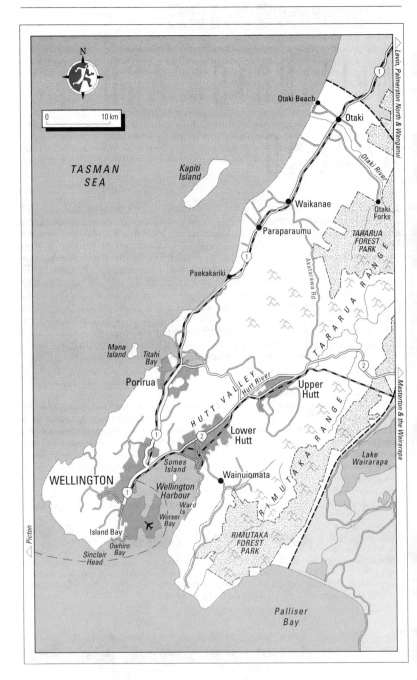

premier **wineries**, with Martinborough (see p.386) only a short scenic drive away through the Rimutaka Range to the Wairarapa, and the sunny Marlborough wineries (see p.466) accessible by boat across Cook Strait.

WELLINGTON

The vibrant city of **WELLINGTON** is the cultural, political and commercial capital of New Zealand, though this is not what most Aucklanders would have you believe. A healthy antipathy exists between the two cities, fuelled by Auckland's conviction that it should be capital. Wellington is by no means a pale shadow of Auckland, though, not least because of the high levels of investment in recent years, aimed at making the city worthy of its capital status and more attractive to visitors. Most of the city is built on precipitous hills overlooking a magnificent harbour, fringed by beaches, marinas and warehouses. The inner city is a mix of historic stone buildings and modern structures, most notably the radical **contemporary architecture** of Ian Athfield, while the sub-urbs are a combination of grand residential villas and unspectacular commercial build-ings. The surrounding hills have provided a natural barrier to the unbridled develop-ment typical of other New Zealand cities, helping to keep central Wellington an easily walkable area with a definite identity.

Wellington is truly **cosmopolitan**, offering a huge range of culinary experiences, alongside nightlife and artistic culture from all over the world. The most exciting months to visit are February and March, when the city hosts three separate **festivals**: the annual Wellington Fringe Festival, a carnival along the lines of the Edinburgh Festival; the biennial International Festival of the Arts, a month-long celebration that draws the best international acts in opera, theatre and music; and the annual Dragon Boat Festival (in late February), which attracts huge crowds to the inner harbour.

Some history

Maori believe that the first Polynesian navigator, Kupe, discovered Wellington Harbour (in 925 AD) and he is said to have camped here for some time on the Miramar Peninsula at the harbour mouth, naming the harbour's islands Matiu (Somes Island) and Makaro (Ward Island) after his daughters. Several *iwi* (tribes) settled around the harbour over the centuries, including the Ngati Tara people, who enjoyed the rich fish-ing areas and the protection that the bay offered. Both Abel Tasman (in 1642) and Captain Cook (in 1773) were prevented from entering Wellington Harbour by fierce winds and, apart from a few whalers, it was not until 1840 that the first wave of **European settlers** arrived, not long after the New Zealand Company had purchased a large tract of land around the harbour. The first settlement, named Britannia, was estab-lished on the northeastern beaches at **Petone**; shortly after, the Hutt River flooded, forcing the settlers to move around the harbour to a more sheltered site known as Lambton Harbour (where the central city has grown up) and the relatively level land at **Thorndon**, at that time just north of the shoreline. They renamed the settlement after the Iron Duke and, finding flat land scarce, began land **reclamations** into the harbour in the 1850s, a process that continued at intervals for more than a hundred years.

By the turn of the century the original shoreline of Lambton Harbour had all but dis-appeared, replaced largely by wharves and harbourside businesses. The growing city, at the hub of coastal shipping, became a thriving import and export centre, and in 1865 it superseded Auckland as the **capital** of New Zealand, largely because of its central location and fine harbour. Wellington has prospered ever since, and these days around seven million tonnes of cargo pass through the wharves each year. Parts of the water-front no longer needed by the modernized shipping industry have been redeveloped for public use, while along the coast a number of **shipwrecks** are further testament to the city's maritime history, victims of the region's notorious high winds. Sailing ships of the 1800s were particularly susceptible, but even as late as 1968 a modern roll-on roll-off ferry, the *Wahine*, foundered at the harbour entrance in the worst storm of the century (see p.398).

Arrival and information

Wellington International Airport is about 5km from the city centre and has two terminals – one used by Qantas and Ansett flights, the other by domestic and Air New Zealand flights. Also operating from here is the smaller airline, Soundsair, that makes the short hop over Cook Strait to the South Island. There is a **visitor centre** in each terminal (daily 7.30am–7.30pm, also open for flight arrivals at the international terminal); the domestic terminal also has **left-luggage** lockers and there's a **bureau de change** in the international terminal (Mon–Fri 9am–4.30pm, and for flights outside these times). Two **shuttle-bus** companies, Super Shuttle (☎04/387 8787) and Johnstons (☎04/569 9017), run a door-to-door service to central Wellington (daily; $5), plus a direct service to Wellington train station (roughly every 30min Mon–Fri; $6). A **taxi** ride from the airport costs around $20.

The main **train station** is in downtown Wellington on Bunny Street, just off Waterloo Quay, and is the last destination on the main north–south rail line from Auckland and the branch line from Napier. Newmans and InterCity **buses** also pull in here (at platform 9), while Mount Cook Landline buses stop at the intersection of Courtenay Place and Cambridge Terrace. Arriving **by road**, SH1 and SH2 merge just north of the city, continuing into the centre, after running briefly along the harbourside and giving excellent views of the city ahead. **Ferries** from Picton on the South Island arrive at the Interislander ferry terminal just off SH1, 2km north of the train station. A free shuttle service operates between the ferry terminal and train station; the Super Shuttle bus (see above) costs $3, and a taxi $5–6.

> For details of sea and air routes from Wellington **to the South Island**, see "Crossing Cook Strait", p.405.

The well-stocked and efficient **visitor centre** is on the corner of Wakefield Street and Victoria Street (Mon–Fri 8.30am–5.30pm; Sat & Sun 9.30am–5.30pm, 4.30pm in winter; ☎04/801 4000, fax 801 3030). They sell city maps for 50¢ and provide a useful free booklet, "Wellington – What's On", published by Jasons and including a central-city map. The **DOC office** is in the Old Government Buildings at the corner of Lambton Quay and Whitmore Street (Mon–Fri 9am–4.30pm, Sat & Sun 10am–3pm; ☎04/472 5821), with stacks of information on walks in the Wellington region, including tramps on Kapiti Island and the forest parks around the city; hut passes are also sold here, as are permits to visit Kapiti Island ($8).

City transport

Wellington has a comprehensive **local bus** service that links the inner city to most of the central suburbs (Mon–Sat 7am–11pm, Sun 8am–11pm). Services depart from the train station or the main city bus stop at Courtenay Place, at the intersection with Cambridge Terrace; free route maps and timetables are available from the visitor centre. Frequent **trolley buses** also trundle around the city, running on overhead cables between the eastern end of Courtenay Place and the train station, along Lambton Quay. Fares are $1 within the inner city, beyond which a zonal system comes into operation, with fares ranging from $1.10 to $3; buy tickets from the driver. "Daytripper" **passes** ($5) are also available from bus drivers, giving unlimited travel for a day (after 9am) and including the cable car to the Botanic Gardens (see p.399). For **information** on all trains and local buses in the Wellington region, call the Ridewell Service Centre (Mon–Sat 7.30am–8.30pm, Sun 9am–3pm; ☎04/801 7000).

Driving around the inner city is easy once you get used to the extensive one-way system and remember to avoid the rush-hour traffic (7–9am & 4.30–6.30pm). Finding a space to **park**, though, is a nightmare. Thankfully at weekends you can park at meters and in car parks for up to two hours for free, after which both cost $3 per hour. The hills around the city are a mecca for **mountain-bike** enthusiasts (pick up the $1 leaflet "Off-road Mountain Biking in Wellington City", containing maps and full descriptions of tracks in the Town Belt), but cycling is also a great way to enjoy the scenic coastal route around the harbour and its bays; most **bike rental** companies (see p.411 for recommended outfits) charge $25 for half a day.

Accommodation

Your best bet is to plump for **accommodation** in the city centre, close to all the action. There are plenty of hostels, B&Bs (many in beautifully preserved Victorian villas) and hotels, but only a few centrally located motels and, curiously for New Zealand, the city has **no campsite**. Instead, pitch a tent in the grounds of *Rowena's Backpackers* (see p.394), or else head all the way out to the Hutt Valley on the harbour's northeastern shore for the *Hutt Park Holiday Village*, 95 Hutt Park Road, Lower Hutt (☎04/568 5913; tent sites $8.50, cabins & units ②–④), about 14km from Wellington's train and bus station.

On the city centre's western fringes, but within easy walking distance of all the attractions, the leafy and characterful suburb of **Thorndon** contains a couple of delightful B&Bs and a pleasant historic hotel, while the inner-city's eastern border, the suburb of **Mount Victoria**, offers a range of accommodation within a stone's throw of the busiest part of town. Finally, if you're after bucolic surroundings within easy **driving distance** of the city, you could do a lot worse than *Braebyre B&B* near Porirua (see p.415).

Availability anywhere in the inner city is limited during the busiest part of the summer (Jan & Feb), so it pays to book as far ahead as possible: for the most popular hostels, you need to allow a week or more. **Prices** are a touch above average: in hostels, most dorms are four- to six-bed and rates hover around $18, while doubles and twins edge just over $40. At the other end of the scale, hotels are expensive during the week, but most offer special weekend deals, sometimes shaving off as much as fifty percent.

Hotels and motels

Abel Tasman, cnr Willis St & Dixon St (☎04/385 1304, fax 385 8416). Extremely central hotel with good weekend discounts and regular rates towards the lower end of this price code. ⑥.

Apollo Lodge, 49 Majoribanks St (☎ & fax 04/385 1849). Central, medium-sized motel, 400m from Courtenay Place. Most units have fully equipped kitchens. ⑤.

Carillon Motor Inn, 33 Thompson St (☎04/384 8795, fax 385 7036). Cheaper prices reflect an average location, about a kilometre south of Courtenay Place, and a communal kitchen simply equipped with a microwave and fridge. ④.

Majoribanks Apartments, 38 Majoribanks St (☎04/385 8879, fax 385 1849). Several big, fully self-contained apartments in a modern block close to the heart of the city; off-street parking. ⑤.

Parkroyal, cnr Grey St & Featherston St (☎04/472 2722, fax 472 4724). The most expensive place in town, this luxurious international hotel in a tower block near Queens Wharf is geared chiefly to businesspeople, but has half-price weekend rates (around $165). Facilities include a gym and a pool, a classy restaurant and an airport limousine service. ⑨.

Plaza International, 148 Wakefield St (☎04/473 3900, fax 473 3929). A gleaming modern corporate hotel on the waterfront near Civic Square, with an a la carte restaurant and brasserie. Marginally cheaper than the *Parkroyal*, especially at weekends. ⑨.

Shepherd's Arms, 285 Tinakori Rd, Thorndon (☎04/472 1320, fax 472 0523). Near the Parliamentary District, this small 1870s hotel (reputedly New Zealand's oldest) is tastefully renovated in period style, but with all mod cons. Bar and restaurant. ⑥.

Trekkers, 213 Cuba St (☎04/385 2153, fax 382 8873). Central, basic but popular hotel-cum-motel-cum-backpackers. Hotel and motel rooms (singles and doubles) are kitted out with private bathrooms, TV, radio and phone. ⑤.

Wellington Motel, 14 Hobson St (☎04/472 0334, fax 472 6825). Small, quiet and well equipped, this is the closest motel to the Picton ferry terminal. ⑤.

B&Bs and guesthouses

Dunrobin House, 89 Austin St, cnr with Derby St, Mount Victoria (☎04/385 0335, fax 385 0336). An elegant turn-of-the-century villa about 1km from Courtenay Place, with three comfortable, big rooms and an abundance of fresh flowers. Mornings begin with a gourmet breakfast which, in fine weather, is served in the sheltered garden. ⑥.

Holdsworth, 292 Tinakori Road, Thorndon (☎04/473 4986, fax 473 9566). An attractive 1890s house in a cottage-garden setting, five minutes' walk from Parliament Buildings, with big, welcoming rooms. Excellent breakfasts; off-street parking. ⑥.

The Mermaid, 1 Epuni St, cnr with Aro St (☎ & fax 04/384 4511). A luxurious guesthouse for women only, set in a restored turn-of-the-century house among bush-covered hills, a ten-minute walk from downtown. Four tastefully furnished rooms (one with private bathroom), each with a view of the garden or hills. Kitchen and lounge. ④.

Talavera, 7 Talavera Terrace (☎04/471 0555). An 1897 villa on a quiet, leafy hill above the central business district, five minutes' walk from Lambton Quay and on the cable-car route. Sweeping views from a self-contained flat with a verandah. ⑥

Tinakori Lodge, 182 Tinakori Rd, Thorndon (☎04/473 3478, fax 472 5554). A well-appointed, big Victorian villa, a short walk from the Parliamentary District, with several airy rooms and a conservatory that looks onto a bushland reserve. ⑤.

Hostels

Downtown Backpackers, 1 Bunny St (☎04/473 8482, fax 471 1073). Huge and rather impersonal hostel occupying a former hotel, opposite the train station but a bit of a walk from the action on Courtenay Place. The doubles are big, dorms are airy, and extra perks include courtesy pick-ups, a very cheap bar and a café serving low-cost breakfasts and dinners. Dorms ①, rooms ③.

Port Nicholson YHA, cnr Cambridge Terrace & Wakefield St (☎04/801 7280, fax 801 7278). Popular, big, modern and fairly luxurious hostel right in the heart of the city, with great harbour views. Most rooms are en suite (singles, doubles, and 4- or 6-bed dorms). To get a double in summer, you'll need to book at least a week in advance. Dorms ①, rooms ③.

Rowena's, 115 Brougham St (☎ & fax 04/385 7872, freephone 0800/801 414). Marginally the cheapest hostel, set on a hill less than a kilometre south of Courtenay Place. It's lively and reasonably well equipped (except for a small kitchen), with doubles and dorms. Pool room; car park and free shuttle service. Dorms ①, rooms ②.

Trekkers, 213 Cuba St (☎04/385 2153, fax 382 8873). Another popular and central backpackers; also a hotel and budget motel. Backpacker rooms (basic singles, 2-bed bunkrooms and slightly shabby doubles with handbasins) share bathrooms, and linen costs an extra $4. The complex has a kitchen, free parking, a spa and sauna, café, bar and a travel centre. Dorms ①, rooms ②.

The City

Wellington's **city centre** is compact and easy to cover on foot, with most of the major attractions within a two-kilometre radius. The heart of the city stretches from the train station in the north to Cambridge and Kent Terraces at the eastern end of Courtenay Place, taking in the waterfront along the way, while the central business district runs along The Terrace and Lambton Quay; the latter is also the main shopping thoroughfare. The main districts for eating, drinking and **entertainment** are Courtenay Place, Cuba Street, Willis Street, and down to the waterfront at Queens Wharf. Cuba Street is also the "alternative" **shopping** district with secondhand bookshops, record stores, retro clothes retailers and quirky cafés.

Meanwhile, the main **sights** are concentrated in four distinct areas: around Civic Square and the waterfront, the Botanic Gardens, the Parliamentary District, and the historic suburb of Thorndon. The nearest **beach** to the city centre is Oriental Bay, skirted by an elegant **esplanade**, Oriental Parade, which is a favourite spot for jogging, walking, swimming, or simply admiring the view of the city and harbour, especially at night. On the hills enclosing the city centre is the **Town Belt** – originally set aside in 1839 by the New Zealand Company for aesthetic and recreational purposes, it contains several good walks and many of the city's best **lookout** points.

Civic Square and the waterfront

Thoroughly modern **Civic Square**, behind the visitor centre, is a good place to start your sightseeing, before making the short walk to the waterfront and Wellington's star attraction, the Museum of New Zealand. A popular venue for outdoor events, Civic Square was revamped in the early 1990s by Wellington architect Ian Athfield (see p.398) and is full of interesting sculptures, with a couple of buildings worth a quick visit.

Just around the corner from the visitor centre and flanked by striking metal nikau palms is the big and refreshingly bold **Wellington Public Library** (Mon–Thurs 9.30am–8.30pm, Fri 9.30am–9pm, Sat 9.30am–5pm, Sun 1–4pm), accessible from both Civic Square and the main entrance around the corner on Victoria Street. Another Athfield design, it's a far cry from the fustiness of most libraries – a spacious high-tech environment of steel, stone and timber. Instead of being concealed, inner workings such as air ducts are exposed to form an integral part of the design, the whole enhanced by strong sculptural forms, colour and plenty of light flooding in. From the upper floor, you get a great view of Civic Square through the curving glass wall.

Across Civic Square from the library and housed in an Art Deco 1939 building is the **City Gallery** (Mon–Fri 11am–5pm, Sat & Sun 11am–6pm; free, except for special exhibitions; ☎04/801 3952), a contemporary art gallery that hosts touring shows of national and international works. Also here is the small arthouse **City Cinema** (details of screenings from the visitor centre or in the local press), with a stylish and expensive café/bar attached. Linking the square with the waterfront is a striking modern **bridge** decorated with timber sculptures of birds, whales and celestial motifs. The work of Maori artist Para Matchitt, completed in 1993, these symbolize the arrival of Maori and European settlers and, by extension, that of present-day visitors from the sea to city.

Just east of the bridge, on Cable Street, is the monolith of the **Museum of New Zealand** (daily: Oct–April 10am–7pm; May–Sept 10am–6pm; free), Wellington's new star attraction and the country's first national museum. A major project (to the tune of $350 million) occupying a purpose-built five-storey building, the museum opened in early 1998. You'll need at least half a day to explore this celebration of New Zealand's people, land and cultures, all brought to life with ambitious state-of-the-art technology. Among the highlights are an earthquake simulator that re-creates the explosive for-

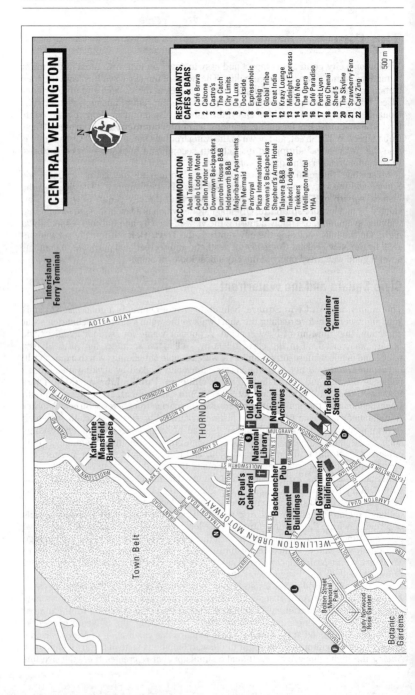

CENTRAL WELLINGTON

N

500 m

Interisland
Ferry Terminal

AOTEA QUAY

Container
Terminal

WATERLOO QUAY

Katherine
Mansfield
Birthplace

HUTT RD

GRANT RD

THORNDON QUAY

HOBSON ST

MURPHY ST

AITKEN ST

MULGRAVE

PIPITEA ST

MOLESWORTH ST

THORNDON

Old St Paul's
Cathedral

National
Archives

Train & Bus
Station

P

KATE SHEPPARD ST

St Paul's
Cathedral

National
Library

Backbencher
Pub

Parliament
Buildings

HAWKESTONE ST

PARK ST

HILL ST

BOWEN ST

Old Government
Buildings

WELLINGTON URBAN MOTORWAY

TINAKORI ROAD

GLENMORE ST

GEORGE

Town Belt

N

L

Bolton Street
Memorial Park

Lady Norwood
Rose Garden

Botanic
Gardens

F

WADESTOWN RD

BOLTON ST

WHITMORE ST

FEATHERSTON ST

LAMBTON QUAY

BUNNY ST

WHITMORE ST

THORNDON QUAY

WESLEY RD

ACCOMMODATION

A	Abel Tasman Hotel
B	Apollo Lodge Motel
C	Carillon Motor Inn
D	Downtown Backpackers
E	Dunrobin House B&B
F	Holdsworth B&B
G	Majoribanks Apartments
H	The Mermaid
I	Parkroyal
J	Plaza International
K	Rowena's Backpackers
L	Shepherd's Arms Hotel
M	Talavera B&B
N	Tinakori Lodge B&B
O	Trekkers
P	Wellington Motel
Q	YHA

RESTAURANTS, CAFES & BARS

1	Café Brava
2	Calzone
3	Castro's
4	The Catch
5	City Limits
6	De Luxe
7	Dockside
8	Expressoholic
9	Fiebig
10	Global Tribe
11	Great India
12	Krazy Lounge
13	Midnight Espresso
14	Café Neo
15	The Opera
16	Café Paradiso
17	Petit Lyon
18	Roti Chenai
19	Shed 5
20	The Skyline
21	Strawberry Fare
22	Café Zing

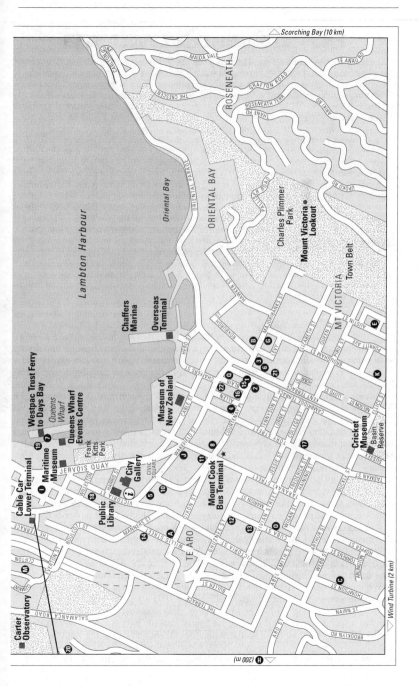

△ Scorching Bay (10 km)

Carter Observatory ■

Cable Car Lower Terminal ■

Maritime Museum

Westpac Trust Ferry to Days Bay

Queens Wharf

Queens Wharf Events Centre

Frank Kitts Park

JERVOIS QUAY

Public Library

City Gallery

CIVIC SQUARE

Mount Cook Bus Terminal

Museum of New Zealand

Chaffers Marina

Overseas Terminal

Lambton Harbour

Oriental Bay

ORIENTAL BAY

Charles Plimmer Park

Mount Victoria ● Lookout

MT VICTORIA

Town Belt

Cricket Museum

Basin Reserve

ROSENEATH

MAIDA VALE

THE CRESCENT

GRAFTON ROAD

ROSENEATH TERR

THANE RD

ARITI RD

TE ANAU RD

UPOKO RD

ORIENTAL PARADE

CARROLL GR

PALLISER RD

TARANAKI STREET

CUBA ST

VICTORIA ST

WILLIS STREET

MANNERS ST

THE TERRACE

CLIFTON

SALAMANCA ROAD

BROOKLYN RD

ARO ST

NAIRN ST

WEBB ST

TASMAN ST

SUSSEX ST

BUCKLE ST

ARTHUR ST

FREDERICK ST

VIVIAN STREET

MARION ST

DIXON ST

WAKEFIELD ST

COURTENAY PL

TENNYSON ST

LORNE ST

CAMBRIDGE TERRACE

KENT TERRACE

ELIZABETH ST

QUEEN ST

BROUGHAM ST

PIRIE ST

HANKEY ST

JESSIE ST

GHUZNEE ST

BOULCOTT ST

WILLISTON ST

HARRIS ST

CABLE ST

HERD ST

CHAFFERS ST

BARKER ST

MAJORIBANKS ST

AUSTIN ST

POBBITT AVE

LLOYD ST

NELSON ST

ELLIS ST

TORRENS ST

HOPPER ST

ARLINGTON

THOMPSON ST

OHIRO RD

GORDON

CLERMONT

THE TERRACE

TE ARO

ALLEN

BLAIR

PHILIP RD

HOMES ST

DRUMMOND ST

COLLEGE ST

ABEL SMITH ST

BLAIR ST

❶ ❷ ❸ ❹ ❺ ❻ ❼ ❽ ⓐ ⓑ ⓒ ⓓ ⓔ ⓖ ⓗ ⓙ ⓚ ⓜ

⑩ ⑪ ⑫ ⑬ ⑭ ⑮ ⑯ ⑰ ⑲ ⑳ ㉑ ㉒

ⓘ

★

H ▽ (200 m)

▽ Wind Turbine (2 km)

THE ARCHITECTURE OF IAN ATHFIELD

The work of New Zealand's most influential and versatile living architect, **Ian Athfield**, generates the kind of love–hate reaction usually associated with the Lloyd's Building in London and the Pompidou Centre in Paris. His principal motif is the juxtaposition of old and new, regular and irregular, as seen in the facade of the **Palmerston North Public Library** (see p.395). However, many of the finest examples of Athfield's work are in his home town of Wellington, where the facade of the **Moore Wilson Building** from 1984 (a food warehouse at the corner of College and Tory streets), explores fractures, while the **Oriental Parade Apartments**, built in 1988 near the start of the Southern Walkway on Oriental Parade (see p.402), have an almost Egyptian facade. Athfield also likes art-work to appear as part of his buildings, as evidenced by the sculptural forms of the **Wellington Public Library** (see p.395). Perhaps the best example of his work is **Logan House** at Windy Point in Eastbourne, across the bay from Wellington (see p.406), where he has cleverly combined an old structure with a new one, making full use of the natural surroundings and revitalizing a disused building. However, many people's favourite Athfield building is a house-cum-office on a hillside in the northern suburb of **Khandallah** (at 105 Amritsar St; closed to the public). Visible from the Wellington motorway and – at some distance – from the ferry to Days Bay, it seems to grow organically down the hill, showing a respect for the environment and a willingness to engage with it that's often lacking in New Zealand architecture. In contrast, the house adjoining the **Te Mata Winery** in Havelock North (see p.375) is a sly backhanded tribute to the modernists of the 1930s and an expression of the architect's humour, though it still manages to look perfectly placed in its surroundings

mation of this volatile land; a journey to the Wellington of the future, some fifty years from now; and virtual-reality experiences of a bungy jump, sheep shearing and diving with whales. The museum also contains an active marae where you can experience a formal Maori welcome and *iwi* (tribal) ceremonies, plus extensive exhibitions on Maori history, art, heritage and navigation.

Retracing your steps a couple of blocks west along the waterfront, you'll come to the **Maritime Museum** on Queens Wharf, beside Jervois Quay (Dec–March Mon–Fri 9.30am–4pm, Sat & Sun 10am–4.30pm; rest of year Mon–Fri 9.30am–4pm, Sat & Sun 1–5pm; $2 donation requested), which brims with artefacts relating to New Zealand and international maritime history. Normally occupying a lovely stone building of 1891 with a lavish interior gleaming with wood and brass, the collection is currently housed in a **temporary facility** nearby, pending refurbishment. Stealing the show are many skilfully made model ships (including a chilling one of the sinking *Titanic*), a scale model of the harbour, and a gripping video that documents Wellington's worst disaster to date: the sinking of the inter-island ferry, T.E. *Wahine*, in April 1968, with the loss of 51 lives. Returning from Lyttelton with 734 people on board, the ferry entered the harbour just as one of the most violent storms ever recorded in New Zealand struck up. Rescue attempts were repeatedly thwarted until, finally, the weather calmed enough for passengers to start abandoning ship, only to find there were insufficient lifeboats. A graphic model depicts the desperation that ensued. When the main building **reopens** (scheduled for the end of 1998), the museum may adopt more of a slant on the city than the seas – check the latest with the visitor centre.

While at **Queens Wharf**, take a few moments to soak up the atmosphere. Bustling and modernized, this T-shaped wharf dating from 1862 is a popular spot for a drink or a bite to eat (see "Eating", p.406) and has a large state-of-the-art Events Centre that functions as a sports stadium and a venue for bands. Past the Events Centre and on the left is **Shed 5**, the oldest building on the waterfront (1886) and one of the last two remaining timber warehouses. In the early 1990s it was sympathetically converted into a restaurant and bar, quickly becoming one of the most popular watering holes in the city.

The Botanic Gardens, Cable Car and the Carter Observatory

Wellington's **Botanic Gardens** (daily dawn–dusk; free) form a huge swathe of green on peaceful rolling hills high above the city and make for a pleasant hour or two's distraction, containing an observatory, a gorgeous rose garden, a begonia house and an atmospheric Victorian cemetery (pick up the useful leaflet and map of the gardens from Wellington visitor centre). There are main entrances on Glenmore Street and Upland Road, but the best way to get there is via the short but scenic **cable-car** ride to Kelburn. The cable car departs every ten minutes from Cable Car Lane, just off Lambton Quay (Mon–Fri 7am–10pm, Sat & Sun 9am–10pm; $1.50 one-way, $2.50 return), climbing an extremely steep incline, making four stops on the way and giving great views over the city and harbour. Operational since 1902, the cable cars were originally driven by steam but succumbed to electricity in 1933; in 1978 the current Swiss system was installed, whereby two shiny red, modern cars, each at either end of a single rope, are propelled by an electric motor at the top station. There's a **lookout** at the top, just inside the Botanic Gardens, offering spectacular views over the city, brought into focus by coin-operated binoculars. At the terminus itself is **Cable Art** (Wed–Fri 10.30am–3pm, Sat & Sun 10.30am–3.30pm; free), a gallery of works by local artists, with one wall devoted to annotated black-and-white photographs recording the history of the cable car. On the other side of the track, the licensed **Skyline Café** (daily 10am–4pm; see "Eating", p.406) is a great spot to sit with a drink, enjoying views of the city through panoramic windows, or, when the wind abates, from an outside balcony.

Once inside the Botanic Gardens, several paths lead back down to the city, meandering through stands of pohutukawa, remnants of dense native forest and ornamental flower beds. It's a two-minute walk from the Kelburn terminus to the 1941 **Carter Observatory**, where, weather permitting, you can view the southern skies at night on Tuesday and Saturday evenings (7pm & 8.45pm; phone ahead for details, ☎04/472 8167; $6). The programme includes a thirty-minute planetarium show, audiovisual presentations, a short talk on astronomy, and telescope viewing from 8pm. During the day (daily 10am–4pm; $3), you can check out the astronomy displays, video screenings, computers and audiovisual shows. Within sight of the Carter Observatory is the recently renovated 1912 **Thomas King Observatory**, which still contains its original instruments. One of the first observatories in the Wellington area, it played a vital role in navigation and time-keeping.

The *tour de force* of the gardens and their most visited section is the **Lady Norwood Rose Garden**, on flat ground at the city end, near the Centennial Entrance on Glenmore Street, and also accessible by car or bus #21 (Mon–Fri only). The fragrant garden blooms throughout the summer, with 300 varieties of roses laid out in a formal wheel shape around a fountain and the whole enclosed by a colonnade of climbing roses. Adjacent is the large **Begonia House** (daily: Oct–March 10am–5pm; April–Sept 10am–4pm; free), which is divided into two areas: the tropical, with an attractive lily pond and a small cage containing carnivorous plants; and the temperate, which has seasonal displays of begonias and gloxinias in summer, changing to cyclamen, orchids and impatiens in winter. Further down from the rose garden, a striking memorial to New Zealand's most lauded politician, Richard Seddon, marks the entrance to **Bolton Street Memorial Park**, an attractive Victorian **cemetery** where many of the city's early pioneers are buried. Old-fashioned roses clamber around the ageing headstones and twist through ironwork in the shade of mature trees. Established in 1840 as three separate cemeteries (Anglican, Jewish and public), in 1892 the cemetery was closed to all except new burials in existing plots. In the 1960s, amid public outcry, it was abandoned altogether, and over 3500 bodies were exhumed and relocated to make way for the motorway that now bisects it.

From Robertson Way, the main pathway through the memorial park, a footbridge crosses the motorway to the smaller half of the cemetery, which comes to an abrupt end where the high-rise buildings from The Terrace back onto it. It's a short walk from here to the Parliamentary District.

The Parliamentary District

On the way north to the Parliamentary District, you'll pass the imposing redbrick Art Deco edifice housing **Wellington Railway Station** (1937), worth a quick look for its sheer scale. Stepping through the unashamedly self-important entrance, framed by two towering stone pillars, you'll find a magnificent marble entry hall, its spectacularly vaulted ceiling decorated with ornate plasterwork.

Beyond, in the Parliamentary District proper, is Wellington's architectural master-piece, the **Old Government Buildings** (Mon–Fri 9am–4.30pm, Sat & Sun 10am–3pm; free), at the corner of Lambton Quay and Whitmore Street. At first glance an opulent Italian Renaissance construction of cream stone, it is, in fact, built from wood, its entrances decorated with grand columns and porticoes. Designed by colo-nial architect William Clayton to mark the country's transition from provincial to cen-tralized government, it was the largest building in New Zealand when completed in November 1876, and today it remains the second-largest timber building in the world. Built on a small block of reclaimed land, it was physically isolated from the rest of the city and dominated Lambton Harbour. This grandiose building housed government ministers and most of the Wellington-based public service for many years, and Cabinet regularly met in the room immediately above the main entrance. As departments grew, they moved to other buildings and by 1975 only the Education Department remained. Fully restored, it is now the home of Victoria University's Law Faculty. At the entrance is a visitor centre, managed by DOC, which provides maps for a free self-guided tour through part of the building, although there's not a great deal to see inside.

Visible across Lambton Quay are the **Parliament Buildings** in use today, a complex of three highly individual structures: the unmistakable **Beehive** (often confused with Parliament House itself, but in fact the executive wing, where ministers and civil ser-vants huddle), the Edwardian Neoclassical **Parliament House**, and the Victorian Gothic **Parliamentary Library**. You can visit all three on a free **guided tour** (depart-ing on the hour: Mon–Fri 10am–4pm, Sat 10am–3pm, Sun 1–3pm; 45min) from the vis-itor centre in the ground-floor foyer of Parliament House, parliamentary meetings and functions permitting (call ☎04/471 9999 to check). The highly informative and anec-dotal tour begins with a short video on the extensive and detailed restoration work that was carried out after a fire in 1992, which began in the library and swept through parts of Parliament House. Incorporated into the restoration is some pretty impressive anti-earthquake work (Parliament House stands a mere 400m from a faultline), which puts it at the cutting edge of earthquake technology. The remainder of the tour highlights some exquisite architecture and a few surprisingly modern areas juxtaposed with the old, before you enter the library. The latter was built in 1899 by Thomas Turnbull, who was famous for designing churches and endowed the library with a strong Victorian Gothic, ecclesiastical feel.

When Parliament is not in session, tours continue into the comfortable-looking Chamber itself, where the first MPs elected by New Zealand's recently introduced sys-tem of proportional representation took their seats on the inauspicious date of Friday, December 13, 1996. On the other side of Parliament House, you briefly enter the foyer of the modernist **Beehive**, designed by British architect Sir Basil Spence, which was started in 1969 and completed in 1982. The story goes that Spence designed this curios-ity on a napkin after dinner, having been inspired by the label on a box of matches. The

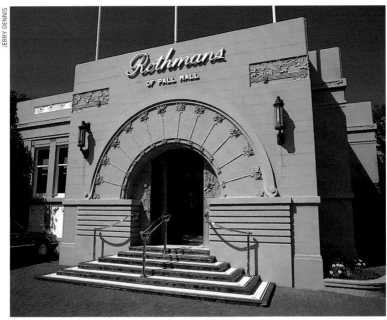

Rothmans Building, Napier

Gannet colony, Cape Kidnappers

Sea kayaking, Abel Tasman
National Park

Beehive and Parliament House, Wellington

Canterbury Plains, seen from a balloon

Art in the Park at the Botanical
Gardens, Christchurch

Cabbage trees, Wairarapa

Civic Centre complex, Wellington

JERRY DENNIS

Lake Rotoiti

JERRY DENNIS

Vineyards, Marlborough

CHRIS WHITEHEAD

Yellow-eyed penguin

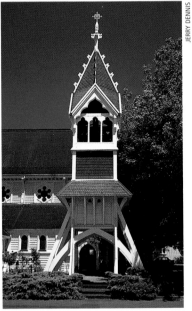

JERRY DENNIS

St Michael's Church, Christchurch

ROBERT NORUM

Moeraki Boulders, Oamaru

building is apparently impractical and hell to work in. Opposite the Parliament Buildings, on Molesworth Street, is the 1893 **Backbencher Pub**, where MPs go to relax, and worth popping into to admire the decor, sporting satirical cartoons and puppets of various Kiwi politicians.

The National Library and Archives

In the next block north from the pub along Molesworth Street is the **National Library of New Zealand**, on the corner with Aitken Street (Mon–Fri 9am–5pm, Sat 9am–1pm; free), the most comprehensive research library in New Zealand and home of the **Alexander Turnbull Library**, a vast collection of volumes, documents, paintings and so on, mostly relating to New Zealand and the Pacific, which was assembled by a wealthy Wellington merchant and gifted to the Crown in 1918. The ground-floor area has a range of reference books that you can take into a reading room, but the rest of the books are off-limits to the public. Also worth checking out is the library's large **gallery** (Mon–Fri 9am–5pm, Sat 9am–4.30pm, Sun 1–4.30pm), which regularly hosts free exhibitions, lectures and events (listed in Wednesday's *Evening Post* and Friday's *Dominion*).

Opposite the library is the pink concrete monstrosity of **St Paul's Cathedral**, a curious mix of Byzantine and Santa Fe styles, designed in the 1930s and 40s by Cecil Wood of Christchurch, a renowned ecclesiastical architect. The cathedral was finally completed in 1972, replacing Old St Paul's, one street away. The interior is cavernous and you can't escape the powder pink or the concrete, but there are some interesting modern stained-glass windows, and a distinctive organ with a set of trumpets jutting out at right-angles from the pipes, which was built in London and first installed in Old St Paul's.

A stone's throw away, at the junction of Aitken Street and Mulgrave Street, are the **National Archives** (Mon–Fri 9am–5pm, Sat 9am–1pm; free), which exhibit a number of important documents relating to New Zealand's social and constitutional development. On permanent display and sealed into an environmentally controlled display case in the centre of the **Constitution Room** (really a vault) is the original **Treaty of Waitangi** (see Contexts, p.764, for more on this landmark document and its repercussions), which barely survived a long spell lost in the bowels of the Old Government Buildings, suffering water damage and the gnawings of rodents before it was rescued in 1908. Other archives on display in the room highlight important milestones on the country's road to independent nationhood. There's a facsimile of an extensive petition for **women's suffrage**, a significant contribution to New Zealand's becoming the first country to enfranchise women (look for Kate Sheppard's signature), and **Maori petitions** dating back to 1909, which complain of broken treaty promises. Outside the Constitution Room is a small container of water, to help Maori neutralize *tapu* (ill-effects caused by a taboo action or object) after viewing the treaty. Mounted on a wall nearby is an enlarged copy of the treaty and a map, showing who signed where; the great Maori chief Te Rauparaha signed it twice, in two different locations, each time receiving muskets and blankets. Other galleries display some great Maori carvings and *tukutuku* (woven leather and flax panels), alongside rotating exhibitions of works by well-known Kiwi artists and of material relating to New Zealand history.

Thorndon

From 1866 to 1964, the modest-looking **Old St Paul's**, at the corner of Mulgrave Street and Pipitea Street (Mon–Sat 10am–5pm; free), was the parish church of **THORNDON**. The church's stunning wooden interior was crafted in early English Gothic style (more commonly seen in stone), the native timbers having since darkened with age to a rich mellow hue. The serried ranks of arches, the pews, pulpit and choral area are all highlighted by fabulous stained-glass windows and the sheen of polished brass plaques on the walls. Consecrated in 1866, the church was the major work of an English ecclesiastical architect, Reverend Frederick Thatcher, who designed it for Bishop Selwyn and was vicar here for a few years.

Head north for about ten minutes, crossing the bridge over the motorway into Thorndon, Wellington's oldest suburb, and you'll reach the **Katherine Mansfield Birthplace**, 25 Tinakori Rd (Mon 10am–2.30pm, Tues–Sun 10am–4pm; $4). A modest wooden house with a small garden, this was the first childhood home of New Zealand's most famous short-story writer and is described in some of her works, notably "Prelude" and "A Birthday". Stuffed with antiques and ornaments, the house has a cluttered Victorian charm and unusual decor, which was avant-garde for its time, inspired by Japonisme and the Aesthetic Movement. This has been beautifully restored and the walls are bright with colour and reprints of original wallpapers. In the kitchen is a doll's house, reproduced from the story of the same name, while an upstairs room is set aside to recount a history of the author's life and career, with some black-and-white photos of Wellington and the people that shaped her life, and an excellent 45-minute video, *A Woman and a Writer*. Born Kathleen Mansfield Beauchamp in 1888, the writer lived here for five years with her parents, three sisters and beloved grandmother before they moved to a much grander house in what is now the western suburb of Karori. At 19, Katherine left Wellington for Europe, where she spent the rest of her short life, before dying of tuberculosis in France in 1923.

WALKS AROUND WELLINGTON

There are several worthwhile walks around Wellington, the most popular being the **Red Rocks Coastal Walk**, beginning about 7km south of the city centre and tracing a shoreline reserve to an unusual volcanic rock formation. Other, **longer tracks** pass through sections of the **Town Belt**. The best of these, and the easiest to reach from the city centre, are the Southern and Northern Walkways, which are described in leaflets from the visitor centre, each with a helpful map. The Town Belt also contains numerous **lesser tracks**, but their layout is confusing, so don't attempt them without a map.

RED ROCKS COASTAL WALK

The easy **Red Rocks Coastal Walk** (4km each way; 2–3hr return) follows a rough track along the coastline from Owhiro Bay to Sinclair Head, passing a quarry and the eponymous **Red Rocks** – well-preserved volcanic pillow lava, formed about 200 million years ago by underwater volcanic eruptions and coloured red by iron oxide. Maori variously attribute the colour to bloodstains from Maui's nose or blood dripping from a paua-shell cut on Kupe's hand, while another account tells how Kupe's daughters cut themselves in mourning, having given up their father for dead. From May to October Sinclair Head is visited by an established colony of New Zealand **fur seals**.

The track **starts** at the **quarry gates** at the western end of Ohiro Bay Parade, where there's a car park. To get there by **bus** you have several options: from the central city take the frequent #1 to Island Bay (daily), get off at The Parade at the corner of Reef Street and walk 2.5km to the start of the walk; at peak times, catch #4 instead, which continues to Happy Valley, only 1km from the track. Otherwise, take a #1 or #4 to Wellington Hospital, at the intersection of Adelaide Road and John Street, and change to the #29 (Mon–Sat), getting off at Happy Valley, again about 1km from the start of the track.

THE SOUTHERN WALKWAY

The **Southern Walkway** (11km; 4–5hr, or as shorter segments) cuts through the Town Belt to the south of the city centre, between Oriental and Island bays, and is fairly easy

Mount Victoria Lookout and southwest to Brooklyn Hill

To the east of the city centre, the **Mount Victoria Lookout** (196m) is one of the best of Wellington's lookout points, offering sweeping panoramic views, day or night. You can get there by car, by bus (#20; Mon–Fri) or on foot as part of the Southern Walkway (see p.402). If you're driving, follow Hawker Street, off Majoribanks Street, then take Palliser Road, which twists uphill through Charles Plimmer Park; on the other side, turn into Thane Road, which snakes up to the lookout. Next to the car park at the top is the **Byrd Memorial**, a triangular construction faced with multicoloured tiles and intended to simulate an Antarctic expedition tent, with the Southern Lights playing across it. The memorial honours the American aviator and Antarctic explorer Richard E. Byrd (1888–1957), who mapped large areas of the Antarctic and was the first man to fly over the South Pole, using New Zealand as a base for his expeditions. From the memorial, there's an impressive view of the city waterfront, the docks and the airport. Up a short flight of steps is the lookout proper, giving magnificent 360-degree views of the surrounding hills, the city and its suburbs, the harbour, Hutt Valley and eastern harbour bays.

Between here and the city's other main lookout point is a treat for ardent cricket fans. Reached along Kent Terrace (entrance on Sussex Street), the small **Cricket Museum** (Nov–March daily 10.30am–3.30pm; April–Oct Sat & Sun only, same times; $3) at Basin Reserve, the city's premier cricket ground, has an exhibition of cricketing memorabilia lurking beneath the old grandstand.

going overall, despite a few steep stretches. The walk offers plenty of **variety**, yielding excellent views of the harbour and central city, shade and tranquillity in the Town Belt forest, and exposed coastline between Houghton and Island bays. Much of the walkway is **shaded**, richly scented by exotic trees, and covered with pine needles; among the birds you might encounter are fantails, grey warblers and wax-eyes. Highlights include the **sweeping views** from the lookout at the Mount Victoria summit (196m) and from Mount Albert (178m), the rugged coastline of Houghton Bay, and the safe and popular **beach** at Island Bay.

The walk can be undertaken in either direction and is clearly marked by posts bearing orange arrows. To **start** at the city end, take the #14 Kilbirnie (via Roseneath) **bus** to Oriental Parade (near Ian Athfield's Egyptian-style Oriental Apartments); the walkway entrance is signposted near the *Hotel Raffaele*, at no. 360. To begin at the other end, take the #1 bus to Island Bay and follow the signs from nearby Shorland Park.

THE NORTHERN WALKWAY

Extending through tranquil sections of the Town Belt to the north of the city centre, the **Northern Walkway** (16km; 4hr, or tackled in sections) offers spectacular views. Stretching from Kelburn to Johnsonville, it covers five distinct areas (Botanic Garden, Tinakori Hill, Trelissick Park, Khandallah Park and Johnsonville Park), which can be accessed from various suburban streets and are served by public transport. Highlights are the **birdlife** on Tinakori Hill (tui, fantails, kingfishers, grey warblers, silver-eyes); regenerating native forest in **Ngaio Gorge** in Trelissick Park; great views across the city and the harbour and over to the Rimutaka and Tararua ranges from a lookout on **Mount Kaukau** (430m); and, in Johnsonville Park, a disused tunnel hewn through solid rock.

From the city end, the track **starts** at the Botanic Garden lookout at the top of the **cable-car** terminus, or you can begin instead at the Tinakori Hill section by climbing St Mary Street, off Glenmore Street, and following the orange arrows through woodland. Starting at the far end means taking a **train** to Raroa station (Mon–Sat), or a #49 Johnsonville **bus** (Sun only).

You can get another fantastic all-round view of the Wellington region from the further-flung **wind turbine** crowning **Brooklyn Hill** in the southwestern part of the city. The turbine, a sort of giant plane propeller loudly whirring atop a mighty tower (31.5m), has generated power for Wellington since 1993, at its maximum capacity supplying over a hundred homes. On a clear day you can see as far as the Kaikoura Ranges on the South Island. To reach the turbine by car, take Brooklyn Road from the end of Victoria Street, turn left at Ohiro Road, then right at the shopping centre up Todman Street and follow the signposts (the road up to the turbine closes at 8pm Oct–April and at 5pm May–Sept). Bus #7 drops you within walking distance.

Wellington Harbour

The sight of multicoloured sails scudding across the water should be enough to convince you that it's impossible to come to Wellington and ignore the lure of the water. On top of that, **Wellington Harbour** and its reliable winds offer excellent sailing experiences. Take your pick between a harbour cruise, a hands-on **sailing** trip, **windsurfing** or a thrilling ride on a **jet ski**.

If you prefer to have a destination in mind, you can take a ferry to **Somes Island**, a hilly little knoll stranded in the northeastern waters of the harbour. Steeped in history and abounding in wildlife, the island enjoys panoramic views across the harbour. You can combine a day-trip here with a stint at the city's favourite beach of **Days Bay**, one of several **beaches** around the harbour that Wellingtonians flock to in good weather. For visitors there's really more fun to be had out on the water or exploring the city, but if you must hit the beach try **Scorching Bay**, a crescent of white sand 13km east of the city centre on the main coastal road, which has safe swimming and a play area. At peak times you can take bus #30 all the way there; otherwise, catch bus #11 to Seatoun (daily) and change onto the #26 (Mon–Fri) or #30 (peak times).

Exploring the harbour

Aimed at novice and experienced sailors alike are the **harbour cruises** run by Mountain Marine (☎04/586 0699; Nov–April daily; rest of year by arrangement). Groups of five to eight are taken out on an 8.5-metre yacht for a short cruise (3hr; $35) or a day-trip (7hr; $70, including lunch); you can either lend a hand or just sit back, and wet-weather gear and lifejackets are supplied. An awe-inspiring way to cruise the harbour, but harder on the pocket, is on board the former Whitbread Round-the-World yacht, *Phantom of the Straits* (☎0800/TO SAIL & 04/499 4221), better known for its adventure trips across Cook Strait (see box on p.405). Options include a jaunt around the inner harbour (10am & 3pm; 1hr 30min; $35), a lunch cruise (noon; 2hr 30min; $65), or a twilight supper cruise (6.30pm; 3hr; $75). The food and drink are great, as are the views, and you'll feel spoilt rotten; you'll need to book ahead for any of these trips, even though they take up to forty people at a time.

Windsurfing is huge here and a popular spot is Kio Bay, to the east of Oriental Bay and around the point towards Evans Bay (bus #24, Mon–Fri). Near the bus stop is good wave-jumping water. For gear rental, try Wildwinds Extreme at the overseas terminal, off Oriental Parade and beside Chaffers Marina (☎04/473 5689; $65 half-day, plus $15 for wetsuit, boots and harness). You can also explore the harbour by **jet ski** with Wet & Wild, based at Frank Kitts Park on the city waterfront (☎04/235 9796): a twenty-minute circuit costs $35 for a solo jet ski, $50 for a double. They also do guided "safari" tours (45min; from $75 solo, $100 double) and trips to Somes Island (1hr; $95 solo, $120 double); wetsuits, life jackets, helmets, booties and goggles are all supplied.

CROSSING COOK STRAIT

From Wellington, planes, ferries and the fast *Lynx* wave-piercer catamaran cross **Cook Strait**, linking the **North and South islands**; the most exciting way to make the crossing, though, is on a sailing trip.

FERRIES
Ferry and catamaran services to Picton depart from Wellington's **Interisland Ferry Terminal**; a complimentary shuttle-bus service runs from the train station 45 minutes before each scheduled sailing. The **ferries** (daily year-round; 3hr) have a standard one-way fare of $44, but this can be reduced by as much as half if you book in advance or take a night or early morning crossing; add $12 each way for a bike, $160 for a car. The *Lynx* **wave-piercer** (Dec–April only) costs $59 each way (plus $15 for bikes, $190 for cars), less in advance or in conjunction with special offers, but be warned that crossings tend to get cancelled in rough weather.

FLIGHTS
Soundsair Shuttle (☎0800/505 005 & 04/388 2594) **fly** daily to Picton (20min; $55 one-way), and twice a week to Blenheim (Fri & Sun; $65). Float Air (☎03/573 6433, fax 573 6511; $70) operate a **seaplane**, making two flights a day between Picton Harbour and Porirua Harbour, north of Wellington, with courtesy bus links to the city and the airport.

SAILING
If you can afford it, the most thrilling way to cross Cook Strait is aboard the 24-metre *Phantom of the Straits* on the **Cook Strait Challenge** (mid-Nov to late April, sailing from Wellington every other day; book as far ahead as possible, ☎ 0800/TO SAIL & 04/499 4221), a full day of action, activity and fun on a majestic ex-racing yacht. As well as a leisurely cruise through the gorgeous waterways of the Marlborough Sounds, chances are that you'll glimpse dolphins, seals, and maybe even whales. As a member of the "guest crew" (20 maximum), you get to participate in the actual sailing, under the expert guidance of the permanent crew. The **crossing** can be undertaken in either direction (7hr 30min between Wellington and Picton, allowing for stopoffs; $275), or as a more energetic **round trip** (11hr 30min, with stopoffs but venturing a shorter distance into the Sounds; $375); a sail-out, fly-back option is also available (6hr; from $495). All gear, meals and drinks are included, luggage is carried for free and you can arrange to stay on board the night before a crossing.

Somes Island and Days Bay

Once a focal point for Maori canoes navigating their way out into the Pacific, **Somes Island** has long held spiritual significance to Maori. Kupe is said to have named it Matiu, meaning "peace", when he sailed into the harbour in the tenth century. The first **Maori** to arrive in the Wellington area settled the island and their descendants lived here until the 1830s. Later, European settlers renamed the island after **Joseph Somes**, then deputy governor of the New Zealand Company which "bought" it. For eighty years it was a **quarantine station** for animals, and until the 1920s travellers suspected of carrying diseases such as smallpox were also quarantined here; subsequently, German, Italian, Turkish, Mexican and Japanese **prisoners of war** were kept in camps on the island during both world wars.

Now managed by DOC, the island is open to the public (daily 8.30am–5pm; free) and permanently staffed by a DOC officer (☎04/472 5821), who can provide further information. Work has recently started in earnest to revitalize native vegetation and plans are afoot to restore several historic buildings. Currently, the island is home to sheep, three species of lizard, a breeding colony of about a thousand black-backed **gulls** and several hundred little blue **penguins**, and **seals** are gradually drifting back to its shores.

A number of **Westpac Trust Ferry** sailings (see below) stop here, enabling you to explore the island for an hour or so before catching a later ferry on to Days Bay. Note that this a protected reserve, so smoking is not allowed. From the wharf at the island's northeastern end, a 500-metre sealed road runs uphill to the **DOC field centre**, in an old hospital, which has maps of the island.

Days Bay

There's not much at **Days Bay** except for the beach (at the foot of sheer bush-covered hills), a single main road lined with a few holiday homes, a park, and a popular café; and a remarkable house designed by Ian Athfield, visible from the harbour as you approach. The cliffside **Logan House** at Windy Point, 500m from the Days Bay wharf, is best viewed from the main road, which runs in front of it. It was built around and within two big old stone chimneys, whose thick walls were punctured by arrow-slit windows, like medieval towers. Athfield then designed the rest of the house to link with not only the chimneys but also the cliff-face directly behind them, so that the new structure fully interacts with its natural surroundings.

A stone's throw from the wharf, on the main road, is *Cobar*, a large glass-fronted bar, restaurant and **café** looking out onto the bay and serving international cuisine and weekend brunches (see "Eating", below). From the Days Bay Boatshed beside the wharf (Boxing Day to mid-Feb daily from 10am; Oct–Christmas Day & mid-Feb to April Sat & Sun from 10am; ☎04/562 8150), you can **rent** jet skis and canoes (both $8 an hour), rowing boats ($10 an hour), windsurfers ($20 an hour) and catamarans ($30 an hour) for use in and around the bay. The nearest shops are at **Eastbourne village**, a kilometre further south along the coast, which also has a few cafés and restaurants. Pre-arranged **bike** rental is available at weekends from Eastbourne Bike Hire on the main road in the village (☎04/569 5994; $6 per hour, $15 half-day; groups of 3 or more only Mon–Fri).

The **Westpac Trust Ferry**, a powerful catamaran (☎04/499 1273), runs daily to Days Bay (Mon–Fri up to 8 daily 6.15am–6.30pm, Sat & Sun 5 daily 10.15am–5pm; 30min; $7 one-way, $14 return, bikes carried free), departing from the end of Queens Wharf, behind the *Shed 5* café/bar. You can also get there and back by **bus** (#81 or #83 daily until 6pm), or by **bike**, taking the SH2 around the harbour.

Eating

The gastronomic centre of New Zealand, Wellington is reputed to have more restaurants and cafés per head of population than New York City. It's a **cosmopolitan** scene, with a plethora of ethnic restaurants catering to all tastes, and new places opening up all the time. There's also a thriving **coffee culture**, and Wellingtonians have a penchant for indulgent **weekend brunches**, especially on Sundays.

During the **day**, Wellington's **food courts** offer bargain grazing from an array of international fast-food outlets: try the licensed *Gourmet Lane*, in the BNZ Shopping Centre on the corner of Willis Street and Willeston Street (Mon–Thurs 9am–5.30pm, Fri 7am–8pm, Sat 10am–4pm); *Cuba Street Foodcourt*, 53 Cuba St (Mon–Thurs 10am–6.30pm, Fri–Sat 10am–late, Sun 6.30am–6.30pm), which also has a bar that's very popular on Fridays; or the *Asian Food Market*, Cable Street, where authentic Indian, Chinese, Malaysian, Middle Eastern and Bengali food is served at weekends (Fri–Sun 10.30am–6pm), albeit in rather dowdy surroundings. In the **evenings**, attention shifts to **Queens Wharf** and **Courtenay Place**, offering a choice between waterfront dining or the buzz of the city.

Cafés and takeaways

Café Brava, 2 Courtenay Place (☎04/384 1159). Next to the Downstage Theatre, this classical, modern and airy café/bar serves all-day breakfasts ($4–14), lunches with Mediterranean flair ($10–20); and scrumptious Sunday brunches. Daily from 7am, until 3am on weekends & show nights. Book for pre-theatre dining; licensed.

Calzone, 1 Courtenay Place, cnr of Cambridge Terrace. Basic and popular Italian café, serving mouth-watering pizzas, pasta and salads at reasonable prices, but marred by extraordinarily slow service. Daily 8am–late; licensed.

Castro's, 12 Majoribanks St, Mount Victoria. Perennially popular intimate all-day café for great coffee, generous cooked breakfasts with spicy sausage ($10), excellent lunches and dinners ($12–20), and weekend brunches ($7–13). Licensed.

The Catch, 48 Courtenay Place. Inexpensive sushi bar with dishes revolving on the counter (colour-coded according to price), to take away or eat in; also side orders and bigger meals (under $15) from a set menu. Closed Sun.

City Limits, 122 Wakefield St. The unpretentious founding father of Wellington's café society, open from early morning until late (Sun till 5pm). Big breakfasts and snacky lunches are served, progressing to a broad dinner menu of well-presented food later in the day. Licensed & BYO ($2 corkage).

De Luxe, 10 Kent Terrace, beside the Embassy Theatre. Cheap, snacky counter food, most of it vegetarian, served in a hip bar that's popular with the post-cinema and theatre crowd. Excellent sandwiches alongside sushi and samosas; and good coffee from their own roasted beans. Daily 8am–midnight.

Expressoholic, 128 Courtenay Place. Seriously hip, graffiti-ridden café, with great coffee, breakfast for $7–15, and big portions of soup, filled focaccia, salad and pasta the rest of the day for $10–15. Also plenty of newspapers and magazines for perusing. Daily 7am till late (Sun–Thurs 1am, Fri–Sat 4am); no alcohol.

Fiebig, 55 Mulgrave St, opposite Old St Paul's. Good coffee and simple, eclectic food for breakfast, lunch and dinner at moderate prices, all in a comfortable rustic setting with a twist. Mon–Fri 7.30am–11pm, Sat 10am–11pm, Sun 10am–3pm; licensed.

Global Tribe, 44 Cuba St. A kind of café-cum-adventure centre, with an 8m rock-climbing wall, skateboard ramp, half-sized basketball court, a wave-simulated surfboard ride, video games, pool tables and an Internet link-up, this radical hangout is mostly frequented by twentysomethings who thrive on a diet of cheap fast food, non-alcoholic drinks – and adrenalin. Mon–Thurs 7am–9pm, Fri & Sat 7am–midnight.

Krazy Lounge, cnr Cuba St & Ghuznee St. This convivial, hip café/restaurant serves pasta and char-grilled mains – including possum ragout – for $10–20. Mon–Fri 8am till the early hours, Sat & Sun 9am–2pm; licensed.

Midnight Espresso, 178 Cuba St. A caffeine junkie's heaven, this mellow coffee-house peddles beans for all palates. Sip a cup on its own, with breakfast or alongside a cheap snack (good toasted sandwiches, foccaccia and pizza), while poring over their reading material. Mon–Fri 8.30am–3am, Sat & Sun from 10am.

Café Neo, 132 Willis St. Extra-quick service and big servings at great prices in a warm bustling atmosphere for breakfast and lunch. Delicious pancakes are filled with banana and covered in maple syrup, or choose from an array of salads, pasta, and foccaccia sandwiches. Closed Sun.

Café Paradiso, 20 Courtenay Place (☎04/384 2675). An icon of Wellington café society, buzzing all day and packed till late (dinner bookings required), offering superb food. Light meals cost under $15, mains set you back around $22–26. Lunch Mon–Fri, dinner daily, brunch Sat & Sun.

Roti Chenai, 120 Victoria St, opposite *McDonalds*. Tiny, simple South Indian and Malaysian café with an open kitchen in the middle where roti are prepared in front of your eyes, as well as delicious dosai, murtabak, curries and rendang. Lunch 11.30am–2pm, dinner 5pm onwards; no alcohol.

Café Zing, cnr Blair St & Wakefield St. Swish café/bar that prides itself on quick service and uncomplicated international food at reasonable prices, served from late morning. They also provide weekend brunches for $10–16.

Restaurants

Cobar, 12 Main Rd, Days Bay. Virtually opposite the wharf, this stylish bar, restaurant and café specializes in seafood and international cuisine; they also do weekend brunches. Mon–Fri from 11am, Sat & Sun from 10.30am.

Dockside, Shed 3, Queens Wharf (☎04/499 9900). High-quality restaurant and bar in a vast converted wooden warehouse with a glass frontage overlooking the harbour, serving lunch and dinner, plus brunch at weekends (10.30am–3pm). Hot on seafood – try New Orleans blackened fish for around $20. Book if you want a window seat; licensed.

Great India, 141 Manners St (☎04/384 5755). The best dinner restaurant for tandoori, biryani or curry (all under $15). Licensed & BYO (corkage $1.50 per person); book for Fri & Sat nights.

The Opera, cnr Courtenay Place and Blair St. Swish theatrical restaurant above a large airy bar, spilling onto a wrap-around balcony. Pasta and salads cost less than $20, with more substantial and varied dishes available for under $25; a downstairs café serves snacks for around $10 and mains for under $20; licensed.

Petit Lyon, 33 Vivian St (☎04/384 9402). A big hit for its imaginative food and original decor, this bistro, salon and café straddles three storeys. Lunches cost around $20, while dinners start at $25, except in the café where prices are nearer $15. Book ahead for bistro and salon. Closed Sun; live jazz Thurs evenings; licensed.

Shed 5, Queens Wharf (☎04/499 9069). Thriving upmarket café, restaurant and bar, proffering great seafood in a stylishly converted 1888 woolshed. Lunch, dinner and weekend brunches are served, and prices start at $23 for char-grilled yellow-fin tuna, rising to $30 for West Coast whitebait. Licensed; book ahead for the restaurant.

The Skyline, 1 Upland Rd, Kelburn, near the Botanic Gardens (☎04/475 8727). Sweeping views over the city enhance this glass-fronted café, bar and split-level restaurant designed by Ian Athfield. The café (10am–4pm) has cheap snacks, while the restaurant lays on good-value lunchtime buffets, with a broad selection of seafood, hot and cold meat dishes, vegetarian alternatives, salads and desserts.

Strawberry Fare, 25 Kent Terrace. Open all day for luxurious desserts at just over $10, washed down by a glass or two of dessert wine. Also serves scrummy breakfasts ($10–13); and Mediterranean-style lunches and dinners ($12–20). Licensed.

Drinking, nightlife and entertainment

The capital city has the best **nightlife** in the country, with a huge array of late-night cafés, restaurants, bars and clubs, all within walking distance of each other, and with new ones constantly joining their ranks. Wellington's playground is **Courtenay Place** and a few streets just off it (Blair, Allen and Dixon streets), extending to Willis Street and Lambton Quay. The scene spreads from there to **Queens Wharf**, ten minutes' walk away, where mostly upmarket **bars** overlook the harbour. The **partying** goes on late into the night, and pumps hardest from Thursday to Saturday. The distinction between pubs, bars and **clubs** is often blurred, since many of the bars have free live music and dancing in the evenings, especially at weekends.

Neither is Wellington short of **live arts performance**, for this is the home of not only four professional theatres but also the Royal New Zealand Ballet, the New Zealand Symphony Orchestra, the Wellington Sinfonia, the Wellington Opera Company and the New Zealand Schools of Dance and Drama. On top of that, there's the month-long **International Festival of the Arts** in March of even-numbered years, which draws the top performers from around the world to the country's biggest cultural event. Celebrating the huge diversity of the arts, performances include classical music, jazz and pop, tragic opera, puppet shows and the Grotesque, cabaret, poetry readings, traditional Maori dance, modern ballet and experimental works – and most of the venues are within easy walking distance of one another. For more information and bookings, call ☎04/473 0149 or email *nzfestival@festival.co.nz*. Originally part of the Arts festival, the vibrant **Wellington Fringe Festival** is now run as a separate event every March, filling the inner city with street and indoor theatre (information and bookings ☎04/384 5141).

The best introduction to **what's on** is the "Wellington – What's On" booklet, free from the visitor centre and from accommodation around the city. There are also weekend listings in *The Dominion* and *The Evening Post*, while bland reviews and more useful **listings** appear in both of the city's free ad-ridden weeklies, *City Voice* and *Capital*

Times, which you can pick up at the visitor centre and from racks around town. The visitor centre also provides **CityLine** (☎04/494 3333, on reply punch in code 1325), which gives a brief rundown of events.

Pubs and bars

Most pubs and bars are **open** daily, from around eleven in the morning until around midnight or later.

Aqua Vitae, cnr Willis St & Manners St. Pleasant wine bar proffering over 100 wines.

The Backbencher, cnr Molesworth St & Kate Sheppard St, opposite Parliament House. Lively, comfortable pub, a bolt hole for MPs who quench their thirst amid satirical cartoons and *Spitting Image*-style puppets. Bar snacks all day and a well-priced café serving unpretentious fare. At its busiest Fri night, when there's free live music from 7.30pm.

Bar Bodega, 286 Willis St. Great atmosphere is the draw in this small bar aimed at a slightly older drinking crowd, which doubles as a venue for bands (see below).

The Blue Room, 20 Courtenay Place. An intimate bar at the back of the buzzy *Café Paradiso*.

Chicago, Queens Wharf, opposite the Events Centre. Huge, American-style sports bar with a dance floor, packed on Fri and Sat nights, when live bands are followed by a DJ. Reasonably priced snacks are available to soak up all that Bud.

Cuba Cuba, 179 Cuba St. Hip café/bar that throbs to live music on Thurs–Sat nights.

Kitty O'Shea's, 28 Courtenay Place. Cosy Irish bar with a mix of live music Tues–Sun (traditional Irish on Thurs).

The Loaded Hog 12–14 Bond St, off Willis St. Big lively bar serving naturally brewed beer and reasonable food. Live music Wed–Sun nights.

The Malthouse, 47 Willis St. Airy, yuppie first-floor bar with table service and a pleasant balcony over the street where naturally brewed Kiwi beers are swilled by suits from the office, especially on Friday evenings. Closed Sun in winter.

Molly Malone's, cnr Taranaki St & Courtenay Place. Hugely atmospheric, loud and in-your-face Irish pub, with foot-tapping live Irish music every evening. Upstairs is the quieter *Dubliner* restaurant and bar, serving snacks, $10 lunches, reasonable dinners and weekend brunches.

The Opera, cnr Courtenay Place & Blair St. Spacious and slick bar with live bands on Thurs.

Clubs and gigs

Live **bands** (usually Kiwi but sometimes international) are a regular fixture, playing in bars or at bigger venues such as the Queens Wharf Events Centre (☎04/472 5021), and supplemented in summer by occasional **free concerts** in the waterfront Frank Kitts Park or in Civic Square.

Bar Bodega, 286 Willis St. Wellington's longest-running musical institution. Every Kiwi band worth its salt has played here; DJs also visit, and it sometimes hosts dance parties.

Escape, upstairs at the *Edward Street Café*, 9 Edward St. Cool dance club that draws the young and hip with DJs playing house, techno and jungle; also one-off raves at weekends.

Global Tribe, 44 Cuba St. A popular alcohol-free hangout for the 18–28s, with dance parties every Fri from 9pm to midnight ($2).

Hole in the Wall, 154 Vivian St. Small, studenty drinking den and club, open nightly till 3am, with all kinds of music (sometimes live), from jazz and reggae to jungle and techno. Beer for $2 on Tues night; pool and pinball.

La Luna Club, Oaks Complex, Dickson St. Popular hideaway for a youngish crowd into pool, hip-hop and light dance music. Bands play regularly and there are two bars.

The Planet, cnr Courtenay Place & Tory St. Late-night, post-pub dancing in an unusual and lively club. Live music every other Wed, DJs Thurs–Sat, and dance shows every weekend, but watch out for the expensive drinks. Mon & Tues till 3am, Wed–Sat till 6am, Sun till 1am.

Tatou, Ground floor, 22 Cambridge Terrace. Upmarket techno bar and dance club attracting smart young professionals to its two bars that stay open until 6am. Gets very busy later on; occasional visiting DJs.

GAY AND LESBIAN WELLINGTON

The **scene** in Wellington is focused in the inner city, woven into the general café/bar mainstream and, though smaller than that of Auckland, it tends to be less cliquey and judgemental. In the centre, at least, gays openly express affection in public, and gays, lesbians, transgender and bi-folk mix freely together. Fairly low-key for most of the year, the scene explodes during Wellington's two annual events for the city's gay, lesbian, bisexual, transvestite and transgender community, plus their friends and families. First off is a huge all-night dance party, **Sprung at Devotion**, a glitteringly glam event in February. Anyone's invited (out-of-towners pay a hefty $60 or so per person for a ticket), as long as they get into the over-the-top spirit of things. November sees a week-long festival called **Devotion** – a celebration of theatre, dance, music and community-based events, which starts with a Saturday **parade**. This spectacular lunchtime carnival takes a couple of hours to wend its way through the city, finishing with a **fiesta** at the waterfront, while the streets heave with hot entertainment, stalls of all sorts, national celebrities, groovy games, and ridiculous competitions. The festival ends with a big Saturday-night **dance party** (again, out-of-towners pay, see above). Book party tickets through NZGLTA (New Zealand Gay & Lesbian Tourism Association) by contacting Chris McKellar (email *operations@gaylink.co.nz*) or the reservations centre (☎04/384 1865, fax 382 8246, email *reznz@gaylink.co.nz*).

For **information** on venues and events at other times, check out the national gay **magazine** *Express* ($2), available from the YHA and Unity Books (see "Bookshops", p.411); the free *City Voice* (which has a Queer City section every six weeks); or the national *OUT* magazine. Other contacts are the Gay Switchboard (☎04/385 0674), the Lesbian Line (☎04/389 8082) or Bisexual Women's Group (☎04/385 1162).

The most established Wellington **venues and meeting places** include *Flipp Brasserie*, RSA Building, 103 Ghuznee St (☎04/385 9493), a café/bar offering continental cuisine to a predominantly business crowd (daily for lunch and dinner, brunch on Sat & Sun; mixed); the *Ruby Ruby*bar at 19 Edward St (☎04/384 5211; Mon–Sat 4pm–3am; mixed); *Afternoons & Coffee Spoons* at Shop 6, 165 Riddiford St, Newtown, a women's shop selling books, videos, music, crafts and the like; *La Strada*, a licensed restaurant at 6 Edward St (Mon–Sat from 5.30pm; mixed); and *Evergreen*, 141 Vivian St, an after-hours coffee lounge (mixed/trannies).

The non-profit New Zealand Gay and Lesbian Tourism Association, PO Box 11–582, Wellington 6001 (☎04/384 1877, fax 384 5187, email *secretariat@nzglta.org.nz*), provides **travel information** aimed at gay, lesbian and bisexual visitors. Gaylink Travel, PO Box 11–584, Wellington (☎04/384 1865 & 0800/429 872, fax 882 8246, email *reznz@gaylink.co.nz*), can advise on gay, lesbian, trans and bi-friendly **accommodation** and offers a **reservations** service; likewise Robert N. Wilson at ☎04/479 8224 (email *rwpacexp@clear.net.nz*).

Classical music, theatre and cinema

The city regularly hosts **orchestral** and other performances, while four professional **theatres** stage Kiwi and international shows. Tickets normally cost around $18–25, but daily discounts bring prices down to $10–15, depending on availability (check with the visitor centre). In addition to its quota of multiplexes, Wellington also has a smattering of arthouse **cinemas**. The cheapest night to head for the movies is Tuesday, when tickets cost $7 all day, instead of the usual $10; tickets are also $7 for screenings before 5pm, Monday to Friday.

You can book **tickets** direct at venues or, for a small fee, through two **booking agencies**: Bass Ticketek, State Opera House, 111–113 Manners St (Mon–Fri 9am–5.30pm, Sat 9am–4pm; ☎04/385 0832), for events throughout the Wellington region; or MFC Ticketing, 111 Wakefield St (Mon–Thurs 9am–5.30pm, Fri 9am–7pm, Sat 10am–1pm; ☎04/801 4263), for shows and events held in the city only.

Theatres and concert halls

Bats, 1 Kent Terrace (☎04/384 9507). Lively theatre concentrating on alternative works.

Circa, cnr Taranaki St & Cable St (☎04/801 7992). One of the country's liveliest and most innovative professional theatres, which has fostered the skills of some of the best-known Kiwi directors and actors. At either of the two spaces in this brand new complex (the main house and a 100-seater studio) you can count on intimate, imaginative productions.

The Downstage, cnr Courtenay Place & Cambridge Terrace (☎04/801 6946). Stages both its own productions and the best touring shows: a mix of mainstream and new drama, dance and comedy, with the emphasis on quality Kiwi work. Cheaper gallery seats available.

Michael Fowler Centre, Town Hall, 111 Wakefield St (☎04/801 4325). Wellington's major venue for orchestral and other performances. More details from their Web site: *www.wcc.govt.nz/wfcc*.

State Opera House, 111–113 Manners St (☎04/384 3840). Hosts opera, ballet and musicals.

Taki Rua Theatre, 12 Alpha St (☎04/384 4531). Original Kiwi works, mostly influenced by Pacific Island culture.

Cinemas

Embassy, 10 Kent Terrace (☎04/384 7657). Mainstream movies on a single giant screen in the city centre.

Hoyts, Manners Mall (☎04/472 5182). Central five-screen complex showing standard general releases.

Paramount, 25 Courtenay Place (☎04/384 4488). A central venue showing both arthouse and mainstream movies on three screens.

Rialto Film Centre, cnr Cable St and Jervois Quay (☎04/382 8555). Independent and avant-garde productions, plus special screenings of New Zealand films from their archives. The ground floor has regular exhibitions on movies, video and television (Mon–Thurs & Sun noon–5pm, Fri & Sat noon–8pm; $2.50).

Listings

Airlines National airlines: Air Nelson/Air NZ Link (☎04/472 6034); Air New Zealand (☎04/388 9900); Ansett (☎04/471 1146); Mount Cook (☎04/388 5020); Soundsair (☎04/388 2594). International airlines: British Airways (☎04/472 7327); Malaysia (☎0800/657 472); Qantas (information ☎04/388 9900, sales ☎0800/808 767); Singapore (☎04/473 9749); United (☎04/472 0470).

Airport buses Shuttles between the central city and airport are operated by *Super Shuttle* (☎04/387 8787; Mon–Fri every 30min 7.15am–9.15am & 3.15–5.45pm; hourly 9.15am–3.15pm; $5), who also offer a door-to-door service ($8; book ahead for weekends), and *Johnstons* (Mon–Fri every 30min 8am–5.30pm; $5; ☎04/569 9017).

American Express Sun Alliance Centre, 280–292 Lambton Quay (☎04/473 7766).

Automobile Association 342–352 Lambton Quay (☎04/473 8738).

Banks and foreign exchange *ANZ* at 75 Courtenay Place (☎04/385 8809), 215–229 Lambton Quay (☎04/496 7000) and 90 Manners St (☎04/473 5635); *BNZ* at 38–44 Courtenay Place (☎04/384 2179), 222 Lambton Quay (☎04/472 3883), 50 Manners St (☎04/473 9021); *National Bank of NZ* at 60–64 Courtenay Place (☎04/382 0780), 120 Lambton Quay (☎04/498 6163), 13–27 Manners St (☎04/802 5550). There's a Thomas Cook bureau de change at 108 Lambton Quay (Mon–Fri 8.30am–5pm; ☎04/473 5167).

Bike rental Pins Cycles Wellington, 126 Willis St (☎04/472 4591; half-day $15, full-day $25); Penny Farthing Cycle Shop, 89 Courtenay Place (☎04/385 2279; full-day $25, or $40 for a full suspension bike). For rental in Eastbourne, see p.406.

Bookshops The biggest general bookshops are London Bookshops, 310 Lambton Quay (☎04/472 9694), 89 Cuba Mall (☎04/384 8179) and at the airport (☎04/388 2072); and Whitcoulls, 312 & 316 Lambton Quay (☎04/472 1921 & 4768 respectively); other options include Dymocks, 366 Lambton Quay (☎04/472 2080), and Unity Books, 119 Willis St (☎04/385 6110), which has the best range of Kiwi literature. The following have good secondhand and book exchange sections: Arty Bee's Bookshop, 172 Cuba St (☎04/384 5339); Bellamys, 106 Cuba St (☎04/384 7770; open daily), which also stocks tapes and CDs; Courtenay Books, 66a Courtenay Place (☎04/385 1819; open daily); and Crossroads, 110 Featherston St (☎04/384 4934). There's a gay-interest section at Unity Books, cnr Manners St & Willis St (☎04/385 6110). New Zealand's largest comics shop is Comics Compulsion, 105 Cuba Mall (☎04/384 2691).

Buses InterCity (☎0800/686 862) head north to Auckland via the Kapiti Coast and Hamilton; and to Rotorua and Tauranga. Heading northwest they link with New Plymouth via Palmerston North and Wanganui; and to the northeast they run to Gisborne. Mount Cook Landline (☎0800/800 287) operate between Wellington and Auckland via the Kapiti Coast, Palmerston North, Taupo, Rotorua and Hamilton. Newmans Coachlines (☎04/499 3261) link Wellington with the west coast, east coast, Rotorua and around, the Bay of Plenty, the Coromandel Peninsula, Auckland and Northland.

Camping and outdoor equipment Mainly Tramping, 39 Mercer St (☎04/473 5353); Kathmandu, 34 Manners St (☎04/801 8755); and Ski & Camping, 181 Wakefield St (☎04/801 8704), who also provide a repair service for tents, backpacks, stoves and lights.

Car parks Council car parks: Civic Centre (entry at Harris St; 7am–midnight); Clifton, Shell Lane (entry off The Terrace; 7am–6pm); Jacobs Place (entry off Tory St; 24hr), James Smith (entry on Wakefield St; 24hr); Michael Fowler Centre (entry on Wakefield St; 24hr; suitable for campervans); Lombard Parking Building (entry off Victoria St; 24hr). Independent car parks: Capital Carpark, Boulcott St (Mon–Thurs till 9pm, Fri till midnight); Midland Carpark, Waring Taylor Street (Mon–Thurs till 7pm, Fri till 10pm, Sat 10am–4pm). Charges are $1.50 Mon–Fri 6am–6pm, $1 outside these hours, free Sat & Sun.

Car rental Multinationals: Avis, at the airport (☎04/802 1088), ferry terminal (☎04/801 8108) and 25 Dixon St (☎04/801 8108); Budget, at the airport (☎04/388 7659) and 81 Ghuznee St (☎04/385 9085 & 0800/652 227); Hertz, at the airport (☎04/388 7070), ferry terminal (☎04/384 3809), and 166 Taranaki St (☎04/384 3809). Mid-range firms: NZ Rent-a-Car, 82 Tory St (☎04/384 2745 & 0800/800 956); Nationwide, 147 Thorndon Quay (☎04/473 1165 & 0800/803 003). Budget rental firms: Rent-a-Dent (☎04/387 9931); Thrifty (☎04/388 5841 & 0800/737 070, fax 388 5842); Shoestring Rentals, 138–140 Adelaide Rd, Newtown (☎04/385 5841); and Welco (☎0800/RENTWELCO).

Embassies and consulates Australia, 72 Hobson St, Thorndon (☎04/473 6411); Canada, 61 Molesworth St (☎04/473 9577); France, 34–42 Manners St (☎04/384 2555); Germany, 90–92 Hobson St, Thorndon (☎04/473 6063); Italy; 34 Grant Rd, Thorndon (☎04/473 5339); Netherlands, cnr Ballance St & Featherston St (☎04/473 8652); UK, 44 Hill St (☎04/472 6049); USA, 29 Fitzherbert Terrace, Thorndon (☎04/472 2068); see the Yellow Pages, under "Diplomatic representation".

Ferries Westpac Trust Ferry (☎04/499 1273) runs daily between Wellington (Queens Wharf) and Days Bay (see p.406 for details); some scheduled sailings stop at Somes Island. The Interislander Ferry (☎0800/802 802) and Lynx (same number) operate services across Cook Strait (see p.405).

Gay and lesbian Wellington See box on p.410.

Internet Email services (around $3) at *Midnight Espresso*, 178 Cuba St (Mon–Fri 8.30am–3am, Sat & Sun from 10am); both email ($3) and Web access (around $5 for 15min) at *Go Global*, 44 Cuba St.

Library Wellington Public Library is on Victoria Street, where it backs onto Civic Square (May–Oct Mon–Fri 9.30am–8.30pm, Sat & Sun 1–5pm).

Market James Smith's Market is a popular flea market on the corner of Cuba St and Manners St, second floor (Mon–Thurs, Sat & Sun 10am–6pm, Fri 10am–8pm).

Medical treatment Call the Free Ambulance (☎04/472 2999) for the nearest on-duty doctor. For urgent night-time medical care, accident treatment and X-rays, contact the After-Hours Medical Centre, 17 Adelaide Rd, Newtown, near Basin Reserve (☎04/384 4944; Mon–Fri 5pm–8am, Sat & Sun 24hr). Wellington Hospital is on Riddiford St, Newton (☎04/385 5999). For dental care, try Central City Dentists, Harbour City Tower, cnr Brandon St & Lambton St (☎04/472 1394), or Graham Symes Associates, 97 Courtenay Place (☎04/801 5551); for emergency dental services, call ☎04/472 7072.

Newspapers The main local daily is *The Dominion*, whose Friday edition has events and entertainment listings, as does *Contact*, a free local rag published every Thursday.

Pharmacy Unichem Eddie Fletcher Pharmacy, 204 Lambton Quay (☎04/472 0362); After-Hours Pharmacy, 17 Adelaide Rd, Newtown (☎04/385 8810; Mon–Fri 5–11pm, Sat & Sun 9am–11pm).

Police Wellington Central Police Station, cnr Victoria St & Harris St (☎04/382 4000).

Post office The main post office is in the train station lobby (☎04/496 4951) and post restante mail can be collected here Mon–Fri 8.30am–5pm (addressed to Post Restante, Wellington Post Office, Wellington Railway Station, Bunny St, Wellington).

Swimming Freyberg Pool and Fitness Centre, 139 Oriental Parade (daily 6am–9pm; ☎04/384 3107), has a 33-metre indoor pool (closes 5.30pm during school terms), plus gym, spas, saunas, steamroom, fitness classes and massage therapy.

Taxis Wellington Combined Taxis (☎04/384 4444 & 0800/809 888) are the biggest company; try also Central City Taxis (☎04/499 4949) or Gold & Black Taxis (☎04/388 8888). Authorized stands are located at the train station; on Whitmore St (between Lambton Quay & Featherston St); outside the *James Smith Hotel* on Lambton Quay; off Willis St on the Bond St corner; outside Woolworths on Dixon St; and at the junction of Willis St & Aro St.

Thomas Cook See Banks and bureaux de change.

Tours Wally Hammond's Wellington City Scenic Tours run a city bus tour, departing from Travelworld Holidaymakers, cnr Mercer St & Victoria St (daily 10am & 2pm; 2hr 30min; $20; ☎04/472 0869), which shows you all the highlights in a relaxed manner; they also run tours to the Kapiti Coast (half-day; $55) and the Wairarapa (full-day; $85). Similar tours (daily from platform 9 at the train station; $30–65) are operated by Dynamic Tours (☎04/801 6900) and Wairarapa Sightseeing Tours (☎04/387 2018).

Trains TRAINS Tranz Metro (☎04/498 3000, ext. 44933; or ☎04/801 7000) operate regular electric trains from Wellington station daily to Johnsonville, Paraparaumu, the Hutt Valley and the Wairarapa. The national Tranz Scenic (☎0800/802 802) provide a daily link with Auckland, via Palmerston North and Hamilton; and with Napier via Palmerston North and Hastings.

Travel agents Air New Zealand Travel Centre, cnr Lambton Quay & Panama St (☎04/471 1616), for all airlines; Budget Travel, Cable Car Complex, Lambton Quay (☎04/472 8342); for national train travel, Tranz Rail Travel Centre at the main train station, Bunny Street (☎0800/802 802); Mount Cook Line Travel Centre, Saatchi & Saatchi Building, cnr Taranaki Street and Courtenay Place (☎04/382 2154). Budget agencies include STA, 233 Cuba St (☎04/385 0561; Mon–Fri 9am–5.30pm, Sat 10am–1.30pm); The Hub in *Trekkers Hotel/Motel*, 213 Cuba St (Mon–Fri 9am–5.30pm; ☎04/385 3580); Lambton Quay Flight Centre, 182 Lambton Quay (☎04/471 2995); and Mid-City Flight Centre, 18 Manners St (☎04/384 4226).

AROUND WELLINGTON

Only two major highways fork from Wellington: SH1, striking north through the satellite city of Porirua and then skirting the Kapiti Coast; and SH2, heading **east** to the Wairarapa, via the built-up commuter settlements of the **Hutt Valley**. To the north and east, the wild scenery of the Rimutaka and Tararua ranges has shrugged off Wellington's advances, leaving the **Rimutaka Forest Park** the sole preserve of weekend picnickers, while the more rugged **Tararua Forest Park**, accessible from Otaki at the northern end of the Kapiti Coast, is largely a place for serious trampers and adventurers.

On SH1 due north of Wellington, the satellite city of **Porirua** holds only a Police Museum and the Colonial Knob Walkway to detain you, and you'll do better to hotfoot it along SH1 to the **Kapiti Coast**. Focused on the wonderful bird sanctuary and marine reserve of **Kapiti Island**, after which this shoreline is named, the coast itself is little more than a string of greyish sand beaches serviced by small communities, which, though popular among Kiwi holidaymakers during the summer season, aren't high on the list of priorities for international visitors.

East of Wellington

Crouched on the northeastern shore of Wellington Harbour, 15km from the city centre, is the **Hutt Valley** and its satellite towns of Upper Hutt and Lower Hutt. Bisected by SH2, this is little more than a transit point to the Wairarapa and the Hawke's Bay region further up the east coast, and barely merits the trip – unless you happen to be staying at Wellington's closest campsite (see p.393), which languishes in Lower Hutt.

Further around the harbour, some respite from suburbia is provided by the **Rimutaka Forest Park**, prime picnicking and tramping territory for weekending Wellingtonians.

The Hutt Valley

Built on the alluvial plains beside the meandering Hutt River are the twin towns of **LOWER HUTT** and **UPPER HUTT**, 15km apart and hemmed in by steep bush-covered hills. Accommodating the overspill from the capital, this urban sprawl stretches from the suburb of **Petone**, site of the first, short-lived European settlement in the Wellington region, up the Hutt Valley to the Tararua Range, 30km north. If you have time on your hands, you could do worse than visit the **Dowse Art Museum**, in the Civic Centre, 45 Laings Rd, Lower Hutt (Mon–Fri 10am–4pm, Sat & Sun 11am–5pm; free), a gallery showcasing high-calibre, contemporary New Zealand art, with a strong leaning towards jewellery, ceramics, textiles and glass. Changing exhibitions are well displayed and there's also a finely carved *pataka* (storehouse).

To get here **by train**, take one of the regular daily TranzMetro commuter services from Wellington train station to Hutt Central, from where the museum is a 1.5-kilometre walk down Knights Road. Eastbourne and Big Red **buses** depart hourly from Courtenay Place to Lower Hutt's Queensgate shopping centre on Knights Road, where there's a small **information** kiosk on the ground floor (Mon–Wed & Fri–Sun 9am–5.30pm, Thurs 9am–7pm), stocking local leaflets and public transport timetables. For more information, contact the main Hutt City **visitor centre** in the train station, on the corner of Hutt Road and Jackson Street, Petone (Mon–Fri 7am–6pm, Sat & Sun 9am–3pm; ☎04/568 9889, fax 568 9838). It's well organized and covers the entire Wellington **region**, taking bookings for transport, accommodation and activities.

Three kilometres north of Upper Hutt, the scenic **Akatarawa Road** branches off SH2 and snakes 35km northwest through the Akatarawa Range and sumptuous bushland **to Waikanae** on the Kapiti Coast (see p.415). Along the way are several roadside picnic and river-swimming spots, before the road climbs a 450-metre pass and descends to Waikanae.

Rimutaka Forest Park

Due south of Lower Hutt is the main entrance to the **Rimutaka Forest Park**, popular among jaded city-dwellers for its series of easy short and **day-walks** in the attractive Catchpool Valley; there's also a well-maintained **campsite**, and picnic and barbecue facilities. Some 20km from Wellington along the Coast Road, a signpost marks the **park entrance** (gates open 8am–dusk), from where Catchpool Road winds a further 2km up the valley to the car park, the starting point for most of the walks. A regular **bus** service (#80) runs between Wellington and **Wainuiomata**, where you can pick up a taxi at Queen Street for the last 12km to the park entrance. Two hundred metres beyond the park entrance is a well-equipped **DOC field centre** (daily: Oct–April 9am–5.30pm; May–Sept 11.30am–4.30pm; ☎04/564 8551), which stocks the useful *Catchpool Valley/Rimutaka Forest Park* leaflet (50¢), detailing walks in the vicinity.

North of Wellington

Separating Wellington from the Kapiti Coast, the small, modern satellite city of **Porirua**, 21km north of the capital on SH1, has a couple of attractions, but little to delay your progress to the short sweep of the **Kapiti Coast**, 24km further north. A narrow coastal plain, bounded on the west by the Tasman Sea and rising steeply in the east to the rugged Tararua Range, its silver sandy beaches make this a summer playground for Kiwis. However, the ravages of overdevelopment have taken their toll, peppering the coast with retirement villages and golf courses. Only **Kapiti Island**, 5km offshore and the area's principal attraction, has escaped this fate. A bush-covered bird sanctuary and marine reserve, the island is open to the public by arrangement, so you'll need to plan ahead. Otherwise, your best option is to pass straight through the Kapiti Coast, using the few sights scattered along the main highway as minor diversions on your journey north or south. The highway, **SH1**, follows an inland route for 35km along the coast, passing through a series of uninspiring small towns that are split between the highway and their beachside communities a few kilometres to the west. The region extends from the seaside village of **Paekakariki**, in the south, to just beyond **Otaki** in the north, passing through **Paraparaumu** and **Waikanae**.

The coastal towns are served by the main north–south rail link between Auckland and Wellington, and by commuter **trains** between Palmerston North and the capital. The main **bus** companies also run to Paraparaumu and Otaki.

Porirua

Built on hills around the small, double-armed Porirua Harbour, the rapidly growing settlement of **PORIRUA** has a population of 46,000, but for the passing visitor holds only a handful of brief distractions, among them **Titahi Bay**, a great little surfing beach, 4km off SH1 along Titahi Bay Road.

More of a curiosity, on a hill just north of Porirua and near SH1, is the **Police Centennial Museum**, in the Royal New Zealand Police College, Papakowhai Road (Tues–Thurs, Sat & Sun 10am–4pm; $5). New Zealand's only police museum, its displays on policing history are reinforced by exhibits from specific cases, an enormous number of handcuffs, and murder weapons and forensic displays to make your hair stand on end. To get there, continue 2km north from the main roundabout on SH1 on the outskirts of the city centre. Turn right onto Whitford Brown Avenue, then onto Papakowhai Road.

For a change of pace, tackle the moderately hard **Colonial Knob Walkway** (7.5km; 3–4hr return), a hill track across the forested hills to the west of Porirua. From the summit of Colonial Knob (468m) there are amazing **views** of Mana and Kapiti islands, Mount Taranaki to the north, Wellington and its harbour, and south as far as the Marlborough Sounds and the Kaikoura Ranges. The walk begins at Elsdon, in the western part of Porirua, from either the car park on Broken Hill Road, off Raiha Street, or from Elsdon Youth Camp on Raiha Street.

Practicalities

Porirua's small **visitor centre** is centrally located in the Page 90 art gallery and cultural centre, on the corner of Norrie Street and Parumoana Street (Mon–Sat 10am–4pm, Sun 1–4pm; ☎04/237 1520). The welcoming **gallery** (same hours; free) shows local works, plus exhibitions by leading contemporary New Zealand artists, and hosts regular Maori and Pacific Island dance performances. If you're looking for somewhere to **stay** that's near the capital but out of the hubbub, then try the upmarket and relaxing *Braebyre B&B*, Flightys Road, Pauatahanui, north of Porirua (call for directions, ☎04/235 9311, fax 235 9345; ⑤), some twenty minutes' drive from Wellington. Set amid rolling hills and incorporating a small mohair-goat farm, this big modern house has a private guest wing with three rooms (one en-suite) and the cooking is great (dinner on request, $30).

To get to Porirua by public transport, take one of several daily TranzMetro trains from Wellington train station to Porirua city centre (Mon–Fri every 30min, more frequently at peak times; ☎04/801 7000; $3.60 one-way).

Paraparaumu and around

The coast's main tourist centre and the only jumping-off point to Kapiti Island (see below), **PARAPARAUMU** lies 45km from Wellington. Paraparaumu's main shopping and business centre is on the highway, while its small beachside settlement, imaginatively named **Paraparaumu Beach**, is 3km west along Kapiti Road. The long sandy beach is safe for swimming and looks directly out onto Kapiti Island. The beach community is small, consisting of just a few holiday homes, cafés and bars, and a shopping centre straddling three main streets, Maclean Street (branching off Kapiti Road and leading to the beach), Marine Parade at the waterfront, and Seaview Road, one block back.

Anyone with a sweet tooth should stop off at **Nyco Chocolate Factory** (daily 9am–5pm), a kilometre or so south of Paraparaumu, on the corner of the main highway and Raumati Road, to visit their shop stuffed with goodies or join a guided tour (Mon–Fri 10.30am & 2.30pm; $2). Up to 90,000 chocolates are made here every day, and the informative tour comprises twenty minutes in the factory itself, with plenty of background on the manufacturing process and a demonstration of melting and moulding, followed by a further fifteen minutes in Kapiti Candies, an adjacent lollipop and fudge factory that makes the fillings. More savoury tastes are catered for at the touristy **Lindale Farm Complex**, about 2km north of Paraparaumu on SH1, where you can sample the French-style **Kapiti Cheeses**, among New Zealand's best, which are made in the complex and sold in a small shop (daily 9am–5pm; free).

A couple of kilometres further north, signposted off SH1 at Otaihanga Road, is the **Southward Car Museum** (daily 9am–4.30pm; $5), a stunningly comprehensive collection of veteran and vintage cars, kept in mint condition and displayed in rotation in a specially built showroom, each accompanied by a detailed history. Gems include Marlene Dietrich's Rolls-Royce, a 1915 Stutz Racer, a gull-winged Mercedes Benz and a Chicago gangster's armour-plated Cadillac.

Practicalities

The **visitor centre** is in the car park of the Coastlands shopping centre, on SH1 (Mon–Sat 9am–4pm, Sun 10am–3pm; ☎ & fax 04/298 8195), and has local and DOC information. All major **bus** companies (InterCity, Newmans and Mount Cook) drop off here, as do local services from Wellington; the **train station** is directly opposite Coastlands and the visitor centre ($7.50 one-way from Wellington). Places to **stay** are limited to a backpackers at the beach and a number of run-of-the-mill motels at the beach and in the main town. Just across from the beach, *Barnacles Seaside Inn*, 3 Marine Parade (☎04/298 4856; singles ①, doubles ②), is a comfortable backpackers with rooms but no dorms.

Eating is best done at Paraparaumu Beach. Top choice is *Brier Patch*, 9 Maclean St (book ahead Thurs–Sat evenings, ☎04/298 5586; BYO & licensed), an intimate restaurant specializing in superb, moderately priced Creole and Cajun food for lunch (Wed–Fri), dinner (daily) and weekend brunch (10am–3pm); there's a separate bar for casual drinking, coffee and desserts. For elegant surroundings and great sea views, try *Chrisy's on the Corner*, 3 Marine Parade (☎04/298 6106; closed Sun; licensed), a restaurant and bar in a stylish colonial house, which serves lunches for under $15 and dinners for $20–27; or settle for the cheap and cheerful *Fagins Eatery*, in the *Copperfield Motel* complex, 7–13 Seaview Rd, a cosy BYO restaurant that dishes up traditional roast beef and Yorkshire pudding. They also do an all-day breakfast for $10, and snacks along the lines of savoury pancakes with brie, avocado and bacon.

Kapiti Island

One of the few easily accessible island **nature reserves** in New Zealand, **Kapiti Island** is a magical spot, its regenerating bush home to birdlife that has become rare or extinct on the mainland. In 1822, infamous Maori chief **Te Rauparaha** captured the island from its first-known Maori inhabitants and, with his people the Ngati Toa, used it as a base until his death in 1849; it's thought that he may be buried somewhere on the island, but the site of his grave is kept secret.

Designated a reserve in 1897, the island is a mere 10km long and about 2km wide. September and October are the best months to visit, when the **birdlife** and bush are at their most abundant. Among the birds you're likely to see are kaka (bush parrots that are apt to land on you head or shoulder), weka, kakariki (parakeets), whiteheads (bush canaries), tui, bellbirds, fantails and robins. The island can be explored on three **walking tracks**, two of them linking up to lead to the island's highest point (521m), which gives spectacular views, though the best variety of birdlife is found along the lower parts of the tracks – take your time, keep quiet and stop frequently (allow about 3hr for the round-trip). The easiest approach is to ascend **Trig Track** and descend the steeper, and sometimes slippery, **Wilkinson Track**. The third track (2–3hr), **North Track**, follows the coast to the island's northern end, climbing quite steeply in places to about fifty metres above sea level and leading to a lagoon thronged with waterfowl.

The exceptionally clear waters of the marine reserve make for great **scuba diving** (see below for operators), particularly to the west and north of the island, where there are some interesting formations, including a rock archway known as the Hole-in-the-Wall. Three types of habitat – a boulder bottom, sheltered reef and sand bottom – are home to a rich variety of marine life, including orange and yellow sponges (some very rare), and luxuriant seaweed beds feeding kina and paua. Visiting ocean fish like moki and kingfish are common, and occasionally you'll see rare and subtropical fish.

Practicalities

DOC manage the island but allow visitors on **day-trips** (Wed–Sun; closed on Wed following public holidays). A maximum of 50 people are allowed onto Kapiti Island each day, having first arranged **landing permits** ($8 per person) with the Department of Conservation in Wellington (see p.392). **Book** as far **ahead** as possible, allowing at least a day, but note that weekends from December to March are booked as much as a year in advance. To arrange **transport** from Paraparaumu Beach, contact any of the following three launch operators: Kapiti Marine Charter (☎04/297 2585), Kapiti Alive (☎06/364 5042), or Kapiti Marine Transport (☎04/298 6085); all charge $30 return per person for the ten- to fifteen-minute trip. On **arrival**, you are greeted by the ranger, who will explain what there is to do and see on the island; a copy of the informative DOC booklet, *Kapiti Island Nature Reserve*, is included in the price of the landing permit.

PADI-qualified **divers** can arrange a full-day trip with either The Dive Spot, 7 The Esplanade, Mana, Paremata (near Porirua; ☎04/233 8238; $55 per person for a full day), or New Zealand Sea Adventures, 65 Omapere St, Wellington (☎04/236 8787; full-day $50). Both companies are members of DINZ (Dive Industry New Zealand) and can supply gear and transport.

Waikanae

WAIKANAE, 7km from Paraparaumu, is another small town divided between the highway and a beach community, 4km away along Te Moana Road. The broad, dune-backed sandy **beach** has no facilities but is safe for swimming.

The Kapiti Coast's main **DOC office** is here, at 10 Parata St, one street west of the main highway (Mon–Fri 8am–4.30pm; ☎04/293 2191), and can advise on Kapiti Island permits. The **train station** is centrally located on SH1 and the **visitor centre** (Mon–Fri 10am–3pm, Sat 9am–noon; ☎04/293 3278) is in the Mahara Place shopping centre, on the corner of the highway and Te Moana Road. **Buses** pull in at the corner of Ngao Road and SH1.

The only real reason to stop is the **Nga Manu Sanctuary**, a large man-made bird sanctuary (daily 10am–5pm; $5), with easy walking tracks and some picnic spots. A 1.5-kilometre loop track cuts through a variety of habitats, from ponds and scrubland to swamp and coastal forest, which attract all manner of birds. There is also a nocturnal house containing kiwi, morepork and tuatara. To get here, follow Te Moana Road off SH1 for just over a kilometre and turn right at Ngarara Road; the sanctuary is a further 3km.

Otaki and around

The northern gateway to the Kapiti Coast, **OTAKI** lies beside a broad, braided section of the Otaki River, in a rich fruit-growing area. For most of the year, this is a quiet place with a strong Maori heritage but, like other towns along this coast, it changes beyond recognition during the high-summer months of December to March, when its population of 4500 swells by a further 2000 or so.

Divided into three parts, the town is announced by a scattering of services on the main highway. Two kilometres towards the sea along Mill Road is the tiny main centre, consisting of little more than a few bars and shops, a post office and a couple of banks. **Otaki Beach**, 2.5km further on, is a long gentle curve of grey sand, backed by dunes and reasonably safe for swimming, being well patrolled by the surf club. There's little here except holiday homes and a small general store.

On Te Rauparaha Street, off Mill Road and 2.5km from the main highway, is the barren site of what was once the finest **Maori church** in New Zealand. Rangiatea Church, begun in 1849, burned to the ground in 1995. All that's left is the graveyard, at the far end of which is a tombstone shaded by two Norfolk pines and bearing the name of Maori chief Te Rauparaha – though it's thought that his remains may have been exhumed by a group of his followers and re-interred on Kapiti Island.

Otaki Gorge and Otaki Forks

A kilometre south of the town, a scenic one-way detour, **Otaki Gorge Road**, branches off from the main highway (signposted just before the bridge). Striking deep into the hills of regenerating bush, the road twists for 19km through the dramatic gorge of the Otaki River to **Otaki Forks**, the main western entrance to the **Tararua Forest Park**, the last 7km being unsealed and narrow. Taxis (☎06/367 9055) from Otaki run to the park for around $12 per person.

Along the road is the **Tararua Recreation Centre** (☎06/364 3110), specializing in adventure activities on the river and in the park. Based on the principle that not all whitewater rafting has to be white knuckle, the team offer **rafting** and other outdoor activities, including abseiling waterfalls, climbing and kayaking. A highlight is the night canyon-rafting (Grade II–III; $80), an exhilarating trip between riverbanks illuminated by flickering glow-worms, with the gorge eerily silent save for the roaring of the rapids. The centre also has **mountain bikes** ($20 per half-day) and **kayaks** ($20 per day) for rent. You can arrange with the centre to be picked up from Otaki train station ($12 per person, minimum 2 people).

Most of the forest park is accessible only to serious trampers, though there are a few shorter and less initimidating **walks** from **Boielle Flat** at the end of the main road, where a resident ranger provides assistance and information, and keeps an intentions book in his house opposite the picnic site; there's also a basic campsite at **Schoolhouse Flat**, partway along the road. The majority of walks in this area take in the remains of old boilers, stone walls, and remnants of abandoned logging and farming endeavours that are gradually being engulfed by regenerating bush. At the Waiotauru car park, at the road-end, is the start of the **Fenceline Walk** (about 3km; 2hr), offering excellent views of the river flowing down the valley to the coast.

Straddling the spine of the southernmost prong of the North Island, the wild terrain of the **Tararua Forest Park** can also be accessed from **Levin** in the west (see p.245) and from **Masterton** in the east (see p.383).

Practicalities

Buses drop off outside the **visitor centre** at Centennial Park, on the corner of SH1 and Mill Road (Oct–April Mon–Fri 8.30am–5pm, Sat & Sun 9–4pm; May–Sept Mon–Fri same times, Sat & Sun 10am–3pm; ☎ & fax 06/364 7620), opposite the **train station**. The visitor centre has free town maps, sells **hut passes** for tracks in the Tararua Forest Park and acts as a booking agency for Newmans, InterCity, Whitestar, Mount Cook, Tranz Rail, and for ferries to the South Island.

There's pleasant backpacker **accommodation** just outside town, on the southern side of the Otaki River, at *Toad Hall Backpackers*, off Addington Road (☎06/364 6906; dorms ①, rooms ②), a carefully renovated manor house set in farmland; they offer a free pick-up service from town. One block back from the beach, the large *Otaki Beach Motor Camp*, 40 Moana St (☎06/364 7107, fax 364 8123; tent sites $7, cabins & on-site vans ②), is well kept and simple. For more trappings, head for *Byron's Resort*, 20 Tasman Rd (☎06/364 8121, fax 364 8123; tent sites $8, tourist flats ③, motel units ④), a multi-faceted complex at the beach with a restaurant and bar, spa and swimming pool.

Eating in Otaki is more or less confined to bland tearooms and takeaways. For an alternative, try *Byron Brown's* in *Byron's Resort* (see above), a licensed restaurant offering good-quality dinners at moderate prices, plus daytime snacks and light meals.

travel details

Buses

From Wellington to: Porirua (9 daily; 25min); Paraparaumu (9 daily; 50min); Masterton via the Hutt Valley (3 daily; 2hr).

From Paraparauma to: Otaki (9 daily; 1hr 5min); Levin (9 daily; 1hr 20min); Palmerston North (9 daily; 2hr 15min).

Trains

From Wellington to: Johnsonville, a suburb of Wellington (every 15min 6am–11.30pm; 21min); Porirua (1 daily; 18min); Paraparaumu (every hour 7am–5.15pm; 1hr); Otaki (1 daily; 1hr 14min); Levin (1 daily; 1hr 34min); Palmerston North (2hr 15min).

Ferries

From Wellington to: Picton (8 daily; 3hr or 1hr 45min; see p.405).

Flights

From Wellington to: Auckland (14 daily; 1hr); Bay of Islands (9 daily; 2hr 45min); Blenheim (24 daily; 25min); Christchurch (29 daily; 45min); Dunedin (12 daily; 2hr); Gisborne (10 daily; 1hr 10min); Hamilton (17 daily; 1hr 10min); Hokitika (5 daily; 2hr 15min); Invercargill (7 daily; 2hr 20min); Kataia (3 daily; 3hr 25min); Milford Sound (3 daily; 4hr 20min); Motueka (2 daily; 1hr 15min); Mount Cook (3 daily 2hr 25min); Napier/Hastings (15 daily; 1hr); Nelson (22 daily; 35min); New Plymouth (8 daily; 55min); Palmerston North (9 daily; 35min); Picton (7–9 daily 25min); Queenstown (8 daily; 3hr 20min); Rotorua (7 daily; 1hr 15min); Taupo (4 daily; 1hr); Tauranga (11 daily; 2hr 20min); Te Anau (2 daily; 4hr 5min); Timaru (7 daily; 1hr 50min); Wanaka (4 daily; 3hr 5min); Wanganui (3 daily; 45min); Westport (2 daily; 55min); Whakatane (12 daily; 2hr 10min); Whangarei (15 daily; 2hr 30min).

CHAPTER EIGHT

MARLBOROUGH, NELSON AND KAIKOURA

Many people's first impression of the South Island is formed when they travel by boat or plane into the northern region, and is crystallized by the intricacy of The Marlborough Sounds, the sweep of the bays as they curl towards Farewell Spit, the splendour of the national parks, the ease of Blenheim and the natural wonders of the Kaikoura. In fact, if you had to choose only one area of New Zealand to visit, this would be a strong contender.

Most visitors travel between the North Island and the South Island by ferry, striking land at the schizophrenic town of **Picton** – drab in the winter, lively in the summer and surrounded by the consistently rugged and beautiful **Marlborough Sounds**. From here you will be within easy reach of some of the country's most spectacular walking tracks and dazzling golden beaches, spread around the lively city of **Nelson**. Each of the national parks in the region has a distinct identity: the most famous is the **Abel Tasman National Park**, while the newest is **Kahurangi**, through which the rugged and spectacular **Heaphy Track** forges a route to the West Coast. Hemmed in by these two national parks, **Golden Bay** is an isolated oasis on the far side of a marble mountain with a strange grassy moonscape pockmarked by grottoes. The curve of the bay culminates in a long sandy bar that juts into the ocean, **Farewell Spit**, an extraordinary and unique habitat. The most neglected of the region's national parks is the **Nelson Lakes**, a superb area with access to Alpine lakes, flora and fauna, as well as being an excellent launch pad for rafting assaults on the Karamea and Buller rivers.

Heading in the opposite direction from Picton, you can slurp your merry way through **Marlborough**, the most famous wine-making region in New Zealand, with **Blenheim** at its heart. The diversity of the region's communities makes for a certain individual outlook, while their rich farmland and coast inspires an easy-going **lifestyle** reminiscent of Mediterranean climes, attracting people from all over the world to settle and perfect their art, brewing techniques, wine, cooking and hospitality. Sated with good living, you can indulge the more spiritual side of your nature by watching **whales** and swimming with **dolphins** in **Kaikoura**. From here, you also have access to a number of challenging skifields – as yet blissfully uncrowded and inexpensive. The Kaikoura coast is a much more desolate-looking landscape which repays the observant traveller with the time to look beneath the surface. The **Kaikoura Ranges**, divided into the landward and seaward, provide a spectacular backdrop to travel along the coast, as

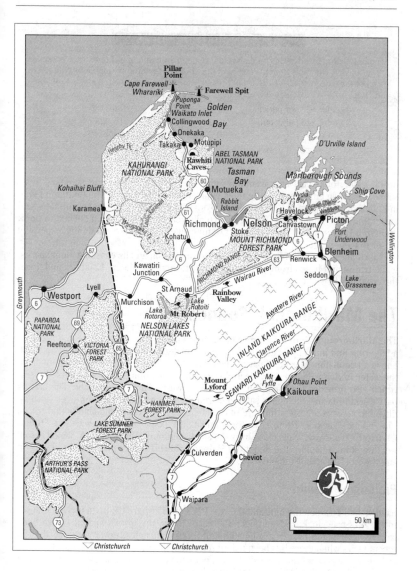

well as superb views from some of the highest peaks and most solitary tracks anywhere outside the Southern Alps.

Marlborough and Nelson enjoy more sunshine than most other parts of New Zealand in the spring and summer and a mild **climate** for most of the year; likewise, the Kaikoura region is generally mild, though often windy. Marlborough and Nelson are both extremely popular from Christmas to early February, with the Abel Tasman and Queen Charlotte **walkways** both attracting big **crowds**. This means solitude,

---

ACCOMMODATION PRICES

Accommodation listed in this guide has been categorized into one of nine price bands, as set out below. The rates quoted represent the **cheapest available** double or twin **room** – except for category ①, which are per-person rates for a dorm bed; fees for **tent sites** and **DOC huts** are also per-person, unless otherwise stated.

① under $20 per person	④ $60–80	⑦ $140–180
② under $40 per room	⑤ $80–100	⑧ $180–240
③ $40–60	⑥ $100–140	⑨ over $240

For more on accommodation, see p.33.

---

beach space, bus seats and accommodation are difficult to find and it makes more sense to visit on either side of the most popular times, if you can. The tourist hot spot in Kaikoura is the town of Kaikoura itself, from where **whale-watching** excursions, and swimming with dolphins and seals run virtually year-round but it is important to **book** them **in advance** and to allow a day or two for cancellation and rescheduling, especially closer to winter.

Buses and **boats** provide access to the Nelson region and its coastal national parks, while **trains** and buses from Picton head east through Blenheim, Kaikoura and down the coast to Christchurch.

The Marlborough Sounds

The **Marlborough Sounds**' pattern of islands is undeniably picturesque and provides a lingering first impression for those travelling by ferry to the South Island. The coastline is a stimulating filigree of bays, inlets, islands and peninsulas rising abruptly from the water to rich wilderness or cleared farmland. Much of it is only accessible by sea, which also provides the ideal vantage point for witnessing its splendour. The area is part working farms, including salmon or mussel farms, and part given over to some fifty-nine reserve areas – a mixture of islands, sections of coast and land-bound tracts. The Sounds' nexus, **Picton**, is the jumping-off point for the rewarding **Queen Charlotte Walkway**, while close by is the small community of **Havelock**, which is well worth a stop to explore the delightful **Pelorus Sound** before pressing on to Nelson and the Abel Tasman National Park.

Picton and around

Sandwiched between the hills and the sea, **PICTON** is where the main **ferries** that ply the Cook Strait dock. Indeed, since the early 1960s, the town's fortunes have been largely determined by the machinations of ferry companies, never more so than in recent years when there has been talk of relocating the ferry terminal to the Blenheim or Nelson areas. The European settlement of Picton dates from 1827, when John Guard established a **whaling** station on its shores. Following the New Zealand Company's purchase of the town site for £300 in 1848, Picton flourished, acting as a port and **service town** for the Wairau Plains to the east.

These days Picton has a population of 4500 and acts as little more than a transit town, but beneath its workaday surface, the town serves as a fascinating introduction to the delights of the South Island, with three **museums**, two focusing on New Zealand's **maritime heritage** and one concerned with Maori, and the whaling, gold, logging, fishing and farming interests that have dominated the lives of people who have settled here.

As you would expect of a port, Picton also boasts an immense range of accommodation and many fine eating houses, trading off the superb seafood found in the area.

Arrival and information

Ferries dock in Picton Harbour, 600m from the town centre, the **train station** is right by the ferry terminal, and **buses** drop off just outside. Koromiko **airport** is 9km from town, from where Corgi Buses or Sounds Link Buses (see "Listings", p.427) will run you into the centre for around $5.

> Details of **transport** between the **North and South islands** are given in Chapter Seven; see "Crossing Cook Strait" on p.405.

The combined **visitor centre** (daily: Oct–Feb 8.30am–8pm; March–Sept 8.30am–6pm, ☎03/573 7477 & 0800/777 477, fax 573 8362) and **DOC office** (daily 8.30am–4.30pm; ☎03/578 9904, fax 578 6084) is on the foreshore, five minutes' walk from the ferry terminal. Here you can accumulate an enormous amount of bumf about the town and the South Island: take your pick from *Picton Walkways*, which details short walks around town; *Queen Charlotte Walking Track*; *Sidewalks and Byways*, which covers historic walks and drives en route to Blenheim and Havelock; *Art and Craft Trail*, which selects the best of the shops and galleries in the Marlborough region; and *Wines of Marlborough* for a rundown of all the wineries and their locations (all free); or the *Marlborough Sounds* leaflet ($1).

Almost directly opposite the official visitor centre and using a deceptively similar logo is The Station (9am–6pm; ☎03/573 8857) in the train station, which is actually a private **booking office** for trips, accommodation and onward travel – one of many in Picton.

Accommodation

As a major **transit centre**, Picton has a disproportionately large number of accommodation options for its size, ranging from backpacker hostels to swanky hotels, and you should have no difficulty finding somewhere to suit your needs within walking distance of the gangplank for most of the year, although **around Christmas** it makes sense to **book** in advance.

HOTELS AND MOTELS

Beachcomber Inn, 27 Waikawa Rd (☎03/573 8900, fax 573 8888). A large hotel complex overlooking the harbour with a swimming pool and spacious comfortable rooms; rates are higher for rooms on the upper floors with better views. ④–⑤.

Bellbird Motel, 96 Waikawa Rd (☎03/573 6912). Set back from the road, these 20-year-old units offer simple self-contained accommodation at a bargain price. ③.

Harbour View Motel, 30 Waikawa Rd (☎03/573 6259, fax 573 6982). Twelve modern, fully self-contained units with views over the harbour. ④.

Jasmine Court, 78 Wellington St (☎03/573 7110, fax 573 7211). Non-smoking throughout, these beautifully kept, luxury motel units are within walking distance of everything. ⑤–⑥.

Tourist Court, 45 High St (☎ & fax 03/573 6331). The best of both worlds – centrally located but quiet, these units (some with fridges and toasters, others with full kitchens), are roomy and comfortable. ③–④.

B&BS AND HOMESTAYS

Echo Lodge, 5 Rutland St (☎03/573 6367). A pretty B&B with simple well-kept rooms, a friendly welcome and delicious home-made bread for breakfast, courtesy car available. ③.

The Gables, 20 Waikawa Rd (☎03/573 6772). An exceptional B&B run by considerate hosts who offer transport to ferries and planes, and cook up superb and filling breakfasts. Rooms are spacious and have private facilities. ④.

Lazy Fish Guest House, in the Sounds (☎03/579 9049). Accessible only by water taxi from Picton (20min; see "Listings" on p.427) or by seaplane from Wellington (Float Air, ☎03/573 6433), this guesthouse offers beautiful views, seclusion and comfort at very reasonable prices. Dorms ①, rooms ③.

Ocean Ridge Homestay, on an unsealed road off the Port Underwood Rd, about 15km from Picton on the way to Blenheim (☎ & fax 03/579 9474). Overlooking Ocean Bay and Robinhood Bay, this homestay enjoys one of the most spectacular settings of any on the South Island. Perched high on a hill, with its own short walking tracks to the sea's edge, there are superb panoramic views from most rooms – which are large and have private bathrooms. There is also a squash court/half basket ball court, stimulating company (the owners make and sell their own jewellery and pewter work) and superb food – dinners by arrangement, $25. ⑤.

HOSTELS

Baden's Picton Lodge, 3 Auckland St (☎03/573 7788, fax 573 8418). This purpose-built hostel is the closest to the ferry terminal, with a range of twins, doubles and dorms. Discounts for VIP and YHA members, $3 extra for linen and towel. Dorms ①, rooms ②.

Bavarian Lodge, 42 Auckland St (☎ & fax 03/573 6536). The smallest hostel in town, this is a friendly, comfortable place run by German speakers, who often turn their hand to home-made apple cake, pretzels and bread. Dorms ①, rooms ②.

The Villa, 34 Auckland St (☎ & fax 03/573 6598). One of the most-often-recommended hostels on the backpackers' grapevine, this 100-year-old house is close to the ferry terminal, offers free pick up, free breakfast, free soup in the winter, and a spa pool, as well as being friendly and a good place to pick up lots of information on things to see and do in the area (they produce their own seasonal newsletter). Dorms ①, rooms ②.

Wedgewood House (YHA Associate Hostel), 10 Dublin St (☎03/573 7797). Central and comfortable hostel in a slightly run-down converted guesthouse. Dorms ①, rooms ②.

CAMPSITES AND MOTOR PARKS

Alexander's Holiday Camp, southeastern end of Canterbury St (☎03/573 6378). This campsite by a creek is about 2km from the ferry terminal, with camping space, cabins and two converted railway carriages that ooze charm. Tent sites $16, cabins & carriages ②–③.

Blue Anchor, 70–78 Waikawa Rd (☎ & fax 03/573 7212). Centrally located campsite with a swimming pool, children's playground, cabins (bedding $1) and motel-style units, in a pleasant spot with trees providing shelter. Tent sites $18, cabins & motel units ②–④.

Waikawa Bay Holiday Park, 302 Waikawa Rd (☎ & fax 03/573 7434). Five minutes' drive from the ferry terminal, this large, sheltered site has views over the water. Tent sites $16, cabins & motel units ②–③.

The Town

The town heads back from the ferry terminal and up the hills that surround it, but most of its most interesting sights are on or near the foreshore, a pretty area with palms, mini golf and picnic benches overlooking the harbour.

Between the ferry terminal and the town centre is the hulk of the **Edwin Fox** (daily 8.30am–5pm; $4), the sole survivor of the fleets that once brought migrants to New Zealand. You access the shell of the ship from the centre alongside, which contains fascinating displays on what remains of this 1853 ship, constructed from saul timber in India, and its colourful life, as well as the mammoth task of restoration that lies ahead. The *Edwin Fox* operated as a troop carrier in the Crimean War and transported convicts to Australia, before bringing free settlers to New Zealand. In later years, the ship was put to service as a merchant vessel, including a spell helping to establish the frozen meat trade in New Zealand. Towed into Shakespeare Bay (just west of Picton), in 1967, for twenty years the *Edwin Fox* received only the attentions of the weather and vandals

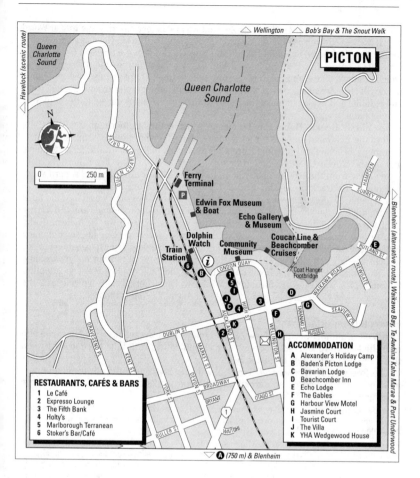

until, in 1986, surprisingly still sound below the waterline, the vessel was floated back to Picton Harbour.

Heading further around the bay, the foreshore area is home to the **Picton Community Museum**, on London Quay (daily 10am–4pm; $3). The main feature of the museum are displays devoted to the Perano Whaling Station, which operated in Queen Charlotte Sound until 1964. There are photographs of the station in its heyday, and a harpoon gun from one of the steamboat chasers. Smaller displays deal with Maori and *pakeha* local history, and there is a finely carved chair inlaid with *paua* (blue-green shell), as well as a large collection of brightly coloured shells from all over the world.

Continuing around the harbour and across the Coat Hanger footbridge, it is a short walk to the unique **Echo Gallery and Museum** (Sept–April daily 10am–6pm; $3), a tribute to the scows and scowmen of New Zealand that's well worth an hour or two of your time. Built in 1905, the *Echo* was a top-sail schooner, with a square bilge scow-type hull, developed to take cargo from the sea upriver to the remote communities of New Zealand. From 1920 she ran river services out of Blenheim, and was the last ship to trade commercially under sail in New Zealand waters, before entering the fray in World War II. Retrieved from a ships' graveyard, she was used by the US Navy as a supply ship for the New Hebrides, Solomon Islands and New Guinea area – a phase in her long history that inspired the 1961 Hollywood film *The Wackiest Ship in the Army*, a copy of which is shown on the shipboard video from time to time. There are also restored home movies of New Zealand scows at work, paintings and photographs around the hull walls and exhibits and explanations of the important role these ships played in the country's development.

The **Shelly Beach/Bob's Bay Track** starts just by the Marlborough Cruising Club, next to the Echo and extends for a kilometre along the shoreline, passing small, safe-swimming beaches and providing great views across the water to the ferry terminal and up the Queen Charlotte Sound before ending at Bob's Bay. From here the path heads away from the bay for about 500m to **Victoria Domain** for more superb views and meets the track on to **The Snout** (5km; 1hr 15min one way), whose evocative Maori name, *Te Ihumoeone-ihu*, translates as "the nose of the sand worm". At the tip of the promontory, you are rewarded with panoramic views of the Sounds and the ferries.

Just over three kilometres from Picton on the Waikawa Road is the **Te Awhina Kaha Marae**, 210 Waikawa Rd (☎03/573 7970), a superbly carved meeting house containing some excellent *tuku tuku* (Maori panel work made of flax and wood); call ahead to see if there are any activities arranged – hangi are sometimes organized for groups, and you may be able to tag along. If you continue along the Waikawa Road for about another kilometre, you will come to a turning for **Waikawa Bay** where, beside a picnic area, the impressive Maori ceremonial *waka* (canoe) *Te Awate Te Hou* is moored.

Eating and entertainment

Picton has a number of typical New Zealand **tearooms** offering cheap and cheerful fare near the foreshore and **cafés** serving snacks and coffee, with little to choose between them; the best of the rest are listed below.

The free weekly *Marlborough Times* newspaper contains **entertainment listings**, most of which is centred on several large old **pubs** along the waterfront that serve drink and cheap food all day.

Le Café 33 High St. Good quality, moderately priced Asian- and European-influenced food, plus salads adorned with a famous dressing, and traditional home-made muffins. Sept–May daily 8am–10pm; June–Aug Wed–Sun 8am–10pm.

Expresso Lounge, 58 Auckland St. Minimalist surroundings are relieved by rimu flooring, New Zealand oak tables and Native American photographs on the walls. Great food spans breakfasts, chicken satay, Greek salads, salmon and brie platters, and crepes served with homemade maple yoghurt; day-time menu under $10, night-time menu under $15. BYO. Sept–March daily 9am–9pm, April–Aug Thurs–Sun 9am–9pm.

The Fifth Bank, 33 Wellington St (book Fri & Sat, ☎03/573 6102). This 1903 building was once a branch of the Bank of New Zealand, but has found a new lease of life as an elegant restaurant serving fine food and wine; the emphasis is on New Zealand produce, but with a touch of Mediterranean (tapas) and Asian (curries) flair. Daily 5.30–11pm.

Holty's, corner of High St & Dublin St. This fast-food emporium occupies a converted garage and serves breakfast, pizzas and charcoal-grilled chicken to eat at the outdoor seating in the old forecourt or take away. Licensed. Daily 7am–midnight.

Marlborough Terranean, 31 High St (☎03/573 7122). The best food in town. Fine dining in comfortable surroundings with a relaxed jazz-soaked atmosphere, and imaginative dishes such as pork fillet with brandy herb butter, fresh fish in a choice of four delicious sauces – and frighteningly good desserts. Evening meals only (main courses $20–30). Licensed & BYO.

Stokers Bar/Café, 5 Auckland St, opposite the visitor centre. Based in the 1914 train station, this is the first and last bar on the South Island, pouring a variety of good Kiwi ales and wines. Impressive meals and blackboard specials justify the bar's motto – "if no one sees you eat it, it has no calories". Occasional live bands.

Listings

Airlines Float Air (☎03/573 6433) and Soundsair (☎03/573 6184 or 04/388 2594) both operate services to Wellington (see box on p.405 for details).

Airport buses Corgi Buses (☎03/573 7125); Sounds Link Buses (☎03/574 2610).

Banks Picton has branches of all the major banks, most of them huddled in Mariners Mall on High Street.

Bookshops Paper World, 28 High St (Mon–Sat 9am–5pm).

Buses InterCity (☎09/357 8400) run to Nelson, Blenheim and Christchurch via Kaikoura; Mount Cook Landline (☎03/573 6687) go to Christchurch and Nelson; Deluxe Travel Line (☎03/578 5467) go to Blenheim; Barry's Buses (☎03/577 9696 & 0800/802 300) serve Nelson and Blenheim; Catch-a-bus (☎0800/508 000) also goes to Nelson. Nelson Lakes Shuttles (☎03/521 1887), go to St Arnaud via Blenheim. Atomic Shuttles (☎0508/108 359) run to Christchurch. Fares are in the region of $10 to Blenheim, $20 to Nelson and $30 to Christchurch.

Car rental Most of the major international and Kiwi companies have offices at the Ferry Terminal: Avis (☎03/573 6363), Avon (☎03/573 6009), Budget (☎03/573 6081), Hertz (☎03/573 7224), New Zealand Rent A Car (☎03/573 7282). Elsewhere, try Pegasus, 5 Auckland St (☎03/573 7733), or Rent-a-Dent, cnr London Quay & Auckland St (☎03/573 7787).

Diving Divers World, corner of London Quay & Auckland St (☎03/573 7323) offer gear rental, dive trips and PADI courses (from $395). Tory Trader, on the water front (☎03/578 1480) will also take you diving. Wreck dives are especially popular, exploring the wreck of the Mikhail Lermontov, a Russian liner which sank in the Sounds in 1986.

Kayaking Marlborough Sounds Adventure Company (☎03/573 6078) rent kayaks, as do Sea Kayaking Adventure Tours (☎03/574 2765); rates are around $35 per day. (See also "Kayaking", p.428, for details of guided trips.)

Medical treatment Picton Medical Centre, 74 High St (☎03/573 6092).

Pharmacy Mc Guires, 3 High St (Mon–Sat 9am–5pm). The free *Marlborough Times* contains a list of after-hours duty pharmacists and emergency services.

Post office The main post office is in the Mariners Mall on High Street (Mon–Fri 9am–5pm, Sat 9am–12.30pm).

Sailing Gateway Sailing (☎03/578 2680) and Paradise Sailing Charters (☎03/578 8236) offer skippered sailing excursions around the Sounds for $35–45 a day (minimum of 2 people); Women's Sailing (☎04/479 2975) operate women-only sailing trips (2–4 days; $250–495).

Taxis Picton Taxis (☎03/573 6207); see also "Water taxis" below.

Tours De Lux Wine Trail (☎03/578 5467 & 0800/500 511) run a day-trip, taking in a number of the better wineries, for $38; Tory Trader (☎03/578 1480) operates diving, fishing and cruising day-trips; The Sounds Connection (☎03/573 8843), offer a number of tours, buses to the skifields and Queen Charlotte Walkway transport; Travelling Women's Network (☎04/479 2975) offer a number of fully-catered, women-only sailing trips, walks and art weekends in the Queen Charlotte Sound.

Trains Tranz Scenic (☎0800/802 802) run to Christchurch once a day, with fares starting at $27 one-way.

Water sports Sunnyvale Motel, 384 Waikawa Road (☎03/573 6800) rents out windsurfers ($25 an hour), dinghies ($10 an hour), and a catamaran ($50 per half-day).

Water taxis Arrow Water Taxis (☎03/573 8229); Cougar Line (☎03/573 7925); Endeavour Express (☎03/579 8465); The Sounds Connection (☎03/573 8843) and Tory Trader (☎03/578 1480) will all run you to various points in the Queen Charlotte Sound or Tory Channel. Beachcomber (☎03/573 6175) run a Picton–Torea Bay ferry ($12), as well as taxi services.

Weaving The House of Glenora, at 22 Broadway(☎03/573 6966, fax 573 7735), is a weaving school set in a beautiful old house; tuition costs $50–80 a day, and a workshop to learn a certain technique will take 5–7 days.

Exploring the Sounds

The Marlborough Sounds enclose moody, picturesque **bays**, deserted sandy beaches, peninsulas of grandeur and great variation, **headlands** with panoramic views and cloistered **islands**. The Sounds offer shelter from the winds and storms in Cook Strait and solitude for the contemplative fisherman, kayaker or tramper. For a taster of the labyrinthine waterways around Picton, by all means take one of the many **day-cruises** available, but to really appreciate their tranquil beauty, you're far better off **kayaking** round the bays or **tramping** the Queen Charlotte Walkway.

Cruises and tours

Several companies run cruises on the Sounds, or you can catch a **water taxi** (see "Listings", p.427) to various points and explore on your own. Beachcomber Fun Cruises (☎03/573 6175), operate four good-value **cruises** from Picton on their state-of-the-art ships: a twice-daily short cruise around the bays (2hr; $28), and a daily luncheon cruise with a stop at Torea Bay (5hr; $32), but the best trips are the **mailboat runs** (Mon, Tues, Thurs & Fri 11.15am; 5hr; $48), which alternate between two routes, either calling at bays in the Queen Charlotte Sound, as well as the Regal Salmon Farm and the Perano Whaling Station, or heading into Endeavour Inlet, Resolution Bay and Ship Cove. Another mailboat runs through Pelorus Sound from Havelock (see p.430); on all the mail trips, tea and coffee is provided, but you must bring your own lunch. The Cougar Line (☎03/573 7925 & 0800/504 090) offers a variety of one-day **walking trips** with drop off and pre-arranged pick up in the bays of the Queen Charlotte Sound ($35), as well as scenic cruises (8am, 10am & 1.30pm; 3hr; $35) to Ship Cove.

A good compromise between the standard cruises and the close-up approach of kayaking is the **eco-tours** offered by Dolphin Watch (☎03/573 8040). From their office by the train station in Picton, they drive you to Port Underwood Marina, about 13km northeast, where you board their small boat for one of two tours. The trip to **Cloudy Bay** (3–4hr; $60), gives you the opportunity to see Hectors dolphins, seals and (sometimes) whales, and visit the site where the Treaty of Waitangi was ratified by some of the South Island chiefs. The other tour focuses on Queen Charlotte Sound (half-day; $55), again with the chance of seeing enormous numbers of sea birds (including penguins), seals and dolphins, before landing at the stunning **Motuara Island**. The island has a superb lookout over Cook Strait – and is home to the South Island bush robin, bellbird, pigeon, blue penguin and the rare saddleback. All the birds are quite fearless, since they live in a relatively predator-free environment, and will rest and fly startlingly close to you. The tour continues to Ship Cove, where you can walk to the waterfall or study the monument to Cook's landing; from here, you can either return to Picton, or stay and tackle the Queen Charlotte Walkway (see below).

Kayaking

Of the many companies offering kayaking, Marlborough Sounds Adventure Company (☎03/573 6078) are the best organized and most professional. Their **guided** kayak **trips** range from one to four days (day-trip $70, including meals; 4 days' camping $550), and are not too strenuous. Another popular jaunt is their twilight paddle, with a barbecue against a background of the sparkling lights of Picton ($55, including barbecue). Sea Kayaking Adventure Tours, Anikawa (☎03/574 2765), offer one-day guided tours ($55), as well as a walk and paddle option which involves walking the Queen Charlotte Walkway, or part of it, and then sea-kayaking back ($55). Both companies also have **rental kayaks** (around $35 per day) for independent paddlers.

The Queen Charlotte Walkway

The **Queen Charlotte Walkway** (67km; 3–5 days) is a spectacular walk through the Marlborough Sounds from Ship Cove to Anakiwa or vice versa. It boasts wonderful views of the Queen Charlotte and Kenepuru sounds and passes through dense coastal forest and golden sandy bays, and lords over it all on skyline ridges. A classified, DOC-administered track, it is broad and relatively easy going – it doubles as a **mountain-**

biking track between March and November (allow 2–3 days). A leaflet outlining the walk and biking dos and don'ts is available from the visitor centre ($1).

Queen Charlotte Sound was an important trade route and provided good shelter and bountiful food for **Maori**, who carried canoes over the low saddles of the walkway to avoid long, unnecessary and hazardous sea journeys. **Captain Cook** stopped at Ship Cove and made it his New Zealand base, spending over 100 days there between 1770 and 1777. The shelter and fresh water made it an ideal spot and its plentiful supplies of (what became known as) Cook's scurvy grass were particularly valued for its vitamin C content, which provided vital relief from scurvy.

The changing seasons are reflected by splashes of colour: karaka groves are laden with bright yellow berries in the summer; native clematis (puawanga) are festooned with creamy-white **flowers** in the spring; and supplejacks and kohia (Kiwi passion fruit) produce red and orange fruits in the autumn. As a result, there is no shortage of **birds**, with tui and bellbirds in profusion, as well as the ever-friendly fantails and little piebald robins. The forests also contain the owls known as moreporks (so named for their cry, which sounds like a request for "more pork"), while the beaches boast an abundance of shags, gannets, terns and shearwaters, as well as the oystercatchers patrolling in pairs. If you are lucky, you may even spot a little blue penguin making its way to the fishing grounds in the morning or home in the evening.

ACCESS AND ACCOMMODATION

Most people walk from Ship Cove to Anakiwa: **water taxis** link with either end of the track and almost anywhere in between, so you can pick and mix sections. Arrow Water Taxis (☎03/573 8229) and Beachcomber (☎03/573 6175) will run you anywhere in the Queen Charlotte Sound or Tory Channel; Cougar Line (☎03/573 7925 & 0800/504 090) will drop you at Ship Cove and then deliver your pack to each night's accommodation ($43); Beachcomber also operates a Picton–Torea Bay **ferry** ($12). Endeavour Express, based in Endeavour Inlet (☎03/579 8465) offer daily departures for Ship Cove (9.30am; $25, pack transfers free), and return trips to Bay of Many Coves, Torea Bay and Anakiwa for **day-trippers** ($10–15 each way); Cougar Line and Beachcomber also cater for day-walks, with several drop-off and pick-up itineraries. In addition, **shuttle** services from Anakiwa to Picton are offered by Barry's Buses (☎03/574 2765), Catch a Bus (☎03/578 9994), Corgi Buses (☎03/573 7125) and Sounds Connections (☎03/573 8843); all charge around $10 per person, although some impose a $25 minimum charge.

Compared with some of the remoter tracks, the Queen Charlotte Walkway has plenty of **places to stay**. The DOC administer seven **campsites** (all $4), which have water and toilets. There are also several privately owned places to stay on or near the track, for which bookings are essential. Most have a range of accommodation, from camping space and **backpacker bunks** to self-contained **resort units** and luxurious rooms; those offering the better deals are listed below.

Anikawa Backpackers, near the trailhead at Anikawa (☎03/574 2174). A straightforward, clean and simple hostel. Dorms ①, rooms ②.

Endeavour Holiday Resort, Endeavour Inlet (☎03/579 8381). A quiet and idyllic place near the water, with a restaurant, shop and safe swimming area. Dorms ①, chalets & units ④.

Furneaux Lodge, Endeavour Inlet (☎03/579 9411). A swanky lodge with a bar and restaurant and some shared accommodation. Dorms ①, chalets ⑤.

Gem Resort, Arthur's Bay (☎03/579 9771). Cabins tucked away in a corner of the Bay of Many Coves. Dorms ①, cabins ④–⑤.

Portage Hotel, Kenepuru Sound, ten minutes' walk along the road from Torea Bay (☎03/573 4309). Resort hotel with a friendly lounge bar and restaurant. Dorms ①, rooms ⑤.

Resolution Bay Cabins, Resolution Bay (☎03/579 9411). The closest accommodation to Ship Cove (4.5km), in a pretty spot offering swimming and canoes. Dorms ①, cabins ②, cottages ⑤.

Te Mahia Resort, Te Mahia Bay, Kenepuru Sound (☎03/573 4089). Close to the walkway with a store – and glow-worms – nearby. Dorms ③, self-contained units ③–④.

THE ROUTE

The track passes through some grassy **farmland** and bleak gorse-covered **hills**, but both ends of the track are **forest** reserves with lush greenery, including nikau palms and climbing keikie, right down to the shoreline. There are a number of **detours** off the main track to places of interest, including a short walk from Ship Cove to a pretty forest-shrouded waterfall, a scramble down to the Bay of Many Coves, or a foray to the Antimony Mines (where there are exposed shafts – stick to the marked tracks). The most spectacular **views** are to be had en route to the mines and at Torea Saddle and Kenepuru Saddle.

Beginning at **Ship Cove**, the track climbs steeply away from the shore through largely untouched forest to a lookout with great views of Motuara Island, before dropping down into **Resolution Bay** (4.5km; 2hr), where there's a DOC camsite and other accommodation, or you can press on along an old bridle path over the ridge into **Endeavour Inlet** (15km; 5hr). From here, you have an easy second day, rounding the inlet, climbing to the **Kenepuru Saddle** and returning to the shoreline; there's a campsite in **Camp Bay** (11.5km; 4hr), but you may decide to push on for another four hours to **Bay of Many Coves**, where there is another campsite and cabin accommodation. Otherwise, day three, the longest and most rewarding stretch, takes you from Camp Bay along the ridge that separates the Kenepuru Sound from the Queen Charlotte Sound to **Torea Saddle** (20.5km; 9hr), where you can follow the road to Cowshed Bay for the DOC campsite or stay at the plush *Portage Resort Hotel*. On day four, you can choose a short ridge walk through beech and manuka forest to **Mistletoe Bay** (7.5km; 4hr) or a long slog high above the water, before descending to the DOC campsite at **Davies Bay** and continuing to the road at **Anakiwa** (20km; 9hr), where you can crash at the *Anakiwa Backpackers*, or meet your prearranged bus or water taxi pick-up.

GUIDED TRIPS

Finally, if you baulk at the thought of lugging a heavy pack, there are several companies willing to take the weight off your shoulders: check out Cougar Line's tempting option of a drop-off at Ship Cove and **transfer** of your pack to each of your intended destinations ($43; ☎03/573 7925); or go the whole hog with Marlborough Sounds Adventure Company (☎03/573 6078, fax 573 8827) on their a four-day **guided walk** along the Queen Charlotte Walkway ($750, fully inclusive). Sea Kayaking Adventure Tours, Anikawa (☎03/574 2765) operate various trips that combine **biking** and walking the track.

Havelock and around

The 28km trip between Picton and **HAVELOCK** is quite spectacular (as is the 75km on to Nelson). Nestled in the heart of the Pelorus Sound, the town itself is tiny and uninspiring – a shortcoming more than made up for by the stunning Pelorus Sound, an exciting maze of sunken seaways with high mountain peaks that can be explored by boat or on foot.

A hundred years ago Havelock was a **boom town**, revelling in the wealth created by an inland gold rush and rampant logging, but it has now reverted to a **sleepy** fishing **village** with a straggle of buildings spread out along the main road and down by the wharf. Havelock is the green-shell mussel capital of the world, and you simply can't leave before you've purchased some choice morsels from the wharf. Until recently its other claim to fame was as the erstwhile home of itinerant author **Barry Crump**. Crumpy, as he was affectionately known, began life as a hunter and bushman, culling deer and pigs in some of New Zealand's roughest country – a way of life he described in a series of humorous, poignant and superbly descriptive novels. The larger-than-life Crump presented television and radio shows and "researched" his books (a euphemism for dedicated drinking) until his demise in 1996. The **Havelock Museum**, on Main Road, near the Shell Garage (Mon–Sat 9am–4pm; if locked, ask at visitor centre or garage for key; donation requested), is housed in two small cream wooden buildings. Among the usual collection of bric-a-brac is a wood-milling display and the honour rolls from Havelock School, which feature Ernest Rutherford, who first split the atom – and went to school here from 1886–1894.

Practicalities

Buses between Picton and Nelson all stop at Havelock, while local bus and **water-taxi** operators offer services to Kenepuru and Pelorus sounds. The **DOC office**, 13 Mahakipawa Rd (Mon–Fri 8am–4.30pm; ☎03/573 7582) is the best place to pick up **information** on the worthwhile tracks and trips in the area. Marlborough Travel Centre, 73 Main Rd (☎03/574 2532), provides some information, but is mostly geared to booking excursions and onward travel; the Outdoor Adventure Centre on Main Road rents out mountain bikes ($30 a day) and rigid-hulled inflatable boats ($120).

Accommodation options include *Havelock Garden Motel*, at 71 Main Rd (☎03/574 2387; ④), with six fully self-contained units and helpful hosts. On the corner of Main Road and Lawrence Street, *Pelorus Motor Inn* (☎03/574 2412; ④), has a few simple units without cooking facilities, though you can get a cheap meal in the tavern attached. *Rutherford YHA Hostel*, 46 Main Rd (☎03/574 2104; tent sites $7, dorms ①, rooms ②), is centrally located in the characterful old schoolhouse, but the rooms are small and soundproofing could be better; the staff are a mine of information on the best trips and things to see. Off the beaten track at **Canvastown**, 10km west of Havelock, *Pinedale Motor Camp* (☎03/574 2349; tent sites $8, cabins & units ②–③) is a delightful spot to relax for a few days, with bushwalks, glow-worms, gold-panning and 1km of river frontage with swimming holes.

Food in Havelock tends to be straightforward – and plenty of it. *Pelorus Jack's Café*, corner of Main Road and Inglis Street, serves breakfast, lunch and dinner (daily 6am–9pm); fresh seafood and large portions make this a good place to stock up on carbohydrate before a walk. For bargain scallops ($18) or **steak and chips** ($15), you can't go past the *Pelorus Tavern* at the Pelorus Motor Inn (see above). Otherwise, try the *Sounds Café*, on the corner of Main Road and Neil Street (daily 8.30am–11pm summer, closes 6pm in winter; licensed & BYO), a small, cheerful place where the infamous **mussels** are $9; a large plate of antipasto is $16, or there's foccacia sandwiches, pizzas, burgers and good ice cream.

Exploring Pelorus Sound

One of the best ways to see the Sound is aboard the delightfully old-fashioned *Pelorus Mail Boat*, run by Beachcomber Fun Cruises (Tues, Wed & Thurs 9.30am; 7hr; $55; ☎03/573 6175), which sets off from Havelock Marina on its leisurely **mail run**, calling at isolated homesteads, a mussel farm and passing countless unspoilt beaches. The same company operates the **French Pass** cruise (8hr; $69) along Pelorus Sound past Maud Island, and around to French Pass, at the entrance to the seething channel where the ship of nineteenth-century French explorer D'Urville was spun by tumultuous whirlpools. On both these trips, you need to bring your own lunch.

Here too, a good way to get into the nooks and crannies of Pelorus Sound is by **kayak**. Te Hoiere Sea Kayaks run **guided trips** ($70; minimum 4 people; ☎03/574 2610) either bird-watching, looking over historic gold workings or paddling to a good spot for a beach picnic. Wild Track and Waters, also offer guided kayaking (from $70 per day, including meals; ☎03/574 2104), with routes tailored to your levels of experience and fitness. Both operators also have **rental kayaks** ($35–40 per day, including safety briefing), so you can do your own thing.

Walks around Havelock

Eighteen kilometeres west of Havelock on SH6 is the **Pelorus Bridge Scenic Reserve**, which contains superb examples of black beech trees and golden green rimu, as well as kahikatea, miro and the blue-green foliage of matai trees. There is also an abundance of tui, grey warblers and bellbirds – and many swimming holes along the trout and salmon-rich, sandy-beached rivers. This fertile area saw a succession of Maori settlements, which prospered until Te Rauparaha conquered the north of the South Island in the 1820s. The misery caused by the casualties of war and the encroachment of European settlers drove most of the Maori away – the few that remained produced flax that Te Rauparaha could trade for rifles.

Facilities include a basic DOC **camping** area (☎03/542 6019; tent sites $7.50, cabins ②) and several walking tracks. The **café** (daily 8am–4pm) at Pelorus Bridge incorporates a **DOC office** and a small **shop**, as well as purveying delicious home-made muffins, pastries and a selection of light meals.

Most of the **walks** in the reserve are fairly flat, well maintained and well marked: the **Totara** (1.5km return; 30min) and **Circle** (1km return; 30min) routes pass through the low-lying woodland for which the area is famous, while the **Trig K** (2.5km one way; 2hr), after a steady climb to 417m, offers stunning views of the whole area. From the summit you can head straight down or follow the **Beech Ridge Track** (3km; 90min), via two waterfalls, which takes the scenic route back to the start of the Trig K track.

Another rewarding tramp near Havelock is the **Nydia Track** (20km; 2 days), which starts at **Kaiuma Bay**, passes Nydia Bay and finishes at **Duncan Bay**. Following a series of bridle paths, the route makes its way through pasture, shrubland and virgin forest, with great views from the Kaiuma Saddle (387m) and Nydia Saddle (347m), as well as along the head of the bay. Maori called Nydia Bay *Opouri*, which means "place of sadness", because when a *hapu* (one faction of a tribe) was preparing to migrate from the North Island to the Sounds, their leader sacrificed a young boy to Tangora the sea god to ensure a safe journey. When the boy's father found out, he sought *utu* or revenge, storming across to Pelorus Sound and slaughtering the disgraced *hapu*.

Kaiuma Bay is 32km from Havelock by road: turn off SH6 12km west of Havelock onto Daltons Road – a car park at the end marks the beginning of the track. For boat **access**, check at the Marlborough Travel Centre or DOC office in Havelock. **Accommodation** is either camping or at the *Nydia Lodge* (①), halfway along the track – but you'll need to get the key at the DOC office in Havelock or from the caretaker, whose house is signposted from the lodge.

Nelson and around

In a broad basin between the Arthur and Richmond ranges lies the pretty city of **NELSON**, which provides easy access to three national parks and Golden Bay. Add to this the universal appeal of sandy beaches and abundant sunshine, and it will come as no surprise that the Nelson region is one of the most popular destinations in New Zealand, with a mass of great activities and opportunities to indulge in the bounty of the land. The small satellite town of **Richmond**, 14km to the west, holds some of the area's most salubrious guesthouses and serves as a suburban retreat for commuters. Located at the junction of SH6 and SH60, it also marks the parting of the ways: south via the market gardens on the flat land of Hope, Brightwater, Spring Grove, Wakefield and Belgrove towards Murchison (see p.463); or northwest via Motueka to the Abel Tasman National Park (see p.445).

Nelson has the air of a bustling go-ahead city, something which can detract from its **historical pedigree** as one of the oldest settlements in New Zealand – a place where many early European immigrants got their first taste of the South Island. By the middle of the sixteenth century, the Ngati Tumatakokiri occupied most of the Nelson area, providing a reception committee for **Abel Tasman**'s long boats at Murderer's Bay, where they killed a number of his sailors. By the time Europeans arrived in earnest, Maori numbers had been decimated by internecine fighting and the nearest pa site to Nelson was at Motueka, although this did little to prevent land squabbles, culminating in the **Wairau Affray** in 1843. Despite assurances from Maori chiefs Te Rauparaha and Te Rangihaeata that they would abide by the decision of a land commissioner, the New Zealand Company went ahead regardless, sending surveyors south to the Wairau Plains. A skirmish ensued, during which Te Rangihaeata's wife was shot. The bereaved chief and his men slaughtered twenty-two people, and only the arrival of industrious German immigrants saved the settlement from complete dissolution.

Today, basking in one of the sunniest and most scenic areas in the country, Nelson has found a new lease of life as a holiday centre, with its busy **fishing port** and a rich fruit- and vegetable-growing **hinterland** scattered with breweries and wineries. It is also a haven for **artists**, who are drawn by the sunlight, the landscape and the unique raw materials for pottery and ceramic art that lurk beneath the rich green grass.

Arrival, information and transport

Flights arrive at Nelson **airport**, 8km west of the centre, and are met by a daily **shuttle** and door-to-door service provided by Super Shuttle Nelson (☎03/547 5782; $6), or **taxis** (☎03/545 1067; $12). All **buses** drop you near the centre of the city, within easy walking distance of most accommodation. InterCity pulls in at 27 Bridge St, while the other companies all stop outside the **visitor centre**, on the corner of Trafalgar Street and Halifax Street (daily 7.30am–5pm; ☎03/548 2304, fax 546 9008). This large and welcoming centre has heaps of leaflets on Nelson and the surrounding region, including guides to the national parks, local studios and workshops; the centre also functions as a booking office for trips, accommodation and onward travel. The **DOC office**, 186 Bridge St (Mon–Fri 8am–4.35pm; ☎03/546 9335), in the Munro Building next to the Courthouse, provides information, hut passes and maps for all the national parks.

Nelson Suburban Bus Company (Mon–Fri 8am–6pm, Sat 8am–12.30pm; ☎03/548 3290) runs between Nelson and its satellite communities from the terminal on Lower Bridge Street, while numerous smaller **shuttle buses** run further afield to Golden Bay, the Abel Tasman, Kahurangi and Nelson Lakes national parks. Otherwise, you can get around most of the sights in the immediate vicinity with the help of a **rental car** or **bike**, while plenty of **tours** take in the highlights of the city and its surroundings (see "Listings", p.442, for details of all these).

Accommodation

The best places to stay, with a few notable exceptions in the shape of some **outlying B&Bs**, are in Nelson itself, where you have a choice of relaxing **beachside** locations or the bustling **centre** within reach of cultural diversions and nightlife. **Camping**, on the other hand, is not such a good option here, and you'll do better to settle for a **hostel** in the city and save camping for prettier areas around Motueka.

Hotels and motels

Carmel Court, 50 Waimea Rd (☎03/548 2234). This motel offers twelve fully self-contained units in a well-kept modern building with off-street parking. ⑤.

Kings Gate, 21 Trafalgar Street (☎03/546 9108, fax 546 6838). Central motel with comfortable well-kept rooms including full kitchens. ⑤.

Quality Hotel Rutherford, Trafalgar Square (☎03/548 2299, fax 546 3003). An international-style hotel with a number of impressive facilities, including a café, bar and excellent Japanese Restaurant, as well as large, well appointed rooms, some with impressive views. It doesn't hurt to try negotiating during the slacker months of March and April. ⑤–⑥.

Riverlodge, 31 Collingwood St (☎03/548 3094, fax 548 3039). One of the better motels, giving value for money in clean and comfortable rooms. ④.

B&Bs and guesthouses

Aloha Lodge, 19 Beach Rd (☎03/546 4000). Beachside accommodation in a hideous building with a tacky pseudo-Japanese gate; inside it's surprisingly comfortable, offering B&B or self-contained units. ④–⑤.

Althorpe, 13 Dorset St, Richmond (☎03/544 8117). A pretty B&B with just two neat bedrooms in an 1880s homestead in the tranquil neighbourhood of Richmond. ⑤.

Cambria House, 7 Cambria St (☎03/548 4681). This 140-year-old weatherboard house boasts a lovely back deck and garden, beautiful fireplaces, and a wide choice of breakfasts – all just ten minutes' walk from town on a quiet road. ⑦.

Cathedral Inn, 369 Trafalgar St South (☎03/548 7369). In the centre of town, this newly restored manor offers elegantly styled, charming rooms and hearty breakfasts. ④.

Harbour House, 371 Wakefield Quay (☎03/548 7430). With comfortable accommodation and friendly hosts, a summertime garden café (see "Eating and drinking", p.440), and kayaks and mountain bikes for guests' use, this is a fine spot. A track at the back of the house leads to the top of a hill, where a seat overlooks Tasman Bay. ⑤.

Kirshaw House, 10 Wensley Rd, Richmond (☎03/544 0957). A large, welcoming B&B in a 1929 house in Richmond, which has been authentically restored – a highlight is the gorgeous dark-stained rimu staircase. All rooms are smartly decorated and have private facilities. ⑥.

Mapledurham, 8 Edward St, Richmond (☎03/544 4210). A beautiful rimu villa encircled by a wide, grey-floored verandah and a well tended garden. The house is light and airy, dressing gowns are provided, and the breakfasts are superb; dinners are available by arrangement ($45, including wine). ⑦.

Hostels

Beach Hostel, 25 Muritai St (☎03/548 6817). An intimate hostel by the beach, with free bikes, a lounge with deck and good views, free pick-up from the city and a twice-daily shuttle service. Dorms ①, rooms ②.

Boots Backpackers, cnr of Trafalgar St & Bridge St (☎03/548 9001). Vibrant and colourful murals and cartoons adorn the walls of this popular hostel, which is full most nights – even though the kitchen is very small and the hostel is in need of some attention. Key deposit $10, linen hire $1. Dorms ①, rooms ②.

Centre of New Zealand Hostel, 189 Milton St (☎03/546 6667). Dorms, twin and double rooms cluster inside this lovely weatherboard house just 500m from the city centre. There's a large kitchen and dining area, plus a balcony with good views over Bridge Street. The entrance to the car park is next to 183 Milton St. ①–②.

Paradiso Backpackers, 42 Weka St (☎03/546 6703). Based in a large 97-year-old house, this hostel has a swimming pool, good facilities and a friendly atmosphere. Dorms ①, rooms ②.

Tasman Towers, 8–10 Weka St (☎03/548 7950). A purpose-built hostel three minutes' walk from town. Good-sized dining and kitchen areas, a large lounge, and clean spacious rooms make this a sound choice. Dorms ①, rooms ③.

YHA, 59 Rutherford St (☎03/545 9988, fax 545 9989). This new purpose-built hostel in a central location is the best in town, with a wide range of accommodation, including connecting rooms for families and two disabled-accessible units. Big kitchens and a bike store add to its appeal, as do very helpful staff and discounted rates in winter. Dorms ①, rooms ③.

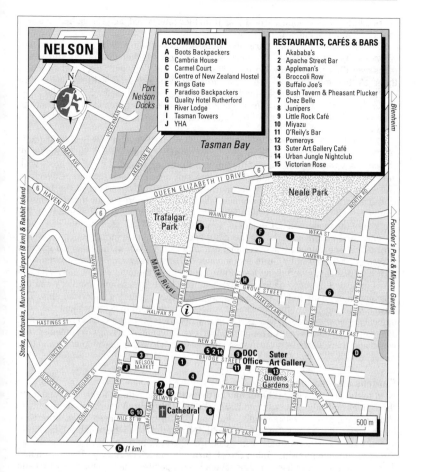

NELSON

ACCOMMODATION

A Boots Backpackers
B Cambria House
C Carmel Court
D Centre of New Zealand Hostel
E Kings Gate
F Paradiso Backpackers
G Quality Hotel Rutherford
H River Lodge
I Tasman Towers
J YHA

RESTAURANTS, CAFÉS & BARS

1 Akababa's
2 Apache Street Bar
3 Appleman's
4 Broccoli Row
5 Buffalo Joe's
6 Bush Tavern & Pheasant Plucker
7 Chez Belle
8 Junipers
9 Little Rock Café
10 Miyazu
11 O'Reily's Bar
12 Pomeroys
13 Suter Art Gallery Café
14 Urban Jungle Nightclub
15 Victorian Rose

The City

The city of Nelson is dominated by the glowering, greystone edifice of the cathedral, perched on a hill with fine views across the harbour and city below, where the streets are laid out in a grid pattern. The liveliest **thoroughfares** are Trafalgar Street and Bridge Street, while the **seafront** to the north is strewn with palm trees and parks where you can hear the thrum of cicadas in summer. And, for respite from the city, there are the long, golden-sand **beaches** and the green oasis and shady paths of the central public **gardens**. To get further away from it on a short day-trip, head for **Rabbit Island**, which is accessible at low tide.

Fortunately, the interior of the Anglican **Christ Church Cathedral** is nowhere near as grim as its exterior. Dazzling stained-glass windows illuminate the building, with ten particularly noteworthy examples tucked away in a small chapel to the right of the main altar. The cathedral has had a chequered history, which may account for its ugliness. English architect Frank Peck's original 1924 design was gradually modified over many years due to lack of money; World War II further intervened, and the cathedral tower looks as if it is still under construction.

The modern city architecture and well-disguised older buildings of Nelson are enlivened by the temporary presence of the **Nelson Market** (Sat 7am–1pm), which takes over the car park between Rutherford Street and Trafalgar Street at the back of the YHA, two minutes' walk from the cathedral. Multicoloured stalls are laden with clothes, jewellery, toys, locally made wood carvings, art and crafts. Food stalls totter under the weight of mounds of fruit, endless varieties of fresh bread and fish, Thai and vegetarian dishes, burgers and hot dogs, coffee and cakes, to sustain you while you browse.

The Bishop Suter Art Gallery, just off Trafalgar Street at 208 Bridge St (daily 10.30am–4.30pm; $3), was built in 1899 as memorial to Andrew Burn Suter, Bishop of Nelson from 1866 to 1891. One of the finest in the South Island, the gallery hosts visiting exhibitions and shows relating to the local area, but its focus is the Suter Collection. Watercolours predominate – especially those of John Gully, a friend of the bishop's whose works largely depict scenes from the surrounding area – but there are also a number of oil paintings and over a hundred works by Sir M. Tossill Woollaston, the founder of the modernist movement in New Zealand art. Woollaston was one of a group of artists and writers who, during the 1930s and 40s, began exploring notions of a New Zealand culture independent of colonial Britain. Pride of place in the gallery is given to a famous 1909 portrait by Gottfried Lindauer of Huria Matenga, a Maori women who, with her husband, saved many lives from the wreck of the *Delaware* in 1863. Her status is indicated by *moko* (facial tattoos), feathers, bone, greenstone jewellery and the ceremonial club she holds; in the background is the foundering American ship. The other significant part of the permanent collection is devoted to ceramics and the work of local potters; the Nelson area is rich in raw materials for potters and ceramic artists. The gallery also showcases a range of Maori art, from early carvings to contemporary work, and there's a 159-seat arthouse cinema (see "Drinking, nightlife and entertainment", p.440).

Gardens and beaches

Next to the Suter Gallery is **Queens Gardens** (daily 8am–dusk; free), hemmed in on three sides by Bridge, Tasman and Hardy streets. This pretty Victorian garden, with its mature trees and a well populated duck pond, is a tranquil haven in an otherwise bustling city. Respite can also be found further out of the city in the delightful, Japanese-style **Miyazu Gardens** (daily 8am–dusk; free). To get here, walk east along Bridge Street to the junction with Milton Street, turn left and follow Atawhai Drive for about 300m. This quiet oasis has a traditional tea house, ponds, azaleas, Japanese irises and flowering cherries; the gardens are at their best during December and January. **Founders Park**, 87 Atawhai Drive (daily 10am–4.30pm; $5), 75m back from the gardens, is less impressive, with a collection of old buildings conspiring to produce a somewhat sanitized version of early colonial history.

For an excellent walk with fine views, head west on Haven Road, past the junction with Queen Elizabeth II Drive, and on to Wakefield Quay. Then walk along Rocks Road (SH6) until you reach the **Tahunanui Beach Reserve**, just past the sea wall, some 5km from the city centre. Grassland and drifting dunes back the long, golden beach, which has safe swimming, a fun park, zoo and children's playgrounds – the place swarms around Christmas time. If you don't feel like walking to the reserve, buses run regularly along SH6 from the city.

Some 18km from the reserve (along SH6 and then northwest on SH60), is Nelson's other beach area, **Rabbit Island**, with golden sands backed by trees. This is much less developed, and all the better for it: the views are stunning, and it is picture-book pretty.

FESTIVAL MANIA

The **Wearable Arts Festival** has become an international event, staged at twelve- to eighteen-month intervals – though the last one was such a success that there are plans to make it an annual event (check with visitor centre for exact dates). This unique fashion show combines elements of sculpture, performance art, theatre, choreography and dance to create an extraordinary spectacle. The bizarre circus lasts for two nights (tickets $35) and is performed on a sparkling 100m catwalk, and afterwards, the best of the costumes go on display at the Suter Art Gallery. Indeed, many of them are more sculpture than haute couture, being fashioned from household junk, food, metal, stone, wood – and a surfeit of imagination. An arts festival has also sprung up around the show, spanning three weeks and including jazz sessions, alternative performances and exhibitions.

The **Taste Nelson Festival**, an annual day-long event held in February, espouses much more conservative ambitions. Essentially a celebration of the quality food, beers and wines that are produced in this area, as well as an excuse for local entertainers and bands to strut their funky stuff, the festival attracts over 10,000 gourmands.

Access is by the Redwood Road (off SH60, just after the Waimea River Road Bridge), but note that the road is barred at 9pm daily.

Stoke

The small satellite town of **STOKE** lying 8.5km southwest of Nelson on SH6, is linked to the city by suburban buses, and hides a couple of attractions.

One of the best diversions around Nelson, not least because it finishes with one of the best beers, is the **Mac's Brewery Tour**, 66 Main Rd (Tues, Thurs & Sat 10.30am & 2pm; 1hr; $5). An interesting tour takes you through the completely natural brewing process: the brewery sits on its own spring, and uses local Motueka Hops. Inevitably though, the highlight is the free tasting of the superior brews – and, just as inevitably, there's a large shop selling brewery products and souvenirs.

Also in the suburb of Stoke, just off Marsden Road (entrance in Hilliard Street), is **Isel Park** (daily 8am–dusk; free) and **Nelson Provincial Museum** (Tues–Fri 10am–4pm, Sat & Sun 2–5pm; $2). The museum celebrates the local human and natural heritage, primarily through its photographic collection of over a million plates, some dating back to the 1870s. Meanwhile in the Maori Gallery you will learn, among other things, that, "By eating a worthy enemy you would increase your own strength and consign their souls to perpetual misery". Even more grisly is the exhibition dealing with the nineteenth-century **Maungatapu Murders**, so-named after the track between Nelson and Pelorus along which a notorious gang of four (Sullivan, Kelly, Burgess and Levy) perpetrated their crimes. One of their more harebrained schemes entailed the use strychnine to murder the staff of the Nelson branch of the Bank of New South Wales, so they could make off with the money. Quite how they intended to administer the poison is less clear, and their plot went badly wrong. Sullivan turned Queen's evidence before the raid even took place and Levy, Kelly and Burgess were all hanged; Levy's death mask is on display here as a gruesome reminder. Also in the museum are two elaborate *waka*, which were salvaged from the sands of Farewell Spit (see p.455).

The grounds also contain **Isel House** (Oct–April Sat & Sun 2–4pm; $1), which dates from 1848. Built as a farmhouse for the Marsden family, it still contains much of the original furniture, china and paintings, and is set in woodland of some grandeur, yet it somehow fails to hold the attention as the museum does.

Activities

A number of companies offer **rafting** trips from Nelson, most venturing onto the **Buller River** via Murchison and the Nelson Lakes National Park or onto the **Karamea River** in Kahurangi National Park. Along both rivers, the scenery is breathtaking, the water swift – and the sandflies omnipresent, so don't forget the insect repellent.

The pick of the operators are Ultimate Descents and The Rapid River Adventure Company. Both offer a variety of trips: with Ultimate Descents (☎03/546 6212), itineraries range from day-long excursions on the Buller ($100, including lunch) to amazing five-day safaris on the Buller and Karamea ($550–650, all inclusive). Their day-trips seem to spend slightly longer on the river than most others, leaving plenty of time for fun with inflatable kayaks and water sledges, as well as for getting your teeth into some serious Grade III and IV rafting and a deceptively high cliff jump. Rapid River (☎03/542 3110) do a good-value day-trip from Nelson ($89, including BBQ lunch) that gets you on the river just after lunch for four hours' rafting on Grade III and IV stretches of the Buller, ending at the Owen River Tavern for a well-earned pint.

You won't escape the buffeting on land, either. Just off Cable Bay Road, about ten minutes' drive east of Nelson on SH6, Happy Valley 4x4 Motorbike Adventures (☎03/545 0304) have a number of **quadbikes** and all-terrain vehicles. With over 4000 square kilometres of forest and 40km of track at their disposal, there is an enormous variety to their **safaris**. Along the way you will see monstrous matai trees as you climb above the tree line for expansive views of Cable Bay and the ocean. Prices range from $25 to $100, and evening forays include glow-worm viewing.

West of Nelson, about 17km along SH6, Haycock Road turns off to the historic Clover Road stables, home to **Stonehurst Horse trekking** (☎03/542 4121). The majority of the shorter treks (1–4hr; $25–70) take place in the foothills of the Richmond ranges and offer great views of the coast and beyond; there are horses to suit all abilities and the routes are challenging but not frightening.

When you've had your fill of Nelson's earthly pleasures, spice things up with a spot of **parachuting**. Tandem Skydiving (☎03/548 7652; $165–210) operate out of Nelson Airport – or, if the weather is unsuitable there, they adjourn to Motueka. You can even get some pictures of yourself trying to look happy as you plummet from an altitude of 3000m. Although you may have other things on your mind, the scenery is excellent and the expert parachuting "buddies" are helpful and friendly. Out in Richmond, Paragliding Tandem Flights offer **tandem paragliding** (☎03/544 1182; $95): a hair-raising drive up the hill to the launch site reveals a spectacular landscape, before you glide off for 15–20 minutes of eerily silent flight, surrounded by stunning views.

Around Nelson

Most of Nelson's attractions, including the wineries, breweries and galleries for which it is renowned, lie beyond the city. The combination of the soil, natural spring water and climate make this area ideal for the production of **wines** or **beers**, and the attractiveness of the scenery will tempt you to linger and sample a glass of either. If the galleries in town whet your appetite for art, make time to investigate the studios of the enormous number of contemporary artists working in the Nelson region, many of whom exhibit in their own small **galleries**, showcasing ceramics, glass-blowing, woodturning, textiles, sculpture and painting. More details can be found in the *Nelson Potters* and *The Coastal Way* leaflets, both free from Nelson visitor centre.

Almost everything worth seeing outside the city of Nelson lie to the south and west: either just off SH6 before it reaches the junction with SH60 or in a slim corridor of land flanking either side of SH60. Nelson Suburban Buses run along SH6, through

Richmond and as far as Wakefield, but do not go along SH60; however, **bus tours** run to the wineries and galleries (see "Listings" on p.443).

Heading west along SH6, you'll reach the **Craft Habitat Centre** (Mon–Fri 9am–5pm, Sat & Sun 10am–5pm), 12km from Nelson on the southernmost edge of Waimea Inlet, opposite the junction with Champion Road. Set up by Jack Laird and his wife, stalwarts of the Nelson pottery scene, the centre was developed by their son Paul, a potter of unusual and engaging pieces inspired by the landscape. As well as pottery, the centre displays glass-blowing by Lynette Campbell (of Höglands fame – see below), jewellery, weaving, spinning and knitting, leadlighting and woodturning. To satisfy more mundane appetites, there's also a very good **café** called, unsurprisingly, *Habitat* (daily 10am–4pm); have the mussel chowder, if it's on. For something to wash down your chowder, press on through the fruit-growing country to the **Perlorus Winery**, on Patons Road in Richmond (Nov–April daily 10am–5pm), where you can sample fine vintages, or just pick up an excellent Chardonnay for later.

Högland's Glass Blowing Studio, Korurangi Farm, Lansdowne Road (daily 9am–5.30pm), is signposted from SH60 just after it leaves SH6. In addition to glass-blowing demonstrations, there's a café, live Irish folk music at weekends, a gallery and park-like gardens inhabited by farm animals. The glass-blowers slickly combine art and entertainment, and may even let you blow a glass bubble. The style of the glassware (mostly tableware) is Scandinavian-influenced, which works best in the bigger, bolder pieces with clean lines and unusual colours. Sticking with the Scandinavian theme, the licensed **café** serves excellent lunches and light snacks; try open sandwiches ($7.50) or the platter of smoked delicacies ($14.50), which is usually enough for two.

The **Seifried Estate Winery**, at the corner of SH60 and Redwood Road, has an excellent restaurant and shop (daily 9am–5pm; wine tasting $3, redeemable against purchases), while the **Silkwood** gift shop (daily 10am–5pm), 4km further along SH60, is famed more for its method of construction than its wares. Made of bails of straw plastered over with concrete – a material originally used in the United States in timber-poor areas – the building is virtually fireproof, safe in earthquakes, cool in summer, and warm in the winter. Inside, among the usual tourist tat, is some beautifully designed knitwear made from the wool of the llama, angora and alpaca that graze the property. The **Bronte Gallery**, at the end of Bronte Road East, which veers east off SH60, is recommended for the diversity of its pottery and painting, and for its selection of tableware by internationally recognized practitioner, Darryl Robertson. The work here provides a useful benchmark for assessing the quality in other outlets; what's more, the gallery enjoys a fine location near the coast, where there are sweeping views across Waimea Inlet to Rabbit Island.

Marpua Wharf is at the end of the Arunui Road, which turns off SH60, 34km from Nelson. Overlooking the west end of Rabbit Island, the wharf is legendary for its hot- and cold-smoked fish, mussels and smoked fish paté, widely acclaimed as the best in the country. The delicious seafood is slowly smoked over manuka wood after being cured in a salt and sugar solution. With a little advance planning (pick up a bottle from one of the wineries en route), you can enoy a simple **fishy feast** right on the wharf. For grease fiends, there's also an excellent fish and chip shop, plus a simple BYO café with a few tables on the boardwalk, serving smoked fish platters ($9–26), accompanied by focaccia and salads. Heading back towards SH60, you'll pass Mapua Village and its **Village Rest**, a licensed café in an impressive modern building with a large deck where you can sup a pint of locally brewed beer (McCashins, Bays and Pink Elephant are all on tap) to wash down the fish.

On the opposite side of SH60, the Seaton Valley Road heads west and inland to the eccentric **Glover's Vineyard** (Mon–Sat 10am–5pm; tastings $2), a small concern that produces fine Cabernet Sauvignon and Pinot Noir (most costing $15 or more); you can draw your own conclusions from the fact that the owner used to tuck a Wagner CD into every package destined for overseas. The **Nuerdorf Winery** (daily, 10am–5pm; free tastings), an altogether more wholesome prospect, is further inland. Once you hit the junction with Moutere Highway, join Nuerdorf Road by heading southeast on the highway for 100m and turning right. The winery is in a low-slung wooden building covered by vines with simple outdoor seating in the shade of some tall ancient trees, where a glass of Chardonnay is complimented perfectly by cheese, bread, olives and other simple fare that is served here ($8–12).

Returning to SH60 on the Seaton Valley Road, head 2km west to the junction with Korepo Road, along which you'll find the idyllic **Ruby Bay Winery** (Oct–April daily 11am–6pm), set on a hill overlooking tiny Ruby Bay. Here you can sit under a vine-covered trellis in a lovely garden and slurp your way through a wine-tasting tray ($4, refundable on purchase of three or more bottles), or try some of the simple but delicious food, such as baked salmon ($13.50), oven-baked blue nose ($13.50), or a vineyard platter of meat, cheese and vegetables ($12). If nothing else, try the Pinot Noir. About 2km from Ruby Bay, back on SH60, is **Steve Fullmer's Gallery** (daily 10am–5pm), near the Tasman Store on Baldwin Road. One of the best galeries in the region, this place is worth a browse even if you can't afford any of the remarkable ceramic art or stunning tableware.

Eating

The enviable lifestyle of Nelson residents is reflected in the **vast choice** of decent places to eat within easy reach of the town centre. And when you tire of these, there's always fine food and wine in gorgeous settings at the **wineries**. If fast food beckons, try out the local **pie cart** that's parked near the central post office on Trafalgar Street most evenings. Don't forget Nelson's pubs (see below) for a quick snack either.

Applemans, 38 Bridge St (☎03/546 8105). Widely regarded as the best fish restaurant in the city, but maintaining moderate prices ($20–30 mains), this place is always busy, the produce is frighteningly fresh and cooked in imaginative ways. Dinner daily from 6pm; licensed & BYO.

Akababa's Turkish Kebabs, 130 Bridge St. Plenty of cheap kebabs and salads ($2–9) to munch in the canopied area out back, or in booth seating on low floor cushions; Turkish decor and music create a lively and casual atmosphere.

Boat Shed, 350 Wakefield Quay (☎03/546 9783). Converted for its new role, this boat shed has large windows offering unimpeded and spectacular sunsets over Tasman Bay. Exceptional seafood and a bustling ambience mean that it suffers somewhat from its own popularity. It's definitely worth coming here, but try to avoid the insanely crowded and rushed Friday and Saturday nights. Mains cost $12–25; licensed.

Broccoli Row, 5 Buxton Square (☎03/548 9621). Morning teas, lunches, afternoon snacks and dinners are all served in generous portions at this vegetarian restaurant, with outdoor dining and blackboard specials ($5–19). Mon–Sat 9.30am–10pm; book for dinner; BYO.

Chez Eelco, 296 Trafalgar St. No visit to Nelson is complete without stopping here. This was the first café/bar in Nelson and is still going strong: the decor might be a little ropy these days, but the mussel chowder is still superb – and prices are reasonable. The food includes fish, steaks and astonishing Chez burgers. Chess sets and newspapers keep you amused, and oiled tablecloths are reminiscent of Amsterdam cafés – a welcome change from the ubiquitous American-style bars. Daily 6am–9pm; licensed.

Harbour House, 371 Wakefield Quay. A delightful garden-café attached to a B&B (see "Accommodation", p.433) and serving an eclectic range of Mediterranean, Greek, Italian and Moroccan food at value-for-money prices. Summer only, daily 10am–3pm. Licensed.

Junipers, 144 Collingwood St (☎03/548 8832). Quite simply, superb food: special favourites ($18–24) are the mesquite-smoked beef and the saltwater duck; equally striking vegetarian dishes prepared on request. Dinner 6.30–11pm; licensed.

Miyazu, Japanese Restaurant in the *Quality Rutherford Hotel*, Trafalgar Square (☎03/548 2299). Predictably expensive but excellent Japanese restaurant; authentic preparation and stylish surroundings make this worth a splurge when nothing but sashimi will do. Licensed.

Pomeroys, 276 Trafalgar St. A quiet and classy restaurant and wine bar, with the Vauxhall motor car crest as its logo (Pomeroy started the company). The food is fresh and attractive, starting with imaginative breakfasts, and moving on to filled focaccia for lunch. Blackboard specials for dinner might include Thai chicken curry, peppered lamb salad or local fish dishes. A full meal will set you back between $12 and $25. Daily 9am–10pm.

Ribbetts, 20 Tahuanui Drive (☎03/548 6911). Despite the tacky frog theme that extends to two dining frogs in the front window, this restaurant serves excellent local produce, prepared with an international slant; main courses cost between $19 and $23. Escape the frogs in the covered, candle-lit courtyard with wooden tables and stone floors. Daily 6.30am–10pm; BYO.

Suter Art Gallery Restaurant, 208 Bridge St. Beautifully placed overlooking Queens Gardens through large windows, this café and wine bar serves Asian-inspired dishes, fresh seafood and meat dishes at fair prices. Try the lamb with sun-dried tomatoes and almond pesto. Lunch daily, dinner Tues–Sat.

Walnut Café, 251 Queen St, Richmond (☎03/544 6187). A classy wine bar and bistro in a conservatory-like setting with modern decor, lots of greenery, glass and white trellising. Lunch and dinner are served (Tues–Sun), with main courses around the $20 mark: their pumpkin puree with fish, coriander and red onions comes highly recommended, as does the Vietnamese calamari; there's also plenty of choice for vegetarians. Service can be slow at busy times.

Drinking, nightlife and entertainment

While most of its neighbours retire early to sip their cocoa, Nelson stays up all night and has a party – most noticeably at various venues on or near Bridge Street. Pubs and **bars** of all sorts dominate, many with **live music** at weekends; check out the Friday edition of the *Nelson Mail* (70¢) to find out **what's on**.

Attached to the Suter Gallery, at 208 Bridge St, is a 159-seat arthouse **cinema**, a superb venue for films you're unlikely to see in the mainstream multiplexes down the road; screenings are generally on Thursday to Sunday evenings (check the local paper for details). The State Cinema Centre, opposite the central post office, shows the latest releases, and movie munchies are available at the Metro Café upstairs.

Apache Street Bar, 145 Bridge St. Live music five nights a week in a sometimes rough, wild west atmosphere. Occasional blues, covers and pop acts offer respite from the staple diet of loud, out of town bands. 6pm happy hour. Daily 6pm–1am.

Buffalo Joe's, 131 Bridge St. Still on the wild west strip, another US-style bar serving large portions of American-influenced food at reasonable prices for lunch and dinner. Slightly incongruous jazz sessions on Sundays. Daily 11am–1am.

Bush Tavern and Pheasant Plucker, 87 Grove St. More along the lines of an English pub, this place has some outdoor seating and good-value bar meals ($3–16) in huge portions. Sun–Thurs 11am–11pm, Fri & Sat 11am–1am.

The Honest Lawyer, 1 Point Rd. A comfortable, country pub with a tree going through the centre and a beer garden overlooking the beach. Pouring Nelson-brewed beers, including Pink Elephant, Bays Ales and Macs, and serving superb pork pies and fresh seafood from a blackboard menu (snacks from $2.50, main meals $10–21). Weekend-evening entertainment is provided by a piano player, Irish folk bands and cover bands. Daily 11am–11pm. Live music Fri, Sat & Sun.

Little Rock Cafe, 165 Bridge St. Piped music and video screens dominate this sports bar adorned with New Zealand icons, including flying ducks and photographs of New Zealand heroes on the walls, industrial-salvage furnishings and 12 tap beers. Very lively, with food ranging from burgers through pizzas to Tex-Mex. Daily 4pm–2.30am.

O'Reilys Bar, in the *Royal Hotel*, 152 Bridge St. More in keeping with the usual spit-and-sawdust Kiwi hotel, complete with obligatory bottle shop. Food ranges from pies, quiche, lasagne, and fish to burgers, with lunch specials for $5. Sky TV entertains you while you eat and drink, augmented by live cover bands and Irish music on Thurs, Fri & Sat.

Urban Jungle Night Club, at the back of *Apache Street Bar*, 145 Bridge St. Outdoor summer-only dance club. No cover charge, good light show, but outshone by the stars. Fri & Sat, 10pm–2am.

Victorian Rose, 281 Trafalgar St. Olde English pub opposite *Chez Eelco*, with a richly deserved good reputation. An excellent atmosphere is enhanced by a wide variety of locally brewed beer, and food at bargain prices ($3.50–11). Jazz sessions on Tuesday evenings. Daily 11am–midnight.

Listings

Automobile Association 45 Halifax St (☎03/548 8339).

Bike rental Fraine Cycles, 105 Bridge St (☎03/548 3877), Greg Traine Cycles, 105 Bridge St (☎03/548 3877) and Stewart Cycle City, 114 Hardy St (☎03/548 1666), all rent out standard bikes for around $10–15 a half-day, mountain bikes for nearer $15–20.

Buses Intercity (☎03/548 1539), Mount Cook Land Line and White Star (book last two through visitor centre) offer daily services to Picton, Blenheim and Christchurch or to Richmond, Motueka, Takaka and Totaranui; Barry's Buses (☎03/546 2300) and Midnight Express (book through visitor centre) run daily to Picton and Blenheim; Abel Tasman National Park Enterprises (☎03/528 7801) and Abel Tasman Express (☎03/528 7014) both offer daily services to the Abel Tasman National Park; Nelson Lakes Transport (☎03/548 6858) and Wadsworth Motors (☎03/522 4248) run to the Nelson Lakes National Park, St Arnaud and Murchison. In addition, the Westcoast Express (☎03/546 6703; $99) is a low-key backpacker bus service that runs to Queenstown and back a couple of times a week.

Campervan rental Kiwi Campervans (☎03/543 2022); Sunrise Holidays (☎03/543 2753).

Camping and outdoor equipment Wet-weather clothing and camping gear can be bought from Rollo's BBQ and Camping Centre, 12 Bridge St, or Basecamp, 295 Trafalgar St.

Car rental Avis (☎03/548 3789), Budget (☎03/548 0169), Hardy Cars (☎03/546 6829), Hertz (☎03/547 2299), National (☎03/546 9232) and Rent-a-dent (☎03/546 9890); daily rates start at $59.

Cruises Nelson Harbour Cruises, Akersten Street boat ramp (☎025/485 617), offer moonlight dinner cruises around Nelson Harbour for $45.

Diving Scuba gear can be rented from Richmond Sportsworld, 213 Queens St, Nelson, Divers World, cnr of London Quay and Auckland St, Picton and Motueka Sportsworld, 201 High St, Motueka.

Medical treatment Nelson Public Hospital, Waimea Road (main entrance on Kawai Street).

Pharmacy Prices Pharmacy, cnr Hardy and Collingwood St, after-hours duty pharmacies are listed in the *Nelson Mail* on Friday.

Post office cnr Trafalgar St & Halifax St, opposite the visitor centre.

Rock climbing Courses at the Airborne Alpine Sports School (☎03/543 2669), range in price from $38 for a half-day to $125 for a full-day course, all amid spectacular scenery.

Scenic flights All based at Nelson Airport, the following companies operate various airborne tours of the region. Scenic Adventure Flights (☎03/547 2378), go as far afield as Golden Bay, with itineraries ranging in price from $60–135. Nelson Aero Club (☎03/547 9643), run a number of half-day tours, starting from $92. Helicopters (NZ) Ltd (☎03/547 5255), offer a variety of trips and landings, as well as drop-offs for mountain biking, for $176–345.

Swimming Riverside public swimming pool (daily 6.30am–6.30pm; $2.20).

Taxis and shuttle services Bluebird Taxis (☎03/546 6681); Nelson Taxis (☎03/548 8225). Bickley Motors (☎03/525 8352), Collingwood Bus Services (☎03/524 8188), Rural Services (☎03/548 6858), Super Shuttle Nelson (☎03/547 5782), Transport for Trampers (☎03/545 1055) and Crown Bus and Shuttle Services (☎03/548 0600) all offer on-demand services.

Tours Agiland conduct tours between Nelson and Motueka (☎03/527 8115); Nelson Art Tour makes an evening visit to Nelson's best gallery (☎03/547 9603); Mail Run Safari (☎03/548 9973) heads to Cable Bay, The Glen, Atawhai Boundary and Dobson Valley. Nelson Day Tours (☎03/545 1055) do the lot – wineries, galleries, beaches, Pupu Springs and Ngarua Cave; while Panoramic Tours (☎03/547 9603) concentrate on parks, gardens, historic sites, beaches, rivers and bushland.

Abel Tasman National Park and around

Abel Tasman National Park is a stunningly beautiful area with an international reputation – resulting in large crowds of trampers, kayakers and day-trippers all through the summer. Don't let this put you off though: within the park are beautiful golden sandy beaches lapped by crystal-clear waters and backed by lush green bushland and forest, all interspersed with granite outcrops and inhabited by a multitude of wildlife.

The goal of most visitors is the **Abel Tasman Track**, combining as it does a picturesque mixture of dense coastal bushwalking with gentle climbs to lookouts and walks across idyllic beaches, but this is also a wonderful place to get into a **kayak** and explore the mercurial coastline and rivermouths.

The park's dearth of settlements means that often all you can hear is birdsong and the gently soporific lapping of the waves on the shore. **Motueka** acts as a gateway and service centre for hungry trampers and locals alike, while the peaceful communities at **Kaiteriteri** and **Marahau**, en route to the park entrance, each have a smattering of places to stay and eat. Marahau, virtually at the park gate, is the base for many kayaking and tramping trips, as well as swimming with seals.

Motueka

Famous for plentiful sunshine, and surrounded by fertile plains, **MOTUEKA**, 47km from Nelson, is really just a jumping-off point for more interesting destinations – most notably the Abel Tasman National Park. The name Motueka means "land of the Weka", a reference to the Maori who lived in the area for over a thousand years, growing kumera in the fertile soil and exploiting the plentiful bird and marine life. However, the arrival of European settlers in 1842 heralded the demise of the community-based traditional Maori lifestyle in the region.

Arrival, information and accommodation

Most of the **bus** companies pick up and drop off on the corner of High Street and Parker Street. Regular **flights** from Wellington land at the grass airfield on College Street, about 3km south of the centre; Motueka Taxis (☎03/528 7900) will take you into town for around $6.50, and will ferry you to the more out-of-the-way places.

The **visitor centre**, 236 High St (Dec–Feb Mon–Fri 8am–5pm; March–Nov Mon–Fri 8am–noon & 1–4.30pm; ☎03/528 6543, fax 528 5663), sells bus tickets, arranges tours and accommodation. Pick up a copy of *Welcome to Motueka* (free), which is well worth getting for the map and descriptions of points of interest. If you're in training for the Abel Tasman Track, there's also a *Motueka District Walks* leaflet ($1), describing many day walks in the surrounding area. The **DOC office**, on the corner of High Street and King Street (Mon–Fri 8am–4.30pm; ☎03/528 9117), is your best bet for information on the national park, and sells tickets for the track. **Camping** and tramping **gear** can be **rented** from Coppins, 255 High St, and Twin Oaks, 25 Parker St.

Accommodation options are limited. *Abel Tasman Motels*, 45 High St (☎03/528 6688; ④), offers six basic but clean units. Other central places are *Motueka Backpackers*, 200 High St (☎03/528 7581; dorms ①, rooms ②), which is in dire need of some sprucing up, and *Twin Oaks*, 25 Parker St (☎03/528 7882; dorms ①, rooms ②, B&B ③), which also rents out camping equipment for the Abel Tasman and Heaphy tracks. The nearest **campsite** is *Fearon's Bush Camp*, 10 Fearon St (☎ & fax 03/528 7189; tent sites $9, cabins & units ②–④), a verdant site with plenty of trees for shelter and clean, well kept facilities just ten minutes' walk from the town centre.

The Town

Motueka is strung along SH60, with quieter streets fanning out from the main highway. The quay and seafront run parallel to SH60 about five minutes' walk down old Wharf Road or along Tudor and Harbour streets.

One of the most interesting diversions in town is provided by a short walk down to the **Motueka Quay**, where the ghost of this once-busy port lingers among the scant remains of the old jetty and store houses. Here too the hulk of the *Janie Seddon* – named after the daughter of Richard Seddon, premier of New Zealand from 1893 until

WALKS AROUND MOTUEKA

A good spot to view Motueka and the surrounding country is the **Mount Arthur Tablelands**, and the various walks that cross them, as detailed in the *Mount Arthur Tablelands Walks* leaflet (available from the visitor centre in Motueka). The numerous tracks in these areas are always quiet, because most visitors are in a mad rush to join the crowds at Abel Tasman.

The starting point for many of the best walks is the Flora car park, on the Graham Valley Road, which leads off SH61 south of Motueka. From here there are commanding views of the lowlands, with Mount Arthur dominating the southern skyline. From the car park you can take a walk (1hr each way) to the **Mount Arthur Hut** (Category 2; $8), from where you can continue on to Mount Arthur in another 3 hours, or tackle the summit of Mount Lodestone (1448m; 2hr).

There are similar tracks up the **Cobb Valley** a little further northwest, starting 28km along the Upper Takaka turn-off; again, leaflets are available from the visitor centre in Motueka. Here too, you can lose yourself in beautiful, forested high country, with panoramic views above the tree line.

his death in 1906 – gracefully decays. Built in Scotland in 1901, then purchased by the New Zealand government and used as a pilot vessel in Wellington, the ship served in both world wars, patrolling the waters of Cook Strait and Wellington Harbour. In 1946 she was bought by the Motueka Trawling Company, but local regulations outlawing steam-powered craft made her redundant, and she was ignominiously beached near the old wharf in 1955.

The tiny **Motueka Museum** (Mon–Fri 10am–3pm, Sat & Sun 10am–1pm; $2), delves into the area's history through copious black-and-white photographs and a few Maori artefacts relating to the area, as well as the *94 Motueka Carvings*, four skilfully carved friezes depicting the livelihoods that have traditionally sustained Tasman Bay.

Eating and drinking

Despite its modest size, Motueka has an abundance of restaurants, cafés and bars, catering to the enthusiastic appetites of fresh-air freaks.

Annabelle's Café, in the Museum Building, High St. Strong coffee, light meals (bacon and eggs) and snacks – a simple formula, but it hits the spot. Mon–Fri 9am–4pm, Sat & Sun 10am–2pm.

The Grain and Grape, 218 High St. A pub/café serving brunch and light meals from 11am–2pm, and dinner from 5.30–10pm. This is the place to satisfy a craving for steak and chips.

Hot Mama's, 105 High St. A brightly hued interior, patio garden and simple furniture create an attractive and intimate ambience in which to enjoy a wide range of Italian, Spanish, French and Mexican-influenced food ($6–18), great coffee – and occasional appearances by touring New Zealand folk, jazz, acoustic and rock acts. Daily 8am–late; licensed & BYO.

The Hop Inn, High St. A café and Motueka's only nightclub cohabit in the Gothic setting of a former church. Food is good quality, with imaginative French and Italian touches at reasonable prices ($6–15). Lunch & dinner daily; licensed.

Jacaranda Park Café and Nursery, 3km southwest of town, just off College St (☎03/528 7777). Commanding views over the countryside and a lovely garden and nursery, provide a suitable backdrop for the exquisite food served at this café-restaurant. Specials might include home-baked flans or chicken apricot roulades ($8–25), there is an extensive wine list and the surroundings and views at sunset make for a memorable evening. Daily 10am–3pm & 6–10pm; bookings advised for dinner.

Theatre Café, 94 High St. This takeaway pizza place is run by an eccentric Dutchman with an infinite variety of chat-up lines; his other weakness – for fine pizzas – is more easily forgiven. His are the best pizzas in Tasman Bay ($15–28). Evenings only; closed June–Aug.

Wholegrain Bakery, Buddens Arcade, High St. The bread here is a must for trampers: superbly baked rye and sourdough bread will last you all along the track (7–10 days), and is made from a nutritious combination of grains, pulses, honey and a starter culture. As well as other breads, there's also a wide variety of filled rolls and savouries. Mon–Fri 8am–5pm, Sat 9am–2pm.

Kaiteriteri

Overlooking Tasman Bay on the beach road as it heads towards the southern end of the Abel Tasman National Park is the tiny resort town of **KAITERITERI**, some 13km from Motueka, just off SH60. There are few **places to stay**, unless you bring a tent, and even fewer places to eat. One of the best for both is the *Kimi Ora Holiday and Health Resort*, a hillside complex on Martin Farm Road, signposted from the beach road (☎03/527/8027, fax 527 8134; ③–⑥, depending on season). Set in a pine forest with views of the bay, this is a comfortable place to stay, or to indulge in the various fitness or therapy sessions they run. The *Kimi Ora Café*, in the resort's comfortable, wood-lined dining room, serves healthy, vegetarian **lunches** and **dinners**. All starters are $6, mains $15, and desserts $6, or you can go the whole hog for $25, rounded off by a range of coffees, teas and juices. Next to the beach is the *Kaiteriteri Motor Camp* (☎03/527 8010, fax 527 8031; tent sites $9, cabins ②), and, slightly further west towards the park, is the *Toslesse Coastal Motel*, on Rowlong Road, Little Kaiteriteri (☎03/527 8063; ⑤–⑥), ten minutes' drive along the beach road, with beautiful views of the area and spacious comfortable units.

Marahau

About 6km further long the beach road from Kaiteriteri, **MARAHAU** is poised right at the southern entrance to the Abel Tasman National Park and is more tourist-orientated, acting as the base for many operators of tours into the park.

The single road that runs through town peters out at the park entrance, where a dirt track, Harvey Road, swerves left to a couple of **places to stay**: *The Barn* (☎03/527 8043; tent sites $10, dorms ①, rooms ②) offers camping and backpacker accommodation, plus secure parking, a mere minute's walk from the park entrance; just beyond, *Old MacDonald's Farm* (☎03/527 8288, fax 527 8289; tent sites $10, dorms ①, rooms ④) is a large and tranquil family-run campsite and farmstay, where you share the grounds with llamas, alpacas and a host of other animals; secure parking and gear storage is also available. The left turn before Harvey Road is the Marahau Valley Road, where, about 200m along, *Abel Tasman Stables* (☎03/527 8181) run **horse treks** into the surrounding area and the fringes of the national park ($15 an hour, $75 per day); they also offer comfortable **B&B** accommodation (④).

The **park entrance** is marked by an unmanned DOC office with an intentions book. Next to the centre is the only **café** in the area, *Park Café* (Oct–April daily 7.30am–10pm; licensed), which serves fine, wholesome food and excellent coffee to an appreciative crowd; try the beef schnitzel or the seafood fettucine, or check out the blackboard for specials. From here, a long boardwalk across marshland leads into the national park.

Abel Tasman National Park

The **Abel Tasman National Park** covers a relatively small area, its boundaries running along the coast from Marahau, about 60km from Nelson, north up to Wainui Bay at the eastern end of Golden Bay, and inland to cover parts of Takaka Hill. Road **access** can only be gained from these three areas; otherwise, you can get here by boat via the many bays or by plane. The main **bases** for forays into the coastal areas of the park are Motueka, Kaiteriteri and Marahau, spread along the road that leads to the park's **southern entrance**, while the rugged inland is best explored from Takaka (see p.451) – or you can stay at *Awaroa Lodge* in the heart of the park and explore in comfort. The

northern entrance to the park is marked by **Totaranui** – little more than a few accommodation options and a lovely beach, from where some water-taxi operators head into the park.

With a range of habitats from sea level to 1000m, Abel Tasman is full of rich and varied **plant life**. In the damp and torpid gullies, shrubs dominate, but elsewhere several species of beech tree hold sway. Kanuka tolerates the wild and windy areas and manuka thrives on land that has been subject to repeated burnings – as this has, at the hands of both Maori and European settlers. At **higher altitudes**, there is a proliferation of silver and red beech mixed with rata, miro and totara. **Birds** you might encounter include tui, native pigeons, bellbirds (their presence betrayed by their distinctive call) and fantails that flutter close by, feeding off the insects you disturb as you walk through the bush. The fresh waterways burbling through the park are invariably the colour of tea (but not drinkable – see below), due to tannin leached from the soil.

The **Maori** presence here dates from about 1500, when for some 500 years, seasonal encampments along this coast and some permanent settlements flourished around the Awaroa Rivermouth. The arrival of **European explorers** was less auspicious: in 1642, **Abel Tasman** anchored his two ships near Wainui in Golden Bay and lost four men in a fight with the Ngati Tumatakokiri; and in 1827, Frenchman **Dumont d'Urville** explored the area between Marahau and Torrent Bay, but it was not for another 23 years that European settlement began in earnest. The settlers chopped, quarried, burned and cleared until nothing was left but gorse and bracken. Happily, few signs of their invasion remain and the vegetation has vigorously regenerated over the years. Named after the first European explorer to experience its shores, the Abel Tasman National Park was **gazetted** in 1942, following the tireless campaigning of one **Perrine Moncrieff**, a determined woman by all accounts. The sanctity of the park and its wildlife is preserved offshore by the **Tonga Island Marine Reserve**, created in 1993 and famous for its fur seal colony, seabirds and plentiful fish.

> The organism that causes **giardia** is present **in the water** supply of the Abel Tasman National Park and many other streams in this area. Basics, p.18, outlines precautions you should take to minimize the risk of infection.

Getting to the park – and information

There are a number of **buses** that run **from Nelson** and **Picton** to the park. These include the big three, InterCity, Mount Cook Landline and White Star, plus Abel Tasman National Park Enterprises (☎03/528 8850) and Abel Tasman Express (☎03/528 7014), both of which leave Nelson at 7.30am daily for Kaiteriteri, Marahau or Totoranui, via Motueka, connecting with launch services deeper into the park. Book-a-Bus (☎03/525 9864) run daily **from Takaka** to Pohara, where they meet the *Spirit of Golden Bay* water taxi into the park, before continuing to Totaranui. From harbours that fringe the park, **water taxis** can take you to remoter areas of the park (for details, see "Trailhead Transport" on p.449).

The **DOC offices** at Nelson, Motueka and Takaka will all book boats, kayaks, track tickets, transport and accommodation; there are also **unmanned** DOC **offices** at the Marahau and Totoranui **park entrances**, with general information about the park, tide times and safety precautions – including intentions books you should fill in before entering and after leaving the park.

Exploring the park

Most people are keen to stick to the park's **coastline**, with its long golden beaches, clear water and spectacular outcrops, and the constant temptation to snorkel in some of

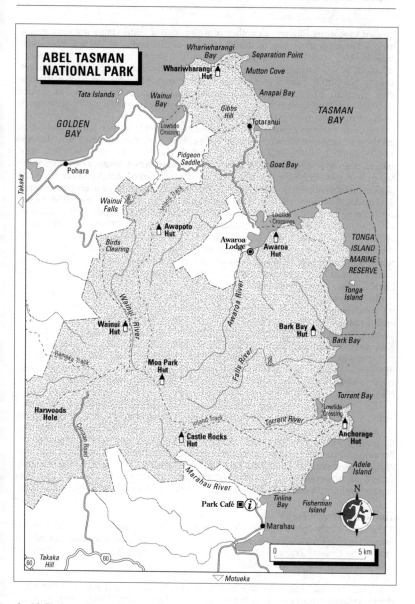

ABEL TASMAN NATIONAL PARK

the idyllic bays. **Tramping** is one of the most popular ways of getting to grips with the park, and the Coastal Track, in particular, provides easy access to a wilderness area of great beauty and varity (see "The Abel Tasman Track" on p.448 for details).

If you have a few days to spare, a **stay** at the *Awaroa Lodge* (☎03/528 8758; dorms ①, units ⑥) is one of the most relaxing ways of experiencing the splendours of the park.

Nestled in Awaroa Bay are a number of well-designed comfortable units, as well as backpacker accommodation (bedding $4 extra) with an outdoor kitchen. The Lodge café (daily 7.30am–8pm) serves all meals in a stylish and relaxed atmosphere, enhanced by an enormous fireplace and unusual wooden furniture. The lodge is accessible by road from Takaka (see p.451), by plane from Motueka and Nelson, by boat from Marahau, Kaiteriteri and Tarakohe Harbour – and, of course, on foot via the Coastal Track. The surroundings are beautiful and peaceful and the owner occasionally lays on barge trips ($5) up the river for guests.

The perfect way to explore the park's remoter shores is by **sea kayak**, and two of the most reliable operators are conveniently close together at Marahau. Abel Tasman Kayaks (☎03/527 8022) run a series of guided trips from one day ($85) to a fully-catered four dayer ($590), while the Ocean River Adventure Company (☎03/527 8266) has guided trips that range from one to five days, the most popular being a day-trip ($85, including barbecue) with a leisurely ride back by means of a sail erected between the kayaks. On the excellent **Paddle and Walk** trip (Tues, Thurs & Sat; $198, including camping and bunkroom accommodation but no meals) you kayak north to camp on a beach, then paddle on to Tonga Island Marine Reserve and further up the coast, before a 45-minute walk to *Awaroa Lodge* where you stay overnight; in the morning, you can walk out whichever way you like, or pick up a water taxi. Both outfits also offer **rental kayaks** to groups of two or more ($90 per person for 2 days, $165 for 5 days). Kayakers must be experienced, water-confident and competent campers; Abel Tasman Kayaks insist on a full day's safety briefing ($20).

Abel Tasman Tours (☎03/528 7497) and Abel Tasman Travel (☎03/528 7801) both offer **sightseeing** trips, scenic **cruises** and guided walks, while **Hydrofoil, Kayak and Cruise** (Dec–March, 9am; 7hr; $90; ☎03/528 7801) offer a hydrofoil ride to Torrent Bay from Kaiteriteri, followed by four hours' kayaking and a launch back to Kaiteriteri, Nelson and Matueka bus connections by arrangement. Approaching the park from its northern end, the motorized catamaran *Spirit of Golden Bay* (☎03/525 9135) runs a number of trips from Tarakohe Harbour; a favourite is the **evening cruise** ($25), with a lesson in the underrated art of scallop catching and a sumptuous barbecue.

This is the best place in New Zealand to **swim with seals**, and the *Abel Tasman Seal Swim*, Marahau (Oct–April, 8.30am &12.30pm; 3hr; book at least 5 days ahead, ☎ & fax 03/527 8136, free-call 0800/527 8136), provides an unforgettable experience. Swimming with seals can be a lot more fun than swimming with dolphins simply because seals are often more curious and, having greater manoeuvrability, are capable of tying a mere human in knots in no time. Underwater visibility in the area is usually superb, and the operators try to minimize the impact on the seals by insisting that seals come to swim with you rather than you just splashing about among them.

The Abel Tasman Track

Although, strictly speaking, the Abel Tasman Track encompasess both the tremendously popular **Coastal Track** and the much less crowded and more arduous **Inland Track**, the Coastal Track is almost universally known simply as the **Abel Tasman Track**. Part of the attraction of this coastal route is that it is the **easiest** of New Zealand's Great Walks, and lack of fitness is no impediment: the track is clear and easy to follow, entry and exit to the beach sections clearly marked and you are never more than four hours from a hut. All of this has made the Abel Tasman Track one of the **most popular** in the country and from December to the end February there is an endless stream of hikers racing to get to the best bunks and campsites. It is possible in the near future that the DOC will **limit the numbers** on the track at any one time, as they have with the Milford Track, which will make it more expensive but possibly more enjoyable.

The **route** traverses broad golden beaches lapped by emerald waters, punctuated by granite pillars silhouetted against the horizon and zig-zagging gentle climbs through tiny stream valleys. As well as the two major tracks, there are a number of shorter **day walks** with access by road or from the major tracks; leaflets (50¢–$1) on all of these are available at local visitor centres.

ACCESS AND ACCOMMODATION

To walk the tracks and stay in the DOC huts or at the campsites in the national park, you must buy a **track pass** and **hut tickets** for the days you will be staying in the national park. These are available from DOC offices, visitor centres, some hostels and travel agents; hut tickets do not guarantee you a bunk and when the track is busy you may feel the need to hurry in order to get one.

Along the **Coastal Track**, the four **DOC huts** (all Category 2; $8) are spaced around four hours' walk apart, and have heating, showers and toilets, but no cooking facilities so you have to carry a stove. Bunks go on a first-come, first-served basis, and you need a sleeping bag; after all the bunks have gone you are consigned to the floor. The other option is camping: there are 21 designated **campsites** ($4) along the coastal route either on or near the beaches or the DOC huts (whose facilities you can use); all sites have a water supply and toilets and you won't have to rush to get a bunk, but you will be carrying more gear. Finally, for a treat midway along the track, book ahead at the *Awaroa Lodge* (see p.445).

Camping is not permitted on the **Inland Track**, but there are four backcountry huts ($4) spaced no more than five hours' walk apart, and there is rarely competition for beds. Water supplies and toilets are provided, but you'll need take a cooking stove.

TRAILHEAD TRANSPORT

The Coastal and Inland tracks share the same starting and finishing points, running between **Marahau** in the south and **Totaranui** or **Wainui** in the north, both of which are well served by transport.

Buses run to the Marahau or Totaranui entrances to the park from Nelson, Motueka and Takaka (see "Getting to the park" on p.446 for details). Several **water taxis** offer drop-off and pick-up services to and from Totaranui for trampers and casual walkers; most also call at the bays en route, catering for those who don't want to walk the whole track. **From Kaiteriterei**, Abel Tasman Travel (☎03/528 7801) run motorized catamarans: one-way fares are Torrent Bay $17, Bark Bay $20, Tonga Bay $23, and Totaranui or Awaroa Bay $28. **From Marahau** to Totaranui, choose between the zippy Abel Tasman Seafaris Aqua Taxi (daily 9am & 2pm; ☎03/527 8083) and the Abel Tasman Water Taxi (daily 8.30am, sometimes also at 12.30pm; ☎03/527 8136 & 0800/527 8136); both charge one-way fares of about $15 to Torrent Bay, $18 to Bark Bay, $20 to Tonga, $25 to Awaroa Bay and $28 to Totaranui. Leaving **from Tarakohe Harbour**, *Spirit of Golden Bay* (daily 9am; ☎03/525 9135) calls at Mutton Cove ($10), Totaranui ($15), Awaroa Bay ($20), Bark Bay ($30), Kaiteriteri ($45) and Nelson ($55); it will also pick up from each of these destinations and drop you back in Golden Bay.

THE COASTAL TRACK

Most trampers walk the **Coastal Track** (51km; 2–5 days) from south to north, starting from Marahau and being picked up at the other end by bus or boat; you can also **kayak** part of the way (see p.448). Before you set off, in addition to arranging your pick-up, you should confirm the **tide times**, since the Awaroa Inlet and Torrent Bay crossings are tide-dependent; there is no alternative at Awaroa and the inland diversion at Torrent Bay adds at least one hour to the walk.

From **Marahau to Anchorage Hut** (11.5km; 4hr), the track follows a wooden causeway crosses the Marahau estuary to the open country around Tinline Bay before rounding a point overlooking Fisherman and Adele islands just off the coast. As the track winds in and out of gullies, the surroundings are obscured by beech forest and tall kanuka trees until you emerge into Anchorage Bay, with its hut and campsite. On the second day, **Anchorage Bay to Bark Bay Hut** (9.5km; 3hr), you have to cross Torrent Bay at low tide, before climbing out of the bay through pine trees and meandering through valleys and a gorgeous inlet before reaching the Falls Rivermouth and the Bark Bay hut, beside the Bark Bay estuary. Day three is a gentle stroll from **Bark Bay Hut to Awaroa Hut** (11.5km; 4hr), overlooking the Tonga Marine Reserve and Tonga Island. The track climbs to the Tonga Saddle before descending to the Awaroa Inlet and the hut, with a campsite alongside; *Awaroa Lodge* is also within easy walking distance.

From **Awaroa Hut**, you must cross the Awaroa estuary (2hr either side of low tide) and head along Goat Bay and up to a lookout above Skinner Point before reaching **Totaranui** (5.5km; 1hr 30min), where there is an extensive campsite, or you can press on over and around rocky headlands as far as Mutton Cove, where the track leaves the coast and climbs to another saddle before descending to **Whariwharangi Hut** (7.5km; 2hr) and campsite. From here it's possible to take a short hike to **Separation Point**, where there is a fur seal colony and a good lookout, or to tackle the strenuous climb up **Gibbs Hill** for even better views. The last day, **from Whariwharangi Hut to Wainui** (5.5km; 1hr 30min), involves crossing Wainui Bay (2hr either side of low tide) or following the road around the bay. If you follow the road, you can also take in the short climb up to the Wainui Falls which heads off the road at the base of Wainui Bay.

THE INLAND TRACK

The considerably less popular **Inland Track** (42km; 3–5 days), is a much more strenuous walk, and should only be attempted by well-equipped and moderately fit trampers. The route climbs from sea level to **Evans Ridge** past many granite outcrops and views of the coast: highlights include the Pigeon Saddle, the moorlands of Moa Park and the moon-like Canaan landscape; you can also link up with the Rameka Track on Takaka Hill and the Harwood's Hole Track (see p.451) along the way.

Starting the walk **from Marahau** in the south, the Inland Track splits away from the Coastal Track at Tinline Bay, following a steady climb through regenerating forest to the **Castle Rocks Hut** (11.5km; 4hr 30min), which is perched near rocky outcrops and has great views of the Marahau Valley and Tasman Bay. From **Castle Rocks to Moa Park Hut** (3.5km; 2hr), is a steeper climb, followed by an undulating section over tussock. The walk from **Moa Park to the Pigeon Saddle** (14.5km; 6–7hr) involves walking along Evans Ridge and descending to the **Awapoto Hut**, while the last day is an easy stroll to **Wainui** (6km; 2hr 15min), with only a short climb to the summit of Gibbs Hill, from where you get some of the most expansive views across the park.

Takaka Hill

From Motueka, SH60 climbs **Takaka Hill**, providing the only **road access to Golden Bay** – and glorious views of the seascape from Nelson north to D'Urville Island. Skirting the inland border of the Abel Tasman National Park, it is possible to explore the hill's fascinating geology from either the Inland Track or from the highway.

The first diversion off SH60, 20km out of Motueka, are the **Ngarua Caves** (Sept–June daily 10am–4pm, guided tours only; 35min; $8), reached along a short bumpy track. A celebration of tackiness, the caves contain numerous examples of stalactites and stalagmites, including some with musical accompaniments and grand illuminated formations such as the Wedding Cathedral. Tour guides also point out bones from moas and regale you with an informative commentary on the caves' history and geology.

A kilometre or so further along SH60 from the caves turn off is the entrance to the unsealed 12-kilometre Canaan Road, at the end of which is the starting point of the forty-minute walk to **Harwoods Hole**, a huge vertical shaft 183m deep (don't get too close to the edge), and a fantastic place to explore and survey the surroundings. The walk begins in an enchanted forest landscape, then follows a dry rock-strewn riverbed through startling country before reaching a viewpoint atop the cliff walls of Gorge Creek, where forests, coastline and sea are all laid out before you. Back on the Canaan Road, you can join the clearly signposted **Rameka Track** (5km; 3hr one-way) for more punishment. This follows one of the earliest surveyed routes into the Takaka Valley, from Canaan to central Takaka, with superb views of the granite outcrops and the surrounding country.

A fine base for your explorations of Takaka Hill is *Marble Park Homestay* (✆03/528 8061; ④–⑤; dinner by arrangement, $25), on the right-hand side of SH60 as you head north, which has twin and double **rooms** in a smart house close to the Ngarua Caves and Harwoods Hole, with stunning walks and views close by.

From here, SH60 twists its way across the mountain before descending in a series of steep, tight switchbacks that eventually straighten out as you roll down into Golden Bay.

Golden Bay

Occupying the northwestern tip of the South Island, **GOLDEN BAY** curves gracefully from the northern fringes of the Abel Tasman National Park to the encircling arm of **Farewell Spit**, all backed by the magnificence of the Kahurangi National Park. A relatively flat area hemmed in by towering mountains on three sides and with waves lapping at its exposed fourth side, its inaccessibility has kept it pristine. The coastline is washed by clear, sparkling water, creating excellent conditions for windsurfing, while its hinterland is home to the country's largest springs, **Pupu Springs**, as well as a number of other curious geological phenomena.

Historically, the bay was also the point where Abel Tasman struck land, guaranteeing his place in history as the first European to encounter the land of New Zealand and the local Maori. Today's bayside communities are small, their growth hindered by **isolation** – the road over Takaka Hill is twisting and treacherous and there is no access from the West Coast, save for a long footslog on the Heaphy Track. This perhaps explains their air of **independence**, self-reliance and stoic forbearance, shot through with an alternative-lifestyle thread and enhanced by a number of artistic endeavours of real merit. Sunny, beautiful and full of fascinating sights, Golden Bay is well worth a few days of your time.

Takaka and around

The small town of **TAKAKA** is situated on SH60, cradled by the sweep of the bay. East of the town and linked to it by road are **Pohara Beach**, where there's safe swimming, and Tarakohe Harbour and Wainui Bay, both providing access to the northern end of the Abel Tasman National Park (see p.445). South of Takaka, **Pupu Springs** emerge from their underground lair, while to the north yawns a considerable stretch of beautiful bay, running parallel to SH60 as it rolls into Collingwood.

Arrival and information

Flights from Nelson and Wellington arrive at the **airport**, 5km from town; Book-a-Bus (✆03/525 9864) run a shuttle service into the centre of Takaka. Most **bus** companies drop off outside the DOC office (see p.452), on Commercial Street, the main thoroughfare. Local shuttle buses will get you to most of the major destinations in Golden Bay, but you can also rent cars or bikes (see "Listings", p.454).

On Willow Street, just south of the main part of town, the **visitor centre** (daily 9am–5pm; ☎03/525 9136) acts as a booking centre for the national parks and tracks, and stocks a number of leaflets detailing local attractions, including a useful one on the Pupu Springs, and walks. The **DOC office**, 49 Commercial St (Mon–Fri 9am–5pm; ☎03/525 9061) also provides hut tickets, leaflets, maps and sound advice.

Accommodation

Golden Bay is a popular holiday spot with both Kiwis and foreign visitors; as a result there is a lot of good quality accommodation in and around Takaka.

Anatoki Lodge Motels, 87 Commercial St (☎03/525 8047). Modern, fully self-contained units close to the centre of town, with great service and helpful staff. ④–⑤.

Elliots Garden, Tukurua, signposted off SH60 17km north of Takaka (☎03/525 9275). One fully self-contained unit overlooking a lovely garden and the sea, with easy beach access. ⑤.

Golden Bay Motel, 132 Commercial St (☎03/525 9428, fax 525 8362). A pretty, well kept little motel with off-street parking and spacious rooms. ④–⑤.

Ka Awetea, East Takaka Rd, 5km south of Takaka (☎03/525 9630). Women-only backpacker-style accommodation and tent sites ($8) in a relaxing setting. Dorms ①, rooms ②.

Marina Motel, Pohara Beach, 10km east (☎03/525 9620, fax 525 8636). Motel units with full cooking facilities, near a safe swimming beach, with an on-site bar and restaurant. ③–④.

Rose Cottage Motel and Homestay, on SH60, 5km from Takaka heading towards Takaka Hill (☎03/525 9048). Three beautifully maintained motel units set in a large, lovingly tended garden, plus a homestay option, all with friendly and helpful hosts. ④–⑤.

Sans Souci Inn, Richmond Rd, Pohara Beach, 10km east (☎03/525 8663). A most unusual and endearing B&B in an architecturally unique building. Reflecting the Mediterranean atmosphere of the bay, the inn has been constructed using mudbricks, with sods as the roofing material and distinctive floor tiles. In keeping with the owners' environmental ethos, the toilets are self-composting and occupy a stunning block that effortlessly combines sanitation and horticulture. Breakfast costs $6.50–12, dinner $20 by arrangment. ④.

Shambhala, Onekaka,16km north on SH60 (☎03/525 8463). Near the infamous *Mussel Inn* (pick-up can arranged), is this relaxed, alternative lifestyle accommodation. Dorms are in the main house, or there are spacious twin and double rooms with good views in a separate block, complete with a solar-heated shower. There is easy beach access and free use of boats, so you can go out and gather your own mussels, or stay home and munch on a lentil pie or a muffin. The only drawbacks are a small kitchen and a $5 charge for bed linen. Dorms ①, rooms ②.

Tukurua Beachfront Lodge, off SH60, about 18km north (☎ & fax 03/525 8644). A lovely house with manicured gardens and swimming pool that offers extremely comfortable rooms, delicious breakfasts, dinner by arrangement ($35), beach access, and is run by friendly and informative people. All in all, a delightful place to kick back for a few days. ⑥.

The Town and around

Despite being the bay's largest settlement, the town itself is a low and architecturally barren affair where three roads, SH60 (Commercial Street as it passes through town), Motupipi Road and Meihana Street, form a triangle.

Close to the centre of town on Commercial Street is the restored old post office (1899), which now houses the **Golden Bay Gallery** (daily 10am–4pm; $1), showing some fairly ordinary paintings and some excellent pottery and woodcraft, all by local artists. The adjacent **Golden Bay Museum** (same hours & admission) contains the usual mish-mash of bits and bobs rooted out of attics or accumulated during travels abroad (usually to wars), along with a small collection of Maori artefacts and informative displays on Abel Tasman and Captain Cook.

Of all the cave trips in the area, the most charming and relaxed is to be had at the **Rawhiti Caves** (tours on demand; 3hr; $12; ☎03/525 9061), reached via a ten-minute drive along Motupipi Road and over the Motupipi Bridge towards Pohara Beach and then a fifty-minute walk from the car park. The pendulous stalactites that hang from the caves' wide mouth are stained by the earth and rain to hues of dirty brown, brightened by the rich green of the moss that covers some of them. Fortified by a cup of tea, you descend into the caves to see the fascinating formations, including transparent stone straws full of water, a discarded billy can now encased in rock deposited from the dripping ceiling and rock pools containing perfectly round stone "marbles".

Where Motupipi Road meets the Clifton Crossroads, turn right to reach the wonderful **Grove Scenic Reserve** (unrestricted access; free), a mystical place in greygreen that could have been transplanted straight from the Lord of the Rings novels or Arthurian legend, where massive rata trees sprout from odd and deformed limestone outcrops. A ten-minute walk from the car park takes you to a narrow slot between two enormous vertical cliffs where a lookout reveals the flat expanse leading to the beaches of Pohara – and the real world.

Back on the Pohara Road, heading west towards the scattered houses of Pohara Beach and Wainui Bay, about 9km from the Clifton Crossroads, you'll see signs for the unsealed 500-metre road to **Wainui Falls**. The falls themselves are a forty-minute return walk from the road, heading up through dense bush and criss-crossing the river on several bridges, with the roar of the falls growing ever louder. Nikau palms shade the banks of the river, and a curtain of spray swathes the rather lovely falls – a great place to just sit and dream.

About five minutes' drive (5km) out of Takaka on SH60 towards Collingwood is **Pupu Springs Scenic Reserve** (unrestricted access; free), New Zealand's largest freshwater springs set in a reserve of old gold workings, regenerating forest and a vestige of mature forest. There are at least sixteen springs in Pupu, with two major vents in the main springs, one major and several minor vents at Dancing Sands (where the sands, pushed by the surging water, literally dance), and about twelve springs in the Fish Creek. The water that emerges from the main springs is cold and the visibility excellent, making for superb viewing of the rich variety of brightly coloured plants beneath the surface – which can be seen by means of a reverse periscope on one of the boardwalks.

Eating

There's a surprising number of places to eat in Takaka, most clustered on Commercial Street. If you're self-catering though, don't miss the *Motupipi Butchery*, at the junction of Glenview Road and the Takaka East Road, about 3km from the town centre (Mon–Fri 8am–6pm, Sat 9am–1pm), which sells the best pork, beef, and beef and garlic sausages in the whole South Island; it is, quite simply, a place of myth and legend.

Junction Hotel, 15 Commercial St. A good, cheap feed ($4–15), but be warned the kitchen tends to close early. Lunch & dinner Mon–Sat, lunch only on Sun.

Milliways, 90 Commercial St. A café/wine bar that serves fantastic lunches and dinners at realistic prices ($25 for a full meal) in charming surroundings. Try the spiced venison and pork sausage or Swahili turkey and pumpkin leaf curry, but leave room for the desserts, which are out of this world.

Mussel Inn, just off SH60, 16km north of Takaka. Do not miss this place – whether you want to eat, enjoy wine or ale (they brew their own), sit and read, play chess or soak up the lively atmosphere of a live band. The purpose-built wooden building is adorned with bits of local art and some clumpy but comfortable wooden furniture. You can always get a simple, fresh and wholesome meal; try a plate of the local mussels for around $10. Daily 10am–midnight.

Whole Meal Café, in the arcade on Commercial St, opposite the supermarket. A Swiss baker churns out superb bread, pizzas and pastries, all served with a variety of colourful and healthy salads, delicious cakes and excellent coffee. Well worth stopping in to look at the blackboard specials, although the regular menu is a little on the pricey side. In the evenings there is sometimes live music. Daily 9am–9pm; licensed.

Listings

Airlines Takaka Valley Air Services, 38 Motupipi St (☎03/525 8613 & 0800/501 901) fly direct to Golden Bay from Nelson ($40 one-way) and Wellington ($135).

Bike rental Quiet Revolution, 7 Commercial St (☎03/525 9555) rent out mountain bikes for $30 a day.

Buses Book-a-Bus, 49 Commercial St (☎03/525 9864, fax 525 8180) run airport buses, plus daily services via Pohara to Tarakohe, connecting with the Spirit of Golden Bay (see below), before continuing on to Totaranui and Motueka (for connections on to Nelson). They also run twice weekly to Christchurch, to Collingwood and to the Heaphy Track by arrangement. Collingwood Services Buses, 98 Commercial St (☎03/524 8188) also serve Collingwood.

Car rental VRLA Rentals, cnr Buxton Lane & Motupipi St (☎03/525 9224).

Tours Quiet Revolution, 7 Commercial St (☎03/525 9555) run mountain-biking day-trips to Takaka Hill and around the historic Aorere Goldfields ($30–55); *Spirit of Golden Bay* (☎03/525 9135) runs day-cruises from Tarakohe Harbour.

Water taxis The fast catamaran *Spirit of Golden Bay* (☎03/525 9135) runs between Tarakohe Harbour and Nelson, dropping off and picking up by arrangement (fares in the range of $10–55).

Collingwood and around

As you might expect from somewhere that marks the end of the road for SH60, **COLLINGWOOD** is a quiet kind of a town, with one store, a café, a friendly pub, a petrol station and a tiny museum. However, its proximity to the Heaphy Track, which traverses Kahurangi National Park (see p.457), and to the wilderness of Farewell Spit, places it firmly on the tourist circuit.

The Town

Over the years, many of the town's older wooden edifices have been burned down, leaving only a few buildings of note on Tasman Street, where the small **Collingwood Museum** (daily 1–4pm; $2) is devoted to the history of the early settlers and the impact of gold mining on the area. The museum also contains exhibits relating to Collingwood's ambitions to be the capital of New Zealand, with plans of the proposed streets and submissions as to why this tiny community, literally at the end of the line, should be the country's principal city.

Collingwood's surroundings, however, offer endless opprtunities for meandering around country galleries and winding roads. Eight kilometres southeast on SH60, winding behind Para Para Beach, is Lookout Road, where you'll find **Decorator Pots** (Dec–April daily 10am–5pm), a gallery and potters' studio situated in manicured gardens with great views. The gallery section displays conservative but high-quality stoneware, porcelain and burnished carved blackware. About 2km further north on SH60, just after the Para Para Estuary, are signs to **Estuary Arts** (Dec–April daily 10am–5pm). Run by Rosie Little and Bruce Hamlin, this is one of the best pottery galleries in the bay, with superb brightly coloured tableware of striking and bold design, some evocative paintings and a great panorama across the bay. Back on SH60, and a couple of kilometres further away from Collingwood, the Tukurua Road heads to the **Tukurua Gallery** (Dec–April daily 10am–5pm), 150m after the turn-off. The gallery contains remarkable tree sculptures hewn by Neil Baker, which spill over in to the grounds, and the delicate, colour-imbued leadlight work of Glenda Walker.

Southwest of Collingwood, on the road to Rockville and the Heaphy Track, is the **Eckert Art Works** (Dec–April daily 10am–6pm), 7km from the centre of town. Here Tim Eckert creates his elemental sculptures, tiles and furniture for the kitchen and garden in natural earthy colours. Eckert derives his inspiration from the twisted and tortured limestone formations that are such a feature of the local landscape. Nearer Rockville is a striking example: two plinths of limestone on either side of the road support bulbous overhangs – and have been dubbed the **Devils Boots** for their resemblance to two feet protruding from the ground.

North to Wharariki Beach

Travelling the 29km to Farewell Spit on SH60, take a detour west to the distinctive **Wharariki Beach**. A twenty-minute walk from the car park at the road end, the beach provides a startling introduction to the rigours of the West Coast: exposed to the harsh winds and waves, Wharariki is backed by striking cliffs gouged with caves. Rock bridges and towering arches are stranded just offshore, while deep dunes have blocked rivermouths, forming briny lakes and islands where fur seals and birds have made a home. The beach is a superb place to swim, explore, watch seals in the rock pools at half-tide and lounge around. Head back towards the car park and join the northeasterly cliff path, which leads after 3km to the **Pillar Point Lighthouse**, perched on the shoulder of the spit, with far-reaching views down the West Coast and over the bay.

Farewell Spit

Farewell Spit stretches out to the very tip of the South Island, with access through Puponga Farm Park, 29km from Collingwood – although the only way you can explore the spit up close and personal is with one of the two licensed tour operators (see box above). The 25km-long spit is a **nature reserve** of international importance, providing a variety of habitats for birds: saltmarsh, open mudflat, freshwater and brackish lakes and bare dunes. Formed by debris sluiced out of West Coast rivers in flood and then carried by coastal currents, an uninterrupted desert of sand inches its way into the ocean and curls back towards Golden Bay, whose shores capture much of the wind-blown sand from the spit's exposed side.

The Farewell Spit **visitor centre**, 26km north of Collingwood (daily 9am–6pm; ☎ & fax 03/524 8454), is in the Puponga Farm Park, on a hill overlooking the spit. The centre has displays and some evocative photographs that recount the history of the area and the sad story of a mass whale-stranding in 1991, and has leaflets on walking tracks. You can also enjoy the spit from a distance in the viewing room (with binoculars), or the **café**, which offers simple meals and snacks – and more views of the spit.

Clustered around the base of the spit is a complex of middens over 50m wide and running for almost 1km, composed mostly of burned shell and evidencing **Maori settlement** over a period of at least 700 years. Puponga Point was the site of a defended pa, with the ditches and house terraces clearly visible, and at Whau Creek there are deep pits and extensive midden spilling down to the stream, indicating a *kainga*, or undefended living area. In 1846 explorer Charles Heaphy reported seeing *waka* (Maori canoes) heading to the ocean beach and down the West Coast, and in 1867 Edmund Davidson collected two *waka*, adorned with elaborate artistic designs, now in the Nelson Provincial Museum in Stoke (see p.437). The spit was named by Captain Cook in 1770. The original **Farewell Spit Lighthouse** was erected in 1870, from materials carried along the spit, and trees were transplanted to the area to provide shelter for the keepers' dwellings.

The most important feature of the spit these days is the **wildlife** it supports. It's a twitcher's paradise, with over ninety **bird species** recorded, ranging from keas to spoonbills; each year thousands of waders, including the bartailed godwit, wrybill, long-billed curlew and mongolian dotteral, fly the 12,000km from Siberia to escape the fearsome Arctic winter. The spit harbours breeding colonies of Caspian terns and gannets, but you might also spot hawks, wekas and skuas, as well as large numbers of black swans. However, the spit also seems to exert a negative influence on some wildlife, as shown by the frequency with which whales beach themselves here: it appears that their navigational system is confused by the unusual shape of the coastline here. If you follow one of the tracks on the spit, you might well come across the wasting carcass of a stranded pilot whale – a sobering sight amid such wild beauty.

There are some interesting **walks** on the spit, restricted to the landward end away from the vehicle tracks and the far end of the sand spit. Starting from the visitor centre, the outer beach track is 2.5km and the inner beach track about 4km; both provide good views of the spit and its wading bird population and offer an undiluted experience of this rather odd landscape.

Practicalities

Buses from Nelson, Motueka and Takaka drop-off in the centre of Collingwood, near the **general store** on Tasman Street (Mon–Sat 9am–6pm), while the **petrol station** (Mon–Fri 7.20am–6pm) is on Haven Road (SH60) as you enter or leave town.

There are a few **places to stay** in town and another en route to Farewell Spit. *Beachcomber Motel*, Elizabeth Street (☎03/524 8499; ③), backs on to the river estuary with lovely views and clean, self-contained units. Also near the estuary is *Collingwood Motor Camp*, William Street, at the junction with Tasman Street (☎03/524 8149; tent sites $8, cabins ②–③), a pretty, sheltered site just two minutes' walk from the shops and pub. One of the nicest homestays in the vicinity is the *Collingwood Homestay*, just off Elizabeth Street (☎03/524 8079; ⑥), a beautiful colonial-style homestead with spacious comfortable rooms, excellent breakfasts and dinner by arrangement ($30, including wine). Finally, halfway between Collingwood and Pakawau, *The Inlet* (☎03/524 8040; dorms ①, rooms ②–③), on Waikato Inlet, offers a variety of accommodation and a series of inexpensive guided trips to underground rivers or kayaking to nearby lakes ($55–110).

The only place worth getting a **drink** in town is the *Collingwood Tavern and Bistro* (closed Sun), opposite the Old Post Office on Tasman Street, which is also a reasonable place to fill up on steak and chips ($16). Close to the pub, *Collingwood Café* serves straightforward **food** every day at no-nonsense prices. At Pakawau Bay, on the way to

Farewell Spit, *The Old School House Café Restaurant* (daily 11am–11pm; licensed) dishes up simple food in a quiet and relaxed atmosphere, concentrating on locally grown veggies, fish and lamb.

Kahurangi National Park

The huge expanse of **Kahurangi National Park**, only designated in 1996, covers 40,000 square kilometres of the northwestern South Island; appropriately enough, its name means "treasured possession". The park enfolds the exposed western side of the Wakamarama Range, which are among the wettest mountains in the country and include the peaks of Mount Owen and Mount Arthur. A remote and beautiful place (presently with relatively few other visitors to distract from your enjoyment), the best way to appreciate its extraordinary landscape is on foot. In fact, this is the only way to get to much of the park and most people come here to walk the **tracks** – primarily the **Heaphy Track**, though its lesser-tramped cousins offer equal rewards and more solitude. The best bases for visiting the Kahurangi National Park are **Collingwood**, Takaka or Motueka, each with buses running to the head of the Heaphy Track. **Motueka** also provides access to the Tablelands, Mount Arthur and the Leslie–Karamea Track from the Flora Saddle car park, while the the Anatoki River Valley can be reached from **Takaka**.

Geologically it is an incredibly diverse area, comprised of sedimentary rocks faulted and uplifted from an ancient sea, as well as limestone and marble riddled with deep caves, bluffs, natural bridges and arches, sink holes and strange outcrops. Over half of New Zealand's native **plant species** are represented in the park, as are most of its alpine species, while the remote interior is a haven for birds and **animals**, including rare carnivorous snails and giant cave spiders.

Around 800 years ago, the area was well travelled by **Maori**, as they made their way to central westland in search of *pounamu* (greenstone) for weapons, ornaments and tools. From Aorere, they traversed the Gouland Downs, crossed the Heaphy rivermouth and headed down the coast, constantly at risk of being swept away. The first **Europeans** to arrive were the Australian sealing gangs in the 1820s, who within 20 years had almost wiped out the entire seal population. In 1856 the first **gold rush** ignited interest in the area and although it had petered out three years later, prospectors tarried on at the Aorere Gold Fields (now a reserve) and deeper into the interior. Ironically, now the area is protected it faces its greatest test as millions of **possums**, which invaded the area in the late 1960s, obliviously munch their way through the native plants and devastate the snail population.

Exploring the park

There are a number of **walking** tracks in the park, the most famous being the **Heaphy Track** (see p.458), all of which offer a taste of this unusual and still relatively unknown area. **Information** on the park and all the walks and activities are available at visitor centres and DOC offices in Takaka, Motueka and Nelson. Local shuttle buses provide **trailhead transport**, and Nelson-based Transport for Trampers, 33 Paremata St (☎03/545 1055), runs a service to all the trailheads in the Kahurangi National Park and the towns along the way.

Two quite arduous but rewarding and uncrowded tracks are the **Wangapeka Track** (60km; 4–5 days), usually walked from Little Wanganui, just south of Karamea on the West Coast (see p.635 for details), and the **Leslie-Karamea Track** (90km; 5–7 days; 1795m ascent), which links the Wangapeka Track with the Mount Arthur Tablelands above Motueka. The Leslie-Karamea Track starts at the Flora Saddle car park near

Motueka (see p.443) and heads south along the Leslie and Karamea rivers and through beech forest before joining the Wangapeka Track near the Luna Hut. There are seven main huts (all Category 3; $4) along the track, which is quite rough in places and should only be attempted reasonably fit and well equipped trampers. A map of the track ($1) is available from DOC offices and visitor centres.

If you're not inclined to tramp the park on your own, then check out the guided walks organized by **Bush and Beyond** (2–4 days; $220–335, all inclusive; ☎03/528 9054). To really get beneath the surface of the park and explore the underground labyrinth, you need the services of **Nelson Caving Experience** (☎ & fax 03/545 1086; day-trips only; $70). On their day-long excursions, you'll spend about three hours underground, admiring the amazing water-sculpted rock formations and looking for enormous cave wetas – insects which apparently provided the inspiration for Ridley Scott's Alien in the eponymous movies.

The Heaphy Track

Crossing the Kahurangi National Park from Golden Bay to Kohaihai Bluff on the West Coast (or vice versa), the **Heaphy Track** (77km; 4–6 days) is one of New Zealand's Great Walks, renowned for the beauty and diversity of landscapes it covers, taking in the confluence of the boiling Brown and Aorere rivers, broad tussock downs and forests, and emerging on the rugged West Coast. The track is named after Charles Heaphy who, with Thomas Brunner, became the first Europeans to walk the route in 1846, accompanied by their Maori guide Kehu.

ACCESS AND ACCOMMODATION

A **map** of the track ($1) is available from visitor centres and DOC offices, whom you should advise of your intentions – and of your safe return. Along the route, there are seven **huts** (Category 1; $12), with heating, water and toilets, and ten designated **campsites** ($6). Before setting off, you must purchase a hut or camp **pass** from DOC offices, visitor centres, some hostels and travel agents in Nelson, Motueka, Karamea and Westport, though this does not guarantee a bunk and there is a two-night limit in each hut. There is nowhere along the track to pick up **supplies** so you must take all provisions with you – and carry out all your rubbish.

TRAILHEAD TRANSPORT

The Heaphy Track is particularly awkward in one respect: if you leave your gear or vehicle at one end, you'll have to re-walk the track or undertake a long journey by road to the place you started. **From Nelson**, Book-a-Bus (☎03/525 9864) run through Motueka, Takaka and Collingwood to the inland head of the track, as do Abel Tasman National Parks Enterprises (☎03/528 8850). Nelson-based Transport for Trampers (☎03/545 1055) charge $35 for a drop-off at the inland trailhead and will also organize transport from the West Coast end of the track to the Wangapeka trailhead for those feeling energetic enough to walk back. **From Blenheim**, Barry's Buses (☎03/577 9696 & 0800/802 300), run via Nelson and Picton to either end of the track ($196.50 for drop-off and pick-up). **From Motueka**, Heaphy Track Transport (☎03/524 8257) run buses to and from the track, via Collingwood.

THE ROUTE

The Golden Bay entrance to the **eastern end** of the Heaphy Track is near **Browns Hut**, at the end of the road that runs (28km) from Collingwood past Bainham; the **West Coast entrance** is at Kohaihai Bluff, 10km north of Karamea.

If you are walking the track from east to west, the hardest day is the first, from **Browns Hut to Perry Saddle Hut** (16km; 5hr), by way of the Flanagans Corner viewpoint – at 915m, the highest point on the track. The second day can either be a very easy walk across the Perry Saddle through tussock clearings to the valley before crossing limestone arches to **Goulands Hut** (7.5km; 2hr), or a more strenuous tramp to **Saxon Hut** (12.5km; 3hr 30min). From Saxon Hut **to Mackay Hut** (11km; 3hr) involves crossing grassy flatlands, winding in and out of small streams as they tip over into the Heaphy River below. If you have the energy, it is worth pressing on to **Lewis Hut** (12km; 3–4hr), a haven for nikau palms – and less welcome sandflies. Next day can either be a long slog **to the Kohaihai Rivermouth** (24km; 8hr), but it's more enjoyable to take your time and stop at the **Heaphy Hut** (8km; 2–3hr), near where you can explore the exciting Heaphy rivermouth: its narrow outlet funnels river water into a torrid sea, resulting in a maelstrom of sea and fresh water. The **final day** (16km; 5hr) is a gentle walk through forest down the coast until you reach Crayfish Point, where you can cross the beach if you are within two hours of low tide; otherwise, take the high-tide track. Once you reach Scott's Beach, you have only to climb over **Kohaihai Bluff** to find the car park on the other side – and hopefully your pre-arranged pick-up.

Nelson Lakes National Park and around

Around 118km southwest of Nelson, the **Nelson Lakes National Park** encompasses tranquil mountains, beech forest and mirror-like lakes, with spectacular tramping in summer and skiing in winter. The park is best known, though, for its two glacial lakes, **Rotoroa** ("long lake"), and **Rotoiti** ("little lake"). Lake Rotoiti is very popular among anglers, kayakers and yachties, and is surrounded by mountains, stands of beech forest and flax, all criss-crossed with fine walks. The vast expanse of deep blue water that is Lake Rotora is rather more rarefied, its enclosing mountains becoming barren and grey at its southern extremity. The park's sub-alpine rivers, lakes, forests and hills are full of bird life, but has offered little solace to man: Maori passed through the area and caught eels in the lakes, but the best efforts of European settlers and gold prospectors yielded little.

The main bases for forays into the park are **St Arnaud**, a small town on SH63, just over 100km southwest of Blenheim and 25km from Kawatiri Junction on the road between Nelson and Murchison (SH6); or **Murchison** itself, 35km further southwest.

Once clear of Murchison, SH6 romps alongside the Buller River through the Buller Gorge to the **West Coast** town of Westport, a route covered in Chapter Twelve (see p.630). If you're heading for the **east**, you can retrace your route along SH6, then cut across to Blenheim (see p.464), 162km away on SH63.

St Arnaud

ST ARNAUD is a tiny place poised on the north shore of Lake Rotoiti, which provides accommodation and food for visitors to the Nelson Lakes National Park, its population of around a hundred swelling with trampers and skiers in season. Little more than a jumble of two-storey buildings on either side of the road, the town has little to detain you, but if you're after some background on the region, the visitor centre (see p.460) shows a fifteen-minute video on the Buller River and its unique ecosystem, which supports giant eels, a variety of bird life (including the endangered blue duck), and abundant brown trout. Displays in the centre also provide information on the Nelson Lakes National Park and its vegetation, including manuka and kanuka trees – the leaves of the latter were used by Cook and other early visitors to supplement their dwindling stocks of tea, giving them their common name of tea trees.

Practicalities

Most **buses** drop you right in St Arnaud, but InterCity and White Star services between Nelson and Murchison drop you at Kawatiri Junction, from where you'll need to pick up a Blenheim-bound bus along SH63, or call Nelson Lakes Shuttles (☎03/521 1887; $14). The commercial hub of St Arnaud is the **service station and store** (daily 7.30am–6.30pm), which also acts as a post office (closed Sun). The **DOC office**, on View Road overlooking Kerr Bay (Mon–Sun 8am–4.30pm, until 7.30pm during summer holidays; ☎03/521 1806, fax 521 1896), is guarded by a red Maori statue depicting Rakaihautu, creator of the lakes. The centre has copious information on the region, including walks and mountaineering around Nelson Lakes – and the exceptional caves to be explored around Mount Owen.

A range of **accommodation** is available in two modern wooden buildings just off the main road (SH60) at *Alpine Chalet and Lodge* (☎03/521 1868, fax 521 1869; dorms ①, rooms ②–⑤); facilities include a licensed restaurant, bar, café and spa pool. *The Yellow House* and *St Arnaud Log Chalets*, 150m from the service station (☎ & fax 03/521 1887; dorms ①, rooms ②, chalets ④), is a small hostel with doubles, twins and shared rooms, kitchen, TV and a wealth of information, plus a few delightful, fully self-contained chalets next door. Around 30km out of town on SH6, near Kawatiri Junction, and signposted from the road, is *Hu ha Backpackers* (☎03/546 9413; dorms ①, rooms ②), an old cottage on a farm which makes a good spot for cyclists, trampers or those who just want to get away from it all; inexpensive breakfasts and dinner can be ordered. Finally, there are two DOC **campsites** (☎03/521 1806; $7), both overlooking the lake, at Kerr Bay and West Bay, with kitchens, toilets and pay showers.

Aside from the homely **snacks** and meals to be had at the service station café (daily 7.30am–5.30pm), the only other place to eat in St Arnaud is at the *Alpine Chalet and Lodge* (see above), whose licensed **restaurant** offers breakfast and dinner (daily 8–9.30am & 6.30–9pm), or you can opt for bar meals (daily noon–2pm & 6–10pm) of burgers, soups, salads and grills.

Getting to – and exploring – the lakes

Lake Rotoiti is the more accessible of the two lakes, easily reached on foot along a short road very close to the settlement of St Arnaud. The Gowan Valley Road to Lake Rotoroa, which veers off SH6 between Nelson and Murchison just after the St Arnaud turn-off, is unsealed; near the end of this road, the **Lake Rotoroa Ranger Station** (Mon–Fri 8am–noon & 1–5pm, Sat & Sun 9am–noon & 1–5pm; ☎ 03/523 9369) offers good advice and literature on the area. Nelson Lakes Shuttles (☎03/521 1887) run a number of park **shuttle services** to Mount Robert car park, Lake Rotoroa, Kawatiri Junction, Howard Valley and Wairau Valley, while Transport for Trampers (☎03/545 1055) runs to most trailheads in the national park. St Arnaud Guiding Services (☎03/521 1028), offer **guided** walks and four-wheel-drive **safaris** in the park (from $55 a half-day).

There are **water taxi** services on both lakes; minimum charges roughly equivalent to four one-way fares apply to all their services. Lake Rotoroa Water Taxis (☎03/523 9199) ply the length of the lake ($20), giving you a chance for a good look around. Lake Rotoiti Water Taxis (☎03/521 1894) run to the head of Lake Rotoiti ($10–12), and between Kerr Bay and West Bay ($8). Alternatively, you can take a scenic cruise around Lake Rotoiti in one of the taxi vessels (1hr 30min; $15); the company also rents out **kayaks**, canoes, row boats ($15 per hour, $35 per day).

There are a few short walks by **Lake Rotoroa**, but although the lake is pretty, there is not much here apart from a few wily fish and some ridiculously expensive accommodation – the exclusive preserve of dedicated anglers and stressed-out executives.

The *Lake Rotoroa Lodge*, at the northern lakeside (☎03/523 9121, fax 523 9028; ⑨) and based in a 1920s building garlanded with US and New Zealand flags, is typical.

Mountain biking

There are a number of mountain-biking possibilities around the national park, including the spectacular **Rainbow Road** (1–2 days; impassable in winter) that connects St Arnaud to Hanmer Springs, 112km to the southeast. The road crosses some private land, for which keys and permission must be arranged at the DOC offices at either end. The highest point on the route is **Island Saddle** (1347m), with panoramic views of the Tarndale Lakes, Lake Tennyson and the surrounding countryside. For **accommodation** en route, there are two Category 3 backcountry huts at Connors Creek and Island Gully ($4) and campsites at Tarndale Lakes and Lake Tennyson, both with a cold water supply and toilets ($4); be sure to boil or filter the water before use.

Walking

There are many walking options in the area, with 270km of track wending their way across the park, served by twenty huts. If you feel the need of a well informed, friendly **guide** to accompany you on your tramps, St Arnaud Guiding Services (☎03/521 1028) are your best bet. The lakes area also provides access to a number of **longer tracks**, two of which – the tramp to the Angelus Hut and the Travers–Sabine Circuit – are particularly recommended. These are alpine tracks so you must be equipped with good boots, and warm and waterproof clothing, as well as the relevant DOC maps and leaflets, and hut tickets from the DOC office in St Arnaud. Both tracks **start** from the **upper Mount Robert car park**, which can be reached by **bus** with Transport for Trampers (☎03/545 1055), Nelson Lakes Transport (☎03/548 6858) and Nelson Lakes Shuttles (☎03/521 1887), for $5 (minimum 4 passengers).

AROUND LAKE ROTOROA

Just before the Rotoroa Bridge on Braeburn Road, close to the **Lake Rotoroa Ranger Station**, is the start of a short section of the **Braeburn Track** (8km; 2hr), which heads along the western shore of the lake, passing through the dense green podocarp forest that surrounds it. The lake's eastern shore is traced by the **Lakeside Track** (28km; 2 days), which heads through the forest to the Sabine Rivermouth at the southern end of the lake and then scrambles up to the Sabine Hut (Category 3; $4), where you'll have to stay overnight before heading back down.

AROUND LAKE ROTOITI

From the shores of **Lake Rotoiti**, a network of tracks explores the edge of the lake, the forests and further afield. There are a number of **leaflets** detailing the various tracks in the area as well as the geology and wildlife, available from the DOC office in St Arnaud (50¢–$1).

Three of the best **shorter walks** are the Peninsula Nature Walk, St Arnaud Range Track and Whiskey Falls Track; you can even avoid backtracking by taking a water taxi across the lake and then walking back. The **Peninsula Walk** (2km; 1hr 30min) is a nature trail around the peninsula that divides Kerr Bay from West Bay, and makes an easy and rewarding introduction to the area. Slightly more strenuous is the **St Arnaud Range Track** (18km return; 5hr; 1650m ascent), also beginning at Kerr Bay, before climbing through beech forest, with spectacular views of the lake and mountain once you emerge from the bushline. Beginning on the Mount Robert Road on the western shore of the lake, a 5-kilometre lakeside track leads to the **Whiskey Falls Track** (4hr return, including lakeside section). Constantly shrouded in mist and fringed by moss and hanging ferns the falls are forty metres high and particularly grand after heavy rain.

SKIING IN MOUNT ROBERT AND RAINBOW VALLEY

The two skifields close to St Arnaud are very different in character. At both, the **season** usually runs from June to October, and Nelson Lakes Shuttles (☎03/521 1887) and JJ's Ski Transport (☎03/544 7081) operate **shuttle services** out to both fields ($10) for the duration.

The **Mount Robert Skifield** (☎03/548 8336), 15km from St Arnaud, is a small ski area that remains quiet due to the ninety-minute walk to the field from the car park, though a helicopter provides lifts at weekends (on demand; $35, minimum 4). Downhill and cross-country skiers enjoy good powdery snow – and two lodges, which provide refreshment. Gear rental is available in St Arnaud village (☎03/521 1850), and lift passes cost $20 per day.

The much more commercial **Rainbow Valley Ski Area** (☎03/521 1861), 32km from St Arnaud, has an enormous variety of runs catering for a wide variety of skiing and snowboarding abilities, with lessons and equipment rental if needed. Access is via a toll road ($8), and the car park is very close to the lifts ($43 daily). Certain days are set aside for **women only**, so call before setting out.

TO THE ANGELUS HUT

The best route **to the Angelus Hut** (14km; 7–8hr), if the weather is fine, is by way of **Robert Ridge**, which involves walking up the face of Mount Robert to 1411m, then tracing the broad ridge, overlooking the whole area. Head southwest across the Julius Saddle, sticking to the ridge until the beautiful Angelus basin with its welcoming hut unfolds before you. The Angelus Lake is really an alpine tarn, a legacy of gaciers that retreated over 10,000 years ago, leaving the characteristic steep-sided valley walls, bluff-ringed creeks, sharp ridges and water-filled basins. From the Angelus Hut, the easiest route is southeast along the **Cascade Track** (14km; 5hr), which descends beside a stream before heading back to Lake Rotoiti, via either the Lakehead Hut on the eastern shore or the Coldwater Hut on the western shore. The longer and tougher option is to head southwest toward Mount Cedric and the Sabine Hut and then follow the **Speargrass Track** (22km; 9hr) back to the Mount Robert car park, a longer and tougher option. From the Mount Robert car park, you can either walk back to St Arnaud (5km) or pre-arrange a pick-up by one of the shuttle bus services.

THE TRAVERS-SABINE CIRCUIT

Not mentioned in the same breath as New Zealand's Great Walks (and, as a consequence, delightfully uncrowded), the **Travers-Sabine Circuit** (80km; 4–7 days) is none the less spectacular for its lowly status.

The track probes deep into remote areas of lakes, fields of tussock and 2000-metre mountains, of which the highlight is the Travers Saddle (1780m), a deep bowl fed by a 20-metre cascade and subject to freezing conditions at any time of year. At the height of summer, the track verges are briefly emblazoned with yellow buttercups, white daisies, sundew and harebells. According to Maori legend, the area's fecundity and peppering of lakes is due to Rakaihautu, a famous chief who travelled the great mountains with his *ko* (digging stick), digging enormous holes that he filled with water and food for those that followed. The circuit requires a good level of **fitness**, though it is fairly easy to follow, with bridges over most streams. You must obtain **hut tickets** at the DOC office in St Arnaud before commencing the walk, as well as stocking up on food, water and the requisite **maps** – DOC's *Sabine-Travers Circuit* ($1) leaflet is quite adequate, but the more detailed and expensive TopoMaps are also available. There are nine huts along the track and **camping** is allowed – but fires aren't, so you must carry a stove and fuel.

Murchison and around

MURCHISON, 35km further along SH6 from Kawatiri Junction, is a service centre for local farmers and beloved of shooting, hunting and fishing types due to its proximity to the Matakitaki and Buller rivers. It also makes a feasible base from which to explore some of the old gold workings and the Nelson Lakes, raft the Buller River (see p.624), or just tramp some of the impressive walks in the area.

Only a few colonial hotels stand as testimony to Murchison's glory days. **Gold** was found in the Murchison district in 1862, though the workings were in remote and rugged areas and difficult to reach. Prospectors flocked to Murchison from Nelson and Collingwood, paddling up the Buller River in Maori canoes to reach the goldfields; the last gold rush was in 1915.

The town itself has little to offer the visitor, except maybe a brief peek at the **Murchison Museum**, on Fairfax Street (daily 10am–4pm; donation requested); if the museum is locked, get the key from the petrol station. This wooden, barn-like building houses the obligatory ancient telephone exchange and, from the gold-rush era, a collection of Chinese pottery, plus opium bottles that once granted temporary oblivion to Chinese gold diggers. There are also newspaper clippings, photographs and various oddities, such as an antique flintlock musket from Afghanistan – and Bob Bunn's bike. A formidable pioneer, who for many years was a forward in the Murchison rugby team alongside his similarly broad-shouldered brother, Bob sold his last timber mill when he was 82 and died eight years later. He is remembered as "a rugged individualist and colourful personality, known for his down-to-earth philosophy of life, his strong political views, and love of cycling" (hence the bike).

Around Murchison

Murchison is surrounded by mountains and river valleys, in a district dominated by rugged escarpments, bush-clad ranges, lakes and many rivers. A good way to explore the area is by **bike**, which can be rented from Pedal Power, 27 Grey Street, just off SH6 ($25 a day; ☎03/523 9425). A leaflet (50¢) detailing several mountain-bike trails (16–85km) is available at the visitor centre; all routes begin and end in Murchison. If you want to try your hand at **gold-panning**, pick up the *Recreational Gold Panning* leaflet (50¢ from the visitor centre): this lists the likely places to strike it rich – Lyell Creek, Ariki Falls and the Howard Valley – and advises on technique.

The **Skyline Walk** (6km return; 2hr; leaflet from visitor centre, 50¢) makes a pleasant diversion. The route starts from the car park 500m past the bridge crossing the Matakitaki River, at the junction of SH6 and Matakitaki West Bank Road. Climbing up through the native forest to the skyline ridge above Murchison, the walk yields views of the township and the confluence of the Buller, Matakitaki, Maruia and Matiri rivers.

Practicalities

Bisected by SH6 (Waller Street or Main Road, as it passes through), everything of note in the town hugs this main thoroughfare. **Buses** drop off close to *Collin's Tearooms* on Fairfax Street, putting you within an easy walk of anywhere in the town. The summer-only **visitor centre**, on Waller Street (Oct–April Mon–Sat 10am–5pm; ☎03/523 9350), has a number of leaflets on walks and other activities in the Murchison area; they can also book bus tickets to other destinations. The town itself contains a **bank** near the junction of Hampden Street and Fairfax Street and a **post office**, on the corner of SH60 and Fairfax Street.

The *Commercial*, on Waller Street (☎ & fax 03/523 9490; dorms ①, rooms ②), is a classic Kiwi **hotel**: the clean, fresh rooms have linen and towels supplied, while the small 8-bed backpacker section has use of a small kitchen; all guest accommodation is away from the pub, so there's no noise problem. On Hotham Street, clearly signposted about 1km from town, *Mataki Motel* (☎03/523 9088; ③–④) is old but clean and quiet; some units have full kitchen, others make do with a kettle and toaster. A kilometre east of town on SH6, the *Riverview Holiday Park* (☎03/523 9315; tent sites $10, on-site vans & cabins ②–③) is a pleasant, shady **campsite** beside the Buller River.

A modern, green-roofed timber construction, the *Beechwoods Restaurant* (daily 6.30–9.30pm; licensed), on SH6 near the bridge over the Maitakitaki River, serves salads, burgers, fish and steak; the Saturday-night **smorgasbord** ($15), is great value. *Collin's Tearooms* (daily 8am–8pm) on Fairfax Street – look for the blue roof – is a large cafeteria-style place that serves up snacks and full meals in no-fuss surroundings. For a quiet pint and a **pie**, head for the *Commercial Hotel* on Waller Street; pub grub is served from 8am–10pm.

Blenheim and around

There are two ways to travel the 27km from Picton to **BLENHEIM:** either the scenic **coastal route**, which takes in the sights of old whaling stations via Port Underwood, as the road winds tightly up and down the bluffs; or the more **direct route** along SH1, which passes one or two wineries and other sights, including the small community of **Korimiko**, where a garage beside the road sells ridiculously cheap, locally smoked salmon. Just up the road and by its side, in the same town, is one of New Zealand's premier cheese factories, with a wide variety available for tasting and purchase.

Blenheim, with a population of 24,000, is a rural **service town** for all the farming and wine-growing activity on the **Wairua Plains**, where the river valleys of Awatere and Wairau rivers create rich land in the shelter of the **Richmond Range**. Like the plains it stands on, Blenheim is a well manicured, slightly sterile town, which makes a good base for visiting the internationally renowned **wineries** of the **Marlborough** region.

Arrival, information and accommodation

The **train station** is on Sinclair Street, about five minutes' stroll from Seymour Square and the centre of town; **buses** also drop off just outside the station. The **airport** is 7km south of town, and flights are met by Airport Super Shuttle (☎03/572 9910; $8). The **visitor centre**, The Forum, Queen Street (Dec–March daily 8.30am–6.30pm; April–June & Aug–Nov daily 8.30am–5.30pm; July Mon–Sat 8.30am–5.30pm; ☎03/578 9904, fax 578 6084), provides a number of useful leaflets, including maps and details of the wineries and art and craft galleries in the area.

Accommodation

Blenheim and the wine region surrounding it attract gourmet travellers, and they are well catered for by **luxury** homestays and **B&Bs** (many of them out of town near the wineries), a well as a couple of stunning **hotels**. If you are looking for reasonably priced accommodation, the centre of town is a better bet, or base yourself in more down-to-earth Picton (see p.422).

Blenheim Backpackers, 29 Park Terrace (☎03/578 6062). In the rather unusual setting of an old maternity home on the banks of the Opawa River, 500m from the centre of town, this hostel is clean and comfortable, and has free bikes for guests' use. Dorms ①, rooms ②.

Blenheim Grove Bridge Holiday Park, 78 Grove Rd, off SH1 2km north of Blenheim (☎03/578 3667). This comfortable riverside campsite has a variety of on-site accommodation. Tent sites $16, cabins & motel-style units ②–④.

Blenheim Motel, 81 Main St (☎03/578 0559). A quiet, comfortable motel with ten self-contained units and two studios, all with off-street parking and Sky TV. ④.

RESTAURANTS, CAFÉS & BARS
1 Barcello's Café
2 China Café
3 The Coral
4 Gino's Italian Restaurant
5 Hotel D'Urville
6 Paddy Barry's Irish Pub
7 Paysanne
8 Redwood Bakery
9 Rocco's
10 Henry Dodson's Wine Bar

ACCOMMODATION
A Blenheim Backpackers
B Blenheim Grove Holiday Park
C Blenheim Motel
D Come In B&B
E Hotel D'Urville
F Koanui Backpackers
G Marlborough Hotel

Charmwood Farmstay, cnr Murrays Rd & Rapaura Rd (☎03/570 5409, fax 574 5110). This beef farm is a homely, welcoming place to stay, with large rooms and hearty breakfasts of home-grown produce. ⑤.

Come Inn, 109 Charles St (☎03/578 2761). Central (2min walk) B&B, with clean, comfortable rooms, off-street parking and enthusiastic hosts. Cooked breakfast costs $5 extra. ④.

Cranbrook Cottage, at the bottom of Giffords Road, off Rapaura Road, about 9km from town (☎03/572 8606, fax 572 8707). Handy for the wineries, this superb self-contained picture-book cottage has the added bonus of breakfast delivered to your door from the main house. ⑥.

Hotel d'Urville, 52 Queen St (☎03/577 9945, fax 577 9946). This former bank right in the centre of town has been turned into a superb, highly individual hotel and restaurant, with each room thematically decorated. ⑧–⑨.

Koanui Backpackers, 33 Main St (☎03/578 7487). A short walk from the visitor centre, this hostel boasts basins in every room and a variety of accommodation. Dorms ①, rooms ②.

Marlborough Hotel, 20 Nelson St (☎03/577 7333, fax 577 7337). Modern, luxury accommodation with Mediterranean decor, two restaurants, a bar and sumptuous large airy rooms with excellent service. ⑥–⑨.

Stonehaven Homestay, 445a Rapaura Rd, 12km south of Blenheim (☎03/572 9730). A modern stone and cedar home with a swimming pool, lots of space and very friendly owners. ⑤–⑥.

The Town

Blenheim is pretty much devoid of tourist attractions and most people use it as a hub from which to visit the wineries and Richmond Ranges. The town retains few of its early buildings, but a stroll following the route in the *Sideways and Byways* leaflet from the visitor centre unearths some vestiges. In the centre of the town is the pretty **Seymour Square** with its flowerbeds and distinctive stone clock tower, a popular lunch spot in fine weather and a useful landmark. About ten minutes' walk north from Seymour Square across Nelson Street (SH6) is **Pollard Park** (7am–dusk, main entrance on Parker St), a charming park area with rose gardens, rhododendrons, native rock garden and ponds – as well as a number of tennis courts, a nine-hole golf course and croquet green catering to more active pursuits.

Some 2.5km south of the town centre, off New Renwick Road, **Brayshaw Park** (Sat 10am–4pm, Sun 10am–1pm; $2) is a reconstruction of an early settlers' community, with many of the historic buildings moved brick by brick from their original sites. The open-air museum also has a formidable collection of vintage farm machinery and vehicles, plus various accoutrements of pioneering life, including a striking array of textiles. At the opposite end of town (north), on SH1, is a small 1860s **Cobb Cottage** (Sat 10am–4pm, Sun 1–4pm; donation requested), which has been restored to house yet more displays on the lives of early settlers.

The wineries

Most of the wineries of note are along the **road** (SH6) **to Renwick** – a small, unremarkable town 10km west – though a couple are out on a limb on SH1 **between Blenheim and Picton**. The region, sheltered by the protective hills of the Richmond Range, records approximately 2400 hours of grape-ripening sunshine a year and is famous for its Sauvignon Blanc, but also produces good Chardonnay and high-quality Methode Champenoise. All the **vineyards** are set up for visitors with **tastings** (either free or for a small charge, which is often deducted from any subsequent purchases), cellar-door sales, gardens and **restaurants** where you can relax and enjoy some excellent food. All the wineries will ship cases overseas – a popular practice is to accumulate bottles from various wineries, filling a case and then arranging shipment at the last winery you visit.

Maps and descriptions of the wineries are available at the visitor centre in Blenheim, but don't be tempted to cram too many into a day; most are more suited to leisurely

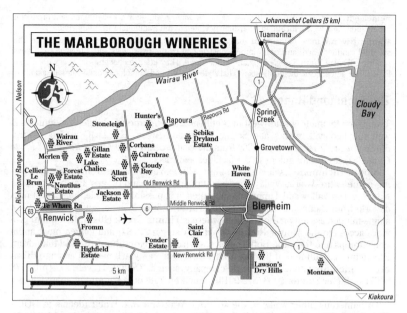

THE MARLBOROUGH WINERIES

vineyard lunches than whistle-stop tours. The only transport to the wineries is with **organized tours**, which may also appeal to drivers keen to avoid the pitfalls of too many tastings; **rental bikes** are also a possibility (see "Listings", p.469, for details of both), though the wineries are fairly spread out.

Cellier Le Brun, Terrace Road, on the outskirts of Renwick (daily 9am–5pm). Producer of extremely high-quality Daniel Le Brun Methode Champenoise offers free non-vintage tastings, reasonably priced bottles and a small café full of simple but wholesome food.

Cloudy Bay, Jacksons Rd (daily 10am–4.30pm). An internationally famous winery offering free tastings and tours around the vineyard.

Highfield Estate, Brookby Rd, between Blenheim and Renwick (daily 10am–5pm). Easily recognizable by its Tuscan-inspired tower, which you can climb for excellent views. It also provides some of the best food in the region, with tapas and antipasto platters for $25 that will easily feed two, plus free tastings.

Hunter's, Rapaura Rd (Mon–Sat 9.30am–4.30pm, Sun 11.30am–3.30pm, restaurant daily noon–2.30pm & 6–9pm). One of the bigger players, *Hunters* offers a broad range of wines (tastings $2) and a fine restaurant specializing in traditional haute cuisine, leavened by Italian snacks such as antipasto and foccaccia.

Johannesdorf Cellars, in Koromiko, 20km north of Blenheim on SH1 (Tues–Fri 10am–4.30pm, Sat & Sun 11am–4.30pm). Famous for its historic underground cellars carved out of the face of the hill (30min tours) and its good-quality cellar door tastings (free) and sales.

Merlen Wines, Rapaura Rd (daily 9am–5pm). A well regarded smaller winery with a German-influenced café and tastings ($5).

Montana Marlborough Winery, 5km south of Blenheim on SH1 (Mon–Sat 9am–5pm, Sun 11am–4pm). One of the oldest and largest in the area, now operating a highly commercial operation, which takes away some of the charm, though they do have some excellent vintages not readily available in the shops.

Ponder Estate, New Renwick Rd, parallel to SH6 (Oct–May only, Mon–Sat 11am–5pm). A comparatively small operation that concentrates its efforts on pressing superb olive oil and producing two very good wines (free tastings). It also showcases the oil paintings of Mike Ponder, which depict typical New Zealand scenes – with his trademark splash of red somewhere in the picture.

Stoneleigh, Jacksons Rd (daily 10am–4.30pm). A winery with stony, well-drained soil producing highly individual wines, including Chardonnay vinted in the traditional Burgundy style.

Wairau River Wines, Rapaura Rd (daily 10am–5pm). At the foot of the Richmond Range, this splendid rammed earth and rimu timber construction by the river deals with the wine from three wineries, *Wairau River*, *Shingle Peak* and *Foxes Island*. They offer free tastings and very good quality lunches and snacks, including spicy Thai-style mussels and Manuka smoked salmon salad.

The Richmond Range

Twenty-six kilometres southwest of Blenheim, the **Richmond Range** of mountains is well supplied with **walks** and Scenic Recreation Areas. The DOC leaflets *Central Marlborough Recreation Areas* (30¢ from the visitor centre) and *Mount Richmond Route Guide* ($1) are useful guides to the facilities and trails.

Mount Richmond itself is 1760m high, with expansive views from its summit, taking in the entire Wairau Valley, the Kaikoura and St Arnaud ranges. Easily accessible from the Top Valley and Timms Creek routes, it is possible to tackle the summit on a day-trip from Blenheim. The **Top Valley route** (7.5km; 3.5hr one-way) is ideal for a single-minded assault on the **summit**, whereas **Timms Creek** (10km; 4hr 30min) provides access to the **Mount Richmond Hut** (Category 3; $4) and longer, more ambitious tramps into the park. Both routes **start** from the **Northbank Road** (16km from Blenheim on SH6) and, if you don't have your own car, you'll need to arrange **drop-off** and **pick-up** with a local shuttle company, such as Deluxe Travel Line (☎03/578 5467) or Super Shuttle (☎03/572 9910), which operate on a flat rate of about $30 per hour.

Of numerous other walks in the area, the **Wakamarina Track** (details in DOC's *Wakamarina Track* leaflet, 50¢) is a useful short cut for trampers and mountain bikers, crossing the Richmond Range from the Wairau Valley to the Wakamarina Valley near Havelock. There are three backcountry **huts** along the track (Category 3; $4), which is best walked or ridden from south to north: trampers should allow two days to cover the 12-kilometre track; bikers should be able to manage it in a day.

Eating, drinking and entertainment

A lot of eating and drinking can be done quite painlessly at the **wineries** (see p.466), but Blenheim itself also has a few restaurants well worth exploring. The free weekly *Marlborough Times* has **entertainment listings**, as does the Friday edition of the daily *Marlborough Mail* (60¢).

Barcello's Café, 67 Queen St. A favourite among the locals, this café offers an extraordinary range of Kiwi, Mexican and Italian meals, gourmet burgers, sandwiches and salads, all at ordinary prices, with good coffee and prompt service. Daily 9am–9pm.

China Café, 70 High St. Excellent teas and coffees from all over the world. Mon–Sat 10am–5pm.

The Coral, 3 Main St. A li'l bit of Texas in Blenheim. Feed on suitably grand portions of highly spiced meat and fish ($8–23), and more traditional appetizers and deserts, in this cowboy-inspired, bar-room setting. Evenings only, Tues–Sun; licensed.

Cork and Keg Inkerman St, Renwick. If you're suffering from winery overload, seek refuge in this comfortable English-style pub that brews its own beer and cider and serves inexpensive bar meals, including proper pork pies. Run by an ex-London cabbie, the bar has a warming stone hearth, and darts, dominoes and bar skittles are played with abandon. Daily 11am–11pm.

Gino's Italian Restaurant, 1 Main St. A simple Italian joint with genuine, rustic cuisine at low prices. BYO.

Henry Dodson's Restaurant and Wine Bar, 1 Dodson St (☎03/577 6634). Stylish mid-range restaurant specializing in fresh, high-quality New Zealand produce – simple lamb, steak and fish dishes, rounded off with rich desserts and excellent wines – served in a comfortable and atmospheric building. Daily, evenings only.

Hotel d'Urville, 52 Queen St. Classy and lively restaurant and wine bar with a Cajun and Mediterranean bent. Try Marlborough mussels steamed in white wine, black bean, tomato and garlic broth ($10) or a Tasman Bay crab wrapped in rice pastry ($13). Lunch & dinner daily.

Paddy Barry's Irish Pub, 51 Scott St. An unassuming log-cabin-style exterior hides the dark wood and lively atmosphere of a popular local boozer, with a Guinness pump to justify the name and reasonably priced bar snacks of pies, hotpots, salads, platters and burgers ($5–12). Occasional live music and regular dedicated drinking at weekends.

Paysanne, 1st floor, The Forum, High St. A café/wine bar with moderately priced Thai, Japanese, Malay and Mediterranean food in pleasant surroundings; try a laksa or chicken breast filled with pesto mousseline. Daily 11.30am–3pm & 5.30–10pm.

Redwood Bakery, 75 Cleghorn St & 69 Queen St. Dutch bakery with great bread and pastries. Mon–Fri 8.30am–4.30pm, Sat 8.30am–1.30pm.

Rocco's, 5 Dodson St (☎03/578 6940). An authentic and enjoyable Italian restaurant, which makes its own fresh pasta daily. For a blowout, order the awesome chicken Kiev alla Rocco – chicken breast filled with ham, garlic butter and cheese, all wrapped in a veal schnitzel. Daily, evenings only. Licensed.

Listings

Airlines Soundsair (☎04/388 2594) operate daily scheduled flights to Wellington.

Airport bus Airport Super Shuttle (☎03/578 9910).

Arts and crafts Art Forum Gallery, in The Forum, is the premier local arts and crafts outlet, (Mon–Thurs 10am–4pm, Fri 10am–7pm, Sat 10am–1pm); Debbie Cave-Higgins (☎03/572 8996), produces very fine silk paintings.

Automobile Association 23 Maxwell Rd (☎03/578 3399).

Bike rental Blenheim Hire Centre, Redwood St (☎03/578 1111), and Spokemans Cycles, Queen St (☎03/578 0433), both charge around $30 a day.

Car rental Hertz (☎03/578 0402); Rent-a-dent (☎03/577 8347).

Cinema West End Cinema, 15 Maxwell St (☎03/578 5812).

Horse trekking Wither Hills Horse Trekking, Taylors Pass Rd, off SH63 (☎03/578 9904), will take you up into the hills for panoramic views of the Richmond Range and Wairau Plains (daily 10am; 2hr $15, 5hr $65, including lunch).

Local produce Taste of Marlborough, cnr Queen St & George St, stocks a large range of regional wines and food and offers tastings; Marlborough Fruit Distillers, Riverland Estate, 6km from Blenheim off SH1, offer a variety of fruit liqueurs and preserves, as does the Prenzel Pacific Distilling Company, also in the Riverland Estate. Prices Traditional Preserves, Selmes Rd, off Rapaura Rd, 5km north of Blenheim, have a small shop peddling multifarious pickles and jams.

Medical treatment Medical Centre, George St, about 100m from junction with Queen St.

Post office Central post office, cnr Scott St & Main St (Mon–Fri 9am–5pm, Sat 9am–1pm).

Rafting Action in Marlborough (☎03/578 4531) offer a number of whitewater rafting trips on the Karamea and Buller rivers (Grade III–V; 1–5 days; $60–695).

Taxis Blenheim Taxis (☎03/578 0225); Red Band Taxis (☎03/578 2072).

Tours and travel Highlight Tours (☎03/578 9904) ply the wine and beer trails, and will arrange gardens, arts and crafts itineraries on demand; Marlborough Travel Centre (☎03/577 9997) offer a number of day-trips and cruises ($30–68) in the Sounds, the surrounding hills or just to the wineries, as well as taking onward travel bookings; Straits Air (☎03/570 5194) operate scenic flights, Cook Strait crossings and wine tours; Super Shuttle Blenheim (☎03/572 9910), offer a shuttle service around town, as well as a customized wine tour ($30 an hour).

Trains The travel centre (☎03/577 8811) in the station has a booking office for onward travel or excursions.

Kaikoura and around

State Highway 1 ploughs south from Blenheim to Kaikoura, with the coast on one side and the Seaward Kaikoura Range on the other. Not long after you pass through the small community of **Clarence**, about 25km from Kaikoura, is the **Ohau Point Seal Colony**, the largest on the South Island and a popular stopping point; although you can see the seals from the road, designated lookout points provide safer viewing.

KAIKOURA, perched on the east coast almost midway between Blenheim (129km away) and Christchurch (180km south), is famous for its whalewatch and swimming with dolphins, but it is also a good spot for bird-watching and tramping on the peninsula and in the **Kaikoura Ranges**, as well as the underrated pleasures of swimming with seals. If you happen to be in the area in the **winter**, the newest and one of the most diverse of New Zealand's skiing areas at **Mount Lyford** is worth investigating.

Kaikoura was named by an ancient **Maori** explorer who stopped to eat crayfish and found it so good he called the place *kai* ("food") *koura* ("crayfish"). Maori legend also accounts for the extraordinary coastline around Kaikoura. A young deity, Marokura, was given the job of finishing the region: first he built the Kaikoura peninsula and a second smaller peninsula (Haumuri Bluff), then he set about creating the huge troughs in the sea between the two peninsulas, where the cold waters of the south would mix with the warm waters of the north and east. Tuterakiwhanoa (the god), realizing the depth of Marokura's accomplishment, said that the place would be a gift (*koha*) to all those who see its hidden beauty – and it is still known to local Maori as Te Koha O Marokura.

The first **Europeans** to settle in the area where whalers, followed relatively quickly by farmers. The trials and tribulations of their existence are recorded in the Kaikoura Museum and the more evocative Fyffe House. Recent history has been kind to the town, the Maori-owned whalewatch and various tourist spin-offs having brought relative prosperity.

Arrival and information

All the **buses** and shuttle services drop off on Westend Parade, in the town car park beside the visitor centre. The *Southerner* **train** between Picton and Christchurch arrives at the station on Whaleway [sic] Station Road, while flights land at the grass Peketa **airfield**, about 8km from the centre of town and served by Bazz's Bus ($4; ☎03/319 5686).

The large **visitor centre**, on Westend Parade (daily: Nov–Feb 8am–7.30pm; March–Oct 8am–5.50pm; ☎03/319 5641, fax 319 6819), is full of helpful information and competent staff. Various activities can be booked here, and there are sometimes video ($2) and slide presentations (Mon–Thurs, 7pm; $4), focusing on the whales and other attractions. The **DOC office** (Mon–Fri 8am–4.30pm, Sat 8am–1pm; ☎ & fax 03/319 5714) is on Ludstone Road, about 500m from the town centre.

Accommodation

Most of the accommodation in Kaikoura is along SH1, just before it veers away from the centre of town, or along Westend and The Esplanade which head out onto the peninsula.

Hotels and motels

Admiral Court, 16 Avoca St (☎ & fax 03/319 5525). Spacious and well kept motel units a little way out of the town on the peninsula. ④–⑤.

Beachcomber Motel, 169 Beach Rd, at the junction with Gillings Lane, 1.5km north of town (☎03/319 5623). A charming small motel with well kept studio units, free use of mountain bikes, and warm and welcoming hosts. ④.

Panorama Motel, 266 Esplanade (☎ 03/319 5053, fax 319 6605). There are superb views from these stripped-pine, clean units with a chalet feel; you'll pay $10 extra for the better view from the first floor. ④.

B&Bs and homestays

Austen Heights B&B, 19 Austin St (☎03/319 5836). The best value in the area, this peaceful homely place has superb views and breakfasts, and a courtesy van to and from the buses. ④.

Dillondale Farmstay, Stag'n'Spey Rd (☎03/319 5205). Forty minutes' drive inland from Kaikoura is this very professionally run farmstay far away from all the world's worries. Rates are for dinner, bed and breakfast. ⑥.

Old Convent B&B, cnr Mount Fyffe Rd & Mill Rd, 4km from town (☎03/319 6603). A character-ful, high-ceilinged, 1912 ex-convent building in spacious grounds with a quiet rural atmosphere and beautiful, individually decorated, colourful rooms. ④.

Hostels, campsites and motor parks

A1 Kaikoura Holiday Park, 11 Beach Rd (☎ & fax 03/319 5999). Close to the bridge and the train station, this motor park offers a variety of accommodation from motel units through five different types of cabin, to backpacker bunks and campsites, all on a smart site that backs onto the river. Tent sites $7.50, dorms ①, cabins & units ②–④.

Cray Cottage, 190 Esplanade (☎03/319 5152). Cosy and comfortable backpacker-style accommodation. Dorms ①, rooms ②.

Dolphin Lodge, 15 Deal St (☎03/319 5842). Excellent, friendly hostel with great views over the town. Dorms ①, rooms ②.

Maui YHA, 270 Esplanade (☎03/319 5931). Much improved by a recent refurbishment, this is now a spacious hostel with excellent facilities and a great view over the beach and up the coast. Dorms ①, rooms ②.

Moby Dix's Backpackers, 65 Beach Rd (☎ & fax 03/319 6699). A large, brightly decorated and friendly hostel about ten minutes' walk from the centre of town. Dorms ①, rooms ②.

Searidge Holiday Park, 34 Beach Rd (☎ & fax 03/319 5362). Handy for the train station, this recently revamped park with trees and upgraded amenities offers a range of accommodation. Tent sites $7.50, units ②–④.

Top Spot Backpackers, 22 Deal St (☎03/319 5540). Tucked away 200m up a (signposted) track next to the post office, this very friendly hostel boasts good views over Kaikoura and the coast, a log-burning fire, mountain bikes, BBQ and sundeck. Dorms ①, rooms ②.

The Town and the peninsula

There is little to be said for the town itself; most visitors are dead-set on seeing whales or swimming with dolphins, and other activities are simply ways of filling in the time until your turn comes.

Some distraction is provided by the **Kaikoura Museum** (also known as "the treas-ures of the Nga Taonga"), at 14 Ludstone Rd (daily 2–4pm; $2), which covers the period from the early moa hunters, through the various groups that have occupied the land since. The Nga Tahu harvested the wealth of the land and seas until they were decim-ated by Te Rauparaha in about 1830. Whaling was established shortly after, in 1843, and immigrants came into the area to fish and farm. The museum contains a large number of argillite and greenstone artefacts, as well as a daunting collection of old photos.

Out on the peninsula, at 62 Avoca St, **Fyffe House** (daily 10am–5pm, 30min guided tours; $3.50) is an old whaler's cottage and the town's oldest building, occupying a great site with views up and down the coast. Fyffe House began as part of the Waiopuka Whaling Station (and still rests on its original whalebone foundations), which was founded by Robert Fyffe in 1842. Originally an unprepossessing two-room cooper's cot-tage, it was extended by George Fyffe in 1860, and looks now much as it did then. While you are on the peninsula, you may be tempted to follow the **Kaikoura Peninsula Walkway** (11km; 4hr 30min; leaflet available from visitor centre, $1), which takes you right round the peninsula, past Fyffe House and back to the town.

Kaikoura Peninsula is made of limestone and siltstone laid beneath the sea sixty mil-lion years ago, with a backdrop of rugged mountains and abundant wildlife. The shore-

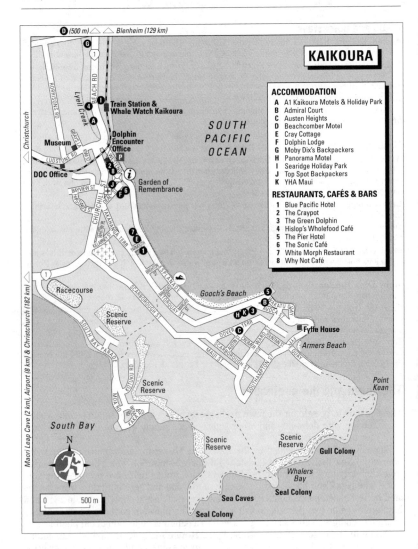

KAIKOURA

ACCOMMODATION
A A1 Kaikoura Motels & Holiday Park
B Admiral Court
C Austen Heights
D Beachcomber Motel
E Cray Cottage
F Dolphin Lodge
G Moby Dix's Backpackers
H Panorama Motel
I Searidge Holiday Park
J Top Spot Backpackers
K YHA Maui

RESTAURANTS, CAFÉS & BARS
1 Blue Pacific Hotel
2 The Craypot
3 The Green Dolphin
4 Hislop's Wholefood Café
5 The Pier Hotel
6 The Sonic Café
7 White Morph Restaurant
8 Why Not Café

line walk from **Point Kean**, just beyond Fyffe House, **to South Bay** (4.5km; 2hr 30min) is particularly fine, revealing gaping sea caves and stacks at Atia Point. This is also a favoured haunt of red-billed and black-backed gulls, oyster catchers, herons and shags, as well as a number of fur seals.

Otherwise, you're stuck with the **Maori Leap Cave**, 2km south of Kaikoura on SH1 (35min tours daily 10.30am, 11.30am, 12.30pm, 1.45pm, 2.30pm & 3.30pm; $7.50; ☎03/319 5023), which contains some remarkable limestone formations. Stalagmites and stalactites sprout from the floor and ceiling of the cave, and translucent stone straws seem to defy gravity by maintaining their internal water level. There are also examples of cave coral and algae that survive in the dank cave by turning darkness into energy – a kind of skewed photosynthesis. There are two rival explanations for the cave's name: one has it that a Maori warrior jumped to his death from the hills above the cave after he was captured by another tribe; the other has two thwarted lovers from different tribes plunging to their deaths.

Whales, dolphins and seals

Off the Kaikoura Peninsula is a complex network of trenches and troughs, forming an underwater canyon system, with unusually deep water very close to the coastline. This provides a rich habitat, constantly replenished from the Antarctic, which supports an enormous amount and variety of marine life.

One of the main reasons people come to Kaikoura is for a chance to see gigantic sperm **whales** (all year), migratory humpback whales (Jun–July) and Orca (Dec–Feb) at relatively close quarters. The Maori-owned and operated Whale Watch Kaikoura (☎03/319 5045, fax 319 6545) runs up to four sailings daily (April–Oct 6am, 8am, 11am & 1.30pm; Nov–March 5.30am, 8am, 10.30am & 1pm; $95), using two different types of rigid-hulled inflatable boat. The larger carries thirty-two people and has an observation deck that enables you to see further and look down on the whales. The smaller carries only twelve people and can often get a bit closer, but the ride is a lot rougher – those with back or heart problems and pregnant women must take the larger craft. Be warned, though, that trips are cancelled if **bad weather** threatens, so if you don't want to miss out, give yourself a couple of days in Kaikoura. And don't forget your camera.

The other way of seeing whales at Kaikoura is from the air, but you'll need a good pair of binoculars. Whale Watch Air (☎03/319 6580) and Air Tours Kaikoura (☎03/319 5986) both offer a number of scenic and whale-spotting flights lasting from twenty minutes ($65) to one hour ($156); prices are based on a minimum of two passengers, and include transfers to the airfield. Kaikoura Helicopters (☎03/319 6609) charge $120 for a twenty-minute spin.

The other main reason people visit Kaikoura is to frolic with **dolphins**. Dolphin Encounter (☎03/319 6777, fax 319 6534) do three trips a day (6am, 9am & 12.30pm; $80 to swim, $55 to watch; book at least 5 days in advance). Many people find being in the water with the dolphins a vaguely spiritual experience. You'll get most out of the experience if you're a reasonably confident swimmer; the more you duck-dive and generally splash around, the more eager the dolphins'll be to investigate. But don't get too carried away: dolphins have a penchant for swimming in ever-decreasing circles until lesser beings are quite dizzy and disorientated, so keep an eye on the boat.

Swimming with seals can be a lot of fun: seals tend to be more curious than dolphins, often coming closer to check you out. There is currently a price war among seal-swim operators, with new ventures constantly entering the fray, so check out the latest deals when you arrive. Among the most reputable outfits when we were in town were Graeme's Seal Swim (☎03/319 6182) and Top Spot Kaikoura (☎03/319 5540). Run by two brothers who are very professional, friendly and knowledgeable, Graeme's offers two-hour trips between November and April ($35, underwater cameras provided on request), as do Top Spot Kaikoura (also $35).

Eating and drinking

The least expensive way to sample the local **crayfish** is to buy them ready-boiled from one of the shacks and caravans advertising their wares alongside SH1 north of town. There are also a number of chip shops in town producing excellent fried-fish **take-**

aways; try the *Continental* on Beach Road or *Food Wonderful Food* on Westend Parade. The **restaurants** in town are all a bit pricey, safe in the knowledge that you're not exactly spoilt for choice.

Blue Pacific Hotel, 114 Esplanade. An evenings-only licensed restaurant that serves truly delicious fish and chips.

Caves Restaurant, 2km south of town on SH1, next to the Maori Leap Cave. Simple and generous meals that concentrate on local sea and farm produce; try the scallops for $12.50 or the massive seafood platter ($20). BYO. Mon–Fri, Sun 7am–8pm, Sat 7am–6pm.

Craypot, 70 Westend Parade. A café/wine bar with polished wooden floors and glass doors, offering breakfast, light meals and dinners with Mediterranean and Cajun influences, including some good seafood (around $18.50) and salads for $12.50. Daily 9am–11pm.

Green Dolphin, 12 Avoca St. A lovely little café on the peninsula, serving superb seafood and grills in a relaxed atmosphere (mains $19–23), with good views out the front. Licensed & BYO. Daily: Nov–Feb 4–11pm, March–Oct 6–10pm.

Hislop's Wholefood Café, 33 Beach Rd. Excellent, healthful café serving teas and coffees, and all-organic meals including superb breakfasts ($7.50), salads, pasta and veggie curries ($8.50–13.50), and delicious poached fish ($17.50). Mon–Wed 8am–6pm, Thurs–Sat 8am–11pm.

Pier Hotel, 1 Avoca St. A large colonial pub/hotel that was moved here from the original wharf opposite Fyffe House. With a wrap-around balcony and two atmospheric bars, they serve large portions of steak, scallops and fish of the day, all with either baked potato or chips, and side salad ($13–18). Daily 11am–11pm, dinner 6–9pm.

White Morph Restaurant, 94 Esplanade. The poshest place in town, with excellent food, especially seafood, at suitably rarefied prices. Licensed & BYO, $2 corkage. Daily 6–9pm.

Why Not Café, 58 Westend Parade. A spot for breakfast, lunch or an early dinner, with delicious pastries, salads and more substantial meals at reasonable prices.

Listings

Airlines Air Direct (☎0800/808 151) fly to Wellington ($120); Whale Watch Air (☎03/319 6580) fly to Christchurch ($95 one-way, $165 return).

Bike rental Westend Motors, 48–52 Westend Parade (☎03/319 5065).

Buses In addition to the services of the major companies, Compass Coachlines (☎03/578 7102) run to Blenheim, Picton and Christchurch; Kaikoura Shuttles (☎03/319 5846) operate a door-to-door service to Christchurch; Ko-op Shuttles (☎03/366 6633) run to Christchurch and Picton via Blenheim; and Southern Link Shuttles (☎03/358 8355) run to Picton and Christchurch.

Car rental Eades Garage, Westend Parade (☎03/319 5036).

Medical Treatment Kaikoura Hospital and Doctors Surgery, Deal St, 50m from cnr Churchill St (☎03/319 5040).

Pharmacy Kaikoura Pharmacy, 37 Westend Parade (Mon–Sat 9am–1pm).

Post office Opposite the visitor centre on Westend Parade (Mon–Fri 9am–5pm, Sat 9am–1pm).

Taxis Bazz's Bus (☎03/319 5686) operates taxi services, sightseeing and trailhead transport.

Around Kaikoura

The Seaward **Kaikoura Ranges** and Mount Fyffe completely dominate the town, creating a bleak and broody atmosphere. Leaflets (50¢–$1, from visitor centre in Kaikoura) outline some of the **walks** in the ranges.

   Mount Fyffe is 1602m high and rewards the climber with views across the Seaward Kaikoura Ranges, the Banks Peninsula and the North Island. The path to the summit (18km return; 8hr) starts about 8km from Kaikoura: head along Postmans Road to the head of the Hinau Track, where there is parking and information. It is also possible to access the Inland Kaikoura Range and the huts of the **Clarence River Conservation Area** from Kaikoura, a journey of about 25km. Head south out of Kaikoura on SH1, then turn inland on the Kaikoura–Waiau Road to the reserve car park at the Kahutara

---

MOUNT LYFORD SKIFIELDS

The **Mount Lyford Skifields** (May to mid-Oct, 9am–4pm; general information ☎03/315 6178, premium-rated snowphone 0900/34 444) are 60km from Kaikoura on the road to Waiau (SH70). The newest and smallest of New Zealand's ski areas, Mount Lyford caters for a broad range of abilities and is rarely crowded. There are two separate fields: **Stella** is ideal for advanced skiers and snowboarders, and **Terako** has a variety of intermediate and beginner runs, as well as some more ambitious routes in the Terako Basin. **Access** is along 4km of unsealed road (toll $5) off SH70, or by Mount Lyford Transport ski bus from Kaikoura (about $30 return; ☎03/319 6182). **Lift facilities** are limited to one fixed grip and two rope tows; heli-skiing is also an option, as is cross-country. Field charges are $30 per day, there's a learners' package for $55, and ski rental is available ($10–25 per day).

Mount Lyford Village, 3.5km from the field, has comfortable **accommodation** at the *Mount Terako Lodge* (☎03/315 6677; B&B ④) and *Graeme Chambers Mount Lyford Lodge* (03/319 6182; dorms ①, rooms ③), while the *Chamois Café* serves snacks and meals at high-altitude prices.

Bridge. The Clarence River Conservation Area offers the opportunity to explore some uncrowded walking tracks in an area with some of the highest mountains outside the Southern Alps and some stunning geological formations.

If this sounds too rugged, the privately owned **Kaikoura Coastal Track** (43km; 3 days) offers an excellent way to explore the area. The track begins 50km south of Kaikoura on SH1, where there's secure parking; Bazz's Bus (☎03/319 5686) will also run you out to the **trailhead**. The trail climbs through farmland and native bush across the Hawkeswood Range and along beaches, with spectacular views of the Seaward Kaikoura mountains and the Southern Alps, ending at *The Staging Post* (see below), where transport can be arranged to your next destination. **Accommodation** is in warm, clean cottages with fully equipped kitchens, baths and showers as well as fresh farm produce, milk, bread and home-cooked meals by arrangement. You must **book in advance** (☎03/319 2715; $90, including 3 nights' accommodation), and only a limited number are allowed to walk the track at any one time. If you want a gentle transition back to civilization after your walk, hole up for a day or two at *The Staging Post*, 2111 Parnassus Rd, Hawkeswood (☎03/319 2898; tent sites $7, dorms ①, cabins ②). This idiosyncratic place right at the end of the coastal track on a large sheep station reflects the personality of its ancient and amusing owner, and is well worth a look even if you don't intend to stay.

South from Kaikoura

Continuing south on SH1, the coastal landscape eventually dissolves into a relatively flat extension of the Canterbury Plains, with little to delay you before you hit the eastern suburbs of Christchurch that face out on to **Pegasus Bay** – a bite out of the coastline bounded by the **Hurunui River** and Banks Peninsula, more than a hundred kilometres further south. The main community along the way is the small town of **Cheviot**, 70km from Kaikoura and 115km from Christchurch, but there's little reason to linger unless you're an angler keen to test your mettle on the trout and salmon in the nearby Hurunui and Waiau rivers or an ardent tramper bound for the Port Robinson Track.

Cheviot and around

Like the other towns between Kaikoura and Christchurch, **CHEVIOT** suffers by comparison with those two destinations and has little to delay the discerning visitor for more than an hour or two. SH1 becomes Main Streeet as it makes its way through the town.

If you're here at a weekend, look in on the **Cheviot Museum**, Main Street (Sat 10.30am–noon, Sun 2–4pm; donation requested), which provides some interesting insights into the origins of the town and its surroundings. The three dominant collections consist of a large number of moa bones; a display devoted to George Forbes, local lad made good, who rose to become prime minister between 1930 and 1935; and a daunting collection of documents relating to land redistribution. Forged in the hills around Cheviot, this policy marked a turning point for land tenure in New Zealand. In 1892 Sir John McKenzie bought, on behalf of the government, the Cheviot Estate (about 16 square kilometres of good land), following a dispute about the tax valuation of the land. He then parcelled the land into small farms and holdings, so the same land could support 650 people, rather than just 80 – a process that was to be replicated across New Zealand, breaking up the enormous landholdings of a few rich and powerful men (as recounted in John Wilson's book, *Cheviot: Kingdom to Country*.

Gore Bay

To dispel driving fatigue or museum ennui, take a walk by the sea at **Gore Bay**, about 8km from Cheviot and well signposted. There's a lovely beach with safe swimming and, at the east end of the bay, adjoining the road, a scenic reserve that shelters dramatic examples of badland erosion. At the southern end of the reserve, siltstone cliffs called **The Cathedrals** have been eroded into huge stalagmite-like fingers that resemble the pipes of a cathedral organ. Also within the reserve is a 2.5km loop track between Cathedral Gully and Tweedie Gully, with a few steep sections that make it ill-advised outside the summer months.

A more rewarding track is the coastal trail from Gore Bay to Port Robinson and then on to the mouth of the Hurunui River, **The Port Robinson Track**. The whole route takes seven hours return, but most of the highlights – the "cathedrals", spectacular bluffs, Port Robinson, Gibson's Point and the lighthouse – are encountered during the **Gore Bay to Manuka Bay** sector, a three-hour round-trip. Beginning at the southern end of the Gore Bay Scenic Reserve, the sector ends on the south side of Gibson's Point, where the track passes the dead end of the road that leads back to Port Robinson and then Gore Bay. The first part of the walkway is along the beach beneath the bluffs, which must be accomplished at low tide; if you miss the tide, the walk can be joined from the Gore Bay Road, turning down to the Port Robinson boat ramps and then round the point and lighthouse. Self-sufficient trampers might want to take advantage of the extremely basic DOC **campsites** ($4) at Gore Bay and the mouth of the **Hurunui River**, though most will be content to explore briefly and then press on to the more tangible rewards of Christchurch or Hanmer.

The road to Waipara

The road veers away from the coast until it reaches **Waipara**, weaving among gently rolling hills that alternate between green and golden brown depending upon the time of the year, and obscure the Pacific Ocean from view. At the tiny hamlet of Waipara, SH1 divides into two, climbing inland towards **Hanmer Springs** as the Lewis Pass Road/SH7 (see p.542), or continuing as SH1 down the coast to **Christchurch** (see p.480).

travel details

Buses

From Blenheim to: Christchurch (3–4 daily; 4hr 55min); Nelson (6 daily; 1hr 50min); Picton (10–11 daily; 30min); St Arnaud (1–2 daily; 1hr).

From Murchison to: Blenheim (1 daily; 4hr 40min); Nelson (2 daily; 2hr 25min); Westport (2 daily; 1hr 30min).

From Nelson to: Greymouth (2–3 daily; 6hr); Kawatiri Junction, for Nelson Lakes (1 daily; 1hr 5min); Motueka (5–6 daily; 1hr 10min); Murchison (2 daily; 2hr 25min); Picton (5–6 daily; 2hr 10min); Takaka (2–3 daily; 4hr).

From Picton to: Blenheim (10–11 daily; 30min); Christchurch (3–4 daily; 5hr 25min); Kaikoura (3–4 daily; 2hr 15min); Nelson (5–6 daily; 2hr 10min).

Trains

From Picton to: Blenheim (1 daily; 35min); Christchurch (1 daily; 5hr 25min); Kaikoura (1 daily; 2hr 20min).

Ferries

From Picton to: Wellington (8 daily; 2hr 15 min–3hr 15min).

Flights

From Blenheim to: Auckland (17 daily; 1hr 55min); Christchurch (31 daily; 1hr 40min); Wellington (35 daily; 25min); Westport (2 daily; 2hr 5min).

From Kaikoura to: Christchurch (1–2 daily; 1hr 20min); Wellington (1–2 daily; 1hr).

From Motueka to: Takaka (2 daily; 30min); Wellington (2 daily; 45min).

From Nelson to: Auckland (33 daily; 2hr); Blenheim (9–10 daily; 55min); Christchurch (18 daily; 1hr); Queenstown (6 daily; 3hr 20min); Wellington (21 daily; 25min); Westport (2 daily; 2hr 20min).

From Picton to: Wellington (7–9 daily; 25min).

CHAPTER NINE

CHRISTCHURCH AND SOUTH TO OTAGO

E ncompassing some stunning and varied scenery, the South Island's east coast perhaps comes closer to most visitors' expectations of New Zealand than any other part of the country. The main hub of the region is New Zealand's third city, **Christchurch**, stretched out between the Pacific Ocean and the agriculturally rich flatlands of the Canterbury Plains, and with the Southern Alps acting as a distant backdrop to the west. A relaxed, green city where parks and gardens rub shoulders with some fine Victorian architecture, it boasts its fair share of urban thrills, provided largely by the cafés, bars and pubs which crowd a busy downtown area. It's also a seaside resort in its own right, with **beach suburbs** like New Brighton and Sumner within easy reach of the centre.

Immediately southeast of Christchurch rise the **Port Hills**, providing welcome relief from the Canterbury Plains. Beyond them, **Banks Peninsula** is a popular escape for city residents, its coastline indented by numerous bays and harbours. Perched above these harbours are the two main communities of the peninsula, the brusque port of **Lyttelton** and the more elegant resort town of **Akaroa**.

South of Banks Peninsula the main road and rail lines forge south across the Canterbury Plains, a patchwork quilt of rich fields and vineyards bordered by long shingle beaches littered with driftwood. Further south the countryside again changes character, with undulating coastal hills and crumbling cliffs announcing the altogether more rugged terrain of **North Otago**. The historic settlements dotted along the coast are a testament to the wealth that farming and mineral extraction brought to the region. The main centres here are the lively port of **Timaru**, close to a series of **Maori rock paintings** that indicate the region has a longer history than the imposed European feel would have you believe; and the quieter **Oamaru**, with an engaging nineteenth-century centre and some captivating **penguin colonies** just outside town.

ACCOMMODATION PRICES

Accommodation listed in this guide has been categorized into one of nine price bands, as set out below. The rates quoted represent the **cheapest available** double or twin **room** – except for category ①, which are per-person rates for a dorm bed; fees for **tent sites** and **DOC huts** are also per-person, unless otherwise stated.

① under $20 per person	④ $60–80	⑦ $140–180
② under $40 per room	⑤ $80–100	⑧ $180–240
③ $40–60	⑥ $100–140	⑨ over $240

For more on accommodation, see p.33.

Beyond here routes lead on towards Dunedin and the south, passing the unearthly **Moeraki boulders**, perfect spherical rocks formed by a combination of subterranean pressure and erosion.

Trains trundle up and down the east coast as rarely as once a day, but otherwise **transport** in the region is pretty straightforward, with numerous buses and shuttle buses plying the main routes out of Christchurch.

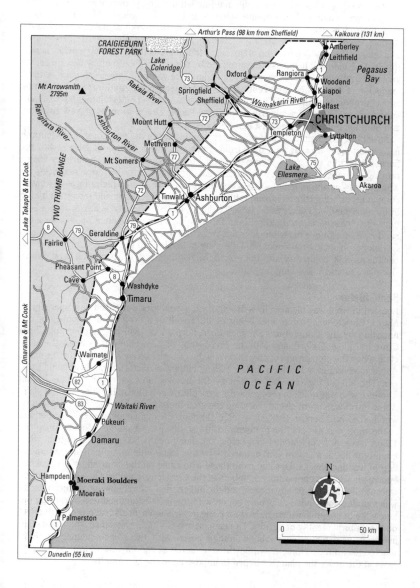

CHRISTCHURCH

Capital of the Canterbury region and the largest city on the South Island, **CHRISTCHURCH** (population 306,000) sports a palpable air of the mother country. Named after an Oxford college and perceived as an outpost of Anglicanism by its first settlers, it still has the feel of a traditional English university town, with its neo-Gothic architecture, winding river, punting students and weeping willows. However, modern Christchurch is also a lively melting pot of cultures, with a continental café scene and a distinct, ever-changing Kiwi identity of its own. Indeed, those who regard Christchurch as a quiet place in which to sleep off jet lag or take a break from the long journey across the South Island will be pleasantly surprised by the city's contemporary face. In recent years its traditional conservatism has gained a more youthful, bohemian edge, with an explosion of lively **bars and restaurants**, the emergence of underground **nightlife**, and a burgeoning of the visual arts, theatre, music and street entertainment. Urban pursuits such as these are nicely balanced by the Pacific Ocean suburbs of New Brighton and Sumner, both of which boast excellent **beaches**.

Straddling the main road and rail routes running down the east coast, Christchurch is used by many tourists as a base from which to explore the South Island, with the fjord-like terrain of **Banks Peninsula** and the **vineyards** of the Canterbury Plains proving the most popular out-of-town destinations. Many of the **outdoor activities** for which New Zealand is famous are accessible from here, with a plethora of city-based companies offering trips involving rafting, paragliding, ballooning and mountain biking in the surrounding countryside (see "Listings", p.503). The city is also within a two-hour drive of several good **skifields** to the west (again, see "Listings", p.503, for a full rundown), making it possible to combine a day on the pistes with an evening in Christchurch's numerous nocturnal watering holes. Indeed the place's only real drawback is its cost: compared with the rest of the South Island, Christchurch is an expensive place to spend any length of time.

Some history

Located in what was historically a dry and windswept area populated only sparsely by Maori, Christchurch came into being as the result of a programmatic policy of colonization by the **Canterbury Association**. Formed in 1849 by members of Christ Church College Oxford, and with the Archbishop of Canterbury at its head, the association had the utopian aim of creating a new Jerusalem in New Zealand; a middle class, Anglican community in which the moralizing culture of Victorian England could prosper. The site of the city was chosen by the association's surveyor Captain Joseph Thomas, who was quick to recognize the agricultural potential of the surrounding plain. A few Europeans were already farming the area (notably the Scottish Deans brothers, who had arrived here in 1843, see p.492), although the main centre of white settlement at the time was the port of Lyttelton to the southeast, a base for whalers since the 1830s. It was at Lyttelton that four ships containing nearly 800 settlers arrived in 1850, bound for the new city of Christchurch – by this stage little more than an agglomeration of wooden shacks. Descent from those who came on the "four ships" still carries enormous social cachet among members of the Christchurch elite. The earliest settlers weren't all Anglicans by any means, and the millenarian aspirations upon which the city was founded soon faded as people got on with the exhausting business of carving out a new life in unfamiliar terrain. However, the association's ideals had a profound effect on the cultural identity of the city. The elegant neo-Gothic architecture which still characterizes Christchurch's public buildings oozes with the self-confidence of these nineteenth-century pioneers, while the symmetry of the city's grid-iron street plan hints at the order the planners hoped to impose upon the community.

Arrival and information

Christchurch Airport is 10km northwest of the city centre, and most Christchurch hotels will provide a free pick-up service from here if you've already booked a room. **City buses** (operated by Canride) connect the airport with the central Cathedral Square at hourly intervals (Mon–Fri 6.30am–8.30pm, Sat & Sun 7.30am–8.30pm; $2.70); while **Super Shuttle** buses (roughly every 20–30 minutes, although departures depend on demand; $8) operate a door-to-door service linking the airport with the Christchurch destination of your choice. There are **taxi ranks** in front of the airport terminal building (otherwise ring Blue Star on ☎03/379 9799 or Gold Band on ☎03/379 5795), with the ride into town costing $15–20.

Trains arrive at Addington Street Station at the southern tip of Hagley Park, just over 2km southwest of Cathedral Square. You can pick up a **shuttle bus** ($3–5) or **taxi** ($7–10) from the station into the centre, although **city buses** don't serve the train station directly – you have to walk down the station access road to the nearby thoroughfare of Blenheim Road to pick up Canride bus #25 into town.

Of the national **bus** companies serving Christchurch, InterCity and Mount Cook Landline drop passengers off either near Cathedral Square or at their respective depots: Mount Cook Landline are based at 40 Lichfield St, 500m south of Cathedral Square; while the InterCity Travel Centre is about 2km southeast of the centre at the junction of Moorhouse Avenue and Fitzgerald Avenue. In addition, Coast to Coast buses operating between Christchurch and Greymouth stop at numerous points throughout the centre, including Cathedral Square; while White Star services on the Nelson–Christchuch and Westport–Christchurch routes stop at 471 Moorehouse Ave. There are also various **shuttle bus** companies (see "Moving on from Christchurch", p.502 for details) linking Christchurch with most destinations on the South Island, picking up and dropping off either in Cathedral Square, at the visitor centre 200m west of the square on Worcester Street, at the airport, or frequently at the destination of your choice for an extra $5 or so.

Cathedral Square itself is within easy walking distance of most of the hostels, major hotels and some of the B&Bs and motels.

Information

The principal visitor centre for Christchurch and the surrounding area is the **Christchurch–Canterbury Visitor Centre**, 200m west of Cathedral Square on the corner of Worcester Boulevard and Oxford Terrace (Oct–April daily 8.30am–7pm; May–Sept Mon–Fri 8.30am–5pm, Sat, Sun & public holidays 8.30am–4pm; ☎03/379 9629, fax 377 2424). You can book most forms of transport as well as trips and activities here; be sure to pick up the free *Christchurch City Central Walks* leaflet, which provides a good introduction to local history, as well as the *Tramway* map, which details the main stops on this popular sightseers' route (see "City transport" p.482). There are also **information desks** at the airport – one in the **international terminal** (open to meet every international flight) and one in the next-door **domestic terminal** (Mon–Fri & Sun 8am–10.30pm, Sat 6.30am–8pm) – where you can book accommodation and pick up literature.

The **DOC** (Department of Conservation) **office** is 1km northwest of Cathedral Square at 133 Victoria St (Mon–Fri 10am–5pm; ☎03/379 9758), and stocks specific information on wildlife and walking routes, as well as booking Great Walks throughout the South Island.

City transport

You can easily see most of what Christchurch has to offer **on foot**, resorting to public transport for the odd trip out to the suburbs or to get from one side of the centre to another.

Bus services are operated by CTL Canride and most run from Cathedral Square or nearby. Tickets cost 80¢ per zone and a large part of the city centre falls within Zone 1; one-day passes cost $5 (for unlimited travel across all zones); 12-trip cards $9; and 24-trip cards $30. All routes run from 6am in the morning until about midnight (slightly longer in the case of some of the more popular routes). The same company operate Big Red buses, which connect Cathedral Square with out-of-town destinations such as New Brighton, Lyttelton and Akaroa. For more information on all routes, timetable and tickets, go to the small CTL kiosk across the square from the cathedral, or call ☎03/366 8855.

Another option for familiarizing yourself with the city is offered by hop-on hop-off **tourist buses**. City Circuit Buses (☎03/385 5386) offer a choice of two routes, both departing from the visitor centre. The Port circuit (departures at 10am, noon & 2pm; $25) runs in a loop around the eastern half of the city; while the Canterbury Plains circuit (Oct–April at 9am, 11am, 1pm & 3pm; June–Sept 10am, 11am, 1pm & 3pm; $25) concentrates on the west. Tickets are valid for two days, allowing you to leave the bus at any designated stop and continue on a later service.

A pleasant and comfortable way of seeing the city centre is provided by the **Tramway** (Oct–April daily 7am–midnight; May–Oct Mon–Thurs & Sun 7am–9pm, Fri & Sat 7am–midnight), whose trams (lovingly restored 1905 originals) operate along a 2.5km circuit which runs past many of the central sights, including Cathedral Square. You can get on or off at any stop, depending upon the time limit of your ticket: a one-hour ticket costs $4 and an all-day ticket $10. Thrown in with the price is a rudimentary commentary that will at least identify landmarks and help you get your bearings.

Driving in Christchurch is pretty straightforward providing you avoid morning and evening rush hours. Most central parking spaces are metered from Monday to Saturday between 7am and 6pm – outside these hours they're free.

Given the city's relatively quiet roads, **cycling** is an ideal way of appreciating some of the more out-of-the-way suburbs. Expect to pay around $20–25 a day for **bike rental** (see "Listings", p.503, for details of outlets). Finally, a sedate way of seeing some of the prettier parts of the city is by **punt** up and down the River Avon (daily 9am–dusk; $12–15 per person; book through the visitor centre); the water-level perspective is a refreshing one.

Accommodation

Christchurch offers a broad range of accommodation, and although prices are by no means extortionate, they're understandably higher than in the South Island's smaller towns and cities.

Most of the hotels and hostels are situated within the **city centre**, as are a number of B&Bs, while many of the budget options are on or near Manchester Street. The majority of hotels are close to Victoria Square, with motels strung out along Papanui Road as it runs through the northwestern suburb of **Merivale** and on Bealey Avenue as it heads towards **Richmond**. Predictably, campsites are scattered outside the city centre, mostly within walking distance of a bus stop. For those who want to wake up **close to the sea**, there's a variety of accommodation in the suburbs facing the Pacific Ocean: New Brighton and Sumner are the best places to aim for – they're about 8km east of the centre and reached by buses #5, #19 and #29 (for New Brighton); and #3 and #28 (for Sumner).

Hotels and motels

There's a broad range of **hotel** and **motel** accommodation in Christchurch, with many conveniently central hotels overlooking Hagley Park or Victoria Square. On the whole, however, the downtown hotels represent the most expensive option, with the more numerous motels – strung out in groups along main thoroughfares like Bealey Avenue and Papanui Road – covering a broader range of prices. Many establishments offer **special deals** for weekend and long-term stays.

City centre
All the following hotels and motels are marked on the map on p.488.

Akron Motel, 87 Bealey Ave (☎03/366 1633, fax 379 1332). A small motel with well kept gardens and cosy units, about ten minutes' walk from Cathedral Square. ⑤.

Cashel Court Motel, 457 Cashel St (☎ & fax 03/389 2768). Very reasonably priced, close to the city centre and next to an indoor pool. Small but comfortable. ④.

Centra Christchurch, cnr Cashel St & High St (☎03/365 8888, fax 365 8822). A modern and bright hotel in the heart of the business and retail precincts, with superb city views and luxurious rooms, but essentially without character. ⑨.

Chateau on the Park, 189 Deans Ave (☎03/348 8999, fax 348 8990). Two-hundred-room hotel, memorable for its lovely surroundings on the edge of Hagley Park, with an outdoor pool, restaurants and cocktail bar. Fifteen minutes' walk from Cathedral Square. ⑦–⑧.

Park Royal, cnr Kilmore St & Durham St (☎03/365 7799, fax 365 0082). This spectacular hotel is one of the outstanding modern architectural features of the city – a sort of Mayan temple with a glass atrium. Overlooking Victoria Square, it has a magnificent lobby and foyer, but disappointing rooms. There are three bars and three restaurants, and it's well worth dropping in for a drink or afternoon tea, even if you're not staying here. ⑨.

Quality Hotel Central, 776 Colombo St (☎03/379 5880, fax 365 4806). Opposite Victoria Square, with a great view of the Park Royal, and close to all major attractions. ⑦.

Tudor Court Motel, 57 Bealey Ave (☎03/379 1465, fax 379 1490). Very small motel in a peaceful environment with simple units. Fifteen minutes' walk to Cathedral Square. ④.

Northwest of the city
All the following hotels and motels are marked on the map on p.494.

Adelphi, 49 Papanui Rd, Merivale (☎03/355 6037, fax 355 6036). A kilometre from the city centre, with spacious units, spa, sauna and playground around a courtyard car park. The best value on Papanui Road. ④.

Airport Plaza, cnr Memorial Ave & Orchard Rd, Burnside (☎03/358 3139, fax 358 3029). A modern unspectacular hotel next to the international airport, 10km from the city centre, with a restaurant and simple rooms. ⑥.

Colonial Inn Motel, 43 Papanui Rd, Merivale (☎03/355 9139, fax 355 5457). A modern well-appointed motel about ten minutes' walk from Cathedral Square. Clean and comfortable units. ⑤.

Diplomat Motel, 127 Papanui Rd, Merivale (☎03/355 6009, fax 355 6007). Situated in the heart of Merivale, 2km from Cathedral Square and 8km from the airport, this is a very smart motel, with swimming pool, spa and large self-contained units with separate kitchens, TV and radio and off-street parking. ⑤.

Strathern Motor Lodge, 54 Papanui Rd, Merivale (☎ & fax 03/355 4411). About fifteen minutes' walk from Cathedral Square with its own spa pool. Each room is airy and equipped with a kitchen. ⑤.

New Brighton
Arcadia Motel, 564 Ferry Road, Woolston (☎ & fax 03/389 4756). Four kilometres from the centre, close to Sumner and the Avon Heathcote Estuary. This is a recently renovated motel containing

studios and one- to three-bedroom units, all with self-contained kitchens. There's a courtesy van to and from the airport and train station. ④–⑤.

Ferry Motel, 330 Ferry Rd (☎03/389 1013 & fax 389 1018). A spacious motel with comfortable and clean units, which range from studios to 2-bedroom apartments, all at very reasonable rates. It's five minutes' walk from the beaches and the Mount Cavendish Gondola. ④.

Golden Sands Motel, 121 Estuary Rd, New Brighton (☎03/388 7996, fax 388 2221). A small motel with six units containing kitchens and TVs. Clean and tidy. ④.

B&Bs and guesthouses

As is the case throughout New Zealand, the standard of **Bed and Breakfast** accommodation is very high in Christchurch. There's a sprinkling of excellent B&Bs in the centre and in the nearby, easily reached suburbs, and another concentration of places in the seaside communities of New Brighton and Sumner. All represent good value for money, and are invariably comfortable and friendly.

City centre
All the following guesthouses are marked on the map on p.488.

Ambassador's B&B, 19 Manchester St (☎ & fax 03/366 7808). A three-minute walk from Cathedral Square and adjacent to Hoyts Cinema complex, this is a cheap and friendly place with unspectacular, but clean rooms. ③.

Croydon Lodge, 63 Armagh St (☎ & fax 03/366 5111). This cheerful, pretty, German-run house, whose facade is brightly painted in red, yellow and green was once a rest home for shell-shocked soldiers from World War II. Twelve comfortable guest rooms with shared facilities. Delicious continental and cooked breakfasts. ⑤.

Melville, 49 Gloucester St (☎03/379 8956). Cheap, no-frills B&B in a central location. ③.

Windsor, 52 Armagh St (☎03/366 1503, fax 366 9796). A century-old former student hall of residence, this renowned B&B is traditional in its approach, with friendly staff and the sort of breakfast that will keep you going all day. The rooms are quiet and comfortable and all have shared bathrooms. ⑤.

Northwest of the city
All the following guesthouses are marked on the map on p.494.

Elm Tree House, 236 Papanui Rd, Merivale (☎ & fax 03/355 9742). A listed historic building on the city-centre edge of the suburb of Merivale, only fifteen minutes' walk north of Cathedral Square. Two charming double rooms, en-suite bathrooms and a heated swimming pool. Dinner by arrangement ($22). ⑤.

Highway Lodge, 121 Papanui Rd, Merivale (☎ & fax 03/355 5418). Beautiful Tudor-style home about ten minutes' walk from the city centre, close to restaurants, shops and Hagley Park, with clean, well equipped en-suite rooms. ④.

Home-Lea Guest House, 195 Bealey Ave (☎ & fax 03/379 9977). Ten minutes' walk from the city centre, this two-storeyed wooden house built in the early 1900s has a quiet family atmosphere and cosy bedrooms. ⑤.

New Brighton and Sumner
Convent Lodge, 97 Lonsdale St, New Brighton (☎ & fax 03/388 3388). A large friendly guesthouse with six shared bathrooms and a separate kitchen and dining room for guests. Tennis court and bikes available. ④.

The Palms B&B, 63 Nayland St, Sumner (☎03/326 7758). Decorated with rimu panelling and leadlight windows. The rooms are spacious and breakfast is served in the garden courtyard, weather permitting. Dinner by arrangement ($20), with great vegetarian options. A bus stops near the end of the drive. ④.

Southshore Homestay, Rockinghorse Rd, Southshore (☎03/388 4067). Between the ocean and the estuary located on a spit, with two clean and cosy bedrooms and views of the sand dunes, close to Mount Cavendish Gondola. Twenty minutes' drive from Cathedral Square. ④.

Sumner Homestay, Panorama Rd, Clifton Hill, Sumner (☎03/326 5755, fax 326 5611). Comfortable accommodation in two rooms, with use of a separate guest lounge and a stunning terraced garden. Dinner by arrangement ($25). Three minutes' drive from the beach. ④.

Villa Alexandra, Clifton Hill, Sumner (☎03/326 6291 or 304 8582). A spacious villa overlooking Sumner Bay with a verandah and turret, offering one bedroom with private bathroom. All meals cooked on a coal range (dinner $20). ④.

Hostels

There are a large number of competing **backpacker** hostels offering a varying range of facilities. Almost all are within easy reach of the city centre, and prices are pretty uniform. As a general rule, hostels closer to the central Cathedral Square cater for a younger, more raucous crowd, while those further out (such as *Cora Wilding* in the suburb of Richmond, see p.486), tend to be more family-oriented. If you are arriving during the peak summer season, try to book accommodation a few days in advance to be sure of getting a bed. Many hostels offer a booking service for events, activities, trips and travel, but rarely at cheaper rates than at the visitor centre.

City centre
All the following hostels are marked on the map on p.488.

Charlie B's, 268 Madras St (☎ & fax 03/379 8429). This one-time YWCA building, in need of a little interior restoration, is two minutes from the city centre and contains 150 beds in dorms and doubles. Sky TV, videos, full cooking and laundry facilities, lockable covered bike storage, free off-street parking, free baggage storage and 24-hour access. Dorms ①, rooms ②.

Christchurch Arts Centre YHA, Rolleston House, 5 Worcester Boulevard, cnr Rolleston Ave (☎03/366 6564, fax 365 5589). The best location of all accommodation in Christchurch, opposite the Arts Centre and full of character. Plenty of dorms but a limited number of doubles, so book ahead if you want a room. Dorms ①, rooms ②.

Christchurch City YHA, 273 Manchester St (☎03/379 9535, fax 379 9537). New, purpose-built and well equipped hostel with a TV room and common room, only three minutes' walk from Cathedral Square. Some of the smaller doubles in the centre of the building are cramped and airless, so ask to have a look at them first. Good discounts on various trips and transport. Dorms ①, rooms ②.

Cokers Backpackers, 52 Manchester St (☎03/379 8580, fax 379 8585). This highly rated backpackers is open 24hr and has 120 beds (free linen); most rooms have a TV and en-suite bathroom. Situated over a pub with a choice of two bars. Dorms ①, rooms ②.

Foley Towers, 208 Kilmore St (☎03/366 9720, fax 379 3014). A more intimate B&B feel, and based only ten minutes' walk from Cathedral Square in a large old house with cosy rooms and a lovely garden. Dorms ①, rooms ②.

Pavlova Backpackers, 50 Cathedral Square (☎ & fax 03/366 5158). A popular *Kiwi Experience* stop-off, this place is full of party animals, attracted by deals on everything from haircuts to car rentals. This was once the *Warners Hotel* and contains 150 beds in doubles, singles and dorms (each room has a toilet and shower), set above two Irish bars offering discounted beer, wine and food each night (live music Thurs–Sat means the first floor is not as peaceful as it might be). Dorms ①, rooms ②.

Round the World Backpackers, 314 Barbadoes St (☎03/365 4363). Brand new, purpose-built modern hostel with clean, spacious rooms and free baggage storage. Dorms ①, rooms ②.

Vagabond Backpackers, 232 Worcester St (☎03/379 9677). Run by the very friendly Jan and Les, this place has only 20 beds, some in a wooden building at the back of the house; all are well kept, quiet, clean and recently redecorated. Free use of bikes, off-street parking, barbecue and garden area. Dorms ①, rooms ②.

YMCA, 12 Hereford St (☎03/365 0502, fax 365 1386). This is state-of-the-art as far as YMCA accommodation goes. Singles, doubles and apartments, all en suite, and equipped with telephone, tea and coffee facilities, and TV. Near the Arts Centre and two minutes' walk from Cathedral Square. Fitness centre, gym, squash courts, climbing wall, sauna and canteen. Dorms ①, rooms & apartments ③–⑤.

Richmond

Christchurch (Cora Wilding) YHA, 9 Eveleyn Couzins Ave (☎03/389 9199). Set in beautiful spacious grounds northeast of the centre and a popular haunt for young families, the hostel offers dorms and a limited number of rooms. Large parking area. Situated a five-minute bus ride or thirty-minute riverside walk from Cathedral Square. Dorms ①, rooms ②.

Campsites

Given the low cost of hostel accommodation in Christchurch, **camping** saves little money, and most of the sites are in any case some distance away from the city centre. There are some well-equipped motor camps within the city limits which are fine for campervans, offer tent sites and have good deals on cabins, but they tend to have a holiday-camp atmosphere.

All Seasons Holiday Park, 5 Kidbrooke St, off Linwood Ave, Linwood (☎03/384 9490). This modern park has a swimming pool, spa pool and large children's playground. Easy access to the beach (good for windsurfing), Linwood shopping centre and Sumner, and only ten minutes' drive from the city centre. Tent sites $7, cabins & on-site vans ②–③.

Amber Park, 308 Blenheim Rd, Upper Riccarton (☎03/348 3327). With easy access from the south and west sides of the city (it's on bus route #21), and handy for the train station, Addington Raceway and Canterbury University, this is a spacious site. Tent sites $8, on-site vans & cabins ②–③.

Meadow Park, 35 Meadow St, St Albans (☎03/352 6153). Situated 4km north of Cathedral Square on SH74 (and reached by bus route #11) this campsite, close to supermarkets and restaurants, covers a large area and has a full range of facilities. Tent sites $10, on-site vans & cabins ②–③.

The City

The city centre, together with many of its more compelling sights, is encased within four avenues: Moorhouse, Fitzgerald, Bealey and Deans. They define a useful border round the downtown area, in the very centre of which is **Cathedral Square**. Scattered in the streets around the square are the city's most attractive buildings, while over on the western edge of the four avenues lies **Hagley Park**, a focal point for leisure activities at weekends. Laid out in a grid pattern, Christchurch is very much a low-rise city, with the cathedral spire serving as a useful landmark. The architecture is predominantly nineteenth-century Gothic, a style which still informs many of the more modern buildings. Beyond the four avenues you pass into suburban districts like Riccarton, Fendalton, Merivale, St Albans, Richmond and Waltham, each characterized by one- and two-storey residential housing and beautifully kept gardens. Further west lie the coastal suburbs of New Brighton and Sumner, which provide access to the beaches of the Pacific Ocean.

Within the four avenues

Christchurch is dominated by its **Cathedral** (Mon–Fri 8.30am–8pm, Sat & Sun 7.30am–8.30pm; free guided tours Mon–Fri 11am & 2pm, Sat 11am, Sun 11.30am) and the square that surrounds it. You can climb the 133-step claustrophobic staircase of the 63-metre spire ($4) for the best panoramic views of the city. Designed by G.G. Scott, the cathedral was begun in the 1860s and completed in 1904 – a Gothic revival Anglican church with a cool and spacious interior. On the left-hand side from the main entrance, look out for the Maori contribution of *Tukutuku* panels made of leather and rimu wood, celebrating the Maori proverb: "What is the most important thing in life? It is people, people, people". Visitors and worshippers contributed many of the stitches. To sample the marvellous acoustics of the building, drop by for choral evensong (Tues & Wed 5.15pm, Fri 4pm).

The **Cathedral Square** is a large, open, paved area peppered with pubs, late-night cafés, bus stops, and the city's largest taxi rank. Bordering it, the **Old Post Office**, an Italianate building constructed in 1879, together with the Palladian-style former **Government Building** (1901), provide a pleasing contrast to the predominantly Gothic architecture on show elsewhere. The **Statue of Robert Godley**, the founding father of Christchurch and agent of the Canterbury Association, stands opposite the **Memorial of the Four Ships** outside the old post office, which shows the vessels sent by the Canterbury Association in 1850 to create a model Anglican community here.

Another less permanent occupant of the square is the **Wizard**, a local eccentric turned national institution. He regales crowds with tales of his battle to stop Telecom painting phone boxes pale blue, or his efforts to alleviate drought in the North Island by performing rain dances – so successfully that the residents of Auckland have complained of flooding. He no longer appears regularly, although the staff at the visitor centre have an uncanny knack of predicting these occasions and carry a healthy stock of his upside-down maps and postcards.

The Arts Centre

A grid of shopping streets and precincts spreads out from the square, to form a downtown area short on specific sights save for the Arts Centre to the west. Before heading out here, however, it's worth taking a look at **New Regent Street** two minutes' walk east of the square along Gloucester Street. Built in 1932, and home to the city's most upmarket cafés and stores, it's one of Christchurch's most attractive streets, with pastel-coloured buildings and trellised balconies recalling the Spanish Mission style of architecture which flourished in eighteenth-century California and New Mexico.

Five hundred metres west of Cathedral Square along Worcester Street, the **Arts Centre** was founded in 1874 as the University of Canterbury and Christchurch Girls' and Boys' High Schools. Today it's a hive of activity, especially at weekends, and is a great place to hang out and watch the world go by. Guided tours of the centre (Mon–Fri 11am & 2pm; $5) consist of a 45-minute whistle-stop excursion through the buildings and their history. The centre's architects included Benjamin W. Mountfort, who also designed the Christchurch Museum, Christ's College and the Provincial Chambers, as well as the neo-Gothic enthusiasts J.J. Collins and his son J.G., whose influence perhaps shines through most clearly. The buildings, constructed from bluestone (a local volcanic rock) mixed with Oamaru limestone, and interspersed with leafy courtyards and grassy quadrangles, evoke the feel of an old and venerated institution. Academic claims to fame include Ernest Rutherford's five-year tenure here, and you can visit the Nobel Prize-winning physicist's cramped basement laboratory. In 1975 the university moved out to a suburban campus and, after a period of some uncertainty, the Arts Centre, with its restaurants, food stalls, shops and galleries, moved in.

The Arts Centre is also home to the **Christchurch Environmental Centre**, which has a reference library that deals with global ecology issues, and also sells a range of ethnic crafts. A **flea market** is held on Saturday and Sunday in the Market Square on the east side of the Arts Centre, and there's an **information centre** (daily 9am–5pm) at the entrance to the clock tower on the corner of Worcester Street and Rolleston Avenue, where you can find out about upcoming events, gallery and shop opening times and concerts.

Hagley Park and around

Across Rolleston Avenue from the Arts Centre lies the entrance to **Hagley Park**. It is whispered by the mischievous priest of St Michael's that the park was put here in order to protect the solidly Anglican districts within the four avenues from the Presbyterians in the suburbs beyond. The park contains the spectacular Botanic Garden, the

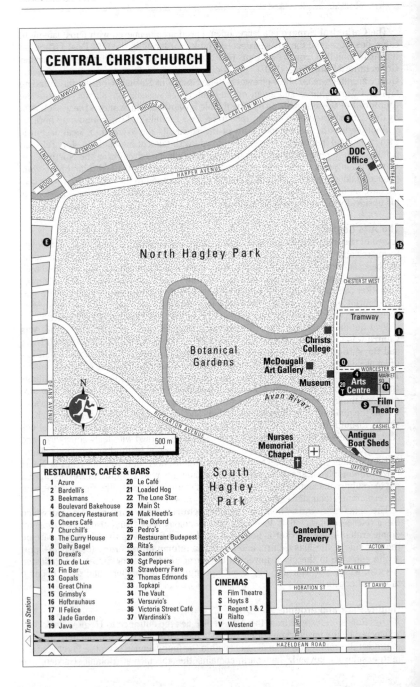

CENTRAL CHRISTCHURCH

North Hagley Park

Botanical Gardens

South Hagley Park

DEANS AVENUE

HOLMWOOD RD

ROSSALL ST

RHODES ST

HELMORES

DESMOND

FENDALTON RD

WOOD

WINCHESTER ST

ANDOVER

HEWITTS RD

CARLTON MILL

HARPER AVENUE

GREENHAM

EXETER

SHREWSBURY

TOMBRIDGE

BASTRICK

PAPANUI RD

ONSLOW

DERBY ST

STONEHURST

KNOX

DUBLIN ST

PARK TERRACE

DORSET

VICTORIA ST

WESTHOW

MONTREAL ST

MARKET

DOC Office

Tramway

Christs College

McDougall Art Gallery

Museum

Avon River

RICCARTON AVENUE

Nurses Memorial Chapel

Arts Centre

Film Theatre

Antigua Boat Sheds

CHESTER ST WEST

WORCESTER ST

CASHEL ST

OXFORD TERR

Canterbury Brewery

ACTON

BALFOUR ST

HORATION ST

ST DAVID

STEWART

ANTIGUA STREET

MONTREAL STREET

HALKETT

HAGLEY AVENUE

WALLER

STUART MILE

HAZELDEAN ROAD

Train Station

0   500 m

RESTAURANTS, CAFÉS & BARS

1	Azure	20	Le Café
2	Bardelli's	21	Loaded Hog
3	Beekmans	22	The Lone Star
4	Boulevard Bakehouse	23	Main St
5	Chancery Restaurant	24	Mak Heeth's
6	Cheers Café	25	The Oxford
7	Churchill's	26	Pedro's
8	The Curry House	27	Restaurant Budapest
9	Daily Bagel	28	Rita's
10	Drexel's	29	Santorini
11	Dux de Lux	30	Sgt Peppers
12	Fin Bar	31	Strawberry Fare
13	Gopals	32	Thomas Edmonds
14	Great China	33	Topkapi
15	Grimsby's	34	The Vault
16	Hofbrauhaus	35	Versuvio's
17	Il Felice	36	Victoria Street Café
18	Jade Garden	37	Wardinski's
19	Java		

CINEMAS

R Film Theatre
S Hoyts 8
T Regent 1 & 2
U Rialto
V Westend

ACCOMMODATION

A Akron Motel
B Ambassador's
C Centra Christchurch
D Charlie B's
E Chateau on the Park
F Cokers
G Croydon Lodge
H Foley Towers
I Melville Hotel
J Park Royal
K Pavlova
L Quality Hotel
M Round the World
N Tudor Court Motel
O Vagabond
P Windsor Hotel
Q YHA Arts Centre
R YHA Christchurch City
S YMCA

McDougall Art Gallery, a golf course, sports centre and playing fields. At weekends you can find what seems like the entire population of Christchurch here, merely strolling around or playing hockey, tennis, cricket, netball, rugby or golf.

The **Botanic Garden** (Rolleston Ave gate; daily 7am until 1hr before sunset; conservatories 10.15am–4pm; free) boasts a collection of indigenous and exotic plants and trees unrivalled on the South Island. Throughout summer and autumn the perennials here give a constant and dazzling display of colour. There is also a herb garden, containing a variety of culinary and medical plants; a rose garden with over 250 types of roses; and the Cockayne Memorial Garden, an area of native bush named after one of New Zealand's greatest botanists. Several conservatories, the largest of which is the galleried Cuningham House, contain tropical and indoor plants.

In fine weather, conducted **tours** of the gardens in tractor-pulled carts (11am–4pm; $4) depart from opposite the *Gardens Restaurant*, which can be found at the gardens' northern end. There's also a range of guided walking tours departing from the same place, of which the most intriguing is the **Te Puna Ora** (Mon–Fri 11am & 3pm; $5), an unusual storytelling tour which incorporates Maori and European myths and legends, as well as pure invention. The gardens are enclosed by a meander of the River Avon and you can explore by water either in a **punt** ($10 per person for 30min) or by paddleboats or canoe ($4 per hour); both are available from Antigua Boat Sheds, 2 Cambridge Terrace (☎03/366 5885).

Also within the grounds of Hagley Park is the **Robert McDougall Art Gallery**, just to the right of the Rolleston Avenue gate (daily 10am–4.30pm; donation requested). Completed in 1932 after designs by Gisborne architect Edward Armstrong, it's a delightful building whose classical Oamaru stone exteriors blend perfectly into their green surroundings. Inside, the gallery contains over four thousand paintings, sculptures, prints, drawings and craft objects, many by New Zealand artists, although only a sample of the gallery's collection is on display at any one time. Most striking among the Kiwi contributions are a series of small ink sketches by Russell Clark and a large number of paintings by Charles F. Goldie, who is known for his serene portraits of Maori. The gradual move away from art heavily influenced by European tradition, and the resulting emergence of an individual New Zealand style, is well reflected in the permanent displays.

Backing on to Hagley Park and just south of the Rolleston Avenue gate is the **Canterbury Museum** (daily 9am–5pm; $5), opposite the Arts Centre. A neo-Gothic structure, the museum was founded in 1870, and its first director was the archeologist Julius Haast (who gave his name to the Haast Pass, see p.663). Its best exhibition is the "Exploration of Antarctica", covering the many expeditions that have used New Zealand as their jumping-off point. Otherwise, this museum has the traditional exhibits on moa hunters, Maori, European settlers, native birds and mammals, fossils and geology.

North of the park gate on Rolleston Avenue, **Christ's College** is the city's most elite private school, a physical embodiment of the English tradition. During term time, you can visit the main quadrangle and use the gate leading into the Botanical Garden, out past the playing fields, while there's the chance for a more leisurely stroll in the school holidays, when visitors can inspect the college's oldest building, Big School (1863), and the Memorial Dining Hall designed by Cecil Wood in 1925.

On the southern borders of Hagley Park stands the Christchurch Hospital and, a little further on, the **Nurses' Memorial Chapel** (Mon–Sat 1–4pm, Sun 10am–4pm; free). Designed by J.G. Collins (son of J.J. of Arts Centre fame), it was constructed after the death of three Christchurch-trained nurses aboard the troopship *Marquette*, torpedoed in 1915. The walls are Oamaru stone with terracotta bricks and the roof is tiled in green slate, but the best feature is the extensively-timbered interior. Windows and doors are framed with matai, and the simply-patterned floors made of blackwood and oak, with redwood sarking and an elaborate oak panel behind the altar. There are nine stained-glass windows, including four by the English glass artist Veronica Whall, all with an uneven texture and a variety of colours set off by the otherwise dark, low-ceilinged interior.

Heading east back into town, along Oxford Terrace, you'll pass the lovely **St Michael and All Angels Church**, overlooking the river (Oct–April Mon–Fri 10am–5pm, Sat & Sun 2–5pm; guided tours on demand; April–Oct open for regular church services only). The church was designed by William F. Crisp and completed in 1875, combining elements of both the French and English medieval Gothic styles. Much of the architectural ingenuity that went into the building can be glimpsed in the impressive, dark-wood interior: the structure is made of matai timber (native black pine) on stone foundations, and supported by monumental pillars carved from single trees. The pine darkens as it grows older, so it is possible to spot new additions by gauging the blackness of the surrounding wood. The stained-glass windows covering both east and west wings are particularly beautiful, their bright colours contrasting with the dark hues of the surrounding timber. Look out also for the **Te Tapenakara o te Ariki** ("The Tabernacle of the Lord") hung from the ceiling over the central aisle, traditionally a container used by Maori chiefs to store *taonga* (treasure such as ceremonial feathers). This one was dedicated by the Bishop of Aotearoa for use as a Christian vessel to contain consecrated bread, and depicts symbols from both Maori and Christian tradition. The rather dainty belfry standing outside the church was designed by Mountfort in 1861, and houses a bell from one of the first four migrant ships. Historically it served as a timepiece for the settlers and was rung on the hour.

Two blocks south of St Michael's, St Asaph Street leads back towards Hagley Park, passing the **Canterbury Brewery Heritage Centre** at no. 30 – a welcome breather from the highbrow culture on display elsewhere. Fifty-minute guided tours (Mon–Fri 9.30am & noon; $5; reservations advised ☎03/379 4940) give you a brief history of brewing in the region, a glimpse of the working brewery itself, and two free beers as a reward at the end.

Victoria Square and around

Overlooking the well-manicured Victoria Square, five minutes' walk northwest of Cathedral Square, and adjacent to the *Park Royal Hotel*, Christchurch's modern **Town Hall** (daily 9am–5pm) is a stark, angular piece of minimalist design, linked by footbridge to the equally radical, glass-fronted Convention Centre on the opposite side of Kilmore Street. The premiere entertainment venue in Christchurch, the town hall harbours a magnificent 2320-seat auditorium (an impressive sight even when empty), which features a flying saucer-like construction above the stage to improve the acoustics. The town hall also contains the Women's Suffrage Commemorative Wall Hanging. Commissioned in 1992 to commemorate Women's Suffrage Year, it depicts aspects of women's lives over the last one hundred years and incorporates *taniko*, a traditional form of Maori finger-weaving. You can enjoy good views of Victoria Square from the *Town Hall Restaurant*, a good place to stop for coffee but too expensive for anything more.

The **Provincial Government Buildings** (1858–65) stand on the corner of Durham Street and Armagh Street, just west of Victoria Square (Oct–April Mon–Sat 10.30am–2.30pm, Sun 2–4pm; donation requested). These are the only provincial government buildings left in New Zealand and are widely regarded as the masterpiece of Christchurch's most renowned early architect, **Benjamin W. Mountfort**. Built in Gothic style with medieval-influenced ornamentation, the older wooden portion of the chambers has a venerable flagstone-paved corridor. The stone council chamber, the high-Victorian Great Hall (1869), is magnificently decorated with an intricate ceiling and elaborate stonework. Masks of the two craftsmen responsible for all this finery appear in the stonework: on the east wall near the fireplace on the ground floor and on the east wall of the public gallery.

Heading northwest from here along Victoria Street, the Victorian **clock tower** houses a clock originally imported from England in 1860 to adorn the government buildings. However, the wooden structure proved too weak to support the weight and the clock went into storage until 1897, when it was mounted on a stone base on the corner of Lichfield, Manchester and High streets, finally being moved to its current home in 1930.

Also on Victoria Street, at no. 30, Christchurch's **Casino** is open 24 hours all year round and contains the usual array of bars, table games and a flood of one-armed bandits. You have to be smartly dressed and aged over 20 to get in.

If you strike it lucky at the casino, you could always survey **Dr Heins Classic Car Collection**, northeast of Victoria Square at 150 Kilmore St (daily 10am–5pm; $4), which features the largest collection of old and vintage Jaguars in the southern hemisphere, each one of which is for sale.

Beyond the four avenues

Just off the eastern end of Moorhouse Avenue (a 2km walk southeast of Cathedral Square), you'll find **Lancaster Park**, home to Christchurch's Sports Museum and the Lancaster Park Stadium. The **Sports Museum** (daily 10am–4pm; $3) is near the stadium's Hadlee Stand, on Stevens Street, and celebrates the twin obsessions of every true (male) New Zealander – cricket and rugby. There's an entire room devoted to Sir Richard Hadlee, the Kiwi fast bowler, and an extensive rugby section which includes much on Grant Fox and the world championship winning side of 1987, as well as the exploits of Jona Lomu in the 1995 world championship in South Africa. If you do visit the museum, don't miss the opportunity to walk around the stadium itself (usually open to casual visitors if no events are taking place), Christchurch's main cricket and rugby venue, and surprisingly atmospheric. While you're in the area, you could do worse than visit the Roman Catholic **Cathedral of the Blessed Sacrament** (daily 8am–4pm), five minutes' walk northwest of Lancaster Park at the southern end of Barbadoes Street. Dating from 1905, it draws heavily on Neoclassical and Renaissance models, and provides a welcome relief to the sometimes overpoweringly neo-Gothic buildings elsewhere in the city. Take a walk around the first-floor balcony to appreciate the elaborate Italianate ceiling design.

To the west of Hagley Park in the suburb of Riccarton, about fifteen minutes' walk down Riccarton Road, is **Deans Bush** (daily dawn–dusk; free), an area of native bush containing several 500-year-old kahikatea trees. The survival of this valuable area of forest is largely due to Scottish brothers William and John Deans, who came to farm the area in 1843 and somehow resisted the temptation to put all their property to immediate agricultural use. Today a concrete path navigates the bush, with signs pointing out the species that still grow here. The **Deans house**, a largely wooden construction next to the bush at 16 Kahu Rd, is currently being restored prior to its opening as a museum celebrating the Deans family and other early settlers. Standing next to the house is the tiny black pine **cottage** built by the Deans brothers upon their arrival in 1843 – the oldest structure on the Canterbury plain.

Also in Riccarton, just beyond the northwest corner of Hagley Park, are the beautiful gardens of **Mona Vale** at 63 Fendalton Rd (grounds open daily Oct–March 8am–7.30pm; April–Sept 8.30am–5.30pm; free; guided tours daily 9.30am & 1.30pm; $35 including tea and souvenir). Originally part of the Deans' estate (see above); the site became the property of the city in 1969 and is now tended by the Canterbury Horticultural Society. The gardens have majestic displays of roses, dahlias, fuchsias and irises, as well as magnolias, rhododendrons and herbaceous perennials. The Bath House has been converted to use as a greenhouse and the old homestead is now a conference centre. You can rent a punt at the homestead and enjoy the gardens from the river ($12 per person for 30min).

Beyond Mona Vale, further to the northwest, lies the airport, where there are one or two attractions worth seeing. The first and most important of these is the **Antarctic Centre**, a large, hangar-like building on Orchard Road (daily: Oct–March 9.30am–8.30pm, April–Sept 9.30am–5.30pm; guided tours 11am & 2pm; $12), about twenty minutes' drive from the city centre and a five-minute walk from the airport stop on bus route #A. Since the mid-1950s the complex has been the base of the US Antarctic programme, which sponsors over 140 flights a year to the icy region. The centre has dynamic exhibitions on Antarctic exploration with continuous video presentations, traditional and interactive displays and plenty of background information. There's also a themed gift shop, and you can buy snacks and drinks at the *60° South Cafe and Bar*.

Less than ten minutes' walk north of the airport is **Orana Park** (daily 10am–5pm; $10), within the McLeans Island Recreational Area, off Johns Road and McLeans Island Road. Sadly there's no regular bus service out here, although the hop-on-hop-off City Circuit sightseeing bus (see p.482) does pass by. This well organized zoological park contains a wide variety of native and imported animals, particularly from Africa. Volunteer guides are on hand, and highlights include endangered New Zealand bird species like kiwi and tuatara, and the chance to observe the feeding of lions and tigers from a treetop viewing balcony.

Smaller and more intimate is **Willowbank Wildlife Reserve**, northwest of the centre on Hussey Road off Gardiners Road (daily Oct–April 10am–10pm; May–Sept 10am–5pm; $8). To get there, ride bus #1 from Cathedral Square as far as the junction of Harewood Road and Gardiners Road, then walk northeast up Gardiners Road for five minutes or so before turning right into Hussey Road. Although nowhere near as exciting as Orana Park, the reserve has some good displays of native birds and a nighttime Kiwi Watch (times vary; phone for details, ☎03/359 6226).

Southwest of Hagley Park and accessible via Blenheim Road is **Air Force World** (daily 10am–5pm; $9), located in the RNZAF base, Wigram, off the Main South Road, about twenty minutes' drive from the city centre. Canride buses #8 to Lincoln or #25 to Templeton, both from Cathedral Square, drop off about ten minutes' walk from the entrance. There are several computer-generated flight simulators, a number of planes to look over, and some cut-away cockpits that you can sit in; it's all presided over by enthusiastic volunteer guides who will give tours on demand for no extra cost. Short flights in an old Tiger Moth biplane can also be arranged here (20min; $155; booking essential).

The Marae of the Four Winds

One of the most rewarding activities in Christchurch is a visit to the **Nga Hau E Wha National Marae** ("Marae of the Four Winds"), 250 Pages Rd (daily guided tours 11am & 2pm, $5.50; "Night of Maori Magic" Tues, Wed & Thurs 7pm, $55; bookings essential for all tours; ☎ & fax 03/388 7685), 3km east of Cathedral Square and on the #5 bus route. Opened in 1990, Nga Hau E Wha symbolizes the meeting of people from all points of the compass. The informal tours explain elements of Maori culture, protocol, history and tradition, as well as taking a look around the compound, which includes the carved gateway (*Waharoa*), the earth oven (*Hangi*), the meeting house (*Whare Nui*) and the house of learning (*Whare Wananga*). The meeting house, one of the largest in New Zealand, is named Aoraki after Mount Cook (see box on p.562), and the carved posts (*poupou*) depict ancient and contemporary ancestors, acting as memory aids encouraging the continuation of oral tradition. A unique feature is the appearance of two European ancestors (one of which is Captain Cook), intended to symbolize the coming together of the two peoples. Between the posts are *tutuku* panels made of flax and representing images of plants, animals and tribal history. During a "Night of Maori Magic", visitors are greeted with a challenge before being invited on to the marae, and

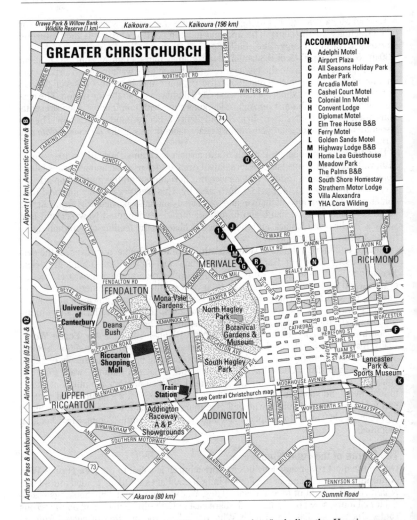

GREATER CHRISTCHURCH

	ACCOMMODATION
A	Adelphi Motel
B	Airport Plaza
C	All Seasons Holiday Park
D	Amber Park
E	Arcadia Motel
F	Cashel Court Motel
G	Colonial Inn Motel
H	Convent Lodge
I	Diplomat Motel
J	Elm Tree House B&B
K	Ferry Motel
L	Golden Sands Motel
M	Highway Lodge B&B
N	Home Lea Guesthouse
O	Meadow Park
P	The Palms B&B
Q	South Shore Homestay
R	Strathern Motor Lodge
S	Villa Alexandra
T	YHA Cora Wilding

are then allowed to take part in traditional ceremonies (including the *Hongi*, or pressing of noses) and partake of a delicious meal cooked in a hangi (earth oven). After-dinner entertainment is provided by performance of songs and dances, including a rendition of the famous haka that's recited by the All Blacks rugby team before matches.

The Christchurch Gondola and Ferrymead

The **Christchurch Gondola**, 10 Bridle Path Rd (Mon–Sat 10am–12.45am, Sun 10am–11.45pm; $6 one-way, $12 return) is a scenic and gentle way of seeing the surrounding countryside. The Gondola terminal is located in the Heathcote Valley about 25 minutes' drive from Cathedral Square, and is serviced by a free Gondola Shuttle operating from the visitor centre, as well as the Lyttelton bus (#28). The Gondola cable

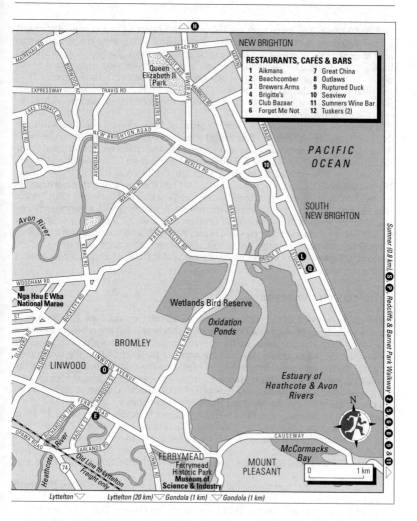

cars climb to the 945m summit of Mount Cavendish, providing views of Christchurch, the Canterbury Plains, the volcanic outcrops of the Banks Peninsula and the Southern Alps. The station at the top contains a "time tunnel" museum (Mon–Sat 10am–12.45am, Sun 10am–11.45pm; free), which covers the geology and geography of the area as well as Maori legends, life aboard early migrant ships and a video about modern-day Canterbury. Also in the station are a viewing deck, souvenir shop, café, bar and restaurant, where you can eat while enjoying fantastic views of the city below – especially at night.

From the summit, you can take one of the footpaths that explore the hills or head straight back down – either by cable car, or the more intrepid methods of paragliding or **mountain biking**. The Mountain Bike Adventure Company (bookings essential,

☎03/384 0006; free pick ups from the visitor centre) offers a number of guided or self-guided descents: the "Mount Cavendish Experience" ($38), for example, allows an hour to explore the station and a choice of three routes down the surrounding Summit Road system, cycling for about an hour; your aching legs will soon be forgotten as you savour bird's-eye views of Sumner's beaches, Lyttelton and the Banks Peninsula. If you're after more thrills, Nimbus (☎03/328 8383) or Phoenix (☎03/384 3131) will **paraglide** you down from near the summit of the gondola, in tandem with an instructor, for about $90.

If you cycle back down to the Gondola terminal in Heathcote, you'll pass through the neighbouring suburb of Ferrymead (also served by bus #3 from Cathedral Square), home to a number of tourist-oriented **arts** and **crafts** outlets (detailed in the *Arts, Crafts and Fine Food by the Sea* map, available free from Christchurch visitor centre) and the **Ferrymead Historic Park**, 269 Bridle Path Rd, Heathcote (daily 10am–4.30pm; $7). The park covers a large area and incorporates a reconstruction of a small Edwardian township, reached by restored engines and tram cars from bygone eras ($2 return). After a walk around the township, mingling with appropriately costumed locals, drop in at the *Kennaway Brothers Tearooms* for a doorstep sandwich or the old bakery for homemade pies and bread. Also within the complex are a mock-up of an airport terminal from the 1960s, indicative of the importance of air travel to New Zealand; a settlers' Cob Cottage, made of mud; and the Hall of Flame, a collection of antique fire engines.

Christchurch's beaches

Eight kilometres east of the centre, the coastal suburbs around **New Brighton** have become seaside playgrounds for residents of Christchurch, but are relatively unknown to visitors. Here you can swim, windsurf, walk or just enjoy the sight of sailing boats bobbing on the water against the hazy backdrop of the Port Hills to the south. New Brighton itself commands a long swathe of sand, running from **Waimari Beach** in the north to **South New Brighton Beach** in the south – the whole area is a great place to swim or simply lounge on a towel. South of New Brighton, a spit of land provides shelter for the waters of the Avon and Heathcote river estuary, which is backed by the quiet suburb of **Bromley** and the **Te Huingi Manu Wildlife Reserve** (daily dawn-dusk; free), a great place for bird watchers. The estuary basin provides an excellent spot for windsurfing and dinghy sailing. Providing access to the whole area is Marine Parade, which runs along the coast and is a thirty-minute bus ride from central Christchurch (Big Red Buses #5, #19 and #29 from Cathedral Square; $1.80 one way, day-pass $5).

About 500m inland from the central portion of Marine Parade, the **Queen Elizabeth II Park** on the corner of Travis Road and Bower Avenue contains the impressive stadium built for the long-forgotten 1974 Commonwealth Games. The complex contains an Olympic-sized swimming pool (daily 6am–9pm; $3) and a children-oriented fun park (same times; expect to pay about $4 per activity), which offers distractions such as mini-golf, mini-racing cars and mini-bikes.

Redcliffs and Sumner

On the south side of the river estuary and served by bus #3 from Cathedral Square, the suburb of **Redcliffs** is the starting point for the 5km-long **Barnett Park Walkway** (1hr 45min round-trip), which begins at a car park just off Main Road. A well-formed track climbs through grassland onto rock outcrops, with steps giving access to a large rock shelter and several caves. The walkway then bisects a copse of native bush and passes a seasonal waterfall, before crossing a creek and descending via bluffs past **Paradise Cave**, home of a Maori family in the 1890s.

WALKS AROUND SUMNER

The *Christchurch Scenic Walk, Nicholson Park and Scarborough* leaflet (free from Christchurch visitor centre) describes a series of **short walks** (each around 15min) that can also be combined to form a **longer route** (2.5km; 1hr 30min).

Mouldeys Track starts just inland from the beach at the junction of Nayland Street and Herberden Avenue. After a short, sharp climb with the sea to the northwest and the head rising to the southeast, the path continues for about fifteen minutes before being crossed by a track to the Boat Shed. Head down this for a great view of Pegasus Bay, stretching away to the northwest (the bay is named after the *Pegasus*, in which Captain Chase sailed the coast looking for sealing grounds), and then join the **Boat Shed to Sumner Head Track**. This ploughs uphill again for about fifteen minutes, skirting the the cliff edge and giving increasingly spectacular views.

From **Sumner Head** you can see the Kaikoura Peninsula in the west, and Godley Head and Banks Peninsula to the east. At this point you have two alternatives for reaching the botanical reserve of **Nicholson Park**: either head straight inland along a clay track to the park ten minutes away; or, more interestingly, continue around the cliffs, climbing quite steeply, for views down the eastern side of the head (20min). On entering Nicholson park the latter track leads onto a small point, from which you can see **Whitewash Head** (so named because of the large number of seabirds that nest on its cliffs), and the **Giants Nose**, a small finger of land behind which is the bay named **Taylor's Mistake**, where according to local lore, a captain named Taylor ran aground during his misbegotten attempt to prove Captain Cook's theory that Banks Peninsula was an island.

Immediately southeast of Redcliffs, #3 buses enter Sumner, a thin strip of a settlement stretching along a long sandy beach. Named after Dr J.B. Sumner, Archbishop of Canterbury and president of the Canterbury Association in the 1850s, it's now a popular seaside resort with a smattering of craft shops, restaurants, cafés, wine bars and a cinema.

Highlight of the beach is **Cave Rock**, a geological anomaly of honeycombed rock – its underside is peppered with little caves like an enormous Swiss cheese – which you can walk through at low tide. You can also clamber up the rock to reach the lifeguard's lookout point on top. More or less opposite Cave Rock on the other side of Main Road, is a small, untidy and much-graffitied **moa cave**, where bones from these now-extinct flightless birds were discovered. Most interesting of all, though, are a series of short walks to and around Sumner Head (see box above) – a must if you lack the time to explore the Banks Peninsula further south.

Eating

Christchurch boasts a healthy variety of **restaurants** offering a wide range of cultural influences and radical new culinary styles. To whet your appetite, buy a copy of the comprehensive *Classic Canterbury Dining Out Guide* from the visitor centre ($4.95). Top-quality gourmet cuisine is fairly thin on the ground, although this is more than made up for by the choice of ethnic restaurants on offer, ensuring that most national cuisines are well represented. There's also a growing number of fun, themed establishments featuring live music. For a more down-to-earth atmosphere, many of the city's **pubs** serve hearty food to soak up their brews.

With more and more **cafés** and **bars** offering substantial food, distinctions between eating and drinking venues are increasingly blurred, and many of the establishments listed under "drinking" (p.500) are perfectly good places in which to enjoy a main meal.

All the places listed below are open daily, unless otherwise stated.

Central Christchurch

You shouldn't have to venture too far from Cathedral Square in order to find a number of widely contrasting food possibilities. The grid of downtown streets around Colombo Street, Cashel Street, Manchester Street and Oxford Terrace harbours a condensed hot pot of cultural influences, with a range of food unmatched anywhere else on the South Island.

Cafés and takeaways

Bardelli's Deli Café, 98 Cashel Mall. A popular spot for Italian-influenced brunches, such as focaccia sandwiches, as well as lunch and dinner at moderate prices. Licensed.

Boulevard Bakehouse, in the Arts Centre, Worcester St. A delightfully simple place where you can get a good bagel, sit outside and watch the world go by; also serves breakfast, lunch and snacks ($5–15).

Le Café, in the Arts Centre, Worcester St (☎03/366 7722). This very popular café is open from 7am to midnight daily – except Saturday, when its stays open round the clock. The atmosphere is very upbeat and the prices are fair. BYO.

Cheers Café & Bar, 196 Hereford St. Specializes in breakfasts and lunches with an international flavour at moderate prices. It is invariably busy at weekends as the late-sleeping city crawls here for brunch and gathers around the lively bar later in the day.

The Daily Bagel, 179a Victoria St. Tiny shop with three tables and a few seats outside that serves authentic bagels with New York-inspired fillings, and superb coffee. Mon–Sat 7am–4pm.

Drexel's, 106 Hereford St (reservations advisable for Saturday and Sunday brunch ☎03/379 8089). An American-style breakfast and lunch diner, with full meals and snacks ($5–20) in surprisingly comfortable surroundings. Mon–Fri 6.30am–2pm, Sat & Sun 7am–2pm.

Gopals, 143 Worcester St. An alcohol-free, strictly vegetarian café run by Hare Krishnas and serving good-quality food at rock-bottom prices ($3–7). Mon–Thurs 11.30am–2.30pm, Fri 11.30am–2.30pm & 5–8.30pm.

Java, cnr High St & Lichfield St. The hippest and most popular coffee bar in town, with great coffee, hot snacks, salads, sandwiches and cakes, served well into the night; the all-day breakfasts are superb. Also a good place to suss out what's on. Daily 6.30am–midnight, until 3am at weekends.

Restaurants

Azure, 128 Oxford Terrace. Moderate to expensive Mediterranean-style brunches, lunches and suppers in chic surroundings. Occasional live jazz or solo piano, plus a DJ at weekends.

Beekman's, 86 Gloucester St. Lunch and dinner in a mellow, relaxing café with live jazz some evenings. The good-value food covers a broad range of European influences, as well as the odd foray into Moroccan cuisine – try the lamb fillets.

Chancery, 98 Gloucester Rd (☎03/379 4317). Traditional, no-nonsense New Zealand restaurant – and that really does mean roast lamb, fried fish or steaks served with potatoes or chips, roast kumara (sweet potato) and possibly another vegetable, all at good-value prices and in tacky surroundings. Licensed.

Churchill's, 441 Colombo St. Another value-for-money lunch and dinner restaurant serving large portions and sticking to traditional Kiwi nosh, with lots of Merrie Olde England memorabilia on the walls; live music on Fri nights. Licensed.

The Curry House, 2 Latimer Square. Unspectacular Indian restaurant with moderately priced food and an "eat till you can't walk" attitude that endears it to the quantity-over-quality fraternity.

Grimsby's, cnr Kilmore St & Montreal St (☎03/379 9040). Fine European/kiwi dining with venison and seafood a speciality, in the historic setting of an old school building filled with stone and stained-glass windows, with prices to match the elegant surroundings. Evenings only.

Hofbrauhaus, 112a Lichfield St (☎03/366 4471). Dinner and late carousing with live German music, large steins, stodgy food and wonderful German bread – all moderately priced and great fun.

Il Felice, 56 Lichfield St (☎03/366 7535). Excellent Italian restaurant, serving Tuscan-influenced cuisine and fresh, homemade pasta at moderate prices (with main courses at $13–16). Evenings only; licensed & BYO.

Jade Garden, 109 Cambridge Terrace (☎03/379 5300). A Cantonese and Szechwan restaurant in atmospheric former library chambers, serving moderately priced lunches and dinners.

Main Street Café & Bar, 840 Colombo St (☎03/365 0421). One of the busiest and friendliest places in town: the café offers a separate bar, lunch and dinner (all vegetarian, all moderately priced and in huge portions), a $2 bottomless coffee cup and the most avant-garde (and least comfortable) bar stools in Christchurch.

The Oxford on Avon, cnr Colombo St & Oxford Terrace (☎03/379 7148). Pub famed for the enormity of the portions as well as the great value. The winning formaula is hearty food in the English tradition on the banks of the Avon and the bar serves the usual stock of native beers. Evenings only.

Pedro's, 143 Worcester St (☎03/379 7668). Spanish place serving predominantly fish and lamb; main course are an expensive $23, but worth it. Proceedings are enlivened by traditional flamenco and Spanish guitar music. Licensed.

Restaurant Budapest, 107 Manchester St (☎03/366 0778). The only Hungarian restaurant on the South Island, which is a pity because the surroundings are fun, the staff friendly and the food of good quality, in generous portions and at moderate prices; with particular specialities being the powerful pork sauerkraut and dreamy chocolate mousse cake. Evenings only; Licensed & BYO.

Rita's Burritas, 818 Colombo St (reservations advisable at weekends; ☎03/379 2387). Popular and intimate Tex-Mex with great-value food and a very good atmosphere, plus a wide selection of veggie dishes. Licensed & BYO.

Santorini Greek Ouzeri, cnr Gloucester St & Cambridge Terrace (☎03/379 6975). Greek restaurant with a live Bouzouki band and dancing to accompany traditional Greek delicacies and barbecued food at moderate prices (with main courses in the $19–22 range). Evenings only; licensed.

Sgt Peppers Steak House, 750a Colombo St. A noisy but fun place for lunches and dinners with karaoke, videos and an overdose of Beatles music; the first floor is a Cavern wannabe where you can get good steaks and a drink from the bar at moderate prices.

Strawberry Fare Dessert Restaurant, 114 Peterborough St. Classy and very correct establishment that's every sweet lover's dream, with over two-thirds of the menu given over to luscious desserts that will harden even the most obstinate arteries, and prices that will hasten a heart attack. Naughty but nice.

Thomas Edmonds Restaurant, cnr Cambridge Terrace & Manchester St (☎03/365 2888). Beautifully located restaurant, overlooking the Avon and resembling a glass-sided bandstand in the middle of a green. The food is premium New Zealand cuisine such as Canterbury lamb cutlets and kumara, and all mains cost $19. Licensed & BYO.

Topkapi Turkish Café, 185 Manchester St. An extremely relaxed and friendly place where you settle into low-slung couches within watching range of the fascinating open kitchen, which emits a wide range of delicious smells and tastes. Lunch & dinner daily; BYO.

Vesuvio's, 182 Oxford Terrace (☎03/365 4183). A mid-range Japanese joint, open for lunch and dinner with a teppanyaki bar at the back, friendly staff and a reputation for being positively riotous at weekends. Licensed.

Victoria Street Café, *Park Royal Hotel*, cnr Durham St & Kilmore St (☎03/365 7799). Overwhelming setting with spectacular views of Victoria square, piano-bar background music, and expensive, largely New Zealand-based cuisine, although there's also a strong Mediterranean influence. Licensed.

Wardinski's, 99 Cashel St (☎03/379 9240). This nautical-style haunt serves excellent seafood, at moderate prices, for lunch and dinner all week and has a lively, well-stocked bar. Dancing and drinking takes centre stage at weekends.

Northwest of the city

When it comes to eateries, suburban Christchurch isn't the best of hunting grounds, although those venturing beyond the four avenues in search of sustenance could do worse than head northwest towards the suburb of Merivale, where there's a handful of excellent restaurants.

Aikmans, 154 Aikmans Rd, Merivale. A moderately priced café with a laid-back atmosphere, and serving breakfast, lunch and dinner with French, Greek, Italian and Mexican variations. Licensed.

Brigitte's Espresso/Wine Bar, Hawkesbury Building, Aikmans Road, Merivale. Conveniently located opposite *Aikmans*, this is a another relaxed place with an open courtyard at the back, and good-quality Mediterranean and Kiwi-style food as well as some wonderful New Zealand-Thai combinations, all at moderate prices. Licensed & BYO.

Great China, cnr Papanui Rd & Bealey Ave (☎03/355 8500). Genuine Cantonese cuisine which you can enjoy inside, or outside in the garden courtyard. The banquet menu is generous and the filet mignon with stir-fry veggies is particularly good. Mains are generally $10–15. BYO.

Sumner and New Brighton

Most of the sophisticated dining options in the seaside suburbs are concentrated in Sumner, while New Brighton tends to make do with cheap-and-cheerful beachfront cafés and takeaways, as well as the obligatory Chinese restaurant.

Beachcomber Restaurant, 25 Esplanade St, Sumner. Excellent seafood dinners (mains start at $13) with a great view of the bay, near Cave Rock. Licensed & BYO.

Club Bazaar Pizzeria, 15 Wakefield Avenue, Sumner. Bar and elaborate balcony where you can sample cheap pasta dishes and pretty acceptable pizzas in a distinctive atmosphere of Kiwi nostalgia. Evenings only. Licensed.

Forget Me Not, 12 Wakefield Ave, Sumner (reservations advisable at weekends ☎03/326 6501). An international brassiere (main dishes from $15) in amenable surroundings; eat in the courtyard or conservatory. Licensed & BYO.

Gilly's Wine Bar, 87a Main Road, Redcliffs (☎03/384 5444). Pleasant little wine bar on the road running through Redcliffs towards Sumner, with local art displayed on the walls. Cuisine is international (try the garlic king prawns), with mains hovering around $14–23. Daily from 11.30am.

Outlaws Café and Saloon, 26 Nayland St, Sumner (reservations advisable at weekends ☎03/326 7388). Reasonably priced steaks and burgers in a "family" atmosphere for lunch and dinner, plus live music at weekends.

Ruptured Duck, 4 Wakefield Ave, Sumner. Pizza palace where a large polystyrene duck watches your every mouthful of such popular fare as the only-in-NZ roast lamb and roast potato pizzas that have acquired cult status. Licensed & BYO.

Seaview Restaurant and Bar, 2 New Brighton Mall, cnr Marine Parade, New Brighton. Chinese restaurant, garishly decorated in red and green, serving dinners and a good value smorgasbord nightly for $19.50, as well as special cocktails.

Sumner's Wine Bar and Restaurant, 29 Wakefield Ave, Sumner. Upmarket Mediterranean food in a modern setting with a lively atmosphere. Daily noon–late; licensed.

Drinking, nightlife and entertainment

Gone are the days when evenings in Christchurch revolved around decaying, male-dominated Edwardian pubs. The modern city harbours enough traditional hostelries, late-night cafés and throbbing music bars to suit most tastes, and many of these offer more than just booze: live music, resident DJs and good food are increasingly taken for granted.

Serious music and drama are centred on venues like the Town Hall and the Arts Centre, while less cerebral entertainment is offered by a concentration of downtown clubs and a clutch of city-centre cinemas. Entertainment **listings** are published in Christchurch's daily newspaper *The Press* (the "What's On" section on Fridays is best for live music and clubbing), and in the free monthly magazines *Volume* and *Presto*.

Drinking

Most drinking venues are to be found within the four avenues, with Colombo and Cashel streets harbouring a particularly dense concentration of watering holes. This is probably the best place to stroll at weekends, when a variety of establishments use loud music and late licences to pull in the crowds.

Pubs and bars

Azure, 128 Oxford Terrace. Live music bar with jazz or a solo pianist on selected evenings, and a DJ and lively atmosphere at weekends.

Baillies in the Square, beneath *Pavlova Backpackers*, 50 Cathedral Square. Typical Irish drinking house with live music (from traditional Irish to rock'n'roll) at weekends and selected nights in the week.

Brewers Arms, 177 Papanui Rd, Merivale. Northwest of the centre, this is a suburban pub with horse brasses, a range of beers, and English-style pub food in large portions at moderate prices. Open from 11am until late.

Dux de Lux, cnr Hereford St & Montreal St. This large pub with outdoor and indoor seating is one of the most popular watering holes in town, with a great atmosphere, moderately priced vegetarian and seafood dishes and, best of all, an on-site brewery serving fine ales in a bar where there's live music or entertainment most days of the week.

Fat Lady's Arms, Manchester St. A popular student hangout for early evening and late-night drinking, with pool tables, music and a wide selection of beers.

Ferg's One Street Over, 165 Hereford St. A barn-like sports bar in the American tradition with big-screen TV, snacks, and a wide range of domestic and imported beers.

Fin Bar, Gloucester St. Traditional Irish pub with occasional live music.

Loaded Hog, 39 Dundas St, just off Manchester St. Comfortable city-centre boozer with ales brewed on the premises.

Clubs and gigs

Christchurch may not be the clubbing capital of the southern hemisphere, but there's a sprinkling of places within the four avenues offering a range of dance-music styles. Some of these are full-on **club venues**, although there's a growing number of bars which transform themselves into dancing venues at weekends by drafting in a DJ or two. There's a surfeit of bars offering **live music**, although most places content themselves with a meagre diet of cover bands or minor local rock acts.

There's a club info line (☎03/363 5000) giving a rundown of what's on from night to night.

Bar Coyote, Cashel St. Mexican-influenced, cacti-ridden dance spot open for café-style drinking during the day, dancing in the evening. Thurs–Sun.

Civic, 186 Manchester St. Popular clubbing venue offering a range of themed nights (eg funk, hip-hop, rare groove, house, techno); check listings in *The Press* to see what's on. 10pm–6am.

The Edge, 85 Hereford St. Open-fronted bar that becomes more clubby as the evening wears on, purveying mainstream techno to a youthful clientele. Occasional spoken word and poetry performances too.

Lone Star, 26 Manchester St. A jumping bar and nightspot that also serves an eclectic mix of Southwestern and Cajun food.

Occidental Pub and Chats Club, Hereford St, opposite Latimer Square. Buzzing spot with live bands on Fridays & Saturdays and dance music.

Palladium, cnr Chancery Lane & Gloucester St. Long-standing disco with conservative reputation, playing anything from the 1960s to the 1990s, and hosting live dance music from time to time. Strict dress code (no trainers, sandals, jeans or T-shirts). Daily 9pm–late.

Rattlesnake Room, Cashel St Mall. Atmospheric bar with resident DJs, which fills up with dancers on Friday and Saturday nights.

Tuskers Bar and Bistro, 3km south of the centre at 155 Colombo St, Beckenham. Live music bar with local bands playing mostly mainstream rock covers. There's another branch at 8 Yaldhurst Rd, Upper Riccarton.

Vault, 90 Lichfield St. Lively and loud late-night bar with dark interior, resident DJs, pool and pinball. Daily from noon until 6.30am.

Wardinski's, Cashel St Mall. Weekend dancing and drinking are on offer in this busy and popular nautical-style haunt.

Entertainment

The Town Hall on Victoria Square (box office ☎03/366 8899) is the main centre for highbrow culture, offering **classical music** in the main auditorium, and serious **drama** in the adjoining James Hay Theatre. There's also a programme of classical music and drama (ranging from fringe theatre to Christmas pantomimes) at the Arts Centre (☎03/366 0989) between Montreal Street and Rolleston Avenue.

Concerts by touring **jazz** and **rock** acts take place either at the Arts Centre, or at the Theatre Royal on Gloucester Street (☎03/366 6326), a fine old Edwardian venue with attracts the glitzier, more mainstream acts. You can catch a host of local jazz and rock performers playing in some of the bars and clubs listed under "Drinking" and "Clubs and gigs", on p.501.

Of the **cinemas** showing first-run international films, the main city-centre multiplexes are the Regent, Cathedral Square; the Westend, Cathedral Square; Hoyts 8, on the corner of Manchester and Moorhouse avenues; and the Rialto, on the corner of Moorhouse Avenue and Durham Street. Arthouse movies are shown at the Academy Film Theatre in the Arts Centre.

Lancaster Park Stadium, southeast of the centre near the junction of Moorhouse Avenue and Ferry Road, is the main venue for the big spectator **sports**, hosting **cricket**

MOVING ON FROM CHRISTCHURCH

Straddling the main road and rail routes down the east coast, Christchurch provides easy access to most parts of the South Island.

The quickest way of getting around the South Island is **by air**, with Air New Zealand (☎03/379 5200) and Ansett New Zealand (☎03/371 1146) operating daily flights to destinations like Invercargill, Dunedin, Queenstown, Blenheim and Nelson.

Trains, by comparison, represent a much cheaper but relatively time-consuming way of getting around, with only one passenger train daily heading south from Christchurch towards Dunedin and Invercargill, calling in at Ashburton, Timaru and Oamaru on the way. Services are equally sparse to Picton at the northern end of the South Island; and to Greymouth on the west coast (although the latter is a classic New Zealand rail journey, crossing the scenic St Arthur's Pass).

Most inter-city journeys are probably best attempted by **bus**, with the major national companies Mount Cook Landline (picking up on Cathedral Square or at their depot at 40 Lichfield St; ☎03/379 0690); and InterCity (picking up on Cathedral Square or at the InterCity Travel Centre at the eastern end of Moorhouse Avenue; ☎03/379 9020) serving the arterial routes north to Nelson, west to Greymouth and south to Dunedin and Invercargill. Smaller companies concentrating on specific routes are Coast to Coast (services to Greymouth; ☎0800 800 847); and White Star, 471 Moorhouse Ave (services to Westport and Nelson ☎03/323 6156).

Shorter hops (as well as a few of the more popular long hauls) can be tackled with the help of the numerous **shuttle bus** companies serving a multiplicity of routes from the city. Many of them will pick you up from or drop you off at your accommodation, although an additional fee is sometimes charged for this. The main companies operating out of Christchurch are Akaroa Shuttles (☎0800 500 929) serving Akaroa; Atomic Shuttles (☎03/322 8883) running from Christchurch to Queenstown, Picton and Dunedin; Catch-a-bus (☎0800 508 000) operating the route south of Christchurch through Timaru, Oamaru and Dunedin; Ko-op Shuttles (☎03/366 6633) serving Picton, Dunedin, and Greymouth; Midnight Express (☎0800 508 400) running to Nelson via Kaikoura, Blenheim and Picton; South Island Connections (☎03/351 6726), which run from Ashburton through Christchurch to Kaikoura, Blenheim and Picton; and Southern Link Shuttles (☎03/358 8355), which go either north to Picton, south to Dunedin or southwest to Queenstown.

in the summer and **rugby** (Canterbury, the big local team, play here) on weekends throughout the winter. **Information** and **tickets** can be obtained from the stadium itself (☎03/366 2961) or from Canterbury All Sports (☎03/366 9688).

Listings

Airlines Air New Zealand, 702 Colombo St, Triangle Centre (☎03/379 5200); Ansett New Zealand, Clarendon Towers, 78 Worcester St (☎03/371 1146); British Airways, Level 18, Price Waterhouse Building, 119 Armagh St (☎03/379 2503); Japan Air Lines, Level 11, Clarendon Towers, 78 Worcester St (☎03/365 5879); Korean Airlines, Christchurch International Airport (☎03/358 0780); Mount Cook Airlines, 91 Worcester St (☎0800 800 737); Qantas, Level 18, Price Waterhouse Building, 119 Armagh St (☎0800 808 767); Singapore Airlines, Level 3, Forsyth Barr Building, cnr Armagh St & Colombo St (☎03/366 1736).

Airport buses A regular Canride service runs to the airport from Cathedral Square roughly hourly (timetables are available from the visitor centre or the CTS kiosk on Cathedral Square). In addition, A1 Shuttles (☎03/775 7755), Carrington Transfer Services (☎03/352 6369), PBS Shuttles (☎03/551 1111) and Super Shuttle (☎03/365 5655) all run from Cathedral Square to the airport ($7). They'll pick you up from your accommodation, although if you're catching a morning flight you should book your transfer the evening before.

American Express Destinations Travel, 485 Papanui Rd (☎03/365 7366); Guthrey Travel, 126 Cashel St (☎03/379 3560); Bureau de Change, 78 Worcester St (☎03/365 7366).

Automobile Association 210 Hereford St (☎03/379 1280).

Ballooning Up Up And Away (☎03/355 7141) offers peaceful and eye-bulging balloon flights over Christchurch (3–4hr; $200).

Banks and exchange Most banks have branches on or near Colombo St and Hereford St. For out-of-hours exchange, try American Express Bureau de Change, 78 Worcester St (Mon–Sat 8.30am–5pm); Thomas Cook Bureau de Change, Victoria Square and cnr Armagh St & Colombo St (Mon–Thurs 8.30am–6pm, Fri 8.30am–8pm, Sat 10am–4pm); and Trustbank Bureau de Change, cnr Hereford St & Colombo St (daily 10am–6pm).

Bike rental Rent-A-Cycle, 141 Gloucester St (☎03/365 7589) and Trailblazers, 96 Worcester St (☎03/366 6033). Expect to pay $20–25 per day.

Bookshops Good high-street bookshops are Editions Book Shop, 16 Colombo St; Kate Shepherd Books, 145 Manchester St; Magazzino, cnr Moorehouse Ave & Colombo St; and Scorpio Books, 79 Hereford St; Liberty Books, 398 Worcester St, are good for secondhand paperbacks; while The Department of Survey and Land Information, Level 2, Torrens House, 195 Hereford St (Mon–Fri 9am–4.30pm), have the best range of walking maps and street plans. Bookshops are open Mon–Thur 9am–5pm, Fri–Sat 10am–6pm unless otherwise stated.

Campervan rentals Expect to pay around $135 per day unless otherwise stated. Outlets include Brits, 18 Rennie Drive, Airport Oaks (☎03/358 0973); Freedom, 166 St Asaph Street (☎03/379 3822); or try Greentours (renting out Toyota van conversions for around $55 per day; ☎0800/399 935); Kombi Kampa, 1013 Ferry Road (with old VW Kombi vans from $35 per day; ☎03/384 4751); Maui, Leisure Port, 530–544 Memorial Ave (☎03/358 4159).

Car rental Avis, 26 Lichfield St (☎03/379 6133); Avon, 166 St Asaph St (☎03/379 3822); Budget, cnr Oxford Terrace & Lichfield St (☎03/366 0072); Herz, 48 Lichfield St (☎03/366 0549); McDonalds, 171 Armagh St (☎03/366 0929); U–Save, 70 Moorhouse Ave (03/379 3492); Welco, 248 St Asaph St (☎03/366 2294).

Emergency services ☎111.

Horse riding Heathcote Valley Riding School, 131 Bridle Path Rd, 500m from the Gondola terminal (☎03/384 1971), offers evening rides (Thurs & Sun 6pm; $30, including BBQ) and other horse treks in the Port Hills.

Internet access and email services Mak Heeth's Café, 150 Manchester St (Mon–Fri 10am–5pm; *petery@nol.co.nz*) offers Internet access ($5 for 30min) and email service; the Email Centre, 69c Worcester Blvd (Mon–Sat 10am–5pm; *petery@sirranet.co.nz*), will also take and keep messages. Future Music Entertainment, 192 Manchester St (Mon–Sat 10am–5pm; *FME@chch.planet.co.nz*), will also take email messages and call you when they are received. Expect to pay a charge of about $2 per email.

Medical treatment Biggest of the hospitals is Christchurch Hospital, cnr Oxford Terrace & Riccarton Ave (☎03/3664 0640). Details of after-hours doctors are published in the local Newspaper *The Press*; otherwise the Riccarton Medical Centre, 59 Division St, Riccarton (☎03/348 8711) can probably fix you up with same-day appointment for non-urgent complaints. In emergencies call ☎111.

Mountain biking The Mountain Bike Adventure Company (☎03/384 0006) offers a range of trips, from just over an hour to a full-day rattling around the hills ($38–59). For renting mountain bikes, see under "bike rental" p.503.

Paragliding Nimbus Paragliding (☎03/328 8383) and Phoenix Paragliding (☎ and fax 03/384 3131) both offer 20-minute tandem flights from around $80 per person.

Pharmacies Late-opening pharmacies include Victoria Square Pharmacy, Victoria St (Mon–Fri 8am–8pm, Sat & Sun 10am–8pm); and Urgent Pharmacy, 931 Colombo St, cnr Bealey Ave (Mon–Thur 6pm–11pm, Fri 9pm–11pm, Sat 1pm–11pm, Sun 9am–11pm). Details of duty pharmacies are published in *The Press*.

Rafting Canterbury Adventure Rafting Company (☎03/318 1813) run rafting expeditions from Christchurch to the Huruni river (one day; $89) or the Waimakariri river (two days including a horse trek and hut accommodation; $190).

Scenic flights Air Adventures (☎03/379 5780); Bellview Flight Centre (☎03/358 7573); and Fly South (☎03/358 8334) operate scenic flights over the Christchurch region. Christchurch Helicopters (☎03/379 6663) offer overflights, heli-skiing or a flying visit to French Farm on the Banks Peninsula (see p.506); while Pionair Adventures (☎0800 733 388) offer nostalgia-oriented flights in Tiger Moths or refitted DC3s. Expect to pay around $65 per 30-minute-flight, more for the nostalgia-oriented flights.

Skiing Christchurch is within a couple of hours' drive of over ten skifields, all of which are covered elsewhere in the guide. They are Broken River (see p.551), Cragieburn (see p.551), Fox Peak (see p.561), Methven (see p.552), Mount Cheeseman (see p.551), Mount Cook (see p.570), Mount Dobson (see p.561), Mount Hutt (see p.551), Mount Olympus (see p.556), Porter Heights (see p.551) and Temple Basin (see p.551). For information on conditions dial the free Infophone number and enter the additional four-digit code for the service required (☎03/363 5000, plus 1101 for weather, 1102 for ski hire, 1103 for transport).

Swimming The main indoor pools are at the Queen Elizabeth II centre in New Brighton (see p.496); the centrally-located Centennial Pool, Armagh St; and Jellie Park Aqualand 4km northwest of the centre at Ilam Rd (bus #9 or #24 from Cathedral Square). Expect to pay $2–3 entry; waterslides may cost extra.

Taxis Blue Star (☎03/379 9799); Gold Band (☎03/379 5795).

Tours The visitor centre runs guided walking tours (daily: Oct–April 10am & 2pm; May–Sept 1pm; 2hr; $8; ☎03/379 9629), which are led by local volunteers who really know their stuff. Grayline offer bus tours of the city centre (9am; 3hr; $27; ☎03/343 3874). Peninsula and Alpine Tours (☎03/384 3576) operate day trips from Christchurch around Banks Peninsula for around $60 per person. Dolphin Adventure (morning tours $40, afternoon tours including cave tour and tea $70; ☎ and fax 03/326 5607) run trips to Sumner and Lyttelton to watch (from a Naiad – a solid-hulled inflatable power boat) Hector's dolphins and birds. For tours of the wineries, see p.505.

Train information ☎0800/802 802.

Travel agencies Canterbury Adventure Centre, in the visitor centre, cnr Worcester Blvd & Oxford Terrace (☎03/379 9629, fax 377 2424); Destinations Travel, 485 Papanui Rd (☎03/352 2612); Guthrey Travel, 126 Cashel St (☎03/379 3560); STA, 90 Cashel St (☎03/379 9098) or Student University Building, Canterbury University (☎03/348 6372); YHA Travel Centre, cnr Gloucester St & Manchester St (☎03/379 8046).

AROUND CHRISTCHURCH

Far too many travellers head straight from Christchurch towards the mountains to the west or Otago to the south, thereby missing out on the many attractions on the city's own doorstep. North of Christchurch are the rich agricultural flatlands of the northern Canterbury Plains, a pleasantly rural area which harbours the sleepy town of **Kaiapoi**, and the vineyards and wineries included in the **Canterbury Wine Trail**, a popular tourist itinerary among more bibulous visitors. However, the city's main vacation area

THE CANTERBURY WINE TRAIL

The **Canterbury Wine Trail** covers some sixteen wineries **around Christchurch**, situated in beautiful and diverse countryside and providing plenty of opportunities to sample **fine wines** and **gourmet food**. Most of these are on the plains north of the city, although there's one winery (*French Farm*, see p.522) on Banks Peninsula to the southeast. For well written descriptions of the wineries and their historical context, pick up a copy of the *Canterbury Wine Trail* leaflet (free from Christchurch visitor centre), by A.K. Grant, one of New Zealand's leading wine writers.

If you would prefer to see the wineries and taste their products without having to drive, there are a number of half- and full-day **tours** to choose from, for around $30–50. *Canterbury Plains Wine Trails* (daily departures 8.30am–10am; book through the visitor centre ☎03/379 9629) offer separate tours to the northern region, southwestern region and Banks Peninsula region, as do *Quality Tours* (☎03/342 9528) and *Canterbury Excursions* (☎03/342 0541).

is **Banks Peninsula**, southeast of Christchurch, an imposing lump of largely volcanic rock penetrated by fiord-like fingers of deep water. At the peninsula's northern end, **Lyttelton** is a hard-edged international cargo port which controls access to the bays and coves of a large inlet known as **Lyttelton Harbour**. Further south, chintzy, French-influenced **Akaroa** is a classic seaside resort, enduringly popular with week-ending city folk. There are some excellent **walking** opportunities in the **Port Hills** between Lyttelton and Christchurch, and around **Mount Bradley** and **Mount Herbert** south of Lyttelton Harbour.

Kaiapoi, Lyttelton and Akaroa are all served **by bus** from Christchurch, although once you stray beyond these centres you'll be largely on your own.

North of Christchurch

North of Christchurch, SH1 heads straight and true along the coast. As you leave the city suburbs, you pass one or two vineyards (see "Canterbury Wine Trail" box above) and a lot of the patchwork-quilt fields so typical of the Canterbury Plains. With flat farm country to its west and Pegasus Bay to its east, the road bisects a series of tiny communities such as **Kaiapoi**, many containing camping facilities for holidaymakers wishing to gaze at the bay or fish the waters.

Kaiapoi and beyond

Nineteen kilometres north of Christchurch, SH1 crosses the braided Waimakariri River, and rolls into the small town of **KAIAPOI**. Once a flourishing port with a reputation for producing high-quality woollen goods, Kaiapoi faded into insignificance after it had been bypassed by the railway. It's now a satellite town for Christchurch commuters, who constitute about sixty percent of the town's population, and has little of note – unless you are an angler keen to flick the rivers for trout or salmon. The best thing to do in Kaiapoi is take a trip on the 80-year-old **MV Tuhoe**, a twin-masted, steam-powered schooner which is moored in the Kaiapoi River near the William Street Bridge. Most weekends, weather and tides permitting, the *Tuhoe* still sails, albeit slowly, up the Kaiapoi until it merges with the Waimakariri River and the sea (1hr 20min; $8; buy tickets an hour before sailings at Williams Street Bridge kiosk; ☎03/327 7146). Tide and sailing times are published in Saturday's edition of *The Press*.

About 32km further north at the junction of SH1 and SH7 is **Waipara**, a town with six **wineries** within a 3km radius, each producing excellent, inexpensive white wines (tastings available on request 11am–5pm; expect to pay $2–5). From Waipara you can either head along SH1, a pretty unexciting haul towards Cheviot (see p.475) on the way to Kaikoura, or turn inland along the SH7 Lewis Pass Road towards Hanmer Springs (see p.542).

Banks Peninsula

Once an island, **Banks Peninsula** was joined to the mainland as a result of violent volcanic activity about 20,000 years ago. The fertile **volcanic** soil of the peninsula's valleys became covered by podocarp forest, mainly totara, matai and kahikatea. After the arrival of the Maori, burning was used to clear the forest, a process accelerated by the European commercial timber milling that ground to a shuddering halt only when the trees ran out in the late 1880s. Today the **vegetation** is characterized by large areas of

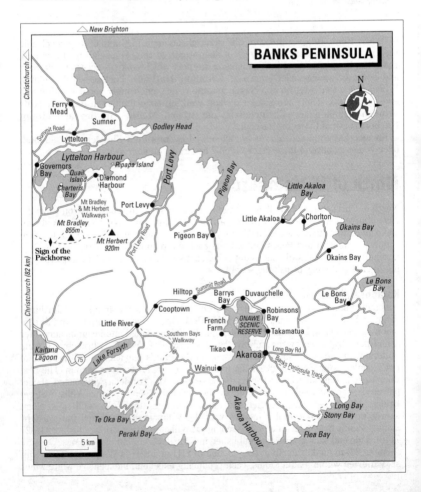

tussock grass on the rolling hills, with tiny pockets of regenerating native bush and small copses of trees. The area was first populated by **moa hunters** a thousand years ago, attracted by the sheltered bays and the abundance of food. The next settlers to leave their mark were **whalers** and **sealers**, who occupied small stations from about 1830 onwards and were in their turn replaced by settlers more interested in **timber** and then sheep **farming**, which now dominates the peninsula.

Nowadays, the main settlements of **Lyttelton** and **Akaroa** have quite distinct characters. Picturesque, French-influenced Akaroa is the more visitor-oriented town, while Lyttelton is a busy port with a rougher, more boisterous feel and a healthy disrespect for its more refined and pretentious neighbour. Between these two centres, there are a number of **scenic walks**, panoramic views, geological features (such as ancient lava flows, or the dykes caused when fissures filled up with molten rock), relics from the earliest Maori and European settlers, and great beaches. As befits a city playground, the peninsula is also well endowed with **country-style accommodation**, especially B&Bs and farmstays, and, particularly in Akaroa, **fine restaurants**.

The peninsula merits at least a day-trip from Christchurch. With more time on your hands, you could enjoyably spend two to three days exploring the quieter nooks and crannies. From Christchurch, the **main route** to Akaroa is the **SH75**, via Lake Ellesmere and Little River, but a more picturesque route follows the **Summit Road** from Sumner via Lyttelton, along the Port Hills and ridges of the peninsula. **Buses** from Christchurch serve only the main towns of Lyttelton and Akaroa, and to reach the smaller communities tucked into the bays you'll need your own transport, whether motorized or pedal-powered (see Christchurch listings for car and bike rental details). If you're planning on cycling, bear in mind that the peninsula is extremely hilly, and the routes linking the summit road with the various bays below can be very steep.

A good way of touring the peninsula's more remote communities if you don't have your own transport is to hop aboard one of the **rural mail runs**, usually run as formal day tours, although they will pick up and drop off by arrangement. At **Diamond Harbour**, you can join the postman on his rounds to Camp Bay and Port Levy (8am; 4hr 30min; $20; only 4–5 passengers taken, so book ahead on ☎03/329 4521), as the long-suffering mail van winds in and out of the bays that cling to the south side of the harbour. You can also get a ride with the **Akaroa** post van (Mon–Sat 8.30am; 4hr 30min; $20; ☎03/304 7207), which follows a 110km rural delivery run, serving the eastern bays of the peninsula, including Okains and Le Bons Bays. A shorter alternative which isn't a mail run is provided by the purely tourist-oriented **Inner Bays Scenic Drive** (daily, depending on demand, at 2pm; 2hr 45min; $20; ☎03/304 7207 or 025/355 249), calling at Barry's Bay, French Farm and other points of interest around the shores of Akaroa Harbour.

Although the peninsula is prone to **sea mists** and storms, both the Port Hills and the peaks across the neck of the peninsula shelter it from the winds that blaze across the Canterbury Plains. The climate tends to be very warm in the summer and extremely cold in the winter but the **weather** is noted for its unpredictability, so it's worth carrying rain gear at any time of year.

Lyttelton

Just 12km from Christchurch city centre, **LYTTELTON** and its harbour create a visual feast of hills, cliffs and water. The Canterbury district's most historic port nestles below a rugged **volcanic crater rim** that was flooded 10 million years ago to form a natural **harbour**, which is now used by cargo ships (and occasionally military vessels) from all over the world – as well as a small local fishing industry.

Once a bustling wharf where countless European migrants disembarked to start their new lives, Lyttelton still retains the raffish glamour that pervades ports the world over. The town itself overlooks the docks and quays, climbing up the Port Hills behind and spreading southwest along the coast toward Governors Bay. Running parallel to the waterfront, the main road of Norwich Quay is fringed by a series of down-at-heel pubs designed to attract dockers, ships' crews and lorry drivers. The web of streets behind are primarily residential, although it's here that the best bars, restaurants, shops and accommodation possibilities are to be found.

Arrival and information

The quickest way to the port **from Christchurch** is along Brougham Road, through the suburb of Sumner and over the Port Hills. The #28 **bus** from Cathedral Square leaves about every half an hour (35min; $4.80 return), with a limited service continuing to Governors Bay for a further $2.40.

The **visitor centre**, 20 Oxford St (Mon–Fri 9am–9.15pm, Sat & Sun 9am–5pm; ☎03/328 9093), is stuffed to the rafters with information. The staff are helpful and it's a good place to learn what lurks behind Lyttelton's workaday facade. You can also obtain a leaflet here describing a **self-guided walk** which takes in Lyttelton's many historic sites. **Guided historic walks** lasting ninety minutes leave from the Signal Box on Norwich Quay (see below; Tues, Thurs & Sun 10.30am, other times by arrangement; $5; ☎03/328 8117). A free weekly newspaper, *The Lyttelton Times*, contains listings and other local information.

Accommodation

Lyttelton's **accommodation** is somewhat limited. Aside from rather grotty pub rooms along Norwich Quay, the choice is between B&Bs, an excellent backpackers and a motor camp. Most of the best places are some way out of town, around Lyttleton harbour.

Harbour View Homestay, 3 Harbour View Terrace, Cass Bay (☎03/328 7250). Three kilometres west of Lyttelton on the way to Governors Bay, this relaxed house has one double and two single rooms with shared facilities, a sun deck around a solar-heated pool and wonderful dinners for an extra $25. ⑤.

Orchard House, Governors Bay (☎03/329 9622). Pleasant accommodation 8km from Lyttelton in a small, address-free settlement (phone ahead if you need directions). The house offers views of the harbour and surrounding farmland; the double room has French doors that open onto a deck where breakfast is served, weather permitting. ④.

Purau Motor Camp, Diamond Harbour (☎03/329 4702; book ahead as a locked barrier blocks the entrance). Situated among tall sheltering trees and across the road from the bay, this site boasts bunkhouse accommodation, a shop, pool and kitchen. Tent sites $7.50 per pitch, dorms ③.

Randolph House B&B, 49 Summer Rd (☎ & fax 03/328 8877). Set in a nineteenth-century wooden villa, this guesthouse has four comfortable rooms with shared facilities, grand views over the harbour, and tasty breakfasts. ④.

Tunnel Vision Backpackers, 44 London St (☎03/328 7576). Without doubt the best place to stay in Lyttelton, this is a brightly decorated, well-maintained, first-class backpackers, occupying a recently renovated old hotel in a central location, close to the town's more interesting bars, cafés and restaurants. Added bonuses are an outside deck and mountain bikes for rent for around $20 per day. Dorms ①, rooms ②.

The Town

There is one attraction above all others for which Lyttelton is famous. The **Timeball Station** (10am–4pm, closed Fri; $3), situated on the eastern side of Lyttelton, above Reserve Terrace, is clearly visible from all over the town. Built by prisoners in 1875–6 and renovated in 1995, it looks for all the world like a Gothic tower that has carelessly lost its castle. On the roof sits a large black ball whose plummet down a black pole registered Greenwich Mean Time at 1pm every day for 58 years. Radio signals replaced the timeball in 1934, though it is still in working order. Inside the station are a number

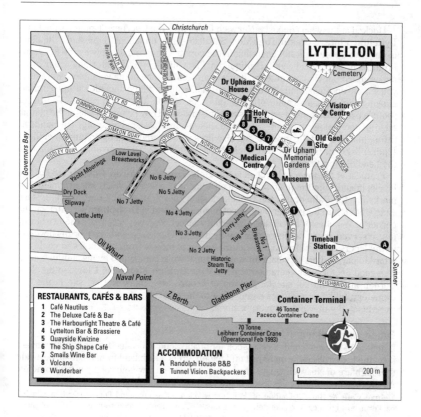

of exhibits on sailors' navigational techniques and the valuable role played by the time-ball.

Another intriguing attraction is **Lyttelton Museum** (Dec–Feb Tues, Thurs, Sat & Sun 2–4pm; March–Jan Sat & Sun 2–4pm; $2), at the eastern end of Norwich Quay where it meets Gladstone Quay. A stuffed penguin greets you at the door of this one-time Seaman's Institute. The nautical flavour lingers in a display of ancient telescopes, which straightfacedly informs visitors that the size and elaborateness of a sailor's telescope denoted his rank. Other exhibits reflect the town's history, while the Antarctic display spotlights Scott and Shackleton, both of whose expeditions set out from Lyttelton. Other curious artefacts have been salvaged from the small shelters built during the nineteenth century on various islands off the New Zealand shore, which were supplied with provisions to cater for unfortunate shipwrecked souls. Overall, the museum has the air of a long-neglected attic filled with a mishmash of collectibles, among which are occasional jewels such as a fossilized crab and watercolours of early Lyttelton personalities.

Opposite the museum is the **Lyttelton Signal Box**. Originally situated at the mouth of the Moorhouse Rail Tunnel on the line to Christchurch, it has been relocated to a heritage precinct on Gladstone Quay and commemorates Lyttelton's days as a rail port until 1963. Above the door of the box a 1902 halfpenny marks the date of the wooden box's construction, and finials on the apex of the roof safeguard against witches.

Docked at the wharf opposite Norwich Quay, over the Overhead Bridge, is the black **Lyttelton Vintage Steam Tug** (Mon–Sat 10am–4pm; donations requested), the older of only two steam tugs still operating in the country. Built in Glasgow by the Ferguson brothers in 1907, this beautiful antique boat is maintained in full working order by an impassioned bunch of volunteers. If you climb aboard, one of the volunteers will escort you on an unofficial and extremely informative tour, which includes a museum occupying the captain's cabin, officers' quarters, saloon and other cabins. The boiler room is particularly impressive: all sparkling brass and oily pistons, it was at the cutting edge of technology in its heyday, with steam-power-assisted steering. On Sundays, throughout most of the year, the tug also fires up for some thrilling round-trip **cruises** (2pm & 3.30pm; 1hr 30min; $10; book ahead on ☎03/322 8911), steaming all the way to the head of the harbour.

Prettiest of the town's churches is the **Holy Trinity Anglican Church** (1860), two blocks inland from the main port area on Winchester Street, which was originally earmarked as the Cathedral of the Diocese, a status never afforded it once building started in Christchurch. Another building of historic interest is **Dr Upham's** (1907), on the corner of Winchester Street and Canterbury Street. For over fifty years the two-storey house served as the home for this saintly doctor, who is remembered for his devotion to the lepers of Quail Island, his refusal to accept money from patients who could not afford to pay, and his penchant for walking the town accompanied by his faithful hound. The good doctor is also commemorated by the **Upham Memorial Clock**, in the Rose Garden at the old jail site (at the top of Oxford St). Above the jail site is the Old Cemetery, full of gravestones dating back to the earliest settlers, except for those who were hanged – they did not merit a stone.

Eating and drinking

Lyttelton has a well-founded reputation for quality food and value for money. The majority of the better places lie on or just off London Street, just inland from the main port-side thoroughfare of Norwich Quay, which itself harbours a few noteworthy establishments. All the restaurants and cafés listed below are open daily, unless otherwise stated.

Deluxe Café & Bar, 18 London St. Polished wooden furnishings and floors provide a relaxing backdrop to high-quality moderately priced meals; their French onion soup is called "NZ onion soup" as a mark of defiance against French nuclear testing in the Pacific. Proceedings are further enlivened by late-evening revelry at the bar as locals play the piano and carouse. Lunch & dinner Mon–Fri & Sun, dinner only on Sat. Licensed & BYO.

Harbour Light Theatre and Café Bar, 24 London St (reservations advisable ☎03/328 8615). Opposite the Supervalue supermarket, this is a charming spot for eclectic dinners ($10–18), accompanied by dance parties, poetry evenings, theatre and live music. Licensed.

Lyttelton Bar and Brassiere, 3 Norwich Quay. An expensive dinner venue situated in the old post office, where well-presented snacks and meals in a city-wine-bar atmosphere are complemented by exceptional harbour views out the back. BYO ($5 corkage).

Café Nautilus, Norwich Quay. Reasonably priced seafood with a nautical theme, served in an unusual circular building overlooking the harbour. Thurs–Mon evenings only; licensed & BYO.

Quayside Kwizine, Norwich Quay, opposite the old post office. A tiny takeaway proffering wholesome fast food, with good veggie choices (lentil burgers for $4.50), fish and chips, beef burgers, satay and Bratwurst; in fine weather you can dine al fresco while enjoying the harbour views. Closed Mon & Tues.

Ship Shape Café, 91 Norwich Quay. Breakfast is served from 7.45am ($7.50 and up), followed by lunch and Devonshire teas ($4); closes at 4pm. Closed Sat & Sun.

Smails Wine Bar and Café, 8 London St (☎03/328 8348). An intimate café/wine bar in an attractive cottage, complete with a herb garden; the fish is especially good, but there are plenty of other choices. Licensed.

Volcano, 42 London St (☎03/328 7077). Fine dinners that have proved a big with locals and Christchurch folk alike. Situated in a historic building with a traditional large-windowed shopfront, its cuisine draws on Cajun, Mexican, Spanish and Italian influences, with all sorts of home-made treats.

Wunderbar, London St. Above the Supersaver supermarket (the entrance is via the car park behind the supermarket and up an iron fire escape). This late-night drinking-hole and club is one of the most original nightspots around. Its decor is idiosyncratic, to say the least, including a gruesome doll's-head lightshade, and a large bar and deck overlook the harbour. Entertainment ranges from 1940s and 50s cabaret nights, through poetry, live bands, stand-up comics, club and disco music, to film noir evenings. Mon–Fri 5pm–late, Sat & Sun 3pm–even later.

Around Lyttelton Harbour

Lyttelton Harbour is a large deep-sea inlet with many small bays, one of which is occupied by Lyttelton itself. The shore of the inlet is served by the harbour road, which heads east from Lyttelton along the northern shore to **Godley Head**, the northern lip of the harbour – a moody, grass- and rock-covered promontory with steep sea cliffs offering excellent views. Heading west out of Lyttelton, the harbour road heads towards **Governors Bay** and out along the southern shore to **Diamond Harbour**, before proceeding to the southeastern lip of Lyttelton Harbour where it meets the next big inlet, Port Levy Harbour (see below). Both **Quail Island** in the centre of Lyttelton Harbour and the tiny **Ripapa Island** just east of Diamond Harbour are havens for birds, as well as offering solitude and superb views. Access to the islands is provided by **ferries** and tourist **cruises** from Lyttelton, although **kayaks** (rented in Lyttelton, see below) allow for a more close-up exploration of the coastline.

Godley Head

At the northernmost tip of the harbour, **Godley Head** stands guard – a spectacular piece of land with high cliffs and excellent views, administered by DOC. Follow the signs east out of Lyttelton to the Summit Road, which takes you out onto Godley Head (about 10km) and the **Godley Head Farm Park**, a delightfully scenic spot for walks and picnics. The walkway network is extensive, in places stumbling across installations left behind after World War II, including dark warren-like tunnels and searchlight emplacements perched like birds' nests on the cliffs. From here, you can also walk

---

LYTTELTON HARBOUR CRUISES AND KAYAKING

A variety of **cruises** depart from the Lyttelton Jetty opposite Norwich Quay, offering a splendid sea-level perspective on the harbour. If you can do without a commentary or simply want more time to explore, check out the regular ferry services to Diamond Harbour and Quail Island (see p.512).

Harbour Cruises operate a straightforward cruise of the **inner and outer harbour** (daily at 2.45pm; 30min; $8; ☎03/328 8368), including a commentary on local history and spectacular views of the harbour mouth, Quail Island, and the workings of the port. If you have more money to spare, Coastline Adventures' pleasure cruiser, *The Fox*, plies the route from Lyttelton as far as Pigeon Bay 20km to the east (daily Boxing Day to May weather permitting; full-day $80; ☎03/326 6833). The cruise takes a good look round Lyttelton Harbour, stopping in Governors Bay for lunch before leaving the Harbour to explore Pigeon Bay and Port Levy. Originally built in 1922, this charming boat is still powered by its original engine and makes for an atmospheric way to see the harbour.

Another peaceful, though rather more energetic way to explore the harbour is by **kayak**. Sea Kayaking Adventures ($35 per person per day; ☎03/328 7228l) demand average fitness and some experience. Once kitted out, you can check out volcanic rock formations, beaches, islands, shipwrecks, bird colonies and caves, with the prospect of seeing Hector's dolphins and other wildlife up close.

down to the tiny coastal settlements of Boulder Bay and Taylors Mistake (see box on p.497).

Diamond Harbour

Diamond Harbour is so named because the bright sunlight on the water sparkles like a million diamonds. Directly across the water from Lyttelton, it serves as a handy short-cut to Camp Bay, the Mount Herbert Walkway and the rest of the peninsula. From Lyttelton, Harbour Cruises (☎03/328 8368) operate passenger **ferries** from the ferry jetty opposite Norwich Quay to Diamond Harbour (sailings every 1–2hr: Mon–Fri 6.15am–6.20pm, Sat 6.15am–5.30pm, Sun 10.30am–5.30pm; $3.60 one-way, $7.20 return), which connect with the #28 bus from Christchurch.

Overlooking the water from a headland just above Diamond Harbour, **Godley House** is a popular vantage point which has attracted visitors from Christchurch and beyond for over a hundred years. Surrounded by gardens and lawns, the house has been co-opted by the conference market in recent years, but it makes a fine place to sit and imbibe a beverage in the licensed café while taking in the panoramic views.

An excellent base from which to explore the area is provided by *Otamahua* **B&B**, Athol Place, Church Bay, 4km west of Diamond Harbour on the way to Charteris Bay (call to arrange pick-up from ferry, ☎03/329 4728; ④). The two en-suite rooms, a double and a twin, both have superb views of the harbour; dinner is also available on request ($25, including wine).

Quail and Riparpa islands

Set in mid-harbour, **Quail Island** was known as *Te Kawakkawa* by the local Maori because it was the place where children collected seabirds' eggs. It was used as a leper colony between 1907 and 1925 (when the afflicted were transported to Fiji), and Scott quarantined his dogs here before his expedition to the South Pole. Although the sheltered waters of Lyttelton Harbour are not known for their treacherous nature, a number of shipwrecks litter the island's shores and can be spied at low tide.

These days it's a venue for day-trips, swimming and walking; it makes a relaxing and fascinating place to spend a day – so long as you remember to pack some provisions, plenty of drinking water (there's none on the island) and rain gear. From Lyttelton Jetty, opposite Norwich Quay, Harbour Cruises **ferries** (☎03/328 8368) run to Quail Island (Nov–March 5 daily; April–Oct 3–4 daily; $8 return). To guide your explorations and get the most from these secluded surroundings, pick up the *Quail Island Walkway* map from the Christchurch DOC office or the Lyttelton visitor centre, which details two circular **walking tracks** (1hr 30min & 2hr 30min), both starting from the wharf.

Further east, just off the southern shore of the Harbour near Diamond Harbour, **Riparpa Island** has a history largely determined by its defensibility. Successively a Maori pa, then the site of a fort built in the 1880s as a measure against a feared Russian invasion that never materialized, it later became a prison camp for Count Felix Von Luckner, a German "sea raider". The island now enjoys some peace as a historic reserve administered by DOC, which can only be visited on guided tours run by Harbour Cruises (Mon–Fri 2.25pm & 4pm, Sat & Sun 2.25pm & 3.45pm; $12; ☎03/328 8368).

The Summit Road

For those with their own transport, the minor roads leading across Banks Peninsula from Lyttelton towards Akaroa (see p.515) provide access to some of the most attractive scenery in the region. The journey begins with the so-called **Summit Road**, which rises from Godley Head and snakes over the Port Hills before skirting around Lyttelton

WALKS ALONG THE SUMMIT ROAD

The best way to get to know this part of the peninsula is in the company of *The Summit Road Map* (from Christchurch visitor centre; $5), which pinpoints sights, historical sites and walks. The map includes a brief description of the **walking tracks** that extend over the peninsula from the road – 39 in all. Among the more worthwhile is the **Crater Rim Walkway** (18.5km; 4hr), a magical walk taking in all of Harry Ell's rest stations (see below) along a part of the crater of the extinct Lyttelton volcano; a DOC leaflet, *Crater Rim Walkway*, has a detailed map and further information. Or, beginning near the Sign of the Bellbird (see below), you can attempt a complex of well-marked, quite steep tracks known as the **Ohinetahi Bush Tracks**. Head south from the Sign of the Bellbird along the Crater Rim for about 150m then turn down towards O'Farrells Track before proceeding east for 30min and then following the switchbacks up the hill. This gives access to several alternatives, including Watlings Track, more of the Crater Rim, Governors Bay and various bush reserves. For more of a challenge, **Mount Herbert Walkway** (16km return; 7hr) offers a demanding climb from Diamond Harbour almost to the summit of Mount Herbert before descending to Charteris Bay; while **Mount Bradley Walkway** (13km return; 6hr) starts from the Summit Road near Gebbie's Pass and heads through open country to the **Remarkable Dykes** and the **Sign of the Packhorse**, before skirting to the west of Mount Bradley through very old native bush and heading down to Diamond Harbour.

Harbour to meet the **Gebbies Pass Road** – which heads south to join SH75 (the more direct route to Akaroa) – and the **Teddington–Purau Road**, which proceeds eastward towards Diamond Harbour, Port Levy and Pigeon Bay. The Summit Road itself continues onwards to the peninsula's eastern outposts of Little Akaroa, **Okains Bay** and Le Bons Bay, finally joining up with SH75 for the descent into Akaroa. Traversing a visibly volcanic area dotted with copses and reserves of regenerating native bush and trees, the route rewards exploration.

The Summit Road was the consuming passion of the public-spirited **Harry Ell**, who dreamed of building a highway with **walking tracks** (see box above) and rest stations along the summit of the Port Hills and right around the peninsula. Ell himself died in 1934, and only four rest stations (named after birds and mammals) were ever built. Follow the Summit Road from Lyttelton towards Dyer's Pass Road to find the first of the Ell's rest stations, **Sign of the Kiwi**, set in the Sugar Loaf Bush Reserve and now a café providing snacks and refreshments for walkers and drivers. If you turn off the Summit Road and head 3km down **Dyer's Pass Road**, in a northerly, Christchurch-bound direction you'll come to **Sign of the Takahe**, a Gothic-style house distinguished by enormous kauri beams, salvaged from a bridge that once spanned the Hurunui River. The house is now a hotel and conference centre, but you can still take a look at some unique friezes fashioned from old packing cases and stone quarried from rocky outcrops on the peninsula, which are kept in a memorial room. Look out for the heraldic embellishments relating to early governors of New Zealand, coats of arms of local families and shields portraying significant events in British history.

Returning to the Summit Road, you can continue 4km southwest to **Sign of the Bellbird**, a stone shelter for trampers with exceptional views, and **Sign of the Packhorse**, a trampers' hut just past the **Remarkable Dykes** on the way to the summits of Mount Bradley and Mount Herbert. These were created by cracks in the volcano formed during eruptions, which were forced wider by the heat of subsequent volcanic activity, forming a receptacle for molten rock. As the molten rock cooled and solidified, it proved more resistant to erosion than the surrounding material, thereby creating the protruding ridges which were subsequently dubbed "dykes".

As you continue around the Summit Road and out onto the Banks Peninsula proper you will see the first of the east coast bays, **Port Levy**, a tiny valley with a beach that once supported the largest Maori population in Canterbury. Continuing over the headlands you will overlook **Pigeon Bay** and **Little Akaloa**, before coming to one of the peninsula's gems, Okains Bay.

Okains Bay

Seventy kilometres southeast of Christchurch, **OKAINS BAY** is a popular holiday and picnic area with a tiny permanent population. No public buses come this far, so those without their own transport will have to use one of the mail run tours (see p.507) operating out of Akaroa. The beach and the placid lagoon formed by the **Opara Stream** are excellent for swimming and boating, but the real reason to come is a remarkable museum containing one of the best collections of Maori artefacts in the South Island. The **Okains Bay Maori and Colonial Museum** (daily 10am–5pm; $4), on the only road going into the bay, was originally the private collection of a Maori-obsessed local man, and is housed in the old cheese factory. Within the same compound, several outbuildings contain the more traditional exhibitions relating to European settlement, including a "slab" stable and cottage – simply constructed from large adzed slabs of totara wood. Among the thought-provoking Maori exhibits are a god stick dating back to 1400, a war canoe from 1867 and various weapons, as well as a valuable *hei tiki* (a pendant with a design based on the human form) recovered in England and brought back to Okains Bay. Beside the Maori exhibition building, there is also a beautiful meeting house (it's *tapu* or sacred, although visitors are allowed to look around it), with fine symbolic figures carved by master craftsman John Rua.

Also on the only road descending to Okains Bay, the *Kawatea Farmstay* (☎03/304 8621; ⑤; dinner on request, $20), is a 90-year-old **homestead** set in lush gardens bordered by 5km of scenic coastline and offering three rooms decorated with native timbers and stained glass. At the end of this road is the *Okains Bay Domain* **campsite**, just behind the beach (office 200m back up the road; $4 per person, dorms ①), which offers a choice of sites or bargain beds in the pavilion which has a fridge and stove. Be sure to bring supplies with you as there is nowhere to eat in the bay.

Le Bons Bay

The last bay before the Summit Road joins up with SH75 is the grassy, verdant **LE BONS BAY**, which contains a number of holiday homes, a small community, and a gorgeous sandy **beach**, framed on two sides by cliffs, that provides safe swimming. For a perspective of the eastern coast of the peninsula and panoramic views of Akaroa Harbour, head along the privately owned **Le Bons Bay to Akaroa Track** (16km; 5hr 30min one-way; advance notice essential, ☎03/304 8533; free to those staying overnight at *Le Bons Bay Motor Camp*, see below; otherwise $2–4 depending on season).

Clearly signposted on the only road into the bay, the friendly *Le Bons Bay* **backpackers** (call to arrange pick-up from Akaroa, ☎03/304 8582; dorms ①, rooms ②), is in a cosy, 120-year-old house situated far enough up the bay to provide spectacular views; breakfast is provided and, on request, generous dinners made from fresh local produce and fish for about $10 a head. It's easy to while away a few days here, taking long walks down the valley or across the hilltops, or joining your host on a **boat trip** to see penguins, dolphins, shags and seals (1hr 30min; $12). At the foot of the road, and about 3km from the shore, the *Le Bons Bay* **farmstay** (☎03/304 8529; cottage ③, B&B ④; dinner on request, $20) has two comfortable rooms with shared facilities in a charming 1880 farmhouse set in extensive gardens; they also own a **self-contained cottage** right next to the beach, with a panoramic sea view and linen supplied. Finally, *Le Bons Bay Motor Camp*, on Valley Road, also at the base of the hill on the opposite side of the road to the farmstay (☎ & fax 03/304 8533; tent sites $8, dorms ①, on-site vans & cabins ②), is a well kept and picturesque **campsite** by a stream, with a store, swimming pool, organized horse trekking, and mountain-bike rental.

Akaroa

The small, sleepy town of **AKAROA** ("long bay") is 82km from Christchurch on SH75, or 90km via the Summit Road and northeastern bays of the peninsula. Both routes join for the scenic descent into Akaroa, overlooking its spectacular harbour. Sitting in a picturesque cove on the edge of the water, and beginning to creep up the crater behind, the town is primarily a Kiwi holiday destination; two-thirds of its houses are baches (holiday homes). What draws these "summer people" and weekenders is the scenery, peaceful atmosphere, water sports, fine cuisine and walks – including the **Banks Peninsula Track**, which starts and finishes nearby (see box on p.518).

This part of the peninsula supported a large **Maori** population and was home of the paramount Kai Tahu chief, Temaiharanui. Akaroa is also one of the oldest European townships in Canterbury, originally settled by **French migrants**. In 1838 a French Commander, Jean Langlois, purchased what he believed to be the entire peninsula for goods to the value of 1000 French francs, and returned to France to encourage settlers to sail with Captain Lavaud and populate a new French colony. However, while the French were making their way to New Zealand, the British sent Captain William Hobson to assume the role of lieutenant-governor over all the land that could be purchased; and just six days before Lavaud sailed into the harbour, the British flag was raised in Akaroa. Lavaud's passengers decided to stay, which meant that the first formal settlement under **British sovereignty** was comprised of sixty-three French – and six Germans who had come along for the ride. The French influence has prevailed, however, and is proudly maintained – a stroll around Akaroa reveals French street names, architecture and cuisine.

You can treat Akaroa as a day-trip from Christchurch, although you'll only have time to scratch the surface of this beguiling spot; far better to spend a night or two in order to appreciate the town and its surrounds.

Arrival and information

Buses take 1hr 40min to get here from Christchurch, dropping passengers on the central Rue Lavaud just outside the efficient and friendly **visitor centre** (Mon–Sat 9am–4pm, Sun 11am–3pm; ☎03/304 8600), which shares a building with the post office and council offices on the corner of Rue Lavaud and Rue Balguerie. Of the many leaflets, maps and brochures available here, be sure to pick up a copy of the free leaflets covering the *Akaroa Historic Village Walk*, a self-guided walking tour, and the *Akaroa Visitors Guide*, which has excellent maps of the town and the peninsula, and lists attractions, shops and restaurants.

Accommodation

There is a wide choice of **accommodation** in Akaroa, most of it relatively expensive, reflecting its resort status. The cheapest option is offered by the three backpacker hostels – two in town and one in Onuku, about 5km south on the main coast road along Akaroa Harbour – though the B&Bs have the edge in terms of home comforts and atmosphere.

Akaroa Holiday Park, Morgan's Rd, off the Old Coach Rd (☎03/304 7471). Sprawling across a terraced hillside overlooking the harbour and the main street running through town, this site has modern facilities, including a swimming pool. Campervan & tent sites $9, cabins & on-site vans ②–③.

Akaroa Village Inn, Beach Rd, next door to *L'Hotel* (☎03/304 7421, fax 304 7423). One of the prettiest hotels in Akaroa, situated in the heart of town opposite the main wharf. Built on the site of the

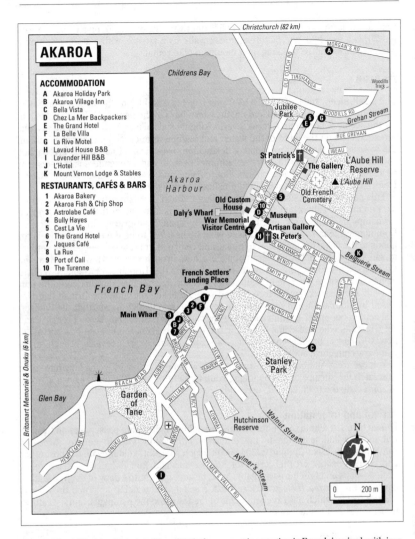

first residential hotel, which dated from 1842, the current incarnation is French-inspired, with iron lacework on the first-floor balconies, 32 comfortable rooms with en-suite bathrooms, a swimming pool and a spa. ⑤.

Bella-Vista, 21b Watson St (☎ & fax 03/304 7137). Comfortable family home containing two double rooms and a single, all with shared facilities. Continental breakfast is served, and there are great views from the veranda. ④.

La Belle Villa, 113 Rue Jolie (☎ & fax 03/304 7084). B&B in a lovely wooden house with spacious light rooms, a large swimming pool and al fresco breakfasts in summer. ⑤.

Chez La Mer Backpackers, Rue Lavaud (☎03/304 7024). Historic building (1871) offering high-quality budget accommodation; friendly staff and some useful hand-drawn maps of local walks and points of interest. Dorms ①, rooms ②.

Grand Hotel, 6 Rue Lavaud (☎03/304 7011, fax 304 7304). Basic singles and doubles, with shared facilities, above a refurbished 1860 pub with bottle shop, restaurant and beer garden. ③.

L'Hotel, 75 Beach Rd (☎03/304 7559, fax 304 7455). French-style guesthouse, with eight clean well-equipped rooms. ⑤.

Lavaud House B&B, 83 Rue Lavaud (☎ & fax 03/304 7121). Historic home overlooking the main swimming beach, with fresh flowers and antique furniture in every room. A comfortable and friendly place, with four bedrooms and a choice of cooked or continental breakfast. ④–⑤.

Lavender Hill B&B, 1 Lighthouse Rd (☎03/304 7082). Pretty house, opposite the lighthouse, with two comfortable rooms sharing a bathroom. The landlady makes leadlight windows, some of which adorn the house itself. ④.

Mount Vernon Lodge and Stables, 500m uphill from the waterfront at Rue Balguerie (☎03/304 7180). A bit of a climb, but well worth the effort for excellent accommodation in purpose-built wooden self-contained chalets, motel units, and budget beds in a dorm hut, all built on a hillside overlooking Akaroa and the bay. Other perks are a swimming pool, nature walks and a courtesy bus to and from from the town centre. Dorms ①, chalets & motel units ③–④.

Onuku Farm Hostel, 6km south of town on the Onuku road (☎03/304 7612). Beside the bay, this secluded and quiet spot has accommodation in the main house or in huts (summer only). Tents $7, dorms ①, rooms ②.

La Rive Motel, 1 Rue Lavaud (☎ & fax 03/304 7651). Large, curiously shaped motel (its open-sided, two-storey conical tower is an allusion to French chateau architecture) in a tranquil garden setting, with a white picket fence at the front and eight units, all containing full kitchens and TVs. ④.

The Town

Akaroa is strung along the shore in a long, easily walkable ribbon. In fact the best way to get acquainted with the place is by following the **Akaroa Historic Village Walk** (free leaflet available from the visitor centre), which pinpoints buildings of interest and architectural note.

The **Akaroa Museum**, opposite the visitor centre on the northeastern corner of Rue Lavaud and Rue Balguerie (daily Oct–April 10.30am–4.30pm; May–Nov 10.30am–4pm; $3), offers something slightly different from the usual small-town New Zealand fare, with several interesting Maori artefacts and a twenty-minute video giving a sketchy account of the remarkable and sometimes violent history of Maori settlement on the peninsula. Also displayed are copies of the Treaty of Waitangi, including a literal English version of the Maori text (see Contexts, p.764). Other exhibits deal with the peninsula's whaling history and settlement, including albums full of fascinating photographs of the original French and German settlers and the British that followed them. The museum also incorporates the **Langlois–Eteveneaux Cottage**, one of the oldest houses in New Zealand and an early "prefab", which was partly constructed in France, then shipped over. Also associated with the museum are the **Court House**, containing a mock-up of the old jail, and the tiny **Custom House**, across Rue Lavaud next to Daly's Wharf, from which glass-wielding officials once kept watch on the port below.

Continuing the Gallic theme is the **French Cemetery** at the northern end of town, reached by a footpath which leads from Rue Pompallier just off Rue Levaud into the L'Aube Hill Reserve. The first consecrated burial ground in Canterbury, the cemetery was sadly neglected until 1925, when the bodies were reinterred in a central plot marked by a single monument, shaded by weeping willows – romantically said to have been grown from a cutting taken at Napoleon's grave in St Helena. Continue about 150m up L'Aube hill for even better views over the town and harbour. At the northern end of Rue Pompallier, the French-inspired **Church of St Patrick** has its origins in the mission station built here by Bishop Pompallier in 1840, but the first two church buildings were destroyed by fire and a storm respectively. The church you see today is a third-time-lucky effort, built in 1864 from large slabs of unplaned totara; the combination of totara, black pine and kauri, and the changing colours of the wood as it ages, fills the church with rich colours, complementing the bold stained-glass in the east window, behind the altar.

THE BANKS PENINSULA TRACK

One of the most popular tracks in the area is the **Banks Peninsula Track**, a 35km private track which must be booked in advance (only 12 trampers are allowed on the route at any one time) – although the entrance fee does include hut-type accommodation along the route. It's open from Oct 15 to May 15, takes four days to walk, and costs $100, including transport and accommodation. There's an $85 standby rate for those ready to take the place of other walkers who cancel, although you'll be expected to step into the breach at short notice (anything from a day to two weeks). **Bookings** can only be made through *Banks Peninsula Track*, PO Box 50, Akaroa (☎03/304 7612). A cheaper option ($60 per person with 2 nights' accommodation) along the same route is also available, although this assumes that you're fit enough to cover the 35km track at twice the normal speed.

The trail starts at Onuku, 5km south of Akaroa – free transport to the trailhead from Akaroa post office is arranged when you book. A reasonable level of **fitness** is required, but because you're guaranteed a bed at each hut, you can walk at your own pace. You will need a good pair of boots, sleeping bag, all-weather gear and, though it is possible to augment your **supplies** with fresh farm produce at Stony Bay and snacks at Otanerito Beach, you should carry provisions for at least the first two days.

THE ROUTE

The **route** traverses spectacular volcanic coastline, verdant farmland, exposed headlands and sandy beaches, as well as the Hinewai Nature Reserve (a marine reserve around the southeastern bays of the peninsula), before reaching the end of the track at Mount Vernon Lodge just east of Akaroa. The first night is spent in **Onuku hut** at the start of the track. There's usually enough time on the following day to explore neighbouring trails before embarking on the first stage of the walk proper from **Onuku to Flea Bay** (11km, 3hr 30min), passing three small waterfalls and providing views of the peninsula's east coast. Accommodation at Flea Bay is in a charming 130-year-old cottage with a veranda overlooking the beach, and comes complete with electric stove, lights and hot showers. The second day, **Flea Bay to Stony Bay** (8km; 2hr 30min) is an exposed hike along coastal cliffs, with a seal colony providing lunchtime distraction around the halfway point. The night is spent in one of the huts-cum-cottages in Stony Bay, where there's also a modest family museum, a bath under the stars, a small shop selling bread, tinned food and beer, and a few short tracks exploring the bay. The walk from **Stony Bay to Otanerita Bay** (6km; 2hr) takes care of the third day, with overnight accommodation provided in a farmhouse just 50m from a great swimming beach, run by New Zealand author Fiona Farrell and her partner. The fourth and final day's walk heads inland, from **Otanerita Bay to Mount Vernon Lodge** (10km; 3hr; 600m ascent), passing two waterfalls and providing a last glimpse of the ocean before descending to the calmer waters of Akaroa Harbour.

Also situated at the northern end of Rue Pompallier is the **Gallery Akaroa** (Oct–April daily 1.30–4.30pm; donation requested), which occupies a former hydro-electric plant, and serves as a venue for national and local exhibitions of arts and crafts, as well as for concerts of various types of music on Sundays – call ☎03/304 7140 for details of current exhibitions and forthcoming events. Also worth a look is the **Artisans Gallery**, 45 Rue Lavaud (daily 10am–5pm), a sales-oriented collection housed in an 1877 cottage and displaying pottery, weaving, silk, jewellery, knitwear, clothing and furniture. Wood-turning demonstrations are given on the premises.

Walks around Akaroa

If you lack the time or inclination to tackle the **Banks Peninsula Track** (see box above), there are some equally rewarding shorter walks starting from Akaroa. The

AKAROA HARBOUR CRUISES AND KAYAKING

For a delightful **cruise** on Akaroa Harbour, where Hector's dolphins often gambol in the boats' spray, head for Akaroa Harbour Cruises, Main Wharf, Beach Rd (Nov–April 11am, 1.30pm & 3.40pm; 2hr; $27; ticket office daily 10am–4pm; ☎03/304 7641). Their large modern **catamaran** cruises to the mouth of the harbour and back via a rookery, a beautiful high-walled volcanic sea cave, colonies of spotted shags and cormorants, Penguin Caves (where Little Blue penguins can sometimes be spotted) and a fish-feeding stop in Lucas Bay.

In an effort to attract their share of the tourist dollar, a number of companies have banded together to offer a variety of watery activities. A popular choice among these is **swimming with dolphins** (Dec–April daily 8.30am; 3hr; $65; bookings essential, ☎03/304 7340), who take you among Hector's dolphins – the world's smallest breed of dolphin, and which is only found in New Zealand waters. The most tranquil and rewarding way of seeing the harbour close up, though, is on a guided **kayaking** trip with Banks Peninsula Sea Kayaks, 114 Rue Jolie (full day $70, including lunch; ☎03/304 8776); they also have kayaks and camping equipment for rent if you want to go it alone.

---

track to Le Bons Bay (16km; 5hr 30min; another privately owned track which needs to be booked in advance; see p.514) heads east over the hills, while the **Round the Mountain Walk** (10km; 4hr return), circumnavigates the hills above Akaroa via the Purple Peak Road – the route is shown on a hand-drawn photocopied map, available for 50¢ from *Chez La Mer Backpackers* on Rue Lavaud.

If you have a day to spare, an interesting walk alongside **Beach Road to Onuku** (5km one-way; 1hr 15min) takes in some of the historical sights, first heading towards Glen Bay and visiting the nineteenth-century white-wood **lighthouse**, which used to stand at Akaroa Head to guide ships into the harbour before being moved to its current location in 1980. Continuing towards Akaroa Head for about fifteen minutes, you'll come to **Red House Bay**, the scene of a bloody massacre in 1830, when the great northern chief Te Rauparaha bribed (with flax) the captain of the British brig *Elizabeth* to conceal Maori warriors about the vessel and invite Te Rauparaha's unsuspecting enemies (led by Temaiharanui) on board, where they were slaughtered. Te Rauparaha and his men then feasted on the victims on the beach. The final part of the walk takes you to **ONUKU**, 5km from Akaroa, where you'll find the **Onuku Marae** and a tiny church, established in 1876–78. Onuku is even quieter than Akaroa: roughly translated, the name means "coming and going though never staying long" – and, sure enough, there's little to keep you here, except maybe more walks and the prospect of a bed for the night at the *Onuku Farm Hostel* (see p.517).

Eating and drinking

With an eager tourist market and its **French heritage**, Akaroa is a very good place to eat, making it popular with people from Christchurch, who think nothing of driving 82km for their evening meal. This does tend to push up prices a little and means that more **expensive** establishments predominate, although there are the usual takeaways and cheaper cafés to fall back on. The reliance on the summer **tourist trade** also means that many places cut back their hours, or even close completely, during winter.

Akaroa Bakery, 51 Beach Rd. Excellent fresh-baked bread, plus a small café, serving sandwiches, pies, cakes, pizza and bottomless cups of coffee. Daily all year, from early morning to 5pm.

Akaroa Fish and Chip Shop, Beach Road, near the harbour. Takeaway "Fush 'n' Chups" with a New Zealand flavour. Daily lunch & dinner.

Astrolabe Café and Bar, 71 Beach Rd. Moderately priced lunches and dinners, including some impressive foccacia sandwiches, as well as mussels steamed in white wine and tomato sauce. Licensed.

Bully Hayes, 57 Beach Rd (☎03/304 7533). Named after a famous local con-man, this place serves reliable, moderately priced dishes alongside great homemade breads – try chicken, leek and kumara soup, Peninsula Pork Fillet, Magnet Bay Crayfish or Lucas Bay Salmon Fillet. Open for lunch and dinner. Licensed.

C'est La Vie, 33 Rue Lavaud (☎03/304 7314). An exceptional, intimate dinner-only restaurant with relaxing live music. The fine French cuisine uses organically grown ingredients and fresh seafood, with plenty of vegetarian choices, all rounded off with delicate pastries. If you order à la carte, main courses are about $25, but you should consider the $65 set menu: a six-course feast of paté, entrée and soup, with a choice of three main courses, dessert buffet, cheese platter and tea or coffee. Evenings only. BYO.

L'Hotel, 75 Beach Rd. Café and wine bar serving modern Mediterranean cuisine that won't break the bank, augmented by a broad selection of beers and spirits. Open for lunch and dinner.

Jacques Café & Wine Bar, *Akaroa Village Inn*, Beach Rd. Reasonably priced snacks and main meals with the emphasis on fresh fish and Mediterranean cuisine, together with some delicious and wholesome salads. Try the warm lamb and avocado salad or the chicken and ham ragout. Open 10am–10pm. Licensed.

The Jolly Roger, *Grand Hotel*, 6 Rue Lavaud. Pleasant and reasonably priced lunch and dinner venue, with particularly tasty fish dishes and a few bar snacks. Licensed.

La Rue, 6 Rue Balguerie (☎03/304 7658). Fresh and well-presented lunches and dinners, with mains from about $17, served in comfortable surroundings. Open for lunch and dinner. Licensed.

The Turenne, 74 Rue Lavaud. Typical New Zealand café, distinguished by home-made pies and cakes – and hearty cooked breakfasts for $10. Daily until early evening.

Listings

Buses In addition to regular Grayline and Mount Cook buses, a couple of companies run summer services between Christchurch and Akaroa: Akaroa Shuttle (twice daily Nov–May; $15 one-way, $25 day-return; book 24 hours ahead, ☎0800/500 929) and French Connection Bus (daily May–Sept; $19 one-way, $38 return; ☎03/377 0951).

Fishing Bluefin Charters (☎03/304 7866) specialize in fishing charters (2–12 passengers; $80 per half day for 2, $130 full day).

Horse riding Horse Trekking Akaroa, Mount Vernon Lodge and Stables, Rue Balguerie (☎03/304 7180), offer various guided treks depending on the amount of time you want to be in the saddle over hilly country ($25 per hour).

Kayaking Banks Peninsula Sea Kayaks, 114 Rue Jolie (☎03/304 8776), rent out single and double kayaks ($35 per person per day), plus camping gear (tents $5 per day, sleeping bag $5 per day); and they also organize guided trips (from $70 per person per day).

Newspaper The *Akaroa Mail and Banks Peninsula Advertiser* carries events listings and advertisements for activities.

Parasailing Akaroa Parasailing (☎03/304 7340) will strap you into a parachute and drag you behind a boat, while you fly above the water for about 10–15min ($50 per person).

Tours Peninsula & Alpine 4x4 Tours, 104 McCormacks Bay Rd (☎03/384 3576) run day-trips for small groups of 4–6, taking in Akaroa, Lyttelton, Barry's Bay Cheese Factory, Okains Bay Maori Museum, a sheep farm and animal park ($60 per person, including refreshments); see also p.507 for details of rural mail runs on the peninsula.

West of Akaroa

Following SH75 from Akaroa towards **Little River** and the west, you have access to the bays around the west side of Akaroa Harbour, **Lake Forsyth**, the spectacular **Lake Ellesmere** and a number of well known (to Kiwis at least) stop-offs that are well worth your time.

The first settlements reached on SH75 are **Takamatua** and **Robinson's Bay**, which are tiny and situated on beaches overlooking the harbour with little to detain you but the views. You may be tempted to linger slightly longer in **DUVAUCHELLE**, where

Relais Rochefort, at Ngaio Point (☎03/304 5832; closed Wed; licensed & BYO), proffers top-quality food for lunch and dinner in a lovely environment. About a kilometre further on along SH75 is a left turn that leads to the **Onawe Peninsula Scenic Reserve** (daily dawn–dusk); situated on a peninsula jutting out into Akaroa Harbour, this at one time offered a highly defensible sanctuary for local Maori. Remains of the pa fortifications, deep ditches and ramparts are still distinguishable, despite years of farming.

Barry's Bay

Back on SH75, 12km from Akaroa, **BARRY'S BAY** is home of the settlers' original dairy factory, **Barry's Bay Cheese**, clearly signposted on the landward side of the road (Mon–Fri 8am–5pm, Sat & Sun 9.30am–5pm; ☎03/304 5809), which is a must for cheese lovers. Accounts of early cheese-making go back as far as 1844, when chessets (the traditional cheese moulds still in use today) were brought from Europe. Ironically, Banks Peninsula was one of the first areas in New Zealand to start producing and exporting cheese to Europe because the clean pastures produced such pure milk. All their cheeses are sold on the premises: try the cheddar, Barry's Bay Sharp, Havarti, Akaroa Mellow, or Port Cooper, with one of the locally made chutneys or mustards on a piece of fresh bread for lunch.

One of the best **B&Bs** in the vicinity is also in Barry's Bay. *Oihitu Estate*, just off SH75 (☎03/304 5804; ④), is a large country house dating from the 1860s. The two luxurious en-suite rooms contain queen-sized beds and the breakfast bacon and eggs are cooked on a wood stove. *Bayview Farmstay* (☎03/304 5875; ⑤), on SH75 6km west of Barry's Bay, has two en-suite rooms and serves a hearty **farm** breakfast – and dinners on request ($20). You can walk around the farm, picnic in native bush, or join in the day-to-day farm activities such as milking cows and feeding livestock. If all this fresh air gives you a thirst, the famous **drinking den** of the *Hilltop Tavern* is only 2km further west on SH75.

THE SOUTHERN BAYS WALKWAY

Advance booking is essential for the **Southern Bays Walkway** (Oct–May; 66km; $112.50, including a $50 deposit; ☎03/329 0007), a **four-day tramp** beginning and ending in Little River, and limited to 12 people at any one time. A cheaper **two-day option** is also available for the super-fit ($80, including a $30 deposit). The cost includes transport from Little River to the start of the track, **hut accommodation** (with cooking facilities, drinking water, hot showers and flush toilets), landowner fees, track registration and information, though not off-road parking in Little River, for which there is a small fee. You'll need good boots, wet-weather gear, a sleeping bag and enough food for four days.

This is a spectacular track, similar in character to the Banks Peninsula Track, but much more physically demanding, with many climbs and one **gruelling** ascent from sea level to 800m. The track crosses beaches, native bush, cliff tops and tussock, rendering views of the peninsula and across to the Canterbury Plains and the Southern Alps. Wildlife sightings might include shag colonies, seals and dolphins. The first day's walk (10km, 2hr 30min) is the least strenuous, taking you from **Little River** to the shores of **Lake Forsyth** near the ocean. Day two (17km, 5hr) has you climbing inland before zigzagging back out to the coast and some impressive cliff-top views. After this, the path heads east and up a couple of switchbacks before arriving at the **Te Oka Bay Valley hut**, which commands splendid views down to the coast. The third day (14km, 4hr) entails a return to the coast and an evocative cliff-top path, before retreating inland to **Robin Hood Bay Spur Hut**. Day four (17km, 7hr) is the hardest, involving a long and strenuous climb before reaching the **Upper Okuti Valley Hut**; and on day five you have a relatively short walk back to Little River (7km; 2hr).

French Farm

If you are interested in more formally presented cuisine, turn down the south fork off SH75 at Barry's Bay and head for **FRENCH FARM**. According to Maori tradition, the heights of French Farm were home to the *patupaiarehe* ("children of the mist"), whose chants can be heard on misty days or in the evenings. Of a more practical nature, the settlers in Akaroa used this fertile and sheltered area to establish orchards and vegetable plots to grow produce that would not otherwise have been available to them.

Some of the latter-day products of these plots can be sampled at the excellent **French Farm Restaurant and Vineyard** (signposted from the main road). Set among native trees is a French-style villa, in which a large open interior with terracotta-tiled floors and simple wooden furniture provides the backdrop for highly acclaimed food, presented with great style to devotees who fly here from all over New Zealand. The seasonally changing menu focuses on international cuisine, made where possible from local produce, and prices are surprisingly reasonable considering the quality (mains range from $20 to $24; salads are $18–20). The vineyard has yet to produce its first vintage, but it is possible to sample other Canterbury wines and to buy chutney and flavoured oils.

Little River and Lake Ellesmere

Back on SH75, the next town of note is **LITTLE RIVER**, which lies next to Lake Forsyth and overlooks Kaitorete Spit, Lake Ellesmere and the sea. The hub of the town is the **Old Railway and Craft Station** on Main Road, which houses a small **visitor centre** (Oct–April daily 9am–5pm; May–Sept Mon–Fri 10am–4pm, Sat 10am–1pm; ☎03/325 1255).

The starting point of the circular **Southern Bays Walkway** (see box on p.521), there is little of interest in the town itself, save for a reminder of the area's Maori heritage. A statue of Tangatahara, the famous chief of the ultimately unsuccessful defence of the Onawe Peninsula (see p.521), stands in the town, alongside a lengthy Maori inscription describing many of his battles. Take time to view, if not visit, **Lake Forsyth** (*Wairewa*), a long finger of water divided from the sea by a narrow shingle bank, **Birdlings Flat**, which leads onto Kaitorete Spit. Traditionally, the lake has been a rich source of food for local Maori, who were granted protected fishing rights off Birdlings Flat in 1896; the accumulated shingle of the sheltering bank also provides a fossicking ground for greenstone and gems.

The 30km-long Kaitorete spit juts southeastwards from Banks Peninsula to join the mainland, separating **Lake Ellesmere** (*Waihora*) from the Pacific Ocean. It's a picturesque area popular with fishermen, although other visitors will probably content themselves with the fine views of the lake to be had from Little River or Lake Forsyth.

If you need somewhere to gather your strength for the Southern Bays Walkway, or a place to rest up afterwards, try the *Little River Holiday Park* (☎03/325 1141; tents $15 per site, backpackers ①, cabins ②). One of the prettiest **campsites** on the peninsula, with cooking facilities and a small shop, it's about 6km from Little River. To get there, leave SH75 in Little River and head southeast on the Te Oka Bay Road for a couple of kilometres, before turning left onto the Okuti Valley Road. The site is inside the Okuti Valley Birdlands Sanctuary. The **sanctuary** itself (Oct–April daily 9am–5pm; May–Sept Mon–Sat 10am–3pm; $5) is dedicated to the preservation of New Zealand bird life, with a variety of paths running through different habitats.

SOUTH TO OTAGO

Heading south from Christchurch both the principal road, SH1, and the rail line forge across the **Canterbury Plains** in an unrelenting straight line, bisecting small service towns catering for the farms on the rich flat land. Weaving across the flood plains are glacially fed braided rivers – liable to overspill their broad gravelly banks after heavy rain – spanned by long narrow bridges that break up the otherwise monotonous landscape. The **Southern Alps** flank the route to the west and in clear weather provide awesome views. The first of the bridges, the 1.8km-long structure spanning the Rakaia River 58km from Christchurch, was the longest in the southern hemisphere at the time of its construction in 1939. It leads into the tiny salmon–fishing and sheep-shearing settlement of **Rakaia**, where a minor road called Thompson's Track heads inland to link with SH77, which in turn grants access to Methven, Mount Hutt and Mount Somers, on the western fringes of the Canterbury Plains (see p.552). A further 27km south is the larger though equally quiet settlement of **Ashburton**, where SH77 joins SH1.

As the road (and the parallel rail line) passes **Temuka** and reaches the southern end of the Canterbury Plains, looming hills force it back to the shoreline at **Timaru**, a small city with a busy port and a fading holiday resort. Timaru is also the point where SH8 strikes inland towards Fairlie, Lake Tekapo and Mount Cook (see p.562). From here on, the trip south is a visual treat, with rolling hills inland and spectacular sea views as you approach SH82 and SH83, which head along opposite banks of the Waitaki River en route to Omarama, Mount Cook and Wanaka. The Waitaki Valley boasts excellent **fishing**, including flounder, yellow-eyed mullet, whitebait (in season), sea-run trout and the particularly sought-after quinnat salmon.

The coastal highway and railway continue south to the pleasing architecture of **Oamaru**, and the unique and fascinating **Moeraki Boulders**. From Moeraki there is little to delay you on your progress toward Dunedin (see p.579), except maybe the small crossroads town of **Palmerston**, where SH85, "The Pigroot" to **Central Otago**, leaves SH1, providing another opportunity to forsake the coast and follow a historical pathway to the goldfields inland (see p.711).

Ashburton and around

The long, thin and stubbornly suburban town of **ASHBURTON** lies 87km south of Christchurch, perched on the north bank of the Ashburton River, with an extension, **Tinwald**, across the bridge on the opposite bank. Few of its buildings stand above two storeys, though some are quite striking brick edifices testifying to the once-extensive ceramic industry (which still thrives in Geraldine, 50km south – see p.557). In tandem with the profits from rich farmland, this short-lived wealth facilitated the building of twenty churches at the turn of the century, servicing a population which even today scarcely rises above 16,000. Although bringing distinction to the town's skyline, few of the churches rate as attractions in themselves. The main highlights of Ashburton today are the various **museums** in and around the town, mostly devoted to local history, arts and crafts.

Arrival and information

Twice-daily Southerner **trains** from Christchurch (booking information on ☎0800/802 802) take sixty minutes to reach Ashburton station, a restored 1920s weatherboard building on East Street (SH1). InterCity **buses** also stop at the train station, while Mount Cook Landlines pull up outside the *Farmer's Corner Tea Rooms* on Havelock Street. Ashburton Shuttles (☎03/308 4889), who run Ashburton–Christchurch services, drop off outside the visitor centre (see below); while most of the shuttle companies serving the Christchurch–Dunedin route (see "Moving on from Christchurch", p.502) also drop off at either the train station or the visitor centre.

The **visitor centre** (Mon–Fri 9.30am–4.30pm, Sat 10am–3pm, Sun 10am–1pm; ☎03/308 1064), also on East Street, between Burnett Street and Tancred Street, stocks timetable information for local buses and shuttles, as well as the free *Ashburton and*

Mid Canterbury Map, which covers all the sights in town as well as the surrounding portions of the Canterbury Plains.

Accommodation

There is a wide range of **accommodation** in the Ashburton area, capitalizing on its proximity both to Christchurch and to the skifields at Mount Somers, Mount Hutt and Methven. The majority of places are either clustered at the south end of East Street, or across the river in Tinwald, although B&Bs and farmstays are a bit more widely spread.

Academy Lodge Motel, 782 East St (☎03/308 5503). Near the racecourse on the northern outskirts of town, this motel offers fully equipped units and a friendly atmosphere. ④.

Adcroft Motels, 13 Main South Rd, Tinwald (☎03/308 3587). A cheerful place with spacious comfortable units set back from the road. ④.

Ashburton Hotel, 200m up Race Course Rd at the northern end of town (☎03/308 3059). The jewel in the Ashburton crown – a large complex of bars, lounges, restaurants and a bottle shop, offering clean and comfortable rooms, one motel-style unit, and campervan sites ($17). ⑤–⑥.

Carradlae Farmstay, Ferriman's Rd, Lagmhor, 8km west of Tinwald (☎03/308 6577). About ten minutes' drive from Ashburton, this pretty, secluded and welcoming farmstay offers the opportunity to join in farm activities and explore the countryside (dinner by arrangement, $20). ④.

Coronation Park, 778 East St, adjacent to the Domain (☎03/308 6603). A good camping area sheltered under trees and tall hedges, with modern facilities. Tent sites $7 per person, dorms ①, on-site vans & units ②–④.

St Ita's Guesthouse, Methven Rd, Rakaia, 27km northeast of Ashburton (☎ & fax 03/302 7546). One of the most popular B&Bs in the area, with large and well decorated en-suite rooms in an old convent schoolhouse. Delicious meals available (dinner $20). ④.

The Town and around

Breaking up the dreary huddle of the town centre to the north is the **Ashburton Domain** (daily 8am–dusk), facing West Street between Walnut Avenue and Wills Street. Fringed by stately hundred-year-old European trees, the parklands contain expertly manicured gardens and an artificial lake, created from the water race of an old mill. Just north of the Domain is the **Ashford Craft Village**, at 429 West St (daily 9am–5pm), a mini-mall comprising clothes shops, a café, the Eastside Gallery, a working pottery, a woodturner, and a massive collection of spinning wheels, looms and accessories, all of which are for sale – though bargains are few and far between. For more authentic shopping, try the **Farmer's Corner Store**, at 208 Havelock St (Mon–Fri 9am–5pm, Sat 9am–1pm), where local farmers shop and discerning bus drivers drop their passengers.

The **Historic Museum and Art Gallery**, 248 Cameron St (Tues–Fri 10am–4pm, Sat & Sun 1–4pm; donation requested), is a cool and airy place with temporary art exhibitions upstairs. The neat museum has an informative display on braided rivers and the bird life they support, such as the endangered black-fronted tern and black-billed gull, and the wrybil plover, which breeds only in this region. The most interesting of the town's other four small museums is the **Museum of Woodworking and Ornamental Woodturning**, tucked away at 103 Alford Forest Rd (open by arrangement, ☎03/308 6611; $2). Housed in a woodturner's workshop, it contains a substantial collection of antique ornamental lathes, with plenty of intricately turned pieces on display. Ashburton's other museums – the Plains Vintage Railway Museum (☎03/308 6252), the Ashburton Aviation Museum (☎03/302 6820) and the Vintage Car Museum (☎03/308 6070) – are primarily for enthusiasts and are only open limited hours or by arrangement.

Continuing south through town, you'll come to the bridge which crosses the **River Ashburton**, an excellent fishing ground for trout, though you'll need a licence to test your luck (check at the visitor centre). Following the river to the sea, the **Ashburton Walkway** (19km; a leisurely 5hr walk one-way) enables you to observe a braided river up close. The waterway is split into small channels, which opportunistically change course across the shingle riverbed. The banks of the river are flanked by cabbage trees, grassland and willows that arch over the river as you approach its mouth, where a short climb is rewarded with views of the coast. Just past the small settlement of **Hakatere**, the path ends at a picnic ground overlooking the sea where there are toilets and a telephone. There is no public transport between Hakatere and Ashburton, so unless you want to slog both ways, arrange for a shuttle or taxi (try Ashburton Shuttles on ☎03/308 4889) there or back.

Eating

Culinary life in Ashburton may not be as sophisticated or adventurous as in Christchurch up the coast, but there's a surprisingly good range of **eating** opportunities in town nevertheless.

Cactus Jacks, Wills St, off East St. One of the liveliest places in town, serving a New Zealand version of Tex-Mex at moderate prices. Daily from 5pm; licensed.

Chandler House, 9 Mona Square, off Kermode St (☎03/308 9983). Very pretty two-storey wooden house, offering upmarket fine dining, including veggie strudel and rich desserts. Lunch Tues–Fri, dinner Mon–Sat; licensed.

Coupland's Family Bakery, cnr East St & Kermode St. Good-value picnic ingredients – traditional pies, sandwiches, biscuits, cakes and bread. Go early: most things sell out by 1pm.

Sharidans Café, 87 Tancred St. The best of the small cafés, serving inexpensive breakfasts, lunches and early dinners, as well as some unusually flavoured monster muffins. Mon–Sat until 6pm.

The Stables, *Tinwald Tavern*, Main South Rd. No-nonsense, "feed 'em fast and ship 'em out" meat and fish dishes at moderate prices, served in stable-like booths. Daily lunches and dinners; licensed.

Tuscany, cnr Burnett St & East St. Styling itself as a brash, big-city café/wine bar, this place serves moderately priced snack food (such as soups, salads and baked potatoes) for most of the day, with a broader menu in the evening. A lively and fun place for a drink, especially at weekends. Daily 11am–11pm; licensed.

Temuka

The town of **TEMUKA**, 90km south of Ashburton on SH1, sprawls unattractively away from the road over a flat plain. Temuka means "fierce oven", and a large number of Maori earth ovens have been found in the area. This light-industrial town's only other claim to fame is that it was the home of aviator Richard Pearse and, with the exception of the town museum, the only other highlight for visitors is a stylish café/bar on the main street (see "Practicalities").

The **Temuka Museum**, in the old court house just off SH1 on the Temuka–Pleasant Point Road (Fri & Sat 2–4pm; $1 donation requested), contains an eccentric array of artefacts, as well as information on Temuka's favourite son, **Richard Pearse** – locally held to be the first man to achieve powered flight in 1902, some months in advance of the Wright brothers. Pearse's plane was technically far in advance of that of his rivals, but Pearse himself did not believe his first powered flight was sufficiently controlled or sustained to justify his townsfolk's claim. He managed a rather desperate 100m, followed by an ignominious landing in gorse bushes. He was a lifelong tinkerer and inventor, although the true gauge of Pearse's genius was his idea for an aircraft that could fly and hover like a modern Harrier jump jet. There's a memorial to Pearse at the site of the legendary flight, about 13km from Temuka on the way to Waitohi; and further reminders of his achievements in the South Canterbury Museum at Timaru (see p.526).

Practicalities

Most buses will drop off and pick up in Temuka, and onward travel can be arranged at the **visitor centre**, which is situated in the Community Centre, 118 King St (Mon–Fri

9am–4pm; ☎03/615 7542). **Accommodation** is limited, but you could do a lot worse than the clean and comfortable *Highway One Motel*, 272 King St (☎03/615 7936, fax 615 7886; ③), or the *Temuka Holiday Park*, 1 Ferguson Drive (☎03/615 7241; tent sites $7 per person; cabins ②), a spacious, well-looked-after site in the Domain, five minutes' walk from King Street.

You'll find a number of **pubs** and bars along King Street and one or two **restaurants**, but none of them beats the ultra-friendly *Benny's* **café/bar** at no. 134 (daily 11.45am–2pm & 5.30pm–late), which has good coffee, cheap and imaginative food including vegetarian options, plus wine and a tempting dessert menu.

Timaru and around

The first major settlement south of Christchurch is the small city of **TIMARU**, with a population of 28,000. After 164km of straight, flat landscape, the city marks the beginning of a subtle change, nestling as it does in gently rolling hills at the edge of Caroline Bay. Timaru has an austere air, due to the unusual volcanic blue-stone used in some of the grand examples of Victorian and Edwardian architecture that characterize the town (the local council insisted on stone and brick construc-tions after a devastating fire in 1868), although attractions such as the fine **Aigantighe Art Gallery** and the **South Canterbury Museum** should not be missed.

Timaru's name is taken from the **Maori** *Te Maru*, meaning "place of shelter", as it provided the only haven for Maori canoes paddling between Banks Peninsula and Oamaru. In 1837 European settlement was initiated by Joseph Price, who set up a **whaling** station south of the present city at Patiti Point. A large part of today's com-mercial and pastoral development can be attributed to Yorkshiremen **George and Robert Rhodes**, who established the first cattle station on the South Island in 1839 and founded Rhodes Town not long after, just north of the existing settlement of Government Town – the towns gradually grew together and merged to form Timaru. Despite an influx of European migrants aboard the *Strathallan* in 1859, it was some years before a safe harbour was established on the rocky coast. A welcome by-product of the land reclamation that created the harbour in 1877 was the fine sandy beach of Caroline Bay. For a time, Timaru became a popular seaside resort, and its annual **summer carnival**, starting at Christmas and running for three weeks, is still well worth dropping in on.

Timaru is a convenient base from which to explore the surrounding countryside. There are six **skifields** within two hours' drive – Dobson, Erewhon, Fox Peak, Mount Hutt, Ohau and Tekapo (see Chapter 10) – as well as plenty of river-based adventure **activities**, parks and **scenic reserves**.

Arrival, information and city transport

The **train station** on Station Street in the centre of the city is the principal drop-off and pick-up point for all trains and most buses. Many buses and shuttles will drop you at your chosen accommodation on their way to the city centre, and most hostels also offer a pick-up service. Inside the train station, the Travellers Rest and Booking Centre (☎03/688 3597) sells bus and train tickets for onward travel.

Just outside the station at 14 Lower George St, the friendly **visitor centre** (Mon–Fri 8.30am–5pm, Sat & Sun 10am–3pm; ☎03/688 6163) provides free maps of South Canterbury, Timaru and Methven, together with details of several historic walks about town. DOC maps can also be bought here. Timaru's **local bus service** is run by CTL Canride, with a flat rate of $1 for all journeys around the city and suburbs, including unlimited transfers within a four-hour period.

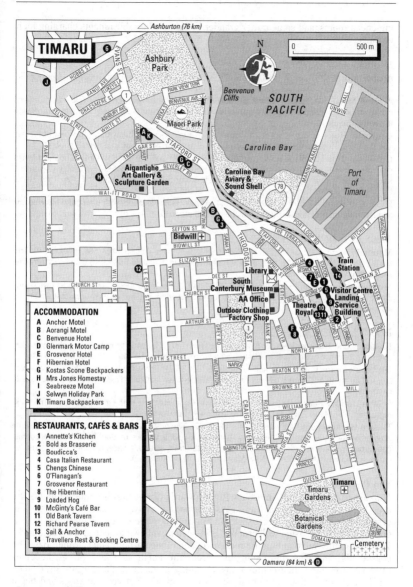

TIMARU

Ashburton (76 km)

Ashbury Park

SOUTH PACIFIC

Benvenue Cliffs

Caroline Bay

Maori Park

Port of Timaru

Caroline Bay Aviary & Sound Shell

Aigantighe Art Gallery & Sculpture Garden

Bidwill +

Library

South Canterbury Museum

AA Office

Outdoor Clothing Factory Shop

Theatre Royal

Train Station

Visitor Centre

Landing Service Building

Timaru Gardens

Botanical Gardens

Cemetery

Timaru +

ACCOMMODATION

A   Anchor Motel
B   Aorangi Motel
C   Benvenue Hotel
D   Glenmark Motor Camp
E   Grosvenor Hotel
F   Hibernian Hotel
G   Kostas Scone Backpackers
H   Mrs Jones Homestay
I   Seabreeze Motel
J   Selwyn Holiday Park
K   Timaru Backpackers

RESTAURANTS, CAFÉS & BARS

1   Annette's Kitchen
2   Bold as Brasserie
3   Boudicca's
4   Casa Italian Restaurant
5   Chengs Chinese
6   O'Flanagan's
7   Grosvenor Restaurant
8   The Hibernian
9   Loaded Hog
10   McGinty's Café Bar
11   Old Bank Tavern
12   Richard Pearse Tavern
13   Sail & Anchor
14   Travellers Rest & Booking Centre

Oamaru (84 km) & D

Accommodation

There's a wide variety of **accommodation** in Timaru, a hangover from the days when it was a more popular Kiwi holiday destination than it is today. Around the **Christmas holidays** and during the **carnival**, you should still book your accommodation well in advance. Most of the better places to stay are on **Evans/Stafford Street**, while around the centre of town you'll find a large number of rather run-down old stone hotels offering cheap rooms, and some rather grander, refurbished establishments charging higher rates.

HOTELS AND MOTELS

Anchor Motel, 42 Evans St (☎03/684 5067). A central, slightly run-down, 1960s two-storey building with off-street parking and nine comfortable units. ④.

Aorangi Motel, 400 Stafford St (☎ & fax 03/688 0097). Located near the new bypass and the town centre, this rather ugly, pragmatic place has nine stacked units, all newly decorated and with kitchen facilities. ④.

Benvenue Hotel, 16–22 Evans St (☎ & fax 03/688 4049). Set on a hill with a good view of the bay and the town. Hotel rooms and studio units as well as a bar, restuarant and heated pool. ④.

Grosvenor Hotel, Cains Terrace (☎03/688 3129 & 0800/106 102, fax 684 8381). The most lavish centrally located accommodation, this imposing white-stone and red-roofed 1875 building was once known as the "Grand Old Lady of the South". It has fifty comfortable rooms, and even if you're not staying here, it's worth a look and a drink in one of the bars. ⑦.

Hibernian Hotel, 4 Latter St (☎03/688 8125). A very central location, with nine quite basic rooms and a restaurant serving breakfasts, lunches and dinners. ④.

B&BS AND HOMESTAYS

Mountain View, 200m along Talbots Rd off SH1, 3km from Timaru (☎03/688 1070). Small farm B&B offering homely rooms with private bathrooms and a cooked breakfast. Dinner by arrangement($20); venison a speciality. ③.

Mrs Jones Homestay, 16 Selwyn St (☎03/688 1400). A lovely late 1920s house with its own tennis court. Rooms share a bathroom, and there's a choice of continental or cooked breakfast; dinner by arrangement ($20). ③.

HOSTELS AND CAMPSITES

Kostas Scone Backpackers, 24 Evans St (☎03/688 0871). Linen is provided, the laundry is free, and the rooms are quite small – although a major revamp is on the cards. Dorms ①, rooms ②.

Glenmark Motor Camp, Beaconsfield Rd (☎03/684 3682). Three minutes' drive from the city centre, and 200m off SH1, this well-kept camp has all the usual facilities. Tent sites $14, on-site vans & cabins ②.

Selwyn Holiday Park, Selwyn St (☎03/684 7690). Campsite close to the golf links and within walking distance of Maori Park. Tent sites $16, cabins & units ②–③.

Timaru Backpackers, 44 Evans St (☎03/684 5067). The best backpackers in town. Highly flexible accommodation – dorms, motel units, homestays and a variety of double and single rooms. Numerous freebies include minibus to and from the train station, towels, tea and coffee, plus discounted dolphin-watching trips (Nov–May). Dorms ①, rooms ②–④.

The City

Looking back down the Canterbury Bight towards Christchurch, Timaru mirrors the crescent shape that SH1 takes as it passes through the city. The place lacks a true geographical focus, largely because it was once two settlements, but also because it doesn't fit into the usual well-ordered grid system, following instead the contours of undulating hills surrounding the reclaimed land of the harbour and Caroline Bay. The coastal highway dips down into town from the north as Evans Street, becomes Stafford Street and then climbs away, changing its name again to King Street. The Stafford Street section is the best place from which to get your bearings and begin your exploration of the city.

The **Landing Service Building** (1870), next to the visitor centre at the eastern end of George Street, is an old bluestone building originally used to store goods unloaded from the small boats that were winched up onto a shingle beach in front – roughly where the railway lines are now. Around the corner on the opposite side of Stafford Street is the **Theatre Royal** (guided tours on demand; $3): originally a stone store, it was converted into an entertainment hall in 1877, at which time it was renowned as the most ornate and lovely in New Zealand. In 1992 a major upgrade replaced the foyer with an imposing Neoclassical facade, quite in keeping with the tall, narrow nineteenth-century buildings that typify the centre of town.

From the Theatre Royal, return to George Street, then head up the hill to the junction with Perth Street and the **South Canterbury Museum** in the Pioneer Hall (April–Jan Tues–Sun 11am–5pm; Feb & March same days 1.30–4.30pm; $1 donation requested). The purpose-built, octagonal building contains a number of well labelled local Maori artefacts, some good examples of **scrimshaw** (intricate etchings on whale teeth and bone) and other memorabilia from the whaling station that occupied Patiti Point in the late 1830s and early 1840s. Look out, too, for the wonderful **E.P. Seally collection** – several cabinets with age-distorted drawers crammed full of butterflies, moths, eggs, minerals, and rare colourful shells. A nineteenth-century naturalist, Seally collected hundreds of butterflies and moths from all over the world, each one conscientiously labelled, including the *Morpho Cypris*, a beautiful blue from Brazil; the smaller electric-aquamarine *Morpho Adonis*; and the (now sadly silent) yodelling cicada. Hanging over the main hall of the museum, and best viewed from the first-floor balcony, is a reconstruction of the 1902 **aircraft** used by Richard Pearse in his attempt to notch up the first powered flight in the world (see p.525). Near the entrance are a number of old arcade machines: try out the 1¢ Kiss-O-Metre to see how sexy you would have been in 1968.

At the opposite end of Perth Street, in a courtyard beside the ANZ Bank at Strathallan Corner, stands the **Bob Fitzsimmons Statue**, a bronze of the Timaru-born world champion boxer who defeated the famous Gentleman Jim Corbett. Fitzsimmons is only one of four sporting champions to emanate from Timaru, the others being **Phar Lap**, the great racehorse and one of the most successful stake winners of all time, beating all comers in the 1920s and 30s, but mysteriously poisoned soon after winning the richest race in America; **Dr John Edward Lovelock**, an athlete who won a gold medal at the Berlin Olympics (1936), and, like many of the winners, was presented by Hitler with an oak tree, which now flourishes in the grounds of his old school, the Timaru Boys' High; and lastly, **Clark McConachy**, world professional billiards champion for two decades in the interwar years.

The **Aigantighe Gallery and Statue Garden**, 49 Wai-iti Rd (Tues–Fri 11am–4.30pm, Sat & Sun 2–4.30pm; admission by donation), is about twenty minutes' walk from Strathallan Corner, up Stafford Street to the junction with Wai-iti Road opposite Caroline Bay. The place was given the evocative name of *Aigantighe* (Gaelic for "Welcome to our home") by the people who owned the house before it became a gallery. The grounds contain an impressive sculpture garden of thirteen works donated by Kiwi and Zimbabwean sculptors (among the most striking are *Baboon*, nearest the house, together with *Cave Spirit* and *Magic Bird*), offset by fine views over the city. Inside the gallery itself is a permanent exhibition, with a growing and excellent collection of works by South Canterbury artists, and usually a temporary exhibition – check the *Timaru Herald* "Arts Diary" on Saturday, or ask at the visitor centre for details.

Providing a contrast to the urban attractions of the city itself are the waterfront sights around Caroline Bay. The Port Loop Road spirals down to the bay from Stafford Street; at the bottom, cross the flat grass to the sandy beach and head north towards the **Dashing Rocks** via Maori Park, passing en route the white wooden **Blackett's Lighthouse** (1878–1970), and the **Benvenue Cliffs**, which gained their name when they witnessed the wreck of the sailing ship *Benvenue* in 1882. The old Timaru Lifeboat which attended this and many other wrecks now rests in Caroline Bay.

Finally, if the weather is fine, you could spend a quiet hour ambling around the **Botanical Gardens**, close to the junction of King Street and Queen Street (daily 8am–dusk, entrance on Queen St; free). The gardens boast an airy conservatory, abun-

---

ROCK ART

Around five hundred years ago, Maori visited the area now known as North Otago, probably hunting moa, and left records of their sojourn on the walls and ceilings of open-sided limestone rock shelters. There are over three hundred **rock drawings** around Timaru, Geraldine and Fairlie: the faded charcoal and red ochre drawings depict a variety of stylized human, bird and mythological figures and patterns. Some of the best cave drawings can be seen in the region's museums (notably the North Otago Museum in Oamaru, see p.534). Those remaining in situ are often hard to make out, but the best examples are at Risk Shelter, Acacia Downs, Blackler's Cave and Hazelburn Shelter, all on Three Mile Bush Road, which can be reached by driving northwest from Timaru along SH8 to Pleasant Point (20km distant), then continuing west along the Ohipi River. You'll need your own transport to explore this area.

The paintings can be hard to find, so don't set off without picking up the *Prehistoric Rock Art Aorangi Region* leaflet (50¢) from the **Timaru Visitor Centre** (see p.532), which shows the sites to visit, how to get to them and what to look for. Access to some of the sites is across **private land**, so check whether you need permission before you set out: the visitor centre will help you plan a route and provide any telephone numbers needed.

---

dant fernery, native bush, herb and rose gardens, an aviary and duck pond, as well as statues of Robert Burns and Queen Victoria. If the weather is not so clement, a fun tour – and product sampling – is offered by the **DB Brewery**, Sheffield Street, Washdyke, 2km north of town on SH1 (Mon–Thurs video 10am, followed by 90min tour at 10.30am; donation requested; no sandals; ☎03/688 2059).

Eating, drinking and entertainment

Timaru's **restaurants**, though numerous, don't offer great variety in terms of decor or ambitious cuisine, but you'll find the usual cache of fish and chip shops, as well as a couple of Italian and Asian eateries. The best of the bunch are listed below, although a couple of purely **fast-food** outlets worth trying are *Southend Takeaways*, 39 King St (Mon–Sat lunchtimes and evenings), for fish and chips; and *Golden Palace Chinese Restaurant*, 84 Evans St, for an oriental takeaway.

Things hot up in Timaru for the three post-Christmas weeks of the **summer carnival**, when there's a circus, a fair, and free concerts in Caroline Bay. Otherwise, Timaru is a pretty quiet place; if there is anything going on in town, then the **entertainment** listings in the daily *Timaru Herald* will provide details.

CAFÉS AND RESTAURANTS

Annette's Kitchen, 5a George St. A stylish restaurant in a green building under a burgundy awning opposite the visitor centre. Inventive lunches ($7–10) and dinner ($10–20) – crispy fish and chips, vegetarian dishes, stir-fry venison and iced chocolate terrine. Licensed.

Bold as Brasserie, 335 Stafford St. Snacks, hearty soups and delicious breads, plus an innovative menu at reasonable prices. Mon–Fri lunch & dinner, Sat & Sun dinner only; licensed.

Boudicca's, 402 Stafford St. Good-quality café specializing in Middle Eastern and Kiwi cuisine. A kebab, salad and a variety of sauces, including delicious sweet chilli, will set you back $7.95, and there's felafel and other meat-free options, as well as mouth-watering, home-made desserts. Tues–Sun 11am till late; licensed.

Casa Italia Ristorante, 2 Strathallan St (☎03/684 5528). Located in the old Customs House, an atmospheric Victorian building, with an Italian owner and chef ensuring delicious, authentic cuisine at affordable prices. Various pastas are made on the premises; and remember to save room for the great desserts. Daily 6pm–late; licensed.

Cheng's Chinese Restaurant, George St. Excellent set menus, good fish dishes, and great chow mein, with main meals hovering in the $8–20 range. Open daily for lunch and dinner; licensed.

Oflanagan's, 18a Hobbs St. Blackboard specials (Mon–Fri, 3 courses $9.50) and an à la carte menu including seafood, satay and burgers ($5–17). Short but reasonably priced wine list. Daily lunch noon–2pm, dinner 5.30–9pm, supper menu 9pm–midnight.

Travellers Rest, in the train station, Station St. The best-value breakfasts in town; also home-made snacks, sandwiches, cakes and pies. Mon–Fri 4am–9pm, Sat & Sun 7am–9pm.

PUBS AND BARS

Grosvenor Hotel, Cains Terrace (☎03/688 3129). A wide variety of cooked breakfasts ($15), lunch and dinner menus abundant with crayfish, salmon, steak and venison ($10–30); and a long but expensive wine list and two bars.

The Hibernian, 4 Latter St. Pub serving enormous portions of Kiwi fare, including generous break-fasts. Carvery buffet Fri 5–10pm, smorgasbord Sun noon–2pm. Live local rock music in the bar on Fri & Sat.

Loaded Hog, opposite the train station on George St. The pleasantest drinking establishment in town, occupying a wonderful stone grain store. The bar serves naturally brewed (on the premises) beers, as well as a broad-ranging, affordable menu. A popular venue for Kiwi bands (Thurs–Sun till 3am) and occasional poetry readings.

McGinty's Café Bar, Variety Lane, Stafford St. Typical New Zealand Irish pub serving snacks, lunches and dinners, and showcasing live Irish music on Saturday. Daily 11am–3am.

Old Bank Tavern, 232 Stafford St. Originally opened in 1876, this popular local haunt was refur-bished two years ago, and now serves pub food for lunch and dinner. Live Irish and folk music Fri & Sat.

Richard Pearse Tavern, 118 Le Cren St. Curious combination of family-style eating establishment and late-night tavern, with a cafeteria-like atmosphere, a carvery ($14–18) and some veggie alter-natives. Try not to listen to the music. Daily 10.30am–3.30am.

Listings

Automobile Association 26 Church St (☎03/688 4189).

Bike rental Howes Cycles, 127 Church St (☎03/684 8900), rents bikes from $20 a day.

Car rental Highfield Service Station, corner of Wai-iti Rd & Otipua Rd (☎03/688 9340); Rental Vehicles Ltd, 37 Sophia St (☎03/684 7179).

Cinema Cinema One, Stafford St (☎03/688 8913); plans are also afoot for a multiplex on Canon St.

Library Timaru District Library, Sophia St (Mon, Wed & Fri 9.30am–8pm, Tues & Thurs 9.30am–6pm, Sat 10am–noon, Sun 1–4pm).

Medical treatment Call ☎03/684 8209 for a duty doctor. Timaru Hospital is on Bidwell St (☎03/684 3089). Rape Crisis line ☎03/684 4666.

Newspaper The *Timaru Herald* has a listings section on Fri & Sat, with details of what's on, and information about late opening pharmacies and emergency numbers.

Outdoor clothing Swandri, Bank St (Mon–Sat 10am–3pm). A great place to pick up factory sec-onds from the manufacturer of the jackets favoured by New Zealand bushmen; also rugs, trusty oil-skins, knitwear and country attire.

Petrol stations Maori Hill Service Station, 43 Evans St, is open 24hr.

Pharmacies Faulks & Jordan, 234 Stratford St; Central Pharmacy, 266 Stratford St. Details of duty pharmacies are listed in the *Timaru Herald*.

Shuttle buses Shuttle bus companies operating Timaru–Christchurch, Timaru–Dunedin and Timaru–Twizel routes include Atomic Shuttles (☎03/322 8883); Catch-a-bus (☎03/477 7900); Ko-op Shuttles (☎03/366 6633); and Southern Link Shuttles (☎03/358/8355).

Swimming There's an excellent summer pool at the Maori Park Aqua Land, Tewaka St (Nov–March; ☎03/688 4504); otherwise try the Century Pool, Craigie Ave (☎03/684 5379), which is open year-round. Precise opening times vary; ask at the visitor centre or consult the *Timaru Herald*.

Taxis Timaru Taxis (☎03/688 8899) and Call-a-Cab (☎03/688 8811) both offer a 24hr service.

Oamaru

Despite some low-slung unattractive suburbs, **OAMARU**, 84km south of Timaru on SH1, is one of the most interesting and attractive cities in the region. A well-preserved core of nineteenth-century buildings forms a renowned **historic district** in the centre, while **penguin colonies** on the outskirts of town provide an unmissable opportunity to observe wildlife. The limestone outcrops throughout the area once provided shelter for Maori and later the raw material for ambitious European builders. As a commercial centre for goldrush prospectors, and shored up by quarrying, timber and farming indus-

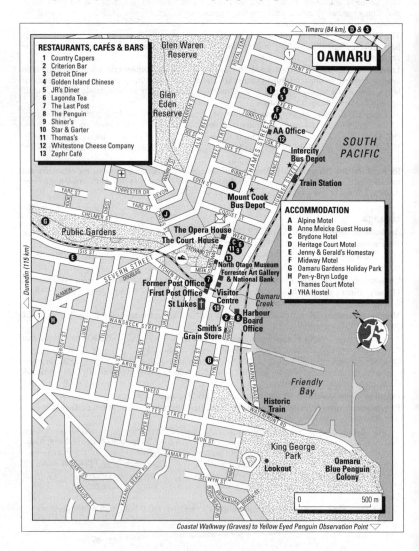

△ Timaru (84 km), **①** & **❸**

OAMARU

RESTAURANTS, CAFÉS & BARS
1 Country Capers
2 Criterion Bar
3 Detroit Diner
4 Golden Island Chinese
5 JR's Diner
6 Lagonda Tea
7 The Last Post
8 The Penguin
9 Shiner's
10 Star & Garter
11 Thomas's
12 Whitestone Cheese Company
13 Zephr Café

Glen Waren Reserve

Glen Eden Reserve

SOUTH PACIFIC

AA Office

Intercity Bus Depot

Train Station

Mount Cook Bus Depot

ACCOMMODATION
A Alpine Motel
B Anne Meicke Guest House
C Brydone Hotel
D Heritage Court Motel
E Jenny & Gerald's Homestay
F Midway Motel
G Oamaru Gardens Holiday Park
H Pen-y-Bryn Lodge
I Thames Court Motel
J YHA Hostel

The Opera House
The Court House

Public Gardens

North Otago Museum
Forrester Art Gallery
& National Bank

Former Post Office
First Post Office
St Lukes

Visitor Centre

Oamaru Creek

Harbour Board Office

Smith's Grain Store

Friendly Bay

Historic Train

King George Park

Lookout

Oamaru Blue Penguin Colony

0   500 m

Coastal Walkway (Graves) to Yellow Eyed Penguin Observation Point ▽

tries, Oamaru grew in wealth, giving shape to its prosperity in the elegant stone buildings that today grace the town centre. The port opened for **migration** in 1874, with three hundred ships arriving that year and a further four hundred between 1876 and 1878, although many foundered on the hostile coastline and wrecks littered the late nineteenth-century shore. After this boom period the fortunes of the town declined, and it's only in recent years that the town has begun to come alive again.

The writer Janet Frame (see Contexts, p.791) spent some of her childhood in Oamaru and lived here on and off in later years, and a **Janet Frame Trail** (a leaflet about which is available from the visitor centre, see below) concentrates on locations used in varying degrees of disguise in her books. Fans of her work may well thrill to the sight of the former subscription library in the Athenaeum that featured in *Face In The Water*, or the rubbish dump that formed the symbolic centre of *Owls Do Cry* – although such sights are hardly essential for the uncommitted.

Arrival and information

Buses drop off at the corner of Eden and Thames streets, while the **train station** is just northeast of the centre on Humber Street. The majority of accommodation is walkable from the bus stop and train station, but if you have heavy bags you can always call for a taxi (see below).

The **visitor centre**, 1 Thames St (Mon–Fri 9am–5pm, Sat & Sun 10am–4pm; ☎03/434 1656), is about ten minutes' walk from the train station and five minutes from the corner where the buses stop. Enthusiastic staff dish out some useful leaflets, including *The Janet Frame Trail*, and *Historic Oamaru*, which focuses on the historic district. Central Oamaru is compact enough to be explored on foot, although there's a local **taxi** firm (☎03/434 8790) should you need them.

Accommodation

Most of the accommodation is on, or near, Thames Street. If your budget will stretch to it, try one of the homestays, which reflect Oamaru's charm.

HOTELS AND MOTELS

Alpine Motel, 285 Thames St (☎03/434 5038, fax 434 6301). Modern building close to the town centre, with ten spacious studio units, some with full kitchens. ③–④ .

Brydone Hotel, 115 Thames St (☎03/434 9892, fax 434 5719). Magnificent old building of Oamaru stone with an ornate Italian facade, dating from 1880. Extensively renovated and redecorated, this is one of the smartest places in town. ④.

Heritage Court Motel, 346 Thames St (☎03/437 2200). Modern, clean and quiet, these units are spacious and comfortable, with cooking facilities. ④.

Midway Motel, 289 Thames St (☎03/434 5388). Opposite the fire station and close to the centre of town, this basic establishment has units with full cooking facilities. ④.

Thames Court Motel, 252 Thames St (☎03/434 6963, fax 434 6982). This friendly place has plenty of facilities, including a free laundry and spacious, fully self-contained units. ④.

B&BS AND HOMESTAYS

Anne Mieke Guesthouse, 47 Tees St (☎03/434 8051). A large suburban house offering B&B close to the town centre and the blue penguin viewing area. Each room has its own washbasin, bathrooms are shared and the rooms at the back of the house have views of the bay. ③.

Jenny and Gerald's Homestay, 11 Stour St (☎03/434 9628). About twenty minutes' walk from the bus stop, this attractive 1920s house contains an ornate staircase, a pleasant double with private facilities and two singles with shared facilities. Jenny and Gerald are very friendly and share an interest in local history, as well as running Slightly Foxed, a secondhand bookshop. Dinner by arrangement ($25). ④.

Pen-y-Bryn Lodge, 41 Towey St (☎03/434 7939, fax 434 9063). A splendid restored Victorian home on a hill overlooking the town, graced with hand-crafted floor-to-ceiling fireplaces, a billiard room, richly carved bookcases and a Florentine-style dining room of rimu timber and English oak. The large and luxurious rooms have private facilities. ⑦.

Tara, Springhill Rd (☎03/434 8187). Worth considering if you have your own transport – getting there involves driving 3km south of town on SH1 followed by a further 6km along the Weston road. Set among rose gardens, native trees and farmland, the B&B has just one twin room with a private bathroom. Good food, including free-range eggs, home-made bread and home-grown veg. Dinner by arrangement ($25). ④.

HOSTELS AND CAMPSITES

Oamaru Gardens Holiday Park, Chelmer St (☎03/434 7666, fax 434 7662). In a lovely sheltered setting, this site offers pitches, tourist flats and cabins, plus scooter rental ($20 per hour, with half- and full-day deals). Tent sites $9, cabins & flats ②–③.

The Red Kettle YHA, cnr Reed St & Cross St (☎03/434 5008). Located near the town centre, but small and rather tired-looking, with cramped dorms and a couple of twin-bunked rooms. Dorms ①, rooms ②.

The Historic District

Thames Street and the web of streets around Tees, Tyne, Itchen and Harbour streets form the ill-defined **Historic District**, designated to make the most of the fact that Oamaru was widely considered the most attractive town on the South Island at the beginning of this century. Such a status was largely due to the cluster of buildings constructed from the distinctive cream-coloured local limestone, which earned Oamaru the title "The Whitestone City". The third weekend in November sees the streets of the historic district become a race track for penny-farthings, cheered on by local residents in Victorian attire and accompanied by a fair.

Moving south along Thames Street from its junction with Severn Street, the first of the nineteenth-century edifices to command attention is the **Courthouse**, an elegant, classically proportioned Palladian building built in 1882 by Forrester and Lemon, the architectural partnership responsible for giving central Oamaru much of its character. Adjacent to the Courthouse is the Athenaeum building, another Forrester and Lemon construction that served as a subscription library (see the Janet Frame Trail, p.533) and mechanics institute before providing a home for the **North Otago Museum** (Mon–Thurs 1–4.30pm, Fri 1–4.30pm & 6–8pm; plus Sun in Jan only 1–4pm; free), an absorbing collection documenting all aspects of North Otago life. The highlight for many visitors is a fine display of **Maori rock art** (see box on p.530), taken from cave sites during the 1850s before the elements had wrought too much damage. The museum archive also has a collection of tracings of other rock drawings that can be viewed on request. Other exhibitions describe the origin of Oamaru stone and its use in the town, and there are rotating displays from the museum's vast collection, only ten percent of which is on show at any one time. A little way south on the junction of Thames Street and Meek Street is the **Former Post Office**, a grand 1883 edifice (again courtesy of Forrester and Lemon) sporting a clock tower added by Forrester's son in 1903. On the opposite side of Thames Street is the **First Post Office** (1864), the only remaining example of the work of W.H. Clayton in Oamaru, whose simple Italianate design houses a very good restaurant and bar (see p.536). Directly opposite the two post offices are the imposing **National Bank**, an 1871 R.A. Lawson building with Corinthian columns; and the **Forrester Gallery** (Mon–Fri 10am–4.30pm, Sat & Sun 1–4.30pm; donations requested), which was designed by Lawson in 1883, and features touring exhibitions of contemporary and traditional art, alongside an extensive permanent collection of works by New Zealand artists.

Continuing southwest along Thames Street to the junction with Itchen Street you'll encounter **St Luke's Anglican Church** (1865), topped by its looming 39m spire. The beautiful dark-wood interior boasts an 1876 Conacher pipe organ and three locally made stained-glass windows (on the left as you face the altar), depicting Christ flanked by saints Luke and Paul. Follow Itchen Street east towards the waterfront and you'll come up against the infinitely more profane 1877 **Criterion Hotel**, with Italianate styling and a quaint bar serving fine ale (see p.537). A few steps further south along Tyne Street, the elegant **Smiths Grain Store**, built in 1881 by stonemason James Johnson, now houses the equally elegant efforts of a tailor, who makes Victorian-style shirts, blouses and petticoats, ably assisted by a collection of old Singer sewing machines. Next door, in the old **Union Offices**, 7 Tyne St, is a traditional bookbinder's workshop (daily 2–6pm; free), where you can watch fine bookmaking, binding and repair work; and see examples of old printing and letterpress machines. A block east of here on the waterfront, Harbour Street boasts the sadly neglected Venetian Renaissance-style **Harbour Board Office**, built in 1876 and one of the first public buildings designed by the prolific Forrester and Lemon. At the opposite end of Harbour Street is the striking **Loan and Mercantile Warehouse** which, when it was built in 1882, was the largest grain store in New Zealand. Look out for the ornamental rope design garlanding the second storey.

The Oamaru Gardens

Five minutes' walk west of Thames Street along either Severn Street or Itchen Street lies the manicured natural beauty of the **Oamaru Gardens** (daily dawn–dusk, glasshouses 9am–4pm; free). These are among the most stunning gardens in New Zealand, dating back to 1876 and indicative of the wealth the town once enjoyed. The main Severn Street entrance leads to the spectacular **Craig Fountain**, built from Italian marble and surrounded by packed flowerbeds. Further on is the hundred-year-old Victorian **summerhouse**, full of bright blooms from around the world, with an extensive collection of cacti in a nearby purpose-built glasshouse. Flanking Oamaru Creek as it flows through the gardens are a **rhododendron dell** and two large ponds, while a splendid red Japanese bridge spans the creek to reach the **Oriental and Fragrant Gardens**. Most popular with younger visitors, though, is an enclosure at the far end of the gardens, full of **wallabies** and alpacas (daily dawn–dusk; admission by donation).

Penguin viewing

Oamaru is unique in having both yellow-eyed and little blue **penguin colonies** within walking distance of the town centre. It is usually possible to see both colonies in one evening, since the yellow-eyes tend to come ashore earlier than the little blues, but check at the visitor centre for expected arrival times. There are some important **guidelines** you must observe when viewing penguins, since these are timid creatures and are easily distressed. Flash photography is banned; you should keep quiet and still; and do not encroach within ten metres of the birds. Once disturbed, the penguins may not return to their nests for several hours, even if they have chicks to feed.

First up, about fifteen minutes' walk southeast of the town centre along Waterfront Road, is the **Blue Penguin Colony** (best visited just before dusk but check for exact times at the visitor centre; tickets available at the visitor centre or the colony entrance; $5). At the viewing platforms, you'll be given a short talk on the history of the colony and information about the penguins. If you come during the breeding season (Aug–Dec), you'll see chicks – and hear them calling to their parents out at sea, hunting for food. When the parents return around dusk, travelling in groups (known as rafts), they climb the steep harbour banks and cross in front of the viewing area to their nests. Outside the breeding season the penguins indulge in much less to-ing and fro-ing, but provide an engaging spectacle nevertheless.

On weekends and public holidays, the **Oamaru Historic Steam Train** (every 30min 11am–4pm; $3 return; ☎03/434 1656) runs from Itchen Street in the centre along the waterfront to Waterfront Road, a short walk from the entrance to the little blue pen-

---

LITTLE BLUE PENGUINS

Found around the coasts of New Zealand and southern Australia, **Little Blue Penguins** have black heads, white chests and indigo-blue tails. Breeding takes place from August to December, and the parents take it in turns to stay with the egg during the 36-day incubation period. The newly hatched chick is protected for the first two or three weeks before both parents go out to sea to meet the increasing demand for food, returning full of krill, squid and crustaceans, which they regurgitate into the chick's mouth. At eight weeks the chicks begin to fledge, but 70 per cent will die in the first year; the juveniles that do survive usually return to their birthplace. At the end of the breeding season the birds moult, losing up to half their bodyweight in two to three weeks.

---

guin colony. The engines and carriages have been lovingly restored by a friendly bunch of fanatics, who also care for the blue penguins that nest in the engine shed at the end of the line.

This stretch of coast is also home to a small number of much larger **yellow-eyed penguins**, which nest on **Bushy Beach**, reached via the **Graves Walkway** (1.25km; 30min each way). Starting just past the blue penguin colony and curving round a headland at the end of Oamaru Harbour, the walk continues to a point overlooking the small cove of Boatman's Harbour. This is worth exploring at low tide when **lava pillows** about 50cm in diameter are exposed in the cliff wall. These were formed millions of years ago when molten lava encased hard fossil-bearing limestone, producing a honeycomb effect with each cell defined by a rim of black lava. The walkway ends overlooking Bushy Beach, where a hide enables you to see the yellow-eyed penguins making their way across the beach.

Eating

Oamaru is hardly an enormous place, but it does have a good selection of **eating** venues catering for a range of pockets. You shouldn't have to stray too far from the central Thames Street to find what you want.

Country Capers, 30 Eden St. Pleasant spot for a snack, with daily changing menus of main courses with salad ($6), and fruit or pastry desserts ($3.50). Mon–Fri 9am–4.40pm, Sat 6–10pm.

Detroit Diner, on SH1, next to the Waitaki Truck Stop 4.5km north of the centre. Retro American-style diner serving breakfasts, snacks, grills and excellent clam chowder. Scallops are only $13 for a plate. Solid and cheap, this place is much favoured by truckies. Daily 5.30am–11.30pm.

Golden Island Chinese Restaurant, 243 Thames St. Dependable and inexpensive Chinese with a good range of set menus for couples or groups, and some generous vegetarian dishes. Daily 6–10pm, Thurs & Fri also noon–2pm; licensed & BYO.

JR's Diner, 301 Thames St. An eat-in and takeaway snack shack, serving burgers, fish and chips, steak and superior Chinese food at reasonable prices ($6–15). Open 24hr.

Lagonda Tearooms, 191 Thames St, cnr Eden St. One of the better greasy spoons in town, open for breakfast, lunch and early dinner.

The Last Post, in the First Post Office building, Thames St. Upmarket bar/restaurant with a beer garden. Snacks and cocktails, as well as good lunch and dinner menus. Mon–Thurs 11am–10pm, Fri & Sat 11am–midnight, Sun 11am–10pm.

Thomas's, *Brydone Hotel*, 115 Thames St. A fairly expensive restaurant with an emphasis on local food. The house speciality is seafood chowder topped with and crumbled Whitestone Farmhouse Cheese. Mon–Sat dinner only. Licensed.

Star and Garter, 9 Itchen St (☎03/434 5246). Oamaru's premier restaurant, with a seventy-year history and vaudeville atmosphere, enhanced by a pianola and the exploits of the Foxy Club, the lively local amateur dramatic group. Great lunch and dinner menus, including fish dishes and huge desserts. This is a great place to stop off for a steamed pudding or Irish coffee on your way back from penguin viewing. Daily 10.30am–2am.

Whitestone Cheese Company, 22 Usk St, between Thames & Humber. A great place for picnic supplies: particularly good are the Farmhouse, a semi-soft cheese with a lemongrass aroma and nutty taste, the Brie, which has a hint of mushroom, the strong Airedale and the Windsor Blue, a creamy soft cheese – all made on the premises. Mon–Fri 8am–4.30pm.

Zephyr Café, 15 Thames St. Hip café serving great coffee, bagels and wholemeal croissants. Exotic muffins pepped up with avocado and feta, olives and sun-dried tomatoes. Work by local artists decorates the walls. Mon–Sat 10am–6pm.

Drinking and entertainment

Criterion Bar, *Criterion Hotel*, Tyne St. The strong Victorian feeling of the wooden bar and stone floors is carried over into an ancient till and barrels of really good beer, including London Porter and Emersons traditional ale, both of which are brewed on the premises.

Penguin Club, off Harbour St. Oamaru's premier back-alley fun house and perhaps the coolest place in town. Next to Willets Furniture Company, an unprepossessing alley with the sign "WFC In", leads to a stone building near the waterfront. Regular poetry, blues, and (on Fridays) jazz; check the *Oamaru Mail* for current happenings. $2 membership fee.

Shiner's, cnr Wear St & Humber St. An imposing, fairly modern bar and popular local haunt, with live music at weekends.

Listings

Bookshops Slightly Foxed, 9 Tyne St (Mon–Sat 1–5pm) sells secondhand books.

Car rental Smash Rentals Palace, 1 Meek St (☎03/434 9699), rents cars for $55 per day.

Cinema The Old Oamaru Opera House, cnr Medway St & Thames St, shows movies for $3; screenings are advertised in the visitor centre, on a noticeboard outside the library, and in the newspapers.

Library Oamaru Public Library, next door to the North Otago Museum on Thames St (Mon, Tues & Thurs 9.30am–5.30pm, Wed & Fri 9.30am–8pm, Sat 10am–12.30pm).

Medical treatment Oamaru Hospital, Forrester Drive, cnr Devon Terrace & Warren St. In emergencies call ☎111.

Newspaper The *Oamaru Mail* has entertainment listings and emergency numbers.

Swimming The Queen Elizabeth II Outdoor Pool is opposite the Oamaru Gardens (Mon, Wed & Fri 6.30am–4.30pm & 5–6pm, Tues–Thurs 10am–8.30pm, Sat 10am–2pm, Sun 1.30–5pm; $1).

Tours Mrs Helen Stead (☎03/434 1173, or book through the visitor centre) takes guided walking tours of the town (1hr; $4).

Moeraki – and the Moeraki Boulders

Forty kilometres south of Oamaru on SH1, a car park and visitor centre (see "Practicalities" below) overlook the beach occupied by the strangely compelling **Moeraki Boulders**. Large, grey and almost perfectly spherical, the boulders (some of which reach 2m in diameter) lie partially submerged in the sandy beach and by the wash of high tide. Their smooth skins hide honeycomb centres, which are revealed in some of the broken specimens. Despite appearances, the boulders did not fall from the sky, nor were they washed up by the sea, but rather lay deep in the mudstone cliffs behind the beach. As the sea eroded the cliffs, out fell the smooth boulders, and their distinctive surface pattern was formed as further erosion exposed a network of veins. The boulders were originally formed around a central core of carbonate of lime crystals which attracted minerals from their surroundings – a process that started sixty million years ago, when muddy sediment containing shell and plant fragments accumulated on the sea floor. The masses formed range in size from small pellets to large round rocks, some with a small void in the middle. There were a large number of these boulders in the area, but many have been removed by collectors over the years. The Moeraki boulders remain simply because they're too heavy to shift.

The **Maori** named the boulders *Te Kai-hinaki* ("food baskets"), believing them to have been washed ashore from the wreck of a canoe whose occupants were seeking the precious greenstone of Te Wai. The seaward reef near Shag Point (see below) was the hull of the canoe, and just beyond it stands a prominent rock, the vessel's petrified navigator. Some of the Moeraki Boulders were *hinaki* ("eel baskets"), the more spherical were water-carrying gourds and the irregular-shaped rocks farther down the beach were *kumara* ("sweet potatoes") from the canoe's food store. The survivors among the crew, Nga tamariki, Puketapu and Paki-hiwi, were transformed at daybreak into hills overlooking the beach.

The large complex beneath a series of domed roofs (supposed to represent the boulders), in the car park overlooking the boulders, acts as a **visitor centre** (Oct–April daily 8am–6.30pm; May–Nov Mon–Sat 9am–4.30pm; ☎03/439 4827), stocking leaflets on the boulders and surrounding attractions. It also contains a restaurant and souvenir shop with a glass front, surrounded by viewing balconies. The **café** serves quite expensive meals and snacks throughout the day and in the evening; there's also a fully licensed bar. The nearest **accommodation** is in Moeraki village (see below).

Moeraki Point and Shag Point

Once you've had a good look at the boulders it's worth walking along the beach to the Moeraki Point whalers' lookout, where there's a view south down the coast to the lighthouse, and the likelihood of seeing Hector's dolphins, which often surf in the breakers off the beach. If you're in the area in the winter (June–Aug), you might chance upon some of the thin, silvery frost fish which beach themselves along the shoreline on frosty nights for no apparent reason.

A number of smaller, odd-shaped boulders can be found at **Shag Point**, 10km south along SH1 (or an 11km walk along Katiki beach if you're feeling energetic). The beach near the point is sometimes visited by fur seals (Oct–March) and yellow-eyed penguins, which usually come ashore between 3.30pm and nightfall – there's a small hide where you can keep watch.

Moeraki village

Across the bay from the boulders, 1km south on SH1, then a further 1.5km down a side road, is the sleepy fishing village of **MOERAKI**, which provides a tranquil place to break your journey – and the only accommodation for ardent boulder viewers.

On the right-hand side of the road just before you enter the village is the **Kotahitanga** ("One People") **Church**, built in 1862 and containing beautiful stained-glass windows, crafted in Birmingham in 1891. Considered unusual for its (at the time rather daring) portrayal of Maori alongside Jesus and Mary, the left light of the window is a portrait based on a photograph of Te Matiaha Tiramoreh of Moeraki, a respected leader of the Ngai Tahu who died in 1881. Be warned that the church itself has already been moved three times in its history and may at some point be relocated to the top of the hill next to the marae, although no date has been proposed.

Of the **accommodation** available in the village, the *Moeraki Motel* (☎ & fax 03/439 4862; ④), on the only road entering the village, is a friendly place located close to a beach with six units and four new two-storey units facing the bay, all with fully equipped kitchens. There's also the *Moeraki Motor Camp* (☎03/439 4759; tent sites $7.50 per person, cabins ②), situated on a hill further into the village, with cooking facilities (camp kitchens and outdoor barbecues) and a store.

Smaller shuttle bus companies will drop you in the village, although services run by the major companies merely drop off at the point where the side road into the village leaves SH1.

Palmerston

The lumber town of **PALMERSTON**, 22km south of Moeraki, is the gateway to Central Otago and the historic goldfields route (see p.711), but there's little reason to stop here for long before pressing on to Dunedin, only 40km further south along the coast road. Most services are strung along SH1, including a **supermarket** and **petrol station** opposite the *Northwestern Hotel*, which serves bar snacks; there's a restaurant next door offering more substantial **meals**. As you enter the town on SH1 you will see *McGregor's* truck stop (6am–8pm) on the right, while on the opposite side of the road the *Postmark Café* (7.30am–10pm) does a works burger that would floor an elephant. For **accommodation**, try *Pioneer Motel*, 56 Tiverton St (☎03/465 1234; ④), with self-contained units, or the *Waihemo Lodge* on SH1 (☎03/465 1700; ③), which serves breakfast and dinner and has a 24-hour bar. About 3km south of town on SH1, an old sanatorium has been converted into the *Paradise Holiday Park* (☎03/465 1370; tent sites $10, dorms ①, cabins ②).

travel details

Trains

Ashburton to: Timaru (1 daily; 1hr).

Christchurch to: Ashburton (1 daily; 50min); Greymouth via Arthur's Pass (1 daily; 4 hour 25min); Picton (1 daily; 5hr 20min).

Oamaru to: Dunedin (1 daily; 2hr 30min).

Timaru to: Oamaru (1 daily; 55 min).

Buses

In addition to the nationwide operators, several smaller companies operate shuttle buses along the east coast and across to the west: Atomic Shuttle (☎03/322 8883), Ashburton Shuttles (☎03/308 4889) and South Island Connections (☎03/308 2366).

Ashburton to Geraldine (2 daily; 40min); Mount Cook (1 daily; 2hr 50min); Timaru (11 daily; 1hr 5min); Twizel (2 daily; 3hr 40min).

Christchurch to: Akaroa (2 daily; 2hr 35min); Ashburton (12 daily; 1hr 10min); Geraldine (3 daily; 2hr); Greymouth via Arthur's Pass (1 daily; 4hr); Hanmer Springs (2 daily; 2hr 30min); Lyttelton (every 30min 8.10am–11.25pm; 35min); Methven (2 daily; 1hr 15min); Mount Cook (2 daily; 5hr 50min); Nelson via Picton (3 daily; 9hr); Picton via Kaikoura and Blenheim (12 daily; 5hr 20min); Twizel (3 daily; 5hr 30min); Queenstown (5 daily; 10hr 35min).

Oamaru to: Dunedin (11 daily; 2hr 15min); Twizel (1 daily; 2hr 15min).

Timaru to: Oamaru (11 daily; 1hr 20min); Twizel (1 daily; 2hr 25min).

Flights

Christchurch to: Auckland (hourly; 3hr); Blenheim (14 daily; 1hr 55min); Dunedin (10 daily; 45min); Invercargill (7 daily; 1hr 15min); Nelson (9 daily; 2hr 5min); Queenstown (12 daily; 50min); Wellington (25 daily; 45min).

CHAPTER TEN

THE CENTRAL SOUTH ISLAND

T he **Central South Island** is one of the most varied and intriguing areas in New Zealand, with extensive pasturelands, dense native forests, and a history rich in tales of human endeavour. The defining feature of the region is however the rugged mountain ridge of the **Southern Alps**, which runs from north to south to form the South Island's central spine. The middle portion of this ridge, which culminates in New Zealand's highest peak, **Mount Cook**, presents an almost insurmountable barrier to travel between east and west coasts. The foothills of the Alps harbour rare and sometimes unique alpine plants and wildlife, including the famous Mount Cook Lilies, the largest white mountain daisies in the world; and the most mischievous of mountain parrots, the kea. A logistical nightmare to Maori and European settlers alike, the region is typical pioneer country, and the communities themselves (often named after the explorers and surveyors that opened the region up; Arthur's Pass and Lewis Pass being two prominent examples) are simple places, tinged with the toughness and idiosyncrasies of the early settlers.

The rugged nature of the terrain ensures that it's impossible to traverse the region on a north–south axis, and access to the area is determined by routes approaching the mountains from the east and west coasts. The most northerly of these routes is the **Lewis Pass Road**, which conveys traffic from the Canterbury Plains north of Christchurch to Westport on the west coast, passing the spa resort of **Hanmer Springs** on the way. Hanmer is a tranquil place surrounded by striking mountain scenery, and a good base from which to visit the neighbouring Amuri skifields, as well as **Hanmer Forest** and **Maruia Springs** further west. South of here, another major cross-mountain route served by both road and rail links Christchurch with the western seaboard town of Greymouth via **Arthur's Pass**, historically an important trade route connecting the coalfields of the west coast with the port of Lyttelton. It's now much

---

ACCOMMODATION PRICES

Accommodation listed in this guide has been categorized into one of nine price bands, as set out below. The rates quoted represent the **cheapest available** double or twin **room** – except for category ①, which are per-person rates for a dorm bed; fees for **tent sites** and **DOC huts** are also per-person, unless otherwise stated.

① under $20 per person	④ $60–80	⑦ $140–180
② under $40 per room	⑤ $80–100	⑧ $180–240
③ $40–60	⑥ $100–140	⑨ over $240

For more on accommodation, see p.33.

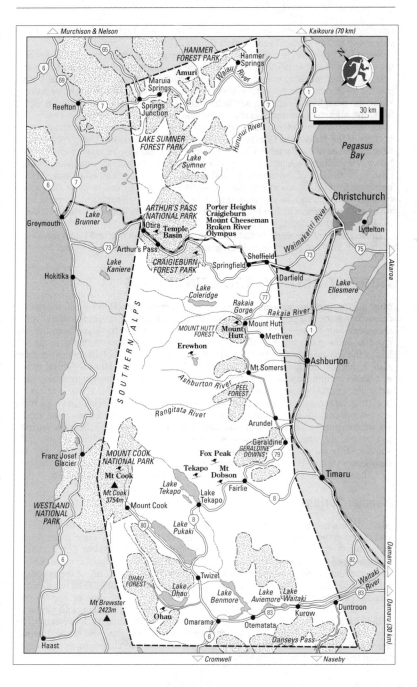

△ Murchison & Nelson
△ Kaikoura (70 km)

HANMER FOREST PARK
Hanmer Springs
Amuri
Maruia Springs
Waiau River
Springs Junction
Reefton
Hurunui River
LAKE SUMNER FOREST PARK
Lake Sumner
Pegasus Bay
Christchurch
ARTHUR'S PASS NATIONAL PARK
Otira
Temple Basin
Porter Heights
Craigieburn
Mount Cheeseman
Broken River
Olympus
Greymouth
Lake Brunner
Arthur's Pass
Lake Kaniere
Hokitika
CRAIGIEBURN FOREST PARK
Sheffield
Springfield
Darfield
Waimakariri River
Lyttelton
Akaroa
Lake Ellesmere
Lake Coleridge
Rakaia Gorge
Rakaia River
SOUTHERN ALPS
MOUNT HUTT FOREST
Mount Hutt
Methven
Erewhon
Mt Somers
Ashburton
Ashburton River
PEEL FOREST
Rangitata River
Arundel
Geraldine
GERALDINE DOWNS
MOUNT COOK NATIONAL PARK
Fox Peak
Tekapo
Mt Dobson
Fairlie
Timaru
Mt Cook
Mt Cook 3754m
Mount Cook
Lake Tekapo
Lake Tekapo
WESTLAND NATIONAL PARK
Franz Josef Glacier
Lake Pukaki
OHAU FOREST
Twizel
Lake Ohau
Lake Benmore
Lake Aviemore
Lake Waitaki
Waitaki River
Mt Brewster 2423m
Ohau
Omarama
Otematata
Kurow
Duntroon
Danseys Pass
Haast
Oamaru
Oamaru (30 km)
0   30 km
▽ Cromwell
▽ Naseby

travelled by tourists, with the Christchurch–Greymouth **TranzAlpine Express** providing one of New Zealand's most spectacular rail journeys.

South of Christchurch, roads lead up from the southern Canterbury Plains towards the small but lively foothill settlements of **Methven**, **Mount Hutt** and **Mount Somers**, which together make up one of the most exciting ski areas on the South Island. It's a popular destination for adventure seekers in summer too, with whitewater rafting, kayaking, paragliding, climbing and ballooning proving the main attractions. South of here, the attractive town of **Geraldine** provides access to the Geraldine Downs, for many the most England-like landscape on the South Island; while **Farlie** stands at the borders of the **McKenzie Country**, an area renowned for massive sheep runs and the beautiful blues of its glacier-fed lakes, **Tekapo** and **Pukaki** – both of which shimmer beneath the Southern Alps' most imperious peak, Mount Cook. **Mount Cook Village**, nestling at the foot of the mountains and the starting point of numerous walks, is the best base from which to explore. Routes south from Mount Cook towards Otago pass through **Twizel**, a strange fledgling settlement of only thirty years; and the rural backwater of **Omarama**, which commands access to the scenic **Waitaki Valley** route east to Oamaru and the coast.

Upland areas of the South Island typically have a wide-ranging and very variable **climate**, with long hot summers, cold crisp winters, and over a metre of rainfall annually.

Hanmer Springs and Lewis Pass

Most northerly of the cross-mountain routes, the **Lewis Pass Road** (SH7) follows the course of a track that provided both Maori and early *pakeha* (European settlers) with a necessary link between the east and west coasts. For those travelling from the east coast the route starts at the town of Waipara, 80km north of Canterbury, where the SH7 leaves the coastal plain and begins its gradual climb between foothills of the Southern Alps. Lying just off this route in a side valley, the spa resort of **Hanmer Springs** acts as a base for summer walks and adventure activities, and as a convienent resting place for winter sports enthusiasts who enjoy the nearby **Amuri Skifield**. It also offers the best range of accommodation in the area, a wooded mountain hinterland, and one of the top ten golf courses in the country. Some 60km further west, the **Lewis Pass** itself is set amidst some exhilarating subalpine terrain and deep forest; while **Maruia Springs**, just beyond the summit of the pass, is another elegant resort in which to soak in the soothing thermal waters. Public **transport** into the region is pretty sparse, with two daily buses making the trip from Christchurch direct to Hamner Springs, and daily services heading from Christchurch over the pass to Westport on the west coast.

Hanmer Springs

About 140km north of Christchurch, a side road leaves SH7 to head north towards the quaint and rather exclusive spa resort of **HANMER SPRINGS**, some 10km distant. Just after the turn-off from SH7, you'll cross the spectacular **Waiau Ferry Bridge**, designed by John Blackett. This was considered a major feat of engineering at the time of its opening in 1887, and the locals threw such a party that the site of the hospitality tent became known as Champagne Flat. The bridge now witnesses the tortured expressions of bungy jumpers as they hurl themselves from its parapet. Hamner Springs itself is pleasantly situated at the edge of a broad, fertile agricultural plain, with steep, forested hills above. As well as the excellent thermal pools, the village offers some charming, if pricey, small café/bars and restaurants, and provides access to the **Hanmer Forest Park**, particularly attractive in autumn when the birch, poplar, sycamore and rowan trees are rich in golden hues.

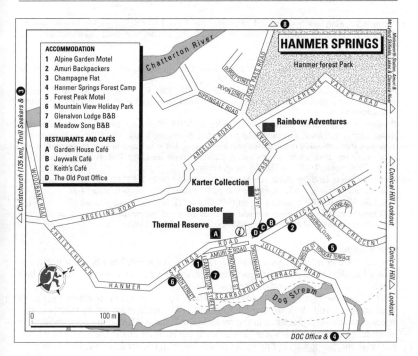

Arrival and information

There are a number of buses to Hanmer, including the Hanmer Connection (☎03/315 7575), which operate a daily service from Christchurch, either as a day-trip (2hr 20min each way; $40 return) or a one-way shuttle (about $25). These and InterCity buses run direct to Hanmer from Christchurch and Kaikoura, and drop off near the visitor centre.

The **visitor centre** on Amuri Road, next to the Thermal Reserve baths (daily: Oct–Feb 10am–6pm; March–Aug 10am–4.30pm; ☎03/315 7128), has helpful staff and a number of displays – including one devoted to varieties of tussock (Eskimos may have many words to describe snow, but Kiwis have tussock) and another on the destruction of the local environment, a sobering illustration of the H.G. Wells quotation "Human history is a race between education and catastrophe". Roughly 1500m northeast of the visitor centre is the **DOC office**, on the forest road known as Jollies Pass Road (Mon–Fri 9am–5pm, Sat 9am–noon), where you can find out more about local tramps.

Accommodation

Given Hanmer's reputation as an elegant resort, accommodation tends to be on the expensive side, although there's a modest sprinkling of backpacker-style dorms and inexpensive cabins. The town is busiest in winter, when it's wise to book ahead.

Alpine Garden Motel, 3 Leamington St (☎03/315 7332). Clean, comfortable, self-contained units, in a quiet setting three minutes' walk from the thermal pools. ④–⑤.

Amuri Backpackers, 41 Conical Hill Rd (☎03/315 7196). Comfortable and friendly place close to the village centre, offering mostly shared rooms, with only one double. Dorms ①, room ②.

Champagne Flat, clearly signposted 200m from the Waiau Ferry Bridge, on the Hanmer side (☎ & fax 03/315 7413). A comfortable homestay with a double and two twin rooms, all with shared facilities; dinner by arrangement ($25). ⑤.

Glenalvon Lodge B&B, 29 Amuri Rd, opposite the visitor centre (☎03/315 7475). Luxury accommodation in eleven rooms, either sharing facilities in the main house, or with private facilities in the separate suites. Dinner on request ($28). ④–⑤.

Forest Peak Motel, 2 Torquay Terrace (☎ & fax 03/315 7132). Five minutes' walk from the visitor centre, this motel has a variety of clean comfortable units, including ten attractive pine cabins, three with open fires. ③–④.

Hanmer Springs Forest Camp, Jollies Pass Rd (☎03/315 7202). Large holiday camp, clearly signposted 2km east of town, surrounded by trees from all over the world, with 150 or so beds, mostly in small cabins. Wood-burning stoves provide heating, hot water and drying areas; there's also accommodation modified for people with disabilities (book ahead for this). A camp track links to several DOC walks. Tent sites $16, dorms ①, cabins ②.

Mountain View Holiday Park, cnr Amuri Rd & Bath St (☎03/315 7113). A variety of motel and cabin accommodation, in a large well-kept area. Tent sites $8.50, cabins & units ②–④.

Meadow Song B&B, 177 Jacks Pass Rd (☎03/315 7577). In a rural setting about fifteen minutes' walk from town, this B&B hosts a maximum of six guests in two rooms with shared facilities and one with an en-suite and spa bath; a delicious cooked breakfast is served. ⑤.

The Village

The main street is Amuri Road, which forks into Conical Hill Road heading north and Jollies Pass Road heading northeast. Amuri Road is divided into two carriageways by a central, tree-shaded reservation that gives the village a quiet, sheltered feel.

The **Thermal Springs**, Amuri Rd (daily 10am–9pm; $6), were discovered in 1859 by William Jones while he searched for stray cattle. The springs are fed by rainwater that seeps down through fractures in the rocks of the Hanmer Mountains, accumulating in an underground reservoir some 2km beneath the Hanmer Plain. After absorbing some minerals and being warmed up by heat radiated from the earth's core, the water rises to the surface via fissures in the greywacke rock. Hanmer became famous in the 1870s for the relaxing and curative powers attributed to its waters; and since then the springs have undergone massive development, thereby losing much of their Victorian charm. The modern pool complex contains seven different-sized, artificially landscaped thermal pools full of light-blue springwater, as well as a standard chlorinated 25m swimming pool. There's also a toddlers' pool, a gym and the *Garden House Café* (daily 10am–9pm; licensed), which provides snacks and light meals at rather extravagant prices. You can also buy "Hanmer Salts" to put in your bath – good for the skin, but not so easy on the nose.

The only other attraction in Hanmer Springs is the small, privately owned **Karter Kollection Museum** (Mon–Sat 10am–3pm; $2), on Conical Hill about two minutes' walk from the Thermal Reserve, which contains a mish-mash of odds and ends that barely justifies the price of admission, unless the weather is awful.

Hanmer Forest Park

Ranged around the village to the north and east, the **Hanmer Forest Park** can be reached by walking along Jacks Pass Road, Conical Hill Road or Jollies Pass Road. It was created in 1901 using convict labour to plant a wide variety of exotic trees, which are now protected from logging. An easy **Forest Walk** (2.5km; 1hr), accessible from Jollies Pass Road leads through some of the oldest of the sycamore, oak, and silver birch. A DOC leaflet, *Hanmer Forest Walks* ($1), details twelve different trails in the forest, ranging in timescale from an hour to half a day.

The forest is also renowned for **mountain biking** and hosts trail-bike races twice a year (Sept–Oct & April–May). **Bike rental** ($25 per day) and **organized trips** (2hr–full day; $19–75) are available at Dust 'n' Dirt, 20 Conical Hill Rd (☎03/315 7233), and you

---

---

can pick up a bike-track map from the visitor centre (10¢). One of the most popular routes follows an old Maori and then European packhorse route to Blenheim (191km), via **Molesworth Station**, one of New Zealand's largest farms: a DOC leaflet, *Molesworth* ($1), sets out information about the **scenic drive/bike ride**, and the cattle station's history. The section through the station is 58km (2hr by car, cycling times vary from 3hr 30min to 6hr), and you must register at either the *Molesworth Cob Cottage* at the northern end of the trail or the *Archeron Guesthouse* at the southern end, both of which offer B&B accommodation as well as camping facilities. This quiet and atmospheric road traverses rugged terrain prone to landslips, washouts and snow; note that caravans, campervans and buses are banned.

Activities

Scenic **rafting** trips on the Clarence, Hurunui and Waiau rivers are offered by Rainbow Adventures on Jacks Pass Road (half-day $58, full day $85; ☎03/315 7444). The same company also offers **fun-yakking** (half-day $65), in which you flop downriver in inflatable two-person kayaks, which are also rather ominously known as "divorce boats"; **canyoning** (half-day $39), which involves walking, jumping and sliding your way through a series of mountain streams and cascades; tandem **paragliding** (25min; $100); and **horse riding** (half-day $45, full day $90). Serious riders should contact Alpine Horse Safaris, based on Waitohi Downs near Hawarden, off SH7 about 60km south of Hanmer, who organize some of the best **horse safaris** in the region (2hr–10 days; $25–$1200; ☎03/314 4293). Longer trips include all food and accommodation, but must be booked at least a month in advance.

For more thrills, go for a **jetboat** ride through the steep-sided gorges of the Waiau River with Amuri Jet (a 20km, 1hr ride costs $55; ☎03/315 7323); or **bungy** with Thrillseekers ($89 per jump; ☎03/315 7046), based at the Waiau Ferry Bridge.

Eating and drinking

Hanmer is full of snug little coffee houses and cafés serving thick, steaming soups to winter sportsmen or low-fat Italian salads to the summer crowd. Unfortunately, they're almost all overpriced. Among the spots still offering good-value, good-quality **food and drink** are *Jaywalk Café and Wine Bar*, Conical Hill Road (daily 6am–late; licensed), offering casual dining from a regularly changing menu, with mains around $18–21 and vegetarian dishes cooked on request; *Keith's Café*, on Amuri Road (daily 9am–8.30pm; licensed & BYO), a rustic-looking place offering a wide range of inexpensive snacks and full meals including full cooked breakfasts and fish and chips; and *The Old Post Office*, Jacks Pass Road (daily 6.30–11pm; licensed & BYO, $2.50 corkage; ☎03/315 7461), a stylish, imaginative restaurant with $20-plus main courses and a surprisingly reasonable wine list.

West to Lewis Pass

West of the Hanmer Springs turn off, SH7 continues on its climb towards the **Lewis Pass** 65km away. The high country around the pass was never actually settled by Maori, although it lay on a trail they tramped in search of greenstone. Later, European pastoralists sought an easier route between east and west coasts, and in 1860, the surveyors Christopher Maling and Henry Lewis stumbled upon the pass. In 1866 a bridle track linking Hanmer Plain with Murchison was finished, and by 1936 a spectacular highway suitable for motor vehicles was finally opened.

ST JAMES WALKWAY

About 4km along SH7 from the Hanmer Springs turn off, just south of the confluence of the Boyle and Lewis rivers, is the start of the **St James Walkway Subalpine Track** (66km; 5 days; outlined in a DOC leaflet of the same name, $1), which provides an alternative route **to Lewis Pass** (and the most secure car parking in the area). There are a number of **bus services** between Lewis Pass and Boyle, so you can get back to your car if you leave it at either end of the walk. This is a subalpine region, so you must be well-equipped with **all-weather gear**. Accommodation is provided by five DOC **huts** (category 2, 20 bunks; $8), all with wood stoves, firewood, intentions book and walkway map. A mixture of riverside walk, forest, farmland, and tussock, this is a quite strenuous tramp: the hardest day is the second, a long climb from the Boyle Flat Hut over the highest point of Anne Saddle (1136m), with spectacular views, to the Anne Hut and valley below.

The land between Hanmer and the squat hills of the **Boyle Bluffs**, which herald the **Doubtful River Valley** (a one-time gold diggers' route), is a rugged area of low-yielding grassland, with broom (a blazing yellow in the summer), spiky matagouri, manuka and kanuka taking hold where the farms have failed. As you approach the pass, red and silver beech forest begins to predominate. Shortly after the tiny cluster of houses that is the settlement of **BOYLE**, 50km out from Hanmer, you will come across **Sylvia Flat**, part of the Lewis Pass National Reserve, where it is possible to park and follow a track beside the Lewis River for about 50m to pools where warm water bubbles up through the rocks, mixing with the cold river water to create refreshing thermal pools. The 907-metre-high **Lewis Pass** itself is just 15km further on, and offers views along the high-sided Cannibal Gorge towards the Spenser Mountains.

Maruia Springs and Springs Junction

Eight kilometres beyond Lewis Pass, **MARUIA SPRINGS** is another thermal spa resort, grouped around a swanky bath complex with **hot pools** (daily 9am–9pm; $3 for the communal pool areas; $15 for private baths) that overlooks the river. The outside pools contain waters whose colours range from black to milky white, depending on the level of minerals they contain. The steaming waters are allegedly good for arthritis – but not so good for jewellery, which gets badly tarnished by the sulphurous fumes. **Accommodation** at the *Maruia Springs Resort* (☎03/523 8840; tent sites $18, dorms ①, units ⑤) ranges from camping to simple en-suite units; if you stay here, you're entitled to free and unlimited use of the springs. Within the complex there's a **café-bar** and two **restaurants**, one Kiwi-style and one Japanese.

Twenty kilometres west of Maruia Springs, there's a parting of the ways at **SPRINGS JUNCTION**, with the SH7 continuing west towards Reefton and the SH65 forging northwards to Murchison. Springs Junction itself has little to recommend it except a **Department of Lands and Surveys visitor centre** (Mon–Fri 8.30am–4.30pm, Sat 10am–12.30pm), with information on local scenic reserves and walks; and essential services such as a petrol station and village shop.

Arthur's Pass and around

Another classic east–west route across the Southern Alps is the one linking Christchurch with Greymouth via **Arthur's Pass**. Traversed by both a highly scenic rail line and the equally breathtaking SH73, the route is easily accessible from Christchurch, making it a popular excursion for city-based travellers eager for a quick taste of the high country.

The pass gets its name from civil engineer **Arthur Dobson**, who "discovered" the pass after hearing about it from local Maori, who had been using it for hundreds of years to bring *pounamu* (greenstone) from the west coast to the Canterbury Plains. Dobson surveyed the pass in 1864, and by 1866 horse-drawn coaches were using it to serve the Westland goldfields. The railway was built in 1923, coinciding with a booming interest in alpine tourism.

From Christchurch to Arthur's Pass

Whether travelling by road or rail, the trip from Christchurch to the pass is an adventure encompassing great geographical contrasts, beginning in the agriculturally rich Canterbury Plains and ending in an earthquake-shaken village 920m above sea level.

Initially both road and rail follow the course of the shingle-lined Waimakariri River, passing though a series of low-lying farm communities before beginning the gradual climb away from the neatly organized fields of the plains. The route ascends gently to **Springfield**, 70km out of Christchurch, at which point the river and the rail line veer away to the northwest, while the road continues climbing steadily past the sources of several rivers and streams to the 923m **Porter's Pass**, at the northern end of Lake Lyndon. As the route winds through increasingly dramatic gorges it passes the **Porter Heights Skifield** (see p.551), and then lakes Pearson and Grasmere to the north, which are directly opposite **Craigieburn Forest Park**, and the **Craigieburn, Mount Cheeseman, Broken River,** and **Mount Olympus** skifields (see p.551). About 6km beyond Lake Grasmere is the small settlement of **Cass**, where the tarmac and track routes rejoin and once again accompany the Waimakariri River along its winding progress through the Southern Alps. On reaching **Bealey**, at the northern foot of the mountain of the same name (1823m), the river once again bids farewell before heading south to its source on the mountain, while the road and railway line push on to Arthur's Pass, in the centre of the national park, with 2271m **Mount Rolleston** to its southern side, and both 1705m **Mount Pfeifer** and the **Temple Basin Skifield** (see p.551) to its northwest. Once over the summit, both road and rail pass through Otira before descending towards the pounding seas of the West Coast.

Springfield

SPRINGFIELD, 70km from Christchurch, is the first place worth stopping for, especially if you fancy a high-speed boat trip down the **Waimakariri Gorge** to blow away the cobwebs. Waimak Alpine Jet, on Rubicon Road, off the Kowahi Bush Road (20min $35, 1hr $55; ☎03/318 4881), operate fourteen-seater jetboats on demand all year round. The gorge is narrow, and the river water as clear as gin, with many waterfalls making for a spectacular and beautiful ride. If you are in need of sustenance, the **Old Springfield Pub** on Main Street is well worth a look, with reasonably priced rustic snacks and substantial main courses.

THE TRANZALPINE RAILWAY

The **TranzAlpine Express** (4hr 30min; $75 one-way, $97 day return) from Christchurch to Greymouth leaves Christchurch train station at 9am every morning. The **train** has large viewing windows and comfortable seats, with an open-sided observation car to aid photographers. Complimentary morning or afternoon tea is served, and snacks are available at only slightly inflated prices.

The scenic, 231km, coast-to-coast journey rises from an altitude of three metres above sea level at Christchurch to 737m at Arthur's Pass (the railway tunnels beneath the 920m summit of the pass), passing through nineteen **tunnels** and crossing numerous **viaducts** spanning picturesque braided rivers. This area is noted for its high rainfall of 1.2m a year, and purple **lupins** festoon the railway embankments, interspersed with yellow broom and beech forest beyond the crest of the pass. If you travel in December you will also see red and white rata in bloom, but the trip is at its romantic, snow-cloaked best in the **winter** months (June–Aug).

The **route** traverses the Canterbury Plain as far as Springfield, after which you start to see the mountains, and reaches the halfway point around Craigieburn, at about the same time as the piped commentary gives way to a TranzAlpine Rail pop song of Lloyd-Webber-like horror. There's a pause at Arthur's Pass itself to allow for a change of locomotive, after which the train dives through the 8.5km-long Otira tunnel. Descending to the west coast, you'll be treated to impressive views of Lake Brunner before trundling into Greymouth (see p.642), having covered in less than five hours a journey that took the horse-drawn coaches of Cobb and Company two days – and shortened the average life expectancy of the draught horses to a mere eighteen months.

Castle Hill Reserve

About 30km west of Springfield, SH73 passes through the **Castle Hill Reserve**, where there are a number of walks among the rising hills and mountains. One of the most interesting is a twenty-minute **stroll** that starts from the old cattle station (just a small building by the side of SH73, 2km south of Castle Hill Village) and heads among large, grey, Stonehenge-like rocky outcrops protruding from mounds of grass and gorse. This rather surreal landscape also offers excellent rock-climbing and good photo opportunities. The lumpy tussock is brightened by mountain daisies (whose leaves are used for weaving by Maori) and Castle Hill buttercups in the summer.

Craigieburn Forest Park – and Bealey

The **Craigieburn Forest Park** lies on the eastern ranges of the Southern Alps, about 15km beyond Castle Hill and 42km before Arthur's Pass, and is chock-a-block with good walking tracks, with longer tramps and climbing opportunities in the more rugged country further west. The park is dominated by mountain beech forest, alpine scrub and tussock grasslands, which are peppered with scarlet native mistletoe flowers from December to February. A variety of native birds streak and squawk through the forest, including bellbird, rifleman, silver eye and kea (alpine parrot), and between October and February, long-tailed and shining cuckoos join the throng. The nearby **Craigieburn skifield**, within the boundaries of the forest park, is one of the most exciting in the vicinity of Arthur's Pass – see box on p.551 for details.

In a signposted car park just off SH73, is the combined **visitor centre** and **DOC office** (Mon–Fri 9am–5pm, Sat 9am–12.30pm), where you can pick up leaflets on walks in the park – the free *Craigieburn Forest Park Walks* details ten of the best shorter walks. Paths up to and around the **Lyndon Saddle** are worthwhile, but if you do nothing else take the **Hut Creek Walk** (2km; 1hr), starting from the car park and winding down to the creek. From the creek, the track continues through mountain beeches and emerges onto a slope of native hebe, dracophyllum (whose leaves shade from green to a reddish-brown in spring and autumn), cassinis and matagouri. The whole walk boasts an abundance of very watchable keas – but watch out for the kleptomanic tendencies of these highly intelligent birds.

If you want to break your journey before the final assault on the pass, the solitary **Historic Bealey Hotel** (☎03/318 9277, fax 318 9014; dorms ③, motel units ④) is around 40km further along SH73, just 14km short of Arthur's Pass Village. Once a stop-off point for the Cobb Coaches that travelled to and from the west coast, it now provides clean and simple backpacker and motel-style accommodation, the *Klondyke Bar*, a bistro and restaurant.

Arthur's Pass Village

Four kilometres south of the actual summit of the pass, **ARTHUR'S PASS VILLAGE** nestles in one of many steep-sided, forest-covered, U-shaped valleys, forming a thin low-rise straggle along the main road (SH73), with power and telecommunication pylons as a fringe. The area receives over a metre of rainfall a year, and the village invariably cowers beneath mist or clouds: there's often a moody contrast between the white clouds that hover halfway up the valley wall, and the rich green trees and vegetation of the valley floor.

The settlement came about in the early 1900s to provide shelter for tunnel diggers and rail workers, and nowadays ekes a living from the tourists visiting the surrounding **national park**. It's a superb base for walking and climbing, with the nearby **Temple Basin skifield** (see box on p.551) providing good skiing and snowboarding opportunities in the winter.

Practicalities

Regular coast-to-coast buses (Coast to Coast ☎0800/800 847, Alpine Coach and Courier ☎025/342 460) stop in the centre of the settlement on the main street. The TranzAlpine train also stops close to the centre of the village. Tickets for both are available at the Arthur's Pass Store, and bookings can be made through the visitor centre. The village is best explored on foot, but Arthur's Pass Taxis (☎03/318 9266) can take you to the start of out-of-the-way tracks, or run you up to look at the actual pass itself.

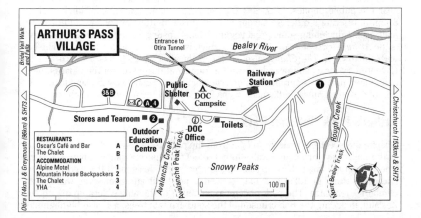

There is an excellent **DOC office** and **visitor centre**, on the main street, diagonally opposite the fire tender (daily 8am–5pm; ☎03/318 9211, fax 318 9271), with numerous walks leaflets and background information on the whole of New Zealand. The visitor centre also has extensive displays on wildlife, plants, geology and local history; and a video about the trail blazed by the stage coaches and the railway is played on request ($1). The only public phones are just outside the YHA. There's a **post office**, a **petrol station** and a couple of stores in the village, but **no banks**.

ACCOMMODATION
There's a wide choice of good-value accommodation in the village, although places fill up quickly during the high season (early Dec to late Feb), when it's a good idea to book in advance. If there's no room at the inn, you could always try the *Historic Bealey Hotel*, 10km to the east (see p.549).

Alpine Motel, on SH73 as you enter the village across Rough Creek, almost immediately on your left (☎03/318 9233). Basic motel units with private facilities, and simpler rooms at slightly cheaper rates. ④.

Sir Arthur Dudley Dodson YHA, on the main street, next to the phone box (☎03/318 9230). The country's first purpose-built hostel, with very helpful and informed staff, contains bunks, a large kitchen and common room, bike shed, gear storage and a constantly warm pot-belly stove. As the best-value central accommodation, this tends to get full, so book ahead. Tent sites $8, dorms ①.

The Chalet, west end of the village on the main road (☎ & fax 03/318 9236). This large alpine chalet offers B&B in eleven clean, individually decorated rooms with central heating and TVs. The guest-house contains lots of woodwork courtesy of the owner's father, and displays paintings by the owner's mother. ⑤.

DOC Campsite, next to Arthur's Pass Public Shelter and backing on to the railway. Basic site with cold water and toilets. Tent sites $3.

Mountain House Backpackers, on the main road through the village, opposite the YHA and next door to the outdoor education centre (☎03/318 9258). Clean bunkroom accommodation, and some doubles and twins in separate units, plus a large common room and kitchen. Tent sites $9, dorms ①, rooms ②.

Outdoor Education Centre, next to the chapel on the main street (book through the visitor centre or the DOC office). Simple bunkroom accommodation available when not fully booked by groups. ①.

EATING AND DRINKING
Due to the small size of the village **eating and drinking** options are somewhat limited, and prices reflect the captive nature of the market. In the centre, on the main street near the public phones, is *Oscar's Café and Bar* (daily 10am–10pm, kitchen closes 8.45pm), offering a different flavour of home-made muffins every day, a full bar, and main meals (including some great veggie dishes) costing $12.50–20. Directly opposite is the *Arthur's Pass Store and Tearooms*, which is cheaper but less salubrious. The best place in town is *The Chalet*, also on the main street, which has a bistro and bar (favoured by locals and open late) with a friendly atmosphere, serving snacks, lunch and dinner, plus a restaurant offering large portions of rustic New Zealand food with a hint of a Mediterranean influence (mains $10–22), and the ubiquitous nachos.

Arthur's Pass National Park

Despite the spectacular views you get from the pass itself, you really need to take one of the many day (or longer) walks to get a feel for this remarkable alpine landscape. The 720 square kilometres surrounding the pass was designated the **Arthur's Pass National Park** in 1929, and has exerted a powerful attraction over walkers and climbers ever since. The park encompasses much of the alpine flora unique to New Zealand, including the rich crimson of the southern rata trees; and also highlights the

SKIFIELDS AROUND ARTHUR'S PASS

There are five skifields in the area around Arthur's Pass, each offering accommodation and equipment rental unless otherwise stated. Although there is not an enormous variety of runs, there are some spectacular views, as well as reliable snow and relatively uncrowded slopes. The fields are described from east to west, heading along SH73 from Christchurch.

Only 96km west of Christchurch is **Porter Heights**, just off SH73 via a 6km unsealed road (☎ & fax 03/318 4731), which boasts the longest single run in the southern hemisphere. Lift passes cost $44 per day, and learners' packages $48 per day.

Just over 100km out of Christchurch along SH73 another 6km-long side road leads to the **Craigieburn Valley skifield** (☎ & fax 03/318 8711 or 365 2514), a challenging area whose extreme slopes make it the best-kept secret in the southern hemisphere. It's only really suitable for intermediate and advanced skiers. Lift passes are $27 per day.

The **Mount Cheeseman skifield**, 112km from Christchurch along SH73, is an exceedingly well appointed club field (☎ & fax 03/318 8794 or 379 5315) with good facilities and a friendly atmosphere. There's a good variety of runs for intermediates, and a wilderness skiing option for those with experience. Lift passes are $35 per day.

The **Broken River skifield** (☎ & fax 03/318 8713) lies 120km out from Christchurch, at the end of a 6km access road from SH73. It's a very well equipped field, offering night skiing and good snowboard terrain. Lift passes are $30 a day.

Mount Olympus (☎ & fax 03/318 5840), 128km from Christchurch, is in the Craigieburn range, set at the end of a road off SH73 only accessible by four-wheel drive. This is a small field with uncrowded slopes suitable for all ability levels. Lift passes are $28 per day, but there's no equipment rental on site (arrange this in Christchurch or at one of the other nearby fields).

Temple Basin (☎ & fax 03/318 9205), is 4km west (45min walk) from Arthur's Pass Village. It's a superb spot for snowboarding, is floodlit for night-skiing and has a variety of runs for all abilities. Lift passes cost $27 a day.

---

contrast between the tussock grasslands and scrub of the eastern South Island and the broad-leaved evergreen podocarp forest of the wetter west.

Although easily accessible, the park can still be a hazardous place: take simple precautions and use your common sense. The weather is highly changeable and often wet, so be sure to bring warm and waterproof clothing, sturdy footwear, a supply of drinking water and (even on the shortest walks) some energy-giving food. If you're embarking on tramps of a day or longer, inform the DOC office in Arthur's Pass Village, or fill in the relevant intentions book, before setting out.

Suggested **short walks** are detailed in the *Walks in Arthur's Pass National Park* leaflet ($1), which is stocked by the DOC office in Arthur's Pass Village. Among the most popular short walks are the circular **Devil's Punch Bowl** (2km; 1hr return), an all-weather track to the base of a 131-metre waterfall, crossing two footbridges and zigzagging up steps, and the **Bridal Veil Nature Walk** (2.5km; 1hr 30min return), which ascends a gentle gradient through mountain beeches then crosses the Bridal Veil Creek before returning along the road. Longer and more strenuous is the climb to **Avalanche Peak** (5km return; 6–8hr; 1000m ascent), which offers wonderful views of the surrounding mountains, but should only be attempted in reasonable weather.

For $5 you can obtain a set of leaflets listing eleven **longer tracks** (ranging from 2 to 5 days) from the DOC office in Arthur's Pass Village, which should be used in conjunction with the *Arthur's Pass National Park Map*. One of the most demanding is the **Harman Pass to Kelly Saddle** (55km; 4–5 days), a rewarding trip mostly along unmarked tracks and involving the crossing of unbridged rivers. Prospective trampers need to be fit and well-equipped; comfortable huts along the way are Category 2–3 ($4–8), and the best views are to be had from the ridges near Kelly Saddle. One of the slightly easier tracks that doesn't skimp on great views is **Casey Saddle to Binser Saddle** (40km; 2 days), a pleasant tramp crossing easy saddles on well-defined tracks through open beech forest, staying overnight in Casey Hut (Category 2; 16 bunks; $8).

For those feeling even more energetic, there is good **rock climbing** at Castle Hill (see p.548) and at the Temple and Speight buttresses on Mount Rolleston.

The South Canterbury foothills

Easily acessible from the east coast and its main artery, SH1, the **South Canterbury foothills** are often ignored by travellers hurrying westwards from Christchurch to Mount Cook (see p.562). Marking the transition from the flat Canterbury Plains to the more rugged and spectacular Southern Alps, the area is primarily known for the ski-fields grouped around the winter resort town of **Methven**, which serves the slopes of **Mount Hutt** and provides a jumping-off point for more distant pistes at **Erewhon**. Things are relatively quiet here in summer, but there's a wealth of natural attractions in the region, with the **Mount Hutt Forest**, the **Rakaia Gorge**, and **walks** around **Mount Somers** rewarding travellers who make the effort to stop. Further south, inland from Timaru, the tiny communities of **Geraldine** and **Fairlie** link the east coast with the mountains and provide bases from which to enjoy either skifields or summer adventure activities. Fairlie is promoted as the "Gateway to the **McKenzie Country**", an area of farmland mixed with tussock and stands of forest, which gives hints of the high country to the west.

Main **routes** into the area from the east coast are the SH72 from near Sheffield on the Arthur's Pass Road, SH77 from Ashburton south of Christchurch, and SH8 from Timaru. **Buses** from Christchurch and Ashburton represent the main means of getting here by public transport, even though services may be limited to one or two per day.

Methven and around

Thirty-four kilometres northwest of Ashburton on SH77, **METHVEN** is the capital of a bustling winter sports area known as the "Snowfed Republic". Scotsman Robert Patton bought land in the area in 1869 and named Methven after his home town. The Scottish influence may also have had some bearing on the building of an outstanding 18-hole golf course, which keeps the thousand-strong population and many visitors entertained once the winter snows have receded.

Being close to Mount Hutt, Erewhon and Mount Somers, Methven makes a good base for some skiing or tramping amid spectacular scenery. Activity operators also offer ballooning, horse riding, jetboating and whitewater rafting, but the **ski season** (May–Oct) is essentially what everyone lives for. In summer the town is much quieter, so much so that many of the restaurants and hotels close down for several months.

Arrival and information

Buses stop on Main Road (SH77), near the visitor centre. Tickets can be bought in the visitor centre or at the nearby Methven Travel Centre and Adventure Shop (☎03/302 8106), also on Main Road; in addition, the Travel Centre can arrange car and scooter rental (from around $50 and $30 per day respectively) and local minibus tours. The town itself is easily explored on foot, and a constantly changing array of companies offer minibus transport **to the skifields** (expect to pay around $15 return); the visitor centre has details of current operators.

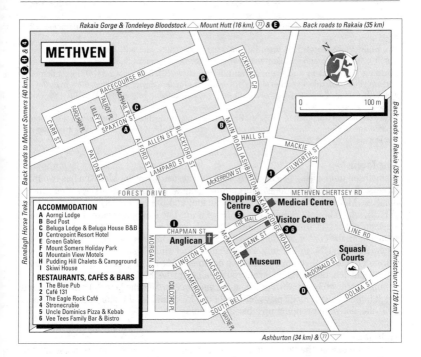

The helpful **visitor centre**, on Main Road, opposite Bank Street (daily 9am–5pm; ☎ & fax 03/302 8955), has lots of information about Methven, the skifields, and guided tramps in the vicinity. The town also has a small shopping centre, off Main Road, including banks, a post shop and several **ski shops** (specializing in gear rental and repairs), the best of which is Big Al's.

Accommodation

During the winter there is a wide variety of accommodation in Methven; in summer much of it disappears, but then so do most of the visitors. The advantage of being here in the summer is the scope it gives you for haggling.

Aorangi Lodge, 38 Spaxton St (☎03/302 8482). A single-storey simple wooden building with twin, double, triple and quad rooms, all with shared facilities. Cooked breakfast ($10) and dinner by arrangement ($15). Summer ②, winter ⑥.

Bed Post, 177 Main Rd (☎ & fax 03/302 8508). Offers twenty beds in twins, doubles and shared rooms, plus cooking facilities. Dorms ①, rooms ②.

Beluga Lodge and **Beluga House B&Bs**, 40 Allen St (☎03/302 8290, fax 302 9290). Luxurious accommodation, much loved by skiers, in two well-kept houses which have retained their original charm and are surrounded by tranquil gardens. Bathrooms are shared, robes are provided, and home-made bread accompanies a breakfast of your choice. Rarely open in summer but it's worth calling to check. ⑦.

Centrepoint Resort Hotel, Rakaia Gorge Rd (☎03/302 8724, fax 302 8870). A modern hotel with good views from its 46 rooms. Set in extensive grounds, guest facilities include a spa, pools, 9-hole golf course, a plush restaurant, ski drying room and nightclub with entertainment on Wed, Fri & Sat. Summer ④, winter ⑦.

Green Gables, 3km north of Methven on SH77 (☎ & fax 03/302 8308). A peaceful rural B&B partly surrounded by a deer farm. Accommodation consists of one en-suite double, and one double and single with shared facilities. Breakfasts are generous, and dinner is available by arrangement ($25). ⑤.

Mountain View Motels, 201 Main Rd (☎03/302 8206). Units with fully equipped kitchens, guest laundry, ski storage, and skifield transport by arrangement. Summer ③, winter ④.

Pudding Hill Chalets and Campground, Forest Drive/SH72 (☎03/302 8416). Five kilometres northwest of town, this upmarket site offers spas and saunas, a drying room, on-site restaurant and well kept cabins. Very busy in winter, but prices are negotiable in summer. Tent sites $9, cabins ②–③.

Skiwi House, 30 Chapman St (☎03/302 8772). Cosy singles, doubles and bunk rooms, a TV lounge, kitchen and drying facilities in a white weatherboard house about five minutes' walk from the centre. Dorms ①, rooms ②–③.

The Town

A small and uninspiring place, widely scattered across the plain, Methven has two main streets: the Ashburton–Rakaia Gorge Road (aka Main Street; or SH77), which heads north to Mount Hutt and south to Ashburton; and the Forest Drive/Chertsey Road (SH72), which bisects SH77 in the centre of town. The shopping centre is on the south-western corner of this intersection. The only outstanding building is the **Anglican Church**, on the corner of Chapman Street and Alington Street, and even that is an interloper. Built in 1880 in the tiny settlement of Sherwood 75km south, the church was transported to Methven by two traction engines in 1884. Turning right down McMillan Street and left on to Bank Stret, you'll come to the **Methven Museum** (open by arrangement, ☎03/302 8391, or ask at the visitor centre for the key; $1). This small red-brick building, with its displays on the Rakaia River and local history, makes a reasonable alternative to propping up a bar if it's raining.

Activities

Aside from skiing, the two most interesting things to do in Methven are horse trotting and ballooning. Both come with a hefty price tag, but the "Adventure Fun Pass" (available from the visitor centre; free) offers discounts ranging from $6 to $40 off a number of activities, including the two above, providing you use the operators participating in the scheme.

Horse trotting happens at the intriguingly named Tondeleyo Bloodstock 20km north of Methven on Lauriston Barrhill Road, off SH77 (daily 9am–4pm; $90 for a full day; ☎03/302 4800). Despite the twee and unstable-looking carts, it's fairly easy to learn the basics of this fast and exciting sport. The most spectacular activity in Methven, though, is **hot-air ballooning** with Aoraki Balloon Safaris (sunrise trip 4hr; $195, including champagne breakfast; ☎03/302 8172): the fine views of the patchwork quilt of the Canterbury Plains and the magnificent Southern Alps make this one of the best balloon flights on the South Island.

If you're an energetic (and wealthy) skiier or snowboarder, Methven Heli-ski ($625 per person, 3–5 passengers; ☎03/435 1834) offers a rather drastic way of finding unsullied snow – by **helicopter**. The company usually operate five runs, with professional guides; and in summer, they switch to helicopter drop-offs for trampers and mountain bikers. Wetter but as much fun is **whitewater rafting** with Max Rafting (☎03/302 8744), whose "Jet/Raft Tour" involves a jetboat ride up the Rakaia Gorge, followed by a fairly gentle guided raft trip down the Grade II river and a light barbecue (2hr; $55).

Eating and drinking

There is more choice in the winter than in the summer, but the prices are correspondingly higher; all but one of the places listed below is open year round.

The Blue Pub, *Methven Hotel*, cnr Kilworth St & Barkers Rd. This 1918 hotel is more of a drinkers' den than somewhere for a civilized meal, though they do produce some cheap lunchtime and evening bar food, including grilled steak for $12. It's crowded in winter, when entertainment is often laid on, although in summer things are fairly quiet.

Café 131, 131 Main Rd. A favourite local haunt with wooden floors and furniture creating a 1920s atmosphere. They serve light meals ($7–15), including delicious gourmet chicken burgers and veggie samosas, plus full breakfasts for $10. The coffee and brandy cake with cream is dreamy. Daily winter 7am–late, summer 9am–5pm. Licensed & BYO.

Centrepoint Resort, Rakaia Gorge Rd (☎03/302 8724). Plush restaurant and carvery, serving high-quality food.

Eagle Rock Café, Main Rd. Passable Italian specialities at pretty reasonable prices, alongside more conventional Kiwi fare (mains $10–25). Dinner daily from 5pm; licensed.

Uncle Dominics's Pizza and Kebabs, 253 Forest Drive, inside the main shopping centre. Surprisingly good pizzas and kebabs, at reasonable prices, to eat in or take away. BYO.

Vee Tee's Family Bar and Bistro, Main St. Evening-only restaurant serving basic, snacky menu weighed down by the 500g Brontosaurus Steak ($18). Sometimes closed in summer. Lively après-ski venue. Licensed & BYO.

Around Methven

Many winter sports enthusiasts choose to stay in Methven because of its easy access to the surrounding skifields. **Mount Hutt**, 26km to the northeast on SH72, is the nearest and most convenient, although **Erewhon**, 75km to the west and serviced by the nearby settlement of **Mount Somers**, is also within striking range (see p.556). The tiny settlements at both Mount Hutt and Mount Somers are little more than feeding stations for the skiers in the winter, and have a ghost-town feel for the rest of the year, although they border on regions of outstanding natural beauty. Around Mount Hutt to the north and west, the **Mount Hutt Forest** provides an opportunity to explore the native flora. Fourteen kilometres southeast of Methven is the **Rakaia Gorge**, offering riverside walks and the chance to fish for salmon or trout.

Mount Hutt Forest

Fourteen kilometres northwest of Methven and accessible via SH77 is the **Mount Hutt Forest**, which covers 444 square kilometres of tall trees on the eastern flanks of the Southern Alps, adjoining the **Awa Awa Rata Reserve** and **Pudding Hill Scenic Reserve**. Mountain beech is the dominant native species of tree, while snow tussock above the scrub line provides a home for a variety of native and introduced birds.

Free leaflets are available about the forest and reserves from local visitor centres, describing the flora and fauna as well as the many **walking tracks** you can explore – most of which can be accessed from the McLennans Bush Road entrance to all three reserves (reached by heading north from Methven on SH77 and turning left onto McLennans Bush Road after about 15km). It is worth taking a little extra time to examine the Mount Hutt flora during the spring and summer: of the **alpine plants** of New Zealand, 94 percent grow only in New Zealand, of which 130 species can only be found on Mount Hutt. One such is the unique vegetable *Sheep Raoulia eximia*, which forms huge grey mounds that look not unlike sheep lying down. There's also the *Ranunculus haastii*, a beautiful species of buttercup with blue-grey leaves and luminous yellow flowers, and ten species of mountain daisies, *Celmisias*, which form huge cushions of flowers.

Rakaia Gorge

Along the northern stretches of the Rakaia River, 14km from Methven, is the **Rakaia Gorge**, a steep-sided defile created by an ancient lava flow and now lined in many places with regenerating forest. The **Maori** account of the gorge's formation tells how a *taniwha* (water spirit) lived nearby, hunting and eating moa and weka; his

---

MOUNT HUTT SKIFIELD

Twenty-six kilometres northeast of Methven, just off SH72, **Mount Hutt** is widely regarded as the best skifield in the southern hemisphere, with a vertical rise of 655m and a longest run of 2km. It also enjoys the longest season and offers a broad range of skiing and snowboarding conditions. A daily lift pass costs $52, and frequent skiers get a $10 reduction. Beginners can take advantage of a one-day starter pack ($60, including equipment); a five-day package ($199); or a one-day learn-to-snowboard package ($75, including 2hr lesson & 1 day's board rental). Mount Cook Landline **buses** run to and from the field from Methven every day, dropping off in the morning and picking up in the afternoon (☎0900 344 44 for times and prices) and a variety of shuttle buses run between the skifield and Methven or Mount Hutt village. There's a Mount Hutt skifield information line on ☎03/302 8811.

---

possessions, because of his status as a spirit, were *tapu*. One cold day he went to find a hot spring, and while he was away the northwest wind demon flattened his property. To prevent this happening again, the *taniwha* collected large boulders and stones from the mountains to block the course of the demon, and in so doing narrowed the Rakaia River so that it flowed between the rocky walls. The spirit became so warm because of his exertions that the heat from his body melted the snow and ice on the mountains, and his perspiration fell on the rocks and formed crystals in the riverbed.

Just off SH72, an information shelter has maps of the area and a list of activities, next to the head of the **Rakaia Gorge Walkway** (15km; 3–4hr return). The path leads through several forest stands and spectacular geological areas, past hardened lava flows of rhyolite, pitchstone and andesite, to the upper gorge lookout.

Mount Somers and around

On SH72, 35km from Mount Hutt, at the junction of the road to Erewhon Skifield (see box below) is the small settlement of **MOUNT SOMERS**. The town itself has little to offer, although those keen on geology and local history might want to look in on the **Foothills Museum** (open by arrangement, ☎03/303 9752; donation requested), in a shabby weatherboard shed on Hoods Road, next to the Anglican Church.

However the **Mount Somers Recreation and Conservation Area**, roughly 10km north of town on Flynn's Road, has some fine tramps (see the *Mount Somers Recreation and Conservation Area* leaflet in local visitor centres and DOC offices; 50¢); and along the road towards Erewhon a proliferation of lakes provide superb scenery, trout-fishing and, on **Lake Clearwater**, superb windsurfing (details from the Methven visitor centre).

EREWHON SKIFIELD

The **Erewhon Skifield** (☎03/308 7091), 40km west of Mount Somers, is a lesser-known club field. Samuel Butler set his utopian novel *Erewhon* in the central South Island, the name being an anagram of "nowhere". The field is based on Mount Potts, and is a small-scale affair, which means you can always find virgin snow and uncrowded slopes. There are rope tows and a learners' lift, and lift passes cost $27 per day. Four-wheel drive transport from Mount Somers can be arranged by phoning the club (see number above). Hot refreshments are available at the day lodge, although the best accommodation is 42km away in Mount Somers.

Walks around Mount Somers

The landscape around Mount Somers differs from its surroundings as it's formed from rhyolite rock, which is harder than greywacke and shows fault lines, exposing columns and fractures of darker andesitic material. As a result the terrain is generally more rugged, with outcrops of rock poking out from patches of regenerating beech forest. The *Mount Somers Recreation and Conservation* leaflet (50¢, from visitor centres) describes in detail the geology and the history of the region, and also gives information on the 17km **Mount Somers Subalpine Walkway**, which passes abandoned coal mines, volcanic formations and a deep river canyon. The walk can be done in ten hours, although it's often treated as a leisurely two-day affair, with the *Mount Somers Hut* (see below) providing overnight accommodation. To get to the start of the walk, you'll have to drive (there's no public transport) west along the Ashburton Gorge for 11km, and turn right at the old trolley wheels, following the Jig Road to **Coalminers Flat picnic area** and the Woolshed Creek car park. From the picnic area, follow the Black Beech Walk to McClimonts Mine; from here, red markers lead to the 934m summit of Mount Somers, with stunning high-country views. The track then goes down a stepladder to the Morgan Stream Junction, under the Spa Pool Waterfall and past the Emerald Pool to **Mount Somers Hut** (2–3hr; category 3; $4). On day two, take the steep steady climb to the 1170m Mount Somers Saddle (3–4hr), then follow the markers to the north face of the mountain and climb to Slaughter House Gulley (named in the days when red deer roamed the area – and were hunted in large numbers) and One Tree Ridge, before descending swiftly to the bushline (2hr). The track then descends around the bluffs to a streambed, before climbing steeply up to Duke Knob (740m), then descending to **Sharplins Fall car park** (3–4hr), where you can arrange to be picked up by local taxi.

There are also a number of **shorter walks**, taking from ten minutes to half a day, from either car park.

Practicalities

InterCity **buses** drop off in the centre of the tiny Mount Somers community, where the best **accommodation** in the area is provided by the pleasant tree-filled campsite of *Mount Somers Holiday Park*, Hoods Road, 1km off SH72 (☎03/303 9719; tent sites $18, cabins ②–③).

The finest **food** in the region is to be had at *Stronecrubie*, just south of Mount Somers on SH72 (Wed–Sat 6.30–10pm, Sun noon–2pm & 6.30–10pm; bookings essential, ☎03/303 9814; licensed), where the Swiss chef uses fresh local ingredients and meat from a Swiss butcher in Auckland to produce mouthwatering dishes. Try the rack of lamb with Provençal herbs and mustard ($21), or filleted grouper on a bed of marinated mushrooms ($18.50), and for dessert don't miss the McRae's whisky cake and whisky sabayon. If you can't tear yourself away after dinner (or can't move), *Stronecrubie* also has five standard **rooms**, and three family rooms, all with kitchens, wicker furniture and views of the mountain (same phone number; ④).

Geraldine and around

The quiet, pretty town of **GERALDINE** lies 45km south of Mount Somers via SH72, and 15km west of the main coastal highway (SH1) along SH79. Set on the Geraldine Downs – gently rolling hills standing out in sharp relief against the craggy, snow-capped Southern Alps – the town is at the centre of a prosperous farming community. Geraldine has a surprising number of **craft shops**, and when you've exhausted the town's limited attractions, the walkways and rafting trips of **Peel Forest** are within easy reach.

Arrival and information

Mount Cook Landline buses drop off at *Oakes Restaurant* on the junction of Talbot Street with SH79, while InterCity services drop off at Orari, 15km away on SH1, where they're met by a shuttle bus into town (Geraldine Community Mini Buses, ☎03/693 8976; $2). Direct bus services from Timaru to Fairlie (40km to the west, see p.560) also connect with shuttle services to Geraldine. Geraldine's **visitor centre**, inside the Pine, Gordon, Guinness Shop on Talbot Street (Mon–Fri 9am–4.30pm, Sat 10am–3pm, Sun 10am–1pm; ☎03/693 8597), is run by helpful volunteers. The regional **DOC office** is also located in town, at the Raukapuka Field Centre, North Terrace (Mon–Fri 9am–4.30pm, Sat 9am–noon; ☎03/693 9994).

Accommodation

There's a small concentration of accommodation in Geraldine, none of it too expensive, and it's rarely a problem getting a bed for the night.

The Crossing, Woodbury Rd (☎03/693 9689, fax 693 9789). This beautiful old English-style manor with a shady verandah houses a fully licensed restaurant and four en-suite guest rooms, each individually and lavishly decorated. Continental breakfast included. ⑥.

Crown Hotel, 31 Talbot St (☎03/693 8458, fax 693 9565). Upmarket pub with eight clean and airy rooms, all with en-suite bathrooms. ④.

Geraldine Backpackers, The Old Presbytery, 13 Jolie St (☎03/693 9644). Clean and well-kept dorm accommodation in a historic building opposite the Talbot Forest Reserve, with helpful hosts and a warm and friendly atmosphere. Dorms ①.

Geraldine Motel, 97 Talbot St (☎03/693 8501). Six pleasant fully equipped units close to the town centre. Complimentary newspaper in the morning. ④.

Geraldine Motor Camp, Hislop St (☎03/693 8860). Surrounded by sheltering trees, this spacious site is inside Geraldine Domain. Tent sites $8 per person, cabins ②–③.

Heron Rose B&B, 29 Cox St (☎03/693 8343). Cosy, renovated 1930s house covered in roses, with leadlight windows and open fires. Three charming guest rooms, with shared facilities and a choice of breakfast. ⑤.

Hislop House B&B, 20 Cox St (☎ & fax 03/693 8890). This single-storey wooden house built in the early 1900s offers two en-suite rooms and a warm welcome. ④.

The Town

In town, the tiny **Geraldine Historical Museum**, on Cox Street (Sun 2–4pm, or by arrangement with the visitor centre), has little of outstanding interest but is housed in a rather quaint blue-and-white stone building with an attractive garden. More extensive is the **Geraldine Vintage Car and Machinery Club**, 174 Talbot St (Nov–Feb daily 10am–noon & 1.30–4pm; March–Oct Sat & Sun only 10am–noon & 1.30–4pm; $4), an amazing and well-kept collection of old cars, tractors and planes.

To check out Geraldine's wealth of **artists and galleries**, pick up the *Art Trail Map, Geraldine District Arts and Crafts Guide* or the *Geraldine* leaflet from the visitor centre. Well worth visiting is Stained Glass Windows, 177 Talbot St (Mon–Thurs 9.30am–4.30pm), where you can browse among the colourful lampshades and stained-glass work, and Allison Arts, 55 Cox St, a frame-shop and gallery specializing in paintings by local artists.

The main attractions lie on the fringes of town. Just 1km from the town centre, at the end of Hislop Street, **Talbot Forest Scenic Reserve** is the last remnant of a once extensive native forest, with the largest radiata pine in the world and plenty of other mature native trees including matai, kahikatea and totara. It's a peaceful place to spend an hour or two with a picnic. **Barker's Winery** (daily 9am–6pm), 8km west from town on SH79 then north on the Te Moana Road, is a well-known local producer of fruit wines, liqueurs and preserves. The winery offers finger-food lunches (for around $15), as well as free tastings of its berry and fortified wines.

Eating and drinking

Given Geraldine's small size, you wouldn't expect to find a wide range of culinary choice in town, but there's something to satisfy most appetites nevertheless.

Berry Barn Bakery and Café, 66 Talbot St. The usual savouries, pies, chips and cakes, served in cheap and cheerful surroundings. Also stocks products from *Barker's Winery* (see p.558). Daily 6am–6pm.

The Crossing, Woodbury Rd (☎03/693 9689). The top restaurant in town, set in an English-style manor house, serving expensive fresh steaks and fish ($20–25), with locally grown vegtables, as well as extraordinarily rich and tempting desserts. The cooking is along traditional Italian and English lines, with hints of Oriental spicing. Tues–Sun lunch & dinner; licensed.

The Oaks, 72 Talbot St, cnr Cox St. Bacon, eggs and chips for $9, great hash browns and the usual café fare. Daily 9am–5pm.

Papillon Chinese Restaurant, Tea Rooms and Takeaway, 40 Talbot St. A peculiar mix of East-meets-New-Zealand café: Chinese food, fish, burgers and chips. Closed Tues; licensed & BYO.

Plum's Café, 44 Talbot St (☎03/693 9770). Good-quality food, home baking and a wood-burning stove. Try the "Plum's Ultimate Snack", a combination of garlic bread, chicken, sour cream, salad and more for $7.50. Delicious lunches daily, dinner Fri & Sat; licensed & BYO.

Totara Bar and Restaurant, *Crown Hotel*, 31 Talbot St (☎03/693 8458). Large restaurant serving reasonably priced Kiwi nosh. The bar is one of the better places in town for a drink.

Around Geraldine: Peel Forest

One of the more beautiful places in the area is **Peel Forest Park**, enclosing a vast expanse of forest, scrub and alpine vegetation 19km northwest of Geraldine. To get there, head north on the SH72 as far as Arundel, before turning west onto the Cooper's Creek/Peel Forest Road. You'll pass through the hamlet of **PEEL FOREST** about 1.5km short of the reserve entrance, a useful spot for stocking up on supplies and picking up information from the **Peel Forest headquarters and DOC office** (Mon–Fri 9am–4.30pm, Sat 9am–noon; ☎03/696 3826), which serves as a campsite booking office and visitor centre, and has displays highlighting natural history, pioneering, walks and picnic areas.

A free leaflet (available at the DOC office) describes the **Peel Forest Tracks**, twelve walking tracks ranging from forty-five minutes to six hours. Of these, the best are the **Acland Falls Walking Track** (1.5km; 45min one way), a steep climb followed by a short streamside walk to a fourteen-metre-high waterfall, and **Allan's Track** (4km; 2–3hr round-trip), a steady ascent past the head of Mils Stream and through podocarp forest which can be extended by joining the **Deer Spur Track** (5km; 2hr return), a steep but well-defined route which climbs above the bushline to a sparkling mountain tarn at an altitude of about 900m. Take time while you walk to admire the huge, ancient totara trees, rata and ferns, and to watch the antics of the fantails and tomtits – these little birds often hover around, feeding on the insects disturbed by trampers and picnickers.

The park is also the home of one of the better **whitewater rafting** operators in New Zealand. Rangitata Rafts, at Peel Forest River Base, about 2km north of Peel Forest Village (☎03/696 3735, fax 696 3534), offer **camping** ($10 per site), very basic bunk **accommodation** in their lodge (①), and, of course, rafting **trips on the Rangitata River** (May–Sept daily at 11.30am; 3hr; $105, including lunch & dinner, or an extra $20 as an overnight trip from Christchurch). The whole operation is very professional: a maximum of six rafts take to the river at once, with a full briefing beforehand and one guide for every nine passengers. The first part of the rafting is Grade I, which gives you a chance to get used to the self-baling boats before the thrilling trip through the high-sided Rangitata Gorge, where you traverse Grade I–V rapids; there's also an optional ten-metre cliff jump near the end. Afterwards, your ordeal by water is rounded off with welcome hot showers and a barbecue dinner.

There is also an Outdoor Pursuits Centre based near the park (☎03/696 3832), which offers an introductory **rock-climbing** course (2 days; $140), introductory **kayaking** (3 days; $140), and a Clarence River rafting expedition (5 days; $270) – all including food and accommodation.

Fairlie and around

Heading west from Geraldine towards the wilds of the McKenzie Country and the mountains around Mount Cook, you first pass through the small town of **FAIRLIE**. Defined by its position at the junction of the two main routes that strike inland from the east coast to Lake Tekapo – SH79 from Rangitata via Geraldine and SH8 from Timaru – Fairlie is a quintessential crossroads town, with a resident population of only 600. Originally called Fairlie Creek, the name was shortened after the telegraph office opened in 1892, the creek having long since dried up. The rail link with Timaru closed in 1960, and the town has pretty much remained in stasis ever since.

Within reach of Fairlie are the **skifields** of Mount Dobson and Fox Peak (see box, p.561).

Arrival, information and accommodation

Daily InterCity and Mount Cook Landline **buses** stop opposite the *BB Stop* café on Main Street, from where everywhere's easily reached on foot. The ad hoc **visitor centre** is housed in The Sunflower Centre, just down the street at no. 31 (daily 8.30am–6pm; ☎03/685 8258), and has a fair stock of leaflets, including the *Fairlie Districts Recreation Map*, which lists four walks in the settlement and three scenic drives. **Accommodation** options in Fairlie aren't particularly exciting or varied, but the town is rarely busy, so you shouldn't have too much trouble finding a bed.

Aorangi Motel, 26 Denmark St (☎ & fax 03/685 8340). This is the most central motel, with seven spacious self-contained units, plus a spa. ④.

Fairlie Lodge, 16 School Rd (☎ & fax 03/685 8452). Well cared for motel offering a very friendly welcome, clean, small units with their own facilities, microwaves, TVs and toasters. ③.

Fontmell Farmstay, 3km southwest of Fairlie on Nixons Rd (☎03/685 8379). Comfortable B&B accommodation in an English-style homestead, surrounded by pastureland and woods. There are two doubles and one single room with shared bathrooms. ④.

Pinewood Motel, 27 Mount Cook Rd (☎03/685 8599). Modern motel with airy, self-contained units close to the town centre. ④.

JAMES MCKENZIE

A Kiwi folk hero, James McKenzie lends his name to the crescent of flat land between Fairlie and Kurow (to the south on SH83) known as **McKenzie Country**. A Scottish immigrant of uncertain background, McKenzie was arrested in 1855 for being a sheep stealer on a grand scale. He stole over 1000 in all, most of them from the the Rhodes brothers' Levels Run station near Timaru (see p.526), grazing them in the basin of rich high-country pastureland which now bears his name. McKenzie escaped from prison three times during the first year of his five-year sentence, and was finally released on condition that he leave the country never to return, which he subsequently did.

It's nowadays difficult to fathom why exactly McKenzie became such an important and popular figure in New Zealand lore. He was certainly a prodigious thief, somehow controlling a vast flock of rustled animals with the assistance of a single dog, Friday – a hound fondly remembered as the prototype for the many hard-working sheepdogs held in deep affection by South Islanders. McKenzie is also regarded as one of the great pioneers, opening up an area of hitherto undiscovered grazing land that contained some of the best sheep runs in the country.

Mount Dobson Motel, 6km west of Fairlie on SH8 (☎03/685 8819). A quiet motel with large units next door to the *Silverstream Hotel* (which serves meals) and bottle shop, and 5km from the Toll Gate to Mount Dobson and Fox Peak skifields. Ski bus pick-ups arranged. ③–④.

Tally-Ho Backpackers, 7 School Rd (☎03/685 8723). Basic accommodation in a small homestead, offering either dorms or cosy twin or double rooms – plus a free spa in the evenings, barbecues, and friendly helpful staff. Tent sites $6.50, dorms ①, rooms ②.

The Town

The centre of the town is marked by the junction of Allandale Road (SH79) and Main Street (SH8), which becomes Mount Cook Road as it heads west out of town. The most interesting sight is the **Mabel Binney Cottage and Vintage Machinery Museum** (daily 10am–5pm; $2), on Mount Cook Road, where three buildings are set back from the road with a Sampson wind pump (a tower surmounted by a wind-powered fan) out front. The display in the cottage remembers the first European settlers, and there's an extensive collection of early photographs. The museum is stuffed with farm machinery, wagons and traction engines. The third building on the site is the old railway station, which was moved here in 1968.

For a little exercise, wander along the **Fairlie Walkway** (3km; 40min one-way). Beginning below the Allendale Road Bridge over the Opihi River, the walkway follows the willow-shaded riverbank past open pastureland and through trees to emerge near Talbot Road. **Guided walks** further afield are offered by Off the Beaten Track (☎03/685 8272; $15 per hour), run by local tramper Louise Wynn. To get an aerial perspective, or for **heli-skiing** jaunts, Skyview Helicopters (☎03/685 8900) operate **scenic flights** and snow landings, while in summer heli-trekking drop-offs at backcountry huts are the order of the day; prices start at around $40 per person for a fifteen-minute flight.

En route to Lake Tekapo or Mount Cook, you could also stop by the **Three Springs Historic Sheep Station** (daily 10am–4pm) 5km west of Fairlie on SH8. Built from local limestone, the woolshed (where the shearing took place) is a magnificent example of early settler farm architecture, while the stable contains displays highlighting the station's history.

Eating and drinking

There's a good choice of eateries in Fairlie, offering a range of culinary styles and some very picturesque locations.

BB Stop, 81 Main St. Variations on a theme of meat, fish, chips and vegetables, followed by a touch of luxury in the form of Irish coffee. Burgers and light meals $4–8, full meals $10–17. Daily 8.30am–10.30pm. Licensed & BYO.

MOUNT DOBSON AND FOX PEAK SKIFIELDS

Mount Dobson Skifield (☎03/685 8039, premium-rated snowphone ☎0900/39 888) is located in a 3km basin 26km north of Fairlie, up a 15km unsealed road off SH8. The mountain is known for its powder snow, long hours of sunshine, uncrowded fields and suitability for all levels of skiing and snowboarding. Equipment rental is available, and there is a lodge serving hot pies and drinks. Lift passes cost $37 per day, beginners' packages $40 including lift passes (equipment rental is extra), and snowboard rental weighs in at around $30 per day. The nearest accommodation is in Fairlie. There are shuttle buses from Fairlie in season; for details call ☎03/693 9656.

The **Fox Peak Skifield** (☎03/685 8539) is 30km northeast of Fairlie, with access from near the Mount Dobson access road. Although a small field it covers a good variety of terrain, catering for all abilities. Lift passes are $25 per day and there's a free learners' tow. There are no ski rental facilities and no accommodation, but refreshments are available. For information on Fairlie–Fox Peak shuttle buses contact ☎03/688 1870.

Old Library Café, 6 Allendale Rd. Originally built in 1914, this café is charming and very comfortable. The menu offers chef's specials, cheap breakfasts, light meals and snacks; there are always veggie choices, Thai curries and T-bone steaks. Prices are moderate, and there's occasional live music Fri & Sat evenings. Daily 8am–late; licensed.

Rimuwhare Country Retreat, 53 Mount Cook Rd (reservations adivisable, ☎03/685 8058). A traditional English-style house in a lovely rustic setting. They do a cracking Spanish omelette ($6.50) for lunch, and a variety of Mediterranean-style dishes ($14–22) for dinner, plus some superb desserts. Daily lunch & dinner; licensed.

The Sunflower Centre, 31 Main St. A wholefood café and health-food shop, offering inexpensive meals and snacks, but be warned – the veggie burgers are enormous. Daily 8.30am–6pm; no licence and no BYO.

Toms, Main St, between Kirke St & School Rd. A sure-fire formula of cheap eats and good value: try Granny's Homemade Soup. Tues–Sun dinner & lunch. Licensed & BYO.

Mount Cook and around

From Fairlie SH8 winds its way westward through the sheep-nibbled grasslands of the McKenzie Country into the Mount Cook area, considered by many to be the most spectacular section of the Southern Alps. Dominating the region to the northwest, the 3764-metre **Mount Cook** is the highest point in New Zealand. Known as Ao-raki by Maori, who passed through the area on their way east or west in search of *pounamu*, it was named Mount Cook by Captain J.L. Stokes of HMS *Acheron* in 1851, although its summit wasn't conquered until 1894.

Mount Cook's permanent cover of snow and ice contrast vividly with the turquoise, glacier-fed **lakes Tekapo and Pukaki**, which stretch beneath its eastern flanks. Both lakes offer abundant fishing, water skiing and ice skating, although it's Lake Tekapo that has the bulk of the tourist facilities. Lake Pukaki is quiet in comparison, even though the view of Mount Cook across its still waters is one of the most memorable in New Zealand. Main access to the mountainous terrain around Mount Cook itself is provided by **Mount Cook Village**, which grew at the base of the mountain purely to cater for nineteenth-century tourists, who were brought here by horse-drawn coaches from Fairlie. You can walk from Mount Cook Village to the glaciers lurking beneath Mount Cook's flanks, most important of which is the 27km-long **Tasman Glacier**, running parallel to the Main Divide and fed by icefalls tumbling from the heavily glaciated peaks. Another good base from which to explore the area is **Twizel**, 70km south on the road to Cromwell and Queenstown, an unexciting modern town, which nevertheless rewards visitors with a glimpse of the extremely rare **Black Stilt**, wading birds that are protected in a reserve nearby. From **Omarama** 30km south of Twizel, SH83 runs eastwards down the **Waitaki Gorge** to Oamaru, providing a quick link between the Mount

HOW MOUNT COOK (AO-RAKI) CAME TO BE

Both the **sky father** (Raki) and the **earth mother** (Papa-tua-nuku) already had children by previous unions. After their marriage, some of the sky father's children came to inspect their father's new wife. Four brothers, Ao-raki, Raki-roa, Raki-rua and Raraki-roa, circled around the earth mother in a **canoe** called Te Waka-a-Aoraki, but once they left her shores, disaster befell them. Running aground on a reef, the canoe was turned to stone. The four occupants climbed to the higher western side of the petrified canoe, where they too were turned to stone: **Ao-raki** became Mount Cook, and his three younger brothers formed flanking peaks. Ao-raki towers over his brother mountains in height, age and spiritual status, as an Atua (Maori god).

Cook area and the east coast. Public transport into the region is meagre but adequate, with Mount Cook Village served by daily **buses** from both Christchurch and Ashburton on the east coast, and three daily services from Queenstown to the south. In addition, Christchurch–Queenstown buses pass through Tekapo, Twizel and Omarama.

Lake Tekapo and around

About 42km from Fairlie on SH8, via Burke's Pass, is **Lake Tekapo** and **LAKE TEKAPO VILLAGE** – little more than a roadside ribbon of buildings, with a population of just 400. It's a popular tour-bus stop for obligatory photo-snapping, and shopping in the string of outlets whose stock leans towards high-priced tourist tat. To make the best of the place, stay overnight and enjoy the scenery and sunset free of the mob, then move on.

At an altitude of 707m, the area is reputed to have the clearest air in the southern hemisphere, and on a good day views really do have sharp edges and vibrant colours, making this is one of the best places from which to photograph the Southern Alps. The most striking thing about the **lake** itself is its colour: the light reflected from microscopic rock particles suspended in glacial meltwater lends its waters a vibrant turquoise hue. Fed by the **Godley** and **Cass** rivers, the lake covers 83 square kilometres and spills into the **Tekapo River**, which tumbles across the McKenzie Basin.

Arrival and information
On their twice-weekly journey between Timaru and Twizel, Canride (☎03/688 5544) **buses** stop at Lake Tekapo Village, as do the daily services of Mount Cook Landline and InterCity. Tekapo is also on the Christchurch–Queenstown route plied by Kiwi Discovery Express and Atomic Shuttles. Timetables and fares for all these services are available from the visitor centre, where you can make bookings and buy tickets.

Buses pull into an area off SH8, opposite the main shops, and you can walk to all the accommodation and worthwhile sights from there. The **visitor centre** is in the *Cassinia Café* in the middle of the settlement (daily 9am–5pm; ☎03/680 6861 or 680 6721).

Accommodation
Most accommodation in this tourist-oriented village is on the expensive side, and the few budget options tend to be oversubscribed – it's a good idea to book ahead.

The Chalets, 14 Pioneer Drive (☎03/680 6774). Six individually decorated, self-contained motel units overlooking the lake and well away from the highway, run by German speakers. ④–⑤.

Lake Tekapo Alpine Inn, in the centre of the village by the Tekapo River Bridge (☎03/680 6848). The original inn building is 33 years old, though several new sections have been added since: old hotel rooms are cheaper than new ones, and motel units are cheaper still. The complex incorporates a variety of restaurants and shops, and various activities are arranged for guests. It might be worth negotiating if things seem quiet. ④–⑥.

Lake Tekapo Motel and Motor Camp, Lakeside Drive (☎03/680 6825, fax 680 6824). Situated among trees at the southern end of Tekapo, this is a large, well-equipped campsite. Tent sites $8, cabins & motel units ②–⑤.

Tailor-made-Tekapo Backpackers, 9–11 Aorangi Crescent (☎03/680 6700). Off SH8, five minutes' walk from the bus stop and shops, this friendly hostel has 30 bunks, plus an organic vegetable garden and a telescope – the clear mountain air makes for great stargazing. ①.

Tekapo YHA, Simpson Lane, just west of the village (☎03/680 6857). This lakeside hostel has doubles and twin rooms, as well as bunks; the common room has a floor-to-ceiling window to make the most of the magnificent view. Dorms ①, rooms ②.

The Village and around

The name Tekapo derives from the Maori *Taka* (sleeping mat) and *Po* (night), suggesting that this place has long been used as a stopover between destinations. Although surrounded by heart-stopping scenery, there is little to the settlement itself – though you should pause long enough to look inside the tiny **Church of the Good Shepherd**, on Pioneer Drive. Overlooking the lake from a small raised platform, the stone church was built as a memorial to the pioneers of the McKenzie Country in 1935. Behind the rough-hewn Oamaru stone altar, a square window perfectly frames the lake and the surrounding hills and mountains; in the stillness of this simple church, the sunset can be quite a moving experience. About 50m east of the church is the perky-looking **Collie Dog Monument**, erected in 1966 by the sheep farmers of the McKenzie Country as a mark of their deep respect and affection for the dogs that make it possible to graze this harsh terrain.

Of a number of good **walks** in the area, the best is to **Mount John Lookout** (10km; 3hr return), starting just past the motor camp on Lakeside Drive and climbing through a larch forest to a loop track which circles the summit of Mount John, with views of the McKenzie Basin, Lake Tekapo and the Southern Alps. Other energetic pursuits include skiing at the Tekapo Skifield (see box below), **ice skating** at the rink (May–Aug only) on Lakeside Drive, and guided **horse treks** through spectacular scenery with Tekapo Trekking (30min–2hr; $15–50; ☎03/680 6882). A more leisurely excursion attempts to recapture the pioneer spirit with Clydesdale-drawn lakeside **wagon rides** run by the Tekapo Wagon Company (15min $8, 30min; $12; ☎03/680 6848).

Finally, determined sightseers short of time can join Air Safaris on SH8, about 6km west of Tekapo (free transfers arranged for customers), for a "Grand Traverse of Mount Cook". This **scenic flight** swoops across the Main Divide to the west coast, providing views of the Franz Josef and Fox glaciers, the Hooker and Muller glaciers, and, of course, Mount Cook (hourly; 50min; $140; ☎03/680 6880).

Eating and drinking

Catering to a relatively captive market, most of the cafés and restaurants in Tekapo are relatively pricey; if you're on a tight budget, your best bet is probably a picnic by the lake. Otherwise, the main street through the village has the *Jade Palace* (lunches 11.30am–2pm, dinner 5pm–9pm; licensed), a modern, airy Chinese **restaurant** with very tasty set menus for $22 a head. The pick of the restaurants in the *Lake Tekapo Alpine Inn* complex, right in the centre of the village by the Tekapo River Bridge is the expensive *Kohan* (evenings only; licensed), specializing in subtle Japanese cuisine, but there's also a Chinese dinner restaurant, and the all-day *Garden Buffet Bar*, so you won't starve. The *Cassinia Café* (daily 9am–5pm), right in the centre of the main drag, serves snacks and coffee, but is on the expensive side.

TEKAPO SKIFIELD

The **Tekapo Skifield** (☎03/680 6700) is on Round Hill, 36km north of the village along the Lily Bank Station Road, which heads along the eastern side of the lake. It's a small field with wide, safe slopes which are good for beginners; and there are plenty of cross-country skiing routes too. Lift passes cost $27 per day. There's no accommodation at the field and equipment has to be rented back in Tekapo. Information on shuttle-bus transport between Tekapo village and the skifield is available from the Tekapo visitor centre or the telephone information line above.

Towards Lake Pukaki

Southwest from Tekapo, SH8 heads towards **Lake Pukaki** some 47km distant, where SH80 branches off northwards towards Mount Cook Village. There's an **Information Shelter** at the road junction, housing several useful and interesting displays on Maori and *pakeha* history, and a beautiful view of the lake – a massive blue-green expanse of water where winds whip up white-capped waves. It's also the starting point for a worthwhile **scenic drive**, which heads up the eastern side of the lake via Hangman Drive and Tasman Downs Road, offering over 40km of scenic lake and mountain views, before eventually petering out at the base of 2035m **Mount Burnett**.

Mount Cook Village

The road from the Lake Pukaki junction to Mount Cook heads north along the west bank of the lake for 55km, squeezed between the shore and an area of gorse- and tussock-covered hills. Thirty kilometres from the junction you'll pass the Glentanner Park campsite (see p.566), closely followed by **Peter's Lookout**, a popular viewing point on the lake side of the road.

On hot days, an atmospheric white mist rises from the plain at the base of the mountain, as you approach the huddle of buildings that make up **MOUNT COOK VILLAGE**. At a height of 760m, this ugly, low-slung settlement is dominated by **The Hermitage**, an alpine-style hotel at the end of the valley that leads to the mountain; there's been a hostelry here since 1886 (though the current incarnation was built in 1958). Mount Cook is something of a company town, since the same people that own *The Hermitage* own just about everything else – and most of the permanent population of 500 work for them. Rain frequently shrouds the village, but the scenery round about more than compensates (see p.567).

Practicalities

All the major operators run **buses** to Mount Cook from Christchurch via Tekapo, or from Queenstown to the southwest. There are additional services from Twizel and Tekapo, and most stop at Glentanner along the way. All the buses drop off in the car park near *The Hermitage*, from where everything is within walking distance. Mount Cook **airport**, 3km south of the village, is served by regular daily flights from Auckland, Christchurch, Queenstown, Rotorua, Taupo, Te Anau, Wanaka and Wellington.

The **DOC office and visitor centre** (daily: April–Sept 8am–5pm; Oct–March 8am–7pm; ☎03/435 1895, fax 435 1080), located among the Hermitage's hotel buildings and chalets, is the best place for information and advice on walks and activities. There are also a number of displays of Mount Cook memorabilia, and a **video** recounting Maori legends, the glacial history of the mountain, and a survey of the people who have, over the years, attempted to climb it (8.30am, 10.30am, 1.30pm & 3.30pm; 20min; $2). Two hundred metres south of here, near the **petrol station**, is a small **Grocery Shop** (daily: Oct–March 8am–7pm; April–Sept 9am–5.30pm), which charges over the odds for a limited variety of goods – fresh produce is usually snapped up at dawn. Banking transactions can be completed at *The Hermitage*, and the nearby pub takes Eftpos. Alpine Guides, close to the grocery store (daily 8am–5.30pm; ☎03/435 1834), offer experienced trekking and climbing guides, stock equipment and rent out **mountain bikes** ($12 per hour).

ACCOMMODATION

There is only a limited amount of accommodation in the area, which means you should book early during the peak season (Oct–April & July–Sept). Conversely, the village is

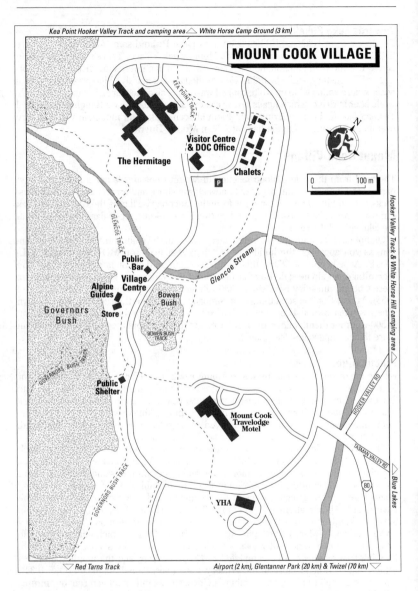

Kea Point Hooker Valley Track and camping area △— White Horse Camp Ground (3 km)

MOUNT COOK VILLAGE

KEA POINT TRACK

The Hermitage

Visitor Centre & DOC Office

Chalets

P

GLENCOE TRACK

Public Bar

Village Centre

Alpine Guides

Store

Governors Bush

Glencoe Stream

Bowen Bush

BOWEN BUSH TRACK

GOVERNORS BUSH TRACK

Public Shelter

Mount Cook Travelodge Motel

GOVERNORS BUSH TRACK

YHA

0 — 100 m

N

Hooker Valley Track & White Horse Hill camping area ▷

HOOKER VALLEY RD

TASMAN VALLEY RD

80

▷ Blue Lakes

▽ Red Tarns Track

Airport (2 km), Glentanner Park (20 km) & Twizel (70 km) ▽

deserted between April and June, a window between the summer tourist and winter skiing seasons, when it is generally possible to negotiate tariffs (with the exception of the
YHA).

Glentanner Park, 20km south on SH8 (☎03/435 1855, fax 435 1854). Well-equipped site with shop,
camping and cabins in a wide open space, giving panoramic views of the mountains and the Tasman
Valley. Tent sites $8, cabins ②–③.

The Hermitage, on the northwestern border of the village (☎03/435 1809, fax 435 1879). This rambling wooden structure topped by a greeny-blue roof has several grades of room, all with a balcony, though not always a view. The complex also includes seven heated and fully self-contained A–frame chalets (often booked out by Kiwi Experience) and twelve very popular motel units. ⑥–⑨.

Mount Cook YHA Hostel, cnr Bowen Drive & Kitchener Drive (☎03/435 1820, fax 435 1820). An excellent hostel with 66 beds in a wooden building and modern, well-kept facilities. Free videos are shown in the evenings or when the weather is rotten. Dorms ①, rooms ②.

White Horse Hill Camping Area, thirty minutes' walk north from the village at the start of the Hooker Track (no advance bookings). A serene and informal camping area with flush toilets and running water; camping spots are indicated by markers. Tent sites $3.

EATING AND DRINKING

The Hermitage will provide **picnics** for all-comers (ask in the lobby; $19–22.50), with a free cooler bag thrown in, and within the hotel complex itself there are four eateries. The *Wakefield Lodge* (Oct–April only; licensed) serves **buffet** meals ($35 a plate, drinks extra), but the real attraction is the excellent view of Mount Cook. Both the *Alpine Room* and the *Panorama Room* are open all year: the former offers breakfast, lunch and dinner, with a full meal costing around $30–40 (or $32 buffet-style; licensed), while the *Panorama Room* specializes in **fine dining**, and also has an excellent view (evenings only; $60–90; licensed). The lower echelons are catered for by *Snackpackers*, a licensed **coffee shop** in the basement (Oct–April only; 8am–7.30pm).

There are also two **bars** in the hotel, the best of which is the *Snowline Lounge*, with panoramic views of the mountain making this an excellent spot to sit and sup a couple of expensive beers as the sun goes down. If you manage to escape the clutches of The Hermitage, you can seek sanctuary at the *Mount Cook Tavern*, a friendly **pub** 200m to the south, where bar food includes pizzas and pies, supplemented by barbecues in summer ($8).

Glentanner Park, on the shores of Lake Pukaki, 20km south on SH8, has the obligatory big-windowed restaurant, *The James McKenzie* (lunch & afternoon tea in winter, all day in summer), and the equally obligatory inflated prices.

Exploring the national park

The 700 square kilometres surrounding the peak and extending to the north and east forms the **Mount Cook National Park**, which was designated a **world heritage site** by UNESCO in 1986. With twenty-two peaks over 3000m, the park contains the lion's share of New Zealand's mountains, mostly made of greywacke laid in an ocean trench 250–300 million years ago. About 2 million years ago the Alpine Fault began to lift, progressively pushing the rock upwards and creating the Southern Alps. These days the process continues at about the same rate as erosion, ensuring that the mountains are at least holding their own, if not getting bigger. Mount Cook is at the heart of a unique mountain area, where the rock of the Alps is easily shattered in the cold, leaving huge amounts of gravel in the valley floors. The inhospitable ice fields of the upper slopes are contrasted by the tussock-cloaked foothills, where Mount Cook Lilies, summer daisies and snow gentians thrive. The weather here is changeable, often with a pall of low-lying cloud liable to turn to rain, and the mountain air is lung-searingly fresh.

There are numerous **walking opportunities** catering for a wide range of abilities, with a variety of scenic trails beginning on the edges of Mount Cook Village itself. Main routes into the mountains from the village are the **Kea Point Track** northwest to the **Mueller Glacier**, the **Hooker Valley Track** northwards to the **Hooker Glacier**, and the **Tasman Valley Road** northeast to the **Tasman Glacier**. Walking as far as these glaciers is well within the capability of any moderately fit recreational walker, and longer walks for the more ambitious branch out from these basic routes. However you shouldn't actually walk on the surface of any of the glaciers unless you've already had experience of such walks and you've sought advice on conditions from the local DOC, or you're in the company of a qualified local guide. A *Walks in the Mount Cook National Park* **leaflet** ($1) is available from the visitor centre.

Although walking is an unbeatable way of exploring the park, the **scenic flights** on offer can provide you with glimpses of areas that you could never dream of reaching on foot. Such flights are extremely popular, and must be booked as far in advance as possible. Remember that flights are cancelled in high winds or if visibility is poor – and the weather can change by the hour, so if you get the chance to go, jump at it. The peak season for flights is from November to March, but in winter (June & July) the weather's often clearer, with better visibility. The Mount Cook region's **ski season** (see box, p.570) lasts from June to September, and the steep, inaccessible slopes (you're delivered to them by helicopter) present an exciting challenge to experienced skiers.

Walks

Walks range from gentle day-hikes to arduous and spectacular alpine treks that take several days. Tramping **information** is available from the DOC office in Mount Cook Village. Most of the trails are suitable for well-equipped independent walkers, but to help you on your way, Alpine Guides (☎03/435 1834) offers experienced **trekking** and climbing **guides**, while On Foot at Mount Cook (based in The Hermitage, ☎03/435 1809) leads gentler **guided walks** (2–5hr; $15–50).

The DOC leaflet *Walks in Mount Cook National Park* ($1) describes the national park and lists twelve excellent **shorter walks** (10min–5hr), all of which can be extended by those with relevant experience. Each of the walks starts in Mount Cook Village and heads out along the banks of one of the two glacier-fed rivers, the Hooker River and the Tasman River. Of these, the most popular is the superb **Hooker Valley Track** (9km; 3hr return). Crossing swingbridges across the Stocking Stream and Terminal Lake, the track heads towards Mount Cook, past the site of the original hermitage (a stone fireplace remains) and the viewpoint at the Alpine Memorial. You can extend your walk (providing you first seek advice on conditions at the DOC centre in the village) by continuing to the 1129m **Hooker Hut** (3hr return; category 1; 12 bunks; $14), staying overnight and returning the following day.

The **Mueller Glacier**, nestling 5km northeast of Mount Cook Village beneath the hanging glaciers and icefalls of Mount Sefton, is reached by the **Kea Point Track** (3hr return), which starts just north of the DOC office. Again, a more gruelling alternative is available to those who first check on weather conditions with the DOC, in the shape of the **Mueller Hut Track** (5km; 5hr one way), which requires moderate fitness. The route leaves the Kea Point Track just before its arrival at the glacier, climbing steeply westwards up the **Sealy Tarn Track** along a route marked by cairns. The final assault is up a loose gravel slope to a skyline ridge, from which you head south towards the 1800m **Mueller Hut** (category 1; 12 bunks; $14). The views are quite startling and you are engulfed by almost perfect silence, interrupted only by the murmur of running water and the twittering of birds.

The trail to the **Tasman Glacier** starts from the Blue Lakes car park, 3km north of the village up the Tasman Valley Road, and leads to the **Glacier Lookout** (500m; 20min one-way; 100m ascent). The glacier is 600m deep at its thickest, 3km across at its widest, and moves at a rate of 20cm a day. A gentleman called Sir Harry Wigley landed an Auster aircraft on the glacier in 1955, paving the way for today's squadrons of tourist flights. Alpine Guides run a sightseers' **walking tour** of the Tasman Glacier (Sept–May daily 10am & 2pm; 2hr; $30; ☎03/435 1834), which includes a guided walk on the glacier surface.

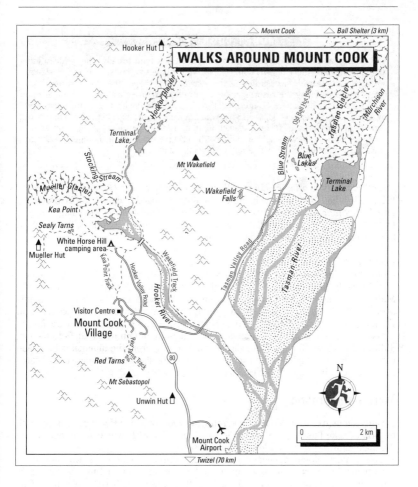

Scenic flights

All the **scenic flights** from the Mount Cook Airfield are operated by **Mount Cook Flights** (☎03/435 1849), who run both fixed-wing and helicopter sightseeing trips. These allow you to see the tops of the mountains and the steepness of the valley walls, and to appreciate the length and mass of the glaciers, and in some instances land on them for a quick walk around. By far the most exhilarating landings and take-offs are in the fixed wing aircraft, when the value of prayer becomes evident.

HELICOPTERS

The best of the **helicopter** trips on offer from Mount Cook Flights takes you the length of the Tasman Glacier in an exciting and bumpy ride, hovering alongside the valley walls and peaks, and the tumbling blocks of the Hochstetter Icefall, and landing on the snow of the glacier when the weather allows. The flight time is forty minutes and the cost $285 per person, with a commemorative glossy booklet in six languages thrown in.

The other flights on offer are shorter: there are thirty-minute ($210) and twenty-minute ($135) trips, both with a snow landing. The only comparable opposition is offered by **The Helicopter Line**, based at Glentanner Park, 20km south of the village on SH8 (☎03/435 1801), who operate three similar scenic trips at similar prices, though since the airbase is slightly further away, they spend less time actually over the mountain.

FIXED-WING PLANES
Mount Cook Flights (see p.569) offer a series of fixed-wing scenic adventures, the best of which is the longest (55min; $291), which circles Mount Cook, crosses (briefly) the Main Divide, then lands and takes off from the Tasman Glacier in a heart-stoppingly short space of time. Of the five shorter flights on offer, two land on the glacier. Mount Cook Flights also offer flights from nearby airfields, including a whizz round the Mount Cook summit from either **Twizel airfield** (45min; $135) or **Omarama airfield** (50min; $145), although you'll be starting slightly further away from the mountains here, and consquently spending less time over them. There are also fly-overs and scenic flights available from the **West Coast** (see p.649).

Twizel and around

Seventy kilometres from Mount Cook, retracing your route on SH80 then veering south on SH8 at Lake Pukaki junction, you'll come upon **TWIZEL**, which sits to one side of the main highway, with a backdrop of alpine scenery.

This modest settlement began life in 1966 as a staff hostel for people working on the local hydroelectric scheme (see box on p.575), and was supposed to have been bulldozed flat after the project was finished. Some think this would have been a kinder fate: Twizel is a windy place, dry and cold in the winter, and dry and hot in summer. The real reason to come here is to take a trip out to the **Black Stilt Colony**, 3km from town, which aims to save these rare wading birds from extinction. Otherwise, you'll have to content yourself with exploring the stark surroundings of **Lake Ohau**.

Arrival and information

Mount Cook Landline and InterCity **buses** drop off at the *High Country Lodge* (see p.571), on the corner of MacKenzie Road and Tasman Road. Canride buses from Oamaru and Timaru, together with **shuttle buses** to and from Mount Cook, use the car park outside the council buildings, just behind the town's central shopping mall. The town's accommodation is all within walking distance of either point of arrival; for exploring further afield, Twizel Hardware, 23–24 Market Place, offers **bike rental** ($10 a day).

The combined **visitor centre** and **DOC office** on Wairepo Road, adjacent to SH8 (May–Sept Mon–Fri 9am–4pm, Sat & Sun 10am–3pm; Oct–March Mon–Fri 8am–6pm,

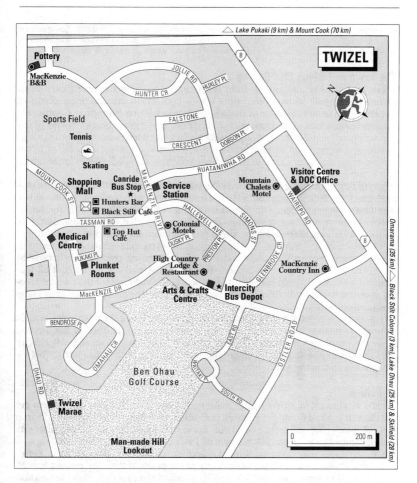

Sat & Sun 9am–3pm; ☎03/435 0802) have heaps of information on the town, Lake Ohau, local walks and wildlife. The town also has a **bank** in the main shopping mall.

Accommodation

Being only half an hour's drive from Mount Cook, Twizel's accommodation tends to be oversubscribed around Christmas, New Year and Easter, when the town is packed with holidaying New Zealanders. **Book ahead** if you plan to be here then.

Colonial Motel, 36–38 McKenzie Drive (☎03/435 0100, fax 435 0499). Superior ground-floor units with full kitchens and facilities, and conveniently close to shops and restaurants. ⑤.

High Country Lodge, McKenzie Drive (☎03/435 0671, fax 435 0747). The former hydroelectric workers' camp, this has retained some of its institutional character, with barracks-like bunk rooms. Hotel and motel rooms are a better bet, with a communal kitchen, restaurant and café-bar. Dorms①, rooms ④.

MacKenzie Hotel B&B, The Old Hospital, MacKenzie Drive (☎03/435 0416). Five rooms and a choice of cooked or continental breakfast. The owners make unusual pots and paintings, all for sale. ③.

Mountain Chalet Motels and Lodge, Wairepo Rd (☎03/435 0785, fax 435 0551). Ten spacious, light-filled, self-contained A-frame chalets. The adjacent lodge section offers simple clean and comfortable backpacker accommodation in dorms and rooms. Dorms ③, rooms ②, chalets ④.

The Town and Black Stilt Colony

These days the low, uninspiring town erupts into a brief summertime frenzy when tourists flock to visit Mount Cook, before lapsing back into its mundane existence as an administrative centre. Circular in design, the **Market Place Shopping Centre** provides the town's focal point. Opposite the visitor centre is a grey concrete statue, which was supposed to be Neptune, though sadly his fork has been removed. Nearby, a section of pipe formed into an arch marks the entrance to a grassed area full of heavy earth-moving machinery used in the hydroelectric project, which passes for an attraction in these parts.

You're best off heading straight out to the **Black Stilt Colony**, which occupies a wetland area 3km south of Twizel on SH8. The colony is attempting to preserve this endangered bird from extinction – an urgent task, with only 120 of them left in the world. Access is by guided tour only (Mon–Fri 10.30am–2pm, Sat & Sun 3pm; 1hr; $10; ☎03/435 0802), but there is a hide where you can watch the birds without disturbing them; binoculars are provided. The long-legged, red-eyed stilts thrived on the banks of braided rivers, feeding on mayfly and exhibiting endearing post-coital behaviour in which the male puts his wing around the female and walks with her. But all this changed when the Waitaki hydroelectric project destroyed many of their winter feeding grounds; to add insult to injury, excess outflows from the dams washed away many nests and chicks.

The centre incubates stilt eggs and hatches them, replacing them with clay models to keep the parents interested, then half the hatchlings are returned to the parents, while the remainder are reared by an electrically heated surrogate stilt. After thirty days the chicks go into aviaries, where they are kept for a further nine months before being released into the wild.

Activities

What Twizel lacks, its surroundings make up for, and there are plenty of ways to get out there. If you're a fit and experienced **trail biker**, Heli Bike (☎03/435 0099) will drop you off somewhere and leave you to bike back; routes take in such diverse places as the Benmore Range, about 50km south of Twizel; Omahau Hill, 15km southwest of town; and the easier Pyramid Circuit (daily on demand, 9.30am & 2pm; 1–4hr; $50–140). If you are intending to **climb** any of the peaks in the area, contact Russell Braddock, 33 Braemar Place (☎03/435 0858), a skilled and experienced guide who also offers introductory, intermediate, and advanced mountaineering instruction. Finally, a branch of Mount Cook Flights operates **scenic flights** over the Mount Cook region from Twizel (see p.570 for details) – and there's always skiing (see box on p.570).

Eating and drinking

Unfortunately Twizel's contagious lack of charm extends to most of its **eating and drinking** options, which tend to be functional and uninspiring – with the notable exception of *Hunters Café Bar*.

Black Stilt Restaurant and Takeaway, 25 Market Place. A regular café serving bacon and eggs ($9.50), light lunches and burgers ($3–9), and main meals (up to $12). Mon–Sat all day, Sun dinner only.

High Country Lodge, McKenzie Drive. A café-bar and restaurant, serving typical Kiwi food in typically large portions (main dishes $13–18). Licensed.

Hunters Café Bar, 2 Market Place. The best place to eat and party in town, run by a Scot with a weak spot for McKenzie Country-themed decoration, such as corrugated iron, barbed wire and wool. Generous well-prepared lunches and dinners ($6–19) include beer-battered fish, locally farmed salmon and merino lamb kebabs, rounded off with good coffee. The buzzy atmosphere is helped along by occasional live music and theme nights, not to mention cocktails such as McKenzie's Dog. Daily 11am–late.

The Top Hut Café and Bar and Woolpack Bistro, 13 Tasman Rd. Pub serving bistro meals such as rump steak or seafood platter (both $14), accompanied by chips, eggs and salad. Occasional discos and live music in a bar with stuffed animals, including an improbable alligator. Daily 9am–3am.

Lake Ohau

Around 25km west of Twizel, **Lake Ohau** is famed for its forest, river and **skifield** (see box below). Renowned for the purity of its water, the lake boasts some distinctive natural features, such as kettles (small depressions left when blocks of glacial ice melt, causing sediment above to subside), and the terracing on its banks that reflects the light of summer sunsets. Although it lacks the colour of Lake Tekapo, it is popular for fishing and kayaking, as are the Dobson and Hopkins rivers that flow into the lake's northern end (contact Twizel visitor centre for details of boat rental).

The **Ohau Forests** lie northwest from the lake, their stands of mountain beech and subalpine scrub criss-crossed by numerous tracks; the *Ohau Forests Recreation Guide* (50¢), available from the DOC office in Twizel, details twenty-odd walks (30min–4hr). The forests flank wide valleys cut by surging rivers and separated by narrow mountain ranges, with short tussock grasslands predominating around the lakes and lowlands.

If you become enamoured with the lake and forests, or simply want to stay and ski or tramp, *Lake Ohau Lodge*, on the southwestern shore of the lake, a 25km drive from SH8 along the Lake Ohau Road (☎ & fax 03/438 9885; dorms ①, rooms & chalets ②–③; camping $7 per person), offers a wide variety of **accommodation**. Breakfast and dinner are available here, too.

OHAU SKIFIELD

Ohau Skifield, about 42km southwest of Twizel, off SH8 (July–Oct; ☎03/438 9885), is a small high-country (1033m) field with powder snow and uncrowded slopes which, as a part of the Main Divide, has reliable snowfall. There are several slopes catering for all standards of skier and snowboarder, with the added bonus of spectacular views of Lake Ohau. The *Lake Ohau Lodge* (see above) provides **accommodation** near the field, while the **Ohau Ski Lodge** on the field has no accommodation but does offer log burners, a sun deck with panoramic views, café and shop. **Equipment rental** is available at the field and lift passes cost $39 per day, with access provided by **bus** from the Lake Ohau Lodge ($15 return); otherwise, transport can be arranged by phoning the skifield information number (see above). Learners' **packages**, with gear rental and passes thrown in, start at $25 for ninety minutes.

Omarama and around

A crossroads town at the heart of the Waitaki Valley, on the edge of the McKenzie Basin, **OMARAMA** lies 30km south of Twizel. Sitting at the junction of SH8, which continues south to Cromwell, and SH83 to Oamaru, it is also on the main tourist route between Christchurch and Queenstown, via Mount Cook. The town itself has little to offer, with the nearby **Clay Cliffs Scenic Reserve** and the excursions offered by the local gliding club providing the main reasons to stop.

Arrival, information and accommodation

Regular Canride **buses** plying the Timau–Twizel–Oamaru loop stop in Omarama, as do services of the major national bus companies, all dropping off at the **visitor centre** in the middle of town at the junction of SH8 and SH83 (Mon–Fri 9am–4.40pm, Sat 10am–4pm; ☎03/438 9610), which provides leaflets, advice, accommodation reservations, bus bookings and trips. The visitor centre also rents out **bikes** for about $10 per hour.

As befits a passing-through kind of town, **accommodation** in Omarama is more geared to stopovers than to kicking back for a few days. The most conducive place is *Buscot Station*, about 8km north of Omarama on SH8 (they'll arrange pick-ups if you book ahead; ☎03/438 9646; dorms ①, rooms ②), a merino sheep farm where **backpacker** accommodation is provided in the old shearers' quarters, surrounded by a beautifully kept garden. Otherwise, you're faced with the usual choice of **campsite**, motel, or the local pub. *Omarama Holiday Park*, at the junction of SH8 and SH83 (☎03/438 9875; tent sites $18 for two, on-site vans & cabins ②–④) is an expansive site with sheltering trees and modern well-kept facilities. A rambling old colonial building on SH83, 200m away from the junction with SH8, the *Omarama Hotel* (☎03/438 9713; ③) has clean basic **rooms** – a good bet so long as you don't mind some noise from the bar below. The most expensive place in town is the *Ahuriri Motel*, on the corner of SH83 and Ahuriri Drive, 500m from the junction with SH8 (☎03/438 9451; ⑤), with comfortable and clean **motel** units in a rejuvenated building.

The Town and around

The name Omarama is Maori, and roughly translates as "place of light", but the town is short and squat with a population of just 300 – maybe it's the wrong kind of light. The settlement is mostly used as a way-station for picking up supplies, but there's one curiosity worth visiting if you're here in summer. Situated 10km back up SH8 towards Twizel then west for 4km up the Henburn Road, the **Clay Cliffs Scenic Reserve** (Nov–Feb only, dawn–dusk; $5 per car; ☎03/438 9428) is a combination of bare pinnacles and angular ridges separated by narrow ravines and canyons. The braided Ahuriri River provides a picturesque backdrop to this eerie landscape of badland erosion – created when a 100m uplift caused by the Ostler Fault exposed gravels, which became differentially weathered.

The Maori name for the clay cliffs is *Paritea*, meaning white or light-coloured cliff, and they were so named by Araiteuru, who brought the *kumara* sweet potatoes from Hawaiki. The cliffs provided natural shelter for moa hunters, with several earth ovens indicative of early Maori settlement. If the weather is wet, four-wheel-drive is advisable to negotiate the road to the cliffs – or join a guided tour run by Omarama Safari Tours (☎03/438 9725; 1hr 30min; $25).

The northwesterly winds that blow across the basin make Omarama a fine spot for **gliding**, and the High Country Gliding Club (20–30min; $125; ☎03/438 9621) takes advantage of the reliable wind and flat surrounds to provide spectacular flights in two-seater gliders. The land and rivers around Omarama are also prime territory for hunting chamois and red deer, and fly fishing for trout and salmon. The fish and the venison are delicious, but no one seems to know what to do with the chamois – except hang their heads on walls. Bookings for fly fishing (2hr 30min; $90, including licence) can be made through Omarama visitor centre.

Eating and drinking

A slightly unusual blackboard menu at the *Oasis Tearooms*, near the SH8–SH83 junction (daily Oct–Feb 7am–9pm; March–Sept 8am–9pm; licensed) includes such exotica

THE WAITAKI VALLEY HYDROELECTRIC SCHEME

The **Waitaki Hydroelectric Scheme** is made up of twelve power stations, built between 1925 and 1981, and currently provides nearly one-third of the nation's power. The scheme has its origins in the work of the engineer Peter Seton Hay, who in 1904 submitted a report to the New Zealand government indicating the extraordinary hydro-electric potential of the country, in particular the headwater lakes of the Waitaki river: Tekapo, Pukaki and Ohau. Construction of the Waitaki Power Station began some 24 years later. Most awesome of the stations are the Benmore, Aviemore and Waitaki, all ranged along the Waitaki River **east of Omarama**.

The nearest to Omarama, 15km away on SH83, is the earth-built **Benmore Dam** (daily 10am–4pm, tours Tues, Thurs, & Sun at 11am, 1pm & 3pm, or on request; 1hr 15min; free; ☎03/3438 7848). The tours take you around the control room and generators, past lots of gushing water and views from the top of the dam. The scale of the dam is quite breathtaking, and you can walk or drive to the top; there is also a loop track with distant views of Mount Cook. **Aviemore Dam**, between Otematata and Kurow, supports SH83, and lay-bys on either side enable you to admire its construction. Alongside the dam is a trout- and salmon-spawning canal, with the lake glinting aquamarine against the mountains. About 20km south of Aviemore Dam on SH83, **Waitaki Power Station** is the oldest station on the river, with good views from a platform just beyond the dam, near an immense grey 17-tonne turbine used in 1941 to drive the generators.

as satay and Asian-influenced soups, as well as pita and foccaccia **sandwiches** and a great-value $9 cooked breakfast. Still in town, both the *Omarama Lodge* and the *Omarama Hotel* have capacious dining rooms that serve up large but uninspiring lunches and **dinners** at reasonable prices.

The Lindis Pass and the Waitaki Valley

Travelling on from Omarama on SH8 towards Wanaka, Cromwell and Queenstown (see Chapter 13), you'll cross the **Lindis Pass**, a rewarding scenic drive on narrow roads through predominantly tussock and grassland, though in bad weather it can feel distinctly foreboding.

The **route to Oamaru** on the east coast is an easier drive, following SH83 as it passes through a string of small settlements, which are surprisingly evenly spaced along the **Waitaki Valley**. The valley itself has been irrevocably changed by a mammoth hydroelectric scheme and the lakes it created (see box above).

The first settlement you come to, 26km from Omamara, is **OTEMATATA**, with little to offer except the *Otematata Motor Hotel* (☎03/438 7899; ⑤), which overlooks Lake Aviemore and provides accommodation, dining and a bar. **KUROW**, 30km further along SH83, is regarded as a fisherman's paradise. Twin wooden bridges (dating from 1880) span the salmon- and trout-filled Waitaki River, and there are a few limestone buildings of some grandeur in the settlement itself. Another 23km on, **DUNTROON** provides another chance to cut across to the goldfields area: a gentler route than the Lindis Pass, **Dansey's Pass Road** to **Naseby** dates from prospecting days. Just off this road, about 9km from Duntroon, are the weird limestone formations of **Elephant Rocks**, which are often used by rockclimbers and abseilers.

Pressing on from Duntroon, the junction with the main east-coast highway (SH1) is just 35km away, and **Oamaru** (see p.532) is a further 8km south.

travel details

Trains

Arthur's Pass to: Christchurch (1 daily; 2hr 5min); Greymouth (1 daily; 2hr 5min).

Christchurch to: Arthur's Pass (1 daily; 2hr 5min).

Buses

Arthur's Pass to: Christchurch (2 daily; 2hr 10min); Greymouth (2 daily; 2hr).

Ashburton to: Fairlie (1 daily; 1hr); Geraldine (1 daily; 50min); Methven (1 daily; 45min); Mount Cook (1 daily; 3hr 10min).

Christchurch to: Arthur's Pass (2 daily; 2hr 10min); Fairlie (1 daily; 3hr 15min); Geraldine (1 daily; 2hr 5min); Hanmer Springs (2 daily; 2hr); Methven (2 daily; 1hr 30min); Mount Cook (1 daily; 5hr 30min); Tekapo (1 daily; 4hr 10min).

Fairlie to: Christchurch (1 daily; 3hr 15min); Tekapo (2 daily; 1hr); Timaru (1 daily; 50min).

Geraldine to: Christchurch (1 daily; 2hr 5min); Fairlie (2 daily; 35min).

Hanmer Springs to: Christchurch (2 daily; 2hr); Murchison (1 daily; 2hr 30min).

Methven to: Christchurch (2 daily; 1hr 30min); Geraldine (2 daily; 1hr 30min).

Mount Cook to: Ashburton (1 daily; 3hr 10min); Christchurch (1 daily; 5hr 30min); Queenstown (3 daily; 4hr); Tekapo (2 daily; 1hr 20min); Twizel (2 daily; 1hr).

Oamarama to: Oamaru (1 daily; 2hr); Queenstown (2 daily; 2hr 20mins); Twizel (3 daily; 35min).

Tekapo to: Christchurch (1 daily; 4hr 10min); Fairlie (2 daily; 1hr); Mount Cook (2 daily; 1hr 20min); Twizel (2 daily; 3hr).

Twizel to: Mount Cook (2 daily; 1hr); Omarama (3 daily; 35 min).

Flights

Mount Cook to: Auckland (1 daily; 2hr 55min); Christchurch (1 daily; 45min); Queenstown (4 daily; 40min); Rotorua (1 daily; 3hr 25min); Taupo (1 daily; 5hr); Te Anau (1 daily; 1hr 25min); Wanaka (2 daily; 1hr 20min); Wellington (8 daily; 1hr).

Church of the Good Shepherd, Lake Tekapo

Foxgloves, Wanaka

Mackay Falls, Milford Track

Hooker sea lions, Catlins Coast

Ski plane, Tasman Glacier, Mount Cook
National Park

Commercial Hotel, Murchison,
West Coast

Fox Glacier

Kea

TranzAlpine train approaching Arthur's Pass

St Paul's Cathedral and Town Hall, Dunedin

Post Office, Arrowtown

Mirror Lakes, Fiordland National Park

Queenstown

Jetboat on the Shotover River

CHAPTER ELEVEN

DUNEDIN TO STEWART ISLAND

The southeastern corner of the South Island contains some of the least-visited parts of New Zealand, yet, hidden away here are a couple of real gems. The first is the attractive city of **Dunedin**, lying 400km south of Christchurch on SH1. Once the commercial and cultural centre of the country, this harbourside city was made prosperous by the discovery of **gold** in the craggy mountains of Otago's hinterland in 1861. Today Dunedin is New Zealand's fourth-largest city, and still a seat of learning and culture, influenced by its university and strong Scottish tradition. From here down to Stewart Island, local accents are marked by a distinctive Scots "burr", the only true regional variation in the country. Within easy reach of the city is the inviting **Otago Peninsula**, an important wildlife haven where you can observe at close range a variety of marine life and seabirds, including **penguins** and even rarer **albatross**. South from Dunedin stretches the second highlight, the wild **Catlins Coast**, a large protected reserve reaching towards New Zealand's southernmost city of Invercargill. This is a magical, virtually forgotten region, home to several rare species and offering dramatically varied scenery, from hills covered with dense native forest to a shoreline vigorously indented with rocky bays, long sweeps of sand and unusual geological formations.

On the South Island's southern tip and bordered by rich pastureland, lies **Invercargill**. Servicing Southland's prosperous farming communities and New Zealand's export industry, it acts as the springboard to the country's third island, the comparatively small **Stewart Island**. Attracting as yet only limited numbers, the island is a growing tourist destination, with its blanket of virgin rainforest offering a tramper's paradise. Others come for a drink in New Zealand's southernmost pub, or to spot kiwi in the wild, on the only organized trip of its kind in the world.

Generally, the **best time to visit** the region is during the summer months (Oct–April), when you're most likely to enjoy warm, though changeable, weather, with

---

ACCOMMODATION PRICES

Accommodation listed in this guide has been categorized into one of nine price bands, as set out below. The rates quoted represent the **cheapest available** double or twin **room** – except for category ①, which are per-person rates for a dorm bed; fees for **tent sites** and **DOC huts** are also per-person, unless otherwise stated.

① under $20 per person	④ $60–80	⑦ $140–180
② under $40 per room	⑤ $80–100	⑧ $180–240
③ $40–60	⑥ $100–140	⑨ over $240

For more on accommodation, see p.33.

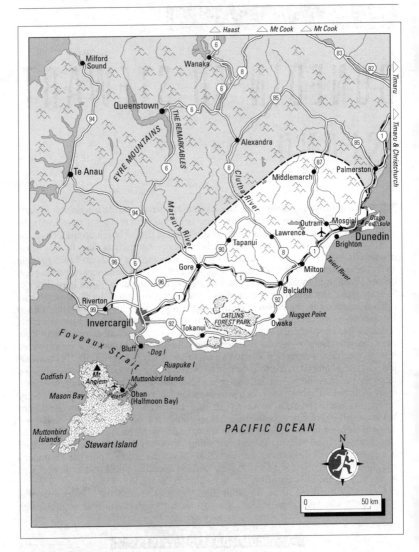

mid-summer temperatures averaging around 19°C in Dunedin. You'll also catch the best of the wildlife, coinciding with the breeding season of many species. Kiwis from more northern parts take great delight in condemning the **climate** of the southern South Island, describing a permanently harsh, cold and rain-lashed landscape – but this is an exaggeration. It's true, though, that the further south you go, the wetter it gets. The Catlins and Invercargill get their highest rainfall in the spring (Sept–Oct), while Stewart Island has showers most days in between bursts of sunshine.

Getting around is a straightforward business. The main east-coast train route connects Christchurch with Invercargill via Dunedin, and regular bus services link all the major towns as well as crossing the island to Queenstown and the West Coast. Stewart Island is served by ferries and planes from Invercargill and by plane from Dunedin. To do the region justice, allow a minimum of three days for Dunedin and the Otago Peninsula, a day or two in the Catlins and at least a couple on Stewart Island.

Dunedin and around

A welcoming and pretty place, **DUNEDIN** is hilly but manageable in size, and blessed with numerous parks and gardens, a temperate, if changeable, climate, and pleasant beaches. Known as the "Edinburgh of the South", its name is a Gaelic translation of its Scottish counterpart, and it shares the same street and suburb names. Despite a compact city centre, Dunedin's official boundaries stretch far beyond its confining hills to accommodate a total population of around 120,000.

The city is home to **Otago University**, the first such institution in New Zealand, founded in 1871 and still occupying a substantial area near the city centre. The presence of eighteen thousand students contributes to a lively arts scene, helping to consolidate Dunedin's long-held reputation as a cultural and intellectual centre. To see the city at its busiest, visit during term time (Feb–June & mid-July to Oct) when the **nightlife**, in particular, takes off, with students packing the bars, pubs and clubs, which foster Dunedin's thriving local music scene, known as the "Dunedin Sound". There are also a number of **festivals** during the year, including two internationally recognized film festivals (April & July); the largest professional craft show in New Zealand (late Sept–early Oct); the two-week-long Dunedin Festival, celebrating the region (February); and Scottish Week, commemorating the city's cultural roots (March). Springtime sees Dunedin ablaze with colour as the many **rhododendrons**, for which it is famous, burst into bloom.

Dunedin's **architecture** is another defining characteristic, dating from the city's foundation in 1848 and, in particular, the boom years of the 1860s gold rush. Its streets brim with elegant and carefully preserved Victorian and Edwardian buildings: mansions and villas (many with whimsical towers and turrets), rows of terraced houses, churches with spires, an ornate cathedral and huge neo-Gothic piles. A variety of local stone was used in construction, ranging from bluestone, a hard, dark volcanic stone quarried near the city to a pleasing creamy limestone originating in Oamaru to the north.

The jewel in Dunedin's crown, though, is its long sheltered **harbour**, site of two working ports and home to a rich variety of wildlife. Dunedin sits at the head of the bay, all but encircled by rugged hills, formed ten million years ago by a series of volcanic eruptions. Halfway along the bay's northern shore lies the small and once-thriving **Port Chalmers**, which still attracts a few container ships and supports a tiny community. Dunedin is also a major jumping-off point for the Otago Goldfields (see p.711) which lie on the way to Queenstown but also make a good day-trip out from the city.

Some history

By the time the first wave of Scottish immigrants arrived at the site of modern-day Dunedin, the area was rich in Maori history. Since about 1100 AD, **Maori** had fished the rich coastal waters of nearby bays, travelling inland to hunt moa, duck and freshwater fish, and initiating trade in *pounamu* (greenstone) with other Maori based further north. Eventually they formed a settlement on both sides of the harbour, calling it *Otakou* (pronounced "O-tar-go") and naming the headland at the harbour's entrance after their great chieftain, Taiaroa. Today a well developed marae occupies the Otakou site. Towards the end of the eighteenth century, the area became the scene of a prolonged feud between three related chiefs of the Ngai Tahu tribe, and a general state of conflict lasted many years. The carnage caused by warfare, however, was nothing compared with the havoc wreaked by European diseases brought by the early nineteenth-century **whalers and sealers**, attracted to the only safe anchorage along this stretch of coast. By 1848 the depredations of measles and influenza had reduced the once-considerable Otakou population to a meagre 110. However, intermarriage between Maori and whalers bolstered numbers and formed a resilient cultural mix.

In 1840, the New Zealand Company (see Contexts, p.764) selected the Dunedin area as a suitable site for a planned **Scottish settlement**. Despite the Treaty of Waitangi (designed to preserve the Crown's right of pre-emption), the company was allowed to deal directly with Maori, who were finally persuaded to sell 1620 square kilometres for a meagre sum. On July 31, 1844, the deed was signed on the site of what later became Port Chalmers. In 1848, the migrant ships *John Wickliffe* and *Philip Laing* arrived, led by Captain William Cargill and the Reverend Thomas Burns, nephew of the Scottish poet, Robert Burns. Most of the 344 passengers were staunch Scots Presbyterians but they were soon in the minority, as the following year another seven hundred people joined them, among them English and Irish. However, Scottish fervour was sufficient to stamp a distinct character on the growing town, bequeathing not only fine churches, but also a passionate enthusiasm for education.

In 1861, a lone Australian prospector discovered **gold** at a creek near modern-day Lawrence, about 100km from Dunedin, in Central Otago. Within three months, gold fever struck and diggers poured in from Australia. As a port of entry, Dunedin suddenly found itself at the forefront of an international gold rush and, requiring a larger port area, it expanded onto land reclaimed from the tidal flats. In six months, its population doubled in size; within three years it trebled again, becoming New Zealand's most important city. This was Dunedin's period of unbridled construction, with the new-found wealth used to establish the university, Otago Boys' High School, and Otago Girls' High School. By the 1870s gold mania had largely subsided, but Otago sustained economic primacy through **shipping**, railway development and the efforts of thousands who stayed on to farm. Decline set in during the early years of the twentieth century, when the opening of the Panama Canal in 1914 rerouted British and European trans-Atlantic shipping away from the great colonial-era port of Otago Harbour to the country's northernmost city, Auckland. In the 1980s, however, the improvement in world gold prices and the development of equipment enabling large-scale recovery of gold from low-yielding soils, re-established **mining** in the hinterland. Today you can visit massive mining operations, including the one at Macraes, an hour's drive from Dunedin (see p.724).

Arrival, information and city transport

Dunedin **airport** is served by domestic flights from Auckland, Christchurch, Queenstown and Wellington, as well as international flights direct from Sydney and Brisbane. The airport is located 30km south of the city centre, just off SH1. Several shuttle bus companies operate from the airport to the city centre ($10), meeting each flight and dropping off at accommodation along the way. A taxi ride to the city centre will also set you back about $10. You can change money at the airport **bureau de change** in the main terminal building, which offers the same rate of exchange as the city's banks. Note that no bureaux de change are open in Dunedin at weekends.

The **train station** is centrally located in Anzac Square, off Stuart Street, a major stop on the Tranz Scenic Southerner Christchurch–Invercargill route.

All the long-distance **bus** companies drop off at various points in the city centre: Intercity at the Intercity Travel Centre, 599 Princes St, and Mount Cook Landline at 205 St Andrew St. The South Island's shuttle bus companies – Atomic Shuttles, Southern Link and Ko-Op – terminate at the visitor centre (see p.582).

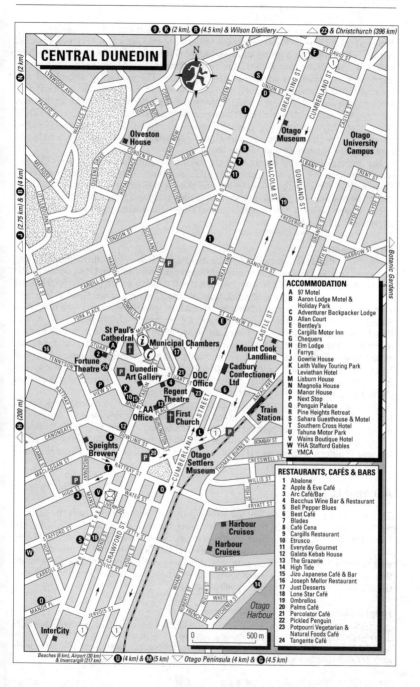

CENTRAL DUNEDIN

9, **K** (2 km), **R** (4.5 km) & Wilson Distillery △   △ **22** & Christchurch (396 km)

△ (2 km)

Olveston House

Otago Museum

Otago University Campus

Botanic Gardens

△ (2.75 km) & **B** (4 km)

P

P

P

St Paul's Cathedral

Fortune Theatre

Municipal Chambers

Mount Cook Landline

Cadbury Confectionery Ltd

Dunedin Art Gallery

Regent Theatre

DOC Office

AA Office

First Church

Train Station

(200 m) **H**

Speights Brewery

Otago Settlers Museum

Harbour Cruises

Harbour Cruises

InterCity

Otago Harbour

| 0 | 500 m |

ACCOMMODATION

- A 97 Motel
- B Aaron Lodge Motel & Holiday Park
- C Adventurer Backpacker Lodge
- D Allan Court
- E Bentley's
- F Cargills Motor Inn
- G Chequers
- H Elm Lodge
- I Farrys
- J Gowrie House
- K Leith Valley Touring Park
- L Leviathan Hotel
- M Lisburn House
- N Magnolia House
- O Manor House
- P Next Stop
- Q Penguin Palace
- R Pine Heights Retreat
- S Sahara Guesthouse & Motel
- T Southern Cross Hotel
- U Tahuna Motor Park
- V Wains Boutique Hotel
- W YHA Stafford Gables
- X YMCA

RESTAURANTS, CAFÉS & BARS

1. Abalone
2. Apple & Eve Café
3. Arc Café/Bar
4. Bacchus Wine Bar & Restaurant
5. Bell Pepper Blues
6. Best Café
7. Blades
8. Café Cena
9. Cargills Restaurant
10. Etrusco
11. Everyday Gourmet
12. Galata Kebab House
13. The Grazerie
14. High Tide
15. Jizo Japanese Café & Bar
16. Joseph Mellor Restaurant
17. Just Desserts
18. Lone Star Café
19. Ombrellos
20. Palms Café
21. Percolator Café
22. Pickled Penguin
23. Potpourri Vegetarian & Natural Foods Café
24. Tangente Café

Beaches (6 km), Airport (30 km) & Invercargill (217 km)   **U** (4 km) & **M** (5 km) ▽ Otago Peninsula (4 km) & **G** (4.5 km)

Information

You can't miss Dunedin's **visitor centre** (mid-Dec to mid-April Mon–Fri 8am–6pm, Sat & Sun 9am–5pm; mid-April to mid-Dec Mon–Fri 8.30am–5pm, Sat & Sun 9am–5pm; ☎03/474 3300) in the grand stone Municipal Chambers that dominate the Octagon, an eight-sided grassland area at the centre of the city. The extremely helpful and well informed staff will book transport, accommodation and tours, and the centre is well stocked with leaflets and maps, including the excellent *Focus on Dunedin* booklet and the *Art and Craft Guide*, which lists the area's many artists and craftspeople. The **DOC** office is at 77 Lower Stuart St (Mon–Fri 9am–5pm; ☎03/477 0677) and has plenty of information on Otago, Fiordland and Mount Aspiring. They also sell hut tickets and passes for the Routeburn and Milford tracks.

For entertainment and events **listings**, the most comprehensive source is the free weekly publication, *Fink*, a complete guide to music, exhibitions and movies in Dunedin. Chiefly aimed at students, it's available all over the city. The parochial *Otago Daily Times* also has a listings section, best in the Friday and Saturday editions, and the visitor centre issues a free monthly paper, *Otago Happenings*, which is full of local attractions and events.

City transport

A number of different companies operate an efficient **bus** system throughout the city – you can pick up free timetables and route maps from the Dunedin City Council on the ground floor of the Civic Centre on the corner of the Octagon and George Street. Most services run daily and on public holidays (except Christmas Day, Good Friday and Easter Sunday), from around 7.30am to 11pm Monday to Saturday and 1pm to 5pm on Sunday. Buses are identified by their route, for example, Octagon–Maori Hill, rather than by numbers. **Fares** are calculated according to the number of zones, with a single one-zone ticket costing $1.10, increasing by about 50¢ per extra zone; concessions are available at off-peak times on inner-city routes. If you're staying a couple of days or longer, it's a good idea to buy a **Multi-trip Ticket**, which gives ten or more journeys for a ten-percent discount. Most bus drivers sell these tickets direct or you can get them during business hours from the City Council in the Civic Centre.

There are several **taxi** ranks in the city centre (see p.594 for locations and details of taxi companies). If you're **driving**, note that strict parking restrictions are enforced in the city centre with meter parking operating Monday to Saturday (see p.593 for details of car parks). A one-way system operates through the inner city, connecting the northern and southern sections of SH1 and affecting Cumberland, Castle, Great King and Crawford streets.

Accommodation

There's a broad choice of accommodation in Dunedin, most of it in or near the city centre. The **hotels** are located in the heart of town, but with a couple of exceptions, are bland affairs designed to attract businesspeople. Several **motels** line George Street, with others dotted around the city, while the best B&Bs and homestays are in the hillside suburbs 2–5km from the centre. The three well equipped **campsites** are no more than a couple of kilometres out of town and two are on bus routes. In summer, **booking ahead** is advisable, wherever you're staying.

Hotels

Bentley's, 137 St Andrew St (☎03/477 0572, fax 477 0293). A fairly luxurious, modern place, right in the heart of the city, offering double rooms, a couple of studios and a family unit, all with private facilities. There's an airy restaurant, a bar and café on the premises, while next door is the lively *Rosie O'Grady's* bar (see p.592), owned by the hotel. ⑥.

Leviathan, 65 Lower High St, cnr of Cumberland St (☎03/477 3160, fax 477 2385). The most atmospheric hotel in Dunedin, and the best value. Built in 1884, it's grand yet comfortable and just a short stroll from both the Octagon and the train station. Accommodation ranges from spacious suites and self-contained studios to standard en-suite and budget rooms. There's also a bar and high-quality, moderately priced licensed restaurant. Off-street parking. ③–⑥.

Southern Cross, cnr of Princes St & High St (☎03/477 0752, fax 477 5776). Huge hotel in the heart of the business district, five minutes' walk from the Octagon. Three fully licensed restaurants and two bars, a fitness centre, Sky TV and off-street parking. ⑧.

Wains Boutique Hotel, 310 Princes St (☎03/477 1155, fax 477 7737). A corporate crowd frequents this central but characterless hotel. Thoroughly modern rooms hide behind an ornate nineteenth-century facade. On-site café, two restaurants and a fully-equipped gym. ⑤.

Motels

Allan Court, 590 George St, cnr of Union St (☎03/477 7526, fax 477 4937). Central, modern, upmarket and comfortable, with cookers in all units and a choice of breakfasts for an extra charge. In-house video and guest laundry. ⑤.

Cargills Motor Inn, 678 George St, near cnr of St David St (☎03/477 7983, fax 477 8098). Adjacent to the business district and university, this stylish place offers a peaceful garden setting and a variety of well-appointed rooms equipped with minibars and fridges. The on-site licensed *Garden Restaurant* serves Kiwi and international cuisine. ⑥.

Chequers, 119 Musselburgh Rise (☎ & fax 03/455 0778). Good-value motel in quiet surroundings, five minutes' drive from the centre and close to the peninsula. Its large units are ideally suited to families and there's a playground on the premises. ④.

Farrys, 575 George St (☎03/477 9333, fax 477 9038). An excellent family motel next to the main shopping area offering one-, two- and three-bedroom units, all fully self-contained, plus a free laundry and small playground. Breakfast available ($7–14.50 extra per person). ⑤.

97 Motel, 97 Moray Place (☎03/477 2050, reservations only 0800/909 797). The best-located, friendliest motel in town with spacious, gleaming units, each equipped with a microwave. ④–⑤.

Sahara, 619 George St (☎03/477 6662, fax 479 2551). A motel section round the back of the guesthouse of the same name (see below); there are ten standard self-contained units, and motel guests can order breakfast for an extra $10–15. ④.

B&Bs and homestays

Gowrie House, 7 Gowry Place, Roslyn (☎03/477 2103). Excellent rural and city views from this small, cosy, turn-of-the-century house set on a hill five minutes' drive from the centre and on the Octagon to Maori Hill/Prospect Park bus route. Two double rooms, both light and airy with big windows and shared facilities. Three-course dinners available for $20 per person, or $35 a couple. ④.

Lisburn House, 15 Lisburn Ave, Caversham (☎ & fax 03/455 8888). Luxurious and beautifully preserved Victorian Gothic house in a suburb ten minutes' drive south of the city. Each of the three distinctly styled and spacious rooms has a four-poster bed, fine linen, fresh flowers and a private bathroom. Not suitable for children. ⑦.

Magnolia House, 18 Grendon St, Maori Hill (☎03/467 5999). A spacious Victorian villa, set in a large garden in the leafy suburb of Maori Hill, 2km north of the Octagon (courtesy car available). Three well appointed doubles with shared facilities, and two house cats. ④.

Pine Heights Retreat, 431 Pine Hill Rd (☎03/473 9558, fax 477 4502). Tranquil rural setting 4.5km from central Dunedin. An inviting blend of Scandinavian and Kiwi hospitality. The two double rooms share facilities and there's a courtesy car and bus connection from the centre (Octagon to Pine Hill). ⑤.

Sahara Guesthouse & Motel, 619 George St (☎03/477 6662, fax 479 2551). Spacious 1863 guesthouse where most rooms have shared facilities. TV lounge, off-street parking. ④.

Hostels

Adventurer Backpacker Lodge, 37 Dowling St (☎03/477 7367). A convivial new hostel in the heart of the city, with off-street parking. Dorms ①, rooms ②.

Chalet Backpackers, 296 High St (☎03/479 2075). Central, comfortable hostel with a great atmosphere and excellent kitchen and dining facilities. Four-bed dorms, plus single and double rooms. Pool room and free bikes. Dorms ①, rooms ②.

Elm Lodge, 74 Elm Row (☎03/474 1872). An airy, clean, 1930s house on a hill near the centre. Free linen and pick-up service. Dorms ①, rooms ②.

Manor House, 28 Manor Place (☎03/477 0484). Well-equipped and beautifully kept colonial house on a hill fifteen minutes' walk south of the Octagon. Free pick-up service. Dorms ①, rooms ②.

Next Stop, 2 View St (☎ & fax 03/477 0447). A slightly spartan converted church hall in an excellent location, just off Moray Place. Dorms ①, rooms ②.

Penguin Palace, corner of Vogel St and Rattray St (☎ & fax 03/479 2175). This friendly place is the biggest backpackers in town, occupying an old building only three blocks from the Octagon. Bike rental and free pick-up service. Dorms ①, rooms ②.

Stafford Gables YHA, 71 Stafford St (☎ & fax 03/474 1919). One of the best YHAs in New Zealand. A large, turn-of-the-century homestead ten minutes' walk from the Octagon. The rooms are large, doubles come with balconies and there are also family rooms. Free linen; bike rental available. Dorms ①, rooms ②.

YMCA, 54 Moray Place (☎03/477 9555). Right in the city centre, with eight fully self-contained flats offering twin rooms and four-bed dorms. Open Dec to mid-Feb only. Dorms ①, rooms ②.

Campsites and motorparks

Aaron Lodge Motel & Holiday Park, 162 Kaikorai Valley Rd (☎03/476 4725). A sheltered, fairly spacious and well-tended site, set in hills 2.5km west of the city centre. Facilities include a spa pool and playground. Tent sites $9, powered sites $10, cabins, units & flats ②–④.

Leith Valley Touring Park, 103 Malvern St (☎03/467 9936). A small, pleasant campsite beside a creek at the foot of bush-clad hills, 2km from the centre. The site is served by the Octagon to Garden Village bus on weekdays and there's a 24hr grocery within walking distance. Tent sites $9, on-site vans & flats ②–③.

Tahuna Motor Park, 41 Victoria Rd (☎ & fax 03/455 4690). Lying alongside St Kilda Beach, this well-appointed park is five minutes' drive from the city centre and served by the Octagon to St Kilda bus. Standard and more comfortable en-suite cabins. There's a seven-day camp store. Tent sites $8, powered sites $11, cabins ②–③.

The City

Day or night, the hub of Dunedin's activity is the **Octagon**, a green, tree-filled space in the heart of the city, bordered by historic buildings and circled by Moray Place. Restaurants, offices, banks, bars, clubs and most of the sights are concentrated around it and the **shopping district** stretches immediately north and south along George Street and Princes Street. Further north lies the **university area** and the expanse of the **Botanic Garden**. To the east, is the head of **Otago Harbour**, a sheltered inlet 22km long and no wider than a river in places. The waters are shared by windsurfers, yachts and sightseeing boats, and occasionally dolphins and whales. Two sandy **beaches** lie a short bus ride south from the city centre in the suburbs of St Clair and St Kilda. For an overview of the city, head for the **lookout points** on the hills around Dunedin (see box on p.588).

The Octagon

The **Octagon** was originally laid out in 1846 by Charles Kettle, the Chief Surveyor of the New Zealand Company, who subsequently died in a typhoid epidemic that swept the city during the 1862 gold rush. Today, following a substantial face-lift in the 1980s, it's a mixture of modern and beautifully preserved buildings overlooking grassland and trees, presided over by a statue of Robert Burns, a potent symbol of Dunedin's Scottish origins and literary associations. Every Friday (10am–4pm; also Sat Oct–Feb & daily in Dec; closed Dec 26–Jan10), the area spills over with **market** stalls selling locally made crafts, such as stained glass, pottery, woodwork and jewellery, while live bands provide free entertainment.

Dominating the Octagon is the **Municipal Chambers** building, a grand, classical structure with a clock tower, which originally opened in 1880. Constructed from limestone dramatically offset against volcanic bluestone, it's a fine example of a recurring combination of materials that's seen throughout the city and also of the handiwork of Scottish architect Robert A. Lawson, who designed many public buildings in Dunedin. Just behind the Municipal Chambers rise the twin white stone spires of **St Paul's Cathedral** (guided tours Mon–Sat 10.30am, also Tues–Thurs 2.30pm; free), one of Dunedin's finest buildings and the seat of Anglican worship in the city. This impressive Gothic Revival edifice, entirely constructed from Oamaru stone was designed by English architect Edmund Spedding and consecrated in 1919. Inside, the 65-metre-high stone-vaulted ceiling is the only one of its kind in New Zealand, and much of the stained glass in the impressive windows is original; the stark modern chancel and altar were added in 1971. One reason for taking a guided tour is to gain access to the passageway high up above the aisles, which gives a superb view of the whole interior.

Across Upper Stuart Street from the Municipal Chambers and just off Princes Street, the spacious and gleaming **Dunedin Public Art Gallery** (Mon–Fri 10am–5pm, Sat & Sun 11am–5pm; $4) was completed in 1996, breathing new life into the Octagon. The gallery occupies six Victorian buildings, refurbished to create an airy, modern, split-level space. Its main strength is a rotated collection of early and contemporary New Zealand works, including many by Frances Hodgkins, though you're hard pressed to find anything truly remarkable. There's also a small international assemblage that boasts a Monet. The gallery regularly hosts temporary international shows.

South, across Princes Street from the art gallery, is the 1874 facade of the **Regent Theatre**, a one-time hotel that was transformed into a cinema in 1928 and, later, into a theatre. Today it's a venue for international shows and the Royal New Zealand Ballet, as well as live music (see p.592). Inside, elaborate nineteenth-century plasterwork and marble staircases blend with colourful 1920s stained-glass windows and geometric balustrades.

Behind the Regent Theatre, near the intersection with Burlington Street, soars the delicate, 54-metre stone spire of the **First Church of Otago**, a landmark easily spotted from many points around the city. The edifice, widely recognized as the most impressive of New Zealand's nineteenth-century churches, was designed in neo-Gothic style by Scottish architect Robert A. Lawson. Two other small, wooden churches had already occupied this site, and when Lawson's version was consecrated in 1873 it was the first Presbyterian church to open in Otago. Of particular interest inside are a wooden gabled ceiling and, above the pulpit, a brightly coloured rose window, while another large window commemorates those who fell in World War I.

South and east of the Octagon

Less than five minutes' walk southeast of the Octagon, a cluster of buildings at 220 Cumberland Street contains the **Otago Settlers Museum** (Mon–Fri 10am–5pm, Sat & Sun 1–5pm; $4), which catalogues two hundred years of social history in Dunedin and Otago, drawing from an exhaustive collection of artefacts, paintings and photographs. Highlights include the chance to sit on a penny-farthing; a restored double-ended Fairlie steam engine, one of the two locomotives that hauled the first Christchurch–Dunedin express train south from Oamaru in 1878; and the "Portrait Gallery", whose walls are plastered with black-and-white photographs of the region's early settler families. Also worth a look is "Window on a Chinese Past", providing an insight into the lives of the legions of Chinese who left their families behind to seek a fortune in the Otago Goldfields, many of them staying for years (see box on p.716 for more on the Chinese experience in New Zealand).

A stone's throw away from the museum, near the junction of Castle Street and Anzac Avenue, **Dunedin Railway Station** is an imposing building, faced with pale Oamaru stone. Opened in 1906, the station was designed by George A. Troup, and constructed on reclaimed swampland, which made it an extraordinary feat of engineering for its day. The exterior, complete with towers, turrets and minarets, is grand enough, but the real surprise lies inside. The main foyer, which has been preserved in its original state, gleams with majolica wall tiles made especially for New Zealand Rail by Royal Doulton, in gentle tones of green, yellow and cream. A fine, classical, china frieze of cherubs and foliage encircles the room, and elaborate tilework decorates the ticket booths. The mosaic floor celebrates the steam engine and consists of over 700,000 tiny squares of Royal Doulton porcelain. Upstairs on the balcony, a stained-glass window at each end depicts an approaching train, whose headlights gleam, no matter which angle you look at them.

Dunedin's three well-established food and drink factories run guided tours and two are in this part of town. The most popular, not least because it's free and offers plenty of opportunities to sample the product, is at **Cadbury Confectionery**, 280 Cumberland St (☎03/467 7800). The hour-long tours run Monday to Friday at 1.30pm and 2.30pm (except for a week or so around Christmas), and it's essential to book at least a week in advance, especially during school holidays. After a short video on confectionery manufacture, you're led through the factory, with frequent chocolate-tasting stops.

Only those seriously interested in the brewing process should bother with a tour of **Speights Brewery**, one of New Zealand's oldest and smallest breweries, at 200 Rattray St (Mon–Thurs at 10.30am; 2hr; $5; book on ☎03/477 9480). The tour is overly long, accompanied by a good deal of walking up and down stairs, and dull hard-sell commentary about the company. The flipside is a chance to see traditional brewing techniques close-up, and your patience is rewarded with two glasses of lager, bitter or ale in the boardroom at the end of the tour. See p.587 for the Wilson Distillery tour.

North of the Octagon

A few minutes' walk north of the Octagon, at 419 Great King St, the **Otago Museum** (Mon–Fri 10am–5pm, Sat & Sun 1–5pm; donations requested) is a large and well-funded museum on three floors. You can easily spend half a day here, ambling through excellent and varied displays of Maori and Pacific Islands anthropology, New Zealand natural history, archeological finds and decorative arts from all over the world. Part of the ground floor contains a separate, hands-on interactive science centre called "Discovery World" ($6, children $3), which is primarily aimed at children. The most impressive exhibits are the huge collection of southern **Maori artefacts** and a group of **moa skeletons**.

OLVESTON

At 42 Royal Terrace, ten minutes' walk northwest of the Octagon, lies Dunedin's showpiece historic home of **Olveston** (guided tours only: daily 9.30am, 10.45am, noon, 1.30pm, 2.45pm & 4pm; 1hr; $10, booking essential; ☎03/477 3320). Contained within the walls of this fine Edwardian house is a treasure trove of art and exquisite antiques collected from all over the world by one family and left just as they were when the last of the lineage passed away.

The collection was gradually assembled by a wealthy, Jewish mercantile family, the **Theomins**, who lived here from 1906 and were passionately interested in travel, art and music. The longest surviving member of the family, Dorothy, outlived her parents and her brother, and on her death in 1966, bequeathed the house and its contents to the City of Dunedin.

Built in 1904–1906 for David Theomin and his wife, Marie, the Jacobean-style **house** is reminiscent of the English Arts and Crafts Movement. London architect Sir Ernest

George filled the house with extraordinary decorative detail, incorporating such features as polished wooden floors, stained-glass windows, wood panelling, fine brass fittings and stairways leading to mezzanine galleries. A particularly striking piece of craftsmanship is the oak staircase in the Grand Hall, made in England and constructed without the use of nails. The house was also a masterpiece of modernity for its time, being among the first to be fitted with the conveniences of central heating, heated towel rails and an in-house telephone system.

THE UNIVERSITY

Less than ten minutes' walk north of the city centre lies New Zealand's oldest university, founded by Scottish settlers in 1869. Based on the design of Glasgow University, the **University of Otago** quickly expanded into a complex of imposing Gothic bluestone buildings, foremost among them the registry building with its **clock tower**, an academic icon and one of the most-photographed landmarks in Dunedin. Today the campus covers several blocks between Albany and Dundas streets in one direction, and Cumberland and Clyde streets in the other, and is set in spacious grounds with the Water of Leith, a small river, winding through it. The **St David Gallery** on St David Street (Mon–Fri 10am–3pm), across the weir from the registry building, acts as an information office for visitors.

Inside the Hocken Building, on the corner of Castle Street and Union Street, is the **Hocken Library** (Mon–Fri 9.30am–5pm, Tues also 6–9pm, Sat 9am–noon; free), which opened in 1910 and is the largest research university library in New Zealand. Its impressive collection of books, manuscripts, paintings and photographs relating to New Zealand and the Pacific was originally assembled by Dr Thomas Morland Hocken, a Dunedin physician and one of the country's first historians. Details of exhibitions held in the library gallery are regularly advertised in the *Otago Daily Times*.

A stroll through the campus from Union Street to Leith Street will take you past the key buildings or you can join **Maur's Guided Walking Tour** (daily by arrangement, ☎03/476 3548; 45min; $5), which departs from the University Union on Cumberland Street, opposite the Otago Museum. This leisurely stroll takes in most of the university, including professorial houses, the original medical and dental schools and the Hocken Library.

THE BOTANIC GARDEN

Established in 1863 at the far northern end of the inner city, the well-tended **Dunedin Botanic Garden** (sunrise–sunset; free) lies at the foot of Signal Hill. The hilly Upper Garden contains an expansive Rhododendron Dell, where well-established specimens grow among native bush, flowering trees and plants. This is the star attraction during the city's annual **Rhododendron Week** in the third week of October. On the hills there's also an arboretum, a native plant collection and a modern aviary complex, home to native birds such as kea and kaka, as well as exotic birds from all over the world. The flat Lower Garden features exotic trees, Winter Garden conservatories (daily 10am–4pm), an Alpine House (daily 9am–4pm), a rose garden and a well-equipped playground. The garden's restaurant (daily 9am–4pm) serves substantial meals for under $10. Access to the Lower Gardens car park is from Cumberland Street, while the Upper Gardens car park is on Lovelock Avenue.

THE WILSON DISTILLERY AND BALDWIN STREET

Near the Botanic Garden, at 8 Willowbank (off Great King Street) is **Wilson Distillers**, New Zealand's only whisky distillery and the southernmost in the world. Book ahead through the visitor centre in the Octagon for the ninety-minute **guided tour** (Mon–Fri 2.45pm; $6). A short video at the start describes the history of whisky making in Dunedin, following Scottish methods, and all stages of distillation. You'll see the process in action in the noisy distillery area, before finally being allowed a drop of "the good stuff" and a taste of whisky liqueur.

Dunedin has the dubious honour of containing the steepest street in the world. In the northern part of town, off North Road, **Baldwin Street** has a maximum gradient of 1 in 2.9, an angle of over 38°. You can walk up to the top in about five minutes, but the views aren't anything special. During the annual "Gutbuster" event in mid-February (part of the Dunedin Festival) contestants run to the top and back down again – the current record is around two minutes.

Baldwin Street is a short **bus** ride from the city centre: take the Normanby bus from outside the Savoy Building in Princes Street to North Road, which drops you near the Gardens Shopping Centre. Head north along North Road for fifteen minutes; Baldwin Street is the tenth street past the shopping centre.

Dunedin's beaches

Four kilometres south of the city centre, the suburbs of St Kilda and St Clair culminate in a long wild sweep of creamy sand enclosed by two volcanic headlands (served by buses from the corner of the Octagon and Princes Street). **St Clair Beach** is excellent for surfing and is patrolled by lifeguards during the summer. For swimming in calmer waters, there's a large, outdoor, heated saltwater pool (Oct–March Mon–Sat 6am–7pm, Sun 8am–7pm; $2.50), beside the rocky point at the western end of the beach. About halfway along the strip, St Clair merges with **St Kilda Beach**, which is reasonably safe for swimming as long as you keep between the flags. At the beach's eastern end, a

---

WALKS IN THE DUNEDIN AREA

From the city, a variety of walks (1–3hr) lead up to and along the skyline ridges surrounding the harbour, giving spectacular views of tussock-covered hilltops, fine bushland, river valleys and beaches. The DOC publishes factsheets describing each walk, 50¢ from the DOC office or visitor centre. Dunedin's weather is notoriously changeable, so equip yourself with warm clothing and wet-weather gear, just in case.

If these suggestions whet your appetite for tramping, see "Walks on the Otago Peninsula" (p.601) for more routes in the vicinity.

SIGNAL HILL

A fairly gentle walk up Signal Hill (6km return; 1hr ascent, 30min descent), a scenic reserve just north of the Botanic Garden, culminates in a magnificent view over Dunedin, the upper harbour and the sea. At the top (393m), the Centennial Lookout sports two powerful bronze figures symbolizing the past and the future, a commemoration of one hundred years of British sovereignty (1840–1940) following the signing of the Treaty of Waitangi. Embedded in the podium is a tribute to Scotland: a chunk of the rock upon which Edinburgh Castle was built.

To reach the hill from the city centre, follow Great King Street to the northern edge of the Botanic Garden and turn right along Opoho Road for 1.25km. Signal Hill Road, which is the fourth on the left, leads to the top of the hill. The Opoho bus from outside the Savoy Building in Princes Street, will take you up and over Signal Hill and there's a stop at the top.

TUNNEL BEACH

One of the best walks – **Tunnel Beach** (1.5km return; 1hr) – is also the shortest and least strenuous, yet offers breathtaking coastal views of creamy sandstone cliffs and islets weathered into curious shapes. Untouched by lava flows, it offers a glimpse of Dunedin's geology before the volcanic eruptions that changed the landscape. A steep path drops down through bush and pasture to impressive sandstone clifftops and a mag-

headland separates St Kilda from the smaller **Tomahawk Beach**, often dotted with horses and buggies preparing for trotting races at low tide. The best swimming beach in Otago is only 15km south of Dunedin, at **Brighton Bay** (Brighton bus from New World supermarket in Cumberland Street), a combination of sand and rocky outcrops.

Taieri Gorge Railway

One of the world's most dramatic rail lines and a feat of Victorian engineering, the **Taieri Gorge Railway** stretches 77km from Dunedin inland to the high country of Otago, penetrating rugged scenery that is only accessible by train. Constructed between 1879 and 1921, the line extended 235km to Cromwell in its heyday, carrying supplies from Dunedin and transporting farm produce, fruit and livestock back to the port and points north.

Today, as well as offering **day-trips** from the city, the rail line is a good way of heading further inland to the Central Otago Goldfields, or even as far as Queenstown. The train departs from Dunedin Railway Station and you need to book well ahead to be sure of a seat (☎03/477 4449). The train itself is comfortable and air-conditioned, with a mix of modern steel carriages with large panoramic windows, and nostalgic, refurbished 1920s wooden cars. Storage space is available for backpacks and bicycles and there's a licensed snack bar on board.

The most frequent trip is to **Pukerangi**, a peaceful spot 58km from the city, arriving back in Dunedin four hours later (Mon–Sat 2.30pm $49 return; Feb & March also Sun 9.30am). On Sundays in summer the train continues a further 19km to the

nificent sea-arch. Additionally, at low tide, you can walk down the steps of a short tunnel carved through the cliff in the 1870s, which leads to a pretty sandy beach on the other side with sandstone buttresses towering above – a pleasant spot for a picnic. The walk crosses private land and is closed during the lambing season (Sept & Oct).

The route starts from the car park at the end of Green Island Bush Road, some 16km from the centre on the city's southwestern outskirts. The Corstophine bus from the corner of the Octagon and Princes Street will drop you within a kilometre of the start of the walk – get off at Stanhope Crescent.

MOUNT CARGILL

Unrivalled panoramic views of the Dunedin area are the reward for making it to the windy summit of **Mount Cargill** on the city's northeastern outskirts. There are in fact three peaks – Cargill, Holmes and Zion – which to the Maori represent the petrified head and feet of an early Otakou princess. European settlers named the dominant peak after their lay leader, Captain William Cargill.

You can either drive to the summit car park – twenty-minutes from the city centre along Pine Hill Road – and just tackle the network of easy tracks around the summit area, or walk the whole track from Bethunes Gully picnic ground, about 7.5km northeast of the Botanic Gardens (8km return; 3hr). This skirts the mountain's northern flank and climbs steadily to 550m before sidling around to the saddle and onto the summit. To reach the picnic ground by bus catch the Normanby bus from outside the Savoy Building in Princes Street and get off at the junction of North Road and Norwood Street. From here it's about 2km northeast along Norwood Street to the picnic ground.

On the slopes of nearby Mount Holmes, an intriguing ancient rock formation called the **Organ Pipes** can be reached on foot, either from the Mount Cargill summit – following the peaks and saddles of Cargill, Buttar and Holmes (3km return; 90min) – or from a steep track starting at the car park on Old Mount Cargill Road (3km return; 1hr), on the mountain's eastern side (not accessible by public transport). Either way, the route passes through colourful remnant forest to a series of rock columns, formed about ten million years ago by molten lava that cracked as it cooled.

old gold town of **Middlemarch**, a five-hour round trip (Oct–March; $55 return). You can stay overnight around Pukerangi where there are various white-water rafting and horse-trekking activities (details from Dunedin Railway Station). In addition, sections of the abandoned line between Middlemarch and Clyde, deep in the gold country, have been developed for walking and mountain biking; check which sections are open to the public at the DOC office in Dunedin. To get **to Queenstown**, you'll need an Otago Central Connection ticket ($80), which links with a bus at Pukerangi or Middlemarch and follows a scenic route via the shores of Lake Dunstan.

Eating

In a city that's undeniably enthusiastic about food, you'll never be at a loss for somewhere to satisfy your appetite, and you'll seldom need to stray far from the **city centre**. Some of the city's **pubs** also serve reasonably priced food (see p.591). Unless otherwise stated, the places listed below are open daily.

Restaurants

Abalone, 1st Floor, 44 Hanover St, cnr of George St, above the BNZ Bank (☎03/477 6877). Slick, yuppie bar-cum-restaurant with modern metal furnishings, terracotta flooring and lots of glass. Moderately priced drinks, snacks and full meals. Seething with people at weekends; book ahead for dinner. Lunch Mon–Fri, dinner daily.

Bacchus Wine Bar & Restaurant, 1st floor, 12 The Octagon, cnr of Lower Stuart St (☎03/474 0824). A great vantage point overlooking the Octagon from a prestigious historic building. Over fifty international wines, accompanied by moderately priced lunch and dinner. Popular office workers' lunch spot. Closed Sun.

Bell Pepper Blues, 474 Princes St (☎03/474 0973). Highly rated à la carte dinner venue, offering great value for money, despite main-course prices that average $25. The food is Pacific-rim, focusing on New Zealand ingredients, such as venison and salmon. Closed Sun; licensed.

Blades, 450 George St (☎03/477 6548). One of the most reliably good restaurants in town. The moderately priced international cuisine features steak, venison and seafood, on a daily-changing menu. You'll need to book ahead. Dinner only. Closed Wed; BYO.

Cargills Restaurant, *Cargills Motor Inn*, 678 George St (☎03/477 7983). Excellent French cuisine – inexpensive at lunchtime and $20–25 main dishes in the evening. An intimate bar opens out into an attractive tree-filled courtyard and there's live music on summer weekends. Book ahead for dinner. Licensed.

Etrusco, 1st floor, Savoy Building, 8a Moray Place, cnr of George St (☎03/477 3737). Authentic Italian fare presented in an airy and lovingly restored building. Moderate prices and friendly service. Dinner only. Good wine list, also BYO (bottled wine only). Closed Mon.

High Tide, 29 Kitchener St (☎03/477 9784). A quietly romantic and friendly waterside hideaway for evening meals, complemented by great views over the harbour and peninsula. The moderately priced menu consists of imaginative seafood, vegetarian and meat dishes, as well as home-made soups and desserts. Closed Sun; BYO.

Joseph Mellor Restaurant, 1st floor, Otago Polytechnic, cnr York Place and Tennyson St, entrance directly opposite Kavanagh College (☎03/477 3014). Unbelievably cheap, high-quality French/New Zealand cuisine prepared by world-class chefs in a bustling restaurant with one of the best city views in Dunedin. Book a few days ahead. Open early Feb to early Dec Tues–Thurs only noon–1.30pm & 6–9pm. Licensed and BYO.

Just Desserts, 29–31 Bath St (☎03/477 5331). Tucked away off Stuart St, by the Octagon, this cosy place is renowned for its sumptuous desserts, which are served from 5pm, each a meal in itself. Lunchtime snacks and moderately priced dinners. No credit cards. Closed Sun; BYO.

Lone Star Café, 417 Princes St (☎03/474 1955). A proliferation of fake cacti, bogus portraits of Native Americans and high prices does nothing to deter families, in particular, from this Tex-Mex diner. Children eat for around $9 a main course, adults for $20-plus. The fully licensed bar serves Jim Beam and a range of beers. Every cowboy's idea of heaven. Dinner only.

Ombrellos, 10 Clarendon St, off Frederick St (☎03/477 8773). An attractive Mediterranean-style courtyard café/bar in the heart of the university area. Open all day, offering breakfast through to dinner and an affordable wine list. Closed Mon, plus Sun & Tues evenings.

Palms Café, 84 Lower High St, Queens Gardens (☎03/477 6534). Something of an institution among locals, who enjoy its leisurely pace and genteel atmosphere; book ahead. From a turn-of the-century setting (complete with enormous windows and high ceiling), you can feast your eyes on the greenery of Queens Gardens, while tucking into hearty vegetarian, seafood and meat dishes. Two courses for $15.00 (Mon–Fri 5–6.30pm) and a moderately priced, à la carte menu. Dinner only; BYO.

Cafés and snack bars

Apple and Eve Café, 199 Stuart St. A student hangout on the hill just above the visitor centre, focusing mainly on vegetarian food, dished up in motherly portions. Lunch only. Closed Sun; BYO.

Arc Café/Bar, 135 High St. A groovy cyber café with panoramic windows looking into a sculptor's studio. Reasonably priced gourmet snacks. Live bands play every night with top Dunedin acts Fri & Sat. Free email access; Internet $2 for 15mins. Lunch and dinner. Licensed.

Best Café, 30 Stuart St. A local legend, despite the spartan decor, and the best spot for fish and chips, which have been served here for over fifty years. Closed Sat & Sun; no alcohol.

Café Cena, 466 George St. Another student haunt and bigger than it looks, serving an imaginative blend of Mediterranean and Asian foods, and speciality coffees. Closed Sat lunchtime & all day Sun; BYO.

Everyday Gourmet, 446 George St. A deli-cum-café stuffed with specialist cheeses, salami and fine meat pies. Substantial sandwiches at $3.50–5 and excellent coffee. Closed Sun.

Galata Kebab House, 126 Princes St. Authentic, cheap Turkish food to eat in or take away, offering the usual mix of vegetarian dishes, falafels and kebabs, from 11am till late. BYO.

The Grazerie, 356 Moray Place. Locally made Evansdale cheese is the big draw at this café. Cheap breakfasts (from 7.30am), lunches and a $10 two-course dinner. Closed Sun evening; licensed & BYO.

Jizo Japanese Café and Bar, Savoy Building, 56 Princes St. Inexpensive sushi, miso soup, rice dishes and noodle soups to take away, or eat in at this small, split-level café. Lunch and dinner Mon–Sat; licensed & BYO.

Percolator Café, 142 Stuart St. A well-established espresso bar open daily from 9.30am till the early hours. Brunch served Sat & Sun morning ($5.50–7.50), plus full lunch and dinner menu.

Pickled Penguin, 50 Dundas St. A spacious café, occupying an old Methodist church. Young, friendly atmosphere and free newspapers to browse through, but very cold in the winter. Emphasis on Italian dishes. Open daily from 11am till the early hours.

Potpourri Vegetarian and Natural Foods Café, 97 Lower Stuart St, near Moray Place. Established veggie venue got up to look like a church. Wholemeal baking, a big salad bar and great frozen yoghurt to eat in or take away. Closed Sun; no alcohol.

Tangente Café, 111 Moray Place. Organic ingredients only at this welcoming spot overlooking the Octagon. Breakfast ($3–13), all-day brunch (around $13), snacks and light lunches (under $10) and dinners (Thurs & Fri only; under $20) featuring gourmet salads, pasta, burgers and seafood. BYO.

Drinking, nightlife and entertainment

As the evening draws in, Dunedin shifts into a higher gear, especially during term time or one of its many festivals. Drinking is taken seriously here and there's no shortage of **pubs and bars**, many of them student hangouts where **local bands** play at weekends (see box on p.592). You can also catch live bands at the Empire, 396 Princes St (☎03/477 8826), and the city is well served with **theatres**, **cinemas** (both arthouse and mainstream) and **concert halls**. For information on what's on, pick up a copy of *Fink* or check the "Entertainments" section of the *Otago Daily Times*. Many bars close early on Sunday or don't open at all.

Pubs and bars

Albert Arms, cnr of George St & London St. Sedate, tartan-decorated pub with live Irish music on Mon and anything from rock to blues on Tues. Bar snacks downstairs, while upstairs the *London Lounge* serves good bistro fare (including steaks and roasts). Closes 8pm Sun.

Captain Cook, cnr of Albany St & Great King St. A favourite student pub, reputed to have the highest turnover of beer in New Zealand. The downstairs bar has pool tables, cheap bar snacks, a pleasant garden bar and a happy half-hour every day 5.30–6pm. Upstairs has regular live bands (Wed) and a DJ and disco (Thurs–Sat till 2.45am), with no cover charge. Closed Sun.

Champions Bar, 140 George St. Focuses on Kiwi sport, with local loyalties expressed through the blue-and-gold colours of Otago. Great atmosphere and toasted "doorstep" sandwiches.

Crossroads, cnr of St Andrew St & Great King St. Slightly upmarket student bar-cum-nightclub in a big, warehouse-like setting. Live bands (usually playing cover versions) start at around 9pm, but the place really gets kicking after midnight, and closes at 2am. No trainers allowed.

Fat Lady's Arms, 157 Frederick St. Popular student haunt and pick-up joint. Dance floor (till 3am Fri & Sat) and occasional live acts. Closed Sun. No trainers.

Inch Bar, 8 Bank St. Tiny hip watering hole with plenty of special beers on tap and a wide range of imported brands. Bar snacks available. Mon–Sat from 5pm.

Rosie O'Grady's, *Bentley's Hotel*, 137 Andrew St. Irish pub with a cosy, dark-wood interior. Varied live music Wed–Sat evenings. Bar meals available.

Statesman, 91 St Andrew St, opposite *Crossroads*. A big party pub where popular Kiwi rock bands play Thurs, Fri & Sat nights. Open till 3am Fri & Sat.

Theatre, cinema and classical music

The Fortune Theatre at 231 Stuart St (box office ☎03/477 8323; tickets around $22.50; closed Jan), in the Neo-Gothic converted Trinity Methodist Church, divides its programme between new works by Kiwi playwrights, fringe theatre, popular Broadway-style **plays** and occasional musicals. The Regent, 17 The Octagon (☎03/477 8597) is the city's largest and most ornate theatre, hosting musicals, ballets, touring plays and performances by popular singers, comedians and groups. The small, intimate Globe, 104 London St (☎03/477 3274) features contemporary plays, classical drama and experimental works. You can catch more **fringe** on campus at Allen Hall on Clyde Street (☎03/479 8896), the showcase for the university's drama students.

Mainstream **films** are shown at Hoyts, a six-cinema multiplex at 33 The Octagon (☎03/477 7019), and at the Odeon, 107 Princes St (☎03/477 1236), while there are international arthouse screenings at the delightful and tiny Metropolis, housed on the ground floor of the 1920s Town Hall on Moray Place (discounted tickets Mon–Fri before 6pm). This is the smallest public cinema in New Zealand, and it's essential to book ahead by leaving a message on their answer machine (☎03/474 3350); collect tickets ten minutes before screening time.

THE DUNEDIN SOUND

In the late 1970s and early 1980s an idiosyncratic style of rock music began to emerge from Dunedin's local pub scene, and it was quickly tagged the "Dunedin Sound". Isolated from the commercial mainstream – the Kiwi music market constitutes a mere three million or so people – the bands indulged in songwriting for the sheer hell of it, which perhaps explains their originality and why so many of the early songs have stood the test of time. Spurred on by local record labels Flying Nun (now based in Auckland) and Xpressway, the bands developed over a number of albums and in relative obscurity until several – notably the Chills, Straitjacket Fits and the Verlaines – started to find a receptive audience in Europe and the States.

The 1990s have brought inventive new bands, among them the 3Ds, Polyps, Age of Dog, My Deviant Daughter and David Kilgour, prompting the *Chicago Tribune* in 1992 to call Dunedin the "Rock Capital of The World". For the latest on the Dunedin Sound, check out the Wednesday Music Page of the *Otago Daily Times*, which keeps track of Dunedin's bands, singers and songwriters.

Regular **concerts** are given by the New Zealand Symphony Orchestra, the Dunedin Sinfonia (a semi-professional orchestra), and chamber music groups at the Town Hall or the Glenroy Auditorium at the Dunedin Centre (☎03/477 4477). The Dunedin Opera Company stages two or three productions a year at the Trust Bank Theatre, 100 King Edward St (☎03/455 4962) and regular public recitals are held by the music department of the University of Otago.

Listings

Airlines The offices of the domestic airlines are in the Octagon: Air New Zealand (☎03/477 5769), Ansett (☎03/479 2146). Southern Air (☎0800/658 876) flies direct from Dunedin to Stewart Island. Freedom Air (☎0800/600 500) offers two international routes, to Sydney and Brisbane.

Airport transport Airport Express Shuttle Service (☎03/476 2519); Airport Shuttle City Taxis (☎03/477 1771); Airport Shuttle Service (☎03/477 9238); Airport Shuttle Service Ltd (☎03/474 1741); Call-a-Cab Shuttle (☎03/477 7800); Dunedin Airport Shuttle (☎03/477 7777); Super Shuttle (☎025/336 951 & after-hours 03/453 6502).

Automobile Association Shopping Centre, Moray Place, near cnr with Burlington St. For road maps and travel and motoring products. Emergency breakdown service ☎0800/500 222. Road reports ☎0900/33222.

Banks and foreign exchange Branches of all major banks are clustered on the George Street side of the Octagon and Moray Place, most of them with ATMs, and some also line Princes Street. Thomas Cook is at 43 Princes St (Mon–Sat 8.30am–5pm; ☎03/477 7204).

Bike rental R & R Sport, 70 Stuart St (☎03/474 1211) has mountain bikes for $20 a day; The Cycle Surgery, 67 Stuart St (☎03/477 7473) offers repairs, and rents bikes for $20 per day; Browns Avanti Pro Cycle Centre, Lower Stuart St (☎03/477 7259) has good-quality mountain bikes for short- and long-term rental, with helmets and locks, and does repairs; Peter Goding Cycles, 78 St Andrew St (☎03/477 2295) offers a full range of bikes and also does repairs.

Bookshops University Bookshop, 378 Great King St, opposite the Otago Museum (Mon–Fri 8.30am–5.30pm, Sat 9.30am–1.30pm), is a comprehensive independent bookshop on two floors, stocking a broad range of New Zealand and international fiction and non-fiction – bargains upstairs; Hyndmans, Civic Centre, George St (just down from the visitor centre) stocks books on New Zealand, fiction, children's books and stationery. Scribes, cnr Saint David St and Great King St (Mon–Fri 10am–4pm) specializes in secondhand books on all subjects.

Buses National bus companies: Intercity Coachlines, Intercity Travel Centre at 599 Princes St, near junction with Andersons Bay Rd (☎03/477 8860) links Dunedin with Christchurch, Queenstown, Te Anau, Wanaka and Invercargill; Mount Cook Landline, 205 St Andrew St, between Castle St & Anzac Ave (☎0800/800 287) runs to Christchurch, Queenstown, Te Anau and Wanaka. Local shuttle buses: Atomic Shuttles (to and from Christchurch and Queenstown; book through the visitor centre, ☎03/474 3300); Ko-Op Shuttles (to and from Christchurch; ☎03/366 6633); and Southern Link Shuttles (to and from Christchurch; ☎03/358 8355) all run from the visitor centre. You can also buy long-distance bus tickets from the train station ticket office.

Camping and outdoor equipment R & R Sport, 70 Lower Stuart St, has the biggest range of camping, skiing, cycling and all sporting equipment; also mountain bike and pack rental. The Wilderness Shop, 101 Stuart St, has mountaineering, skiing and kayaking gear for rent and for sale; also tramping and alpine gear for sale.

Car parks City centre ($1 per hour): off Upper Moray Place, opposite View St; Lower Moray Place, near Stuart St; Filleul St, between St Andrew & Hanover; Great King St, between St Andrew & Hanover; Anzac Ave, at junction with Castle St; Crawford St, at junction with Castle St, and another between Water & Liverpool; High St, near junction with Broadway.

Car rental Avis, 36 Moray Place (☎03/477 5973 & 0800/655 111), also at Dunedin Airport (☎03/486 2780); Budget, 330 Moray Place (☎03/474 0428) and Dunedin Airport (☎03/486 2660); Hertz, 121 Crawford St (☎03/477 7385 & 0800/654 321), also at the airport (☎03/486 2778), Reliable Rentals, 20 Carroll St (☎03/477 7671), for cars and minibuses; Rhodes, 124 St Andrew St (☎03/477 9950) for cars, vans, minibuses and 4WDs; Thrifty, 366 Princes St (☎03/477 7087 & 0800/737 070), also at the airport; and Welco, 8a Reid Rd, South Dunedin (☎03/455 5064. Cheapest of all are Rent-a-Dent, 212 Crawford St (☎03/477 7822) for cars, station wagons, vans and minibuses; and Jackies, 23 Cumberland St (☎03/477 7848).

Dentist Raymond J. George, 7th floor, National Mutual Building, cnr The Octagon & George St (24hr; ☎03/477 7993, after hours 474 1277).

Laundry The only one in Dunedin is Sudz Laundry Washin, 4 Howe St, near the university (daily 8.30am–5pm & 5.30–10pm).

Library Dunedin Public Library, cnr of John St & Stewart St (Mon–Fri 10am–5pm, Sat 10am–noon, also Tues 7–8pm & Fri 6.30–8.30pm; ☎03/474 3690), has excellent facilities, newspapers and Internet access.

Medical treatment Dunedin Hospital, 201 Great King St (☎03/474 0999). For general practice medical care, try Bell Hill Health Centre, 399 Moray Place (Mon–Fri 8.30am–6pm; ☎03/477 9183).

Petrol stations Mobil Downtown 24hr Service Centre, 99 Crawford St.

Pharmacy After-hours service at 95 Hanover St (Mon–Fri 6–10pm, Sat, Sun & public holidays 10am–10pm; ☎03/477 6344).

Police Dunedin police station is at 25 Great King St (☎03/477 6011). In an emergency call ☎111.

Post office Dunedin Post Shop, John Wickliffe Plaza, 243 Princes St; Moray Place Post Shop, 233 Moray Place; Dunedin North Post Shop, 366 Great King St; South Dunedin Post Shop, 166 King Edward St. Poste restante held at Dunedin Post Shop (Mon–Fri 8.30am–5pm, from 9am Wed).

Swimming Moana Pool, cnr of Stuart St & Littlebourne Rd ($3;☎03/474 3400) is a leisure complex with a fifty-metre heated indoor pool, outdoor paddling pool, hydroslide, gym and sauna; St Clair Hot Saltwater Pool and Toddlers Pool (Nov–March Mon–Sat 6am–7pm, Sun 8am–7pm; ☎03/455 2668) is accessible from St Clair Beach (see p.588).

Taxis You'll find taxi ranks in the Octagon, between George & Stuart; on St Andrew St, between George & Filleul; and on Frederick St, between George & Filleul. Radio cabs include Call a Cab (☎03/477 7800) and City Taxis (☎03/477 1771; 24hr service).

Tours The visitor centre has information on the vast array of tours from Dunedin. Newtontours (☎03/477 5577) runs city tours (daily 10am & 3.30pm; $15) and trips out to the Otago Peninsula, while the Otago Peninsula Express (book through the visitor centre) minibus runs to various points on the peninsula. Wings of Kotuku (☎03/473 0077) takes small groups to see the wildlife on Otago Peninsula (daily Oct–March), and also runs daily trips north to the Moeraki Boulders (see p.537). Harbour and wildlife cruises on the *Monarch* leave from Dunedin Wharf, cnr of Wharf St & Fryatt St (1–4hr; from $20; ☎03/477 4276), giving close-up views of royal albatross, seals, penguins, cormorants and waders on the peninsula. An excellent full-day tour of the Catlins Coast is offered by Catlins Coastal Link (Mon, Wed, Fri & Sat; $65 one way; see box on p.604 for details). Gold Trail Mini Tours (book through the visitor centre) runs various tours to the largest open-cast gold mine in the southern hemisphere at Macraes Flat ($57–127.50). The Southern Explorer backpacker bus (☎03/249 7820) operates a hop-on-hop-off service one way to Queenstown and Te Anau, stopping at sights in the Otago Goldfields (Tues Nov–May only; Queenstown $35, Te Anau $45).

Trains The Tranz Scenic Southerner train between Christchurch and Invercargill stops at Dunedin Train Station, Anzac Square, off Stuart St (☎03/477 4449). The Taieri Gorge train to Pukerangi leaves from here, too (see p.589).

Travel agents Amo & Holmes Travel, 233 Stuart St (☎477 2233); STA, 32 Albany St (☎03/474 0146); Stars Travel International, cnr Princes St & Rattray St (☎03/477 7496) for all flight bookings; Thomas Cook, 43 Princes St (☎03/477 7204); Winston Darling, 138 Princes St (☎477 0449) for Ansett and Air New Zealand bookings.

Port Chalmers

The attractive, historic town and modern container port of **PORT CHALMERS**, on a tiny peninsula 12km from Dunedin, is worth a half-day trip for its magnificent harbour views offset by bush-covered hills, its fine nineteenth-century buildings and its thriving artistic community.

The site was chosen in 1844 as the port to serve the proposed Scottish settlement of New Edinburgh, later called Dunedin. The first settlers arrived on the *John Wickliffe* in March 1848 and named the port after the Reverend Dr Thomas Chalmers, who had led the split between the Presbyterian and Free churches of Scotland. Development was slow until the Otago **gold rush** of the 1860s, which heralded a boom for Port Chalmers. Later, it served as the embarkation point for several **Antarctic expeditions**, including those of Captain Scott, who set out from here in 1901 and, ill-fatedly, in 1910. The first trial shipment of **frozen meat** to Britain was sent from Port Chalmers and today the export of wool, meat and timber is the port's chief business.

The Town

The main street, **George Street**, connects the docks with SH88 and is lined with several old stone buildings containing shops, galleries, a few cafés and a bank. Most of the town crawls up hills on either side, where two churches dominate. On Mount Street stands the tall stone spire and clock tower of **Iona Church**, completed in 1883 and once Presbyterian but now United (Presbyterian Methodist), and on the opposite side, on Grey Street, sits the squat Anglican **Holy Trinity** (1874), designed by Scottish architect R.A. Lawson and built from local bluestone (volcanic rock).

On the George Street waterfront, you'll find the small, rather atmospheric **Museum**, in the old post office building. Run by volunteers, its hours vary considerably (Oct–March daily; April–Sept by arrangement only; donations requested; ☎03/472 8233). Brimming with maritime artefacts and some local settler history, the highlights include a history of navigational equipment with splendid models and photographs. Downstairs is a large working electric model of a **gold dredge**, built in 1900 by a boiler-maker apprentice. Staff can fill you in on local walking trails, and can also arrange escorted historical walks along the nearby beaches.

On the corner of Grey and George streets is the private studio of artist **Ralph Hotere**, one of New Zealand's best-known abstract artists. The rest of George Street is lined with **art galleries** and **craft shops**. Port Chalmers Aero Club (Thurs–Sun; free), at no. 10, a delightful 1884 building, has contemporary works by local artists displayed over several floors and there's a café downstairs serving cheap lunches and snacks. Next door, occupying an old bank, The Crafty Banker (Mon–Sat 9am–5pm) is a pleasant gallery and craft shop, while further up, Portfolio has a good selection of rugs and local pottery.

For a spectacular panorama of the harbour and Otago Peninsula, a **coastal walk** (4km; 45min–1hr) starts from Wickliffe Terrace, at the junction with George Street. After crossing the rail line, the road takes you past Mussel Bay to the commanding headland. Continuing around the coast, home to a wide variety of sea birds including terns, oystercatchers, shags, gulls, herons and ducks, you reach Back Beach, and can return to George Street via a log-storage area or detour up to Flagstaff Lookout, above the headland.

Practicalities

By **car** from Dunedin, it's a ten-minute scenic harbourside drive along SH88, or you can take the longer scenic route, following Mount Cargill and Upper Junction roads. From the north on SH1, take the road to Port Chalmers from Waitati. **Buses** from Dunedin to Port Chalmers leave from Stand 4 in Cumberland Street, dropping you off in George Street about 25 minutes later (Mon–Sat). Courtesy Tours (☎03/472 7100) also run a shuttle service on demand.

Eating options are limited to cafés and takeaways, the best being *Café Giardino*, 10 George St, which serves cheap soups, sandwiches, bagels and quiches, and *Port Stables Bar & Café*, 56 George St, in tastefully converted stables with a pool table and a roaring fire in winter. You'll find scenic picnic spots along Peninsula Beach Road, just around from the harbour.

The Otago Peninsula

Jutting out to the east of Dunedin and dividing its harbour from the Pacific Ocean, the **OTAGO PENINSULA** is a lightly populated undulating area of natural beauty and exceptional wildlife. Its grass-covered hills afford excellent views of the harbour, the open sea and the spread of Dunedin against its dramatic backdrop of hills. Served by well-kept roads, the peninsula is easily accessible from the city, the trip from one end to the other taking an hour by car.

The chief reason for visiting the peninsula is to appreciate, at close range, the intriguing variety and abundance of **marine wildlife** that is drawn to its shores year round. At its tip is the small headland of **Taiaroa Head**, a protected area where several colonies of mammals and sea birds congregate. Unique among these is the majestic **royal albatross**, which breeds here in the only mainland colony of albatross in the world. Also concentrated on the headland's shores are **penguins** (little blue and the rare yellow-eyed) and **southern fur seals**, while the cliffs are home to other sea birds including three species of **shag**, **muttonbirds** (sooty shearwaters) and various species of gull. The peninsula's other beaches and inlets play host to a great variety of wading and waterfowl and, occasionally, New Zealand **sea lions**, while offshore, orca and other **whales** can sometimes be spotted.

Although there's ample opportunity to see much of the wildlife without having to pay for the privilege, it's well worth forking out for one or more of the several official **wildlife tours** (see below for details), since they take you up close, yet cause minimal disturbance to the animals.

On the way to Taiaroa Head there are a handful of other sights, including the large woodland gardens and walks of **Glenfalloch**, particularly renowned for their rhododendrons, azaleas and camellias; the bizarre **Larnach Castle**, which is little more than an overblown folly; **Fletcher House**, a delightfully restored small Edwardian villa; and an intimate **aquarium**. A number of **scenic walks** cross both public and private land to spectacular views and unusual land formations created by lava flows.

Around Taiaroa Head

The peninsula's marine wildlife is mostly concentrated around **Taiaroa Head**, where a rich and constant food source is created by cold waters forced up by the continental shelf. Other than taking a tour, the best opportunities for seeing animals are on the beaches and inlets on either side of the headland. Southern fur seals can be seen at **Pilots Beach**, on the western side (follow the main road to the shore as it snakes past the Royal Albatross Centre) and from the **cliff tops** on the eastern side of the headland. Pilots Beach is also home to a small colony of little blue penguins, which are best visited around dusk. A short signposted walk from the Royal Albatross Centre car park to a **cliff-edge viewing area** unfolds spectacular scenes of a spotted shag colony, while royal albatross in flight can be spotted all year round from anywhere on the headland.

When **observing wildlife**, respect the animals by staying well away from them (at least 5 metres), and keeping quiet and still. **Penguins** are especially timid and easily frightened by people getting too close. They will be reluctant to come ashore (even if they have chicks to feed) if you are on or near the beach and visible. In summer, stay well away from them and keep to the track as they're extremely vulnerable to stress while nesting and moulting. Never get between a **seal** and the sea; these animals can be aggressive and move surprisingly quickly.

The Royal Albatross Centre

Serving as the gateway to the only mainland colony of albatross in the world, the **Royal Albatross Centre** (daily: Oct–April 9am–dusk; May–Sept 10am–dusk; free), 33km from Dunedin's city centre at Taiaroa Head, also operates as the peninsula's **information** centre and booking office. Its galleries contain displays on local wildlife and history, and there's a comfortable café with panoramic windows. The centre's excellent

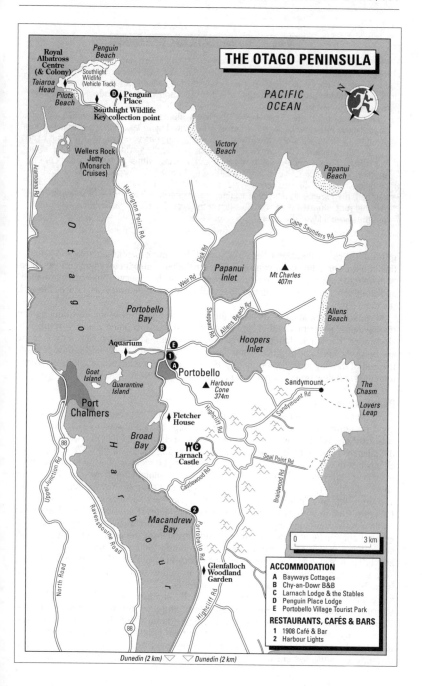

THE OTAGO PENINSULA

PACIFIC OCEAN

Royal Albatross Centre (& Colony)

Penguin Beach

Taiaroa Head

Pilots Beach

Southlight Wildlife (Vehicle Track)

Penguin Place

Southlight Wildlife Key collection point

Wellers Rock Jetty (Monarch Cruises)

Victory Beach

Papanui Beach

Aramoana Rd

Harington Point Rd

Dick Rd

Weir Rd

Cape Saunders Rd

Papanui Inlet

Mt Charles 407m

Allens Beach Rd

Sheppard Rd

Allens Beach

Portobello Bay

Aquarium

Hoopers Inlet

Goat Island

Quarantine Island

Port Chalmers

Portobello

Harbour Cone 374m

Sandymount

The Chasm

Lovers Leap

Sandymount Rd

Fletcher House

Broad Bay

Larnach Castle

Seal Point Rd

Braidwood Rd

Upper Junction Rd

Ravensbourne Road

North Road

Castlewood Rd

Highcliff Rd

Macandrew Bay

Portobello Rd

Highcliff Rd

Glenfalloch Woodland Garden

O t a g o   H a r b o u r

0   3 km

ACCOMMODATION
A Bayways Cottages
B Chy-an-Dowr B&B
C Larnach Lodge & the Stables
D Penguin Place Lodge
E Portobello Village Tourist Park

RESTAURANTS, CAFÉS & BARS
1 1908 Café & Bar
2 Harbour Lights

Dunedin (2 km) ▽   ▽ Dunedin (2 km)

THE ROYAL ALBATROSS

The magestic and mysterious **albatross**, one of the largest seabirds in the world, has long been the subject of reverence and superstition. A solitary creature that regularly circumnavigates the globe, the albatross spends most of its life in flight or at sea, and is traditionally held to be the embodiment of a dead sea captain's soul, condemned to wander the oceans for ever.

The largest of all the albatrosses is the **royal albatross** – a stunning sight, with an impressive **wing span** of up to 3.5 metres. They travel up to 190,000km a year, at speeds of 120kph and have a **life expectancy** of 45 years. The albatross mates for life, but male and female separate to fly in opposite directions around the world, returning to the same **breeding** grounds once every two years, and arriving within a couple of days of one another. The female lays one egg (weighing up to 500g) per breeding season, and the parents share incubation duty over a period of eleven weeks. Once the chick has hatched, the parents take turns at feeding it and guarding it against stoats, ferrets, wild cats and rats. Almost a year from the start of the breeding cycle, the fledgling takes flight and the parents leave the colony and return to sea.

guided tours (daily except Sept 17–Nov 23; booking essential on ☎03/478 0499 or through the Dunedin visitor centre; $15–27) include an introductory film and talk, plenty of time to view the birds from an enclosed area in the reserve (binoculars provided) and an optional but uninspiring visit to the labyrinthine tunnels of Fort Taiaroa beneath the nature reserve.

At Taiaroa Head, adult birds arrive for the new season in September. Courting and mating takes place in October and eggs are laid and incubated from November to December. The chicks hatch in January and February. The **best months** for viewing are between April and August, when parent birds leave the nests and return towards the end of the day to feed their chicks. By September the chicks and adults are ready to depart and new breeding pairs start to arrive.

Penguin-viewing

Two companies on the peninsula run markedly different yet equally appealing **yellow-eyed penguin** tours. The best months for viewing are mid-August to early March.

Southlight Wildlife, whose booking office is on Harington Point Road, 2.5km before the albatross colony (daily dawn–dusk; $7.50; booking essential, ☎04/478 0287), is the cheaper of the two tour operators, and allows repeated viewings on the same day at no extra cost, but you need your **own car** to reach the colony hidden away on the eastern shore. You'll be given a key to a signposted gate opposite the Royal Albatross Centre and after fifteen minutes' drive you reach a car park. The nearby cliffs overlook **Penguin Beach** with its colonies of yellow-eyeds (*hoiho*) and little blues. Viewing is unobstructed and aided by telescopes (including a powerful self-focusing coin-operated one) and shelters. Penguins emerge and head across the swathe of sand to a high sandy bank, which they laboriously climb to reach their nests hidden in the grass above. There's also a large signposted seal colony further along the coast and a spotted shag colony five minutes' walk beyond the seals, in the cliff face. The best viewing spot is the hide directly above one of the nesting areas.

Employing a very different approach are the carefully controlled and extremely informative **guided tours** run by an award-winning penguin-conservation project. At **Penguin Place**, McGrouther's Farm, Harington Point Road, 3.5km before the albatross colony (daily; 90min; $20; book ahead on ☎03/478 0286 or through Dunedin visitor centre), you are given the rare privilege of entering a protected **nesting area** through a unique system of hides and tunnels. The best months to visit here are

THE YELLOW-EYED PENGUIN (HOIHO)

Considered the most ancient of all living penguins, the **yellow-eyed penguin**, or *hoiho*, evolved in forests free of predators. Found only in southern New Zealand, it is an endangered species, numbering around four thousand birds, due to introduced predators (ferrets, stoats and cats), the loss of its forested habitat, disturbance by humans and livestock, and recurring food shortages. The small mainland population of just a few hundred occupies nesting areas dotted along the wild southeast coast of the South Island (from Oamaru to the Catlins); other smaller colonies inhabit the coastal forest margins of Stewart Island and offshore islets, and New Zealand's subantarctic islands of Auckland and Campbell.

Male and female adults are identical in colouring, with pink webbed feet and a bright yellow band that encircles the head, sweeping over their pale yellow eyes. Standing around 65cm high and weighing 5–8kg, they have a **life expectancy** of up to twenty years. Their **diet** consists of squid and small fish and hunting takes them up to 40km offshore and to depths of 100m.

Maori gave this rare penguin the name of **hoiho**, meaning "the noise shouter", because of the distinctive high-pitched calls (an exuberant trilling) it makes at night when greeting its mate at the nest. Unlike other penguins, the yellow-eyed does not migrate after its first year, but stays close to its home beach, making daily fishing trips and returning as daylight fails.

The **breeding season** lasts for 28 weeks, from mid-August to early March. Eggs are laid between mid-September and mid-October, and both parents share in the duties of incubation, a period of about 43 days. The eggs hatch in November and for the next six weeks the chicks are constantly guarded against predators. When the down-covered chicks are six or seven weeks old, their rapid growth gives them voracious appetites and both parents must fish daily to satisfy them. The fledglings enter the sea for the first time in late February or early March and journey up to 500km north to winter feeding grounds. Fewer than fifteen percent of fledged chicks reach breeding age, but those that do return to the colony of their birth.

between early November and May, but at any time of year, cold wet days make for especially good viewing. Tours begin with a talk about penguins and their conservation, before a guide takes you to the beachside colony, where well-camouflaged trenches and hides among the dunes allow an extraordinary proximity to the penguins and excellent photographic opportunities. Proceeds from the tours are used to fund the conservation work. If you want **to stay** overnight, budget accommodation is available on the farm (see "Accommodation" on p.600).

The rest of the peninsula

Lying between Dunedin and Taiaroa Head are four sights worthy of a brief diversion, most of them strung along the harbourside on Portobello Road. Eleven kilometres from Dunedin, the peaceful **Glenfalloch Woodland Garden**, at 430 Portobello Rd (daily dawn–dusk; donations requested), contains 120 square kilometres of rambling mature garden and bush, surrounding a homestead built in 1871. The garden is at its best between mid-September and mid-October, when it is resplendent with rhododendrons, azaleas and camellias and, to a lesser extent, magnolias, fuchsias and roses. Near the entrance, a licensed café (daily 10am–4.30pm) serves snacks and drinks, and also stocks leaflets on the peninsula.

Set high on a hill above the harbour, 16km from the centre of Dunedin and signposted off Castlewood Road, is a bizarre nineteenth-century Gothic Revival building. The so-called **Larnach Castle** (daily 9am–5pm; grounds only $4, grounds and castle

$10) was the sumptuous residence of William Larnach, an Australian banker politician, who spent a fortune on its construction and decoration. Completed in 1871, it was designed by Scotsman R.A. Lawson, architect of the First Church and the Municipal Chambers in Dunedin. Most impressive is the sheer scale of the project. The very best local and overseas craftsmen were employed to build the family home entirely by hand, using materials shipped from all over the world: glass from Venice, marble from Italy and tiles from England. On arrival, these were punted across the harbour and then laboriously dragged up the hill by ox-drawn sleds. Today the castle is owned by a family who bought it in 1967 and renovated it, providing accommodation (see opposite) in two of the castle's buildings. Without your own transport, you'll have to take the Portobello **bus** either to Company Bay, from where it's a five-kilometre (signposted) walk, uphill all the way, or to Broad Bay from where you'll have a steeper but shorter walk (2km).

Back on the coast, about halfway along the peninsula, **The Fletcher House**, 727 Portobello Rd, Broad Bay (daily 11am–4pm; April to mid-Oct Sat, Sun & public holidays only; $3) is an attractive small Edwardian villa, lovingly restored to its original state and furnished in period style. Built entirely of native wood in 1909, it was the family home of the Broad Bay storekeeper. Inside the house, the absence of restricting ropes allows you to appreciate fully the furniture and fine woodwork, including the tongue-and-groove panelling in the small kitchen and richly coloured rimu ceilings and floors.

Further east, at Portobello, Hatchery Road leads 2km along a headland to the **Aquarium** (Dec–Feb daily noon–4pm; March–Nov Sat & Sun, public & school holidays noon–4.30pm; $3), displaying marine life found in New Zealand's southern waters. The fun part is sticking your hands into the several shallow "touch tanks" to feel the small sea creatures. As part of a marine laboratory run by the University of Otago, this is a well run venture, and staff are always available to answer questions. Visitors are also invited to participate in **fish feeding** (Sat 2–3pm; Dec–Feb also Wed 2–3pm).

Practicalities

With your own transport, access to the peninsula from Dunedin is easy, either via the snaky **Portobello Road**, which hugs the western shoreline overlooking the harbour or the inland **Highcliff Road**, which heads up and over the hills. The public **bus** (Mon–Sat) from Cumberland Street in Dunedin runs halfway along the peninsula, as far as Portobello (35min), from where it's still another 14km to Taiaroa Head. Several hop-on, hop-off **tour buses** depart daily from Dunedin visitor centre ($20–43), and there are daily harbour wildlife **cruises** on board the *Monarch*; see p.594 for details.

The Dunedin visitor centre can also help with tour bookings and accommodation, and stocks plenty of leaflets about the peninsula, including maps of various walking tracks. On the peninsula itself, the Royal Albatross Centre at Taiaroa Head also supplies information and tickets for tours and attractions.

Accommodation and eating

There's a limited amount of accommodation on the peninsula, and you'll find it pricier than in Dunedin. **Camping** is permitted only at the small *Portobello Village Tourist Park*, 27 Hereweka St, Portobello (☎03/478 0359; ②–③), which has on-site caravans and cabins, as well as tent sites ($8.50). **Budget accommodation** is available at Taiaroa Head at the simple *Penguin Place Lodge*, McGrouther's Farm, Harington Point Rd (☎03/478 0286; ②), 3.5km before the albatross colony, with single and double rooms, shared showers and kitchen. Mid-range options include several fully self-contained **cottages** at *Bayways Cottages*, Highcliff Rd, Portobello (☎03/478 0181; ④),

---

WALKS ON OTAGO PENINSULA

A free map from the Dunedin visitor centre, *Otago Peninsula Tracks*, briefly describes several walks on the peninsula. Bear in mind that they cover hill country and that though most tracks are well defined, some are pretty steep. Also, the weather here can turn cold or wet very quickly, even on the sunniest days.

The most rewarding walks include the easy loop track to **Lovers Leap and the Chasm** (3km; 1hr; closed Aug–Oct) which crosses farmland to sheer cliffs dropping 200m to the sea, with collapsed sea caves and rock faces of layered volcanic lava flows visible. The track begins from the end of Sandymount Road, a 25-minute drive from the centre of Dunedin. Also good is the track along **Sandfly Bay** (3km; 80min) which leads to sweeping dunes visited by yellow-eyed penguins and, occasionally, New Zealand sea lions. There's a penguin hide at the far end of beach. This walk begins at the end of Seal Point Road, a twenty-minute drive from the city.

---

and the *Chy-an-Dowr* **B&B**, 687 Portobello Rd, Broad Bay (☎03/478 0306; ⑤), a spacious house with a sunroom giving a panoramic view of the harbour. You can also stay in a couple of buildings in the grounds of Larnach Castle (☎03/476 1616, fax 476 1574), but you pay a premium for the tranquil garden setting high above the harbour. The converted *Stables* (③) contains six basic rooms, while the *Larnach Lodge* (⑦), refurbished to imitate a two-storey colonial farm building, has twelve rooms, each individually decorated in period style and all with private facilities. All guests get a free tour of the castle during opening hours and you can also book for dinner in the castle's dining room.

Eating is limited to two reasonable waterfront venues, both cashing in on the harbour views and rustling up seafood, meat and vegetarian dishes. Closest to the city is the modern, glass-fronted *Harbour Lights*, 494 Portobello Rd, MacAndrew Bay (☎03/476 1604), which is open daily for dinner (plus lunch on Sunday) and combines a bar, expensive licensed restaurant and cheaper café. Further along, in Portobello, the elegant *1908 Café & Bar*, 7 Harington Point Rd (☎03/478 0801; licensed & BYO – wine only), serves pricey lunches and dinners daily, in a converted turn-of-the-century house, enhanced by excellent views of the harbour and city against a backdrop of hills. The varied menu includes enormous desserts.

South from Dunedin: Balclutha and the Catlins Coast

The dramatic, rugged coastal route linking Dunedin and Invercargill, part of the **Southern Scenic Route** that continues on to Fiordland, is one of the least travelled highways in New Zealand, and traverses some of the country's wildest scenery along the **Catlins Coast**. Within this significant region is the largest area of native forest on the east coast of the South Island, most of it protected as the **Catlins Forest Park**, and consisting of rimu, rata, kamahi and silver beech. Roaring southeasterlies and the remorseless sea have shaped the coastline here into plunging cliffs, windswept headlands, white sand beaches, rocky bays and gaping caves, much of this accessible on a number of short bushwalks. Not surprisingly, this relatively untouched area abounds with **wildlife**, including several rare species of marine bird and mammal. The only major stop-off point between Dunedin and the Catlins Coast is **Balclutha**, which is a good place to stock up before entering the wilderness beyond. At Balclutha, SH1 turns inland, skirting the Catlins region before turning south to Invercargill at the town of **Gore**, a centre for brown-trout fishing.

> The **western continuation** of the **Southern Scenic Route**, from Invercargill to Te Anau via Tuatapere, is covered in the *Fiordland* chapter, starting on p.754.

Maori hunters once thrived in the Catlins region, one of the last refuges of the flightless moa, but by 1700 they had moved on, to be supplanted by European **whalers and sealers** in the 1830s. Two decades later, having decimated whale and seal stocks, they too moved on. Meanwhile, in 1840, Captain Edward Cattlin arrived to investigate the navigability of the river that bears his (misspelled) name. He purchased a tract of land from the chief of the Ngai Tahu and soon after, boatloads of **loggers** began to arrive, lured by the great podocarp forests. Cleared valleys were settled, bush millers supplied Dunedin with much of the wood needed for housing and, in 1872, more timber was exported from the Catlins than anywhere else in New Zealand. From 1879, the rail line from Balclutha began to extend into the region, bringing with it sawmills, schools and farms. Milling continued into the 1930s, but gradually dwindled and today's tiny settlements are shrunken remnants of the once-prosperous logging industry.

Although the 126-kilometre stretch of road through the Catlins should present no problems for vehicles, be aware that a fifty-kilometre section is **unsealed**, as are smaller roads edging out to the sea. For this reason, none of the major bus companies operates through the Catlins and there is no train either. Without your own transport, or if you just want to make a day-trip, you can take one of several **guided tours** (see box opposite) which operate from Dunedin, Balclutha and Invercargill.

Balclutha

Located on SH1, 80km southwest of Dunedin and 185km from Invercargill, **BALCLUTHA** lies in the heart of South Otago, amid rich pastures. Nicknamed "Big River Town", Balclutha occupies both banks of the mighty **Clutha River**, with the town centre on the southern shore linked to SH1 by an unmissable, arched concrete bridge. The river was once a source of alluvial gold but today is used to generate hydroelectricity. Anglers are lured to Balclutha by the river's substantial stocks of brown trout and salmon; for non-fishing folk, there are few attractions in the small township and the main reason to stop is to pick up information and supplies for the trip south.

InterCity **buses** stop outside the visitor centre (see below), and the centrally located **train station** is at the junction of Scotland Street and Baxter Street. The Southerner passes through once a day, in each direction.

Balclutha's well-organized **Clutha visitor centre** is beside the bridge at 4 Clyde St (Mon–Fri 9am–5pm, Sat 10am–1pm; ☎03/418 0388) and has plenty of information on the Catlins, including the excellent *Visitors Guide to the Catlins* ($2) and two DOC pamphlets, *Southern Scenic Route* ($1) and the comprehensive, *The Catlins: Walks and Tracks Information* ($2.50).

There's a small selection of **accommodation** in town. The best campsite is the small *Naish Park Motor Camp*, 56 Charlotte St (☎03/418 0088), five minutes' walk from the town centre and set in pleasant parkland with excellent modern facilities. There are plenty of tent sites ($7 per person), powered sites ($8 per person) and five cabins (②). Among the motels, try the friendly *Helensborough Motor Inn*, 23 Essex St (☎ & fax 03/418 1948; ④), north of the bridge, with fully self-contained units, or the more upmarket *Rosebank Lodge*, 265 Clyde St (☎03/418 1490, fax 418 1493; ⑤), a quiet new complex with eighteen units, three bars, a restaurant, spa and sauna. Twelve kilometres north of Balclutha is the luxurious *Garvan Homestead B&B* (☎ & fax 03/417 8407; ⑥), a large tudor-style retreat in rambling gardens with a good licensed restaurant.

Places to eat are strung along Clyde Street. *The Captain's*, a centrally located and pleasant **pub** at no. 13, serves reasonable and well-priced bar food, from snacks to steaks, and there's a good Chinese, *Gins*, at no. 27 (closed Tues; BYO). The moderately priced à la carte **restaurant** at *Rosebank Lodge* is the best place for something special.

The Catlins

The best way to enjoy the **CATLINS COAST** is to take it slowly, absorbing its unique atmosphere over at least one or two days. If you can visit during the week you'll avoid most of the day-trippers from Dunedin. From Nugget Point in South Otago (just southeast of Balclutha) to Waipapa Point in Southland (60km northeast of Invercargill), the wild scenery stretches unbroken, with dense rainforest succumbing to open scrub as you cut through deep valleys and past rocky bays, inlets and estuaries. The coast is home to **penguins** (both little blues and yellow-eyed), **dolphins**, several types of sea bird and, at certain times of year, migrating **whales**. Elephant **seals**, fur seals, and increasingly, the rare New Zealand **sea lion**, are found on the sandy beaches and grassy areas, and within the mossy depths of the forest are abundant **birds**: tui, resonant bellbirds, fantails, grey warblers and colourful tree-top dwellers such as kakariki and mohau.

The most awe-inspiring natural features scattered along the way are **Nugget Point**, a rugged, windswept promontory favoured by seals and sea lions; the **Purakaunui Falls**, among the most photographed in New Zealand; the impressive **Cathedral Caves**, their high "ceilings" and deep chambers carved out of the cliffs by the sheer force of the sea; and **Curio Bay**, where an intriguing forest has been captured in stone.

The main settlement is **Owaka** (Place of the Canoe), a farming town 38km from Balclutha and inhabited by less than two hundred people. It has a small selection of accommodation, services and shops, including a pub, supermarket, store/diner/backpackers, pharmacy and a 24-hour medical centre. Elsewhere, there are general stores at **Kaka Point**, **Papatowai** and at **Curio Bay** Camping Ground. **Petrol** stations are few

TOURS OF THE CATLINS

If you don't have your own transport, **guided tours** are really the only way of exploring the Catlins; trips start from Dunedin, Balclutha and Invercargill.

An excellent guided minibus tour, **Catlins Coastal Link**, regularly shuttles in both directions along the Southern Scenic Route, from Dunedin to Te Anau via the Catlins, allowing you to get on and off where you want and pick up a later bus; the trip from Dunedin to Invercargill takes about ten hours, including five hours off the bus for bush and beach walks. The guides really know their stuff and the tour is extremely friendly and relaxed. Dunedin–Invercargill departs Mon, Wed & Fri at 8.30am; Invercargill–Dunedin departs Tues, Thurs & Sat at 8.30am (book ahead through visitor centres or direct on ☎03/471 0292; Dunedin–Invercargill $65; Dunedin–Te Anau $109).

Also highly recommended is an inspirational eco-tour run by **Catlins Wildlife Trackers**. Fergus and Mary Sutherland offer an intimate overnight or three-day round trip ($200 & $490 respectively) for groups of up to eight, from Balclutha, which explores remote beaches and rich rainforest. All meals, accommodation, transport and equipment are provided and a shuttle service to and from Dunedin can be arranged for an extra $50 (advance bookings essential ☎03/415 8613, email *catlinw@es.co.nz* or through Clutha visitor centre, see p.602).

From Invercargill only, flexible return tours of the Catlins highlights are run by **Lynette Jack Scenic Sights** (book ahead on ☎025/338 370, after hours 03/215 7741; full day tour $130 per person, including food and drink).

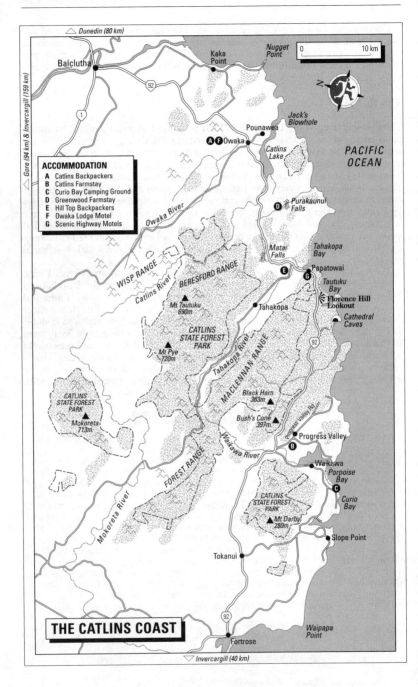

Dunedin (80 km)

Gore (94 km) & Invercargill (159 km)

Balclutha

Kaka Point

Nugget Point

PACIFIC OCEAN

Jack's Blowhole

Pounawea

A **F** Owaka

Catlins Lake

ACCOMMODATION
A Catlins Backpackers
B Catlins Farmstay
C Curio Bay Camping Ground
D Greenwood Farmstay
E Hill Top Backpackers
F Owaka Lodge Motel
G Scenic Highway Motels

Owaka River

D Purakaunui Falls

Matai Falls

Tahakopa Bay

WISP RANGE

Catlins River

BERESFORD RANGE

E Papatowai

G Tautuku Bay

Florence Hill Lookout

Mt Tautuku 690m

Tahakopa

Cathedral Caves

CATLINS STATE FOREST PARK

Mt Pye 720m

Tahakopa River

MACLENNAN RANGE

CATLINS STATE FOREST PARK

Mokoreta 713m

Black Horn 363m

Bush's Cone 397m

Progress Valley Rd

B Progress Valley

FOREST RANGE

Waikawa River

Waikawa

Porpoise Bay

C Curio Bay

Mokoreta River

CATLINS STATE FOREST PARK

Mt Darby 280m

Slope Point

Tokanui

THE CATLINS COAST

Waipapa Point

Fortrose

Invercargill (40 km)

and far between, so fill up before you set off, then at Kaka Point, Owaka, Papatowai or Tokanui (before pumps close at around 5pm). Note that there are no **banks** within the Catlins.

Kaka Point to Owaka

First stop inside the Catlins is **Kaka Point**, a tiny beachside community 22km from Balclutha (turn off SH92 at Romahapa). There's a general store here that doubles as café, petrol station and postshop, as well as a pleasant backpackers on Moana Street (☎03/412 8834; dorms ①, rooms ②) and a quiet, modern campsite (☎ & fax 03/412 8800; tent sites $7 per person; cabins ②). The beach's golden sands are patrolled by lifeguards, so it's a good spot for swimming as well as surfing. Just behind the township a fine scenic reserve of native forest is accessible on an easy loop track (2.5km; 30min; signposted from the top of Marine Terrace).

Nine kilometres further down the coast, accessed from SH92 along a track, is **Nugget Point**, a steep-sided, windswept promontory rising 133m above the sea. Just offshore lie jagged stacks of rock, whose layers have been intriguingly tilted over time. A lighthouse dating from 1870 still operates here and from the high-level track beside it you can see southern fur seals, elephant seals (on the only mainland breeding site in the world), penguins and a variety of seabirds, including gannets and three species of shag. On the beach (Roaring Bay) are a colony of New Zealand sea lions and a hide from where you can watch yellow-eyed penguins as they leave their nests (early morning) or return to them (two hours before dark).

As you approach the farming town of **OWAKA**, you'll see totara growing in abundance. On the main street is the tiny **Catlins Museum** (Dec–Feb daily 1–4pm; March–Nov Sun 1.30–4.30pm or by arrangement ☎03/415 8490; $1), focusing on local pioneer history, early settlement, sawmills, dairy factories and shipwrecks. The **Catlins visitor centre**, located in the diner on Main Road (daily 9am–5pm; ☎03/415 8371) has plenty of leaflets, and there's also a **DOC Field Centre** at 20 Ryley St (Dec–Feb Mon–Fri 8.30am–5pm; March–Nov Mon, Tues, Thurs & Fri 10am–3.30pm; ☎03/415 8341), with good displays of Catlins history, marine habitats, flora and fauna. The *Catlins Diner* (daily 9am–7pm) also runs *Catlins Backpackers*, 3 Main Rd (☎03/415 8392; ①), a tiny and basic place with kitchen, laundry, and rental bikes. Alternatively, *Owaka Lodge Motel*, 12 Ryley St (☎03/415 8728; ③), opposite the DOC Field Centre, has four fully self-contained modern units.

Owaka to Papatowai

About 15km south of Owaka, the road seal runs out and stays that way for a further 50km or so, the road narrow and winding in places. This section contains an impressive blowhole and two sets of striking **waterfalls**, close to one another.

Jack's Blowhole (closed Sept & Oct), signposted 6km from Owaka, was created when the roof of a subterranean cave fell in and is pretty spectacular at high tide. It lies about 13km from the main road and you have to walk the last two kilometres along a track. The renowned three-tiered **Purakaunui Falls** lie in a scenic reserve of silver beech and podocarp, signposted off the main road 17km from Owaka. There's a picnic area here and an easy track (10min) through the forest to a viewing platform. Just before the falls, *Greenwood Farmstay* (☎ & fax 03/415 8259; ④), a beautifully kept house on a sheep, cattle and deer farm offers accommodation and dinner on request. Two kilometres south of the Purakaunui turn-off, are the exquisite **Matai Falls**, best viewed late in the morning. The track to the falls (10min) cuts through regenerating podocarp forest, including fuchsia trees.

Across the estuary of the Maclennan River, the small settlement of **PAPATOWAI** offers several forest and beach walks, a general store (Mon–Fri 9am–5pm, Sat

10am–1pm), and three good **places to stay**. *Hill Top Backpackers* (☎03/415 8028; ①), on a farm off the Tahakopa Road, just before the bridge near Papatowai is small and nicely kept, with astounding sea views; in town, at *Scenic Highway Motels* (☎03/415 8147; ④), next to the general store there are three newish units with fully equipped kitchens; and at the beach, there's a self-contained cottage (☎03/415 8259; ③) which sleeps four.

Papatowai to Waipapa Point

Just south of Papatowai is **Tautuku Bay**, a magnificent crescent beach of pale sand backed by extensive forest, with a great view point, Florence Hill Lookout, on the main road, offering a complete panorama of the bay, forest and coastline. The grandest and most accessible of about fifteen caves along this part of the coast are the **Cathedral Caves**, signposted 36km south of Owaka. Two connecting caverns with massively high walls have been created by furious sea action against the cliffs. They can only be entered one hour before or after low tide; times are published by the DOC at Owaka and are also posted at the turn-off from the highway. There's a picnic area and a pleasant, easy forty-minute walk to the caves. At the fishing village of **WAIKAWA**, 40km from Papatowai, an old church houses a dolphin information centre (Mon–Fri 10am–4pm, Sat 10am–1pm), and in summer, **Hector's dolphins** come close to the shore to rear their young. Koramika Charters operates regular one-hour dolphin encounter trips from Waikawa Jetty ($35 per person, $45 to also swim with the dolphins; book ahead on ☎03/216 5931); on their evening cruises, you'll also see yellow-eyed penguins.

    CURIO BAY, 10km further south, is home to an international treasure, a fine example of a Jurassic **fossil forest** that's clearly visible at low tide. Over 180 million years ago, when most of New Zealand still lay beneath the sea, this would have been a broad, forested floodplain. Today, the seashore, composed of several layers of forest buried under blankets of volcanic mud and ash, is littered with fossilized tree stumps and fallen logs. The region's prime **campsite**, the *Curio Bay Camping Ground & Store* (☎03/246 8443; tent sites $4, powered sites $7.50, on-site vans & units ②–③), is located here, spread across a peninsula between Curio Bay and Porpoise Bay, with wonderful views on all sides, a store, and sites sheltered by long grass and shrubs; avoid the three-week Christmas and New Year period when the site is inundated. However, just fifteen-minute's drive northeast of Curio Bay is the best place to stay in the Catlins – *Catlins Farmstay*, Progress Valley Road (☎03/246 8843; ②). A comfortable **homestead** on a large, secluded sheep, deer and cattle farm, it also provides home-cooked meals ($20 per head for a three-course dinner). Two kilometres away, the farm also owns a four-bed **backpacker cabin** (①), hidden away in the bush and equipped with a pot-bellied stove and cooker, but no electricity.

    At the southern end of the Catlins, 22km south of Curio Bay along the unsealed road to Otara, **Waipapa Point** saw New Zealand's worst civilian shipwreck in 1881, three years before the erection of a lighthouse, when 131 lives were lost on SS *Tararua*. Nowadays it's the haunt of **seals and sea lions** that bask on the golden beach and rocky platform. Back on the main road, once past the windswept trees of Fortrose, it's a clear run of 60km along a bland inland stretch of SH92 to Invercargill.

Gore

Seventy-one kilometres west of Balclutha on SH1 is **GORE**, a pleasant enough transit point at the intersection of routes from Dunedin to Te Anau and Invercargill. Dominated by the Hokonui Hills, Gore spans the Mataura River ("reddish swirling water"), which is renowned for its plentiful brown trout. Apart from breaking your journey for a night or grabbing a bite to eat, there's little reason to linger unless you're heavily into fishing or country music. This is the **brown trout** capital of the world (celebrated by an enormous fish statue in the town centre), and New Zealand's centre of **country music**. For eight days during late May and early June, this normally quiet rural town is the scene of the **Gold Guitar Awards**, during which hundreds of would-be Country and Western stars and a few established performers congregate to celebrate their art.

The only attractions worth a brief visit are the small museum and a tiny art gallery. The **museum**, on Main Street, just north of the town centre (Sun 2–4.30pm; donation), provides an insight into the region's gold-dredging days and colonial history, with a passing nod at local Maori history. Opposite the museum, in the Coronation Library, the **Eastern Southland Art Gallery** (Sat & Sun 2–4pm; free) has short-term local art and travelling exhibitions. If you're here during the **fishing** season (Sept–April), and want to pit your wits against a wily brown trout you'll need a licence from the visitor centre (around $15 for a week). Tackle can be rented from B&B Sports, 4 Medway St.

Practicalities

Gore is served by the Southerner **train** service between Dunedin and Invercargill and lies on the major **bus** route between the two cities. Buses drop off at the **visitor centre** on the corner of Medway and Ordsal streets (Oct–April Mon–Fri 9am–7pm, Sat & Sun 10am–7pm; May–Sept Mon–Fri 9am–5pm, Sat & Sun 10am–3pm; ☎03/208 9908), opposite the giant trout, where you can book accommodation and transport and pick up information on the town and surrounding area.

ACCOMMODATION

Croydon Lodge Hotel, cnr of SH94 and Waimea St (☎03/208 9029). A modern hotel-cum-motel with two bars and restaurans, set in extensive grounds, including a golf course. ⑤–⑥.

Dellmount , Woolwich Street, East Gore (☎03/208 1771). A super-friendly B&B-cum-farmstay on a small Arabian horse stud 2km from Gore town centre on the banks of the Mataura River. Dinner on request $20. ④.

Gore Motor Camp, 35 Broughton St (☎03/208 4919). Well-run and fairly central campsite with tent sites for $9 per person, powered sites $10 per person, and cabins. ②.

Riverlea Motel, 46–48 Hokonui Drive (☎03/208 3130). About $15 more expensive than the town's other motels, but worth it for the well-equipped units and breakfast on request. ⑤.

Xavier House, Ardwick Street (☎03/208 1545). Four rooms are rented out in this central, converted 1920s convent next door to St Mary's School. Dorms ①; rooms ②.

EATING

Café 1901, cnr Main St & Ashton St. A fairly upmarket licensed café and wine bar, open daily for reasonably priced lunches and dinners. Pricey wine list.

Croydon Lodge Hotel, cnr of SH94 and Waimea St. There are two licensed restaurants in this hotel on the outskirts of town, serving moderately priced lunchtime grills, à la carte dinners and a popular Sunday-night smorgasbord.

Gore Pie Cart, Main St. A blue and white caravan that serves cheap fish and chips and fry-ups, including steak. Eat on board or take away.

Jokers, Norfolk Street, off Hokonui Drive, beside *Traffers Hotel*. A popular lunch and dinner venue for pizza and pasta.

Table Talk, 70 Main St. Friendly café, offering a broad range of coffees, teas, big muffins and sumptuous cakes. Closed Sun.

Taste Buds, 51 Main St. Good-value breakfasts served daily (from 5am Mon–Fri). Also snacks and simple lunches.

Invercargill and around

For most visitors, the southern city of **INVERCARGILL** is little more than a transit point for some of New Zealand's most remote regions. Southland's thriving economic and cultural centre, with a population of 57,000, it was settled in the mid-1850s, and has, like Dunedin, a predominantly Scottish character. Here the legacy is demonstrated through streets named after Highland rivers, and a few fine old stone buildings in the city centre, ornately carved from white Oamaru stone.

Regularly lashed by harsh winds and rain, Invercargill sprawls over an exposed, broad expanse of flat land at the head of an estuary, the monotony compounded by a low skyline, but relieved by the city's huge parks and friendly people. Jutting out into the Foveaux Strait beyond, and partially enclosing the estuary, is a small peninsula with a couple of sights worth a brief visit. At its tip sits the busy island port of **Bluff**, linked to the city by a southbound finger of SH1. A short distance across the choppy Foveaux Strait is the island retreat of **Stewart Island** (see p.614), twenty minutes away by plane and one hour by ferry.

Arrival, information and city transport

Invercargill's **airport** is 2.5km from the city centre and receives domestic flights from New Zealand's main cities as well as Stewart Island. Spitfire Shuttles ($5) and taxis ($6–7) provide transport into town. The Southerner train service from Christchurch arrives every evening at the centrally located **train station** in Leven Street, on the corner of Esk Street. Arriving by **bus**, InterCity will drop you at the train station. The city is laid out in a grid system of wide streets which is easy to negotiate by **car**. The main highways entering the city, SH1 from the east (Tay Street) and SH6 from the north (Dee Street), meet at right angles in the city centre. See "Listings", p.612, for locations of car parks.

The city's excellent **visitor centre** is in the foyer of the Southland Museum and Art Gallery, Victoria Avenue (Mon–Fri 9am–5pm, Sat & Sun 1–5pm; ☎03/218 9753), and stocks free street maps and leaflets on Invercargill and Southland in general. The **DOC office**, in the State Insurance Building on Don Street, near the junction with Dee Street (Mon–Fri 8am–5pm; ☎03/214 4589), is the best place to go for information on the Catlins, Stewart Island and Fiordland. For local events listings, check out *The Southland Times*.

There are ten **city bus routes**, most of them circular (Mon–Fri only, 7.10am–5.45pm; timetables available from the visitor centre; information ☎03/218 7108). One-way fares to the inner suburbs cost 90¢; to the outer suburbs $1.20.

Accommodation

Accommodation prices this far south are very reasonable and there's a good choice in the centre close to the transport links. Bluff also has a couple of places to stay if you want to avoid Invercargill altogether on your way to or from Stewart Island.

Aachen Motel, 147 Yarrow St (☎ & fax 03/218 8185). Central motel with cosy studio and spacious two-bedroom units. There's a children's play area and breakfast is available. ④–⑤.

Admiral Court Motel, 327 Tay St (☎ & fax 03/217 1117). Ten spotless, fully self-contained units with extras including breakfast delivered to your door and transport to and from the airport, train and bus stations. ④–⑤.

Balmoral Lodge, 265 Tay St (☎03/217 6109, fax 217 5755). Just outside the centre, this upmarket motel has 27 luxurious units with queen-sized beds. Breakfast available. ⑤.

Gerrards, corner of Esk and Leven streets (☎03/218 3406, fax 218 3003). Nostalgic hotel right in the heart of the city, offering well-appointed budget rooms, B&B and suites; also a pleasant bar and licensed restaurant. ③–⑤.

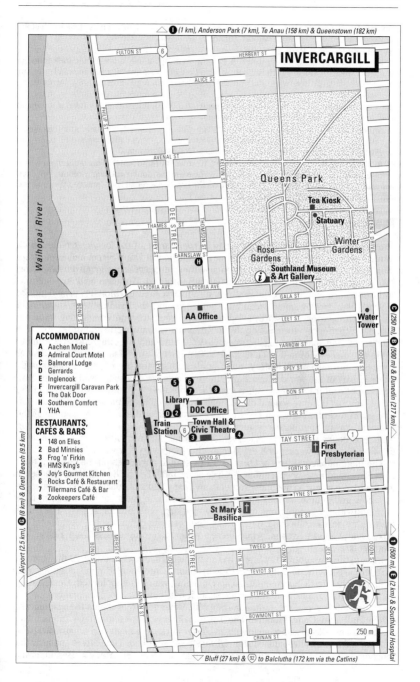

△ **I** (1 km), Anderson Park (7 km), Te Anau (158 km) & Queenstown (182 km)

INVERCARGILL

FULTON ST

HERBERT ST

ALICE ST

PHILIP ST

AVENAL ST

Queens Park

Tea Kiosk

Statuary

DEE STREET

THAMES ST

THOMSON ST

LIFFEY ST

EARNSLAW ST

H

Rose Gardens

Winter Gardens

QUEENS DRIVE

Waihopai River

BOND ST

F

VICTORIA AVE

VICTORIA AVE

i **Southland Museum & Art Gallery**

GALA ST

AA Office

LEET ST

Water Tower

G (250 m),

YARROW ST

A

SPEY ST

KELVIN ST

DEVERON ST

JED ST

DOON ST

G (500 m) & Dunedin (217 km) ▷

LEVEN ST

5 **6**

7

8

DON ST

Library

D 2

DOC Office

ESK ST

Train Station

6

3

Town Hall & Civic Theatre

4

TAY STREET

First Presbyterian †

WOOD ST

FORTH ST

TYNE ST

St Mary's Basilica †

EYE ST

BUTE ST

BOND ST

MERSEY ST

CLYDE STREET

LIDDEL ST

NITH ST

TWEED ST

CONON ST

JED ST

DOON ST

▷ **I** (500 m),

E (2 km) & Southland Hospital

TEVIOT ST

ETTRICK ST

AINNAN ST

N

BOWMONT ST

1

CRINAN ST

0   250 m

Airport (2.5 km), **G** (8 km) & Oreti Beach (9.5 km)

ACCOMMODATION

A Aachen Motel
B Admiral Court Motel
C Balmoral Lodge
D Gerrards
E Inglenook
F Invercargill Caravan Park
G The Oak Door
H Southern Comfort
I YHA

RESTAURANTS, CAFÉS & BARS

1 148 on Elles
2 Bad Minnies
3 Frog 'n' Firkin
4 HMS King's
5 Joy's Gourmet Kitchen
6 Rocks Café & Restaurant
7 Tillermans Café & Bar
8 Zookeepers Café

▽ Bluff (27 km) & (92) to Balclutha (172 km via the Catlins)

Inglenook, 2 Seddon Place (☎03/216 1232). An inviting homestay four minutes' drive south of the centre and five minutes from the airport. Dinner by arrangement ($22). ④.

Invercargill Caravan Park, 20 Victoria Ave (☎03/218 8787). The most central campsite situated in the expansive treeless and exposed A & P Showgrounds, but only a five-minute walk from the Southland Museum, Queens Park and train station. Free bikes are available and you can leave your car and store luggage here while you visit Stewart Island. Tent & powered sites $7, dorms ①, on-site vans & cabins ②.

The Oak Door, 22 Taiepa Rd, Otatara (☎ & fax 03/213 0633). A modern, airy B&B in a tranquil bush setting, three minutes' drive west of the centre, close to Oreti Beach. ④.

Southern Comfort, 30 Thomson St (☎03/218 3838). The best of the city's hostels is this beautifully kept Art Nouveau villa set among manicured lawns. Pleasant, clean dorms and double rooms, an excellent kitchen, large dining room and free bikes. Dorms ①, rooms ②.

YHA, 122 North Rd, corner with Bullar Street, Waikiwi (☎03/215 9344). This modern and comfortable hostel is in a suburb 3.5km north of the centre. Dorms, double and family rooms, free linen and excellent amenities, including a barbecue on the lawn, bike rental and a shuttle service to and from the city centre. Dorms ①, rooms ②.

The City

The best place for an overview of the city is from the top of the forty-metre-high brick **water tower** (1889), centrally located at the junction of Doon Street and Leet Street (Sun & public holidays 1.30–4.30pm; outside these times collect a key from next door; $1). Invercargill's chief attraction is the large **Southland Museum and Art Gallery**, at the southern entrance to Queens Park on Victoria Avenue (Mon–Fri 9am–5pm, Sat & Sun 1–5pm; free). Capped with a huge white pyramid, the building houses a well laid out collection, over two storeys. Upstairs, the extensive and imaginative "Roaring Forties Experience" focuses on New Zealand's **subantarctic islands**, the tiny windswept land masses lying between New Zealand and the Antarctic. A 25-minute audio-visual show (Mon–Fri 11.30am & 3.30pm, Sat & Sun 11am, noon, 2pm, 3pm & 4pm; $2) introduces the history, flora, fauna and marine life of this extraordinarily exposed part of the world. Downstairs, there's coverage of a successful breeding programme of **tuatara**, reptilian relics from the dinosaur age found nowhere else in the world. You can observe several of the small, well-camouflaged tuatara in simulated natural environments, but you'll need to peer hard to spot them. The remainder of the museum covers Southland's history, both human and natural, with exhibits ranging from moa bones to Maori artefacts and Victoriana. The **art gallery** displays international and national works, with exhibitions changing every few weeks.

The huge public gardens of **Queens Park** stretch north behind the museum from Gala Street and have been a public reserve since 1869. Today there are showhouses, a formal rose garden, a rhododendron dell, an aviary and a statuary, as well as an eighteen-hole golf course, various sports grounds and the biggest aquatic centre in New Zealand (with three pools, one of them Olympic-size, see p.613 for details). The park's main entrance is on Queens Drive; other entrances (with car parks) are located off Gala Street and Victoria Avenue, while there's pedestrians-only access from Kelvin and Herbert streets.

Back in the city centre, Tay Street has some distinctive **architecture**. At the junction with Jed Street is the so-called **First Presbyterian Church** of 1915 (in fact the second, built after the First Church of Otago, in Dunedin), which is kept locked. Designed by architect John T. Mair, in Romanesque style, it has impressive ornamental brickwork, fashioned into a mosaic. Near the corner with Deveron Street stands the magnificent **Town Hall and Civic Theatre**. The Town Hall was completed in 1906 and is a fine example of neo-Renaissance style with its plasterwork, pediments and ornamental parapets carved from white Oamaru stone. Two streets south, on Tyne Street and near the junction with Nith Street, the striking Roman Catholic **St Mary's Basilica** was designed by F.W. Petre, its brick exterior concealing a sumptuous interior lining of Oamaru stone, unfortunately only visible when the church is open for services. Its elegant copper dome can be spotted for miles around, but the best vantage point is from the gardens flanking the Otepuni Stream on the other side of the road.

Anderson Park and Oreti Beach

On the outskirts of Invercargill, 7km north of the city centre are the beautifully preserved grounds and stately home of **Anderson Park**. Donated to the city in 1951, the house contains an atmospheric gallery set amid extensive **grounds** (unrestricted access; free). The Georgian-style mansion was built in 1925 as the family home of a local businessman. Designed by Christchurch architect Cecil Wood, it was constructed from reinforced concrete and set against a backdrop of forest. The delightful **gallery** (Tues–Sun 1.30–4.30pm; free except during special exhibitions) displays a permanent collection of traditional and contemporary New Zealand art. During the month of October, a spring exhibition of recent Kiwi art replaces the permanent collection, and there are recitals each Sunday, when classical music drifts around the gardens. Behind the gallery, **The Maori House**, also built in the early 1920s, was used for dances, its doorway and porch decorated with carvings by Tene Waitere, a renowned Rotorua carver. Anderson Park is a three-kilometre drive along McIvor Road, via North Road/SH6, or during daylight hours through Donovan Park, off Bainfield Road. There is no bus service to out here; a taxi will cost you about $15 one way.

Oreti Beach, 9.5km west of the city centre, is a beautiful broad expanse of fine sand, sweeping 30km right around to the seaside resort of Riverton to the west (see p.756), and giving great views of Stewart Island and Bluff. In summer, it's popular for swimming (surf patrols operate), yachting and water-skiing, but there are sometimes shark alerts, and windy days cause violent sandstorms. Use the entrance off Dunns Road (the others are pretty rough going); there's no bus service to the beach.

Eating, drinking and entertainment

The culinary revolution already well under way elsewhere in New Zealand is only just beginning in Invercargill. As a result there are a few really good places to eat, but hardly any cosmopolitan cafés. A strength, though, is the local **seafood**, including excellent blue cod and Bluff oysters. Another local delicacy is **muttonbird**, though the oily and rather fishy flavour is something of an acquired taste. Serious **drinking** doesn't generally start until Friday night.

148 on Elles, 148 Elles Rd (☎03/216 1000). An elegant upmarket restaurant, serving large portions of local seafood, steak and venison in a restored 1912 building. Main courses will set you back $20–30. Dinner only.

Bad Minnies, 38 Dee St, Piccadilly Lane (☎03/218 3551). Tucked away near the library, this intimate evening spot on two levels has a café feel, background R & B music and an extremely hospitable host. Imaginative, consistently good main courses ($20–25) are accompanied by Australian and Kiwi wines. Try their homemade pâté and "Drunken Duck", followed by sticky toffee pudding. In season, they catch their own muttonbirds and prepare them in a traditional Maori fashion by preserving in salt. Closed Sun; BYO & licensed.

Frog 'n' Firkin Café & Bar, Dee St, next door to the cinema. Good, economical pub food for lunch and dinner. Live entertainment Thurs nights and a good dance spot (with DJ) till 3am at weekends.

HMS King's Restaurant, 80 Tay St (☎03/218 3443). Jauntily decorated to look like an old wooden ship, this restaurant is *the* seafood spot in town. Blue cod, crayfish, oysters (in season) and whitebait are served up for $20 and under. Mon–Fri lunch and dinner, Sat dinner only, closed Sun; BYO & licensed.

Joy's Gourmet Kitchen, 122 Dee St. A reliable breakfast place open daily from 7am.

Rocks Café & Restaurant, Courtville Place, 101 Dee St (☎03/218 7597). A small and trendy café-cum-wine bar where voices and background music reverberate, reaching headache-inducing levels on Fri and Sat nights. Lunches for $10 or less; dinner around $20 a main course. Theme nights on the second Sun of each month, and jazz or blues on the second Fri.

Tillermans Café & Bar, 16 Don St (☎03/218 9240). This excellent-value local institution offers high-quality cosmopolitan food (lunch for under $10, dinner for under $20). The atmosphere is relaxed, and large vibrant paintings adorn the brick walls. Upstairs is a popular bar with pool tables, a focal point for live music on Sat nights. Closed Mon eve and all day Sun.

Zookeeper's Café, 50 Tay St. A zany, inexpensive, split-level café and bar easily identified by its ironwork giraffe in the window. From 10am till late they serve bar food, snacks and a wide-ranging menu with generous portions – nothing over $16.

Entertainment

Local bands play at several of the city's hotels on Friday and Saturday nights (check *The Southland Times* for details) and there are three **dance venues** worth trying. *The Colosseum* nightclub is 3km north of the city centre, on Gimblett Street, Waikiwi (Thurs–Sun from 9.30pm and occasional Sun from 8.30pm), while in town you can dance the night away at the *Frog 'n' Firkin* (see p.611) and *Sgt. Pepper's Café/Bar* in the *Don Lodge Hotel* on Don Street.

For details of productions at the Civic Theatre in Tay Street and the State Insurance Theatre in Don Street, check the *The Southland Times* **arts** page on Tuesday. The four-screen Movieland **cinema** at 29 Dee St (☎0900/900 77) has reduced ticket prices on Monday and Tuesday and any day before 5pm.

Listings

Airlines Air New Zealand (☎03/214 4737); Ansett ☎03/214 4644); Southern Air (for daily scheduled services to Stewart Island; ☎03/218 9129 or 0800/658 876).

Automobile Association 47 Gala St (☎03/218 9033).

Bike rental Gladstone Cycles, 430 Dee St (☎03/218 8822), $15 a day; Wensley's Cycles, cnr Tay St and Nith St (☎03/218 6206), $10–20 a day, and bike repairs too.

Buses InterCity (☎03/214 0598) operate daily from the train station to Dunedin, Christchurch, Queenstown & Te Anau. Shuttle bus services include the daily door-to-door Catch-a-Bus (☎03/477 7900) to Queenstown, Cromwell, Wanaka & Dunedin, and Spitfire Shuttle Service (☎03/214 1851) to Te Anau, via the Southern Scenic Route. Campbelltown Passenger Service (☎03/212 7404) run regular buses to Bluff for the ferry to Stewart Island.

Car parks There's a multistorey car park at the rear of the library, with access off Leven St. Pay-and-display car parks are located in Don St, Deveron St and Esk St.

Car rental The multinational firms have branches in the city: Avis, 73 Airport Ave (☎%03/218 7019); Budget, Airport Ave (☎03/218 7019); Hertz, 109 Spey St (☎03/218 2837). Cheaper alternatives include: Crawford Rentals, 166 Clyde St (☎03/218 3870); Inner City Rentals, cnr Clyde St & Tweed St (☎03/214 4483); Rent-a-Dent, 259 Mersey St (☎03/214 4820); Riverside Rentals, 90 Preston St (☎03/215 9030); and Waikiwi Rentals, 376 North Rd (☎03/215 7328).

Ferry The *Foveaux Express* (☎03/212 7660) departs Bluff for Stewart Island Aug 24–May 20 Mon–Sat 9.30am & 5pm, Sun 5pm; May 21–Aug 23 Mon–Fri 9.30am & 4pm, Sun 4pm.

Laundry Wunda Wash Laundromat, Glengarry Shopping Centre, Yarrow St. Open daily.

Library Invercargill Public Library is in Dee St (Mon–Fri 9am–8.30pm, Sat 10am–1pm; ☎03/218 7025).

Medical treatment Southland Hospital, on Kew Rd (☎03/218 1949), has a 24hr accident and emergency department. For illness and minor accidents outside surgery hours, contact the Urgent Doctor Service in The Crescent (Mon–Fri 5pm–9am, Sat, Sun & public holidays 24hr; ☎03/218 8821).

Pharmacy Inside the Countdown supermarket (daily Mon–Fri 8.30am–10pm, Sat & Sun 9am–7pm); Urgent Pharmacy, 90 Kelvin St (Mon–Wed 7–10pm, Sat 10am–noon, 2–4.30pm & 7–10pm, Sun 11am–12.30pm, 2–3pm & 7–10pm).

Police The central police station is in Don St (☎03/214 4039).

Post office The main post office is in Don St, near the junction with Kelvin St (Mon–Fri 8.30am–5pm).

Swimming Splash Palace, Elles Rd (Sat 6am–9pm, Sun 8am–8pm) is an aquatic centre in Queens Park, with three pools, a hydroslide, spa and steam room.

Taxis Blue Star (☎03/218 6079); Catch-a-Bus (☎03/214 1414); The Taxi Co (☎03/214 4478).

Tours Invercargill Passenger Service (☎03/218 7108) run a two-hour city tour ($30 per person) taking in the Southland Museum, Queens Park, Anderson Park and a few historic landmarks. They also offer 3hr trips to Bluff ($40). Lynette Jack Scenic Sights (☎025/338 370, after hours 03/215 7741) operate similar tours of Invercargill, but include Oreti Beach ($30 per person); also tours of Bluff ($45), Riverton ($45), Western Southland ($120) and the Catlins Coast ($130). For more on tours to the Catlins, see box on p.603. Scenic flights to Stewart Island can be arranged with South East Air (☎03/214 5522) and Southland Air Charter (☎03/218 6171); see p.618 for more details.

Trains The Southerner departs for Christchurch every morning from the train station in Leven St (☎0800/802 802), returning in the evening.

Bluff

Twenty-seven kilometres south of Invercargill, perching at the tip of a peninsula, is the small fishing town of **BLUFF** and its man-made port. Offering great views across Foveaux Strait, Bluff is the departure point of the **Stewart Island ferry**, and you may choose to avoid Invercargill altogether and stay here in the local B&B or hotel. You won't need more than half a day to get a good look at the place, but without a car this involves a good deal of walking as the town spreads along the shoreline for about 6km.

Bluff is the oldest European town in New Zealand, having been continuously settled since 1824. These days it's still struggling to recover from the 1980s recession, and has a rather tired feel about it. The **harbour**, however, flourishes, exporting Southland's meat, timber, aluminium, fish and wool, and importing a variety of goods from overseas. In addition the Foveaux Strait yields a highly sought-after delicacy – the **Bluff oyster**. This deepwater shellfish has a sweet and succulent taste, and is dredged from the beginning of March until the end of August, then processed in oyster sheds at Bluff before being sent all over the country. Between June and August you can watch them being processed at Johnson's Oyster Factory (daily 8am–5pm; free; bookings ☎03/212 8665). Across the harbour, at Tiwai Point, is the sprawl of a giant aluminium smelter, Southland's biggest employer.

Bluff's small **Maritime Museum** (Mon–Fri 10am–4.30pm, Sat & Sun 1–5pm; $2), on Foreshore Road as you enter town from Invercargill, has historical displays focusing on whaling, the harbour development, oyster harvesting and shipwrecks. Pride of place is given to a vast triple-expansion steam engine, taken from a steam tug, TST *Awarua*, which spent most of its life working the harbour. Back on the main road, you'll pass the ferry wharf and, three streets further, on the corner with Henderson Street, the kitsch **Paua Shell House** (daily 9am–5pm; free). This is the home of Fred and Myrtle, a couple who have spent years amassing a collection of shells from all over the world – most noticeably iridescent paua shells gathered from local beaches, which are plastered all over their living-room walls, creating a wall-to-wall shimmer in blue and green.

From here it's another 1.5km to the end of the road, and **Stirling Point**, which feels rather like the end of the earth, with its many-armed signpost marking the distance to major international cities. The views are impressive and, on a clear day, you can see as far as Stewart Island, 35km away. From the car park at the end of the road you can set out on a couple of easy walks: the **Foveaux Walkway** (6.6km; 2hr one way) and, branching off it, the **Glory Track** (3.8km; 1hr return). The first is an exposed walk skirting Bluff Hill's rugged coastline, with some magnificent views, before cutting back across open farmland to the main road at the other end of town, near the old freezing works. The second is a loop track, mixing forest and coastal scenery. Short sections of the Glory Track are very steep, but the surface is sealed.

The turning to another good viewpoint, **Bluff Hill Lookout**, leaves the main road in town at Lee Street, opposite the ferry wharf. From here it's a three-kilometre drive, or a thirty-minute walk, to the car park and viewing platform beyond. From 267m up you get a 360-degree view of Stewart Island and the other, smaller islands in Foveaux Strait, Southland's estuaries and the harbour. The sunsets here are astonishing.

Practicalities

Bluff is a twenty-minute drive down SH1 from central Invercargill. Local **buses** run a regular daily service between the city and Bluff ($6, same-day return $10), to connect with the ferry. For details on sailings to Stewart Island, see p.612.

Good **accommodation** in Bluff is limited to the *Foveaux Hotel*, 40 Gore St (☎03/212 7196; ④), whose rooms are all en suite, with breakfast included in the price, and the four en-suite B&B rooms above the *Land's End Wine Bar and Café* at Stirling Point (☎ & fax 03/212 7575; ⑤). The *Land's End*, perched high on the hill, also serves **breakfast, lunch**, Devonshire teas and **dinner** daily, with specialities including pan-fried blue cod ($15.50) and oysters. Back in town, the *Harbour Lights Café*, at 158 Gore St, is popular among locals, especially for its seafood. The *Captain's Retreat* in the *Foveaux Hotel* is a rather pricey, licensed seafood and grill restaurant (evenings only) with a good reputation and a comfortable bar.

Stewart Island

New Zealand's third main island is the small, rugged triangle of **STEWART ISLAND**, separated from the mainland by Foveaux Strait and largely ignored by tourists. Its lack of pulling power is understandable: it's fairly expensive to get to; most of the island is uninhabited and covered in dense native bush and coastal rainforest; the climate is mild but wet; and mainstream attractions are limited. Apart from some serious wilderness tramping and great sunsets (hence the island's Maori name of *Rakiura*, meaning "Land of the Glowing Skies"), the chief reasons to visit are to go **kiwi spotting** in the wild, and to visit **Ulva Island**, a haven for native New Zealand birds. In addition, Stewart Island boasts one of New Zealand's Great Walks, **The Rakiura Track** (3 days), not to be confused with the island's mud-ridden North–West Circuit Track, only suited to the most experienced (and masochistic) tramper.

Inhabited by Maori from the thirteenth century and erroneously recorded as a peninsula by Captain Cook in 1770, the island was named after William Stewart, the first officer on a sealing vessel that visited in 1809. The island is characterized by bush-fringed bays, sandy coves, windswept beaches and a rugged interior of tall rimu forest and granite outcrops. The only settlement is tiny **Oban**, its uniformly bland buildings huddling around Halfmoon Bay and creeping uphill towards the airfield.

The mainstay of the economy was once rimu milling, with three thousand people living on the island in the boomtime of the early 1930s, but the main industries today are **fishing** (crayfish, blue cod and paua) and **fish farming** (salmon and mussels) in Big Glory Bay. The liveliest time to visit is during **Marine Mardi Gras** (Labour weekend, at the end of October). Bear in mind that there are **no banks or bureaux de change** on Stewart Island, although most businesses take credit cards.

Island practicalities

The *Foveaux Express*, a sixty-seater catamaran **ferry**, leaves regularly from Bluff (☎03/212 7660; $37 one-way, $74 return), usually taking one hour to cross the choppy Foveaux Strait. It departs twice daily Monday to Friday and once on Sunday, with two Saturday services (Aug 24–May 20). The ferry docks at the wharf in Oban, a stone's throw from the town centre. A far easier journey is in the nine-seater Southern Air **plane**, which leaves three times daily from Invercargill Airport (☎03/218 9129 & 0800/658 876; $68 one-way, $123 return; student and YHA standby discounts). Shuttle-bus transfers between central Oban and the airfield are included in the price of your ticket. Alternatively, you can catch a Southern Air flight direct from Dunedin (Mon, Wed, Fri & Sun 1pm; $190 return, YHA & student standby $120; 1hr).

Since it's easy to walk around the inhabited part of the island, you're unlikely to need much **road transport** once you've arrived, although Oban Taxis & Tours (☎03/219 1456) operate a daily shuttle service. Alternatively, try Sam Sampson, based at Stewart Island Travel on Main Road in Oban (☎03/219 1269; after hours 219 1406). You can also rent **motor scooters** from Oban Taxis & Tours and Stewart Island Travel ($16 an hour, or $60 per day). **Mountain bikes** are rented out by Innes Backpackers on Argyle Street ($10 per day; ☎03/219 1080), or you can rent a Mazda station wagon from Stewart Island Travel ($70 a day). **Water taxis** operate between Stewart Island and Ulva Island departing from Golden Bay, a ten-minute walk from central Oban; both Seaview Tours (☎03/219 1014 or 219 1078) and Stewart Island (☎03/219 1394 or 219 1414), charge around $20 return per person. **Charter launches** are available for tailor-made diving, fishing or nature trips (Oban visitor centre – see below – has a list); see box on p.618 for other Stewart Island **tours**.

Accommodation ranges from backpacker hostels to B&Bs and hotels, some of them in Oban and some in neighbouring bays. It's always advisable to book ahead, especially during summer; in general, accommodation here is more **expensive** than on the mainland. Several people on the island **rent** out spare **rooms** in their homes, but these can be cramped and claustrophobic, becoming especially difficult during pro-longed bad weather. If you're staying for a week or more, and travelling as a couple or in a group, then consider renting a self-contained **holiday home** from Stewart Island Holiday Homes (☎03/217 6585 or 219 1057) or The Agency (☎03/219 1171, fax 219 1116).

Oban and around

It doesn't take long to get to grips with **OBAN**, which is enclosed by hills of dense bush and bisected by Main Road, linking the airfield with the other principal road on the island, the waterfront Elgin Terrace. This, in turn, extends in one direction to Horseshoe Bay and in the other to Leask Bay. The southeastern part of town is bound-ed by Golden Bay, the jumping-off point for boat trips to Paterson Inlet. The township consists of little more than a few houses, a hotel (very much the social centre), the vis-itor centre, a tiny museum, a couple of stores and a café.

Oban's combined **visitor centre** (daily 9am–5pm; ☎03/219 1218) and **DOC office** (☎03/219 1130) is centrally located on Main Road and has excellent displays on Stewart Island's tracks and natural history. Staff are helpful and have free maps of Oban and neighbouring bays, and can advise on accommodation, activities, island flora and fauna, tracks and transport; they also sell hut passes for the two major Stewart Island tracks. There's also an independent booking office at the town end of the wharf, The Agency (☎03/219 1171), which organizes various outdoor activities. The **post office** is in the Southern Air depot, on the waterfront, near the junction with Ayr Street (daily: Oct–March 7.30am–6.30pm; April–Sept 7.30am–4.30pm), where stamps are still can-celled by hand.

Oban offers a couple of **short walks** (listed in the DOC pamphlet *Halfmoon Bay Walks*), one of which takes you up to a lookout point and the other through bird-filled bush. Definitely worthwhile is the stroll up to the hilltop vantage point of **Observation Rock** (15min). From here the panorama laid out below (best seen at sunset) includes Golden Bay and the island's highest point, Mount Anglem, on one side, and Horseshoe Bay on the other, as well as the expanse of Paterson Inlet, broken by the long strip of Ulva Island and the blobs of other islets. To reach the summit, follow Ayr Street past the Rakiura Museum, crossing Dundee Street and continuing up along Golden Bay

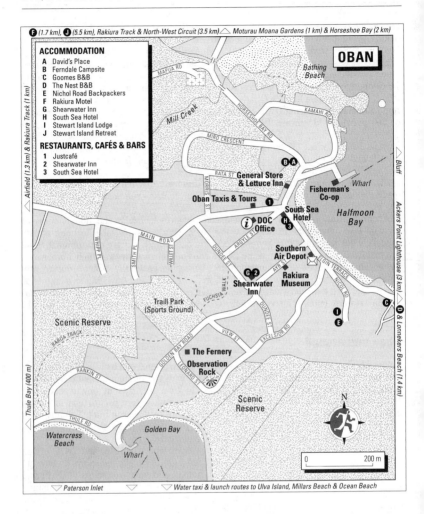

Road. Near the summit of the hill is a small gallery, The Fernery (Oct–March Mon–Sat 9am–5pm), which sells a cornucopia of souvenirs and gifts, all inspired by the island and hand-made by New Zealand artists and craftspeople. Just past the gallery, Observation Rock is signposted up Leonard Street and along a short forest track on the left to the lookout point.

For a taste of some stunning bush, first dominated by fuchsia, then by rimu, follow the signposted **Fuchsia Walk,** which begins at Dundee Street and emerges a few minutes later at Traill Park. In summer the foliage rings with the birdsong of tui, bellbirds and pigeons. From the end of the Fuchsia Walk, you can follow the **Raroa Track** down through fine rimu forest to Watercress Bay (15min). Thule Road and Golden Bay Road lead back to town from the bay (1km; 30min).

Accommodation

Ferndale Campsite, Horseshoe Bay Rd (☎03/219 1176). The only official campsite on the island and just 200m north of the wharf. Facilities include coin-operated showers and a washing machine. Tent sites $5.

David's Place, Horseshoe Bay Rd (☎03/219 1078, no advance bookings taken). A small, friendly backpackers in relaxed surroundings 200m from the wharf, with TV, microwave and fridge. Dorms ①, rooms ②.

Goomes B&B, Leask Bay Rd (☎03/219 1057). About 300m from the *South Sea Hotel*, this is the cheapest of the B&Bs, but nevertheless offers good-quality accommodation with great views. Dinner by arrangement; free pick-up. ⑤.

The Nest B&B, Lonnekers Beach (☎03/219 1310). Two kilometres from the wharf (free pick-ups), this big, bright house perched on a hill overlooking a small bay has plenty of character. Two double rooms with shared facilities; dinner (an optional extra) is often seafood. ⑥.

Nichol Road Backpackers, Nichol Rd (☎03/219 1328). Friendly, warm, spacious and new, this backpackers is just 500m from the wharf. Dorm ①, rooms ②.

Rakiura Motel, Horseshoe Bay Rd (☎03/219 1096). Great views over Halfmoon Bay from a hill just outside Oban, 2.5km from the wharf (a 25-minute walk, or $7.50 taxi ride). Five well maintained units sleeping four to six people. ④.

Shearwater Inn, cnr of Ayr St & Dundee St (☎03/219 1114). Central, large and basic, with shared facilities. Communal kitchen and lounge; breakfast available. ③.

South Sea Hotel, cnr of Main Rd & Elgin Terrace (☎03/219 1059, fax 219 1120). Clean rooms above the waterfront pub, in a hundred-year-old building, but can be a little noisy (especially Room 6 right above the bar). TV lounge. ④.

Stewart Island Lodge, off Nichol Rd (☎03/219 1085). A grandiose luxury lodge with five airy suites, offering panoramic views of Halfmoon Bay and the surrounding hills. Lavish home cooking, featuring fresh local seafood. Either B&B rates or full board; courtesy pick-up. ⑧.

Stewart Island Retreat, Horseshoe Bay (☎ & fax 03/219 1071). An ideal place to unwind, 6km from Oban wharf (free pick-up), is this spacious and comfortable B&B on the shore of the bay. Large rooms with shared facilities; excellent dinners and packed lunches by arrangement. ⑥.

Eating and drinking

Oban has only a few places to **eat** and even these close early in the evening. If you're cooking for yourself, you can buy basic foodstuffs, fruit and vegetables at the Ship to Shore **general store** and *Lettuce Inn* next door, whose prices compare well with those on the mainland. Fresh fish and crayfish can be bought from the Fishermen's Co-op on the wharf, the *Lettuce Inn* or Southern Seafoods at Horseshoe Bay, or direct from the locals.

The only decent **café** in Oban is the *Justcafé*, up from the hotel on Main Road, which serves fresh coffee. Don't bother with the cheerless tearooms further up the road. The *South Sea Hotel* has a simple **restaurant** that serves lunchtime snacks and unpretentious early-evening meals (closes 8pm), while the *Shearwater Inn* serves inexpensive and hearty meals in its bistro (Oct–April). Just outside Oban, at Horseshoe Bay, the tiny café adjoining the *Stewart Island Retreat* serves coffee and cake, and with prior arrangement will provide lunchboxes ($10).

Drinking is confined to the two bars at the *South Sea Hotel*, the focus of most social activity in these parts, and the small house bar upstairs at the *Shearwater Inn* (Oct–April only). The local ale, once brewed on the island but now produced in Invercargill, is the powerful and aptly named "Roaring Forties".

Around Oban

North of Halfmoon Bay, twenty-minutes' walk along Horseshoe Bay Road, are the attractive and secluded **Moturau Moana public gardens**, which were donated to the island in 1940. Picnic tables, barbecues and a viewing platform looking out across the bay to Oban are set amid lawns, native plants and dense virgin forest.

STEWART ISLAND TOURS

The best tour on the island is the **kiwi-spotting trip** which takes you to a remote area
to see the Stewart Island brown kiwi (a sub-species of the mainland birds) in the wild.
Bravo Adventure Cruises (book as far ahead as possible on ☎ & fax 03/219 1144; $50)
runs atmospheric four-hour trips every other night, picking up from central Oban
accommodation around dusk. You'll need warm clothing, sturdy footwear and a flashlight. The adventure entails a short boat trip and a brief bushwalk to a windswept beach,
where the kiwi feast on tiny crustaceans. Great care is taken to avoid disturbing these
timid birds.

General tours of the island are run by an irrepressible island character, Sam, who drives "Billy the Bus". A naturalist and historian, he humorously imparts his intimate knowledge of local history, flora and fauna and the islanders' way of life on a short tour leaving
from Stewart Island Travel on Main Road (most days at 11.30am; 1hr; $15; book ahead
on ☎03/219 1269). Also worthwhile are his longer afternoon excursions, which include
guided walks (2hr 30min; $25), and trips to **Ackers Point** (see below), picking up and
dropping off at Oban (Mon, Wed & Fri; other days by arrangement; 3–4hr; $30). There
are also more prosaic bus tours with Oban Taxis & Tours (daily 11am & 1.30pm; 1hr
30min; $15; book ahead on ☎03/219 1456), departing from their office on Main Road,
opposite the visitor centre, and with **Sunset Bus Tours** (Apil–Oct only; 7.30pm; 2hr;
$16).

Scenic flights can be arranged with Invercargill-based South East Air (☎03/214 5522),
who will drop you off for sightseeing, tramping and diving in inaccessible parts of the
island, such as Mason Bay ($130 one-way). Southland Air Charter (Stewart Island
☎03/219 1090, Invercargill ☎03/218 6171) also offer over-flights and operate as air taxis,
dropping-off trampers, picnickers and day-trippers.

Tours of **Ulva Island** and its plant and birdlife are arranged through DOC. Moana
Charters (☎03/219 1202) offers an enjoyable half-day scenic boat excursion ($40 per
person), which includes stops for fishing and a visit to salmon farms on the way to the
island, where you're dropped off and collected later. See p.620 for details of **kayaking**
trips.

One of the more interesting historical sites on the island is an abandoned
Norwegian whaling base near **Millars Beach** at Prices Inlet, about 6.5km west of
Oban. The only access is by boat, so you'll need to charter a launch or water taxi
from Golden Bay to Millars Beach (15min; $40), from where an easy twenty-minute
coastal walk heads north from the beachside picnic shelter through native bush to
the whaling base. Several eerie relics remain from 1923–33, when a fleet of
Antarctic whaling ships was repaired here, and the beach is littered with objects left
behind: old drums, cables, giant iron propellers, a boiler out in the water and, at the
far end, a wrecked sailing ship deliberately sunk by the whaling company to create
a wharf.

A good coastal walk, the **Harrold Bay to Ackers Point Lighthouse** track (1.25km;
20min), starts at the end of Leask Bay Road, 2.5km east of the post office along the
waterfront, and gives you the chance to see **little blue penguins** and **muttonbirds**
returning to their nests at dusk (Nov–Feb). Near the start of the track, you can follow
a brief diversion to Harrold Bay, the site of a simple stone house built in 1835, making
it one of the oldest European buildings in New Zealand. The main track continues
through coastal forest to a lighthouse and lookout point from where you can watch the
penguins arduously climbing to their nests hidden in the bush. You'll need a flashlight
to find your way around after dusk, but keep the beam pointed to the ground to avoid
disturbing the birds. Guided tours also come out here, often staying late into the night
(see box above).

Ulva Island and Paterson Inlet

Well worth a visit for its astonishing bird life, pleasant walks, beaches and rich natural vegetation is the scenic reserve of **Ulva Island**, the largest of several islands in **Paterson Inlet**, a flooded valley cutting deep into Stewart Island. **Water taxis** ply out here regularly from the wharf at Golden Bay ($15–20 return) and you should allow a

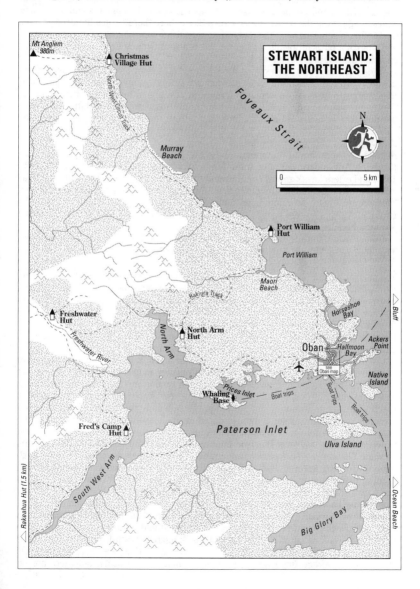

STEWART ISLAND: THE NORTHEAST

full day (bring a packed lunch) to explore the several gentle tracks around the island; see box on p.618 for details of **guided tours**.

Clearly visible from Oban, the long, low island has largely escaped the effects of introduced predators and is full of birdsong. Thriving in its dense vegetation are weka, bellbirds, oystercatchers, kaka, yellow- and red-crowned parakeets, tui, fantails and pigeons, who fearlessly approach visitors out of curiosity. Plant life includes many species of fern and orchid, and the forest floor is covered in mosses and liverworts. Tracks begin from the wharf at Post Office Bay (where there's still a hundred-year-old post office, a remnant from the days when the island was the hub of the community) and there's a pleasant picnic shelter on the beach at Sydney Cove nearby. Note that camping overnight is not allowed.

One of the best ways to explore the sheltered waters of Paterson Inlet is in a **sea kayak**. Scattered around the inlet's margins are several navigable rivers and four DOC huts where you can stay overnight (arrange in advance with the DOC field centre in Oban). Frequent visitors to these waters are bottle-nosed dolphins and fur seals, while the tidal flats attract wading birds, including herons, oystercatchers, godwits and the New Zealand dotterel. Bear in mind that the waters around Stewart Island can be changeable and May to August brings the most settled weather; only extremely experienced kayakers should venture into these waters unaccompanied. Stewart Island Sea Kayaking Adventures operates from *Innes Backpackers* on Argyle Street (☎03/219 1080) and offers kayak **rental** (single kayaks $30 a day, double kayaks $60), as well as guided **tours** with flexible itineraries (from $65 per person per day). They also rent out waterproofs, tents, sleeping bags and stoves. Completely Southern Sea Kayaks (☎03/219 1275) also rent kayaks ($40 per person per day), and their guided trips cost $35 for a half-day, $55 full day.

The Rakiura Track and North–West Circuit

You need to be well equipped for both of Stewart Island's major walks both of which fan out from Oban. As the weather is changeable, often mixing sunshine and rain within an hour, take several layers of clothing for warmth, good waterproofs (including gaiters) and don't forget sandfly repellent. The DOC office has a helpful video and leaflets on the tracks, and you must buy hut or campsite passes before you set out. You'll need a Great Walks pass for the Rakiura Track and for part of the North–West Circuit. Both tracks are usually deserted except for the Christmas period.

One of New Zealand's Great Walks, the **Rakiura Track** (29km, plus a further 7km of road walking to complete the circuit; 3 days) makes an excellent introduction to the island's history, forest and birdlife. Starting and ending in Oban, the circuit can be walked in either direction, and at any time of the year, since boardwalk covers most of the track's boggy sections. Staying within the bushline, the track follows the open coast, before climbing over a three-hundred-metre forested ridge and traversing the shores of Paterson Inlet. The highlight is a lookout tower on the summit ridge, which provides excellent views of Paterson Inlet and beyond to the Tin Range. The two huts en route (30 bunks; $8 per person) are equipped with mattresses, wood stoves for heating only, running water and toilets, but you'll need your own stove. Camping is allowed at three designated areas ($6 per person) along the way – Maori Beach, Port William and Sawdust Bay – and sites have water supply and toilets.

Only the hardiest and most experienced tramper should consider attempting the **North–West Circuit** (130km; 10–12 days) around the island's northern arm. Mud on the tracks is the main problem, usually widespread and often deep and thick. One option is to walk as far as the second hut (at Bungaree, 17km from Oban) and then hook up with the Rakiura Track. Ten huts (6–30 bunks; $4–8) are spaced at intervals suited to an average day's tramping, most of them on the coast, but there are no campsites. The track itself alternates between open coast and forested hill country, offering highlights of a side trip to the 980-metre summit of Mount Anglem (5.5km; 6hr return) and the chance to see kiwi in the wild at Mason Bay.

travel details

Trains

Dunedin to: Balclutha (1 daily; 1hr 10min); Gore (1 daily; 2hr 23min); Invercargill (1 daily; 3hr 18min); Oamaru (1 daily; 2hr 25min).

Invercargill to: Balclutha (1 daily; 2hr 8min); Dunedin (1 daily; 3hr 18min); Gore (1 daily; 55min).

Buses

Dunedin to: Alexandra (4 daily; 3hr); Balclutha (6 daily; 1hr 35min); Cromwell (4 daily; 3hr 30min); Gore (6 daily; 2hr 35min); Invercargill (6 daily; 3hr 10min); Lawrence (4 daily; 1hr 30min); Oamaru (5 daily; 1hr 30min); Queenstown (4 daily; 4hr 25min).

Invercargill to: Gore (2 daily; 55min); Queenstown (4 daily; 2hr 40min); Te Anau (2 daily; 2hr 25min).

Ferries

Invercargill to: Stewart Island (2 daily; 1hr).

Stewart Island to: Invercargill (2 daily; 1hr).

Planes

Dunedin to: Auckland (12 daily; 2hr 40min); Blenheim (9 daily; 3hr 5min); Christchurch (10 daily; 45 min); Gisborne (6 daily; 3hr 15min); Hamilton (7 daily; 2hr 30min); Hokitika (4 daily; 1hr 45min); Invercargill (2 daily; 30min); Kaitaia (3 daily, 4hr 20min); Napier/Hastings (6 daily; 3hr); Nelson (12 daily; 2hr); New Plymouth (5 daily; 4hr); Palmerston North (7 daily; 2hr 40min); Rotorua (7 daily; 3hr 50min); Stewart Island (four times weekly; 1hr); Taupo (4 daily; 3hr 50min); Tauranga (9 daily; 3hr); Wanganui (3 daily; 3hr); Wellington (12 daily; 1hr 10min); Westport (2 daily; 3hr); Whakatane (6 daily; 4hr 5min); Whangarei (8 daily; 3hr 45min).

Invercargill to: Auckland (8 daily; 3hr 30min); Blenheim (6 daily; 4hr); Christchurch (8 daily; 1hr 40min); Dunedin (3 daily; 30min); Gisborne (4 daily; 5hr); Hamilton (4 daily; 7hr); Hokitika (4 daily; 6hr); Kataia (2 daily; 4hr 40min); Napier/Hastings (4 daily; 4hr 30min); Nelson (7 daily; 4hr 30min); New Plymouth (4 daily; 4hr); Palmerston North (6 daily; 3hr 25min); Rotorua (4 daily; 4hr 25min); Stewart Island (6 daily; 20min); Taupo (3 daily; 3hr 45min); Tauranga (4 daily; 3hr 30min); Wanganui (3 daily; 4hr); Wellington (8 daily; 2hr); Westport (2 daily; 7hr); Whakatane (5 daily; 8hr); Whangarei (6 daily; 4hr 30min).

Stewart Island to: Dunedin (four times weekly; 1hr); Invercargill (6 daily; 20min).

CHAPTER TWELVE

THE WEST COAST

T he Southern Alps run down the backbone of the South Island, both defining and isolating **the West Coast**. A narrow, rugged and largely untamed coastal strip of turbulent rivers, lush bushland and crystal lakes that's seldom more than 30km wide, it comes fringed by astonishing surf-pounded beaches backed by the odd tiny shack or, more frequently, nothing at all. What really sets "the Coast" apart is the interaction of settlers with their environment. **Coasters**, many descended from early gold and coal miners, have long been proud of their ability to coexist with the wild primeval landscape – a trait mythologized in their reputation for **independent-mind-edness** and intemperate beer-drinking, no doubt fuelled by a heavy admixture of Irish drawn to the 1860s gold rushes. Stories abound of late-night drinking sessions in pubs way past their closing times, and overall, your fondest memories of the West Coast might well be chance encounters one evening in the pub, rather than the sights.

Cook sailed up this way in 1770, when he described the Coast as "… an inhospitable shore, unworthy of observation, except for its ridge of naked and barren rocks covered with snow. As far as the eye could reach the prospect was wild, craggy and desolate". Little here then for early **European explorers** such as Thomas Brunner and Charles Heaphy, who made forays in 1846–47, led by Kehu, a Maori guide. They returned without finding the cultivable land they sought, and after a shorter trip in 1861 Henry Harper, the first Bishop of Christchurch, wrote, "I doubt if such a wilderness will ever be colonized except through the discovery of **gold**". Prophetic words: within two years reports were circulating of flecks of gold in West Coast rivers and a year later Greymouth and Hokitika were experiencing full-on gold rushes. The boom was soon over, but mining continued into the twentieth century, with huge dredges littering the

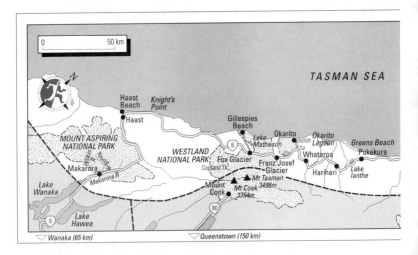

landscape, looking like beached galleons as they worked their way up the gravel riverbeds, scuttling through spent tailings.

As gold was worked out, longer-lasting **coal** took its place (the West Coast still produces a third of the country's coal), laying the foundation for more permanent towns. Many of these have since foundered and a shrinking economy has tapped the resourcefulness of the people – you'll still find individual miners hacking away at a single coal seam or running a sawmill in the bush single-handed. Abundant open space and low land prices have also nurtured a thriving **alternative culture**, and you may well spot the smoke stack of some purple bus sticking out from behind the trees. In the last ten years or so, everything has been turned upside down by the challenge of increasing **tourism** and a greater awareness of the the Coast's **fragile ecosystems**.

No discussion of the West Coast would be complete without mention of the torrential **rainfall**, which falls with tropical intensity for days at a time; every rock springs a waterfall and the bush becomes vibrant with colour. Such soakings have a detrimental effect on the soil, retarding decomposition and producing a peat-like top layer with all the minerals leached out. The result is **pakihi**, scrubby, impoverished and poor-looking paddocks that characterize much of the West Coast's cleared land. But the abundant sunshine that alternates with the downpours produces excellent conditions for **dope-growing**, a significant component of the local economy. Enthusiasm for marijuana growing is matched only by the springtime rush to catch **whitebait**, when fishers line the tidal riverbanks on rising tides trying to net this epicurean holy grail of Kiwi angling.

The boom-and-bust nature of the West Coast's gold- and coal-mining past produced scores of ghost towns, but also spawned its three largest towns – the harbour town of **Westport**, and the former ports of **Greymouth** and **Hokitika**. The real pleasure of the West Coast, though, lies in smaller places more closely tied to the countryside, where the Coasters' indomitable spirit shines through: places such as **Karamea**, on the southern limit of the Kahurangi National Park, the strike town of **Blackball** at the foot of the Croesus Track on the Paparoa Range, the gold town of **Ross** and windswept **Okarito**. With the exception of a couple of decent museums and a handful of sights, the West Coast's appeal is in its scenic beauty. The **Oparara Basin**, near Karamea, and the **Paparoa National Park**, south of Westport, exhibit some of the country's finest limestone formations, including huge arched spans and the famous Pancake Rocks, while

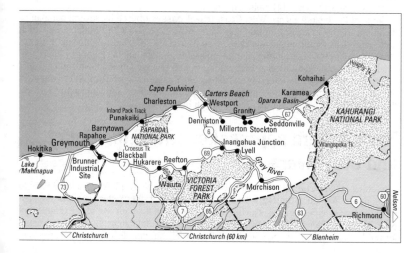

in the Westland National Park the frosty white tongues of the **Franz Josef and Fox
glaciers** career down the flanks of the Southern Alps into dense emerald bush almost
to sea level.

Most people visit from November to April, and you might expect that a place with
such a damp reputation is a bad place to visit in **winter**, but temperatures are not as low
as you might think and the greater number of clear days make for cloud-free viewing.
Pesky sandflies are also less active in the winter. The West Coast never feels crowded
but in the off-season you'll have even more room to move and accommodation will be
cheaper; the downside is that **whitewater rafting, caving** and **scenic flights**, which
require minimum numbers to operate, may be harder to arrange.

The simplest way to get around the West Coast is with your own **vehicle**. Likewise,
cycling isn't such a chore: the coast road is undulating but the distances between towns
aren't off-putting and you can always find somewhere to camp in between. Public transport, on the other hand, is fairly restrictive. **Trains** only penetrate as far as Greymouth;
bus services are infrequent and, though they call at all the major towns, they won't get
you to most of the walks. Having said that, with patience and a degree of forward planning it is possible to see much of interest, especially if you are prepared to walk a little.
The major bus **route** along the coast is the combined InterCity (☎03/768 1435) and
Mount Cook Landline (☎0800/800 287) service, which runs once a day in each direction; this is referred to in this chapter just as InterCity. For service frequencies and journey times, consult "Travel Details" on p.665.

Some of the best deals are West Coast **travel passes** offered by several companies
including the backpacker tour-bus operators, Kiwi Experience and Magic Bus, which
both run daily southbound services (see Basics, p.28). The Westcoast Express
(☎03/546 6703; $99) is designed along similar lines but with a more low-key approach,
smaller numbers and a slower pace, running from Nelson to Queenstown and back just
a couple of times a week. InterCity's **West Coast Passport** (Nov–April $114; May–Oct
$99) is good for travel (in one direction only) between Nelson and Queenstown over a
three-month period with as many stops as you like.

The northern approaches: along the Buller and Grey rivers

Stretching 169km from its source at Lake Rotoiti in the Nelson Lakes National Park to
its mouth at Westport, the **Buller River**'s blue-green waters reflect sunlight dappled
through riverside beech forests as they swirl and churn through one of the grandest of
New Zealand's river gorges between the Lyell and Brunner ranges. The Maori name
for the Buller is *Kawatiri*, meaning "deep and swift", a fitting description of its passage

THE BULLER GORGE AND REEFTON/625

through a region which, in the national consciousness, is associated with two devastating **earthquakes**. The first, registering 7.8 on the Richter Scale, was centred on Murchison in 1929; the other had its epicentre near Inungahua and struck in 1968. Landslides associated with these catastrophic events have combined with the natural geology to soften the curves of rocky bluffs that shelter white-sand beaches inaccessible from the road but frequently used by rafting parties. Gold was discovered along the Buller in 1858, sparking a gold rush centred on Lyell, now a ghost town whose outlying remains can be visited on the Lyell Walkway.

The Buller is traced by SH6 from Kawatiri Junction to Westport through Inungahua Junction, where Greymouth-bound travellers turn south towards Reefton. From Reefton, SH7 hugs the **Grey River**, a far less dramatic watercourse than the Buller, as it flows through a wide valley to the east of the granite tops of the Paparoa Range past more evidence of long-dead gold and coal industries, principally at laidback Blackball and the Brunner Industrial Site.

The Buller Gorge

SH6 from Nelson passes through Murchison (see p.463) and follows the Buller River 11km to **O'Sullivan's Bridge** where you turn right to remain on SH6 as it enters the Upper Buller Scenic Reserve. After 6km, the road passes the **Buller Bridge** ($2 toll), the longest example of the swaying pedestrian footbridges known in New Zealand as swing bridges; crossing high above the Buller River, the 110m span has a hair-raising 145m-long flying fox alongside.

Fifteen kilometres on, a lay-by provides a "**View of Earthquake Slip**" which, thirty years after the Inungahua earthquake, is gradually being recolonized but still bears the scars of the huge landslide that completely dammed the Buller River for several days. Following a 4km bend in the river, the road passes the grassy site of **Lyell**, a former gold-mining town named after the great geologist Charles Lyell. The town sat high above the Buller on flats beside Lyell Creek and, in its 1890s heyday, supported five hotels, two banks, two churches and even its own newspaper, all serving a population of three thousand spread between here, Gibbstown and Zalatown, further up the Lyell Creek. Fires and the gradual decline in gold mining saw off all three settlements, but a few mementoes remain, and can be visited via the short but fairly strenuous **Lyell Walkway**, which passes terraces where huts once stood, the sobering slabs that stand askew in the cemetery (15min return), and the ten-hammer Croesus quartz stamping battery (1hr 30min return). The roadside site of the former township itself is now a peaceful DOC **campsite** ($4).

The next town, 17km to the west, is **INUNGAHUA JUNCTION**, which is little more than a service station attached to a café and grocery shop, an excuse for a brief stop only, unless you want to stay at the rustic but pleasant *Inwoods Farm Backpacker*, Inwoods Road (☎03/789 0205; ①), signposted 400m down Inwoods Road which spurs off beside the general store.

West of Inungaha Junction the river approaches Westport through the **Lower Buller Gorge**, the narrowest and most dramatic section. The road hugs the cliff-face in places, most notably at **Hawks Crag**, where the rock has been hewn to form a large overhang – the fact that the water level rose several metres above this carved-out section during a 1926 flood will give you some idea of the volume of water that can surge down the gorge.

Reefton and around

Located beside the Inungahua River at the intersection of roads from Westport, Greymouth and Christchurch, **REEFTON**, as its name suggests, owes its existence to rich gold-bearing quartz reefs, which were exploited so heavily in the 1870s that this was considered by some "the most brisk and businesslike place in the colony". This frenzy of financial speculation put Reefton in the vanguard, and it became the first place in New Zealand, and one of the first in the world, to install electric street lighting powered by a hydroelectric generator. Such forward-looking activity soon abated and, despite decades as an important coal-mining town, moribund Reefton hasn't weathered well. The town is pleasant enough, but after a couple of hours you'll want to explore the Victoria Forest Park to the north or press on down the Grey Valley.

Specific points of interest around town are linked by two walks, both the subject of brochures available from the visitor centre (see "Practicalities", p.627). The elegiac **Historic Walk** (40min) meanders around Reefton's grid of streets, bidding farewell to the dilapidated exteriors of once-grand buildings – the Masonic Lodge, the School of Mines and the Court House – all ripe for preservation. The pleasant **Powerhouse Walk** (40min) also recalls a more illustrious past but succeeds in being more uplifting, perhaps because of its course along the Inungahua River.

The water race for Reefton's original hydroelectric scheme was diverted 2km from Blacks Point, where the **Blacks Point Museum**, Springs Junction Road (Oct–April Wed–Fri 9am–noon & 1–4pm, Sat & Sun 1–4pm; $2; ☎03/732 8808), occupies a former Wesleyan Chapel. The museum charts the district's cultural and mining history through engaging photos and a large collection of lamps, moustache cups, clunky old typewriters and the like. Outside, parts from two ancient stamper batteries have been knitted together to form one five-hammer battery hydro-driven by a Pelton wheel; the whole ensemble is cranked into action on Sunday afternoons and during school holidays. **Walks** along mining trails through the regenerating bush to the mine shafts and stamping batteries of the Murray Creek Goldfield start from behind the museum and range from half an hour to a day; pick up the informative *Walks in the Murray Creek Goldfield* leaflet from the visitor centre or museum.

Coal- and gold-mining heritage combines with a vast area of bushland in the **Victoria Forest Park**, which cloaks the ranges right around the western side of Reefton. The park is well off the traditional tourist itinerary and is consequently little-visited, making it all the more appealing for wilderness freaks. Day-walks are possible, but most require overnight stays in DOC huts; the visitor centre in Reefton can fill you in on all the options.

WESTLAND'S ENDANGERED FORESTS

If gold and coal built the West Coast's foundations, then the **timber industry** supports the structure. Ever since timber was felled for sluicing flumes and pit props, Coasters have relied on the seemingly limitless forests for their livelihood. As coal and gold were worked out, miners became loggers, felling trees which take from three hundred to six hundred years to mature and which, according to fossil records of pollen, have been around for 100 million years.

Few expressed any concern for the plight of Westland's magnificent stands of **beech** and **podocarp** until the 1970s, when the magnitude of the threat to the forests became clear. Environmental groups rallied around a campaign to save the Maruia Valley, east of Reefton, which became a touchstone for forest conservation, but it wasn't until the 1986 **West Coast Accord** between the government, local authorities, conservationists and the timber industry that some sort of truce prevailed. With the benefit of hindsight, the accord is considered by many to be far too weak: felling of the south Westland rimu forests stopped in 1994, but continues apace in Buller, and will do so under the terms of the accord until 2006. The effect on New Zealand's endangered **birds** – particularly kaka, kakariki (yellow-crowned parakeet), morepork (native owl) and rifleman – and long-tailed **bats**, all of which nest in holes in older trees, is incalculable.

Practicalities

Buses all stop on Broadway, Reefton's main street, within sight of the helpful combined **visitor centre** and **DOC office**, 67–69 Broadway (daily: Nov–March 8.30am–5.30pm; April–Oct 8.30am–4pm; ☎03/732 8391), which rents out gold pans for $2 a day, should you want to try your luck.

Almost all Reefton's **accommodation** is on, or just off, Broadway, the cheapest beds being bunks and small, old-fashioned doubles at *Wilson's Hotel*, 32 Broadway (☎03/732 8445; dorms ①, rooms ②–③). Slightly more modern rooms can be found at *Hotel Reefton*, 75 Broadway (☎03/732 8406; ③), and the best of the **motels** is the *Bellbird*, 93 Broadway (☎03/732 8444; ④), but Reefton's nicest rooms are at the central *Quartz Lodge B&B*, 78 Sheil St (☎0800/302 725, fax 03/732 8383; ④), which also serves $15 dinners. **Campers** should make for the *Reefton Domain Motor Camp*, 1 Ross St, at the top of Broadway (☎03/732 8477; tent sites $6, cabins ②), where there's good swimming in the Inungahua River, or head 10km south down the Grey Valley to DOC's *Slab Creek* campsite ($4).

About the only culinary relief from rural tearoom hell is *Alfresco Outside Eatery* (closed Sun), on Upper Broadway, with light **meals** and decent pizza served at lunch and on summer evenings.

The Grey Valley

Southwest of Reefton, SH7 follows the Grey Valley, cut off from the Tasman Sea by the rugged Paparoa Range and hemmed in by the Southern Alps. From both sides, the bush is gradually reclaiming the mine workings that characterized the region for a century. Nothing has stepped in to replace them, and the small communities tick over, a few eking a living from inquisitive tourists keen to explore the former mining towns of **Waiuta** and **Blackball**, and to walk the **Croesus Track**.

Waiuta

The first diversion of any consequence lies 21km south of Reefton where **Hukarere** marks the junction for **WAIUTA**, a ghost town seventeen partly-sealed kilometres east. This was the last of the West Coast's great gold towns, attaining a population of 6000 in the 1930s.

The end came for Waiuta when a mine shaft collapsed in 1951, burying large deposits of gold-bearing reef-quartz 879m down, where it was uneconomic to extract them. Miners left for jobs on the coast, much of the equipment was bought by Australian mining companies and even many of the houses were carted off, but the town wasn't completely abandoned; four or the remaining five cottages are occupied and there are several more buildings scattered around, including the original post office. The rolling country pocked by waste heaps is slowly being colonized by pioneer species like gorse and bramble, but the cypresses and poplars that once delineated gardens and the fruit trees that filled them remain; the rugby field, whippet track, croquet lawns and swimming pool are faring less well.

The whole place is wonderfully atmospheric for just mooching around, guided by the invaluable *Waiuta* leaflet (available from Reefton visitor centre) and strategically placed interpretive panels. You can see the lot in a couple of hours, but Waiuta is an ideal place for well-equipped **campers**, who can pitch their tent just about anywhere. For the less hardy, there's the open-plan thirty-bunk *Waiuta Lodge* (book through the Reefton visitor centre; ①), with a fully equipped kitchen, TV and video and a public phone. There's no other accommodation, no public transport and nowhere to buy food, so come prepared.

Blackball

Both the Grey River and SH7 meander through inconsequential small towns until they reach **Stillwater**, 11km short of Greymouth, where side roads lead to Blackball and Lake Brunner.

Refugees from the blistering pace of Greymouth gravitate to languid **BLACKBALL**, a former gold- and coal-mining village spread across a plateau at the foot of the Paparoa Range, 8km northeast of Stillwater. Here, commuters, neo-hippies and gnarled folk still hunting and prospecting in the bush seem to coexist fairly harmoniously. Blackball owes its existence to alluvial gold discovered in Blackball Creek in 1864, but gold returns diminished by the early twentieth century and it was left to coal, also mined from 1889, to save the day. Coal supported Blackball until the mine's closure in 1964, along the way staking the town's place in New Zealand's history as the birthplace of the **labour movement.**

During the first three decades of the twentieth century, the whole of the Grey Valley was a hotbed of doctrinaire socialism, as organizers moved among the towns, pressing unbending mine managers to address the atrocious working conditions. Anger finally came to a head, resulting in the crippling 1908 "cribtime strike", when Pat Hickey, Bob Semple and Paddy Webb requested an extension of their "crib" (lunch) break from fifteen to thirty minutes. Management's refusal sparked the longest strike in New Zealand's history. After three years of enormous sacrifice and deprivation, the strike was eventually broken and the workers returned to the mine. Though they lost the struggle, they succeeded in forming the Miners' Federation, which later transformed itself into the Federation of Labour, the country's principal trade union organization. Eric Beardsley's historical novel *Blackball 08* (see "Books" in Contexts) gives an accurate and passionate portrayal of the 1908 strike, but the most powerful evocation of the labour spirit is in the TV room at *Formerly the Blackball Hilton* (see below), with its relics and press cuttings from the strike and red flags bearing rousing slogans.

Ironically, these days Blackball's tranquillity is the main draw, abetted by excellent walking through the gold workings of Blackball Creek and up onto the wind-blasted tops of the Paparoa Range along the **Croesus Track** (see box opposite).

PRACTICALITIES

Blackball's social life revolves around the welcoming and wonderfully low-key *Formerly The Blackball Hilton*, Hart Street (☎03/732 4705; tent site $9, dorms ①, rooms ②), the last of the mining-era hotels which opened as the Dominion in 1910 and subsequently operated as the Hilton – ostensibly named for the former mine manager remembered in Hilton Street nearby – until challenged by the international hotel chain of the same name. Apart from lively drinking with quirky local characters, the hotel offers **accommodation**, a hot tub for guests, gold panning in local rivers (2hr; $12), horse riding (half-day; $45) and a hatful of suggestions for walks and exploration. Self-caterers should feast on venison sausages from the *Blackball Salami Co.* across the road; everyone else is limited to no-nonsense bar **meals** at the hotel and **takeaways** from the local dairy.

There is no public transport but the hotel can often organize a ride from Greymouth.

Lake Brunner

From Stillwater another sealed road runs 25km southeast to Lake Brunner, or *Moana Kotuku*, a filled glacial hollow celebrated for its trout fishing (the lake is also accessible off SH73 between Greymouth and Arthur's Pass). Immediately before the lake, the **Moana Kiwi House and Conservation Park**, Stillwater–Jacksons Road (daily: Dec–March 9am–7pm; April–Nov 9am–5pm; $8), boasts the country's largest kiwi house. The centre participates in the nationwide captive breeding programme and presents exotic and other native birds in something akin to their natural surroundings. The 2km **Velenski Walkway** meanders through unspoilt native bush beside the Arthur River nearby.

The only facilities are a couple of kilometres further on at the lakeside village of **MOANA**, where the TranzAlpine **train** makes a regular newspaper stop on Saturdays

THE CROESUS TRACK

DOC's informative Croesus and Moonlight Walks pamphlet shows adequate detail for walkers. The NZMS's 1:50,000 AhauraTopomap is the one for map enthusiasts.

Prospectors seeking new claims gradually pushed their way up the Blackball Creek, cutting paths to get their reef-quartz rock down to stamping batteries and to get supplies back up to their shelters in the bush. The scant remains of decades of toil now provide the principal interest on the **Croesus Track**, the first half easily explored in a day from Blackball, the whole track over the 1200m Paparoa Range to Barrytown on the coast north of Greymouth taking two relatively gentle days or one eight-hour slog.

ACCESS AND ACCOMMODATION

The track **starts** at Smoke-Ho car park, at the end of a rough but passable road 5km north of Blackball and **finishes** opposite the Barrytown Tavern on SH6, where southbound and northbound buses pass twice daily. There are two **huts** along the track: the free Category 4 Garden Gully Hut, with two sack bunks and an open fire, and the Category 2 Cec Clarke Hut (24 bunks; $8), with panoramic views, pots and a good coal-burning stove; the adjacent Top Hut is now abandoned.

THE TRACK

Much of the track was designed to accommodate tramways and the requirements of a gentle, steady grade characterize today's track. The route wends through hardwood and native podocarps interspersed with ferns and mosses and vines, gradually giving way to hardier silver beech and eventually alpine tussock and herbfields above the tree line. Sea mist commonly cloaks the tops during the middle of the day.

The trail from **Smoke-Ho** begins along a well-graded track, gradually descending to cross Smoke-Ho Creek then rising gently to a clearing (reached in half an hour), from where a ten-minute return path leads to the former site of the **Minerva Battery**. Immediately after the clearing, the path crosses Clarke Creek on a new wire bridge above the remains of an old wooden bridge. Another half hour on, a side track leads to two more clearings that once contained **Perotti's Mill** (10min return) and the **Croesus Battery** (50min return), respectively. After almost an hour, another side path leads to the primitive **Garden Gully Hut** (5min return) and the **Garden Gully Battery** (40min return). The main track turns sharply west before reaching the **Cec Clarke Hut** on the tree line in around an hour. The top of the ridge near Mount Ryall (1220m) lies two undulating hours beyond, a little more if you run off to climb **Croesus Knob** (1204m) along the way. If it isn't cloaked in cloud, the broad ridge offers wonderful views down to the coast, which is reached in under three hours by a steep but well marked path that dives down into the bush.

An alternative for experienced and fit trampers is to follow a loop that joins the Croesus Track with **The Moonlight Track**, detailed in DOC's *Croesus and Moonlight Walks* leaflet.

and will halt on request at other times. **Accommodation** extends to the drab but serviceable *Moana Hotel*, Ahau Street (☎ & fax 03/738 0083; dorms ①, rooms ③, units ④), and the neighbouring *Moana Motor Camp* (☎03/738 0600; tent sites $8, cabins ②). The *Station House Cafe*, Koe Street (☎03/738 0158), has the best **eating** around about, with lunches from $10, dinners from $16 and excellent lake views.

Brunner Industrial Site

Back on SH7, a couple of kilometres past Stillwater, a tall brick Tyneside chimney marks the **Brunner Industrial Site** (unrestricted access). Roadside information panels mark the path to a fine old suspension bridge (now relegated to foot traffic only), which crosses the swirling river to the few remaining buildings and the largely intact ruins of distinctive beehive coking ovens.

On his explorations in the late 1840s, Thomas Brunner noted the seam of riverside coal. By 1885, the mine site was producing twice as much coal as any other mine in the country and exporting firebricks throughout Australasia, but in 1896 New Zealand's worst mining disaster (with 69 dead) heralded its decline. The site was finally abandoned in the 1940s, and only exhumed from dense bush in the early 1980s. Half an hour wandering around the foundations and the fifty-minute bushwalk to some of the old mine sites evoke a long-gone era.

Westport and around

WESTPORT runs Greymouth close for the dubious honour of being the West Coast's most dispiriting town, a drab low-slung place of wide streets and slim opportunities which nevertheless warrants a visit for the nearby sights, principally the seal colony of **Cape Foulwind** and the former coal towns of the **Rochford Plateau** to the north. Besides, as this is a principal transport interchange, you may well end up spending a couple of nights here, which is made tolerable by reasonable accommodation, some decent restaurants and pubs – and a few adventure activities to keep you entertained.

Westport was the first of the West Coast towns, established by one **Reuben Waite** in 1861 as a single store beside the mouth of the Buller River. He made his living provisioning the few Buller Gorge prospectors in return for gold, but when the miners moved on to richer pickings in Otago, Waite upped sticks and headed south to help found Greymouth. Westport turned to the more dependable coal and, while the mining towns to the north were becoming established, engineers channelled the river to scour out a **port**, which fast became the largest coal port in the country but now lies idle. Westport battles on, with a respectable-sized fishing fleet and the odd ship laden with the produce of New Zealand's largest cement works at Cape Foulwind, which is fuelled by coal from open-cast Stockton, the only large mine left.

Arrival, information and transport

Almost everything of consequence in Westport happens around Palmerston Street. The helpful **visitor centre**, 1 Brougham St (Christmas–Jan daily 9am–7pm; rest of year Mon–Thurs 9am–5pm, Fri 9am–6pm, Sat & Sun 9am–4pm; ☎03/789 6658, fax 789 6668), is just off Palmerston Street, a few steps from the **DOC office**, at 72 Russell St (Mon–Fri 8am–noon & some weekday afternoons; ☎03/789 7742); both handle Heaphy Track **hut tickets**.

Bus stops are scattered around town. Barry's Buses stop outside the visitor centre; Cunningham's Motors from Karamea pull up at their depot at 179 Palmerston St; and all other services stop outside the Caltex service station, 197 Palmerston St. The **airport**, with a direct daily flight to Wellington, is 8km south of the centre (around $12 by taxi).Westport is compact enough for you to **get around** on foot, though to reach the nearby attractions you'll need your own transport or the services of Karaka Tours, 50 Mill St (☎03/789 5080) who, in addition to a seal colony trip (see p.632), run flexible **tours** to Denniston (5hr; $40), the Stockton Mine (5hr; $50) and the Charming Creek Walkway (5hr; $40). **Bike rental** is available from Becker's Sports World, 204 Palmerston St ($15 a day; ☎03/789 8787).

Accommodation

Accommodation is surprisingly abundant in Westport, so it isn't usually hard to find somewhere to stay. **Backpackers** are well catered for, and there's a cluster of decent **motels** along The Esplanade, but a limited choice of more luxurious places.

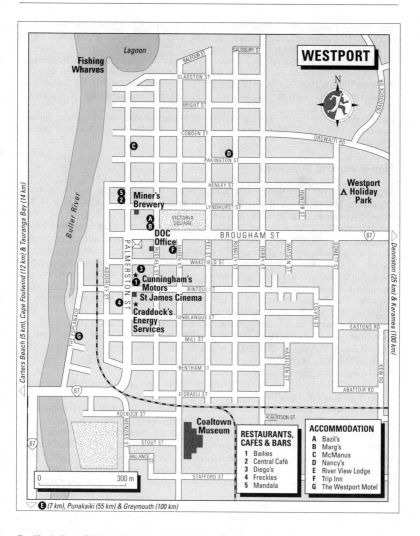

Bazil's, 54 Russell St (☎03/789 6410, fax 789 6240). Attractive, airy house converted to backpacker accommodation, with a nice garden and bike rental ($10 a day). Dorms ①, rooms ②.

Marg's Hostel, 56 Russell St (☎03/789 8627 & 0800/808 627, fax 789 8396). Associate YHA hostel that's a little impersonal but tidy and well run. Tent sites $9, dorms ①, rooms ②.

McManus Hotel, 39 Palmerston St (☎03/789 6304). A budget alternative without the backpacker scene is offered by old-fashioned but pleasant rooms tucked in behind the pub. ③.

Nancy's, 42 Romily St (☎03/789 6565). The quietest of the backpacker places, in a fine old house with comfortable lounge and gardens. Tent sites $8, dorms ①, rooms ②.

River View Lodge, Buller Gorge Rd, 7km south of Westport (☎ & fax 03/789 6037). Attractive homestay overlooking the Buller River. En-suite facilities, continental breakfast ($8–10) and dinners ($20) are all available. ⑤.

Seal Colony Tourist Park, Marine Parade, Carters Beach, 5km west (☎03/789 8002, fax 789 6732). Spacious, fully equipped site with some very comfortable motel units fronting onto a broad golden beach on the way to Cape Foulwind. Tent sites $9, cabins ②, motel units ⑤.

Trip Inn, 72 Queen St (☎03/789 7367, fax 789 6419). A big old rambling backpackers, with small dorms, videos, barbecue area and all the usual features. Tent sites $9, dorms ①, rooms ②.

Westport Holiday Park, 37 Domett St (☎03/789 7043, fax 789 7199). Smallish, low-key site partly hemmed in by native bush ten minutes' walk from the town centre. Tent sites $7–8, dorms ①, chalets ②.

The Westport Motel, 32 The Esplanade (☎03/789 7575 & 0800/805 909). The best of the downtown motels, with well-appointed rooms, complete with modern kitchens; cooked and continental breakfast is also served. ④.

The Town and activities

Anyone with even the vaguest interest in Westport's coal-mining past should visit **Coaltown**, Queen Street (daily: mid-Dec to mid-Jan 8.30am–5.30pm; rest of year 9am–4.30pm; $6), an imaginatively presented museum concentrating on the Buller coalfield. Scenes of the workings in their heyday pack a fascinating video, which complements remnants salvaged from the site – a coal wagon on tracks angled, as it was in situ, at an unsettling forty degrees, and a huge braking drum – and a mock-up of a mine tunnel, complete with musty smells and clanking sound effects. Fascinating photos of the inclined tramways in operation, a scale model of the plateau and a collection of miners' hats and lamps round out this engaging exhibition. The museum also tries to fulfil the role of a pioneer museum, with less compelling exhibits on gold dredging, the Buller earthquakes, brewing and the town's maritime history.

Before leaving town, try the preservative- and chemical-free beers made by the co-operatively run **Miner's Brewery**, 10 Lyndhurst St (Mon–Fri 8.30am–5.30pm, Sat 10am–5.30pm; ☎ & fax 03/789 6201), which distributes its beers throughout the West Coast and Marlborough. They'll give you a quick tour, let you sample their draught and dark beers and sell you some to take away.

Once again we have Captain Cook, battling heavy weather in March 1770, to thank for the naming of Westport's most dramatic and evocatively titled stretch of coastline, **Cape Foulwind**, 12km west of town. Cook's name has stuck, and also lends itself to the undulating four-kilometre **Cape Foulwind Walkway**, which runs over exposed headlands, airing superb coastal views – perfect for sunset ambling between the old lighthouse, a replica of Abel Tasman's astrolabe and the **Tauranga Bay Seal Colony**, where platforms overlook New Zealand's most northerly breeding colony of fur seals. The seals are at their most active and numerous from October to January, often numbering three hundred or more, a sign of the welcome recovery from the decimation of 150 years of sealing.

The quickest access to the seals is from the sandy but treacherous beach of Tauranga Bay, accessible by road and at the southern end of the walkway, ten minutes along from the seals. To save retracing your steps all the way back, look for a marker around the halfway point, indicating an alternative route around the foot of the cliffs. Karaka Tours (☎03/789 5080) run two-hour **Seal Colony Tours** for $20, the same price as trips out here with Buller Taxis (☎03/789 7719).

Wet and wild activities

As the largest town hereabouts, Westport has become the base for a couple of adventure companies, both operating trips some distance from town. The bread-and-butter trip for Norwest Adventures (☎03/789 6686 & 0800/116 686) is **Underworld Rafting** (4–5hr; $90), which starts with a minibus trip 28km south to the Charleston Tavern (where you can also join the trip) and a bushwalk through a dramatic valley of fine limestone bluffs within the Paparoa National Park. The trip proper involves an informative guided walk through the Metro cave system; you'll be decked out in wetsuit and caver's helmet, and lugging a rubber inner tube, which comes into play for the final drift down a flooded glow-worm cave and out through a gorgeous ravine into the Nile River. None of it is tremendously arduous; if you like caves and water, you'll like this. Novice descenders might try the easier of the two **abseiling** trips (3hr; $45), typically down sheer sea cliffs, but fit and active adrenalin addicts should fork out for the **Adventure Caving** (4hr; $150).

Rafting and jetboating are run by Buller Adventure Tours (☎03/789 7286, fax 789 8104). Throughout the year they run the six major rapids of the Grade IV "earthquake" section of the **Buller River**, 4km either side of Lyell, spending over two hours on the water for $75. Trips to more isolated rivers reached by helicopter are run less often and are dependent on numbers, so booking in advance is recommended. The most exciting is the stupendous Grade V **Karamea River** (Dec–March; 1 day; $195), while longer trips include the Grade IV+ **Mokihinui River** (Dec–March or April; 2 days; $295), which reaches the sea near Seddonville. Buller Adventure Tours also offer **jetboat rides** through the Lower Buller Gorge (1hr; $50) or as far as the riverside Berlins Hotel for a drink (2hr; $80). Other options include **horse trekking** through bush and along a river beach (from $35) and **gold panning** ($5).

Eating, drinking and nightlife

Westport has fewer decent **places to eat** than the other towns on the West Coast, but enough to satisfy for a short visit. **Pubs** are plentiful, most following the West Coast tradition, with those towards the northern end of Palmerston Street exhibiting a raw edge. **Nightlife** is limited to occasional bands at *Bailies* and second-run **movies** at the St James, 193 Palmerston St (☎03/789 8936).

Bailies, 187 Palmerston St. Westport's attempt at an Irish pub – only Guinness, pint glasses and the odd folk-music tape distinguishing it from the others. Pretty lively though, and with decent bar lunches, a cook-it-yourself barbecue and occasional live music.

Bay House Café, Tauranga Bay (☎03/789 7133). Superb restaurant and café out towards the seal colony at the southern end of the Cape Foulwind Walkway. Coffee, lunch and Westport's best dinners (around $20) – including Malaysian seafood curry, roast lamb in tamarillo and port sauce and vegetarian cannelloni – are served in the cosy interior or on the terrace of this former surf-lifesaving hut with excellent sea views. Closed Mon & Tues; BYO.

Central Café, 124 Palmerston St. Fairly scruffy place in the Kiwi tearoom tradition, but with inexpensive dishes of the steak, egg and chips variety.

Diego's Restaurant & Bar, 18 Wakefield St (☎03/789 7640). The best of Westport's downtown restaurants features an imaginative and varied menu (mains around the $20 mark), including delicious fresh fish dishes, many with an Asian twist.

Freckles, 216 Palmerston St. Decent daytime café with hearty and straightforward sandwiches, quiches and cakes.

Mandala, 110 Palmerston St (book for dinner, ☎03/789 7931). An airy licensed restaurant with sofas for relaxing over coffee, cakes and newspapers, as well as a more formal area for inexpensive burgers, pizzas and quiches. From 5pm, moderately priced à la carte dishes such as poached mussels and venison in cranberry sauce are served. Open for breakfast from 7am.

Around Westport: coal country

Westport's role as a service town was entirely dependent on trade from the coal-mining towns to the north, towns often sited in such inhospitable spots that fresh vegetables were hard to grow and sheep were almost impossible to raise. Foremost among them was **Denniston**, for years New Zealand's most productive coalfield, located high on the Rochfort Plateau. Coal hasn't been mined here in any quantity for thirty years; houses have been carted away and the bush is rapidly engulfing what remains of the mining machinery. It makes an intriguing place to explore for half a day, or longer if you want to tackle the **Denniston Incline Walk**. All the other deep mines have gone the same way, leaving a legacy of inclines, tramways and rusting machinery that can be visited on a number of walks, the **Charming Creek Walk** being the best.

Denniston and its incline

The Karamea Road runs north from Westport 15km to Waimangaroa, the junction for a steep 9km road that wends its way 600m up to the lonely Rochford Plateau and the semi-ghost-town of **DENNISTON**, the finest and best-preserved example of once-numerous isolated mining communities. There old schoolhouse here has been turned into a small **museum** (Sun only 10am–3pm; free; check opening on ☎03/789 9755), containing historical photos and old mining machinery, which also acts as the local information centre. On a fine day the views across the coastal plain down to Westport and north towards Karamea are impressive, but even the vaguest suggestion of bad weather brings a blanket of cloud and damp fog down over the town, adding a suitably ethereal quality to this desolate landscape. At its peak, around 1910, the plateau supported three mining villages, Denniston, Coalbrookdale and Burnetts Face, which were home to over 2500 people, served by a post office, three hotels and numerous shops. After limping by on a skeleton staff for several years, the last coal was extracted in 1995, leaving the post office, a fire station, half a dozen scattered houses, twenty-two people and a treasure trove of industrial archeology centred on a gaunt winding derrick.

The Coalbrookdale Seam was first discovered by one John Rochford in 1859, and the plateau was soon humming with activity, though the difficult access slowed development until the construction of the **Denniston Self-acting Incline** in 1879. Regarded as something of an engineering marvel in its time, and still impressive today, this gravity-powered tramway was the steepest rail-wagon incline in the world, lowering coal-filled wagons 518m over 1.7km, while hauling up empty wagons. Throughout its 88-year lifespan, over a thousand tonnes of coal a day would rattle at a prodigious 70km an hour down to Conn's Creek, where a water-driven braking system would stop them for marshalling onto rail tracks for the trip into Westport. Initially everything destined for Denniston – goods, machinery and people – also came up the incline but after four people were flung to their death from careering wagons, a path was constructed in 1884 and sixteen years later the road was put in, finally easing some of the hardship of living up on the plateau.

Fit and ambitious visitors to Denniston can approach on the **Denniston Walk** (2km; 2–3hr; 520m ascent), starting at Conn's Creek, 2km inland from Waimangaroa. The route follows the 1884 path roughly parallel to the incline, but the most interesting section is close to the top and can more easily be reached from Denniston. From Denniston to Middle Brake (1hr 30min return), the incline can still be seen among the bush, as can the midway point where wagons where disconnected from one hauling cable and connected to another for the lower half of the journey.

Considering how recently the mines were abandoned, there is surprisingly little left, save for foundations of mine workings and the remains of a few horse-drawn tramways. The greatest pleasure is in just rambling about (exercising some care not to disappear down mine shafts), seeing what you can turn up, though there is more structured activity with Back & Beyond (☎03/789 9008), who run a variety of four-wheel-drive bike **tours** (Nov–April only) visiting abandoned mine sites, typically going to the top of Mount Rochford; trips cost $30 an hour and most run for two hours.

Minor roads continue beyond Denniston to the sites of Burnetts Face and Coalbrookdale, neither of which have much to detain you, but you can pass a day exploring the backroads and walkways then repair to *The Railway Tavern* in Waimangaroa to admire the photos of Denniston.

North to Seddonville

The road north of Waimangaroa passes a turn-off running 1km to the **Britannia Track** (3hr each way), which leads to the Britannia Battery and other remnants of the gold-mining era. **Granity**, 6km further on, marks another junction, this time of a road that sweeps up the range to **MILLERTON**, an old coal town with a few houses still inhabited, and **Stockton**, the site of a vast open-cast mine, which is still worked and therefore inaccessible. It's worth going as far as the **Millerton Incline Railway Walk** (10min loop), a pleasant, gently graded stroll which starts 3km off the main highway and passes the 4.7km-long Millerton Incline; though less impressive than Denniston, this one is easier to visit.

At **Ngakawau**, 2km north of Granity, the coal depot signals the start of the lovely **Charming Creek Walk** (4km; 2hr one-way; 100m ascent), which follows an old railway that was used for timber and coal extraction between 1914 and 1958. The first half hour is the least interesting, but things improve dramatically after the S-shaped Irishman's Tunnel, with great views of the boulder-strewn river below and, after a swing-bridge river crossing, the Mangatini Falls. From here to the picnic stop by the remains of Watson's Mill is the most interesting section of the walk and is commonly the furthest people get (2–3hr return). The walk finishes among the manuka and gorse scrub and post-industrial wasteland of Charming Creek Mine, which is also accessible by 12km of mostly dirt road through **SEDDONVILLE**, itself little more than a pub, a shop and a **campsite** (☎03/782 1816; tent sites $6, dorms ①) 3km off SH6.

The best **eating** between Westport and Karamea is at *The Cow Shed* (Oct–March daily; ☎03/782 1826), beautifully sited at the mouth of the Mokihinui River, 3km west of SH6, with outdoor seating and croquet on the lawn. Wholesome snacks, cakes, burgers, savoury pancakes, enchiladas and the like are served in a much-converted cow shed, and there is also **accommodation** in bunkrooms (①).

Karamea and the Oparara Basin

The northwestern corner of the South Island competes with Fiordland as the least developed and most inaccessible region in the country, a fact sanctioned by the formation of the **Kahurangi National Park** in 1996. The second-largest park in the country, it embraces a vast wilderness of spectacular hill country supporting alpine meadows, the high Matiri ("Thousand Acre") Plateau, fifteen river catchment areas, New Zealand's finest karst landscape, dramatic windswept beaches and a coastal strip warm enough to support extensive stands of nikau palms. Charles Heaphy and Thomas Brunner surveyed the region in 1846, paving the way for European and Chinese gold-miners, who came a couple of decades later and sporadically took thin pickings as late as the Depression years of the 1930s. Pioneers followed, establishing themselves at **Karamea**, now the base for visiting the fine limestone country in the southern half of the park – and the first sign of civilization for walkers coming off the Heaphy Track (see p.458); other activities in the area are concentrated in the **Oparara Basin** and the final straight of the track.

The road north from Westport mostly runs parallel to the coast, pinched between the pounding Tasman breakers and bush-clad hills as it passes through meagre hamlets with barely a shop or a pub. The journey takes roughly two hours if you don't stop, though there are plenty of opportunities to do so, not least at the coal towns around Westport (see p.630). North of the **Mokihinui River**, the road leaves the coastal strip to climb **Karamea Bluff**, before descending again into a rich apron of dairying land. Rainfall begins to drop off and humidity picks up, promoting more subtropical vegetation, characterized by marauding cabbage trees and coastal nikau palms. At the foot of the bluff, **Little Wanganui** marks the turn-off for the start of the **Wangapeka Track**

(60km; 4–5 days), which traverses the southern half of the Kahurangi National Park to Matariki, 50km west of Nelson. Though it lacks the coastal scenery of the more famous Heaphy Track, it easily compensates with dramatic mountain terrain. Trampers searching for something quieter than the Heaphy should pick up DOC's *Wangapeka Track* leaflet (50¢), and be prepared for Category 2 and 3 huts; *The Last Resort* in Karamea (☎03/782 6617) and Transport Trampers in Nelson (☎03/545 1055) run transport to the trailheads.

The **Heaphy Track**, which is generally walked from north to south, is covered in Chapter Eight; our account starts on p.458.

Karamea

Diminutive **KARAMEA**, 100km north of Westport, is one of those places where doing nothing seems just right. This peaceful and isolated spot is virtually at the end of the road; to continue any distance north, you'd have to go on foot along the Heaphy Track. At the same time there is no shortage of things to do in the vicinity, the southern section of the Kahurangi National Park easily justifying a day or two of exploration.

Back in 1874, when land grants lured pioneers to a dense and isolated patch of bush at the mouth of the Karamea River, this was very much **frontier territory**, with the port providing the only link with the outside world. Settlers on the south shore of the Karamea River eked a living from **gold** and **flax**, but after a couple of fruitless years realized that the poorly drained pakihi wouldn't support them. Haunted by ill fortune, they moved upstream and north of the river to the current town site which, sure enough, soon after their move, was devastated by **floods**. Determinedly they pushed on, opening up the first road to Westport just in time for the upheavals of the 1929 Murchison **earthquake**, which altered the river flow and permanently ruined the harbour. Life hasn't been much better since: one sawmill remains, but **tourism** is increasingly the town's lifeblood.

Only devoted fans could spend more than ten minutes among the pioneering and sawmilling paraphernalia inside the **Karamea Centennial Museum**, SH67 (Christmas–Feb Mon–Fri 10am–4pm, Sat & Sun 1–4pm; other times by arrangement; donations requested; ☎03/782 6812). Otherwise there's **swimming** and **fishing** in the Karamea River, or **rafting** further upstream run by *The Last Resort* (☎03/782 6617); they negotiate the relatively gentle lower reaches (2.5hr; $22) and heliraft some magnificent Grade IV–V water far inland (1 day; $150).

Practicalities

Only one scheduled **bus** service makes it as far as Karamea: Cunningham's Motors (in Karamea ☎03/782 6761, in Westport ☎03/789 7177) run to Westport on weekday mornings ($15 each way, bikes $5), returning in the afternoon. Minibus **charter services** at fairly competitive prices are also run by Karamea Motors (☎03/782 6757) and *The Last Resort* (☎03/782 6617), the latter pretty much the hub of all Karamea activity.

The **visitor centre** at Market Cross, 2km east of the centre (Christmas–Jan daily 9am–5pm; Feb–Easter daily 9am–4pm; rest of year Mon–Fri 9am–4pm, Sat 10am–noon; ☎03/782 6652), has information about exploring the local area. The **DOC office** (Mon, Wed & Fri 9am–1pm and sporadically at other times; ☎03/782 6852), on SH67 midway between *The Last Resort* and the *Karamea Tavern*, issues **hut passes** for the Heaphy Track, as do *The Last Resort*, *Karamea Tavern* and the visitor centre.

Accommodation is limited. *The Last Resort*, unmissable on SH67 (☎03/782 6617, fax 782 6820; dorms ①, rooms ②–④), is where most people stay. This modern accommodation and restaurant complex consists of a cluster of turf-roofed buildings and low-profile salvaged-timber constructions, providing a full range of backpacker dorms and doubles to comfortable en-suite hotel rooms. Elsewhere, there are shared rooms with kitchen facilities at the *Karamea Tavern*, SH67 (☎ & fax 03/782 6800; ①); very simple but adequate and extraordinarily cheap backpackers accommodation and camping at *Karamea Domain* (no phone, enquire at adjacent caravan; tent sites $4, dorms ①); and the *Arapito Valley B&B* (☎03/782 6600; ③), 3km east of town, on the south bank of the Karamea River.

The only **places to eat** are the licensed bistro at *The Last Resort*, which does filling grills, tasty fish dishes and snacks, the *Karamea Tavern*, for straightforward bar meals, and the *Karamea Tearooms and Takeaway* across the road.

The Oparara Basin and Kohaihai

Kahurangi's finest limestone formations lie east of the Karamea–Kohaihai Road in the **Oparara Basin**, a compact area of **karst** topography characterized by numerous sinkholes, underground streams, caves and bridges created over millennia by the action of slightly acidic streams on the heavily jointed rock. This is home to New Zealand's largest native **spider**, the gradungular spider (found only in caves in the Karamea and Collingwood area, where it feeds off blowflies and cave crickets), and to a rare species of ancient and primitive carnivorous **snail** that grows up to 70mm across and feeds on earthworms. Tannin-stained rivers course gently over bleached-white boulders and, in faster-flowing sections, the rare whio or blue duck swims for its supper. Even if your interest in geology is fleeting, the Oparara Basin makes a superb place for an afternoon **swim** or a **picnic** by one of the rivers.

Ten kilometres north of Karamea, North Beach marks the turn-off for the steep and narrow 16km dirt road to the **Honeycomb Caves**, only discovered in the 1970s and a valuable key to understanding New Zealand's fauna. The lime-rich sediment on the cave floor has helped preserve the ancient skeletons of birds, most of them killed when they fell through holes in the cave roof. Bones of over fifty species have been found here including those of the Haast Eagle, the largest eagle ever known with a wingspan of up to four metres. In total there are 15km of passages through the cave system, some of which are visited on the excellent and educational **Honeycomb Caves Tour** (5hr; $60, including lunch; run by *The Last Resort*, ☎03/782 6617). The tour is the only way you can get into the caves, but if you are exploring under your own steam you can join the tour group at the entrance (2hr; $30), so long as you book in advance. If you don't fancy the caves but want transport to the Oparara Basin area, they'll carry you for $20 return, provided they have space. As is common in limestone areas, the watercourses alter frequently, leaving behind dry caves, such as the adjacent **Crazy Paving and Box Canyon caves**, both accessible on a five-minute track from the road-end car park and good for spider-spotting; details and a map are available from the Karamea visitor centre.

The two most spectacular examples of limestone architecture lie at the end of beautiful, short bushwalks signposted from a car park 3km back down the road towards Karamea. The largest is the **Oparara Arch** (40min return), a vast two-tiered bridge 45m high, 40m wide and over 200m long, which appears magically out of the bush but defies any attempt at successful photography. The **Little Arch** (1hr return) is more easily captured on film but harder to reach, requiring a short fixed-rope descent and a good deal of mud, though the untouched, high-canopy native forest and a magnificent cavern make it all worthwhile. A short path to the deep black reflections in **Mirror Tarn** (20min return) spurs off the road nearby.

Kohaihai

Visitors with no aspirations to tramp the full length of Heaphy Track can sample the final few coastal kilometres from the mouth of the Kohaihai River, 17km north of Karamea, where there is good river (but not sea) swimming, a basic DOC **campsite** ($4) and an abundance of sandflies. In the heat of the day, you're much better off across the river in the cool of the **Nikau Walk** (40min loop), which winds through a wonderfully shaded grove dense with nikau palms, tree ferns and magnificent gnarled old rata dripping in epiphytes. When it cools off, stick to the southern side of the Kohaihai River and the **Zig-Zag Track** (35min return), which switchbacks up to an expansive lookout.

Paparoa National Park and around

South of Westport lies the Paparoa Range, a 1500m granite and gneiss ridge inlaid with limestone that separates the dramatic coastal strip from the valleys of the Grey and Inungahua rivers. In 1987, the limestone country of the South Island's western flank was designated the **Paparoa National Park**, still one of the country's smallest and least-known parks. The highlight is undoubtedly the **Pancake Rocks**, where crashing waves have forced spectacular blowholes through a stratified, pancake-like stack of weathered limestone. But to skip the rest would be to miss out on a mysterious world of disappearing rivers, sinkholes, caves and limestone bluffs best seen on the **Inland Pack Track**, but also accessible on shorter walks up river valleys close to Punakaiki.

Fertile limestone soils always support distinctive flora and fauna, a trait exaggerated here by the Tasman Convergence, a current warmed in the Coral Sea off Queensland, Australia. Striking this stretch of coast, the current creates a balmy microclimate favoured by the **Westland black petrel** and insects such as the **Captain Cook cicada**, the largest and noisiest of native cicadas.

The mild climate provided a bounty for **Maori**, who named the area Punakaiki, meaning "a spring of food, in abundance". Groups of Maori travelling the coast in search of *pounamu* (greenstone) often stopped here, as did early **European explorers** seeking agricultural land. Charles Heaphy, Thomas Brunner and two Maori guides came through in 1846, finding little to detain them, but within twenty years this stretch of coast was alive with **gold** prospectors at work on the quartz veins at **Charleston** and **Brighton**, the former barely hanging on, the latter long gone.

Visitor interest is centred on **Punakaiki**, close by the Pancake Rocks where bus passengers get a quick glimpse and others pause for the obligatory photos. But a couple of days spent here will be well rewarded with a stack of wonderful walks, horse riding, canoeing up delightful limestone gorges and just slobbing about.

Westport to Punakaiki

South of Westport, SH67 crosses the Buller River and picks up SH6, the main West Coast road. There's little reason to stop before you reach the **Little Totara River** and *Jack's Gasthof* (☎ & fax 789 6501), 20km south of the junction. This simple **café** and bar serves an array of meals and toasted sandwiches on excellent sourdough rye bread, which is also sold by the loaf. The whole setup is pretty laid-back, with a couple of basic **rooms** (②), free **camping**, a sauna and swimming in the creek. A couple of kilometres further along SH6 is **Mitchells Gully Gold Mine** (usually open daily 9 or 10am–3 or 4pm; $5; call ☎03/789 6553 to check hours), a family-run mine working dating back to 1866, which has been reopened mainly to demonstrate the time-honoured methods used to extract fine gold held in a cement-like mass of oxidized ironsand. Along with a predictable collection of mining paraphernalia, you can see a restored overshot wheel driving a stamping battery, and water races and tunnels still in use.

The most intensive mining went on 3km to the south at **CHARLESTON**, then a rollicking boom town of around 18,000 people, but now with a mere thirty residents. The dozens of **hotels** that thrived on the gold spoils have collapsed or been burned down, leaving only the modern *Charleston Tavern*, which dishes up suitably modern fare of nachos and grills; Norwest Adventures convene here for their Underworld Rafting and abseiling trips (see p.632 for details). There really isn't much to be seen here, though there are a couple of short coastal walks and free **camping** beside the lovely little Constant Bay. Other **accommodation** consists of the modest *Charleston Motel* (☎03/789 7599; ③) and the *Charleston Motor Camp* (☎03/789 6773 tent sites $8–9, cabins ②).

Some 20km south of Charleston, the Fox River marks the site of the classic boom-and-bust town of **Brighton**, which experienced just four months of frantic activity in 1867, temporarily eclipsing Charleston for gold exports. Immediately to the south rise the 50m cliffs of Te Miko – tagged Perpendicular Point by Charles Heaphy, who in 1846 recorded climbing the cliff on two stages of ladders constructed of shaky and rotten rata vines while his dog was hoisted on a rope. The vines were later replaced by a chain ladder, but Te Miko remained an impenetrable barrier to pack animals until 1866, when the combined needs of traders and the new Westport–Greymouth telegraph line prompted the forging of the **Inland Pack Track**, a path now followed by the tramp of the same name (see box on p.640).

The coast road, finally completed in 1927, now climbs over Te Miko, passing the **Iraiahuwhero Point Lookout**, with stupendous coastal views extending to the Te Miko cliff and layered rocks similar to those at Punakaiki, 6km ahead.

Punakaiki and Pancake Rocks

The **Pancake Rocks** and blowholes at **PUNAKAIKI** are often all visitors see of the Paparoa National Park, as they tumble off the bus outside the visitor centre and shop that pretty much constitute the village. A ten-minute paved track leads from the road to Dolomite Point, where layers of limestone have been weathered to resemble an immense stack of giant pancakes created by **stylobedding**, a chemical process in which the pressure of overlying sediments creates alternating durable and weaker bands. Subsequent uplift and weathering has accentuated this effect to create wonderfully photogenic formations. The edifice is undermined by huge sea caverns where the surf surges in, sending spumes of brine spouting up through vast **blowholes**. The rocks are magnificent even in calm conditions, but at high tide with a good swell from the south or southwest the performance is stunning.

More shapely examples of Paparoa's karst landscape are on show on a number of walks. The **Punakaiki Cavern Track** (5min return), 500m north, leads into a glow-worm cave (torch essential), and 2km beyond that, the **Truman Track** (30min return) runs down from the highway to a small beach hemmed in by a wave-sculpted rock platforms.

No matter how slight your interest in birds, you could hardly fail to be impressed by the sight of **Westland black petrels** bundling through the trees at dusk to the world's only breeding colony of this, the largest of the burrow-nesting petrels. These relatives of the albatross glide effortlessly at sea, where they live most of their lives, but are less gainly when they leave their offshore rafts to crash land at their burrows. Birds arrive nightly from March to December, but activity reaches fever pitch from April to June, when the single egg is laid and hatched. Paparoa Nature Tours schedule **guided visits** for dawn and dusk (April–late Dec daily; 2hr; $25; ☎03/731 1826), using a viewing platform right in the middle of a sub-colony.

Kiwa Sea Adventures run excellent sea trips (Oct–March daily; 2–4hr; $85–165; ☎03/731 1813), combining a fun-seeking **speedboat ride** with a chance to see the shag colony on Seal Island and a close look at the blowholes from sea level; the longer trips offer opportunities to swim with **dolphins**. More conventional **swimming spots** are rare along the West Coast but relatively abundant here, with good river swimming in the Pororari and Punakaiki rivers, sea bathing at the Punakaiki Rivermouth and point-break surfing at the southern end of Pororari Beach.

Practicalities

Southbound InterCity **buses** stop outside the *Punakaiki Tearooms* at 12.20pm, pausing long enough for a quick look at the Pancake Rocks across the road; northbound services do the same an hour and a half later. Barry's Buses pass northbound at 9.50am and southbound at 8.10pm, making a day-trip from Greymouth feasible.

Close by, the extensive **Paparoa National Park visitor centre** (daily 9am–4pm, until 7 or 8pm in summer; ☎03/731 1895) houses the DOC office, and has excellent displays on all aspects of the park, information on activities and walking maps and leaflets. Punakaiki Canoe & Cycle Hire (☎03/731 1870) **rent** out **kayaks** ($10 an hour, $30 a day) and **bikes** ($15 a day).

Most of Punakaiki's **accommodation** is clustered by the Pororari Beach close to the rivermouth, around 800m north of the visitor centre. Here you'll find the comfortable *Punakaiki Cottage Motel*, Mabel Street (☎03/731 1008, fax 731 1118; ④), with some

---

PAPAROA WALKS AND THE INLAND PACK TRACK

The 1:50,000 Paparoa National Park *map covers the region in great detail, but DOC's* Inland Pack Track *leaflet (50¢) provides enough information for that tramp.*

The best way to truly appreciate the dramatic limestone scenery of the Paparoas is on the **Inland Pack Track** (17km; 1–3 days). Most of the terrain is easy going with only one pass to negotiate, but there are no bridges for river crossings and you need to be aware of the possibility of flash floods. With less time or greater demand for comfort, some of the best can be seen on two **day-walks**. The delightful **Punakaiki–Pororari Rivers Loop** (12km; 4–5hr; 100m ascent) follows the initial stretch of the Inland Pack Track as far as the Pororari River, which is then followed downstream between some magnificent limestone cliffs to return to Punakaiki. The **Fox River Caves Track** (12km; 4–5hr; 100m ascent) traces the last few kilometres of the Inland Pack Track from the Fox Rivermouth as far as the caves and returns the same way.

PRACTICALITIES

The Inland Pack Track can be walked in either direction, though by going from south to north (as described below) you eliminate the risk of missing the turn-off up Fossil Creek. There are **no huts** along the way and you're advised carry a tent. This isn't absolutely necessary, as trampers can shelter under the rock **bivvy** known as The Ballroom at the end of a long first day; by carrying full **camping gear**, though, you get protection from bugs, earn the freedom to break the walk into more manageable chunks and, perhaps most importantly, avoid a night in the open if the rivers flood. Choose a spot well away from flood risk areas and take care off the main track, as there are unmarked sinkholes. **Campfires** are permitted, but DOC recommends carrying a stove, particularly for stays at The Ballroom, where most of the usable wood has already been burned. The latest **weather forecast** is available from the DOC office in Punakaiki, where you should fill out an **intentions form**, remembering to check in on your return.

THE INLAND PACK TRACK

The starting point of the Inland Pack Track is 1km south of the Punakaiki visitor centre at the end of a 1.5-kilometre track that follows the south bank of the Punakaiki River to

units overlooking the breakers; the relaxed and vibrantly painted *Punakaiki Beach Hostel*, Webb Street (☎03/731 1852; dorms ①, rooms ②), where guests can buy freshly baked bread and rent bikes; and the spacious and grassy, DOC-run *Punakaiki Motor Camp*, SH6 (☎03/731 1894, fax 731 1888; tent sites $7–8, dorms ①, cabins & units ②–④). Ranking among the most relaxing backpackers in the country is *Te Nikau Retreat* (☎03/731 1111; dorms ①, rooms ②–④), which lies off SH6 a couple of kilometres north. Carved out of bush peppered with nikau palms, the retreat offers small dorms, rustic huts for couples, double rooms in the wooden main house, studio units, free use of bikes, and breakfast and dinner on request.

Eating options are limited to the *Punakaiki Tearooms* by the visitor centre and the more appealing *Nikau Palms Café* next door, which serves the likes of lasagne, toasted sandwiches and, appropriately, pancakes. Don't expect to find anything open after around 8pm and if you're **self-catering**, you'll do better to bring **supplies** from Westport or Greymouth.

Punakaiki to Greymouth

The road from Punakaiki to Greymouth is a spectacular drive, sometimes pushed onto the seacliffs by intrusive ramparts of the Paparoa Range, but there's little to stop for

a car park. From **Punakaiki River to Pororari River** (3.5km; 2hr 30min; 120m ascent, 100m descent), the track crosses to the right bank then cuts northeast, gradually rising to a low saddle then descending to the Pororari River, which is forded a couple of hundred metres upstream. From **Pororari River to Bullock Creek** (6km; 2hr; 100m ascent), the track climbs to an excellent viewpoint over the Pororari Gorge before reaching Bullock Creek, which should be forded with some care – in flood conditions a wall of water courses down the creek's usually dry lower section. Camping is possible on the DOC-owned farm by the Bullock Creek crossing. From **Bullock Creek to Dilemma Creek** (8km; 2hr 30min; 100m ascent, 100m descent), the farm track soon becomes a path, skirting swampland then climbing to a ridge. Descend gradually to Fossil Creek, where you wade downstream from pool to pool, occasionally clambering over fallen tree trunks. After half an hour of this, Fossil Creek meets the main tributary of the Fox River, Dilemma Creek, by a small sign – keep your eyes peeled. Heading **downstream to Fox River** (2km; 1hr; gradual descent) is the most dramatic section of the trip but potentially the most dangerous, with 18 fords to cross between gravel banks in the bed of Dilemma Creek: if you have any doubts about the first crossing, turn back, as they only get worse. The lower river carves out a deep canyon between gleaming white vertical cliffs and, if you can find a patch of sun, this makes a great place to rest awhile. The track resumes by a sign on the left bank just above the confluence with the Fox River; a steep bluff on the right makes a useful landmark.

Even if you don't plan to stay, the vast limestone overhang of **The Ballroom** (1km; 30min each way; negligible ascent) is worth a look. A signposted track crosses to the right bank of the Fox River below the confluence, then crosses several more times higher up. There's no chance you'll miss the 100m-long lip, which easily provides shelter for a hundred or more campers; long-drop toilets have been installed and a huge fire ring has developed. Return the same way to **the confluence**, from where the track **to the Fox Rivermouth** (5km; 2hr; 100m descent) follows the left bank. A short distance along, a sign points across the river to the **Fox River Caves** (30min); the safest and most impressive of the caverns is the upper leftmost of the three. Meanwhile, the Inland Pack Track crosses to the car park by the Fox Rivermouth, some 12km by road from your starting point; the southbound InterCity **bus** currently passes around noon, or you can walk back along SH6.

until you get close to Greymouth. The former gold town of **BARRYTOWN**, 16km from Punakaiki, is no more than a scattered shock of houses and the *Barrytown Tavern* (☎03/731 1812; dorms ①, motel units ③), with a self-catering kitchen and good meals of locally caught fish; the tavern is principally used by those who stagger in from the **Croesus Track** (see p.629), though you might want to stop by for the occasional live music at weekends.

The next settlement of any consequence is **RAPAHOE**, which boasts about the safest bathing beach on the coast and has a reputation for gemstones among those in the know. Seven Mile Creek meets the sea here, by the beginning of the **Point Elizabeth Track** (5km; 3hr; 100m ascent), a walk along former gold-miners' trails and through dense bush that ends 5km north of Greymouth at the end of Domett Esplanade, though you can go just as far as the excellent vantage of Point Elizabeth (2hr return).

Greymouth and around

The Grey River forces its way through a break in the coastal Rapahoe Range and over the treacherous sand bar to the sea at workaday **GREYMOUTH**, which ranks as the West Coast's largest town but still claims under ten thousand residents. Greymouth is hardly going to be a highlight on most visitors' itineraries, though there's a pleasant enough walk along the riverwall a couple of kilometres out to **Blaketown Beach** and a few worthwhile **adventure activities**. Best to do what you need to and move on, especially in winter when you might be plagued by **The Barber**, a razor-sharp cold wind that whistles down the Grey Valley and envelops the town in a thick icy fog.

The town began to take shape during the early years of the **gold rush** on land purchased in 1860 by James Mackay, who bought most of Westland from the Poutini Ngai Tahu people for 300 gold sovereigns. The deal was finalized on the site of their Mawhera pa, where the river bridge across to the suburb of Cobden now stands; a plaque beneath the bridge marks the spot. Several respectably **grand buildings** from the prosperous later decades of the nineteenth century pepper Greymouth's gridplan streets but there's nothing to give the place any defining character except for the river, which is deceptively calm and languid through most of the summer, but awesome after heavy rains. Devastating **floods** swept through Greymouth in 1887, 1905, 1936, 1977 and 1988; since the last great flood, the Greymouth Flood Protection Scheme, completed in 1990, has successfully held back the waters.

Arrival, information and transport

The stylish way to arrive in Greymouth is on the daily TranzAlpine **train** from Christchurch (see box on p.548), which pulls in at the station on Mackay Street and is met by InterCity **buses** (agency inside the station; Mon–Fri 10am–5pm, Sat & Sun noon–3pm; ☎03/768 1435) running south to Hokitika and Franz Josef, and north to Westport and Nelson. Greymouth is also served by **shuttle buses** from Christchurch, Nelson and Hokitika. Greymouth's nearest **airport** is at Hokitika; Greymouth Taxis (☎03/768 7078) charge about $15 each way.

The **visitor centre**, inside the Regent Cinema, on the corner of Mackay Street and Herbert Street (Nov–Easter daily 9am–6pm; Easter–Oct Mon–Fri 9am–5pm, Sat & Sun 10am–4pm; ☎03/768 5101, fax 768 0317), will provide a free street map, which is all you need for **getting around** the town on foot. Longer forays may demand the services of Mann Security and Cycles, 173 Tainui St (☎03/768 0255), who rent bikes from around $25 a day and stock spares for long-distance cyclists. Avis and Budget both have **car rental** offices but local outfit Value Rentals (☎03/762 7503) is cheaper, starting at around $50 a day with unlimited kilometres.

Accommodation

Visitor demands seldom put much pressure on Greymouth's modest collection of **places to stay**, except during the Coast to Coast Race (around the second weekend in February), when everything is packed to the gills. At other times there is a fair choice of hostels, moderately priced motels and a couple of comfortable B&Bs.

Ardwyn House, 48 Chapel St (☎03/768 6107). Appealing and very welcoming homestay in a comfortable 1920s house surrounded by a quiet garden and close to the town centre. ④.

Greymouth Seaside Holiday Park, Chesterfield St (☎03/768 6618, fax 768 5873). The more central of the two motor parks, right by the beach. Tent sites $8–9, dorms ①, cabins ②, units ③.

Kainga-ra YHA Hostel, 15 Alexander St (☎ 03/7684951, fax 768 7276). Relaxed, low-key and central hostel, with all the usual facilities and good views over the town. Dorms ①, rooms ②.

Noah's Ark Backpackers, 16 Chapel St (☎ & fax 03/768 4868). The most rumbustious and gaudily painted of Greymouth's hostels, occupying a two-storey villa originally built as a monastery, with great verandahs, a spacious lounge and satellite TV. Dorms ①, rooms ②.

Oak Lodge, SH6, 3km north of town (☎03/768 6832). Swanky modern B&B with olde-worlde styled rooms set among gardens enhanced by a nice outdoor pool. Dinners go for $26. ⑥.

Revingtons Hotel, Tainui St (☎03/768 7055, fax 768 7605). Spanish Revival-style hotel built in the 1930s with traditional hotel doubles and budget twin rooms. ③–④.

Sanford's Guest Lodge, 62 Albert St (☎03/768 5605). Excellent-value small hotel with simple, fresh and airy rooms, complete with colour TV and the option of a cooked breakfast. ③–④.

Willowbank Pacifica Lodge, SH6, 3km north of town (☎0800/668 355, fax 03/768 6022). Sprawling motel with a good range of modern and older en-suite rooms and use of a small indoor swimming pool and spa. ⑤.

The Town and around

It is difficult to wander for long around central Greymouth without stumbling on the **Jade Boulder Gallery**, 1 Guinness St (daily: Nov–March 9am–9pm; April–Oct 9am–5pm), a sales outlet for a vast range of carved greenstone pieces. Even if you have no intention of buying, pop in to watch the cutting, grinding and polishing processes in the glass-panelled workshop at the back, and to take a look at the raw material – huge, water-polished boulders – lying strategically around the showroom in a kind of Zen garden arrangement. Greymouth's local museum, the **History House**, Gresson Street (Mon–Fri 9am–5pm; $2) is harder to find. Hidden in the former Grey County Chambers out towards the fishing harbour, the museum makes a good shot at relating the Grey District's history through piles of maritime memorabilia and a stack of photos depicting the town's heyday. The townspeople's long struggle to combat the floods is also given thorough and diverting treatment.

Rainy and sweltering days both provide equally good excuses to join the free tastings and **brewery tours** at Monteith's Brewing Company, corner of Turumaha Street and Herbert Street (Mon–Fri 10.30am & 1.30pm; book through the visitor centre, ☎03/768 5101), where age-old recipes have recently been revived to produce some deep-brown, flavoursome brews popular all down the Coast.

Greymouth also makes a good base for the **Point Elizabeth Track** (see p.642), beginning over the river north of the suburb of Cobden and returning from Rapahoe by one of the twice-daily buses. If you're looking for a short walk and somewhere to watch the sun go down, try the ten-minute **Lions Walk**, starting up Weld Street in Cobden and meandering through the bush to a panoramic viewpoint over the city and the Southern Alps.

Activities

If you're looking for something more thrilling, Wild West Adventures (☎0800/223 456) can oblige. Their **Dragons Cave Rafting** (5hr; $85) is a challenging caving trip

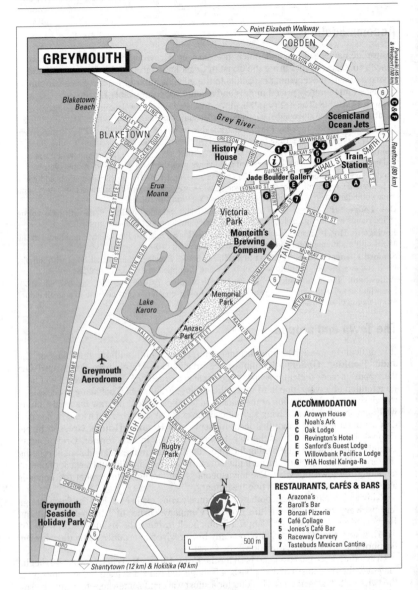

GREYMOUTH

△ Point Elizabeth Walkway

COBDEN

NELSON QUAY

Blaketown Beach

BLAKETOWN

COLLINS ST

COAKLEY ST

Grey River

Scenicland Ocean Jets

▷ Punakaiki (45 km) & Westport (100 km)

△ C & F

GRESSON ST

History House

JOHNSTON ST

MAWHERA QUAY

❶❸

❷❹

❺

MACKAY ST

▷ Reefton (80 km)

Erua Moana

GUINNESS ST

ℹ

SMITH ST

Train Station

Jade Boulder Gallery

ARNEY ST

LEONARD ST

HERBERT ST

CHAPEL ST

WHALL ST

MOUNT ST

A

❻

HIGH ST

❻

❼

E

G

PUKETANI ST

Victoria Park

Monteith's Brewing Company

TAINUI ST

TURUMAHA ST

LORD ST

ALEXANDER ST

MURRAY ST

Memorial Park

Lake Karoro

FRANKLIN ST

WHANE ST

FREYBERG TERR

❻

Anzac Park

COWPER STREET

BALEIGH ST

BUCKTHORN ST

Greymouth Aerodrome

SHAKESPEARE STREET

PALMERSTON STREET

LYDIA ST

MARSDEN RD

ACCOMMODATION
A Arowyn House
B Noah's Ark
C Oak Lodge
D Revington's Hotel
E Sanford's Guest Lodge
F Willowbank Pacifica Lodge
G YHA Hostel Kainga-Ra

WATER WALK ROAD

MARLBOROUGH ST

Rugby Park

RESTAURANTS, CAFÉS & BARS
1 Arazona's
2 Baroll's Bar
3 Bonzai Pizzeria
4 Café Collage
5 Jones's Café Bar
6 Raceway Carvery
7 Tastebuds Mexican Cantina

Greymouth Seaside Holiday Park

CHESTERFIELD ST

NELSON ST

BYRON ST

MILTON RD

JOYCE CR

ASMAN ST

MIRO

N

0   500 m

▽ Shantytown (12 km) & Hokitika (40 km)

into the Taniwha cave system; wetsuits and cavers' lamps are the order of the day for muddy scrambling down a fairly steep underground streambed, floating along deep sections on inner tubes and squeezing through tight sections. The far more restrained **Chasms Underworld Whitewater Tunnel Rafting** ($95) has elements of its racier cousin, with a short spell underground in proper rafts, but more time spent above ground in a 4WD, learning about the gold-mining history of the region, European explorers and something of the local flora and fauna. Other options include whitewater **rafting** trips, which must be booked a day or two ahead, on the Grade III Taipo River (half-day; $125), **jetboating** (2hr; $75), and trips to Pancake Rocks at Punakaiki (4hr; $35). Scenicland Ocean Jets (☎03/768 9770 & 0800/929 991) seek to combine the thrill of jetboating with **seal- and dolphin-watching** using their nippy jetboat; three tours ($50–85) chance the Grey Bar and head up the coast in search of Hector's dolphins.

Shantytown

The replica 1880s West Coast gold-mining settlement of **Shantytown** (daily: mid-Oct to mid-March 8.30am–7pm; rest of year 8.30am–5pm; $8), 8km south of Greymouth and 4km off the main highway, is unashamedly a tourist trap, frequented by a near-constant stream of visitors who pile off tour buses. Although mostly constructed since the early 1970s, the complex incorporates rescued older buildings: the 1902 Coronation Hall from Ross, an 1865 church originally from No Town in the Grey Valley, and a hotel cobbled together from parts. With the exception of the pristine church, though, even these have been insensitively restored, with scant regard for authenticity. The most interesting buildings to wander through are the printing shop, with its faded billboards advertising the latest films; the wonderful 1837 Colombian Press, which found its way here from Philadelphia via London, Auckland and Napier; the hospital, identical to one built in Greymouth; and the Gem Hall, with its collection of minerals. At the replica train station, your entry ticket entitles you to a 2-kilometre round-trip ride behind the 1887 steam engine *Kaitangata*, calling at a mine site and sawmill, where boards are cut on summer days and, of course, sage prospectors will help you pan for "colour" in salted tanks. As if that weren't more than enough schmalz, a mock hotel serves sandwiches, bar meals and beer in saloon surroundings.

No public transport runs to the site, but Kea Tours (☎03/768 9292) finish their **Goldstrike Tour** (2–3 daily; 2.5hr; $20) around various gold rush sites at Shantytown.

Eating and drinking

You'll soon exhaust Greymouth's scope for eating and drinking, but there are enough places serving tasty and hearty dishes to last the night or two you're likely to stay.

Arazona's Cafe Bar, 19 Mackay St. Decent spot for toasted sandwiches, nachos and delicious gateaux, though the pizzas are better at Bonzai.

Barroll's Bar, 9 Tainui St. Lively downtown bar with occasional live music.

Bonzai Pizzeria, 29 Mackay St. Cheerful licensed restaurant with a broad range of reasonably priced and tasty pizzas served daytime and evening.

Café Collage, 115 Mackay St (book in summer & at weekends, ☎03/768 5497). Greymouth's best, and priciest, food is served upstairs in this wooden-floored Art Deco room. The menu concentrates on French treatments of seafood and game dishes. BYO & licensed; closed Mon.

Jones's Cafe Bar, 37 Tainui St. One of Greymouth's trendier places for coffee and cake or moderately priced full meals.

Raceway Carvery, *Union Hotel*, 20 Herbert St. Huge plates of grilled and roast meat.

Tastebuds Mexican Cantina, 84 Tainui St. Inexpensive, brightly muralled restaurant and takeaway, serving variations on the taco and tortilla theme, plus delicious desserts. Daily until 8pm, later at weekends. BYO.

Hokitika and around

South from Greymouth, SH6 hugs a desolate stretch of coast that's fine for long moody beachcombing walks, but there's little of abiding interest until **HOKITIKA**, 40km away.

On initial acquaintance "Hoki", as it is known to its friends, appears no more interesting than Greymouth – its jumble of mundane modern buildings interspersed with crumbling edifices from the town's golden days – but its proximity to the beach and good bushwalks, and a couple of quality restaurants give it the edge. Besides, it is a long way to the next place of any size.

Like the other West Coast towns, Hokitika owes its existence to the **gold rushes** of the 1860s. Within months of the initial discoveries near Greymouth in 1864, fields had been opened up on the tributaries of the Hokitika River, and Australian diggers from Ballarat and Bendigo and Irish hopefuls all flogged over narrow passes from Canterbury to get their share. Hokitika boomed and within two years it had a population of 6000 (compared with today's 4000), streets packed with hotels, and a steady export of over a tonne of gold a month, mainly direct to Melbourne. Despite a treacherous bar at the Hokitika Rivermouth, the **port** briefly became one of the country's busiest, with ships tied up four deep along Gibson Wharf. As gold became harder to find and more sluicing water was needed, the enterprise eventually became uneconomic and was replaced by dairying and the timber industry. The **railway** started to transport the region's produce and the port closed in 1954, only to be smartened up in the 1990s as the focus for the town's Heritage Trail.

Arrival and information

Although a rail line comes as far as Hokitika, there are no passenger services. InterCity, Barry's Buses and Coast to Coast **buses** all stop outside the Hokitika Travel Centre, 65 Tancred St (☎03/755 8134), which sells tickets. Only InterCity heads south from here, leaving at 3pm for Fox Glacier. Air New Zealand Link **fly** daily to Hokitika from Christchurch, arriving 2km east of the centre.

Hokitika's **visitor centre**, on the corner of Weld Street and Sewell Street (Dec–March daily 8.30am–5.30pm; April–Nov Mon–Fri 8.30am–5pm, Sat 10am–1pm; ☎03/755 8322, fax 755 8026), is staffed by helpful folk. Just a few paces away, the **DOC office**, at the corner of Hamilton Street and Sewell Street (Mon–Fri 8am–4.30pm; ☎03/755 8301), is stocked with leaflets on local walks.

While here, you may need to make some preparations for the long drive south. Though there are EFTPOS facilities in Franz Josef, Fox Glacier and elsewhere, the **banks** and ATMs here are the last before Wanaka, more than 400km away over the Haast Pass. **Cyclists** can obtain spares at the well-stocked Hokitika Cycles and Sports, 33 Tancred St (☎03/755 8662).

Accommodation

Apart from during the Wildfoods Festival (second weekend in March), **accommodation** is seldom hard to find.

Beach House Backpackers, 137 Revell St (☎03/755 6859). Slightly cramped but decent, fun and friendly hostel right by the beach. There's free use of dilapidated bikes, fishing gear and gold pans, and they'll put you in touch with folk selling well-priced greenstone. Tent sites $10, dorms ①, rooms ②.

Blue Spur Lodge, Cement Lead Rd (☎03/755 8445). Spacious, modern and airy pine house in a tranquil setting 5km from town but close to bushwalks, and with free pick-ups from town and free use of bikes. They'll also drop off and pick up at trailheads, and rent kayaking gear (even full whitewater sets to the experienced) for $30 a day. Dorms ①, rooms ②.

Goldsborough Motels, 252 Revell St (☎ & fax 03/755 8772). Spacious motel ten minutes' walk from the centre, with a swimming pool, spa and complimentary morning newspaper. ④.

Hokitika Holiday Park, 242 Stratford St (☎03/755 8172). Hokitika's only campsite, neither spacious nor particularly appealing. Tent & powered sites $8–9, dorms ①, cabins & flats ②–③.

Jade Court Motor Lodge, 85 Fitzherbert St (☎0800/755 885, fax 03/755 8133).Well-equipped, if somewhat characterless motel five minutes' walk from town with in-house video and some rooms with private spa baths. ⑤.

Riley's Roost, Golf Links Road, Southside, 3km south (☎03/755 6018). Relaxed farmstay with great sea views and a squash court. Breakfast is continental and $25 dinners are available. ④.

Teichelmann's B&B, 20 Hamilton St (☎0800/743 742, fax 03/755 8239). Comfortable, well-appointed and central B&B, with friendly hosts and a hearty continental breakfast. ⑤.

The Town

Hokitika's leading role in the West Coast gold rushes rightly occupies much of the **West Coast Historical Museum**, Tancred Street (daily 9.30am–5pm; $3, gold panning $5 extra) and, along with greenstone and pioneering life, forms the focus for an interesting audio-visual presentation every half hour. The photos of the submerged horrors of the Hokitika River bar and the pleasures of the hundred or so bars of another kind that once lined Tancred Street are highlights among a predictable collection of firefighting and shipping paraphernalia.

With interest suitably kindled, grab the free **Hokitika Heritage Trail** leaflet, which details the remaining landmarks from the town's past, including the centrepiece **clock tower** commemorating the Boer War, a statue of **Richard Seddon**, local boy made good to become prime minister from 1893 to 1906, and the Gibson Quay area. This former riverside dock has been tarted up in recent years and makes a pleasant place for an evening stroll from the 1897 **Custom House**, past an ugly concrete memorial to ships lost on the bar, to the spit-end **Signal Station Lookout**, where coloured flags and raised balls used to help guide ships into the rivermouth. The Heritage Trail also crosses the river to a plaque marking the site of the Southside Aerodrome where, in 1934, one Bert Mercer started New Zealand's first licensed air

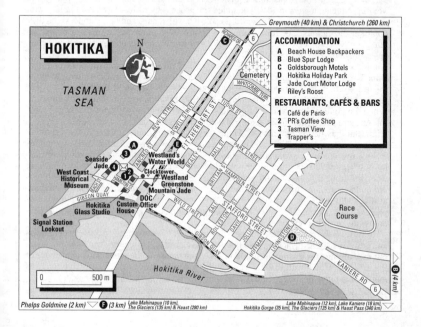

service to the glaciers, using a de Haviland Fox Moth, a replica of which stands outside Hokitika Airport.

Only those with kids to entertain and real fisheries buffs will get much out of **Westland's Water World**, Sewell Street (daily: Nov–March 9am–8pm; April–Oct 9am–5pm; $10), which concentrates on Westland's river and sea fish and gives you a chance to catch your own from indoor tanks. A better bet is **Phelps' Goldmine**, 2km south on SH6 (daily 9am–5pm; $5, gold panning $4 extra), where a huge and still-worked open-cast pit stands in dramatic contrast to ancient workings, which are enthusiastically demonstrated. Reproduction miners' huts and original riffle boxes mark the entrance to a 300m bushwalk to old tunnels.

Hokitika is **crafts** mad. Everywhere you look there is someone trying to sell you carved wood, blown glass, woven wool or a greenstone pendant, preferably with gold embellishments; and if you are in buying mode, there are quality pieces to be found. **Greenstone** (see box below) is big business, and the shops with the best ranges are Mountain Jade, 41 Weld St, and Westland Greenstone Ltd, 22 Tancred St; both lay on stone-cutting and shaping demonstrations. Seaside Jade, 67 Revell St, is one of the best of the smaller businesses, which often ask lower prices without sacrificing quality. Glass blowing is another long-standing Hoki tradition, and can be observed at the Hokitika Glass Studio, 2 Tancred St.

GREENSTONE

Maori revere **pounamu** (hard nephrite jade) and **tangiwai** (the softer, translucent bowenite), usually collectively known as **greenstone**. In Aotearoa's pre-European culture, it took the place of durable metals for both practical, warfaring and decorative uses: adzes and chisels were used for carving, *mere* (clubs) were used for hand-to-hand combat, and pendants were fashioned for jewellery. Charles Heaphy observed a group of Maori producing a *mere* in 1846, and noted the process by which they "saw the slab with a piece of mica slate, wet, and afterwards polish it with a fine sandy limestone which they obtain in the vicinity. The hole is drilled with a pointed stick with a piece of Pahutanui flint. The process does not appear so tedious as has been supposed; a month sufficing, apparently, for the completion".

In Maori, the entire South Island is known as **Te Wahi Pounamu**, "the place of greenstone", reflecting the importance of its sole sources, the belt from Greymouth through the rich Arahura River area near Hokitika south to Anita Bay on Milford Sound – where the beautifully dappled tangiwai occurs – and the Wakatipu region behind Queenstown. When the Poutini Ngai Tahu arranged to sell most of Westland to James Mackay in 1860, the Arahura River, their main source of pounamu, was specifically excluded.

Its value has barely diminished. Mineral claims are jealously guarded, the export of raw greenstone is prohibited and no extraction is allowed from national parks; penalties include fines of up to $200,000 and two years in jail. **Price** is heavily dependent on quality, but rates of $50,000 a tonne are not unknown in the raw state – and the sky's the limit when the stone is fashioned into sculpture and jewellery. Many of the cheaper specimens are quite crude, but pricier pieces (and we're talking a minimum of $100 for something aesthetically pleasing, and closer to $1000 for anything really classy) exhibit accomplished Maori designs executed to perfection; at the other end of the scale, simple pendants can be picked up for as little as $10.

Hokitika is the main venue for greenstone shoppers: bear in mind that the larger **shops** and **galleries** are firmly locked into the tour-bus circuit and prices are consequently high, but they are fine for learning something about the quality of the stone and competence of the artwork. Armed with this knowledge, check out the smaller places, which often have more competitive deals. Specific **recommendations** are given above.

The Hokitika year ticks by peacefully until the annual **Wildfoods Festival**, held on the second Saturday in March ($10 at the gate, $7.50 in advance; ☎03/755 8322). The town quadruples its population for this celebration of bush tucker, which takes place around Cass Square, where up to fifty stalls sell such delicacies as stir-fried possum, golden-fried huhu grubs, marinated goat kebabs and smoked eel wontons, all washed down with home-brewed beer and South Island wine. The gorging is followed by a hoe-down in the evening.

Activities

Few of the dramatically steep rivers spilling out of the alpine wilderness inland from Hokitika have any road access, and hardly any had been kayaked or rafted until recent years when helicopters were co-opted to reach them. Now, Alpine Rafts (☎03/755 8156) go **helirafting** on some of the most scenic and exciting stretches: trips include half a day on the Grade III **Taipo River** ($110), a full day on the Grade IV–V **Wanganui River** ($185), complete with a midway soak in a hot pool, and a full day on the wild, Grade V **Frisco Canyon**; full-day trips end with a big barbecue. Families are also catered for with a scenic drift down the **Hokitika Gorge** ($49, kids $25). Hokitika Nature Tours (☎03/755 8225) run gentle **kayaking trips** on Lake Mahinapua (see below; 3hr; $35) or in the coastal wetlands and tidal channels of the Totara Lagoon (full-day; $70).

Out at the airport, Wilderness Wings (☎03/755 8118) and Westair (☎03/755 7767) both do a number of **scenic flights** (from $160), principally around Mount Cook and the glaciers, while Skydive New Zealand (☎03/755 7575) offer **tandem skydives** ($165), with wonderful scenery and the possibility of a beach landing.

Eating and drinking

In *Trapper's* and the *Café de Paris*, Hokitika is fortunate in having a couple of the best **restaurants** on the Coast – reason enough to make this an overnight stop before heading south. Neither are prohibitively expensive but if you are counting the pennies there are cheaper cafés and snack bars, with little to choose between them. The most pleasant places to **drink** are the restaurants, though Hokitika has its share of beer barns. Evening entertainment is limited to a stroll to an attractive glow-worm dell about a kilometre north of the centre beside SH6.

Café de Paris, 19 Tancred St (☎03/755 8933). This fine restaurant is tastefully decorated and has a relaxed atmosphere that doesn't rule out a daytime snack. An extensive selection of moderately priced breakfasts gives way to bistro lunches and more formal evening dining with a Mediterranean theme (from around $18 for a main course). Licensed & BYO.

PR's Coffee Shop, 37 Tancred St. Popular and well-priced all-day café serving light lunches, dinners, cakes and coffees.

Tasman View, 111 Revell St (☎03/755 8344). Predominantly seafood restaurant with great sea views, mains from around $15 and a good-value smorgasbord on Friday evenings. Licensed.

Trapper's, 79 Revell St (☎03/755 5133). Try to block out the laboured theme and the heads of stuffed beasts around the walls and concentrate instead on the food: excellent chicken, salmon and vegetarian dishes are cooked in imaginative ways and prices under $20; trademark crocodile, kangaroo, wild boar and, in season, whitebait, cost a little more. Licensed.

Around Hokitika

Some of the best bush scenery and the finest **walks** hereabouts lie among the Taharoa Forest, where the dairying hinterland turns into the foothills of the Southern Alps some 30km inland along Stafford Street. Minor roads make a good 70km scenic drive (shown in detail on a free *Visitors' Guide to Hokitika* leaflet available from the visitor centre), passing the fishing, water skiing and tramping territory of **Lake Kaniere**, a glacial lake

18km from Hokitiki with several picnic sites and primitive camping ($4) along the eastern side. The most popular walk is the **Kaniere Water Race Walkway** (9km one-way; 3hr; 100m ascent), which starts from the lake's northern end and follows a channel that used to supply water to the goldfields, through stands of regenerating rimu. Close by is the **Lake Kaniere Walkway** (11km one-way; 4hr; flat), which traces the western lake margin by way of the basic Lawyer's Delight Hut (free) – more of a lunch stop than a place to stay. The eastern-shore road passes the attractive **Dorothy Falls** and continues to a spur leading to the **Hokitika Gorge**, 35km from Hoki, where a short path leads to a swing bridge over the tranquil Hokitika River as it eases through a deep gorge.

Immediately south of Hokitika, SH6 runs inland for 15km before meeting the old coastal Rautapu Road near Lake Mahinapua. Take the old road to visit the **Lake Mahinapua Scenic Reserve**, from where there are a number of short walks plus the easy **Mahinapua Walkway** (12km return; 3hr; mainly flat), detailed in a free leaflet available from the Hokitika DOC office. There's a DOC **campsite** ($4) here, and the *Mahinapua Hotel* (☎03/755 8500; dorms ①, rooms ②), opposite the reserve, serves **meals**, good beer and has backpacker-style **accommodation**. Gentle paddle-boat **cruises** along the Mahinapua Creek to the lake (Dec–April 10.30am, 2pm & 6pm; 1hr 30min; $20; ☎03/755 7239) start 5km south of Hokitika.

From Hokitika to the glaciers

The main highway leaves the coast **south of Hokitika** and snuggles in close to the Southern Alps for most of the 135km to the glacier at Franz Josef, the next town of any size. The journey through pakihi and stands of selectively logged native bush is broken by a series of **small settlements**, none of which warrant a long stay, though you may find yourself seduced by the sultry charms of **Okarito** and its lagoon.

Ross

The tiny village of **ROSS**, 30km south of Hokitika at the base of the bush-clad Mount Greenland, lies right on top of one of New Zealand's richest alluvial **goldfields**. The mining company is still chewing away at the large hole on the edge of town and would dearly love to get at the gold-bearing gravels underneath.

Once all the claims had been staked along the West Coast's original gold river, the Greenstone River near Hokitika, prospectors descended on the **Totara River** and soon there were over 3000 people here, digging down into the rich gravel layers of ancient riverbeds. By the early twentieth century, waterlogging and the lack of power for pumping put an end to a lengthy boom time, but just as things were winding up in 1909 a couple of diggers prospecting less than 500m from the current visitor centre turned up the largest gold nugget ever found in New Zealand, the 2.83kg "**Honourable Roddy**", named after the then Minister of Mines. The nugget was eventually bought by the government and given as a coronation gift in 1910 to Britain's George V, who melted it down to make royal tableware. A replica of the fist-sized lump of gold resides in the 1885 **Miner's Cottage**, Bold Street (daily 9am–4pm; free), surrounded by gold rush photos.

DOC leaflets (from the visitor centre – see below) detail the **Jones Flat Walk** past the source of the "Honourable Roddy" and the more popular **Water Race Walk**, which passes the remains of fluming designed to supply water for gravel washing.

Practicalities

The **visitor centre**, 4 Aylmer St (daily 9am–4pm, sometimes to 7pm in summer; ☎03/755 4077), presents an interesting show ($2) on the 1865 gold rush and subsequent sawmilling and farming history, and stocks DOC leaflets on local walks (50¢

each). For a little more information on different methods of gold extraction, call in at the so-called Tourist Centre, 11 Main St (daily 9am–5pm; free), with its tearooms and small museum.

Accommodation is limited to the *Historic Empire Hotel*, 19 Aylmer St (☎03/755 4005; tent sites $7–8, dorms ①, rooms ③), which has spacious verandahed doubles (some en-suite), four-person backpackers cabins and tent and campervan sites, and the basic but functional *Ross Motel*, Gibson Street (☎03/755 4022; ③). If there's nobody at the motel, ask at *Manera's General Store*. For sustenance, the *Empire Hotel* does good bar **snacks and meals**, including a cook-it-yourself barbecue, and the Tourist Centre hosts *Romeo's Pizza*.

Pukekura

The roadside south of Ross is dotted with places that process sphagnum moss, which grows readily around here and is much appreciated by Japanese and Korean orchid growers for its absorptive properties. The moss is also noted for being sterile and was used during the two world wars for swabs. The industry is covered in some detail at the **Bushman's Museum**, inside the **Bushman's Centre**, (Dec–March 9am–6pm; April–Nov 9am–5pm; free, museum $5), which is marked by a giant sandfly at **PUKEKURA**, 25km south of Ross. The whole centre takes a pretty light-hearted approach to showing how people make a living from the forest through timber milling and possum trapping, with opportunities to try knife- and axe-throwing. Once you've fed the captive possums, you can go next door to the *Wildfoods Restaurant* and eat their cousins, then buy a possum-fur trappers hat at the gift shop. The *Lake Ianthe Tavern*, across the road (☎03/755 4032; ②), has decent **cabins** and double rooms with TVs.

Rest areas around beautiful **Lake Ianthe**, 4km south, make good picnic stops, but exploring the region in any more depth is for the committed only. An unsealed road winds 10km through the Lake Ianthe Forest to the exposed **Greens Beach**, from where it is an hour and a half's walk south to a seal colony; there's also a DOC **campsite** at the beach and opportunities for swimming and boating if you have your own gear.

Harihari

Lake Ianthe feeds a tributary of the Wanganui River, crossed just before the village of **HARIHARI**, 20km further south. Harihari's chief claim to fame is its proximity to the marshy landing site of **Guy Menzies'** aircraft when he flew from his home town of Sydney to New Zealand, becoming the first to do the trip solo, only three years after Charles Kingsford Smith and his team made the original crossing; he bettered Kingsford Smith's time by two and a half hours. Menzies' plane, the *Southern Cross Junior*, crash-landed in the La Fontaine swamp, leaving Menzies strapped in upside down in the mud. There's little reason to actually stop in Harihari but you might want to turn onto Wanganui Flat Road and drive 20km coastwards to the start of the **Harihari Coastal Walkway** (8km; 2–3hr; negligible ascent), which follows a track used by miners heading south in the 1870s. The route runs through kahikatea forest to a spectacular piece of coastline, a sandy beach and the Doughboy Lookout, with great views of the Southern Alps.

Harihari **accommodation** is limited to a couple of places on the main road (SH6): the old but pleasant *Tomasi Motel* (☎03/753 3116; cabins ②, motel rooms ④) and the *Harihari Motor Inn* (☎03/753 3026; dorms ①, rooms ④), which also has a caravan site and a spa; and the excellent *Wapiti Park Homestead* (☎ & fax 03/753 3074; ⑥), a farmstay on the southern exit from town. Most **eating** happens at the *Harihari Motor Inn*, where there are good bar meals, or at the *Glenalmond* tearooms on SH6.

Whataroa and the herons

From November to February, New Zealand's entire population of the graceful white heron (*kotuku*) arrives to breed at the Waitangiroto Sanctuary, by the northern end of the Okarito Lagoon. The sanctuary is near **WHATAROA**, 35km south of Harihari, but access is strictly controlled and the only way to visit is on the DOC-officer-accompanied **White Heron Sanctuary Tours** (Nov–Feb 3–6 daily; 2.5hr; $66; booking advised ☎03/753 4120, fax 753 4087), which include a twenty-minute bus journey, a twenty-minute jetboat ride on the narrow Waitangitaona River, and half an hour observing the birds from a well-placed hide.

The White Heron Sanctuary Tours office on the main highway acts as the local **visitor centre** (no set hours; ☎03/753 4120) and also has **motel** units (④), cabins (②) and backpacker bunks (①). The *Whataroa Hotel* (☎03/753 4076; ③) does B&B, has a bit of wasteland out the back for campervans ($15), serves **dinners** and is the focal point of the town. *Country Fare Tearooms* caters to daytime snackers.

Okarito

In 1642, Abel Tasman became the first European to set eyes on Aotearoa at **OKARITO**, a hamlet scattered around the southern side of its eponymous lagoon and reached by a 13-kilometre side-road, 15km south of Whataroa. Two centuries later, the discovery of gold sparked an eighteen-month boom that saw fifty stores and hotels spring up along the lagoon's shores. Timber milling and flax production stood in once the gold had gone but the community foundered, leaving a few holiday homes and around thirty permanent residents – including author Keri Hulme, who used Okarito as the setting for much of her Booker Prize-winning novel, *The Bone People*.

The best of the **Okarito Lagoon** is hard to fully appreciate from the shore, but Okarito Nature Tours (☎ & fax 03/753 4014) run excellent-value and well-organized **kayaking trips**. On the two-hour trip ($15), you get to paddle around the sheltered lagoon, but best of all is the overnight trip to Lake Windemere ($50), where you camp at a remote beach and maybe visit the White Heron Sanctuary. Some experience is needed for the overnight trip, and all trips are tide-dependent: call ahead to check times. Kayaking aside, Okarito seems to draw people in, mainly just to laze about and take long strolls along deserted beaches, the most popular being the **Okarito Trig Walk** (1hr 30min return; 200m ascent) at the southern end of town, which climbs to a headland with fabulous mountain and coastal views. An extension to the Trig Walk, the **Coastal Track Walk** (3hr return from Okarito; negligible ascent), should only be tackled on a receding tide.

Practicalities

There's no fancy **accommodation** here, but a good range of budget places. A memorial commemorating Tasman's sighting stands next to the associate YHA, The Strand (☎03/753 4082; ①), a primitive two-room affair in the former schoolhouse, with an open fire and bunks but no bedding. Just along the street is the welcoming *Royal Motel & Hostel* (☎03/753 4080 & 0800/398 080; dorms ①, motel unit ②), comprising one motel unit, a house converted for backpacker use and a garden where you can pitch a tent for $5; fishing gear is available and there are sometimes locally grown vegetables to be had. If you don't need to be right in Okarito, then try *The Forks Bunkhouse*, 11km back towards SH6 (☎03/753 4122; tent sites $8, dorms ①), a lovely little spot at the confluence of the Okarito and Zolas rivers, with cheap bikes and gold-panning equipment for rent. There's also a fine DOC **campsite** ($4) at Lake Mapourika on SH6, just south of the Okarito turn-off. Note that there is **no shop** in Okarito, so bring everything with you.

The glaciers

Around 150km south of Hokitika, two blinding white rivers of ice force their way down towards the thick rainforest of the coastal plain – ample justification for inclusion of this region in *Te Wahipounamu*, the South West New Zealand World Heritage Area. The glaciers are stunning viewed from a distance, but are even more impressive close up, generating a palpable connectedness between the coast and the highest peaks of the Southern Alps, a sensation heightened by being able to walk on the glaciers on guided trips. Within a handful of kilometres the terrain drops from over 3000m to near sea level, bringing with it **Franz Josef glacier** and **Fox glacier**, the two largest and most impressive of the sixty-odd glaciers that creak off the South Island's icy backbone, together forming the centrepiece of the rugged **Westland National Park**.

The park is equally characterized by the West Coast's prodigious **precipitation**, which here reaches its greatest expression, with five metres being the typical yearly dump. These conditions, combined with the rakish angle of the western slopes of the Southern Alps, produce some of the world's **fastest-moving** glaciers; stand at the foot for half an hour or so and you're bound to see a piece peel off. But these phenomenal speeds haven't been enough to completely counteract melting, and both glaciers have **receded** over 3km since Cook saw them at their greatest recent extent, soon after the Little Ice Age of 1750. Since 1985 the trend has reversed though, with a series of high-snowfall winters looking to set both glaciers **advancing** into the next millennium.

Art critic and arbiter of public taste in **Victorian** England, John Ruskin, once postulated that glaciers retreat "on account of the vulgarity of tourists", and Franz Josef and Fox had certainly turned their tail when contemporary **travellers** battled their way down the coast to observe these wonders of nature, initially named "Victoria" and "Albert" respectively. In 1865, geologist Julius von Haast renamed Franz Josef after the Austro-Hungarian Emperor, and following a visit by prime minister William Fox in 1872, the other glacier was bestowed with his name.

GLACIERS FOR BEGINNERS

The existence of a glacier is always a balancing act between competing forces: snowfall at the **névé**, high in the mountains, battles with rapid melting at the **terminal** lower down the valley, the victor determining whether the glacier will **advance** or **retreat**. Snowfall metres thick gradually compacts to form clear **blue ice**, which accumulates to the point when it starts to flow downhill under its own weight. Friction against the valley walls slows the sides while ice in the centre charges headlong down the valley, giving the characteristic **scalloped effect** on the surface, which is especially pronounced on such vigorous glaciers as Franz Josef and Fox. Where a riverbed steepens, the river forms a rapid: under similar conditions, glaciers break up into an **ice fall**, full of towering blocks of ice known as **seracs**, separated by **crevasses**.

Visitors familiar with grubby glaciers in the European Alps or American Rockies will expect the surface to be mottled with **rock debris** which has fallen off the valley walls onto the surface; however, the glaciers here descend so steeply that the cover doesn't have time to build up and they remain pristine and white. Rock still gets carried down with the glacier though, and when the glacier retreats, this is deposited as **terminal moraine**. Occasionally retreating glaciers leave behind huge chunks of ice which, on melting, form **kettle lakes**.

The most telling evidence of past glacial movements is the location of the **trim line** on the valley wall, caused by the glacier stripping away all vegetation. At Fox and Franz Josef, the advance associated with the Little Ice Age around 1750 left a very visible trim line high up the valley wall, separating mature rata from scrub.

Activity in the glaciers focuses on two small **villages**, which survive almost entirely on tourist traffic. Both lie close to the base of their respective glacier and are near the start of numerous walks, and both offer a comparably wide variety of plane and heli-copter **flights** and **guided glacier walks** (see box on p.657). Franz Josef has margin-ally better facilities, while Fox Glacier is the quieter, with a more rural aspect; with your own transport, it makes sense to base yourself in one of the two villages and explore both glaciers from there.

To avoid confusion between the **villages** and the **glaciers** from which they derive their names, we've used a capital "G" for the Franz Josef Glacier (*Waiau*) **village**, and a lower-case "g" for the Franz Josef **glacier**; the same goes for the village of Fox Glacier (*Weheka*), which lies close to the foot of the Fox glacier.

Franz Josef Glacier

Historically there has been little to choose between the two glacier villages, but in recent years **FRANZ JOSEF GLACIER** has edged ahead, with a wider range of places to stay and an improving culinary scene. The Franz Josef glacier almost licks the fringes of the village, the Southern Alps tower above and developers have done what they can with steeply pitched roofs and pine panelling, but the village somehow lacks alpine character, perhaps owing to the encircling rain-soaked bush. It is an appealing place though, and small enough to make you feel almost like a local if you stay for more than a night or two – something that's easily done, considering the number of fine walks hereabouts and the proximity of the glaciers.

Arrival and information

Daily InterCity **buses** in both directions arrive in the evening and leave the following morning: the southbound bus drops off around Franz Josef then continues to Fox Glacier, where it spends the night; the northbound bus does the reverse, dropping off in Fox Glacier first.

First stop in Franz Josef should be the excellent combined **visitor centre** and **DOC office** on SH6 (daily: Nov–April 8.30am–7pm; May–Oct 9am–5pm; ☎03/752 0796, fax 752 0797), which has stacks of leaflets on walks in the area and first-class displays on every aspect of glaciation and the region's geology. Twenty-minute performances (daily 9am–4pm; $2.50), with actors imitating nineteenth-century tourists, are distinctly cringe-worthy, but the evening slide shows (8pm; $4) are almost always worth attending.

Pretty much everything else you are likely to need is within a couple of hundred metres along, or just off, SH6. There are **no banks** or cash machines either here or in Fox Glacier, but several places have EFTPOS facilities.

Accommodation

As a consequence of the bus schedules and the tendency of backpacker buses to spend two nights here, accommodation is very tight throughout the summer. Between December and March, you should aim to **book** at least a couple of days **in advance**. The better backpacker places are all clustered at one end of Cron Street, just along from a couple of decent motels; guesthouses are a better bet than the large motor lodges.

A1 Rata Grove Motel, 6 Cron St (☎03/752 0741). Central and fairly modern motel with kitchen-less studios and fully equipped self-catering units just nudging into the next price code. ④–⑤.

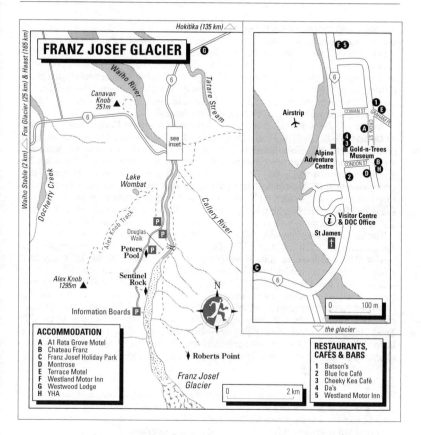

Chateau Franz, 8 Cron St (☎ & fax 752 0738). Well-organized and justifiably popular backpackers with an easy-going atmosphere, a wide selection of videos and a pool table. Tent sites $8, dorms ①, rooms ②.

Franz Josef Holiday Park, 1km south on SH6 (☎03/752 0766). Large riverside campsite with the usual range of facilities plus lodge bunks. Camping $16 per site, dorms ①, cabins ②–③.

Montrose, 3 Cron St (☎03/752 0188, fax 752 0750). Slightly cramped but perfectly decent hostel in a re-sited house. Dorms ①, rooms ②.

Terrace Motel, 1 Graham Place (☎03/752 0130, fax 752 0190). Brand new, high-quality motel with all mod cons, close to the centre of town. ⑤.

Waiho Stables Country Stay, Docherty Creek, 6km south (☎03/752 0747, fax 752 0786). Comfortable homestay with a strong environmental slant. Modern wood-panelled rooms come with bathroom and full continental breakfast, vegetarian dinner costs $30 and there is horse riding on the property. ⑥.

Westland Motor Inn, SH6 (☎0800/100 729, fax 752 0709). The pick of Franz Josef's large hotels, with bland but comfortable rooms, and firmly on the tour-bus circuit. ⑧.

Westwood Lodge, 1km north on SH6 (☎ & fax 03/752 0111). The best Franz Josef has to offer: a spacious and comfortable guesthouse with a cosy alpine lodge feel, well-appointed en-suite rooms, a billiard room and a buffet continental breakfast. ⑥.

YHA, 2–4 Cron St (☎ & fax 03/752 0754). Modern, airy hostel with a spacious kitchen, a sunny lawn out the front and nightly videos, plus bike rental for $20 a day. Dorms ①, rooms ②.

Walks – and more sedentary diversions

Top of everyone's list of **walks** is the one from the information kiosk and car park, 5km south of the village, **to the face of the Franz Josef glacier** (3km; 1hr return; flat), a roped-off and ever-changing wall of ice beside an ice cave where the Waiho River issues from beneath the glacier. The rough track crosses gravel beds left behind by past glacial retreats, giving you plenty of opportunity to observe the glacier-scoured hump of Sentinel Rock just downstream, small kettle lakes, the trim line high up the valley walls and a fault line cutting right across the valley (marked by deep gullies opposite each other).

Worthwhile walks off this access road include one to **Sentinel Rock** (10min), the circular **Douglas Walk** (1hr) past Peter's Pool, a serene lake left by a retreat in the late eighteenth century, and the **Alex Knob Track** (12km; 6–8hr return; 1000m ascent), which climbs high above the glacier through several vegetation zones and offers fine views up the valley. The first few metres of the Douglas Walk are shared with the spectacular **Roberts Point Track** (9km; 5hr return; 600m ascent) which climbs up through dripping rainforest on the opposite (northern) side of the valley, high above the glacier. Slippery stream crossings and occasional rockface ladders make this an entertaining, though not especially strenuous walk. The only way to actually walk on the glacier surface is with a guide (see box on p.357).

The shortest walk from town follows SH6 for a couple of hundred metres south to **St James Church**, which once framed the glacier in the altar window. The ice retreated from view in 1953, and the church itself nearly did so in 1995, when the flooded Waiho River scoured away the alluvial bank and left the church precariously poised on a cliff.

If you can't face the real thing, there's always the twenty-minute *Flowing West* widescreen film (3–5 showings daily; 20min; $10) at the Alpine Adventure Centre, an overproduced journey around the region with all the spirit of a failed fizzy-drink commercial. As a wet-day substitute, you're probably better off across the road at **Gold-N-Trees** (daily: Dec–April 8am–10pm; May–Nov 9am–5pm; $2), a small but perfectly formed display of gold-extraction equipment and photos of local workings, plus a thinly disguised promo for the company that's logging the local forests.

Eating and drinking

With the opening of an innovative **restaurant** in recent years, a couple of days in Franz Josef doesn't mean culinary deprivation, and there's even a central **bar**. The relatively remote location keeps prices high though, and even if you are self-catering you can expect to pay over the odds for a limited stock of **groceries**.

Batson's, cnr Cowan St & Cron St. The best and most convenient of Franz Josef's two pubs – the other is out at the Franz Josef Glacier Hotel, 1km north of town – with a convivial atmosphere, pool table and a range of bistro meals for $12–15.

Blue Ice Café, SH6. A modern, airy and much-needed addition to the Franz Josef scene, with café-style all-day dining, and the best coffee in town. Imaginative and beautifully presented mains start at around $20, but they also do $7 light-meal-and-a-beer backpacker specials. There's an ambitious range of New Zealand wines by the bottle or glass and the bar stays open until 2am, making good use of an upstairs area fitted with futon sofas and a pool table.

Cheeky Kea Café, SH6. Cheerful and inexpensive BYO café serving a middle of the road selection of grills, burgers, sandwiches and tearoom favourites.

DA's, SH6. Tolerable café and takeaway with a few Asian dishes to add spice to your diet.

Westland Motor Inn, SH6 (☎03/752 0729). Formal dining in a cavernous restaurant with well-cooked food from a predictable menu along the lines of grilled salmon and rack of lamb. Mains start around $20.

Fox Glacier

FOX GLACIER, 25km south of Franz Josef, lies scattered over an outwash plain of the Fox and Cook rivers, and supports the local farming community, as well as sightseers. Everything of interest is near SH6 or Cook Flat Road, which passes the scenic Lake

GLACIER FLIGHTS AND GUIDED WALKS

The range of flights, glacier walks and activities available from Franz Josef Glacier and Fox Glacier are almost identical.

FLIGHTSEEING

On any fine day the skies above both villages are abuzz with choppers and light planes. Safety demands that specific **flight paths** must be followed, limiting what can be offered and forcing companies to compete on price; ask for youth, student, senior or just-for-the-sake-of-it **discounts**, most readily given if you can band together in a group of four to six and present yourselves as a ready-to-go plane or chopper load. **Plane** flights tend to be longer for the same money, but apart from the Mount Cook Airline ski planes, only the **helicopters** land, usually on a snow saddle high above the glacier where the rotors are left running – hardly a serene setting. Of the **plane operators**, Westair (☎03/752 0716) run overflights of both glaciers (25min; $90) and circuits of Mount Cook (40min; $145); Mount Cook Airline (☎03/752 0714) do the same flights for similar prices and also do snow-landing flights (conditions permitting; 30–60min; $100–180). **Helicopter operators** Fox and Franz Josef Heliservices (☎03/752 0793), Glacier Helicopters (☎03/752 0755) and The Helicopter Line (☎03/ 752 0767 & 0800/807 767) all charge similar prices for flights, including snow landings: one glacier (20min; $90–100), two glaciers (30min; $140–150), and two glaciers plus Mount Cook (40min; $220–230).

WALKING ON GLACIERS

The only people licensed to take visitors on **Franz Josef glacier walks** are Franz Josef Glacier Guides, SH6 (☎03/752 0763, fax 752 0102), who undertake a **half-day trip** (daily 9.15am & 2pm; $35) that involves a trudge across the braided riverbed below the glacier in hobnail boots then an hour on the ice, snaking up ample ice steps cut by your guide. Although you're steadied by a fixed rope, it can be unnerving balancing beside deep blue crevasses – vertigo sufferers beware. For a more tangible sense of adventure, fork out for the full-day **Icefall Climb** (daily 9.15am; $70), which gives around five hours on the ice, with the hobnail boot supplemented by an ice axe for additional purchase on far smaller ice steps. If you are also thinking of doing a helicopter flight, combine the two as a **Heli-Hike** (on demand; 2hr 30min; $175), involving two flights and an hour on the ice among ice caves, pinnacles and seracs.

Glacier walking is perhaps more rewarding on the **Fox glacier**, where entry is from the side, giving more immediate access to crevasses and seracs. Alpine Guides (☎03/751 0825, fax 751 0857) lead half-day walks (9.30am & 2pm; $34), with around an hour on the ice, and do **longer trips** (Dec–March only 9.30am; $45), giving around three hours on the ice. For serious ice addicts, there are even **Ice Climbing Instruction Days** ($115 each for 4, $195 for 2).

Matheson on the way to the former gold settlement and seal colony at Gillespies Beach. The foot of the Fox glacier lies around 8km away, although it's creeping closer at a rate of around 150m a year.

Arrival and information

The village of Fox Glacier suffers from the same **bus** schedule as Franz Josef (see p.654) and consequently has similar problems with accommodation through the summer months. If you come unstuck, seek help at the combined **visitor centre** and **DOC office**, SH6 (daily: mid-Nov to mid-April 8.30am–7.30pm; rest of year 8.30am–4.30pm; ☎03/751 0807, fax 751 0858) which, besides providing information about the region, has displays concentrating on lowland forests. You can rent **bikes** for $30 a day from Alpine Guides (☎03/751 0825).

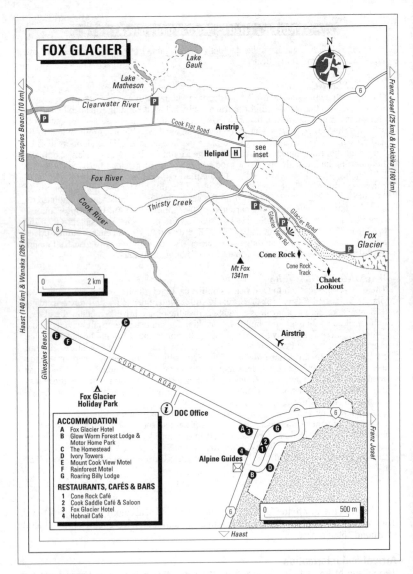

Accommodation

Fox Glacier's range of places to stay is more limited than Franz Josef's but is generally pretty good and well priced; **booking** as far ahead as you can is a good idea if you are determined to stay in the village.

Fox Glacier Holiday Park, Cook Flat Rd (☎03/751 0821, fax 751 0813). Spacious campsite with standard facilities with tent sites, a bunkhouse and a range of cabins and flats. Camping $18 per site, dorms ①, cabins & flats ②–③.

Fox Glacier Hotel, Cook Flat Rd (☎03/751 0868). Ageing hotel with faded but still elegant public areas and widely varying rooms, ranging from economy twins to modern en-suites. ③–⑥.

Glow Worm Forest Lodge and Motor Home Park, SH6 (☎03/751 0888). An unusual but excellent set-up in a pine-lined alpine chalet with simple, attractively furnished rooms sharing bath and self-catering facilities. There's also bike rental for $15 a day and campervans can be hooked-up outside for $10 per person, but there are no tent sites. ③.

The Homestead, Cook Flat Rd (☎03/751 0835). Friendly homestay in a lovely old house with views of Mount Cook and attractive en-suite rooms. ⑤.

Ivory Towers, Sullivan's Rd (☎03/751 0838). Clean and reasonably spacious backpackers with bunks in small dorms and doubles; bikes can be rented for $25 a day. Dorms ①, rooms ②.

Mount Cook View Motel, Cook Flat Rd (☎03/751 0814, fax 751 0803). High-standard motel with characterful older units and more luxurious newer units, some with spa baths. ⑤–⑥.

Rainforest Motel, Cook Flat Rd (☎03/751 0140, fax 751 0141). Log cabin exteriors belie the clean interior lines of smallish but attractive studio units and larger one-bedroom units. ⑤.

Roaring Billy Lodge, SH6 (☎ & fax 03/751 0815). Friendly homestay in the centre of Fox Glacier with simple rooms and a comfortable lounge area; venison sausages are on offer for breakfast. Billy also runs nature-guiding trips to order. ④.

Walks and glacier views

It would be a shame to miss the Fox glacier just because you have already seen the Franz Josef glacier: the **approach walks** are quite different and their characters are very distinct, the Fox valley being less sheer but with more impressive rock falls. The approach, imaginatively named Glacier Road, crosses the wide bed left by glacial retreats and is occasionally re-routed as "dead" ice under the roadway gradually melts. From the car park, 8km from the town, a track leads to the foot of the glacier in half an hour, crossing a couple of small streams en route. Part way back along Glacier Road, **River Walk** (2km; 30min) crosses a historic swing bridge to the Glacier Valley Viewpoint on Glacier View Road, which runs along the south side of the Fox River. From here, the **Cone Rock Track** (7km; 2hr 30min return) climbs steeply for stupendous glacier and mountain views.

It's difficult to imagine a New Zealand calendar or picture book without a photo of Mount Cook and Mount Tasman mirrored in **Lake Matheson**, 6km west of town along Cook Flat Road. A well signposted lakeside boardwalk through lovely native bush encircles the lake, which was formed by an iceberg left behind when the Fox Glacier retreated 14,000 years ago. It takes around an hour and gives everyone, but particularly those who venture out before breakfast, a chance for that perfect image.

Continue 15km along Cook Flat Road to reach **Gillespies Beach**, a former gold-mining settlement where a small cemetery, the remains of a dredge and piles of tailings can be seen. Several **walks** fan out from there, the most celebrated leading along the beach north to a **colony of fur seals**; aim to leave a couple of hours before low tide (consult the visitor centre for times), allowing at least four hours for the round trip.

Eating and drinking

For its diminutive size, Fox Glacier does a reasonable job of catering to hungry walkers coming off the glacier-side paths, with a small selection of reasonably priced **cafés**, a restaurant and a couple of lively **bars**.

Cone Rock Café, SH6. Fine café selling wholefood snacks and meals either outside or inside on mismatched and ageing furniture. Pizzas, nachos, main meals, cakes and coffee are all delicious.

Cook Saddle Café and Saloon, SH6. Hearty drinking in a mountain-lodge atmosphere.

Fox Glacier Hotel, Cook Flat Rd. Upmarket restaurant following the Kiwi taste for Mediterranean and Pacific Rim cuisine, adjacent to a noisy and fairly scruffy public bar.

The Hobnail Café, SH6. Adequate café in the same building as Alpine Guides, with a standard range of pies, sandwiches, cakes and coffee in alpine-chalet surroundings.

THE COPLAND TRACK TO WELCOME FLAT

The three-to-four-day **Copland Track** over the spectacular 2150m Copland Pass has long been regarded as the pinnacle of tramping achievement, on the cusp of real mountaineering. It requires competent use of an ice axe and crampons but is currently highly dangerous on account of unstable rock rubble beside the Hooker Glacier on the Mount Cook side. Guided crossings are currently suspended, though DOC continues to issue an instruction leaflet and Alpine Guides in Fox Glacier and Mount Cook will rent out equipment. Conditions do change though, so ask locally.

At present, the best compromise is to tackle just the sector from the foot of the **Copland Valley to the thermal pools** (17km; 6–7hr; 400m ascent), near **Welcome Flat Hut** (Category 2; $8; 30 bunks). It is pleasant bushwalking all the way and the open-air pools are a wonderful incentive. The track starts by a car park just off SH6, 26km south of Fox Glacier, and follows the right bank all the way to Welcome Flat, crossing numerous streams by hopping from rock to rock or wading. If the creeks are high, as they commonly are, you may have to use the flood bridges, which will add an hour or so; after really heavy rain, the track becomes impassable.

South Westland and Makarora

South from the glaciers, the West Coast feels remoter still. There wasn't even a road through here until 1965 and the final section of tarmac wasn't laid on the Haast Pass until 1995. SH6 mostly runs inland, passing the start of the ambitious **Copland Track** (see box above), through kahikatea and rimu forests as far as **Knight's Point**, where it returns to the coast along the edge of the Haast Coastal Plain, with its stunning **coastal dune systems** sheltering lakes and some fine stands of kahikatea. The plain continues south past the scattered township of **Haast** to the site of the short-lived colonial settlement of **Jackson Bay**. From Haast, SH6 veers inland over the Haast Pass to the former timber town of **Makarora**, not strictly part of the West Coast but moist enough to share some of the same characteristics and a base for the excellent **Gillespie Pass** Tramp.

South to Haast

Many visitors do the glaciers to Wanaka or Queenstown run in a day, missing out on some fine country that makes up for its relative lack of comforts with its sheer sense of remoteness. Facilities aren't completely absent: the majority of the accommodation and eating places are clustered around Haast, but there are a few pitstops along the way. Some 60km south of Fox Glacier, the road crosses the **Paringa River**, where a plaque marks the southern limit of Thomas Brunner's 1846–48 explorations. He recorded in his diary the desire to "once more see the face of a white man, and hear my native tongue", and it is doubtful whether Brunner ever saw **Lake Paringa**, 10km further south. By the northern side of the lake, the *Lake Paringa Heritage Lodge* (☎03/751 0894; cabins ②, motel units ④) has fully self-contained **accommodation** and a beautifully sited and moderately priced café overlooking ponds where salmon are bred. Towards the southern side of the lake, the *Lake Paringa Café* is worth a stop for its $10 **meals**, including venison pie, quiche and, in season, whitebait omelettes. The DOC **campsite** ($4) by the lake is primitive, but driftwood fires are permitted.

Around 10km south of Lake Paringa, the **Munro Beach Walk** (5km; 1hr 30min return) leads through lovely forest to one of the best places for spotting rare **Fiordland** crested penguins – mainly during the breeding season (July–Dec), but also occasionally in February, when they come ashore to moult. Nature lovers with ample wallets can gain a deeper appreciation of the fragile ecosystems of south Westland by staying nearby at the exclusive *Lake Moeraki Wilderness Lodge* (☎03/750 0881, fax 750 0882; ⑨) where, for just under $200 per person per day, you get lodge **accommodation**, all meals, free canoe use and all manner of guided nature walks and safaris.

The highway finally returns to the coast at **Knight's Point**, where a roadside marker commemorates the linking of Westland and Otago by road in 1965; a dog belonging to one of the surveyors lends his name to this dramatic bluff fringed by magnificent seascapes where, with binoculars, seals can often be picked out on the rocks below. Ahead lies the **Haast Coastal Plain**, which kicks off at the tea-coloured **Ship Creek**, where a picnic area and information panels by a beautiful long surf-pounded beach mark the start of two lovely walks: a twenty-minute walk up the river through kahikatea forest to a lookout and the **Dune Lake Walk** (2km; 30min return) along the coast to the dune-trapped Lake Mataketake.

From Ship Creek it is only another 15km to the 700m-long Haast River Bridge, the longest single-lane bridge in the country, immediately before Haast Junction.

Haast

HAAST is initially a confusing place, with three communities all taking the name: Haast Junction, at the intersection of SH6 and the minor road to Jackson Bay, Haast Beach, 4km along the Jackson Bay Road (see below) and Haast, the largest settlement 2km along SH6 towards the Haast Pass and Wanaka.

The first stop is Haast Junction, site of the distinctive **Haast World Heritage Centre** (daily: mid-Nov to mid-April 8.30am–6pm; rest of year 8.30am–4.30pm; ☎03/750 0809), which serves as the local visitor centre but is much more, with highly informative displays on all aspects of the local environment. Half an hour in here may well induce you to spend longer in what they are at pains to point out is part of the Southwest New Zealand World Heritage Area. If you're won over, there are economy and considerably better standard **rooms** across the road at the *World Heritage Hotel* (☎03/750 0828, fax 750 0827; ④/⑤), which is also the region's social centre, with hearty **meals** and a lively public bar.

Buses stop 2km east at tiny Haast, which has a reasonable **café-cum-shop** and a couple of **places to stay**, the best being the brand new and highly-rated *Wilderness Backpackers*, Pauareka Road (☎0800/750 029; tent sites $8, dorms ①, rooms ②).

The road to Jackson Bay

A real sense of isolation soon sets in on the 50km **dead-end road** south to the fishing village of Jackson Bay. A modest number of inquisitive tourists make it down this way, to discover a place hanging on by its fingernails. Leaving Haast Junction, the canopies of windswept roadside trees are bunched together like cauliflower heads down to and beyond **Haast Beach**, 4km south, where there's a small shop, petrol and the decent *Erewhon Motel* (☎03/750 0803, fax 750 0817; ④). At **Okuru**, 12km further south, a onetime Maori fishing and greenstone-gathering settlement, dating back to around 1300, now comprises a strip of beach housing set back from a wild coastline and the *Haast Motor Camp* (☎03/750 0860; tent sites $8, dorms ①, cabins ②–③). Opposite the motor camp, the **Hapuku Estuary Walk** (20min loop) follows a raised boardwalk over a brackish lagoon and through kowhai forest that gleams brilliant yellow in October and November. Old sand dunes support rimu and kahikatea forest, and there are occasional views out to the **Open Bay Islands**, noted by Cook in 1770 and later gainfully employed as a sealing base away from the sandflies of the coast. They are now a **wildlife sanctuary** and a major breeding colony for fur seals and Fiordland crested penguins.

The road continues 35km to **Jackson Bay**, a former sealing station tucked in the curve of Jackson Head, which protects it from the worst of the westerlies. In 1875 it was chosen as the site for a "Special Settlement", a significant port and commercial centre to rival Greymouth and Hokitika. Assisted migrants – Scandinavians, Germans, Poles, Italians, English and Irish – were expected to carve a living from tiny land allocations, with limited and irregular supplies. Sodden by rain, crops rotted, and people were soon leaving in droves; a few stalwarts stayed, their descendants providing the core of today's residents, who eke out a meagre living from lobster and tuna fishing.

If you can bear the sandflies, try the **Wharekai Te Kau Walk** (20min return) across the low isthmus behind Jackson Head, the **Smoothwater Track** (1hr 30min return), with great coastal views on the way to the Smoothwater River, or the longer **Stafford**

GILLESPIE PASS: THE WILKIN AND YOUNG VALLEYS CIRCUIT

DOC's Tramping Guide to the Makarora Region ($2) has all the detail you need for this walk, though the 1:150,000 Mount Aspiring National Park and the 1:50,000 Wilkin maps are useful.

This tramp over the 1490m **Gillespie Pass** links the upper valley of the **Young River** with that of the **Siberia Stream** and the **Wilkin River**. The scenery is superb, the match of any of the more celebrated valleys further south, but is tramped by a fraction of the folk on the Routeburn or the Greenstone tracks; perhaps the biggest gripe for the tramping purist is the disturbance caused by **planes** flying into the Siberia Valley. The tramp can be divided up into smaller chunks, using the Siberia Experience's planes and jetboats (see p.664), but the full circuit (60km) takes **three days**.

ACCESS AND ACCOMMODATION

All the **huts** (Category 2; $8) in the Wilkin and Young valleys are equipped with mattresses and heating (but not cooking) stoves; hut **tickets** and annual hut **passes** are available from the DOC office in Makarora (see p.664). The walk is typically done up the Young Valley and down the Wilkin – the way we've described it here. **Access** at both ends of the walk is a question of **wading** the broad **Makarora River**. If it hasn't rained substantially in the last five days and you can pick your spot well (the river changes course frequently, so ask locally), you'll barely be in up to your knees but if you have any doubt, band together with other trampers and get a **jetboat** to drop you at the confluence of the Young and Makarora rivers (around $15 per person); it's also a good idea to arrange a **pick-up** from Kerin Forks at the far end of the walk, unless you want to take your chances with river crossings or a stand-by flight out of Siberia Valley.

THE ROUTE

The walk proper starts on the northern bank of the confluence of the Young and Makarora rivers; from Makarora, walk 3km upstream, find a good crossing place upstream of the confluence then walk down the right bank of the Makarora to the bush-side marker. From the **confluence to Young Hut** (15km; 7–9hr; 700m ascent), the easy-to-follow track traces the left bank through beech forest then, after a fork, follows the left bank of the South Branch, climbing steeply with some difficulty over

Bay Walk (10hr return), with the possibility of a night at the Stafford Bay Hut (Category 3; $4). Details and tide tables are available from the Haast World Heritage Centre.

Haast Pass and Makarora

From Haast it is nearly 150km over the **Haast Pass** (at 563m, the lowest road crossing of the Southern Alps) to Wanaka – a journey from the verdant rain-soaked forests of the West Coast into the parched, rolling grasslands of Central Otago. Ngai Tahu used the route as a greenstone trading route and probably introduced it to gold prospector Charles Cameron, who became the first *pakeha* to cross in 1863; he was closely followed by the more influential **Julius Von Haast**, who immodestly named it after himself. The pass was finally opened as a vehicular road as far as Haast in 1960, linked through to Fox Glacier in 1965 and completely sealed in 1995.

The road starts beside the broad **Haast River** which, as the road climbs, narrows into a series of churning cascades. Numerous short walks, mostly to waterfalls on tributaries, spur off at intervals. The most celebrated include the **Thunder Creek Falls**

---

several bad slips. It eases after a while and the track continues, sometimes indistinctly, through ever more stunted bush and occasional clearings to the tree line. Collect firewood here – you're now less than half an hour from the Young Hut (20 bunks), which is wonderfully sited on the right bank in a magnificent avalanche-scoured rock cirque crowned by 2202m Mount Awful, apparently named in wonder rather than horror.

Suitably rested, you've another fairly strenuous day ahead from **Young Hut to Siberia Hut** (9km; 6–7hr; 500m ascent, 800m descent) over the Gillespie Pass. Keep to the right bank until you reach a rock cairn, which marks the start of a steep and lengthy ascent, following snow poles to a saddle; it'll take two or three hours to reach this fabulous, barren spot with views across the snow-capped northern peaks of the Mount Aspiring National Park. Grassy slopes marked by more snow poles lead steeply down to Gillespie Stream, which is followed to its confluence with the Siberia Stream, from where it's a gentle, undulating hour downstream to Siberia Hut (20 bunks), though keen types might tag on a side-trip to **Lake Crucible** (4hr return) before cantering down to the hut. Those with more modest aspirations can spend two nights at Siberia Hut and do the **Lake Crucible side trip** (13km; 6–7hr return; 500m ascent) on the spare day. From the Siberia Hut, retrace your steps to the confluence of the Siberia and Gillespie streams, ford the Gillespie Stream and continue along the left bank of the Siberia Stream a short distance until you see Crucible Stream cascading in a deep gash on the far side. Ford Siberia Stream and ascend through the bush on the right bank of the stream. It is hard going, and route-finding among the alpine meadows higher up can be difficult but the deep, alpine lake tucked under the skirts of Mount Alba and choked with small icebergs is ample reward.

Planes fly in and out of the **Siberia Valley airstrip**, and you can take your chance on "backloading" **flights out** ($25). To continue tramping from **Siberia Hut to Kerin Forks** (6km; 2–3hr; 100m ascent, 300m descent), enter the bush at the southern end of Siberia Flats on the left bank of Siberia Stream and descend away from the stream then zigzag steeply down to the Wilkin River and the **Kerin Forks Hut** (10 bunks), where many trampers arrange to be met by a jetboat. If it has rained heavily, fording the Makarora lower down will be impossible, so don't forgo the jetboat lightly. The alternative is to walk from **Kerin Forks to Makarora** (17km; 6–7hr; 100m ascent, 200m descent), following the Wilkin River's left bank, then crossing the Makarora upstream of the confluence.

(10min), the roadside **Fantail Falls**, and the **Blue Pools Walk** (30min return), where a stream issues from a narrow gorge.

Makarora

The hamlet of **MAKARORA** lies roughly midway between Haast and Wanaka, on the northern fringe of the Mount Aspiring National Park. If you're aching for the relative comforts of Wanaka and Queenstown there's little reason to stop, but keen trampers with a few days to spare should consider tackling Gillespie Pass.

In the nineteenth century the dense **forests** all about and the proximity of Lake Wanaka made Makarora the perfect spot for marshalling cut logs across the lake and coaxing them down the Clutha River southeast to the fledgling North Otago **gold towns** of Clyde and Cromwell. The creation of the national park in 1964 paved the way for Makarora's increasing importance as the main northern access point to a region of majestic beauty, alpine vegetation and dense beech-filled valleys.

About all you'll find here is a motor camp, a shop and a **DOC office** (Dec–Feb daily 8am–5pm; March–Nov Mon–Fri 8am–5pm; ☎03/443 8365), the place to go for information and hut tickets for tramps. The main justification for stopping here is to head out on the Gillespie Pass tramp (see box on p.662) or to join Southern Alps Air's **Siberia Experience** (mid-Oct to mid-April; 4hr; $132; ☎03/443 8372), an excellent combination of flying into the remote Siberia Valley, tramping to the Wilkin River and jetboating back to Makarora; the same operator also offers overflights of Mount Aspiring (around $100), and just about anywhere else if they can get the numbers. The **jetboating** can also be tackled separately with Wilkin River Jet (1hr; $42; ☎03/443 83651). Finally, if the Gillespie Pass seems a little daunting, there are a couple of **shorter walks** close to Makarora, the **Makarora Bush Nature Walk** (20min), which starts near the visitor centre and, branching off this, the **Mount Shrimpton Track** (4–5hr), which climbs up through silver beech to the bushline, then to a knob overlooking the Makarora Valley.

InterCity and some of the backpacker **buses** stop at Makarora, and almost everyone **stays** at the *Makarora Tourist Centre*, SH6 (☎03/443 8372, fax 443 1082; tent sites $8, chalets ②–④), a collection of self-catering and simpler A-frame chalets in a clearing. It is all very peaceful and there's a pool, making it a good place to hole up for a day or two, provided you are well supplied – the tearooms are only open until around 5pm and the shop has fairly limited supplies. The other alternative is *Larivee Homestead*, SH6 (☎03/443 9177; ③–⑤), a lovely house hidden behind the visitor centre, with B&B in the main house and a cheaper cottage, plus dinners for $25.

travel details

The only passenger **train** services to the West Coast are from Christchurch over Arthur's Pass to Greymouth. All other public transport is **buses**. The majors (InterCity and Mount Cook Landline) run a joint service between Nelson and Queenstown along the coast once a day in each direction, with an overnight stop in the glacier villages en route. Smaller **minibus** operators run **feeder services** to the main West Coast towns, running one or two services a day in each direction and sometimes give a small fare saving over the majors; visitor centres have the latest details.

Trains

From Greymouth to: Christchurch (1 daily; 4hr).

Buses

From Fox Glacier to: Franz Josef (2 daily; 45min); Makarora (1 daily; 4hr 15min); Wanaka (1 daily; 5hr 15min).

From Franz Josef Glacier to: Fox Glacier (2 daily; 45min); Haast (1 daily; 3hr 15min); Hokitika (1 daily; 2hr 30min); Makarora (1 daily; 5hr); Queenstown (1 daily; 8hr); Wanaka (1 daily; 6hr).

From Greymouth to: Arthur's Pass (1 daily; 1hr 30min); Blenheim (2–3 weekly; 4hr 45min); Christchurch (2 daily; 4hr 15min); Fox Glacier (1 daily; 4hr 30min); Franz Josef (1 daily; 3hr 40min); Hokitika (2 daily; 30–40min); Murchison (2–3 daily; 3hr–3hr 30min); Punakaiki (2 daily; 40min); Reefton (2–3 weekly; 1hr); St Arnaud (2–3 weekly; 3hr 45min); Westport (2 daily; 1hr 40min–2hr).

From Hokitika to: Arthur's Pass (1 daily; 1hr 45min); Christchurch (1 daily; 4hr 30min); Franz Josef (1 daily; 2hr 30min); Greymouth (2 daily; 30min); Ross (1 daily; 25min); Whataroa (1 daily; 1hr 30min).

From Westport to: Christchurch (2 daily; 4hr 30min–6hr); Greymouth (2 daily; 1hr 40min–2hr); Karamea (1 daily; 1hr 30min); Murchison (2 daily; 1hr 15min–1hr 30min); Nelson (2 daily; 3hr 40min–4hr); Punakaiki (2 daily; 1hr); Reefton (2 daily; 1hr–1hr 15min).

Flights

From Hokitika to: Christchurch (2–3 daily; 35min).

From Westport to: Wellington (1 daily; 50min).

CHAPTER THIRTEEN

QUEENSTOWN, WANAKA AND THE GOLD COUNTRY

Wedged between the sodden beech forests of Fiordland, the fertile plains of south Canterbury, the city of Dunedin and the sheep country of Southland lies Central Otago, a region encompassing **Queenstown**, **Wanaka** and the surrounding **gold country**. Rolling, deserted hills to the east give way to the sharper profiles of the mountains around Queenstown and Wanaka, which rub shoulders with the final glaciated flourish of the Southern Alps. Meltwater and heavy rains course out of the mountains into the 70km lightning bolt of **Lake Wakatipu**, which in turn drains through the Kawarau River, carving a rapid-strewn path through the Kawarau Gorge. Along the way it picks up the waters of the Shotover River from the gold fields of Skippers and Arrowtown. To the north the pristine, glassy lakes of Wanaka and Hawea feed the **Clutha River**, which joins forces with the Kawarau at Cromwell and high-tails it to the coast through the heartland of the Otago gold country.

Queenstown is undoubtedly the region's jewel, with a legendary setting, looking across Lake Wakatipu to the craggy heights of the Remarkables range. New Zealand's self-professed adventure capital, it offers the chance to indulge in just about every adrenalin-fuelled activity imaginable: numerous competing operators have honed bungy jumping, jetboating, rafting and paragliding into well-packaged, forcefully marketed products – although they're no less exciting for all that.

No matter how abiding the appeal of Queenstown, you'll soon be looking for a break. The great outdoors presents the perfect antidote to the town, and some of the country's most exalted multi-day tramps start from the nearby town of **Glenorchy** at the head of Lake Wakatipu. Well organized track transport will drop you at the trailheads of the magnificent **Routeburn Track**, the match of any in the country; the less challenging **Caples** and **Greenstone** tracks, which can be combined with the Routeburn to make a satisfying five-day circuit; and the rugged **Rees–Dart Track**, which opens up the arduous Cascade Saddle Route towards Mount Aspiring.

The glacially scoured, three-sided pinnacle of "the Matterhorn of the South" forms the centrepiece of the **Mount Aspiring National Park**. This permanently snow-capped alpine high country is linked by the Matukituki valley to the peaceful resort of **Wanaka**, slung around the placid waters of its eponymous lake. Wanaka's laid-back atmosphere stands in marked contrast to the frenetic bustle of Queenstown, though there's no shortage of operators keen to take you canyoning, stunt flying, rock climbing or on any number of other pursuits.

Queenstown and Wanaka lie on the fringe of the **Otago Goldfields**, which stretch east towards the coast at Dunedin. Most of the gold has long since gone and the area is largely deserted, but there are numerous interesting reminders of New Zealand's gold-rush days, including old workings set amidst rugged scenery. **Arrowtown** – a popular day-trip destination from Queenstown – remains the best preserved of them all,

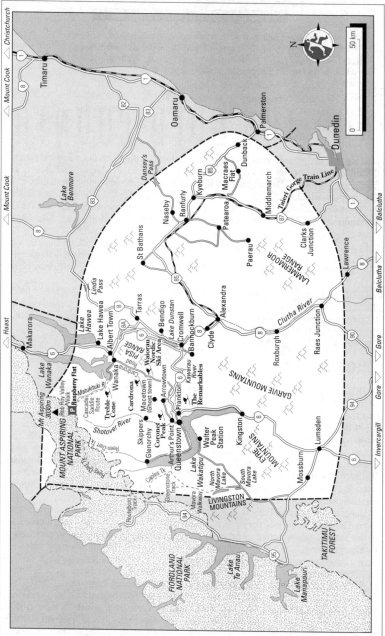

ACCOMMODATION PRICES

Accommodation listed in this guide has been categorized into one of nine price bands, as set out below. The rates quoted represent the **cheapest available** double or twin **room** – except for category ①, which are per-person rates for a dorm bed; fees for **tent sites** and **DOC huts** are also per-person, unless otherwise stated.

① under $20 per person	④ $60–80	⑦ $140–180
② under $40 per room	⑤ $80–100	⑧ $180–240
③ $40–60	⑥ $100–140	⑨ over $240

For more on accommodation, see p.33.

---

offering the intriguing remains of a former Chinese settlement and a day-long walk to the defunct gold mines around **Macetown**. To the east the larger, and duller, gold towns of **Cromwell**, **Alexandra** and **Roxburgh** are scattered along the banks of the Clutha River, which once provided Maori with the easiest path to the *pounamu* fields of the West Coast. Gold miners subsequently used the same paths, fanning out to found tiny and now moribund towns such as **Bannockburn**, **St Bathan's** and **Naseby**, the most enjoyable places in which to idle among the mouldering boomtime remains.

From June to October the region's focus switches to **skiing**, with Queenstown acting as a base for the downhill resorts of Coronet Peak and the Remarkables, while Wanaka serves the Cardrona and Treble Cone fields, as well as the **Waiorau** Nordic field.

Getting around the region is easily done on the reasonably frequent buses linking the main towns, supplemented by shuttle buses to trailheads, and minibuses transporting you from your hotel out to the various adventure activities. For more detailed coverage of route frequencies and times, consult "Travel Details" on p.727.

Queenstown

QUEENSTOWN is in many ways the victim of it own popularity. Kiwis and visitors seduced by New Zealand's tranquil rural beauty can often be overheard complaining that the country's main centre for adventure sports is getting overcrowded and too big for its boots. Don't believe a word of it. There is no doubt that it is one of New Zealand's most popular and commercialized year-round resorts, but it remains an idyllic spot, attractively set beside the deep blue Lake Wakatipu and hemmed in by craggy mountains. Furthermore, it offers the best selection of restaurants outside Auckland, Wellington and Christchurch, and some of the finest accommodation in the country. Even the string of new hotels blighting the foreshore can't ruin its appeal, although they certainly jeopardize its small-town intimacy.

Queenstown is nevertheless best taken in small doses, either as a base from which to plan lengthy forays into the surrounding countryside, or as a venue for sampling one of the many outdoor activities on offer. The most prominent of these is undoubtedly **bungy jumping**. The town's environs now boast four of the world's most gloriously scenic bungy sites, visited either in isolation or as part of a multi-thrill package, perhaps including **whitewater rafting** and **jetboating** on the Shotover River, or a helicopter flight into the dilapidated former gold workings of **Skippers Canyon**.

Visitors after a more sedate time are equally spoilt for choice, with lake cruises on the elegant TSS *Earnslaw*, the last of the lake steamers; the **gondola ride** to Bob's Peak, which commands magnificent vistas over Queenstown and The Remarkables range; and a **wine tour** around some of the world's most southerly wineries. Formal lakeshore gardens and hillside viewpoints provide the focus for easy local **walks**, with the heartier multi-day tramps all starting at Glenorchy (p.689) at the head of the lake.

Even the frantic summers are nothing in comparison to winter, when Kiwi and international skiers descend on **Coronet Peak** and **The Remarkables**, two fine skifields within half an hour of Queenstown which are at their peak during the annual **Queenstown Winter Carnival** towards the end of June.

Arrival, information and city transport

Buses all arrive in the centre of Queenstown, from where it's less than fifteen minutes' walk to most hotels and hostels; better still, most of the smaller bus companies will drop you off outside your chosen accommodation. Mount Cook Landline and the West Coast InterCity buses pull in to the Mount Cook Coach Terminal on Church Street, while all other InterCity buses arrive at The Top of the Mall, the intersection of the Mall and Camp Street. Kiwi Discovery stop outside their office at 37 Camp St, but also do pickups and drop-offs around Queenstown – as do Atomic Shuttle, Southern Link Shuttles, Southern Explore, Magic Bus and Kiwi Experience.

Queenstown's **airport** is just outside Frankton, 7km northeast of central Queenstown; the Shopper Bus runs at least hourly (15min; $2.50), and the Super Shuttle ($5) meets most flights. **Taxis** (☎03/442 6666 or 442 7788) charge around $15 for the ride into town.

Information

Queenstown's main downtown area is concentrated around Rees Street, Shotover Street, Camp Street and the pedestrianized Mall, which runs from the Main Town Wharf eastwards to Ballarat Street. The main **visitor centre**, on the corner of Camp Street and Shotover Street (daily: Nov–April 7am–7pm; May–Oct 7am–6pm; ☎03/442 4100, fax 442 8907), is the place to go for all manner of impartial advice, something not offered by the handful of booking agents which masquerade as information centres in order to push their own tours and products (see box on p.679).

The best unbiased information on walks in the area comes from the **DOC office** at 37 Shotover St (Dec–April daily 8am–7pm; May–Nov Mon–Sat 8am–5pm; ☎03/442 7933, fax 442 7932), which is stacked with leaflets on DOC activities, operates a **Great Walks Booking Desk** (July–April daily 9am–4.30pm) for aspiring Routeburn, Kepler and Milford track walkers, and runs a Summer Visitors' Programme of full- or half-day walks (generally for a couple of weeks in Dec & Jan).

City transport

Pretty much everywhere you are likely to want to go in central Queenstown can be reached **on foot**. Most of the activities – bungy jumping, whitewater rafting, mountain biking and the like – take place out of town, although all operators run courtesy buses from the centre of town to the site, usually picking up from accommodation en route. There's a **taxi rank** on Camp Street at the top of the Mall, or call ☎03/442 6666 or 442 7788. On the lake, Queenstown Water Taxis, Lake Esplanade (☎03/442 8665), run twelve-seater speedboats at $150 an hour.

Circuit Shuttles, at the top of the Mall (daily departures every 1hr 15min 9am–3.15pm; ☎025/449314), make a circuit of the Shotover Jet, Millbrook Resort, Arrowtown, the Kawarau bungy and Gibbston Winery, charging $25 for the day with as many stops as you wish.

More personalized transport comes in the form of **rental cars** and **bikes**, which are available from several outlets around town (see "Listings", p.686). It pays to shop around – especially for one-day or overnight rentals to Milford Sound, which can work

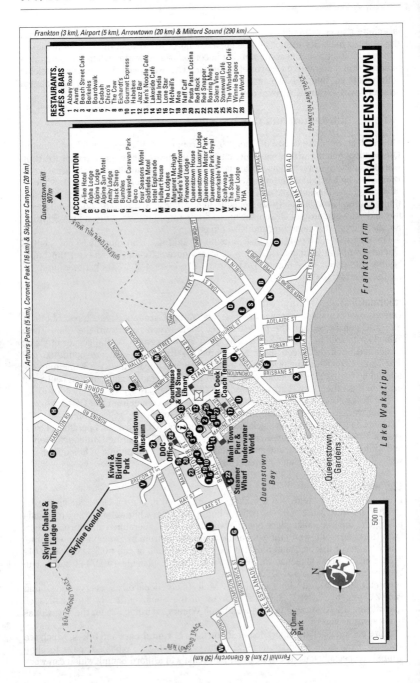

CENTRAL QUEENSTOWN

Frankton (3 km), Airport (5 km), Arrowtown (20 km) & Milford Sound (290 km)

Arthurs Point (5 km), Coronet Peak (16 km) & Skippers Canyon (20 km)

QUEENSTOWN HILL WALK

Queenstown Hill 907m

RESTAURANTS, CAFÉS & BARS

1 Abbey Road
2 Avanti
3 Beach Street Café
4 Berkeles
5 Boardwalk
6 Casbah
7 Chico's
8 The Cow
9 Eichardt's
10 Gourmet Express
11 Habebes
12 Jazz Bar
13 Ken's Noodle Café
14 Lakeside Café
15 Little India
16 Lone Star
17 McNeill's
18 Moa
19 Naff Caff
20 Pasta Pasta Cucina
21 Red Rock
22 Red Snapper
23 Roaring Meg's
24 Solera Vino
25 Stonewall Café
26 The Wholefood Café
27 Winnie Bagoes
28 The World

ACCOMMODATION

A A-line Hotel
B Alpha Lodge
C Alpine Lodge
D Alpine Sun Motel
E Amity Lodge
F Black Sheep
G Bumbles
H Creekside Caravan Park
I Deco
J Four Seasons Motel
K Goldfields Motel
L Hotel Esplanade
M Hulbert House
N The Lodges
O Margaret McHugh
P McFee's Waterfront
Q Pinewood Lodge
R Queenstown House
S Queenstown Luxury Lodge
T Queenstown Motor Park
U Queenstown Park Royal
V Remarkable View
W Scallywags
X The Stable
Y Turner Lodge
Z YHA

Frankton Arm

PANORAMA TERRACE

FRANKTON ARM TRACK

FRANKTON ROAD

Lake Wakatipu

ADELAIDE ST
HOBART
BRISBANE ST
PARK ST

THE TERRACE

Queenstown Gardens

MELBOURNE ST
STANLEY ST
Mt Cook Coach Terminal
Courthouse & Old Stone Library
Queenstown Museum
DOC Office

Kiwi & Birdlife Park

Skyline Chalet & The Ledge bungy

Skyline Gondola

BEN LOMOND TRACK

GORGE RD
ROBINS RD
HAMILTON RD
BRECON ST
ISLE ST

Main Town Pier & Underwater World

Steamer Wharf

Queenstown Bay

St Omer Park

LAKE ESPLANADE
BRUNSWICK ST
THOMPSON ST
LOMOND CR

Fernhill (2 km) & Glenorchy (50 km)

N

500 m

0

out to be real bargains, with companies sometimes offering a group of four a car plus petrol and a Milford cruise for under $60 per person.

Drivers will have no problem negotiating Queenstown's relatively quiet streets, but may fall foul of stringent parking restrictions. Parking meters in the central streets (checked daily until 9pm) cover several spaces and it is easy to inadvertently pay for someone else's vehicle; there's usually some free parking to be found within a couple of hundred metres in any case.

Accommodation

Queenstown has the widest selection of **places to stay** in this corner of New Zealand, but such is the demand in the middle of summer and at the height of the ski season that rooms can be hard to come by and prices are correspondingly high.

With a few exceptions, all the accommodation is packed into a compact area less than fifteen minutes' walk from the centre of town. Good deals are sometimes offered by the big **hotels** in what passes for Queenstown's off season (essentially April, May & Nov) but in general you'll do better in smaller places, particularly the **B&Bs and home-stays**, of which there are some fine examples. Families, groups and keen self-caterers might consider **motels**, which match the Kiwi standard but tend to charge a little more than in less popular resorts. The best budget deals are to be found at the many **hostels** and backpackers, which compete fiercely for trade. They generally offer a similar range of services – free activity booking, free luggage storage and the like – for much the same rates. The Queenstown district also has abundant **campsites** with attendant cabins, though only a couple of these are within walking distance of town.

If a less frantic atmosphere – and lower prices – appeal, it's also worth considering **Arrowtown** as a base for exploring the Queenstown area – see p.714 for reviews of places to stay in the vicinity.

Hotels

A-Line Hotel, 27 Stanley St (☎03/442 7700, fax 442 7755). A cluster of nicely furnished rooms in A-frames with good lake views. This place is firmly on the tour bus circuit, but some discreet haggling when business is slow can bring rates down considerably. ⑧.

Aspen on Queenstown, 155 Fernhill Rd (☎03/442 7688 & 0800/427 688, fax 442 8906). A sprawling hotel with a small indoor pool and great lake views. The abundantly equipped rooms and apartments are overpriced in high season but can be an off-peak bargain – especially the very comfortable two-bedroom apartments, whose rates drop by as much as a third. The hotel is 2km from the centre of Queenstown, so phone ahead to check discounted prices. ⑦.

Hotel Esplanade, 32 Peninsula St (☎03/442 8611, fax 442 9635). Dowdy but good value en-suite rooms in a traditional Kiwi hotel with an indoor pool, sauna and views over Frankton Arm. ③.

Queenstown Luxury Lodge, cnr Frankton Rd & Melbourne St (☎03/442 5999 & 0800/654 999, fax 442 5998). Tasteful, luxuriously appointed apartments close to the centre of Queenstown, each equipped with a full kitchen, TV, CD and cassette player, spa baths and with free access to two saunas and a full gym. ⑦.

Motels

Alpha Lodge, 42 Frankton Rd (☎03/442 6095, fax 442 8010). Good value, low-cost motel close to town with all basic amenities and a range of budget and studio units. ④.

Alpine Sun Motel, 14 Hallenstein St (☎03/442 8482, fax 442 6432). Good-value basic motel units with TV, kitchenettes, spa and off-road parking. ④.

Alpine Village Motor Inn, 325 Frankton Rd (☎03/442 7795, fax 442 7738). Large place midway to Frankton (the Shopper Bus passes by) and frequented by tour groups. Most rooms and chalets come with views of the Remarkables, and all have the run of two restaurants, a tennis court and the jacuzzi. ⑥.

Amity Lodge, 7 Melbourne St (☎03/442 7288, fax 442 9433). Pricey but well maintained one-bedroom units, all fully self-contained and with microwaves. ⑥.

Four Seasons Motel, 12 Stanley St (☎03/442 8953, fax 442 7233). Reasonable downtown motel with off-street parking, good kitchens, mountain views, an outdoor swimming pool and a spa. ④.

Goldfields Motel, 41 Frankton Rd (☎03/442 7211, fax 442 6179). A range of decent chalets all equipped with TV and fridge. ⑤, without kitchen ④.

The Lodges, 8 Lake Esplanade (☎03/442 7552, fax 442 6493). Top-quality lakeside three-bedroom apartments with full kitchens, laundry and parking. Good value for groups of four or more. ⑦.

B&Bs and homestays

Bush Creek Health Retreat, 20 Bowen St (☎03/442 7260). This wonderfully secluded house 1km from central Queenstown is surrounded by beautiful organic gardens tended by Ileen Mutch, a renowned iridologist and holistic healer. A relaxing and rejuvenating place to stay. ⑤.

Highview, 17 Wakatipu Heights (☎03/442 9414). Something between a homestay and a motel, *Highview* enjoys stunning lake views, and is just a $5 cab ride from town (20min walk). En-suite rooms are separate from the main house, but you are welcome to join the friendly hosts, who also deliver breakfast each morning. ⑤.

Hulbert House, 68 Ballarat St (☎03/442 8767). In a rambling century-old Victorian villa built on the hill behind Queenstown Bay, this opulent but tasteful B&B has a large library, idyllic gardens and great breakfasts. ⑦.

Margaret McHugh, 9 Panorama Terrace (☎03/442 8512, fax 442 6080). One of Queenstown's better homestays, five minutes' walk from town with lake views from the lounge,. The entertaining and helpful host is a whiz with dinners ($25). Just a couple of comfortable rooms, one with a water bed. ⑤.

Queenstown House, 69 Hallenstein St (☎03/442 9043, fax 442 8755). Professionally run B&B with nicely decorated and well-equipped rooms, plus a welcome beer or wine on arrival. ⑦.

Remarkable View, 22 Brecon St (☎03/442 9542). Friendly, traditional homestay with simple rooms. Guests share the family facilities, and are offered continental or cooked breakfast. ④.

Scallywags, 27a Lomond Crescent (☎03/442 7083, fax 442 5885). Pitched somewhere between an off-beat homestay and an upmarket backpackers' hostel, this suburban house is a stiff ten-minute walk up from town. It has great views and a very laid-back muck-in atmosphere, with use of a kitchen and free tea and coffee. Dorms ①, rooms ③, including towels & bedding. ④.

The Stable, 17 Brisbane St (☎03/442 9251, fax 442 8293). Cosy and popular homestay stacked with books and housed in a former stable. Cooked or continental breakfasts are served, as are dinners ($30) if ordered in advance. ⑥.

Turner Lodge, 2 Turner St (☎03/442 9432, fax Mon–Fri only 442 6816). Central, relaxed and modern place that operates as a comfortable homestay serving a cooked breakfast, and has three additional rooms which are let on a self-catering basis, sharing kitchen facilities, a lounge and a sun deck. Room only ④, B&B ⑤.

Hostels

Alpine Lodge, 13 Gorge Rd (☎03/442 7220, fax 442 7038). Small, welcoming and central hostel which can be a little cramped when full. Ask about the self-contained unit that's sometimes let separately to groups. Dorms ①, rooms ②.

Black Sheep, 13 Frankton Rd (☎03/442 7289, fax 442 7361). Converted motel that's spacious enough to cope with the backpacker tour-bus crowd who frequently pack out the four- to ten-bed dorms. Everything is very well organized with barbecues nightly, a spa pool, mountain bikes ($25 a day) and sea kayaks ($30 a day) for rent and booking facilities for just about everything; there's a $1 charge per night for storing luggage. ①.

Bumbles, 2 Brunswick St, cnr Lake Esplanade (☎03/442 6298). Good, rambling hostel down by the lake with heaps of parking space, a central lounge and barbecue area, and plentiful cooking and washing facilities. Dorms ①, rooms ②.

Deco Backpackers, 52 Main St (☎03/442 7384, fax 442 7403). This hostel in an Art Deco-style house is an uphill trudge from town. Office closed 2–4pm and after 8pm. Dorms ①, rooms ②.

McFee's Waterfront Hotel, 48a Shotover St (☎03/442 7400, fax 442 7403). Large hostel with good communal areas overlooking the lake; accommodation is in four-bed dorms, budget doubles with TV, and flashier en-suite rooms. Dorms ①, budget rooms ③, en-suites ④.

Pinewood Lodge, 48 Hamilton Rd (☎03/442 8273, fax 442 9470). Located on the edge of Queenstown ten minutes' walk from the centre, each cluster of these ageing but comfortable rooms is surrounded by lawns and has its own lounge, cooking area and bathroom. There's also a spa bath ($10 per half-hour), bike rental ($25 per day) and bargain four-wheel-drive vehicle rental ($60 a day). Dorms ①, rooms ②.

Round the Bend, Meilejohn Bay, 28km along the Glenorchy road (☎03/442 6196). A kind of home-stay and backpackers close to the lake and with good walking and fishing nearby. Almost everything is made from logs cut by the Swiss owner and part-time forester, Thomas. Accommodation ranges from bargain backpacker bunks and standard rooms to a charming en-suite chalet. Dorms ①, rooms ②, chalet ③.

Scallywags; see "B&Bs and homestays" on p.672.

YHA, 80 Lake Esplanade (☎03/442 8413, fax 442 6561). Always bustling, particularly in the ski sea-son, this is one of New Zealand's flagship YHAs, ten minutes' walk along the waterfront from town. Accommodation is in spacious, mostly six-bed dorms – which have better views than the double rooms. Good-value meals ($8) are served nightly. Dorms ①, rooms ②.

Campsites and motorparks

Arthur's Point Camping Ground, close to the Shotover Jet site at Arthur's Point (☎03/442 9306). Smallish, quiet and fully equipped site with a small pool. Tent and powered sites $9–9.50, standard cabins. ②.

Closeburn Alpine Park, 8km south of Queenstown on the Glenorchy road (☎03/442 6073). Sylvan, lakeside campsite with tent and powered sites ($12–17 for two people), plus on-site caravans (②).

Creeksyde Campervan Park, 54 Robins Rd (☎03/442 9447, fax 442 6621). This highly organized and spotlessly clean site ten minutes' walk from town is primarily aimed at campervanners who (along with tenters) pay $22 per couple. A central building houses a spa bathroom ($5 per half-hour for two), sauna ($10), ski store, drying rooms and motel rooms. ④.

Kawarau Falls Lodge & Camping, 7km north of Queenstown on SH6, near Frankton airport (☎ & fax 03/442 3510). Very attractive lakeside campsite that's ideal for exploring the region. Excellent facilities extend to spacious tent sites ($9), a backpacker-style lodge and three different grades of cabins, some with their own facilities. In peak season, the Shopper Bus comes to within 500m; with-in 1km out of season. Dorms ①, cabins ②.

Queenstown Motor Park, Man St (☎03/442 7252, fax 442 7253). Enormous site that sprawls over the base of Bob's Peak and seems to swallow just about all of Queenstown's campers. Facilities are extensive and accommodation runs the gamut from grassy tent sites ($9) to self-contained motel units, but it can hardly be considered peaceful. ②–⑤.

Twelve-Mile Creek Reserve, 5km south of Queenstown, off the Glenorchy road (no phone). DOC campsite with facilities limited to basic toilets and water. Tent sites $2.

The Town and around

The best all-round views of the Queenstown region and Lake Wakatipu are undoubtedly those from **Bob's Peak**, which rises up immediately behind the town and can be reached on one of Queenstown's gentler rides. The four-minute **Skyline Gondola**, Brecon Street (daily 9am–midnight; $12 return), deposits you at the Skyline Complex, where a fair proportion of passengers are herded into **Kiwi Magic** (daily 11am–9pm; 30min; $7), a well produced and engagingly corny promotional film that's beginning to show its age, not least because the lead, comedian Billy T. James, died some years ago. Everyone else either peels off to The Ledge bungy (see p.680) or makes straight for the viewing balcony, getting their bearings off The Remarkables and Cecil and Walter peaks beyond Lake Wakatipu. The *Skyline Restaurant* (☎03/442 7860) serves good buf-fet lunches ($25) and dinners ($35), or there's outdoor seating at the reasonably priced *Skyline Café*, from where you can watch paragliders launch themselves from the conifer-clad slopes. If you're overcome by a sudden impulse to join their ranks, you can book an introductory paraglide ($110) at the *Kiwi Magic* reception in the Skyline

Complex. The complex can also be reached on foot in under an hour by following Kent Street up from town.

The base of the gondola is reached along Brecon Street, which passes Queenstown's **cemetery** – the final resting place of Queenstown pioneer Nicholas von Tunzelmann, as well as Henry Homer, discoverer of the Homer Saddle on the Milford Road. Almost opposite, the **Queenstown Museum**, 25 Brecon St (daily 9.30am–5.30pm; $7), contains a run-of-the-mill collection of much-loved cars, motorbikes and a MiG21 fighter. A spare half-hour is better spent close by at the **Kiwi and Birdlife Park**, on Bevan Street (daily: Nov–Feb 9am–7.30pm; March–Oct 9am–5pm; $9), an expanse of ponds, lawns, stands of bush and aviaries that are home to some of New Zealand's rarest birds. The effect is more zoo than wildlife park but does a good job of presenting morepork, kea, kereru (native pigeons), kakariki (native parakeets) and little owls, alongside the products of captive breeding programmes for the North Island brown kiwi, and the black stilt, one of the world's ten most endangered bird species.

Down in the town centre there's very little left of gold-rush Queenstown. At the top of the Mall, Ballarat Street crosses a small stream spanned by an 1882 stone bridge to reach the **Courthouse** and **Old Stone Library**, both built in the mid 1870s and since dwarfed by century-old giant sequoias. At the opposite end of the Mall, the waterfront **Eichardt's Hotel** dates partly from 1871 when the Prussian Albert Eichardt replaced

---

WALKS AROUND QUEENSTOWN

All the hard-sell on adventure activities in Queenstown can become a bit oppressive, and a few hours away from town can be wonderfully therapeutic. The majority of the walks outlined below – listed in ascending order of difficulty – are well covered by DOC's *Queenstown Walks and Trails* leaflet ($1), which also includes a sketch map. Serious multi-day tramps in the region are centred on Wanaka and Glenorchy (see p.698 and p.687, respectively).

One Mile Creek Walkway (1hr 30min return; 6km; 50m ascent). Fairly easy walk through a gully filled with beech forest and following a 1924 pipeline from Queenstown's first hydroelectric scheme. The route starts on the lakefront by the Fernhill roundabout, and offers a good opportunity to acquaint yourself with fuschia, lancewood and native birds – principally fantails, bellbirds and tui.

Queenstown Hill Track (2–3hr return; 5km; 600m ascent). Starting from the top of Edgar Street, this is a fairly steep climb up through mostly exotic trees to panoramic views from the 907m Queenstown Hill.

Frankton Arm Track (1hr–1hr 30min oneway; 7km; flat). This easy path is ideal for an early-morning or sunset stroll. Start from Peninsula Street in Queenstown, follow the lakeside to Frankton, and continue a further 2km round to the Kawarau River outlet.

Ben Lomond Summit Track (6–8hr return; 11km; 1400m ascent). A full-day, there-and-back tramp scaling the 1748m Ben Lomond, one of the highest mountains in the region and consequently subject to inclement weather, especially in winter when the track can be snow-covered. Start by the One Mile Creek Walk or use the Skyline Gondola and walk up past the paragliding launch site to join the track, which climbs through alpine tussock to reveal expansive views. Gentler slopes approach Ben Lomond Saddle, from where it's a steep final haul to the summit.

Ben Lomond–Moonlight Track (8–10hr one-way; 16km; 1400m ascent). A demanding and occasionally difficult-to-follow route which combines the ascent to Ben Lomond Saddle (see above) with a poled sub-alpine route to the site of the former gold town of Sefferstown and the eastern section of the Moonlight Track to Arthur's Point. Organize someone to pick you up at Arthur's Point or be prepared for a 5km slog back to Queenstown.

the Queen's Arms, a bar William Rees created from a woolshed in 1862. Around the corner on Marine Parade, **Williams Cottage** dates from around 1866 and is currently in a rather sorry state, though there are plans to open it as some kind of museum.

Nearby, at the foot of the Mall, lies the Main Town Pier, home base for a number of jetboating and parasailing trips, and the feeble **Queenstown Underwater World** (daily 9am–5pm; $5), where those desperate for distraction can scour the waters for longfin eels, the occasional diving scaup duck, and lake trout lured to the underwater windows by regular feeding. Marine Parade continues east past the cottages to **Queenstown Gardens** (unrestricted entry), an attractive parkland retreat which covers the peninsula separating Queenstown Bay from the rest of Lake Wakatipu. Two English oaks were planted when the land was first designated as a reserve in 1867; they're still going strong, as are sequoias and a stack of other exotics – ornamental cherry, maple, sweet chestnut and the like – lavished around the rose gardens and bowling lawns.

The Shotover River and Skippers Canyon

The churning **Shotover River** is inextricably linked with Queenstown. The majority of the town's adventure-based trips – bungy jumping, rafting, jetboating, mountain biking and more (see "Activities", p.679) – take place on, in or around the river and, if you are prepared to drive the treacherous road, there's also a stack of gold workings to explore.

The Shotover rises in the Richardson Mountains north of Queenstown and picks up speed to surge through its deepest and narrowest section, **Skippers Canyon**, and into the Kawarau River downstream from Lake Wakatipu. Tributaries run off Mount Aurum, beneath which is the mother lode of the Shotover goldfields – first discovered when a couple of pioneer shearers, Thomas Arthur and Harry Redfern, found gold in 1862 at what is now Arthur's Point, on the banks of the Shotover 5km north of Queenstown. Word spread that prospectors were extracting the equivalent of over ten kilos a day, and within months thousands were flocking from throughout New Zealand and Australia to work what was soon dubbed "The Richest River in the World". The river-edge gravels had been all but worked out by 1864, necessitating ever more sophisticated extraction techniques. With the introduction of gravity-fed water chutes, mechanical sieves and floating dredges, the construction of a decent road became crucial. From 1863, Chinese navvies spent over twenty years hacking away with pick and shovel at the Skippers Road; those who stuck out the harsh conditions began building quarters more substantial than the standard-issue canvas tents. Meanwhile, entrepreneurially-minded pioneers began to exploit the boom, building 27 hotels along the 40km of road, and selling fresh fruit and vegetables at extortionate prices to miners as often as not suffering from scurvy. By the turn of the century the river was worked out, though a few stayed on; even today there are a couple of die-hards who make part of their living from gold panning and sluicing.

The narrow and winding **Skippers Road** is best left to experienced drivers. Locals who know the road like the back of their hand tend to hare around, leaving little space for oncoming traffic; besides, rental cars aren't insured for Skippers. Being driven into either the Pipeline or Skippers Canyon Bridge bungy sites or to the Skippers Canyon Jet (see p.680 for more on all of these) gives you a good chance to see the valley. By far the best way, though, is on a **tour** with The Riches of Skippers Canyon (☎03/442 9434; 4hr; $69), who take in most of the highlights, including the Skippers Canyon Jet, and also produce a useful, and widely available, free leaflet and map.

The Skippers Road, which follows the Shotover River only in its upper reaches, branches off Coronet Peak Road 12km north of Queenstown. It is approached along Malaghans Road through **Arthur's Point**, 5km north of Queenstown, marked by the historic *Arthur's Point Hotel*, the only one of the Skippers Road hotels still operating, adjacent to where Thomas Arthur first struck gold. Half a kilometre on, the Edith

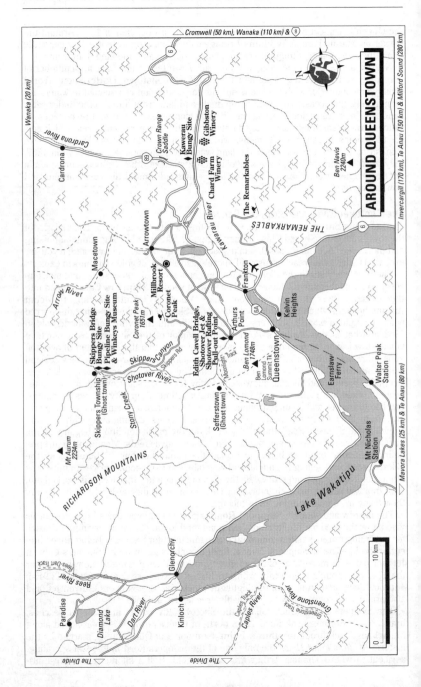

AROUND QUEENSTOWN

△ Cromwell (50 km), Wanaka (110 km) & ⑧

Wanaka (20 km) △

Invercargill (170 km), Te Anau (150 km) & Milford Sound (280 km) ▷

Cardrona River

Cardrona

Crown Range Saddle

Kawerau Bungy Site

Gibbston Winery

Chard Farm Winery

Kawarau River

The Remarkables

Ben Nevis 2240m

Arrowtown

THE REMARKABLES

Macetown

Arrow River

Millbrook Resort

Frankton

Kelvin Heights

Coronet Peak 1651m

Coronet Peak

Skippers Bridge Bungy Site

Pipeline Bungy Site & Winkeys Museum

Skippers Canyon

Skippers Rd

Edith Cavell Bridge, Shotover Jet & Shotover Rafting Pull-out Point

Arthurs Point

Shotover River

Stony Creek

Moonlight Track

Ben Lomond 1748m

Ben Lomond Summit Tk

Queenstown

Earnslaw Ferry

Walter Peak Station

Skippers Township (Ghost town)

Sefferstown (Ghost town)

Mt Aurum 2234m

RICHARDSON MOUNTAINS

Mt Nicholas Station

Lake Wakatipu

Glenorchy

Rees-Dart Track

Rees River

Dart River

Diamond Lake

Paradise

Kinloch

Caples Track

Caples River

Greenstone Track

Greenstone River

Mavora Lakes (25 km) & Te Anau (80 km) ▷

The Divide △

The Divide △

N

10 km

0

Cavell Bridge spans a gorge where the Shotover Jet performs its antics, its upstream progress limited by the Mother-in-Law rapid and the 1911 **Oxenbridge Tunnel**. After three years of drilling, this 200m-long bore – designed to absorb the flow of the Shotover while the gold-bearing riverbed was worked – reaped meagre rewards, returning only 2.5kg of gold.

Skippers Road soon begins to shadow the river, negotiating Pinchers Bluff, where Chinese and European navvies cut the road from a near-vertical cliff face. Upstream, the 1901 **Skippers Bridge**, now used for bungy jumping, was the first high-level one built – and consequently survived the winter floods which had swept away all past efforts. For the first time, the township of Skippers had reliable access, though this did little to prevent the exodus that saw a population of 1500 dwindle to nothing once the gold ran out. The old schoolhouse has been restored and there are the ruins of a few more buildings scattered around, but otherwise it is a bleak, haunted place.

The wineries

Grapes have been grown commercially in the **Central Otago** district – essentially Wanaka, Queenstown and Alexandra – only since the 1980s, but local winemakers have already garnered a shelf-full of awards. Widely billed as "the world's most southerly wine-growing region", the vineyards lie close to the 45th Parallel – in country which detractors pooh-poohed as too cold and generally unsuitable for wine production, despite the fact that the Rhône Valley lies on a similar latitude. A continental climate of hot dry summers and long cold winters prevails, which tends to result in low yields and high production costs, and wines from these small boutique wineries are relatively expensive.

The steep schist and gravel slopes on the southern banks of the **Kawarau River** were first recognized as potential vineyard sites as early as 1864, when French miner Jean Désiré Feraud, by now bored of his gold claim at Frenchman's Point near Clyde, planted grapes from cuttings brought over from Australia. His wines won awards at shows in Australia (though standards were none too exacting at the time), but by the early 1880s he'd decamped to Dunedin. No more grapes were grown commercially until 1976, when the Rippon vineyard was planted outside Wanaka (see p.703). It was another five years before the Kawarau Gorge, with its long summer days of intense light followed by cool nights, was recognized as ideally suited to the cultivation of Pinot Gris, Sauvignon Blanc, Chardonnay and particularly Pinot Noir grapes. As an added bonus, the dry conditions inhibit growth of fungus and mildew, so the dreaded phylloxera has been kept at bay and, to keep it that way, strict protocols exist about bringing vines into the district. No such strictures apply to the import of grapes, however, and in poor years, fruit is brought in from other areas – leading some critics to question Central Otago's credibility as a distinct wine-growing region.

Only two local vineyards are currently open for tasting, both on the southern slopes above the Kawarau Gorge, around 20km northeast of Queenstown. The closest is **Chard Farm Winery** (daily 11am–5pm), reached down a long and precipitous dirt road off SH6 opposite the Kawarau bungy bridge. They don't conduct tours but do offer free tasting of current vintages, most notably the Chardonnay and Pinot Noir, though the Sauvignon blanc and Gewurztraminer can be good too. **Gibbston Valley Winery** lies 5km further northeast towards Cromwell and is better geared to visitors, with a **Wine Cave Tour** (hourly 10am–4pm; 30min; $8.50, refundable with a minimum six-bottle purchase) which explores cellars burrowed into the hillside. This is not especially impressive, but the tour includes an informed and generous tasting session – highlights are the Chardonnay and Pinot Noir, but don't miss the Pinot Gris. All these wines are also sold in the highly regarded vineyard restaurant, which is open for lunches and snacks throughout the day. Both vineyards are included on the **Queenstown Wine Trail**, which picks up from accommodation around town, starting from the Information and Track Centre, 37 Shotover St (daily 12.30pm; 4hr; $48; ☎03/442 7640); the tour stops at Gibbston for lunch, and drops by the Millbrook Resort, near Arrowtown, for a blind tasting.

Cruising on Lake Wakatipu

The coal-fired twin-screw steamship **TSS Earnslaw**, the last of the lake steamers, is one of Queenstown's most enduring images. Wherever you are, the encircling mountains echo the haunting sound of the steam whistle, as this beautifully restored relic glides gracefully out from Steamer Wharf. Before the lakeside roads were built, almost all commerce in and out of Queenstown was conducted by boat, with a fleet of four steamers serving the large sheep stations at the top of the lake and the southern railhead at Kingston.

Originally prefabricated in sections in Dunedin, the *Earnslaw* was transported on the now defunct railway to Kingston, where its steel hull was riveted together. Launched in 1912, the 51-metre-long craft was the largest steamer to ply the lake – and surely one of the most stately. Burnished brass and polished wood crown its gleaming white hull, and its vertical prow cuts a dash through the lake, reaching a top speed of thirteen knots. The *Earnslaw* usually runs five or six trips throughout the day. The **Walter Peak Farm Tour** (Oct–March daily 9am & 2pm; 3hr; $43) combines two forty-minute lake crossings with a visit to the Walter Peak homestead, a tourist enclave carved out of Walter Peak Sheep Station, nestling in the southwestern crook of Lake Wakatipu. The house itself, a convincing replica of an original building which burnt down in 1977, is beautifully sited among lawns that sweep down to the lakeshore, creating an elegant setting for tea and scones after the farm tour – an entertaining if sanitized vignette of farm life, with demonstrations of dog handling and shearing. The **Midday Cruise** (daily 12.30pm; 1hr; $21) chugs around Queenstown Bay and Frankton Arm, while the **Evening Cruises** (daily: Oct–March 5.30pm, 7.30pm & 9.30pm; Sept, April & May 5.30pm & 7.30pm; July & Aug 5.30pm; 1hr 45min; $26) make wider lake circuits. The most enjoyable of these evening cruises is the **Walter Peak Evening Dining** cruise (daily: Oct–March 5.30pm & 7.30pm; April–Sept 5.30pm; $65), which involves a Kiwi buffet in the Walter Peak homestead's dining rooms. Tickets for all these are available at the Steamer Wharf: up to eight hundred people can cram the decks of the *Earnslaw*, though there are usually far fewer, giving passengers the freedom to peer down at the gleaming steam engine or cluster around the piano at the back of the boat for a surprisingly popular music-hall sing-song. In June each year the *Earnslaw* is overhauled and replaced by a launch.

There are other ways to get a ride on the *Earnslaw*: if you have your own bicycle, take a one-way trip to Walter Peak (departure times as above; $25, plus $5 for a bike), where you'll have the freedom of the remote and unsealed 80km road up the Von River to SH94 at Burwood, 27km east of Te Anau. Alternatively, you could tag along for an hour's **horse trekking** at Walter Peak (daily: Nov–March 9am & 2pm; mid-Aug to Oct, April & May 2pm; $92), or join the **Milford Backroad Adventure** (see p.746). If you don't mind trading a water taxi ride for the *Earnslaw*, the back way to Te Anau can be covered on the Southern Explorer's **Wednesday Back Road Special** (Nov–April; $45; ☎03/249 7820).

An equally fine way to see the lake is under sail on the *City of Dunedin* (bookings on ☎03/442 7390), a modern schooner based at Steamer Wharf. Passengers are encouraged to assist in sailing the vessel during its three daytime sailings (Oct–April daily 10.30am, 12.30pm & 3pm; 2hr; $45) and the dinner-inclusive Captain's Table (6.30pm; 2hr 30min; $66) – though the last doesn't run if there is enough interest in the excellent **Overnight Cruise** ($50). Leaving at around 5pm for the two- to three-hour sail to the mooring in Bob's Cove, 20km to the north, there's time for a short bushwalk, dinner and a campfire, before bedding down on board (take a sleeping bag); an early start gets you back to Queenstown by 9am the next morning.

Activities

Queenstown has a vast array of operators running every conceivable type of **adventure** trip. Almost all hotels and hostels in Queenstown will make reservations for you, but the best deals can often be obtained by shopping around the town's booking agents (see box below). Whatever you want to do you'll be picked up in Queenstown, often from your hotel. **Photos** of your jump, jetboat ride or rafting trip are pretty much de rigueur, so you'll frequently encounter photographers demanding a cheesy grin; the results are available for purchase within a couple of hours.

To get the most action for the least money, check out one of the numerous **combination deals** knitting together two, three or four of the main activities – rafting, bungy jumping, jet-boating and helicopter rides – and tending to focus on either the Shotover or the Kawarau. Basic triple combinations include the **Shotover Triple Challenge** (4hr 30min; $189), which takes in the Shotover Jet, a helicopter ride into Skippers Canyon and rafting down the Shotover, and **Three of the Best** (4hr; $220), combining the Shotover Jet, Kawarau Bungy, and rafting down the Kawarau. Quad combos all sound pretty much like the **Awesome Foursome** (6hr; $289): a four-wheel-drive trip into one of the Skippers Canyon bungy sites, the jump itself, followed by a spin on the Jet, a short helicopter ride and rafting the Shotover.

BOOKING AGENTS

Many of Queenstown's adventure and tour companies essentially run their companies by mobile phone and don't operate an office as such, though most are directly associated with one of the following **information** and **booking centres**, pretty much all of which will also book accommodation and transport. **Shop around** to get the best deals. Almost all cluster around the junction of Camp and Shotover streets and **open daily**, usually to around 9pm in summer, 8pm in winter. The following list gives a rundown of the main places but is by no means exhaustive.

The Backpacking Specialists, 18 Shotover St (☎03/442 8178). Master agents for Gravity Action mountain biking, Magic Bus, Westcoast Express.

Fiordland Travel, Steamer Wharf (☎03/442 7500 & 0800/656 503). Tickets and information for all Fiordland Travel trips and activities around Queenstown and Fiordland.

Information & Track Centre, 37 Shotover St (☎03/442 7038). Backpacker-oriented booking office and the main stopping point for Kiwi Experience. Master agents for Action Flight, Rosco's Milford Sound Kayaks and Queenstown Wine Trail.

Pipeline Bungy, Pipeline Iglu, 27 Shotover St (☎03/442 5455). Pick-up point and booking office for the Pipeline bungy and main agent for Flying Cow parapente.

Queenstown Travel & Information Centre, cnr Camp St & Shotover St (☎03/442 7319). The main visitor centre, with all the usual travel and accommodation booking facilities plus a bureau de change.

Queenstown Rafting, 35 Shotover St (☎03/442 9792 & 0800/100 792). Home turf for Queenstown Rafting and main agents for Wilderness Jet, Moonlight Stables, Shotover Jet, MV *Tutoko* and more.

Raging Thunder Information Centre, cnr Camp St & Shotover St (☎03/442 7318). The main office for Raging Thunder's rafting operation.

The Sightseeing Shop, cnr Camp St & The Mall (☎03/442 7640). Master agents for Nomad Safaris and Renegade Parapente.

The Station, cnr Camp St & Shotover St (☎03/442 7100 & 0800/105 550). A.J. Hackett's nerve centre with a big bungy shop, booking desks for The Helicopter Line, the BBQ Bus, Atomic Shuttle and many more, and the main pick-up spot for Hackett bungy and the Shotover Jet.

Bungy jumping

Even visitors who never had any intention of parting with a large wad of money to dangle on the end of a thick strand of latex rubber find themselves **bungy jumping** in Queenstown. A combination of peer-group pressure, magnificent scenery and hard-sell promotion eventually gets to most people and, let's face it, historic bridges high above remote rivers beats a crane over a supermarket car park any day.

The original, most famous and most frequently jumped of the bungy venues is A.J. Hackett's 43m **Kawarau Suspension Bridge** beside SH6, 23km northeast of Queenstown (daily 9am–dusk; $129; ☎03/442 7100 & 0800/105 550). The price includes a certificate, T-shirt, photo (an extra $10 gets you a short video recording your fifteen seconds of fame), and transport if required. At busy times the whole scene resembles a rather ghoulish production line, as bungy initiates are trundled out, and tour buses disgorge spectators to fill several viewing platforms. For those with more time, an eye for the scenery and an even steadier head for heights, A.J. Hackett also operates the 71m **Skippers Canyon Bridge**, 25km up Skippers Canyon (same hours & booking numbers; $110). For your money, you effectively get a four-wheel-drive tour of the historic Skippers Road, the jump itself, the sought-after T-shirt and the return journey – about three hours in all; videos cost an additional $30, though the footage of your jump is less sophisticated at this low-key venue than at the more hyped sites. Subsequent same-day jumps at either of the Hackett sites go for a bargain $25. In addition, the Hackett operation have recently started the 35m **Ledge** (9am–dusk; $89, including T-shirt and gondola ride), from the top of the Skyline Gondola, where it feels like you are diving out over Queenstown; they've even got all manner of "toys" (surf boards, bikes and the like) to add an extra dimension to your jump. A.J. Hackett plans to resume 300m bungy jumps from a helicopter (minimum of 4 people; $299 each) some time soon.

Otherwise the big, pricey and truly knee-trembling jump is the 102m **Pipeline Bungy** (9am–dusk; $130 jump only, same-day repeat jumps $70, video $49; ☎03/442 5455), spanning the Shotover 3km downstream from the Skippers Canyon Bridge, where the jumping platform is atop a reconstructed 1864 sluice-water pipeline. The setup is similar, with the price including a four-wheel-drive trip in to the jump site.

Jetboating

Second in the adrenalin hierarchy of Queenstown activities is **jetboating**, and almost a dozen operators would love to relieve you of fifty bucks or so for a quick spin. Aside from the excellent and scenic trips on the Dart River (based in Glenorchy, but also offering Queenstown pick-ups – see p.689), only two rivers are negotiated directly from Queenstown: the **Kawarau**, usually reached by a fifteen-minute buzz across the Frankton Arm of Lake Wakatipu; and the **Shotover**, accessed either at Arthur's Point, 5km north of Queenstown, or from the Skippers Canyon Road. Jetboat trips fall into two main categories – those dedicated solely to thrills, spills and close encounters with canyon walls; and those which take a more traditional approach, exploiting the boats' ability to negotiate shallow, braided rivers.

The most celebrated of all the jetboat trips is undoubtedly the **Shotover Jet** (daily 9am–5pm; $65; 30min; ☎03/442 8570), a slick operation and the only company to run thrill-a-second trips down Shotover Canyon downstream from the Edith Cavell Bridge. Battered boats attest to a lifetime of close shaves with rocks and canyon walls. Though more expensive than most other trips, this is undoubtedly the most thrilling, and half an hour of 360-degree turns and periodic dousings is quite enough. Courtesy minibuses run from The Station throughout the day.

The only other company with exclusive use of a section of the Shotover is the **Skippers Canyon Jet** ($69 as part of the Riches of Skippers Canyon tour; 40min; ☎03/442 9434) which runs a couple of trips every day in the upper section of Skippers Canyon. Small, nimble jetboats are used to negotiate the rapids and tight turns, offering occasional glimpses of the canyon's gold-mining heritage, such as the rusting hulk of an abandoned dredge, long-disused bridge supports and twisted metal sheets which once diverted the water around gold-bearing gravels.

The remainder of the trips work the braided sections of the Kawarau and lower Shotover from either Queenstown or Frankton. None is as thrilling as the Shotover Jet, as interesting as the Skippers Canyon Jet, or as scenic as the Dart River trips, and there's little to choose between them.

Whitewater rafting

The majority of jetboat operators stick to fairly flat water, leaving the rough stuff for **whitewater rafting**. The same two rivers – the Kawarau and the Shotover – are commercially rafted from Queenstown. The easier of the two is a 7km section of the large-volume **Kawarau River**, negotiating four Grade III–IV rapids (exciting but not truly frightening; see "Basics", p.53, for details of river grading) and culminating in the potentially nasty Chinese Dog Leg, said to be the longest commercially rafted rapid in New Zealand. Being lake-fed, its flow is relatively steady, though it peaks in spring and drops substantially towards the end of summer.

In contrast, the 14km rafted section of the Grade III–V **Shotover River** flows straight out of the mountains and its level fluctuates considerably, thereby affecting its raftability. In winter the lack of sunlight reaching the depths of the canyon makes it too cold for most people (though some companies do run shorter and more expensive helicopter-access trips), while in late summer the flow can be too insubstantial to safely raft some rapids. If one operator deems the river to be unsafe for rafting, then no trips are run – the upshot of an agreement reached after seven deaths had occurred on the river since 1990. During subsequent investigations, the whole industry was condemned for its appalling standards of **safety** and training. Standards are undoubtedly improving – and, of course, thousands of people do these trips every year without incident – but you should bear in mind that rafting, in common with other adrenalin-charged sports, always entails a degree of risk. The Shotover in particular is a demanding river: revelling in names such as Mother Rapid and Oh Shit, the rapids reach their apotheosis in the Mother-in-Law rapid, often bypassed at low water by diverting through the 170m Oxenbridge Tunnel (see p.677).

Trips on the Kawarau River take around three and a half hours with around an hour on the water; those on the Shotover last an hour longer, with most of the extra time given over to more rafting. All Queenstown's rafting companies operate on both rivers and offer pretty much the same **package**, ferrying punters by bus to an out-of-town base where they kit you out in a wetsuit and provide showers afterwards; the pricier operators also throw in a simple barbecue or a restorative beer. Competition is cutthroat and **prices** vary considerably; expect to pay $65–79 for Kawarau trips and $85–99 to ride the Shotover. Note that rafting is usually limited to those **over 13** years of age. **Booking** tends to be done directly with the main operators: Queenstown Rafting Co. (☎03/442 9792) and Raging Thunder (☎03/442 7318).

Both companies have concessions to run infrequent two- to three-day wilderness trips on the Grade II–III **Landsborough River** (Oct–April only), which runs south off the southwestern flank of Mount Cook to the Haast Highway north of Makarora (see p.663). Given a minimum of six people, Raging Thunder run a two-day trip ($500 with helicopter access, $350 by plane) with all meals included, while Queenstown Rafting Co. offer a similar two-dayer ($490) plus a more leisurely three-day trip ($675).

River surfing and sledging

Through the summer months (roughly mid-Sept to mid-May) the rafted section of the Kawarau River becomes a playground for the parallel sports of whitewater sledging and river surfing. In both cases, small groups are equipped with a board or sledge, a padded wetsuit, a helmet and fins, then led downstream and encouraged to view their independence and freedom of movement as virtues rather than hazards.

River surfing involves floating downstream, grasping a foam boogie board and surfing as many as possible of the rapids' standing waves. While rafters bob around high up on their inflatable perches with little water contact, river surfers get right in the thick of it: what look like ripples to rafters become huge waves and the serious rapids can be thoroughly daunting, as froth engulfs you on all sides. Three- to four-hour trips, with an hour in the water, are run by Serious Fun ($95; ☎03/442 5262), who also offer second-timers a more technically demanding 6km section of the Kawarau ($95 including T-shirt), a four-hour round trip from Queenstown with an hour spent on the river.

Largely the same techniques are used in **whitewater sledging**. Suited primarily to shallow, rocky rivers, this involves grasping the handles of a foam or plastic "sledge" and snuggling arms and upper body down into a streamlined shape. The extra buoyancy gives a better roller-coaster ride over the waves and greater manoeuvrability for catching eddies. Trips are run by Raging Thunder ($95; 1hr on the water; ☎03/442 7318) in conjunction with Wanaka-based Frogz Have More Fun (see p.705), who run fractionally cheaper trips and will pick up from Queenstown on demand.

Paragliding, hang-gliding, skydiving and scenic flights

A fine day with a little breeze is all it needs to fill the skies above Queenstown with people **paragliding**. Jump site of choice is Bob's Peak, immediately above town and reached by the Skyline Gondola. Flying Cow (☎03/442 8638), Maxair (☎03/442 7770, after hours 442 6202), Queenstown Tandem Parapente (☎03/442 7318), Icarus (☎03/442 8178) and Renegade Tandem (☎03/442 7640) all offer the same package – a gondola ride up and one tandem jump, typically lasting ten to fifteen minutes – for $110. How many acrobatic manoeuvres are executed is largely down to you, your jump guide and the conditions. Identically priced tandem paragliding flights off Coronet Peak are run from the Flight Park on Malaghans Road (☎03/442 1586), where you can also learn to solo paraglide. Options range from one-day introductory sessions with a solo flight at the end of the day ($180) to a three-day course ($390) leading to a limited licence, and the fifteen-day full licence course ($1100).

The only company in New Zealand currently doing commercial **tandem hang-gliding** is Skytrek Hanggliding (☎03/442 6311; $135 for 12–15min in the air); flights launch from Coronet Peak and, in winter, from the Remarkables.

Paragliding while being towed behind a boat goes by the name of **parasailing**, an activity offered by Parafly, Main Town Pier (Aug–May daily 10am–5pm; ☎03/442 8507), who run a large motorboat saddled with a small helipad. For $55 each, you (and a buddy if you wish) are winched out on a rope until you reach a height of 80m above the lake surface and, after ten minutes admiring the scenery, winched back in again, theoretically still dry.

Queenstown is an expensive place to go **tandem skydiving** but the scenery does go some way in compensation. Ultimate JumpSkydive Tandem ($245; ☎021/325 961) take twenty minutes to reach an altitude of 2500m, from where you get around 25 seconds' freefall over Lake Wakatipu, landing by the foot of the Remarkables some five minutes later. Another airborne possibility includes a 25-minute spin in a Pitt Special **stunt plane** with Actionflite ($150; ☎025/360 264).

The majority of Queenstown visitors who take scenic **helicopter flights** do so as part of a combination deal alongside rafting or bungy jumping, though there are some trips worth doing in their own right if you have the cash to spare. Southern Lakes Helicopters (☎03/442 3016) operate flights to the top of the Remarkables ($96; 15min), plus the "Skippers Helichase" ($185; 30min), a rollicking half-hour ride from the airport at Frankton into Skippers Canyon and back, with a stop at the Skippers Canyon bungy bridge; The Helicopter Line (☎03/442 3034 & 0800/500 575) do similar trips for a few dollars more.

Horse riding and mountain biking

Superb scenery makes Queenstown a great place to go **horse riding**. Good-value trips are run from Shotover Stables on Malaghans Road, 7km north of town (☎03/442 7486); their treks ($45; 1hr 30min) emphasize local history, exploring gold-mining relics down by the Shotover riverbed and often visiting the old mining tunnel on St Kilda Hill. The Meadow Park Equestrian Centre, 14km further north on Malaghans Road, is more convenient for Arrowtown and Macetown, though a courtesy bus does run from Queenstown (see pp.686 & 727 for details).

If pedals appeal more than stirrups, Gravity Action (mid-Nov to March; book through Backpacking Specialists ☎03/442 8178) run exhilarating **mountain-biking** trips ($50, with over 2hr in the saddle), descending almost 600m down a narrow track which, until a better road was pushed through in 1888, was the only route into Skippers Canyon.

WINTER IN QUEENSTOWN

Two substantial ski fields – **Coronet Peak** and **the Remarkables** – within easy striking distance of numerous quality hotels, good restaurants and plenty of apres ski combine to make Queenstown New Zealand's **premier ski destination**. Both fields have interchangeable lift tickets, giving you the freedom to pick your mountain. The highlight of the season is the week-long **Queenstown Winter Carnival**, usually around the third week in June, which, as well as all the conventional ski events, has dog racing on snow and a great line-up of entertainment. Of the various other events, the Remarkables' family-oriented **Spring Ski Carnival**, in the first week of the September school holidays, is one of the best.

Neither field has **accommodation** on site, but frequent shuttle buses run down to Queenstown, where the supply is plentiful – except during school holidays. See "Listings", p.687, for details of **ski rental**.

CORONET PEAK

Coronet Peak (☎03/442 4620, premium-rated Snowphone ☎0900/99766), 18km north of Queenstown, opened in 1947, making it New Zealand's first real ski destination. The field boasts sophisticated snow-making equipment which extends its season into spring, when cobalt blue skies and stunning scenery earn it an enviable reputation. Its range of **runs** for skiers of all abilities, and over 400 vertical metres of skiing, only add to its popularity – get here early to avoid long waits for the tows. Throughout the season, which typically starts in early June and sometimes makes it into October, **buses** from Queenstown shuttle back and forth along the sealed access road (no toll). **Passes** for daytime skiing (9am–4pm) currently cost $58 a day ($264 for a 5-day anytime pass); from mid-July to mid-September there's also floodlit night skiing (4–10pm) for $30 per session.

THE REMARKABLES

The Remarkables (☎03/442 4615, premium-rated Snowphone ☎0900/99766), 20km east of Queenstown, is one of the newest commercial fields, occupying three mountain basins tucked in behind the wrinkled face of the Remarkables. It is most renowned as learner and intermediate terrain but there are also good runs for advanced skiers, plus some excellent country for off-piste ski touring. Current **day pass** rates are $55 ($264 for a 5-day anytime pass). Though the bottom of the tows is 500m higher than at Coronet Peak, more snow is required to cover the tussock, giving a slightly shorter season (late June to early Oct). At 320m, the total vertical descent from the tows is also less than at Coronet, but you gain an extra 120m by taking the Homeward Run – a long stretch of powder with sparkling scenery – to the access road, where frequent buses shuttle you back up to the chairlift. Cars pay $9 to use the 14km unsealed **access road**, which is also plied by shuttle **buses** from Queenstown.

Eating

You can eat well in Queenstown. Some restaurants try, and usually fail, to be all things to all people, but those that concentrate on one cuisine shine, with **prices** to match. An increasing number of places are making the most of Queenstown's summer climate, spilling out onto the pedestrianized streets or stretching out along the waterfront, where you can sit and watch the *Earnslaw* glide in. **Breakfast** and **snack** places generally close by 6pm, though some serve early **dinners**, while restaurants often double up as bars as the evening wears on.

Grocery prices are up to thirty percent higher here than in the cities and some locals do weekly trips to Alexandra, though most visitors are content to make do with the local **supermarkets** along Shotover Street.

Breakfasts, cafés and snacks

Beach Street Café, 23 Beach St. Easy-going café that's strong on inexpensive breakfasts, serving all-day fry-ups, bottomless coffee and scrumptious muffins. In the evening burgers and nachos shore up a reasonable menu of standard dishes for around $15. Closed Sun.

Gourmet Express, Bay Centre, Shotover St. About the nearest you'll get in New Zealand to a genuine American diner, with pancakes, French toast, burgers and sandwiches at reasonable prices. BYO & licensed.

Habebes, Wakatipu Arcade, Beach St. Hole-in-the-wall vegetarian and Lebanese daytime café serving Queenstown's best felafel, tabouleh and Kiwi variations on Middle Eastern dishes, as well as juicy lamb and chicken kebabs and the thickest of smoothies.

Jazz Bar, 24 Camp St. Excellent dive of a place where you can (just about) eat inside or take away great plates of penne, fettuccine, slices of spanakopita and other filo pies, and a Thai green curry to remember. Real fruit smoothies come as thick as anything and there's (usually) jazz while you wait.

Ken's Noodle Café, 37 Camp St. Small and hectic east Asian joint serving an inexpensive menu of miso soup, tempura and a stack of noodle dishes daily until 9pm.

Lakeside Café, Wakatipu Arcade, Beach St. Lively breakfast and lunch spot with excellent muffins, sandwiches, soups and cakes served in bright folk-art surroundings.

Naff Caff, 1/62 Shotover St. Relaxed daytime café with a good range of muffins and Danishes for breakfast and some of the best coffee in town, notably the *mega mucho* strong cappuccino. At lunch they do pies, quiches and salmon and cream cheese bagels.

Stonewall Café, 17 The Mall. Casual daytime café with fine coffee, quiches, muffins and salads at good prices; give the evening meals a miss.

The Wholefood Café, Plaza Arcade, between Beach St & Shotover St. An "almost vegetarian, almost healthy" place tucked away and serving wholesome salads, pies, quiches, soups, plus less healthy cakes and decent coffee.

Restaurants

Avanti, 20 The Mall. Cheery Italian place whose reasonable food at modest prices ($13–16 for main courses) guarantees popularity, especially on Wednesday fish nights. Gourmet pizzas and bowls of pasta go for $7–10.

Berkeles, 5/19 Shotover St. Spacious but cosy restaurant serving excellent full breakfasts ($8), and gourmet burgers ($10) which are meals in themselves – try the chicken and camembert or the Mexican spicy. Licensed.

Boardwalk, Steamer Wharf (☎03/442 5630). Swanky, expensive restaurant that serves the freshest seafood in town, imaginatively prepared and often with delicate Asian touches. Dress smartly and expect to pay $25 for mains.

The Cow, Cow Lane. Reasonably priced ($16 a head) and popular pizzeria that fails to live up to its exalted reputation. A small range of fairly mainstream dishes are served in a cosy stone house; be prepared to share a table. BYO & licensed.

Gantley's, Malaghans Rd, Arthur's Point (☎03/442 8999). Fancy restaurant serving beautifully cooked modern Kiwi food with French leanings in an 1863 former inn 7km north of Queenstown.

Mains start at $25 and the wine list is extensive. Reservations are essential, and courtesy transport from Queenstown is laid on.

Little India Bistro & Tandoori, 11 Shotover St (☎03/442 5335). Tastefully decorated restaurant drawing influences from all over the sub-continent. Enormous banquets with spiciness adjusted to your taste are available ($20–27 per head), as are takeaways and home delivery. Licensed.

Lone Star Café and Bar, 14 Brecon St. Cajun, Southern and Mexican dishes of immense proportions ($20–25) are served in a rowdy "saloon"; see also "Drinking and nightlife" below.

Moa Bar & Café, 5 The Mall (☎03/442 8372). Queenstown's most fashionable and cosmopolitan restaurant and bar, serving $5 tapas and an extensive blackboard menu of imaginative dishes. Eat early if you want to avoid the inevitable smoke and clamour as the place transforms itself into a lively wine bar (see "Drinking and nightlife" below).

Pasta Pasta Cucina, 6 Brecon St (☎03/442 6762). Simply decorated Italian restaurant serving wonderful crisp pizza from the manuka-fired oven and great pasta dishes such as baby octopus in a sweet chilli sauce or vegetable ravioli with walnut and chives for lunch and dinner. Desserts and coffee are equally superb. Takeaway service too. Licensed.

The Red Snapper, Steamer Wharf. First-rate sushi and sashimi and daily $15 fish specials are served at the bar or at your table, all washed down with sake or something from the excellent list of wines by the glass.

Roaring Meg's, 57 Shotover St (☎03/442 9676). Candlelit dining in an original Skippers gold-miners' cottage reconstructed here in 1922. The lamb comes highly praised and this is one of the few places you'll find baked muttonbird alongside salmon en papillote or filet mignon on the menu. Mains $20–25. Licensed.

Solera Vino, 25 Beach St (☎03/442 6082). This small, informal and classy evening-only restaurant showcases Spanish/western Mediterranean cuisine, served either in the smoke-free restaurant or upstairs in the bar. Main courses ($20) are modest but beautifully done, and you can always supplement your meal with $5 tapas from the blackboard selection. Closed Mon. Licensed.

Winnie Bagoes, 7–9 The Mall. Boisterous bar (see "Drinking and nightlife" below) noted for its excellent gourmet pizzas and pasta.

Drinking and nightlife

Despite its high profile and large number of visitors, Queenstown is still essentially a small town. Touring **bands** are relatively rare, there isn't much in the way of highbrow **culture** and even the **clubs**, though great fun, aren't exactly cutting-edge. That said, there is no shortage of lively places to drink (see below), many doubling as restaurants early in the evening, when there are often a couple of **happy hours** to help get things going. Free newspapers – *Mountain Scene* and the *Mirror* – distributed around town give up-to-date **listings**, including the **movies** shown at the Embassy Theatre, 11 The Mall (☎03/442 9990).

About the only regular entertainment is the **Maori Concert and Feast**, 1 Memorial St (Wed–Sat; $45; reservations essential on ☎03/442 8878), a five-course hangi buffet followed by an hour-long cabaret-style concert that takes a tongue-in-cheek romp through potted Maori mythology, the haka, poi dances and stick games. Yes, it is as corny as it sounds, but if you enter into the spirit of the thing, it can be fun.

Bars and clubs

Abbey Road, 66 Shotover St. Loosely Beatles-themed bar that is one of Queenstown's cheaper drinking haunts and hence very popular with the backpacker tour-bus crowd.

Casbah, 54 Shotover St. Late-night venue that plays crowd-pleasing dance favourites to the post-*Abbey Road* fraternity. Bargain drinks before 11.30pm, plus bungy and paragliding freebies.

Chico's, 15 The Mall (☎03/442 8439). The latest-closing of all Queenstown's late bars, this joint starts to jump when the others close around 2am. Some form of live music most nights.

Eichardt's Tavern, 1 The Mall. (☎03/442 8369). Popular and unpretentious public bar in one of Queenstown's most historic hotels. Frequent blues and rock cover bands.

Lone Star Café and Bar 14 Brecon St (☎03/442 9995). The upstairs *Rattlesnakes* bar is a rowdy spot for an early-evening drink with a happy hour (4–7pm); this is also the main venue for touring Kiwi bands.

McNeill's Brewery Café, 14 Church St. Micro-brewery built into an 1880s stone building and usually selling at least three beers – a lager, a malty bitter and a dark stout-like brew – in the cosy bar or outside. They also serve a good selection of wines by the glass and run a happy hour (5–7pm), featuring their own brews at $2.50 per pint.

Moa Bar & Café, 5 The Mall. This early-evening restaurant subsequently undergoes a transformation into a trendy bar with a grand selection of wines.

Red Rock, 48 Camp St (☎03/442 6850). Popular town bar with hints of a ski-lodge atmosphere and a good range of beers including Red Rock, which is usually discounted during happy hours (5–7pm & 9–11pm). Later on, the downstairs bar becomes a chill-out zone, while upstairs at Club Station DJs plough a deep techno groove.

Winnie Bagoes, 7–9 The Mall. Italian eating joint (see "Restaurants", p.685) with occasional bands, happy hours (4.30–7.30pm & 10–11pm) featuring $2 pints, and pool tables. The scene gets louder and distinctly less restaurant-like as the evening wears on; open until 3am most nights.

The World, 27 Shotover St. The latest and hottest late-night venue, with a dedicated budget clientele here for the happy hours and adventure give-aways.

Listings

Airlines Air New Zealand/Mount Cook Airlines (☎03/442 4600 & 0800/800 737); Air Queenstown (☎03/442 6300 & 0800/838 828); Ansett New Zealand (☎03/442 8146).

Automobile Associaton Travel Centre, 37 Stanley St (daily: Nov–March 8.30am–7pm; April–Oct 8.30am–5.30pm; ☎03/442 5155).

Banks and foreign exchange All major banks are represented with a branch and ATM somewhere around the centre of Queenstown. Best bets for exchange services are Thomas Cook, cnr Camp St & The Mall (daily: Oct–May 8am–8pm; June–Sept 8am–7pm; ☎03/442 8600), and the ANZ Bank, 28–30 The Mall (daily 9am–9pm; ☎03/442 8287), though Travelex, in the main visitor centre (same hours) also have reasonable rates.

Bike rental Outside Sports, cnr The Mall & Camp St (9am–9pm; ☎03/442 8883), rents out serious, suspension-equipped mountain bikes with local track information for $50 a day and $30 a half-day – and also serves as a meeting place for keen off-roaders. More straightforward bikes go for $38 a day, or you can rent one-person **scooters** ($48 a day, $38 a half day), which require no licence and are fine for most purposes, but deemed unsuitable for Skippers Road. Bikes, tandems and scooters are also available from Queenstown Bike Hire, 25 Beach St (☎03/442 6039), at similar prices.

Buses Atomic Shuttles (☎03/442 8178) run to Christchurch and Dunedin; Catch-a-Bus (☎03/442 8178) operate a door-to-door service to Dunedin; InterCity (☎03/442 8238) operate the most extensive services to all major destinations; Kiwi Discovery (☎03/442 7340 & 0800/505 504) run a fast service to Christchurch and minibuses to the major trailheads and Milford Sound; Kiwi Experience (☎03/442 9708) add a special Milford Sound run to their backpacker tour-bus setup; Magic Bus (☎03/442 8178) run through Queenstown en route from the West Coast to Dunedin; Mount Cook Landline (☎03/442 4641 & 0800/800 287) vie with InterCity for the broadest coverage; Southern Explorer (☎03/249 7820) run a sparse circuit around Southland and Central Otago; Southern Link Shuttles (☎03/442 8725 & 0800/502 522) run to Dunedin, Christchurch and Picton; and Super Shuttle (☎03/442 9803) meets planes from Queenstown's airport.

Camping and outdoor equipment At the Small Planet Recycling Co, 3 Athol St (☎03/442 6393; daily 10am–6pm), you can pick up used gear, including snowboards, ski gear, wetsuits, bikes, camping and tramping gear and books – all at good prices and with competitive buy-back deals. If you've got something to get rid of, they'll hawk it for 20 percent commission. See also "Ski rental", p.687.

Car rental Typical summer rates from the major firms start at $90 a day, rising to around $150 for four-wheel-drive vehicles. Smaller companies generally offer better deals, with rates for cars of $45–60 a day for week-long rentals, and around $80 per day for four-wheel-drive vehicles with snow chains included. Budget, cnr Camp St & Shotover St and the airport (☎03/442 9274); NZ Rent a Car, cnr Camp St & Shotover St (☎03/442 7465); Queenstown Car Rental, 18 Shotover St (☎03/442 9220); Reg's Rentals, 25 Beach St (☎03/442 6039); Rent-a-Dent, 48 Shotover St (☎03/442 9922 & 0800/736 822).

Childminding Caring Bears (☎03/442 6540); Fairy Godmothers (☎03/442 8787); or 24hr baby-sitting for all ages with Kids K (☎03/442 6037).

Dentist 24hr coverage on ☎03/442 8580 and ☎03/442 7274.

Laundry Can usually be done where you're staying, but Brilliant Laundry Services (☎03/442 9592) charge $10 for a 5kg bag collected and returned on the same day to most hotels, motels and backpackers. Alpine Coin Operated Laundrette, 10 Shotover St (daily 7.30am–9pm), do a $3 wash.

Library Malaghan Library, 44 Stanley St, Queenstown.

Medical treatment Queenstown Medical Centre, cnr Stanley St & Shotover St (☎03/442 7301, 442 3053 for after-hours doctor), and Lakes District Hospital, 20 Douglas St, Frankton (☎03/4423053).

Pharmacy Wilkinsons Pharmacy, The Mall (☎03/442 7313), is open daily from 8.30am to 10pm.

Police 11 Camp St (☎03/442 7900).

Post office Main post office, cnr Camp St & Ballarat St (Mon–Fri 9am–5pm); poste restante is here, too.

Scenic flights Air Fiordland (☎03/442 3404); Air Wakatipu (☎03/442 4148); Milford Sound Scenic Flights (☎03/442 3065 & 0800/101 767).

Ski rental Outdoor Sports, cnr The Mall & Camp St (☎03/442 8883), rent skis, boots and poles from $30 per day for the basic kit to $45–50 for top-quality "executive" gear; snowboards go for $30 a day, as does telemark equipment. The excellent Brown's, 39 Shotover St (☎03/442 4003) offer similar rates on new gear, deliver to your hotel and also do overnight tuning; while Steep & Cheap Snowboard Shop, 49 Camp St (☎03/442 9870), specialize in snowboard gear for around $40 a day.

Taxis Alpine Taxi (☎03/442 6666 & 0800/730 066); Queenstown Taxis (☎03/442 7788 & 0800/477 888).

Thomas Cook cnr Camp St & The Mall (daily: Oct–May 8am–8pm; June–Sept 8am–7pm; ☎03/442 8600).

Tours and booking agencies In Queenstown, the frenzied tour industry means that pretty much anywhere in the southern half of the South Island is fair game for a flight or a bus trip. Stewart Island and Mount Cook are both possibilities for visitors in a massive hurry, but those with a little more time on their hands will find trips to the Milford Sound area (see p.738) or a mosey around the old gold towns (see p.711) more rewarding. Tour-booking agencies are listed in the box on p.679.

Glenorchy and the major tramps

The tiny town of **GLENORCHY**, at the head of Lake Wakatipu 50km northwest of Queenstown, is quiet and supremely picturesque, making it a perfect retreat for a couple of days. For the majority of visitors, though, this still isn't remote enough, and for them Glenorchy is simply a staging post en route to some of the finest **tramping** New Zealand has to offer – a circuit of the Rees and Dart Rivers, the Routeburn Track and the Greenstone and Caples **tracks**.

Glenorchy and around

The Glenorchy region's fantastic scenery owes a debt to beds of ancient sea-floor sediments laid down some 220–270 million years ago and metamorphosed into the grey-green schists and *pounamu* (greenstone) of the Forbes and Humboldt mountains. The western and northern flanks of the Forbes Mountains were shaped by the Dart Glacier, now a relatively short tongue of ice which, at its peak 18,000 years ago, formed the root of the huge glacial system that gouged out the floor of Lake Wakatipu.

In pre-European times the plain beside the combined delta of the Rees (*Oware*) and Dart (*Oturu*) rivers was known as **Kotapahau**, "the place of revenge killing", a reference perhaps to fights between rival *hapu* over the esteemed *pounamu* littering an area centred on the bed of the Dart River. There's still greenstone up there, but most is protected within the bounds of the Mount Aspiring National Park, including a huge, 25-tonne boulder estimated to be worth some $15 million.

The first **Europeans** to penetrate the area were gold prospectors, government surveyors, and nearby runholders in search of fresh grazing. James McKerrow finished the first reconnaissance survey in 1863, about the same time as a party of five miners led by Patrick Caples made their way up the Dart River. The fledgling community of Glenorchy served these disparate groups, along with teams of sawmillers and workers from a mine extracting sheelite, a mineral used in the manufacture of arms. Despite the lack of road access to Glenorchy, **tourists** began to arrive early this century, cruising across Lake Wakatipu on the TSS *Earnslaw*, before being decanted into charabancs for the 20km jolt north to the Arcadia homestead at **Paradise**. Disappointingly drawing its name from the locally abundant paradise ducks rather than its idyllic qualities, Paradise has nevertheless been deemed stunning enough to emulate the Rockies or the European Alps in numerous movies.

The **road from Queenstown** was eventually pushed through in 1962, opening up a fine lakeside drive that passes **Bob's Cove**, the best place to observe the lake's seiche, an ill-understood phenomenon which causes the lake level to cycle by around 150mm every five minutes. Glenorchy has remained defiantly rural, with only a few tourist-oriented ventures disturbing the bucolic atmosphere but, given that the road was only sealed all the way in 1997, it remains to be seen if the town can withstand the likely increase in tourist-bus traffic.

Arrival and information

Summer-only backpacker **buses** ply the Queenstown–Glenorchy route, charging around $15 for the one-hour run. Most frequent are those run by Backpacker Express (3–5 daily; ☎03/442 9939), though there are competing, and often cheaper, buses run by Kiwi Discovery (☎03/442 7340) and Upper Lake Wakatipu Tours (☎03/442 9986).

The Backpacker Express is operated from the *Glenorchy Holiday Park*, at 2 Oban St (☎03/442 9939), which is also the best source of **general information** and the place to go for post-tramp **transport bookings**. For the lowdown on tramping information, see p.692.

Accommodation

After the rigours of the tramp, Glenorchy is a welcome sight and, considering its size, there is a reasonable range of accommodation to suit most budgets.

Comfort's Place, 50 Oban St (☎ & fax 03/442 8307). Highly regarded bed-and-breakfast establishment right in the centre of town, offering lovely cooked breakfasts to set you up for the day and $20 dinners when you return. ⑤.

Glenorchy Holiday Park & Backpackers, 2 Oban St (☎03/442 9939, fax 442 9940; ②). This well-organized campsite is the cheapest place in town, with spacious tent ($7) and powered sites ($8), plus bunks, basic double or twin cabins. Non-residents can shower here for $2.50. Dorms ①, cabins ②.

Glenorchy Hotel and Backpackers' Retreat, cnr Mull St & Argyll St (☎03/442 9902, fax 442 9912). Good backpacker-style dorms, with communal kitchen and lounge, are hidden behind this hotel. From November to April, plain double rooms – but with great views up the Dart Valley – are also available. Dorms ①, rooms ③, en-suite rooms ④.

Glen Roydon Lodge, cnr Mull St & Argyll St (☎03/442 9968). Good modern rooms with a nod to ski-lodge style, all sharing the comfortable guest lounge with its open fire, TV and videos. ⑤.

Paradise Backpackers, Paradise Rd, 5km north of Glenorchy (☎ & fax 03/441 8177). Backpacker beds in two-bed dorms or rooms let on a homestay basis, plus transport into Glenorchy on request. Dorms ①, rooms ③.

The Town and nearby activities

Glenorchy itself doesn't amount to much – a petrol station, a post office, a couple of pubs and cafés, some accommodation and a grocery shop. To get a feel for the area and its geography, follow the 2km loop of the **Glenorchy Walkway** from the wharf at the end of Islay Street along the edge of Lake Wakatipu and through the wetlands around the town's lagoon, a pleasant way to soak up the mountain scenery at either end of the day.

Almost all the non-tramping visitors are here for the excellent **jetboating** trips up the **Dart River**, a two-and-a-half-hour journey which fully utilizes the jetboat's shallow-water capabilities, picking routes through braided river beds and finally entering a short gorge before turning round at Sandy Bluff on the edge of the Mount Aspiring National Park. The usual jetboating antics are duly performed, but the real star is the magnificent scenery, featuring snowcapped mountains and dense bush, which is most easily appreciated from the middle of the river. The highlight is the visit to **Rockburn Chasm**, where a small tributary of the Dart has carved out a narrow, twisting canyon filled with calm, clear water. When the river is high the jetboat can get in here, but in summer you'll probably have to walk in. Dart River Jetboat Safari (☎03/442 9992) run trips from Glenorchy ($119); round-trips from Queenstown ($129) last about six hours and leave two or three times daily.

Better still, combine the upstream section of the Dart River Jetboat Safari with **canoeing** back downstream in Fun Yaks (☎03/442 7374), two- or three-person inflatable canoes carried upriver in the jetboats, then paddled down. Suitable even for absolute beginners, this is a gentle trip with no rapids and very little likelihood of an enforced swim. Trips run on demand and cost $149 ($159 from Queenstown), including jetboat, canoeing downstream, lunch and a snack in the pub afterwards.

All this fabulous scenery can be viewed from the air on **flights** operated by Glenorchy Air (☎03/442 2207), who do short flights locally for $80 and Milford Sound overflights for $150. **Horse treks** with either High Country Horses (☎03/442 9915) or Dart Stables (☎03/442 5688), both on the Queenstown road as you enter Glenorchy, cost $20 for one unguided hour, $50 for an unguided day or $70 all day with a guide.

Eating

The best **daytime** haunt is undoubtedly the *Glenorchy Café* on Mull Street (closed Tues), which serves good pies, delicious cakes, quiches, salads, coffee and Danishes in a cosy wood-panelled café complete with dried flowers, newspapers, chess and backgammon. They also sell good solid rye bread, which feels heavy in your pack but lasts the distance. Most **evenings** hungry and thirsty trampers gravitate towards the *Glenorchy Hotel*, which serves a good selection of Kiwi staples, with bar snacks from $8 and main dishes from $15. Dinners are more formal across the road at the "Rod and Rucksack" in the *Glen Royden Lodge*, where substantial mains cost $18–22.

The widest selection of **tramping food** is to be found in Queenstown, where prices are also slightly lower, but you can always pick up some last-minute supplies from The Chocolate Shop on Mull Street or the store at the *Glenorchy Holiday Park*.

The major tramps: preliminaries

The fame of the **Routeburn Track** is eclipsed only by that of its westerly neighbour, the Milford Track (see p.742). Many justly claim that the Routeburn is superior, citing its more varied scenery, longer time spent above the bushline away from sandflies, and better spacing of huts. It can't be denied that the Routeburn is one of New Zealand's finest walks, straddling the spine of the Humboldt Mountains and providing access to many of the southwestern wilderness's most archetypal features: forested valleys with rich bird life and plunging waterfalls are combined with river flats, lakes and spectacular mountain scenery. In the past the Routeburn was treated as a cheaper and less regimented alternative to the Milford Track, but overcrowding and the consequent introduction of a booking system have redressed the balance. The Routeburn is usually promoted as an easy tramp, a rating influenced more by the short distance between huts than the moderate terrain. Fit hikers might consider doing it in two reasonably long days, though that doesn't leave much time for soaking up the scenery and wallowing in the relative solitude.

Both the **Greenstone and Caples tracks** are easy walks, following gently graded, parallel river valleys where the wilderness experience is moderated by grazing cattle from the high-country stations along the Lake Wakatipu shore. The Greenstone occupies the broader, U-shaped valley carved out by one arm of the huge Hollyford Glacier, but despite the grandeur of the surrounding mountain scenery, it is sometimes criticized for being dull. Its detractors prefer the track over the sub-alpine McKellar

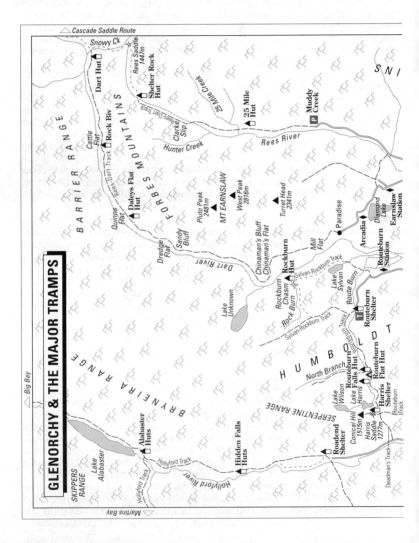

Saddle and down the Caples Valley, where the river is bigger and the narrow base of the valley forces the path closer to it.

As the Routeburn reaches maximum capacity, the **Rees–Dart Track** is now being primed for wider usage; in parts the path is being graded, the track is being re-routed to avoid a hairy stepladder and the huts are slowly being improved. Nonetheless, it remains the toughest of the major tramps in the area, covering some fairly rugged terrain and requiring six to eight hours of effort each day. It follows the standard Kiwi tramp formula of climbing one river valley, crossing the pass and descending into another, but adds an excellent side-trip to the Cascade Saddle and the choice of a jet-boat or inflatable kayak trip to complete the final day.

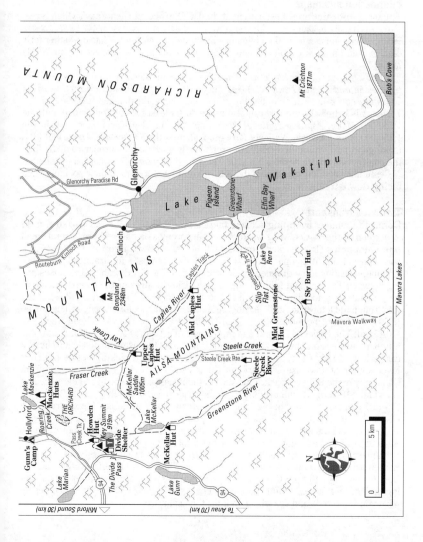

In **winter** the Routeburn takes on a different character and becomes a much more serious undertaking. The track is often snowbound and extremely slippery, the risk of avalanche is high and the huts are unheated. Return day-trips from Routeburn Shelter to Routeburn Falls Hut and from The Divide to the Lake Mackenzie Hut are much better bets. The lower-level Greenstone and Caples tracks also make a less daunting prospect – not least because the huts are heated by wood-burning stoves which can be used throughout the year – though the McKellar Saddle is often snow-covered. Only experienced, knowledgeable and well-equipped trampers should venture onto the Rees–Dart Track in the winter.

Information and maps

Tramping **information** is best sought at the **DOC office** on Glenorchy's Oban Street (Nov–April daily 8.30am–5pm; May–Oct Mon–Fri 8.30am–5pm; ☎03/442 9937, fax 442 9938), where you can fill in the obligatory intentions forms, get the latest weather forecast, gen up on track conditions and either rent ($3, plus $10 deposit) or buy ($11) maps.

DOC's leaflets on *The Routeburn Track* (free with hut booking – see below) and *The Greenstone and Caples Tracks* ($1), together with the 1:75,000 *Routeburn/Greenstone Trackmap* cover these three walks. For real route-finding, the detailed 1:50,000 *Eglinton Topomap* is better, though you can also make do (at least for the Routeburn) with the 1:150,000 *Mount Aspiring National Park* map. For the Rees–Dart Track, again the 1:150,000 *Mount Aspiring National Park* **map**, along with DOC's *Rees–Dart* leaflet ($1), make good background material, but aren't really adequate for proper route-finding; the considerably more detailed 1:50,000 *Tutoko* and *Earnslaw* Topomaps are far better.

Remember that any mention of the **left or right bank** refers to their position when **facing downstream**.

Trailhead transport

During the summer **tramping season**, there is little difficulty with transport to or from either end of the tracks. Most walkers use Glenorchy as a base, where several small **bus companies** (Backpacker Express ☎03/442 9939; Kiwi Discovery ☎03/442 7340; and Upper Lake Wakatipu Tours ☎03/442 9986) compete for trailhead business. Trampers wanting to be dropped off or picked up at The Divide can hop on buses plying between Te Anau and Milford Sound (ask visitor centres or the companies above for schedules); in addition, Fiordland Tracknet (☎03/249 7777) operate a daily loop service from mid-October to April, leaving Te Anau at 7.30am, before calling at The Divide (8.30am), Milford Sound (9.30am), The Divide (10.15am), Hollyford Road track end (10.45am), The Divide (11.30am) and returning to Te Anau by 12.30pm. For Rees–Dart trampers, those same three companies run from both Queenstown and Glenorchy to a car park at Muddy Creek, the start of the Rees Track, and pick up beside the Dart River, either at Paradise car park or Chinaman's Bluff. Expect to pay $15 from Glenorchy to the Rees car park at the start of the Rees–Dart Track, $15 to Paradise Flat at its end, $10 to the Routeburn Shelter at the eastern end of the Routeburn Track, and $15 to Greenstone Wharf at the end of the Greenstone and Caples tracks; from The Divide the fare is $20 to Te Anau, $16 to Milford.

To save backtracking, trampers can also arrange to have their bags sent on to Te Anau for a small fee through the Backpacker Express people.

Numerous **round-trip deals** and **packages** are also available, such as a bus to Routeburn Shelter with a pick-up at Greenstone Wharf, or vice versa, for around $20 from Glenorchy, $40 from Queenstown; or Rees–Dart track access with either jetboating or Fun Yak (see p.689 for more on these activities) for $60–80. Basically, decide what you want to do and see who'll do it for the best price.

Hut and campsite bookings

The **Routeburn Track** has a compulsory system of booking **accommodation passes** for all four Category 1 huts and two campsites for the duration of the **tramping season** (Nov–April). It's a reasonably flexible system, allowing people to walk in either direction, retrace their steps and stay up to two nights in a particular hut. Numbers are limited, so you'll need to book as far ahead as possible – three weeks if you can be adaptable, three months if you need a specific departure date or are part of a large group. This does have the huge advantage of guaranteeing you a bed, so you don't have to get up at the crack of dawn and almost sprint to the next hut to be sure of a bunk. Huts are all equipped with flush toilets, running (but not drinkable) water, heaters and gas rings, but you'll need to carry your own pans and plates. The cost is $28 per person per night; families get a thirty percent discount, and in October, November and April the price of huts is reduced by thirty percent for everyone. A limited number of simple **campsites** (with long-drop toilets and water; $9) exist close to the Routeburn Flats and Mackenzie Huts.

Credit-card phone or mail **bookings** are taken from July 1 for the following season: contact the Great Walks Booking Desk in Glenorchy, in Te Anau, or PO Box 811, Queenstown (May–Oct Mon–Fri 9am–4.30pm; Nov–April daily 9am–4.30pm; ☎03/442 8916, fax 442 7932). Accommodation passes can be collected from Te Anau or Glenorchy between one and five days before departure. If the track is closed due to bad weather or track conditions, full refunds are given – but new bookings can only be made if there is space. Changes can be made to existing bookings ($5 per alteration) either before you start or with the wardens at each hut, but again only if there is space. **Outside the season** the Mackenzie and Howden huts revert to backcountry Category 3 status and, like the campsites, cost $4 a night. Routeburn Falls and Flats huts become Category 2 ($8) as they have heating. Bookings are not required and annual hut passes are valid.

The **Greenstone and Caples tracks** are far less popular, and bookings are not necessary at any time of year. Each trail has two Category 2 huts ($8), but none of them have gas rings. One warden patrols each valley and may be inclined to sell you hut tickets, although you should really buy them in advance unless you have an annual hut pass (see "Basics", p.51). Free camping is allowed in both valleys along the fringes of the bush (but not on the open flats), but you are encouraged to camp close to (but at least 50m away from) the huts and use their outside facilities – long-drop toilets and water – for which you'll pay half the hut fee.

The three **Rees–Dart** huts (all Category 2; $8) currently cannot be booked in advance. Trampers should carry an annual hut pass or two hut tickets per night.

Guided walks

Routeburn aspirants who aren't confident about their level of fitness or who prefer not to lug heavy backpacks should consider joining a **guided walk**. The pace is fairly leisurely and walkers have to carry only their personal effects (no food or camping equipment); daily hikes are still typically 5–6 hours, occasionally on rough terrain, so anyone unused to hill walking should still do a good deal of preparatory hiking.

Accommodation is in clean, plain huts which are by no means luxurious, but do have hot showers, duvets on the bunks, and you'll be served cooked breakfasts and three-course dinners with wine. All you have to do is walk – but there's a **price** to pay for all this pampering: the **Routeburn Guided Walk**, PO Box 568, Queenstown (Nov–April; ☎03/442 8200, fax 442 6072), including return transport from Queenstown and three days' walking with two nights' accommodation in huts costs $860; while **The Grand Traverse**, a five-day, six-night walk combining the Routeburn and Greenstone tracks, will set you back $1160.

> Note that all **times** and **distances** given in the following accounts are **one way**, unless otherwise stated.

The Routeburn Track

Most people walk the **Routeburn Track** (32km; 2–3 days) westwards from Glenorchy towards The Divide; it can also be combined with the Greenstone and Caples tracks to make three- to five-day loops. The Routeburn isn't for everyone, though. The terrain is sometimes rough and the paths steep, but anyone of moderate fitness who can carry a backpack for five or six hours a day should have little trouble. That said, the track passes through sub-alpine country and snowfall and flooding can sometimes close it, even in summer.

The first day on the Routeburn is an easy one. Trailhead buses offer mid-morning and mid-afternoon start times, both leaving enough time to reach either Routeburn Flats or Routeburn Falls huts, and the earlier one giving ample opportunity to explore the North Branch of Route Burn. From **Routeburn Shelter to Routeburn Flats Hut** (7km; 2–3hr; 250m ascent) the route follows Route Burn steadily uphill on a metre-wide track, though it's never strenuous and has an even shingle surface. Because Route Burn is a tributary of the Dart River, you are following a side valley and will have experienced a wide variety of scenery – river flats, waterfalls and open beech forest – by the time you reach the Routeburn Flats Hut. The nearby Routeburn Flats campsite is superbly sited on the edge of wide alluvial flats at the end of a short path a couple of hundred metres beyond the hut. Only a few tents are permitted so there is plenty of space to spread out, and campers can make use of an open fireplace and a small shelter, the run-off from which provides water for cooking. Hut users are better off making the first day a little longer and tackling the next leg, **Routeburn Flats Hut to Routeburn Falls Hut** (2km; 1hr–1hr 30min; 300m ascent), which is considerably steeper and rougher, but the extra exertion is rewarded by a stay at the well-sited Routeburn Falls Hut, perched on the bushline above a precipice with east-facing verandahs looking back to Routeburn Flats and Sugar Loaf (1320m).

The second day is the longest, continuing from **Routeburn Falls Hut to McKenzie Hut** (11km; 4–7hr; 300m ascent, 250m descent) on the most exposed section of the track. Most of the day is spent above the bushline among the sub-alpine snow tussock of the Harris Saddle (1277m) and passing through bog country, where sundews, bladderworts and orchids thrive. You might even catch sight of chamois clambering on the rocks to either side of the saddle. The track climbs gradually enough to the Harris Saddle Shelter (2–3hr), which offers respite from the wind and has toilets; on a clear day, drop your pack here and climb up to the summit of **Conical Hill** (1515m; 2km return; at least 1hr; 240m ascent) for superb views down into the Hollyford Valley and along it to Martin's Bay and the Tasman Sea. Continuing from the Harris Saddle Shelter you cross from the Mount Aspiring National Park into the Fiordland National Park and skirt high along the edge of the Hollyford Valley, before switchbacking down through silver beech, fuchsia and ribbonwood to Mackenzie Hut. The bush beside the hut hides a campsite, a cramped affair that comes as a big disappointment after the Routeburn Flats site.

From **Lake McKenzie Hut to Howden Hut** (8km; 3–4hr; 300m descent), the track continues along the mountainside through a grassy patch of ribbonwood known as The Orchard and past the cascading Earland Falls to the Howden Hut at the junction of three tracks. The Routeburn continues from **Howden Hut to The Divide** (2.5km; 1hr–1hr 30min; 170m net descent), initially climbing for fifteen minutes to a point where you can make a half-hour excursion to Key Summit for views of three major river systems, the Hollyford, the Eglinton and the Greenstone. From the **Key Summit**

(919m) turn-off, the track descends through silver beech to the car park and shelter at The Divide.

The Greenstone Track

Trampers starting on the **Greenstone Track** (35km; 2–3 days) at The Divide first cover the short section to Howden Hut (described in reverse, above), then walk south from **Howden Hut to McKellar Hut** (6km; 2hr–2hr 30min; 50m descent), passing (after 20min) a free primitive campsite where fires can be lit. The Greenstone continues beside Lake McKellar to McKellar Hut (Cat 3; $8), just outside the Fiordland National Park.

The easy track from **McKellar Hut to Mid-Greenstone Hut** (12km; 4–6hr; 100m descent) starts by crossing the Greenstone River and follows the left bank down a broad, grazed valley mostly along river flats and through the lower slopes of the beech forests. A swingbridge then crosses Steele Creek, and the track continues for another half-hour to the Mid-Greenstone Hut, located on the edge of a grassy expanse.

It is eminently possible to finish the Greenstone in a day from here, though you might want to walk from **Mid-Greenstone Hut to Sly Burn Hut** (5km; 1hr–1hr 30min; 30m descent) and use the hut (Cat 3; 10 bunks) as a base for exploring the gentle **Mavora Walkway** to the south, taking two to three days through open tussock country and beech forest to Mavora Lakes (see p.697); a couple of Category 3 huts provide accommodation en route.

From **Sly Burn Hut to Greenstone Wharf** car park (10km; 3–5hr; 100m descent), the track follows the left bank as the valley narrows and the river heads into a long gorge. The river soon meets the Caples River, an enticing series of deep pools that make great swimming holes. A swingbridge give access to the left bank of the Caples River and the Caples Track; turn left to Greenstone Wharf (20–30min), or right to Mid Caples Hut (see below).

The Caples Track

The **Caples Track** (27km; 2 days) follows the Greenstone Track from **The Divide to Howden Hut** and then the first half of the section from Howden Hut to McKellar Hut, turning off an hour south of Howden Hut and beginning the very steep bush-clad zig-zag up the **McKellar Saddle** (1005m). Try to asses your capabilities beforehand as many find the walk from The Divide to Upper Caples Hut (11km; 5–7hr; 550m ascent, 600m descent) too much for one day, but are obliged to push on, as camping is neither pleasant on the saddle's bogland nor permitted on what is very fragile open tussock. The descent mostly follows snow poles, crossing and recrossing the infant Caples River before regaining beech forest and the **Upper Caples Hut** (Cat 2; $8; 20 bunks).

Greenstone Wharf is within a day's walk of here, though you can break it up into two sections: from **Upper Caples Hut to Mid Caples Hut** (7km; 2hr–2hr 30min; 50m descent) you cross easy grassland, finishing up by a short but dramatic gorge right outside the Mid Caples Hut (Cat 2; $8; 12 bunks); then from **Mid Caples Hut to Greenstone Wharf** car park (9km; 2–3hr; 150m descent) the path crosses the gorge and follows the left bank, continuing alongside the bush edge and crossing grassy clearings before arriving at the junction with the Greenstone Track, from where it is only twenty minutes to Greenstone Wharf.

The Rees–Dart Track

The standard approach to the Rees–Dart Track is to walk up the Rees and down the Dart, an anticlockwise circuit which leaves open the option of finishing off with either a Fun Yak or a jetboat ride (see p.689). The track from **Muddy Creek car park to Shelter Rock Hut** (16km; 6–8hr; 450m ascent) follows a four-wheel-drive track across grass and gravel flats on the left bank of the braided lower Rees and requires a couple of foot-soaking stream crossings. After 6km, at the end of the four-wheel-drive track, you pass Twenty-five Mile Hut (emergency use only) and press on across Twenty-five Mile Creek and over more river flats for another hour or so, with Hunter Creek and the peaks of the Forbes Mountains straight ahead. Just past the confluence of Hunter Creek, the Rees valley steepens appreciably and becomes cloaked in beech forests. Soon after, the track crosses a swingbridge to the right bank and climbs above river level, eventually coming out on the grassy flats of Clarke Slip. The track is bush-bound again up to just below the tree line, where it passes the site of the old Shelter Rock Hut then continues for a kilometre until you hit tussock country. One final crossing of the Rees River, now a large stream, takes you back to the left bank and the new Shelter Rock Hut (Cat 2; $8; 20 bunks).

The second day, from **Shelter Rock Hut to Dart Hut** (7km; 4–6hr; 500m ascent, 500m descent) is the shortest but one of the toughest, scaling the 1447m Rees Saddle. Stick to the left bank of the Rees over sub-alpine scrub and gravel banks for a couple of kilometres before crossing the river and gradually climbing up to a tussock basin and the saddle. Descend rapidly and then more steadily across snow grass following the left bank of Snowy Creek, which churns down a narrow gorge to your right. A kilometre or so later the track crosses a swingbridge to the right bank, commencing a loose and rocky descent past a long series of cascades to another crossing of Snowy Creek, just above its confluence with the Dart River. Grassy areas on the right bank provide camping spots and the Dart Hut (Cat 2; $8; 20 bunks) sits on the left bank; this is the pinch point for Rees–Dart accommodation, with tramper numbers swelled by those staying two nights to explore the Cascade Saddle route (see "Walks in the Matukituki Valley" box on p.708).

The track from **Dart Hut to Daleys Flat Hut** (16km; 6–8hr; 430m descent) initially climbs high above the river and stays there for 3km, passing through beech forest before dropping to Cattle Flat, 5km of grassed alluvial ridges traced by a winding and energy-sapping but easy-to-follow route. At the end of Cattle Flat the track returns to the bush and runs roughly parallel to the river until it reaches the beautiful grassy expanse of Quinns Flat (perfect in the late afternoon light), where the track turns inland. Within half an hour you reach the sandfly-ridden **Daleys Flat Hut** (Cat 2; $8; 20 bunks), redeemed by its pleasant location on the edge of a clearing.

Trampers planning to pick up a jetboat or Fun Yak to Glenorchy at 10.30am will need to leave around 8am for the **Daleys Flat Hut to Sandy Bluff** section (7km; 2hr–2hr 30min; 100m ascent, 110m descent). The walk skips through the bush for around 4km until Dredge Flat, where you make your own track, looking for markers on the left that indicate where you re-enter the bush. The track then climbs steeply up Sandy Bluff to reach a belvedere high above the river before dropping down to river level and the jetboat and Fun Yak pick-up point.

If you are determined to walk all the way, you'll find the section from **Sandy Bluff to Chinaman's Bluff** (12km; 3hr; negligible descent) fairly easy, crossing the flats south of Sandy Bluff and following the river to Chinaman's Bluff. Pick-ups from here can be arranged, though you can continue on foot from **Chinaman's Bluff to Paradise car park** (6km; 2hr; negligible descent) through Dan's Paddock and along either the four-wheel-drive track or a more direct walking track.

The Lake Sylvan and Rockburn tracks

Ambitious trampers wanting to combine the Rees–Dart Track with the Routeburn Track without returning to Glenorchy, can link the two using either the Lake Sylvan Track or the tougher Rockburn Track. Note that **river levels** must be low enough to safely ford the Dart River south of Chinaman's Bluff, so that you can reach Rockburn Hut (Cat 4; free; 4 bunks). The hut is unmarked on the Mount Aspiring Park map, but is located on the edge of the bush on the right bank of Rock Burn where it enters the Dart; the Rockburn Chasm (see p.689) is close by. **Daleys Flat Hut to Rockburn Hut** (20km; 5–6hr; 100m ascent, 150m descent) makes a sensible day's walk. There are two possible routes from **Rockburn Hut to Routeburn Flat Hut**: the more arduous goes west **via Rock Burn** (14km; 7–10hr; 800m ascent, 700m descent) to Sugarloaf Pass then south and steeply down Sugarloaf Stream; the longer but easier path heads south **via Lake Sylvan** (17km; 6–7hr; 300m ascent), a brownish lake surrounded by regenerating forest.

Kingston and the road to Fiordland

Most people travel from Queenstown to Fiordland by road, making the 170km journey to Te Anau in under three hours. It is an attractive if unspectacular route that follows the lakeshore road, hugging the foot of the Remarkables then striking out across open Otago and Southland farming country.

As the Dart glacier retreated at the end of the last ice age, Lake Wakatipu formed behind the terminal moraine at what is now **KINGSTON**, a scattered community 46km south of Queenstown on SH6. The lake's waters formed the Mataura Valley to the south, but successive terminal moraines raised the lake level to the point at which it was able to carve out a new passage down the bed of the Kawarau, out of the Frankton Arm. In the 1860s the Mataura Valley provided a perfect route from the populated coast to new gold fields on the Shotover and Arrow rivers. Kingston became a major transit centre, accommodating up to five thousand people while they waited for boats across the lake or bullock carts to transport their spoils to Dunedin or Invercargill. By 1878, the railroad had reached Kingston, and the pre-fabricated parts for ever-larger steamers could be brought in and assembled on the lakeshore. The 1936 completion of the lakeside road to Queenstown drove the last nail into the coffin of the steamer freight trade, and goods trains went the same way, but the line has managed to struggle on thanks to the **Kingston Flyer** tourist train, Kent Street (daily Oct–April 10.15am & 3.45pm; $15 one-way, $20 return; ☎03/248 8586). Initially it plied the 60km to Lumsden and was much eulogized in those halcyon days before Kiwi tourism went ballistic, but since 1982 the cut-down forty-minutes-each-way service only runs 15km to the nowhere town of Fairlight. Gleaming black steam engines haul creaky but sumptuous turn-of-the-century first-class carriages with embossed steel ceilings and brass gas lamps: arrive early to avoid being shunted down to the less exalted second-class seats, which are charged at the same rate.

The only **accommodation** in Kingston, and for some distance either side, is at the roadside *Kingston Stream Holiday Camp*, 10 Kent St (☎ & fax 03/248 8501; tent & powered sites $9, dorms ①, cabins & motel units ③).

Beyond Kingston there's little to delay your progress to Te Anau. Just short of the dull Southland farming town of **Lumsden**, a signposted short-cut diverts you to **Mossburn** and SH94. Some 14km west of Mossburn a narrow road cuts north towards **Mavora Lakes**, a very popular summertime retreat; the southern lake is reserved for quiet pursuits like fishing and canoeing while the larger North Mavora Lake hosts rowdy boats. Trails through the surrounding beech forests make great mountain-biking territory, and trampers can head north along the Mavora Walkway (see p.695) and link up with the Greenstone Track (see p.695).

Back on SH94 you soon enter the Red Tussock Conservation Area, named for a type of grass essential to the livelihood of the takahe (see Contexts, p.782), and before long you'll find yourself in Te Anau, perched on the brink of Fiordland (see p.730).

Wanaka

WANAKA, 55km northeast of Queenstown, languishes in the shadow of its brasher southern sibling, but offers a similar combination of beautiful surroundings and robust adventure activities. Situated at the point where the hummocky, poplar-studded hills of Central Otago rub up against the dramatic peaks of the Mount Aspiring National Park, it commands a wonderful spot on the shores of the willow-girt Lake Wanaka, with the jagged summits of the Southern Alps as often as not mirrored in its waters.

Founded in the 1860s as a service centre for the local run-holders and itinerant gold miners, the town didn't really take off until the prosperous middle years of the twentieth century, when camping and caravanning Kiwis discovered its warm, dry summer climate and easy-going pace. Today it is gradually picking up speed, but Wanaka remains a small and eminently manageable place, with the tenor of a village and an overwhelming feeling of light and spaciousness. It continues to promote itself as an adventure destination in its own right, and it's an excellent place in which to relax for a couple of days and eat well in some fine cafés and restaurants.

A half-day spent exploring Wanaka's intriguing **maze** and absorbing **museums** will leave plenty of time to go kayaking, jetboating, rock climbing, horse riding or, best of all, canyoning. Wanaka is also the perfect base from which to explore the surrounding region, notably the Mount Aspiring National Park and the Cardrona Valley. During the winter months, Wanaka's relative calm is shattered by the arrival of **skiers and snowboarders** eager to explore the downhill skifields of Treble Cone and Cardrona, and the Nordic terrain at Waiorau.

Arrival, information and transport

Daily direct **buses** from Christchurch, Dunedin, Queenstown and Franz Josef all arrive centrally: InterCity stop outside The Paper Place, 84 Ardmore St, while Mount Cook, Catch-a-Bus and Southern Link Shuttles pull up in front of Wanaka Travel & Booking Agency, 99 Ardmore St (☎03/443 7414, fax 443 9434). You'll usually have to book in advance through these agencies or direct with the company, particularly for the Catch-a-Bus and Southern Link services, which will drop off and pick up at your hotel.

The best source of general and tramping **information** is the combined **Wanaka visitor centre** (Mon–Fri 8am–4.45pm, Sat & Sun 8am–3.45pm; ☎03/443 1233, fax 443 9238) and DOC's **Mount Aspiring National Park visitor centre** (same hours; ☎03/443 7660, fax 443 8776), 500m east of central Wanaka on SH89 at the corner of Ballantyne Road. They'll give impartial advice on activities and transport in the region – though you're just as well served at The Adventure Centre, 99 Ardmore St (Nov–April daily 8.30am–6.30pm; ☎03/443 9422 & 0800/684 468, fax 443 8876), which acts as the booking agent and central radio contact for many of the adventure travel companies both here and in Queenstown, and books flights to Milford. There are several **banks** around town, with foreign-exchange facilities and ATMs.

Wanaka is so compact that you can **walk** everywhere in the centre, and most accommodation is less than fifteen minutes' away on foot. Longer excursions are best made with **bicycles** or **cars** rented from several shops around town (see "Listings", p.707); for short trips into the surroundings, there's always Wanaka Taxis (☎03/443 7999).

Accommodation

For such a diminutive town, Wanaka has a splendid range of accommodation, and **rates** are generally a fair bit lower than in Queenstown. You should have no problem finding a place to suit, except during the peak months of January and August, when **booking** is essential – and some establishments respond to the surge in demand by raising their rates.

Hotels and motels

Altamont Lodge, Mount Aspiring Rd, 2km west of Wanaka (☎ & fax 03/443 8864). The perfect ski lodge, with a pine-panelled alpine atmosphere, communal cooking and lounge areas, drying rooms, and ski-tuning facilities. Rooms are functional but attractive, with shared bathrooms and good rates for singles, reduced if you use your own bedding. The spa pool is open only during the winter season, but the tennis court is available year round. ③.

Aspiring Lodge, cnr Dungarvon St & Dunmore St (☎03/443 7816, fax 443 8914). Spacious and attractive wood-panelled studio units and executive suites, with full kitchens and drying room for ski gear. Continental and cooked breakfasts available. ⑥.

Bay View Motel, Mount Aspiring Rd (☎03/443 7766, fax 443 9194). Well-appointed motel with lake and mountain views, a spa pool ($2 per person), and a pleasant site well back from the road, just over 1km west of Wanaka up the Matukituki Valley. ⑤.

Cardrona Hotel, 26km along the sealed section of the Cardrona road south towards Queenstown (☎ & fax 03/443 8153). Characterful, restored gold-rush hotel. Decent bathless doubles are in a new extension and are very popular with skiers from the nearby Cardrona and Waiorau slopes. ③.

Lakeview Motel, 68 Lismore St (☎ & fax 03/443 7029). Well-placed en-suite studios, and slightly pricier but better-value larger units – all with good views. ④.

Manuka Crescent Motel, 51 Manuka Crescent (☎03/443 7773, fax 443 9066). Pleasant, good-value motel with a mix of modern and older units and a small pool. Twenty minutes' walk from town, but there's a courtesy minibus and guests can rent bicycles ($20 a day) and scooters ($35 a day). Breakfasts available. ④.

Matterhorn South Lodge, 56 Brownston St (☎03/443 1119, fax 443 8379). This upmarket section adjoining the hostel of the same name (see below) has modern, nicely furnished en-suite rooms with TV and fridge, and access to an excellent kitchen and comfortable lounge area. ③.

Midtown Motel, 50 Brownston St (☎ & fax 03/443 1265). The cheapest of the motels, centrally located with perfectly serviceable en-suite units that languish at the bottom of this price category for most of the year. ③.

Wanaka Motel, 73 Helswick St (☎ & fax 03/442 7545). Spacious two-bedroom units with huge lounges, a full-size kitchen and all mod cons. ⑤.

B&Bs and homestays

Aspiring Images, 26 Norman St (☎ & fax 03/443 8358). Comfortable suburban homestay, with nice rooms, each with a terrace. Free use of bicycles; dinner by arrangement. ⑤.

Bremner Lodge, 311 Lakeside Rd (☎03/443 8585, fax 443 1499). Quality homestay in a spacious modern house close to Eely Point and Bremner Bay. Continental breakfast is served and dinners are available. ⑤.

Margaret and Alan Jolly, 9 Redwood Lane (☎03/443 7072). Very welcoming and spacious home on the outskirts of Wanaka with a fine garden and a couple of rooms with shared facilities. Continental breakfast is included ($5 extra for cooked), and guests are encouraged to stay for dinner ($25). Per-person rates make this a good place for those travelling alone. ⑤.

Rippon Lea, 15 Norman Terrace (☎ & fax 03/443 9333). Longstanding and welcoming homestay comprising a two-bedroom apartment which is ideal for families. A generous continental breakfast is served, and they'll pick you up from central Wanaka, 2km away. ④.

Te Wanaka Lodge, 23 Brownston St (☎0800/926 252, fax 443 9246). Wanaka's finest B&B inn, with twelve luxurious and quiet en-suite rooms, communal TV, and a cedar hot tub during winter. The sumptuous buffet breakfast is a mellow affair centred on a huge dining table, and there are also self-catering facilities. ⑥.

Tirohanga, 102 Lismore St (☎03/443 8302). Friendly homestay with stupendous views across the lake to Mount Roy. Sleep in either the modest twin room or the self-contained unit and eat a light breakfast with the family. Evening meals available. ⑤.

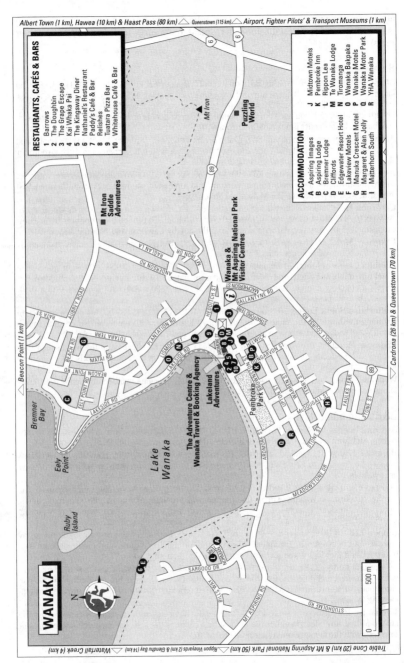

Albert Town (1 km), Hawea (10 km) & Haast Pass (80 km) △ Queenstown (115 km) △ Airport, Fighter Pilots' & Transport Museums (1 km)

RESTAURANTS, CAFÉS & BARS

1 Barrows
2 The Doughbin
3 The Grape Escape
4 Kai Whaka Pai
5 The Kingsway Diner
6 Nathaniel's Restaurant
7 Paddy's Café & Bar
8 Relishes
9 Tuatara Pizza Bar
10 Whitehouse Café & Bar

ACCOMMODATION

A Aspiring Images
B Aspiring Lodge
C Bremner Lodge
D Cliffords
E Edgewater Resort Hotel
F Lakeview Motels
G Manuka Crescent Motel
H Margaret & Alan Jolly
I Matterhorn South
J Midtown Motels
K Pembroke Inn
L Rippon Lea
M Te Wanaka Lodge
N Tiromanga
O Wanaka Bakpaka
P Wanaka Motels
Q Wanaka Motor Park
R YHA Wanaka

Mt Iron

Puzzling World

Mt Iron Saddle Adventures

Wanaka & Mt Aspiring National Park Visitor Centres

The Adventure Centre & Wanaka Travel & Booking Agency

Lakeland Adventures

Pembroke Park

Lake Wanaka

Bremner Bay

Eely Point

Ruby Island

Beacon Point (1 km)

WANAKA

N

500 m

0

Treble Cone (20 km) & Mt Aspiring National Park △ Rippon Vineyards (2 km) & Glendhu Bay (14 km) △ Waterfall Creek (4 km)

Cardrona (26 km) & Queenstown (70 km)

Hostels

Cliffords, Ardmore St (☎03/443 7826, fax 443 9069). Functional backpacker beds in single or double rooms with a communal lounge, kitchen and bathroom. Located at the back of a large town hotel of the same name. Dorms ①, rooms ②.

Matterhorn South, 56 Brownston St (☎03/443 1119, fax 443 8379). Small, slightly cramped but appealing hostel right in the centre of town with a log fire surrounded by scatter cushions. Smallish dorms ①, rooms ②.

Wanaka Bakpaka, 117 Lakeside Rd (☎03/443 7837). Low-key hostel five minutes' walk from town and with great lake and mountain views, a peaceful atmosphere, summer barbecues and rental of canoes ($24 a day) or sea kayaks ($16 a day). Cabins & dorms ①, rooms ②.

YHA, 181 Upton St (☎ & fax 03/443 7405). Decent all-day hostel ten minutes' walk from the centre with small dorms, bargain bike rental ($10 per day), and a good garden in which you can camp ($9). Dorms ①, rooms ②.

Campsites and motorparks

Albert Town Recreation Reserve, 6km northeast of Wanaka on SH6 (Mount Aspiring visitor centre ☎03/443 7660, fax 443 8776). Open, informal camping area with water and toilets on the banks of the swift-flowing Clutha River. $5 per site.

Glendhu Bay Motor Camp, Mount Aspiring Rd, 15km west of Wanaka (☎03/443 7243). Popular lakeshore family campground with fabulous views across to Mount Aspiring, boat-launching facilities, canoe and bike rental. Tent & powered sites $7/$8 per-person, cabins ①.

Pleasant Lodge Holiday Park, Glendhu Bay Rd, 3km west of Wanaka (☎ & fax 03/443 7360). Sprawling, family-oriented site with tent sites ($8.50), a range of cabins and heaps of amenities, including mountain-bike rental. Cabins ②, tourist apartments ③, motel units ④.

Wanaka Motor Park, 212 Brownston St (☎ & fax 03/443 7883). The most convenient of the campsites, ten minutes' walk from central Wanaka, with $9 tent sites and all the usual facilities. Dorms ①, cabins & apartments ②–③.

The Town, its maze and museums

The solid lump of Mount Iron rises immediately east of town, pointing the way to **Stuart Landsborough's Puzzling World**, almost 2km away on SH89 (daily 8.30am–5.30pm; $6). Star attraction is "The Great Maze", a complex wooden structure comprising 1500m of dead-end passageways packed into a dense labyrinth, with overhead bridges linking the four sections. Should you choose to accept it, your mission is to reach all four corner towers, either in any order (30min–1hr) or in a specific sequence (at least 1hr), then to find your way out again; if it all goes horribly wrong, you can cheat by using escape doors. Put aside a couple of hours to appreciate this prototype for the Eighties maze-building boom that swept New Zealand and Japan – where Stuart Landsborough briefly enjoyed a fanatical following. The ticket price includes entry to the dubious attractions of "Hologram Hall", full of the usual numbing circus of 3-D images, and the "Tilted House", which revels in tricks of perspective produced by the floor being fifteen degrees off the horizontal. Skip both in favour of half an hour in the café, playing with the puzzles scattered over the tables.

Wanaka's airport, 4km east of Puzzling World on SH6, is the base for a number of aerial activities (see "Activities", p.703) and the **New Zealand Fighter Pilots' Museum** (daily: Christmas to mid-Feb 9.30am–6pm; rest of year 9.30am–4pm; $6), which honours Kiwi pilots and ground crew who fought in the two world wars. This homage to the New Zealand contingent contains hagiographic profiles of the men and blow-by-blow descriptions of the major battles and campaigns, all accompanied by rousing war anthems. Star exhibits are a North American Harvard adapted to look like a Mitsubishi Zero for the Pearl Harbor re-enactment film *Tora, Tora, Tora*, New Zealand's oldest Tiger Moth, Spitfires, Messerschmitts, Hurricanes, a P-51D Mustang and a Soviet YAK-3. If any of this strikes a chord, then you might want to time your visit to coincide with

WALKS AROUND WANAKA

Visitors shy of the beard-and-Goretex walks in the Mount Aspiring National Park to the west might reap greater rewards from these more modest expeditions. No special gear is required, just robust shoes, wet-weather gear and sun protection.

MOUNT IRON

The most accessible of Wanaka's hilltop walks is up the 527m **Mount Iron** (2km; 1–2hr; 240m ascent), a glacially sculpted outcrop, its western and northern slopes ground smooth by the glacier that scoured its southern face. The path through farmland and the bird-filled manuka woodland of the Mount Iron Scenic Reserve starts 2km east of Wanaka on SH89, climbing the steep southern face to the summit. Here you can enjoy magnificent panoramic views of Wanaka and the nearby lakes, before following the path down the east face of Mount Iron towards the entrance to Puzzling World (see p.701).

MOUNT ROY

Mount Roy Walking Track (16km; 4–6hr; 1100m ascent) is a much more ambitious prospect, winding up to the 1581m summit of Roy's Peak for wonderful views over Lake Wanaka and surrounding glaciers and mountains. The path starts 7km west of Wanaka on the Mount Aspiring Road, but is closed during the lambing season (Oct to mid-Nov).

DIAMOND LAKE WALKING TRACK

The long vistas from Mount Iron and Mount Roy are only really challenged by those on the **Diamond Lake Walking Track** (7km; 2hr 30min; 400m ascent), a community project which requests a $2 donation. From the car park 18km west of Wanaka on the Mount Aspiring Road there are several short variations – but to get the views, you'll need to tackle the 775m summit of Rocky Hill.

BEACON POINT–CLUTHA OUTLET CIRCUIT

This is a long but undemanding riverbank and lakeside walk which starts from Wanaka and follows the shore to **Eely Point** (15min), a sheltered bay popular for boating and picnics. Beyond Eely Point is Bremner Bay and the continuation of the waterfront path to **Beacon Point** (a further 30min). Either return the same way or continue along Beacon Point Road to the Outlet Motor Camp and pick up the **Outlet Track**, which runs 1km to the Albert Town bridge. By following SH6 this can be turned into a loop back to Wanaka (16km in all), passing Puzzling World (see p.701) and the base of Mount Iron (see above). The map in DOC's *Walks around Wanaka* leaflet (50¢) makes the route a little clearer.

WATERFALL CREEK TO DAMPER BAY

The westbound equivalent of the Beacon Point–Clutha Outlet Circuit leaves Roy's Bay along the **Waterfall Creek and Damper Bay Track** (5km one way; 1hr; negligible ascent), heading through Wanaka Station Park and past Rippon Vineyard to Waterfall Creek (35min). It continues along lakeside terraces to a high point on the Wanaka side of Damper Bay.

the biennial, four-day **"Warbirds over Wanaka"** air show. At Easter each even-numbered year all manner of airborne craft – but predominantly small and vintage planes – take to the air; details and tickets ($10–15 per day) are available from the Wanaka visitor centre.

A similar theme is explored in the adjacent **Wanaka Transport Museum** (daily: Nov–April 8.30am–6pm; May–Oct 9am–5pm; $5), an engaging hoard of cars, trucks and bikes preserved by Wanaka's dry climate. There should be something here to titillate anyone with even a passing interest in motor vehicles. Some machines are just well-kept examples of stuff still puttering around New Zealand roads, but there's also exotica such as a Centurian tank, a ten-seater Lockhead Lodestar used by the US Army in the 1950s, Velocette and BSA bikes, and the Solar Kiwi Racer, an aluminium and glass-fibre bullet-shaped car powered by solar panels on its roof.

The perfect antidote to the museums is a trip to the small but perfectly formed **Rippon Vineyards**, 3km west of Wanaka on the Mount Aspiring Road (Aug–April daily 11.30m–5pm). The dry, stony and sun-soaked slopes running down to Lake Wanaka were planted in 1974 and produced their first, fully organic vintage in 1989. Five of their wines can be tasted for $3 – the typically excellent Pinot Noir and the Sauvignon Blanc come particularly recommended – while a bottle of the good stuff will set you back $20–30. The best approach to the vineyard from Wanaka is on foot, along the lakefront Waterfall Creek Walking Track (see box on p.702).

Activities

Wanaka's relatively low profile and the absence of the hard sell and conveyor-belt style that characterizes some of Queenstown's slicker operations add up to a more relaxed approach – and frequently better value for money. Many, but not all, activities can be booked through The Adventure Centre, 99 Ardmore St (Nov–April daily 8.30am–6.30pm; ☎03/443 9422 & 0800/684 468, fax 443 8876), which acts as their booking agent and pick-up point.

On land

If abseiling down thirty-metre waterfalls and sliding down eighty-degree polished rock chutes into deep green pools appeals, then **canyoning** should fit the bill. You don't need any special experience, just a sense of adventure and water confidence – once you start into the canyon, there is only one way out. Deep Canyoning Experience (mid-Nov to April or May; book through The Adventure Centre or on ☎03/443 7922) take up to five canyoners with each guide, who secures all abseils with safety ropes and provides enough warm, protective clothing to ease the sense of vulnerability. First-timers usually tackle **Emerald Creek** ($145 for a full day), a narrow fissure where fern-draped verdure envelops you, in complete contrast to the parched landscape of the surrounding Matukituki valley. Half-time tea and biscuits are served on a huge slab wedged high above a cascade, and the day is rounded off with a fine picnic and strong camp-brewed coffee. The season typically runs from mid-November to March; the warmer, more open **Speargrass Creek** (also $145) is roped into service at the cooler ends of the season. Experienced abseilers or canyoners are catered for by the 400-metre **Twin Falls** ($300).

Wanaka's dry, sunny climate is ideal for **rock climbing**, and two local companies offer tuition and guiding. The Wanaka School of Rock Climbing (contact The Adventure Centre) run half-day top-roping, seconding and abseiling courses for two to four people ($85 each), and full-day outings ($125 per person), inclusive of all transport and equipment. Out on a Thread, based at Wanaka Gym, 155 Tenby St (☎03/443 9418), run comparable trips; the gym also houses a fairly basic bouldering wall (daily except Sat 5–9pm; $5). If you want to get out onto the Matukituki valley schist and gneiss unsupervised, pick up a copy of *Wanaka Rock Climbing*, published by Wanaka Tourist Craft ($12, available from Good Sports – see p.708).

If the idea of performing gymnastics on roadside crags tends to pale beside the prospect of getting up into the ice and snow of the Southern Alps, then you can always try one of the expensive but professional **mountaineering** packages offered by Mount Aspiring Guides (☎03/443 9422). Their guided five-day alpine ascents (minimum two people) of Mount Aspiring ($1600 each), Mount Cook or Mount Tasman ($2400 per person) require a high degree of fitness and some mountain experience. Private mountain guiding will set you back just over $200 per person per day, plus the cost of equipment rental, hut fees, transport and food. Mountain Recreation (☎03/443 7330) offer similar deals; both outfits also do guided multi-day treks, ski mountaineering and alpine skills courses.

Wanaka abounds with shops renting out all-terrain bikes, but for a day's guided **mountain biking**, join Alpine Biking (The Adventure Centre or mobile ☎025/331 714) on one of their jaunts along ridges of the lakeside mountains (4hr; $85) or biking to a hut in the Pisa Range (overnight; $125). Saddles of a different cut are employed by Mount Iron Saddle Adventures (☎03/443 7581), which runs **horse-riding** treks (2hr; $40) over farmland and through kanuka forest on the easy northern slopes of Mount Iron from their stables on Anderson Road, five minutes' drive northeast of Wanaka. A wider range of rides are offered by Backcountry Saddle Expeditions (☎03/443 8151; 2hr–2 days; $45–150) from their stables 25km south of Wanaka in the Cardrona Valley; they'll pick you up from Wanaka if you book in advance.

To explore some of the less accessible parts of Wanaka and its environs, try the **four-wheel-drive tours** organized by Edgewater Adventures at the Edgewater Resort (☎03/443 8311; 3hr; $80); or the **photographic tours** of Aspiring Images (☎03/443 8358; $50 per hour, maximum 4 people), who tour the prime viewpoints and provide professional cameras.

In the air

Magnificent scenery, clear skies and competitive prices make Wanaka an excellent place to get airborne. Bi-Plane Adventures (☎03/443 1000) will pick up in town and run you 6km east to Wanaka airport for any of a number of one-pilot-one-passenger **scenic and stunt flights**. Cheapest (both $140) are the twenty-minute joyride in the open-cockpit 1920s Tiger Moth bi-plane and fifteen minutes in a closed-cockpit Pitt Special, which is designed specifically for aerobatics. For adrenalin junkies with money to burn there's also the 1940s-designed Mustang, which combines aerobatic agility with neck-snapping acceleration (20min; $2000). A twenty-minute scenic flight can be combined with a thirty-second freefall on a **tandem skydive** with Tandem Skydive Wanaka, Wanaka Airport (mobile ☎025/796 877; $225). Mount Roy and Treble Cone provide the launch pads for **paragliding** with Wanaka Paragliding (☎03/443 9193), who offer tandem flights for $98–118 and various learn-to-fly courses ($138–1400).

Flights to Milford (for a description of Milford Sound, see p.738) from Wanaka tend to be a few dollars more expensive than those from Queenstown, but you're in the air longer and fly over a wider range of scenery including Mount Aspiring, the Olivine Ice Plateau and the inaccessible lakes of Alabaster, McKerrow and Tutoko. Most local accommodation receives daily bulletins on Milford weather and flight conditions. Both Aspiring Air (☎03/443 7943 & 0800/100 943) and Wanaka Aviation (☎03/443 1385 & 0800/104 431) do an extensive range of flights, the most popular being an overflight of Milford Sound (1hr 30min; $200), an overflight of Mount Aspiring (50min; $120), and a circuit of Mount Cook (1hr 50min; $220).

On the water

With a beautiful lake, a number of decent rivers and a friendly, low-key approach, there's plenty of opportunity for getting wet in style. Lakeland Adventures, Main Wharf (☎03/443 7495), lay on all manner of waterborne activities, the most leisurely being the twice-daily hour-long **lake cruise** ($30) around Ruby Island, Glendhu Bay, Pigeon Island and the lake outlet, and half-day trips landing on Pigeon Island and making the short walk to Arethusa Pool, a lake within a lake ($50). For kicks there's **water skiing** and banana boat rides, plus kayaks, windsurfers and sailing dinghies for rent. For thrills and spills, try the fifty-minute **jetboat rides** onto the upper reaches of the Clutha with Clutha River Jet, Main Wharf (same phone; $50).

From October to April, Alpine River Guides (book through The Adventure Centre or on ☎03/443 9023) will take you on a number of different **kayaking** trips on the Matukituki River (3hr; $96); the Clutha or Hawea (both 3hr; $91); and full-day trips on the Makarora (prior experience required; price dependant on numbers); independent paddlers may also be able to rent kayaks, depending on their abilities and intended route. A far cry from Queenstown's boisterous Kawarau and Shotover rivers, the **rafting trips** run by Pioneer Rafting (Sept–April; ☎03/443 1246; half-day $75, full-day $95) are pitched at families, the emphasis being on appreciating the scenery, swimming and gold panning as you drift down the Upper Clutha or follow the historic timber-rafting route down the Makarora in oar-rigged rafts. No-holds-barred thrill-seekers need look no further than **whitewater sledging** with Frogz Have More Fun (☎0800/338 737), who sledge a twelve-kilometre stretch of the Upper Clutha (Grade I–II; 2hr on water; $70), the Hawea (Grade II–III; 2hr; $75) and 7km of the popular Kawarau with its four major rapids (Grade II–IV; 1hr 30min; $89). The season runs from October to April, though by late summer the low water levels mean that the rapids have lost much of their might.

Wanaka and Hawea lakes and the rivers flowing into them are popular territory for brown and rainbow **trout fishing**. There's a maximum bag of six fish per day and you'll require the southern lakes fishing licence ($12 a day, $25 a week). Unless you really know your bait, you'll have a better chance of catching your supper with Lakeland Adventures, who are confident enough to offer a "No Fish, No Pay" guarantee (excluding the licence fee). Charter rates start at $200 for two hours on a six-metre cabin cruiser (maximum 4 passengers), or they'll rent you a rod, reel and lures for $12 a day and a four-metre runabout carrying five adults for $50 an hour.

Eating and drinking

The sophisticated tastes and open wallets of Wanaka's skiers, combined with a healthy influx of summer tourists, have together fostered an abundance of decent places to eat. The town's drinking dens are less appealing, but you can always take refuge in the restaurant bars.

Barrows, 20 Ardmore St. Fairly typical Kiwi bar that is fine for straightforward drinking but poor for meals.

The Doughbin, Pembroke Mall. Home-style bakery with good cakes and pies, including vegetarian versions.

The Grape Escape, 2 Brownston St (☎03/443 9488). The dreadful pun conceals a good and moderately priced restaurant, al fresco café and wine bar with an informal atmosphere. The small, well-chosen menu features the likes of sweet chilli chicken and blue-eyed cod. Licensed, with many excellent New Zealand wines, but few available by the glass. Bookings recommended in the evening.

Kai Whaka Pai, Pembroke Mall, hidden behind Snack Shack. Undoubtedly Wanaka's essential eating spot and a hot favourite with the locals, who come here for Danish pastries and croissants for breakfast, damn fine coffee and fabulous meals through the day. It's a casual place, is often packed and the service can be slow when you do manage to get a table, but these quibbles soon evaporate when you're faced with such gargantuan portions. Soups are hearty and the mains – shrimp and avocado fettuccine, hapuku and scallop crepes, pepperoni and jalapeño pizza – are always generous. Pizzas and snacks are also available to take away. BYO.

The Kingsway Diner, 21 Helwick St. Cavernous and airy place that styles itself somewhere between an upscale American diner and a chic restaurant, with burgers and melts ($9), steaks, seafood and vegetarian dishes ($15–19) either to take out or served on newsprint-covered tables. Sumptuous American breakfasts served from 8.30am. Licensed.

WINTER IN WANAKA

May signifies the end of the summer season, and Wanaka immediately starts gearing up for winter. Mountain-bike rental shops switch to ski rental (see "Listings", p.708), water-sports instructors don their salopettes, pot-bellied stoves replace parasols at restaurants, and frequent shuttle buses run up to the skifields, calling at the hotels, hostels and sports shops along the way. Reports on snow conditions can be heard on the premium-rated Snowphone (☎0900/34444), or by listening to local radio at around 6.45am. If you plan to drive up to the skifields, you'll need tyre chains, which can be rented at petrol stations close to the fields and in Wanaka.

CARDRONA

Cardrona Ski Resort (☎03/443 7411) sprawls over three basins on the southeastern slopes of the 1934-metre Mount Cardrona, the 12km unsealed access road branching off 24km south of Wanaka and just short of the hamlet of Cardrona. Predominantly a family-oriented field – they run a junior ski school and a crèche – Cardrona is noted for dry snow and an abundance of gentle **runs** ideally suited to beginners and intermediates. Currently there are two quads, a double chair and learner tows, giving a maximum vertical descent of 390m and, though there is little extreme terrain, snowboarders have the run of a half-pipe. As you would expect, there's a full programme of lessons, ski packages and gear rental, plus full restaurant and bar facilities. Beginners can spend the day on the learner field for less than half the $56 adult **lift pass**.

Through most of the long season (June to early October), you'll need snow chains to negotiate the access road which drops you at the base facilities halfway up the field. Non-drivers can get **buses** from Wanaka and, less conveniently, Queenstown, an hour and a half away.

Cardrona is unique in offering **accommodation** actually on the mountain – in luxury, fully self-contained three-bedroom apartments (☎03/443 7341; ④–⑥).

TREBLE CONE

More experienced skiers tend to frequent the excellent steep slopes of **Treble Cone** (☎03/443 7443), 20km west of Wanaka, where recently installed additional snow-making equipment has extended the season, which now lasts from mid-June to early October. Its appeal lies in open uncrowded slopes, spectacularly located high above Lake Wanaka, and a full 610 vertical metres of skiing, served by New Zealand's first detachable six-seater chair, a couple of T-bars and a learner tow. The **terrain** is very varied with moguls,

Nathaniel's Restaurant, Sargood Drive (☎03/443 8311). Highly rated and expensive lakeside restaurant within the Edgewater Resort complex, serving innovative New Zealand cuisine. Licensed & BYO; reservations recommended.

Paddys Café & Bar, Pembroke Mall. Ersatz Irish bar with occasional live music – but more frequent karaoke nights. Suitably stodgy burgers and carvery meals are also available.

Relishes, 99 Ardmore St. Bustling, cheery BYO and licensed restaurant with tables outside and indoors, by the fire. Popular for daytime sandwiches and light meals, before the chef moves on to eclectic dinners – from burritos to Cajun cod. Wines include some from the local Rippon winery. Closed 3–6.30pm.

Tuatara Pizza Bar, 72 Ardmore St. Licensed eat-in and take-out evening-only pizzeria – but more renowned for its pool table and lively bar.

White House Café & Bar, 33 Dunmore St (☎03/443 9595). One of Wanaka's best: a classy yet casual licensed restaurant in a flamboyantly nautical blue and white open-plan house with a sunny patio. The cuisine is Mediterranean with strong Mahgrebi and Greek leanings, accompanied by wonderful fresh breads and great strong coffee. Mains are around $18, and you can BYO or take your pick from an extensive wine list, most sold by the glass or by the bottle.

powder runs and plenty of natural and created half-pipes; the limited extent of wide, groomed slopes makes it hard work for beginners, but snowboarders should find plenty to do. Day **lift passes** go for $55 and there's a first-time package for $40 including a lower lift pass, ski rental and instruction.

Lessons, gear rental and food are all on tap, and the field is easily reached along a 7km toll-free access road. Morning **buses** leave from Wanaka, and a shuttle bus takes skiers from the start of the access road on Mount Aspiring Road up to the tows.

WAIORAU NORDIC SKI AREA

With so many Kiwi skiers committed to downhill, it comes as a surprise to discover the **Waiorau Nordic Ski Area** (☎03/443 7542), 24km south of Wanaka, just before Cardrona. At around $20 for access to the field, $25 for the T-bar and $15 for ski rental, it is a relatively inexpensive way to get on the snow; and Nordic skiing – essentially lowland tramping on skis – is beginning to catch on. From July to September, exponents negotiate the 35km of marked and groomed Nordic trails designed to cater to beginners and experts in both the Nordic and telemark disciplines. The ski school caters to all levels with improvers' clinics and children's programmes run throughout the season, though more frequently at weekends.

HELI-SKIING

No one is going to fool you into believing that **heli-skiing** is cheap, but there's no other way of getting to runs of up to 1200 vertical metres across virgin snow on any of six mountain ranges. From June to October, Harris Mountain Heli-skiing (☎03/443 7930), New Zealand's biggest heli-skiing operator, offers almost 400 different runs on 150 peaks – mainly in the Harris Mountains between Queenstown's Crown Range and Wanaka's Mount Aspiring National Park.

Strong intermediate and **advanced skiers** generally get the most out of the experience, though those with more limited skills can still participate provided they meet the minimum standard determined by an ability questionnaire. **Conditions** are more critical than at the skifields, but on average there's heli-skiing on seventy percent of days during winter, typically in four- to five-day weather windows separated by storms. From mid-July to mid-September, prices are a little higher than during the shoulder seasons (3–4 weeks either side). Of the multitude of packages, the most popular have to be "The Classic" ($670 high, $600 shoulder), with five runs in a day, and "Maximum Vertical" ($845/$770), comprising seven runs for advanced skiers only; **bookings** should be made well in advance and accompanied by a substantial deposit (around 40 percent).

Listings

Bike rental Mountain Bikes Unlimited, 99 Ardmore St (☎03/443 7882), rent out the latest off-road machines for around $40 a day ($25 per half-day) during the summer season, complete with a local map indicating prime mountain-biking routes. Less exalted specimens are available across the road at Lakeland Adventures, Main Wharf (☎03/443 7495), for $8 an hour or $35 a day; if you're sick of pedalling, they also rent out 30cc motorized bicycles for $15 an hour, $50 a day. The bargain deal is from the YHA, 181 Upton St (☎ & fax 03/443 7405), which rents out basic bikes for $10 a day to all-comers.

Buses Catch-a-Bus (☎03/477 7900) runs to Dunedin; InterCity (☎03/443 7885) stop in Wanaka on the Queenstown to Franz Josef and Queenstown to Christchurch runs, and go to Dunedin; Mount Cook Landline (☎03/443 7414) mimic InterCity; and Southern Link Shuttles (☎03/358 8355) run to Christchurch.

Camping and outdoor equipment Good Sports, Dunmore St (☎03/443 7966), rents out fishing tackle ($10 a day), hiker tents ($10 a day), alpine tents ($15 a day) and a whole heap of other stuff.

Car rental Pegasus (☎03/443 8801) have cars for around $50 a day, with unlimited kilometres and insurance.

Medical treatment Wanaka Medical Centre, 39 Russell St (☎03/443 7811).
Pharmacy Wanaka Pharmacy, 33 Helwick St (☎03/443 8000).
Police Helwick St (☎03/4437272).
Post office Ardmore St (☎443 8211).
Ski rental Harris Mountain Heliskiing, 99 Ardmore St (☎0800/684 468), and Racers Edge, 99 Ardmore St (☎03/443 7882), rent out skis and snowboards for $25–42 per day, and also run a ski tuning and repair service – as does Good Sports on Dunmore St (☎03/443 7966).
Taxis Wanaka Taxis (☎03/443 7999).

Around Wanaka

Wanaka is the only town of any size within a huge area of western Central Otago, and the only resort with easy access to tramps in the **Mount Aspiring National Park**. Consequently, it's a popular base for exploring the surrounding countryside, principally the open and mountainous areas to the north and west, the Haast Pass road over to the West Coast (see p.663), and the tortuous **Cardrona Road**, the most direct route to Queenstown.

WALKS IN THE MATUKITUKI VALLEY

The 1:150,000 *Mount Aspiring National Park* map is recommended for these walks, along with DOC's *Matukituki Valley Tracks* and *Rees–Dart Track* leaflets ($1 each). The considerably more detailed 1:50,000 *Earnslaw Topomap* is better for the Cascade Saddle Route.

These walks can be tackled by relatively fit and experienced trampers; all times and distances given are one-way, and remember that any reference to the left or right bank of a river assumes you're facing downstream. The climatic differences in the park are extreme, and the half-metre of rain that falls each year in the Matukituki Valley is no indication of the six metres that fall on the western side of the park; as ever, go prepared.

RASPBERRY FLAT TO ASPIRING HUT

The popular day walk from **Raspberry Flat to Aspiring Hut** (9km; 2hr 30min–3hr; 100m ascent) starts along a four-wheel-drive track which climbs gently from the Raspberry Flat car park beside the western branch of the Matukituki River, only heading away from the river to avoid bluffs en route to Downs Creek, from where you get fabulous views up to the Rob Roy Glacier, Mount Avalanche and Mount Aspiring. Bridal Veil Falls is only a brief distraction before **Cascade Hut** (Cat 2; 4 bunks; $8), followed thirty minutes later by the relatively luxurious **Aspiring Hut** (Cat 1; 26 bunks; Nov–April $14 with gas; May–Oct $7 without), a common base camp for mountaineers off to the peaks around Mount Aspiring, which can be seen from the picture windows.

ROB ROY VALLEY

The **Rob Roy Valley Walk** (6km; 2hr 30min; 400m ascent) is shorter and steeper than the walk to Aspiring Hut but just as spectacular, striking through some magnificent alpine scenery, snowfields and glaciers. From the Raspberry Flat car park, follow the right bank of the Matukituki for fifteen minutes to a swingbridge; cross to the left bank of the Rob Roy stream, which cuts through a small gorge into the beech forest. Gradually the woods give way to alpine vegetation – and the Rob Roy glacier nosing down into the head of the valley.

ASPIRING HUT TO THE HEAD OF THE VALLEY

An excellent day out from Aspiring Hut involves exploring the headwaters of the Matukituki River to the north. The **Aspiring Hut to Pearl Flat** (4km; 1hr 30min; 100m ascent) stretch follows the still-broad river as it weaves in and out of the bush to Pearl

The Cardrona Valley

Though designated a state highway (SH89), the road through the **Cardrona Valley** from Wanaka to Queenstown is one of New Zealand's highest public roads, reaching an **altitude** of 1120m, and many consider it little more than a track. The road is closed altogether in winter; even when it's open, caravans are banned and car-rental agencies forbid travel over one unsealed twenty-kilometre section. On a fine day, however, its twists and precipitous drops present no more of a problem than any other dirt road in New Zealand. The effort expended is rewarded by a shorter if slower alternative route from Wanaka to Queenstown – 70km as against 120km by SH6 – and a drive past the detritus of the valley's gold-mining heyday.

Rumours of William Fox's unwitting discovery of gold in the Arrow River at Arrowtown in 1862 sparked a frenzy of activity. Prospectors spread far and wide, quickly moving north along the Crown Range and stumbling into the Cardrona Valley, where **gold** was discovered later that year. Five years on, the Europeans legged it to the new fields on the West Coast, leaving the dregs to Chinese immigrants, who themselves had drifted away by 1870.

Flat. From **Pearl Flat to the head of the valley** (3.5km; 1hr 30min; 250m ascent) the path follows the right bank, crosses a huge avalanche chute off the side of Mount Barff and climbs high above the river through cottonwood and into open country. Scott Rock Bivvy, marked on some maps, is little more than a sheltering rock 50m east of the river and reached by a sometimes tricky ford.

CASCADE SADDLE ROUTE

The most challenging and most satisfying of the local tramps connects the Matukituki Valley to the Rees–Dart Circuit centred on Glenorchy (see p.695), via the arduous **Cascade Saddle Route**, (4–5 days one-way) a magnificent alpine crossing with fine panoramic views of the Dart Glacier and the Barrier Range. Long stretches of exposed high country and a finishing point 150km from the start mean that the route is not one to be undertaken lightly, though it is usually possible to **send your excess gear ahead** to the Mount Cook Landline depot in Queenstown through Wanaka Travel & Booking Agency, 99 Ardmore St (☎03/443 7414; $5 per bag). For most of the year, Cascade Saddle can be negotiated without specialized mountaineering equipment, but requires sound route-finding skills, totally waterproof clothing and a compass, while a tent gives you the option of breaking the longest day by spending a night in the alpine meadows at the saddle.

The first part of the route follows the track from **Raspberry Flat to Aspiring Hut** (9km; 2hr 30min–3hr; 100m ascent – see description above). From **Aspiring Hut to Dart Hut** (13km; 8–11hr; 1350m ascent) views of Mount Aspiring improve as you rise above the tree line onto the steep tussock and snowgrass ridge above. The route is now marked by orange snow poles which lead you to a steel pylon (1835m) that marks the top of the ridge, down to Cascade Creek and across it before climbing gently to the meadows around Cascade Saddle (1500m); four to six hours so far. Non-campers will have to press on another four or five hours to the somewhat oversubscribed Dart Hut, some 500m lower down, along the upper **Dart Valley**. The initial steep descent beside snow poles is treacherous when wet, but on a warm afternoon enjoys expansive views towards the mouth of the rubble-topped Dart Glacier, where chunks of ice periodically crash into the milky river that surges beneath it. In 1914, the terminus of the glacier had crept to within a kilometre of Dart Hut, but is retreating an average of 50m a year and could all but disappear within eighty years. After following lateral moraine, rounding bluffs and fording streams, you eventually reach the **Dart Hut** (Cat 2; $8; 20 bunks; see also box on p.668), from where it is two days to Glenorchy, following either the Dart or Rees river valleys.

From Wanaka the road is sealed for the first 26km, past the Cardrona and Waiorau Nordic ski areas (see "Winter in Wanaka" box on p.706) to the few cottages and long-forgotten cemetery that make up the hamlet of **Cardrona**. Here, the *Cardrona Hotel* (see "Accommodation", p.699) stands in a state of arrested decay. Built in 1868, it survived the floods of 1878 that destroyed most of the old town, battling on until 1961. After years of neglect it was reopened in 1984, with its original facade and a completely renovated interior opening onto a great beer garden; it's now a popular watering hole for skiers in winter, and a good spot for bar and restaurant meals ($8–18) at any time.

South from here, the surfaced section ends, heralding 20km of twisting dirt road through grassy flanks of bald, mica-studded hills to a great viewpoint overlooking Queenstown and Lake Wakatipu. Here the tarmac resumes, just in time for the steep switchback down towards SH6 and Queenstown.

The Matukituki Valley and Mount Aspiring National Park

The **Matukituki Valley** is very much Wanaka's outdoor playground, a 60km tentacle reaching from the parched Otago landscapes around Lake Wanaka to the steep alpine skirts of Mount Aspiring, which at 3030m is New Zealand's highest mountain outside the Mount Cook National Park. Extensive high-country stations run sheep on the riverside meadows, briefly glimpsed by skiers bound for Treble Cone, rock climbers making for the roadside crags, Matukituki-bound kayakers, and trampers and mountaineers hot-footing it to the **Mount Aspiring National Park**.

The park, first mooted in 1935 but not created until 1964, is one of the country's largest, extending from the Haast Pass (where there are tramps around Makarora, see p.664) in the north, to the head of Lake Wakatipu (where the Rees–Dart Track and parts of the Routeburn track fall within its bounds, see p.694) in the south. The pyramidal Mount Aspiring undoubtedly forms the centrepiece of the park, rising with classical beauty over the ice-smoothed, broad valleys and creaking glaciers. It was first climbed in 1909 using heavy hemp rope and none of the modern climbing hardware used by today's mountaineers, who still treat the mountain as one of the grails of Kiwi mountaineering ambition. Travelling along Mount Aspiring Road beside the Matukituki River, the peak hoves into view just outside Wanaka, and remains tantalizingly present all the way to the **Raspberry Flat**, where a car park and public toilets mark the start of a number of magnificent tramps (see box on p.708) into the heart of the park.

Buses operated by Mount Aspiring Express (Nov–April daily; $25 one-way, $40 return; book through Wanaka Travel & Booking Agency or on ☎03/443 8802) run 55km along Mount Aspiring Road to the national park's main trailhead at Raspberry Creek; Matukituki Services (☎03/443 7980) run a similar but less frequent operation. Both also run a charter service, which gives you greater flexibility and works out cheaper if you can get at least five people together.

Towards the West Coast: Lake Hawea and Hawea

Mountain-backed **Lake Hawea**, immediately east of Lake Wanaka, receives a fraction of the attention of its western neighbour. With its milky, azure waters this might seem surprising, but much of its appeal was shorn away in 1958 with the completion of a small dam, which raised the lake level by twenty metres, in the process drowning the lake's beaches and gently shelving shoreline. Nevertheless, the lake is still popular with anglers intent on bagging landlocked rainbow and brown trout, and salmon. Otherwise there is little reason to spend time here – except to recharge your batteries in the peace and quiet of **HAWEA**, a village that clings to the lake's southern shore 15km northeast of Wanaka. The Lake Hawea Store (Mon–Sat 8am–7.30pm, Sun 9am–7pm), right in the centre of the village, sells one-day fishing licences ($12) and can put you in touch with local angling experts; expect to pay $300–400 a day for fly-fishing guides.

If you stay, you'll find **camping** and basic **accommodation** in the cabins of the spacious, leafy *Lake Hawea Motor Camp* (☎03/443 1767; ②–③) right by the lakeshore. The *Lake Hawea Hotel*, 1 Capell Ave (☎03/443 1224, fax 443 1024; dorms ①, motel units ④), is optimally sited for uninterrupted lake and mountain views; the backpacker-style lodge has pleasant four-bunk dorms complete with bedding, but inadequate self-catering facilities. There are decent, fully equipped units a kilometre east of the Hawea store at *Glenruth Lakeview Motel*, 45 Lakeview Terrace (☎03/443 1440, fax 443 1709; ④, ③ if you provide your own bedding and towels), while the best of the **B&Bs** is at 3 Bodkin St (☎03/443 1343; ④), where a couple of balconied rooms tucked atop a craft-filled A-frame boast fine mountain views.

Eating is best done in the B&Bs if that's where you are staying; otherwise, make for the substantial bar meals and beer garden at the *Lake Hawea Hotel* or the takeaway and small café at the Lake Hawea Store.

The Otago goldfields

Though Queenstown's gold-rush heritage has largely been swamped by adventure tourism, the mining past remains the main attraction of the **Otago goldfields**, a historically rich but now almost deserted region covering much of the country east from Arrowtown to the coast at Dunedin. This barren, rugged and peculiarly beautiful high-country hinterland is where, from the 1860s to the end of the century, gold was panned from the streambeds, dredged from the deeper rivers, and eventually mined and blasted from the land. Small-time panners still extract a little "colour" from the streams and a few commercial mines still operate, but for the most part the gold has turned its back on the country it built. The landscape is now littered with abandoned mines, perilous shafts and scattered bits of mysterious-looking machinery, while shingle banks in the rivers occasionally reveal the remains of huge dredges, or the detritus of hare-brained schemes to divert the waters and reveal the gold-bearing riverbed.

Towns which boomed in the 1860s were mostly moribund by the early years of the twentieth century, but a few either struggled on as way-stations between the coast and the farmlands of the interior, or developed into prosperous service towns for the stone-fruit orchards which thrive in the region's crisp, dry winters and searingly hot summers. A shortage of water to irrigate these fertile lands was subsequently addressed by building a couple of controversial hydro dams on the Clutha River, drowning many of the orchards in the process.

Many of the significant locales in the gold country fall under the auspices of DOC's **Otago Goldfields Park**, which encompasses a score of diverse sites scattered throughout the region – all of which are listed in the free *Otago Goldfields Heritage Highway* leaflet, available from local visitor centres. When out exploring, **take precautions**: deep shafts and heavy machinery are potentially hazardous, so at recognized sites, keep to marked paths and heed safety barriers; elsewhere tread extremely carefully.

Arrowtown is far and away the most visited of the gold towns, easily accessible from Queenstown and a good base for exploring the nearby ghost town of Macetown. The reconstructed nineteenth-century boom town at **Cromwell** probably won't delay you long, but the town is a good jumping-off point for the former mining settlements of **Bannockburn** and **Bendigo**. Cromwell's Lake Dunstan is actually a reservoir backed up behind a dam, adjacent to the attractively sited town of **Clyde**. **Alexandra** acts mainly a service town at the fork of two roads penetrating deep into the less-visited part of the gold county: SH85 heads northeast skirting the dilapidated former gold towns of **St**

Bathan's and Naseby on the way to workaday Ranfurly, and the only accessible working mine at Macraes Flat; while SH8 dives southeast towards the coast through dull Roxburgh and Lawrence, where the gold rush initially started.

Major bus and shuttle companies run fairly regular services along SH8 between Queenstown and Dunedin, but to really explore this region you need your own vehicle.

Some history

New Zealand's greatest gold rush kicked off in 1861 when Gabriel Read, an Australian who had previously worked the Californian fields, unearthed flakes of the precious metal beside the Tuapeka River, south of Lawrence. Within weeks Dunedin had all but emptied and thousands were camping out on the **Tuapeka Goldfield** around Gabriels Gully. The excitement at Tuapeka soon fizzled out, although by the winter of 1862 Californian prospectors Horatio Hartley and Christopher Reilly teased their first flakes out of the Clutha River, bagging a 40kg haul in three months. This sparked off an even greater gold rush, this time centred on Cromwell, which mushroomed as wagon trains made their way over the rough muddy trails from the coast into the interior. Tent cities sprung up, soon to be replaced by more permanent buildings as merchants moved in founding banks, hotels, shops, bars and brothels. Later in 1862, Thomas Arthur and Harry Redfern struck lucky at what is now Arthur's Point on the Shotover River, sparking a mass exodus for the fresh fields of what soon became known as "the richest river

---

GOLD FROM DIRT

The classic image of the felt-hatted old-timer **panning** merrily beside a stream is only part of the story of gold extraction, but it's a true enough depiction of the first couple of years of the Otago gold rush. Initially all a miner needed was a pick and shovel, a pan, and preferably a special wooden box known as a "rocker" for washing the alluvial gravel. Periodic droughts lowered the river levels to reveal unworked banks, but as the easily accessible gravel beds were worked out, all manner of ingenious schemes were devised to gain access to fresh raw material. The most common technique was to divert the river, and some far-fetched schemes were hatched, especially on the Shotover River: steel sheets were driven into the river beds with some success, landslides induced to temporarily dam the flow, and a tunnel was bored through a bluff.

When pickings got thinner miners turned their attentions to the more tightly packed banks of the gorges. Hillside dams were constructed and water was piped under pressure to **sluicing** guns that blasted the auriferous gravel free, ready for processing either by traditional hand-panning or its mechanical equivalent, where "riffle plates" caught the fine gravel and carpet-like matting trapped the fine flakes of gold. Eventually the scale of these operations put individual miners out of business and many pressed on to fresh fields.

To get at otherwise inaccessible gravel stock, larger companies began building **gold dredges**, great clanking behemoths anchored to the riverbanks but floating free on the river. Buckets scooped out the river bottom, processed the gravel and spat the "tailings" out of the back to pile up along the riversides.

Otago's alluvial gold starts its life underground embedded in reefs of quartz, and when economic returns from the rivers waned, miners sought the mother lode. **Reef quartz mining** required a considerable investment in machinery and whole towns sprang up to tunnel, hack out the ore and haul it on sledges to the stamper batteries. Here, a series of water-driven (and later steam-powered) hammers would pulverize the rock, which was then passed over copper plates smeared with mercury, and onto gold-catching blankets, before the remains were washed into the berdan – a special kind of cast iron bowl. Gold was then separated from the mercury, a process subsequently made more efficient with the use of cyanide.

in the world". Miners flooded into Skipper's Canyon, but a few months later some of the heat was taken from its banks by discoveries on the Fox River near Arrowtown, the last of the major gold towns to be built and still the best preserved. Within a few years, returns had dwindled and many headed off to investigate reports of richer finds on the West Coast. As fortunes waned and traders saw their profits diminishing, Chinese miners were co-opted to pick over the tailings (discarded bits of rock and gravel) left behind by Europeans, and were occasionally allowed to work unwanted claims.

Though the boom and bust cycle was as rapid here as in gold country elsewhere, some form of mining continued for the best part of forty years, and the profits fuelled a South Island economy which, for a time at least, dominated New Zealand's exchequer. Dunedin's economy boomed, and the golden bounty funded the majority of that city's grand civic buildings.

Many claims were eventually abandoned not for lack of gold but because of harsh winters, famine, war, a dip in the gold price, lack of sluicing water, or just disinterest. Although returns are far from spectacular, there are still people out there eking out a living from gold-mining; stakes are still claimed and you'll find small- and medium-scale operations all over the province. There's very little appliance of science and despite a fair bit of sophisticated machinery, these are very much backyard operations where instinct counts for much and fancy mining theories not at all. Bigger capital-intensive companies occasionally gauge the area's potential, and as one mining engineer pithily put it, "there's still a shitload of gold out there".

Arrowtown

The former gold-rush settlement of **ARROWTOWN** seems perched on the brink of tour-bus hell as groups swarm around the sheepskin, greenstone and gold of its souvenir shops. But Arrowtown manages to retain the spirit of a living community, with the grocers' shops, pubs and post office fitfully coexisting alongside the gift-wrapped centre. The best way to appreciate Arrowtown is to linger on after the Queenstown-based day-trippers have gone, leaving behind a peaceful farming town at the confluence of the Arrow River and Bush Creek. The sheltering hills give Arrowtown parched summers and snowy winters, thrown into sharp relief by autumn, when the deciduous trees planted by the mining community cast golden shadows on a central knot of picturesque miners' cottages.

Arrowtown's permanent population is only around 1200 but in summer, when holiday homes are full and tourists arrive in force, it comes close to regaining its 7000-strong peak attained during the **gold rush**. There is some debate as to whether American William Fox was actually the first to discover alluvial gold in the Arrow River in 1862, but there is no doubt that he dominated proceedings hereabouts, managing to keep the find secret while he recovered over 100kg of gold. Jealous prospectors tried to follow him to the lode, but he gave them the slip, on one occasion leaving his tent and provisions behind in the middle of the night. The town subsequently bore his name until Foxes gave way to Arrowtown. The eponymous river became known as the richest for its size in the world – a reputation which drew Chinese miners, who lived in the now partly restored **Arrowtown Chinese Settlement**, and enticed prospectors to the surrounding hills, where brothers Charley and John Mace set up **Macetown**, now an appealing ghost town.

As prospectors pushed further up the Arrow and Bush Creek, they began to populate **the valleys**; scattered communities sprang up along the banks, but were abandoned just as suddenly, leaving telltale poplar, rowan and willows to be reclaimed by nature. Where settlers' cottages once stood, **fruit** trees have colonized the riverbanks, and in autumn apples, pears and plums weigh down the branches, and bushes of blackberry, blackcurrant, gooseberry, raspberry and elderberry become rampant. There are few specific sights, but you can easily spend a lazy afternoon gorging on fruit and trying to identify the overgrown sites of houses. The surrounding hills are speckled with **rose bushes**: according to folklore, these were planted by miners seeking vitamin C (rosehips are one of the richest sources); others contend that they were planted primarily for their root systems, which could be fashioned into briar pipes.

Arrival and information

Three **buses** run from Queenstown to Arrowtown, both departing from the Top of the Mall on Camp Street in Queenstown and stopping outside the library on Buckingham Street in Arrowtown. The **scheduled** Arrow Express (3–4 daily; June & July Mon–Fri only; 25min; $4; ☎03/442 1535) runs via Frankton and Queenstown airport. The Double Decker uses a red London bus to operate Queenstown-based **tours** (daily 10am & 2pm; 2hr 30min; $25; ☎03/442 6067), visiting the Kawarau bungy bridge and the Gibbston winery en route and spending an hour in Arrowtown. In addition, Circuit Shuttles (5 daily; ☎025/449 314) do a circuit around the Shotover Jet, Arrowtown, the Kawarau Bungy Bridge, Gibbston Winery and Queenstown, allowing you to get on and off as often as you like in a day for $25; if you want more time to explore, catch the morning bus out and the afternoon one back.

Arrowtown has no visitor centre, but there is a useful **information** counter in the foyer of the Lakes District Museum at 49 Buckingham St (daily 9am–5pm; ☎03/442 1824), where you can pick up the *Historic Arrowtown* leaflet and buy the informative *Arrowtown Chinese Settlement* booklet ($2.50).

Accommodation

To see Arrowtown without the maddening crowd, you really need to **stay** the night; happily, there's plenty of accommodation, much of it especially affordable for lone travellers, with single rooms just over half the price of doubles.

HOTELS AND MOTELS

Golden View Motel, 48 Adamson Drive (☎ & fax 03/442 1833). Fairly standard motel with well-equipped rooms, an outdoor pool and mountain bikes to rent for $6 an hour. ④.

Millbrook Resort, Malaghans Rd, on the outskirts of town (☎03/441 7000 & 0800/800 604, fax 442 1145). A fledgling 18-hole golf course, several bars and restaurants, and luxury accommodation in suites and chalets make this one of New Zealand's more exclusive resort complexes – and account for its popularity with Queenstown tour groups. ⑨.

Settlers Motel, 22 Hertford St (☎ & fax 03/442 1734). New lace-and-Laura Ashley place that has earned numerous plaudits. Studios and one- and two-bedroom units are all fitted out to a high standard, with decorations based on traditional pioneer motifs, and rates include continental breakfast. ⑤.

Viking Lodge Motel, 21 Inverness Crescent (☎ & fax 03/442 1765). One of Arrowtown's best-value motels, featuring an outdoor pool and a cluster of one- and two-bedroom A-frame chalets with well-equipped kitchens and VCRs. ④.

B&BS AND HOMESTAYS

Caernarvon Homestay, 25 Caernarvon St (☎03/442 1227). The lowest-priced and one of the best of Arrowtown's homestays, in a large modern house with two attractive rooms – one en suite, the other with French windows opening onto the garden. Dinner by arrangement ($25). ④.

Anne & Arthur Gormack, 18 Stafford St (☎03/442 1747). Comfortable, well-appointed rooms in a spacious modern homestay five minutes' walk from the town centre, with a pool, badminton court and long views over the Arrow Basin. Evening meals ($20) available on request. ⑤.

Polly-Anna Cottages, 43 Bedford St (☎03/442 1347). Homestay in a tidily restored hundred-year-old miner's cottage with a sun deck and manicured lawns; close to the centre. ④.

Postmasters Guest House, 50 Buckingham St (☎ & fax 03/442 0272). An appealing, friendly and very central B&B in the former postmaster's residence of 1907, with two cosy rooms in the house (one en suite) and a separate en-suite studio. An evening glass of wine and a continental breakfast are included; a cooked breakfast is available for an extra $12. Rooms ④, studio ⑤.

Speargrass Lodge, Speargrass Flat Rd, 5km from Arrowtown (☎ & fax 03/442 1417). One of the most attractive, spacious and luxurious country B&Bs around, surrounded by landscaped lawns and mature exotic trees. Simply decorated rooms are all en suite and there's free use of mountain bikes and a dinghy on nearby Lake Hayes. Breakfast is included, dinner costs $28. ⑥.

HOSTELS AND CAMPSITES

Arrowtown Camping Ground, 11 Suffolk St (☎& fax 03/442 1876). Marginally the handiest and largest of the town's two campsites with tent ($8) and powered sites ($9), standard cabins (②), showers available to non-guests ($3) and a tennis court.

Arrowtown Caravan Park, 47 Devon St (☎03/442 1838). Smaller and more appealing of the two campsites, about ten minutes' walk from the centre, with tent ($8) and powered sites ($9).

Royal Oak Hotel, 46 Buckingham St (☎03/442 1700). Recently renovated old hotel in the centre of town with well-priced beds in simple rooms sharing facilities. Soap and towels are provided and there's a reduction if you provide your own bedding. Dorms ①, rooms ②.

The Town

Twin rows of sycamores and oaks planted in 1867 have grown to overshadow the tiny miners' cottages along the photogenic **Avenue of Trees**, Arrowtown's most recognizable image. Most of the sixty or so cottages were built towards the end of the nineteenth century and they're unusually small and close together, the chronic lack of timber undoubtedly being a factor.

A visit to the informative nearby Lakes District Museum (see below) is probably the best preparation for a stroll around the **Arrowtown Chinese Settlement** (part of the Otago Goldfields Park; unrestricted entry). This string of heavily restored buildings hugging a narrow willow-draped section of Bush Creek at the western end of Buckingham Street is easily the best-preserved of New Zealand's Chinese communities, and provides an insight into a fascinating, if shameful, episode in the country's history (see box on p.716). Many of the buildings were originally built as temporary retreats from peripatetic prospecting and to provide shelter during the harsh winters, only becoming permanent homes as miners aged. With tin, sod and timber the principal building materials, little was left standing when an archeological dig was begun in 1983, and most of the dwellings languish in a state of graceful decay. Some schist, mortar and corrugated-iron buildings fared rather better and five of these have been restored. The best is **Ah-Lum's Store**, built in typical Canton delta style in 1883 for Wong Hop Lee and leased from 1909 to 1927 to Ah-Lum, one of the pillars of the Chinese community in its later years. By this time integration was making inroads: Ah-Lum sold European as well as Chinese goods, and operated an opium den and bank. Wood panelling divides the store into low-roofed rooms with mezzanine areas above, perhaps used for opium smoking. Beyond that it is mostly stone plinths and chimney breasts fleetingly brought back to life by interpretation panels.

Artefacts found during the 1983 Chinese Settlement dig are displayed inside the former BNZ building of 1875 that now operates as the **Lakes District Museum**, 49 Buckingham St (daily 9am–5pm; $4), a bits and bobs museum which nevertheless succeeds in bringing local history to life. Not surprisingly, it mainly covers the lives of the gold-miners and their families, with a particular emphasis on the Chinese community and the archeological excavations. There's also a feature on opium smoking, which remained legal in New Zealand until 1901, some twenty years after games of chance – fantan and pakapoo – were proscribed. Technophiles also gets a look in, with displays on the quartz-reef mining used at Macetown and on the country's earliest hydro scheme, which once supplied mining communities in Skippers and Macetown with power.

ARROWTOWN'S HIDDEN CHINESE HISTORY

The initial wave of miners who came to Arrowtown in the early 1860s were fortune-seekers intent on a fast buck. When gold was discovered on the West Coast, most of them hot-footed it to Greymouth or Hokitika, leaving a much-depleted community that lacked the economic wherewithal to support the businesses which had mushroomed around the mining communities.

The solution, as it had been ten years earlier on the Victorian goldfields of Bendigo and Ballarat in Australia, was to import **Chinese labour**. The first Chinese, who principally came from the Canton delta region of Kwangtung (now known as Guangdong), arrived in Otago in 1866, their number reaching 5000 by 1870. The community settled along Bush Creek, its **segregation** from the main settlement symptomatic of the inherent racism of the time – something which also manifested itself in working practices that forced the Chinese to pick over abandoned mining claims and work the tailings of European miners. Even Chinese employed on municipal projects such as the Presbyterian church were paid only half the wages paid to Europeans doing the same job.

A ray of light is cast amid the prevailing bigotry by contemporary newspaper reports, which suggest that many citizens found the Chinese conduct of their business "upright and straightforward" and their demeanour "orderly and sober" – perhaps surprisingly in what was an almost entirely male community. Most came with starry-eyed dreams of earning their fortune and returning home so, initially at least, few brought their **families**; a process of chain migration later brought wives, children and then members of the extended family. Few realized their dreams, but around ninety percent did return home, many in a box, driven into an early grave by overwork and poor living conditions. Many more were driven out in the early 1880s when recession brought racial jealousies to a head, resulting in the enactment of a punitive poll tax on foreign residents. There was little workable gold by this time and those Chinese who stayed mostly became market gardeners or merchants and drifted away, mainly to Auckland, though the Arrowtown community remained viable into the 1920s. Once the Chinese had left or died, the Bush Creek settlement was **abandoned** and largely destroyed by repeated flooding.

Around Arrowtown: Macetown

As gold fever swept through Otago in the early 1860s, prospectors fanned out, clawing their way up every creek and gully in search of a flash in the pan. In 1862, alluvial gold was found at Twelve Mile, sparking the rush to what later became known as **Macetown** (part of the Otago Goldfields Park; unrestricted entry), now a ghost town of three buildings and a popular destination for mountain bikers, horse trekkers and trampers (see box on p.717). On first acquaintance, it isn't a massively exciting place, but the grassy plateau makes a great free camping spot, sheltered by low stone walls and willow, sycamore and apple trees. The only facilities are long-drop toilets and river water, but walking in here with tent and provisions, and spending a day or two exploring the old mines and grubstake claims, is the best way to experience the place's unique atmosphere.

Macetown's story is one of boom and bust: at its peak, it boasted a couple of hotels, a post office and a school; but when the gold ran out, it couldn't fall back on farming in the way that Arrowtown and Queenstown did and, like Skippers, it died. All that remains of the town itself are a couple of stone buildings – the restored schoolmaster's house and the bakery – and a smattering of wooden shacks. The surrounding creeks and gullies are littered with the twisted and rusting remains of gold batteries, making a fruitful hunting ground for industrial archeology fanatics; the area is covered in some detail in the *Macetown and the Arrow Gorge* booklet ($3, available from the Lakes District Museum in Arrowtown).

THE ARROWTOWN–MACETOWN CIRCUIT TRAMP

The 16km four-wheel-drive road up the Arrow Creek from Arrowtown to Macetown is the district's premier biking and trekking route, but walkers have the edge by being able to include the road as part of the fairly strenuous, full-day **Arrowtown–Macetown Circuit** (8hr; 32km).

The walk is best done in the months from **Christmas to Easter**, after the winter snows have melted and the swollen Arrow River has subsided a little, making the 22 river crossings on the Arrow Creek a little easier – though even in summer, access can be problematic after rain. The *Macetown and the Arrow Gorge* booklet makes a good companion for the route, interpreting sights along the way.

The walk starts by the confluence of the Arrow River and Bush Creek, following the northern bank of the latter westwards, then skirting the base of German Hill and branching up the Sawtooth Gully. The gully emerges through open hill country to Eichardt's Flat, a terrace named after a local farmer and brother of the Queenstown hotelier. At this point, about an hour out of Arrowtown, you can pursue the **Sawpit Gully variation** east down Sawpit Gully to meet the Arrow River road and Arrowtown, thus making a two- to three-hour circuit.

From the Sawpit Gully junction, the Macetown path contours gradually around to the **Big Hill** saddle, with its expansive views back to Lake Hayes and the Remarkables. The route then drops steeply towards Eight Mile Creek, the path becoming indistinct – marked by infrequent poles – as it traverses soggy and potentially ankle-twisting country. After three to four hours, you stumble across the Arrow Creek road, just a couple of kilometres short of **Macetown**.

When you've had your fill of Macetown, follow the Arrow Creek road back to Arrowtown, occasionally diverting on to paths that run parallel to the road for respite from the dust.

Macetown is a full-day (or overnight, if you want to camp among the ruins) outing either on foot (see box above), by **mountain bike** (you'll need to rent one from Queenstown unless you have your own), or on **horseback** from Meadow Park Equestrian Centre on Malaghans Road, 3km west of Arrowtown (☎03/442 1937); full-day treks from Meadow Park to Macetown ($98) are really only for experienced riders, though beginners can take a preliminary lesson for an additional $35, or go for the less arduous Arrow Trek ($45; 1hr). Outback Tours (4–5hr; $65; ☎03/442 7386) cover the Arrowtown–Macetown route in **four-wheel-drives**.

Eating and entertainment

Sadly, Arrowtown's range of eating establishments doesn't match the choice of accommodation. If you're at a homestay, then **eating in** may well be your best bet. Otherwise, you could try the **bar meals** at one of the pubs; or settle for a snack from the Arrowtown Bakery, in the Ballarat Arcade on Buckingham Street, which produces a prodigious range of tasty pies and wonderful **breads** – from Italian and sourdough to gluten-free and organic; try their "football", a kind of soft-bread calzone. The best **lunches** in town can be had at the *Wind in the Willows*, in Ramshaw Lane: this combined bookshop and licensed café does pizza, quiche, soup, cakes and good coffee, all at decent prices.

More refined **dining** experiences await at the *Gibbston Valley Winery*, 14km away on SH6 (☎03/442 6910), whose fine restaurant is open for lunch and snacks throughout the day; or splash out at one of the **swanky restaurants** in the *Millbrook Resort* complex on Malaghans Road (☎03/441 7000), a few kilometres outside Arrowtown. Far and away the best (and most expensive) of the town's restaurants, though, is *The Stables*, 28 Buckingham St (☎03/442 1818; closed Mon), where you can feast on classy bistro-style dishes, such as Thai chicken or stuffed capsicum, and soak up the atmosphere of this beautiful old stone building.

Finally, if your visit is during the week leading up to Easter, you can partake in the **Autumn Festival** (enquiries on ☎03/442 1211), with all manner of historic walks, street theatre and hoe-downs, much of it free.

Cromwell and around

East of Arrowtown, SH6 runs for 40km through the scenic Kawarau Gorge, past the Kawarau Gorge Mining Centre (see below), to **CROMWELL**, a deracinated town with its gold-mining roots waterlogged below the shimmering surface of the **Lake Dunstan** reservoir. Formed by the Clyde Dam 20km downstream (see p.720), Lake Dunstan swamped much of Cromwell's historic core, and the present-day town centre is uninspringly modern. Civic boosters hope that the crisp, dry climate and inchoate waterborne leisure facilities will lure visitors, but on current evidence they don't have a hope: for the moment Cromwell is a soulless place only marginally viable as a base for exploring the gold diggings hereabouts.

Soon after Hartley and Reilly's 1862 discovery of **gold** beside the Clutha River, a settlement sprouted at "The Junction" at the fork of the Kawarau and Clutha rivers. Local stories tell that it was later renamed when a government survey party dubbed it Cromwell to spite local Irish immigrant workers. Miners low on provisions planted the first fruit trees in the region, little expecting that Cromwell would become the centre of the Otago orchard belt. Its location, further from the sea than any other town in New Zealand, dictates an extreme temperature range – hot and arid in summer with still, cool, dry winters – making it perfect for growing dripping, toothsome **stone fruit**.

Tour buses disgorge their load at the dozen or so fruit stalls beside SH8, which skirts Cromwell passing the giant glass fibre fruity confection by The Mall. The combined visitor centre (see below) and **museum** (donations welcome) is packed full of gold-mining memorabilia, together with material on the construction of Clyde Dam. Free leaflets outline the self-guided **Cromwell Tour**, mind-numbingly dull but for the section around **Old Cromwell Town** (unrestricted entry), a kind of historic reserve on Melmore Terrace, where Lake Dunstan now laps the old shopfronts. In the mid-1970s when the Clyde Dam was planned and the death knell sounded for the heart of old Cromwell, the preservation instinct kicked in, but in the wrong gear. Cromwell missed a perfect opportunity to preserve an 1870s town as it was in the 1970s and opted instead for a dull "Historic Town" re-creation. A dozen buildings due to be submerged were dismantled stone by stone and are now being rebuilt on the water's edge, ready to house tacky tourist shops. **Aquatic activities** are still in their infancy here, currently geared only towards people bringing their own tackle.

Practicalities

Queenstown- or Wanaka-bound **bus** travellers may well have to change in Cromwell, using the stop outside the petrol station on Murray Terrace right by The Mall, Cromwell's civic centre and home to the **visitor centre** (daily 10am–4pm; ☎03/445 0212, fax 445 1649), which provides an abundance of leaflets on the gold region.

The cheapest **place to stay** is at the *Cromwell Holiday Park*, Alpha Street (☎ & fax 03/445 0164), which has tent sites for $16, and a range of cabins and flats (②–③). Across town, there's the low-cost *Anderson Park Lodge*, Gair Avenue (☎03/445 0321; ③–④), and for a few dollars more you can stay by the water at *Gateway Lakeside Motel*, Alpha Street (☎03/445 0385, fax 445 1855; ④). About the only homestay around is at *Cottage Gardens*, Alpha Street (☎03/445 0628; ④), surrounded by an orchard, yet right in town.

The Mall has several places for reasonable **meals**, though *The Ferryman Family Restaurant and Bar* (☎03/445 0607) on Melrose Terrace in "Old Cromwell Town" has more atmosphere.

Around Cromwell

The appropriate response to the lack of diversions in Cromwell is to get out and explore the remains of the gold country diggings. Hype is reserved for the **Kawarau Gorge Mining Centre** (daily 9am–5.30pm; $14; ☎03/445 1038), approached by footbridge over the brooding Kawarau 7km west of Cromwell on SH6. The extensive site occupies a long-standing though not especially lucrative alluvial mining site where ground-sluicing eventually gave way to Californian-style water jets used to loosen the shingle beds. Museum pieces are stations on a self-guided tour, or you can view the lot on gentle guided horseback rides ($30). Though this was an authentic site, there is an overriding staginess about the whole affair; the stamper battery has been brought in, a turbine was recovered from the river before Lake Dunstan filled and the Chinese Village was constructed as a film set in the early 1990s. As well as the usual opportunity to extract a flake or two you can ride the flying-fox over the gorge ($5), or sample the only Otago-based jetboat ride which actually negotiates rapids: Goldfields Jet ($60; ☎03/445 1038), which runs thirty-minute trips on the Kawarau just below the site. A short distance upstream from the Goldfields site the small **Roaring Meg** power station marks both an important rapid occasionally run by rafters, sledgers and river surfers, and the "**natural bridge**", a point where the river narrows into a twisting gorge below cliffs which almost touch. Maori moa hunters and nineteenth-century gold men used the narrows as their main crossing point until ferries and bridges were constructed elsewhere.

Dedicated ruin-hounds should call in at the visitor centre in Cromwell and pick up the *Cromwell and District: Guide to Walks and Outings* leaflet which details minor gold sites within a few minutes' drive of Cromwell. Pioneering spirits can head out to remote clusters of cottage foundations such as those in the Carrick Range or the Nevis Valley (both south of Cromwell), but for most the best bet is **BANNOCKBURN**, a scattered hamlet 9km southwest of Cromwell which has the *Cairnmuir Camp* (☎03/445 0164) down by Lake Dunstan and the *Bannockburn Hotel*. Once home to two thousand people, this tortured landscape now serves to illustrate the effect of gold-mining operations on the landscape. A two-hour **self-guided trail** (unrestricted entry except for lambing season, Aug 20 to Oct 20) starts 1.5km along Felton road and weaves around huts, tailraces sluicing and tunnelling operations following numbered stakes.

If venturing slightly further afield, consider the quartz-mining district of **BENDIGO**, 15km north of Cromwell towards the Lindis Pass, and its acolytes Logantown and Welshtown. None comprises much more than a few scattered remains and deep mine shafts, but a (careful) amble among the ruins makes a fine way to pass a summer evening.

Clyde

SH8 cuts southeast from Cromwell through 20km of the bleak and windswept **Cromwell Gorge**, hugging the banks of Lake Dunstan through what used to be New Zealand's most fertile apricot growing country. The orchards are now all submerged below the waters of the lake, which are held back by the dam at **CLYDE**. This is a tiny but beautifully situated town huddled beside the deep-green Clutha River, its streets lined with ornate stone buildings and simple cottages left over from the gold-mining days of the 1860s. Originally known as Dunstan, the town sprang up just downriver from the spot where Hartley and Reilly made their big find in 1862. As tens of thousands of fortune-seekers flooded in from Dunedin and Lawrence, it quickly became the centre of the Dunstan goldfields, but by 1864 waning fortunes and swift river currents forced out the miners in favour of river dredges.

Since the mid-1980s, the town has been dominated by the giant grey hydroelectric **Clyde Dam**, 1km north of town on SH8, which apart from power generation, provides water for irrigation. Initially controversial, the dam is nevertheless considered something of an engineering marvel, with special "slip joints" providing the dam wall with flexibility in case of earth tremors. The Dunstan Information Centre (see "Practicalities" below) is stacked with displays and audio-visual presentations on the topic, and is the starting point for free hour-long **tours** (daily 11am & 1pm, extra tours Dec 26–Jan 31; bookings essential all year, ☎03/449 2056) around the dam and power station.

Clyde's other attractions are limited to the panoramic views from the **Clyde Lookout** hill (500m from town; 30min walk) and three small but well-kept museums within easy walking distance of one another. The 1864 stone courthouse on Blyth Street now operates as the **Clyde Museum** (Tues–Sun 2–4pm or by arrangement; $1; ☎03/449 2092), worth a peek for its intriguing coverage of Clyde's Great Gold Robbery of 1870. One George Rennie made off with £13,000 in bullion and banknotes, but his horse was so weighed down with the gold that he left a trail of bags hidden behind rocks at intervals. Unfortunately the co-conspirator for whom this trail had been intended had already ratted on Rennie to the police, and the ill-fated villain was easily tracked down and arrested. The **Briar Herb Factory Complex**, corner of Fraser Street and Fache Street (Tues–Sun 2–4pm; $2), was established in the 1930s as New Zealand's first herb factory, and thrived for several decades, making use of the common thyme which still grows wild hereabouts, with entire hillsides flowering purple throughout November. The factory closed in the 1970s but lives on as an exhibition space, housing well maintained displays of drying trays, presses and home-made machines used for processing the herbs. Other parts of the factory are given over to horse-drawn vehicles, a rabbiter's hut and an early hospital full of ghoulish medical instruments. The former Clyde Railway Station next door houses the **Stationary Engine Museum** (Sat & Sun 2–4pm; $1), enabling rail fanatics to pore over its varied collection of well kept locomotives.

Practicalities

Pre-booked InterCity and various shuttle **buses** stop in Clyde on demand, pulling up outside the Clyde Food Centre on the main Sunderland Street, just a short walk from the **Dunstan visitor centre**, on the corner of Blyth Street and Fraser Street (daily 10am–4pm; ☎03/449 2056). Despite its small size, Clyde does boast a couple of good **places to stay and eat** and you may prefer its easy charm to the larger, more suburban Alexandra (see p.721). *Dunstan House B&B*, 29 Sunderland St (☎03/449 2701; ④), a fine house dating from 1900, offers a wraparound verandah on the first floor, spacious comfortable rooms, dinner by arrangement ($20) and a hearty breakfast that's also available to non-guests for $12. The relaxing and extremely atmospheric *Olivers Lodge*, 34 Sunderland St (☎03/449 2860, fax 449 2862; ⑥–⑧), has a range of individually styled luxury rooms in rustic rural-style buildings that were once part of a large general store catering for the gold-miners. There's also a pleasant campsite, *Clyde Holiday and Sporting Complex*, Whitby Street (☎03/449 2713; vans ②), surrounding a cricket ground and equipped with tent sites ($6), power sites ($7), a fully self-contained cabin and several on-site caravans, plus a swimming pool and book exchange.

Olivers also has an excellent and characterful, award-winning **restaurant** serving breakfast and wholesome lunches (both around $15) and dinners ($20–30; book ahead especially at weekends), featuring the likes of rabbit, venison and pickled walnut pie. There's also a welcoming upstairs bar and mellow live music on Friday and Saturday nights. Cheaper snacks such as bacon and brie open sandwiches and barbecue food cooked out in the garden can be obtained at the attractive *Post Office Café*, on the corner of Blyth and Matau streets, built into the former 1865 post office and with a bar serving a delicious ale, "Post Office Dark".

Alexandra and around

A huge and ugly white clockface – visible from as far away as 8km – looms out of the cliff which backs **ALEXANDRA** (affectionately known as "Alex"), 10km southeast of Clyde. A prosperous service town for the fruit-growing heartland of Central Otago, it's the largest place for some distance, and its modest clutch of sights and stark mountain scenery may well persuade you to stop. Alexandra sprang up during the 1862 gold rush, and flourished for four frenzied years before settling into decline, although the gold-dredging boom at the end of the century breathed some life back into the town.

A huge waterwheel marks Alexandra's main point of interest, the **Alexandra Museum and Art Gallery** on the corner of Walton Street and Thomson Street (Mon–Sat 11am–5pm, Sun 1–4pm; donations welcome), which houses exhibitions on the glory years of the 1890s, along with an entertaining display on the sorry tale of rabbits, which were introduced into the area in 1909 and did what rabbits do – so well that they soon became a major menace throughout the South Island. To combat the problem, the town holds an Easter Bunny Shoot every year, and hunters from all over New Zealand congregate on Good Friday to slaughter as many as they can.

In the early years, the only way across the Manuherikia River was by unstable punt, but in 1879 the town built the **Shaky Bridge**, a suspension **footbridge** – originally wide enough for wagons but since narrowed – now crossed to reach a **lookout point** (1.5km; 30min one-way) high above the town on Tucker Hill, which affords great views of the whole area.

With its long hours of hot sun, the region is slowly gaining a reputation for its wines. **Black Ridge Vineyard**, Conroys Road, 6km southwest of Alex (free tasting daily 10am–5pm; ☎ & fax 03/449 2059), produces award-winning white wines from the world's most southerly vineyard, and **William Hill Vineyard**, 2km west of Alex on Dunstan Road (tastings Sat & Sun 11am–5pm, sales daily Oct–April; ☎03/448 8436), also produces high-quality whites; pick up the free *Central Otago Wine Trail* leaflet from the visitor centre (see p.722), which locates and briefly describes the region's wineries.

Activities

Alex makes a good base from which to explore some impressive mountain ranges and the Roxburgh Gorge, either on a guided tour or under your own steam. This is a great area for **mountain biking**, with plenty of trails to tackle on your own or with a trail guide recommended by the visitor centre. You can rent a mountain bike from MCS Services, 21 Shannon St (☎03/448 8048), or Henderson Cycles, 17 Limerick St (☎03/448 8917); both charge around $15 for a half-day, $22 for a full day. Several operators run **tours** from Alex into the surrounding mountain ranges: you can go **horse trekking** in the thyme-scented hills of the Dunstan Trail (1hr; $20), with longer treks by arrangement (☎03/449 2445 evenings or 7.30–8am); on a **four-wheel drive safari** up the Dunstan Mountains, the Old Man Range or other remote gold-mining areas, with John Douglas (☎03/448 7474, or through the visitor centre; around $35 for half-day, $50 full-day), who also organizes day or night **rabbit shooting** for up to three people at a time (half-day daytime shoot $40–70, depending on numbers; full-day $65–130 per person; 3hr night-time shoot $45–80). Alternatively, the reasonably fit can try a one-day guided trip paddling a **Canadian canoe** down the Roxburgh Gorge and mountain biking back, with Central Outdoor Adventures (Oct–April; ☎03/448 6360; 3 people maximum; around $90 per person). During the winter months there's ice skating on local lakes, cross-country skiing and trips by snow **skidoo** into the mountains (for more information, contact the visitor centre).

Practicalities

InterCity **buses** drop off at the monument at the intersection of Tarbert Street and Centennial Avenue; Atomic and Southern Link **shuttles** stop at the visitor centre, while Catch-a-Bus offer a door-to-door service. The **visitor centre**, 22 Centennial Ave (Mon–Fri 9am–5pm, Sat & Sun 10am–3pm; ☎03/448 9515, fax 448 9516), has free leaflets on a number of walks in the local mountains, and the *Mountain Biking* pamphlet detailing five local trails that are open all year. You can also book here for guided four-wheel-drive tours of the surrounding rugged terrain (see "Activities", p.721).

There's plenty of low-cost **accommodation** in Alexandra, including the *Riverside*, 4 Dunorling St (☎03/448 8152; dorms ①, rooms ②), an associate YHA hostel with bikes for rent, located in a quiet spot overlooking the Clutha, a five-minute stroll from the centre of town. Among the **motels**, try the soothing *Alexandra Garden Court*, Manuherikia Road (☎03/448 8295, fax 448 8200; ④), a fifteen-minute walk from the centre, with five fully self-contained units and a swimming pool set in extensive landscaped gardens; or the slightly more central, small and friendly *Kiwi Motel*, 115 Centennial Ave (☎03/448 8258, fax 448 6201; ④). The French provincial-style *Czerny Lodge*, 2km south of town, signposted off SH8 (☎ & fax 03/448 6150; ⑤), is the luxury pick, perched high on a hill amid schist outcrops with stunning panoramic views; dinner can be arranged for an extra $50. **Campers** need to head for the *Alexandra Holiday Camp* on Manuherikia Road/SH85 (☎03/448 8297, fax 448 8294; huts ①, cabins ②), a large well kept and tree-sheltered site offering tent sites for $8, single-bed huts and cabins, as well as mountain bikes for rent; or the pleasant *Pine Lodge Holiday Camp*, 31 Ngapara Street (☎03/448 8861, fax 448 8276; tent sites $8, cabins ②, motel units ③), beside a deer park; both are fifteen minutes' walk from the centre.

The best place to **eat** in town is the licensed *Briar & Thyme*, 26 Centennial Avenue (Oct–April daily; May–Sept Tues–Sat; book for dinner ☎03/448 9189), which specializes in classy lunches like camembert and vegetable turnovers or oven-baked blue cod (around $10 each), as well as elegant dinners ($15–25), in a comfortable historic house with a wine bar. For a more intimate café/wine bar feel, try *Dandelion*, Limerick Street (closed Mon), which serves light meals (around $12) until around 11pm. The *Red Brick*, in the Supervalue car park on the corner of Limerick Street and Ennis Street, is a mellow café, licensed and open daily for a good range of lunch ($10–20) and dinner ($20–25) dishes, plus great desserts.

North of Alex: St Bathans, Naseby, Ranfurly and around

Providing you have your own transport and the time to explore, the most interesting route to the east coast from Alexandra is the SH85 to Palmerston (see p.539), a good road commonly known as "The Pigroot". It began life as the easiest route from the east coast to the Central Otago Goldfields, a more sheltered, steadier climb than the shorter but gruelling Old Dunstan Road, which crossed several mountain ranges.

Scattered on the way are a handful of old gold-mining communities, among them **St Bathans**, **Naseby** and **Ranfurly**, each worth a brief visit for their laid-back atmosphere, calm seclusion and subtle reminders of how greed transforms the land. The latter lies on the Maniototo Plain, a vast agricultural basin sheltered on all sides by barren glaciated mountains, and separating inland Central Otago from the coast.

These days the highway also provides access to a rugged route further northeast to the Waitaki Valley (see p.575), via Dansey's Pass.

St Bathans

The first place with genuine appeal is the minute yet strangely attractive former gold town of **ST BATHANS**, 80km north of Alexandra and accessed 17km along a mainly unsealed loop road from Becks. St Bathans began life as a boom town called Dunstan Creek in 1863, following a gold strike at the foot of Mount St Bathans. Within six months two or three hundred miners were working the area, and the tent town comprised twenty stores, four pubs and a bank. The population peaked at 2000, but when the gold ran out in the 1930s, everything went with it. These days it's virtually a ghost town, its buildings strung in a crooked line along a single road, with just one **pub**, the atmospheric (and haunted) 1882 *Vulcan Hotel* (daily 11am–11pm), where local farmers and the town's thirteen residents prop up the old wooden bar. The pub offers good cheap snacks and dinners (Mon–Sat till 8pm), as well as simple B&B accommodation (☎03/447 3629; ③). The prettiest thing about the area is the striking **Blue Lake** right beside the town, where mineral-rich water has flooded a crater left by the merciless sluicing of Kildare Hill, which used to be 120m high until it was entirely washed away. A short track leads from the *Vulcan* to a vantage point over the intensely azure lake, now used for water-skiing, swimming and picnics.

Naseby

The small settlement of **NASEBY**, 25km east of St Bathans and 14km off SH85, clings to the Maniototo Plain some 600m above sea level. Surrounding the town, the dark-green swathe of **Naseby Forest** stands out from the tussock-covered hills to the north and the farmland plains to the south. Managed for its exotic timber – mainly European larches, Douglas firs and pines – it is the highest forest of its kind on the South Island. A number of pleasant picnic spots and forest **walks** (750m–3km one-way; 30min–90min; or a circuit walk of 10km, 6hr) are easily accessible from Naseby, signposted throughout the forest with times, distances and destinations, and also listed in the *Naseby Forest* leaflet and map available free from the Timberlands HQ in the middle of town on Derwent Street, which also acts as a **visitor centre** (Mon–Fri 9am–4pm; ☎03/444 9995). To witness the effects of former sluicing at their most dramatic, follow the **One Tree Hill Track** (1.6km; 1hr return), starting only five minutes' walk north of the visitor centre, which snakes uphill along the eastern side of Hogburn Gully, past dramatic honey-coloured cliffs entirely carved by water; a free sheet on the walk is available from the visitor centre.

At its 4000-strong peak in 1865, Naseby was the largest gold-mining town on the Maniototo, but today numbers have dropped to around 150. It functions as a quiet holiday town in summer and the country's centre for the Scottish sport of curling (a sort of bowls on ice played on a local dam) in winter, but is little more than a collection of small houses (many of them originally built by miners from sun-dried mud brick), with a shop, a garage, a couple of hotels, a café, a great campsite and a good pub. There are also a swimming dam, an impressive ice rink for winter use, and a couple of tiny museums, both at the junction of Earne Street and Leven Street. The **Maniototo Early Settlers Museum** (Nov–April Tues–Sun 1.30–3.30pm; $2) features a large number of black-and-white photos of past residents' lives alongside a small collection of items left by Chinese miners, while the **Watchmakers Museum** (daily 10am–5pm; $1) houses the remains of an old watchmaker's shop together with displays on the local gold rush of the 1860s and 1870s. On the northwestern outskirts of town, just outside the forest boundary and about ten minutes' walk from the centre, is the **swimming dam**, a popular cooling-off spot in summer, surrounded by mature Douglas fir and larch trees. The **Maniototo Ice Rink** (May–Sept; $10 including skate rental) at the southern end of town on Channel Road is New Zealand's largest outdoor rink, and is a popular venue for skating, curling and ice hockey; curling equipment is available for rent ($6 for a stone and broom).

If you want to break your journey here, the *Ancient Briton* pub in Leven Street (☎03/444 9992; dorms ①, rooms ④) has a number of neat, good-quality motel units, a backpackers and power sites ($10), all in a quiet spot out the back. The pub serves breakfast for around $10 and hearty cheap dinners in enormous portions. There's also the *Naseby Larchview Camping Park* (☎03/444 9904; tent sites $7, powered sites $8, cabins & vans ②–③), in the forest about five minutes' walk from town. This is one of the prettiest and most tranquil campsites anywhere, surrounded by tall trees. The only café in town is the *Stables Café* on Earne Street (Oct–April daily 9am–9pm), where you can get snacks for under $10, to eat in or takeaway, and simple dinners for around $10.

Dansey's Pass

The metalled Kyeburn Diggings Road, running east out of Naseby, continues as a narrow rugged route climbing northeast across the Kakanui Mountains via **Dansey's Pass** (about 40km from Naseby), to eventually emerge in the Waitaki Valley, where SH83 gives access to Mount Cook in the west and the coast in the east. Though reasonably well maintained, the route is sometimes closed in summer and always unsafe in winter, so check in Naseby before setting out and fill up with petrol. Old gold workings are visible from the roadside, where water jets from sluices have distorted the schist and tussock landscape, leaving rock dramatically exposed. At Kyeburn Diggings, 16km from Naseby, you'll come across the charming **Dansey's Pass Coach Inn** (☎ & fax 03/444 9048; ⑤–⑥), a comfortable lodge high up in the middle of nowhere, built from local schist stone in 1862 and the only remnant of a 2000-strong gold-rush community. The stonemason was reputedly paid a pint of beer for each stone laid. The inn offers good beer and affordable food, as well as expensive modernized accommodation, which is booked up most weekends throughout the year. They also rent out mountain bikes ($8 per hour, $24 a half-day) and organize horse treks ($25 per hour). There's **budget accommodation** at the far end of the route, about 15km from the pass itself, at the small and quiet *Dansey's Pass Holiday Camp* (☎03/431 2564; tent & powered sites $7–8, cabins ②), down by the riverside.

Ranfurly, SH87 to Dunedin, and Macraes Gold-Mine

Back on SH85 and 5km beyond the Naseby turn-off lies the compact town of **RANFURLY**, the largest settlement on the Maniototo Plain, though with precious little to show for it except for a few places to stay and eat. The elegant former train station now houses the **Maniototo visitor centre**, Charlemont Street East (Oct–April Mon–Fri 10am–2pm, erratic hours at weekends; May–Sept Mon–Fri 10am–noon; ☎03/444 9719), which has a free audio-visual show on the region and pictorial displays tracing the history of the town and the Central Otago Railway. The line arrived here in 1898, making Ranfurly the railhead for the district until the last train ran in 1976. In the meantime the decline of Naseby saw Ranfurly's ascendancy as the new administrative centre of the Maniototo. In summer, anyone with a four-wheel-drive or high-clearance vehicle can set out from here to explore part of the magnificent **Old Dunstan Road** (unsafe May–Sept), the original route to the Central Otago goldfields before the Pigroot was opened. Traversing the Rock and Pillar and Lammerlaw ranges fills you with admiration for those gold prospectors who guided their horse-drawn drays and bullock wagons through some of the harshest land in the country, all for the sake of a dream. From Ranfurly head 20km south to Patearoa and from there a further 25km to Paerau (aka Styx), where a 50km section of the Old Dunstan Road begins its gruelling journey to Clarks Junction and the easier SH87 heads towards Dunedin.

You'll find a range of budget **accommodation** in Ranfurly. In the centre the large colonial *Ranfurly Lion Hotel*, on the corner of Charlemont Street East and Pery Street (☎ & fax 03/444 9140; dorms ①, rooms ③–④), offers a range of single and double rooms (some en-suite) plus a pleasant backpackers across the road. There's a bar, a good but fairly cheap restaurant, and guests get free use of a spa pool. The clean and sheltered *Ranfurly Motor Camp*, Reade Street, off Pery Street, two minutes' walk from the town centre (☎03/444 9144; tent sites $6, dorms ①, cabins ②), has a covered swimming pool. About ten minutes' walk west of the centre, in a park-like setting, is the small and quiet *Ranfurly Motel*, Davis Avenue, off Caulfield Street (☎03/444 9383; ④). Twelve kilometres east from Ranfurly and on the road to the tiny settlement of Waipiata is *Peter's Farm Hostel* (phone for directions and free pick-up from Ranfurly, ☎03/444 9083; tent sites $10, dorms ①, rooms ②), a comfortable and relaxing farm with horse treks and free use of bikes, kayaks and gold pans. The best **eating** in town is at the restaurant in the *Ranfurly Lion Hotel*, which turns out respectable roasts, burgers and salads, and even does takeaways.

At Kyeburn, 15km east of Ranfurly, the slow **route to Dunedin** (SH87) branches south off SH85 and twists through the eastern Maniototo, a barren yet scenic landscape squeezed between the towering Rock and Pillar Range and the Taieri River. Fifty kilometres south of Kyeburn you'll pass **Middlemarch**, where the **Taieri Gorge Train** sets out for a spectacular two-hour trip to Dunedin (see p.589 for details).

The most renowned of Otago's operating gold mines, the huge opencast **Macraes Gold Mine**, lies on windswept hills between Ranfurly and Palmerston and can be visited on a two-hour tour (Sept–May Sat & Sun 1.30pm; $10; bookings essential, ☎03/465 2400), which also takes in a historic reserve and a fully operational stamper battery. Tours leave from *Stanley's Hotel* at Macraes Flat, most quickly reached by following SH85 63km east from Ranfurly and cutting 17km west just before Dunback. Viewing platforms allow you to see the gold-processing plant and the earth-moving equipment at work in the mining pit, but it's not especially fascinating. Should you want to **eat or stay** in the area, the historic and cheap *Stanley's Hotel* (☎ & fax 03/465 2400; B&B ②), another schist-stone construction, has a restaurant and bar, a few rooms with shared bathrooms, and a swimming pool.

Back on SH85 it's a further 14km from Dunback to Palmerston, where SH1 heads south to Dunedin and north towards Oamaru.

Southeast along SH8: Alexandra to Dunedin, via Roxburgh

The fastest route from Alexandra to the coast is SH8, partly because it's a better road than the SH85, but also because there are fewer enticing stop-offs en route. The road follows the meandering course of the Clutha River, passing through rugged hill country between the Old Man and Lammerlaw ranges to the east, and the Knobby Blue Mountain range to the west. Along the way are a couple of mildly interesting gold towns, Roxburgh and Lawrence, both served by the major **bus** companies and **shuttles** (notably Atomic Shuttle and Catch-a-Bus) running between Queenstown or Alexandra and Dunedin.

Roxburgh and Lawrence

Thirteen kilometres south of Alexandra you pass through the ironically named **Fruitlands**, a tiny settlement where orchards were once planted in the hope that they'd flourish, only to fail and be replaced by grazing sheep. From the ridge to the west of the road you get a good view of the 27-metre-tall **Old Man Rock**, an extraordinary stone obelisk from which the Old Man Range takes its name. A characterful reminder of the gold-mining days, the roadside **Fruitlands Gallery** (daily 10am–5pm), occupies a restored stone pub of 1866 and functions as a fully licensed and BYO café exhibiting local arts and crafts.

Some 15km further on, a signposted turn-off leads to an **observation point** high above the immense **Roxburgh Dam** and power station, which, when built in 1962, was

New Zealand's most massive, and is still only pushed into second place by its cousin upriver at Clyde. From the lookout you get a great view over the shimmering turquoise of Lake Roxburgh, which backs up for over 30km.

Eight kilometres south of the dam, and hemmed in by orchards, farmland and open-cast coal mines, the bland former gold town of **ROXBURGH** occupies the flat western bank of the Clutha River at the foot of a precipitous hillside, in turn dominated by the parched Umbrella Mountains further west. Soon after the discovery of gold here in 1862, Roxburgh turned its attention to fruit growing. The vast orchards now yield bountiful crops of peaches, apricots, apples, raspberries and strawberries, all harvested by an annual influx of seasonal pickers; the season's surplus is sold from a phalanx of roadside stalls from early December through to May. Roxburgh is one of the only towns of significant size between Alexandra and Dunedin, and there are a couple of budget **places to stay**: the *Roxburgh Family Motor Camp*, 11 Teviot St (☎03/446 8093; tent sites $7, dorms ①, cabins ②), in a quiet spot near the town centre; and the central *Villa Rose*, 79 Scotland St (☎03/446 8761, after-hours ☎446 8211; dorms ①, rooms ②), a delightful backpackers in a villa equipped with dorms and several doubles.

From Roxburgh SH8 runs 24km south to **Raes Junction** (where SH90 spurs off southwest to Tapanui and Gore, see p.606), and continues 26km to **LAWRENCE**, Otago's original gold town. It's hard to believe that this sleepy farming town, with its population barely nudging 550, was once the scene of frenetic activity, as 14,000 gold-seekers scrambled to try their luck in the gold-rich Gabriels Gully, discovered by Gabriel Read on May 23, 1861 (see p.712). This short-lived boom (it was over in barely a year) is recalled in a scattering of Victorian buildings, hastily constructed in a variety of materials and styles.

The combined **visitor centre** and **Goldfields Museum** on Ross Place/SH8 (Mon–Fri 9am–4.30pm, Sat & Sun 11am–3pm; ☎03/485 9222) brings something of those heady days to life through imaginative displays, rents out gold pans ($10 per day), and dispenses information on the town. An occasionally steep road walk to **Gabriels Gully** (8.5km round trip; 2.5hr return) is signposted nearby and leads through old gold workings before returning along a ridge with broad views of the town and its surroundings. Along the way the **Pick and Shovel Monument** commemorates Read and the pioneer miners, and a noticeboard illustrates how the area would have looked in its gold-mining heyday. A climb up the steep rise of **Jacob's Ladder** gives a good view of the gully, long since filled with tailings that reach nearly 20m in depth. From here the road follows the ridge, dips into the gully once more and returns to town.

Accommodation is scarce in Lawrence save for a couple of budget options: *Oban Guest House*, 1 Oban St (☎03/485 9600; dorms ①, rooms ②), is a pleasant backpackers in a big old house; while the creekside *Gold Park Motor Camp*, 1km south of the main road on Harrington Street (☎03/485 9850; tent sites $8, cabins ②), is a fairly basic campsite with cabins in a picturesque setting. As for **eating**, your best bet is the *Coach and Horses Tavern*, in Ross Place, which has simple bistro meals, though only from Friday to Sunday.

From Lawrence it's another 33km southeast to the junction with SH1 on the east coast, which strikes north towards Dunedin or south to Balclutha (see p.602).

travel details

The following lists the direct scheduled **bus** services in the area and doesn't include the scores of tour buses which ply the Queenstown to Milford Sound route daily – see the relevant accounts for details of these.

Apart from scheduled services to the South Island's main centres, most **flights** are geared towards the lucrative Milford Sound market (see p.738), with nearly a dozen fiercely competitive companies flying out of Wanaka and Queenstown daily.

Buses

Alexandra to: Lawrence (2 daily; 1hr 40min); Queenstown (2 daily; 1hr 40min); Dunedin (2 daily; 3hr).

Arrowtown to: Queenstown (10 daily; 40min).

Lawrence to: Alexandra (2 daily; 1hr 40min); Cromwell (2 daily; 2hr 20min); Dunedin (2 daily; 1hr 30min).

Cromwell to: Alexandra (2 daily; 45min); Lawrence (2 daily; 2hr 20min); Queenstown (8 daily; 50min); Wanaka (6 daily; 45–60min).

Glenorchy to: Queenstown (3–7 daily; 1hr).

Queenstown to: Alexandra (2 daily; 1hr 40min); Arrowtown (10 daily; 40min); Christchurch (5 daily; 7hr–10hr 30min); Cromwell (8 daily; 50min); Dunedin (4 daily; 4–5hr); Franz Joseph Glacier (1 daily; 8hr); Glenorchy (3–7 daily; 1hr); Invercargill (2 daily; 3hr); Kingston (1 daily; 45min); Invercargill (1 daily; 2hr 15min); Milford Sound (2 daily; 5hr 15min); Mount Cook (3 daily; 4hr); Te Anau (3–5 daily; 2hr 15min); Wanaka (1 daily; 1hr 40min).

Wanaka to: Christchurch (2 daily; 6hr 30min); Cromwell (4 daily; 45–60min); Queenstown (1 daily; 1hr 40min).

Flights

Queenstown to: Auckland (3 daily; 2hr 30min); Christchurch (10 daily; 1hr); Milford Sound (5 daily; 35min); Mount Cook (2 daily; 40min); Te Anau (3 daily; 30min); Wanaka (3 daily; 20min).

Wanaka to: Queenstown (3 daily; 20min).

CHAPTER FOURTEEN

FIORDLAND

For all New Zealand's scenic grandeur, no single region quite matches the concentration of stupendous landscapes found in its southwestern corner. Almost the entirety of **Fiordland** falls within the generous boundaries of the Fiordland National Park, a land of superlatives, boasting New Zealand's two deepest lakes, its highest rainfall and some of the world's rarest birds. This hasn't gone unnoticed at the United Nations, which has gathered pretty much the whole region – along with the Mount Aspiring National Park and parts of south Westland and the Mount Cook area – into the **Te Wahipounamu World Heritage Area**.

The **Fiordland National Park**, New Zealand's largest, stretches from Martin's Bay, once the site of New Zealand's remotest settlement, to the southern forests of Waitutu and Preservation Inlet where early gold prospectors set up a couple of short-lived towns. The 12,500 square kilometres of the park embraces breathtaking scenery, a raw and heroic landscape with deep, icy and mountain-fringed lakes in the east and a western coastline of fourteen hairline fiords gouged out over the last two million years by glaciers creaking off the tail of the Southern Alps.

Maori legend tells how the **fiords** were formed at the hands of the great god Tu-te-rakiwhanoa (see box on p.731), while scientific explanations point to a complex underlying geology, which evolved over the last 500 million years. When thick layers of seabed sediment were compressed and heated deep within the earth's crust, hard crystalline granite, gneiss and schist were formed. As the land and sea levels rose and fell, layers of softer sandstone and limestone were overlayed; during glacial periods, great ice sheets deepened the valleys and flattened their bases to create the classic U-shape, invaded by the sea lapping at their mouths.

After a few days in the inhospitable conditions created by Fiordland's copious rainfall and pestilent **sandflies** (*namu*), you'll appreciate why there is little evidence of permanent **Maori settlement** in these parts, though they certainly spent summers hunting here and passed through in search of greenstone (*pounamu*). **Cook** was equally suspicious of Fiordland when, in 1770, he sailed up the coast on his first voyage to New Zealand. Anchorages were hard to come by: the glowering sky put him off entering Dusky Sound; slight, shifting winds hardly encouraged entry into what he dubbed Doubtful Harbour; and, uncharacteristically, he missed Milford Sound altogether.

Paradoxically, for a region that's now the preserve of hardy trampers and a few anglers, the southern fiords region was once the best-charted in the country. Cook returned in 1773, after four months battling the southern oceans, and spent five weeks in Dusky Sound. His midshipman, George Vancouver, returned in 1791, with the first bloodthirsty sealers and whalers hot on his heels. Over the mountains, **Europeans** seized, or paid a pittance for, land on the eastern shores of lake Te Anau and Manapouri for the meagre grazing it offered, while **explorers** headed for the interior. More egotistical than their seafaring kin, they conferred their own names on the passes, waterfalls and valleys they came across – Donald Sutherland lent his name to New Zealand's highest waterfall and Quentin McKinnon scaled the Mackinnon Pass (but failed to persuade cartographers to spell his name right).

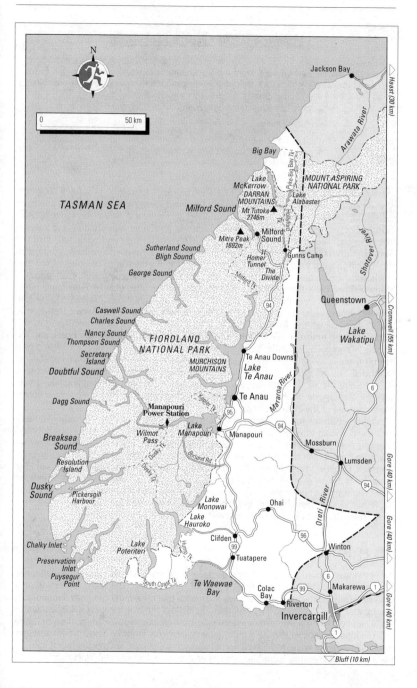

Accommodation listed in this guide has been categorized into one of nine price bands, as set out below. The rates quoted represent the **cheapest available** double or twin **room** – except for category ①, which are per-person rates for a dorm bed; fees for **tent sites** and **DOC huts** are also per-person, unless otherwise stated.

① under $20 per person	④ $60–80	⑦ $140–180
② under $40 per room	⑤ $80–100	⑧ $180–240
③ $40–60	⑥ $100–140	⑨ over $240

For more on accommodation, see p.33.

One feature of Fiordland you can't miss is the **rain**: the region is sodden for much of the year. Milford Sound is particularly favoured, being deluged with up to seven metres of rainfall a year – the second-highest in the world (after the mountains of Tahiti). Fortunately the area's settlements are in a relative rain shadow and receive less than half the precipitation of the coast. Despite its frequent soakings, **Milford Sound** is undoubtedly the most popular destination: wherever you look, ribbons of water plunge from hanging valleys directly into the fiords, where colonies of red and black coral grow and dolphins, fur seals and Fiordland crested penguins gambol. Many visitors on a flying visit from Queenstown see little else of Fiordland, but a greater sense of remoteness is gained by driving along the dramatically scenic **Milford Road** between the sound and the lakeside town of **Te Anau**. Better still, trudge here along the **Milford Track**, widely promoted as the "finest walk in the world", though others in the region – the **Hollyford Track**, the **Kepler Track** and the **Dusky Track** – constantly threaten to steal this title. A second lakeside town, **Manapouri**, is the springboard for trips to the West Arm hydroelectric power station, **Doubtful Sound** and the isolated fiords to the south. From Manapouri, the Southern Scenic Route winds through the western quarter of Southland through minor towns such as **Tuatapere**, a base for exploration of the **Waitutu Tracks** along the south-western coast of the South Island.

Almost all **buses** in Fiordland ply the corridor from Queenstown through Te Anau to Milford Sound: most are tour buses (in various guises), stopping at scenic spots and regaling passengers with a jocular commentary, but others are scheduled services that disgorge trampers at the **trailheads**. Elsewhere, services are skeletal. Drivers are well disposed to giving **lifts**, though the Milford Road from Te Anau to Milford Sound is notoriously fallow ground for hitchers and, bearing in mind the number of diversions along the way, teaming up with like-minded souls and renting a car for the day, or joining a tour bus, is a much better bet. The only **flight** you are likely to take is the scenic jaunt from Milford Sound to Queenstown.

Te Anau

The growing town of **TE ANAU** straggles along the shores of its eponymous lake, one of New Zealand's deepest and most beautiful. To the west, the lake's watery fingers claw deep into bush-cloaked mountains so remote that their most celebrated inhabitant, the takahe (see box on p.734), was thought extinct for half a century. Civilization of sorts can be found on the lake's eastern side, predominantly in Te Anau, though this is still the kind of place where the Sunday papers arrive on Monday. The town is the major way station on the route to Milford Sound and serves as base and recuperation spot for the numerous **tramps**, including several of the most famous and worthwhile in the

---

TU-TO-RAKIWHANOA AND TE NAMU

Fiordland came into being when the great god **Tu-to-Rakiwhanoa** worked with his axe to carve the rough gashes of the southern fiords around Preservation Inlet and Dusky Sound, leaving Resolution and Secretary islands where his feet stood. His technique improved further north, where he formed the more sharply defined lines of Nancy Sound, Caswell Sound and, the most famous of all, Milford Sound (Piopiotahi), the acme of Tu's skill.

After creating this spectacular landscape, Tu was visited by Te-Hine-nui-to-po, the goddess of death, who feared that the vision created by Tu was so wonderful that people may wish to live in Piopiotahi forever. To remind humans of their mortality, she liberated *namu*, or **sandflies**. The place of this liberation, Te Namu-a-Te-Hine-nui-te-po, at the end of the Milford Track, is now known as Sandfly Point. And the pesky critters have certainly had the desired effect. In 1773, when James Cook entered Dusky Sound, he was already familiar with the sandfly:

The most mischievous animal here is the small black sandfly which are exceedingly numerous and are so troublesome that they exceed everything of the kind I ever met with, wherever they light they cause swelling and such an intolerable itching that it is not possible to refrain from scratching and at last ends in ulcers like the small Pox. The almost continual rain may be reckoned a nother ilconveniency attending this Bay.

---

country. Top of most people's lists is the Milford Track, which is reached across the lake from here, as is the newer **Kepler Track**. To the north, the Milford Road passes The Key, the western end of the Routeburn, Greenstone and Caples tracks (see p.741), and beyond that there's the Hollyford Valley and its tramp to the Tasman Sea.

Arrival, information and transport

Buses either drop off around town or stop on the town's main shopping and restaurant street, known as Town Centre. The **visitor centre**, at the junction of Town Centre and Lake Front Drive (daily: Oct–March 8am–6pm; April–Sept 8.30m–5pm; ☎03/249 8900), is adjacent to the offices of **Fiordland Travel** (☎03/249 7416 & 0800/656 501), who operate a number of cruises on Lake Te Anau, Lake Manapouri and Milford Sound. The **Fiordland National Park visitor centre** is 500m south along Lake Front Drive (daily: Christmas–Feb 8am–8pm; March–Easter 8am–6pm; Easter–Oct 9am–4pm; ☎03/249 7921, fax 249 7613), and has a **Great Walks Booking Desk** (July–late April 9am–4.30pm; ☎03/249 8514, fax 249 8515), as well as plenty of general information. From here, DOC run an excellent summer programme of hour-long evening talks ($3) plus half-day ($7–35), full-day ($40–85) and evening ($30) conservation-themed trips, all of which need to be booked in advance. Bev's Tramping Gear Hire, 16 Homer St (9am–8pm; ☎03/249 7389) is the place to **rent** any **gear** you need: individual items are charged by the day, or you can save a few dollars with special packages aimed at Great Walks trampers.

Getting around Te Anau is no problem: everywhere in town is easily walkable, and there's a plethora of transport to the various trailheads. If you yearn for pedals, though, **bikes** can often be rented from your accommodation or, failing that, from Fiordland Mini Golf & Bike Hire, 7 Mokonui St (☎03/249 7435; $20–25 per day), whose tandems ($8 an hour) make exploring fun. For ranging slightly further afield (Manapouri springs to mind), rent 50cc one-person **scooters** from Solly's Red Bike Hire, 28 Mokonui St (☎03/249 8554; $47 half-day, $70 full day). These aren't robust enough for trips to Milford Sound, for which you'll need a **car**: Rent-a-Dent (☎03/249 8363) does a good 24-hour deal aimed at Milford Sound trippers, including 250km and a cruise ($83 per person for 2 people, $60 each for a group of 4).

Accommodation

Good motels string the length of Lake Front Drive, while slightly more downmarket places line Quintin Drive a block back. At more expensive places, **rates** tend to drop dramatically between June and August, and may be negotiable in the shoulder seasons (mid-April to May & Sept).

Hotels and motels

Alpenhorn Motel, 35–37 Quintin Drive (☎ & fax 03/249 7147). Well-priced concrete-block motel with full kitchen, in-house video and courtesy pick-up. ④.

Campbell Autolodge, 42–44 Lake Front Drive (☎03/249 7546, fax 249 7814). Quite attractive place with lake views and flower-bedecked one-bedroom units, each with bath, shower and full kitchen, microwave, TV and phone. Bargain rates June–Aug, rest of the year. ⑥.

Edgewater XL Motel, 52 Lake Front Drive (☎03/249 7258, fax 249 8099). Fairly basic waterfront motel with one- and two-bedroom units, full kitchen, TV, barbecue and free use of canoes. ④.

Explorer Motor Lodge, 6 Cleddau St (☎03/249 7156, fax 249 7149). These spacious studios and one-bedroom units come complete with microwaves. The decor is slightly faded and quirky, with walls at weird angles. Discounts during the off-season. ⑤.

Lakefront Lodge, 58 Lake Front Drive (☎ & fax 03/249 7728). Brand new, luxurious motel units, some with spa bath and all with every convenience, including room service. Prices drop considerably outside the Oct–April season. ⑥.

Rainbow Downs Country Lodge, Mount Yorke Rd, 8km south at Rainbow Reach (☎ & fax 03/249 8006). En-suite units with excellent views in a lovely lodge handbuilt from natural timbers and with a licensed à la carte restaurant and bar on site. Horse trekking along the Waiau River is also available. ④.

B&Bs and homestays

Arran House, 64 Quintin Drive (☎ & fax 03/249 8826). Attractive en-suite rooms and the opportunity for guests to meet up over continental breakfast. ⑤.

The Cat's Whiskers, 2 Lake Front Drive (☎ & fax 03/249 8112). Excellent and very welcoming lakeside guesthouse with three pleasantly decorated en-suite rooms, one with a bath, and all with TV and full cooked breakfast. ⑤.

House of Wood, 44 Moana Crescent (☎03/249 8404, fax 249 7676). Four tastefully decorated, modern rooms, one with bathroom, make up this fine homestay, which takes its design cues from an alpine chalet. Guests share the welcoming hosts' cosy lounge and it is only two minutes' walk from the town centre. ⑤.

Bob & Nancy Marshall, 13 Fergus Square (☎ & fax 03/249 8241). Pleasant, peaceful homestay rooms and a self-contained apartment five minutes' walk from town. Cooked breakfast is accompanied by fresh home-made bread and dinners are available by prior arrangement. Homestay ④, apartment ⑤.

Hostels and campsites

Fiordland Holiday Park, Milford Rd, 2km east (☎ & fax 03/249 7059). Small attractive site with a range of well-priced cabins and tourist flats. A courtesy bus does daily Kepler Track drop-offs and there's free gear storage. Tent & powered sites $7.50, cabins & flats ②–③.

Mountain View Holiday Park, 128 Te Anau Terrace (☎ & fax 03/249 7462). Cramped, central park that's most in demand for its fine on-site accommodation. Tent & powered sites $10, cabins & units ②–④.

Te Anau Backpackers Lodge, 48 Lake Front Drive (☎03/249 7713, fax 249 8319). Shabby former motel saved by a friendly atmosphere and small dorms, mostly with their own bathroom and kitchen. They're well set up for trampers, being five minutes' walk from the DOC office; what's more, pots and cutlery are available on free loan, gear is stored at no charge, and baggage can be sent on to Queenstown for about $5 per piece. As well as dorms, there are nice doubles and free use of shonky bikes. Dorms ①, rooms ②.

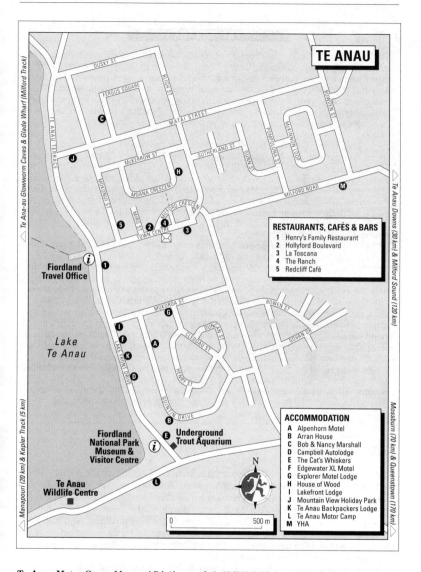

TE ANAU

Te Ana-au Glowworm Caves & Glade Wharf (Milford Track)

Te Anau-au Glowworm Caves & Glade Wharf (Milford Track)

Te Anau Downs (30 km) & Milford Sound (120 km)

Manapouri (20 km) & Kepler Track (5 km)

Mossburn (70 km) & Queenstown (170 km)

DUSKY ST

FERGUS SQUARE

BLIGH ST

MATAI STREET

C

SUTHERLAND ST

POMPOLONA ST

McKINNON LOOP

BOWEN ST

TE ANAU TERRACE

McKERROW ST

J

MOKONUI ST

MOANA CRESCENT

H

QUINNS ST

MILFORD ROAD

M

MIRO ST

MILFORD CRESCENT

TOWN CENTRE

5 **2** **4** **3**

Fiordland Travel Office (i) **1**

Lake Te Anau

MOKOROA ST

G

BOWEN ST

DUNCAN ST

CLEDDAU ST

GOVAN DR

I

F

A

LAKEFRONT DRIVE

K

HENRY ST

D

QUINTIN DRIVE

B

RESTAURANTS, CAFÉS & BARS
1 Henry's Family Restaurant
2 Hollyford Boulevard
3 La Toscana
4 The Ranch
5 Redcliff Café

Fiordland National Park Museum & Visitor Centre (i)

E **Underground Trout Aquarium**

Te Anau Wildlife Centre ◼

L

N

ACCOMMODATION
A Alpenhorn Motel
B Arran House
C Bob & Nancy Marshall
D Campbell Autolodge
E The Cat's Whiskers
F Edgewater XL Motel
G Explorer Motel Lodge
H House of Wood
I Lakefront Lodge
J Mountain View Holiday Park
K Te Anau Backpackers Lodge
L Te Anau Motor Camp
M YHA

0   500 m

Te Anau Motor Camp, Manapuri Rd, 1km south (☎03/249 7457, fax 249 7536). Te Anau's largest site, with spacious camping areas, dorms, and a range of cabins and units. There are also basic bikes for rent ($5 an hour), a sauna ($5 for 30min) and the *Jintz* bar and grill (Oct–April) to keep you fed and amused. Tent sites $9.50, powered sites $11, dorms ①, cabins ②, motel units ④.

YHA, 220–224 Milford Rd (☎ & fax 03/249 7847). Modern hostel over a kilometre out of town, with large dorms, double rooms, free gear storage and a good lawn for camping; the lack of a TV-free communal area may be off-putting to some. Tent sites $9, dorms ①, rooms ②.

THE TAKAHE

For half a century the flightless blue-green **takahe** (*Notornis mantelli*) was thought to be extinct. These plump, turkey-like birds – close relatives of the ubiquitous pukeko – were once common throughout New Zealand. By the time Maori arrived, however, their territory had become restricted to the southern extremities of the South Island. When Europeans came, only a few were spotted by early settlers in Fiordland. No sightings were recorded after 1898; the few trampers and ornithologists who claimed to have seen its tracks or heard the takahe's call in remote Fiordland valleys were dismissed as cranks.

One keen birder, **Geoffrey Orbell**, pieced together the sketchy evidence and concentrated his search on the 500 square kilometres of the **Murchison Mountains**, a virtual island surrounded on three sides by the western arms of Lake Te Anau and on the fourth by the Main Divide. In 1948, he was rewarded with the first takahe sighting in fifty years. However, the few remaining birds seemed doomed: deer were merrily chomping their way through the grasses on which the takahe relied. Culling of the deer population averted the immediate crisis and management programmes brought takahe numbers to 160 by the early 1990s, but a couple of harsh winters and a plague of stoats have since knocked them back by about a third.

Meanwhile, studies at the **Burwood Bush** rearing facility (closed to the public), in the Red Tussock Conservation Area east of Te Anau, have shown that takahe often lay three eggs but seldom manage to raise more than one chick. DOC officers now enter the Murchison Mountains each November to manipulate the **egg quota** so that each pair has only one viable egg to hatch. Any "surplus" eggs are removed to Burwood Bush, where rearing techniques pioneered here and at the **Te Anau Wildlife Centre** (see below) are employed to raise takahe for release back into the wild. Taped takahe noises encourage the chicks to hatch; then, to prevent them imprinting on their carers, the chicks are fed using **hand puppets** designed to look like adult takahe. And to help them hold their own against marauding stoats, young birds have their defensive instincts reawoken by watching DOC "Punch and Judy" shows, featuring stuffed stoats and juvenile takahe glove puppets.

Fear of having all their eggs in one basket has prompted DOC to establish several takahe populations on predator-free **sanctuary islands** – Maud Island in the Marlborough Sounds, Mana Island and Kapiti Island (both northwest of Wellington), and Tiritiri Matangi in Auckland's Hauraki Gulf – where the birds appear to be breeding well.

Sights and activities

There is little in Te Anau itself to distract you from simply admiring the scenery across the lake and taking gentle strolls along its shore. Ten minutes' walk south, a statue of Milford Track explorer Quintin McKinnon heralds the Fiordland National Park visitor centre (daily: Christmas–Feb 8am–8pm; March–Easter 8am–6pm; Easter–Oct 9am–4pm), where a short video (20min; $3) introduces the **Fiordland National Park Museum** (same hours; free), with its fascinating displays on the construction of the Homer Tunnel and the undersea life of the national park, including an eighteenth-century cannon salvaged from Dusky Sound.

Across the road you can drop $1 in a turnstile to view the dismal tank of fish which masquerades as the **Underground Trout Aquarium**, or press on a kilometre or so along the lakeside path to DOC's **Te Anau Wildlife Centre**, on Manapouri Road (unrestricted entry; donations appreciated), where you can amble through the park-like setting and see parakeets, morepork and other bush birds, notably the takahe (see box above for more on the centre's ground-breaking work).

Te Anau's only real paying attraction is the **Te Ana-au Glow Worm Caves** (guided tours only: Sept–May daily 2pm & 8.15pm; June–Aug daily 2pm & 7.45pm; $33), although even this is rather ad hoc and old-fashioned in its approach, with obtrusive concrete gangways and exposed electrical junction boxes obstructing the views. True, there are a couple of nice waterfalls and the glow-worm grotto is impressive, but its main appeal lies in its ability to occupy long evenings in Te Anau. A thirty-minute boat trip takes you across to the western side of Lake Te Anau where you are herded into a visitor centre and taken through the caves in small groups on punts, spending thirty minutes in a 200-metre length of the Aurora cave system which tunnels under the Murchison Mountains.

Lake cruises and flights

Having exhausted the limited possibilities on shore, it pays to get **cruising** on the lake. If you're going tramping, this can best be accomplished en route to the start of the Kepler or Milford tracks (see below & p.742). The operators who provide trailhead transport also run a number of other trips: Sinbad Cruises (☎03/249 7106) take the ketch *Manuska* across the lake to let you walk up to the Mount Luxmore Hut on the Kepler Track and back ($25), run day-trips to secluded coves ($50) and evening cruises ($40). Fiordland Bird & Bush Wilderness Guiding (☎03/249 7078) run a number of fishing, wilderness camping and scenic trips, while Fiordland Wilderness Experiences (☎03/249 7700) will get you paddling either on guided trips or independently.

For an aerial view of southern Fiordland, try fixed-wing **flights** with Waterwings Airways, Lake Front Drive (☎03/249 7405), who run float planes into Supper Cove and fly just about anywhere – from local runs (10min; $39) to Kepler Track overflights (20min; $72) and Doubtful Sound overflights (40min; $139). Air Fiordland (☎03/249 7505) concentrate more on Milford Sound, offering various combinations of flights, bus rides and cruises ($150–225).

The waterside helipad of Southern Lakes Helicopters, Lake Front Drive (☎03/249 7167), launches several **scenic flights** (from $85) and flights to Doubtful Sound with landings in a narrow canyon known as Campbell's Kingdom. They're also responsible for the **Triple Buzz** ($85–145), a flight/walk/cruise combination taking you over the lake to Mount Luxmore Hut or Forest Burn, both on the Kepler Track, followed by a downhill walk to Brod Bay and a boat ride back to Te Anau.

The Kepler Track

The **Kepler Track** (67km; 3–4 days), finished in 1988, was intended to take some of the load off the Milford and Routeburn tracks. Tracing a wide loop through the Kepler Mountains on the western side of Lake Te Anau, the track takes in one full day of exposed sub-Alpine ridge walking and some lovely virgin beech forest, and has the added advantage of being easily accessible (on foot if you are keen) from Te Anau. Throughout its length it is well graded and maintained but the long haul up to Mount Luxmore Hut makes this a strenuous tramp, and sections can be closed after snowfalls. DOC's *Kepler Track* leaflet ($1) is adequate, but for more detailed information, consult the 1:50,000 *Kepler Track Trackmap*.

Access and accommodation

The Kepler Track is one of the Great Walks and through the summer season (Nov to mid-April) its three main **huts** – Mount Luxmore (60 bunks), Iris Burn (60 bunks) and Moturau (40 bunks) – are all designated Category 1 ($15), and come with a warden, gas rings and flush toilets. You don't need to book specific nights in particular huts, but a Great Walks hut **pass** for the required number of nights must be bought in advance from the Great Walks Booking Desks in Te Anau, Glenorchy or Queenstown. During the winter, these huts lose their warden and their gas rings and revert to Category 3 ($4). In addition there is the simple Shallow Bay Hut (free), just off the track beside Lake Manapouri.

Camping ($6) is permitted at only two places, Brod Bay and Iris Burn, making for one very short and two very long days – assuming you walk the track anti-clockwise – but getting the bulk of the climbing over with on the first long day.

Trailhead transport

It is possible to start the Kepler from Te Anau, but most people avoid the 5km walk around the southern end of Lake Te Anau by taking the Fiordland Tracknet **shuttle bus** (mid-Oct to April; $5; ☎03/249 7777), which picks up at accommodation around town at 8.30am and 9.30am and drops off at the Control Gates, the source of the Waiau River. On the return leg, most trampers stop 11km short of the Control Gates at the swingbridge over the Waiau's Rainbow Reach. Fiordland Tracknet pick up here at 10am, 3pm and 5pm and charge $8 back to Te Anau.

You can skip another 5km of lakeside walking by cutting across Lake Te Anau to Brod Bay: Lakeland Boat Hire (☎03/249 8364) operate an early **boat** departing from the Te Anau wharf at 8.30am and 9.30am; and Sinbad Cruises (☎03/249 7106) sail the *Manuska* across at 9am. Both services charge $15.

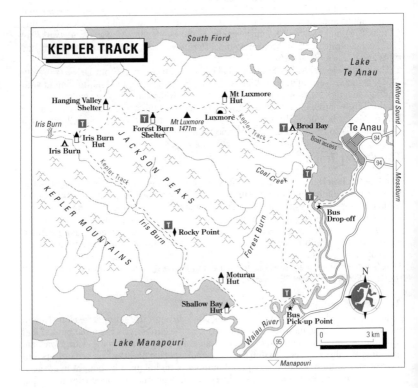

The route

If you're setting out from Te Anau, head south along Lake Front Drive, then right, following the lakeshore and taking the first right to the Control Gates. From the **Control Gates to Brod Bay** (5.5km; 1hr–1hr 30min; flat) the track follows the lakeshore around Dock Bay and over Coal Creek, passing through predominantly beech and kamahi forests but with a fine stand of tree ferns. Brod Bay has good swimming off a sandy beach and makes a lovely place to camp. Non-campers must press on from **Brod Bay to Mount Luxmore Hut** (8.5km; 3–4hr; 880m ascent), following a signpost midway along the beach. The path climbs fairly steeply for a couple of hours to limestone bluffs, from where it is almost another hour to the bushline and fine views over Te Anau and Manapouri lakes and the surrounding mountains. The hut is almost an hour from the bushline.

With the hard ascent done, the section from **Mount Luxmore Hut to Iris Burn Hut** (19km; 5–6hr; 300m ascent, 900m descent) is only gently undulating but makes a long day, and this is an exposed, high-level section where any hint of bad weather should be treated seriously. The track climbs to just below the summit of Mount Luxmore (from where you can scramble up to the 1471m peak), then descends to Forest Burn Shelter before following a ridge to Hanging Valley Shelter and turning sharply south to trace another open ridge towards Iris Burn. The Iris Burn is reached by zigzagging west into the forested Hanging Valley then following the stream to the hut and campsite in a large tussock clearing.

The track from **Iris Burn Hut to Moturau Hut** (17km; 4–6hr; 300m descent) starts behind the Iris Burn Hut and makes a steady descent through beech forest and riverside clearings beside Iris Burn. About halfway you pass toilets at Rocky Point, then enter a short gorge before hugging the river for several magical kilometres. Just before Iris Burn spills into Lake Manapouri, the track swings east and skirts Shallow Bay to the pleasant lakeside Moturau Hut. The hut is seldom full since some trampers prefer the simpler and older **Shallow Bay Hut** (Cat 4; free; 6 bunks) about forty minutes further on, while others continue from **Moturau Hut to Rainbow Reach** (6km; 1hr 30min; flat) through gentle beech forest to catch the last shuttle bus.

Walkers who persevere with the final stretch along the Waiau River from **Rainbow Reach to the Control Gates** (11km; 2–3hr; negligible ascent) are in for an easy forest walk with opportunities for fishing and swimming.

Eating and drinking

Diners have little culinary genius to look forward to in Te Anau but there are plenty of **no-frills places** selling decent food at reasonable prices. The **drinking** picture is much the same, and entertainment is BYO.

Henry's Family Restaurant, Lake Front Drive. Standard pub meals, enlivened by the Sunday all-you-can-eat buffet for $20.

Hollyford Boulevard, Town Centre. Reasonably priced pseudo-American burger and grills joint which, under threat of litigation, was recently forced to change its name from the infinitely more catchy Planet Hollyford.

Kepler's Restaurant, Town Centre. This down-home family restaurant offers succulent open burgers with fries ($9–15), grills and seafood mains ($18–22). Licensed.

The Ranch, Milford Rd. Rumbustious place for expensive but expansive ribs and grills; better as a lively place to drink.

Redcliff Café, 12 Mokonui St (☎03/249 7431). Highly regarded evening favourite serving a limited but excellent range of modern Kiwi variations on Pacific Rim cuisine, and in quantities to satisfy trampers' appetites. Their imaginative warm salads are a speciality. The cosy bar area acts as a local meeting spot and is a good place to drop by for a coffee. Licensed.

La Toscana, 108 Town Centre. Reasonable Italian restaurant that tries hard to please with a wide range of good pizza and pasta dishes. Licensed & BYO.

Milford Sound and around

Milford Sound is the most northerly and most celebrated of Fiordland's fifteen fiords, with vertical sides towering 1200m above the sea and waterfalls plunging from hanging valleys. While many of the other fiords approach Milford for their spectacular **beauty**, none come close for **accessibility**. Before the road was pushed through in 1952 visitors had to arrive by boat or walk the much-lauded **Milford Track** to reach the head of the fiord, but the opening of the Homer Tunnel paved the way for the phalanx of tourist buses that disgorge patrons onto fiord cruises. Around the middle of the day the crowds can certainly detract from the grandeur of the spot but don't let that, or anything else for that matter, put you off. Even torrential rain adds to the atmosphere of this magical place, as an ethereal mist descends, periodically lifting to reveal the waterfalls at their thunderous best.

Like the other sounds, Milford is a drowned glacial rather than a river valley, making it technically a fiord. Maori know it as **Piopiotahi** ("the single thrush"), and attribute its creation to the god Tu-to-rakiwhanoa, who was called away before he could carve a route into the interior, leaving high rock walls. These precipitous routes are now known as the Homer and Mackinnon passes, but were probably first used by Maori who came here to collect *pounamu*. The first European to sail into Piopiotahi was probably sealer John Grono who, in 1823, named the fiord Milford Haven after his home port in south Wales. The main river flowing into the Welsh Milford was the Cleddau, so naturally the river at the head of the fiord took that name too.

The earliest settler was Scot **Donald Sutherland**, who arrived with his dog, John O'Groat, in 1877; he promptly set a series of thatched huts beside the freshwater basin of what he called the "City of Milford", funding his explorations by guiding the small number of visitors who had heard tell of the scenic wonder hereabouts. By 1890 Sutherland had married a Dunedin widow, Elizabeth Samuel, and together they built a twelve-room hotel to serve the growing number of steamer passengers – "ashfelters" (city dwellers) and "shadow catchers" (photographers) – who flocked to admire the beauty of his remote home and to walk the newly opened Milford Track.

The predations of today's influx of visitors and the operation of a small fishing fleet have necessitated strategies to preserve the fiord's **fragile ecosystem**. Like all fiords, Milford Sound has an Entrance Sill at its mouth, in this case only 70m below the surface as compared to the deepest point of almost 450m. This effectively cuts off much of the natural recirculation of water and hinders mixing of sea water and the vast quantities of fresh water that pour into the fiord. A less-dense tannin-stained surface layer (up to 10m deep) builds up, further diminishing the penetration of light, which is already reduced by the all-day shadow cast by the fiord walls. The result is a relatively barren inter-tidal zone that protects a narrow – but wonderfully rich and extremely fragile – band of light-shy red and black **corals**; these normally grow only at much greater depths, but thrive here in the dark conditions. Unfortunately, Milford's fishing fleet use crayfish pots, which tend to shear off anything that grows on the fiord's walls. A marine reserve has been set up along the northeastern shore, where all such activity is prohibited, but really this is far too small and conservation groups are campaigning for its extension.

The road to Milford Sound

The 120-kilometre road from Te Anau to Milford Sound has to be one of the world's finest, though this hasn't stopped folk from hatching outlandish plans to circumvent it (see box on p.739). This two-hour drive can easily take a day if you grab every photo opportunity. Anywhere else the initial drive beside Lake Te Anau would be considered

SHEEP STATIONS, MONORAILS AND SOGGY ROADS

A visit to **Milford Sound** is undoubtedly one of the highlights of most visitors' South Island experience. For most, the **journey** to this remote spot is half the enjoyment, but tour operators catering to short-stay-must-see tourists are constantly on the lookout for new ways to get punters in and out quickly. Milford Sound's topography largely prevents much development of the airport, so developers have concentrated on two **hare-brained schemes**: shortening the Queenstown to Milford journey by means of a monorail; and linking the Hollyford Valley with Jackson Bay and Haast to the north. If either of these schemes goes ahead, the dynamics of the whole region will be drastically changed.

The **monorail** plan was originally mooted by the Ngai Tahu *iwi*, which claims land rights over much of the Greenstone Valley, the shortest route from Queenstown to The Divide, just 40km east of Milford Sound. An alliance of greenies and outdoor enthusiasts – recognizable from their bumper stickers proclaiming "Hands off the Greenstone Valley" – raised enough public concern to force the shelving of the plans in 1994. But by 1996 a **second** and more feasible **proposal**, again backed by the Ngai Tahu, was on the table: a $120-million state-of-the-art monorail would link Mount Nicholas Station, at the southwestern crook of Lake Wakatipu, with the Milford Road 50km north of Te Anau, via the Von and Mararoa valleys. Detractors claim that the inconvenience of transferring between catamaran, monorail and bus would offset any time gains, while investors still need to obtain consent for a 30-kilometre section of the route which passes through the DOC-managed Snowdon State Forest. For every supporter of the venture in Queenstown, there is an opponent in Te Anau – a town that relies heavily on Milford-bound traffic for its livelihood.

The **road proposal** seems less likely to go ahead. The current **Hollyford Valley Road** was approved in 1936, but only 16km of it were built as a spur off the SH94 to Milford. Between the Hollyford end of this spur and existing roads around Jackson Bay lie around 80km of valley floor, across which a new toll-road could be constructed. In its favour, the route is generally flat, but the region is prone to extreme flooding. In this case it is businesspeople in Queenstown who oppose the plans, fearing that tourists would travel the West Coast, see Milford Sound and visit Queenstown briefly – if at all.

obscenely scenic, but it is nothing compared to the Eglinton Valley, where the road penetrates into steeper, bush-clad mountains and winds through a sub-alpine wonderland to the bare rock walls of the seemingly impassable head of the Hollyford River. The Homer Tunnel then cuts through to the steep Cleddau Valley, the home straight down to Milford Sound.

Maori parties must have long used this route on their way to seek *pounamu* at Anita Bay on Milford Sound, but no road existed until two hundred unemployment-relief workers with shovels and wheelbarrows were put on the job in 1929. The greatest challenge was to puncture the headwall of the Hollyford Valley: work on the 1200-metre-long **Homer Tunnel** began in 1935, but was badly planned from the start. Working at a one-in-ten downhill gradient, the builders soon hit water and were forced to pump out continuously; a pilot tunnel allowing the water to drain westwards was finished in 1948 – when the whole project was relegated to the too-hard basket until 1952. After a concerted push, the road was finally completed in 1953, and officially inaugurated the following year, opening up Milford Sound to road traffic for the first time.

Despite recent improvements, such as passing bays for buses, the tunnel remains **rough-hewn**, forbiddingly dark and is often choked with diesel fumes (which make the headlights of oncoming vehicles appear to change from red to yellow to white). The sub-alpine section of the road is one of the world's most **avalanche-prone**. Since the last death on the road, in 1984, there has been a sophisticated avalanche-monitoring system in place and, if necessary, explosives are dropped from helicopters to loosen dangerous accumulations of snow while the road is closed. This mostly happens between May and November, when motorists are required to carry chains (available from service stations in Te Anau for around $25). Whatever the season, drivers should bear in mind that there is heavy bus traffic, which tends to be Milford-bound from around 11am to noon and Te Anau-bound between 3 and 5pm. Apart from the store in the Hollyford Valley, 8km off your route, there is nowhere to buy **food** until you reach Milford, so be prepared.

Along the road there are a dozen simple DOC **campsites** ($4), almost all with giardia-free stream water, long-drop toilets and fireplaces. Two are between Te Anau and Te Anau Downs, and the remaining ten pack into the next 50km, either on the grassy flats of the Eglinton Valley or in the bush nearby. Mackay Creek, Totara Creek and East Branch Eglinton, all around 55km north of Te Anau, are particularly good.

Heading north from Te Anau, there's little reason to stop in the first 30km to **Te Anau Downs Harbour**, where boats to the start of the Milford Track depart. The road then cuts east away from the lake, before veering north into the **Eglinton Valley** through occasional stands of silver, red and mountain beech interspersed with open flats of red tussock grass. Surprisingly in a national park, these plains are grazed, an anomaly resulting from longstanding leases which had to be honoured. The mountains that hem in the valley are picturesquely reflected in the roadside **Mirror Lakes**, 56km north of Te Anau, just before you hit the underwhelming **Avenue of the**

THE HOLLYFORD TRACK

DOC's Hollyford Valley leaflet ($1) is fine for following the track, though the 1:75,000 Hollyford Track Trackmap is more detailed.

The **Hollyford Track** (54 km; 4 days) is long, but mostly flat, following Fiordland's longest valley from the end of the Hollyford Valley road to Martins Bay. The track suffers from being essentially a **one-way tramp**, requiring four days' backtracking – unless you're flash enough to fly out from the airstrip at Martins Bay or tough enough to continue around a long, difficult and remote loop known as the **Big Bay–Pyke route** (9–10 days total; consult DOC's *Big Bay–Pyke Route* leaflet for details). The joy of the Hollyford is not in the sense of achievement that comes from scaling alpine passes, but in the appreciation of the dramatic mountain **scenery** and the kahikatea, rimu and matai **bush** with an understorey of wineberry, fuchsia and ferns. At Martins Bay, Long Reef has a resident **fur seal** colony, and from September to December you might spot rare Fiordland crested **penguins** nesting among the scrub and rocks.

Trampers who hate carrying a big pack, prefer more comfortable lodgings and having hearty meals cooked for them should consider a **guided walk** with Hollyford Valley Walk, PO Box 360, Queenstown (☎03/442 3760 & 0800/832 226): small groups are led by knowledgeable guides, and nights are spent at the relatively luxurious Martins Bay Lodge and the simpler Pyke Lodge (3–5 days; $950–1175); those in a mad rush can even fly from Queenstown, see the seal colonies, jetboat upriver for a night at the Martins Bay Lodge and fly back to Queenstown for $395.

ACCOMMODATION AND ACCESS

The six Category 3 DOC **huts** ($4) are each equipped with platform bunks, mattresses, water and toilets and do not need to be booked, though hut tickets or an annual hut pass should be bought in advance.

Buses on the Te Anau–Milford run will drop off at Marian Corner, where the Hollyford and Milford roads part company, and some, such as the BBQ Bus (☎03/442 1045), go as far as Gunns Camp. That still leaves you an 8-kilometre walk to the start of the track, so

Disappearing Mountain where the road slopes up, creating the illusion of the mountain ahead growing smaller as you approach.

As you get nearer to the head of the valley the road steepens to **The Divide**, at 532m the lowest east–west crossing of the Southern Alps. From the car park, with its toilets and walkers' shelter, you can walk to **Key Summit** (919m; 2–3hr return) for fine panoramic views over three valley systems. For those travelling by bus, a noticeboard details the times of passing services (Kiwi Discovery come through at 11.20am Milford-bound & 4.30pm Te Anau-bound; ☎03/442 7340), though it's best to book a pick-up beforehand. Pressing on towards Milford, you descend into the valley of the Hollyford River, which is best seen from a popular viewpoint just before the Hollyford Road shoots off north. The Milford Road continues west towards the Hollyford's source, a huge glacial cirque in which an Alpine Club hut marks the start of a walk to the Gertrude Saddle (4hr return), where you'll be rewarded by great views of the Darran Mountains and Mount Tutoko (2756m), Fiordland's highest point.

A kilometre further on, the **Homer Tunnel** forges through the rock, emerging at the top of a long switchback down to the Cleddau River. Roughly 10km on from the tunnel all buses stop at **The Chasm**, while their passengers stroll (15min return) to the near-vertical rapids where the Cleddau has scoured out a deep, narrow channel. Tantalizing glimpses through the foliage reveal sculpted rocks hollowed out by churning stones or tortured into free-standing ribs that resemble flying buttresses.

a better bet is to contact Hollyford Valley Walk (☎03/442 3760 & 0800/832 226) which, most mornings from November to May, runs a bus from Te Anau right to the Road End, as does Fiordland Tracknet (☎03/249 7777) from mid-October to April; both charge $30. From Martins Bay, Hollyford Valley Walk also operate **flights** (which must be pre-booked), the most useful being to Gunns Camp or Milford Sound (both $265); better still, since many people fly out from Martins Bay, you can often fly standby from Milford Sound – and walk the track in reverse – for under $100.

Finally, you can avoid most of the long day's walk beside the attractive but samey Lake McKerrow with Hollyford Valley Walk's **jetboat service** (4–7 people; $40 each) along the lake from McKerrow Island Hut to Martins Bay Lodge; if you're really pushed for time, a similarly priced run up the Hollyford River can further reduce the walk by a day.

THE ROUTE
The track from **Road End to Hidden Falls Hut** (9km; 2hr 30min–3hr; negligible ascent) follows a disused section of road which soon crumbles into a track with some riverbank walking to the Hidden Falls Hut (20 bunks). Keen walkers will probably want to push on from **Hidden Falls Hut to Alabaster Hut** (11km; 3–4hr; 100m ascent) through ribbonwood and beech to Little Homer Saddle and past Little Homer Falls. From **Alabaster Hut to Demon Trail Hut** (13km; 3–4hr; negligible ascent), you soon pass a side track to the nicely sited McKerrow Island Hut (20 bunks), before continuing beside Lake Alabaster to Demon Trail Hut (12 bunks). The section from **Demon Trail Hut to Hokuri Hut** (10km; 5–6hr; 100m ascent) is probably the toughest on the walk, following the shore of Lake McKerrow on rough ground with some tricky stream crossings, to Hokuri Hut (12 bunks). The path continues from **Hokuri Hut to Martins Bay Hut** (11km; 4–5hr; negligible ascent), by way of the scant remains of Jamestown, a cattle-ranching settlement that prospered briefly in the 1870s. Passing the small airfield served by Hollyford Valley Walk's flights, you'll stumble across some of the dozen dwellings that comprise Martins Bay; no one lives here permanently, but they are used by opportunistic whitebaiters and hunters. Continuing parallel to Martins Bay, and occasionally glimpsing the Hollyford River through wind-shorn trees, you reach the new Martins Bay Hut (20 bunks).

The Hollyford Valley

The Milford Road drops down from The Divide into the Hollyford Valley, which runs 80km from its headwaters in the Darran Mountains north to the Tasman Sea at Martins Bay. A 16km spur road (originally planned to reach Haast – see box on p.739) provides access to the Hollyford Track (see box on p.730) and a couple of other diversions. The first of these is a walk to **Lake Marian** (5km return; 2–3hr; 400m ascent), which starts 1km along the Hollyford Valley spur road and climbs to a beautiful alpine lake, passing some wonderful cataracts (30–40min return) where boardwalks are cantilevered out from the rock wall.

The only settlement is 8km along the valley road at **Gunns Camp**, home to Murray Gunn, who operates a small shop (daily 8.30am–8pm) packed with all you need for tramping and a lot more besides – postcards, good books, maps and tacky souvenirs. Murray also runs the *Hollyford Camp* (no phone; bunks ①, rooms ②), a huddle of rough 1930s cabins which served as married men's quarters for the long-suffering road-builders. Each cabin has a double room and a four-berth bunk room, linked by a kitchen/lounge area equipped with a wood-burning range and cold water supply. The **museum** (shop hours; $1, free to *Hollyford Camp* guests) is yet another Murray Gunn venture – a collection of photos and paraphernalia relating to the building of the Milford road and the Homer Tunnel, the one-time community at Martins Bay, and the devastating floods that periodically afflict the region.

The road runs 8km beyond Gunns Camp to the Road End – the beginning of the Hollyford Track and a shorter walk to **Humboldt Falls** (20–30min return), a three-step cascade leaping some two hundred metres.

The Milford Track

More than any other Great Walk, the Milford Track has become a Kiwi **icon** and it sometimes seems that walking it is the dream of every New Zealander. Unlike other major tramps where foreigners, and particularly Europeans, predominate, Kiwis are in the majority here.

Its exalted **reputation** is partly accidental and partly historical. It seems likely that southern Maori paced the Arthur and Clinton valleys in search of *pounamu*, but there is little direct evidence. The first Europeans to explore this section of Fiordland were Scotsmen **Donald Sutherland** and **John Mackay** who, in 1880, blazed a trail up the Arthur Valley from Milford Sound. The story goes that while working their way up the valley they came upon the magnificent Mackay Falls and tossed a coin to decide who would name it, on the understanding that the loser would name the next waterfall. Mackay won the toss but rued his good fortune when, days later, they stumbled across the much more famous and lofty Sutherland Falls. They may well have climbed the adjacent Mackinnon Pass, but the honour of naming it went to **Quintin McKinnon** who, with his companion Ernest Mitchell, reached it in 1888 after having been commissioned by the Otago Chief Surveyor, C. W. Adams, to cut a path up the Clinton Valley.

The route was finally pushed through in mid-October 1888 and the **first tourists** came through the next year, guided by McKinnon. The greatest fillip came in 1908 when a writer submitted her account of the Milford Track to the editor of London's *Spectator*. She had declared it "A Notable Walk" but, in a fit of editorial hyperbole, the editor retitled the piece "The Finest Walk in the World". From 1903 until 1966 the **government**, through its Tourist Hotel Corporation (THC), held a **monopoly** on the track, allowing only guided walkers; the huts were supplied by a team of packhorses, which weren't finally retired until 1969.

Wider **public access** was only achieved after the Otago Tramping Club challenged the government's policy by tramping the Milford in 1964. Huts were built in 1966 and the first independent parties came through later that year.

Preliminaries – and maps

The **Milford Track** (54km; 4 days) has become a victim of its own **hype**. There is no doubt that it is a wonderful route through some of Fiordland's finest scenery, but many trampers disparage it as over-regimented, expensive, and not especially varied, while other complaints focus on the huts, which are badly spaced and lurk below the tree line among the sandflies. While these criticisms aren't unfounded – the tramp costs $200 in hut and transport **fees** alone – the track is extremely well managed and maintained, the huts are clean and unobtrusive, and, because everyone's going in the same direction, you can go all day without seeing a soul. The Milford is also **tougher** than many people expect, packing the only hard climb and a dash for the boat at Milford Sound into the last two days. Nevertheless, almost anyone of any age can walk the track, though DOC recommends that unfit aspirants build up to it over 6–8 weeks.

DOC's *Milford Track* **leaflet** (provided free when you book – see below), is adequate for route-finding, though the 1:75,000 *Milford Track Trackmap* provides much more information. The 1:250,000 *Fiordland National Park* **map** is too small a scale to be of much use.

Booking and accommodation

Independent walkers tackling the Milford Track during the November to mid-April tramping season are subject to a rigid system of advance-booking **accommodation passes** – use DOC's Great Walks Booking Desks in Queenstown, Glenorchy and Te Anau – for the three special category huts. Bookings are made for specific days and you can only walk the track from south to north, spending the first night at Clinton Forks Hut, the second at Mintaro Hut and the third at Dumpling Hut. No backtracking or second nights are allowed and there is strictly **no camping**. **Numbers** are **limited** to forty per day, so you'll need to book as far ahead as possible (a month or more if you are adaptable, six months if you need a specific departure date or are part of a large group), but this does have the huge advantage that you are guaranteed a bed. Huts all have wardens and are equipped with flush toilets, running (but not drinking) water, heaters and gas rings, but not pans and plates; the **cost** is $90 for the three nights, and family discounts of thirty percent apply throughout the season. **Credit-card** phone or mail **bookings** are taken for the following season from July 1 and can be made through the Great Walks Booking Desk, DOC, PO Box 29, Te Anau (Nov–April daily 9am–4.30pm; May–Oct Mon–Fri 9am–4.30pm; ☎03/249 8514, fax 249 8515); pick up your accommodation passes from Te Anau before 11.30am on the day of departure. If the track is closed due to bad weather or track conditions, full refunds are made but new bookings can only be taken if there is space.

Outside the season the huts revert to Category 3 ($4). They are unstaffed and have no heating, clothes-drying or cooking facilities; bookings are not required and annual hut passes are valid.

Trailhead transport

Both ends of the Milford Track can only be realistically approached **by boat**. There are several possibilities, but all must be arranged and paid for before, or at the same time as, accommodation passes are issued. Most independent walkers catch the 1.15pm bus ($11) from outside the Mount Cook Lines office in Te Anau, which meets the *Tawera* launch (Nov to mid-April; $40; Fiordland Travel) at Te Anau Downs, 30km north of Te Anau. The launch departs at 2pm for the journey across Lake Te Anau (1hr 45min) to the start of the track at Glade Wharf. At the Milford end of the track, the majority catch either the 2pm or the 3pm *Anita Bay* launch from Sandfly Point (Nov to mid-April; $20) for the journey to Milford Sound (20min). **Buses** back to Te Anau can be picked up at 3pm and 5pm (3hr; $35).

Other operators offer different ways to approach and leave the track. They can all be booked individually, but most have combined to marginally undercut the total price you'd pay for independent arrangements. Probably the best way to start from Te Anau is on the *Manuska*, a wooden ketch run by Sinbad Cruises (10.30am; 5–6hr; $50; ☎03/249 7106), which **sails** under canvas when possible to Glade Wharf. A package deal costs $98, including a short **paddle** back from Sandfly Point with Rosco's Milford Sound Sea Kayaks ($18 when booked separately; ☎03/249 8840) and a bus from Milford to Te Anau.

Trampers wanting an **early start** should go with Fiordland Bird & Bush Wilderness Guiding ($50; ☎03/249 7078), who'll take you to Te Anau Downs and powerboat to a beach for a brew, before depositing you at Glade Wharf by 2pm. They also do a $98 boat-kayak-bus combo in conjunction with Fiordland Kayaks ($19 individually; ☎03/249 7700) – note that this is the only drop-off and pick-up service to operate **year-round**.

If money is no object, you can **fly** in to Glade Wharf with Waterwings Floatplane ($99; ☎03/249 7405) or one of the several companies who fly out of Milford Sound, Te Anau or Queenstown.

Guided walks

For many years, the only way to walk the Milford Track was on a **guided walk**. Some would argue that this is still the case, with just your personal effects to carry and comfortable beds to sleep in. Accommodation is in clean, plain huts which aren't exactly luxurious, but do boast hot showers, duvets on the bunks, three-course dinners with wine and cooked breakfasts. Staff prepare the huts, cook the meals, make up the lunches and tidy up after you. All you have to do is walk, but there's a price to pay for all this pampering. The **Milford Track Guided Walk**, PO Box 185, Te Anau (Nov to mid-April; ☎03/249 7411 & 0800/659 255, fax 249 7590) is a six-night, five-day affair and costs $1490. For that you get an introductory talk with dinner and a night at the *Te Anau Travelodge*, transport to the trailhead, accommodation and food on the track, a night at the *Milford Sound Hotel*, a cruise and a return bus ride to Te Anau.

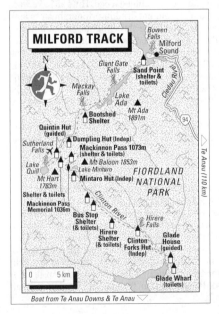

Boat from Te Anau Downs & Te Anau

Anyone wanting a taste of the track without having to walk more than a couple of kilometres can stay overnight at **Glade House**, the first of the guided walkers' huts on the track. Bus and boat transport are scheduled to leave time to explore the Clinton River and eat a three-course dinner – all for $195 (book through Milford Track Guided Walk).

The route

The track starts at the head of Lake Te Anau and follows the Clinton River into the heart of the mountains, climbing over the spectacular Mackinnon Pass before tracing the Arthur River to Milford Sound.

The first day is a doddle. **Glade Wharf to Clinton Forks Hut** (8km;

2hr; 50m ascent) starts along a 2km 4WD track which serves Glade House. The path then crosses a long swingbridge to the right bank of the gentle, meandering Clinton River; keen anglers can spend an hour or two fishing for trout in the deep pools. The track runs through dense beech forest, only occasionally giving glimpses of the mountains ahead beyond Clinton Forks Hut.

From **Clinton Forks Hut to Mintaro Hut** (13.5km; 4–5hr; 350m ascent), the track follows the right bank of the Clinton River to its source, Lake Mintaro, right by the Mintaro Hut. Again this is easy going, and, by the time you reach a short side track to Hidden Lake, the Mackinnon Pass should be visible ahead. The track steepens a little to Bus Stop Shelter, then flattens out to Pompolona Hut. From here it's a further hour to Mintaro Hut where, if it looks like it will be a good sunset, it pays to drop your pack and head up the Mackinnon Pass.

The walk so far does nothing to prepare you for the day from **Mintaro Hut to Dumpling Hut** (14km; 5–6hr; 550m ascent, 1030m descent). Though the surface of the broad path is firm and well graded, bushwalking neophytes will find the haul up to Mackinnon Pass (1hr 30min–2hr) very strenuous. Long breath-catching pauses provide an opportunity to admire the wonderful alpine scenery, notably the headwall of the Clinton Valley, a sheer glacial cirque of grey granite. As the bush drops away behind you, the slope eases to the saddle at Mackinnon Pass, a great place to eat lunch, though you'll have the company of kea and the incessant buzzing of pleasure flights from Milford. A memorial to McKinnon and Mitchell marks the low-point of the saddle, from where the path turns east and climbs to a shelter (with toilets and a gas ring) just below the dramatic form of Mount Balloon. From there it is all downhill, and steeply too, initially skirting the flank of Mount Balloon then following a recent re-routing of the path beside the picturesque Roaring Burn and down to the Arthur River. The confluence is marked by **Quintin Hut**, which was originally built by the Union Steamship Company as an overnight shelter for sightseers from Milford visiting the Sutherland Falls. Though it remains a private hut, toilets and shelter are provided for independent walkers – who mostly dump their packs for the walk to the base of the 560m **Sutherland Falls** (4km; 1hr–1hr 30min return; 50m ascent), the highest in New Zealand. Quintin Hut has an airstrip and anyone with $50 to spare can take a **scenic flight** (minimum 4 people; 20min) to view Lake Quill (which feeds the Sutherland Falls), the Mackinnon Pass and the Clinton Valley. Dumpling Hut is another hour's walk from Quintin Hut.

After a tiring third day, you're in for an early start and a steady walk from **Dumpling Hut to Sandfly Point** (18km; 5–6hr; 125m decent) to meet your launch or kayak at 2pm. After rain this can be a magnificent walk, as the valley walls stream with waterfalls and the Arthur River is in spate. The track follows the tumbling river for a couple of hours to the Boatshed (toilets), before crossing the Arthur River on a swingbridge and cutting inland to the magnificent MacKay Falls. More a steep cascade than a waterfall, they are much smaller than the Sutherland Falls but equally impressive, particularly after rain. Don't miss Bell Rock, a water-hollowed boulder that you can crawl inside. The track subsequently follows Lake Ada, created by a landslip 900 years ago, and named by Sutherland after his Scottish girlfriend. A small lunch shelter midway along its shore heralds Giant Gate Falls, which are best viewed from the swingbridge that crosses the river at the foot of the falls. From here it is roughly an hour and a half to the shelter at Sandfly Point.

Milford Sound

After all the superlatives feted on Milford Sound, initial impressions can be a little deflating. The smattering of buildings that comprise the small settlement are hardly in keeping with such magnificent surroundings and the best of the fiord can only really

TRIPS TO MILFORD SOUND

As **Milford Sound** is on most visitors' itineraries, there's no shortage of operators willing to get you there from almost anywhere in the country. **From Queenstown**, a stream of luxury **buses** make the four-to-five-hour drive via Te Anau to Milford, complete with frequent photo-opportunity stops and a relentless commentary, decanting their passengers for a cruise on the fiord then running them back again. Trips **from Te Anau** involve the middle (and most interesting) section of Queenstown-based trips and are appreciably shorter, generally taking a leisurely eight rather than a hurried twelve hours. Most tours also include a **cruise** on the sound once you get there – see p.749 for a run-down of the various vessels that ply its waters.

FROM QUEENSTOWN

Trips typically start between 7am and 8am and seldom get back before 8pm. Many shy away from such a long day and opt instead for a package involving the forty-minute **flight** to Milford's small airfield, a **cruise** and a **return flight**. A good compromise is to combine the two: flying there and bussing back is the most economical option (from around $165 with Kiwi Discovery; ☎03/442 7340), since flights back are oversubscribed by people who have booked a bus/cruise/bus trip but simply can't face the return journey, sending prices up to nearer the $240 mark. Travellers locked into the Kiwi Experience or Magic Bus circuit have to pay extra to do the Milford Sound leg; if you can get a group of four or five together, you can get here as cheaply, and with greater flexibility, by renting car from Queenstown (see p.686).

Prices for the **bus/cruise/bus trips** kick off at $99 with Mount Cook Landline (Nov–April; ☎03/442 4640 & 0800/800 287); Kiwi Discovery and Kiwi Experience (☎03/442 9708) both run comparable trips on smaller buses for $105; but, best value of all, the BBQ Bus ($130; ☎03/442 1045) run full-day trips, with stops for short bushwalks and a barbecue in the Hollyford Valley. More upmarket tours using air-conditioned vehicles, complete with prerecorded multilingual commentary, are offered by several companies, including Mount Cook Landline ($143); and Fiordland Travel ($143; ☎03/442 7500 & 0800/656 503), whose unusual wedge-profiled coaches give the best all-round views. Fiordland Travel also run the best trip for those with a couple of days to explore Milford. The backpacker-orientated **Milford Backroad Adventure** (mid-Oct to March Mon, Wed & Fri; $194), which takes the early sailing across Lake Wakatipu on the TSS *Earnslaw* (see p.678), then a minibus along 80km of dirt roads through the Walter Peak

---

be seen from the water. Nevertheless, it is a fine spot on the edge of a basin where the Cleddau and Arthur rivers surge into the fiord, and the whole scene is dominated by the triangular glaciated pinnacle of **Mitre Peak** (1694m), named for its resemblance to a bishop's mitre when viewed from this angle.

Arrival and getting around

The most worthwhile way to get here, and the one which conveys the greatest sense of place, is to **walk** the **Milford Track** (see p.742), though **drivers** and **cyclists** do get the freedom to stop, sightsee and camp at the numerous basic campsites along the dramatic road from Te Anau (see p.738). Failing either of those, you can **fly**, hop on a **bus**, or do a combination of both, often with a cruise on the fiord thrown in (see box above for a run-down of the options).

There isn't much to Milford Sound. The airport, fishing harbour, new cruise terminal, post office and an expensive petrol station are scattered along the shore. Though none is more than a few hundred metres apart, there is a sporadic free **shuttle bus** connecting them all.

and Mount Nicholas high-country stations and on up the scenic Von Valley to Mavora Lakes (see p.697). The bus eventually meets SH94 and continues through Te Anau to Milford Sound in time to catch the *Milford Wanderer* for its overnight sailing. The return journey the following morning is generally broken by a brew up at Mavora Lakes, before catching the early-evening *Earnslaw* sailing back to Queenstown.

Magnificent though it is, the Milford road scenery is upstaged by the aerial views of the top end of Lake Wakatipu and the Routeburn and Greenstone tracks from the **flights to Milford**. Mount Cook Airlines do a four-hour fly/cruise/fly package for $256; other operators include Air Fiordland (☎03/442 3404), Air Wakatipu (☎03/442 4148), and Milford Sound Scenic Flights (☎03/442 3065 & 0800/101 767). Finally, if the thought of hundreds of people crammed onto Milford's cruise boats leaves you cold, consider the **Big Bay Wilderness Adventure** ($195; ☎03/442 6228), a five-hour trip for two or three people to the remote Big Bay, 40km north of Milford Sound. Departure times are dictated by low tide, which reveals the landing zone, from where you spend a few hours exploring the bush and canoeing. In some respects the flights out this way are more spectacular, as they overfly the Olivine Ice Plateau and the Red Hills.

FROM TE ANAU

The **cheapest** trips are those which don't include cruises – good value if you're going kayaking: try Southern Explorer ($45 return; ☎03/249 7820 & 0800/252 000) or the track-transport specialists Milford Sound/Te Anau Shuttle (Nov–May; ☎03/249 7777), who will get you there and back for $40, but you'll have to put up with detours to the trailheads. The big boys such as Fiordland Travel (☎03/249 7416 & 0800/656 510), InterCity (☎03/249 7559 0800/731 711), Milford Explorer (☎03/249 7516 & 0800/800 904) and Mount Cook Landline (☎03/249 7516 & 0800/800 287) all run luxury **bus and cruise** packages for $80–90, though there are small reductions for backpackers and substantial standby **discounts** outside the peak season.

The **most interesting** possibilities include trips with Fiordland Wilderness Experiences ($80; ☎03/249 7700), involving four hours' kayaking on the fiord; Kiwi Discovery ($75; ☎03/442 9792 & 0800/100 792), with a bus and MV *Tutoko* cruise combo; the BBQ Bus (☎03/442 1045; $85), stopping for a barbecue as well as a cruise; Milford Sound Scenic Tours (☎03/249 7227; $86), who run a cycle and bus trip, including the observatory cruise; and Trips 'n' Tramps ($86; ☎03/249 7081 & 0800/305 805), concentrating on short bushwalks along the way before meeting up with the *Milford Wanderer*.

Accommodation and eating

There are only two **places to stay** in town and neither of them are particularly good value, so if you're keen to stay the night and can afford it, book on one of the overnight cruises. The *THC Milford Sound Hotel* (☎03/249 7926 & 0800/657 444, fax 249 8926) has fairly ordinary back-facing rooms (⑤) and considerably better fiord-view rooms (⑦); all are en suite. The unappealing *Milford Sound Lodge* (☎ & fax 03/249 8071; tent sites $8, dorms ①, rooms ②–③) is on the approach to Milford Sound, almost 2km from the wharf and linked to it by a courtesy bus.

Eating is equally limited. *Milford Sound Lodge* sells filling meals for under $10 and is the only place to buy groceries – at inflated prices, due to transport costs. The *THC Hotel* has the expensive *Lobster Pot Restaurant*, serving hefty main courses at around $20, snackier lunches from $8, and a huge breakfast for under $10; in bad weather, their lounge, with its picture windows and open fire, makes a good place to bide your time over a coffee, watching the weather sweeping along the fiord. The hotel also runs the spartan *Shark in the Bar* **pub** next door, which does pies and toasted sandwiches, and the basic *Mitre Peak Café* (daily 9am–4pm), which follows the Kiwi tearoom tradition.

Around Milford

You are pretty much surrounded by water here, and you should waste little time before getting out on it. If tales of his pioneering days have inspired you, pay homage at **Donald Sutherland's grave**, hidden among the staff accommodation behind the pub. Otherwise, there's a five-minute stroll up to a **lookout** behind the *THC Hotel*, or a boardwalk and track beside the cruise terminal leads to the 160m **Lady Bowen Falls** (15min return), named after the wife of George Bowen, New Zealand's governor in the 1860s. Though most impressive in spate, when the upturned lip sends a spume out across the fiord, the falls are worth the walk at any time to observe the village's source of water and hydroelectricity. Three old graves at the foot of the falls guard the remains of nineteenth century sealers and whalers.

The only other sight attached to terra firma is the **Milford Sound Underwater Observatory** (9.30am–4.30pm; $32, including water taxi from the wharf; or on a Red Boat cruise – see below), a floating platform moored to a sheer rock wall in Harrison Cove, part of the marine reserve about a third of the way along the fiord. A series of explanatory panels on the surface prepare you for the main attraction, a spiral staircase which takes you nine metres down through the relatively lifeless freshwater surface layer to a circular gallery where windows look out into the briny heart of the fiord. Sharks and seals have been known to swim by, but most of the action happens immediately outside in window-box "gardens", which have been specially grown from locally gathered **coral** and plant species. Lights pick out colourful fish, tubeworms, sea fans, huge starfish and rare red and black coral (see p.738). This might all sound a little naff – but unless you're an experienced diver, this is the only chance you'll get to see these corals, which elsewhere in the world grow only at depths greater than forty metres. Cruises only stop for around twenty minutes, which isn't really long enough, so if you're really interested, a water taxi's your best bet.

Seeing the fiord: cruises, kayaks and flights

Dramatic though it is, the view from the shore of Milford Sound pales beside the incomparable spectacle from the water, with waterfalls plunging hundreds of metres into the fiord. It is still difficult to grasp the heroic scale of the place, unless your visit coincides with that of one of the great cruise liners – even these formidable vessels are totally dwarfed by the cascades and cliff faces.

The majority of cruises explore the full 22km of Milford Sound, all calling at waterfalls, the seal colony, and overhanging rock faces; at Fairy Falls, boats nose up to the base of the fall, while suitably attired passengers are encouraged to edge out onto the bowsprit and collect a cup of water. Longer trips sometimes anchor in Anita Bay (*Te-Wahi-Takiwai*, "the place of Takiwai"), a former greenstone-gathering place at the fiord's mouth, but still sheltered from the wrath of the Tasman Sea. In short, having come this far, it's essential to get out on the water by some means or other – even if it means putting up with corny cruise commentaries. There are three main options, all of which should be booked a few days in advance: a two- to four-hour cruise around the fiord, an overnight cruise, or kayaking. All boats leave from a cavernous new building at the wharf.

Two large companies and one single-boat operator run **cruises on the fiord**. Red Boat Cruises (☎03/249 7926 & 0800/657 444) operate five well-appointed boats, some carrying several hundred passengers and all bombarding you with a running commentary. Most cruises go to the Tasman Sea (2–6 daily; 1hr 45min; $38), but the longer **cruise to the observatory** (daily 12.25pm; 2hr 30min; $45) is preferable, taking you out to the mouth of the fiord and returning to Harrison Cove for a quick look at the underwater observatory. Apart from the lack of any observatory visits, Fiordland Travel (☎03/442 7500) run similar cruises to the Tasman Sea (2–4 daily; 1hr 45min; $38) and longer ones on the *Milford Wanderer* (Oct–April 2 daily; 2hr 30min; $43). Fiordland Adventures (☎03/442 9792 & 0800/100 792) operate the small but perfectly formed MV *Tutoko* between November and April; daytime cruise options are a scenic trip out to the Tasman Sea (daily 9.45am; 2hr 30min; $40) or a slightly longer trawl around the fiord, with time for a little fishing (daily 12.30pm; 3hr; $40).

All three companies operate **overnight trips**, the **classiest** being on *Red Boat's Lady of the South Pacific*, a large double-decker catamaran: "A" deck has comfortable en-suite double and twin rooms with large windows (Oct–April $199 per person; May–Sept $159); while "B" deck is kitted out with good two- and four-bunk cabins ($119 per person year-round). Everyone is greeted with scones and champagne, then there's an excellent three-course dinner, and breakfast the following morning. A courtesy bus leaves the *THC Hotel* in Milford at 4pm and takes you to the wharf. After a trip out to the Tasman Sea, the vessel anchors in Deep Water Basin, returning you to the wharf around 10am. The other two are more determinedly **backpacker-orientated**. Fiordland Travel run the *Milford Wanderer* (Oct–April daily 5pm–9am; $118), a motor-driven, seventy-berth replica of a sailing scow. It makes an impressive sight as it ploughs along the fiord to Anita Bay for some fishing, canoeing and bushwalking before spending the night in Harrison Cove. On-board accommodation is somewhat institutional, with cramped four-bunk rooms equipped with sheets, sleeping bags and towels, but a hearty three-course evening meal is served (drinks extra). Much smaller numbers (max 12 passengers) contribute to the more intimate feel of the MV *Tutoko* (Nov–April daily 5pm–8.30am; $118, including meals), which follows much the same itinerary.

Fine though the cruises are, the elemental nature of Milford Sound can best be appreciated without the throb of an engine. The most extensive range of **kayaking** trips are run by Rosco's Milford Sound Sea Kayaks (☎03/249 8840), who take single and double sea kayaks on a range of trips to Harrison Cove and Sandfly Point (mid-Oct to mid-April; $49–95). Fiordland Wilderness Experiences run full-day kayaking trips on Milford Sound, with an ecological slant ($75; ☎03/249 8833). Both companies organize transport from Te Anau and will pick up trampers coming off the Routeburn, Greenstone or Caples tracks at The Divide.

Scenic **flights** over Fiordland's magnificent alpine terrain are run by numerous companies. Mount Cook Airlines (☎0800/800 737) are typical, running flights to the mouth of the sound (10min; $49), Sutherland Falls (20min; $74) and a grand tour (Oct–March only; 40min; $123). Milford Sound Helicopters (☎03/249 8384), offer a circuit of Mitre peak (10min; $90), a jaunt to Sutherland Falls (30min; $160) and a Grand Tour (55min; $275).

Manapouri and the southern fiords

There is no shortage of contenders for the title of New Zealand's most beautiful lake, and **Lake Manapouri** is definitely among them, with its long and indented bush-clad shoreline contorted into three distinct arms. The lake has a vast catchment area, guzzling all the water that flows down the Upper Waiau River from Lake Te Anau and unwittingly creating a massive hydroelectric generating capacity – something which almost led to its downfall.

The one good thing to come from the hydroelectric project has been the opening up of **Doubtful Sound**, following the construction of the Wilmot Pass supply road.

A TALE OF ELECTRICITY, ALUMINIUM AND BRICKBATS

Lake Manapouri's **hydroelectric** potential had long been recognized, but nothing was done to realize it until the 1950s. Consolidated Zinc Pty of Australia wanted to smelt their Queensland bauxite into **aluminium** – a tremendously power-hungry process – as cheaply as possible, and their beady eyes alighted upon **Lake Manapouri**. They approached the New Zealand government, who agreed to build a power station on the lake, at taxpayers' expense, while Consolidated Zinc's subsidiary Comalco built a smelter at Tiwai Point, near Bluff, 170km to the southeast.

The scheme entailed blocking the lake's natural outlet into the Lower Waiau River and chiselling out a **vast powerhouse** 200m underground beside Lake Manapouri's West Arm, where the flow would be diverted down a 10km tailrace tunnel to Deep Cove on Doubtful Sound. By the time the fledgling **environmental movement** had rallied its supporters, the scheme was well under way, but the government underestimated the anger that would be unleashed by its secondary plan to boost water storage and power production by raising the water level in the lake by 12m. The threat to the natural beauty of the lake sparked **national protests**, culminating in the presentation to parliament of a 265,000-signature petition, after which the plan was reluctantly dropped. The full saga is recounted in Neville Peat's book *Manapouri Saved* (see "Books" in Contexts, p.793).

The **West Arm Power Station** took eight years to build. Completed in 1971, it remains one of the most ambitious projects ever carried out in New Zealand. Eighty percent of its output goes straight to the **smelter** – which consumes something like fifteen percent of all the electricity used in the country, and yet Comalco are charged only a third of what domestic users pay. It is widely perceived to be an unnecessary drain on the country's resources and every time a new power station is proposed, the cry goes up for the plug to be pulled on the smelter. Nevertheless, a second parallel tailrace tunnel is now being drilled to **increase** the station's **capacity**.

What was previously the preserve of the odd yacht and a few deerstalkers and trampers is now accessible to anyone prepared to take a boat across Lake Manapouri and a drive over the Wilmot Pass. Costs are unavoidably high and you need to be self-sufficient (no burger joints or corner shops here), but any inconvenience is easily outweighed by glorious isolation and pristine beauty. Wildlife is a major attraction, not least the resident pod of bottlenose dolphins, who frequently come to play around ships' bows and gleefully cavort near kayakers. Fur seals slather the outer islands, Fiordland crested penguins come to breed here in October and November, and the bush, which comes right down to the water's edge, is alive with kaka, kiwi and other rare bird species.

Cook spotted Doubtful Sound in 1770 but didn't enter as he was "doubtful" of his ability to sail out again in the face of winds buffeted by the steep-walled fiord. The breeze was more favourable for the joint leaders of a Spanish expedition, Malaspina and Bauza, who in February 1793 sailed in and named Febrero Point, Malaspina Reach and Bauza Island.

In fact, Cook seemed more interested in **Dusky Sound**, 40km south, where he spent five weeks on his second voyage in 1773, while his crew recovered from an arduous crossing of the Southern Ocean. At Pickersgill Harbour, Cook endeavoured to ward off scurvy by using manuka leaves to brew a kind of "spruce beer" which, helped along with a touch of brandy, apparently tasted like champagne; obviously, the captain hadn't supped champagne for some time. On Astronomer's Point nearby, it is still possible to see where Cook's astronomer had trees felled so he could get an accurate fix on the stars; not far from here is the site where 1790s castaways built the first European-style house and boat in New Zealand. Marooned by the fiord's waters, Pigeon Island shelters the ruins of a house built by Richard Henry, who battled from 1894 to 1908 to save endangered native birds from introduced stoats and rats.

Manapouri

The scattered community of **MANAPOURI**, 20km south of Te Anau, drapes itself prettily around the shores of the lake of the same name which, in the 1960s became a cause célèbre for conservationists opposed to the raising of the lake level as part of the massive West Arm hydroelectric power scheme (see box on p.750). With the power station complete, the lake left at its original level and the passage of three decades, there is little tangible evidence of the passions that once threatened the community's cohesion, but scratch below the surface and you'll find a lingering antipathy between economic rationalists and environmentalists.

Arrival and information

To get to Manapouri without your own transport, hop on the Spitfire Shuttle (contact Fiordland Travel ☎03/249 7416), which leaves Te Anau at 8.30am and returns from Manapouri around 4pm, or try the Fiordland Travel **buses** ($5 each way) plying the West Arm and Doubtful Sound runs, who'll take you if their cruise passengers don't fill the bus.

The road from Te Anau reaches Manapouri as Cathedral Drive and then becomes Waiau Street, passing almost everything of interest on the way to the offices of **Fiordland Travel**, Pearl Harbour (daily 8am–4pm; ☎03/249 6602 & 0800/656 502, fax 249 6603), the closest thing the village has to an **information** centre, and the jumping off point for lake cruises. The sole **shop** and the **post office** both occupy the same building as the Cathedral Café on Cathedral Drive – find one and you've found the lot.

Accommodation and eating

There is a reasonable selection of **places to stay** in Manapouri (see below) but not much choice for **eating** – so, if you are staying at either of the B&Bs listed, take advantage of their excellent meals. Failing that, the *Manapouri Motor Inn* dishes out ordinary bar meals, while the *Pearl Harbour Coffee Bar* produces standard New Zealand tearoom fare. Your best bet is the *Cathedral Café*, Cathedral Drive (☎03/249 6619), which serves teas and snacks, but also stays open for $15 evening meals until 8pm, later if you make a reservation.

The Cottage, Waiau St (☎03/249 6838 & 0800/677 866). Attractive en-suite rooms in a cutesy house with a cottage garden close to the wharf. Continental breakfast is included and $25 dinners are available. ④.

Deep Cove Hostel, Deep Cove, Doubtful Sound (☎03/249 6602). This two- and four-bed bunkroom accommodation overlooking Doubtful Sound is available only during school holidays. There are mattresses, all eating and cooking utensils and good hot showers, but the nearest place to buy food is Manapouri, so bring everything you'll need. The one-way fare with Fiordland Travel's Doubtful Sound service from Manapouri is $48. ①.

Lake View Motels and Motor Park, 50 Manapouri–Te Anau Highway, 1km from the wharf (☎03/249 6624). Fully equipped motor park with spa and swimming pool. Tent and powered sites cost around $8 or there are cabins and units. Cabins ②, motel units ④.

Manapouri Glade Motel and Motor Park, Murrell Ave (☎03/249 6623). Appealingly old-fashioned, peaceful and neatly tended motor park located right where the Waiau River meets the lake. Tent and powered sites go for $7.50. Cabins ②, motel units ④.

Murrell's Grandview House, 7 Murrell Ave (☎ & fax 03/249 6642). The finest of Manapouri's B&Bs, this wide-verandahed house was built in 1889 by the present owner's grandfather. Gracious rooms and spacious grounds exude a country-sports ambience. Swanky dinners making the most of local ingredients go for $50. ⑦.

Possum Lodge Manapouri Backpackers, Cathedral Drive (☎ & fax 03/249 6660). Very homely and central place catering to only a dozen or so guests in a tastefully renovated house overlooking the lake. Beds are in small dorms or doubles, and all have free use of the well stocked kitchen, comfortable lounge warmed by a log-burning stove, and bikes. They'll even pick you up from Te Anau if you've booked in advance. Dorms ①, rooms ②.

Ruth and Lance Shaw, 1 Home St (☎ & fax 03/249 6600). Self-contained flat let by the folk who operate Fiordland Ecology Holidays. Continental breakfast is included, and dinner is available for $20. ④.

Around town

The several dozen houses that constitute Manapouri cluster at the outlet of the Waiau River, which the hydroelectric shenanigans have turned into a narrow arm of the lake now known as Pearl Harbour.

Apart from cruises and kayak trips (see below), the only thing to do in Manapouri is to saunter along some of the **walking trails** detailed in DOC's *Manapouri Tracks* leaflet ($1, from some accommodation and the Fiordland Travel office). On the Manapouri side there's the **Pearl Harbour to Fraser's Beach** trail (25min), which follows an easy track through lakeshore beech forest with fantails and silvereye flitting about the thin understorey. For all the other tracks, you'll need to rent yourself a row boat to get across the Waiau River: Adventure Charters (daily 8am–6pm; ☎03/249 6626), at the Mobil station on Waiau Street, are happy to oblige. Boats cost $5 per person per day, or you can pay another $3 each and stay on the other side overnight, either camping or in one of the two DOC huts (both Category 3; $4).

The most frequently walked is the **Circle Track** (3hr loop; 7km; 330m ascent) initially contouring west around the lake then turning southeast to climb the ridge up to a point with stupendous views over the lake then north back the to start.

The lake: cruises and kayaking

Most of the lake cruises are operated by Fiordland Travel (☎03/249 6602 & 0800/656 502), who run four-hour trips across Lake Manapouri to the impressive, if controversial **West Arm Power Station** (1 daily; $43 ex-Manapouri, $53 ex-Te Anau); work on a second tailrace over the next few years is likely to disrupt tour schedules, so check the latest with Fiordland Travel. The ride across the lake terminates at a visitor centre, which highlights the European "discovery" of Fiordland, its flora and fauna and, more predictably, the construction of the power station. A bus then takes you down a narrow, 2km-long tunnel to a viewing platform in the Machine Hall. All you can see are the exposed sections of seven turbines, but there's an interesting model of the whole system and some panels assaulting you with yet more statistics; read quickly before you're whisked back to the bus for the return trip.

For greater independence, you'll need **kayak rental**: Adventure Charters (daily 8am–6pm; ☎03/249 6626) rent reasonable-quality single and double sea kayaks for $35 per day; or Fiordland Wilderness Experiences, 66 Quintin Drive, Te Anau (☎03/249 7700), rent out better boats for a little more.

The southern fiords

To fully appreciate the beauty and sense the isolation of the **southern fiords**, you really need to spend a few days among them, travelling either by boat or kayak. If time is limited, plump for a full-day trip to Doubtful Sound; with more time to spare, a few days weaving between these mystical waterways is an unforgettable experience.

Fiordland Travel run a full-day trip to **Doubtful Sound** (1–2 daily; $145 ex Manapouri, $155 ex Te Anau; lunch $10 extra; ☎03/249 6602 & 0800/656 502): after the inevitable power-station treatment on Lake Manapouri, you're transferred onto a bus

THE DUSKY TRACK

DOC's Dusky Track leaflet *($1) is the best single resource for this walk, though tricky route finding makes the 1:50,000* Wilmot *(S148) and* Heath *(S157) maps invaluable adjuncts.*

At its most extensive, the **Dusky Track** is one of the **longest** and **most remote** tracks in New Zealand. The high cost of transportation and the commitment involved make it one of the least-walked tracks, but anyone with sufficient experience and stamina shouldn't miss this opportunity to walk from one of New Zealand's largest lakes (Manapouri) to its longest fiord (Dusky Sound).

There are three basic elements, each following a major river valley and connecting to form an inverted Y. Any two of these can be combined to make a tramp of **four to six days**, or all three can be attempted in **eight to ten days**. On a tramp of this length it is especially important to have plenty of spare food and stove fuel in case of bad weather or flooding. In **summer**, be prepared for a lot of stream crossings and precarious walkwires to negotiate. In **winter** you can also expect snow and ice, which often render the track impassable, though you will be advised of conditions when you **notify** either the Tuatapere or Te Anau DOC office of your **intentions**; remember to **check in** on your return from the track.

ACCOMMODATION AND ACCESS
There is no need to book **huts** on the Dusky, all eight huts are Category 3 ($4) and operate on a first-come-first-served basis. All have twelve bunks (except the 6-bunk West Arm Hut), tank water and long-drop toilets; only Halfway Hut lacks mattresses.

Most trampers enter the region **by boat** across Lake Hauroko with Lake Hauroko Tours (Nov–April; $48; ☎03/226 6681), who'll also drive you in from Tuatapere (see p.755) at 9.30am on Mondays and Thursdays. For walkers coming in the opposite direction, pick-ups from **Hauroko Burn** Hut are on the same days at noon, but must be confirmed in advance.

From Lake Hauroko, it's three days' walk to Loch Maree Hut, which is poised at the junction of the three "legs". Some trampers then turn west to **Supper Cove** (1 day) and **fly out** with Waterwings Airways' scheduled service (Nov–April daily 11am; $148; ☎03/249 7405), while others head north to **West Arm** (3 days) to pick up the daily Fiordland Travel **launch** across Lake Manapouri ($45; ☎03/249 6602 & 0800/656 502).

THE ROUTE
You won't want to hang around the Hauroko Burn Hut, and mid-morning boat drop-offs leave you plenty of time to walk from **Hauroko Burn Hut to Halfway Hut** (12km; 4–6hr), following Hauroko Burn as it runs through a short gorge and gradually steepens to Halfway Hut. The second day from **Halfway Hut to Lake Roe Hut** (7km; 3–5hr) goes easily for a couple of hours then climbs above the bushline and follows snow poles to the magnificently sited Lake Roe Hut. On the third day, from **Lake Roe Hut to Loch Maree Hut** (10km; 4–6hr), the track veers west along the tops of the Pleasant Range, with spectacular views to Dusky Sound, before descending very steeply to Loch Maree Hut.

Trampers wishing to walk from **Loch Maree Hut to Supper Cove Hut** (12km; 6hr) continue west from Loch Maree following the Seaforth River. At low tide, the last rough section of track can be avoided by cutting across the flats to Supper Cove Hut – where it is traditional to take out the dinghy and fish for your supper. Anyone not flying out has to retrace their steps to Loch Maree Hut.

From **Loch Maree Hut to Kintail Hut** (11km; 4–5hr), you follow the Seaforth River upstream on fairly difficult ground that can be boggy and becomes impassable when the river is high. The next day, the route from **Kintail Hut to Upper Spey Hut** (7km; 5–6hr) involves a steep ascent to the scenic sub-alpine Centre Pass, then an equally precipitous descent to Upper Spey Hut. The last day takes you fairly painlessly from **Upper Spey Hut to West Arm Hut** (11km; 4–5hr), down the Spey River to the Wilmot Pass road between West Arm and Doubtful Sound. Forty minutes walk brings you to the wharf at West Arm – hopefully in time to catch the last launch (usually at around 4pm). Otherwise you'll have to spend the night at West Arm Hut 200m east of the power-station visitor centre.

for the 20km ride over Wilmot Pass – said to be the costliest stretch of road in the country and completely unconnected to any other road – to Deep Cove, where the tailrace tunnel spews out vast quantities of lake water. Here you board a three-hour cruise to the mouth of the fiord, where fur seals loll on the rocks, and into Hall Arm, where bottlenose dolphins often congregate.

For a more in-depth encounter with the fiords, join one of the superb multi-day trips organized by Fiordland Ecology Holidays (3–6 days; $145 per day; ☎03/249 6600). The **motor-sailer** *Breaksea Girl* is skippered by Lance Shaw, who spent twelve years running DOC's research vessel in these waters and holds passionate views on the non-extractive use of the fiords. Fishing is out and, though snorkelling and scuba diving are in, care is taken to minimize the impact on this fragile environment. Trips typically take in **Doubtful**, **Dusky** and **Breaksea** sounds, spending time with dolphins and seals and calling at places frequented by Cook and by turn-of-the-century bird conservationist Richard Henry.

A similar ethical vein flavours the **kayaking trips** run by Fiordland Wilderness Experiences (☎03/249 7700), who sometimes run joint trips with Fiordland Ecology Holidays which enable kayakers to reach unsullied waters by hitching a ride aboard the *Breaksea Girl* (around $200 per day). Otherwise, their regular guided trips involve kayaking on Doubtful Sound and camping out in one of its remote arms (Tues & Sat departures; 2 days; $220).

During the **winter months** (May–Sept), the *Milford Wanderer* (☎03/249 6602 & 0800/656 502) leaves its beat on Milford Sound and indulges in some leisurely cruises around the southern fiords: prices range from $315 for a two-day jaunt to $1195 for a week-long saunter around Preservation Inlet and Dusky Sound.

The Southern Scenic Route

The vast majority of visitors to Te Anau and Manapouri retrace their steps to Queenstown and miss out on the fringe country, where the fertile sheep paddocks of Southland butt up against the remote country of the Fiordland National Park. The minor towns of the region are linked by the **Southern Scenic Route**, small roads where mobs of sheep are likely to be the biggest cause of traffic problems. From Te Anau it runs via Manapouri to SH99, following the valley of the Waiau River to the cave-pocked limestone country around **Clifden**. A minor road cuts west to Lake Hauroko, access point to both the Dusky Track and the Hump Track, while the Southern Scenic Route continues south through the service town of **Tuatapere** to estuary-side **Riverton** and on to Invercargill.

Southern Explorer shuttle **buses** do the trip through Manapouri, Tuatapere and Riverton on Saturday (8am from Te Anau, arriving at Invercargill around 5pm; $40), making plenty of stops along the way.

The **eastern continuation** of the Southern Scenic Route through the Catlins to Dunedin is covered in Chapter Eleven, starting on p.601.

Borland Road and Lake Monowai

Some 35km south of Manapouri, **Borland Road** cuts west to Lake Manapouri's South Arm. Built in 1963, it provides hunting, fishing, mountain-biking and tramping access to a huge swathe of untouched country south of Lake Manapouri.

Passing the dam which controls the flow of water from Lake Manapouri down the Waiau River, the road runs 8km to the *Monowai River Lodge* (☎ & fax 03/225 5191, freephone 0800/877 222; dorms ①, rooms ③), a superb lagoonside retreat geared to both the rod-and-gun set and backpackers. The fully self-contained lodge – complete with piano – sleeps twelve, and when not booked by groups, individual rooms are rented out; failing that, there are beds in rustic but comfortable bunkhouses. The lodge also operates Fiordland Adventures (same phone & fax numbers), offering mountain bikes for rent ($25 per day), 4WD trips and advice on walks off Borland Road.

Immediately past the lodge, a spur runs 6km to **Lake Monowai**, the water level of which was artificially raised as part of an early, small-scale hydro scheme in 1925. The scars can still be seen on its shores, where there's a primitive **campsite** ($2) with long-drop toilets and barbecues. Monowai is a popular for fishing – mostly done from boats to avoid snagging lines in the submerged skeletons of drowned trees. Back on Borland Road it is another 4km west to *Borland Lodge* (☎03/225 5464; ①), a youth adventure centre where you can stay in twin chalets (bring your own bedding). They also rent out reasonably-priced tents and stoves to those wanting to explore the excellent **walking** country and huts hereabouts, all detailed in DOC's *Lake Monowai/Borland Road* leaflet (50¢).

Beyond *Borland Lodge*, the increasingly narrow, steep and landslip-prone road can be driven another 40km to **Lake Manapouri's South Arm**, where there is a shelter and toilets (Oct–May; key from DOC in Tuatapere or Te Anau). Close to the end of the road, a spur (open to trampers only) leads 15km over the Percy Saddle to **West Arm** and eventually to Doubtful Sound.

Clifden and Lake Hauroko

Back at the junction with the main highway, it is 32km further south to **CLIFDEN**, barely a town at all but of some interest for the historic **Clifden Suspension Bridge**, one of the longest in the South Island, built over the Waiau River in 1899 and in use until the 1970s. The north abutment overshadows a free campsite and barbecue area. Clifden most likely gets its name from low cliffs made of the same limestone that is riddled with the **Clifden Caves** (unrestricted access, signposted off Clifden Gorge Road), where Maori once camped on summer foraging trips. Suitably equipped with torches and treading carefully, you can explore the stalactite and glow-worm grottos at your leisure, using ladders installed in the steepest sections.

Languishing at the end of a dirt road, 30km west of Clifden, **Lake Hauroko** is New Zealand's deepest lake (462m). Low bush-clad hills surround the lake, leaving it open to the "sounding winds" immortalized in its name. There are no facilities at First Bay, the road end, just a primitive campsite midway between Clifden and Lake Hauroko and, at the north end of the lake, the Hauroko Burn Hut (accessible by boat, or on foot via the Dusky Track – see p.753).

To explore the lake and its environs, call the Wairaurahiri Jet (☎03/225 8318) or Wairaurahiri Wilderness Jet (☎03/225 8174), both of which run day-trips across Lake Hauroko, followed by **jetboating** 27km of the Grade III Wairaurahiri River down to the coast, and exploring the bush around Percy Burn. Transport can be arranged from Tuatapere (see below) or Clifden, and trips are priced by the boat-load ($400 for up to 3 people, $500 for 4 or 5).

Tuatapere and around

Two sawmills and one feeble stand of beech and podocarp forest is the only evidence that **TUATAPERE**, on the banks of the Waiau River 14km south of Clifden, could once have justified its epithet of "The Hole in the Forest". As the largest town in southwestern Southland, it makes an obvious base for exploring the very southern limits of Fiordland.

The Town

Maori legend records the great war canoe Takitimu being wrecked on the Waiau River bar at Te Waewae Bay some six hundred years ago. Maori set up summer foraging camps along the river and used these as way-stations on the route to the *pounamu* fields around Milford Sound, but it wasn't until European **pioneers** arrived around 1885 that Tuatapere came into being. By 1909 the **railway** had arrived from Invercargill, bringing with it increasingly sophisticated steam-powered haulers that made short work of clearing the surrounding bushland. More recently, foresters' attention shifted west to the fringes of the Fiordland National Park where, in the 1970s, the Maori owners proposed clear felling stands of rimu. Environmentalists prevailed upon the Conservation Minister who eventually, in 1996, agreed to pay compensation in return for a sustainable management policy. The bush's last stand – a riverside clump of beech, kahikatea and totara on the Domain – forms one station on the **Tuatapere Walkway**, a 5km stroll around town guided by a leaflet from DOC.

Practicalities

For such a small town, Tuatapere is thinly spread. The riverside town centre holds the **DOC office**, 21 Orawai Rd (Mon–Fri 8am–4.30pm; ☎03/226 6607) and the Tuatapere **visitor centre**, 18 Orawai Rd (daily 9am–5pm; ☎03/226 6393).

The pick of the limited **accommodation** is the simple *Tuatapere Motel*, 41 Orawia Rd (☎ & fax 03/226 6593; ④). Otherwise, the *Five Mountains Holiday Park*, 14 Clifden Rd (☎03/226 6418 & 025/342 898), has cheaper, basic units (②), a primitive bunkhouse (①), and a spacious camping area ($6), though **campers** are better served at the *Tuatapere Domain Motor Camp*, Erskine Street (☎03/226 6474), where tent ($6) and powered sites ($8) are surrounded by native bush, or the compact *Mikaela Motor Camp*, Peace Street (☎03/226 6626), with similarly priced sites and cabins (②).

The best **eating** around is to be found at the *South Coast Café*, on the corner of Clifden Road and Half Mile Road (☎03/226 6665), or settle for a bar snack at the *Waiau Hotel*, 47 Main St.

Around Tuatapere

This is no real reason to spend much time in Tuatapere itself, though you might use it as a base for jetboat trips on Lake Hauroko (see p.755) or as a springboard for **Te Waewae Bay**, a large bite out of the Southland coastline 10km to the south where Hector's dolphins frequently frolic and the occasional southern right whale drifts past. **Bluecliffs Beach**, at its western end, 28km from Tuatapere, is the start of the South Coast Track (see box on p.757).

Colac Bay and Riverton

South of Tuatapere, SH99 follows the wind-ravaged cliffs behind the wide and moody Te Waewae Bay, where fierce southerlies have sculpted some much-photographed macrocarpa trees into compact forms not unlike giant broccoli. Beyond the small town of Orepuki, the road cuts inland, regaining the sea 45km southeast of Tuatapere, at the quiet community of **Colac Bay** – a name eighteenth-century whalers derived from the name of the local Maori chief, Korako. Swimming aside, there's little reason to stop here, and you might as well press on a further 12km to **RIVERTON** (*Aparima*), one of the country's oldest settlements. Used by whalers from New South Wales as early as the last decade of the seventeenth century, the town was formally established in 1836 by another whaler, John Howell – who is also credited with kick-starting New Zealand's now formidable sheep-farming industry.

Strung along a spit between the sea and the Jacob's River Estuary (actually the mouth of the Aparima and Pourakino rivers), where fishing boats still harbour, Riverton

THE WAITUTU TRACKS

The map on DOC's Waitutu Tracks *leaflet ($1) is adequate for these walks.*

The Waitutu Tracks is the combined name for two historic paths that slice through the largest area of lowland rainforest in New Zealand: the predominantly easy-going and well graded **South Coast Track** from Bluecliffs Beach on Te Waewae Bay southwest to Big River, and the tougher **Hump Track** which rises above the bushline en route from Bluecliffs Beach to Lake Hauroko. For **history** buffs, the South Coast Track in particular is one of the country's most interesting. The route follows a portion of the 100km track cut in 1896 to link Orepuki, 18km southeast of Tuatapere, with Cromarty and Te Oneroa, gold-mining settlements in the southernmost fiord of Preservation Inlet. This paved the way for wood cutters, who arrived en masse in the 1920s. Logs were transported to the mills on tramways, which crossed the burns and gullies on **viaducts** built of Australian hardwood – four of the finest have been faithfully restored, including the one over Percy Burn that spans 125m.

Bluecliffs Beach **trailhead access** is by road from Tuatapere with Lake Hauroko Tours (☎03/226 6681; $30) or by jetboat (Wairaurahiri Jet, ☎03/225 8318; or Wairaurahiri Wilderness Jet, ☎03/225 8174). Expect to take **a week** to explore all of the South Coast Track; it takes the best part of four days to reach Big River and you'll just have to turn around and walk back, unless you prearrange a **jetboat** out of Wairaurahiri Hut. A popular alternative is to make a **three-day excursion**, staying at Port Craig Hut for two nights and exploring the environs on the second day. Three huts (Cat 3; $4), spaced four to seven hours' walk apart, provide **accommodation** on the South Coast Track and camping is free. Following the accidental razing of the Hump Hut in 1994, the Hump Track has only one hut (Cat 3; $4), around nine hours' walk from Bluecliffs Beach.

THE SOUTH COAST TRACK

The first day's walk is typically **Bluecliffs Beach to Port Craig Hut** (20km; 5–7hr; negligible ascent), a relatively easy walk following either the old logging road or, tide permitting, the beach – which should shave an hour off your walking time. The section from **Port Craig Hut to Wairaurahiri Hut** (16km; 4–6hr; 200m ascent) the track follows the old tramway, crossing all four of the restored viaducts, before dropping down to the Wairaurahiri River. The path from **Wairaurahiri Hut to Waitutu Hut** (13km, 4–6hr, negligible ascent) largely follows the coastal flats across Maori land. Fit trampers with camping equipment might want to continue from **Waitutu Hut to Big River** (12km; 5–7hr; negligible ascent), the boundary of the Fiordland National Park and the end of the track; note that there are no facilities of any kind at Big River.

THE HUMP TRACK

The lack of huts makes camping equipment a real boon on the Hump Track. From **Bluecliffs Beach to Teal Bay Hut** (17km; 9–10hr; 600m ascent, 300m descent), you pick up the old logging road for about 7km to the remains of an old hut and a path branching north. This gradually climbs a ridge, which is followed for around five hours to the site of the burned-out Hump Hut, just below the bushline. The track soon ascends into open country; follow the ill-defined path and the line of orange snow poles, keeping an eye out for a large marker where the path cuts left into the bush and follows another ridge down to the Teal Bay Hut, on the shore of Lake Hauroko. The track from **Teal Bay Hut to Hauroko car park** (18km; 9hr; 300m ascent) hauls steeply up a spur to a ridge that runs parallel to Lake Hauroko for 7km, then descends to Second Bay, which is followed eastwards. The final stretch climbs a headland to First Bay before following an easy shoreline path to the finish, where there is a very basic shelter.

has a relaxed, airy feel that might just tempt you to stay for a day or so. The town is trying to pitch itself as some kind of paua capital, with a giant paua shell at the eastern entrance to town, buildings painted in shell-like colours and there are even plans to inlay the streets with bits of shell. You should reserve an hour or so for the interesting local history and hoard of knick-knacks in the **Early Settlers Museum**, 172 Palmerston St (daily 2–4pm; donation requested; ☎03/234 8520). Otherwise, you'll have to seek diversion on the water: one-hour scenic and historic rides up the Pourakino River are offered by Pourakino Jet Boat Tours ($60; ☎03/234 6130); or let Riverton Fishing Service (☎03/234 8907) take you out trout or saltwater **fishing**.

Local **information**, including a leaflet detailing leisurely beach and hilltop walks, is available in the foyer of *The Riverton Rock*, at 136 Palmerston St (☎03/234 8886 & 0800/248 886, fax 234 8816) – which is also easily the best **place to stay**. Beautifully decorated standard (③) and en-suite (④) rooms occupy a recently renovated 1870s building, and there's also a bunkroom (①); campervans can park outside for $18, and everyone gets to use the well-equipped kitchen area and spacious, comfortable lounge overlooking the lagoon. If they're full, make for the *Riverton Caravan Park and Holiday Homes* on Roy Street (☎03/234 8526; tent sites $8, bunkhouse ①, cottages & chalets ②–③). Of the limited range of **places to eat**, the most appealing is the *Nostalgia Country Café*, 108 Palmerston St (closed winter weekday evenings), which is good for coffee, light meals and predominantly seafood specials.

Beyond Riverton, SH99 heads into the hinterland of Invercargill, 40km away.

travel details

Buses

From Manapouri to: Clifden (1 weekly; 1hr 30min); Te Anau (2 daily; 20min); Riverton (1 weekly; 5hr); Tuatapere (1 weekly; 3hr).

From Milford Sound to: Te Anau (2–5 daily; 2hr 15min); The Divide (2–5 daily; 1hr 30min); Queenstown (2 daily; 5hr 15min).

From Te Anau to: Dunedin (1 daily; 5hr); Manapouri (2 daily; 20min); Milford Sound (2–5 daily; 2hr 15min); Invercargill (1 daily; 3hr); Manapouri (2 daily; 20min); Queenstown (3–5 daily; 2hr 15min); Te Anau Downs (2 daily Nov–April; 30min); The Divide (2–5 daily; 1hr 20min).

From The Divide to: Milford Sound (2–5 daily; 1hr 30min); Te Anau (2–5 daily; 1hr 20min).

From Tuatapere to: Invercargill (1 weekly; 2hr 30min); Riverton (1 weekly; 1hr 30min).

Flights

From Milford Sound to: Queenstown (5–20 daily; 35min).

From Te Anau to: Queenstown (3 daily; 30min).

PART THREE

THE

CONTEXTS

A BRIEF HISTORY

White New Zealanders have long thought of their country as a model of humanitarian colonization. Most Maori take a different view, however, informed by generations of their ancestors witnessing the theft of land and erosion of rights that were guaranteed by a treaty with the white man. Schoolroom histories have long been faithful to the European view, even to the point of influencing Maori mythology, but in the last couple of decades revisionist historians have largely discredited what many New Zealanders know as fact. Much that is presented as tradition, on deeper investigation turns out to be late nineteenth-century scholarship, often the product of historians who bent what they heard to fit their theories and, in the worst cases, even destroyed evidence. What follows is inextricably interwoven with Maori legend and can be understood more fully with reference to the section on *Maoritanga* (see p.773).

PRE-EUROPEAN HISTORY

Humans from southeast Asia first started exploring the South Pacific around five thousand years ago, gradually evolving a distinct culture as they filtered down through the islands of the Indonesian archipelago. A thousand years of progressive island hopping got them as far as Tonga and Samoa, where a distinctly Polynesian society continued to evolve, the people honing their seafaring skills and navigational skills to the point where lengthy sea journeys were possible. Around a thousand years ago, Polynesian culture reached its classical apotheosis in the Society Islands, a group west of Tahiti. This was almost certainly the hub for a series of migrations heading southwest across thousands of kilometres of open ocean, past the Cook Islands, eventually striking land in what is now known as **New Zealand** (Aotearoa).

It is thought that the first of these Polynesian people, the ancestors of modern **Maori**, arrived in double-hulled canoes between 1000 and 1100 AD, as a result of a migration that was planned to the extent that they took with them the *kuri* (dog) and food plants such as taro (a starchy tuber), yam and kumara (sweet potato). It seems likely that there were several migrations and there may have even been two-way traffic, although archeological evidence points to a cessation of contact well before 1500 AD. The widely believed story of a legendary "**Great Fleet**" (see p.775) arriving in 1350 AD seems most likely to be the product of a fanciful Victorian adaptation of Maori oral history, which has been readopted into contemporary Maori legend.

Arriving Polynesians found a land so much colder than their tropical home that many of the crops and plants they brought with them wouldn't grow. Fortunately there was an abundance of large quarry in the form of marine life and flightless birds, particularly in the South Island, where most settled. The people of this **Archaic Period** are often misleadingly known as "Moa Hunters" and while some undoubtedly lived off these birds, they didn't exist in other areas. By 1300, settlements had been established all around the coast, but it was only later that there is evidence of horticulture, possibly supporting the contention that there was a later migration bringing plants for cultivation. On the other hand, it may just signal the beginning of successful year-round food storage allowing a settled living pattern rather than the short-lived campsites used by earlier hunters. Whichever is the case, this marks the beginning of the **Classic period** when *kainga* (villages) grew up close to the kumara grounds, often supported by *pa* (fortified villages) where the people could retreat when under attack. As tasks became more specialized and hunting and horticulture began to take up less time, the arts – particularly carving and weaving (see p.776) – began to flourish and warfare became endemic, digs revealing an armoury of *mere*, *patu* and *taiaha* (fighting clubs) not found earlier. The decline of easily caught birdlife and the relative ease of growing kumara in the warmer North Island marked the beginning of a northward population shift, to the extent that when the Europeans arrived, ninety-five percent of the population was located in the North Island, mostly in the northern reaches, with coastal settlements reaching down to Hawke's Bay and Wanganui.

EUROPEAN CONTACT AND THE MAORI RESPONSE

Ever since Europeans had ventured across the oceans and "discovered" other continents, many were convinced of the existence of a *terra australia incognita*, an unknown southern land thought necessary to counterbalance and the northern continents. In 1642, the Dutch East India Company, keen to dominate any trade with this new continent, sent Dutchman **Abel Tasman** to the southern oceans where he became the first European to catch sight of the South Island of Aotearoa. He anchored in Golden Bay, where a small boat being rowed between Tasman's two ships was intercepted by a Maori war canoe and four sailors were killed. Without setting foot on land Tasman turned tail and fled up the west coast of the North Island and went on to add Tonga and Fiji to European maps. He named Aotearoa "Staten Landt" later renamed Nieuw Zeeland after the Dutch maritime province.

New Zealand was ignored for over a century until 1769 when Yorkshireman **James Cook** sailed his *Endeavour* into the Pacific to observe the passage of Venus across the sun. He continued west arriving at "the Eastern side of the Land discover'd by Tasman" where he observed the "Genius, Temper, Disposition and Number of the Natives" and meticulously charted the coastline – the only significant errors were to show Banks Peninsula as an island and Stewart Island as a peninsula – and encouraged his botanists, Banks and Solander, to collect numerous samples.

Cook and his crew found Maori a sophisticated people with a highly formalized social structure and an impressive ability to turn stone and wood into fabulously carved canoes, weapons and meeting houses – and yet they were tied to Stone Age technology, with no wheels, roads, metalwork, pottery or animal husbandry. Cook found them aggressive, surly and little inclined to trade, but after an initial unfortunate encounter near Gisborne (see p.354) and another off Cape Kidnappers, near Napier (see p.366), he managed to strike up friendly and constructive relations with the "Indians". These "Indians" now found that their tribal allegiance was not enough to differentiate them from the Europeans and subsequently began calling themselves *maori* (meaning "normal" or "not distinctive") while referring to the newcomers as *pakeha* ("foreign").

Offshore from the Coromandel Peninsula, Cook deviated from instructions and unfurled the British flag, claiming formal possession without the consent of Maori, but was still allowed to return twice in 1772 and 1776. The French were also interested in New Zealand, and on his first voyage Cook had passed **Jean Francois Marie de Surville** in a storm without either knowing of the other's presence. Two years later, **Marion du Fresne** spent five amicable weeks around the Bay of Islands, before most of his crew were killed, probably after inadvertently transgressing some *tapu* (taboo).

The establishment of the Botany Bay penal colony in neighbouring Australia aroused the first commercial interest in New Zealand and from the 1790s to the 1830s New Zealand was very much part of the Australian frontier. By 1830 the coast was dotted with semi-permanent **sealing** communities which, within thirty years, had almost clubbed the seals into extinction. Meanwhile the British navy was rapidly felling giant kauri trees for its ships' masts, while others were busy supplying Sydney shipbuilders. By the 1820s **whalers** had moved in, basing themselves at Kororareka (now Russell, in the Bay of Islands), where they could recruit Maori crew and provision their ships. This combination of rough whalers, escaped convicts from Australia and all manner of miscreants and adventurers combined to turn Russell into "the Hellhole of the Pacific", a lawless place populated by what Darwin, on his visit in 1835, found to be "the very refuse of Society".

Before long, the Maori way of life had been entirely disrupted. Maori were quick to understand the importance of guns and **inter-tribal fighting** soon broke out on a scale never seen before. Hongi Hika from Ngapuhi *iwi* of the Bay of Islands was the first chief to acquire firearms in 1821, adding 300 muskets to his stock by trading the gifts showered on him by London society when he was presented to George IV as an "equal". Vowing to emulate the supreme power of the imperial king, he set about subduing much of the North Island, using the often badly maintained and inexpertly aimed guns to rattle the enemy, who were then slaughtered with the traditional *mere*. Warriors abandoned the old fighting season – the lulls between hunting and tending the crops – and set off to settle old scores, resulting in a massive loss of life. The quest for new territory fuelled the actions of Ngati Toa's **Te Rauparaha** (see p.204), who soon controlled the southern half of the North Island.

The huge demand for firearms drove Maori to sell the best of their food, relocating to unhealthy areas close to flax swamps, where flax production could be increased. Even highly valued tribal treasures – *pounamu* (greenstone) clubs and the preserved heads of chiefs taken in battle – were traded. Poor living conditions allowed European **diseases** to sweep through the Maori population time and again, while alcohol and tobacco abuse became widespread, Maori women were prostituted to *pakeha* sailors, and the tribal structure began to crumble.

Into this scene stepped the **missionaries** in 1814, the brutal New South Wales magistrate, **Samuel Marsden**, arriving in the Bay of Islands a transformed man with a mission to bring Christianity and "civilization" to Maori, and to save the souls of the sealers and whalers. Subsequently Anglicans, Wesleyans and Catholics all set up missions throughout the North Island, playing a significant role in protecting Maori from the worst of the exploitation and campaigning in both London and Sydney for more policing of *pakeha* actions. In return, they destroyed fine artworks considered too sexually explicit and demanded that Maori abandon cannibalism and slavery; in short Maori were expected to trade in their Maoritanga and become Brown Europeans. By the 1830s, self-confidence and the belief in

Maori ways was in rapid decline: the *tohunga* (priest) was powerless over new European diseases which could often be cured by the missionaries, and Maori had started to believe the *pakeha*, who were convinced that the Maori race was dying out. They felt they needed help.

THE PUSH FOR COLONIZATION

Despite Cook's "discoverer's" claim in 1769, imperial cartographers had never marked New Zealand as a British possession and it was with some reluctance – informed by the perception of an over-extended empire only marginally under control – that New South Wales law was nominally extended to New Zealand in 1817. The effect was minimal; the New South Wales governor had no official representation on this side of the Tasman and was powerless to act. Unimpressed, by 1831 a small group of northern Maori chiefs decided to petition the British monarch to become a "friend and the guardian of these islands", a letter that was later used to justify Britain's intervention.

Britain's response was to send the pompous and less-than-competent **James Busby** as British Resident in 1833, with a brief to encourage trade, stay on good terms with the missionaries and Maori, and apprehend escaped convicts for return to Sydney. Feeling that New Zealand was becoming a drain on the colony's economy, the New South Wales governor, Bourke, withheld guns and troops, and Busby was unable to enforce his will. Busby was also duped by the madness of Baron de Thierry, a Brit of French parents, who claimed he had bought most of the Hokianga district from Hongi Hika and styled himself the "sovereign chief of New Zealand", ostensibly to save Maori from the degradation he foresaw under British dominion. In a panic, Busby misguidedly persuaded 35 northern chiefs to proclaim themselves as the "**United Tribes of New Zealand**" in 1835. As far as the Foreign Office was concerned, this allowed Britain to disclaim responsibility for the actions of its subjects.

By the late 1830s there were around two thousand *pakeha* in New Zealand, the largest concentration around Kororareka in the Bay of Islands, where there were often up to thirty ships at anchor. Most were British, but French Catholics were consolidating their tentative toehold, and in 1839 James Clendon was appointed American consul. Meanwhile, land

THE TREATY OF WAITANGI: IN ENGLISH AND MAORI

The main points set out in the **English treaty** are as follows.

• The chiefs cede sovereignty of New Zealand to the Queen of England.

• The Queen guarantees the chiefs the "full exclusive and undisturbed possession of their Lands and Estates Forests Fisheries and other properties which they may collectively or individually possess".

• The Crown retains the right of pre-emption over Maori lands.

• The Queen extends the rights and privileges of British subjects to Maori.

However, the **Maori translation** presents numerous possibilities for misunderstanding, since Maori is a more idiomatic and metaphorical language, where words can take on several different meanings. The main points of contention are as follows.

The preamble of the English version cites the main **objectives** of the treaty being to protect Maori interests, to provide for British settlement and to set up a government to maintain peace and order. On the other hand, the main thrust of the Maori version is that the all-important rank and status of the chiefs and tribes will be maintained.

In the Maori version, the concept of **sovereignty** is translated as *kawanatanga* ("governorship"), a word Maori linked to their experience of the toothless reign of British Resident James Busby. It seems unlikely that the chiefs realized just what they were giving away.

In the Maori text, the Crown guaranteed the *tangata whenua* ("people of the land") the possession of their properties for as long as they wished to keep them. In English this was expressed in terms of **individual rights** over property. This is perhaps the most wilful mistranslation and, in practice, there were long periods when Maori were coerced into selling their **land**, and when they refused, lands were simply taken.

Pre-emption was translated as *hokonga* – a term simply meaning "buying and selling", with no explanation for the Crown's exclusive right to buy Maori land, which was clearly spelled out in the English version. This has resulted in considerable friction over Maori being unable to sell any land that the government didn't want, even if they had a buyer.

The implications of British **citizenship** may not have been well understood: it is not clear whether Maori realized they would be bound by British law.

speculators and colonists were taking an interest for the first time. The Australian emancipationist, William Charles Wentworth, had "bought" the South Island and Stewart Island for a few hundred pounds (the largest private land deal in history, subsequently quashed by government order) and British settlers were already setting sail. The British admiralty finally began to take notice when it became apparent that the Australian convict settlements, originally intended simply as an out-of-sight, out-of-mind solution to their bulging prisons, looked set to become a valuable possession.

It was a combination of these pressures and Busby's continual exaggeration of the Maori inability to control their own affairs that goaded the British government into action. The result was the 1840 **Treaty of Waitangi** (see box above, and also p.401), a document that purported to guarantee continued Maori control of their lands, rights and possessions in return for their loss of sovereignty, a concept poorly understood by Maori. The annexed lands became a dependency of New South Wales

until New Zealand was declared a separate colony a year later.

SETTLEMENT AND THE EARLY PIONEERS

Even before the Treaty was signed, there were moves to found a settlement in Port Nicholson, the site of Wellington, on behalf of the **New Zealand Company**. This was the brainchild of **Edward Gibbon Wakefield**, who desperately wanted to stem American-style egalitarianism and hoped to use New Zealand as the proving ground for his theory of "scientific colonization". This involved preserving the English squire-and-yokel class structure by encouraging the settlement of a cross-section of English society, though without the "dregs" at the bottom. It was supposed to be a self-regulating system, whereby the company would buy large tracts of land cheaply from the government then charge a price low enough to encourage the relatively wealthy to invest, yet high enough to prevent labourers from becoming landowners. The revenue from land sales was then to fund the transportation of cheap labour to work the land, but the system ended up encouraging absentee landlordism as English "gentlemen", arriving to find somewhere altogether more rugged and less refined than they had been promised, hot-footed it to Australia or America.

Between 1839 and 1843 the New Zealand Company dispatched nearly 19,000 settlers and established them in "**planned settlements**" in Wellington, Wanganui, Nelson and New Plymouth. This was the core of *pakeha* immigration, the only substantial non-Wakefield settlement being **Auckland**, a scruffy collection of waterside shacks which, to the horror of New Zealand Company officials, became the capital after the signing of the Treaty of Waitangi. Maori welfare and social justice had no place in all this, despite the precarious position of *pakeha* settlements, which were nothing but tiny enclaves in a country still under Maori control. Transgressing the protocols of the local *iwi* was likely to have graver implications than offending the *pakeha* government.

The company couldn't buy land direct from Maori, but the government bought up huge tracts and sold it on, often for ten or twenty times what they paid for it. Maori must have been well aware that they were being swindled and could have negotiated better prices themselves, but sold almost the whole of the South Island in a number of large blocks. Some was bought by two more organizations expounding the Wakefield principle: the dour Free Church of Scotland founded **Dunedin** in 1848, while the Canterbury Association established **Christchurch** in 1850, fashioning it English, Anglo-Catholic and conservative. In 1850 the New Zealand Company foundered, leaving well-established settlements which, subject to the hard realities of colonial life, had failed to conform to Wakefield's lofty theories and were filled with sturdy workers from labouring and lower middle-class backgrounds.

In 1852 New Zealand achieved self-government and set about dividing the country into six **provinces** – Auckland, New Plymouth, Wellington, Nelson, Canterbury and Otago – which took over land sales and encouraged migrants with free passage, land grants and guaranteed employment on road construction schemes. The same people drawn to the

Wakefield settlements heeded the call, hoping for a better life away from the oppression and drudgery of working-class Britain. The new towns were alive with ambitious folk prepared to work hard to realize their high expectations, but many felt stymied by the low-quality land they were able to buy. At this point Maori still held the best land and were doing quite nicely growing potatoes and wheat for both local consumption and export to Australia, where the Victorian gold rush had created a huge demand. *Pakeha* were barely able to compete, and with the slump in export prices in the mid-1850s, many looked to pastoralism. The Crown helped out by halving the price of land, allowing poorer settlers to become landowners but simultaneously paving the way for the creation of huge pastoral runs and putting further pressure on Maori to sell land.

MAORI DISCONTENT AND THE NEW ZEALAND WARS

The first five years after the signing of the Treaty were a disaster, first under governor Hobson then under the ineffectual FitzRoy. Relations between Maori and *pakeha* began to deteriorate immediately, as the capital was moved from Kororareka to Auckland and duties were imposed in the Bay of Islands. The consequent loss of trade from passing ships precipitated the first tangible expression of dissent, a famous series of incidents involving the Ngapuhi leader **Hone Heke**, who repeatedly felled the most fundamental symbol of British authority, the flagstaff at Russell (see p.160). The situation was normalized to some degree by the appointment of **George Grey**, the most able of New Zealand's governors and a man who did more than anyone else to shape the country's early years. He was economical with the truth and despotic, but possessed the intelligence to use his deceit in a most effective (and often benign) way. As Maori began to adapt their culture to accommodate *pakeha* in a way that few other native peoples have – selling their crops, operating flour mills and running coastal shipping – Grey encouraged the process by establishing mission schools, erecting hospitals where Maori could get free treatment, and providing employment on public works. In short, he did what he could to uphold the spirit of the Treaty, thereby gaining enormous respect among Maori. Sadly, he failed to set up any mechanism to perpetuate his policies after he left for the governorship of Cape Town in 1853. Under New Zealand's constitution, enacted in 1852, Maori were excluded from political decision-making and prevented from setting up their own form of government; although British subjects in name, they had few of the practical benefits and yet were increasingly expected to comply with British law.

By now it was clear that Maori had been duped by the Treaty of Waitangi: one chief explained that they thought they were transferring the "shadow of the land" while "the substance of the land remains with us", and yet he now conceded "the substance of the land goes to the Europeans, the shadow only will be our portion". Growing **resistance** to land sales came at a time when settler communities were expanding and demanding to buy huge tracts of pastoral land. With improved communications *pakeha* became more self-reliant and dismissive of Maori, who progressively began to lose faith in the government and fell back on traditional methods of handling their affairs. Self-government had given landowners the vote, but since Maori didn't hold individual titles to their land they were denied suffrage. Maori and *pakeha* aspirations seemed completely at odds and there was a growing sense of betrayal, which helped to replace tribal animosities with a tenuous unity. In 1854, a month before New Zealand's first parliament, Maori held inter-tribal meetings to discuss a response to the degradation of their culture and the rapid loss of their land. The eventual upshot was the 1858 election of the ageing **Te Wherowhero**, head chief of the Waikatos, as the Maori "King", the leader of the **King Movement** behind which Maori could rally to hold back the flood of *pakeha* settlement. Initially just the Waikato and central North Island *iwi* supported the King, but soon Taranaki and some Hawke's Bay *iwi* joined in a loose federation united in vowing not to sell any more land. This brave attempt to challenge the changes forced upon them gave Maori a sense of purpose and brought with it a resurgence of ancient customs such as tattooing. While some radical Maori wanted to completely rid the country of the white menace, most were moderates and made peaceful overtures that *pakeha* chose to regard as rebellious.

By now, most settlers felt that the Treaty of Waitangi had no validity whatsoever and sided with the land sellers to drive the government to repress the Maori landholders. There had been minor skirmishes over land throughout the country, but matters came to a head in 1860, when the government used troops to enforce a bogus purchase of land at Waitara, near New Plymouth. The fighting was temporarily confined to Taranaki but soon spread to consume the whole of the North Island in the **New Zealand Wars**, once known by *pakeha* as the Maori Wars and by Maori as *te riri pakeha* (white man's anger). Maori were divided: most of the supporters of the King movement, particularly the Waikatos, traced their *whakapapa* (genealogy) back to the Tainui canoe and some others chose this opportunity to settle old grievances by siding with the government against their traditional enemies. Through the early 1860s the number of *pakeha* troops was tripled to around 3000, providing an effective force against Maori who failed to adopt a co-ordinated strategy. The warrior ethic meant there was no place for more effective guerrilla tactics, except in the east of the North Island, where **Te Kooti** (see box, p.362) kept the government troops on the run. Elsewhere Maori frequently faced off against ranked artillery and, though there were notable successes, the final result was inevitable. Fighting had abated by the end of the 1860s but peace wasn't finally declared until 1881, when the Maori fastness of the "King Country" (an area south of Hamilton which still goes by that title) was finally opened up to *pakeha* once again.

British soldiers had been lured into service with offers of land and free passage and, as a further affront to defeated Maori, many of them were settled in the solidly Maori Waikato. Much of the most fertile land was **confiscated** – in the Waikato, the Bay of Plenty and Taranaki – with little regard to the owners' allegiances during the conflict. By 1862 the Crown had relinquished its right of pre-emption and individuals could buy land directly from Maori, who were forced to limit the stated ownership first to ten individuals and later to just one owner. With their collective power smashed, there was little resistance to voracious land agents luring Maori into debt then offering to buy their land to save them.

Throughout this period, Maori tradition was ignored by settlers and an Anglo-Saxon world view came to dominate all aspects of New

Zealand life; by 1871 the Maori language was no longer used for teaching in schools. A defeated people were widely thought to be close to extinction: Anthony Trollope in 1872 wrote "There is scope for poetry in their past history. There is room for philanthropy as to their present condition. But in regard to their future – there is hardly a place for hope."

Meanwhile, as the New Zealand Wars raged in the North Island, **gold fever** had struck the South. Flakes had been found near Queenstown in 1861 and the initial rushes soon spread to later finds along the West Coast. For the best part of a decade, gold was New Zealand's major export, but the gold provinces never had a major influence on the rest of the country, nor does the gold era retain the legendary status it does in California and Victoria. The major effect was on population distribution: by 1858 the shrinking Maori population had been outstripped by the rapidly swelling horde of *pakeha* settlers, a number which doubled during the first three years of the gold rush, most settling in the South Island where relations with Maori played a much smaller part. The South Island prospered, with both Christchurch and Dunedin consolidating their roles, serving the surrounding farms and more distant sheep stations. Dunedin became the largest town in the country, the influx of the "New Iniquity" radically changing the city's staunch front of the "Old Identity".

CONSOLIDATION AND SOCIAL REFORM

The 1870s were dominated by the policies of **Julius Vogel**, an able Treasurer who started a programme of borrowing on a massive scale to fund public works. Within a decade what had previously been a land of scattered towns in separately governed provinces was transformed into an single country unified by improved roads, an expanding rail system, 7000 kilometres of telegraph wires and numerous public institutions. Almost all the remaining farmable land was bought up or leased from Maori and acclimatization societies sprang up with the express aim of anglicizing the New Zealand countryside and improving **farming**. New Zealand quickly began to realize the agricultural expectation created by fertile soils, a temperate climate and relatively high rainfall. Arable farming was mostly abandoned and

pastoralism was taking hold, particularly among those rich enough to afford to buy and ship the stock. With no extensive market close enough to make perishable produce profitable, **wool** became the main export item, stimulated by the development of the Corriedale sheep, a Romney-Lincoln cross with a long fleece. Wool continued as the mainstay until 1882, when the first refrigerated shipment left for Britain, signalling a turning point in the New Zealand economy and the establishment of New Zealand as Britain's offshore larder, a role it maintained until the 1970s.

From 1879 until 1896 New Zealand went into the "long depression", mostly overseen by the conservative "Continuous Ministry" – the last government composed of colonial gentry. During this time **trade unionism** began to influence the political scene and bolstered the Liberal Pact (a Liberal and Labour alliance), which, in 1890, wrested power from those who had controlled the country for two decades and ushered in an era of unprecedented social change. Its first leader, **John Ballance**, firmly believed in state intervention and installed **William Pember Reeves**, probably New Zealand's most radically socialist MP, as his Minister of Labour. Reeves was instrumental in pushing through sweeping reforms to working hours and factory conditions that were so progressive that no further changes were made to labour laws until 1936. On his own initiative, with no apparent demand from workers, he introduced the world's first **compulsory arbitration system**, which went on to award numerous wage rises, so increasing the national prosperity. He had become too radical for most of his colleagues, however, and only remained in office until 1896. When Ballance died in 1892 he was replaced by **Richard "King Dick" Seddon**, a blunt Lancastrian who became, along with Grey, one of the country's greatest, if least democratic, leaders. Following Ballance's lead he introduced a graduated income tax and repealed property tax, hoping to break up some of the large estates (something eventually achieved much later, as technological changes made dairying and mixed farming more prosperous). New Zealand was already being tagged the "social laboratory of the world", but more was to come.

In 1893, New Zealand was the first nation in the world to enact full **female suffrage**, undoubtedly in line with the liberal thinking of the time, but apparently an accident nonetheless. The story goes that Seddon let an amendment to an electoral reform bill pass on the assumption that it would be rejected by the Legislative Council (an upper house which survived until 1950), thus diverting the ill will of suffragists. Others contend that female suffrage was approved not for any free-thinking liberal principle but in response to the powerful quasi-religious temperance movement, which hoped to "purify and improve the tone of our politics", effectively giving married couples double the vote of the single man who was often seen as a drunken layabout. In 1898 Seddon further astonished the world by weathering a ninety-hour continuous debate to squeeze through legislation guaranteeing an **old age pension**. Fabian Beatrice Webb, in New Zealand that same year, allowed that "it is delightful to see a country with no millionaires and hardly any slums".

By early this century, the radical impetus had faded along with the memory of the 1880s depression, and *pakeha* could rest easy in the knowledge that their standard of living was one of the highest in the world. But things were not so rosy for Maori, whose numbers had dropped from an estimated 200,000 at Cook's first visit to a low of 42,000 in 1896. However, as resistance to European diseases grew, numbers started rising, accompanied by a new confidence buoyed by the rise of Maori parliamentary leadership. **Apirana Ngata**, **Maui Pomare** and Te Rangi Hiroa (**Peter Buck**) were all products of Te Aute College, an Anglican school for Maori, and all were committed to working within the administrative and legislative framework of government, convinced that the survival of Maoritanga depended on shedding those aspects of the traditional lifestyle that impeded their acceptance of the modern world.

Seddon died in 1906 and the flame went out of the Liberal torch, though the party was to stay in power another six years. This era saw the rise of the "**Red Feds**", international socialists of the Red Federation who began to organize Kiwi labour. They rejected the arbitration system that had kept wage rises below the level of inflation and prevented strikes for a decade, and encouraged **strikes**, the longest at Blackball (see p.628) on the West Coast,

where prime movers in the formation of the Federation of Miners, and subsequently the Federation of Labour, led a three-year stoppage.

The 1912 election was won by William Massey's Reform Party, with the support of the farmers or "cow cockies". Allegiances were now substantially polarized and 1912 and 1913 saw bitter fighting at a series of strikes at the gold mines of Waihi, the docks at Timaru and the wharves of Auckland. As workers opposed to the arbitration system withdrew their labour, the owners organized scab labour, while the hostile Farmers' Union recruited mounted "specials" to add to the government force of "special constables". All were protected by naval and military forces as they decisively smashed the Red Feds. The Prime Minister even handed out medals to strike-breaking dairy farmers. Further domestic conflict was only averted by the outbreak of war.

COMING OF AGE: 1918–1945

Though New Zealand had started off as an unwanted sibling of Mother England, it had soon transformed itself into a devoted daughter who could be relied upon in times of crisis. New Zealand had supported Britain in South Africa at the end of the nineteenth century and was now called upon to do the same in **World War I**. Locally born *pakeha* now outnumbered immigrants and, in 1907, New Zealand had traded its self-governing colony status for that of a Dominion, giving it control over its foreign policy; but the rising sense of nationalism didn't dilute a patriotism for the motherland far in excess of its filial duty. Altogether ten percent of the population were involved in the war effort, 100,000 fighting in the trenches of Gallipoli and elsewhere. Seventeen thousand failed to return, more than were lost in Belgium, a battleground with six times the population.

At home, the **Temperance Movement** was back in action, attempting to curb vice in the army brought on by the demon drink. Plebiscites in 1911, 1914 and 1919 narrowly averted national prohibition but the "wowsers" succeeded to the point that from 1917 pubs would close at 6pm for the duration of the war. Six o'clock closing entered the statute books in 1918: not until 1967 did its repeal end half a century of the "**Six o'clock swill**", an hour or so of frenetic after-work consumption in which the ability to tank down as much beer as possible was raised to an art form. This probably did more to hinder New Zealand's social development than anything else: pubs began to look more like lavatories, which could be hosed down after closing, and the predilection for quantity over quality encouraged breweries to churn out dreadful watery brews.

The wartime boom economy continued until around 1920 as Britain's demand for food remained high. Things looked rosy, especially for *pakeha* returned servicemen, who were rehabilitated on newly acquired farmland; in contrast, Maori returned servicemen got nothing. These highly mortgaged and inexperienced farmers began to suffer with the rapid drop in produce prices in the early 1920s, fostering a sense of insecurity which pervaded the country. Political leadership was weak and yet New Zealand continued to grow with ongoing improvements in infrastructure – hydroelectric dams and roads – and enormous improvements in farming techniques, such as the application of superphosphate fertilizers, sophisticated milking machines and tractors. New Zealand remained a prosperous nation but was ill prepared for the **Great Depression**, when the Wall Street Crash sent shock waves through the country. The already high national debt skyrocketed as export income dropped and the Reform government cut pensions, health care and public works' expenditure. The budget was balanced at the cost of producing huge numbers of unemployed. Prime Minister Forbes dictated "no pay without work" and sent thousands of men to primitive rural relief camps for unnecessary tasks such as planting trees and draining swamps in return for a pittance. With the knowledge of the prosperous years to come it is hard to conjure the image of lines of ragged men awaiting their relief money, malnourished children in schools and former soldiers panhandling in the streets.

Throughout the 1920s the Labour Party had gradually watered down some of its socialist policies in an attempt to woo the middle-ground voter. In 1935 they were swept to power and ushered in New Zealand's second era of massive social change, picking up where Seddon left off. Labour's leader **Michael Joseph Savage** felt that "Social Justice must be the guiding principle and economic organi-zation must adapt itself to social needs", a sentiment translated by a contemporary commentator as aiming "to turn capitalism quite painlessly into a nicer sort of capitalism which will eventually become indistinguishable from socialism". State socialism was out, but "Red Feds" still held half the cabinet posts. Salaries reduced during the depression were restored; public works programmes were rekindled, with workers on full pay rather than "relief"; income was redistributed through graduated taxation; and in two rapid bursts of legislation Labour built the model **Welfare State**, the first in the world and the most comprehensive and integrated. State houses were built and let at low rental, pensions were increased, a national health service provided free medicines and health care, and family benefits supplemented the income of those with children.

Maori welfare was also on the agenda and there were moves to raise their living standards to the *pakeha* level, partly achieved by increasing pensions and unemployment payments. Much of the best land had by now been sold off but legal changes paved the way for Maori land to be farmed using *pakeha* agricultural methods, while maintaining communal ownership. In return, the newly formed **Ratana Party**, who held all four of the Maori Parliamentary seats, supported Labour, keeping them in office until 1949.

New Zealand's perception of its world position changed dramatically in 1941 when the Japanese bombed Pearl Harbor. The country was forced to recognize its position half a globe away from Britain and in the military sphere of America. As in World War I, large numbers of troops were called up, amounting to a third of the male labour force, but casualties were fewer and on the home front the economy continued to boom. Foreign wars aside, by the 1940s New Zealand was the world's most prosperous country, with a fabulous quality of life and the comfortable bed of the Welfare State to fall back on.

MORE YEARS OF PROSPERITY

The Reform Party and the remnants of the Liberals eventually combined to form the **National Party** which, from the late 1940s until the mid-1980s, became New Zealand's natural party of government, disturbed only by two three-year stints with Labour in power. The conservatism always bubbling under had now found its expression. Most were happy with the government's strong-arm tactics, which emasculated the militant unions and the country settled down to what novelist C.K. Stead viewed as the Kiwi ideal: "to live in a country with fresh air, an open landscape and plenty of sunshine; and to own a house, car, refrigerator, washing machine, bach, launch, fibre-glass rod, golf clubs, and so on." While the egalitarian myth still perpetuated by many Kiwis had never have existed, by most measures New Zealand's wealth was evenly spread, with few truly rich and relatively few poor.

The exception at least in economic terms were Maori, many now migrating in huge numbers to the cities, especially Auckland, responding to the urban labour shortages and good wages after World War II. By the 1970s the deracination of urban Maori was creating social unrest which, left unchannelled, resulted in high Maori unemployment and a disproportionate representation in prisons. Increasing contact between Maori and Europeans exposed weaknesses in the *pakeha* belief that the country's race relations were the best in the world. *Pakehas* took great pride in Maori bravery, skill, generosity and good humour, but were unable to set aside the discrimination which kept Maoris out of professional jobs.

On the economic front the major changes took place under **Walter Nash**'s 1957–60 Labour government, when New Zealand embarked on a programme designed to relieve the country's dependence on exports. A steel rolling mill, oil refinery, gin distillery and glass factory were all set up and an aluminium industry was encouraged by the prospect of cheap power from hydroelectric project on Lake Manapouri (see box, p.749). When **Keith Holyoake** took over at the helm of the next National government, Britain was still by far New Zealand's biggest export market but was making overtures to the economically isolationist European Common Market. New Zealand was becoming aware that Britain was no longer the guardian she once was. This was equally true in the **military** sphere, where New Zealand began to court its Pacific allies, signing the anti-Communist SEATO (South-East Asia Treaty Organization) document, and the ANZUS pact, which provided for mutual defence of Australia, New Zealand and the US.

DITHERING IN THE FACE OF ADVERSITY: 1972–1984

In a landslide victory, the third **Labour government** took control in 1972. Again it was to only last a single three-year term, largely due to the difficulties of having to deal with international events beyond its control. Most fundamental was the long expected entry of Britain into the Common Market. Some other export markets had been found but New Zealand still felt betrayed. Later the same year oil prices quadrupled in a few months and the treasury found itself with mounting fuel bills and decreasing export receipts. The government borrowed heavily but couldn't avoid electoral defeat in 1975 by National's obstreperous and pugnacious **Robert "Piggy" Muldoon**, who denounced Labour's borrowing and then outdid them. In short order New Zealand had dreadful domestic and foreign debt, unemployment was the highest for decades, and the unthinkable was happening – the standard of living was falling. People began to leave in their thousands and the "brain drain" almost reached crisis point. Muldoon's solution was to "**Think Big**" a catch-all term for a number of capital-intensive petrochemical projects designed to utilize New Zealand's abundant natural gas to produce ammonia, urea fertilizer, methanol and synthetic petrol. Though undoubtedly self-aggrandizing it made little economic sense. Rather than use local technology and labour to convert New Zealand vehicles to run on compressed natural gas (a system already up and running), Muldoon chose to pay international corporations to design and build huge prefabricated processing plants which were then shipped to New Zealand for assembly, mostly around New Plymouth.

Factory outfalls often jeopardized traditional Maori shellfish beds, and where once *iwi* would have accepted this as inevitable, a new spirit of protest saw them win significant concessions. Throughout the mid-1970s Maori began to question the philosophy of *pakeha* life and looked to the Treaty of Waitangi (see box, p.764) to correct the grievances that were aired at occupations of traditional land at Bastion Point in Auckland (see p.89), and Raglan), and through a petition delivered to parliament after a march across the North Island.

Maori also found expression in the formation of **gangs** – Black Power, the Mongrel Mob and the bike-oriented Highway 61 – along the lines graphically depicted in Lee Tamahori's film *Once Were Warriors*, which was originally written about south Auckland life in the 1970s. Fortified suburban homes still exist and such gangs continue to be influential among Maori youth, a position now being positively exploited to bring wayward Maori youth back into the fold.

Race relations were never Muldoon's strong suit and when large numbers of illegal **Polynesian immigrants** from south Pacific islands – particularly Tonga, Samoa and the Cook Islands – started arriving in Auckland he responded by instructing the police to conduct random street checks for "over-stayers", many of whom were deported. Muldoon opted for a completely hands-off approach when it came to sporting contacts with South Africa and in 1976 let the pig-headed rugby administrators send an All Black team over to play racially selected South African teams. African nations responded by boycotting the Montreal Olympics, putting New Zealand in the unusual position of being an international pariah. New Zealand signed the 1977 Gleneagles Agreement requiring it to "vigorously combat the evil of apartheid" and yet in 1981 the New Zealand Rugby Union courted a **Springbok Tour**, which sparked New Zealand's greatest civil disturbance since labour riots of the 1920s.

MODERN NEW ZEALAND: A MATURING NATION

Muldoon's big-spending economic policies were widely perceived to be unsuccessful, and when he called a snap election in 1984, Labour were returned to power under **David Lange**. Just as National had eschewed traditional right-wing economics in favour of a "managed economy", Labour now changed tactics, addressing the massive economic problems by shunning the traditional left-of-centre approach. Instead, they grasped the baton of Thatcherite economics and sprinted off with it. Under Finance Minister Roger Douglas's **Rogernomics**, the dollar was devalued by twenty percent, exchange controls were abolished, tariffs slashed, the maximum income tax rate was halved, a Goods and Services Tax was introduced, Air New Zealand and the Bank of New Zealand were privatized, and state benefits were cut. Unemployment doubled to twelve

percent, a quarter of manufacturing jobs were lost, and the moderately well-off benefited at the expense of the poor; nevertheless, market forces and enterprise culture had come to stay. As one of the world's most regulated economies became one of the most deregulated, the long-standing belief that the state should provide for those least able to help themselves was cast aside, a policy dubbed "Ruthanasia" after its perpetrator Ruth Richardson.

In other spheres Labour's views weren't so right-wing. One of Lange's first acts was to refuse US ships entry to New Zealand ports unless they declared that they were nuclear-free. The Americans would do nothing of the sort and withdrew support for New Zealand's defence safety net, the **ANZUS** pact. Most of the country backed Lange on this but were less sure about his overtures towards Maori who, for the first time since the middle of the nineteenth century, got legal recognition for the Treaty of Waitangi. Now, Maori grievances dating back to 1840 could be addressed.

The rise in apparent income under Rogernomics created consumer confidence and the economy boomed until the **stock market crash** of 1987, which hit New Zealand especially hard. The country went into freefall and all confidence in the reforms was lost. Labour's position, consolidated in the 1987 election, now became untenable, and in the 1990 election National's **Jim Bolger** took the helm. Throughout the deep recession National continued Labour's free-market reforms, cutting welfare programmes and extracting teeth from the unions by passing the Employment Contracts Act, which established the pattern of individual workplaces coming to their own agreements on wages and conditions. By the middle of the 1990s the economy had improved dramatically and what for a time had been considered a foolhardy experiment is now seen by monetarists as a model for open economies the world over. Meanwhile, the gap between the rich and the poor continues to widen and New Zealand's classless society is increasingly exposed for the myth it always was.

Ever since New Zealand achieved self-government from Britain in 1852, it had maintained a first-past-the-post Westminster style of parliament, with the exception of the scrapping of the upper house in 1950 and the provision for four (later five) Maori seats. Effectively the country is divided into a large number of general constituencies and into four or five Maori constituencies. Maori can chose to vote for their general or Maori candidate but not both. In 1987 and 1990 Labour and National had both made election promises to hold a plebiscite on electoral reform. This was finally held in 1993 in the depths of the recession and, perhaps inevitably, produced a mandate for change: most wanted Mixed Member Proportional representation (MMP), a system which purports to give smaller parties an opportunity to have some say. In the first **MMP elections**, held in 1996, National and Labour shared the majority of the vote, but the balance of power was held by **New Zealand First**, a new Maori-dominated party headed by former National MP, **Winston Peters**, who shaped their policies of reducing Asian immigration, increasing government spending and accountability and getting long-term unemployed back to work. After two months of playing National off against Labour, they finally formed a coalition under Bolger and introduced a new Maori spirit in parliament. There are far more Maori than ever before and maiden speeches of new MPs were received with a *waiata* (song) from their *whanau* (extended family group) in the public gallery. A year or so on, National probably regret striking the deal, as New Zealand First MPs – many of them political neophytes – have never been out of the critical spotlight. Jim Bolger's poor handling of numerous scandals saw his support wane, and his attendance at a Commonwealth leaders' conference left the field open for a palace coup, in which the formidable **Jenny Shipley** became New Zealand's first female prime minister. Her time in charge of the social welfare and health ministries has left her with a reputation for offering Thatcherism without the warmth, so it remains to be seen whether her blend of right-wing economics and more liberal social views will hold the coalition together.

Until a recent slight downturn, New Zealand's economy has remained strong through much of the 1990s, and many have relished the good life, but social welfare remains under siege. In her resignation speech, **Cath Tizard**, the most popular and charismatic Governor-General New Zealand has had for years, levelled a thinly veiled attack at the government for its record on health care, but succeeded only in raising anti-monarchist hackles at her vice-regal intervention. Nonetheless, the kind of republican rabble-rousing championed across the Tasman in recent years largely falls on deaf ears in Aotearoa, where, despite the maturing of the nation in the last decade or so, and a progressive realignment with the Pacific and Asia, most seem happy to maintain links with Britain. Meanwhile, Maoritanga looks set to play an ever increasing role in the life of all New Zealanders as Maori consolidate the gains of the past few years. In the twenty-first century the number of New Zealanders who consider themselves Maori may well surpass the number of *pakeha*, and it can only be hoped that such a point will become completely insignificant.

MAORITANGA

When the Pakeha first came to this Island, the first thing he taught the Maori was Christianity. They made parsons and priests of several members of the Maori race, and they taught these persons to look up and pray; and while they were looking up the Pakehas took away our land.

Mahuta, the son of the Maori King Tawhiao, addressing the New Zealand Legislative Council in 1903.

The term **Maoritanga** embodies Maori lifestyle and culture – it is the Maori way of doing things, embracing social structure, ethics, customs, legends and art, as well as language (see p.795). In the Anglo-European dominated society that New Zealand has always been, and to a large extent still is, it has been easy to see Maori culture as harping back to some fond-remembered idyll of the past, but Maoritanga has remained very much alive, and in the last couple of decades has seen a dramatic resurgence. By most measures, Maori make up over ten percent of New Zealand's population, but Maori–*pakeha* marriage since the early nineteenth century has left a complex inter-racial pool; many third- or fourth-generation *pakeha* can claim a Maori forebear or two, and some contend that there are no full-blooded Maori left. Maori ancestry remains the foundation of Maoridom, but a sense of Maori belonging is increasingly a question of cultural identity as much as bloodlines.

Until very recently, white New Zealanders liked to promote the image of the two races living in harmony as one people, citing scenes of Maori and *pakeha* elbow to elbow at the bar and Maori rugby players in the scrum alongside their *pakeha* brothers. *Pakeha* prided themselves on successful integration that seemed a world away from the apartheid of South Africa or the virtual genocide exacted on North American and Australian aboriginal peoples; after all, Maori could claim all the benefits of *pakeha* plus dedicated seats in parliament, extra university grants and various other concessions. Yet this denied the undercurrent of Maori dissatisfaction over their treatment since the arrival of the first Europeans; the policy of **assimilation** relied entirely on Maori

conforming to the *pakeha* way of doing things and made no concession to Maoritanga. Maori adapted incredibly quickly to *pakeha* ways but were rewarded with the loss of their **land**. It is impossible to overestimate the importance of this: Maori spirituality invests every tree, every hill and every bay with a kind of supernatural life of its own, drawn from past events and the actions of the ancestors. It is by no means fanciful to equate the loss of land with the diminution of Maori life-force; little surprise, then, that much of the spirit went out of Maori people.

It is only really in the 1980s and 1990s that the *pakeha* paternal view has been challenged, with the country reacting by adopting **biculturalism**. As Maori rediscover their heritage and *pakeha* open their eyes to what has been around them for generations, knowledge of Maoritanga and some understanding of the language is seen as desirable and even advantageous. The government has increasingly channelled resources towards the "flax roots" of Maoridom, fostering a rapid take-up in the learning of Maori language, a resurgence in interest in Maori arts and crafts and a growing pride in Maoridom. At the same time, Maori have won back customary rights to fisheries and resources, and parcels of land have been returned to Maori ownership. Nonetheless, there is a sense in some quarters that Maori are only getting as much as the *pakeha*-dominated government feels it is prepared to give back.

For many *pakeha*, however, there is considerable unease over what is perceived as the government's soft stance on Treaty of Waitangi land claims (see box on p.764). Some envisage a future where Maori will own the land (including private land not currently up for redistribution under Treaty claims), will reclaim the rights granted them by the Treaty, and will have more influence than *pakeha*. Quite frankly, they're afraid. So far, reaction to the strengthening Maori hand in this climate of conciliation has only been voiced quietly, and just how this scenario will pan out remains to be seen. True power-sharing and biculturalism seems a long way off, and Maori aspirations for "sovereignty" – a separate Maori government and judiciary – look far-fetched at present, but the Maori juggernaut is moving fast.

MAORI LEGEND

Maori culture remains highly oral, with chants, storytelling and oratory central to ceremonial and daily life. This was doubly so when Europeans arrived and first recorded the traditions and legends normally passed down verbally. Different tribal groups often had different sets of stories, or at least variations on common themes, but European historians with pet theories to promote often distorted the stories they heard and even destroyed conflicting evidence, creating their own Maori folklore. This generalizing trend served the purpose of creating a common Maori identity, and many of the stories have been accepted back into the Maori tradition, leaving a patchwork of authentic and bowdlerized legends. Nonetheless, there are a few fixed themes common to most.

CREATION

From the primal nothingness of **Te Kore** sprang **Ranginui** the sky father and **Papatuanuku** the earth mother. They had numerous offspring, principally the major gods: **Haumia Tiketike**, the god of the fern root and food from the forest; **Rongo**, the god of the kumara and cultivation; **Tu Matauenga**, the god of war; **Tangaroa**, the god of the oceans and sealife; **Tawhirimatea**, the god of the winds; and **Tane Mahuta**, the god of the forests. Through long centuries of darkness the brothers argued over whether to separate their parents and create light. Tawhirimatea opposed the idea and fled to the skies where his anger is manifested in thunder and lightning, while Tane Mahuta succeeded in parting the two, breaking their primal embrace and allowing life to flourish. Rangi's tears filled the oceans and even now it is their grief which brings the dew, mist and rain.

Having created the creatures of the sea, the air and the land, the gods turned their attentions to humans and, realizing that they were all male, had to create a female. They fashioned clay into a form resembling their mother and the responsibility again fell to **Tane**, who breathed life into the nostrils of the first woman, the Dawn Maiden, **Hinetitama**. It is from their union that the whole human race is descended.

MAUI THE TRICKSTER AND KUPE THE NAVIGATOR

Maori mythology is littered with half-human demigods, and none is more celebrated than **Maui-Tikitiki-a-Taranga**, whose exploits are legend throughout Polynesia. With an armoury of spells, guile and boundless mischief, Maui gained a reputation as a trickster, using his abilities to turn any situation to his advantage. Equipped with the powerful magic jawbone of his grandmother, he set about taming his world, believing himself invincible. He even took on **the sun**, which had taken to passing so swiftly through the heavens that the people had no time to tend their fields before it disappeared back into its fiery pit. Maui vowed to solve the problem and, with the aid of his older brothers, plaited super-strong ropes which they tied across the sun's pit before dawn. As the sun rose into the net, Maui set upon the sun with his magic jawbone, beating him and imploring him not to go so fast. The sun was weakening rapidly and, in return for his release, agreed to do as Maui asked.

In the New Zealand context, Maui's master work was the creation of **Aotearoa**. With his reputation for mischief, Maui's brothers would often leave him behind when they went fishing, but one morning he stowed away under the seats. Far out at sea he revealed himself, promising to improve their recent poor catch. Maui egged them on until they were well beyond the normal fishing grounds before dropping anchor. In no time at all Maui's brothers filled their canoe with fish, but Maui still had some fishing to do. They scorned his hook (secretly armed with a chip of his grandmother's jawbone) and wouldn't lend him any bait, so Maui struck his own nose and smeared the hook with his own blood. Soon he had hooked a fabulous fish which, as it broke the surface, could be seen stretching into the distance all around them. Chanting an incantation, Maui got the fish to lie quietly on the surface where it became the North Island, known as *Te ika a Maui*, the fish of Maui. As Maui went off to make an offering to the gods, his brothers began to cut up the fish and eat it, hacking mountains and valleys into the surface. To fit in with the legend, the South Island is often called *Te waka a Maui*, the canoe of Maui, and Stewart Island is the anchor, *Te punga o te waka a Maui*.

With more historical veracity, Maori trace their ancestry back to **Hawaiki**, the semi-legendary source of the Polynesian diaspora, for which the Society Islands and the Cook Islands are the most likely candidates. According to legend, the first visitor to Aotearoa's shores was **Kupe**, the great Polynesian navigator. In one version of the tale he was determined to kill a great octopus that kept robbing his bait; drawn ever further out to sea in pursuit, he finally reached landfall on the uninhabited shores of *Aotearoa*, the "land of the long white cloud", around 950 AD. He named numerous features of the land, then returned to Hawaiki with instructions on how to retrace his voyage. Generations later his descendants set sail in the **Great Fleet** of seven canoes, which arrived in 1350 AD, laying the foundation for Maori society. All Maori trace their *whakapapa* back to one or more of these canoes.

SOCIAL STRUCTURE AND CUSTOMS

Maori society remains **tribal** to a large extent, though the deracination resulting from the widespread move from the tribal homelands to the cities has eroded some of the closer ties. The finer points of Maoritanga are no longer strictly adhered to, especially in urban situations, but the basic tenets remain strong and formal protocol still reigns for ceremonies as diverse as funeral wakes, meetings and Maori exhibition openings.

The most fundamental and tightest division in Maori society is the extended family or **whanau** (literally "birthing"), which extends from immediate relatives to cousins, uncles and nieces several times removed. A dozen or so *whanau* jointly form a localized sub-tribe or **hapu** (literally "gestation or pregnancy"), perhaps the most important tribal group, comprising perhaps 500 people of common descent. *Hapu* were originally economically autonomous and today continue to conduct communal activities, typically through their *marae* (see p.776). Neighbouring *hapu* are likely to belong to the same tribe or **iwi** (literally "bones"), a looser association of several thousand Maori spread over a fairly large geographical area. The thirty-odd major *iwi* are even more tenuously linked by their common ancestry traced back to the

seven **waka** (canoes) of the Great Fleet, and in troubled times, especially during the eighteenth-century New Zealand Wars, *iwi* from the same *waka* would band together for protection. Together these are the **tangata whenua** (literally "the people of the land"), a term that may refer to Maori people as a whole, or just to one *hapu* if local concerns are being aired.

The literal meanings of *whanau*, *hapu* and *iwi* can be viewed as a metaphor for the Maori view of their relationship with their ancestors or **tupuna**, who are considered to exist through their genetic inheritors; the past is very much a part of the present. Evidence of this is seen in the respect accorded the **whakapapa**, an individual's genealogy tracing descent from the gods via one of the migratory *waka* and through the *tupuna*. The *whakapapa* is often recited at length on formal occasions such as **hui** (meetings).

Maori traditional life is informed by the parallel notions of **tapu** (taboo) and **noa** (mundane, not *tapu*). These are not superstition but a belief system designed to impose a code of conduct: transgressing *tapu* brings ostracism and ill fortune and is thought to cause sickness. Objects, places, actions and even people can be *tapu*, demanding extra respect – for example, the body parts of a chief, especially the head; menstruating women; sacred items to do with ritual; earrings, pendants and hair combs; burial sites; and the knowledge contained in the *whakapapa* are all *tapu*. There is a practical aspect too, with the productivity of fishing grounds and forests maintained by imposing *tapu* at critical times. The direct opposite of *tapu* is *noa*, a term applied to ordinary items which, by implication, are considered safe; a new building is *tapu* until a special ceremony renders it *noa*.

People, animals and artefacts, whether *tapu* or *noa*, possess **mauri** (life force), **wairau** (spirit) and **mana**, a term loosely translated as prestige, but embodying wider concepts of power, influence and charisma. Birthright brings with it a degree of *mana* which can then be augmented through battle or brave deeds, and lost through inaction or defeat. Wartime cannibalism was partly ritual but by eating an enemy's heart a warrior absorbed his *mauri*; likewise personal effects gain *mana* from association with the *mana* of their owner, accruing more as they are passed down to descendants. Any slight on the *mana* of an individual was felt by the whole *hapu*, which must then exact **utu** (retribution or revenge), a compunction which often led to bloody feuds, sometime escalating to war and further enhancing the *mana* of the victors. *Pakeha* found this a hard concept to grasp and deeds which they considered deceitful or treacherous could be correct in Maori terms.

The responsibility for determining *tapu* falls to the **tohunga** (priest or expert), the most exalted of many specialists in Maoritanga, who is conversant with tribal history, sacred lore and the *whakapapa*, and considered to be the earthly presence of the power of the gods.

MARAE

The rituals of *hapu* life – *hui*, **tangi** (funeral wakes) and **powhiri** (formal welcomes) – are conducted on the **marae**, a kind of combined community, cultural and drop-in centre (and much more), where the cultural values, protocols, customs and vitality of Maoritanga find their fullest expression. Strictly, a marae is simply a courtyard, but the term is often applied to the whole complex, comprising the **whare runanga** (meeting house, or *whare nui*), *whare manuhiri* (house for visitors), *whare kai* (eating house) and possibly even an old-fashioned **pataka** (raised storehouse). Marae belonging to one or more *hapu* are found all over the country, though they're concentrated in rural areas where a larger number of Maori live. In recent years, pan-tribal urban marae have started up, partly to help wayward Maori youth find their roots but also to cope with the growing awareness of Maoritanga on the part of urban Maori, many of whom have lost their *whakapapa*.

Visitors, whether Maori or *pakeha*, may not enter marae uninvited, so unless you have Maori friends, you're only likely to visit on a commercially run **tour**. Invited guests are expected to provide some form of **koha** (donation) towards the upkeep of the marae, but this is included in tour fees. Remember that the marae is sacred and due reverence must be accorded the **kawa** (protocols) governing behaviour. There's no need to feel intimidated, though, as you aren't expected to know *kawa* and will be instructed as to what is required of you.

Following long tradition, **manuhiri** (visitors) approaching the marae are ritually challenged to determine friendly intent. This **wero** might involve a fearsome warrior (often the teenager you see driving away after the show) bearing down on you with twirling **taiaha** (long club), flickering tongue and bulging eyes. The women then make the **karanga** (welcoming call), which is followed by their *powhiri* (sung welcome), which breaks the *tapu* and acts as a prelude to ceremonial touching of noses or **hongi**, binding the *manuhiri* and the *tangata whenua* both physically and spiritually. On commercial trips, the welcoming ceremony is followed by a concert comprising songs, dances and chants, and a **hangi** (a feast cooked in an earth oven).

ARTS AND CRAFTS

Although the origins of **Maori art** lie in the traditions of eastern Polynesia, over half a millennium of isolated development has resulted in a unique richness and diversity. Eastern Polynesia has no suitable clay, so Maori forebears had already lost the skills of pottery and focused their talents on wood, stone and weaving, occasionally using naturalistic designs but most often the highly **stylized forms** that make Maori art unmistakable.

As with other *taonga* (treasures), many superb examples were taken out of the country by Victorian and later collectors, but there is a determined move on the part of *iwi* and the Department of Maori Affairs to restore as many *taonga* as possible to New Zealand, including over a hundred severed heads which are scattered through museums all over the world.

WOOD CARVING

Maori handiwork finds its greatest expression in **wood carving**, a discipline applied with as much care to a water bailer or ornamental comb as it is to the pinnacles of Maori creativity, *waka* (canoes) and *whare whakairo* (carved houses).

The earliest examples of wood carving feature the sparse, rectilinear styles of ancient eastern Polynesia, but by the fifteenth century these had been replaced by the cursive style still employed by more traditional carvers today. In the Northland forests, kauri wood was used, but in the rest of the country the durable yet easily worked totara was the material of choice. Carvers worked with shells and sharp stones in the earliest times, but the artist's scope increased dramatically with the invention of tools fashioned from **pounamu** (greenstone, a form of jade; see box on p.648), and again with the transition to steel tools. Some would say that the quality of the work declined with the coming of the Europeans: not just through the demand for quickly executed "tourist art", but as a consequence of pressure to remove the phallic imagery that the missionaries considered obscene. As early as 1844, carving had been abandoned altogether in areas with a strong missionary presence, and it continued to decline into the early years of the twentieth century, when Maori pride was at its lowest ebb. By the end of the 1920s there were only two experienced carvers outside the Arawa region around Rotorua. In response to this lamentable situation, Maori parliamentarian Apirana Ngata established Rotorua's pantribal **Maori Arts and Crafts Institute**, viewed as the foundation on which Maoritanga could be rebuilt. As a consequence, the Arawa style became the national standard, and the institute remains the guardian of what is now a much more secure art.

The role of a carver has always been a highly respected one, with seasoned and skilled exponents having the status of *tohunga* and travelling the country both to carve and to teach. The work is a *tapu* activity and *noa* objects must be kept away – cooked food is not allowed near, and carvers have to brush away shavings rather than blow them – though women, previously banned, have now become carvers.

Maori carving exhibits a distinctive **style**, not just in its visual elements but in the approach to the material. Typically, relief forms are determinedly hewn from a single piece of wood with no concession to the natural forms, shapes and blemishes of the material. There is no attempt to represent perspective and no landscapes are depicted – figures stand alone. Unadorned wood is rare, carvers creating a stylistic rather than symbolic bed of swirling spirals, curving organic forms based on fern roots or sea shells, and interlocking latticework. Superimposed on this are the key elements, often inlaid with paua shell. The most common is the ancestor figure, the **hei tiki**, a grotesquely distorted, writhing human form,

either male, female or of indeterminate gender, often stylized to the point of unrecognizability except for the challenge of a protruding tongue and the threat of a hand-held *mere*. Almost as common are the mythical *manaia*, a beaked birdlike form, often with an almost human profile. Secondary motifs such as the *pakake* (whale) and *moko* (lizard) also occur.

While the same level of craftsmanship was applied to all manner of tools, weapons and ornaments, it reached its most exalted expression in *waka taua* (**war canoes**), sleek and formidable vessels that were the focus of community pride and endeavour. Gunwales, bailers and paddles would all be fabulously decorated, but the most detailed work was reserved for the prow and sternpost, usually a matrix of spirals interwoven with *manaia* figures. As guns and the European presence altered the balance of tribal warfare in the 1860s, the *waka taua* was superseded in importance by the *whare whakairo* (**carved meeting house**). Originally the chief's residence, the *whare* gradually adopted the symbolism of the *waka* – some even incorporated wood from *waka*. Each meeting house could be seen as the tangible manifestation of the *whakapapa*, usually representing a synthesis of the ancestors: the ridgepole is the backbone; the rafters form the ribs, enclosing the belly of the interior; the gable figure is the head; and the barge boards represent arms, often decorated with finger-like decoration. Inside, all wooden surfaces are carved and the spaces are filled intricate woven panels known as *tukutuku*.

GREENSTONE CARVING

When not using wood, Maori carvers work in **pounamu** (greenstone). In pre-European times complex trade routes developed to supply Maori throughout the land from the sources on the West Coast and in Fiordland; the South Island even became known as *Te Wai Pounamu*, the Water of Jade. The stone was fashioned into adzes, chisels and clubs for hand-to-hand combat; tools which soon took on a ritual significance and demanded decoration. Pounamu's hardness dictates a more restrained carving style and *mere* and *patu* in particular tend to be only partly worked, leaving large sweeping surfaces ending in a flourish of delicate swirls. Ornamental pieces range from simple drop pendants worn as earrings or neck decoration, to *hei tiki*, worn as a breast pendant and, for women, serving as a fertility charm and talisman for easy childbirth. Like other personal items, especially those worn close to the body, an heirloom *tiki* posesses the *mana* of the ancestors and absorbs the wearer's *mana*, becoming *tapu*.

TATTOOING

A stylistic extension of the carver's craft is exhibited in *moko*, an ornamental and ceremonial form of **tattooing** that largely died out with European contact. Women would have *moko* just on the lips and chin, but high-ranking men often had their faces completely covered, along with their buttocks and thighs; the greater the extent and intricacy of the *moko*, the greater the status. A symmetrical pattern of the traditional elements – crescents, spirals, fern-root and other organic forms – were painfully gouged into the flesh with an *uhi* (chisel) and mallet, then soot rubbed into the open wound. In the last decade or so the tradition of full-face *moko* has been revived by Maori street gangs, as both as an initiation into the group and as an identification with Maoritanga.

WEAVING AND CLOTHING

While men were busy carving, the women dedicated themselves to weaving and the production of clothing. When Polynesians first arrived in these cool, damp islands their paper mulberry plants didn't thrive and they were forced to look for alternatives. In time, they found *harakeke* (New Zealand **flax**), which became the foundation of all Maori fibre-work. The strong, pliable fibres were used as fishing lines and cordage for lashing axe-heads onto hafts, and most importantly for protection from the elements and floor matting. With the arrival of the *pakeha*, Maori quickly adopted European clothes, but they continued to wear cloaks on formal occasions and these now constitute the basis of contemporary design.

Flax will grow on marshy land all over the country and so the long, spindly leaves were almost always on hand. They were used in something close to their raw form for *raranga* (plaiting) into *kete*, handle-less baskets used for collecting shellfish and kumara, triangular canoe sails, sandals and *whariki*, patterned floor mats still used in meeting houses. For finer work, the flax must be treated by trimming, soaking and beating, a laborious process that produces a wonderfully strong and pliable fibre. Most fibre is used in its natural form, but Maori design requires some **colouring**: black is achieved by soaking in a dilute extract of the bark from a *hinau* tree then rubbing with a black swamp sediment known as *paru*; the red-brown range of colours requires boiling in a dye derived from the bark of the *tanekaha* tree then fixed by rolling in hot ashes; and the less popular yellow tint is produced from the bark of the Coprosma species. Economic necessity and consideration for the tree species concerned have seen the introduction of synthetic dyes, but traditional dyes are still used whenever possible.

Natural and coloured fibres are both used in *whatu kakahu* (**cloak-weaving**), the crowning achievement of Maori women's art, the finest cloaks ranking alongside the most prized *taonga*; the immense war canoe now in the Auckland Museum was once exchanged for a particularly fine cloak. The technique is sometimes referred to as finger-weaving as no loom is used, the women working downwards from a base warp strung between two sticks. Complex weaving techniques are employed to produce a huge array of different textures, often decorated with *taniko* (coloured borders), cord tags tacked onto the cloth at intervals and, most impressive of all, **feathers**. Feather cloaks (*kahu hururu*) don't appear to have been common before European contact, though heroic tales often feature key players in iridescent garments undoubtedly made from bird feathers. The appeal of the bright yellow feathers of the *huia* probably saw to its demise, and most other brightly coloured birds are now too rare to use for cloaks, so new feather cloaks are very rarely made. Existing examples have become the most prestigious of garments, and you'll come across some fine examples in museums, the base cloth often completely covered by a dense layer of kiwi feathers bordered by zig-zag patterns of tui, native pigeon and even parakeet feathers. More robust *para* (rain capes) were made using the water-repellent leaves of the cabbage tree, and a form of coarse canvas which could reportedly resist spear thrusts was used for *pukupuku* (war cloaks). Some *pukupuku* were turned into *kahu kuri* (dog-skin cloaks) with the addition of strips of dog skin, arranged vertically so that the natural fur colours produced distinctive patterns.

As with other aspects of Maoritanga, weaving and plaiting have seen a resurgence. Cloaks are still an important element of formal occasions, whether on the marae for *hui* and *tangi*, or elsewhere for receiving academic or state honours. Old forms are reproduced directly, and also raided as inspiration for contemporary designs, which interpret traditional elements in the light of modern fashion, sometimes incorporating non-traditional colours and designs.

THE HAKA AND MAORI DANCE

Opposing rugby teams quiver as the New Zealand All Blacks perform the ferocious, thigh-slapping, foot-stomping, tongue-poking, eye-bulging chant *Ka mate, Ka mate, Ka ora, Ka ora* (It is death, it is death, It is life, it is life), the first line of the intimidating Te Rauparaha Haka. This is just the best known of many posture dances (often wrongly referred to as war dances) designed to demonstrate the fitness and prowess of warriors. It was supposedly composed by Te Rauparaha himself (see p.204) as he lay in a kumara pit trying to avoid detection by his enemies. Its use by what are often predominantly *pakeha* sides might seem inappropriate, but it is so entrenched that there was considerable backlash when in 1996 the All Black coach suggested the haka may be changed to mollify southern Maori who were decimated by Te Rauparaha.

At commercial **Maori concerts** (predominantly in Rotorua but also in Christchurch, Queenstown and elsewhere) there will always be some form of haka, usually the Te Rauparaha version, which is almost always performed by men. Though women aren't excluded from the haka, they normally concentrate on **poi dances**, where balls of *raupo* (bulrush) attached to the end of strings are swung around in rhythmic movements originally designed to improve co-ordination and dexterity.

The drums of eastern Polynesia don't appear to have made it to New Zealand, and both chants and the haka go unaccompanied. To the traditional bone flute, *pakeha* added the guitar, which now accompanies **waiata** (songs), relatively modern creations whose impact comes as much from the tone and rhythm as from the lyrics (which you probably won't understand anyway). The impassioned delivery can seem at odds with music that's often based on Victorian hymns: perhaps the most well known are *Pokarekare ana* and *Haere Ra*, both post-European contact creations.

WILDLIFE AND THE NATURAL ENVIRONMENT

New Zealand is still perceived as a green and pleasant land, as it has been by many thousands of immigrants, first from the Polynesian Islands, then Europe and now the Pacific rim of Asia. Although relatively small it boasts an enormous diversity: unspoiled sub-tropical forest, rich volcanic basins (and volcanoes), mudpools and geysers, intricate and rugged coastline with golden sand beaches and spectacular alpine regions. This diverse landscape supports an extraordinary variety of animals and plant life, with almost ninety percent of the flora not found anywhere else in the world. Thanks to the efforts of a vociferous minority, since the late 1800s, examples of the many habitats, plants and wildlife are still easily accessible, protected within national parks and scenic reserves. For more on green issues, see p.787.

BEGINNINGS

Land has existed in the vicinity of New Zealand for most of the last 500 million years: the earliest rocks found in the country are thought to have originated in the continental forelands of Australia and Antarctica, part of

Gondwanaland, the massive continent to which New Zealand belonged. The oceanic islands were created by continental drift, the movement of the large plates that form the earth's crust, which created a distinct island arc and oceanic trench about 100 million years ago.

Around 26 million years ago, the land that makes up New Zealand rose further from the sea, and the landscape you see today was formed by **volcanic** activity and continuous movement along fault lines, particularly the Alpine Fault of the South Island. The essential geology of the two islands is different: the North Island is at the edge of two tectonic plates, where one has slid beneath the other, resulting in prolific volcanic activity; the South Island is the site of two tectonic plates crashing into each other, causing rapid **mountain** building. Today New Zealand experiences about four hundred **earthquakes** every year, roughly a quarter of them strong enough to be noticeable. The volcanoes on the North Island, some still impressively active (the last eruption was Ruapehu in 1996), extend from the Bay of Plenty to the dormant volcanic cone of Mount Taranaki on the West Coast.

Isolated from man and other mammals, New Zealand would have been the perfect place to study the **evolution** of species. It's hardly surprising that so many botanists considered the oceanic islands as laboratories where they could perfect their theories. The country was separated from all other land masses for so long that, uniquely, **birds** occupied the position in the food chain usually held by mammals. Darwinism would suggest that with no predators the birds became fearless, learning to walk amid the dense bush, gradually becoming flightless and growing in size. If allowed to develop unhindered, perhaps they would have evolved into a serious competitor to mammals, but their perfect adaptation to the environment brought their downfall with the arrival of man and other aggressive, fast-moving mammals.

No ground-based mammals colonized the islands until Maori gave rats and dogs passage in their canoes in about 1000 AD. Maori were also responsible for hunting the large, flightless **moa** into extinction, and clearing great swathes of **bush**. At that time both islands were almost entirely covered in dense **forest** composed of over a hundred species of tree, the floor carpeted by moss and lichen with a thick tangled undergrowth of tree fern, some species over ten metres high. Amongst the trees and ferns were twining creepers, nikau palms and palm lilies, all intermingled and forming an impenetrable bush alive with native birds.

The changes to the land brought by Maori pale in comparison with the incursions of the Europeans. Right from Cook's first exploratory visits, when he brought with him the pig, the sheep and the potato, Europeans tampered with the delicate balance of New Zealand in an attempt to turn it into a "New England". In the early 1800s whalers and sealers bloodied the coastal waters, while logging campaigns cleared vast swathes of native trees, leaving land suitable only for grazing cattle; later, gold prospectors diverted streams and carved chunks out of hillsides. Perhaps the greatest environmental changes were made by immigrant farmers, who had introduced over fifty species of **mammal** to New Zealand by the start of World War I, including rabbits, weasels, mountain goats, cats, dogs, frogs, mice, possums and wallabies. These animals decimated native animal and plant life in the increasing competition for food. Imported plants, such as blackberry, pine and gorse, had just as much effect: allowed to grow wild, they choked and destroyed hundreds of unique plants vital to the ecology of the islands.

THE COAST, ISLANDS AND SEA

New Zealand's indented coastline, battered by the Tasman Sea and the Pacific Ocean, is a meeting place of warm and cold currents, which makes for an environment suited to an enormous variety of **fish**. **Tropical** fish species such as barracuda, marlin, sharks and tuna are attracted by the warm currents, locally populated by **hoki**, **kahawai**, **snapper**, **orange roughy** and **trevally**. The cold Antarctic currents bring blue and red **cod**, blue and red **moki**, and fish that can tolerate a considerable range of water temperatures, such as the **tarakihi**, **grouper** and **bass**, all avidly sought after by an army of weekend anglers.

Many people visit New Zealand with the express intention of seeing the sea mammals that grace the waters, and most leave satisfied. The rare **humpback whale** is an occasional visitor to the shores of Kaikoura and Cook Strait, while **sperm whales** are common year round in the deep sea trench near Kaikoura. **Orca** are seen regularly wherever there are dolphins, seals and other whales, namely Banks Peninsula, Kaikoura, Dunedin, Stewart Island, the Marlborough Sounds, Cook Strait, the Bay of Plenty and the Bay of Islands. One frequent visitor is the **pilot whale**: up to 200 pass by Farewell Spit each year and many strand themselves there. Despite the efforts of the locals to refloat them, some die nearly every year. Pilot whales are also seen in Cook Strait and the Bay of Plenty.

Common dolphins congregate all year round in the Bay of Plenty, Bay of Islands and around the Coromandel Peninsula. Of the three other species seen in New Zealand, **bottlenose** dolphins hang around Kaikoura and Whakatane most of the year, while **dusky** dolphins, the most playful, can be spotted near the shore of the Marlborough Sounds and Kaikoura, from October to May. At any time of year you might get small schools of tiny **Hector's** dolphins accompanying your boat around Banks Peninsula, as far down as Invercargill.

Until recently there were few opportunities to see the Hooker's (now called New Zealand) **sea lion** except on remote Antarctic islands; now these rare animals with their round noses and deep, wet eyes are appearing once more around the Catlins and Otago Peninsula. If you do see them, though, be careful: they bite and can move fast over short distances, so don't go any closer than ten metres and avoid getting between them and the sea. The larger New Zealand **fur seal** is in much greater abundance around the coast, easily spotted basking on rocks or sand and gracefully turning in the waters, their broader, pointy heads popping above the surface. You're most likely to come across them in the Sugar Loaf Marine Reserve, the Northland Coast, the Bay of Plenty, near Kaikoura, the Otago Peninsula and in Abel Tasman National Park. Both seals and sea lions can become aggressive during the breeding season (Dec–Feb), so remember to keep your distance (at least 30m) at these times. If you are lucky enough to visit the Nuggets in the Catlins, you may be rewarded by a sighting of one of the few **elephant seals** still breeding on the New Zealand coast; more extensive colonies exist on the offshore islands.

Also drawn by the fish-rich waters of the coast are a number of visiting and native sea birds, the most famous being the graceful and solitary **royal albatross**, found on the Otago Peninsula, and, just offshore, the smaller **wandering albatross**. A far more common sight are **little blue penguins**, which you're almost guaranteed to see on any boat journey, all year round. The large **yellow-eyed penguin** is confined to parts of the east coast of the South Island, from Christchurch to the Catlins, while the **Fiordland crested penguin** with its thick yellow eyebrows is rarely seen outside Fiordland and Stewart Island. Other common sea birds include **gannets**, their yellow heads and white bodies unmistakable as they dive from great heights into shoals of fish; and **cormorants** and **shags** (mostly grey or black), usually congregating on cliffs and rocky shores. On and around islands you're also likely to see the **sooty shearwater**, *titi* (also known as "mutton birds"), while the black and white **variable oystercatchers** with their orange cigar beaks and stooping gait can be spotted searching in pairs for food on the foreshore almost everywhere.

THE HIGHLANDS

Thanks to the impact of introduced species on the environment (see p.781), to really appreciate the picture that greeted first the Maori and then the European immigrants, you need to visit one of New Zealand's many scenic reserves or national parks. In the Tongariro, Whanganui, Taranaki, Nelson Lakes, Arthur's Pass and Mount Cook national parks, all **highland forest** areas, **tawhairauriki** (mountain beech) grow close to the top of the tree line, straight trees up to 20m high, with sharp dark leaves and little red flowers. Also at high altitudes, often in mixed stands, are **tawhai** (silver beech), whose grey trunks grow up to 30m. Slightly lower altitudes are favoured by the other members of the beech family, the black and red varieties. Often mixed in with them is the thin, straggly **manuka** (tea tree), which grows in both Alpine regions and on seashores.

New Zealand has five hundred species of flowering alpine plant that grow nowhere else in the world. Most famous are the large white mountain daisies, **Mount Cook lilies** – the largest in the world, and a white-flowered yellow-centred member of the buttercup family. Another interesting plant found on the high ground of the South Island is the **vegetable sheep**, a white hairy plant that grows low along the ground and, at a distance, could just about be mistaken for grazing sheep.

One of the oldest of New Zealand's unique creatures inhabits caves and rock crevices above the snow line: the **weta** (also known as the "Mount Cook flea"), an insect that has changed little in 190 million years. There are several species, the most impressive being the giant weta, which is the heaviest insect in the world, weighing up to 71g and about the size of a small thrush. Weta aren't dangerous, despite their vicious-looking mandibles (they're said to have been the model for Ridley Scott's *Alien*). Though weta also inhabit the bush, they're hard to spot and you're most likely to see them in museums and zoos.

The red-beaked, green **takahe**, a close relative of the more common pukeko, is one of the most famous of the country's flightless birds. Thought to have been extinct until 1948, its survival is currently in the hands of DOC, who have set up protection programmes in a few highland regions (see p.134). Another highland forest bird to watch out for is the **New Zealand falcon** or bush hawk, seen sometimes in the north of the North Island and more often in the high country of the Southern Alps, Fiordland and the forests of Westland. It has a heavily flecked breast, chestnut thighs and a pointed head.

New Zealand boasts the only flightless **parrot** in the world, the green and blue, nocturnal **kakapo**. Once widespread, it's now very rare and predominantly seen in the forests and highlands of Fiordland. You're much more likely to come across the **kea**, regarded as the only truly alpine parrot in the world (see p.549), though its range encompasses both lowland and highland forests. Known for killing sheep (a recently acquired habit), making off with people's possessions and then ripping them apart or eating them, the kea is green with distinctive orange patches on the underside of its wings and a crimson abdomen. Finally, of the smaller birds in the sub-alpine areas, the yellow and green **rock wren** and the **rifleman**, a tiny green and blue bird with spiralling flight, are commonly seen in the high forests of the South Island.

THE LOWLANDS

These days the majority of New Zealand is covered by grazing land, grasslands and plains that are dominated by tall and low **tussock**. Fortunately, there remains a great variety of native trees in the **mid to lowland forests** of Northland, the Coromandel Peninsula, along the west coasts of both islands, around Wellington and on Stewart Island. There are also sixty different endemic native flowering plants in lowland areas, whose blooms mostly range from white to yellow, their relative lack of colour due to the fact that there were no bees to cross-pollinate until the Europeans arrived. Much colour in gardens, parks and mixed forest comes from introduced species such as roses, azaleas and rhododendrons.

New Zealand's best known tree, the **kauri**, is found in mixed lowland forest, particularly in Northland (see p.176). With a lifespan of two to four thousand years, this magnificent king of the forest rises to thirty metres, two-thirds of its height being straight, branchless trunk. Maori canoe-builders treat the kauri with great reverence and have always enacted solemn ceremonies before hacking them down for transformation into giant canoes; European shipbuilders coveted the trees for making oceangoing traders and warships. The tree is also the source of the kauri gum, dug from ancient forests and exported in the late eighteenth and early twentieth century.

Open spaces along forest edges and river banks are often alive with tui (see below) sucking nectar from golden clusters of **kowhai**, the national flower, which hangs from an eponymous tree whose wood was once fashioned into Maori canoe paddles and adze handles. Another useful tree, the **maire** stands up to 20m tall and is covered with whitish bark, thick narrow leaves and tiny pink flowers that look like open umbrellas. Its wood is heavy and close grained, ideal for war clubs, and when burned it gives off very little smoke. Now quite rare, the 30m **matai** was also once used by Maori, as a source of timber for canoe prows and settlers' buildings; it can be identified by a thick, dark grey bark that flakes off .

North of Banks Peninsula and on the North Island grows New Zealand's only native **palm**, the **nikau**, whose slender branchless stem bears shiny leaves of up to 30cm, long pink spiky flowers and red fruit. Early European settlers used to use the berries as pellets in the absence of ammunition.

The **pohutukawa** is an irregularly branched 20m tree found as far south as Otago, seen in forests around the coast and at lake edges.

Bearing bright crimson blossoms from November to January, it's often known as "New Zealand's Christmas tree". Another well-known red-blooming tree is the gnarled **rata**, found in quantity in South Island forests and in ones and twos around the North Island. It starts out life as a climber, its windblown seeds establishing it high in other trees, and then its aerial roots gradually take over the host, eventually draining it of life.

One native pine which was heavily milled for its timber and yet is still widespread throughout mixed forests is the majestic **rimu** (red pine), growing to 50–60m with small green flowers, red cones and tiny green or black fruit. Charcoal from rimu used to be mixed with oil and rubbed into tattoo incisions.

A common shade-loving tree found in stands in the forests is the **tawa**, with a long, thin blackish trunk and spear-shaped leaves. The tree produces black berries which, although initially unpleasant, develop a better flavour some time after picking. Also common throughout the country's mixed forests is the **totara**, which usually lives for a thousand years and was often used by Maori to make war canoes. The tree's thick brown bark was also used: it peels in long lengths, suitable for weaving baskets.

The **ti kouka** grows beneath the forest canopy, usually in moist areas and often along the edges of farmland. These 10- to 20m trees with long, thin grey trunks and spear-shaped leaves are also known as "cabbage trees", a reference to the shoots that were eaten by Captain Cook and his men. The tree also produces hundreds of white flowers in spectacular clusters. Below, on the forest floor grow an enormous variety of **ferns**, many of them hard to tell apart. The most famous, adopted as a national emblem, is the **ponga** (silver fern). Reaching about 10m in height, it has long fronds that are dull green on top and silvery white underneath.

LOWLAND WILDLIFE

Next to the sea, the mid to lowland forests contain the broadest range of **wildlife**. One of the country's oldest inhabitants is the **tuatara**, a lizard-like reptile dating back at least 260 million years, making it, to all intents and purposes, a dinosaur, although admittedly a small one. It's nocturnal so you're unlikely to see one in the wild, although they have been reintroduced to many pest-free offshore islands – your best chance of spotting one is in a zoo or kiwi house. Tuatara are about sixty centimetres in length and live for over a hundred years, feeding off insects, small mammals and birds' eggs.

New Zealand's national bird, the flightless **kiwi** (see box below) is also mostly found in the mid to lowland forests. It has been on the endangered list for many years, and these days the only place you're likely to see one in the wild is on Stewart Island; however, they can be seen in specially designed kiwi houses all over the country, such as Otorohanga (see p.205) and Napier (see p.366). Of the other flightless birds in New Zealand the most common is the **weka**, which has four subspecies found in a variety of

habitats throughout the country. The North Island bird flourishes in Poverty Bay and has been reintroduced around Auckland and in the forests. The South Island bird is found on the west coast of the South Island and Fiordland; and the bluff weka has thrived on the Chatham Islands and is being reintroduced in Canterbury. The last sub-species is ever present on Stewart Island. The bird is slimmer than the kiwi, and dark brown with marked golden flecks, especially on the heavily streaked breast. Like the kiwi, the weka grubs around at dusk but can be seen regularly during the day: many are bold enough to approach trampers and take titbits from their hands. The bird's whistle is a loud and distinctive "kooo-li".

KIWI

The **kiwi** is a member of the ratite family, which includes the ostrich, emu, rhea, cassowary and the long-extinct moa. A stout muscular bird, shy and nocturnal, which inhabits the forest floor. Sadly there are probably fewer than 15,000 wild birds left in the country. It sleeps for up to twenty hours a day, which probably explains why it normally lives to the age of 20 or 25. The females are bigger than the males and lay huge eggs, equivalent to around a fifth of their body weight. After eighty days, the eggs hatch and the chicks live off the rich yolk; neither parent feeds them and they emerge from the nest totally independent.

The kiwi is one of the few birds in the world with a well-developed sense of **smell**. At night you might hear them snuffling around in the dark, using the nostrils at the end of their bill to detect earthworms, beetles, cicada larvae, spiders and also koura (freshwater crayfish), berries and the occasional frog. Armed also with sensitive bristles at the base of its bill and a highly developed sense of hearing, the kiwi can detect other birds and animals on its territory and will readily attack them with its claws.

The **Brown Kiwi** (*Apteryx australis*), the largest species, is famous for its big nose, bad temper and for being a tough fighter against intruders on their territory. They live in a wide range of vegetation, including exotic forests and rough farmland on the North Island. In 1993 the **Tokoeka**, which is almost identical, was identified as a separate species. Inhabiting the South Island and Stewart Island, the southern tokoeka are the most communal of the kiwi family and can be seen poking about along the tideline

within a few metres of one another. A subspecies, the **Haast Tokoeka**, are found only in Fiordland.

The **Little Spotted Kiwi** or *Kiwi Pukupuku* (*Apteryx owenii*) is the smallest and rarest of the kiwi, found on only six offshore islands, including Kapiti Island. Predators and land clearance are largely responsible for the low numbers, although a programme to remove predators from the offshore islands has seen their fortunes revive. This species is mellow and docile by nature and pairs often share daytime shelter, going their separate ways to feed, grunting to one another as they pass. Little Spotted Kiwi rarely probe for food, instead finding prey on the ground or in the forest litter. In spring, during courtship, birds stand with bills crossed and pointing downwards while shuffling around each other, grunting, for up to twenty minutes. The best time to hear them is just after dark from high points around an island. Listen carefully for the male's shrill whistle and the female's gentle purr.

Great Spotted Kiwi or *Roa* (*Apteryx haastii*) inhabit regions of snow-covered peaks, herb fields, with rocky outcrops, valleys of red tussock and mountains clothed in beech forest and alpine scrub. Their severe living conditions account for the many legends that surround them. Early European explorers told stories of remote kiwi the size of a turkey with powerful spurs on its legs, whose call was louder than any other of the species. Their harsh home has also helped preserve these big handsome birds, keeping them safe from the pigs, dogs and stoats that have killed so many other kiwi species.

The **kaka** is a member of the parrot family and closely related to the kea, though it does not venture from its favoured lowland forest environments in Northland, around Nelson, the Marlborough Sounds, the West Coast and Stewart Island. You can recognize the bird by its colour: bronze with a crimson belly and underside of the tail and wings.

When walking among the forests of New Zealand, it is not unusual to hear the cry of the **morepork**, an owl that's named after the distinctive sound of its call. A small brown bird, it sometimes appears in town and city gardens. Alongside the morepork is the distinct musical "mackmacko" of the **bellbird**, a shy green and blue, curve-billed bird. In contrast, the **fantail**, another common forest dweller, is more likely to be seen than heard, constantly opening and closing the tail that gives it its name. Often flying alongside walkers on trails, the bird is not keeping you company but feeding on the insects you disturb.

The **tui**, with its white throat and mostly green and purple velvet-like body, is renowned for mimicking the calls of other birds and the copious consumption of nectar and fruit. Its song has greater range than the bellbird and contains some rather unmusical squeaks, croaks and strangled utterances. Just as noisy is the **saddleback**, a rare but pretty bird, mostly black except for a tan-coloured saddle, whose chattering call welcomes you if you stumble into its patch of the forest. The thrush-sized saddleback belongs to the endemic family of wattle birds, of which the North Island kokako is also a member – see below.

Among the smaller birds regularly glimpsed as they flit around the forest the most distinctive are the **robin** family, which range from black with a cream or yellow breast to all black, depending on how far south you have travelled. They have a prolonged and distinctive song lasting for up to thirty minutes with only brief pauses for breath.

The New Zealand pigeon, the **kereru**, was a favourite Maori food but these days it is prohibited to kill and eat them. It is a very ancient New Zealand species, which seems to have no relatives elsewhere. A handsome large bird with metallic green, purple and bronze colouring and a pure white breast, you'll often see it flashing along in the low-lying forests. Another of New Zealand's oldest birds is the **kokako**, an abysmal flyer that lives around the Pureora Forest, Little Barrier Island (see p.135) and Rotorua (see p.258). If you're lucky you'll see it grouchily walking around the forest floor or climbing trees for another crack at flying, or catch a glimpse of its distinctive bright blue wattle.

RIVERS, LAKES AND WETLANDS

New Zealand is riddled with **rivers**, most of them short and flowing rapidly down to the sea. There are some slower, meandering rivers on the east coast of the South Island, however, which create for a unique environment. The braided rivers in Canterbury and the Waitaki/Mackenzie Basin have distinctive wide shingle beds and multiple channels, providing a breeding ground for many birds, insects, fish and plants. Numerous **lakes** provide rich habitats for fish and birds; many of New Zealand's **wetlands**, on the other hand, have been drained for agriculture and property development, although some areas are preserved as national parks and scenic reserves. It's in low wetland areas that you're likely to come across the tallest of the native trees, the **kahikatea** (white pine), which reaches over 60m. There's a particularly fine stand in the central western North Island close to Te Awamutu.

One bird you're bound to see in the vicinity of a lake is the takahe's closest relative, the **pukeko**, a bird which is still in the process of losing the power of flight. The pukeko is mostly dark and mid-blue with large feet and an orange beak, and lets out a high-pitched screech if disturbed.

New Zealand is renowned for its great freshwater fishing, with massive brown and rainbow **trout** and **salmon** swarming through the fast-flowing streams. All introduced species, these fish have adapted so well to their conditions that they grow much larger here than elsewhere in the world; as a result, many native species have been driven out. Another delicacy commonly found in New Zealand's waters are native **eels**, much loved by Maori who built complicated eel traps along many rivers.

Keeping the fishermen company along the river banks of the Mackenzie country and Canterbury are **black stilt** or *kaki*, one of the world's rarest wading birds. A thin black bird with red eyes and long red legs, the stilt is incredibly shy – if you do see one in the wild, keep well away. Usually found in swamps and beside riverbeds, the best place to see them is in the specially created reserve near Twizel (see p.570). A slightly more adaptable member of the family is the **common pied stilt**, a black and white bird that has been more successful in resisting the attentions of introduced mammals, particularly feral cats.

Another inhabitant of the Canterbury braided riverbank is the **wrybill**. This small white and grey bird uses its unique bent bill to turn over stones or pull out crustaceans from mud. In winter the species migrates to Auckland and the mudflats of Kaipara, Manukau and the Firth of Thames. The wrybill's close cousin, the **banded dotterel**, favours the sides of rivers, lakes, open land with sparse vegetation and coastal lagoons and beaches. It is a small brown and white bird with a dark or black band around its neck and breeds only in New Zealand, though it does briefly migrate to Australia.

The **blue duck** is one of four endemic species with no close relatives anywhere in the world. Its Maori name, *Whio*, is a near perfect representation of the male bird's call. You can spot it by its blue-grey plumage, with chestnut on both breast and flanks; it also has an unusual bill with a black flexible membrane along each side, and beady yellow eyes. Mountainous areas are where it makes its home, preferring the swift mountain streams and approaching the coast only where the mountains are close to the sea. Unfortunately this is now an endangered species, preyed upon by mammals and forced to compete for food with the salmon and trout in the rivers.

GREEN ISSUES

The fact that New Zealand is, at least by European standards, apparently both clean and green is more by accident than design, a result of its isolation and relatively short human history. And although many New Zealanders are trying to preserve the country's environment, their efforts are often hampered by a vacillating government and the paramount interests of big business – wildlife has had to pay the price for some short-sighted and flagrant profiteering.

Traditionally meat, wool and dairy products have been New Zealand's main exports, but today a greater proportion is made up of forestry, machinery, aluminium and chemicals, all of which take their toll on the environment in terms of land usage, pollution and energy demands. Today none of the animals or crops and few of the trees harvested is endemic to New Zealand: the countryside is a confusion of native, European and Australian birds, exotic and indigenous trees, and a profusion of plants and animals from each hemisphere. Since human habitation began, ninety indigenous birds have been consigned to the ranks of the extinct and New Zealand now accounts for eleven percent of the world's endangered bird species.

LAND USAGE

People came to New Zealand to build a new, green land and visitors today arrive with the same images in mind. With a population of only 3.6 million, you would expect human interference to be limited but the country is in fact one of the most bizarre ecological disasters in the history of man. **Forest cover** has been reduced from about 50 percent to 25 percent in the last 150 years, while nearly three-quarters of the land area is given over to the production of food and commercial forestry, the latter essential to the national economy. Most of the trees are quick-growing **radiata pine**, an introduced species that is more profitable than any native variety; these days just five percent of native forest remains.

The increase in demand for forestry land goes unabated, even though commercial timber milling turns areas into virtual lunar deserts dot-

ted with tree stumps. A by-product is added air pollution from fume-spitting, eighteen-wheeler logging trucks.

On both North and South Islands, there are further problems on the land. Despite a sustained programme to eradicate pests like **possum**, wild deer, goats and rabbits (all of which if unchecked threaten the country's economic welfare), possums still outnumber other animals – pushing sheep into second place – consuming 21,000 tonnes of vegetation every 24 hours.

POLLUTION

Influenced by commerce, the government still has some decidedly unfriendly environmental policies. Despite a past record of admirable moral stands, such as banning ships and submarines carrying nuclear warheads from its shores (see p.771), the government has managed to disregard environmental initiatives related to **air pollution** and **industrial emissions**. New Zealand has the second worst record for CO_2 emissions in the OECD. Although it's perceived abroad as a country with enviably clean air, the quality of air in many cities, if measured, is shocking (check out Christchurch in the winter), and there have been massive increases in asthma and other respiratory problems among the young. Greenpeace rates the pollution from the Tasman pulp and paper mill in Kawerau as one of the country's worst problems. The mill is apparently responsible for the largest discharge of toxic organochlorine chemicals in the country and the nearby Tawera River has been contaminated by some of the most harmful chemicals known to man. New Zealand also scores badly on waste disposal and the monitoring of chemical usage and contaminated sites – with 700 potentially contaminated sites, it is on a par with the USA. Every day more than a billion litres of **sewage** and **industrial waste** is discharged into rivers and the sea.

Further short-sightedness is sadly evident in the use of intensive **farming** techniques and the massive amounts of **phosphates** piled onto soil that has been heavily exploited this century. Some rivers and lakes, in regions such as the Waikato, are either polluted by high nitrate levels or have few natural features left. Thankfully there is a strong groundswell of informed opinion leaning towards organic smallholdings that become increasingly profitable with the rising consumer demand for natural, untreated food. Recently the food industry has introduced a carefully monitored "eco-label", where rigorous standards provide an independent endorsement of the quality of food production.

ENERGY

New Zealand is about 70 percent energy self-sufficient, but the known reserves of gas and oil are thought to be good for only another twenty to thirty years and coal will also run out some-time in the next century. Demand for energy is currently on the increase, thanks to energy intensive processes like aluminium smelting (near Invercargill) and the Taranaki petrochemi-cal industry, together with a general increase in energy demand of 57 percent, despite only a 17 percent population rise over the last 25 years.

Although the nation is surrounded by sea water and buffeted by high winds, the efforts to exploit **alternative power sources** have been token at best. Hydroelectricity is, on the face of it, an environmentally friendly way of coping with the demands for power from an ever increasing population, but the flooding of unique environments to create lakes and grand dams has destroyed numerous natural habitats. Perhaps the most important environments at risk are the riverbanks, where several threat-ened species of bird live, nest and feed.

PRESERVING THE ENVIRONMENT

With only about 28 percent of the country not taken up with farming and forestry, and land constantly swallowed up by urban sprawl, what remains of pre-colonized New Zealand is under increased pressure.

As early as the 1880s it was realized that humans were having a detrimental effect on the land and that measures needed to be taken to preserve the environment. Pressure was exert-ed by the eco warriors of the time to conserve the forest, wetlands and volcanic areas by gazetting them as **national parks**. In this way, native flora and fauna could be preserved, encouraging regeneration and restocking. In 1887 Te Heuheu Tukino IV (Horonuku) set the ball rolling by giving the nucleus of the Tongariro National Park to the nation, in order to preserve the integrity of a venerated tribal area. The newest national park is the Kahurangi, formed in 1996 to ensure the preservation of an area of great natural beauty at the northwest-ern tip of the South Island.

A further effort to take back land and allevi-ate pressure on the national parks has seen the creation of small **scenic reserves**, areas given over to preserving or regenerating native bush. There are hundreds of them dotted around the country, each concerned with regenerating a particular aspect of the local environment so that it can sustain native fauna. The process requires great vigilance as the stands grow slowly and are constantly under threat from development and introduced animals. It takes about a hundred years for the bush to grow to maturity.

In another positive step, the Department of Conservation has made efforts to clear pests from **offshore islands**, in order to restock them with native species. The creation of these envi-ronmental havens saves many animals from extinction and provides an opportunity to build up depleted stocks of endangered species. Once the native birds become familiar with their new environment and realize that there are no predators, they become almost fearless and allow their curiosity full rein, inspecting all visi-tors at close quarters – just as they would have done when Maori first arrived over a thousand years ago.

BOOKS

Kiwis are avid readers, and almost equally keen writers, producing more glossy picture books and wildlife guides than you would think possible. Some excellent novels have come out of New Zealand too, despite the tiny home readership and the near impossibility of breaking into the international market.

Almost all of the following titles can be easily found in bookstores. Where two publishers are given, these refer to UK and US publishers respectively; titles that are published only in New Zealand are denoted NZ. Note that Hodder Headline titles are published by Hodder Moa Becket in New Zealand.

TRAVEL AND IMPRESSIONS

Mark Lawson, *The Battle for Room Service: Journeys to all the Safe Places* (Picador). On the basis that Timaru is rumoured to be the most activity-challenged city in New Zealand, itself the world's most differently-interesting place, Lawson selects this modest South Island city as the first port of call, and first chapter, of his wonderfully entertaining world tour of such dull places.

Austin Mitchell, *The Half-gallon, Quarter-acre, Pavlova Paradise* (OUP). A humorous and insightful vision of 1960s New Zealand as seen through the eyes of a British Labour MP and self-declared Kiwi commentator. Though wildly out of date, in many ways the lifestyles and values he describes still have the ring of truth, and the book stands as a measure of how much New Zealand has progressed, and at the same time how little.

Paul Theroux, *The Happy Isles of Oceania* (Penguin). Another misanthropic diatribe from Mr Theroux, and one which really put Kiwi noses out of joint. This time he kicks off in New Zealand and subsequently rides a clutch of hobby-horses through the Pacific. Some worthwhile observations on trekking in the South Island and a little historical context on the Polynesian migrations go some way towards saving the book.

HISTORY, SOCIETY AND POLITICS

James Belich, *The New Zealand Wars* (Penguin). An extraordinary, well-researched, and in-depth demolition job on the received version of the course and outcome of the colonial wars, which re-examines the Victorian and Maori interpretation of the conflict. A book for committed historians and those fanatically interested in the subject, since it gives more detail than most people will ever need to know.

A.K. Grant, *Corridors of Pua* (Hazard Press, NZ). A light-hearted look at the turbulent and fraught political history of the country from 1984 to the introduction of MMP.

Tom Hewnham, *By Batons and Barbed Wire* (o/p). A harrowing account of the 1981 Springbok Tour of New Zealand that stirred up more social hatred than any other event and proved conclusively that there is more to New Zealand society than just a bunch of good blokes and "Hail fellow well met".

Hineani Melbourne, *Maori Sovereignty: The Maori Perspective* (Hodder Headline); and its companion volume *Maori Sovereignty: The Pakeha Perspective* by **Carol Archie** (Hodder Headline). Everyone from grass-roots activists to statesmen get a voice in these two volumes, one airing the widely divergent Maori visions of sovereignty, the other covering the equally disparate *pakeha* view on the subject. They assume a fairly good understanding of Maori structures and recent New Zealand history, but are highly instructive nonetheless.

Claudia Orange, *The Story of the Treaty* (Bridget Williams Books, NZ). A concise, illustrated exploration of the history and myths behind what many believe to be the most important document in New Zealand history, the Treaty of Waitangi. Well written but probably more than the casual traveller needs to know.

Much the same criticism applies to the author's *The Treaty of Waitangi* (Allen & Unwin, NZ), which covers the lead-up to the signing, and the treaty's first sixty years.

Jock Phillips, *A Man's Country? The Image of the Pakeha Male* (Penguin). Recently updated version of a classic treatise on mateship and the Kiwi bloke. This thorough exploration ranges through the formative pioneering years, rugby, wartime camaraderie, the development of the family-man ideal and now includes Nineties man. It comes to life with the partial dismantling of the stereotype in the light of developments of the last twenty years.

Keith Sinclair, *The History of New Zealand* (Penguin). A highly readable general history of New Zealand with comprehensive coverage of the social factors that have shaped the country, as well as the prime movers. Maori oral history gets a brief and informative look-in, and there's plenty on uneasy Maori–*pakeha* relations, but it's not been updated to take into account recent political changes and the Maori renaissance.

D.C. Starzecka (ed), *Maori Art and Culture* (British Museum Press). A kind of Maori culture primer, with concise and interesting coverage of Maori history, culture, social structure, carving and weaving, spiced up by excellent colour photos of artefacts from the British Museum's collection.

Ross Wiseman, *The Spanish Discovery of New Zealand in 1576* (Discovery Press, NZ). Wiseman puts the case for pre-Abel Tasman European discovery based on wreckage from ships, Spanish-sounding Maori names and a clutch of other circumstantial but convincing evidence.

FICTION

Barbara Anderson, *All the Nice Girls* (Vintage, NZ). A short, insightful comedy of manners-cum-romance about a naval officer's wife who goes off the rails in 1960s Auckland, by a writer known for her clarity and vibrancy.

Anonymous, *The Spin* (Hodder Headline). Allegedly written by a government insider, hence the anonymity. Though Kiwis were shocked at the antics of barely disguised current politicians, it's all pretty tame by world standards, and only mildly revealing about the behaviour of elected representatives behind closed doors.

Graeme Aitken, *Fifty Ways of Saying Fabulous* (Headline). An extremely funny book about burgeoning homosexuality in a young farm boy, who lives in a world where he is expected to clean up muck and play rugby. Brilliant and touching, but it loses its way in the final third and serves up an anticlimactic ending.

Eric Beardsley, *Blackball 08* (Collins, NZ). Entertaining and fairly accurate historical novel set in the West Coast coal-mining town of Blackball during New Zealand's longest ever labour dispute.

Samuel Butler, *Erewhon* (Penguin). Gulliver's Travels-style journey to a utopian land, initially set in the Canterbury high country (where Butler ran a sheep station) but increasingly devoted to a satirical critique of mid-Victorian Britain.

Barry Crump, *A Good Keen Man; Hang on a Minute Mate; Bastards I Have Met; Forty Yarns and a Song* (Hodder Headline). Just a few of the many New Zealand bushman books by the Kiwi equivalent of Banjo Patterson, who writes with great humour, tenderness and style about the male-dominated world of hunting, shooting, fishing, drinking, and telling tall stories. Worth reading for a picture of a New Zealand and a lifestyle that have now largely disappeared.

Sigrid Crump, *Bushwoman* (Reed Books, NZ). Light, fresh and highly evocative account of a young German woman's solo travels on foot in New Zealand's backcountry during the 1960s and 70s. Infusing each page with her deep love of the Kiwi bush and fiercely independent spirit, Barry Crump's sister-in-law leaves you full of admiration.

Alan Duff, *Once Were Warriors* (Virago/Random House). A shocking and violent book in the social realism, kitchen-sink drama style, set in 1970s south Auckland and adapted in the 1990s for Lee Tamahori's film of the same name. At its heart are good intentions concerning the predicament of urban Maori, but at times this is a clumsy book with an oddly upbeat ending. Duff has recently published a sequel, *What Becomes of the Broken Hearted* (Virago/Random House).

Fiona Farrell, *Six Clever Girls Who Became Famous Women* (Penguin). A second novel of some quality and style has the girls of the title reunited in mid-life to confront what they have achieved and come to terms with their present and the possibilities of the future.

Janet Frame, *An Angel at My Table* (Random House). Though undoubtedly one of New Zealand's most accomplished novelists, Frame is perhaps best known for this three-volume autobiography, dramatized in Jane Campion's film which, with wit and a self-effacing honesty, gives a wonderful insight into both the author and her environment. Her superb novels and short stories use humour alongside highly disturbing combinations of events and characters to overthrow readers' preconceptions. For starters, try *Faces in the Water*, *Living in the Maniototo* and *Scented Gardens for the Blind* (all The Women's Press).

Maurice Gee, *Crime Story*; *Going West*; *Prowlers* (Penguin). Three from an underrated but highly talented writer. Despite the misleadingly light titles, Gee's focus is social realism, taking an unflinching, powerful look at motivation and unravelling relationships.

Patricia Grace, *Potiki* (Penguin). Poignant and poetic tale of a Maori community redefining itself through a blend of traditional and modern values, while its land is threatened by coastal development. Exquisite writing by an outstanding author who ranks among the finest in New Zealand today. She has also written several other novels and short-story collections.

Peter Hawes, *Leapfrog with Unicorns* (Vintage Press, NZ) and *Tasman's Lay* (Hazard Press, NZ). Two from the unsung hero, cult figure and probably only member of the absurdist movement in New Zealand, who writes with great energy, wit and surprising discipline about almost anything that takes his fancy.

Keri Hulme, *The Bone People* (Picador). Celebrated winner of the 1985 Booker Prize, and a wonderful first novel set along the wild beaches of the South Island's West Coast. Mysticism, myth and earthy reality are transformed into a haunting tale peopled with richly drawn characters.

Witi Ihimaera, *Bulibasha – King of the Gypsies* (Penguin). The best introduction to one of the country's finest Maori authors. A rollicking good read, energetically exploring the life of a rebellious teenager in 1950s rural New Zealand, where two mighty sheep-shearing families are locked in battle. It's an intense look at adolescence, cultural choices, family ties and the abuse of power, culminating in a masterful twist.

Phil Kawana, *Dead Jazz Guys* (Huia Publishers, NZ). A relatively new kid on the block, writing short stories about the young urban Maori, family, drugs and sex. Poignant and intelligent writing in a collection of mixed quality.

Fiona Kidman, *The Book of Secrets* (Picador). Historical novel tracing one family's heritage through the reclusive granddaughter of a Scot who left the highlands with commanding preacher Norman McLeod, eventually ending up in Northland's Waipu.

Shonagh Koea, *The Grandiflora Tree* (Penguin). A savagely witty yet deeply moving study of the conventions of widowhood, with a peculiar love story thrown in. First novel from a journalist and short-story writer renowned for her astringent humour.

Katherine Mansfield, *The Collected Stories of Katherine Mansfield* (Penguin). All 73 short stories sit alongside 15 unfinished fragments in this 780-page tome. Concise yet penetrating examinations of human behaviour in apparently trivial situations, often transmitting a painfully pessimistic view of the world, and startlingly modern for their time.

Ngaio Marsh, *Opening Night*; *Artists in Crime*; *Vintage Murder* (Fontana). Just a selection from the doyenne of New Zealand crime fiction. Since 1934 she has been airing her anglophile sensibilities and killing off innumerable individuals in the name of entertainment, before solving the crimes with Inspector Allen. Perfect mindless reading matter for planes, trains and buses.

Ronald Hugh Morrieson, *Came a Hot Friday* (OUP). Superb account of the idiosyncrasies of country folk and the two smart spielers who enter their lives, in a comedy thriller focusing on crime and sex in a small country town.

John Mulgan, *Man Alone* (Penguin). Seminal and soberly written boy's-own novel about one man's restless and peripatetic times working the New Zealand back blocks between the wars, as the country lurched from its pioneering days into the modern world. First published in 1939, it is often regarded as one of the first truly Kiwi novels and had a huge influence on New Zealand writing, its evocation of the Kiwi male quickly becoming an archetype.

Vincent O'Sullivan, *Let the River Stand* (Penguin). Deftly conjuring the minutiae of homestead and rural school life in a Waikato farming community of the 1930s, Sullivan weaves disparate tales around the life of his gawky anti-hero, Alex. Tragic, humorous and captivating.

Emily Perkins, *Not Her Real Name* (Picador). Sub-Mansfield short-story writer who inexplicably picked up an award for this. Though lacking the subtlety and incisiveness of the master, this uneven collection shows definite promise.

Frank Sargeson, *The Stories of Frank Sargeson* (Penguin). Though not well-known outside New Zealand, Sargeson is a giant of Kiwi literature. His writing, from the 1930s to the 1980s, is incisive and sharply observed, at its best in dialogue, which is always true to the meter of New Zealand speech. This work brings together some of his finest short stories. *Once is Enough*, *More than Enough* and *Never Enough!* (all Penguin) make up the complete autobiography of a man sometimes even more colourful than his characters; **Michael King** has written a fine biography, *Frank Sargeson: A Life* (Viking).

Maurice Shadbolt, *Strangers and Journeys* (Hodder/Atheneum). On publication in 1972 this became a defining novel in New Zealand's literary ascendancy and its sense of nationhood, putting Shadbolt in the same league as Australia's Patrick White. A tale of two families of finely wrought characters, whose lives interweave through three generations. Very New Zealand, very human and not overly epic. Later works, which have consolidated Shadbolt's reputation, include *Mondays Warriors*, *Season of the Jew* and *The House of Strife* (Hodder/Atheneum).

Paul Thomas, *Old School Tie* (Hodder Headline). Smart thriller with some neat comedic touches but a bit clichéd, just like his last book *Inside Dope* (Hodder Headline), and lacking any really sympathetic characters. Another relaxing read, ideal while waiting for a bus.

C.K. Stead, *The Singing Whakapapa* (Penguin). Highly regarded author of many books and critical essays who is sadly little known outside New Zealand and Australia. A combination of a powerful historical novel about an early missionary, and a dissatisfied modern descendant

who is searching for meaning in his own life by exploring the past. An excellent and engaging read.

Damien Wilkins, *The Miserables* (Faber). One of the best novels to come out of New Zealand, shorn of much of the colonial baggage of many writers. It is surprisingly mature for a first novel, sharply evoking middle-class New Zealand life from the 1960s to the 1980s through finely wrought characters.

ANTHOLOGIES

Fergus Barrowman (ed), *The Picador Book of Contemporary New Zealand Fiction* (Picador). A good combination of extracts and short stories from most of the best living writers in the country.

Warwick Brown, *100 New Zealand Paintings* (Godwit Publishing, NZ). As the title suggests, with some excellent reproductions and a good bit of information.

Warwick Brown, *100 New Zealand Artists* (Godwit Publishing, NZ). The companion to the above but also allowing room for sculptors, printmakers, photographers and graphic artists.

Bill Manhire (ed), *100 New Zealand Poems* (Godwit Publishing, NZ). A very manageable selection of Kiwi verse which provides an excellent introduction to the poetry of the nation.

C.K. Stead (ed), *Contemporary South Pacific Stories* (Faber and Faber). A great collection from authors as diverse as European Kiwi, Maori, Fijian-Indian, Samoan, Tongan and Cook Islanders, with a brilliant introduction.

Ian Wedde and Harvey McQueen (eds), *The Penguin Book of New Zealand Verse* (Penguin). A comprehensive collection of verse from the earliest European settlers to contemporary poets, and an excellent introduction to Kiwi poetry; highlights are works by James K. Baxter, Janet Frame, C.K. Stead, Sam Hunt, Keri Hulme, Hirini Melbourne, and Apirana Taylor.

REFERENCE AND SPECIALIST GUIDES

Les Hill & Graeme Marshall, *Images of Silver* (The Halcyon Press, NZ). Inspirational fishing picture book with great shots of anglers in action all over the country.

Rosemary George, *The Wines of New Zealand* (Faber and Faber). Entertaining and informative look at New Zealand's most important wine regions, the history, the people and the product.

John Kent, *North Island Trout Fishing Guide* and *South Island Trout Fishing Guide* (Reed, NZ). Laden with information on access, seasons and fishing style, and illustrated with maps of the more important rivers.

Terry Sturm (ed), *The Oxford History of New Zealand Literature* (Oxford University Press). A massive and comprehensive guide to non-fiction, novels, plays and poems by a variety of academics, which is fascinating for anyone with an academic interest in the subject but otherwise as dry as an old stick.

J & J Thomas, *The New Zealand Bed & Breakfast Book* (Moonshine Press, NZ). Annually updated listing of member B&Bs, homestays and farmstays, covering almost 1000 places all over the country. The guide is available from bookshops or direct from Moonshine Press, PO Box 41022, Eastbourne, Wellington (☎ & fax 04/562 7667), for NZ$20, though the larger car-rental firms often supply customers with a free copy. Bear in mind that entries are submitted by the owners, so a little reading between the lines is advisable.

TRAMPING

Pearl Hewson, *New Zealand's Great Walks* (Hodder Headline). Pearl is a no-nonsense DOC Officer working out of the Wellington Office and what she doesn't know about the Great Walks isn't worth knowing. This is a practical, concise guide which concentrates her experiences into a useful aid to trampers.

Mark Pickering, *Wild Walks* (Shoal Bay Press, NZ). Sixty short and easily accessible walks on the North Island, mixed in with historical anecdotes and precise descriptions of the local environment.

Philip Temple, *BP Pocket Tramping Guides* (BP). A series of inexpensive, lightweight paperback guides giving handy and informative track notes, with information on the history, flora and fauna, for the major New Zealand tramps. Titles cover the Routeburn, Milford, Copland, Hollyford and Abel Tasman tracks.

FLORA, FAUNA AND THE ENVIRONMENT

D.H. Brathwaite, *Native Birds of New Zealand* (Caxton Press, NZ). Brilliant colour photographs and lots of information pinpointing thirty rare birds that, with a little effort and some patience, you can observe while travelling around.

Andrew Crowe, *Which Native Tree?* (Viking Pacific, NZ). Great little book, ideal for identification of New Zealand's common native trees – though not tree ferns – with diagrams of tree shape, photo of leaves and fruit, and an idea of geographic extent.

John Dawson, *New Zealand Coast and Mountain Plants* (Victoria University Press, NZ). A luxuriant book filled with colourful and unusual illustrations.

Geoff Moon, *The Reed Field Guide to New Zealand Birds* (Reed, NZ). Excellent colour reference book, with ample detail for species identification

Geoff Moon, *The Reed Field Guide to New Zealand Wildlife* (Reed, NZ). Separate chapters, stuffed with colour photos, cover forest, open country, the coast and offshore islands, but facts are too thin on the ground for it to succeed as a reference work.

Rod Morris & Hal Smith, *Wild South: Saving New Zealand's Endangered Birds* (Century Huchinson/TVNZ). A fascinating companion volume to a 1980s TV series following a band of dedicated individuals trying to preserve a dozen of New Zealand's wonderfully exotic bird species, including the kiwi, kakapo, takahe and kea.

Murdoch Riley, *New Zealand Trees and Ferns* (Viking Sevenseas, NZ). An excellent, pocket-size guide with colour illustrations identifying the most often seen trees and ferns.

Neville Peat, *Manapouri Saved* (Longacre Press, NZ). Full and heartening coverage of one of New Zealand's earliest environmental battles when, in the 1960s, a petition signed by ten percent of the country succeeded in persuading the government to cancel its hydroelectric plans for Lake Manapouri.

Susanne & John Hill, *Richard Henry of Resolution Island* (John McIndoe, NZ).

Comprehensive and very readable account of a man widely regarded as New Zealand's first conservationist. The book serves as a potted history of this underpopulated area of Fiordland, peopled by many of the key explorers.

ADVENTURE SPORTS

Mike Bhana, *New Zealand Surfing Guide* (Reed, NZ). Pragmatic handbook to the numerous prime surf spots around the New Zealand coast, with details on access, transport, the best wind and tide conditions and expected swells.

Graham Charles, *New Zealand Whitewater: 100 Great Kayaking Runs* (Craig Potton, NZ). An indispensable, comprehensive and entertaining guide to New Zealand's most important kayaking rivers. River maps and details on access are supplemented by quick reference panels with grades, timings, and handy tips like which rapids not to even think about running.

Marty Sharp, *A Guide to the Ski Areas on New Zealand* (Random House). Exactly what you'd expect, with full descriptions of the fields complete with tow plans and information on access, local towns and ski rental.

Ken Sibly and Mark Wilson, *4 Wheel-drive South Island* (Shoal Bay Press, NZ). A book for adventurous drivers who know how to use their off-road vehicles, covering seventy public, but treacherous, roads.

LANGUAGE: KIWI ENGLISH AND MAORI

English and *te reo Maori*, the Maori language, share joint status as New Zealand's official languages, but on a day-to-day basis all you'll need is English, or its colourful Kiwi variant. All Maori speak English fluently, often slipping in numerous Maori terms which in time become part of everyday Kiwi parlance. You may find television, radio and newspaper articles – especially those relating to Maori affairs – initially confusing without a basic grounding, but with the aid of our glossary (see p.798) you'll soon find yourself using Maori terms all the time. A basic knowledge of Maori pronunciation will make you more comprehensible and some understanding of the roots of place names can be helpful. You'll need to become something of an expert, though, to appreciate much of the wonderful oral history, and stories told through *waiata* (songs), but learning a few key terms will enhance any Maori cultural events you may attend.

To many Brits and North Americans, **Kiwi English** is barely distinguishable from its trans-Tasman cousin, "Strine", sharing much of the same lexicon of slang terms, but with an accent marginally closer in tone to South African English. Australians have no trouble distinguishing the two accents, repeatedly highlighting the vowel shift which turns "bat" into "bet", makes "yes" sound like "yis" and causes "fish" come out as "fush". This vowel contortion is carried to new levels in remoter country areas, but there is really very little regional variation, only Otago and Southland – the southern quarter of the South Island – distinguishing themselves with a rolled "r", courtesy of their predominantly Scottish founders. Throughout the land, Kiwis add an upward inflection to statements, making them sound like questions; most are not, and to highlight those that are, some add the interrogative "eh?" to the end of the sentence, a trait most evident in the North Island, especially among Maori.

MAORI

For the 50,000 native speakers and 100,000 who speak it as a second tongue, Maori is very much a living language, gaining strength all the time as both Maori and *pakeha* increasingly appreciate the cultural value of *te reo*, a language central to Maoritanga and forming the basis of a huge body of magnificent songs, chants and legends, lent a poetic quality by its hypnotic and lilting rhythms.

Maori is a member of the Polynesian group of languages and shares both grammar and vocabulary with those spoken throughout most of the South Pacific. Similarities are so pronounced that Tupaia, a Tahitian crew member on Captain Cook's first Pacific voyage in 1769, was able to communicate freely with the Aotearoa Maori they encountered. The Treaty of Waitangi was written in both English and Maori, but *te reo* soon began to lose ground to the point where, by the late nineteenth century, its use was proscribed in schools. Maori parents keen for their offspring to do well in the *pakeha* world frequently promoted the use of English, and Maori declined further, exacerbated by the mid-twentieth-century migration to the cities. Though never on the brink of extinction, the language reached its nadir in the 1970s when perhaps only ten percent of Maori could speak their language fluently. The tide began to turn towards the end of the decade with the inception of *kohanga reo* **pre-schools** (literally "language nests") where Maoritanga is taught and activities are conducted in Maori. Originally a Maori initiative, it has now crossed

MAORI PLACE NAMES

The following is a list of some of the most common words and elements you will see in town and place names throughout New Zealand. A.W. Reed's *A Dictionary of Maori Place Names* (Reed) gives more detailed coverage of the same field.

AO Cloud.
ARA Road or path.
AWA River or valley.
HAU Wind.
IKA Fish.
ITI Small.
KAI Food, or eat.
KAINGA Home, village.
KARE Rippling.
KINO Bad.
MA White, clear.
MANGA Stream.
MANU Bird.
MATA Headland.
MAUNGA Mountain.
MIHI Speeches.

MOANA Sea, lake.
MOTU Island or anything isolated.
MURI End.
NUI Big.
O The place of.
ONE Sand, beach.
PA Fortified settlement.
PAE Ridge.
PAPA Flat, earth, floor.
PATERE Chants.
PUKE Hill.
PUNA Spring.
RAKI North.
RANGI Sky.
ROA Long, high.

ROTO Lake.
RUA Hole, cave, pit, two.
RUNGA Top.
TAHU Light.
TAI Sea.
TANE Man.
TAPU Sacred.
TARA Peak.
TE The.
TOMO Cave.
WAI Water.
WAKA Canoe.
WHANGA Bay, body of water.
WHENUA Land or country.

over and *pakeha* parents are increasingly introducing their kids to biculturalism at an early age. Fortunate *kohanga reo* graduates can progress to the small number of state-funded Maori-language primary schools known as *kura kaupapa*. For decades, Maori has been taught as an option in secondary schools, and there are now two state-funded tertiary institutions operated by Maori, offering graduate programmes in Maori studies.

The success of these programmes has bred a young generation of Maori speakers frequently far more fluent than their parents who, shamed by the loss of their heritage, are beginning to attend Maori evening classes. Legal parity means that Maori is now finding its way into officialdom too, with government departments all adopting Maori names in recent years and many government and council documents being printed in both languages. The increasing knowledge and awareness has spawned Maori TV and radio broadcasts, notably the nightly news, *Te Karere*.

In your day-to-day dealings you won't need **to speak Maori**, though both native speakers and *pakeha* may well greet you with *kia ora* (hi, hello), or less commonly *haere mai* (welcome). On ceremonial occasions, such as *marae* visits, you'll hear the more formal greeting *tena koe* (said to one person) or *tena koutou katoa* (to a group).

Maori words used in place names are listed in the box above, while those in common use are listed in the general glossary (see p.796). If you are interested in learning a little more, the best handy reference is Patricia Tauroa's *The Collins Maori Phrase Book* (HarperCollins; $15) which has helpful notes on pronunciation, handy phrases and a useful Maori–English and English–Maori vocabulary.

PRONUNCIATION

Laziness and arrogance have combined to give *pakeha* – and consequently most visitors – a distorted impression of Maori pronunciation, which is usually mutated into an Anglicized form. Until the 1970s there was little attempt to get it right, but with the rise in Maori consciousness through the 1980s and 1990s, coupled with a sense of political correctness, most *pakeha* now make some attempt at Maori pronunciation. As a visitor you will probably get away with just about anything, but by sticking to a few simple rules and keeping your ears open, the apparently unfathomable place names will soon trip off your tongue. The key to **pronunciation** is in knowing where to split long compound words; scanning the place name elements in the box (see above) should help a great deal, and it is worth remembering that all syllables end in a vowel. Each syllable is then stressed equally, so that, for example,

Waikaremoana comes out as a flat Wai-ka-re-mo-ana. The other trick for the unwary is that Maori words don't take an "s" to form a plural, so you'll find many plural nouns in this book — kiwi, tui, kauri, Maori — in what appears to be a singular form; about the only exception is Kiwis (as people), a Maori word wholly adopted into English.

Maori was solely a spoken language before the arrival of British and French missionaries in the early nineteenth century, who transcribed it using only fifteen letters of the Roman alphabet. The five **vowels** come in long and short forms; the long form is sometimes signified in print by a macron — a flat bar above the letter — but usu-ally it is simply a case of learning by experience which sound to use. When two vowels appear together they are both pronounced, though sub-stantially run together. For example, "Maori" should be written with a macron on the "a" and be pronounced with the first two vowels sepa-rate, turning the commonly used but incorrect "Mow-ree" into something more like "Maao-ri".

The eight **consonants**, **h**, **k**, **m**, **n**, **p**, **r**, **t** and **w**, are pronounced much as they are in English. Finally, there are two digraphs: **ng**, pronounced much as in "sing", and **wh**, which sounds either like an aspirated "f" as in "off", or like the "wh" in "why", depending on who is saying what and in which part of the country.

GLOSSARY OF KIWI TERMS, PHRASES AND SLANG

ACC Accident Compensation Commission.

ANZAC Australian and New Zealand Army Corps; every town in New Zealand has a memorial to ANZAC casualties from both world wars.

Aotearoa Maori for New Zealand, the land of the long white cloud.

Ariki Supreme chief of an *iwi*.

Bach (pronounced "batch") Holiday home, originally a bachelor pad at work camps and now something of a Kiwi institution that can be anything from shack to palatial waterside residence.

Back-blocks Remote areas.

Biddy-bid A burr-bearing bush (from Maori *piripiri*).

Blat Travel at great speed.

Bludger Someone who doesn't pull their weight or pay their way, a sponger.

Boomer Excellent.

Bro Brother, term of endearment widely used by Maori.

Captain Cooker Wild pig, probably descended from pigs released in the Marlborough Sounds on Cook's first voyage.

Chilly bin Insulated cool box for carrying picnic supplies and beer to the beach or cricket match.

Chook Chicken.

Choice Fantastic.

Chuddy Chewing gum, also "chutty".

Chunder Vomit.

Coaster (Ex-) resident of the West Coast of the South Island.

Cocky Farmer, comes in "Cow" and "Sheep" variants.

Crib South Island name for a bach.

Cuz or **Cuzzy** Short for cousin, see "bro".

Dag Wag or entertaining character.

Dairy Corner shop selling just about everything, open seven days and sometimes 24 hours.

Dally Semi-derogatory name for descendants of Dalmatian immigrants from the Balkans.

Dob in Reporting one's friends and neighbours to the police; there is currently a dobber's charter encouraging drivers to report one another for dangerous driving.

Docket Receipt.

Domain Grassy reserve, open to the public.

Fizz boat Small powerboat.

Flicks Cinema, movie theatre.

Flog Steal.

Footie Rugby, usually union rather than league, never soccer.

Freezing works Slaughter house.

Give it a burl Try it.

Godzone New Zealand, short for "God's own country".

Gorse in your pocket To be slow to pay your share.

Good as (gold) First rate, excellent.

Good on ya Expression of approbation or encouragement, frequently appended with "mate".

Greasies Takeaway food, especially fish and chips.

Greenstone A type of nephrite jade known in Maori as *pounamu*.

Haka Maori dance performed in threatening fashion before All Black rugby games.

Handle Large glass of beer.

Hangi Maori feast cooked in an earth oven (see p.776).

Hapu Maori sub-tribal unit. Several make up an *iwi*.

Hard case See "dag".

Hard yacker Hard work.

Hollywood A faked or exaggerated sporting injury used to gain advantage.

Hongi Maori greeting, performed by pressing noses together.

Hoon Lout, yob or delinquent.

Hori Offensive word for a Maori.

Hui Maori gathering or conference.

Iwi Largest of Maori tribal groupings.

Jandals Ubiquitous Kiwi footwear, thongs or flip-flops.

Jug Litre of beer.

Kai Maori word for food, used in general parlance.

Kaimoana Seafood.

Karanga Call for visitors to come forward on a *marae*.

Kaumatua Maori elders, old people.

Kawa-Marae Etiquette or protocol on a *marae*.

Kete Traditional basket made of plaited flax that is seeing something of a resurgence in popularity.

Kiore Polynesian rat.

Koha Donation.

Kohanga Reo Pre-school Maori language immersion (literally "language nest").

Kumara Sweet potato.

Kuri Polynesian dog, now extinct.

Lay-by Practice of putting a deposit on goods until they can be fully paid for.

Log of wood Slang for the Ranfurly Shield, New Zealand rugby's greatest prize.

Mana Maori term indicating status, esteem, prestige or authority, and in wide use among all Kiwis.

Manaia Stylized bird or lizard forms used extensively in Maori carving.

Manchester Linen section of a department store and its contents.

Manuhiri Guest or visitor, particularly to a marae.

Maoritanga Maori culture and custom, the Maori way of doing things.

Marae Literally "courtyard" but much more. Place for conducting ceremonies in front of a meeting house. Also a general term for a settlement centred on the meeting house.

Mauri Life force or life principle.

Mere War club, usually of greenstone.

Metalled Graded road surface of loose stones found all over rural New Zealand.

MMP Mixed member proportional representation – New Zealand's new electoral system.

Moko Old form of tattooing on body and face that has seen a resurgence among Maori gang members.

Ngati Tribal prefix meaning the descendants or people of. Also *Ngai* and *Ati*.

No fear Expression indicating refusal or disagreement.

OE Overseas experience, usually a year spent abroad by Kiwis in their early twenties.

Pa Fortified village of yore, now usually an abandoned terraced hillside.

Paddock Field.

Pakeha A non-Maori, usually white and not usually expressed with derogatory intent. Literally "foreign" though it can also be translated as "flea" or "pest" . It may also be a corruption of *pakepakeha*, which are mythical human-like beings with fair skins.

Pashing Kissing or snogging.

Patu Short fighting club

Paua Abalone, a type of shellfish with a wonderful iridescent shell.

Pavlova Meringue dessert with a fruit and cream topping.

Pike out To chicken out or give up.

Piss Beer.

Pissed Drunk.

Piss head Drunkard.

Plunkett rooms Childcare centre.

Poms Folk from Britain; not necessarily offensive.

Powhiri Traditional welcome onto a *marae*.

Puckerooed Broken. Derived from the Maori for broken, *pakaru*.

Puku Maori for stomach, often used as a term of endearment for someone amply endowed.

Queen Street farmer City businessman owning rural property.

Ranch slider Sliding glass door giving onto the garden or decking.

Rangatira General term for a Maori chief.

Rapt Well-pleased.

Rattle your dags Hurry up.

Root Vulgar term for sex.

Rooted To be very tired or beyond repair, as in "she's rooted mate" – your car is irreparable.

Rough as guts Uncouth, roughly made or operating badly, as in "she's running rough as guts, mate".

Scroggin Trail mix, essentially nuts and raisins.

Sealed road Bitumen-surfaced road.

Section Block of land usually surrounding a house.

She'll be right Everything will work out fine.

Shoot through To leave suddenly.

Shout To buy a round of drinks or generally to treat folk.

Skull To knock back beer quickly.

Slutted Greatly annoyed.

Smoko Tea break.

Snarler, **snag** Sausage.

Spinner A jerk.

Squiz A look, as in "Give us a squiz".

Station wagon Estate car.

Stoked Very pleased.

Taiaha Long-handled club.

Tall poppy Someone who excels. "Cutting down tall poppies" is to bring overachievers back to earth – every Kiwi's perceived duty.

Tane Man.

Tangata whenua The people of the land, local or original inhabitants.

Tangi Mourning or funeral.

Taniwha Fearsome water spirit of Maori legend.

Taonga Treasures, prized possessions.

Tapu Forbidden or taboo. Frequently refers to sacred land.

Te reo Maori Maori language.

Tiki Maori pendant depicting a distorted human figure.

Tiki tour Guided tour.

Togs Swimming costume.

Tohunga Maori priests, experts in Maoritanga.

Tukutuku Knotted latticework panels decorating the inside of a meeting house.

Tupuna Ancestors; of great spiritual importance to Maori.

Ute Car-sized pick-up truck, short for "utility".

Varsity University.

Wahine Woman.

Waiata Maori action songs.

Wairau Spirit.

Waratah Stake, a term used to describe snow poles on tramps.

Waka Maori canoe.

Wero Challenge before entering a *marae*.

Whakapapa Family tree or genealogical relationship.

Whanau Extended family group.

Whare Maori for a house.

Whare runanga Meeting house.

Whare whakairo Carved house.

Within cooee Within reach.

Wop-wops Remote areas.

Yahoo To be or act like a lout.

INDEX

Stay in touch with us!

ROUGH*NEWS* **is Rough Guides' free newsletter.**
In three issues a year we give you news, travel
issues, music reviews, readers' letters and the
latest dispatches from authors on the road.

I would like to receive ROUGH*NEWS*: please put me on your free mailing list.

NAME . . . .

ADDRESS . . . .

Please clip or photocopy and send to: Rough Guides, 1 Mercer Street, London WC2H 9QJ, England
or Rough Guides, 375 Hudson Street, New York, NY 10014, USA.

the perfect getaway vehicle

low-price holiday car rental.

rent a car from holiday autos and you'll give yourself real freedom to explore your holiday destination. with great-value, fully-inclusive rates in over 4,000 locations worldwide, wherever you're escaping to, we're there to make sure you get excellent prices and superb service.

what's more, you can book now with complete confidence. our £5 undercut* ensures that you are guaranteed the best value for money in holiday destinations right around the globe.

drive away with a great deal, call holiday autos now on **0990 300 400** and quote ref RG.

holiday autos miles ahead